DS

DISCARD

D0207913

THE CAMBRIDGE HISTORY OF PHILOSOPHY 1870–1945

The Cambridge History of Philosophy 1870–1945 comprises over sixty specially commissioned essays by experts on the philosophy of this period, and is designed to be accessible to non-specialists who have little previous familiarity with philosophy. The first part of the book traces the remarkable flowering of philosophy in the 1870s, with the start of German Neo-Kantianism, American pragmatism, and British idealism, through to the beginnings of the phenomenological movement and analytical philosophy in the early years of the twentieth century. After a brief discussion of the impact of the First World War, the second part of the book describes further developments in philosophy in the first half of the twentieth century, looking, for example, at some of the new ideas associated with Wittgenstein, Heidegger, and the Vienna Circle. As with other volumes in the series, much of the emphasis of the essays is thematic, concentrating on developments during the period across the range of philosophical topics, from logic and metaphysics to political philosophy and philosophy of religion. Several chapters also discuss the changing relationship of philosophy to the natural and social sciences during this period. The result is an authoritative survey of this rich and varied period of philosophical activity, which will be of critical importance not only to teachers and students of philosophy but also to scholars in neighbouring disciplines such as the history of science, the history of ideas, theology, and the social sciences.

The Cambridge History of Philosophy 1870–1945

EDITED BY

THOMAS BALDWIN

University of York

CAMBRIDGE
UNIVERSITY PRESS

PUBLISHED BY THE PRESS SYNDICATE OF THE UNIVERSITY OF CAMBRIDGE
The Pitt Building, Trumpington Street, Cambridge, United Kingdom

CAMBRIDGE UNIVERSITY PRESS
The Edinburgh Building, Cambridge, CB2 2RU, UK
40 West 20th Street, New York, NY 10011-4211, USA
477 Williamstown Road, Port Melbourne, VIC 3207, Australia
Ruiz de Alarcón 13, 28014 Madrid, Spain
Dock House, The Waterfront, Cape Town 8001, South Africa

http://www.cambridge.org

First published 2003

Printed in the United Kingdom at the University Press, Cambridge

Typeface Bembo 10.25/12.5 pt.   *System* LaTeX 2_ε [TB]

A catalogue record for this book is available from the British Library

ISBN 0 521 59104 X hardback

CONTENTS

CONTRIBUTORS

CHRISTOPHER ADAIR-TOTEFF
Mississippi State University

WALTER ADAMSON
Department of History
Emory University

JAMES ALLARD
Department of History and
    Philosophy
Montana State University

R. LANIER ANDERSON
Department of Philosophy
Stanford University

LESLIE ARMOUR
University of Ottawa

DAVID BAKHURST
Department of Philosophy
Queen's University, Kingston,
    Ontario

THOMAS BALDWIN
Department of Philosophy
University of York

DAVID BELL
Department of Philosophy
University of Sheffield

RICHARD BELLAMY
Department of Politics
University of Reading

JAMES BOHMAN
Department of Philosophy
Saint Louis University

LUCIANO BOI
Université de Québec à Montréal

JAMES BRADLEY
Department of Philosophy
Memorial University of
    Newfoundland

ALEX CALLINICOS
Department of Politics
University of York

JONATHAN DANCY
Department of Philosophy
University of Reading

JOHN DAWSON
Department of Philosophy
Penn State University

CORNELIUS DELANEY
Department of Philosophy
University of Notre Dame

LUCIANO FLORIDI
Wolfson College
University of Oxford

GEORGE GALE
Department of Philosophy
University of Missouri

SEBASTIAN GARDNER
Department of Philosophy
University College London

MANUEL GARRIDO
Department of Logic
   and Philosophy of Science
Madrid University

RAYMOND GEUSS
Faculty of Philosophy
University of Cambridge

SIMON GLENDINNING
Department of Philosophy
University of Reading

RHIANNON GOLDTHORPE
Emeritus Fellow
St Anne's College, Oxford

PAUL GUYER
Department of Philosophy
University of Pennsylvania

MICHAEL HALLETT
Department of Philosophy
McGill University

ROM HARRÉ
Department of Psychology
Georgetown University

ROSS HARRISON
King's College
University of Cambridge

GARY HATFIELD
Department of Philosophy
University of Pennsylvania

GEOFFREY HAWTHORN
Faculty of Social and Political
   Science
University of Cambridge

DAVID HOLDCROFT
Department of Philosophy
University of Leeds

CHRISTOPHER HOOKWAY
Department of Philosophy
University of Sheffield

THOMAS KASULIS
Comparative Studies
Ohio State University

THOMAS LEAHEY
Department of Philosophy
Virginia Commonwealth
   University

DANIEL LEDUC-FAYETTE
Centre d'Etude des Philosophes
   Français
Université de Paris-Sorbonne IV

JAMES LIVINGSTON
Department of Religion
The College of William and Mary
Williamsburg, VA

MICHAEL MARTIN
Department of Philosophy
University College London

MARIE McGINN
Department of Philosophy
University of York

BRIAN McLAUGHLIN
Department of Philosophy
Rutgers University

F. C. T. MOORE
Department of Philosophy
University of Hong Kong

PETER NICHOLSON
Department of Politics
University of York

STANLEY L. PAULSON
School of Law
Washington University

HERMAN PHILIPSE
Department of Philosophy
University of Leiden

CHRISTIAN PILLER
Department of Philosophy
University of York

EDUARDO RABOSSI
Department of Philosophy
University of Buenos Aires

ALAN RICHARDSON
Department of Philosophy
University of British
   Columbia

RICHARD H. ROBERTS
Department of Religious
   Studies
University of Lancaster

ARTUR ROJSZCZAK
Department of Epistemology
Institute of Philosophy
Jagiellonian University

THOMAS RYCKMAN
Department of Philosophy
University of California,
   Berkeley

MERRILEE H. SALMON
Department of History and
   Philosophy of Science
University of Pittsburgh

MICHAEL SCANLAN
Department of Philosophy
Oregon State University

MARGARET SCHABAS
Department of Philosophy
University of British Columbia

PETER SIMONS
Department of Philosophy
University of Leeds

EDGAR SLEINIS
Department of Philosophy
University of Tasmania

BARRY SMITH
Department of Philosophy
SUNY at Buffalo

JAN VON PLATO
Department of Philosophy
University of Helsinki

JAN WOLEŃSKI
Department of Epistemology
Institute of Philosophy
Jagiellonian University

ELI ZAHAR
Emeritus Reader
London School of Economics

INTRODUCTION

THOMAS BALDWIN

This volume begins in 1870, the year in which the Prussian army defeated the French at Sedan; it ends in 1945, the year of German defeat in the Second World War. During this period Germany became the most powerful state in Europe and, indeed, twice sought to achieve control of Europe. This is also a period during which the work of German philosophers, including those of the Austrian tradition, was widely regarded as making the most important contributions to the subject. After 1945 no one could sensibly continue to maintain such a claim; so there is also a sense in which this volume covers the period of the rise and fall of the influence of German philosophy.

The early chapters of this volume describe and discuss the main currents of philosophical debate in 1870 and the following decade, during which there was a remarkable flourishing of new philosophical activity – the German Neo-Kantian movement, the idealist movement in Britain, the start of pragmatism in the United States, the work of Brentano and his followers in Austria, and so on. I shall attempt to set the scene for these chapters by briefly sketching the political and cultural world of the 1870s.

The Franco-Prussian war of 1870, followed by the fall of Paris in 1871, precipitated several important developments. The Prussian victory finally persuaded the south German states to join with Prussia in establishing a new German empire, which was consummated when Wilhelm I was crowned Kaiser in Versailles in 1871 and Bismarck was appointed chancellor of the newly unified Germany that he had for so long sought to create. At the same time the French assembly, meeting in Bordeaux, put an end to the second empire of Napoleon III and created the Third Republic. Since the French had earlier withdrawn their garrison from Rome to protect France, Pius IX (who had just established the doctrine of Papal Infallibility at the Vatican Council) was no longer able to prevent the Italian annexation of Rome, which completed the unification of Italy. So by 1871 Germany, France, and Italy had acquired the frontiers and constitutions which were to last until 1914.

Elsewhere in Europe the troubles in the Balkans that were to lead to the First World War were beginning to fester, with a three-way struggle between Turkey, Austria-Hungary, and Serbia for control of Bosnia-Herzegovenia and Macedonia – regions whose complex history and divided loyalties have returned to haunt us. Not far in the background, of course, were the Russians, but by the early 1870s they had troubles of their own. Alexander II had started the previous decade by emancipating the serfs in 1861, but by 1870 it was clear that his will to reform had ceased and repression set in, exacerbated by the activities of the socialists and anarchists. Britain, of course, tried to keep clear of the conflicts in continental Europe. But conflict was stirring at home: discontent with British rule in Ireland led to the foundation in 1870 of the association to restore Home Rule. The British government, however, was more concerned to reinforce and extend its overseas possessions, one part of which was converted into an empire when Queen Victoria accepted Disraeli's invitation to become Empress of India in 1876.

This British imperialism was not exceptional. In 1871 the journalist Henry Stanley had famously greeted the missonary David Livingstone at Ujiji on the shore of Lake Tanganyika; soon the European exploration of central Africa was complete, and the scramble for Africa followed, with Britain, France, Belgium, Portugal, and Germany dividing up the continent at the Conference of Berlin (1884–5). The period this volume covers, 1870 to 1945, is indeed that of the high noon of European imperialism, which involved not only overseas empires but also massive European emigration at the expense of native peoples across North and South America, Australia, and New Zealand.

Turning now away from political history to natural science, two of the fundamental ideas of twentieth-century science began their long course of development at this time. In 1873 Clark Maxwell published his *Treatise on Electricity and Magnetism*, thereby providing the theory of electro-magnetism that was to guide the development of physics for the next fifty years. The most influential scientific idea of the nineteenth century, however, had been Charles Darwin's thesis of the evolution of species by natural selection. Darwin had presented this thesis in *The Origin of Species* (1859); but debate on the subject persisted into the 1870s when Darwin published his book *The Descent of Man* (1871). Nonetheless, by this time, thanks to the writings of Herbert Spencer and others, the general conception of evolutionary progress had gained currency and was being applied across a wide field, as in Edward Tylor's work in anthropology (*Primitive Culture* 1871) and in Engels's judgement that in *Capital* (vol. I, 1867) Marx had achieved for the study of society what Darwin had achieved in biology. What was not noticed at the time, however, was the publication in 1869 of Gregor Mendel's 'gene' theory of the inheritance of characteristics, based on his work on the crossing of different types of pea. This was the first detailed study to propose and substantiate a system for inheritance which confirmed Darwin's thesis, and, when Mendel's work was discovered in 1900, it was recognised to have laid the foundation of twentieth-century genetics.

The latter part of the nineteenth century was in fact a period of rapid technological change rather than one of theoretical discoveries. Many devices upon which we still rely were introduced – the typewriter was invented in 1867 and mass production by Remington with the familiar 'qwerty' keyboard followed in the 1870s; Alexander Graham Bell patented the telephone in 1876, and the following year Thomas Edison patented the first phonograph, or record player. Most important developments involved electricity in one way or another, which had become more readily available thanks to the development by Siemens in 1867 of large-scale generating equipment. Swan's invention of the light bulb in 1860 was turned into a commercial product by Edison in 1879, enabling him to construct the first public lighting system in New York in 1881. Although steam locomotives were familiar by 1870, urban transport was transformed during the 1870s by another Siemens invention, the electric motor, which was rapidly applied in tramway systems and underground railways. Finally, the curse of modern life, the internal combustion engine, was soon to appear: Daimler invented the petrol engine in 1883 and, with Benz, put it on wheels to create the first motor vehicle with a petrol engine in 1885.

While technology was creating in the 1870s much of the physical structure of the urban world of the next century, many of the familiar institutions of the twentieth century were also taking shape, such as the limited liability company and the trades union movement. Even the English Football Assocation, the first in the world, has its origins at this time: it was founded in 1867, with the FA Cup first competed for in 1871. Meanwhile composers, writers, and artists were exploring the limits of traditional forms. In Vienna Brahms began his symphonies, in St Petersburg Tchaikovsky created his ballets, and in Bayreuth Wagner performed his Ring cycle (which was written earlier) in his special new theatre. The novel reached its peak with masterpieces such as Tolstoy's *War and Peace* (1869) and George Eliot's *Middlemarch* (1872), while on the stage Ibsen's dramas broke new ground, exploring themes of social disintegration and personal despair. Despite the tragedy of the Paris Commune of 1871, the great centre of artistic innovation at this time was Paris: the poetry of Mallarmé, Rimbaud, and Verlaine inspired the 'symbolist' movement while the paintings of Monet and others launched the 'impressionist' movement (the term was first applied in 1874, supposedly as a criticism, to one of Monet's paintings).

Several of the great literary works of the period explored the position of women (e.g. *Middlemarch* and Ibsen's *The Doll's House*). J. S. Mill's attempt in

1866 to achieve votes for women in Britain failed, and in Britain, as elsewhere, this question was largely set aside until the suffragette movement took up the fight at the beginning of the twentieth century. But in other areas of life women did begin to make some headway in the 1870s, for example, in the legal and medical professions. Most notably, in North America and across Europe university education was opened up to women, generally in separate institutions set up alongside established universities (as at Cambridge and Oxford). This change was part of a massive expansion of higher education during the 1870s. The model adopted across the world was that of the German university. In his famous *Addresses to the German Nation* of 1807–8, following the defeat of Prussia by Napoleon, Fichte had identified the university as the institution which represented all that was best about the German nation; and in the decades that followed most German states had taken pride in encouraging the development of universities in which research was conducted in an atmosphere of remarkable academic freedom (*Lehrfreiheit*). The result was that by the 1870s Germany contained much the best universities in the world. Students from all over the world (but especially from the USA) travelled to Germany to engage in advanced studies, and when they returned home, it was the German model that they sought to replicate.

Fichte had, not surprisingly, placed the study of philosophy at the heart of his idealised German university, and even if the German universities of the 1870s did not entirely fulfil this ideal, the study of philosophy did enjoy a status there which it did not possess elsewhere. There were certainly more professors of philosophy in Germany in 1870 than anywhere else in the world, and perhaps more even than everywhere else put together (although it is not easy to gather the evidence to test this hypothesis). So, not surprisingly, it was to Germany (and Austria) that students of philosophy came, to study with Lotze in Göttingen, Cohen in Marburg, Brentano in Vienna, Wundt in Leipzig, and so on; and from Germany they returned, familiar not just with the latest varieties of German idealism, but also with the positivism of Haeckel and Mach, with Brentano's conception of the distinctive intentionality of psychological phenomena, or with Wundt's conception of a scientific psychology.

Thus much of the work discussed in the first part of this book has its roots in German philosophy. But, of course, once established outside Germany, the academic study of philosophy quickly built up local institutions, and one way to track the development of the subject during the last half of the nineteenth century is through the growth across the world of distinctively philosophical journals (unlike, say, the *Westminster Review*). Not surprisingly, the three oldest philosophical journals are all German, of which one, *Ratio* (founded in 1847) still survives (the others were *Zeitschrift für Philosophie und philosophische Kritik*

(1837–1918) and *Zeitschrift für Philosophie und Pädagogik* (1861–1914)). Then comes the first journal in English, the *Journal of Speculative Philosophy*, which was published in St Louis from 1867 until 1893. This was followed in 1868 by two journals which still survive, *Archiv für Geschichte der Philosophie* and the oldest journal in French (though published in Lausanne), *Revue de théologie et de philosophie*, and soon after in 1870 by the first Italian journal, *Rivista di filosofia*. In 1876, two famous journals commenced publication: *Mind* and *Revue Philosophique*. There is then a gap until nearly 1890, when a host of familiar names appeared – *The Monist* (1888), *Ethics* (1890), *The Philosophical Review* (1892), *Revue de métaphysique et morale* (1893), *Revue Philosophique de Louvain* (1894), *Kant-Studien* (1896). From its base within the German university system, the study of philosophy was by 1900 spreading out across the world.

Part I

1870–1914

SECTION ONE

POSITIVISM, IDEALISM, AND PRAGMATISM

POSITIVIST THOUGHT IN THE NINETEENTH CENTURY

ROM HARRÉ

INTRODUCTION

The positivist impulse, to accept only what is certain and to reject anything in any degree speculative, from its earliest intimations in classical Greece to its most recent revival in contemporary anti-realist philosophy of science, expresses itself in two main ways. It appears as a doctrine about the limits of what human beings can legitimately claim to know, displayed as an austere epistemological attitude. This leads to a foundationalism according to which only what is immediately given by the senses can be known for certain. It also appears as a doctrine about what can legitimately be taken to exist, displayed as an austere ontological attitude. This leads to a scepticism about the existence of unobservables of all sorts, from God to the material substance thought by many philosophers and scientists to account for common experience. Positivism is at root driven by an impulse, attitude, or frame of mind, which expresses itself in a variety of philosophical theses and arguments. That positivistic arguments and analyses are found convincing has perhaps more to do with an attitude of austerity and scepticism, than with their intrinsic worth. Always ready to wield Ockham's Razor against the proliferation of kinds of entities which people are tempted to believe in, positivists could be said to hold that it is better to accept less than one perhaps could, for fear of believing more than perhaps one should.

The topic of this chapter, the rise of positivism in the nineteenth century, picks out just one of the high points of a repeated cycle of waxing and waning enthusiasm for positivist austerity. Harsher and more relaxed attitudes to what one should reasonably believe have come and gone since antiquity. In the sixteenth century the debates about astronomy turned on an opposition between positivism and realism in science. Should one believe in the reality of the heliocentric theory or was it just a convenient calculating device for predicting the comings and goings of 'lights in the sky'? Considerations rather like those canvassed in the contemporary controversies in philosophy of science were advanced by the protagonists of each position, such as the positivist Osiander and the realist Kepler. In the eighteenth century the positivist impulse led some authors, especially Berkeley, to a kind of idealism, at least with respect to our knowledge of the material world. Only that which was perceptible should be held to exist. But in the nineteenth century positivism stood in opposition to idealism, yet in paradoxical ways. Its most powerful and influential nineteenth-century advocate, Ernst Mach, seemed to share a great deal with Berkeley. Both thought that the human senses provided not only the only proper grounding for claims about material reality, but also exhausted the realm of the real. Berkeley's hypothesis of a spiritual, that is, non-material, power to account for what people experience, might have been anathema to Mach, but was revived by another influential nineteenth-century adherent to the positivist attitude, Herbert Spencer.

For expository purposes one can divide the dramatis personae of the philosophical advocacy of positivism into three national groups. In Germany a form of positivism developed among physical scientists, consciously in opposition to the prevailing idealism of German philosophy. To some extent these overtly academic debates reflected important disputes about the hegemony of disciplines in the German universities. The positivist philosophers, such as Mach, were professional scientists. For them such Hegelian definitions as 'This *vanishing* and *self-generation* of space in time and time in space, a process in which time posits itself spatially as *place*, but in which place too, as indifferent spatiality, is immediately posited as temporal: this is *Motion*' (Hegel 1830 [1970]: 41) were not far short of insulting. In France the positivists were part of the anti-clerical movement which was expressed in the revolution of the late eighteenth century. Auguste Comte formulated positivism in the context of a history of the emancipation of the intellect from the superstition and myth he found in the institutionalised religion of his time. The scientific roots of French positivism were in the human sciences. In England the authors who advocated and defended something like positivism were united only by their positions in certain methodological controversies in the philosophy of science. William Whewell's Kantian defence of the priority of concepts over facts was famously disputed by J. S. Mill in a defence of a strong empiricism which had affinities to Comtian thought, and seemed to anticipate much that was argued for by the German physicists of the last half of the century. But there was no political commonality among English positivists. Mill was a man of the left, while Pearson held views that in our times would have been thought close to fascism.

In the nineteenth century the positivist attitude appeared first in France (Comte's *Cours de Philosophie Positive* began to be published in 1830), then in England (Mill's *A System of Logic* appeared in 1843) and finally in Germany

(Mach's *Science of Mechanics* appeared in 1883). Not surprisingly it was the writings of Mach that, in hindsight, can be seen as having the most influence in the twentieth century.

POSITIVISM IN FRANCE: REINVENTING MORALITY IN A SECULAR WORLD

While there is no doubt that French positivism grew out of the critical philosophies and anti-clerical sentiments of the eighteenth century (Comte himself professed Saint Simon as his mentor), as Charlton (1959) points out in his comprehensive study of French thought in the middle of the century, those we might lump together as positivists, in their reliance on the senses as the exclusive sources of knowledge, held rather diverse views on how moral and political principles were to be created to replace those which their criticisms of religion would have eliminated. Yet, unlike the arrogant 'puritanical' reductionism of Ernst Mach, most acknowledged the existence of irresolvable mysteries, *inconnaissables*, and all recognised the difficulties of constructing a plausible and satisfying positivist ethics.

Auguste Comte (1798–1857), very much in the manner of his times, built his philosophy on the idea of a three-phase development of ways of understanding. Rather than describe these phases or styles as stages, he prefers to call them states or attitudes of mind, since he saw around him examples of people thinking in all three of the main ways he discusses. In the 'theological state of mind' a person looks for explanations in terms of the 'continuous and arbitrary actions of supernatural agents' (Comte 1830–42 [1864]: 5). The next, more advanced, state of mind is only a modification of the first, replacing supernatural agents by 'abstract forces . . . capable of giving rise by themselves to all the phenomena observed' (p. 5). In the third or positive state the human mind 'endeavours now to discover by a well-combined use of reasoning and observation, the actual *laws* of phenomena . . . that is to say, their invariable relations of succession and likeness'.

In a striking passage (Comte 1830–42 [1864]: I, 23) Comte slips from a repudiation of the search for first or final causes to a rejection of an interest in causes at all: 'we do not pretend to explain the real causes of phenomena, as this would merely throw the difficulty further back' (p. 23). All that Newton's Law of Gravity can do is to show us a great variety of phenomena as 'only a single fact looked at from different points of view . . . the weight of a body at the earth's surface' (p. 26). So stringent was Comte's empiricism that he famously and unwisely chose the chemical composition of the stars as a prime example of unattainable knowledge.

A historian would see much of Hume in Comte's writings on the positive philosophy when applied to the natural sciences. But on psychology Comte was quite opposed to the Humean project of psychology as the study of the relations of ideas. He denied that we 'can discover the fundamental laws of the human mind, by contemplating it in itself'. The way forward was the 'physiological study of our intellectual organs'. French positivism was fiercely materialist. Not only were explanations to be reduced to laws of correlation of phenomena, but the phenomena too were exclusively material.

The laws of society ought to be discoverable by exactly the same methods as those by which the laws of material nature had been arrived at. It should be possible to devise a scientific sociology. By the four methods of Observation, Experiment, Comparison, and History we could arrive at laws of society without positing any unobservable causes. But these too will only be available to those whose 'state of mind' has passed from the theological through the metaphysical to the positive, seeking only correlations among social phenomena. Since not everyone can aspire to this degree of perfection Comte advocated the fabrication of a suitable religion to take the place of superstitious faiths of the time. But how was this to engender a morality? As Charlton (1959: 49) puts it: how can one be a positivist and yet provide an 'objective, authoritative ethical system'? If we are confined to phenomena how can we make the passage to such a system? From whence comes an 'ought' from a world of 'is'? Progress, according to the threefold scheme of 'states of mind', must pass from the theological to the positive, and this will of itself engender the new social morality. In the positive state of mind the true decency and generosity of human nature will come to dominate social relations. This is the 'law of progress'. Sociology is like a medicine for the ills of the state, letting natural health shine through. Since the main bar to progress is the persistence of primitive attitudes of mind, the cure is at hand – change the attitudes. But Comte certainly respected the role that religion had had in supporting morality, and he published a catechism for those who would 'take instruction' in the new religion (Comte 1852).

The next generation of positivistically oriented philosophers in France is typified by Hippolyte Taine (1828–93). In his own time Taine was famous, perhaps one could say notorious, for his attack upon the characters and the motives of the main figures of the French Revolution. His philosophical writings were also uncompromisingly critical of received opinion, in particular on those aspects of human life where spiritual or non-material entities and processes had been given a central role. Along with his criticisms of the revolutionaries went a reductionist treatment of moral qualities. In his *D'Intelligence* (1870) he set out an account of those aspects of human life that had been assigned to a mental substance, especially by Descartes, wholly in terms of the contents of conscious experience. He declared that both the 'self' (*le moi*) and material 'substance' were illusions. 'There is nothing of reality in the self but a stream of events' (quoted in Charlton 1959: 137). His metaphysical austerity is very much in the Comtian style. 'All reality', he declared, 'is perceived experientially by man'.

But his critical account of Mill's philosophy, *Le positivisme Anglais* (Taine 1864), shows how much his positivism differed from the strictly empiricist 'archetype', according to which natural regularities might have been otherwise, and hence their expression in empirical generalisations must be contingent. Causality was not a natural necessity, but merely a psychological product of the constant experience of experiential regularities. However, according to Taine, laws of nature and of psychology were indeed discovered by abstraction from catalogues of facts, but they were necessary causal truths. This allies him with the 'Kantians' like Whewell and Helmholtz, both of whom played important parts in the English and German versions of positivism.

In applying his positivist psychology, Taine was especially critical of the idea that works of art were the product of a special faculty, an individual spiritual teleology, and in his *Philosophie de l'art* (1865) he offered a systematic account of artistic excellence in the same manner as he had earlier dealt with other intellectual, mental, and moral qualities of human beings. The circumstances, not the artist, were responsible for the production of works of art. In the first place a work of art was an imitation of its model, but not too much. To understand a work of art 'it is necessary that it represents exactly the general spirit and customs (*moeurs*) of the time at which it appears' (Taine 1865: 7). He remarks that these constitute the primitive cause that determines all the rest. But there are secondary conditions, and these amount to the existence of a cultivated public who can recognise the work as according with the spirit of the times. Furthermore a work of art expressing a certain emotion will affect only those who have already experienced such an emotion. Culture is like the geographical conditions that determine what sorts of plants will grow in a certain place and time. This account is worth a fairly detailed exposition since it brings out another strand in positivist thought, the tendency to look for the sources of psychological phenomena in the environment rather than in the workings of an individual mind.

In summary, we can see that French positivism was anti-theoretical, strongly empiricist in the sense that the only legitimate source of knowledge was human sensory experience. However, the writings of Comte and Taine illustrate the extent to which French philosophers of the period were well aware that the sensationalism and environmentalism that they favoured in psychology left questions of great moment still unanswered. Above all they pondered the question 'How to live?'

POSITIVISM IN ENGLAND: WHAT IS SCIENTIFIC KNOWLEDGE?

The positivist quest for a firm basis for knowledge led back always to what could be discerned by the use of the five senses. Yet data derived in this fundamental way were local and particular. The known laws of nature and the anticipated laws of human thought and social action were evidently universal and general in scope. How could the one be related to the other? Two answers had been proposed in the late eighteenth century. According to Hume the generalisation of patterns of concomitance in experience were at best guides to practical action, but, from the limited evidence available, they could not be certified as necessary truths. According to Kant the basic laws of nature were synthetic a priori propositions expressing the forms within which human experience had to be framed. Comte took the Humean stance while Taine's views were Kantian. The same opposition characterised English philosophy of science in the nineteenth century.

John Stuart Mill (1806–73) published his *System of Logic* in 1843. Its influence was immediate and long lasting. It became a standard textbook in the universities and was generally taken to be a definitive account of scientific method for the rest of the century. In Book III Mill presented a set of principles by the use of which reliable knowledge of material causes could be arrived at. Mill's philosophical outlook owed a great deal to his youthful enthusiasm for the ideas of Saint Simon and, from these, to the writings of Comte. The principles upon which Mill proposed to found an Inductive Logic, to set alongside Deductive Logic as a method of proof for the empirical sciences, are the famous Canons of Induction. Clearly influenced by Bacon's *Novum Organon* (1620), Mill based his system on the distinction between ephemeral and permanent causes (Mill 1843 [1862: 258]). Finding a regular concomitance between paired types of events gives us a hint that the one might be the cause or part of the cause of the other. This hint is confirmed, usually by deliberate experiment, if it is found that in the absence of the putative cause no event of the correlated type occurs. For permanent causes like gravity one must look to see if variations in the one are correlated (or anti-correlated) with variations in the other. Mill describes his Canons as 'the only possible modes of experimental enquiry – of direct induction *a posteriori*, as distinguished from deduction' (Mill 1843 [1862: 266]). Not only were the laws of physics and chemistry arrived at by induction, but so were the laws of arithmetic and geometry. The laws of logic were the laws of thought. This was a thoroughgoing empiricism. To the objection that all this was based on data that were local in both space and time Mill answered that the Uniformity of Nature upon which the formal validity of his 'inductions' depended was itself a 'complex fact' arrived at by the same methods (Mill 1843 [1862: 206]), an application of the 'boot-strap principle'.

The dominant figure in British philosophy of science at the time Mill published his *System of Logic* was William Whewell, Master of Trinity College, Cambridge, friend and mentor of Michael Faraday, and of whom it was said 'his foible was omniscience'. Whewell had argued, with a multitude of examples, that facts could only be discovered by the application of prior hypotheses to inchoate experience. Such hypotheses were initially relative to their immediate applications, but refined as a kind of dialectic between ideas and facts unfolded through the pursuit of experimental programmes, driven by the newly revised ideas (Whewell 1847: I, 42). Hence, Whewell declared, Mill's four methods or canons were not and need not be employed in the process of discovery.

Mill, granting that his four methods might not be methods of discovery, insisted that they were the indispensable methods of proof. For Whewell new facts brought forth new hypotheses leading to a gradual refinement of hypotheses. For Mill something like proof was called for. According to Mill it is modes of thought that produce errors. 'Hence it is that, while the thoughts of mankind have on many subjects worked themselves practically right, the thinking power remains as weak as ever . . . in what relates to the invisible world . . . and to the planetary regions, men of the greatest scientific achievement argue as pitiably as the merest ignoramus' (Mill 1843 [1862: 285]). Of course what they need is Mill's Canons, a strict method of proof. 'The business of Inductive Logic is to provide rules and models . . . to which, if inductive arguments conform, those arguments are conclusive, and not otherwise' (Mill 1843 [1862: 283]).

It seems that Mill was not seriously troubled by the problem that had been much in the minds of the French philosophers of the positivist frame of mind: namely, how is it that from a basis of the sensations of individual human beings, we, those human beings collectively, arrive at a common material world, a commonality obvious in even the simplest activities that we engage in, individually and collectively? The methods Mill advocated were not techniques for bridging the gap between sensation and reality, but for bridging the gap between local and general facts about that common world.

Despite the success of Mill's point of view with many scientists, and the popularity of a strict empiricism with chemists, many of whom rejected the reality of chemical atoms, the necessity for some a priori principles in science was still felt by some positivists, in particular Karl Pearson (1857–1936). Pearson virtually created the modern mathematical science of statistics. His enthusiasm for it led him into both philosophy of science and politics. In the latter he became the academic leader of the eugenics movement. From his eponymous Galtonian chair in the University of London he advocated the state control of human

breeding. In philosophy of science his rejection of the idea of any real unifor-
mities behind observable variations led him to a kind of positivism. The idea
of natural homogeneities is a metaphysical conceit. Pearsonian statistical curves
were mental constructs summing up the data and no uniform underlying causes
could be inferred from them. His book, *The Grammar of Science* (Pearson 1892),
coming decades after Mill's empiricism, served to boost the positivistic point
of view against the rising tide of British idealism. Since all we have are simple
sensory experiences, how could the complex material world, as we perceive it
and as the natural sciences seem to reveal it, be possible objects of a common
discourse? Here again is the same problem that troubled the French positivists.
Pearson resorted to a Kantian solution.

such an [external] object [for example a blackboard] must be recognised as largely constructed by ourselves; we add to a greater or lesser store of immediate sense-impressions
an associated group of stored sense-impressions. (Pearson 1892: 41)

But the things-in-themselves which the sense-impressions symbolise, the 'reality' as the
metaphysicians wish to call it, at the other end of the [sensory] nerve, remain unknown
and unknowable. (Pearson 1892: 63)

The fact that the human reflective faculty is able to express in mental formulas the routine
of perceptions may be due to this routine being a product of the perceptive faculty itself.
(Pearson 1892: 112)

Indeed Pearson's views were described by Peirce (1892) as 'Kantian nominalism'.
The laws of nature were not just generalisations or abstractions from catalogues
of simple experiential facts. They were 'products of the perceptive faculty'. 'The
logic man finds in the universe', said Pearson, 'is nothing but the reflection of his
own reasoning faculty.' There is no knowable reality (in both senses of 'know',
savoir and *connaître*) other than the sensations of the individual consciousness. The
motivation for science as the abstraction of statistical regularities is 'economy
of thought'. There was a shared common world only because each mind was
furnished with the same a priori principles.

   The influence of Hume can surely be discerned in Pearson's remark that 'what
I term "myself" is only a small subdivision of the vast world of sense-impressions'
(Pearson 1892: 66). Significantly Pearson reproduced Mach's famous drawing of
his own field of vision, looking down his lounging body to his feet. It is not
surprising that Pearson remarked that matter, force, and action at a distance 'do
not express real problems of the phenomenal world'.

POSITIVISM IN GERMANY: PHYSICISTS AS PHILOSOPHERS

In the German story we have a grand opposition between claims to knowledge
based on scientific research, positive science, and what were seen as not much

short of mystery mongerings, claims to knowledge based on Neo-Kantian philo-sophical speculation. Here we have German positivism in conflict with German idealism. But within the German-speaking scientific community another di-vision appeared. On the one hand were those scientists who adopted a strong reductive empiricism, such as Mach, and on the other those who took the-ory to be a source of reliable knowledge, as good as or better than experiment and observation, physicists such as Hertz and Boltzmann. Here we have a more tightly defined kind of positivism in opposition to scientific realism. To make the 'internalist' history of the movement even more complicated one of the major figures, Herman Helmholtz (1821–94), developed a strongly Kantian account not only of the natural sciences, but also of the very possibility of perception. But at the same time, and almost within the same breath, he eschewed any projection of the conceptual basis of physics onto the material world.

The breadth of Helmholtz's contributions to science is astonishing (Turner 1980). He contributed not only to the physiology of both visual and auditory perception, but also to hydrodynamics and to electromagnetism. He was sceptical of metaphysics and committed to a theory of science according to which the mathematical generalisation of empirical observations and experimental results was the ultimate aim of research. Laws of nature were summaries of facts and their utility was practical. So far he would seem to have been more or less of the same opinion as Mach and Mill. But his neurophysiological work, developing Müller's law of specific energies – that it was the perceptual organ that determined how a stimulus would be experienced – was strongly Kantian. Indeed, he claimed that his work on the neurophysiology of perception confirmed Kant's general thesis as to priority of concepts, in particular the concept of causality. The causal order in experience was imposed by the human mind. His empiricism was very unlike that of Mill. Indeed, had he been asked, he would probably have sided with Whewell in the great controversy.

Helmholtz was well aware of the problem that has dogged positivism in all its various manifestations. If the ultimate source of reliable knowledge is imme-diate sensory experience of individual people, how can it give rise to impersonal knowledge of the kind the natural sciences seem to provide? Helmholtz's solution invoked the a priori law of causality. Everyone believes that external objects are the cause of our perceptions. Why? The experiential ground is that they change without our volition. But we do not pause, as it were, and try to work out why this might be so. Rather we make instantaneous 'unconscious inferences' (*unbewusste Schlusse*) so that our sensory experience is taken to be of a real, material world. These inferences are driven by the a priori law of causality. But, unlike Kant, Helmholtz held that space and time, as empirical givens, were constructions, the result of unconscious inferences under the influence of the law of causality of the same sort that gave us material things.

Of all the positivistically inclined writers of the nineteenth century there is
no doubt that Ernst Mach (1838–1916) was the most influential on subsequent
generations of philosophers and scientists. His three most influential works, *The
Science of Mechanics* (1883), *The Analysis of Sensations* (5th edition, 1906) and
Popular Scientific Lectures (1894) were widely read, quickly translated, and often
quoted in the decades that followed. Many of the most characteristic theses of
the Logical positivists of the Vienna Circle can be found explicitly formulated
in Mach's writings.

Mach's positivism did not emerge from philosophical reflections on epistemology, but from his long-running programme to rework the foundations of
physics in such a way as to eliminate the unobservable domain from the ontology
of the natural sciences, and particularly to eliminate any traces of reference to
absolutes. He described his project very clearly:

My definition [of 'mass'] is the outcome of an endeavour to establish the interdependence
of phenomena and to remove all metaphysical obscurity, without accomplishing on this
account less than other definitions have done. (Mach 1883 [1893: 267])

His method was simple. He set out to show that all concepts in physics that
purported to refer to unobservable properties, entities, or relations, including
'quantity of electricity' and 'temperature', could be defined in terms of observable properties of material set-ups, such as the mutual accelerations of visible
and tangible bodies. Newtonian mass, as the quantity of matter in a body, was
not only an absolute, but also, in Mach's terms, metaphysical since unobservable.

Perhaps his best known 'reduction' of absolutes is his criticism of Newton's
famous thought experiments – the rotating globes and the spinning bucket –
which seemed to show that there could be an experimental proof of the existence
of absolute space and time. The arguments turned on the principle that if the
relevant *concept* can be parsed out of the discourse then that to which it seems to
refer is redundant. The concept of 'mass' can be eliminated from the discourse
of mechanics, so mass as quantity of matter can be dropped from our ontology.
Similarly with absolute space and time. It is a mistake, so he claimed, to substitute
a 'mechanical mythology' for the 'old . . . metaphysical scheme'. 'The atom must
remain a tool for representing phenomena, like the functions of mathematics'
(Mach 1894: 205).

Summing up his point of view, Mach claimed that the laws of nature were
nothing but devices for 'the communication of scientific knowledge, that is a
mimetic reproduction of facts in thought, the object of which is to replace and
save the trouble of new experience' (Mach 1894: 192).

But what were the phenomena, the facts? Examining a 'province of facts'
'we discover the simple permanent elements of the mosaic' (Mach 1984: 194).

According to Mach the only positive knowledge one can have is knowledge of one's own sensations. How does this escape a charge of solipsism? This leads him to a strongly reductive account of material objects:

> In mentally separating a body from the changeable environment in which it moves what we really do is to extricate a group of sensations on which our thoughts are fastened and which is of relatively greater stability than the others, from the stream of our sensations . . . It would be better to say that bodies or things are compendious mental symbols for groups of sensations – symbols that do not exist outside of thought. (Mach 1894: 200)

This sounds very much like subjectivism. Mach's escape route from the threat of solipsism is via the concept of uniform 'elements'. Only when considered 'in connection and relation to one's own body' are elements sensations. Considered in relation to each other they are properties of material things. But things are not substances. Substance words simply name groups of elements that remain together in experience.

A parallel path was taken by Richard Avenarius (1843–96). His work added little to the core of Machian positivism. However he did influence one important 'philosopher-king' of the twentieth century, V. I. Lenin. Avenarius introduced the term 'empirio-criticism' to describe his version of positivism and it was against that that Lenin wrote his most important philosophical tract in support of his pragmatist scientific realism (Lenin 1920). Like Mach, Avenarius restricted knowledge to 'pure experience', saw scientific method as driven by the need for economy of thought and argued for the complete elimination of metaphysical categories. He phrased this as a stricture on the process of 'introjection' – the imposition of metaphysics on to experience – which was just the very thing that Helmholtz had required in order to make sense of human experience, of our universal conviction that there was a material world which was other than our individual experiences. Despite the rejection of introjection, Avenarius too needed to find a solution to the threat of solipsism. His 'assumption' was less metaphysical than that of Helmholtz but served the same purpose. Each human being assumed that he or she was confronted by a material world, and that there were other human beings who were making assertions about it.

Here the path from the rejection of German idealism to an extreme anti-theoretical stance to the physical sciences reaches its logical terminus. But there were important dissenting voices in the German-speaking scientific establishment to this slide. Perhaps the two most prominent were Heinrich Hertz and Ludwig Boltzmann.

Heinrich Hertz (1857–94) is best known to philosophers for the preface to his *The Principles of Mechanics* (1894). Adopting an empiricist approach to metaphysics, Hertz was not at all averse to entertaining hypotheses about unobservable realms of the natural world, nor to devising a methodology by the use of which such hypotheses might be assessed for their verisimilitude. He was also the inventor, at least for the physical sciences, of the later-to-be-famous 'picture theory of meaning'. According to Hertz, laws of nature were pictures (*Bilden*) of facts, and it was this that endowed them with meaning. The science of mechanics could be reduced to the laws of interaction of elementary masses. However, when the totality of observable masses did not allow for the creation of an adequate picture, physicists were entitled to add more elementary masses to their scheme to enrich their picture of nature until it was adequate to the laws of phenomena. In the terminology of twentieth-century philosophy of science, physicists were entitled to create realistic models of aspects of reality that were unobservable:

We become convinced that the manifold of the actual universe must be greater than the manifold of the universe which is directly revealed to us by the senses. (Hertz 1894 [1899]: 25)

Hertz and Mach were roughly contemporaries, but their ways of realising the anti-idealist strand in German thought was very different. Hertz's early death from an infected tooth deprived the German scientific community of an advocate of a 'positivism' which stood in sharp opposition to Machian anti-realism. The contrast between the two was well summed up by Helmholtz in his preface to Hertz's *Principles of Mechanics* (p. xx). Helmholtz says:

For my part, I must admit that I have adhered to the latter (Machian) mode of representation [of phenomena] and have felt safe in so doing; yet I have no essential objections to raise against a method [modelling unobservable states of nature] which has been adopted by three physicists [Kelvin, Maxwell, and Hertz] of such renown.

Both Mach and Ostwald (the most influential chemist of the era) were opponents of realist interpretations of atomic theories in the physical sciences. Though both later abandoned their resistance Boltzmann felt himself to have been personally victimised by the anti-atomism of these influential men. Ludwig Boltzmann (1844–1906), along with James Clark Maxwell, had pushed forward the schematic molecular theories of the behaviour of gases that had been proposed in the late eighteenth century, mainly by mathematical analyses of the possible behaviour of swarms of molecules, relatively elementary bodies great numbers of which were the constituents of gases. Did the overwhelming power of the mathematically developed molecular theory to explain the behaviour of gases justify a belief in the existence of unobservable molecules? A strict Machian would have to say that it did not. A strict Hertzian would have to say that it did. Like Hertz, Boltzmann believed that it was both scientifically fruitful and philosophically respectable to make claims about unobservable states and processes in the material world, on the basis of the explanatory power that hypotheses of this sort gave to the mathematical abstractions from observations and experiments. This attitude did not meet with the approval of the Machian physicists of the Austrian scientific establishment. Boltzmann felt himself, rightly or wrongly, to have been persecuted by the hard-line positivists (Blackmore 1995).

The German physicist-philosophers, while insisting on a strictly empiricist account of the sources of knowledge, were not agreed on the ultimate scope of the materialist view of the world. The positivism of Mach and Avenarius restricted the ontology of physics to persisting clusters of sensations. The scientific realism of Hertz and Boltzmann advanced that ontology into a reality given to experience only in its effects.

BIOLOGISTS AS PHILOSOPHERS: THE NATURE OF LIFE AND THE REINVENTION OF MORALITY

If one thinks of philosophy in the broader sense, reflections on the Nature and Destiny of Man must surely count amongst its proper tasks. Many Victorian scientists, usually actively engaged in research projects in biology, wrote very influential works on these larger themes. In Germany, as Passmore (1957: 31) puts it, philosophically minded biologists like Haeckel, quite as much as the physicists discussed above, stood in opposition to the 'official philosophy' of the German universities, which was 'dedicated to the defence of "the spiritual life" against the inroads of natural science and of the state against radical reform'. This is something of an exaggeration. In Paulsen's (1893 [1895]) account of the German universities he remarks on the unfettered academic freedom of lecturing and research though, he concedes, in the first half of the nineteenth century 'interference was sometimes practised [by the state]; for instance about 1820 in favour of Hegelian philosophy, about 1840 against it'. In England the opposition between established religion and scientific radicalism was more muted. Most scientists, even Darwin himself, went no further than declarations of agnosticism. It is well to remember that most of the writers of the pro-science, positivist persuasion were publicists as much as they were philosophers in their commentaries on and discussions of scientific method.

Two issues commanded attention. On the matter of the origins of life and in particular the origins of the human race, Darwin and other biologists, particularly Thomas Henry Huxley, seemed to have established that the existence of human beings had a naturalistic explanation and required no special creation.

Among physiologists the dominant opinion, especially stemming from Germany, was equally uncompromising. The processes of life were at root 'mechanical' and required no special life force to explain them.

Just as positivism displayed a spectrum of views so too did the naturalistic philosophy of the biologists and those influenced by them. On the key question of the grounds of scientific knowledge, Huxley (1863) argued not only that consciousness was not a material property of the human organism but that one was forced to the epistemological conclusion that 'our one certainty was the existence of the mental world'. How this seemingly 'idealist' principle was to be reconciled with the generally materialist line of scientific thought Huxley never revealed. Huxley had published a book on Hume's philosophy. He seems to have interpreted Hume's sensory impressions as mental. Ernst Haeckel (1834–1919), on the other hand, had no hesitation in taking a strongly monistic position. The universe displays a development towards the complexity and sophistication of human life, but the whole many-layered and hierarchical reality is based firmly on nothing but the 'mechanics of atoms' (Haeckel 1899). He was also uncompromisingly against the agnosticism popular in England. There is no place for God in the story of the origins of the human race (Haeckel 1874 [1905]). Evolution is a 'mathematical necessity of nature'. Haeckel was the first to formulate the famous aphorism 'Ontogeny [individual development] is a recapitulation of phylogeny [the history of the species].' He based his arguments for an evolutionary origin for human beings on a detailed comparison between stages in the development of the human embryo and the anatomy of earlier life forms (Haeckel 1874 [1905]: 2). Haeckel's book on the evolution of the human race caused an uproar in Germany, at least as great as Darwin's *Origin of Species* had raised in England. It was described by one commentator as 'a blot on the escutcheon of Germany'.

At least in the popular mind, the most influential philosopher of the nineteenth century in England, and in the United States, was not J. S. Mill, but Herbert Spencer. His books, mostly published as sections of his enormous *System of Synthetic Philosophy* published in eight volumes between 1862 and 1896, sold tens of thousands of copies. His influence extended into political philosophy (Social Darwinism) and into education. He too drew his inspiration from biology, and in particular the general idea of evolution. This was not Darwin's cautiously phrased conception of development without a teleology of ascending value. Spencer applied the idea of development, in the sense of improvement, to every aspect of the universe, inorganic and organic, cosmic and local.

But it was a development that was wholly material. Volume II of the *System*, devoted to the Principles of Biology, begins with a firm statement of materialism.

Organic bodies consist almost wholly of four elements: oxygen, nitrogen, hydrogen, and carbon. Evolution, in biology as elsewhere in the natural order, is just the redistribution of Matter and Motion. Philosophy, he thought, sought the most general principles of science, and the principle or law of evolution was the most general of these. This law states that there is constant change 'from a [relatively] indefinite, incoherent homogeneity to a [relatively] definite, coherent inhomogeneity' (Spencer 1862 [1996: 396]). Darwinian application to organic evolution was only a particular case of the general movement of the whole world. And, of course, the same principle applied to human society, which, according to the dictates of the law would improve indefinitely. This optimistic outlook on the world goes some way to explain the enormous popularity of Spencerian philosophy in his own time. It has been suggested that the horrors of the First World War so contradicted the principle that Spencer's philosophical reputation fell with it.

Equally important, perhaps, in explaining that popularity was Spencer's explicit attempt to find a reconciliation between science and religion, and so bring the most tendentious topic of Victorian debate to an end. 'We must find', he says (Spencer 1862 [1996: 22]) 'some fundamental verity in defence of which each [that is, science and religion] will find the other its ally.' It cannot be a specific doctrine or fact of either. The common principle is the inscrutability of the world. From the standpoint of all religions, 'the Power which the Universe manifests to us is utterly inscrutable' (Spencer 1862 [1996: 22]). And 'the ultimate scientific ideas . . . are all representative of realities that cannot be comprehended' (Spencer 1862 [1996: 66]).

Unlike Huxley, Spencer did have an account of the world to experience relation, an account that harks back to Thomas Reid in the previous century, and forward to recent ontological suggestions in attempts to interpret contemporary physics. But it must have seemed thin indeed. Science, says Spencer, leads to the Unknowable. As the sciences progress, for example biology, despite finding an exhaustive catalogue of material substances involved in Life, 'its essence cannot be conceived in physico-chemical terms' (Spencer 1862–96: II, 120). 'The Ultimate Reality behind this manifestation . . . transcends conception . . . even simple forms of existence are in their ultimate natures incomprehensible.' Spencer is very critical of vitalism, the interpretation of the essence of life in terms of primitive animism. We do not know, indeed cannot know what the Ultimate Reality could be. But our sensations must be produced by something. This 'something' can only be, from our point of view a Power, some primordial activity.

Finally it is worth remarking on Spencer's ambitions for Philosophy. 'Science is *partially-unified* knowledge.' The work of Philosophy is to abstract such principles from that level of knowledge as to arrive at '*completely-unified* knowledge' (Spencer, 1862 [1996: 134]). The abstraction of a general law of evolution from chemistry, biology, and human history is just such a work of philosophy.

Some commentators, for instance Passmore (1957), have been scathing in their judgement of the philosophical quality of the scientist-philosophers such as Huxley and Spencer, who so dominated English popular thought in the nineteenth century. It is true that such key concepts as 'Power' were not treated to the kind of analysis that had been popular in the eighteenth century and would be so again in the twentieth. But the style of thinking, centred on scientific insights, raised profound questions ignored, ridiculed or treated quite superficially by the analytical philosophers of the twentieth century.

SUMMARY

Though the scientifically oriented authors in each of the three main centres of philosophical activity were materialists, reductionists, and empiricists by inclination and conviction, few, if any, managed to balance the paradoxes and inconsistencies that quickly emerged. A strict empiricism left them struggling with the problem of how correlations of types of sensations can lead a scientist to reliable and general knowledge of the material universe which is presumably the origin of these very sensations. It was also difficult to account for the strength of the laws of nature if they were nothing but summaries of and abstractions from sensory experience. In many cases recourse was had to some form of the Kantian a priori. Those who resisted this way out, like Mach and Mill, had the traditional 'problem of induction' to deal with, and it cannot be said that either made a good job of resolving it.

It has often been remarked that the five centuries since 1500 have seen a progressive demoting of human beings from a privileged and unique place in the order of things. The biologist-philosophers of the second half of the nineteenth century realised this transformation very well. Having abandoned a transcendental source for morality, they looked for one from within the biological realm itself. Evolution as progress was seized upon as a way of forging a morality not so much for a secular, as for a molecular world. The impressive 'rise of science' in the public regard in this period (one commentator remarked that the locomotive was all that was needed to convince the general public of the authority of physical science) ensured that the influence of authors like Comte, Darwin, Huxley, Mach, and Spencer was very widespread, filtering through to moral, political, and economic attitudes to life itself.

NEO-KANTIANISM: THE GERMAN IDEALISM MOVEMENT

CHRISTOPHER ADAIR-TOTEFF

WHAT IS NEO-KANTIANISM?

For contemporary philosophers it is safe to say that much, if not most, of recent philosophy is either directly or indirectly indebted to Kant. Paul Guyer and Allen Wood write in their introduction to the new Cambridge translation of the *Critique of Pure Reason*: 'all modern thinkers are children of Kant, whether they are happy or bitter about their paternity' (Kant 1781, 1787 [1998: 23]). Although this sentiment has been prominent for some time, it has not always been the case. Indeed, some of Kant's contemporaries prophesied that he would be soon forgotten, and his German speculative idealist successors appeared to go so far beyond Kant that he was no longer recognisable – hence Kant was almost forgotten. That philosophers of the late nineteenth century and the twentieth century not only remember him, but also maintain that philosophy since Kant is the attempt either to build upon him or refute him, is due in large measure to the German idealist movement of the last decades of the nineteenth century and the first several decades of the twentieth century. This is the movement known as Neo-Kantianism.

Despite the significant role that the Neo-Kantians played in emphasising Kant's importance, there has been little work done on this movement. Writing in 1967 Lewis White Beck observed that 'There is very little material in English on Neo-Kantianism' (Beck 1967). This is still true today, although there have been several recent German scholars who have attempted to draw attention to certain figures, or to certain aspects of the movement as a whole.[1] This neglect is

---

[1] In English there have been three attempts to help draw some attention to the Neo-Kantian movement: Willey (1987), Köhnke (1986), and Oakes (1986), as well as Oakes's translations of other Neo-Kantian works. However, these attempts suffer from being more historical and less philosophical; this is understandable because much of the work done on Neo-Kantians has been by non-philosophers. Köhnke's book is further marred because there is little documentation and almost two hundred pages of important material found in the original German work is missing from the English translation. This is troubling because there is nothing in the English edition to indicate that this material is omitted. Besides Köhnke, Hans-Ludwig Ollig, and Helmut Holzhey are two other German scholars who have contributed substantially to the renewal of interest in Neo-Kantianism.

unfortunate because members of the movement were serious Kantian scholars whose discussions contain much that would still be helpful in understanding Kant today. But there are a number of difficulties which make this neglect understandable.

The first obstacle is the question as to what is meant by 'Neo-Kantianism'. In a general sense 'Neo-Kantianism' includes all Kant's successors, including Fichte, Schelling, Hegel, and probably Schopenhauer. But in the specific sense with which we are primarily concerned here the Neo-Kantian movement is the 'Back to Kant' movement that flourished in Germany from 1860 to the First World War. One important general feature of this movement is that its adherents were frustrated with the state of German philosophy around the middle of the nineteenth century. The great German idealist systems of the previous generation had collapsed under their own weight; the revolutionary movement of 1848 and its aftermath had prompted thinkers to embrace revolutionary social questions and then to abandon them; and many of the natural scientists of the time had a naïve materialistic philosophy which accompanied their scientific successes. These three points provided a starting point for these philosophers of the second half of the nineteenth century. First, most of the Neo-Kantians had learned that system building was an exercise in futility and instead they sought to concentrate on incremental improvements in understanding. Second, while there is a tendency to see Neo-Kantianism as primarily a movement that emphasised problems of knowledge, this is to ignore the fact that many of the movement's members were active in looking at social questions; indeed, a number made the attempt to right social, political, and religious wrongs. And, third, while they rejected materialism, most, if not all Neo-Kantians, had learned enough from Hume and Marx to have a healthy respect for empiricism, while rejecting any form of scepticism.

Another obstacle to discussing Neo-Kantianism is its magnitude and diversity. The movement lasted for at least seventy years, and some scholars have gone so far as to suggest that it lasted almost a century. Even within a short period, the numbers involved are large: Klaus Christian Köhnke lists dozens of philosophers who lectured on Kant between 1862 and 1890 (Köhnke 1986). Further while some of the schools centred on certain topics for investigation, there were considerable differences both in the interests of the members of the schools as well as the changes in the 'membership' in them. It is usual to focus on the two major schools: the Southwest school, named for the Neo-Kantians in the Southwest German universities of Heidelberg, Freiburg, and Strasburg, and the Marburg school located further north at the university in Marburg. As an overgeneralisation, members of the Southwest school tended to gravitate to questions of culture and value, while members of the Marburg school leaned towards issues of epistemology and logic. Naturally, there was some crossover in interests.

Many schools founded their own journals in order to put forward their contentions and combat rival theories. At Marburg, Hermann Cohen and Paul Natorp founded the journal *Philosophische Arbeiten* (1906). They published not only their own writings, but also those of Ernst Cassirer, Nicolai Hartmann, and later Heinz Heimsoeth. At Heidelberg, a number of prominent thinkers established the journal *Logos* (1910/11) which focused primarily on questions of culture. The founding members included the Heidelberg philosopher Wilhelm Windelband, the philosopher/theologian Ernst Troeltsch, and the Freiburg philosopher Heinrich Rickert. Another founding member was Max Weber, a friend of Rickert when they were colleagues at Freiburg in the late 1890s, who moved to Heidelberg before retiring early because of ill-health. Weber's friend from Berlin, Georg Simmel, was another member, but what is especially intriguing was the inclusion also of Edmund Husserl, the founder of phenomenology, for we tend to think of Husserl as interested in founding philosophy (phenomenology) as a strict science, not concerned with questions of culture. Besides these journals connected with specific schools, there were also independent journals such as *Kant-Studien*. Hans Vaihinger founded this in 1897 with the express purpose of allowing freedom of discussion without the partisanship of the earlier school journals, and alone among all of these journals it has not ceased publication but continues to be a primary source for work on Kant.

Despite all their differences and the lengthy and sometimes personal quarrels it is safe to say that virtually all of the Neo-Kantians subscribed to the movement's battle cry, which came from Otto Liebmann's *Kant und die Epigonen* (*Kant and the Epigones*): 'So muß auf Kant zurückgegangen werden' ('So [we] must return to Kant') (Liebmann 1865). But members had two different approaches to Kant. One was an attempt to determine what Kant actually *did* say; in effect, Kant philology: Hermann Cohen's three commentaries, one on each of the *Critiques*, are examples of this. Other examples include works from the 1880s devoted to Kant's unpublished writings. These include the work by Benno Erdmann on Kant's *Reflexionen* and that by Rudolf Reicke on Kant's so-called *Lose Blätter* from Kant's *Nachlass*. Another example is Hans Vaihinger's massive commentary, of which more will be said below. Around the turn of the century major efforts were also begun to provide textually correct editions of Kant's writings. Ernst Cassirer with his brother Bruno published a ten-volume edition, but it was the Royal Prussian Academy edition, begun in 1900 under the general editorship of Wilhelm Dilthey, that has provided Kant scholars with the definitive edition of Kant's works, ranging from his major and minor published pieces, to his letters, lectures, and notes.

The other approach to Kant was the attempt to set out what Kant *should* have said. The great speculative idealist systems of Fichte, Schelling, and Hegel were attempts to improve on Kant's philosophy, and the members of the Neo-Kantian movement were just as tempted to follow suit. However, in contrast to their system-building predecessors, the Neo-Kantians attempted to adhere more to both the spirit and the letter of Kant's teachings. Thus, rather than simply using Kant's texts as points of departure for new philosophies, the Neo-Kantians wished to return to Kant in order to use his principles and methodologies to answer both old and new philosophical problems. For example, according to Kant's famous 'Copernican Revolution' it is our subjective epistemological constitution which guarantees the objectivity of cognition, and this in turn implies that mathematics and the natural sciences exemplify the twin cardinal characteristics of knowledge: universality and necessity. Many Neo-Kantians wanted to use this methodology to demonstrate that there could be new sciences applicable to man, for despite their reverence for Kant, many saw Kant's limitations, especially in the respect of not dealing with the so-called human sciences, including what we know as sociology and even history. Kant had been interested primarily in mathematics and natural sciences. That is why the 'Transcendental Aesthetic' of the *Critique of Pure Reason* was designed to demonstrate the validity of the sciences of Euclidean geometry and mathematics, and the 'Transcendental Analytic' was intended to prove the validity of Newtonian science. And however much Kant was interested in man as a rational and moral agent, he was not really intrigued by the various changes that make up human culture. One might indeed suggest that Kant's attempts to provide justifications for the universal and necessary conditions of knowledge blinded him to the varieties of human cultures and to the contingencies of the individual human beings. In light of this, it should not come as a shock to come across Wilhelm Windelband's dictum: 'to understand Kant means to go beyond him' (Windelband 1884). Lest any one think that this is irreverence, bear in mind that in the *Critique of Pure Reason* Kant maintained that we understand Plato better than he understood himself.

Scholars generally agree that the Neo-Kantian movement more or less dissolved just prior to or during the First World War, though some suggest that it continued, if in altered form, into the 1920s and 1930s. But there is significant disagreement on the question of when it began and who started it. Some hold that it was F. A. Lange with his *Geschichte des Materialismus* (*History of Materialism* – 1866), others hold that it was Otto Liebmann with his *Kant und die Epigonen* (1865), and still others suggest that it was Eduard Zeller's paper 'Über Bedeutung und Aufgabe der Erkenntnistheorie' ('On the Significance and Task of the Theory of Knowledge' – 1862 [1865–84]). Yet even from 1860 there was considerable interest in Kant, which was generated by Kuno Fischer's two works on Kant, both of which were published that year. Indeed, Liebmann was Kuno Fischer's student at Jena and Windelband, another of Fischer's students, proclaimed that 'the new impetus in Kantian teaching' began with Kuno Fischer in 1860 (Windelband 1904).

Kuno Fischer's first work on Kant was *Kants Leben und die Grundlagen seiner Lehre* (*Kant's Life and the Foundations of his Teaching*) (Fischer 1860a). It consists of three lectures with the first providing a sketch of Kant's life. In the second Fischer focuses on human cognition, which he takes to be the first question of philosophy. His concern with epistemology prompts him to take up the notions of time and space as found in the first *Critique*'s section entitled 'The Transcendental Aesthetic'. It is this section that provoked the long-running feud with the Berlin Aristotelian, F. A. Trendelenburg. This issue will be addressed below. Fischer continued to try to make Kant accessible and in the same year he published a two-volume work *Geschichte der neuern Philosophie (History of Modern Philosophy)* (Fischer 1860b), which was part of his larger attempt to provide a history of modern philosophy. In the second volume Fischer attempted to set out the fundamental tenets of Kant's philosophy. It is clear that Kuno Fischer saw that his task was to make Kant comprehensible, which he did with remarkable success. Thomas Willey contends that 'by all accounts' Fischer's books were of paramount importance in renewing interest in Kant (Willey 1978: 63). Further, his lectures on Kant were justly famous. He sought to engage his audience, which tended to be packed with students, and he continued to lecture when he returned to Heidelberg in 1872, as he said, 'to live and to die'.

THE SPACE CONTROVERSY

When Kant published the *Critique of Pure Reason* it generated both interest and controversy. One charge that his critics levelled dealt with the notion of space and the thing-in-itself. In the 'Transcendental Aesthetic' Kant claimed that space was a pure form of intuition and applied exclusively to things as they appeared to us. This claim can be regarded as the 'exclusivity claim'. Yet he also held that we can never have knowledge of the thing-in-itself. This claim can be called the 'unknowability thesis'. Some critics argued that as these are mutually exclusive positions Kant must give up one or the other. Others granted that Kant was correct to insist that space is a pure intuition of sensibility and that it is subjective; but, they argued, Kant never considered the possibility that space might also apply to the things-in-themselves. This last charge began a controversy which lasted some forty years and included some fifty participants (Vaihinger 1882–92). It was often personal and petty and was the epitome of

Neo-Kantian quarrels which Vaihinger described using Hobbes's phrase as 'a war of all against all'. It began when F. A. Trendelenburg took up this criticism in his *Logische Untersuchungen* (*Logical Investigations*) (1840), but it was not until twenty years later that Kuno Fischer published a spirited defence of Kant (Fischer 1860a). He devoted the third section of his first book on Kant to this issue and argued that because space is the first condition of human knowledge it must be purely subjective. A few years later Fischer published his *System der Logik und Metaphysik oder Wissenschaftslehre* (*System of Logic and Metaphysics or the Doctrine of Science*), where he opined that if Trendelenburg were right and space was something real, then mathematics would lose its universality and certainty; hence, it would cease to be a science (Fischer 1865).

In 1867 Trendelenburg again took up the challenge when he published 'Über eine Lücke in Kants Beweis von der ausschliessenden Subjectivität des Raumes und der Zeit. Ein kritisches und antikritisches Blatt' ('On a Gap in Kant's Proof of the Exclusive Subjectivity of Space and Time. A Critical and Anti-critical Page'). The subtitle gives more than a hint on how personal this major disagreement was becoming. Trendelenburg insisted that if space were merely subjective then we are led to scepticism. Fischer offers a few defensive remarks in the preface to his *Kant's Vernunft Kritik* (*Kant's Criticism of Reason*). He defends his approach as a historian of philosophy who pays close attention to Kant's arguments, and insists that Kant is simply right and Trendelenburg is wrong. Trendelenburg responded with *Kuno Fischer und sein Kant* (*Kuno Fischer and his Kant*) (Trendelenburg 1869) and the next year Fischer published *Anti-Trendelenburg* (Fischer 1870). By now the debate had hopelessly degenerated – both works consist mostly of personal attacks and the notion of space is practically ignored. But the controversy continued to draw interest. Hermann Cohen published an article (Cohen 1870) in which he seemed to side with his teacher Trendelenburg; however, the following year he appeared to move away from him in his *Kants Theorie der Erfahrung* (*Kant's Theory of Experience*) (Cohen 1871). C. Grapengiesser published *Kant's Lehre von Raum und Zeit* (*Kant's Doctrine of Space and Time*) (Grappengiesser 1870) and the same year Emil Arnoldt published *Kants Transzendental Idealität des Raumes und Zeit* (*Kant's Transcendental Ideality of Space and Time*) (Arnoldt 1870). Both defended Kant, but the latter made it obvious with his subtitle: 'For Kant Against Trendelenburg'. Later philosophers tended to change sides. Johannes Volkelt criticised Kant in his *Immanuel Kants Erkenntnistheorie* (*Immanuel Kant's Theory of Cognition*) (Volkelt 1879) and later Vaihinger, in his *Kommentar* (*Commentary*) (Vaihinger 1881 [1970]), would criticise Kuno Fischer. Indeed, Vaihinger provides a splendid survey of the long-running controversy and with his opinion the debate began to subside.

THE MARBURG SCHOOL

Although there are many philosophers associated with the Marburg school there is only room here to discuss three of them: F. A. Lange, Hermann Cohen, and Paul Natorp. That all three were interested in a wide range of issues belies the claim that the Marburg school devoted its talents only to questions of knowledge. While this may have been the primary focus, many of the Marburg philosophers were concerned with political, social, and religious issues. This is clearly evident with Lange. Friedrich Albert Lange did not become a professor until 1870 when he was forty-two years old. Before that time he was a Gymnasium (upper-level secondary school) teacher, a writer and editor of newspapers and articles, and the equivalent of head of the chamber of commerce. During these years he discussed issues of political and social importance. In particular, he wrote on the question of work for the working class and his book *Die Arbeiterfrage* (*The Question of the Worker*) (Lange 1865) had a Marxist twist. He was also much involved in political questions, first in Germany, then in Switzerland, and again when he returned to Germany in 1872 to take up the chair of philosophy at Marburg. In fact, his stand on a matter of principle almost cost him his earlier teaching position at Cologne, but he resigned first. The issue at stake there was his insistence that teachers should have full political freedom, including the freedom to criticise the state when it is warranted.

It is for his *Geschichte des Materialismus* (*History of Materialism*) (Lange 1866 [1887]) that Lange is chiefly remembered. He began work on it in 1857, but it was not published until 1866. It is a wide-ranging book, dealing not only with Greek, Roman, and modern philosophy, but also with such subjects as music and even mysticism. He then revised the first volume, dealing with materialism up to Kant, and published this revised volume in 1873 before extensively revising the second volume, devoted to Kant and his successors, which was published in 1875, shortly before his death. Despite the fact that he was in considerable pain because of cancer, Lange evidently believed that he needed to rework the second volume. Two matters prompted him to undertake the effort: the important scientific achievements of the years following the book's first appearance, and, secondly, his belief that, following, Hermann Cohen's *Kants Theorie der Erfahrung*, he needed to revise radically his views on Kant.

Lange's *Geschichte des Materialismus* is an intriguing work. Despite the title, it is primarily a denunciation of materialism from a Kantian standpoint. Lange allows that empiricists are correct to believe that experience is, as Hume held, the basis of knowledge of all matters of fact. However, empiricists err by not realising that there must be a priori workings of the mind for us even to have experience. Thus although experience and the theory of induction are important scientific tools, they are no substitute for the mind's ability to employ a priori categories. Lange, however, was hostile to abstract metaphysical speculation; hence because the thing-in-itself is beyond experience, he questioned whether Kant was justified in maintaining its existence and sought to turn Kant against himself by insisting that, properly speaking, metaphysics is restricted to the theory of knowledge. Yet Lange is not content to say that knowledge is all there is. He believes that he follows Kant in insisting that there are other worthwhile human endeavours. While we cannot have knowledge of ethics, religion, and poetry, these are nonetheless extremely valuable human activities. In particular, Lange had a fondness for Schiller's philosophical poetry which comforted him in his final years of illness. He endorsed a specifically Kantian type of idealism, which he believed demonstrated the optimistic side of human nature that emphasised the artistic impulses and the freedom of morality in contrast to the deterministic and pessimistic philosophy of materialism. It is to Lange's credit that philosophers as diverse as Cohen and Vaihinger paid tribute to him. Cohen dedicated the second edition of *Kants Theorie der Erfahrung* to Lange; and Vaihinger, not one eager to pay homage, claimed with some pride that his philosophy of 'as if' was based in large measure on the 'Standpoint of the Ideal' with which Lange ends his *Geschichte des Materialismus.*

Hermann Cohen owed much to his friend and mentor Lange, and it would have been interesting to see how things turned out had Lange lived longer. As it was, their three-year relationship had a profound impact on both of them. At an earlier stage Cohen had turned from an interest in Judaism to Platonic and Aristotelian studies, which is why he went to Berlin to study with Trendelenburg. Trendelenburg's criticism of Kant then prompted Cohen to begin his own study of Kant, which in turn induced him to seek employment with Lange at Marburg. He arrived there and was *habilitiert* (allowed to have a university position) in 1873, became an *Extraordinarius Professor* (associate level) in 1875, and *Ordinarius Professor* (full professor) a year later and took over the recently deceased Lange's chair of philosophy. Besides their shared interest in Kant they had a number of other things in common. Both believed that art, religion, and politics were important; both believed in helping the common person to seek social and economic gains, and both tackled religious problems. Lange's father was a well-known Protestant minister and later professor of theology; Cohen's father was a teacher at the local Jewish school. Both fathers had lasting influences on the religious outlooks of their sons.

Hermann Cohen has a reputation in religious circles, especially Jewish, but he is best remembered because of his commentaries on the three *Critiques: Kants*

Theorie der Erfahrung (1871); *Kants Begründung der Ethic* (*Kant's Foundations of Ethics*) (1877); and finally *Kants Begründung der Aesthetik* (*Kant's Foundations of Aesthetics*) (1889). These three commentaries covered what Cohen took to be important from Kant: thinking, willing, and judging.

Cohen was considered one of the best Kantian scholars. However, friends and critics alike complained about his obscure style and his penchant for apparent paradoxes; Georg Simmel once remarked that Cohen's commentaries were among the best but doubted that there was anyone who could decipher them. One feature of his style was his tendency to collapse distinctions. An example of this was his way of combining historical analysis with philosophical criticism: thus, he tried both to explain what Kant said and what he should have said. He did this in his commentaries, but also in his later and more original works, especially *Logik der reinen Erkenntnis* (*Logic of Pure Knowledge*) (1902), *Ethik des reinen Willens* (*Ethics of Pure Will*) (1904), and *Asthetik des reinen Gefühls* (*Logic of Pure Feeling*) (1912). He also sought to collapse the fundamental Kantian distinction between the two faculties of Sensibility and Understanding, arguing that Kant suggests that these two stems have a common, if unknown, root (Lange and Heidegger are two others who follow Cohen's claim). And he later argued that thinking and being were essentially the same.

Cohen may have felt lonely at Marburg after Lange's death in 1875 and he welcomed the arrival of Paul Natorp in 1881, who came there as a Privatdozent to study Kant with him. Despite Natorp's friendship and support, however, Cohen remained rather isolated at Marburg because of his opinionated behaviour and contentious theories. So when Cohen retired and fought to have his favourite pupil, Ernst Cassirer, as his successor, only Natorp sided with him (the position went to a now-forgotten experimental psychologist). Cohen was disheartened by this and moved to Berlin in 1912 where he threw himself even more into problems of religion and especially into the so-called Jewish question. He appeared to have somewhat abandoned his 'objective' philosophical stance in favour of polemics against what he perceived was anti-semitism. Kuno Fischer, in a moment of tactlessness, even suggested that Cohen was more interested in the question of race than he was in being a philosopher. His defence of the Jews and his attempt to demonstrate that the Jews were superior as a people to German citizens was bound to cause consternation; and his conviction that the relation between God and Jew was ultimately a highly personal one was equally certain to cause concern among Jews. Like Lange, Cohen was not afraid to hold controversial opinions, whether on Kant, politics, or religion. Whereas many of the philosophers of the early 1930s were scholars who either tolerated or even aided the Nazis in order to escape personal difficulties, Cohen, Lange, and other Neo-Kantians had been more than ready to pay the price for defending unpopular positions.

Although Cohen and Paul Natorp enjoyed a long relationship which was marked both by warm friendship and joint philosophical efforts, one scholar has suggested that there are important differences between their approaches to philosophy (Holzhey 1986). Despite the fact that Natorp went to Marburg to study Kant with Cohen, Natorp's early work was not on Kant but on Descartes. And, while Cohen continued to concentrate primarily on Kant (and religious questions), Natorp was just as interested to work on other figures in the history of philosophy, notably Plato. Again there are differences in their attitudes to historical scholarship. While some scholars criticised Cohen for taking some liberties with his reading of Kant, all appeared to agree that his historical examination of Kant's writings was fundamentally correct. Natorp, however, was thought to take considerable liberties with his 'historical' work. In perhaps his best work, *Platons Ideenlehre* (*Plato's Doctrine of Ideas*) (1902), he departs from the traditional reading of Plato on the issue of Plato's thesis that 'ideas' or the 'Forms' are the only real entities. It had been the received view that for Plato the 'Forms' are the only ontological things worthy of being called 'Beings' and are accordingly the only objects of knowledge. Departing from this view Natorp maintained that Plato's major discovery was in showing that ideas are not things, but are instead laws and methods. This prompted him to claim that Plato was a 'Kantian before Kant, indeed a Marburg Neo-Kantian before Marburg' (Natorp 1902: 462). This Kantian approach to Plato generated considerable controversy but it was based upon years of research and Natorp continued to defend it.

In 1912 Natorp published a paper in *Kant-Studien* entitled 'Kant und die Marburger Schule', in which he argued a number of points. First, he maintained that the school did not have a constant reading of Kant; but, instead, the members were always engaged in new research and interpretations. Second, the Marburgers were not only interested in Kant but also in ancient and modern philosophy, and in the scientific developments from Galileo and Newton to recent work in mathematics and the natural sciences. And, third, speaking primarily of himself, Natorp rejected the fixed ideas of Plato's middle dialogues (such as the *Republic* and the *Symposium*) in favour of the 'movement' of the later dialogues (e.g. the *Sophist*). Here again Natorp stresses change coupled with the twin notions of law and method. Natorp continued to side mostly with Cohen even after the latter's resignation and departure to Berlin in 1912. But, after Cohen's death in 1918 Natorp reassessed his philosophical relationship with him, and from this time there is a noticeable movement away from his old friend and mentor, Cohen.

THE SOUTHWEST SCHOOL

There are, of course, fundamental similarities between the Marburg school and the Southwest school but what is of interest here are the dissimilarities. The members of the Marburg school did not take up theoretical questions of value until Ernst Cassirer started to investigate them long after the turn of the century, though many of them, especially Lange and Cohen, were extremely active in pursuing practical matters involving questions of value. In contrast, the Southwest school was preoccupied with abstract questions of value from the 1880s. These theoretical investigations concerned a wide range of issues, but mention can be made here only of one – the problem of history. If natural science provides rational accounts of the universal laws of the real world, what kind of account should history provide of that which is singular and unrepeatable? Only a sketch can be offered here, and it must be accompanied with significant limitations; in particular the discussion must, unfortunately, omit the contributions of Simmel and Troeltsch. In the latter's case this is unfortunate because he not only contributed to the debate, but also wrote an important history of it. This work, *Der Historismus und seine Probleme* (*Historicism and its Problems*) (1922) runs to 777 pages and sheds numerous insights on the debate and the people who contributed to it.

First and foremost, the Southwest Neo-Kantians rejected two opposing conceptions of history – Hegel's idealistic, rationalist conception and Ranke's later 'realism', according to which history simply recounted the past 'as it happened'. Despite building on his predecessors it was Wilhelm Windelband who gave the main clear exposition of the problem and sketched a means of overcoming it. He had learned from Hermann Lotze the limitations of the natural sciences and from Kuno Fischer the importance of history, specifically the history of philosophy. But he repudiated (temporarily) Fischer's reliance on Hegel: Windelband was above all a Kantian and he even insisted that all nineteenth-century philosophers had been fundamentally Kantians (Windelband 1924: iv). He began working on the problem early in his career but it was not until he moved to Strasburg to take over the chair of his deceased friend Otto Liebmann in 1882 that he began work in earnest, and he continued even when he moved to Heidelberg in 1903 to take Kuno Fischer's chair.

While he had learned much from Fischer, he parted from him in significant ways. One such issue concerned the approach to the history of philosophy: instead of providing a chronological account of the history of philosophy, Windelband provided one based upon problems (Windelband 1884). He also propounded an extremely influential distinction between nomothetic and ideographic science, between the natural scientist's interest in universals and the historian's concern with particulars. In his speech 'Geschichte und Natur-wissenschaft' ('History and Natural Science') which he delivered as rector at Strasburg in 1894, Windelband developed the traditional contrast between the natural and the 'moral' sciences, following Dilthey's distinction between the natural sciences and the *Geisteswissenschaften* (the 'cultural' sciences, including history). Windelband spells out the situation as follows: the natural sciences deal with universal laws of the external material world, so natural scientists have little regard for the singular – what they are interested in is experiments that can be repeated; and while they must be satisfied with inductive reasons, what they are really seeking is the apodeictic certainty of universal laws. By contrast, the historian, as a cultural scientist, is interested in the single, individual fact. This reflects the human revulsion towards the concept of the *Doppelgänger*, and the belief that mankind has been saved by the single occurrence of Christ's resurrection. Thus where the natural scientist wants to find the causal and determined *laws of nature*, the historian seeks to explore the *individual's moral freedom*. Windelband suggests that, as a consequence, the discipline of history has a connection to Belle Lettres and aesthetics. In this he is very close to Dilthey, and the charge brought against both of them is that this thesis leads history away from objective knowledge towards a point of view which is merely subjective, relative, and irrational.

Max Weber and Heinrich Rickert emphatically objected to points of view which are merely subjective and relative. Both scholars are remarkable figures, but Weber is the more controversial one. He had studied philosophy at Heidelberg but claimed not to be a philosopher. Yet he was keenly aware of philosophical movements: he once commented that Marx and Nietzsche were the two most influential thinkers of the nineteenth century. His reputation now rests primarily on his sociological writings; however, his close friend Ernst Troeltsch counted him, along with Windelband and Rickert, as one of the three main figures in the Southwest school (Troeltsch 1922: 565). The intellectual relationship between Rickert and Weber was close, though it is a matter of debate as to who most influenced whom. In a letter of 1902 to his wife Weber wrote of Rickert: 'He is *very* good' (Oakes 1986: 7). But for Rickert, Weber was not a philosopher: instead he was the embodiment of the independent scholar, ready to take on any opponent and fierce in denouncing dilettantes. Certainly there are many points of similarity: both Rickert and Weber were concerned with the logic of the cultural sciences; both believed that Windelband's and Dilthey's approaches led ultimately to subjective aestheticism, both wanted to answer the question of relationship between concepts and reality, and finally, both wished to find some means for securing the objectivity of the cultural sciences.

Rickert's main work was *Die Grenzen der Wissenschaftlichen Begriffsbildung* (translated as *The Limits of Concept Formation in Natural Science* – Rickert 1986). Where the first two books of this work are primarily negative (and were published in 1896), the last three books are primarily positive (and were published in 1901; the entire work appeared in 1902). Rickert's approach here is twofold. One aspect concerns the natural sciences. Rickert argued that the traditional account of natural sciences was faulty. According to this account there is just one method for solving the problems of the natural sciences; but the reality is that there is a multiplicity of methods; so there is no such thing as *the* method of science. Further, Rickert argued, this account of the natural sciences also underestimates the problem of abstraction. Rickert shared with his mentor Windelband the conviction that natural scientists regard concrete particulars as of no intrinsic interest and are primarily concerned to find abstract universal laws. Rickert then argued that this gives rise to a problem when natural scientists seek to validate the abstract concepts which occur in their universal laws, since their position implies that there is a considerable gap between these abstract universal laws and the behaviour of concrete particulars. Thus far Rickert's approach is broadly similar to that of Windelband, but he then diverges from Windelband in holding that philosophy must go beyond the limitations of both natural science and historicism as Windelband conceived it. If the natural sciences overlooked the importance of the particular, Windelband's historicism led only to relativism and nihilism. Rickert's conclusion was, therefore, that the true dichotomy between the natural and the cultural sciences is between the natural scientist's efforts to find general laws, which may be rational but are unreal because they are abstractions; and the historian's, and philosopher's, investigation into concrete particulars, which are real, but because of their very particularity, may also be irrational.

Rickert maintained that in several other respects too there are fundamental differences between the natural and the cultural sciences. First, for the natural scientist the spatiality and temporality of particular instances is irrelevant, but for the historian all that really matters is that the event has occurred at some particular time. Secondly, where the natural scientist utilises general observations as a guide to universal laws, the historian uses them to lead back to its proper object – the individual. Thirdly, where natural science is inherently value free, the historian's approach is inescapably value relevant even if he does not evaluate directly. Rickert clarifies this final contrast by several interrelated points. History deals not just with individuals but with important ones, and these individuals must be seen in context, which implies that there is some degree of coherence between the individuals in the group. So, like Weber, Rickert thinks that the appearance of values in the cultural sciences is permitted; indeed, unlike the natural sciences, it is a necessary part of them. What matters is that these value judgements should not be 'hidden' but should be made openly.

Emil Lask was friendly with Rickert and Weber and was influenced by both. Lask wrote his *Habilitationsschrift* on the philosophy of law for Windelband but primarily under Weber's influence. Before that, he had earned his doctorate at Freiburg under Rickert's direction. This work is on Fichte's philosophy of history, but in it he also touches on the problems facing the general philosophy of history. Thus, he builds upon the work that Rickert finalised in *The Limits of Concept Formation in the Natural Sciences*. For Lask, as for Rickert, the crucial difficulty is overcoming the gap between abstract concept and concrete reality. Like Rickert, he never closes this gap, but, perhaps unlike Rickert, Lask faced the problem head on. He believed that there were two approaches to developing a real science of history, both of which were problematic: either some way must be found to close the gap between concept and reality, or, to show that despite this gap, history could still be possible.

VAIHINGER, SIMMEL, AND NEW DIRECTIONS

Hans Vaihinger holds a crucial place in the annals of Neo-Kantianism for two important reasons: his work on Kant, and his use of Kant and others to found his philosophy of 'as if'. On the centennial anniversary of the publication of the *Critique of Pure Reason* (1881), Vaihinger published the first volume of a projected four-volume commentary on the *Critique*. This was a commissioned work which Vaihinger took very seriously. The second volume did not appear until 1892, largely because of Vaihinger's illnesses and his decreasing ability to see. He never did write the projected third and fourth volumes but he maintained that much of what he would have published was already in print in his articles and pamphlets. Indeed, while he was certainly often indisposed he continued to organise and write with great zeal. His *Kommentar* is a fascinating work. In the 1,066 pages of the two volumes Vaihinger not only writes a commentary on the *Critique* but also on Kant's commentators, ranging from Kant's contemporaries to the latest writings of the Neo-Kantians. For an exhaustive work and an indication of the Neo-Kantians' work on Kant philology, Vaihinger's commentary will probably never be superseded. Besides the *Kommentar* he published a monograph on the difficult 'Transcendental Deduction' of the *Critique* in which he argued that the disunity and apparent contradictions were a result of its being a 'patchwork': he argued that Kant finally patched together notes in a hurry from different stages of his eleven-year effort to write the *Critique*. Vaihinger performed additional services for the furthering of interest in Kant. He founded *Kant-Studien* in 1897 and served as general editor, often contributing short commentaries and book reviews, and in 1904 he founded the Kant-Gesellschaft (Kant Society) dedicated to the funding and furthering of the Kant research.

Vaihinger was not content with these endeavours. Much earlier he had begun work on a lengthy project. Influenced by Kant and Nietzsche, this effort would finally be in print in 1911 – *Die Philosophie des Als-Ob* (*The Philosophy of As-If*). In a dedication he claims that the cornerstone could be found in Lange's work. Drawing from his predecessors Vaihinger maintained that much that we take to be ethics and religion does not, and cannot, pass for knowledge. Moral and religious creeds are heuristic fictions; they are beneficial and undoubtedly necessary, but as fictions they can never be tested for validity. Instead, they are useful for helping us confront the irrationality of the world. It is to Vaihinger's credit that he attempted to bring together the optimism and rationality of Kant with the pessimism and irrationality of the early Nietzsche. Vaihinger's interest in Nietzsche prompted him to publish a work on him (1902b). This is a rather scholarly work written during the time that Nietzsche was mostly considered a madman and simply dismissed by his critics or adored by his 'disciples' who usually distorted their 'master's' theories.

Vaihinger was not the only one to publish a book on Nietzsche; Georg Simmel also wrote on Nietzsche. Besides this Simmel was noted for a number of things, of which two will be mentioned here. In 1904 he published his book on Kant. In contrast to Cohen, Simmel's Kant work is accessible; being both correct and understandable it is easy to see why Simmel was so popular. He is also important in that he, along with Ferdinand Tönnies and Max Weber, was the philosophical founder of classical German sociology. His numerous writings on questions of social interaction, culture and value should be consulted by those interested in the history of sociology as well as those interested in modern social theory.

Vaihinger and Simmel are just two examples of the new directions for the Neo-Kantians. Work on other figures in the history of philosophy prompted some of them to become Neo-Fichteans and Neo-Hegelians or to develop novel interpretations of older philosophical figures. In other ways, too, the movement survived the death of its members. Thus the influence of Natorp and Lask on the young Heidegger is well attested (it may have been their Platonic theories or their methodologies that influenced Heidegger, or perhaps both): Heidegger once referred to Natorp as his 'congenial opponent' and apparently continued to hold this view after Natorp's death. Thus even when Neo-Kantianism began to fade as a movement, the ideas and methods of its members lived on in the work of later philosophers.

A study of the Neo-Kantians is worthwhile because they demonstrated the importance of the study of Kant's philosophy, and, more generally, the value of the study of the history of philosophy. Research on the movement is also rewarding because the Neo-Kantians were among the brightest, most innovative, and prolific of nineteenth-century and early twentieth-century philosophers. Whether one wants to study phenomenology, deconstruction, hermeneutics, or even analytical philosophy, one cannot avoid study of the Neo-Kantians, since all of these movements have their antecedents in the great German idealist movement known as Neo-Kantianism.

3

IDEALISM IN BRITAIN AND THE
UNITED STATES

JAMES ALLARD

In 1856 the leading Oxford philosopher of his generation, Henry Longueville Mansel, later Waynflete Professor of Moral and Metaphysical Philosophy, Canon of Christ Church, and Dean of St Paul's, gave a lecture on the philosophy of Kant in which he described the value of studying German philosophy, particularly that of Schelling and Hegel. 'Presumptuous', he said, 'as [their] conceptions must appear to us, daringly profane as their language must sound to one who believes in a personal God, their study is not without its value in the *reductio ad absurdum* which it furnishes of the principles from which such conclusions spring' (Mansel 1856 [1873: 181]). Despite this backhanded recommendation in one of the first serious discussions of German absolute idealism in English, within twenty years English-speaking philosophers were on their way to domesticating what they had learned from Kant and Hegel and using it to supplant the two previously dominant philosophies in Britain and North America, British empiricism and Scottish common-sense realism. The sudden rise of idealistic philosophy, with its wide influence through religion and politics, does not seem explicable except as a response to the nineteenth-century crisis of faith. English-speaking philosophers found in idealism a defence of religious emotions which they were able to enlist in the cause of social reform (Richter 1964: 134).

1. EARLY BRITISH IDEALISM

In Britain, the nineteenth-century crisis of faith was produced by a confrontation between evangelical Christianity and seemingly incompatible forms of knowledge, particularly higher criticism of scripture and Darwin's biology. Evangelical Christianity was grounded in a belief in the literal truth of scripture. Beginning in the late eighteenth century, an evangelical revival had by the nineteenth century carried this belief into most aspects of Victorian society. When higher criticism showed that the Gospels were not the simple eyewitness stories they purported to be and when biologists rejected the literal truth of the creation story in Genesis, the fabric of Victorian life came under attack. Thoughtful

Victorians found themselves caught between their commitment to a way of life and its intellectual basis. Victorian novelists and poets testify to the depths of this crisis, a crisis reflected in science and inevitably in philosophy as well. Yet neither of the two established philosophies, Scottish common-sense realism or British empiricism, seemed able, in the words of one contemporary writer, 'to present its leading principle bent as one would like to see it into the curves and junctures of the most anxious thought of our time' (Masson 1865 [1877: 196], quoted in Bradley 1979: 16).

Even prior to the Darwinian controversy interest in German philosophy was growing. William Whewell and Sir William Hamilton had both been stimulated by Kant, Benjamin Jowett had prepared a translation (never published) of Hegel's shorter *Logic* (Wallace 1874 [1894: x–xi]), and James F. Ferrier and John Grote had developed their own versions of idealism. But more widespread interest in German idealism only caught hold with the work of a Glasgow physician, James Hutchison Stirling, whose *The Secret of Hegel* was published in 1865. This large, uneven work, mixing introduction, translation, and commentary, first indicated how Hegel might be exploited to deal with the British crisis of faith. Stirling attributed to Hegel Kant's project of reconciling religion and science. Kant did this, Stirling assured his readers, by arguing that the familiar objects of everyday experience are partially constituted by the experiencing subject. For Stirling this meant that sensations, contributed by a source external to minds called 'the thing-in-itself', are converted into objects by a priori subjective functions in minds (Stirling 1865 [1898: 156–8]). Hegel corrected Kant's account, Stirling thought, by arguing that sensations are actually products of the divine mind in which individual human minds participate. Stirling thus took Hegel to have completed Kant's 'Copernican revolution' in philosophy by eliminating the thing-in-itself, the source of objects external to minds. That objects are materialisations of the divine mind was for Stirling the secret of Hegel (Stirling 1865 [1898: 84–5]). Since the world is a materialisation of divine thought, no study of the objects in the world, no scientific investigation properly conducted, can cast doubt on God's existence. Hegel's philosophy showed that any scientific study had to presuppose it.

Stirling's argument for this conclusion, however, was not compelling. Rather than providing a defence, he announced a strategy. Employing that strategy effectively was the work of academically placed idealists, particularly William Wallace and the brothers John and Edward Caird. Wallace translated Hegel's *Logic* from *The Encyclopaedia of the Philosophical Sciences* (1874) and this became the main Hegelian text for the British idealists. Furthermore, in his detailed introduction Wallace showed how the dialectical progression of categories in Hegel's *Logic* could be seen as a struggle for survival among the 'fittest' ideas and so a counterpart to natural selection (Wallace 1874: clxxx). John Caird's *Philosophy of Religion* (1880) provided a systematic idealistic account of Christianity as well as a version of the ontological argument inspired by Hegel. In two long books (Caird 1877, 1889) Edward Caird presented Kant as a philosopher who had almost reconciled philosophy with religion. Unfortunately, in Caird's view, Kant persisted in treating reason as subjective and so separated thought from reality. Caird loosely followed Hegel in arguing that thought and reality are both fragments of a larger whole, objective reason or what Caird called the Absolute. This enabled Caird to treat science as a study of the manifestations of the Absolute. In his *Evolution of Religion* (1893) he argued that religion progressively understands God as the Absolute. Since he regarded Christianity as the most developed religion, this allowed him to reconcile Christianity with science. By their translations and scholarly studies Wallace and the Cairds showed how a loosely Hegelian revision of Kant's philosophy could deal with the Victorian crisis of faith. That many Victorians saw it as providing a solution was a result of the work of T. H. Green, who more than anyone else made idealism a force in British culture.

2. T. H. GREEN

Although strongly sympathetic to Kant and Hegel, Green's gifts were not those of an expositor. The tenor of his work is invariably critical. This is apparent in his first major work, his dense, demanding, 371-page introduction to David Hume's *Treatise of Human Nature* (1874). Surprising as it may seem, Green intended this work to help resolve the religious crisis of his age. He traced this crisis, 'the modern unsettlement' (Green 1868 [1888: 97]), to a widespread mode of thinking which he called 'the popular philosophy'. This was not an articulated philosophy but a widely held set of beliefs loosely derived from John Locke. Green thought that this philosophy was incapable of resolving the religious crisis because it had an inadequate conception of both knowledge and morality (Green 1868 [1888: 93]). It could not explain how either was possible. This fact was not, however, generally appreciated. Green thought this was because the philosopher who had shown it, David Hume, was no longer studied in detail. To remedy this situation Green wrote his introduction for a new edition of Hume's *Treatise of Human Nature*. His aim was to show that Hume had demonstrated that empiricism cannot explain how knowledge and morality are possible. It can only be explained, Green thought, by adopting a new philosophy, one inspired by Kant and Hegel (Green 1874 [1885: 1–3, 371]).

To show this, Green examined the roots of the popular philosophy in Locke. Locke's aim, according to Green, was to explain the origin of ideas in individuals and the connections between ideas which constitute knowledge. Locke proposed to do this by examining the ideas in his own mind which, he said, were either products of sensations or of the operations of his mind reflecting on ideas derived from sensations (Green 1874 [1885: 6]). Among the problems Green found here was a crucial ambiguity in Locke's treatment of sensations. Locke alternatively treated them as feelings and as felt things (Hylton 1990: 25–6). By so doing he confused having sensations with making judgements about objects (Green 1874 [1885: 13, 19]). We can only make judgements about objects, according to Green, if we have certain a priori concepts – Green particularly emphasised concepts of relations like identity and causation – which enable us to distinguish the way things seem to us from the way they are. Treating sensations as judgements allowed Locke to presuppose in consciousness the ideas which he then so laboriously attempted to derive from sensations (Green 1874 [1885: 12]). Because of this procedure, Green pronounced Locke's programme a failure.

On Green's interpretation, Hume was aware of Locke's failure and attempted to remove the ambiguity from Locke's treatment of 'sensations' and so to carry out his programme. Hume's goal was to reduce all ideas to sensations or, barring this, to explain why we think we have ideas that we do not in fact have (Green 1874 [1885: 161–3]). Green thought that since Hume could not reduce ideas of relations to sensations, on Hume's account knowledge was impossible. Nevertheless, Hume did attempt to explain why people believe that they have ideas of relations, particularly ideas of causation and identity, in terms of propensities to feign. In doing so, however, he made a mistake related to one made by Locke (Green 1874 [1885: 182]): he treated impressions both as feelings and as felt things. As a result, he confused sensations and judgements, just as Locke did (Walsh 1986: 30).

Green provided his own account of how knowledge and morality are possible in his most comprehensive work, his posthumously published *Prolegomena to Ethics* (1883a). He began the book with the question, 'Can the knowledge of nature be itself a part or a product of nature?' (Green 1883a [1907: 13]). His answer was that it cannot. Knowledge of nature, he claimed, is knowledge of objects of consciousness (Green 1883a [1907: 13]). But in order to identify an experience as an experience of an object, Green continued, we must be able to distinguish our experience of objects from our way of experiencing them, from our sensations. We do this, Green argued, by conceptualising our experiences, by judging them either to be or not to be experiences of the unalterable order of relations defining reality. As a result, experiencing objects presupposes a priori concepts of relations. Green concluded that knowledge of objects of nature presupposes an a priori or spiritual principle that enables us to distinguish ourselves from objects while relating ourselves to them (Green 1883a [1907: 16–23]).

Furthermore, since reality as we know it is constituted by an unalterable order of relations, it too must be the product of a spiritual principle (Green 1883a [1907: 33]). Like Stirling, Green rejected as incoherent Kant's claim that this principle supplies the form of reality while the matter is supplied by unknown things-in-themselves (Green 1883a [1907: 57]). From this he concluded that the spiritual principle constitutes not merely the form of nature, but nature as it is. Green identified this principle with God, an eternal consciousness which reproduces itself 'piece-meal' over time in finite knowers (Green 1883a [1907: 41]).

This principle, Green argued, also makes ethics possible by enabling us to have desires (Green 1883a [1907: 140–1]). The language used to describe desire, Green thought, is misleading. We say we desire food or wealth, when in fact we desire ourselves to be eating food or acquiring wealth. What is desired is not merely an object, but the desiring agent enjoying or having the object. As a result, only self-conscious beings, beings that can distinguish themselves from objects and then relate themselves to those objects in virtue of a spiritual principle, have desires (Green 1883a [1907: 97–9]). We decide to satisfy a desire by identifying our personal good with its satisfaction. We then will it and in so doing further realise ourselves. Since acts of will are determined by our characters, our actions are self-determined (Green 1883a [1907: 113–15]). As a result, Green's spiritual principle also explains how free action and hence ethics is possible.

Green derived the content of his ethics from practical reason. As moral agents having conflicting desires, it is rational for us to act on those desires which will enable us to achieve, in Green's phrase, 'the abiding satisfaction of an abiding self' (e.g., Green 1883a [1907: 274]; cf. Thomas 1987: 181–4). Although Green thought that this sort of satisfaction, and hence moral goodness itself, can only be realised in individuals, he also thought that self-realisation requires society. But societies can only exist, Green contended, if their members share a common conception of the good. Because of this, Green thought we can only satisfy ourselves by giving up our private ends for the common ends embodied in our social institutions. These ends provide the common good necessary for defining the moral ideal (Green 1883a [1907: 208–10]). This is necessary because the common good prescribes rules that often interfere with our inclinations. As a result, we come to value the will to do good for its own sake (Green 1883a [1907: 221–4]). This defines Green's moral ideal: being a person who wills the good for its own sake. This ideal depends for its realisation on a prior morality specified by the rules of one's social institutions (Green 1886 [1986: 13–14]). But from the point of view of the moral ideal, institutional rules may be criticised with a view to improving them. Green believed that this sort of criticism leads to the progressive improvement of social institutions (Green 1883a [1907: 356–8]).

Green's moral theory allowed him to transform Christian dogma into philosophy by treating the revealed portion of Christianity as a description of how we become moral persons (Green 1883b [1888: 182]). We give up our private conceptions of the good and identify our individual goods with the good for all as it is embodied in our social institutions. When we do this, Green said, we are realising the fundamental Christian idea of sacrificing ourselves, or dying to self, in order to live. This, Green thought, is the core meaning of the story of Jesus's life, death, and resurrection (Green 1883b [1888: 236–7]). Revealed Christianity thus describes the fundamental structure of the moral life in mythical form.

Green's political theory, presented in his posthumously published *Lectures on the Principles of Political Obligation* (1886), complements his moral theory. Here he argues that the function of the state is to maintain through law the conditions that make morality possible (Green 1886 [1986: 16]). Laws cannot enforce morality but they can require the performance of acts which are minimum conditions under which individuals can progressively realise the moral ideal (Green 1886 [1986: 17, 20]). The obligation to obey the law is grounded in the fact that only through law am I able to realise my moral ends. This fact also justifies giving individuals rights, since rights for Green are conditions for reaching moral ends (Green 1886 [1986: 26]).

Like classical liberals, Green defended property rights, but unlike them, he was willing to limit these rights in the interests of liberty. This is particularly obvious in his essay, 'Liberal Legislation and the Law of Contract'. Here he argued that the state has the function of preserving individuals from outside interference. But he went beyond this by saying that the state should also confer on individuals 'freedom in the positive sense' (Green 1881 [1986: 200]). It should act to enable them to achieve the common good and this, in some cases, requires the state to limit freedom of contract. This aspect of Green's philosophy was once interpreted as mildly socialistic but is now more often regarded as a halfway house to the new liberalism of the early twentieth century (e.g., Freeden 1996: 179).

Green, Wallace, and the Cairds provided the basis for a school of idealism. Green persuaded many younger philosophers that progress in philosophy could only be made by turning from the study of Locke and Hume to that of Kant and Hegel, while Wallace and the Cairds provided much-needed introductions to the obscurities of the German idealists. In the process they showed how idealism, unlike its competitors, could reconcile a liberal version of Christianity with science. Furthermore, Green's moral and social philosophy, resting on the notions of self-realisation and the common good, enjoined putting philosophy into practice and so provided an outlet for religious emotion. The achievement of this school of philosophy was not in producing professional philosophers, but in putting idealism into practice in service to society. Prominent members of the school included D. G. Ritchie (1853–1903), Sir Henry Jones (1852–1922), John Henry Muirhead (1855–1940), Richard Burdon Haldane (1856–1928), and John Watson (1847–1939). Ritchie, Jones, and Muirhead were all active in universities and in social life in Britain, Haldane held a number of official positions in his distinguished intellectual and political career, while Watson emigrated to Canada where for many years he was professor of philosophy at Queen's University in Kingston, Ontario.

This school has been frequently called Hegelian and this is not misleading if it is understood as a description of one of its prime sources of inspiration. But it did not follow Hegel blindly. Green, for example, accepted the Hegelian identity of thought and reality, but he was critical of what he took to be Hegel's way of demonstrating it. As Green saw it, Hegel's argument for the identity of thought and reality seemed to involve an equivocation. It purports to be based on an analysis of thought. But thought as normally understood is contrasted with another mental element, feeling. So the argument seems to proceed by analysing thought defined by contrast with feeling, only to reach the conclusion that thought includes feeling. Green was not sure that this was a real failure in the argument, but he was convinced that it prevented it from being convincing. He claimed that avoiding this difficulty would require an new account of thought (Green 1880 [1888: 141–3]). The felt need to examine the nature of thought was a starting point for the next generation of British idealists, a generation dominated by F. H. Bradley and Bernard Bosanquet.

3. F. H. BRADLEY

Bradley was ten years younger than Green and his first important work, *Ethical Studies* (1876), defended an ethics of self-realisation similar to Green's in content although not in style. Bradley's forceful rhetoric, love of irony, and vigorous prose contrast sharply with Green's stiff and sometimes turgid sentences. Bradley's aim in *Ethical Studies* was to show how ethics is possible although, characteristically, he placed more emphasis on criticising views he thought made it impossible (Bradley 1927: viii). One condition for its possibility, that moral agents are responsible, gave Bradley his starting point. Like Green, Bradley thought that when we act responsibly it is because we are acting to realise ourselves (Bradley 1876 [1927: 64]). Although all responsible actions realise a self, Bradley thought he could define the good self as one that had realised itself harmoniously

(Bradley 1876 [1927: 303]). From his overwhelmingly negative examinations of utilitarianism, and what seems to be a travesty of Kant's ethics, he drew the conclusion that a good self must will a particular good for its own sake (Nicholson 1990: 21–3). Bradley admitted that this thesis required a metaphysical defence, a defence he did not provide, either in *Ethical Studies* or in his later work (Bradley 1876 [1927: 65]). His later work does, however, provide a psychological ground for self-realisation in what he called 'the law of individuation': 'Every mental element (to use a metaphor) strives to make itself a whole or to lose itself in one, and it will not have its company assigned to it by mere conjunction in presentation' (Bradley 1935 [1969: 212]).

Bradley elaborated his moral thesis in the most celebrated (some would say 'notorious') essay in *Ethical Studies*, 'My Station and Its Duties'. Here he argued that the good self can be realised by willing for its own sake the requirements of one's position in society, by acting 'as an organ in a social organism' (Bradley 1927: 163). Although sometimes taken as his final view, Bradley saw morality as developing through a series of stages of which this is only one (MacNiven 1987: 149–50; Bradley 1927: 190). He made it clear that the doctrine of 'My Station and Its Duties' leaves out important aspects of the good self. No society is perfect, and some aspects of the ideal self are not social (Bradley 1876 [1927: 202–6]). To remedy this defect Bradley described a stage higher than 'My Station and Its Duties', a stage he called 'Ideal Morality'. The self of this stage is the ideal self of moral theory, the self which realises itself as a comprehensive and harmonious whole (Bradley 1876 [1927: 219–20]). Even though this is the highest stage in moral theory, it is still problematic. Morality commands us to suppress our bad selves in order to realise our good ones (Bradley 1876 [1927: 215]). The problem is that if we were to succeed in doing this, we would have undermined morality since it requires the existence of a bad self. Morality consequently fails to specify the final goal of self-realisation (Bradley 1876 [1927: 313–14]). This is supplied, Bradley argued, by religion, which in Bradley's secularised Christianity commands one to die to self in order to live (i.e., to realise one's ideal) (Bradley 1876 [1927: 325]).

Ethical Studies was the only book in which Bradley's position coincided with Green's. Even though Bradley began his next book, *The Principles of Logic* (1883), by accepting the account of judgement implicit in Green's critique of Locke and Hume, Bradley developed it in a way that partially undermined Green's metaphysics. He began with the premises of inferences, the true or false entities he called 'judgements'. While he used traditional terminology in describing judgements as composed of ideas, he also accepted Green's criticisms of empiricism. This led Bradley to distinguish two distinct kinds of ideas: mental images which are particular mental events, and ideal contents which are symbolic and universal.

He denied that mental images are constituents of judgements (Bradley 1883 [1928: 5–10]). Judgments, he said, are mental acts which refer an ideal content to an object (Bradley 1883 [1928: 10]). By defining 'judgement' in this way Bradley separated logic from psychology and rejected the psychologism of the British empiricists.

Bradley developed his account of judgement by distinguishing between the grammatical and logical forms of judgements. His analysis proceeds at several levels which are not always easy to distinguish. At a relatively high level Bradley treated simple negative judgements, like 'This tree is not green', as asserting that the tree named by the subject term lacks the quality named by its predicate term. For this to be true, however, requires that the object named by the subject term have a different quality that excludes the quality named by the predicate term. As Bradley put it, 'negation presupposes a positive ground' (Bradley 1883 [1928: 114]; Stock, 1985: 470–4). At a deeper level, however, Bradley treated all judgements as conditionals. A universal categorical judgement like 'All animals are mortal' asserts that if any individual is an animal, then that individual is mortal (Bradley 1883 [1928: 47–8]). More radically, Bradley treated singular categorical judgements as conditionals. The subject term of a judgement like 'This tree is green' describes more than one actual or possible individual and so fails to specify which individual the judgement is about. As a result the judgement is 'defective'. Its predicate term does not qualify its subject term except under further conditions. But this is to say that it is a conditional judgement (Bradley 1883 [1928: 97–100]). From this Bradley concluded that all judgements have the logical form of conditionals.

This is particularly striking because Bradley used counterfactual judgements as a model for treating universal conditionals. For example, Bradley analysed the judgement 'If you had not destroyed our barometer, it would now forewarn us' by saying, 'In this judgement we assert the existence in reality of such circumstances, and such a general law of nature, which would, *if we suppose* some conditions present, produce a certain result' (Bradley 1883 [1928: 87]). In other words, judgements like this can be treated as metalinguistic. They assert that the argument formed by premises describing the circumstances, describing the relevant scientific law, and asserting the negation of the antecedent, entail the consequent. Conditionals, in other words, are condensed arguments. For this reason, if they are true, they are necessarily true.

On this analysis judgements are true if the arguments they condense are sound. Determining the truth value of a conditional requires determining the truth of its premises. But since the premises must also be conditionals, this requires determining the truth of their premises and so on *ad infinitum*. Since the arguments that judgements condense can be specified differently, Bradley later concluded that all judgements have ambiguous truth values. They are true and false only to a degree (Bradley 1914: 252).

Although Bradley's treatment of judgement has been the most influential part of *The Principles of Logic*, it is preliminary to his main concern, defending deductive logic against John Stuart Mill by specifying the principles that make informative deductive inferences possible. His explanation is that the conclusions of valid inferences are present in the premises, but not asserted in them. The conclusion becomes informative by asserting them (Allard 1998: 70–6). But this defence is bought with a price. Since reality is fully determinate while thought is essentially conditional and incomplete, thought can never constitute reality (Bradley 1883 [1928: 590–1]).

But if thought does not constitute reality, how then does it stand to reality? Answering this question was Bradley's main concern in his major work, *Appearance and Reality* (1893). Even more obviously than in his other books, Bradley's constructive conclusions in *Appearance and Reality* emerge from criticism. Much of this criticism is found in Book I, where he argued that as described by many ordinary ideas the world is contradictory and hence appearance, not reality. The most important ideas Bradley discussed were relation and quality. Bradley argued that they presuppose each other yet are mutually inconsistent. His two arguments supporting this conclusion are his most famous and one or the other of them is usually what philosophers have in mind when they refer to 'Bradley's regress'. The first, the 'internal diversity argument' (Mander 1994: 88), begins from the fact that qualities depend on relations for their existence. But if this is the case, then every quality has at least two distinguishable aspects: it is and it is related. Each of these aspects must in its turn be and be related, and so on *ad infinitum*, a result fatal to the unity of any quality (Bradley 1893 [1930: 26–7]). The second argument, the 'chain argument' (Mander 1994: 92), asserts that if a relation R relates its terms A and B, then there must be additional relations between R and A and R and B and so on *ad infinitum* (Bradley 1893 [1930: 27–8]). By treating both of these regresses as vicious, Bradley concluded that relations and qualities are inconsistent and so appearance and not reality. Even though he examined a number of additional ideas in Book I including space, time, motion, causation, activity, things, and the self, he advised his readers that if they have understood 'the principle of this chapter they will have little need to spend . . . time on those [in Book I] that succeed it'. They 'will have condemned, almost without a hearing, the great mass of phenomena' (Bradley 1893 [1930: 29]).

In Book II Bradley built his constructive metaphysics on his criticisms which, he said, presuppose a criterion of reality. The criterion he proposed was 'Ultimate reality is such that it does not contradict itself' (Bradley, 1893 [1930: 120]).

From his account of negative judgements in *The Principles of Logic*, Bradley inferred from this criterion that reality has a positive ground for excluding self-contradictions. Its character is to include its content harmoniously (Bradley 1893 [1930: 121–3]). Since relations are not independently real and since what appears in some sense is real, Bradley concluded that reality has the form of a whole including as its matter all appearances, blended harmoniously. The content of this harmonious whole is experience (Bradley 1893 [1930: 124–7]; Sprigge 1993: 273).

On this basis Bradley confronted 'the great problem of the relation of Thought to Reality'. He posed this problem as a dilemma. On one hand thought is made true by an object other than thought. On the other, completed thought as fully determinate is identical to reality (Bradley 1893 [1930: 492]). His solution is that thought is inconsistent on its own terms since it fails to satisfy its own ideal of being completely 'coherent and comprehensive'. To the extent that thought fails to satisfy this ideal, it fails to be identical to reality. But if it were to satisfy it, then it would have transcended itself so as to include feeling (Bradley 1893 [1930: 145–8]). At this ideal limit, thought is thus made true by reality, which is identical to it (Candlish 1989: 338–9). In this mitigated form Bradley defended the Hegelian identity of thought and reality.

In the remainder of *Appearance and Reality* Bradley asked whether anything fails to find a place in this system of reality. Through examining such topics as nature, body and soul, goodness, Bradley concluded that nothing did. In his later work, especially the papers collected in *Essays on Truth and Reality* (1914) and in the 'Terminal Essays' in the second edition of *The Principles of Logic* (1922) Bradley elaborated, occasionally modified, and defended his position without alternating it in any fundamental way.

4. BERNARD BOSANQUET

That the reality of the self was an important concern among idealists was indicated by Andrew Seth (who later changed his name to 'Andrew Seth Pringle-Pattison') in his book *Hegelianism and Personality* (1887). Seth accused Green and Hegel of being unable to accommodate in their philosophies the reality of persons, both human and divine (Seth 1887: 221–2). By emphasising the theistic elements he found lacking in absolute idealism, Seth formulated a version of personal idealism, a philosophy that became increasingly popular in the wake of *Appearance and Reality*. The adherents of personal idealism included Andrew's brother James Seth, W. R. Sorley, Hastings Rashdall, and possibly even James Ward, whose final metaphysical views are often difficult to determine precisely. Yet even though absolute idealism denied the reality of selves, it retained its power as a philosophy of religion. This was demonstrated by Bernard Bosanquet, who used Bradley's ideas to reaffirm Green's project of reconciling religion and science.

Bosanquet's longest and most important book was *Logic or the Morphology of Knowledge* (1888). Bosanquet considered judgements to be the fundamental units of knowledge. He accepted Bradley's view that judgements are true or false entities composed of ideas referred to reality. The task of logic, as he conceived it, was to explain how valid inference is possible (Bosanquet 1883: 70). Bosanquet thought it was possible because reality, and hence knowledge of it, forms an interconnected whole or 'system'. The judgements which form the premises of inferences derive their meaning from their place in the totality of judgements which determine reality. Valid inference is then possible because valid inferences make explicit what is implicit in their premises in virtue of their place within the system of judgements as a whole (Bosanquet 1888 [1911: 2]). Logic demonstrates this by examining different forms of judgement (categorical, hypothetical, etc.) and the extent to which they depend on other forms of judgement. Although Bosanquet said he accepted Bradley's account of the relation between thought and reality, he subtly shifted the meaning of 'thought'. Unlike Bradley who sharply separated feeling and thought, Bosanquet blurred the line between them by treating 'simple apprehension', Bradley's immediate experience, as something that was defined by relation to thought (Bosanquet 1911: 292–9). Thus for Bosanquet, as for Green, thought is all inclusive, although Bosanquet employed Bradley's arguments to show this. This allowed him to follow Green in identifying thought with reality and logic with metaphysics.

Bosanquet thought the best indication of his expanded understanding of thought was found in beauty (Bosanquet 1912: 62). This was one of the themes he developed in his aesthetic writings, particularly *History of Aesthetic* (1892) in which he described the history of the Western aesthetic consciousness from ancient Greece through the nineteenth century. His aim was to show how the formal Greek view of beauty was given content by nineteenth-century idealists. They did this, Bosanquet thought, by showing that beauty involved reason in sensuous form, thereby further blurring the line between thought and feeling (Bosanquet 1892: 462–3).

The enhanced significance Bosanquet attributed to thought enabled him to use Bradley's ideas in restating Green's reconciliation of religion and science in the face of personal idealist criticisms. The particular problem he faced was combining Bradley's metaphysical denial of the ultimate reality and value of individual persons (or 'finite individuals' as Bosanquet called them) with Green's insistence that moral goodness can only be realised in individuals. Bosanquet did this by arguing that while finite individuals are ultimately unreal, the only true individual, the Absolute, has characteristics analogous to those found in finite individuals. Bosanquet then argued that what is of value in individuals is preserved in the Absolute.

Bosanquet's rather informal argument for the existence of the Absolute in *The Principle of Individuality and Value* (1912) drew heavily on his *Logic*. Bosanquet thought that the standard for reality and value was provided by the central or higher human experiences which include experiences of satisfaction (Bosanquet 1912: 3). Like Bradley, he thought that what satisfies the intellect is real and that whatever does this is complete and self-contained and hence 'individual' (Bosanquet 1912: 52, 68). Most of the things we experience, however, lack this feature. What we immediately experience, for example, contains elements that are universal in the sense that they have significance for other experiences. As a result, immediate experience is not complete in itself. It leads us to consider further experiences (Bosanquet 1912: 9, 13, 31–2]). The ideal goal of this process, Bosanquet thought, was an experience whose different aspects are interdefined and make no reference to anything outside of the experience. Bosanquet called anything that can be interpreted this way a 'concrete universal' and argued that concrete universals can only be embodied in a world including thought and feeling. There is no way to reach ultimate satisfaction, Bosanquet claimed, short of admitting that the whole of reality is one such world. Bosanquet called this world 'the Absolute' (Bosanquet 1912: 68).

A consequence of this is that as finite individuals we are not complete, but rather self-contradictory and hence ultimately unreal, just as Bradley thought (Bosanquet 1912: 221). We can nevertheless become more complete by defining ourselves by means of our interactions with objects and with other finite individuals. In so doing we expand ourselves and experience satisfaction as a consequence. As one of our higher experiences, Bosanquet argues, this is an indication of the character of the Absolute. It must contain something like the satisfaction we achieve by resolving contradictions. Since this is a fundamental experience of self-hood, the Absolute must be analogous to a self (Bosanquet 1912: 250). As finite selves, we can never experience this completeness, yet we experience some of the satisfaction of overcoming our finite selves as members of harmonious societies or in religion (Bosanquet 1912: 270). In particular, we can never overcome the contradiction between thought and sense, yet by seeing beauty as reason we can understand that in principle it can be overcome (Bosanquet 1912: 258–9).

Although this philosophy of religion did not quiet the personal idealists, it was Bosanquet's political philosophy that became the focus of his most intense critics, particularly during and after the First World War. Despite his critics' charges of authoritarianism, Bosanquet basically restated Green's political philosophy with somewhat different emphases (Nicholson 1990: 199). His work with the Charity Organisation Society convinced him that the times required a clearer account of the limits of state action and he wished to fill in the psychological background of Green's theory more fully (Bosanquet 1899 [1965: viii–x]). Like Green, Bosanquet argued that human beings are only able to realise themselves in communities (Bosanquet 1899 [1965: 102]). Human beings rationally will to achieve their own ends and because these ends differ at different times, they rationally will an end that will harmonise their various desires. Since the ends of different individuals conflict, they rationally will ends that will harmonise their separate ends and these are the ends of the community (Bosanquet 1899 [1965: 112]). Following Rousseau, Bosanquet said that they are willed by the general will, the end of which is freedom. This then provided a rational ground for political obligation since the most comprehensive system defined by the general will is the state. Bosanquet did not, however, identify this with government, which is simply one of the important ways in which this will is manifested in a society (Bosanquet 1899 [1965: 139–40]).

5. JOSIAH ROYCE AND AMERICAN IDEALISM

In the United States, as in Britain, the desire to reconcile science, particularly evolutionary biology, with religion was the main impetus behind the development of idealism. But the story of that development was different. German immigrants, such as Frederick A. Rauch and J. B. Stallo, introduced Hegel to American audiences in the 1830s and 1840s, but it was the Civil War rather than Darwin's work that made it initially attractive. Hegel's account of history as the development of liberty through struggle provided a potent rationale for political union and it was a group of committed unionists, the Philosophical Club of St Louis (better known as the St Louis Hegelians), who in 1867 founded the first philosophy journal in the United States, *The Journal of Speculative Philosophy*. Besides containing translations of German idealists, it provided a forum for young philosophers to exchange ideas. Its editor, William Torrey Harris, eventually became United States Commissioner of Education. As universities grew in the reconstruction following the Civil War, Harris's journal helped popularise idealism as an attractive way of harmonising liberty with union and religion with science. The latter task became increasingly important after the Civil War as Americans turned their attention to the theory of evolution. Idealism only established itself in American universities in the decades following the Civil War. By the end of the century forms of absolute idealism were represented by George Sylvester Morris at the University of Michigan and James Edwin Creighton at Cornell University, while forms of personal idealism were represented by Borden Parker Bowne at Boston University and G. H. Howison, who finally settled at the University of California at Berkeley. But the only American idealist with an international reputation was the Harvard philosopher Josiah Royce.

Like other Anglo-American idealists, Royce attempted to find a place for religion in a world of scientific facts. He defined his way of doing this in his first book, *The Religious Aspect of Philosophy* (1885), and then spent the rest of his career elaborating and defending it. Royce's goal in this book was to determine the nature and worth of reality. He pursued this goal by defining a moral ideal and determining the extent to which it is found in reality. The fact that different ideals have been proposed, Royce thought, suggests that scepticism between ideals is necessary. Royce claimed, however, that scepticism results from attempting to harmonise incompatible but equally attractive aims. From this he concluded that even scepticism accepts harmony among ends as its ideal (Royce 1885: 138). This ideal enjoins us to extend the moral ideal of harmony to others and to realise it in the organisation of our own lives (Royce 1885: 172–3). It requires us to seek the unity and harmony of all life. Royce later reformulated his moral philosophy in his most popular work, *The Philosophy of Loyalty* (1908), in which he argued that we create moral wills through loyalty to a cause. As individuals become loyal to the same cause, they constitute communities. Since there are different communities defined by different causes, Royce argued that one should be loyal to loyalty; that is, one should further the spirit of community in such a way as not to interfere with the formation of communities which do the same thing (Royce 1908: 118–19).

Royce relied on a metaphysical argument to show that the moral ideal is real. Consider, Royce said, the judgement 'Error exists'. If it is true, then error exists, but error also exists if it is false since in this case the judgement 'Error exists' is an error. What makes error possible, Royce continued, is a judgement disagreeing with its intended object. But how, Royce asked, can a judgement do this? We can intend only what we know, and we know only our own ideas, but we are not in error about them (Royce 1885: 398–9). The only way out of this difficulty, Royce urged, is to see that our ideas sometimes fail to correspond to their intended objects from the point of view of a third consciousness, one which includes both our ideas and our objects. Since we can be in error about virtually anything, this consciousness must be an infinite, all-inclusive consciousness. Royce called it 'The Absolute'. From its point of view our ideas fail to correspond to their objects by being incomplete embodiments of the purpose they embody in their fully developed form in the absolute mind (Royce 1885: 422–3). Royce took this argument to establish the reality of the moral ideal, since the Absolute unifies and harmonises all life.

Although Royce said that he 'never could bear to read Green with any continuity' (Royce 1970: 347), his position resembles Green's in combining Absolute idealism with a belief in the reality and value of individual selves and it is vulnerable to similar criticisms. To defend his position, Royce attempted to explain why finite individuals experience the Absolute as an objective, external world (Royce 1892: 411). In *The World and the Individual*, volume I, Royce reformulated his argument in terms of the internal and external meanings of an idea. The internal meaning is the purpose the idea embodies, while its external meaning is the object to which the internal meaning refers. Royce then asked how it is possible for an internal meaning to refer to an external object (Royce 1899: 32–3). His answer, once again, was that it is possible if finite consciousnesses are parts of a larger consciousness, the Absolute, which includes them (Royce 1899: 352–4). Reformulating his position in this way enabled Royce to confront Bradley's charge that selves, because relational, are inconsistent and unreal and to describe further the relation between minds and the external world. The focus of Royce's response to Bradley was the latter's claim that relations produce an 'endless fission' which is inconsistent. Drawing on the work of Richard Dedekind and Georg Cantor, Royce argued that infinite internally self-representative systems, systems represented by portions of themselves, are consistent embodiments of a single purpose and so have the form of a self (Royce 1899: 544–54). This, he concluded, reconciled the reality of finite individuality with the Absolute. To describe further the relation between minds and the natural world, Royce speculated that the natural world is a mind. Its seemingly constant laws are the habits it has so far formed (Royce 1901: 224–6). This was Royce's version of panpsychism.

After *The World and the Individual* Royce continued his study of mathematical logic. He was particularly interested in the work of Alfred Bray Kempe, a British logician who tried to derive geometry from a more basic logical system (Kempe 1889–90). Royce developed Kempe's ideas in several essays, particularly 'The Relations of the Principles of Logic to the Foundations of Geometry' in which he tried to show that geometry could be derived from a more general, a priori system of logic which defined order. Had this derivation been successful, Royce could have shown that the spatial order of the external world is a special case of the necessary order of thoughts in the mind of the Absolute (Kuklick 1972: 200–1).

Royce's last metaphysical work was *The Problem of Christianity*. Although Royce's main concern in this book was to determine in what sense a modern, educated person could be a Christian (Royce 1913 [1968: 62]), it also featured a further restatement of his idealism. Christianity for Royce had two aspects: it was a way of life lived first by an individual person, Jesus, and it was an interpretation of that life by the early church and particularly by Paul (Royce 1913 [1968: 65]). Royce emphasised the second aspect by arguing that according to Christian doctrine salvation can only be found in a community of interpretation, the ideal form of which is the kingdom of heaven (Royce 1913 [1968: 71, 318–19]). The key term here is 'interpretation' which Royce, following Peirce, is treating as a triadic relation: it requires an interpreter, something to be interpreted, and someone to whom one interprets it (Royce 1913 [1968: 286]). Royce argued that we define ourselves by self-interpretation just as we define others whom we interpret as selves to make our experience coherent. By so doing we create a community of interpreters. The Absolute is such a community and by the argument of *The Religious Aspect of Philosophy* Royce concluded that it is real (Royce 1913 [1968: 361]).

Although Royce influenced some of his students, most notably C. I. Lewis, he did not succeed in creating a school of idealism. But even though idealism maintained its popularity longer in Britain than in the United States, its later developments lacked the cohesion of the philosophers here considered. The legacy of the school was a defence of deductive logic primarily against Mill. It was this legacy which led Royce to mathematical logic and led Russell, who defined logic differently, to proclaim that it was the essence of philosophy. Idealism was unable to adapt itself to the new conception of philosophy as a discipline concerned with certain problems, a conception common to both American pragmatism and British analytical philosophy, and one which proved to be more suitable for a secular and increasingly professionalised age.

4

IDEALISM IN RUSSIA

DAVID BAKHURST

Idealism flourished in Russia in the last quarter of the nineteenth century. The most significant thinker in this movement was Vladimir Soloviev (1853–1900), whose ideas influenced an entire generation of philosophers and inspired the Russian religious-philosophical renaissance of the early twentieth century. In the post-Soviet era, Soloviev's thought is again much discussed, as religious philosophy returns to prominence in Russia.

At first sight, Soloviev's contribution seems remote from most nineteenth-century Russian philosophy, written by men of letters and political activists preoccupied with the social issues raised by the backwardness and brutality of Russian life. Yet although Soloviev was a scholar, he was equally concerned with practical matters of human wellbeing. His work shares the predominant theme of all Russian philosophy: the search for a conception of regenerated humanity, where human beings live harmoniously as parts of an integral whole and the forces that alienate and divide us are overcome. Soloviev is admired for his critique of positivism (Soloviev 1874 [1996]), but it would be misleading to portray the Russian scene as dominated by a confrontation between positivism and idealism. At issue was a broader conflict between naturalism and supernaturalism, between secular and religious visions of humanity's destiny. To appreciate the significance of Soloviev's thought, and the tradition it created, it must be seen in historical context.

THE INTELLECTUAL CLIMATE IN 1870: POPULISM

At the outset of Soloviev's career, the principal secular vision of Russia's salvation was offered by populism, a political movement which flourished among the radical intelligentsia who had lost confidence in European conceptions of progress. Influenced by Marx, the populists viewed capitalism with moral repugnance, though they rejected the view that the commune, or *mir*, could immediately be established in Russia. The years 1873 and 1874 saw an extraordinary 'Go to the people' movement, in which hundreds of young radicals, often dressed up in peasant clothes, went to the villages to demonstrate their enthusiasm for the *mir* and to spread socialist ideas. The peasants reacted with suspicion, sometimes turning their visitors over to the police. Yet the crusade inspired populism and led to the rebirth of the revolutionary Land and Freedom Organisation, which had previously existed in the early 1860s.

The main theorists of populism were Pëtr Lavrov (1823–1900) and Nikolai Mikhailovskii (1842–1904). Both reacted to the postivistic materialism, or 'nihilism', that had dominated Russian radicalism in the 1860s. They argued that scientific methods are unable fully to explain psychological and historical phenomena, and injected various moderate idealist themes into a broadly positivist vision. They denied that iron laws govern historical development and stressed the importance of ethical ideals. Ideals, they argued, influence both the course of history, and how historians portray the past. Nothing dictates the path Russia must take, for history has no objective logic or meaning. We read meaning into history and conceptions of 'progress' are relative to our ideals. We must recognise that the study of society is a normative endeavour, a 'subjective sociology' in which questions of what is and what ought to be cannot be disentangled. Lavrov and Mikhailovskii upheld the individual as the primary value, though they recognised that the proper social setting is a precondition of the flourishing of 'integral personality', an insight which fuelled their romantic communitarianism and Mikhailovskii's scathing critique of the division of labour.

Guilt was a central component of populist ideology. Lavrov (1870 [1967]) stressed the intelligentsia's debt to the masses, whose untold suffering made possible the conditions in which an educated minority could engage in intellectual reflection. The intelligentsia, he argued, was not so much an intellectual elite as a moral voice. Its tragic fate was to precipitate a revolution destined to destroy the very conditions of its own possibility. As hopes of reform foundered, this self-destructive activism infected rank-and-file populism. Underground terrorist factions gained prominence, inspired by the 'Jacobinism' of Lavrov's most outspoken critic, Pëtr Tkachev (1844–86). In 1882, populists assassinated Alexander II. The killing precipitated an era of extreme reaction that effectively destroyed populism as a political movement. Populist ideas survived, however, as a component of Russian Marxism.

SOLOVIEV AND THE RISE OF METAPHYSICAL IDEALISM

The theorists of populism reacted to the materialism of the 1860s by weaving idealistic elements into a broadly naturalistic worldview. Soloviev's philosophy was also a response to materialism, which he had embraced fervently in his youth, but his reaction was more drastic. Adopting the concept of 'integral wholeness' from the Slavophile Ivan Kireevsky (1806–56), Soloviev argued that all things are organically interconnected and that the principle of their unity is divine. We must see the cosmos as a living organism standing in intimate relation to God. God and world are not one, for the world has fallen from God and taken material, particular, and temporal form. Happily, the evolution of the world tends towards reintegration, though only human agency striving for reunion with God can restore all-unity. This is the task entrusted to Christians. It is not a matter of particular souls uniting with God, but a process, collectively realised, of the transfiguration of the corporeal.

Soloviev saw the relation between the divine and the natural as one between two worlds, the former concrete and real, the latter 'the nightmare of sleeping humanity' (quoted in Frank 1950: 10). Yet the divine is present in material nature, and human beings, as inhabitants of both worlds, are simultaneously divine and insignificant. The supernatural is for us a possible object of awareness, though not by empirical or rational means. Empirical cognition is essentially fragmented and particular, and unifying principles supplied by reason are abstract and empty. The divine may be glimpsed only by mystical intuition (Soloviev was prone to visions), and integral knowledge thus requires a proper balance of empirical, rational, and intuitive cognition.

The restoration of all-unity is ultimately not an epistemic matter but a practical act. Crucial here is Soloviev's concept of 'Godmanhood', an idea that expresses God's unity with humanity as a whole (Soloviev 1948 [1877–81]). Soloviev argues that in Christ God is revealed to be neither transcendent, nor immanent in all, but present in man. The figure of Christ is not an object of passive faith but a call to humanity to become 'the receptacle of universal divine Incarnation', as S. L. Frank puts it (1950: 16). Soloviev thus represents humanity – indeed the whole of creation – as a feminine principle, striving to receive divinity. Soloviev explored this idea through the concept of Sophia, the eternal feminine, which he portrayed in diverse ways: as the soul of the universe, the Word made flesh, pure and perfect humanity, and as a mystical being (who, he claimed, had appeared to him on three occasions). The idea of all-unity as achieved through a union of masculine and feminine principles lends Soloviev's work a mystical-erotic dimension. The envisaged union is not, however, analogous to physical sex, which Soloviev portrayed as a tragic affirmation of our mortality, of the 'bad infinity' of one generation succeeding another. His idea is rather one of a union in unconditional love where individuality and particularity are transcended (Soloviev 1985 [1892–4]).

For Soloviev, the reunion of God and world was a real historical process that required the agency of a universal Church. Accordingly, he argued strenuously that the rift between Eastern and Western churches should be healed. Soloviev was attracted to many Catholic doctrines, endorsing the idea of the Pope as the divinely ordained head of the Church, and the doctrine of the Immaculate Conception. He was often attacked as a papist, though, as his Orthodox admirers are quick to argue, he never became a Catholic (see Frank 1950: 249–52; Lossky 1951: 84–6). Rather, he viewed the schism between the Churches as a mistake on both sides.

Soloviev saw theocracy as a necessary consequence of his philosophy. In the mid-1880s, he envisioned a theocratic utopia, a 'tri-unity' of papal, imperial, and prophetic forces representing a temporal manifestation of the Trinity. After the reunification of the Churches, world government was to be united under the Pope and the Russian Tsar, while prophets, moving out in the world, would mediate between the people and the state. Although Soloviev quickly lost confidence in this colourful vision, that he entertained it at all might suggest that his political sensibilities were naïve and reactionary. This, however, was not so. In the 1890s, Soloviev published frequently in liberal journals. Despite his messianic view of Russia as the Third Rome, he was an outspoken critic of the pan-Slavism of Nikolai Danilevsky (1822–85), and of those forms of patriotism and nationalism he took to conflict with Christian commitments. He vehemently opposed anti-semitism. His ethical views, though framed by his religious philosophy, were remarkably secular in content. He sought empirical foundations for morality in feelings of shame, compassion, and religious adoration, which he supplemented by a rational ethic based on the categorical imperative. Despite his commitment to theocracy, he argued that state institutions must administer an impersonal system of legal rules and not appeal to religious authority. A society governed by the rule of law secures minimum morality and thereby furthers freedom and dignity. Soloviev also defended the idea that natural rights have priority over rights we bear as citizens. The latter are all too fragile, the former absolute. There are thus interesting parallels between Soloviev's views and those of liberal jurist Boris Chicherin (1828–1903), though the latter had no time for theocracy.

Soloviev always portrayed the transfiguration of the flesh as a real event, a view that made him sympathetic to Nikolai Fedorov's (1828–1903) bizarre idea that humanity's common task is to resurrect the bodies of the dead. But towards the end of his life, he became increasingly preoccupied with eschatology and beset with premonitions and foreboding. One of his last works contains a fictional portrayal of the end of the world, in which Antichrist, in the form of a brilliant and charismatic writer, becomes world leader. At the point of his assuming all earthly powers, secular and ecclesiastical, Antichrist is challenged by the leaders of the (still fragmented) Christian Church, but he destroys them. He is eventually vanquished, as first the Jews, and then the remaining true

Christians, defeat his armies with the help of divine intervention. The Church leaders are resurrected, the Church united, Christ returns, and the righteous dead return to life and reign with Christ for a thousand years (Soloviev 1950: 229–48).

Though no more fanciful than, say, much contemporary science fiction, these final phantasmagorical speculations are hardly a fitting coda to Soloviev's philosophy, though they speak volumes about the mythology that inspired it.

RUSSIAN IDEALISM AFTER SOLOVIEV

Soloviev's influence was paramount in the remarkable renaissance of Russia religious philosophy in the early twentieth century. Many thinkers of the 'silver age' embraced the metaphysics of all-unity, the idea that the divine is a possible object of mystical–intuitive awareness, the concepts of Godmanhood and Sophia, and the quest for a cultural and religious transformation of world-historical significance. Such notions figure in the work of Pavel Florenskii (1882–1937), one of the most characteristic philosophers of the period, and the thinkers collectively known as 'Godseekers', who participated in the religious–philosophical societies of St Petersburg and Moscow.

The Godseekers comprised two groups. The first group consisted of symbolist poets and literary theorists, including Dmitrii Merezhkovskii (1865–1941), Andrei Belyi (1880–1934), Alexander Blok (1880–1921), and Vyacheslav Ivanov (1866–1949). The symbolists despised rationalism, which they took to undermine religious faith, and advanced an epistemology in which the natural world is a reflection of a deeper reality that can be reached through art and other modes of intuitive awareness. They supplemented Solovievian ideas with the old Slavophile concept of *sobornost'* (the idea of the mystical unity of all believers), and various Nietzschean themes, particularly the Superman, whom they identified with Christ (they took Nietzsche's hostility to Christianity to apply only to traditional Christian conceptions). They were trenchant critics of socialism, though their own political visions were absurd; Ivanov, for example, proposed a 'mystical anarchism' requiring the abolition of all authorities and a social union based on myth, faith, and self-sacrifice.

The other group comprised idealist philosophers, including Nikolai Berdiaev (1874–1948), Sergei Bulgakov (1871–1944), Semën Frank (1877–1950), and Pëtr Struve (1870–1944). They were contributors to two influential collections, *Problemy idealizma* (*Problems of idealism*) (Novgorodtsev 1903) and *Vekhi* (*Signposts*) (1909). Many thinkers in this group were former 'legal Marxists' who had rejected historical determinism as ethically bankrupt. They turned first to Neo-Kantianism, then to metaphysical idealism, in order to assert the autonomy of value and the sanctity of the individual. Those among them with utopian leanings, such as Berdiaev and Bulgakov, sought a new metaphysics of integral personality and tended to see potential in the efforts of those socialists, such as Anatoly Lunacharskii (1875–1933), who viewed socialism as a kind of humanist religion. In contrast, liberals like Struve and Frank represented the religious yearnings of the socialists as a dangerous perversion. *Vekhi* provoked enormous controversy and was denounced by liberals and Marxists alike. The latter, of course, won the debate in practice, if not in theory. In 1922, Berdiaev, Bulgakov, and Frank were among many thinkers expelled from Russia by the Bolsheviks. They became influential figures in the émigré philosophical community.

Not all species of idealism that flourished in early twentieth-century Russia were so heavily influenced by Soloviev. Vasili Rozanov (1856–1919), for example, was an original and disturbing thinker with very different sensibilities. Like many of his contemporaries, Rozanov was influenced by Nietzsche and Dostoevsky, but he also admired the arch-conservativism of Konstantin Leontiev (1831–91), with its hostility to the homogenising effects of modernity and its aesthetic immoralism which accorded beautiful objects greater value than 'faceless' people. Although steeped in Orthodoxy, Rozanov was contemptuous of Christianity's preoccupation with transcending the flesh, which he saw as a denial of earthly existence. He advanced a 'metaphysics of sex', and maintained, memorably, that there is more theology in a bull mounting a cow than is found in the seminaries. Scurrilous, cynical, and sometimes anti-semitic, Rozanov was not unduly preoccupied with consistency, nonchalantly publishing at once in both the ultra-right and liberal-left presses.

A form of pan-psychism, Leibnitzian in influence, also flourished in Russia. Its originator was Aleksei Kozlov (1831–1901), who held that reality is an infinite plurality of interacting spiritual substances, or monads, all mutually related. Our categories and forms of thought are merely symbols of a deeper reality, the development of which is logical not temporal. Kozlov was concerned with pure philosophy, but his pupil Nikolai Losskii (1870–1965) introduced into the system religious themes owing much to Soloviev. The result was, however, very obscure. Losskii imputes agency to all monads, explaining natural events as the outcome of their choices, and argues that even though everything is immanent in everything, there is an ontological rift between the natural and the divine. Losskii was, however, a fine historian of Russian philosophy, who worked tirelessly to preserve Russian religious philosophy in exile (see Losskii 1951).

CONCLUSION

The blossoming of Russian idealism between 1870 and 1917 was a fascinating and refreshing development. Both the moderate social idealism of Lavrov and Mikhailovskii, and the more dramatic metaphysical idealism of Soloviev and his followers, contain impressive insights and challenging visions. With the collapse of communism, religious philosophy is once again hotly debated in Russia, and Soloviev is as popular as ever. That his kind of religious philosophy might be considered a worldview of contemporary relevance is a sobering, even frightening, thought. Russian metaphysical idealism is important not because of its truth, but because of what it reveals about the characteristic quest of Russian thinkers (a quest found equally within the Russian Marxism that displaced idealism): the search for an all-embracing vision to facilitate the renewal, even deification, of humanity through apocalyptic transformation, and a burning desire for all-encompassing unity, equality, and the transcendence of the commonplace.

5

BERGSON

F. C. T. MOORE

At times of transition in the history of thought, we find thinkers who open and close doors, often in exploratory or surprising ways, and others who map out whole new programmes of enquiry. The sketch of Bergson's work in this chapter will set it in context, and show it as opening and closing doors, rather than as providing a manifesto for a new philosophical programme.

ANALYSIS IN PHILOSOPHY

Nineteenth-century debates over positivism and idealism were displaced in time by other themes, in which a renewed interest in analysis had a major part. The analytic method had played a central role in European thought since Descartes. His invention of analytic geometry, and the later invention by Leibniz and Newton of the calculus, had been inseparable from major advances in natural science, as well as leaving their imprint upon philosophical work more generally.

But analysis, while not indifferent to the temporal dimension, treats it on the model of spatial dimensions (indeed, Descartes had described his physics, which was, after all, destined to give an account of physical change over time, as nothing but pure geometry). Now the nineteenth century had seen a new concern with diachronic explanation, whether as an idealist project in the wake of Hegel, or as a disciplinary project in linguistics (historical linguistics), in economics (Marx), in biology (Darwin, Mendel), in textual criticism, and so forth. This had, for the time, displaced the analytic method from its central (though contested) position as the key to our understanding of the phenomena of our world.

As the twentieth century dawned, both Russell and Bergson perceived anew the importance of analysis. But where Russell emphasised its liberating power, Bergson emphasised its tricky limits. This contrast provides a key to understanding the work of Bergson in particular and the philosophical developments of the first half of the twentieth century in general.

ANALYSIS REVIVED: RUSSELL

In order to establish the strategic contrast with Bergson, a brief sketch of Russell's position is required. As with Descartes, mathematics played a key role. Since antiquity, mathematics had often been conceived as having two distinct objects: number (in arithmetic), and space (in geometry). Descartes had achieved the partial arithmetisation of geometry, a process advanced by the later invention of the calculus. Thus, it seemed, geometry could be reduced to arithmetic. It was the new idea of Frege that arithmetic itself could be analysed as nothing but pure logic: that is, arithmetical statements could be fully explicated in a way which would retain no reference to numbers. Though Russell detected a crucial defect in Frege's approach, he not only recognised its revolutionary character, but attempted (with Whitehead) to achieve the analysis which Frege had been unable to carry through (it is an insufficiently explored paradox that Whitehead's later philosophical work had more in common with Bergson's views than with those of Russell).

The work of Russell and Whitehead work was technical in its details, but its guiding ambitions provided a template for subsequent philosophical work by many thinkers in areas far removed from mathematics, and *Principia Mathematica* (Russell and Whitehead 1910–13) is commonly regarded as an initiating moment for that varied family of philosophical movements widely known as 'analytic philosophy'.

ANALYSIS REVIVED: BERGSON

Bergson was as unorthodox as Russell *vis-à-vis* the philosophical establishment of his youth, and he too acquired a fame which went far beyond the academic world. Furthermore, he too started from mathematics. But where Russell was fired by the great analytic project of Frege, Bergson started with a puzzle: 'It was my mathematical studies which stirred my interest in durance,[1] at a time when I had no pretensions to doing metaphysics. At first, this was no more than a kind of puzzlement at the value given to the letter t in the equations of mechanics'[2] (Maire 1935: 219).

What was this puzzle? Analysis gives us what seems a clear picture, for instance, of the motions of celestial bodies, under classical mechanics. But suppose that we transpose these motions to a human scale. Suppose that we try to re-enact the

---

[1] 'Durance' is my preferred translation of Bergson's word *durée* (more usually rendered 'duration'). See Moore 1996: 58–9.

[2] This, and all translations from Bergson in this chapter, were made by the author. Accordingly, page references are given to the original French versions, rather than to published translations.

motions of sun, earth, and moon by human action, as Wittgenstein is reported to have done (Malcolm 1958: 51–2). It turns out that this cannot be achieved (Moore 1996: 59–62). Is this a trivial, or a deep problem? Is there something in the sense of time or the experience of time which escapes mechanics and its analytic procedures?

It seems that we need to take a second look at mechanics. 'Metaphysics and even psychology were of much less interest to me than work in the philosophy of science, especially mathematics. What I wanted to do in my doctoral thesis was to make a study of the basic concepts of mechanics' (Du Bos 1946–61: 63–8).

TIME AND DURANCE

In trying to resolve this puzzle, Bergson was led both to emphasise and to limit the operations of human reason (our thought and our language), and to adopt a pragmatic and evolutionary view of them, in a way which was to lead to a sharp divergence from the views of Russell.

We may go here to the reasonings of McTaggart, a late English idealist, though they postdated the work of Bergson. McTaggart pointed to two views of time, one represented by the relation *before and after*, the other by the relation *past/present/future* (McTaggart 1908: 457–74). He argued that these two kinds of relation were incompatible, and drew idealist conclusions. Bergson offered a different and deeper account. A distinction of the kind made by McTaggart presupposes an analysis of the temporal evolution of the world (and our experience of it) into discrete events. But for Bergson, this analysis is not imposed by any logical, methodological, or metaphysical imperative (as so many have thought, from Hume to Davidson). Instead, it is a pragmatic imperative. For active creatures like ourselves, such an analysis of the changing world is indispensable: without the evolved capacity for analysis, we should be helpless. In this sense, Bergson gives great importance to analysis, but in a more focused and restricted way than philosophy has traditionally accorded to our intelligence:

Human intelligence, as we conceive of it, is in no way the kind of intelligence depicted by Plato in the allegory of the cave. It does not have the function of watching vain shadows pass by any more than of turning round and contemplating the blazing sun. It has other things to do. Yoked, like plough-oxen, to a heavy task, we feel the play of our muscles and joints, the weight of the plough and the resistance of the soil: the function of human intelligence is to act and to know that it is acting, to enter into contact with reality and even to live it, but only in so far as it is concerned with the job being done, and the furrow being ploughed. (Bergson 1907 [1986: 192])

Thus Bergson's epistemology gives priority to action. Human beings, he claims, have 'virtual actions', provided by instinct or learning. It is these which carve out the world for use, and effect an indispensable segmentation of our experience into items which can also be classified and regimented for the purposes of action. But this heritage of atomism also falsifies the world and our experience of it. Our intelligence and our capacity for language which instantiates it are evolved capacities, whose importance to us is beyond question, but whose tendency to create a kind of mental paralysis when we step beyond the need to act, in order to reflect, is represented by an array of philosophical problems, which need to be dissolved, rather than solved: 'habits formed in the sphere of action, when they go up into the sphere of speculation, create factitious problems' (Bergson 1896 [1985: 9]).

PHENOMENOLOGICAL APPROACHES

Thus Bergson rejected an atomism which makes discrete events the basic furniture of the temporal order, out of which processes are, as it were, to be reconstructed. The event-ontology is no more nor less than a pragmatic fiction enabling active beings to act. However, we do require a positive account of temporal becoming, and the first step is to attend to the phenomenology of past, present, and future. If we no longer allow ourselves to describe this in terms of *events* passing in experience from past, to present, to future, what better account can be found?

Melody and speech are examples of temporal entities. It seems, furthermore, that an event-ontology naturally imposes itself. Is not a melody simply a sequence of notes, or a speech a sequence of words? No doubt, we do need this view, in order, for instance, to learn to play or sing a melody. But a melody is not a sequence of notes (Bergson 1934 [1987: 164]). For instance, I might hum 'Three blind mice', and I might hum the opening melody of the *Largo* from Bach's Double Concerto in D minor. And the first three hummed notes of 'Three Blind Mice' could be identical in all respects to the second, third, and fourth hummed notes of the *Largo*. But when I hum the *Largo*, I am not thereby also humming 'Three Blind Mice', nor does a proper part of the 'Three Blind Mice' melody form a part of the *Largo* melody. Similarly, I might say 'The wife of John Lennon is Japanese' – but 'John Lennon is Japanese' is not a proper part of this saying, even though it is the same string of words.

But if the melody as a whole (or the speech as a whole) is phenomenologically prior to its individual notes (or words), it remains true that one note (or word) does follow another, and that I can be aware that I am now singing a particular note (or saying a particular word) of the sequence. How to accommodate this plain fact of experience? One approach is to insist that there is no awareness of a pure present (something which goes against the epistemological priority which Russell was led to give to 'this here now'). William James, whose personal and intellectual affinities with Bergson should be emphasised, was one of the philosophers who held that 'the only fact of our immediate experience is . . . "the specious present"' (James 1890: 608–9). He held that this had a certain duration (up to at most twelve seconds), and was the 'unit of composition' of our perception of time. Bergson went much further. He held that what we are aware of *now* is a complexity, a 'rhythm', of evolving processes to which no general procedure can assign a beginning in measurable time. 'When I utter the word *causerie*, I have before my mind not only the beginning, the middle, and the end of the word, but also the words which came before it, also the whole of the sentence which I have so far voiced; otherwise, I should have lost track of what I am saying' (Bergson 1907 [1986: 9]).

In his earlier works, this phenomenological approach was pursued in various ways, in line with Bergson's claim that precision in philosophy had to be subject-specific (Moore 1996: 14–17). He discussed perception, the mind/body problem, free-will, images, memory, laughter, dreams, intellectual effort, creative thought, in each case combining a phenomenological approach with a distrust of conventional metaphysics. The 'mind/body problem', for instance, was a family of factitious puzzles: apart from attending to the phenomenology of action, we should try to advance our understanding of the mental and the cerebral by studying phenomena like amnesia and aphasia. In this way, 'a capital problem of metaphysics is shifted over into observation on the ground, where it can be progressively resolved, instead of endlessly feeding disagreement between schools in the closed field of sheer disputation' (Bergson 1907 [1986: 9]).

INTUITION

In 1903, Bergson systematised his earlier work by introducing a general distinction between two forms of knowledge, *intuition* and *analysis* (Bergson 1903). If I raise my arm, I am aware of doing so 'from the inside'. This intuition is *simple*. But one who observes my action can properly apprehend or analyse it as a complex of elements, set in relation to others. The object of intuition is absolute, while that of analysis is relative. But Bergson does not now confine this distinction to the phenomenological realm. It opens up the possibility of a new metaphysics in which intuition of the absolute might be a key to understanding in domains beyond the psychological.

This decisive change of direction in Bergson's work is the one to which Russell took strong exception (Russell 1914), not only because of its challenge to the role of analysis, but also because of the importance it attached to intuition. In *L'Evolution créatrice (Creative Evolution)* (Bergson 1907), Bergson tried to supplement scientific evolutionary theory with the *élan vital*, envisaging a sort of ultra-phenomenology for life itself. In *Durée et Simultanéité (Duration and Simultaneity)*, he tried to supplement relativity theory by reintroducing (the intuition of) absolute simultaneity (Bergson 1922). And in *Les Deux Sources de la morale et de la religion (The Two Sources of Morality and Religion)*, he ventured into views of morality and religion which combined a brilliant analytic power with a kind of mysticism (Bergson 1932).

These attempts brought Bergson his greatest fame, and they are often penetrating. Yet there are signs that he had misgivings about them. Four years after *Creative Evolution*, he gave a lecture in which he said: 'How can the profession of philosophy entitle a practitioner to go further than science? . . . Such a conception of the role of the philosopher would be injurious for science. But how much more injurious for philosophy!' (Bergson 1911 [1987: 135–6]). As for his foray into relativity theory, Bergson would not allow further reprints in the thirties, since he doubted whether he could defend the technical parts of the work. And in 1934, the collection of earlier pieces published as *La Pensée et le mouvant* included a new introduction, in which Bergson attacked philosophical system-making, and insisted that precision in philosophy consists in proper adaptation of methods of enquiry to the subject-matter: 'Philosophical systems are not made to the measure of the reality in which we live. They are too big' (Bergson 1934 [1987: 1]).

BERGSON'S 'PROJECT'

It is an occupational hazard of historians of thought to assume that the work of a thinker must form a system. It is tempting to believe that we should be able to find a key to reconcile writings which are sometimes various, even conflicting, and which may change and develop over time, into a single doctrine.

The massive secondary literature about Bergson is not lacking in such approaches. Some, for instance, taking their cue from Bergson's late religious philosophy, have attempted to read his entire œuvre as a concerted theism, even though theism is not envisaged at all in his early works (e.g. Hude 1989–90). Possibly the best indication that such approaches to Bergson's work are erroneous is the fact that, despite Bergson's fame and influence, it cannot be said that he fathered a school of philosophy. There was nothing which bore the same relation to Bergson's work as 'analytic philosophy' bore to that of Russell. He was, perhaps, too individual and adventurous a thinker for that. Here was a person in whose work are substantial, sometimes elegant and limpid, sometimes tough and rebarbative, forays into the philosophy of science and mathematics, into pragmatism, into moral philosophy and mysticism, into phenomenology, into defusing traditional philosophical debates.

ANALYSIS AND ACTION:
THE GREAT BUT MODEST ROLE OF REASON

Bergson is not the only philosopher to have given priority to action over cognition. But this puts philosophy into an awkward position. For what instruments does it have but reason, intelligence, language? But since these were created by evolution for the needs of action, and may mislead us if we step back to take stock, all we can do is to use our intelligence for purposes contrary to those for which it came into being: analysis must be turned against itself: all we can do, in Bergson's expression, is to 'think backwards' (Bergson 1934 [1987: 214]; for the translation, see Moore 1996: xii, note 4).

But how does Bergson's theoretical emphasis on action fit in a historical volume? As a small boy, Bergson lived as a boarder, far from his parents, through the dramatic events of the *commune*, when French troops eventually massacred the *communards* in Paris with the German troops standing by. He lived through the First World War, and, as an old man, he died under the German occupation in the Second.

Did he avoid taking action, as opposed to theorising about it? Not so. He played a prominent international role between 1917 and 1925 for the causes of peace and international cooperation. And, close to death, he avowed that his personal itinerary had led him towards becoming a member of the Catholic Church. He did not do so, he said, because this would have been, at that time and place in a world of total war and multiple barbarisms, an abandonment of those threatened fellow-beings who were also of Jewish descent.

It should be added that Bergson himself would not have liked these biographical remarks. He insisted that 'the life of a philosopher throws *no light* on his or her doctrine, and is not the concern of the public' (Soulez 1997: 288). Nevertheless, we know the scene of his death in occupied France, the France which he so much loved. He spoke of philosophy, and then said to those present: 'Gentlemen, it is five o'clock. The course is ended.' So speaking, he died.

PRAGMATISM

CHRISTOPHER HOOKWAY

1. INTRODUCTION

Pragmatism entered public debate in 1898, when William James (1842–1910) lectured on 'Philosophical conceptions and practical results' to the Philosophical Union at Berkeley. His book *Pragmatism: A New Name for some Old Ways of Thinking* appeared in 1907, a record of lectures delivered in Cambridge, Massachusetts, a year or two earlier (James 1907). Charles Sanders Peirce (1839–1913) delivered a series of lectures entitled *Pragmatism* in Harvard in 1903 (Peirce 1934), and spent much of the following decade attempting to distinguish his version of pragmatism from James's and trying to establish its truth. However, although James's lecture may have been the first public statement of pragmatism, the philosophical outlook which he presented was already two or three decades old, dating to philosophical discussions in Cambridge in the early 1870s. The roots of James's pragmatism can be seen in writings from that decade which culminated in his *Principles of Psychology* (1890); an early classic statement of Peirce's pragmatism is found in a series of papers entitled *Illustrations of the Logic of Science* which appeared in the *Popular Science Monthly* in 1877–78, and James's readers were further prepared for his pragmatism by works such as *The Will to Believe* (1897).

Although pragmatism is a distinctively American contribution to philosophy, we should not lose sight of the degree to which both Peirce and James were engaged in debates growing out of European philosophy. Indeed this European connection continued: both Peirce and James identified F. C. S. Schiller in Oxford and Italian thinkers such as Giovanni Papini and Giovanni Vailati as important fellow pragmatists. Educated at Harvard, where the prevailing orthodoxy had tried to reconcile the claims of science and religion by relying on ideas drawn from the Scottish common-sense philosophers, Peirce and James both reached maturity as this reconciliation was rocked by Darwinism and by John Stuart Mill's critique of Sir William Hamilton's defence of the Scottish position. James's *Pragmatism* was dedicated to Mill, 'from whom I first learned the pragmatic openness of mind and whom my fancy likes to picture as our leader were he alive today' (James 1907 [1975a: dedication]). Peirce, by contrast, despised Mill's psychologistic approach to logic, and self-consciously developed a philosophical position which he described as 'but a modification of Kantism' (1905–6 [1998: 353]). These differences may reflect their other interests: James came to philosophy from psychology; and Peirce made innovative contributions to formal logic, developing, independently of Frege, a logic of relations and quantifiers in the early 1880s.

It is easy to see that the pragmatist 'tradition' has many strands – especially when we note that the views of the third of the classic pragmatists, John Dewey, were shaped by his early Hegelianism. However, we can sketch some themes that are common to all versions. The first of these explains why many have seen the school as allied to positivism. Peirce's pragmatism was formulated as a principle or tool for clarifying the meanings of propositions, concepts, and hypotheses. This has a verificationist flavour: we clarify a concept by showing what difference it would make to experience if some object fell under it. Although he emphasised the role of such clarifications in enabling us to clarify scientific hypotheses and test them against experience, the principle was also used to show that some claims and concepts, including those of 'ontological metaphysics', were empty. Thus he claimed that, taken literally, the Catholic doctrine of transubstantiation is 'senseless jargon' (1877–8 [1986: 266]). James, too, introduced his pragmatism as a device for defusing metaphysical questions: appealing to Peirce's principle, he approached traditional metaphysical debates by asking 'what difference it would practically make to anyone if this notion rather than that notion were true?' If there is no difference, then the 'alternatives mean practically the same thing, and all dispute is idle' (1907 [1975: 28]). Although these remarks have a strong positivist flavour, Peirce and James were both far more receptive to religious belief than other positivists and far more open to the possibility that there are intelligible and valuable forms of metaphysics.

A second theme is that both pragmatists defended distinctive theories of truth which have led many readers to ally pragmatism with idealism and anti-realism. Indeed on occasion, James insisted that his pragmatism *was* a theory of truth, and it was the slogans James used to express this doctrine which most encouraged the perception that pragmatism was a crude and immoral doctrine. The truth is what is 'expedient in the way of belief' or what it is good to believe; a proposition is true in so far as it puts us into a satisfactory relation to our experience and so on. Cases such as terminally ill patients whose lives may be improved by the belief that a cure is possible were taken to show that James held that this was enough to make the belief true. Peirce's theory was different: a true proposition is one that would be an matter of 'fated' or 'destined' long-run consensus or agreement among those who investigated the matter. This too appeared to conflict with the realist doctrine that there may be facets of reality that will forever be beyond our grasp, that the truth may outstrip what we can discover. Truth is defined by reference to human enquiry and experience rather than in terms of correspondence to an independent reality. Hence the view that pragmatism is not a realist doctrine. This makes it surprising that, from the 1860s, Peirce linked his view of truth to realism. Later he declared himself a 'realist of a somewhat extreme stripe', and a 'Scotistic realist', claiming that pragmatism such as his could never have entered the head of someone who did not endorse realism.

A third cluster of views supports the first two. James's psychological writings contained a distinctive view of thought. Conceptualisation and theorising are explained in teleological terms: we attend to specific features of experience, and employ concepts which emphasise particular saliencies and similarities, in the light of our needs and interests. Theories and concepts are cognitive instruments which are judged by how well they enable us to achieves our goals and find our way around the world. In defending this view, James challenged the claim of Herbert Spencer that the function of thought was to provide us with beliefs and theories which corresponded to, or 'mirrored' an external reality. Thus concepts are empty unless they have a role in enabling us to deal with our surroundings; and beliefs are true if they perform their intended function effectively.

Peirce's *semiotic*, his theory of signs, introduced a related perspective. Signs stand for objects only through being understood or 'interpreted' as so doing: the content of a belief or hypothesis is explained by reference to the ways in which it is used in inference and enquiry. The pragmatist principle guided interpretation, and also drew attention to cases where our assurance that some form of words had a use, could genuinely be interpreted or understood, was an illusion. Much of Peirce's later work was an attempt to prove that the pragmatist principle could serve this role, an attempt which drew on an increasingly complex and sophisticated account of the ways in which signs relate to their objects and of the variety of ways in which they are understood.

The final theme in pragmatism is relevant to questions about realism. The views we have described have an empiricist flavour. Earlier empiricists tended to adopt an austere conception of experience. Hume, for example, defended an atomist picture of impressions and ideas, and he faced the task of explaining how we could develop ideas of external existence, law, and causation out of sensory materials which lacked these features. Both our pragmatists claimed that experience was far richer than other empiricists had claimed. Peirce insisted that we have direct experience of external things, of causal interactions between them and of the causal potentialities which they embody: experience is, in many ways, 'theory laden'. James's 'Radical Empiricism' also held that the elements of experience are linked together by relations which are themselves part of experience. This rich notion of experience explains many of the differences between pragmatists and positivist philosophers whose views might otherwise seem similar to theirs.

The first chapter of James's *Pragmatism* presents the doctrine as a way of overcoming 'The Present Dilemma in Philosophy' (James 1907 [1975: 9–26]): it offers a middle way between scientistic positivism and idealism. Remarking on the role of temperament in shaping philosophical views, James contrasts two philosophical outlooks. The tough-minded philosopher is a materialist, a determinist who rejects free will, and an empiricist, who tends to be sceptical, irreligious, and pessimistic. The tender-minded philosopher, by contrast, embraces principles and values, holds to religious belief and to free will, and is optimistic in the face of the future. The tough-minded, who include positivists, are driven into pessimism because they want their views to be answerable to experience and to accord with science, with what is evidently our best knowledge. They are led to reject ideas which are fundamental to morality and personal fulfilment. The tender-minded idealist is less alienated from her surroundings, but is likely to employ methods of enquiry which smack of wishful thinking: she trusts reason to discern fundamental principles and values which are not tested against experience. The task of reconciling these outlooks, remaining optimistic while taking seriously what science teaches about the world, was to be completed by James's pragmatism. The empiricist strain was to show how our views are disciplined and sensitive to the way things are; but this would still allow room for religion, for belief in free will and for taking values seriously. It offers a middle way between positivism, which is one embodiment of the tough-minded philosophy, and the varieties of idealism that appeal to the tender minded. This search for a middle way is characteristic of pragmatist philosophy in general. Peirce, too, saw positivists as committed to a flawed conception of reality which led inevitably to scepticism; and he shared James's hope for an empirically grounded philosophy which would find room for values and religious belief.

What is the source of the name 'pragmatism'? It did not appear in print or even in manuscripts before 1898, but Peirce and James agreed that it was employed in the discussions of a 'metaphysical club' that met in Cambridge for several years around 1870. This group included lawyers such as Oliver Wendell Holmes and Nicholas St John Green, and, as well as James and Peirce, the philosopher Chauncey Wright. Wright was a powerful figure, referred to by Peirce as his philosophical 'boxing master', and influenced by John Stuart Mill. He was anxious to explore the philosophical importance of Darwinian ideas. Peirce later claimed that 'pragmatism' came from Kant's *pragmatisch*, meaning empirical or experimental: the pragmatist urges that *all* concepts and hypotheses can be explained in terms of their relation to experience. James may have understood the term differently, suggesting that we should understand concepts in terms of their relevance to our practical needs; after 1905, alarmed at seeing his word adopted to label some philosophical outlooks that he found unpalatable, Peirce referred to his own version as 'pragmaticism' a name, he said, which was 'ugly enough to be safe from kidnappers' (1905–6 [1998: 332–5]).

INQUIRY, PRAGMATISM AND TRUTH

In 'The Fixation of Belief' and 'How to Make Ideas Clear', the first two of the 'Illustrations of the Logic of Science' (1877–8 [1984: 242–75]), Peirce introduced his pragmatism as part of an anti-Cartesian framework for epistemology and the philosophy of science. These were his most influential papers and had an important impact upon James and later pragmatists such as Dewey. The central notion in this epistemology is *enquiry*, a controlled activity of problem solving: we pose a question, and we seek to arrive at a state of settled belief in which we accept an answer to it. 'The Fixation of Belief' is a discussion of the methods we should employ for carrying out enquiries, for moving from a state of doubt to a state of belief. The conclusion that the 'method of science' is the only defensible method sets the agenda for the remaining papers in the series which explore this method in more detail.

Some ten years earlier, Peirce had urged: 'Let us not pretend to doubt in philosophy what we do not doubt in our hearts.' This claim that Cartesian doubt is self-deception is echoed in 'The Fixation of Belief' (1868–9 [1984: 212]): 'the mere putting of a proposition into the interrogative form does not stimulate the mind to any struggle after belief' (1877–8 [1986: 248]). Doubt requires a reason: we doubt propositions, and thus begin to enquire into them, only when experience or other confident beliefs conflict with them. Peirce similarly rejects the Cartesian demand that enquiry should rest upon 'ultimate and absolutely indubitable propositions'. We can rely upon all those things we actually believe when we start out in enquiry, and the fact that some of these may prove to be mistaken is not an insuperable obstacle to cognitive progress. Doubts arise in the course of our enquiries, and when they arise they must be addressed and settled; so long as a proposition is not doubted, we should trust it while acknowledging the fallibility of our trust. Although Peirce later acknowledged the value of *trying* to doubt propositions as an aid to rational self-control, he retained his sympathy with the common-sense tradition. Philosophers' reasons for doubt are often insensitive to the mass of experience and shared knowledge which supports our views of the world.

This idea that enquiry is a problem-solving activity was developed in much more detail in John Dewey's *Logic: The Theory of Inquiry* (1938). Peirce's own paper moves quickly to considering the standards we should follow in our enquiries, comparing four methods for 'the fixation of belief'. If we adopt the 'method of tenacity', we simply choose an answer to our question, dwelling on considerations that support it, and avoiding anything that might shake our resolve. Defenders of the 'method of authority' also allow the correctness of an opinion to be grounded in the will, but in this case the will of the state or of some religious or intellectual authority which is allowed to fix the matter and to control our environment to ensure that the belief remains secure. The 'a priori method' denies that the correctness of an opinion can depend upon the will, and enjoins us to accept what is 'agreeable to reason' after 'reflection and conversation' (1877–8 [1986: 248–54]). These methods all fail: doubt will re-emerge when we encounter those who have chosen other opinions or who accept different intellectual authorities. And, as the history of metaphysics shows, the a priori method makes opinion a matter of fashion or taste: this method is likely to appeal to the 'tender minded' and to encourage wishful thinking. Any method which makes the correctness of opinion something subjective is unsatisfactory, and Peirce concludes by defending the method of science which rests on the 'fundamental hypothesis' that:

There are real things, whose characters are entirely independent of our opinions about them; those realities affect our senses according to regular laws, and, though our sensations are as different as our relations to the objects, yet by taking advantage of the laws of perception, we can ascertain by reasoning how things really are, and any man, if he have sufficient experience and reason enough about it, will be led to the one true opinion. (1877–8 [1986: 254])

Peirce probably supposed that this hypothesis is implicit in our common-sense view of things: if this were not so, we would neither worry about which methods we should adopt, nor be dissatisfied by the first three methods as we evidently are.

Later papers in the series give more details of the rules and methods that can be derived from this hypothesis. Pragmatism is presented in 'How to Make Our Ideas Clear' as a procedure for clarifying ideas: 'Consider what effects, which might conceivably have practical bearings, we conceive the object of our conception to have. Then, our conception of those effects is the whole of our conception of the object' (1877–8 [1986: 266]). This means that we clarify a conception or proposition by listing the experiential consequences we would expect our actions to have if the concept applied to something or the proposition were true: if something is soluble, then, if it is added to water, we will

observe it dissolve; if something is hard, then if we try to scratch it, we will see no
change; and so on. Although Peirce acknowledges that this enables us to dismiss
some metaphysical concepts as 'empty', its immediate relevance to his epistemological work is different from this and is twofold. First that the whole content
of hypotheses can be explained in terms of the experiential consequences of
our actions and interventions is an important premise in explaining how experimental science can take us to the truth. Second Peirce applies his principle
in order to clarify important logical concepts such as *probability* and, especially,
reality.

Since the 1860s Peirce had blamed the errors of most modern philosophy
upon a 'nominalist' conception of reality: we think of real things as the efficient
causes of our sensations and truth as correspondence to a wholly independent
reality. Since this view allowed that reality might be utterly different from the
sensations that it causes and might thus be unknowable, it led inevitably to
nominalism about laws and classifications, to scepticism and to an anti-realist
view of science (see Peirce 1871 [1984: 467–72]). Moreover, its concept of reality
could not be clarified using the pragmatist principle. Peirce preferred the 'realist'
conception: truth is explained through final causation as the opinion we are fated
or destined to reach if only we enquire into the matter long enough and well
enough. In 'How to Make Our Ideas Clear', he initially defines the real as 'that
whose characters are independent of what anybody may think them to be' and
turns to his pragmatism to clarify just what this means. He finally identifies the
'great law' that 'is embodied in the conception of truth and reality':

The opinion which is fated to be ultimately agreed upon by all who investigate, is what
we mean by the truth, and the object represented in this opinion is the real. (1877–8
[1986: 273])

Although this forges a connection between truth and human enquiry, he insists
that it retains the mind independence of truth expressed in the more abstract
definition. Truth is always independent of what any particular person or group
takes it to be; we always allow that further enquiry might reveal that we were
mistaken. Eventually we shall reach the fated or destined opinion.

The pragmatist principle is a tool for reflective self-controlled reasoning, and
Peirce was suspicious of placing too much trust in reflective rationality outside
the realm of science. Indeed, and this is an important point of contrast with
James, the fundamental role of his pragmatism lay in explaining the importance
and character of scientific knowledge and the life of the scientist. A major
concern in defending his principle was thus to defeat the claim that science
itself made use of concepts – drawn from mathematics or articulating ideals of
explanatory coherence – which lacked pragmatic meaning. His argument for

his pragmatism in the 1870s depended upon a theory of belief taken from the Scottish logician and psychologist Alexander Bain: beliefs are habits of actions; thus we can clarify the content of a proposition by describing the habits of action and expectation that would result from believing it. Application of the pragmatist principle does just that. He subsequently decided that a psychological theory of belief is too controversial and flimsy a basis for a fundamental logical principle, and his last decade was devoted to the search for a new argument, one that grounded pragmatism in Peirce's systematic theory of reference and understanding, or one that depended upon an exhaustive taxonomy of the kinds of arguments and inferences involved in science.

WILLIAM JAMES: RATIONALITY AND TRUTH

In the light of the verificationism involved in the pragmatist principle and his defence of the method of science as the best method for fixing belief, it is unsurprising that Peirce was interpreted as a kind of positivist. One would expect him to accept the fundamental principle of W. K. Clifford's positivist 'ethics of belief': 'it is wrong, always, everywhere, and for everyone, to believe anything upon insufficient evidence' (Clifford 1877: 309). But James feared that accepting this maxim – in a 'tough-minded' spirit – would deprive us of the truths which were necessary for a fulfilling life. Clifford's maxim may help us to avoid error, but at the cost of excessive agnosticism: fear of error can deprive us of truth. One of his most famous papers, 'The Will to Believe', presented a still controversial argument against Clifford's view: rather than following Clifford into agnosticism about religious matters, James urged us to believe on 'inadequate' evidence in certain special circumstances. In fact, Peirce's views were closer to James than to Clifford on these issues.

Suppose I am genuinely uncertain about whether to believe in God (or in freedom of the will). Moreover this is a matter of vital importance, it is a 'momentous choice'. Postponing a decision is not a real option: the agnostic, just as much as the atheist, misses out on the possible benefits of religious belief. In such cases, James urged, we must allow non-evidential considerations to guide our opinion: indeed, any decision about how to weight the avoidance of error against possible loss of truth will itself be a 'passional' decision. If we allow that the experience which confirms religious belief may be vouchsafed only to those who already believe – as elsewhere, experience is theory-laden – the force of James's argument against Clifford can seem strong. The same holds for cases where believing in a proposition can contribute to making it true: belief in my possession of capacities required for achieving my life's goals may be required for me to have the confidence required to exercise those capacities. Whether to believe a proposition, in cases where evidence does not settle the matter, can be sensitive to the expected benefits or harms that can come from getting it right or wrong. This is James's doctrine of the 'will to believe': affective considerations have a legitimate role in settling belief (James 1897: ch. 1).

Peirce's resistance to Clifford's style of positivism was evident from his earliest writings but takes a slightly different form. Purely as a matter of logic, he allowed that when the truth of some proposition is required for achieving vital projects, it is rational to *hope* that it is true and to act on that hope. Indeed, in marking one difference between himself and Kant, he urged that all the fundamental laws of logic were regulative ideas (hopes) rather than propositions whose role as presuppositions of enquiry justified us in *believing* them. Of course in the case of religious belief, *hope* is too detached and uncommitted an attitude to meet our needs. So in connection with 'vital matters', including matters of religious belief, Peirce denied that our tentative theorising possessed any authority against the instinctive sentimental certainties that formed part of our common-sense inheritance (see Peirce 1992: lect. 1). If religious belief – or confidence in moral judgements or in the freedom of the will – is natural and provides vital benefits, we would be irrational to reject it on the basis of reasoning which shares all the fallibility of our other scientific and intellectual activities. In 'A Neglected Argument for the Reality of God' (1908), he defended religious belief by showing that it was natural and evolved through a kind of 'scientific testing': if religious belief were true, then those who hold it should find that it gives meaning and direction to their lives.

James's pragmatism took him further in this direction. He claimed that 'thought distinctions' all consist in possible differences of practice (James 1907 [1975: 29]); and he described his pragmatism as a 'philosophical attitude', which leads away from 'principles' and 'categories' and towards 'fruits, consequences, facts' (James 1907 [1975: 32]). Major differences between Peirce and James reflect views about how such differences in practice should be understood. This becomes evident when we turn to the pragmatist account of freedom of the will. We naturally suppose that this issue concerns the 'mechanisms' of choice and action: are our actions determined by their physical antecedents and our upbringing? Or do we have the power to interrupt the laws of nature and initiate wholly new chains of causality? James looks instead at what practical difference it would make if we did or did not possess freedom; and he denies that the fundamental issue concerns whether, and how, we can be held accountable for our actions. We learn that 'free will pragmatically means *novelties in the world*, the right to expect that in its deepest elements as well as in surface phenomena, the future may not identically imitate the past'. He concludes that it is a '*melioristic* doctrine': 'it holds up improvement as at least possible'. This gives it a role as a 'doctrine of relief': we can believe that if we exert ourselves, things will get better. Believing that we are free grounds a sort of 'metaphysical optimism' and this 'practical significance', James suggests, captures all the content that the idea has. He began by asking what difference it would make if the doctrine of free will were true or false; and he concludes with an interpretation of its content which suggests that we can free ourselves of the metaphysical error of supposing that our actions can be both 'our own' and yet in a way that escapes from physical causation and from the influence of our character and experience. The practical consequences of free will seem to lie in the feelings, hopes, and reactions that it sustains.

The most famous and important application of James's pragmatism is his account of truth. In *Pragmatism* he offered an account which is widely misread: *'The true is the name of whatever proves itself to be good in the way of belief'* (James 1907 [1975: 106]). This supports the interpretation seized upon by critics like Russell and Moore: if it is useful ('expedient') to believe in the existence of Santa Claus, then it is true that he exists; if the belief is a useful instrument, then it is true. Although James continues 'Expedient in almost any fashion', it is important to note how the paragraph finishes:

. . . and expedient in the long run and on the whole of course; for what meets expediently all the experience in sight won't necessarily meet all farther experiences equally satisfactorily. Experience, as we know, has ways of boiling over, and making us correct our present formulas.

James agrees that true propositions will 'agree with reality'; but this must mean that we are 'guided straight up to it or into its surroundings' or we are 'put into such working touch with it as to handle either it or something connected with it better than if it had disagreed' (James 1907 [1975: 102]). 'Expedience' and 'agreement' are explained in ways that fit a verificationist reading better than the interpretation that was adopted by James's earliest critics. Expedient, yes: but expedient as a way of dealing with, and acting on the basis of, our experience. How far James's account of truth differs from Peirce's is a difficult question: many of his slogans and statements suggest something far more radical and implausible. But having endorsed a largely Peircean account of what he called 'absolute truth', he concluded: 'other content of truth than this, I can find nowhere'. As Peirce himself saw, the major difference between them involved how we should understand the practical consequences of belief. James saw the relief provided by belief in freedom of the will as 'truth relevant'; Peirce adopted a more traditional experimentalist's conception of experience.

The chief legacy of James's writings on truth is his emphasis on the importance of recalling that *truth* is an *evaluative* notion. Truth, he writes, 'is one species

of good: *The true is the name of whatever proves itself to be good in the way of belief* '
(1907 [1975: 42]). The difficulties in assessing his position arise because beliefs
can be good in many different ways: false beliefs, it seems, can shield us from
unpleasant facts that we are better not knowing, or can provide comfort in
the face of an uncertain future. In that case a belief can be good even if it
does not 'agree with reality'. James sometimes seems to waver between a broad
understanding of doxastic goodness and a narrower more verificationist notion.
Occasionally he allows that since a belief can be good at one time and not
another, its truth value can also change. When speaking more carefully, he tries
to avoid such relativism about truth, holding to a more qualified view of how
beliefs can be good. The less careful formulations were responsible both for
the scorn that his theory received from the likes of Moore and Russell and the
appeal it has had for many other thinkers.

REALISM AND EXPERIENCE

Both Peirce and James insisted that earlier philosophers had employed an impoverished and inadequate conception of experience. James's 'radical empiricism'
was defended in the preface to his collection *The Meaning of Truth* (1909b). Subsequently it was made the basis of a sophisticated metaphysics and philosophy of
mind which was subsequently transformed into Russell's 'Neutral Monism'. He
began with a 'postulate': 'the only things that shall be debatable among philosophers shall be things definable in terms drawn from experience'. He then drew
attention to the fact that 'the relations among things, conjunctive as well as
disjunctive, are as much matters of direct particular experience, neither more
so nor less, than the things themselves'. And then a generalised conclusion: the
parts of experience are 'held together from next to next by relations that are
themselves parts of experience' (James 1909b [1975: 6–7], and also James 1912
[1976: *passim*]).

　　Hume's empiricism was atomistic: items of experience (impressions) were all
distinct existences. Impressions of red and of green stood in objective relations;
they are rivals and no idea or impression can possess both characters. But there
are no necessary connections (such as relations of causality) between them;
although *we* can relate impressions by bringing them together in our minds,
their relations are not *there to be recognised*. James's radical empiricism breaks with
Humean empiricism at this point: experience is a unity, spread out in time and
with a relational structure which can itself be experienced. Where Hume tried
to build up our experience of a unified world from experiential atoms, the
pragmatists abstracted the 'parts' of experience from a unified structured whole.
Thus James could conclude the 'directly apprehended universe . . . possesses in its

own right a concatenated or continuous structure'. The reference to continuity is important. For Peirce, in particular, the doctrine of *synechism* – the tendency to take real continuity seriously – was to be the key to reconciling pragmatism with realism about laws and possibilities.

In a doctrine that reflected the Kantian affinities of his thought, Peirce – from his very earliest writings – attached great importance to a theory of categories, and sought to derive his system of categories from a logical account of the forms of propositions, thoughts, and arguments (see Peirce 1867). He frequently argued that a language that was adequate for our cognitive purposes would have to contain general terms or predicate expressions of three fundamental kinds. It must contain monadic predicates such as '. . . is red', dyadic relational expressions such as '. . . hits . . .' and triadic relational expressions such as '. . . gives . . . to . . .'. He argued that primitive expressions of all three kinds were necessary for science and cognition – thus there are triadic relations which cannot be defined in terms of simpler expressions; he also claimed that no more complex primitive relations were required. These predicates and relational expressions express forms of *firstness*, *secondness*, and *thirdness* according to the number of 'unsaturated bonds' that they contain. Peirce thought that earlier philosophers had erroneously neglected the need for irreducible triadic relations. The most important such relations were semantic and psychological: representations, for example, refer to an object only because they are understood or interpreted as so doing in subsequent thought and inference. Understanding or use *mediates* between the representation and what it refers to. In later work Peirce also insisted that notions such as law and causation involved mediation or thirdness. After 1880, he developed a system of 'scientific' metaphysics which was supposed to explain how realism about laws and other nomological modalities and forms of thirdness was possible (see Peirce 1891–3).

After 1900, concerned to show that his pragmatism and theory of science did not commit him to using any concepts which were not themselves pragmatically respectable, Peirce defended his categories through a phenomenological enquiry (Peirce 1934 [1998: 145–78]). Reflecting on the totality of all that appears, upon the 'phaneron', we find that firstness, secondness, and thirdness are all elements of experience. Continuity was an important form of thirdness – 'ultimate mediation' – and was required to ground the reality of 'would-be's, of subjective conditionals, nomological modalities and 'generals'. Indeed he took this commitment to realism to be the main point of difference between himself and James, renaming his own doctrine 'pragmaticism' to mark its distinctness.

A further application of the categories, developed in the 1880s, enabled Peirce to claim that we have direct knowledge of the external world. This emerged in the course of an attempt to respond to the challenge presented by Josiah Royce's version of absolute idealism, a challenge that was also extremely important for the development of James's thought.

In 1885, Josiah Royce published *The Religious Aspect of Philosophy*. As well as containing a thinly disguised critique of Peirce's account of truth, this argued that only absolute idealism could make sense of the possibility of false belief. Suppose I falsely believe that *this purse contains money*. The *object* of my belief is a particular purse but what determines that this is the object? If my belief does not fit the purse, if it does not contain money, then it is hard to see what it is about the belief that puts it in touch with *that* object. The argument appears to rest upon the assumption that a thought or belief relates to a particular object by containing a correct description of it, and the challenge is to show how I can be in cognitive contact with an object which I falsely describe. Royce concluded that finite human thoughts must all be fragments of the thought of an absolute mind in which the object is completely and correctly conceived. Royce considered a 'Peircean' solution: a belief is false if, were we to enquire into the matter long enough, we would change our mind about its truth value. He concluded that we cannot appeal here to a bare 'would be': there must be something in virtue of which this convergence of opinion would occur, and he denied that Peirce could meet this demand. We need to understand how the belief is anchored to reality, to understand what determines how it should or could be reassessed. Royce found the required basis in the contents of the absolute mind.

Both Peirce and James responded to this argument, each doing so in a way that reinforced realism and identified a similar flaw in Royce's idealist position. Peirce's response was in an unpublished review of Royce's book (Peirce 1958). The moral he drew was that the fundamental kind of reference to external things was not mediated through our descriptive characterisations of things. Instead, we exploit demonstrative, indexical signs, which exploit the secondness of our experience of external objects. This enables us to track objects of reference through enquiry while revising and developing our descriptions of them. Once we allow that our cognitive contact with things exploits the brute 'secondness' of external facts, the fact that they *react* with us, he felt able to claim that we have fallible direct perceptual knowledge of external things. I can recognise that *that* object, which I took to be a sheep on the hillside is in fact a bush. And I can defend that claim by reference to my knowledge of how bushes can resemble sheep in poor lighting conditions. The role of indexical representations in perceptual judgements provides a clue to richness in experience which suggests a way to vindicate realism. James too saw Royce's argument as raising problems about reference and intentionality, as raising the question what it is that makes one part of the world a representation of (or *about*) some other part. Although he did not share Peirce's categories or his semiotic ideas, James claimed that a feeling knows 'whatever reality it resembles, and either directly or indirectly operates on' (James 1909b [1975: 28]). My thoughts enable me to 'operate on' objects which they misdescribe, and this provides an anchorage enabling me to revise or correct the descriptions. The views of James and Peirce are thus not so very different.

Although both James and Peirce rejected Royce's style of absolute idealism, Peirce, at least adopted idealism of a different kind, one that can also be described as somewhat extreme realism. Although the physical world exists independently of human knowers, Peirce's system of scientific metaphysics claimed that the fundamental categories to be used in thinking of the material world are 'psychological' ones. His account of laws of nature and their operation entailed that final causation was involved in the operation of the external world. Where materialist philosophers argue that mental phenomena are complex material processes, Peirce argued that physical processes were best understood as inflexible and non-conscious mental ones: 'matter is mind become hidebound with habits' (Peirce 1891–3 [1992: 331]). His conclusion that the entire universe is a vast mind perfecting itself through time may have been crucial to his attempt to reconcile science and religious belief. James's metaphysical view, by contrast, flowed from his radical empiricism. A world of 'pure experience' contains segments which are mental or physical according to the relations that are salient to us at any particular time. Although Russell was disdainful of James's pragmatist account of truth, the 'neutral monism' which he defended around 1920 was directly derived from this metaphysical side of the latter's radical empiricism.

EUROPEAN PRAGMATISTS

Although pragmatism was born in the United States, it had affinities and links with contemporary movements in European philosophy.[1] We have already mentioned the responses to James's work by Moore and Russell. Peirce also influenced English thought. This was partly through his important contributions to formal logic. But his lengthy correspondence about signs and representation with Victoria, Lady Welby, helped to introduce his work to C. Ogden and I. A. Richards who included an appendix on his theories in their influential book *The Meaning of Meaning* (1923). After 1920, Frank Ramsey lamented the lack of pragmatism in Wittgenstein's *Tractatus Logico-Philosophicus* and exploited Peirce's writings on truth and enquiry in his writings on probability and induction. Since

---

[1] A more detailed account of the development of European pragmatism is to be found in Thayer (1968), part III.

conversations with Ramsey at this time influenced the changes in Wittgenstein's thought in the late 1920s, it is plausible to see an indirect pragmatist influence upon his later thought.

The chief exponent of pragmatism in England, however, was F. C. Schiller (1864–1937) in Oxford. A lively writer and a keen polemicist, Schiller's philosophical prominence in the early decades of the twentieth century is hard to appreciate given the speed with which his star subsequently fell. Before encountering James's work, he had formulated a philosophy of 'humanism' which was used to challenge the 'absolutist' idealism which then dominated the subject in Oxford. After 1900, he welcomed pragmatism as an ally in his campaigns. Humanism, and Schiller's pragmatism, was an anthropocentric doctrine which treated the self as agent as the key to all philosophical problems: once we see that all things are 'of like nature with the mind that knows them' we shall reach a state where knowledge is 'perfect and perfectly humanised'. This humanism encouraged a psychologistic mistrust of logic which pragmatists such as Peirce can only have deplored.

As we have already noticed, there was a substantial group of Italian pragmatists whose work was taken seriously by both Peirce and James. Centred on the journal *Leonardo*, they fell into two groups. Giovanni Papini advocated the romantic or 'magical' version of pragmatism: Peirce was particularly scathing about his major discovery that pragmatism was 'indefinable'. James was the major influence upon these thinkers, and he responded very positively to their boldness and their lively witty style of writing: he admired their 'frolicsomeness and impertinence', and their hope that pragmatism should serve as a collection of methods for 'augmenting the power of man'. Vailati and Calderoni owed more to Peirce (and Dewey) than to James; Vailati in particular worked on logic and the foundations of mathematics. While taking seriously the role of values and interests in shaping our theories, they both worked out an account of scientific knowledge which increasingly came to resemble the view of science to be found later in the work of the logical positivists. Nonetheless, their contacts with Lady Welby ensured that they took account of some of the issues about signs and representations that were fundamental to Peirce's later writings.

There were also connections between pragmatism and the French philosophy of action which came from Maurice Blondel (1861–1939). The similarities between the positions were probably not great, although for a while Edouard Le Roy called his version of the philosophy of action *pragmatisme*. These French philosophers were generally more taken by James's doctrine of the 'will to believe' than by his pragmatism; and the respect for *experience* which is largely characteristic of American pragmatism was largely absent. There were also parallels between pragmatism and other themes in European thought, although in most cases the similarities are not evidence of any direct influence. Thus Hans Vaihinger defended an instrumentalist view of science in his *Philosophy of As-If* (1911). Rather than asking whether theories are *true*, we should ask whether it is rational to act as if they are true. Although this instrumentalist view resembled some of James's claims about science, it is unlikely that the pragmatists influenced his position; indeed the book was probably in draft by 1877 and was mainly shaped by Vaihinger's scholarly work on Kant.

SECTION TWO

PSYCHOLOGY AND PHILOSOPHY

PSYCHOLOGY: OLD AND NEW

GARY HATFIELD

INTRODUCTION

Psychology as the study of mind was an established subject throughout the nineteenth century in Britain, Germany, France, and the United States. This established psychology was in part a school discipline, conveyed in textbooks and lectures surveying the theory of mind. Standard topics included the senses, imagination, memory, intellect, emotions, will, bodily motion, the nature of mind, and the question of mind-body interaction.

During this time, psychology was also an object of research and speculation by physicians and independent scholars. James Mill, John Stuart Mill, George Henry Lewes, Francis Galton, and George Romanes, none of whom held university appointments, published general works or specialist treatises on psychological topics. From early in the century physicians conducted empirical research on sensory perception, drawing on their own perceptual experience and clinical observation. Textbooks on human and comparative physiology contained psychological chapters, and medical journals published psychological work (e.g., Carpenter 1837, Dunn 1858). Early on J. F. Herbart (1816 [1891], 1824–5) and F. E. Beneke (1833) in Germany, and later Alexander Bain (1855: v) and Lewes (1857: 621) in Britain, renewed the call for a genuinely scientific psychology or 'science of mind' (a call issued earlier by Bonnet 1755 and Krüger 1756, among others).

By the middle of the century quantitative studies, found sparsely but regularly in eighteenth-century works on vision, were becoming common in sensory physiology and psychology. At universities, the discipline of psychology was variously located within faculties or schools of philosophy. 'Philosophy' at this time had both broad and narrow senses. Broadly, it was roughly equivalent to the 'arts and sciences'; narrowly, it might be restricted to logic, metaphysics, moral philosophy, and natural philosophy (though the latter was becoming separate as 'natural science'). Psychology was variously positioned under these rubrics, sometimes in metaphysics (Lotze 1881 [1886]), sometimes as an autonomous division of philosophy (J. S. Mill 1846: 532), but most often as an empirical natural science (Beneke 1845: 5; Wundt 1863: I, iv). It was known under various titles, including 'moral science', 'mental science', 'theory of the mind', 'physiology of the mind', and '*Seelenlehre*' (theory of the soul).

During the period from 1870 to 1914 the existing discipline of psychology was transformed. British thinkers including Herbert Spencer, Lewes, and Romanes allied psychology with biology and viewed mind as a function of the organism for adapting to the environment. British and German thinkers called attention to social and cultural factors in the development of individual human minds. In Germany and the United States a tradition of psychology as a laboratory science soon developed, which was called a 'new psychology' by contrast with the old, metaphysical psychology (Ribot 1879 [1886: 1–15]; Scripture 1897). Methodological discussion intensified. New syntheses were framed. Chairs were established and departments founded. Although the trend towards institutional autonomy was less rapid in Britain and France, significant work was done by the likes of Galton and Alfred Binet. Even in Germany and America the purposeful transformation of the old psychology into a new, experimental science was by no means complete in 1914. But while the increase in experimentation changed the body of psychological writing, there was considerable continuity in theoretical content and non-experimental methodology between the old and new psychologies. This chapter follows the emergence of the new psychology out of the old in the national traditions of Britain (primarily England), Germany, and the United States, with some reference to French, Belgian, Austrian, and Italian thinkers.

While the division into national traditions is useful, the psychological literature of the second half of the nineteenth century was generally a European literature, with numerous references across national and linguistic boundaries, and it became a North Atlantic literature as psychology developed in the United States and Canada. The order of treatment, Britain, Germany, and the United States, follows the centre of gravity of psychological activity. The final section considers some methodological and philosophical issues from these literatures.

BRITISH PSYCHOLOGY 1870–1914

In 1870 the French philosopher and psychologist Théodule Ribot surveyed British psychology, hoping to transplant a non-metaphysical empirical psychology to France to replace the dualistic 'science of the human soul' (1870 [1874: 17]). He praised the British tradition stemming from Locke, Hartley, and Hume and now embodied in the empirical and non-metaphysical psychologies of Bain, Spencer, Lewes, and J. S. Mill (and soon represented in France by Taine

1870 [1871]). British psychology was indeed flourishing in 1870, as the ensuing quarter century reveals (see Hearnshaw 1964: chs. 1–11).

In 1876 Bain founded the journal *Mind*, subtitled 'A Quarterly Review of Psychology and Philosophy' until 1974, long after properly psychological work was excluded. At first about half of its pages were devoted to psychology, including some experimental and statistical reports. While the journal was international in coverage, it reflected the two major trends in English psychology, towards a biological psychology on the one hand, and towards phenomenological analysis of mental phenomena on the other. The traditional associationist psychology was represented by Bain, by James Mill (annotated edition, 1869), and then by Sully (1884, 1892). It treated psychology as a science of mental phenomena or of consciousness. Indeed, J. S. Mill contended that unconscious mental states (as postulated by Hamilton) are a contradiction in terms (J. S. Mill 1865: ch. 15). Associationists adopted the usual classification of mental phenomena under intellect, feeling, and will, but denied that it revealed underlying discrete mental faculties. Their main explanatory strategy was to discern or posit elements of consciousness and then show how the laws of association, operating on such elements, can explain mental abilities and mental phenomena more generally. The associative laws usually included a law of spatial or temporal contiguity and a law of similarity.

Biological psychology was developed in England by medical physiologists such as William Carpenter and Henry Maudsley, by biologically inspired intellectuals such as Spencer and Lewes, and by research naturalists including Charles Darwin, Romanes, and C. Lloyd Morgan. Carpenter's *Principles of Mental Physiology* (1874) emphasised the mutual interaction of mind and body. Following a chapter on the nervous system, it was organised into psychological topics, including the usual coverage of the senses, attention, higher cognition, and motor action, together with medical topics such as intoxication and delirium. Carpenter, who adopted a comparative perspective, recognised psychologically relevant instincts in animals, but argued that in humans there are no instincts beyond those involved in basic maintenance, such as the beating of the heart. He relied on associationist theory to explain all other apparently instinctual behaviour in humans as 'automatic' behaviour acquired through experience (1881: 191). The book built a strong case, using clinical evidence and ordinary observation, that much mental activity occurs automatically as 'unconscious cerebration' (1881: ch. 13). Carpenter nonetheless maintained that a certain 'fact of Consciousness' available in immediate experience, namely, 'that we have within us a self-determining Power which we call will', was sufficient to refute materialism and show that two sorts of forces (mental and material) operate, and interact, in organic life (1881: 28; see also 4–5, 26–7).

Maudsley published his *Physiology of Mind* in 1876 (separated from Maudsley 1867). He held mental states to be identical with brain states. Mental phenomena are grouped together because they are (partly) accessed through 'inner sense' as opposed to outer sense (1876: 39). But he disparaged the reigning method of introspection in psychology, citing several grounds, including: lack of agreement among observers; the disturbing effect of the introspective act on the phenomena to be observed; its restricted applicability to the developing mind of the child or to minds of other species; and its failure to reveal the basis for the laws of association, which must be physiological (1876: 16–50). He also denounced introspection's inability to reach the great majority of mental states and processes which, he contended, are unconscious (1876: 24–40). Hence he recommended that introspection be replaced with 'objective' methods, including physiological, comparative, and developmental observations, and the study of pathological cases, biography, and history – the latter because (as with Comte) 'the individual is a social unit and cannot be comprehended independently of the social medium in which he lives' (1876: 53).

Maudsley was one of the few materialistic monists (1876: ch. 2) who contributed to the new psychology. Spencer and Lewes pursued a slightly different approach, promoting a biological psychology that regarded mind as a means of adjusting or adapting the organism to environmental circumstances. In 1855 Spencer defined life as 'the continuous adjustment of internal relations to outer relations' and intelligence as 'the adjustment of inner to outer relations' (1855: 374, 486). In the enlarged (and widely cited) second edition of 1870–2, he distinguished 'objective' psychology, dealing with material organismic processes, from the study of 'subjective' processes available to consciousness (pt 1, ch. 7). Objective psychology concerns the adaptive adjustment to external states of affairs of relations between states internal to the organism. If its explanations are restricted to 'actions' or 'conduct', that is, to behaviour, they need appeal only to 'objective' factors (see also Mercier 1888). Such explanations hypothesise that nervous states become adapted to external situations, as when the nervous action initiated by the sight of an apple comes to trigger reaching for the apple (an internal relation that now 'corresponds to' the *de facto* external relation between the physical shape and colour of the apple and its nutritional composition). Subjective psychology describes consciously available mental states that correspond (by a parallelism between mental and physical, both expressing a single unknown reality) to some of the processes of objective psychology. Lewes's *Problems of Life and Mind* (1874, 1877, 1879, 1880) similarly treated mind as a biological function of the organism, and recognised an essential social condition on mind in humans (which accounted for the observed differences between humans and their biologically similar primate relatives). Spencer and Lewes both made association the engine of psychological development, but they also recognised a fixed organic component in psychological responses. Typical associationists restricted innate factors to sensations and associative laws, but Lewes saw that evolutionary theory supported attribution of a wider range of innate mental adaptations to organisms, including humans (1879: chs. 1, 9), a point of view developed more extensively by Romanes (1883, 1888) and Morgan (1891: 336–8).

James Ward brought psychology back to phenomenology in his influential survey for the *Encyclopedia Britannica* (1886). He drew widely on the established literature, including Herbart, Lotze, Wundt, Hamilton, Mill, Bain, Spencer, and Lewes. But for Ward the standpoint of psychology is individual consciousness and scientific psychology is agnostic about the metaphysics of realism or idealism. Ward contended that an active self or ego must be recognised in psychology, apart from representations or 'presentations' to that self. He endorsed attention as the fundamental psychological activity, more important in thinking than association, which he saw as having its primary effect in memory. He adopted a developmental or 'genetic' view, according to which instincts arise from psychological habits that become fixed through inheritance of acquired characteristics (a mechanism endorsed by Darwin [1859: 209; 1872: 29] and stressed by Spencer and Lewes). Ward's student, G. F. Stout, also criticised the atomising tendency of associationism, stressing the phenomenal unity and directed activity of mental life (1896) and introducing a British audience to the early phenomenological tradition in psychology, including the work of Stumpf, Brentano, Ehrenfels, and Meinong.

University laboratories arose late, founded in the mid-1890s at Cambridge and in 1897 at University College London. But from the 1870s onwards there was frequent discussion of the relations between 'subjective' and 'objective' methods and subject matter in psychology. The method of introspection, attacked by Maudsley (and, earlier, Comte 1830–42 [1855: 33, 383–4]), was widely defended as the only access to the 'subjective' side of psychology's subject matter, the conscious states of the individual, and its scientific (hence, 'objective' in the sense of true, or properly established) credentials were affirmed (Lewes 1879: chs. 3, 5; Ward 1886: 42–3). Many objective factors were listed for inclusion in psychology's methodology, including physiological observations, comparative psychology, the outward expression of emotions, the development of language, historical records of human actions, and 'natural experiments' afforded by mental and neural pathology (Maudsley 1876: ch. 1; Lewes 1879: ch. 8; Stout 1896: 1: 9–16). Among these the focus was on (largely speculative) physiological factors, evolutionary hypotheses, and comparative observations. Spencer (1855 [1870–2: pts. 3–5]), and his follower the mental pathologist Charles Mercier (1888), appealed to such objective factors in elaborating explanations of behaviour, the 'objective' subject matter of psychology. For this subject matter Mercier especially eschewed all reference to consciousness and appealed only to hypothesised internal physiological states adjusted and adapted to the environment. By contrast Ward, who took consciousness to be the sole subject matter of psychology, questioned whether physiological knowledge was sufficiently advanced to be of any help (1886: 90). On that score he was not in disagreement with Spencer (1855 [1870–2: I, 140–1]), and presaged the later assertion by Stout that psychological results must guide any investigation of the physiological conditions of mental processes (1896: I, 26–35).

GERMAN PSYCHOLOGY 1870–1914

Whereas in 1870 Ribot credited British psychology with initiating a 'new epoch' of scientific psychology (1870 [1874: 44]), nine years later he said it was the Germans who had created a 'new psychology' (Ribot 1879 [1886: 9–15]). He now characterised British psychology as 'descriptive' next to the physiological and experimental psychology of the Germans. The crucial factor was the introduction of experimental techniques into psychology from sensory physiology, by figures including Johannes Müller (founder of the experimental tradition according to Ribot 1879 [1886: 21]), as well as E. H. Weber, Rudolph Hermann Lotze, G. W. Fechner, Wilhelm Wundt, Hermann Helmholtz, and Ewald Hering (see Hatfield 1990: chs. 4–5).

In the period 1850 to 1875 Lotze was the foremost German academic philosopher and psychologist (Brentano, Stumpf, and G. E. Müller were among his students). He analysed spatial perception in his *Medizinische Psychologie, oder Physiologie der Seele* (1852), where he introduced the doctrine of 'local signs'. He contended that the merely physical spatial order of the retinal receptors and optic nerve could not itself explain the spatial order of perception. Instead, the sensation from each nerve fibre must receive a qualitative marker peculiar to that fibre, from which the spatial order of retinal stimulation might be reconstructed through a psychological process, whether innate (Lotze's early view, 1852: 330–7, 354–60) or learned (Helmholtz's view, 1867 [1924–5: 185–6], and later Lotze's, 1881 [1886: 56]).

The problem of deriving spatially ordered perceptions from discrete nerve fibres had long been discussed (James 1890: II, 157). In 1834 the physiologist Weber published what became known as Weber's Law. This law concerned the just noticeable differences between intensities of a stimulus, that is, the amount by which a stimulus dimension, such as weight, had to be increased in order to produce a noticeable difference. Weber found that within limits this amount varies as a constant fraction of the stimulus value, at least for pressure on the skin, weights lifted by hand, line lengths perceived by sight, and the pitches of tones. The physicist Gustav Fechner developed Weber's result into a fundamental law of psychophysics (1860 [1966]). Fechner argued that the relation between physical stimuli needed to produce a noticeably different sensation yields an indirect measurement of the sensation itself. His argument explicitly assumed that the just noticeable difference is a constant unit of sensation, that is, that the differences between each pair of just noticeably different sensations are equal; and it treated the threshold of sensation – that is, the smallest perceivable value, e.g., the smallest pressure that can be felt on the skin – as defining the zero point for the scale of sensations, and the unit value for the physical stimulus. Using these assumptions he produced his famous psychophysical law, according to which sensation varies as the log of the stimulus value times a constant (which means that felt intensity goes up arithmetically while the stimulus intensity increases geometrically). (For discussion, see Delboeuf 1883a and b, Fechner 1882, G. E. Müller 1878.)

Psychophysical measurements became the pride of the new psychology; Weber and Fechner were widely cited in the German, British, French, and American literatures. The empirical investigation of mental phenomena blossomed. Wundt (1862), Hering (1861–4, 1868), and Helmholtz (1867) investigated spatial perception, including binocular stereopsis. Careful quantitative observations were made to determine the empirical horopter, that is, the imaginary line along which a point, when viewed with two eyes, appears single, and off which (by some distance) the point appears doubled. Helmholtz, Hering, and their students also investigated colour perception, carrying out precise quantitative investigations of colour matches for stimuli of known wavelength, colour contrast phenomena, and colour deficient or 'color blind' individuals (see Turner 1994). In 1879 Wundt established in Leipzig the first regular psychological laboratory. Many students and visitors worked there, on visual, auditory, and tactile psychophysics, and on reaction time, attention, and feeling. In 1883 he began a journal, *Philosophische Studien*, which, despite its title, largely served as the house organ of the Leipzig laboratory. In the meantime Georg Elias Müller (1878, 1904) took Lotze's place at Göttingen in 1881, establishing an important and productive laboratory there. In 1885 Hermann Ebbinghaus published his epoch-making experimental work on memory (1885 [1913]), gaining him a professorship in Berlin the following year.

Wundt gave new voice to the call for a scientific psychology. In 1863 he published his lectures on human and comparative psychology, and in 1874 his *Grundzüge der physiologischen Psychologie*. The latter became the herald of the new experimental psychology (French translation, 1886; open emulation by

Ladd 1887). Wundt's conception of psychology as a science changed over time (see Hatfield 1997). In 1862–3 he treated psychology as a natural science that would be supplemented by other methods, including historical study of the cultural development of human mentality. He saw human cognition as unified by logical acts of synthesis, exemplified in unconscious inferences that synthesise perceptions out of sensations (1862: 422–45). In 1874 Wundt regarded psychology as intermediate between natural science and the mental or human sciences (*Geisteswissenschaften*). He rejected unconscious mental processes, saying that any such processes must be conceived physiologically and nonmentally. And while he retained the basic view that the elements of experience are sensations varying only in quality and intensity, he abandoned logical form as the unifying element of cognition, arguing that psychological processes are prior to any mental appreciation of logical structure (1874: ch. 18). These processes of psychical synthesis combine elements to create 'ideas' (*Vorstellungen*) having new attributes, not found in any element, as when nonspatial sensations are synthesised to create spatial perceptions (chs. 11–12).

Wundt distinguished passive association from 'apperception', an active mental process, allied to attention, which forms new mental connections. The enlarged second edition (1880: chs. 15–17) expanded the role of apperception as the central cognitive act. Wundt increasingly emphasised the variety of influences on apperception. To understand the apperceptive process in an adult human in the nineteenth century, Wundt believed, one would have to consider her cultural context, which would have to be approached through the historical development of the belief system of the culture in question, together with the personal development of the individual. He thus came to think that the processes of higher cognition could best be approached through *Völkerpsychologie*, or ethnographic psychology, which he regarded as on a par with the physiological or experimental branch (1887: I, 5–6), or as likely to replace it (1908: viii). In one of the few attempts actually to distil 'objective' materials for psychology from history and culture, Wundt (1900–20) sought to reveal the developmental laws of human thought through the history of language, myth, and morals. Many German experimental psychologists rejected Wundt's claim that higher mental processes could not be subjected to experiment, and many regarded psychology as properly a natural science (see Kusch 1999: chs. 1–2).

Wundt (1894) held that his (ontologically agnostic) psychophysical parallelism entailed that mental and physical phenomena form two distinct but parallel causal realms. He advocated a 'pure' psychology according to which psychological states can be caused only by other psychological states. His students Oswald Külpe (1893 [1895: 4–6]) and the British-American Titchener (1909b: 13–15) also endorsed parallelism and avoided positing direct causal relations between

mental and physical. But their parallelism did not preclude physiological processes from playing an explanatory role in psychology (see Danziger 1979). They
found it obvious that psychological phenomena are 'dependent on' or 'correlated
with' nervous states which have resulted from processes that are unavailable to
consciousness. Külpe postulated 'unconscious' purely physiological states (1893
[1895: 291, 450]), while Titchener described his nonconscious physiological
states psychologically, as carriers of 'meaning' over time (1909b: 369).

The early experimental psychologists knew and discussed Franz Brentano's
(1874) descriptive psychology of consciousness. Ribot (1879 [1886: 295]) classed
it with the 'new psychology' because it was empirically based and left aside metaphysics. Brentano argued that psychological states are characterised by their directedness towards a phenomenally available object. His book did not fulfil the
aim of establishing a common theoretical framework for scientific psychology,
but it did influence discussions of mental content and judgement in Germany
and Austria (see chapter 12), and it found appreciation in England (Stout 1896:
I: 40–2) and America (Titchener 1909a: lect. 2). The work of Brentano's students, especially Carl Stumpf and Christian von Ehrenfels, provided materials
for Gestalt psychology.

AMERICAN PSYCHOLOGY 1870–1914

In 1870, psychology in America was a school discipline largely under Scottish
influence (Upham 1841; McCosh 1886). This 'old psychology' was usually allied with religion and generally taught by the Provost, who also taught moral
philosophy (see Evans 1984). The United States was late in developing a 'new
psychology', perhaps because it had neither Britain's thriving gentlemen scholars
nor Germany's research universities. But once it took hold, the new psychology
developed more rapidly in the United States than elsewhere, benefiting from
late-century foundation of new research universities and graduate schools. By
1900, laboratories had been established at forty-two North American colleges
and universities. Many American psychologists had passed through Wundt's laboratory as visitors or students (Hilgard 1987: 31–4, 79), but some took PhDs in
the United States, including George T. Ladd and James M. Baldwin under
James McCosh at Princeton, and G. Stanley Hall under William James at
Harvard. During the 1880s Hall founded laboratories at Johns Hopkins and
Clark and started *The American Journal of Psychology*. Baldwin was a major force
in the 1890s, publishing an important handbook (1889, 1891), establishing laboratories, and co-founding *The Psychological Review* in 1894 (with J. M. Cattell).

The new American psychology gained textual presence through books by
Ladd and James. Both authors were advocates of a new psychology, but neither

was convinced that experiment would be its defining feature. Ladd (1887) was the first systematic textbook of the new physiological psychology in English. It defended the importance of the physiological and experimental approach, provided considerable coverage of the nervous system, summarised primary results in psychophysics, and devoted a chapter to chronometric studies. It also contained an argument for the reality of the mind as a spiritual being, presented as a scientific hypothesis to explain the unity of consciousness (1887: 668–88). Ladd later elaborated a distinction between a descriptive, explanatory, empirical psychology of consciousness (1894) and a rational or metaphysical psychology (1895). As a framework for psychology he defended a provisional dualism, leaving it to philosophy to establish his preferred Lotzean monism, with Absolute Being underlying both body and mind (Ladd 1895: 409–12).

James's two-volume *Principles of Psychology* (1890) put a phenomenalist and functionalist stamp on theoretical psychology in America. It synthesised and appraised the main theory and findings concerning sensation and perception, cognition, and will. James defined psychology as 'the Science of Mental Life, both of its phenomena and of their conditions' (1890: I, 1), the latter including nervous processes, behavioural consequences, and environmental conditions. With a hint of irony, he labelled both 'spiritualist' and 'associationist' theories as metaphysical, because each attempts 'to explain our phenomenally given thoughts as products of deeper-lying entities', among which he included not only 'Soul', but also 'Ideas' or 'Elementary Units of Consciousness' (James 1890: I, vi). He was not opposed to explanation in general, but he rejected appeals to mind-stuff or to atomistic sensations (as posited by Hume, Mill, Helmholtz, and Wundt) to explain conscious experience. James's own explanations appealed to physiology, acquired habit, and the function of mind in adjusting the organism to its environment. He considered the main methods of psychology to be introspection, experiment, and the 'comparative method' applied to children and across cultures, to 'madmen, idiots, the deaf and blind, criminals, and eccentrics', and to the history of science, politics, and culture (I, 194). James also reported the new experimental findings from Germany but was not much impressed by them, proclaiming that in many cases great effort had 'as yet borne little theoretic fruit', while admitting that more work would be done and allowing that it might well yield theory (I, 193).

The Englishman Edward Bradford Titchener, who studied philosophy at Oxford, psychology at Leipzig, and then went to Cornell University in 1892, was a leading presence in American experimental psychology. Titchener (1908, 1909a and b) adopted Wundt's elementalism and the Leipzig laboratory's interest in chronometry. But he deviated from Wundt in treating attention not as an independent mental activity but as a property of sensation (1908: lect. 6), and in accepting physiological processes as explanatory in psychology (1909b: 38–41). In pursuing the Wundtian project of resolving mental life into its elements, he adopted the method of analytic introspection. Other American psychologists, including John Dewey (1896) and James Rowland Angell (1907), focused on the function of mental processes. Titchener (1898) himself divided psychology into 'structuralist' and 'functionalist' camps, initiating the American practice of classifying psychologies into various 'schools' or 'systems' (see Heidbreder 1933). Despite these divisions, the experimental tradition grew rapidly in America, soon supplemented by other empirical techniques, including questionnaires and mental testing. So when Boring wrote his history of experimental psychology in 1929, he wanted to consolidate the identity of American psychology as an emphatically experimental science, divorced from philosophy and speculation (see O'Donnell 1979). Through the efforts of Boring and others this conception held sway through much of the twentieth century.

PSYCHOLOGICAL METHOD, SUBJECT MATTER, AND THEORY

Psychological works contained discussions of psychology's subject matter, its methods, its relation to philosophy and metaphysics, the existence of unconscious mental states, and the plausibility of attributing innate faculties or representational capacities to the mind. These philosophical topics were addressed sometimes out of necessity, as in the debates on method or subject matter, sometimes because philosophy and psychology had a shared interest, as in the question of mental faculties, and sometimes to assure that a clear boundary was maintained between fields. Those like Wundt, James, or Ladd, who were both philosophers and psychologists, nonetheless recognised psychology as an independent subject matter or discipline.

Conceptions of psychology's subject matter developed and changed. Early on, some authors held that psychology could settle the metaphysical question of the substantiality of the soul. Although McCosh (1886: 7) tried to establish the soul's existence through direct introspection, the most common argument posited an immaterial soul as a scientific hypothesis needed to explain the unity of consciousness (Waitz 1878: 24–36, 119–20). Others used similar arguments to support a monism of causally interacting simple beings, including some dubbed as 'souls' (Lotze 1881 [1886: 91–104]). Increasingly, metaphysical questions about mind–body interaction and substantiality were bracketed. The motivation varied, from positivism and critical idealism to a plain attitude that the sciences cannot answer metaphysical questions, which are left to philosophy. Most authors considered psychology to be a natural science, which meant ceasing to talk of 'the mind' as its subject matter, or perhaps regarding 'mind' as a natural activity of the organism (without necessarily endorsing materialism).

The new psychology was, in Lange's oft-repeated phrase, a 'psychology without a soul' (1866 [1925: III, 168]). With talk of a unitary mental substance banned, new formulations of psychology's subject matter had to be developed. We have seen that Spencer and Mercier took one branch of psychology to focus on explaining behaviour. But most authors made mental phenomena the sole subject matter of psychology, and saw behaviour merely as an expression of mind. These authors variously described psychology's subject matter as 'phenomena of mind' (Sully 1884: 1–2), 'phenomena of consciousness' (Baldwin 1889: 8), or 'immediate experience' (Wundt 1901 [1902: 3]). This subject matter was to be studied with both 'subjective' and 'objective' methods, including direct reports of experience, behavioural manifestations, and physiological conditions. Supposing that the object of description and explanation in psychology is conscious experience, there was further division over the type of entities or states to be admitted into psychological explanations. Some insisted that only conscious mental states be admitted. Others posited unconscious mental states that produce conscious mental states, while still others posited physiological states (not directly correlated with consciousness) as causes or explanatory conditions. Some considered such physiological states to be psychological, others not.

In the days of realism about immaterial mind, theorists readily posited unconscious ideas or representations that were 'below threshold' (in Herbartian terms) – though Ladd, an immaterialist of sorts, later protested on behalf of 'psychological science' (1894: 30, 258). Some anti-metaphysical empiricists viewed such posits as tantamount to the self-contradiction of unconscious conscious states (J. S. Mill 1865: ch. 15), though others happily referred to unconscious sensations and mental processes (Helmholtz 1867 [1924–5: III:4]). By the century's end the chief defender of the latter position among German academic psychologists was the panpsychist Theodor Lipps (1903). In the 1880s and 1890s, a majority understood 'subconscious' and 'unconscious' states in relation to attention (see Cesca 1885). On this view, all mental states have some degree of consciousness, but some are least attended and so least salient, and these may be called subconscious or unconscious (Ward 1886: 52–4). A sensory state could be mental only if it had the qualitative character of experienced sensations (Wundt 1880: II: 195). Truly unconscious (as opposed to unnoticed or forgotten) sensations or mental operation were rejected; any mentally relevant processes and states that fall outside consciousness were assigned to pure physiology and considered nonmental (Brentano 1874 [1973]: bk 2, ch. 2; Stout 1899: 8–9; Wundt 1901 [1902: 227–8]; Ziehen 1891 [1892: 20–36]).

From this perspective, some physiological states have psychological concomitants and some physiological states without such concomitants are explanatorily relevant for psychology; but there are no purely physiological, nonconscious mental or psychological processes. The English mental physiologists and biological psychologists, materialist and anti-materialist, took the opposite stand. Maudsley proposed 'that all the operations which are considered mental and to belong to psychology may be performed as pure functions of the nervous system, without consciousness giving evidence of them' (1876: 245). Carpenter offered as examples of possibly unconscious mental activity playing music, reading aloud while thinking about something else, and thinking about writing while also dipping the pen and spelling the words right (1881: 526). Lewes wrote extensively on the relations among conscious, subconscious, and unconscious mental states (1877: prob. III, ch. 4; 1879: 19–25, 91–9; 1880: prob. II, ch. 10). Subconscious states are merely conscious states not under attention, whose existence he took for granted. He was keen to gain recognition for genuinely unconscious states and operations, including the process of assimilating present experience to the 'residua' or 'traces' of previous experience (1880: 54). Lewes posited a great number of unconscious factors, some cognitive, such as habits arising from repeated excitation, and some visceral, such as emotional episodes:

Besides the residual effect of multiple excitations through the senses, there is the influence of some recurrent stimulation from the viscera, or from some emotional shock which has left behind its persistent tremors. Deep down in the recesses of the organism there are thus influences at work, which only emerge into consciousness at intervals, but which are always modulating the mental state. (1880: 112)

Lewes was a dual-aspect monist (1877: prob. III, ch. 3) who held that organic processes can be at once physiological and psychological (1880: 149). Those organismic states having a mental aspect need not be conscious. A state is mental because it enters into the organism's overall mental functioning, not because it is accessible to consciousness.

Around the turn of the century many psychologists endorsed the notion that physiological states could be psychological without being accompanied by consciousness (Müller and Pilzecker 1900: 78–82, 271; Titchener 1909b: 38–41, 369). The functionalist Angell defended regular appeal to physiological processes in psychology on the grounds that psychological activity is a form of biological adjustment; he decried the usual parallelism as 'insipid, pale, and passionless' (1907: 81) and invoked an instrumentalist attitude towards the mind-body distinction itself, suggesting that mind be seen as an activity of organisms.

Of all the theoretical and methodological issues attending the new psychology, the place of introspection is most notorious. Despite widespread acknowledgment of 'objective' methods, the main experimental and observational methods of the new psychology relied on introspection, loosely defined. Introspection as defended by Brentano (1874 [1973: 29–30]) involved retrospective verbal reports of one's recent mental phenomena. Introspective analysis might include attempts by trained observers to discern the elements of mental life, such as the dimensions of feeling or emotion. In psychophysical experiments subjects reported their phenomenal responses to physical stimuli. Stout, describing successful cases of introspection, observed that in such experiments subjects are not asked 'What process do you, by introspection, find to be going on in your mind?' but rather 'What do you see?' (1896: I, 12). But even as Stout wrote, psychologists interested in mental functions or acts (as opposed to static contents) were using retrospective reports in an attempt to discern process, instigating the controversy between Wundt and the Würzburg school over proper experimental method (Kusch 1999: chs. 1–2). Introspection got a bad name, since even trained observers as preferred by Wundt disagreed among themselves, a result Titchener (1909a: 6–7) suggested might partly reflect individual differences.

Leaving aside behaviourism (see chapter 52), reports of experience were not wholly abandoned when 'introspective methods' were rejected after 1914 for psychological research into mental phenomena, as in Gestalt work on perception and cognition (see chapter 53); what was abandoned was the analytic introspective search for psychological elements. Thus by 1900 psychology as an experimental natural science had been born, though scientific psychology was not as yet equated with experimental psychology.

THE UNCONSCIOUS MIND

SEBASTIAN GARDNER

INTRODUCTION

The concept of the unconscious is now associated so firmly with Sigmund Freud that an alternative conception of the unconscious, one which is not in some way dependent on or derived from that of psychoanalysis, is hard to imagine. Yet, as studies of the prehistory of psychoanalysis emphasise, by no means did Freud introduce the concept from scratch: already by 1900, when *Die Traumdeutung* (*The Interpretation of Dreams*) appeared, the unconscious was a well-established intellectual topic (the classic studies of psychoanalysis's ancestry are Ellenberger 1970 and Whyte 1979; see also Brandell 1979: ch. 8, Decker 1977: ch. 9, and Ellenberger 1993: chs. 1–2; Freud's debts are acknowledged in Jones 1953: I, 435–6). Throughout the period 1870 to 1914 the concept of the unconscious was, however, in comparison with its psychoanalytic version, indeterminate in several respects. This reflects its deep involvement with two broader issues in later nineteenth-century philosophy, namely the disentangling of psychology as an autonomous discipline from philosophy, and the opposition between ascendant materialistic naturalism and the contrary impulse to preserve something of the metaphysical systems which had dominated the first three decades of the century (for a different suggestion as to why the unconscious appeared in Western thought, see Foucault 1966 [1974: 326–7]).

THE CONCEPT OF THE UNCONSCIOUS

The concept of the unconscious entered the scene in the latter half of the nineteenth century from two directions. First, unconscious mental entities and processes were postulated explicitly many times over in the context of nascent empirical psychology. Unconscious ideas were affirmed in Johann Friedrich Herbart's dynamic conception of ideas as inhibited but not destroyed by mental conflict, and as reaching consciousness on the condition of adequate strength and clarity (Herbart 1816 and 1824, esp. §§41–3; on Herbart, see Boring 1929

[1950: 245–61]; another early and influential source is Stewart 1792: ch. 2). Subsequently they appeared in Gustav Theodor Fechner's elaboration of the notion of a threshold of awareness and theory of its relation to the intensity of sensation (Fechner 1860: I, esp. ch. 10; on Fechner, see Boring 1929 [1950: ch. 14]). Decisively, the concept of unconscious inference, which goes a step beyond the postulation of mere unconscious ideas, was introduced by Hermann von Helmholtz in his analysis of perceptual knowledge, where it is made the key to spatial awareness, and it played a central role in the early writings of Wilhelm Wundt.[1] And in many other contexts theorists saw the need to refer to mental states and processes that exceed the immediate given data of intro-spective consciousness. As the discipline of psychology defined and consolidated itself, the references became more frequent.[2] In most of these writings, how-ever, unconscious mental states are thought of as states which are not objects of consciousness, rather than, as in Freud, states which cannot become such. A distinctive school of psychological theory formed around Janet's notion of *désagrégation* (dissociation), although it was unclear what relation the concept of dissociation bears to that of the unconscious, Janet preferring the term sub-conscious (*sous-conscience*) (see Janet 1889, esp. pp. 190ff. and pt. II, ch. 1, and 1907–8; and Münsterberg *et al.* 1911; on Janet, see Ellenberger 1970: ch. 6). It is safe to assume that most if not all of these authors would have been known to Freud, whether directly or indirectly. For example, Freud says in letters of 1898 that he is reading Lipps (Freud 1954: Letters 94, 95, 97), whom he discusses in *The Interpretation of Dreams* (Freud 1800 [1960: V, 611–15]).

Notions of the unconscious were also introduced in metaphysical contexts, the chief and most spectacular instance being Eduard von Hartmann's *Philosophie der Unbewußten (Philosophy of the Unconscious)* – a work no longer read, but which, measured in terms of its reception by the broader public, must be counted as one of the most successful in the history of nineteenth-century philosophy. Here the unconscious was associated with a very different cultural tendency, namely the surge of interest in Schopenhauer and the recrudescence of romanticism (in a novel, pessimistic form) in the late nineteenth century (on Schopenhauer's growing fame in the second half of the nineteenth century, see Henry 1988 and

---

[1] Helmholtz 1855, 1856–67, vol. III, and 1894, and Wundt 1862, p. 65 and ch. 6; on Helmholtz, see Boring 1929 [1950: ch. 15], and Mandelbaum 1971: 292–8: on Wundt, Boring 1929 [1950: ch. 16]; the idea of unconscious inference goes back to J. S. Mill: see Mill 1843: II, bk. 6, ch. 4, discussed in Reed 1997: ch. 7.

[2] See Baldwin 1891: 93ff.; Butler 1880; Clifford 1878; Galton 1883: 203ff.; Lewes 1875: 126–7, 139ff., and 1874: I, 134–46 and II, problem 3, ch. 2; Lipps 1883 and 1897; Lotze 1854–64: I, bk. II, ch. 3, §§12–14 and bk. III, ch. 3, §5 [1885: I, 196–214 and 324–32] and 1884: pt. I, ch. 3, pt. II, ch. 6; Maudsley 1867: ch. 1; Prince 1906, 1907–8, and 1914 (esp. Lecture 8); Ribot 1881: ch. 1 and 107ff. 1889 [1890: 112–17] and 1914; Taine 1870 (e.g. I, 165ff. and 332ff.), and Ward 1893.

Wallace 1890: 189ff.; public interest in Schopenhauer in Britain began with a review of his œuvre in the *Westminster Review* 1853: 388–407).

With qualification, these two sources can be thought of as giving rise respectively to psychological and philosophical conceptions of the unconscious. Qualifications are needed, first because psychologists, particularly in Germany, conceived their theories as integral to the philosophical task of analysing the conditions of human knowledge (Helmholtz for example was a Neo-Kantian, psychological enquiry being on his account the correct means of effecting the Copernican Revolution); and second because the conception of metaphysics in Hartmann, inherited from Arthur Schopenhauer (most clearly exemplified in Schopenhauer 1836), allowed metaphysical results to be based upon those of the natural sciences, which meant that a metaphysical concept of the unconscious could be supported by psychological research. The distinction between psychological and philosophical grounds for postulating the unconscious had no firm place in the self-conceptions of the time.

The use made by Helmholtz and others of the concepts of unconscious ideas and inferences belongs, strictly, to the history of psychology (see Boring 1929 [1950: chs. 13–18]; Littman 1979; Murray 1983: chs. 5–8; Reed 1997: chs. 4–7, 10; Robinson 1981: ch. 11). Essentially its theoretical motivation is the same as that of contemporary sub-personal cognitive science. Once it had been resolved that the mind should be made an object of scientific study on the model supplied by the material natural sciences, it was inevitable that psychological concepts defined with indifference to consciousness, in some cases by explicit analogy with the theoretical entities of physics, would be introduced. The immediate background to nineteenth-century psychology was supplied chiefly by the legacy of Locke, and the limitations of what could be achieved within the empiricist framework of associationism were well known; they had been exposed, albeit in highly abstract terms, by Immanuel Kant (even though Kant's warnings against confusing epistemology with empirical investigation were ignored by Helmholtz, as they had been by Herbart). Hence, given the undeveloped state of physiology until late in the nineteenth century, which ruled out direct explanation of conscious events by neurological causes, some investment in psychological entities outside consciousness would be needed if psychology were to make headway and not to remain a merely descriptive discipline.

Hartmann's philosophy of the unconscious, by contrast, requires considerable historical reconstruction in order to become intelligible from a late twentieth-century perspective. The sub-title of his main work – *Versuch einer Weltanschauung* (*Attempt at a World-View*) (1869) – signals his distance from the comparatively circumscribed project of empirical psychology. Hartmann's overarching intention is to allow the opposing systems of G. W. F. Hegel and Schopenhauer, each of which he regards as expressing a partial truth, to be rendered consistent and fruit-fully integrated.[3] Accordingly, the world is envisaged by Hartmann as a teleologi-cal whole with two interdependent but mutually irreducible aspects. On the one hand, the world is, as in Schopenhauer, will, a process of striving which mani-fests itself in the kinds and particulars of organic nature. Hartmann argues (1869 [1931: I, 30, 117ff.]), however, that will presupposes an end, which is supplied by the Hegelian Idea, the unity of will and idea comprising in Hartmann's lan-guage, borrowed from F. W. J. von Schelling, the Unconscious (1869 [1931: I, 4–5, 28–9, II, 55–61]; see Schelling 1800 [1993: 58–9, 75–9, 203–36]).

Hartmann's construction of his picture follows what he calls an 'inductive' method (1869 [1931: I, 6–15]), whereby the existence of the unconscious is established initially through a wide-ranging survey of natural phenomena, in-cluding instinctual behaviour in animals and physical pathology, extending to an analysis of human sexual and moral behaviour, language, aesthetic experi-ence, and so on (1869 [1931: I]). In each case Hartmann argues that mechanical causality fails to provide a complete explanation, which requires reference to ends which must be represented and yet are not conscious (1869 [1931: I, 98, 113]). On the basis of this empirical warrant, Hartmann differentiates the hy-pothesised unconscious into several kinds (physiological, psychic, metaphysical), culminating in the absolute unconscious, which shares in the attributes of God (1869 [1931: II, 245ff.]).

At one level, Hartmann's system appears to have advantages over those of Hegel and Schopenhauer. The (frequently supposed) difficulty of understanding Hegel's conception of a development of thought which is at the same time the development of reality – of understanding in what sense concepts can 'move' – does not arise for Hartmann, because of his interpretation of this process on the model of agency (Hegel's Idea is assimilated to a subject with practical reason). Similarly, a question which arises for Schopenhauer, as to why the world-will should objectify itself in individuated nature, is answered by the Hegelian com-ponent of Hartmann's system, the dependence of will on representation. To that extent, Hartmann uses Hegel and Schopenhauer to solve one another's prob-lems. At another level, however, Hartmann's own system faces a problem, since it provides no answer to the question why the absolute Unconscious should give rise to a world (see 1869 [1931: II, 271–5]: the Unconscious has no attributes apart from that of the individuals in which it manifests itself). Hartmann cannot, like Schopenhauer, appeal to the a-rational character of will to bring explana-tion to an end, nor can he take over Hegel's claim that this end is supplied by

---

[3] See the preface to the eighth edition, 1869 [1931: xxx; see also III, 147]; Hartmann offers detailed accounts of his relations to his predecessors, 1869 [1931: I, 16–42, and III, 147–59].

the self-explaining Concept. Instead, Hartmann effectively seeks to translate the metaphysical problem of explaining the existence of the represented world into the ethical problem of explaining the existence of evil, to which he responds with a doctrine of philosophical pessimism, more thoroughgoing than Schopenhauer's in so far as it teaches that the Unconscious is pure suffering and that the world's telos – for which consciousness evolved – is its own self-abolition (1869 [1931: II, 256–9, III, 123ff.]).

SCHOPENHAUER AND BERGSON

The use which Hartmann intends for the concept of the unconscious is highlighted by comparison with, first, Schopenhauer, and, second, another philosopher of a slightly later period who also had affinities with Schopenhauer and made explicit use of the concept of unconscious mental states, Henri Bergson.

Schopenhauer is widely noted as a precursor of Freud. In volume II of *Die Welt als Wille und Vorstellung* (*The World as Will and Representation*) Schopenhauer sketches many of the key elements of Freud's metapsychology, including the limited scope of consciousness, the subservience of consciousness and cognition to the will, the fallibility of self-knowledge, the existence of repression, the aetiology of madness, and the importance of sexuality (Schopenhauer 1844: chs. 14–15, 19, 22, 32, 42, 44; see Assoun 1976: pt. II, and Gardner 1999). Yet, the concept of the unconscious itself does not appear in Schopenhauer: there is nothing in his philosophy comparable to the explicit discussion of the Unconscious found in Schelling. The explanation for this lies in the fact that his concept of will, together with his conception of the world as a 'cryptograph' in which natural phenomena, human psychology included, could be interpreted as manifesting the constitution of an underlying reality (Schopenhauer 1844: II [1966: II, 182–5]), allowed Schopenhauer to arrive at a disenchanted view of the human psyche similar to that of Freud. The same programme – of interpreting human beings in terms that stand on the border of metaphysics and naturalistic explanation – is pursued in Friedrich Nietzsche, again with results that famously approximate to those of psychoanalysis and which became increasingly well known towards the turn of the century (Nietzsche's most sustained attempt in this direction is *Zur Genealogie der Moral* (*On the Genealogy of Morals*), 1887; on his relation to Freud, see Assoun 1980 and Lehrer 1995, esp. ch. 14).

Bergson, though well acquainted with empirical psychology and prepared to appropriate its results for philosophical ends, arrived at a conception of the unconscious on the basis of uniquely metaphysical considerations, and the claim that there are unconscious mental states has for him a quite distinctive meaning (Bergson 1896 [1991: 140–9; see also 67, 171, 176]). Consciousness, according to Bergson, is the mark of the present, and so, on his analysis of the structure of time and the nature of mind, essentially an action-directed function. Hence it is an illusion (though an intelligible one, in so far as it reflects a more general illusion of the autonomy and priority of theoretical cognition) to suppose that consciousness is necessary to psychological states: in fact, for Bergson, consciousness is merely a condition enjoyed by states that engage with our practical interests. Representations, he holds, exist outside awareness in a manner precisely analogous to objects in space. Memory has this status.

Redolent though this may be of the atemporal Freudian unconscious – a comparison drawn by Bergson himself (1934 [1946: 75]: 'my idea of integral conservation of the past has more and more found its empirical verification in the vast collection of experiments instituted by the disciples of Freud') – the distance between the two conceptions is in fact enormous: not only does Bergson's account imply that unconscious states are ineffective, he also holds (due to his idealism) that the reality of the unconscious is equivalent to that of the material world at large. Bergson's conception of the unconscious evidently stands or falls with his philosophical system as a whole, and is disengaged from the problems of psychological explanation addressed by Freud (the 'ontological', non-psychological character of Bergson's unconscious is stressed in Deleuze 1966 [1991: 55–6, 71–2]).

The comparison with Schopenhauer and Bergson puts in focus the reason why Hartmann's vast system is not a living survivor in the history of philosophy. Hartmann's aim of synthesising the philosophies of the Idea and the Will requires them to be brought under a single principle which possesses an independent content and justification. There is, however, nothing in Hartmann's system comparable to Schopenhauer's account of will or Bergson's account of time which might give philosophical substance to his notion of the Unconscious. It remains the wholly indefinite concept of whatever it is that would provide a unitary ground for Hegelian and Schopenhauerian metaphysics, and his philosophical system reduces to an eclectic compendium (criticism of Hartmann by his contemporaries may be found in Brentano 1874 [1973: 103–9], and Lange 1873 [1925: bk. 2, 71–80]; on Hartmann, see Darnoi 1967 and Windelband 1892: §§44, 46).

CRITICS OF THE UNCONSCIOUS

It would be a mistake to suppose that the concept of the unconscious met no resistance in the pre-Freudian era. Examples of systematic critical discussions of the unconscious are found in Franz Brentano and William James. Each argues at length, with reference to writings of their contemporaries, that a broadly empirical approach to psychological questions fails to uncover good reasons for hypothesising unconscious mental states. Brentano's discussion of unconscious mental phenomena (Brentano 1874: bk 2, ch. 2 [see also 1973: 56–9]) considers four possible lines of defence, the most familiar and promising being inference to unconscious mental phenomena as causes of conscious mental phenomena. Speculations of this form – Brentano cites instances from Sir William Hamilton, G. H. Lewes, Henry Maudsley, Hartmann, and Helmholtz – fail to fulfil the conditions of a successful inference, Brentano argues, in most cases because of the failure to rule out alternative explanations, in terms of dispositions to conscious mental states or the activation of pre-established associative connections (Brentano 1874 [1973: 105–16]; see e.g. Hartmann 1869 [1931: I, 98]). Brentano also stresses (here anticipating a standard criticism of psychoanalysis) the tension between the homogeneity of conscious and unconscious states which arguments of this form must presuppose, and the heterogeneity of conscious and unconscious mental processes which is characteristically asserted by theorists such as Hartmann who appeal to the unconscious for explanation of what cannot be explained by consciousness alone (Brentano adds a further, independent criticism of Hartmann's metaphysics as wholly lacking in rigour, 1874 [1973: 108–9]). Another, less familiar attempted justification of the unconscious considered by Brentano is an a priori argument turning on the claim that if all mental phenomena are conscious, i.e. objects of other mental phenomena, then an infinite (and vicious) regress of mental acts is generated (Brentano 1874 [1973: 121–37]). To this Brentano opposes his doctrine that each mental act is its own (secondary) object (1874 [1973: 127–8]), a reflexive conception of the mental which persists in the phenomenological tradition and underpins the criticism of Freudian ideas in phenomenology and existentialism (in addition to the well-known discussion in Sartre 1943 [1958: 50–4, 568ff.], see Merleau-Ponty 1945 [1962: 157–8], Scheler 1923 [1954: 196–209], and Henry 1985: ch. 9).

James covers similar territory to Brentano. The classic argument of G. W. Leibniz, that conscious perception of a whole presupposes unconscious perception of its perceptible parts (Leibniz 1765 [1981: 53–6 and 164–7]), is rejected by James as exemplifying the 'fallacy of division', and cases of habitual, automated intelligent behaviour are accounted for by him in terms of either conscious states which are instantly forgotten, or split-off consciousness (James 1890: I, ch. 6 [1950: 162–76]; James's discussion is very similar to that in Mill 1878: ch. 15). James regards Janet's conception of split consciousness as providing also the explanation of somnambulism and of the purported unconsciousness of hysterics (James 1890: I, ch. 6 [1950: 202–13]; see also ch. 10 [1950: 373ff.]). Where these forms of explanation come under pressure or give out, as in sequences of thought where links are absent from consciousness, James (here departing from Brentano) refers to brain traces and the operations of the nervous system in place of unconscious ideation – 'there are all kinds of short-cuts in the brain' (James 1890: I [1950: 167]). Quasi-Freudian cases, where we seem to retrospectively self-ascribe motives and emotions previously unrecognised by us, are on James's analysis simply ones in which our mind has changed: the motive or emotion which we are now aware of did not in fact exist earlier (though some conscious fact closely related to it may have done so), and so need not be assumed to have previously taken an unconscious form. (James, however, later takes a different view of the unconscious in the context of religious experience: see James 1902 [1982: 233ff., 483ff., 511ff.].)

FREUD

Freud is sometimes said to have rendered the concept of the unconscious 'scientific' (e.g. Robinson 1981: 380), or at any rate to have made an attempt in the direction of genuine science, but this is not an especially helpful way of characterising the difference between psychoanalysis and earlier theories which gave application to the notion of unconscious mentality. The latter were no less guided by considerations of systematicity and empirical proof (Hartmann included, within his own terms). Rather, what Freud did was to take the idea that unconscious mental states and activities can be postulated legitimately in accordance with the demands of psychological explanation, and give it a novel, very much broader sphere of application, one that encompassed not only psychopathology but also the normal functions of dreams, sexuality, child development, adult motivation and so on – all of this material being subjected to a highly original form of holistic, interpretative scrutiny, anchored in the new clinical practice of the psychoanalytic session. Freud's primary innovation thus lay in the development of a new plane of psychological explanation, one that goes beyond common-sense psychology, not by appeal to experimental methods modelled on those of natural science, but by radically innovating selected elements taken from within everyday psychological knowledge and practice (see Wollheim 1991: Preface).

The image of Freud as having discovered the unconscious has a justification, therefore, in so far as he gave the concept a stability and empirical determinacy which it lacked previously. To the extent that any narrowly philosophical development may be associated with Freud, it lies in his having developed a conception of the unconscious mind as something more substantial than a mere aggregate of unconscious ideas or representations, yet which does not amount to a second mind as such, and so does not (like Pierre Janet's theory of dissociation) take us full circle to a theory of split-off (subliminal, secondary, etc.) consciousness. (Freud's own philosophical defence of the concept of unconscious mentality recapitulates what had been said before by Herbart, Hartmann, and others: see Freud 1912, 1915, and 1940: pt IV.)

The objections to talk of unconscious mentality levelled by Brentano and James could certainly, in principle, continue to be pressed against Freud, but not nearly as straightforwardly: the explanatory detail and integration of psychoanalytic theory, together with its reliance on a hermeneutical method which is only obliquely related to familiar instances of inductive reasoning, made it harder to refute the claim that postulation of the Freudian unconscious satisfies the conditions of inference to the best explanation. In fact, the bulk of the criticism directed at psychoanalysis in Freud's lifetime (when it did not revert, rather disingenuously, to a flat repudiation of the notion of the unconscious as absurd) took issue with his account of the content of human motivation, especially regarding the role of sexuality (see Decker 1977: chs. 3–4, esp. 95ff. and 123ff.); Freud's contemporary opponents did not in general seek to counter psychoanalytic claims directly by advancing explanations of the same phenomena in competing (neurophysiological or other psychological) terms.

Though Freud discarded all pretensions to metaphysical truth, and aligned himself unequivocally with the endeavour to make the human mind a topic of objective scientific knowledge, he may be regarded as having persevered, in contrast with the other major schools of empirical psychology in this century, with the philosophical, Schopenhauerian, or Hartmannian, task of providing an interpretation of human existence (Decker 1977: 322ff., suggests that this aspect of psychoanalysis played a role in its negative reception). To the extent that psychoanalysis supports a *Weltanschauung* (see Freud 1933: Lecture 35), it may be said that the philosophical and psychological conceptions of the unconscious were brought together in Freud. That the traditional philosophical task of providing a synoptic account of man's situation should have been taken over by what is essentially an empirical theory of the individual mind is a measure of the degree to which, by the end of the nineteenth century, speculative ambition had faded from philosophy, and, lying immediately behind this development, natural science had achieved a cultural authority which allowed it to influence significantly the terms of intellectual enquiry – such that it now seems inevitable that a fully naturalistic conception of the unconscious such as Freud's would eclipse the compromised, scientific-cum-metaphysical sort advanced by Hartmann (for a contrasting view of the significance of the Freudian unconscious, see Henry 1985).

SECTION THREE

LOGIC, MATHEMATICS, AND JUDGEMENT

LOGIC: REVIVAL AND REFORM

PETER SIMONS

From the end of the Middle Ages to the nineteenth century, logic languished in stagnation and neglect. At the end of the eighteenth century Kant declared it incapable of further improvement. Yet within a hundred years of the first stirrings in the early nineteenth century it had undergone the most fundamental transformation and substantial advance in its history. Between 1826 and 1914 logic was irreversibly changed, leading in the 1930s to the metalogical limitation results of Gödel, Church, and Turing which rocked mathematics, while laying the foundations for the coming computer revolution. The story of this transformation is one of the most astonishing in the history of ideas.

1. NEW INTEREST, NEW FORMS

Ironically, the revival of logic began as a retrospective movement. Dismayed by the deadening influence of Locke on Oxford, in 1826 Richard Whately (1787–1863), assisted editorially by John Henry Newman, published his *Elements of Logic*. It was not an innovative work, being based in good part on Henry Aldrich's (1647–1710) *Artis Logicae Compendium* (1691), an Aristotelian Latin crammer for Oxford students, but the mere fact of its publication was significant. Whately also restricted logic deliberately to the study of deduction, in contradistinction to the emphasis on induction among empiricists. Whately's work went through many editions and became an established textbook in England. Thus logic, albeit in a form much impoverished by comparison with the Middle Ages, re-entered the syllabus. John Stuart Mill, in his *System of Logic* of 1843, defended the empiricist preoccupation with inductive methods, and his careful linguistic preliminaries to logic, including the influential though by no means novel distinction between the denotation and connotation of terms, were to be widely copied, but his rather negative attitude to deduction was to have little influence on the development of logic.

Semantic analysis lay at the heart of the most considerable logical text of this period, the massive four-volume *Wissenschaftslehre* (1837) of the Bohemian

polymath Bernard Bolzano (1781–1848). Bolzano's many subtle analyses anticipate, often uncannily exactly, developments which came a century later with
Tarski and Quine, and his semantic Platonism resembles that of Frege (whom he
did not influence) and Husserl (whom he did). But Bolzano's work, unwieldily
huge and obscurely published, lay undiscovered and without significant influence throughout most of the period.

The standard logic, against the background of which the nineteenth century
was to bring a host of innovations, was categorical syllogistic, with a minimal
discussion of its components of terms, judgements, and inferences, together
with such addenda as fitted it easily: sorites, enthymemes, and some fallacies.
Logicians in the nineteenth century in part rediscovered the lost variety and
riches of medieval logic – modal logic, propositional logic, insolubilia – but
they went much further than this. Traditional logic nevertheless continued to
be taught as all or part of the syllabus in many places well into the twentieth
century.

Novelty first emerged through some logicians questioning the fixity of the
traditional logical forms. In *Outline of a New System of Logic* (1827), the later
outstanding botanist George Bentham (1800–84), raised the possibility of quan-
tifying the predicate in categorical propositions, for example in replacing *All A
are B* by *All A are all B* and *All A are some B*. The point of this not linguistically
obvious modification was to turn categorical propositions into equations between total or partial extensions of terms. Bentham's discovery was made again
by Sir William Hamilton (1788–1856), but Hamilton's interpretations were inept and his claims exaggerated: they were decisively and wittily refuted by the
mathematician Augustus De Morgan (1806–71).

2. SYMBOLS, RELATIONS, ALGEBRA

De Morgan was the first of many mathematicians who were to change and ultimately appropriate logic. De Morgan's major works were *Formal Logic* (1847) and
'Syllabus of a Proposed System of Logic' (in De Morgan 1966). Exploiting hints
of inadequacy from earlier logicians, he became convinced that the Aristotelian
logic was too restrictive. He introduced a number of new symbols to represent
different categorical forms, and represented the negation of a term by a switch
from upper to lower case and back. The form *Every X is Y* was represented as
$X)) Y$, so *No X is Y* becomes $X)) y$ or *Every X is non-Y*, while *Some X is Y* is
$X ( ) Y$ and so on. A copula may be negated by placing or removing a dot
between its two brackets, and negative terms may appear in 'subject' position.
Symbolisation in syllogistic in English dated from a little earlier – from the work
A Syllabus of Logic (1839) of Thomas Solly (1816–75), but his work remained un-
regarded at the time except for an interchange of letters with De Morgan. On the

European continent, the use of symbols to expedite the formulation of propositions and inference was pressed first by Herbart and then by Moritz Drobisch (1802–96), whose *Neue Darstellung der Logik* (1836) went through three editions.

De Morgan's name is now best known for the laws expressing the duality of disjunction and conjunction, though historically this is inaccurate as they were known to William of Ockham and indeed to the Stoics. But De Morgan's more important development was to broach the logic of relations, the copula of syllogistic being seen by him as just one instance among many, so that the syllogism *Barbara* becomes a particular instance of the general idea of the transitivity of a relation. He introduced notions such as the converse of a relation, transitivity, and the relational product, and notations for them. The introduction of relations was one of the most far-reaching developments in nineteenth-century logic and was ultimately to transform the subject from a quaint relic into a powerful tool for formalising inference and representing the substance of mathematics.

The most significant development came from another mathematician, the English autodidact genius George Boole (1815–64). In his revolutionary *Mathematical Analysis of Logic* (1847, published on the same day as De Morgan's *Formal Logic*) Boole took the step – conceived earlier in the 1830s and with hindsight so seemingly simple – of not only using symbols to represent propositions as equations between terms but introducing operations of sum and product between terms and exploiting the laws of algebra, familiar from arithmetic, governing addition (interpreted as the disjoint union of classes) and product (interpreted as the intersection of classes). By treating the numerals 1 and 0 as symbols for the universal and empty classes respectively, Boole could treat equations true in arithmetic such as $x(1 - x) = 0$ as representing truths connecting terms: the term $(1 - x)$ standing for the negation (complement) of the term x, the whole equation means that the intersection of a class with its complement is empty. At one stroke logic is freed from the Aristotelian straitjacket of four categorical forms and a rich storehouse of equations becomes available for interpretation. This algebraisation of logic is its most important advance since the Stoics and can only be rivalled in significance by the subsequent invention of the quantifiers and the idea of a formal system.

Boole observed that his novel interpretation of algebraic equations as an algebra of classes led to new laws, such as $xx = x$, which are not valid in arithmetic. He was thus the first to develop a non-arithmetical algebra with laws at variance with those of arithmetic, the crucial first step in the liberation of mathematics (outside geometry) from exclusive preoccupation with number and quantity. By confining the values for the variables to just two values, 1 and 0, Boole further observed that one could obtain an interpretation of his calculus of equations which was adequate to represent the ideas of equivalence, disjunction, conjunction, and negation among propositions, with '1' being interpreted as truth and 'o' as falsity. Nevertheless Boole inadvisedly chose to regard the interpretation of his algebra in terms of classes as primary and that in terms of propositions, artificially conceived as classes of times at which something is true, as secondary. It took MacColl and Frege to overturn this mistake and irreversibly establish the logic of propositions as the primary branch.

In his interpretation of the syllogism Boole abandoned the assumption, prevalent since Aristotle, that the subject term of every proposition is referential, or has existential import. Boole's simplification exposed as invalid syllogisms relying on existential import, namely all subaltern moods and all syllogisms with a 'p' in their name, relying on *conversio per accidens*. Aristotle's twenty-four valid syllogisms are thus reduced to fifteen, and the square of opposition denuded to its diagonals. This in retrospect rather small step prompted an unreasonably strong reaction from traditionalists: the lost inferences could after all be restored by making existential assumptions explicit as additional premises.

Boole's work had flaws, notably the emphasis on equation-solving with little logical motivation, and the unfruitful explanation of particular propositions as involving an indeterminate part vx of a term x. Of much more minor significance was his slightly unfortunate choice of exclusive rather than inclusive disjunction as the meaning for '+'. This small point was adjusted with exaggerated rhetoric by the English economist-logician William Stanley Jevons (1835–82), whose *Pure Logic* of 1864 also attempted to reduce the merely symbolic manipulation of Boole by rightly insisting that all steps in a string of equations should be interpreted as are the endpoints. Jevons's perspicuous work, which deserves more attention than it gets, succeeded in making Boole's ideas palatable to philosophers not at home with algebra. Jevons also has the distinction of having designed and caused to be made the world's first logical computer, a piano-like construction using keys, wires, and wooden slats with pins, enabling inferences with up to four terms and their negations to be resolved to a conclusion. Jevons thus anticipated not only the later electronic automation of much inference but expressed by his construction his confidence in the mechanical solvability of term-logical inferences, a confidence shown to be justified in 1922 by Behmann's proof of the decidability of monadic predicate calculus.

3. PERFECTION OF THE ALGEBRA

Algebra was also applied to logic by the German mathematician Robert Grassmann (1815–1901), son of the mathematician Hermann Grassmann; but Grassmann's *Formelbuch der Formenlehre oder Mathematik* (1895) was less radical a break with Aristotle than Boole's work. Boole's innovations were however taken further by the American polymath Charles Sanders Peirce (1838–1914) and the

German mathematician Emst Schröder (1841–1902). Advancing beyond the equational form, Peirce introduced a sign for inclusion or subordination —≺, which could equally stand for class-inclusion or for implication (see Peirce 1933). Schröder, who gave the first lecture about mathematical logic in Germany in 1876, used a different symbol for inclusion but made it the basis of his formulation of the algebraic laws of logic in his 1877 *Operationskreis des Logikkalküls*, where equality is defined as mutual inclusion. In his three-volume *Vorlesungen zur Algebra der Logik* (1890–1905) he gave the definitive statement of the algebraic approach to formal logic. The laws for this algebra, which Schröder expressed for the first time as a set of axioms, have come to be termed 'Boolean algebra', and form the basis of a vast subject of mathematical enquiry. Peirce and Schröder continued to understand their formulas, like Boole, as standing either for classes or for propositions, but not at the same time: this variation of interpretation is characteristic of the algebraic approach to logic and contrasts with the logistic approach of Frege and Russell later.

Schröder, like everyone before Frege and Peano, failed to distinguish between an object and the unit class containing it, and this led him into a paradox. If we express the predication *a is b* as $a \subset b$, say the null class o is a subclass of every class, so that $o \subset a$, and express the idea that a class is universal U by saying it is equal to 1, then since $o \subset U$ it follows that $o = 1$ and all distinctions are erased. Schröder evades the paradox by postulating a hierarchy of classes of individuals, classes of classes of individuals, and so on, with distinct null and universal classes at each level, thereby introducing the first system of types. Schröder reasoning was strongly criticised by Frege, whose own logic ironically fell prey to a more subtle paradox in due course, to be remedied again with a theory of types by Russell. The algebra of logic was brought to axiomatic perfection in 1904 by the American mathematician Edward V. Huntington.

Peirce continued and extended De Morgan's logical treatment of relations, understanding them extensionally as classes of ordered pairs. His treatment was taken further by Schröder, and led to the perfection of the algebra of relations at the hands of Tarski in the twentieth century. Boole's non-arithmetical algebras served as examples, along with Hamilton's quaternions and Grassmann's calculus of extension, in the survey *Universal Algebra* (1896) by the English mathematician Alfred North Whitehead (1865–1947).

4. TRADITIONAL LOGIC IN ITS FINAL PHASE

It was perhaps natural that many philosophers would resent and resist the intrusion of mathematicians into 'their' subject. Philosophers had had custody of logic since its inception, and despite their collective neglect of it in the previous centuries were not always willing to let it be spirited away. The first blundering steps of Hamilton were easily ridiculed, and the equations of Boole were so alien as to be dismissible. The resistance to mathematisation was particularly strong in Germany, where 'philosophical' logicians clung to an intensional interpretation of the terms as referring to concepts, belittling the extensional interpretation of terms as referring to classes by the 'English logicians' as philistine misunderstanding. Such a Luddite attitude to mathematisation could be combined with dissatisfaction with the tradition, as it was in the work of the German philosopher Franz Brentano (1838–1917), whose reform of logic owed something to Jevons but more to Brentano's own theory of judgements as fundamentally existential rather than predicational. Brentano's modest but interesting proposals dating from 1870 were summarised by Hillebrand (1891).

German logicians continued to produce large and wordy textbooks of traditional logic, importing at the same time a pseudo-empirical or psychological justification for the valid inferences as 'laws of thought'. This traditional term was intended to give logic scientific respectability in an empirical age. The intrusion of psychology into logic was bemoaned by mathematically inclined logicians, most notably Frege, and later Husserl, who castigated the position as 'psychologism'. Nevertheless, German logicians produced respectable works, most notably the large logic treatises of Christoph Sigwart (Sigwart 1873–8) and Benno Erdmann (Erdmann 1892).

The innovations introduced by Boole were more equably received by British logicians, who were less attached to the intensional approach to propositions. They passed in a modest way into widely used and less bluntly mathematical textbooks, such as the *Symbolic Logic* (1881) of John Venn (1834–1923). Venn is a cautious moderniser: 'I think . . . that the Common Logic is best studied on the old lines, and that the Symbolic Logic should be regarded as a Development or Generalization of it' (1881: xxvii). Venn was also an early and astute historian of his subject, declaring his suspicion that Kant 'had a disastrous effect on logical speculation' (1881: xxxvii), noting Lambert's neglected anticipation of Boole's use of algebraic symbols, and bemoaning the historical ignorance of innovators Robert Grassmann and Frege (whose *Begriffsschrift* he remarkably cites, though with the wrong year of 1877 – cf. his 1881, p. xxxi). Venn also wrote on probability, but is best known today for his diagrammatic representation of categorical propositions and inferences about classes, Venn diagrams, which represent classes by overlapping circles. The use of diagrams as an aid to represent propositions and inferences about classes had a modest prehistory with Leibniz, Euler, and Gergonne, but it was Venn who elevated the method to exactness and in so doing provided an easily grasped decision procedure for syllogistic and some of its extensions, putting an end to the tedious memorisation of rules which had plagued logic students since the Middle Ages. Venn's advance over Euler consisted in using the same diagrammatic scheme or framework for all inferences, representing the different forms by additional graphical devices such as shading out (to represent the emptiness of a class) or placing a cross (to represent its non-emptiness).

In this representation, syllogistic and basic class algebra is within the grasp of small children, and one logician was quick to realise this and seize the opportunity to present logic as a game. Charles Lutwidge Dodgson (1832–98), mathematician at Christ Church, Oxford, better known as a pioneer photographer and above all as the writer Lewis Carroll, published *The Game of Logic* in 1887 and Part I of his *Symbolic Logic, a Fascinating Recreation for the Young* in 1896. Logic was a late interest for Dodgson but he took to it with gusto, modifying Venn's diagrams into a more flexible rectangular format, and introducing a perspicuous symbolism for representing categorical propositions and propositional connectives. He clarified the distinction between implication and inference in a famously witty *Mind* article, 'What the Tortoise Said to Achilles' (1895). Dodgson is the undisputed king of the sorites, his typically whimsical examples sometimes running to over thirty premises. Dodgson's approach to logical form was conservative: he remained within standard categorical logic of terms and even retained existential import. At his death the second part of *Symbolic Logic* remained unpublished, but its rediscovery and reconstructed publication in 1977 reveals Dodgson to have been exuberantly innovative in method, introducing tables and trees to test the validity of his horrendously complex puzzle inferences, thereby anticipating semantic tree methods by more than half a century.

Just as in technology the last examples of an obsolete kind are often the most elegant – one thinks of steam locomotives or clippers – so in logic the last major examples of traditional logic textbooks show rare balance and sum up, positively, the centuries of traditional logic before them. *Studies and Exercises in Formal Logic* by John Neville Keynes (1852–1949) was first published in 1884 and saw its fourth edition in 1906, the year which saw the publication of *An Introduction to Logic* by H. W. B. Joseph (1867–1943). Keynes acknowledges the influences of De Morgan, Jevons, Venn, and Sigwart, but he resists all but minimal symbolisation, and uses Venn diagrams only briefly. His touch is light: he proposes an elegant solution to the problem of existential import: letting positive formulas (A and I) have it and negative ones (E and O) lack it he retains a full square of opposition. He sets psychologism gently aside with the remark that although 'Psychological and logical discussions are no doubt apt to overlap one another at certain points', nevertheless 'Logic has thus a unique character of its own, and is not a mere branch of psychology' Keynes (1884 [1928:6]). With two sentences he neatly avoids the pitfalls of excess on either side. Keynes's examples and explanations are models of clarity and hardly to be bettered. Joseph's work, as to be expected of a Oxford man, is more prosy, contains more Greek, and no exercises, but it is notable for the balance of his survey of traditional themes and for its sensible discussion of the principles of classification, a subject soon to disappear from logic books.

Logic books were also published in England by members of the philosophically predominant neo-Hegelian movement, notably *The Principles of Logic* (1883) by Francis Herbert Bradley (1846–1924) and *Logic or the Morphology of Knowledge* (1888) by Bernard Bosanquet (1846–1923). Though both reject formal logic, of the two, Bradley's book is incomparably more rewarding philosophically because of his interesting comments on indexicality, universals, on the unity and primacy of judgements over concepts, and his clear rejection of psychologism, in the last two respects converging with Frege. Bosanquet, who chided Bradley from a more orthodox Hegelian idealistic position, prompted Bradley to an inferior revised edition (1922). Bradley's *Principles* had been influenced by the *Logik* (1874) of Rudolf Herman Lotze (1817–81), which Bosanquet translated into English. Lotze rejected formal as distinct from philosophical logic, but he was not an orthodox Hegelian. In fact Lotze influenced a broad range of philosophers including Brentano, Husserl, and Russell, none of whom would consider himself a Lotzean. For the history of logic, however, Lotze is chiefly of interest now as the only philosophy teacher of Frege, and it is likely that Frege read the *Logik*, though its influence on him, if such can be discerned, must have been slight.

5. PROPOSITIONAL LOGIC

There had been propositional logic since the Stoics, and it flourished in the medieval schools, but the traditional logic of the nineteenth century had lost any knowledge of that. Boole reintroduced consideration of propositional logic along with its operations of conjunction, disjunction, and negation, with implication symbolised by Peirce and Schröder. Nevertheless the idea that a logic of propositions should be conceptually prior to a logic of classes or terms was made difficult to achieve by the algebraists' insistence on using the same symbolism for two different purposes. This decisive advance first came from an unlikely quarter, a Scottish schoolteacher of mathematics living in Boulogne, Hugh MacColl (1837–1909). In 1877, two years before Frege's *Begriffsschrift*, he published the first purely symbolical presentation of a version of propositional logic in the first article in a series called 'The Calculus of Equivalent Statements'. It was MacColl's fate to be persistently overlooked as a pioneer of mathematical logic, and a modicum of belated recognition came to him only after 1900, when Russell came across his work and corresponded with him. Propositional logic, though present implicitly as a calculus of judgement contents in Frege's logic, became a subject in its own right only after being highlighted as the 'theory of deduction' in *Principia Mathematica* (Whitehead and Russell 1910–13), and then isolated for metalogical research in the 1920s by Łukasiewicz (see Łukasiewicz 1970).

FOUNDATIONS OF MATHEMATICS

MICHAEL HALLETT

I. INTRODUCTION

It is uncontroversial to say that the period in question saw more important changes in the philosophy of mathematics than any previous period of similar length in the history of philosophy. Above all, it is in this period that the study of the *foundations* of mathematics became partly a mathematical investigation itself. So rich a period is it, that this survey article is only the merest sketch; inevitably, some subjects and figures will be inadequately treated (the most notable omission being discussion of Peano and the Italian schools of geometry and logic). Of prime importance in understanding the period are the changes in mathematics itself that the nineteenth century brought, for much foundational work is a reaction to these, resulting either in an expansion of the philosophical horizon to incorporate and systematise these changes, or in articulated opposition. What, in broad outline, were the changes?

First, traditional subjects were treated in entirely new ways. This applies to arithmetic, the theory of real and complex numbers and functions, algebra, and geometry. (a) Some central concepts were characterised differently, or properly characterised for the first time, for example, from analysis, those of continuity (Weierstrass, Cantor, Dedekind) and integrability (Jordan, Lebesgue, Young), from geometry, that of congruence (Pasch, Hilbert), and geometry itself was re-cast as a purely synthetic theory (von Staudt, Pasch, Hilbert). (b) Theories were treated in entirely new ways, for example, as axiomatic systems (Pasch, Peano and the Italian School, Hilbert), as structures (Dedekind, Hilbert), or with entirely different primitives (Riemann, Cantor, Frege, Russell). (c) Moreover, established subjects were often generalised and/or combined, for example, analysis was generalised to point-set, then general, topology (Cantor, Hausdorff); arithmetic to analytic and algebraic number theories (Dirichlet, Kronecker, Kummer, Dedekind), geometry to geome*tries*, and these into a combination of function theory and algebra (Klein's *Erlanger Programm*), and Riemann created a general theory of manifolds as a framework for geometry; algebra itself moved away from the specific algebraic structures of the number systems, and algebra and geometry combined in algebraic topology (Poincaré, Brouwer); complex function theory was systematised and massively expanded (Cauchy, Weierstrass). (d) Entirely new subjects were first articulated and introduced into the core of mathematics in a way which profoundly changed conceptions of what mathematics is about. Some of these were the result of new combinations of old subjects, some were entirely new, such as the theory of transfinite numbers (Cantor), logic and mathematical logic (Frege, Peirce, Schröder, Peano, Hilbert, Russell), set theory (Cantor, Dedekind, Zermelo).

Second, as some of the examples mentioned above indicate, mathematics in the nineteenth century became more abstract and more general, partly as the result of the freedom wrought by treating established theories in new ways, partly by striving for systematisation and unification. That mathematics should move in the direction of conceptual abstractness was stressed earlier in the century by Dirichlet, Gauss's successor in Göttingen, and the teacher of Kronecker, Riemann, and Dedekind. In a lecture on Dirichlet in 1905, Minkowski referred to Dirichlet's 'other Principle' (the allusion is to Dirichlet's Principle in analysis, so-called by Riemann), namely that mathematics should try to solve problems by a minimum of 'blind calculation and a maximum of clear thoughts [*sehenden Gedanken*]' (see Minkowski 1905 [1911: 460–1]), a principle which Minkowski sees as characteristic of modern mathematics. It is not clear precisely what Dirichlet meant, but one reading is that mathematics should concentrate less on particular cases (particular infinite series, functions; special cases of continuity, convergence, etc.), and instead seek out general conditions and conceptual frameworks, and that one gains deeper insight into a field by generalising it, or by finding a conceptual framework which unites it to another. One example was the development of a general conception of a function of a real variable in the nineteenth century (partly due to Dirichlet himself) and the consequent investigations of the conditions a function must satisfy to be continuous or differentiable or integrable or representable by a Fourier series expansion, and what properties are preserved or lost when functions are combined in infinite sequences and series (see e.g., Hawkins 1970). Klein's *Erlanger Programm* (1872 on) is another important example, which proposed a unifying framework for the study of Euclidean, non-Euclidean, and projective geometries alike, founded on a combination of algebra and function theory, and the classification of geometries according to the groups of automorphisms allowed.

This burgeoning of new mathematics led to questions which dominate the period under consideration: 'What is the relationship between the new developments and established mathematics?', and more generally, 'What is the relationship of a given theory to others?' It is often stressed that this period was dominated by an interest in rigour: witness the development of mathematical logic and concentration on axiomatic and then (later) formal systems, partly as a reaction to the set-theoretical and logical antinomies discovered at the end of the nineteenth century (see section 7, below). But the interest in greater rigour is best seen as part of an attempt to deal with the new conceptual developments quite independently of any concern with particular contradictions.

2. THE ISSUES

The most basic approach to the general questions outlined was conceptual as-similation. There were at least two important forms of this, *generalisation* and *reductionism*. *Generalisation* is characterised by the attempt to reveal that the central laws governing an established area are restricted instances of general laws which govern some new or different theory, which can thus be assimilated to the first. By *reductionism* is meant primarily the attempt to explain the central concepts of a theory by characterising it as using the conceptual apparatus of another (usually better-established) theory; versions of central theorems or principles of the first are then proved in the second. Reductionism was often appealed to in nineteenth-century mathematics; but in practice reductionist arguments often tacitly invoked more general concepts and principles, in fact generalisation. But generalisation raises the question of the coherence of the more general concepts and principles, their exemplification, and more generally their consistency, in short, demands a demonstration/argument that the new general theory is acceptable on its own terms, or represents a *possibility*.

The best-known examples of reductionism appear in the movements to *arith-metise* mathematics, the purpose here being to give precise definitions of impre-cise notions using concepts from the standard number systems. Continuity in analysis provides one example, with the elimination of appeal to concepts of the infinite using a clear definition of the limit process. Klein (1895) saw arithmeti-sation as essentially the search for increased rigour, presumably because without accurate characterisation concepts cannot be properly appealed to in deduc-tions, a point made by Dedekind in 1872. (The search for rigour in this sense has nothing to do with the formalisation of reasoning, nor with *logical* reduction.) Geometry furnishes another example. Geometry (as the science of space) was often conceived as more a natural science than pure mathematics, a conception which, according to Gauss, was strengthened by the discovery of non-Euclidean geometry (letter from Gauss to Bessel, 9 April 1830; see Ewald 1996: I, 302). Consequently, the dependence of central theorems of analysis (e.g., that every convergent sequence converges to a limit) on geometrical intuition was doubly suspect; it predicates analysis on something intrinsically vague (and unusable in a deductive framework), and simultaneously challenges analysis's status as a 'product of the intellect'. Some (e.g., Dedekind, Cantor) saw the correct way to proceed as being to give a purely arithmetical analysis of continuity; thus, to assert that *physical* space is continuous is to assert the 'axiom' that the *analytical* structure of continuity can be imposed on the manifold of physical points.

These issues are tied to a type of 'purity of method' question of great foundational importance at the end of the nineteenth century, namely, to show positively that certain goals can be achieved by using *only* specified conceptual means. This form of the 'purity' issue, which goes back to Euclid, was also closely tied to one of the central occupations with rigour, for one way to show that a limited stock of concepts and principles is adequate is to show that all the central concepts/principles can be defined/derived from these without admixture of anything 'foreign' (a term used by Dedekind). Concentration on the 'purity' of the means of derivation itself is then entirely natural, common both to those movements which applied a formal logic (e.g., Frege), and to those which did not (e.g., some of the arithmetisation movements, or Pasch in geometry). For example, Pasch put as much stress as Frege on the 'rigour' of proofs, insisting that no assumptions *extra* to the axioms should play a role. Pasch's purpose – like Frege's – was epistemological in arguing that geometry is an *empirical* science studying certain properties of physical bodies. To sustain this, Pasch specified a small number of axioms from which all the basic results of (projective) geometry could be derived, arguing that these axioms have an empirical character. *If* this is accepted, the further argument only works if one is certain that the means of derivation itself are epistemologically neutral, that proofs allow no room for anything like geometrical intuition to creep in, for example, via the inspection of diagrams. Pasch's claim is ultimately that it must be the syntactic (logical) structure of the steps in a proof, and not semantic considerations, which determines the correctness of the derivation, a claim which was intrinsic to Pasch's general argument for the Duality Principle (see below). This point was to have profound implications for the development of logic, though neither Pasch nor Frege realised the force of it.

Interest in reductive analysis not only led to reflection on the deductive mechanisms used in mathematical theories, but more generally to an interest in precise specifications of the conceptual foundations (sometimes concepts, sometimes concepts *and* axioms) of the central theories, without which such analysis is of limited value. But to illustrate the connection between reductionism and generalisation, let me turn to two examples where reduction cannot be kept separate from appeal to more abstract concepts and general laws. One is the work of Frege (1879, 1884, 1893/1903), the other is the foundational work of Dedekind.

3. FREGE

Like Pasch, one of Frege's motives was epistemological, for he wanted to show that arithmetic is *analytic* since it can be *derived* from (reduced to) logical laws alone. The claim was in conscious opposition to Kant's claim that arithmetic is *synthetic*, although it involves a significant alteration of Kant's conception of the analytic: it does not claim that the 'basic laws' of arithmetic are 'contained in' logical laws in any obvious sense (see 1884, §88), just that it can be derived from them given the right definitions and system of derivation, in effect, full second-order logic. The fulfilment of Frege's project involves two things. (1) Giving definitions of central number-theoretic notions using only the conceptual machinery of pure logic. This Frege does (1884) for the concepts of (cardinal) number; 'following in an *R*-series' for any relation *R*; the relation of 'immediate successor'; the number 0; natural number. (2) Proving that the central arithmetical laws can be derived from more basic logical laws, which involves specifying, and using, a fully developed deductive system, which Frege was the first to do. What are the basic laws? This is not a straightforward question to answer. In 1884, Frege defends the principle that numbers are (abstract) *objects*. (The philosophical question, 'What are abstract objects?' first arises in Frege.) (Cardinal) numbering is then the association of an object with a concept, the number of things which fall under that concept. (Thus, the concepts 'moon of Venus' and 'book of Euclid's *Elements*' are assigned the objects 0 and 13, respectively.) The fundamental principle governing correct assignments has come to be known (since Boolos's work in the 1980s) as *Hume's Principle* (*HP*): the number objects assigned to concepts *F* and *G* are the same if and only if the extensions of *F* and *G* can be put into one-one correspondence. Call two concepts *F*, *G equinumerous* (written '$Fx \approx Gx$') if this latter holds. Frege then does two things. First, he shows that if 'the number of *F*s' (abbreviated here by *NxFx*) is defined as the extension of the (higher-order) concept '$\approx Fx$', then *HP* can be *proved*. Second, he shows that all the central principles of arithmetic (basically the Dedekind-Peano axioms, including mathematical induction) can be derived (in second-order logic) from *HP*, this second step being quite independent of the first. Thus, the 'more basic principle' in the *Grundlagen* (1884) in effect is *HP*. However, *HP* on its own is quite compatible with the thesis that numbers are *primitive* objects, and not generated by the *general* apparatus of pure logic. Logic, as conceived by Frege, is the most general of sciences, governing the operation with concepts. So, if the numbers were primitives, then arithmetic would be a 'special science', not completely general, hence *a fortiori* not part of logic. It is for this reason that Frege defines *NxFx* as he does, treating the extensions of concepts as 'logical objects'. Thus, Frege's use of extension-objects assumes that logic permits the general switch between concepts and their extensions.

The presence of a technical principle corresponding to this is therefore essential in the (simple) proof of *HP*. In the *Grundgesetze* (1893), Frege introduces his Basic Law V as just such a principle, governing the existence and behaviour of very general objects, as befits its classification as a logical law. It is at this point we see that Frege's system is not the reduction of arithmetic to anything well known at all, but rather a form of generalisation. In form, Law V is somewhat similar to *HP*, for it says that the extension of *F* is the same as the extension of *G* just in case *F* and *G* are co-extensional. It is a powerful existence principle because it implies the existence of the extension of *F* for any *F* whatsoever. Too powerful, in fact: in 1902, Russell showed that it is inconsistent, since it implies Russell's Antinomy (see Russell's letter to Frege in van Heijenoort 1967). Law V is close to what has become known as the *Set Comprehension Principle* (*SCP*) of set theory, which asserts that the extension of every concept is a set (object), and which easily engenders Russell's Antinomy (see section 7). Frege employs a regimented type hierarchy for concepts which is strict in its distinction between objects and concepts and about what sorts of things can fill 'gaps' in concepts. But the hierarchy goes wrong because Law V allows that the extension of any concept, no matter how complex, is an object, that is, of the lowest level, thus rendering the type hierarchy largely otiose. Frege had generalised to a logically *impossible* theory.

Can Frege's system be rescued? Work in the 1980s by Wright and Boolos suggests that to some extent it can. *HP* is all Frege requires (with second-order logic) to derive arithmetic. Boolos showed that *HP*, unlike Law V, is consistent, that therefore Frege's technical achievement can be restored in much the form envisioned (see the papers in Boolos 1998). Wright has argued that *HP* itself is *analytic*, thus restoring the philosophical part of Frege's project, too (see Wright 1997). But this claim is much more contentious.

4. DEDEKIND

Another important body of foundational work in which reductionism appears to play a significant part is Dedekind's (1854, 1872, 1888). The context for the reductionist sympathies expressed in Dedekind 1888 is provided by Dirichlet, Dedekind's teacher and mathematical inspiration.

One of Dirichlet's important theoretical innovations in arithmetic was the use of complex function theory to prove facts about the natural number sequence (analytic number theory). For example, Dirichlet in 1837 proved in this way that any arithmetic progression of natural numbers whose initial term and difference are relatively prime contains infinitely many primes. This systematised various special assumptions that had been made, for example, by Euler and Legendre. Riemann went further, establishing a connection between the distribution of primes and the complex zeta-function, which has been subsequently been of great importance in number theory. (The Riemann zeta-function is the subject of one of the most famous unproved hypotheses in mathematics, the Riemann Hypothesis, the conjecture that the real part of all arguments to which the zeta-function assigns 0 is 1/2; proving the Riemann Hypothesis is the 8th Problem on Hilbert's famous list from 1900b, and is unsolved.) The power of these methods is epitomised by the Prime Number Theorem (*PNT*); this was conjectured by Gauss and Legendre around 1800, and proved by Hadamard and de Vallé-Poussin (independently) in 1896 using properties of the zeta-function, and says that the number of primes $\leq x$ tends to $x/log\ x$ as x tends to infinity. In any case, this powerful new conceptual tool yields a striking example of the general question: what is the relation between the expanded framework and the old one? There is also a specific purity of method question: can the same results be proved without recourse to analytic number theory?

Dirichlet himself (see Cantor 1883a, 1883b, Dedekind 1888) stated the thesis that all facts about analysis and function theory will ultimately reduce to facts about natural numbers. There are two obvious ways in which this can be taken. One is to regard the new conceptual material as merely auxiliary, and to seek proofs which avoid it. (For example, in 1948, Selberg, and then Selberg and Erdos, found elementary proofs of both Dirichlet's Theorem and *PNT*.) The other is to show that the basic concepts of the extended domains can be constructed out of the very conceptual material employed by the theory of natural numbers itself. In so far as Dedekind 1888 provides support for Dirichlet's claim, it is for this latter. This view, so expressed, sounds close to that of the 'arithmetisation' project of Kronecker, who stated his conviction that all of pure mathematics must have the same 'necessity' as the simplest arithmetic because it ought to be possible to 'arithmetise' it, to found it on 'the number concept alone' taken 'in the narrowest sense' (Kronecker 1887: 253). However, the closeness is only apparent. The argument must turn on the means adopted in reducing theories to arithmetic, and Kronecker objected to those employed by Dedekind. Kronecker was right in this at least: Dedekind's work does rest on something conceptually novel, and thus the reduction cannot be considered as straightforward (see Kronecker 1887). The origins of the constructivist (predicativist) movements later developed by Weyl and others can be seen in Kronecker's foundational views. (For a summary, and further references, see Ewald's Introduction to Kronecker 1887 in Ewald 1996: II.)

Consequently, it is important to disentangle the reductionist strains in Dedekind from the explicit appeal to generalisation. The three works 1854, 1872, 1888 must be seen as a whole, in which Dedekind adumbrates a series of conceptual connections between the elementary arithmetic of the natural numbers and higher arithmetic and analysis, and then attempts to reduce the natural number structure to something more primitive.

The 1854 essay advances an explanation of how the various number systems (the positive integers, the natural numbers, the integers, the rationals) can be regarded as natural extensions of each other, as *number* systems. The explanation is this: one isolates general laws which hold only in a restricted form in (say) the positive integers, and then looks for an extended domain in which these laws hold in full generality. (In effect, it appeals to the existence, or actually the *creation*, of the smallest domain satisfying the general laws.) For example, in extending the natural numbers to the integers, the subtraction operation is extended; if we regard $a - b$ as a shorthand for *the x such that* $x + b = a$, then we want $\exists x[x + b = a]$ to be true for any choice of a, b. In short, the structural laws take precedence over the objects.

Dedekind's essay of 1872 on the irrational numbers continues this theme, part of the point being to show that one does not have to rely on geometrical intuition for a guarantee that the real 'line' is continuous and complete (thus it is a purity investigation of the Euclidean type). Again, Dedekind starts with a domain (and its arithmetic), the rationals, and then considers what would have to be added to this to make it continuous. His analysis isolates the *Dedekind Cut Property* (*DCP*): a 'line' L satisfies the *DCP* if, for any Cut (C_L, C_U) in L, there is always an r in L which 'produces' (C_L, C_U). (A Cut in a simply ordered 'line' L is a division of L into two parts, a 'lower', C_L, and an 'upper', C_U, such that if $x \in C_L$ (C_U) and $y \le x$ ($y \ge x$), then $y \in C_L$ (C_U), too. A Cut (C_L, C_U) is 'produced' by r if r is the least element in C_U.) The rationals *fail* to possess *DCP*, whereas the real line, ordinarily conceived, is the smallest extension of the rationals which does possess it. Dedekind points out, however, that the collection of all Cuts in the rationals *itself* has the *DCP* (and satisfies the right field laws, given naturally defined ordering and field operations). Consequently, he proposes that corresponding to each rational Cut which is not actually produced by a rational we 'create' an irrational which produces that Cut. Thus, we have our 'law', and creation according to it. Other analyses of continuity were given by Weierstrass (never published) and Cantor (1872), the latter using equivalence classes of Cauchy sequences. This analysis, along with Dedekind's, became standard. All achieve two of Dedekind's central aims, avoiding appeals to geometry and providing a conceptual analysis precise enough for use in deductions.

Frege (later) made the general point that the coherence of laws has to be shown before it makes sense to say we 'create' according to them. At a minimum, the laws have to be shown to be consistent; Frege argues that the only way to show this is to exhibit objects which exemplify them, rendering creation, and the claim about the primacy of laws, otiose (see 1893, §§139–44). Hilbert later simplifies this problem, first (1899, correspondence with Frege in Frege 1976 [1980]) by *identifying* existence with syntactic consistency, and then later by insisting on the search for direct syntactic consistency proofs, without requiring the exhibition of a model. But Dedekind *does* exhibit objects satisfying the right laws, e.g., the Cuts in the rationals. The problem is that this depends on a central set existence principle: if the set of rationals exists, so does the set of all subsets of rationals, for the law that *DCP* yields begins 'For every Cut in $\mathbb{Q}$ (the rational field), there exists an x such that . . .'. Thus, one is dependent on quantification over the Cuts of $\mathbb{Q}$ whether or not one takes 'creation' or exhibition as primary. In short, Dedekind's procedure cannot show that the theory of the irrationals (let alone analysis) can be reduced to that of the rationals: not only does this require generalisation according to a law, the very statement of that law depends in turn on another (unarticulated) law governing collections.

A similar combination of generalisation and reduction is found in Dedekind 1888 (which presents work of earlier vintage), and concerns the natural number structure N. What characterises N is that it forms what Dedekind calls a *simply infinite system*, i.e., that is there is a one-one map ϕ from N into itself (thus, N is infinite), where some privileged element of N ('1', the first element) is the only element omitted by ϕ. Call a subset X of N a *chain* under ϕ if it is such that $\phi(X)$ is a proper subset of X, and then call a_0 the intersection of all chains under ϕ which have a as a member; 1_0 is then N itself. Dedekind then gives definitions of the arithmetical operations, and a demonstration of what amount to the Dedekind-Peano postulates governing N. As with Frege, central principles like that of mathematical induction are *proved* for simply infinite systems, and so not taken as primitive methods of inference. Dedekind states that one can arrive at the notion of *the* natural number structure from the simply infinite systems (all isomorphic) by a creative act of abstraction.

Dedekind's argument is designed to show that arithmetic 'is an immediate emanation of pure laws of thought', 'a part of logic' (1888: III). Precisely what he means by this is not clear. However, what is shown is that the natural number structure (with the appropriate arithmetic) can be characterised using the concept of a one-one mapping, which corresponds, says Dedekind, to a fundamental, and quite general, intellectual capacity characterised as one 'without which no thinking is possible' (Dedekind 1888: iii–iv), exemplified, says Dedekind (§2), in naming, thus associating certain things (objects) with others (names). Hence, the drift of Dedekind's foundational argument is that the mathematics of the central number systems is reduced to fundamental intellectual capacities, so is 'nothing but the product of our intellect'. But what we actually see in Dedekind is the reduction of arithmetic to some form of set theory, about which Dedekind begins to be more explicit in 1888, though not fully. Is the relevant set theory a 'product of our intellect', too? Is it simply 'logical', part of intellectual equipment? Or do these concepts require clarification and elucidation in turn? The general appeal to set theory was perhaps regarded by Dedekind as straightforward, based, no doubt, on his experience with algebra and number theory, although he later came to see this reliance as ill-advised.

Dedekind's work therefore fails to support Dirichlet's reductive thesis. Dedekind himself says that, though one might believe in the Dirichlet reduction in principle, conceptual innovation will be necessary to circumvent long and involved reductions, and that the greatest progress in mathematics has come through the 'creation and introduction of new concepts' (1888: vi). Thus, what really counts for Dedekind is some version of the Second Dirichlet Principle, and not the Dirichlet belief in reducibility in principle. Dedekind's analyses are indeed classic examples of conceptual generalisation and unification.

In 1888, Dedekind says that his reduction of arithmetic is to the 'laws of thought'; one illustration of his belief that these embrace the principles of set construction he employs is the following. Dedekind recognises that one has to *prove* that there exist infinite collections, and indeed gave a proof (1888: Theorem 66). This is the construction of an infinite set in the *Gedankenwelt* of a conscious subject, namely 'the totality S of all things which can be objects of my thought' (Dedekind 1888: 14): if s is an element of S, then s', the thought that s is an element of S, is also an element of S, apparently establishing the required iteration. But it is not clear what the proof proves; it is not obvious that something distinct is acquired at each stage, casting doubt on the iteration, and it is irredeemably subjective. That it is meant to illustrate the power of the mind (thought) in *creating* sets is indicated by the fact that it is structurally very similar to a proof of Bolzano's (1851: §13), differing from it mainly in that it *does* employ a subjective element. (Bolzano uses 'propositions in themselves'.)

Frege's work and Dedekind's (1888), although technically similar, make an interesting contrast. Both succeeded in *deriving* the basic principles of arithmetic, both showed how the vagueness of intuition could be avoided, both made essential use of some form of the set concept, both support the abstractness of arithmetic and higher mathematics. But Frege was opposed to the psychological elements in Dedekind's foundational work, specifically the appeal to the 'creative' and 'active intellectual', stressing instead the abstract and non-mental character of mathematical objects. Frege's 'anti-psychologism' is a crucial philosophical component of his work (see, above all, 1884), and Frege provides a general *philosophical* justification for treating abstract objects as real, as real as concrete (or 'actual') objects. The further exploration of this led to a series of works (e.g., 1892) which are the first in a new philosophical discipline, the philosophy of language. (For surveys, see Dummett 1991, 1994.)

5. CANTOR

When we move to Cantor's work, we see generalisation at work without any appeal to reductionism. Whereas Dedekind and Frege sought a general foundation for concepts of established mathematics, Cantor's work concerned genuinely new mathematics, the mathematical theories of the infinite and of transfinite numbers. The work of Cauchy and Weierstrass on the limit concept apparently showed that the potential infinite is the only way the infinite enters higher mathematics. However, Cantor argued that the concept of potential infinity is not self-sufficient, since potential infinities presuppose infinitely large domains of variation, that is, actual infinities. Moreover, the characterisation of real numbers (through Cauchy sequences or Dedekind Cuts) reveals that an ordinary finite real number is (or rests on) an actually infinite collection (as do the natural numbers in the Frege-Russell conception). Cantor's work (1872–99) is an extended theory of actually infinite domains, which is the central generalising concept, and of their numerical representations, which are generalisations of the natural numbers. Like Dedekind, Cantor argued that progress in mathematics depends on conceptual innovation, the central constraints being the 'integration' of the new concepts with already accepted concepts and the condition that the concepts be consistent.

Before Cantor, there were two standard objections to a theoretical treatment of actual infinity, one conceptual (well-known since at least Galileo) and the other metaphysical. The conceptual objection is exemplified by the following. If the natural numbers and the even numbers are regarded as two distinct, actually infinite collections, then the former seems obviously bigger than the latter. But one can easily construct a one-one correspondence between them which seems to indicate that they are of the same size, each element of each collection being uniquely paired with an element of the other. Thus, talk of size is incoherent. There are analogous difficulties if one takes numerical representation: impossible that a cardinal number when added to itself should remain the same, or that a number be both even and odd. The metaphysical objection (which Cantor took from Scholastic philosophy) is that the treatment of actual infinity violates a theological injunction against intellectual subjugation of the actual infinite when taken as a representation of the Almighty (such actual infinity Cantor terms the *Absolute* Infinite).

However, Cantor argued (1883a) that there is nothing *self*-contradictory about actual infinites (domains or numbers). The putative demonstrations of contradictoriness invariably have one (or both) of two starting points: (a) an implicit assumption that infinites have the standard properties that finites have; or (b) a conflation of two different methods of comparing size, either by comparing extension or by using one-one correspondence (or order-isomorphism). Only when at least one of two collections is finite is it the case that a broader extension implies that the two cannot be put into one-one correspondence. (Like Dedekind and Frege, Cantor took the basis of the theory of cardinality to be the notion of one-one correspondence.) As for the theological objection, Cantor divided the actual infinite into the *increasable* (i.e., the numerable) and the *unincreasable*, and he takes only this latter as the true Absolute which is beyond numbering and mathematical determination. The former, Cantor calls the *transfinite*, which is left as a legitimate realm of mathematical investigation.

The transfinite is only mathematically important if it can be shown that there are distinct increasable actual infinities with essentially *different* properties. However, this had been made clear by Cantor himself before 1883, that is, showing that, while the collection of all algebraic numbers and the natural numbers N can be put into one-one correspondence (1874), there cannot be such a correspondence between N and that of all reals, R; that is, R is *non-denumerable*. Thus, there are at least two sizes among the number systems. In 1878, Cantor showed that there is a one-one correspondence between R and the points in a plane (of any dimension, even simply infinite dimension), so that here there is no increase in size. In 1892 he gave a different argument that R is non-denumerable, which generalises to show that the collection of all subsets of *any* given collection (finite or infinite) is of a larger size (or 'higher power') than the collection itself. Thus, the collection of all real functions *is* of greater size than R. Since infinite collections of different size are fundamental to *ordinary* mathematics, the study of the fundamentals of mathematics must include a theory of infinite collections and of mathematical infinity. The generalising element is indispensable.

The distinction discovered in 1874 between the types of infinity represented by N and by R rapidly became fundamental to mainstream mathematics, for example, in the study of the negligibility of point-sets and the theory of integration (Hawkins 1970). The discoveries of 1874 and 1878 also gave rise to the following natural question: are the infinities represented by N and R the *only* infinities in R itself, or are there finer distinctions? (Cantor's 1878

conjecture that they *are* the only infinities is the famous Continuum Hypothesis, *CH*.) These questions underline the need for a general theory of the infinite
in mathematics, and Cantor's direct achievement is the provision of such a theory, which has descended to modern mathematics as the theory of sets.

At the centre of Cantor's work are *transfinite numbers*. The size properties
of finite collections are represented by the familiar natural numbers; Cantor
developed a generalisation presenting a theory of *infinite* cardinal number to
represent the size properties of infinite sets, and with them an arithmetic which,
he thought, might help to settle the *CH*. At this point, a second factor in Cantor's
work becomes important, the theory of transfinite *ordinal* numbers.

By 1879, Cantor had come to the realisation that the solution of a basic
problem in analysis concerning Fourier series representations of functions and
the 'negligibility' of certain sets of exceptions can be achieved only via an
extension of the indexing properties of the natural numbers involving 'symbols
of infinity', thus ∞, $\infty + 1$, $\infty + 2$, etc. (see Hawkins 1970, Hallett 1984).
These 'symbols of infinity' enabled Cantor to prove a significant generalisation
of the representation theorem. In 1883a, Cantor argued that these 'symbols of
infinity' are actually transfinite *numbers*; both these and the natural numbers
represent a certain kind of ordering on the underlying sets (or the underlying
processes) being analysed, a *well-ordering*. (To be well-ordered a collection has to
be linearly ordered, to have a first element, and every element with a successor
has a *least* or *immediate* successor. Obviously, well-orderings are generalisations
of the ordering on the natural numbers.) When they are used for counting the
natural numbers are ordinal numbers, since counting imposes a well-ordering.
The difference between these ordinal and cardinal numbers in the finite realm
is blurred by the fact that any two well-orderings on a given finite set are order-
isomorphic, so a finite set can be assigned only one ordinal number; this can then
be identified harmlessly with the cardinal number, so one can measure *cardinal*
size by counting. But among infinite collections, cardinal size and well-ordering
do not fall neatly together; for example, the same denumerable collection can
be well-ordered (counted) by non-denumerably many ordinals. Moreover, the
transfinite ordinals, like the transfinite cardinals, display quite different numerical
properties from their finite counterparts; thus $1 + \alpha = \alpha \neq \alpha + 1$, for transfinite
ordinal numbers α. Hence, any expectation that transfinite numbers behave like
finite numbers effectively rules out a theory of the former.

Thus, Cantor's work represents two generalisations governing number: the
correct arithmetical laws for finite and infinite cardinals depend on the behaviour of one-one correspondence; the correct arithmetical laws for finite and
infinite ordinal numbers depend on the behaviour of (well-)order isomorphisms
(one-one correspondences which also mirror the order). What we get from this

in the *finite* realm is the familiar finite arithmetic, but the same laws do not apply in the infinite realm. Cantor also generalised the use of ordinal numbers as *counting* numbers, under the assumption that every set can be put into well-ordered form, thus amalgamating the theories of transfinite ordinals and cardinals, too (see Hallett 1984: §2.2). This gave him the sequence of *aleph* ($\aleph$) *numbers* (the cardinals of well-ordered sets) as the infinite cardinals, and in effect set down the core of modern set theory. Cantor's *CH* becomes the conjecture that the cardinality of *R* is $\aleph_1$, the second infinite aleph (the cardinal number of denumerable sets, like *N*, is $\aleph_0$), represented by Cantor's second number-class (of all denumerable ordinals). The *Continuum Problem* (if not the first aleph, then which?) was of enormous importance in the development of Cantor's work, and has assumed a central place in foundational studies ever since, being the first in Hilbert's list of 24 central mathematical problems given in a celebrated address in 1900 (Hilbert 1900b). It is now widely thought to be insoluble. *CH* was shown to be independent of the standard axioms of modern set theory in two steps; Gödel showed its consistency in 1938, and Cohen showed the consistency of the negation in 1964. Work stemming from Cohen's shows that it is consistent to assume that the cardinality of the continuum can be represented by almost any of the vast sequence of $\aleph$-numbers.

The assumption that every set can be well-ordered, which Cantor called (1883a) a 'law of thought', is crucial to his theory. To prove it was also a part of Hilbert's First Problem. The problem was solved, in a sense, by Zermelo (a colleague of Hilbert's) in 1904 by showing that the Well-Ordering Theorem (*WOT*) follows from a principle Zermelo called the Axiom of Choice (*AC*). The isolation of this principle sparked one of the severest controversies in the history of mathematics, involving debates about the obviousness, the legitimacy, and even the meaning of *AC*, debates which spread to other features of set theory, such as the use of impredicative definitions and non-denumerable collections. (For a taste, see Zermelo 1908a, and Borel *et al*. 1905.) Zermelo included *AC* in the first axiomatisation of set theory in 1908b, and it has been regarded as a standard axiom of set theory ever since. (The same works of Gödel and Cohen referred to above together showed the independence of *AC*, too.) It quickly emerged that the inclusion of the axiom is necessary in the limited sense that *no* reasonable general theory of infinite size at all is possible without it, let alone Cantor's (see also Moore 1982, Hallett 1984).

Cantor's work had a profound effect on the philosophy of mathematics, for at least four reasons. (a) It contributes substantially to the view that the foundations of mathematics must themselves become objects of mathematical study. (b) It emphasises that classical mathematics involves infinity in an essential and variegated way, and it thus renders study of many philosophically important concepts vacuous without some knowledge of the mathematical developments Cantor wrought. (c) In Cantor, one sees a liberation of mathematics from its traditional foci (arithmetic and geometry), and the introduction of a genuinely new conceptual element, not just the reconceptualisation of traditional subjects. The traditional concepts had been stretched, for example, in the work of Riemann and Klein on more generally conceived manifolds. But Cantor's generalisation goes much further. After Cantor, there is no longer any question of a 'reduction of all of mathematics to arithmetic', in no matter how attenuated a sense. Sets generally are mathematical objects, and there is an essential arbitrariness about the set concept, since it is not essential that there be any 'form' holding the elements of the set together. (Cantor famously suggested that the term 'free mathematics' is more appropriate than 'pure mathematics'.) Among other things, this had a productive effect on well-established areas of mathematics, revolutionising, for example, the theory of integration. (d) Cantor, however, saw limits to the conceptual freedom in mathematics, both mathematical (there must be conceptual links to existing theories, and the new concepts must be self-consistent), and external (the Absolute remains outside mathematical determination), but even so there were challenges to this alleged freedom. The most important were provoked by the *set-theoretic antinomies*, of which more in section 7.

6. CREATION, POSSIBILITY, AND CONSISTENCY

The mathematician who extended Cantor's appeal for 'free' mathematics, and also developed important insights of Dedekind's, was Hilbert (his views also show significant traces of those of Gauss, Kronecker, and, later, Frege and Russell). Hilbert had more influence over the modern foundational study of mathematics than any other thinker. Much of the influence stems from 'Hilbert's Programme' developed, with Bernays's help, in the 1920s (sometimes misleadingly called 'formalism'; for a survey, see Bernays 1967, Mancosu 1998). For example, Gödel's work, both technical and philosophical, is best seen in the context of Hilbert's. Although Gödel's main results in logic have negative consequences for some aims of Hilbert's foundational programme, it is not a straightforward refutation; there is much in Hilbert's work which remains of genuine importance. Above all, Hilbert was the first who explicitly adopted the axiomatic method as an investigative framework for the study of the foundations of mathematics, where abstract, ideal mathematics forms the very subject matter. The axiomatic method is foreshadowed in Dedekind's foundational analyses, specifically in the insistence that it is the laws which determine the subject matter, not vice-versa. The axiomatic method generalises the generalisation arguments, but without

Dedekind's appeal to 'creative abstraction' to single out a unique domain, it being accepted instead that there will be many structures which satisfy the given properties. For Hilbert, axiomatised mathematics is constrained above all by consistency, understood not just as the demand that concepts be *self*-consistent (as with Cantor), but that it be impossible to derive a contradiction from the whole deductive structure. Under this view, abstract theories themselves become the objects of mathematics, and consistency demonstrates their existence.

The concern with consistency is not solely an extension of Cantor's criterion of self-consistency, but also an extension of the concern with *possibility* brought to the fore in the work of Gauss, Beltrami, Helmholtz, and Klein on non-Euclidean geometry. Non-Euclidean geometry was first considered viable primarily because of the work of Saccheri, Lambert, and others in the eighteenth century. Gauss (in private) and Bolyai and Lobatchevsky later showed that one can create coherent and rich geometrical theories in which the Euclidean parallel postulate is negated which give explicit (analytic) treatments of measurement and trigonometry, and thus elaborated (analytic) geometrical theories. These theories were thereby shown to be *possible*, perhaps as the geometry of physical space (Gauss, Riemann), and certainly as theoretically sustainable. However, in later work Beltrami, Helmholtz, Klein and Poincaré appeal in turn to extended senses of possibility (see Bonola 1912, Stillwell 1996, Torretti 1978). Beltrami's work showed that non-Euclidean constructions can be correctly represented in Euclidean geometry. This shows that non-Euclidean geometry is *conceivable* on the basis of Euclidean geometry, or is 'only a part of ordinary geometry' (Poincaré 1891). Helmholtz takes this further, for he attempts to describe in phenomenological detail what would be experienced in worlds like Beltrami's (see Helmholtz 1870, 1878).

However, models such as Beltrami's, when viewed as a *translation* of non-Euclidean geometry into Euclidean, can be used to make a logical point, showing the *independence* of the Parallel Postulate from the other Euclidean assumptions, and the *consistency* of non-Euclidean geometry relative to Euclidean, thus the *logical* possibility of the former (see Poincaré 1891). With this, intuition, conceivability and phenomenology are left behind altogether. The importance of relative consistency in modern foundational settings hardly needs stressing. One (modern) way to view the relative consistency proof of which Poincaré speaks is as an *inner model* proof (modelling non-Euclidean geometry within Euclidean geometry). But what Poincaré considers is really a translation from the language of non-Euclidean geometry into the interpreted language of Euclidean geometry which preserves logical structure, hence guaranteeing that proofs will always transform into proofs. This procedure does not depend on the fact that the non-Euclidean geometries share most of their basic assumptions with Euclidean, or on the actual construction of *models* at all, but solely on a mapping of one theory into another which preserves syntactic structure. In Hilbert's work on geometry (in the later 1890s) this kind of syntactic mapping becomes a form of *reinterpretation*. In Hilbert, the models of geometry are constructed in quite different theories (mostly theories of number), so are not inner models at all. However, full clarification of the cogency of this procedure had to await clarification of syntactic and logical structures and deducibility.

Hilbert's work on geometry had a profound effect on modern foundational investigation. Before Hilbert, two standard attitudes towards geometry were either that it was subsumed under analysis (e.g., Klein, Dedekind, Cantor), or that it was a natural science, thus not part of pure mathematics in the way that arithmetic is (Gauss, Kronecker). However, there were very important movements in the nineteenth century which revived *synthetic* geometry built on purely geometrical primitives, like 'point', 'line', 'plane', unimpeached by arithmetical principles. Building partially on the work of Monge and Poncelet, von Staudt constructed independently of analysis a system of projective geometry, which even contained a replacement for the idea of coordinatisation. But there were some prickly questions: how much of the development is free of continuity assumptions, through which a *numerical* element threatens to creep in? Is congruence based on assumptions about the movement of lines or figures, as it is ultimately in Euclid? Or on equality of *size* (length, angle)? The status of the widely invoked Duality Principles was also unclear. For example, it was accepted as obvious that in ordinary 3-dimensional projective geometry, theorems remain correct when the terms 'point' and 'plane' are interchanged, 'line' remaining unaltered. But there was nothing like a general argument given for the correctness of such principles. Moreover, the fact that there were no clear axioms made it difficult to settle these issues, or to determine the central theorems around which projective geometry can be organised.

Pasch (1882) provided a system of axioms for projective geometry which included genuinely synthetic congruence axioms, dispensed with continuity, and which established the central theoretical shape of pure geometry. (He also gave the first general argument for Duality.) Hilbert's axiomatic study of geometry in the 1890s (presented in lectures in the 1890s, culminating in the book Hilbert 1899) relied significantly on Pasch's axioms. Yet this study was highly original and radically different. (For surveys of geometrical work before Hilbert, see Nagel 1939, Freudenthal 1957, Gray 1998.)

Hilbert's axiom system was divided into five groups, governing incidence, order, congruence, parallels, and continuity. He was motivated not at all by proving new Euclidean theorems, but more by general 'purity of method' concerns, which aimed: (i) to show that certain theories *can* be developed using only restricted means (cf. Frege, Dedekind); (ii) when this is not possible, to *prove* that it cannot be done; (iii) to prove that key theorems *within* a theory can be proved without specified axioms, but do depend on others; (iv) to prove that geometries other than the standard Euclidean or non-Euclidean (e.g., non-Desarguesian, non-Archimedean) are possible. His grouping of the geometrical axioms is a crucial part of this refined analysis, especially in establishing the role of various central theorems. In short, Hilbert generalises from the proof of the unprovability of the Parallel Axiom, turning the construction of models which interpret some sentences as true and a designated sentence as false into an art form. (The best descriptions of the aims of Hilbert's geometrical work are Hilbert's letter to Frege of 29 December 1899 in Frege 1976 [1980], and Bernays 1922.) Hilbert clearly recognised that answering these possibility/impossibility questions had become *de facto* part of modern mathematics, in which one mathematical theory is used to prove something decisive about another; witness the demonstrations that e and π are not algebraic numbers, the latter showing that the circle cannot be squared by elementary geometric constructions. In the Conclusion to his 'Grundlagen der Geometrie' (1899), Hilbert states that the 'purity' question is the 'subjective side' of what he calls a *Grundsatz* of foundational investigation, to elucidate every question by examining whether it is possible to answer it 'in a prescribed way with restricted means or not' (p. 89). Thus, we have a new kind of mathematical investigation, which concentrates systematically on the search for *proofs* of unprovability, and then focuses on the reasons for the unprovability. This had a very important effect on the shape of modern logic (not least because it was the beginning of *proof theory*), and 'purity' questions became of central importance in foundational investigation in the twentieth century. Four examples come to mind: (a) Gödel's invention of a general method for finding unprovable statements (1931); (b) Gödel's demonstration that there cannot be 'elementary' proofs of the consistency of arithmetic; (c) the unprovability of the *CH* from the usual axioms of set theory, and the proliferation of models of set theory following the invention of Cohen's forcing method in 1963; (d) the special cases of propositions like the Paris-Harrington Theorem, simple enough statements about the natural numbers, whose proof nevertheless uses conceptual means not duplicable within standard arithmetic.

Hilbert did not pursue 'purity' considerations for reductionist motives. Indeed, as mentioned, his strategy relies intrinsically on the cooperation of various, often apparently disparate, mathematical fields. (The paradigms are: the translation of the question about squaring the circle from geometry into algebra, then showing that π cannot be 'constructible'; the use of algebraic theories for the provision of the models that underlie the geometrical independence proofs.) The philosophical questions ('Is geometrical knowledge *synthetic*, or derived

from spatial intuition?', 'Is arithmetic *analytic*, and in what sense?') are not only
put to one side, but lose much of their point. Hilbert was *not* concerned with
the epistemological status of geometry (see Bernays 1922: 95–6), as were Pasch,
Frege, and Russell (1897). Hilbert did not deny that the basic axioms of synthetic
geometry are 'about the world', and repeatedly said that geometry is the oldest,
most basic natural science, many of whose axioms are 'confirmed' by experiment. Geometry for Hilbert starts from a loose background of 'facts' formed by
a complex mixture of what the mathematical science of geometry bequeaths,
experience of the physical world, including the results of clever experimenting,
and what we take involuntarily to be obvious. But he was interested, not so much
in geometrical theory as the garnering of facts, but in the foundational organisation of the theory, the primary tool for which is the axiomatic method. He
systematises the body of facts, revises it, reshapes it, relates it to other branches of
mathematics (primarily algebra and analysis), and investigates the logical interrelations between various central propositions. Moreover, Hilbert knew, even in
the 1890s, that experimental or theoretical results could undermine Euclidean
geometry's pre-eminent position, and also saw nothing sacrosanct about the
choice of primitive concepts. There is no trace of Russell's interest (see below)
in 'getting the foundations right', in isolating the 'right' set of primitives. For
Hilbert, there is no 'right' set of primitives; some might be better than others
for certain purposes, but there is never really any final word, even for relatively
simple theories. (This foreshadows Hilbert's doctrine of the *Tieferlegung der Fun-
damente* of Hilbert 1918.) Even the commitment to *synthetic* geometry was not
absolute; for Hilbert, there is nothing in itself wrong with pursuing geometry
analytically, as Riemann, Klein, and Lie did. Far more important is the study of
the relationships *between* theories, and the use of one to study another.

As stated, Hilbert's approach depends on the use of varying interpretations
of theories. This can be seen even *within* the apparently restrictive view that
'geometry is a natural science': lines can be taken both as stretched threads or as
light rays, points as pin marks or distant 'points' of light or 'point' masses. Hilbert
stressed that any theory is only a 'schema of concepts'; it is 'up to us' how to fill
it with content. Thus, once a theory is axiomatised, the full 'meaning' of the
primitives is given by the axioms and only the axioms; we cannot say what a
point is independently of stating axioms which govern points, lines and planes,
and this is *all* we can say in general (this is the real generalisation of Dedekind);
there is no prior notion of 'point' using which we can judge whether the axioms
are true, and different sets of axioms governing 'point' might present different
concepts. (This was a major bone of contention between Frege and Hilbert; see
the correspondence in 1899/1900 in Frege 1976 [1980].) The closest a theory
comes to possessing a unique interpretation is by being categorical, that is, where

all its interpretations are isomorphic. (Hilbert recognised that this is sometimes a criterion we should impose on an adequate axiomatisation, e.g., of the real numbers.) It follows that the means of deduction used within a theory must be *invariant under different interpretation*, thus that deduction operates independently of the meaning of the substantive terms (cf. Pasch). (Note that the appeal to varying interpretations is also a generalisation of the views of various British algebraists in the nineteenth century: see Ewald 1996: I, chs. 8–12.)

Much of Hilbert's study of geometry itself reveals generalisations, but he generalised again from this: the axiomatic method is to be the central pillar of investigation of the foundations of mathematical theories, investigating how they are constituted, organised, internally structured, and how they relate to other theories, whether cognate or remote. Indeed, such investigation is hardly possible while a theory remains at an informal level (see Hilbert 1900a). Axiom systems are not completely arbitrary, but must satisfy certain adequacy conditions. (a) Axiomatisations should only be attempted once theories have achieved a certain level of maturity, stability, and precision, and are thus always based on (but not tied to) a bedrock of 'facts'. (b) Hilbert sometimes demands that an axiomatised theory be *complete*, meaning that the axiom system be able to derive all the important facts, or all facts of a certain sort. (E.g., 'Can synthetic geometry derive all the geometrical "facts" derivable in analytic geometry?') This was not quite the modern concern with complete axiomatisations, but there is a clear relation. (c) Lastly, axiom systems must be syntactically consistent (one cannot derive both *P* and *not-P*, for otherwise they are trivial). This is a clear generalisation of Cantor: 'non-contradictoriness of concepts' becomes 'consistency of the theory (the axioms that govern the concepts)'.

7. PARADOXES

If one thinks that axioms are selected partly because they are true, then consistency is a trivial criterion; otherwise not. That it is indeed non-trivial was highlighted by the famous *set-theoretical/logical antinomies* or *paradoxes*. These brought a halt to the period of bold generalisation, and issued in more precise foundational reflection on basic theories.

In retrospect, the set-theoretic antinomies were first alluded to in Cantor's distinction (in correspondence with Hilbert in 1897 and Dedekind in 1899) between what he called 'consistent' (i.e., legitimate) and 'inconsistent' sets, whose elements cannot be taken together without engendering a contradiction (see Ewald 1996: II, ch. 19, E, and Ewald's prefatory remarks). Cantor stated a proof that every cardinal number must be an aleph, based on an argument that the sequence of all ordinal numbers (and hence that of all alephs) is 'inconsistent'. If we take them to be legitimate sets, then they must be numerable, so represented by an ordinal number/aleph respectively. These numbers would then be both *bigger than* any number in the sequence yet necessarily *in* the sequence; which is a contradiction. The sequences are thus 'beyond numerability', so Absolute and not legitimate, transfinite sets. This argument contains a core which is very similar to what is now known as 'Burali-Forti's Paradox' (for Burali-Forti's own argument, see his 1897 paper in van Heijenoort 1967): assume C is a legitimate infinite cardinal number, but no aleph, representing a legitimate set X. Then, for any aleph, we can choose a well-ordered sub-collection from X whose size is that aleph. Hence, C must be greater than all alephs, and the aleph sequence can be projected into X, contradicting its legitimacy. A well-ordering principle is at work here underlying Cantor's various projection (or successive selection) arguments. (In modern settings, the proposition that every infinite cardinal is an aleph requires AC, or WOT, *and* the Replacement Axiom.)

Cantor saw no contradiction here, just the basis of various *reductio* arguments that certain collections are not legitimate sets. Neither did Burali-Forti see a contradiction, but (in his case) just a (faulty) argument that the ordinals cannot be well-ordered. Cantor's division of collections into proper sets and 'inconsistent totalities' (a transformation of the older division between transfinites and Absolutes) is a creative way to exploit contradictions and indeed suggestive. It indicates a move from the self-consistency of concepts to the consistency of theories, a move which Hilbert made explicitly. Moreover, it ties the existence of specific mathematical objects to such consistency, and this, too, is contained in Hilbert's declaration that mathematical existence amounts to the consistency of theories (see, e.g., his correspondence with Frege). In effect, this means that it is the existence of the *domain* of appropriate objects which is in question, not that of individual objects (see Hilbert 1900a, 1900b). Nevertheless, Cantor's position is unsatisfactory since it did not give enough *positive* criteria as to what is to count as a legitimate set. This problem comes to the fore in Russell's paradox, the first such argument explicitly recognised as an antinomy (see Russell 1903: 101).

The argument is simple: look at the collection $A = \{x : x \notin x\}$; then $A \in A$ if and only if $A \notin A$; contradiction. In the case of Burali-Forti's argument, there are many assumptions on which the antinomy can be blamed (the premises were all challenged at one time or another, by Russell among others). Russell's antinomy, however, simplifies matters: the problem definitely resides in presuming that A is a set, or that the universal set U is a set, presumptions which (as Russell pointed out, 1903, section 102) rest on SCP, that is, the extension of any property (or concept) forms a set. Now the problem is this: If SCP is to be rejected, what is to replace it as a basic predicate-to-set conversion principle?

Zermelo's first axiomatisation of set theory (1908b; there was a second in 1930) seeks to replace *SCP* with a more restrictive principle, the Separation Axiom: any collection of objects all satisfying a given 'definite' property, and itself contained in a *set*, forms a set. Zermelo's axiomatisation avoids Russell's Antinomy and the Antinomy of the Greatest Set (it has no way of representing the general notions of ordinal and cardinal, so it cannot express the other antinomies). (Zermelo sees the *SCP* as implicit in Cantor's 1895 characterisation of a set as 'any collection to a whole of definite, properly differentiated objects of our intuition or our thought'. However, it is unlikely that Cantor adhered to *SCP*; in 1882, he appeals to a set existence principle close to the Separation Axiom, and in any case his theory of the Absolute Infinite from 1883 on makes it improbable, as the argument above about the aleph sequence suggests. See Hallett 1984: ch. 1.)

Zermelo's axiomatisation is in the spirit of Hilbert's use of the axiomatic method to tackle foundational problems. The 'facts' here are constituted by all the standard results of the theory of sets, minus the contradictions. But Zermelo's theory does this inadequately: it cannot deal with sets of power $\geq \aleph_\omega$ nor with ordinals $\geq \omega + \omega$; hence it cannot show that every well-ordered set is represented by an ordinal, the fundamental theorem of ordinal number theory. Partly for this reason, alternative axiomatisations were presented in the 1920s by Skolem, Fraenkel and von Neumann, axiomatisations which gave rise to the ones now standard (see Hallett 1984).

There was a more immediate problem with Zermelo's axiomatisation. The Separation Axiom appeals to the notion 'definite property', but Zermelo cannot make perfectly explicit what 'definite properties' are; there is certainly no mechanism within the theory to clarify or define the notion. It was clear by 1905 that choosing an inappropriate property leads to contradiction, as shown by Richard (1905). The problem also highlights a serious gap in Hilbert's axiomatic method, the lack of an explicit framework in which axiom systems can be set. It was partially solved by Weyl in 1910, with a definition close to that standard now: assume membership and equality are the two basic relations of set theory, then the 'definite properties' are just the one-placed predicates defined from these recursively using the basic logical operations. This gave the basis of the now standard logical framework (language, plus system of deduction) into which Hilbert's characterisation is naturally incorporated. (Here, as opposed to its treatment in Russell's system, Richard's antinomy is dissolved by the linguistic framework rather than by any mathematical theory itself.)

Richard's antinomy was an instance of 'intensional' or 'semantic' antinomies (Ramsey's term: 1926), involving notions like truth, denotation or definition, the most famous (and oldest) being the Liar Paradox. Many of these are gathered in Russell 1908. Antinomies of definition were particularly worrying, since they, too, prejudice normal mathematical specifications. Indeed, some mathematicians thought that these must be sharply circumscribed. In particular, the semantic paradoxes all involve what came to be known as *impredicative definitions*, i.e., definitions of an object a by a predicate ϕ which makes direct or indirect reference to, or presupposes the existence of, a collection to which a belongs. To one who thinks that mathematical objects have no existence until they have received proper definition, impredicative definitions are unacceptable. Poincaré was one such; he argued (e.g., 1909) that the use of impredicative definitions can only be accepted as legitimate by one who accepts the existence of a pre-existing mathematical realm, a supposition Poincaré decisively rejects. (Since impredicative definition is held responsible for contradiction, the contradictions are thus assimilated to a distinctive philosophical position.) However, barring impredicative definitions wholesale involves rejecting a great deal of set theory; the whole theory of non-denumerable infinity rests on their use (cf. the proof of Cantor's Theorem), and so does classical analysis (e.g., the Least Upper Bound Theorem). But Poincaré, like a number of other French mathematicians (see Borel *et al.* 1905, Borel 1908), was suspicious of non-denumerable infinity, and advocated its avoidance. They developed no systematic positive account of mathematics, though Weyl later did (1917), on lines sympathetic to them. Poincaré's dismissal of the realistic attitude towards Cantorian set theory was vigorously opposed by Zermelo (1908a), who was willing to *accept* the legitimacy of impredicative definitions for the very reason Poincaré gives (definitions describe, not create), and also points to the apparently consistent development of the full range of Cantor's set theory (including AC) axiomatically (see also Gödel 1944). Nevertheless, Gödel's work on incompleteness in the 1930s shows that generally one can only expect to prove the consistency of a theory by using means *stronger* than those embodied in the theory itself, which bars a decisive answer to Poincaré along these lines.

Reactions to the antinomies were many and various. Some adopted the relatively sanguine view that what they reveal is simply imprecision in the formulation of concepts or principles – the Hilbert School's attitude. Some took them to be (further) evidence of something profoundly amiss with classical mathematics – Poincaré, the French analysts, Borel, Lebesque, the English philosopher Russell, and, most extremely, the Dutch topologist Brouwer (later supported by Weyl). Brouwer saw the paradoxes as a confirmation of something wrong with the basic principles of mathematical reasoning, particularly the Law of Excluded Middle (*LEM*) applied to infinite totalities (see Brouwer 1908). According to Brouwer, the correctness of a mathematical proposition must be supported by a *construction*. In particular, to exist is to be constructed; it is not enough to show that the assumption that there is no such object leads to a contradiction. What exercised Brouwer most was the theory of the continuum, conceived of, not as a discipline with a fixed subject matter, but as a growing body of knowledge driven by certain underlying (and imprecise) intuitions which are the basis of all mathematical constructions. (Hence the term 'intuitionism' for the mathematics which Brouwer advocated.)

Brouwer's position is complicated by the fact that he conceived of mathematics as essentially 'languageless', and thus distorted by its objectification in propositional formulation. It follows that reasoning for Brouwer is not 'logical' in the traditional sense, that is, concerning the mediation of relations between linguistic propositions. If it makes sense to speak of logic, it is as a summary of the basic mathematical reasoning in a given discipline; for instance, the use of logical constants is determined by principles about the combination and manipulation of constructions. However, one of Brouwer's pupils, Heyting, later attempted to codify the logical principles supported by Brouwer, giving rise to *intuitionistic logic* (*IL*), which became the most significant alternative to classical logic, and its study has been enormously important in the twentieth century. (Dummett developed an important line of argument in favour of *IL* which avoids Brouwer's idealistic and solipsist standpoint: for a summary of *IL* and Dummett's philosophical approach, see Dummett 1977.) Brouwer's positive theory was only embryonic in the period covered by this article, and we therefore cannot discuss it, except to remark that later work of Glivenko, Gentzen, and Gödel showed that it is really the theory of the continuum which is especially coloured by Brouwer's approach, and not ordinary arithmetic. (For discussion, and some original papers, see Mancosu 1998.)

The most systematic reaction to the paradoxes is to be found in the work of Russell, culminating in Russell 1908 and the monumental Whitehead and Russell 1910–13. Russell perceived a single cause behind all the known antinomies, residing in the misuse of 'all':

our contradictions have in common the assumption of a totality such that, if it were legitimate, it would at once be enlarged by new members defined in terms of itself. (Russell 1908, p. 155)

Thus, he concluded, the definition of such totalities cannot be real definitions, for 'all' has no stable meaning through the process: the definitions claim to isolate a collection containing *all* the objects satisfying a certain predicate ϕ; but the collection turns out to satisfy ϕ, hence the original claim to be gathering *all* ϕ-objects is chimerical. (This diagnosis is similar to Poincaré's: see Poincaré 1909; Goldfarb 1988, 1989. It can also be found in Russell 1906, though there the diagnosis is only one among several.) This leads to a negative doctrine, stated in 1908 as the rule:

'Whatever involves *all* of a collection must not be one of the collection'; or conversely: 'If, provided a certain collection has a total, it would have members definable only in terms of that total, then the said collection has no total.' (Russell 1908: 155)

This is the first version of what Russell later called 'the vicious-circle principle' (*VCP*) (see Whitehead and Russell 1910–13: ch. II, section I). In 1906, Russell termed 'predicative' those propositional functions which properly define totalities; hence the propositional functions involved in the contradictions are *impredicative*. (This explains the modern use of 'impredicative': sets *a* defined impredicatively *do* invoke a predicate ϕ which, directly or indirectly, refers to *a*, if only through a universal quantifier.) As is obvious, Russell's position, like Poincaré's, relies on the implicit assumption that sets (Russell's term is *classes*) do not exist until they are defined.

Since about 1900 (see Russell 1903), Russell had been a logicist, holding that 'mathematics and logic are identical' (1937, p. v). The original project has much in common with Frege's (though most of 1903 was written in ignorance of Frege), relying rather freely on class formation. Russell discovered his famous antinomy before 1903 was published, and saw some of the difficulty which this presents, but it was only afterwards that he sought to introduce a greatly revised logical framework. The *VCP* is negative, stating what is not permitted. But, with *VCP* as a guide, Russell produced a positive theory governing the admissibility of definitions and objects, the *theory of logical types*, according to which logical formulas are arranged into a hierarchy of increasing complexity. This theory was first introduced in mature form in 1908, and assumed a central place in Whitehead and Russell's *Principia Mathematica* (1910–13). A basic illustration is as follows. Elementary propositions are formed by combining (elementary) concepts (or relations) and individuals, all these being assumed to be 'destitute of logical complexity'. The individuals form the lowest type. Propositional functions can now be formed from these elementary propositions by putting variables in place of individuals; quantification over these variables generates new propositions, and these propositions Russell calls *first-order propositions*, which form the next type. For example, if *a*, *b*, and *c* are individuals, and ϕ is a 3-place (elementary) relation, then $\phi(a,b,c)$ is an elementary proposition, $\phi(x,b,c)$ an elementary propositional function in *x*, while $\forall y,z\phi(a,y,z)$ is a first-order proposition, and correspondingly $\forall y,z\phi(x,y,z)$ is a *first-order* propositional function in *x*, whose quantifiers presuppose the existence of the totality of individuals. Clearly, first-order propositions (propositional functions) have logical complexity, and we have assumed that individuals do not; hence, these types do not overlap. Consider now a more complex propositional function, $f(\phi,x)$, which can be used to assert something both of ϕ and an individual. If we turn ϕ

into a variable and universally quantify over it, we get $\forall X f(X,x)$, again a propositional function of x. This function involves a universal quantifier, so it must 'presuppose' a totality (of functions), in fact, the totality of first-order functions. According to the *VCP*, the function just defined must lie outside this totality, and will in fact be a function of x of *second-order*, thus giving a new domain of quantification, and so on. According to Russell, the contradictions result precisely from confusion (or conflation) of these domains of quantification. For instance, the Liar says 'Every proposition I utter is false'; for Russell, this can only mean 'Every proposition of type t I utter is false', and this proposition is not of type t, so does not fall in the original range of quantification, that is, is not one of the propositions indirectly mentioned. If we regard sets as specified by propositional functions, then not only is $A = \{x: \phi x\}$ not an individual (where the xs are restricted to range over individuals), but A is to be assigned an order branded on it by the order of the function used to specify it. Thus, the sets of xs defined by $\forall y,z\phi(x,y,z)$ and $\forall X f(X,x)$ respectively are of different order.

With this we reach the heart of Russell's philosophical approach: all is dictated (or should be) by the recursive construction (and consequent complexity) of propositional functions. The approach is therefore in a certain sense a *linguistic* one, though Russell was unclear where the linguistic framework stops and the mathematics begins. In classical set theory, one is accustomed to assume that sets are again just individuals, like their elements, and that the complexity of the predicate or (concept) used to single them out is irrelevant; this holds, too, of Frege's extensions of concepts. Russell's approach rejects this. Russell actually goes further; he does not allow sets into his system at all, although he provides contextual definitions of all the standard set-theoretical vocabulary: there are just propositions and propositional functions. Given this, it is undoubtedly more natural to insist that these carry the marks of their type and order distinctions with them. (To say 'This pillar-box is red', and 'Red is a colour' are both natural; but to say 'This pillar-box is a colour' is nonsensical. Linguistic intuitions, however, do not run to quantification: 'All things are red' is certainly not nonsensical, but is the 'all' a genuinely universal quantifier, or is the quantification just over things of which it is meaningful to assert colour properties?)

Is Russell's account of mathematics adequate? He himself immediately recognised difficulties, for there are manifold cases in mathematics where one does really want to quantify over *all* propositional functions of a given variable, and not just those of some fixed order. In 1908, Russell singles out the definition of natural number by 'inductive property' and the definition of identity ('the identity of indiscernibles') as two such. He adopts the *Axiom of Reducibility* as a way around this. This says that for any propositional function of nth-order, there exists an extensionally equivalent one of *first-order* (in Russell's *Principia* terminology, *predicative*). Thus, *de facto*, the quantification can proceed, restricted, of course, to the functions of first-order (the predicative functions), but effectively without loss of generality. (There are similar reducibility axioms for relations.) Russell's reasons for the adoption of Reducibility are twofold: (1) If it were the case that for any function ϕ of whatever order there is a class $A = \{x : \phi x\}$, then the function $x \in A$ is in fact of the first-order and extensionally equivalent to ϕ. Thus Reducibility performs this important function of classes. (2) Much important mathematics is facilitated which would otherwise be blocked, and proofs of much else are greatly simplified. Reducibility was duly adopted in Russell and Whitehead 1910–13, too.

However, the axiom points to a severe conceptual difficulty, for its *existential* nature clashes with the constructive nature of the theory of functions it supposedly supplements, and this strains even the pragmatic logicism of *Principia*. (Something similar might be said of Russell's Axiom of Infinity and the Multiplicative Axiom, i.e., *AC*.) In the Introduction to the second edition of *Principia*, Russell repudiated Reducibility as 'clearly not the sort of axiom with which we can rest content' (Russell and Whitehead 1927, p. xiv). Without it, as he recognised, standard classical analysis falls by the wayside. (For example, it will not always be true that an infinite, bounded set of reals all of the same order has a least upper bound of that order.) This genuinely constructive route (beginning with Weyl 1917), which allows classical logic, but only predicative definition/set formation, has been of great philosophical significance. Nevertheless, Russell's own system without Reducibility was rendered incapable of achieving its main purpose, as Russell admitted, since this logical framework does not permit the reconstruction of standard mathematics. However, it does show how a great deal of conceptual machinery can be reconstructed in general logical vocabulary without incurring the known contradictions.

Ramsey (1926) pointed out that one can simplify Russell's theory of types if one does not insist on solving all the contradictions simultaneously. He singled out contradictions such as the Liar as having to do with the operation of the linguistic framework, and not, like Russell's contradiction, the mathematics or logic, and noted that a *simple* (and non-constructive) *theory of types* will prevent the latter contradiction without requiring the ramifications of the constructive theory of orders used to deal with the Liar. Indeed, the simple theory of types is not far removed from Zermelo's set theory (Quine 1963). Ramsey's distinction between different kinds of antinomies has been largely followed, although one topic of enduring interest (following Gödel's and Tarski's work) is the investigation of how much of a theory's *semantics* can be reproduced in that very theory (on pain of contradiction, not all can), and to examine just how the theory has to be supplemented to provide this.

CONCLUSION

What impact did the work described here have on foundational work in the twentieth century? There are four important legacies.

The first great legacy is the theory of sets. Work of Grassman, Riemann, and others suggested that something like the set concept was necessary in generalised mathematics. The work of Cantor emphasised this and provided a general framework theory. The work of Frege and Dedekind further stressed its importance in foundational analysis, especially given the requirements of a theory of infinity, and even Russell was not entirely successful in avoiding it. The first concern, which Zermelo's work began, was the formulation of an adequate axiom system; the second was to settle the Continuum Problem. In both respects, the meta-mathematical investigations of Gödel and Cohen were of the greatest importance. Set theory exhibits, roughly, Hilbert's pattern of development for a maturing axiomatic theory; however, it also became (gradually) the basic framework for foundational work, not just for those of a reductionist bent, but also as the provider of material for abstract mathematical structures, and finally as the theoretical basis for the central notion of logical consequence. With this, even Hilbert's belief in the diversity of abstract structures succumbs to a measure of set-theoretic reductionism.

The second important legacy was left by the antinomies. They had a considerable impact on foundational investigation, for example, largely destroying the attempt to show that mathematics is nothing more than elaborated logic. While they did not have anything like the great revisionary impact on the substance of mathematics as the work of Poincaré and Brouwer might have suggested, they did undoubtedly invoke sharper formulations, and these ensured that the great generalising movements of the nineteenth century survived, if a little curtailed. In addition, the attempt to produce diagnoses and satisfactory solutions of the antinomies, especially of the semantic antinomies, remains a standing project (witness Tarski's, and more recent, work on the Liar Antinomy and truth-definitions).

The third great legacy was Hilbert's 'axiomatic method', and the kind of foundational question which Hilbert was the first to ask, questions which only make sense once theories are cast in axiomatic form. 'Purity of method' questions especially became a standard part of foundational investigation.

The fourth great legacy was the amalgamation of philosophical and mathematical analysis, where we see philosophy's reflection on mathematics and the mathematical creativity of that reflection.

Mathematical logic was in its infancy in 1914; one could argue that study of it transformed the foundations of mathematics once it reached maturity in the

1920s and 1930s. Perhaps; but it did not transform it beyond recognition. For one thing, logic itself was indelibly shaped by such things as Hilbert's recognition, and use, of varying interpretations. Secondly, logic eventually enabled some of Hilbert's questions about theories (e.g., concerning completeness) to be posed, and answered, in a precise way. Thirdly, the use of logic in foundational studies became a striking example of Hilbert's strategy of using mathematics to analyse mathematics. The genuine novelty wrought by mathematical logic was that it led to the discovery of certain limitations in the logical formulation of axiomatic theories, a consequence of which was the revelation that formal, axiomatic set theory surely cannot be a final foundational theory for mathematics, and that nothing else could be.

THEORIES OF JUDGEMENT

ARTUR ROJSZCZAK AND
BARRY SMITH

1. THE COMBINATION THEORY OF JUDGEMENT

1.1. Introduction

The theory of judgement most commonly embraced by philosophers around 1870 was what we might call the 'combination theory'. This was, more precisely, a theory of the *activity* of judging, conceived as a process of combining or separating certain mental units called 'concepts', 'presentations', or 'ideas'. Positive judging is the activity of putting together a complex of concepts; negative judging is the activity of separating concepts, usually a pair consisting of subject and predicate, related to each other by means of a copula.

The combination theory goes hand in hand with an acceptance of traditional syllogistic as an adequate account of the logic of judging. In other respects, too, the theory has its roots in Aristotelian ideas. It draws on Aristotle's intuition at *Categories* (14b) and *Metaphysics* (1051b) to the effect that a conceptual complex may reflect a parallel combination of objects in the world. It had long been assumed by the followers of Aristotle that the phenomenon of judgement could be properly understood only within a framework within which this wider background of ontology is taken into account. The earliest forms of the combination theory were accordingly what we might call 'transcendent' theories, in that they assumed transcendent correlates of the act of judgement on the side of objects in the world. Such views were developed by Scholastics such as Abelard (e.g. in his *Logica Ingrediendibus*) and Aquinas (*De Veritate* 1, 2), and they remain visible in the seventeenth century in Locke (*Essay* IV, V) as well as in Leibniz's experiments in the direction of a combinatorial logic, for example at *Nouveaux Essais*, IV.5.

By 1870, however, there were few if any followers of Aristotelian or Leibnizian transcendent theories. For, by then, in the wake of German idealism, an immanentistic view had become dominant according to which the process of judging is to be understood entirely from the perspective of what takes place within the mind or consciousness of the judging subject. The more usual sort of idealism in Germany in the second half of the nineteenth century conceives the objects of knowledge as being quite literally located in (as 'immanent to') the mind of the knowing subject. Windelband, for example, can define idealism in this sense as 'the dissolution of being into processes of consciousness'. Combination theories in this idealist spirit were developed in Germany by, among others, Gustav Biedermann, Franz Biese, Eduard Erdmann, Kuno Fischer, Ernst Friedrich, Carl Prantl, and Hermann Schwarz.

1.2. Bernard Bolzano's sentences in themselves

A somewhat exceptional case is provided by the *Wissenschaftslehre* of Bernard Bolzano, published in 1837. While Bolzano's work appeared some forty years before the period which here concerns us, its importance for the theory of judgement makes a brief exposition indispensable. Bolzano, too, defended a combination theory of judgement, but of a Platonistic sort. Bolzano tells us that all propositions have three parts, a subject idea, the concept of having, and a predicate idea, as indicated in the expression <A has b> (Bolzano 1837 [1972]: par. 127). Bolzano's theory of judgement distinguishes between (1) the *Satz an sich* (sentence in itself) which would now standardly be described as the 'proposition' and (2) the sentence thought or uttered. The former is an ideal or abstract entity belonging to a special logical realm; the latter belongs to the concrete realm of thinking activity or to the realm of speech or language.

A judgement, according to this theory, is the thinking of an ideal proposition, an entity outside space and time: 'By proposition in itself I mean any assertion that something is or is not the case, regardless whether or not somebody has put it into words, and regardless even whether or not it has been thought' (Bolzano 1837: par. 19 [1972: 20–1]). This Platonistic theory of judgement plays an influential role in the story which follows, and it is to be noted that theories similar to that of Bolzano were embraced later on in the nineteenth century by Lotze and by Frege in Germany, as well as by G. F. Stout in England.

According to Bolzano, truth and falsity are timeless properties of propositions, and every proposition is either true or false, though the property of having a truth value does not in Bolzano's eyes belong to the definition of the concept of a proposition (Bolzano 1837 [1972]: pars. 23, 125). Since judgement is the thinking of a proposition, the act of judgement can also be called true or false in an extended sense, and truth and falsehood can further be predicated of speech acts in which judgement is expressed.

Bolzano's theory serves to secure the objectivity of truth. First, truth is independent of consciousness; it obtains independently of whether it is ever thought or recognised. Second, truth is absolute; it does not depend on time or times. Third, the truth or falsehood of a judgement does not depend upon the context in which it is made (Bolzano 1837 [1972]: par. 25). This Bolzanian understanding of the objectivity of truth and knowledge was influential first of all in Austria (see Morscher 1986), and has had a wide influence thereafter.

1.3. Problems arising from the combination theory of judgement

As philosophical idealism itself began to be called into question around the middle of the nineteenth century so, by association, did the combination theory begin to be recognised as problematic. The first problem for the combination theory turned on the problematic character of existential and impersonal judgements like 'cheetahs exist' or 'it's raining'. Such judgements seem to involve only one single member, and so for them any idea of 'combination' or 'unification' seems to be excluded.

A further problem turned on the fact that, even in those cases where judging might be held to involve a combination of concepts or presentations, the need was felt for some further moment of affirmation or conviction, some 'consciousness of validity' in the idealist's terminology, or some 'assertive force' in the language of Frege. For otherwise the theory would not be in a position to cope with hypothetical and other logically compound judgements in which complex concepts or presentations seem to be present as proper parts of judgements without themselves being judged.

Other problems centred around the notion of truth. One important mode of valuation of a judgement is its truth value. It became clear to a number of philosophers around 1900 that to do justice to the truth of judgements it is necessary to recognise some objective standard, transcendent to the judgement, against which its truth could be measured. This marked a challenge to the assumption that conceptual combination provides all that is needed for an account of judgement. Even if judging involves a combination of concepts, the truth of a judgement must involve also something on the side of the object to which this conceptual combination would correspond. Attempts were therefore made to come to terms with such objectual correlates, to establish what the objectual something is, to which our acts of judging correspond.

2. FRANZ BRENTANO

2.1. The concept of intentionality

It was Franz Brentano who was responsible for the first major break with the combination theory of judgement through the doctrine of intentionality set forth in his *Psychologie vom empirischen Standpunkt* (Brentano 1874/1924 [1973: 77–100, esp. 88–9]). Knowledge, for Brentano, is a matter of special types of judgement. The psychological description and classification of judgements in all their modes of occurrence is thus in his eyes a necessary precursor to the theory of knowledge as a branch of philosophy. First, however, it is necessary to find a firm foundation for the science of psychology itself, and this requires a coherent demarcation of the proper object of psychological research. For this we need some unique property which would distinguish mental from other types of phenomena. Hence Brentano's much-mooted *principle of the intentionality of the mental*, which states that each and every mental process is *of* or *about* something.

Brentano distinguishes three basic types of mental or intentional phenomena: *presenting, judging*, and *phenomena of love and hate*. Each of these three types of mental phenomenon is determined by its own characteristic intentional relation or intentional directedness. A *presentation* is any act in which the subject is conscious of some content or object without taking up any position with regard to it. Such an act may be either intuitive or conceptual. That is, we can have an object before our mind either in sensory experience (and in variant forms thereof in imagination), or through concepts – for example when we think of the concepts of colour or pain in general. Presentations may be either (relatively) simple or (relatively) complex, a distinction inspired by the British empiricists' doctrine of simple and complex ideas. A simple presentation is for example that of a red sensum; a complex presentation that of an array of differently coloured squares (Brentano 1874/1924 [1973: 79f., 88f.]).

2.2. The existential theory of judgement

On the basis of presentation, new sorts or modes of intentionality can be built up. To the simple manner of being related to an object in presentation there may come to be added one of two diametrically opposed modes of relating to this object, which we call 'acceptance' (in positive judgements) and 'rejection' (in negative judgements). Both, for Brentano, are specific processes of consciousness.

Brentano's concept of acceptance comes close to that which is expressed by the English term 'belief'. Brentano did not distinguish clearly between judging and believing as he did not draw a clear distinction between mental *acts* and mental *states*. Acceptance and rejection are, however, to be distinguished from what analytic philosophers have called 'propositional attitudes'. The object of the latter is a proposition or abstract propositional content and Brentano has no room in his ontology for *entia rationis* of this kind.

A judgement for Brentano is either the belief or the disbelief in the existence of an object. Hence all judgements have one or other of the two canonical forms: 'A exists', 'A does not exist.' This is Brentano's famous *existential theory of judgement*. Its importance consists not least in the fact that it is the first influential alternative to the combination theory, a theory which had for so long remained unchallenged. The judgement expressed in the sentence 'Franz sees a beautiful autumn leaf that is wet and has the colour of lacquer red' ought, according to the existential theory, to be expressed as follows: 'The seen-by-Franz-lacquer-red-wet-beautiful-autumn-leaf is.' The judgement expressed in the sentence 'Philosophy is not a science' should be transformed into: 'Philosophy-as-science is not.' The universal judgement expressed in the sentence: 'All people are mortal' should be represented as: 'There are no immortal people' or 'Immortal-people are not.' Judgements can be further classified into probable/certain, evident/not evident, a priori/a posteriori, affirmative/negative, and so on. Brentano holds that each of these distinctions represents an actual psychological difference in the judgements themselves. As we shall see, the same cannot be said about the classification of judgements into true and false.

Like almost all philosophers in the nineteenth century, Brentano follows Aristotle in holding that a judgement's being brought to expression in language is a secondary phenomenon only – it is the act of judgement itself that is primary. It is not ultimately important what you say; it is important what you think. Yet the central role of linguistic analysis in the work of Brentano and his followers is remarkable. Crucial to Brentano's analysis of linguistic expressions is the distinction between *categorematic* and *syncategorematic* expressions. Syncategorematica are words that have meaning only in association with other words within some context. 'True', for example, is syncategorematic. This means *inter alia* that there is nothing real in virtue of which a true judgement differs from a mere judgement (as there is nothing real in virtue of which an existing dollar differs from a dollar). There is no property of judging acts to which the predicate 'true' refers. Brentano's successors applied this same kind of analysis to other cases, for example to the deflationary analysis of words like 'being' and 'nothing'.

2.3. The object of the judging act

If judging is the acceptance or rejection of something, then we still need to determine what this something is, which is accepted or rejected. This Brentano calls the judgement's *matter*. The mode in which it is judged (accepted or rejected) he calls the *quality* of the judgement. To understand these terms we need to look once again at Brentano's concept of intentionality. Unfortunately, the famous passage from his *Psychology* leaves room for a variety of interpretations (Brentano 1874/1924 [1973: 88–9]). One bone of contention concerns the relation between the objects of the three different types of mental acts. Are we to assume that all acts are directed towards objects *in their own right*? Or is it acts of presentation that do the job of securing directedness to objects in every case? Judgements, emotions, and acts of will, according to the latter view, would be intentional only because of the underlying intentionality of the presentations on which they are founded.

A second point of dispute concerns relational and non-relational interpretations of the expression 'being directed towards an object' as a gloss on the phrase 'being intentional'. The relational interpretation of intentionality sees all mental acts as directed towards objects as their transcendent targets. That this is a somehow problematical interpretation can be seen by reflecting on the acts involved in reading fiction, or on acts which rest on mistaken presuppositions of existence. The thesis that all mental acts are directed towards objects in the relational sense, to objects external to the mind, seems in the light of such cases to be clearly false, unless, with Meinong, we admit other modes of being of objects, in addition to that of existence or reality.

In fact, however, a careful reading of Brentano's work dictates a non-relational (nowadays sometimes called an 'adverbial') interpretation of intentionality. This sees intentionality as a one-place property of mental acts, the property of their being directed in this or that specific way. When Brentano talks of directedness towards an object, he is not referring to putative transcendent targets of mental acts, to objects without the mind (a thesis along these lines has nonetheless repeatedly been ascribed to Brentano: cf. esp. Dummett 1988 [1993]: ch. 5). Rather, he is referring to immanent objects of thought, or to what, fully in the spirit of Brentano's treatment in the *Psychology*, can also be called 'mental contents'. The act of thought is something real (a real event or process); but the object of thought has being only to the extent that the act which thinks it has being. The object of thought is according to its nature something non-real which dwells in (*innewohnt*) a mental act of some real substance (a thinker) (Brentano 1930 [1966: 27]).

2.4. The theory of evident judgement

Brentano's theory of judgement is subjective in two senses. First, it is immanentistic as far as the objects of judging are concerned. Second, judgements are real events; they are mental states or mental episodes, a view which leaves no room for any view of truth and falsity as timeless properties along Bolzanian lines.

How, then, are we to tie the subjective realm of mental acts of judgement to the objective realm of truth? One solution to this problem would appeal to the traditional conception of truth as correspondence. Brentano, however, came to reject this idea; this was, among other reasons, because the correspondence theory does not yield a *criterion* of truth, and Brentano believed himself to have found such a criterion in relation to what was for him a large and important class of judging acts, namely acts pertaining to the sphere of what he called inner perception (Brentano 1930). Hence Brentano moved to a so-called epistemological conception of truth, a move supported also by his view according to which 'truth' and 'false' are syncategoremata, that is, they do not refer to properties of acts of judging.

The central role in Brentano's theory of truth is played by the concept of evidence, and here we encounter an important Cartesian strain in Brentano's thinking. He divides all judgements into *judgements of fact*, on the one hand, and *axioms* or *judgements of necessity*, on the other. The former are of two types: judgements of inner perception (for example, when I judge that I am thinking, or in other words that *my present thinking exists*), and judgements of outer perception (for example, when I judge that there is something red, that *a red thing exists*). Evidence attaches to our judgements, Brentano holds, when there is what he refers to as an identity of judger and that which is judged. An experience of such identity is so elementary that it can be clarified only so to speak 'ostensively' in one's own particular acts of judging (Brentano 1928: par. 2 [1981: 4]). Such identity, and thereby our experience thereof, is ruled out for judgements of outer perception, but it is guaranteed for judgements of inner perception. 'Inner perception is evident, indeed always evident: what appears to us in inner consciousness is actually so, as it appears' (Brentano 1956: 154). Axioms, for Brentano, are illustrated by judgements such as: a round square does not exist. Such judgements have as their objects conceptual relations, and they, too, are always evident. Axioms are such that their truth flows a priori from the corresponding concepts (Brentano 1956: 141 ff., 162–5, 173; Brentano 1933 [1981: 71]). They are 'a priori' in the sense that they do not rely on perception (or on any judgements of fact). His favourite examples of the objects of axioms are, in addition to *a round square*, *a green red* and *a correct simultaneously accepting and rejecting judger*. All axioms, Brentano now insists, are negative, and are of the form 'An A that is B does not exist', 'An A that is B and C does not exist', and so on.

The judgements which are evident for beings like us include only inner perceptions and axioms. Brentano holds that we can judge truly also about the external world, but he insists that our judgements must remain 'blind' (a matter of hunch or guesswork) and that such judgements do not belong to our knowledge in the strict sense. Even true judgements that are not evident for us must however still be evident to a being (like God), that is able to judge about the same objects and in the same ways but in such a way that its judgements are accompanied by the experience of evidence.

3. ACT, CONTENT, AND OBJECT OF JUDGEMENT

Truth, on Brentano's epistemological theory, is subjective in that it depends on the subjective experience of evidence. At a deeper level, however, it is objective in the sense that the experience of evidence can at any given time be gained only in regard to the members of a restricted class of judgements that is fixed independently of the judging subject. (On Brentano's theory of truth see Brentano 1930, Baumgartner 1987, and Rojszczak 1994.)

What, now, of logic? Do logical laws enjoy an atemporal validity? This question pertains to what has come to be called the problem of *psychologism*. Brentano's solution to this problem was to argue that the objectivity of logic should be guaranteed by evidence, in exactly the same way that evidence guarantees the objectivity of truth. But such a concept of truth can reasonably be held to be related always to single cognitive acts and thus to a single judging subject. How, on this basis, are we to explain the fact that logic serves to yield a shared normative system of rules that every process of thinking is called upon to satisfy? Brentano himself provided no ultimately satisfactory answer to this question. His successors addressed the problem in two ways: on the one hand via close-grained investigations of the mental side of the acts of judgement, and on the other by a move from psychology to ontology: a move which led to the postulation of special *objects* of judging acts along lines already anticipated on the one hand in the work of the Scholastics and on the other hand in Bolzano's doctrine of the proposition in itself (see Nuchelmans 1973, Smith 1992).

3.1. *Herman Lotze and Julius Bergmann: the concept of the Sachverhalt*

It is above all in connection with the term *Sachverhalt* that the theorists of judgement towards the end of the century began once more to rediscover elements of the older, transcendent (realist) theories of the Scholastics. The term itself is derived from phrases in standard German usage like *wie die Sachen sich zueinander verhalten* (how things stand or relate to each other). The phrase occurs, albeit only in passing, in 1874 in Herman Lotze's *Logik*. He introduces his treatment of judgement by contrasting relations between presentations, on the one hand, with *relations between things* (*sachliche Verhältnisse*), on the other (Lotze 1880). It is only 'because one already presupposes such a relation between things as obtaining', Lotze writes, 'that one can picture it in a sentence (*in einem Satz abbilden*)'. It is in talking of this relation between things as the transcendent target of judging that Lotze employs the term *Sachverhalt*, a term used in a systematic way by Julius Bergmann, a philosopher close to Lotze, in his *Allgemeine Logik* of 1879. For Bergmann, knowledge is that thinking 'whose thought content is in harmony with the *Sachverhalt*, and is therefore true' (Bergmann 1879: 2–5, 19, 38). The *Sachverhalt* or state of affairs in the hands of Lotze and Bergmann thus serves as the objective component to which the judgement must correspond in order to be true.

Lotzean ideas on the objects of judgement were developed also in England through the influence of James Ward, who studied under Lotze after the appointment of the latter in Göttingen in 1844. Lotze's lectures were attended, too, by another close disciple of Brentano – Carl Stumpf.

3.2. Carl Stumpf: act and content of judgement

To understand what Stumpf achieved, we must recall Brentano's existential theory of judgement. The prototypical ontological correlates of judgement, in Brentano's eyes, are simply the immanent mental objects of presentation, for example the sense data, that are accepted or rejected in positive and negative judgements. Brentano's immediate followers, however, were inspired at least to some degree by Bolzano and by Lotze to seek ontological correlates of judging acts which would be categorially distinct from those of acts of presentation. But Stumpf, Marty, and others still saw these ontological correlates in terms that were in harmony with Brentano's existential theory. For the ontological correlate of the positive judgement 'A exists' they used terms like: 'the existence of A'; for the correlate of the corresponding negative judgement terms like: 'the non-existence of A'. Other types of judgement-correlate were also recognised: *the subsistence of A* (as the correlate of judgements about ideal objects and fictions), *the possibility of A, the necessity of A* (as the correlates of modal judgements), and so on. In 1888 Stumpf fixed upon the term *Sachverhalt* to refer to judgement correlates such as these, establishing a usage for the term which proved more influential than that of Lotze and Bergmann. The relevant passage appears in Stumpf's logic lectures of 1888, notes to which have survived in the Husserl Archive in Louvain, where we read: 'From the matter of the judgement we distinguish its content, the *Sachverhalt* that is expressed in the judgement. For example "God is" has for its matter God, for its content: the existence of God. "There is no God" has the same matter but its content is: non-existence of God' (MS Q 13, p. 4). The *Sachverhalt* is, then, that *specific content of a judgement* 'which is to be distinguished from the content of a presentation (the matter) and is expressed linguistically in "that-clauses" or in substantivized infinitives' (Stumpf 1907: 29f.).

Sachverhalte or states of affairs are assigned by Stumpf to a special category of what he calls *formations* (*Gebilde*), entities he compares to the constellations of stars in the heaven, which we pretend to find in the sky above but which are in fact creatures of the mental world. We can begin to make sense of this idea if we reflect that Stumpf's idea of a science of formations (Stumpf 1907: 32) was almost certainly influenced by the theory of manifolds developed by Georg Cantor, a colleague of both Stumpf and Husserl in the University of Halle. Recall Cantor's definition of a set (*Menge*) as 'any collection into a whole of definite and well-distinguished objects of our intuition or our thought' (Cantor 1895/1897: 282 [1915: 85]). Just as Cantor's work sparked a new sort of sophistication in the ontology of sets or collectives, so Stumpf's work on states of affairs represents an important milestone on the road to an ontologically more sophisticated theory of judgements of a sort which, as we shall see, would be fruitful for the purposes of modern logic.

3.3. Kazimierz Twardowski: content and object

It is Kazimierz Twardowski, a Polish student of Brentano, who makes the crucial break with the immanentistic position that had proved so fateful for theories of judgement throughout the nineteenth century. This occurs in his *Zur Lehre vom Inhalt und Gegenstand der Vorstellungen* (*On the Content and Object of Presentations*) of 1894, where Twardowski puts forward a series of arguments in defence of a distinction between the *contents* of presenting acts on the one hand, and their *objects*, on the other.

Twardowski begins his investigation with an analysis of the distinction between 'presentation' (*Vorstellung*) and 'that which is presented' (*das Vorgestellte*) as these terms had been used by the earlier Brentanists. Both terms are ambiguous. The first refers sometimes to an act or activity of presenting, sometimes to the content or immanent object of this act. The second refers sometimes to this immanent object (roughly: to an image of the real thing), sometimes to this real thing itself as it exists in independent reality. To prevent this confusion, Twardowski argues, we need to subject the distinction to a more precise analysis.

First, there are properties which we ascribe to the object that are not properties of the content: my image of the red rose is not itself red. Second, objects and contents are distinguished by the fact that the object can be real or not real, where the content lacks reality in every case. This thesis turns on Twardowski's distinction between 'to be real' and 'to exist'. The former applies only to spatio-temporal entities which stand in causal relations to each other. The latter applies also to putative *irrealia*, for example, to numbers and other abstract entities. Third, one and the same object can be presented via distinct presentational contents: thus, the same building can be seen from the front and from the back. Fourth, it is possible to present a multiplicity of objects via one single content, for example, via a general concept such as *man*. And finally we can make true judgements

Table 1

Presenting act (a thinking of an apple)	Content of presentation (an image of an apple)	Object of presentation (the apple)
Judging act (a positive judging [acceptance] of an apple)	Judgment-content (the existence of the apple)	State of affairs (an apple exists)

even about non-existent objects, as, for example, when we judge truly that Pegasus has wings. If there were no real distinction between content and object, then it would be impossible that the content of such a judgement could exist while the object did not. Twardowski defines the content of a presentation as the 'link between the act and the object of a presentation by means of which an act intends this particular and no other object' (Twardowski 1894 [1972: 28–9]). The object Twardowski characterises as follows:

> Everything that is presented through a presentation, that is affirmed or denied through a judgement, that is desired or detested through an emotion, we call an object. Objects are either real or not real; they are either possible or impossible objects; they exist or do not exist. What is common to them all is that they are or they can be the *object* . . . of mental acts, that their linguistic designation is the name . . . Everything which is in the widest sense 'something' is called 'object', first of all in regard to a subject, but then also regardless of this relationship. (Twardowski 1894 [1972: 37])

In *On the Content and Object of Presentations*, Twardowski sees the act of judgement as having a special *content* of its own, but as inheriting its *object* from the relevant underlying presentation. For Twardowski as for Brentano and Stumpf, therefore, the content of the judgement is *the existence of* the relevant object. Three years later, however, in a letter to Meinong, Twardowski suggests that one should recognise also a special object of the judging act, in addition to the judgement-content (Meinong 1965: 143f.). He thereby effected a generalisation of the content–object distinction to the sphere of judging acts, in a way which yields a schema (see table 1).

Once the distinction between these three elements in the realm of judgement had been granted, a range of different types of investigations concerning judgement became possible. There arise, in the work of Meinong, Ehrenfels, Husserl, Marty, and other successors of Brentano, ontologies of states of affairs, and of related formations such as values and Gestalt qualities. Twardowski himself was interested primarily in the act and content of judging in relation to linguistic expressions, and he thereby initiated a tradition in Poland which led naturally to the work of Tarski and others in logic and semantics in the present century (Woleński and Simons 1989, Woleński 1989, 1998, 1998, Rojszczak 1998, 1999). At the same time he revived among his Polish followers an interest in the classical correspondence-theoretic idea, a revival which was possible because he had acknowledged, in addition to the act and content of judging, also its truthmaking transcendent target.

4. EDMUND HUSSERL: JUDGEMENT AND MEANING

Of all works on the psychology and ontology of judgement produced in the wake of Brentano, it is Husserl's *Logische Untersuchungen* (*Logical Investigations*) of 1900/1 which stands out as the consummate masterpiece. Husserl, like Twardowski, distinguishes the immanent content and the object of a judging act (Husserl 1894, 1900/1: VI, par. 28, 33, 39). He recognises also the Brentanist concept of the quality of the act, but sees it as including not only the positive or negative factor of acceptance or rejection in an act of judgement, but also that factor which determines whether a given act is an act of judgement, of assumption, of doubt, and so on. At the same time he lays great emphasis on the fact that this moment of the act may vary even though its content remains fixed (Husserl 1900/1: V, par. 20). Thus I can *judge that* John is swimming, *wonder whether* John is swimming, and so on. This content is that moment of the act which determines the relevant object, as it also determines *in what way* the object is grasped in the act – the features, relations, categorial forms, that the act attributes to it (Husserl 1900/1: V, par. 20).

All of this is familiar from the writings of Brentano and Twardowski. Husserl's theory also has its counterparts in the writings of Frege, where the threefold theory of act, content, and object is translated into the linguistic mode, yielding the familiar distinction between expression, sense, and reference. Husserl's 'quality' corresponds to what, in Frege's theory of judgement, is called 'force' (Frege 1879: pars. 2–4). The more orthodox Brentanists had focused on psychology, on act-based approaches to the theory of judgement. Frege, notoriously, had difficulties integrating this psychological dimension into his language-based approach (see Dummett 1988 [1993], esp. ch. 10, 'Grasping a Thought'; Smith 1989a). It is Husserl who first succeeds in constructing an integrated framework in which the theory of linguistic meanings is part and parcel of a theory of acts and of the structures of acts. Indeed, Husserl's handling of the relations between language, act and meaning manifests a sophistication of a sort previously unencountered in the literature of philosophy (see Holenstein 1975).

In order to understand the originality of Husserl's views, it is important to note that the older Brentanists had an insufficient appreciation of the dimension of *logical syntax* – a price they paid, in part, for their rejection of the combinatorial aspects of the older combination theory of truth and judgement. Thus they lacked any recognition of the fact that acts of judgement are distinguished from acts of presentation not only by the presence of a moment of assertion or belief (Brentano's acceptance/rejection), but also by a special *propositional form*. A judgement must, in other words, have a certain special sort of complexity. This complexity expresses itself linguistically in the special form of the sentence and is reflected ontologically in the special form of the state of affairs. To give an account of this complexity, of the way in which the various dimensions of the judgement are unified together into a single whole, Husserl utilises an ontological theory of part, whole, and fusion along lines set out in the third of his *Logical Investigations*.

According to Husserl, when we use a linguistic expression, the expression has meaning because it is *given* meaning through an act in which a corresponding object is given intentionally to the language-using subject. 'To use an expression significantly, and to refer expressively to an object', Husserl tells us, 'are one and the same' (Husserl 1900/1 [1970: 293]). An act of meaning is 'the determinate manner in which we refer to our object of the moment' (Husserl 1900/1 [1970: 289]). The object-directed and the meaning-bestowing component of the act are thereby fused together into a single whole: they can be distinguished only abstractly, and are not experienced as two separate parts in the act. Thus, the bestowal of meaning does not, for example, consist in some deliberate cognitive association of a use of language with some ideal meaning of a Platonistic sort. Husserl – in contrast to Bolzano or Frege – does not see meanings as ideal or abstract objects hanging in the void in a way that would leave them set apart from concrete acts of language use. Like Bolzano and Frege, however, Husserl needs some ideal or abstract component as a basis for his non-psychologistic account of the necessity of logical laws. He also needs to find some way of accounting for the fact that the meaning bestowed on a given expression on a given occasion can, in being communicated, go beyond the particular acts involved on that occasion. How can the same meaning be realised by different subjects at different places and times? Husserl's answer to this question is both elegant and bold: he develops an Aristotelian conception of the meanings of linguistic expressions as the *kinds* or *species* of the associated meaning acts.

To see what is involved here, we must first note that Husserl divides meaning acts into two classes: those associated with *uses of names*, which are acts of presentation, and those associated with *uses of sentences*, which are acts of judgement. The former are directed towards *objects*, the latter towards *states of affairs*. A meaning act of the first kind may occur either in isolation or – undergoing in the process a certain sort of transformation – in the context of a meaning act of the second kind (Husserl 1900/1 [1970: 676]). The meanings of names, which Husserl calls concepts, are *species of acts of presentations*; the meanings of sentences, which Husserl calls propositions, are *species of acts of judgement*. And the relation between meaning and the associated act of language use is in every case the relation of species to instance, exactly as between, say, the species *red* and some red object. To say that my use of 'red' means the same as your use of 'red' is to say that our corresponding acts exhibit certain salient similarities. More precisely, we should say that, just as it is only a certain part or moment of the red object – its individual accident of redness – which instantiates the species *red*, so it is only a certain part or moment of the meaning act which instantiates any given meaning-species, namely that part or moment which is responsible for the act's intentionality, for its being directed to an object in just this way (Husserl 1900/1 [1970: 130, 337]; see also Willard 1984: 183f., Smith 1989b and references there given). The meaning *is* this moment of directedness considered *in specie*. The identity of meaning from act to act and from subject to subject is then the *identity of the species*, a notion which is to be understood against the background of that type of immanent realist theory of species and instances that is set forth by Aristotle in the *Categories*.

Meanings so conceived can become objects or targets of special types of reflective act, and it is acts of this sort which make up (*inter alia*) the science of logic. Logic arises when we treat those species which are meanings as special sorts of *proxy objects* (as 'ideal singulars'), and investigate the properties of these objects in much the same way that the mathematician investigates the properties of numbers or geometrical figures. Just as geometrical figures are what result when concrete shapes are treated *in specie*, disembarrassed of all contingent association with particular empirical material and particular context, so the subject-matter of logic is made up of what results when concrete episodes of using language are treated in abstraction from their material and context of use. And just as terms like 'line', 'triangle', 'hemisphere' are equivocal, signifying both classes of factually existing instantiations and ideal singulars in the geometrical sphere, so terms like 'concept', 'proposition', 'inference', 'proof' are equivocal: they signify both classes of mental acts belonging to the subject matter of psychology and ideal singulars in the sphere of meanings.

5. ALEXIUS MEINONG: OBJECTIVE AND ASSUMPTION

As we have seen, judgement, for Brentano, is a purely psychological phenomenon. The judging act is an act of consciousness in which an object of presentation is accepted or rejected. For Brentano, 'judgement' and 'belief' are synonymous terms, which means that Brentano has a problem in explaining those complex hypothetical judgement-like phenomena which appear for example in our consideration of alternative possible outcomes of decision or choice and in other 'what if' scenarios. It was Meinong who filled this gap in his *Über Annahmen* (*On Assumptions*, 1902).

Consider, for example, the case where we assume that such and such is the case in a proof by *reductio*. Here no conviction is present, and it is the moment of conviction which distinguishes judging from assuming, in Meinong's eyes (Meinong 1902 [1983: 10–13]). But assuming is distinguished also from presenting; for assuming is, like judging, either positive or negative (Meinong 1902 [1983: 13–21]). Presentation is in a way passive in comparison with assuming and judging. Assumptions, often called by Meinong 'judgement–surrogates', thus form a class of psychic phenomena which lies between presentation and judgement (Meinong 1902 [1983: 269–70]).

Meinong's *On Assumptions* offers not only a new view of the psychology of judgemental activity but also, with its theory of *objectives* (Meinong's counterpart to Stumpf's *states of affairs*), a new contribution to the ontology of judgement. Objectives are, Meinong holds, the objects to which we are intentionally directed in both true and false judgements and in assumptions. Thinking is that kind of mental activity which refers to objectives. Objectives are objects of higher order, which means that they are built up on the basis of other, lower-order objects in the same sort of way that a melody is built up on the basis of individual tones. Some objectives are themselves built up on the basis of other objectives, as for example in the case of a judgement like 'If the meeting takes place, then we shall need to fly to Chicago.' The objective, as that towards which I am intentionally directed in a given act of judgement, is thus distinct from the object *about which* I judge. Thus in the judgement 'The rose is red' the object about which I judge is the rose, and the objective of the judgement is *the rose's being red*. The object about which I judge in the judgement 'Pegasus does not exist' is Pegasus; the objective of this judgement is *the non-existence of Pegasus*. Pegasus himself, as Meinong puts it, is a pure object, inhabiting a realm 'beyond being and non-being'. Truth, possibility, and probability are, according to Meinong, attributes not of objects but of objectives, and it is objectives, finally, which provide the subject matter for the science of logic. (See Meinong 1902 [1983]. This view makes itself felt in the early writings of Łukasiewicz, who studied for a time with Meinong in Graz. See for example Łukasiewicz 1910 [1987].)

6. ADOLF REINACH: STATES OF AFFAIRS, LOGIC, AND SPEECH-ACTS

As Adolf Reinach pointed out in 1911, however, there is a fundamental objection which must be raised against Meinong, namely 'that his concept of objective runs together the two completely different concepts of proposition (in the logical sense) and state of affairs' (Reinach 1911 [1982: 374]). In his writings, Meinong refers to objectives as the *objects* (targets) of mental activities like judging or assuming, but equally as the *meanings* of the corresponding expressions. It was Reinach's contention that these two concepts should be pulled apart, that where propositions are the meanings of judgements, states of affairs are objectual *truthmakers*, in virtue of which judgements are true.

Reinach conceives the totality of states of affairs as an eternal Platonic realm comprehending the correlates of all possible judgements, whether positive or negative, true or false, necessary or contingent, atomic or complex. A state of affairs gains its foothold in reality through the objects it involves; a state of affairs is *of* or *about* these objects. But where objects may come and go, states of affairs are immutable. In this way Reinach is in a position to conceive states of affairs as the locus of existence of the past and of the future, that is, as truthmakers for our present judgings about objects which have ceased to exist or have yet to come into existence. He is by this means able to guarantee the timelessness of truth while at the same time avoiding that sort of running together of truth-bearer and truthmaker which is characteristic of the work of Bolzano and Meinong.

Reinach's ontology of states of affairs constitutes one further sign of the fact that, by 1911, the subject matter of logic had been expelled once and for all from the psyche. As a result, however, it became necessary for logicians to provide some alternative account of what this subject matter ought to be. Frege himself, along with Bolzano and, on some interpretations, also Husserl, had looked to ideal meanings; but ideal meanings have something mystical about them and they bring with them the problem of how they can be 'grasped' or 'thought' by mortal thinking subjects. Reinach, by contrast, looked neither to ideal meanings nor to the expressions of meanings in language, but rather to states of affairs, the objectual correlates of judging acts, as that which would serve as the subject matter of logic. A view of logic along these lines could serve as an alternative to psychologism, however, only if it could somehow guarantee the objectivity and necessity of logical laws. This Reinach achieved by viewing states of affairs in a Platonistic way: he granted them a special status of the sort that was granted to propositions by Bolzano and Frege or sets by Cantor. Yet because the objects involved in states of affairs are ordinary objects of experience, he is able to show how our everyday mental acts of judgement and our associated states of belief or conviction may relate, in different ways, to states of affairs as their objectual correlates. He is thus able to show how such mental acts and states may stand in relations parallel to the logical relations which obtain (as he sees it) among these state of affairs themselves. One of Reinach's most original contributions is in fact his account of the different sorts of acts in which states of affairs are grasped and of the various kinds of attitudes which have states of affairs as their objects, and of how such acts and attitudes relate to each other and to the acts and attitudes which have judgements and propositions as their objects (see also Smith 1978 and 1987).

In his 1913 monograph on 'Die apriorischen Grundlagen des bürgerlichen Rechts' ('The A Priori Foundations of the Civil Law') Reinach extended this ontological treatment to uses of language of other, non-judgemental sorts, beginning with the phenomenon of promising and ending with an ontology of social acts which includes *inter alia* an account of sham and incomplete and otherwise defective acts, of acts performed jointly and severally, conditionally and unconditionally, and of that sort of impersonality of social acts that we find in the case of legally issued norms and in official declarations such as are involved in marriage and baptismal ceremonies. He thus elaborated the first systematic account of what would later be called the theory of 'speech acts'.

7. CONCLUSION

It has become a commonplace that Bolzano, Frege, and Husserl, by banishing meanings from the mind, created the preconditions for the objectivisation of knowledge and for the development of logic in the modern sense. By defending a view of thoughts or propositions as ideal or abstract entities, they made possible a conception of propositions as entities capable of being manipulated in different ways in formal theories. Just as Cantor had shown mathematicians of an earlier generation how to manipulate sets or classes conceived in abstraction from their members and from the manner of their generation, so logicians were able to become accustomed, by degrees, to manipulating propositional objects in abstraction from their contents and from their psychological roots in acts of judgement.

However, it is important to note that the achievements of Bolzano, Frege, and Husserl were part of a larger historical process, in which not only Lotze and Bergmann, but also Brentano, Stumpf, Meinong, Reinach – and Twardowski and his students in Poland – played a crucial role. In the period from 1870 to 1914, both logic and epistemology underwent a transformation both in object and method. The theory of judgement was transformed from being a theory of the processes of thinking (as a branch of psychology) into a theory of the meanings or contents of cognitive acts, a theory not of mental acts, but of what these acts are about, and this transformation served in its turn as an important presupposition of twentieth-century developments in logic and semantics.

THE LOGICAL ANALYSIS OF LANGUAGE

DAVID BELL

The aim of this chapter is to chart the emergence and early development, particularly in the works of Gottlob Frege and Bertrand Russell, of a revolutionary approach to the solution of philosophical problems concerning the nature of human understanding, thought, and judgement. That approach has been hugely influential and, perhaps more than any other single factor, has determined the subsequent course of twentieth-century Anglophone, 'analytic' philosophy, as a result of the developments and modifications it subsequently underwent in the hands of Wittgenstein, Carnap, Quine, Tarski, Ryle, Davidson, Kripke, Dummett, and those whom they, in their turn, have influenced. Amongst the elements of this new approach to have emerged during the period from 1879 to 1914, emphasis will here be placed on those involving new conceptions of logic, logical analysis, linguistic analysis, meaning, and thought, in the context of an overall anti-psychologism, and a commitment to taking what came to be called 'the linguistic turn'.

1. BACKGROUND

The nature of our conceptual, discursive, rational abilities – the nature, that is, of human concepts, ideas, representations, understanding, reason, thought, and judgement – has been a perennial and central focus of philosophical concern since at least the time of Plato. And for over two thousand years, from the appearance of the works comprising Aristotle's *Organon* to the publication of Frege's *Begriffsschrift* and *Grundlagen* (Frege 1879, 1884), that concern typically relied upon an intuitively attractive, indeed apparently inescapable set of general assumptions concerning the nature of the phenomena (for a detailed account of this tradition, see Prior 1976).

One such widespread assumption was that terms like 'thought', 'understanding', 'assertion', 'concept', and 'judgement' stood for psychological states, acts, or capacities, which, as such, should be studied, at least in part, via whatever methods were deemed most appropriate for the study of mental phenomena. Of course, in so far as such phenomena were construed as capable of representing objective states of the world, or as susceptible to purely rational evaluation, it was commonplace to distinguish between a mental act, on the one hand, and its content or object on the other – between a mental act of judging, for instance, and that which is thereby judged to be the case. Traditionally the discipline charged with investigating and codifying whatever is rational and responsible in human thought was logic, a discipline about which Kant expressed a not uncommon view when he observed that 'since Aristotle it has not required to retrace a single step', and moreover that 'to the present day this logic has not been able to advance a single step, and is thus to all appearance a closed and completed body of doctrine' (Kant 1787: viii).

Now according to Aristotle, and to those, like Aquinas, Leibniz, Locke, Kant, Mill, Hegel, Jevons, Boole, and Brentano who followed him in this, logic inevitably comprises three sub-disciplines which in order of priority are:

1. Doctrine of terms
2. Doctrine of propositions
3. Doctrine of syllogism (or inference).

The intuitive attraction of an approach of this kind is obvious: the elements comprising a syllogism are propositions, and the elements comprising a proposition are terms, and just as it is not possible to grasp a proposition without first grasping the terms of which it is composed, so it is impossible to understand an inference without first grasping its component propositions. In the natural order of things, therefore, one needs first to provide an account of individual terms considered in isolation, then of how they come together to form propositions, and only then of how the latter come together to form valid arguments.

This ordered, tripartite division of logic, in so far as it dealt with the contents of rational discursive or conceptual acts was generally taken to determine the appropriate taxonomy for two further kinds of entity. The investigation of linguistic phenomena, that is, was generally taken to concern the nature of:

1. Words
2. Sentences
3. Arguments,

in that order. And likewise, the relevant mental acts were themselves subject to an analysis of the same form. As one nineteenth-century logician wrote: 'If . . . there be three parts of logic, terms, propositions, and syllogisms, there must be as many different kinds of thought or operations of the mind. These are usually called:

1. Simple apprehension
2. Judgement
3. Reasoning. . . .' (Jevons 1875: 11)

(There is, however, one historically significant line of development which constitutes an exception to this broad generalisation which can be traced back to Kant's emphasis in the *Critique of Pure Reason* on the primacy of judgement, that is, on the claim that 'all categories are grounded in logical functions of judgement', and in general, that 'the only use that the understanding can make of concepts is to judge by means of them' (Kant 1787 [1933: 152 and 105]). This line of development is discernible in the writings on logic, judgement, and understanding by, amongst others, T. H. Green, R. H. Lotze, F. H. Bradley, and W. E. Johnson. For further details, see Passmore 1957, chs. 6–10.)

With only occasional exceptions, those who subscribed to this view also accepted the inevitability of a particular explanatory ordering of the different categories of phenomena: the prior, primitive phenomena were taken to be mental acts and states (grasping, apprehending, judging, inferring, and the like); their contents (ideas, concepts, propositions, and so forth) were then to be isolated via a process of abstraction; and linguistic phenomena (names, subject expressions, predicate expressions, the copula, sentences, etc.) were typically construed as merely a collection of devices by which mental acts and their contents could be expressed and communicated. Within this framework, crudely speaking, ideas, concepts, and the like are both intrinsically and transparently significant: an idea is, in and of itself, meaningful; and to 'have' an idea is to have grasped that meaning, to have that meaning in mind. Language, like the postal system, is of considerable use when we wish to communicate our ideas and thoughts to others, but it is quite inessential to the intrinsic nature of those thoughts and ideas themselves.

The revolution in philosophy inaugurated by Frege overturned virtually every explicit commitment and every tacit assumption present in the foregoing approach to problems concerning the nature of human understanding, thought, judgement, and reason. In effect, that is, Frege succeeded in reversing each of the priority relations upon which that approach relies. He took linguistic phenomena to be fundamental, and to hold the key to questions concerning content, meaning, understanding, thought, and the like. Merely psychological considerations he saw as coming a poor third: appeal to them is, he believed, almost always irrelevant in philosophy, when it is not actually pernicious. Moreover, rather than taking sub-sentential elements of language as basic, Frege's syntactic and semantic theories took inference as the primitive phenomenon and appropriate starting point. By investigating what is necessary for deductive inference, he maintained, we can understand the nature and composition of propositions, and thus, finally, the nature of the conceptual elements which comprise them. To this end Frege invented a *Begriffsschrift* or conceptual notation, that is, a formal, artificial language whose function was to represent perspicuously the objective content of human thought and judgement. This language was designed to meet just one requirement: 'in my formalized language . . . only that part of judgements which affects the *possible inferences* is taken into consideration. Whatever is needed for a valid inference is fully expressed; what is not needed is for the most part not indicated either' (Frege 1879: 3).

Purely logical requirements determine the syntax and semantics of language, which then comprise or yield solutions to problems concerning logical form, sense, meaning, truth-conditions, and reference. These, in their turn, yield an account of the contents, the objects, and the rationality of human thought. We have here, for the first time in distinctively modern guise, the analytic programme that was in various forms to dominate Anglophone philosophy for the next century, and which aimed to establish conclusions concerning, ultimately, the essence of thought, mind, and reality on the basis of a logical analysis of language.

2. FREGE'S LOGICISM

Intellectually, the 1870s was a remarkable decade in the German-speaking world. In 1872 Weierstrass, Cantor, and Dedekind published revolutionary works that were to inaugurate a new era in number theory and analysis. In the same year both Klein and Riemann published works that changed geometry perhaps more radically than at any time since Euclid. Again in the same year, Mach published his influential study of the conservation of energy. Two years later, in 1874, Wundt's *Grundzüge der physiologischen Psychologie* appeared, as did Brentano's *Psychologie vom empirischen Standpunkt*. And five years later, in 1879, Frege published his *Begriffsschrift*. What we witness here is the virtually simultaneous emergence of a number of new disciplines, or at least of old disciplines in what is, for the first time, a recognisably modern, contemporary form. In addition to the new logic, the new geometry, and the new mathematics of the infinite, the works of Wundt and Brentano heralded, respectively, the establishment of experimental psychology as a discipline in its own right, and of descriptive psychology, which was to constitute the basis both of the phenomenological tradition in philosophy and of the Gestalt movement in psychology.

As a professional mathematician, Frege was greatly exercised by the questions to which contemporary developments in geometry and number theory gave rise – questions such as, for instance, what is a number? If numbers cannot be perceived, how can we have any awareness of them? Are the statements of

arithmetic actually true? And, if so, are they contingent, empirical generalisations (Mill), or trivial analytic truths (Hume), or synthetic a priori statements
(Kant)? What is the nature of arithmetical functions? And what is the nature of
arithmetical proof? Frege wished to provide explicit, substantiated answers to
these questions which would not only (i) clarify and explain the fundamental
basis of contemporary mathematical practice, and thus capture (as he saw it)
the timeless, a priori, objective, necessary, knowable, and indeed purely rational status of arithmetical truths, but also (ii) avoid all forms of contamination
which would result from appeal to the merely contingent, empirical, subjective, and relativistic considerations which characterised (he thought) the new
developments in psychology.

The intellectual programme, to the implementation of which Frege single-
mindedly devoted some thirty years of his professional life, and the purpose of
which was to answer all of the above questions while conforming to all of the
above requirements, is a form of logicism – a reductive programme according to
which number theory in its entirety can be reduced, without remainder, to pure
logic. This required Frege to demonstrate that the only concepts employed in
number theory are purely logical concepts, that the truths of number theory are
without exception logical truths, that the proofs of number theory are merely
deductively valid proofs of pure logic, and that, ultimately, our knowledge of
arithmetical entities and truths is a form of epistemic access that requires merely
the exercise of pure reason alone. By far the greatest single obstacle to stand
in Frege's way at the outset was the weakness of the available logic which he
inherited, ultimately, from Aristotle. Consequently the first task he undertook
(Frege 1879) was a radical strengthening of logic. 'Logic is an old subject',
Quine has written, 'and since 1879 it has been a great one' (Quine 1974: 1); and
according to an authoritative history of logic, the date on which the *Begriffsschrift*
was published 'is the most important date in the history of the subject' (Kneale
and Kneale 1962: 511).

Having at his disposal a logical system of sufficient power, Frege next began to
implement his logicist programme. *Die Grundlagen der Arithmetik* (Frege 1884)
is in many ways Frege's manifesto. It presents an informal, discursive, and highly
plausible defence of the claim that the foundations of arithmetic are purely
logical in nature, and it formulates often devastating objections to a variety of
competing empiricist, formalist, psychologistic, and Kantian alternatives. For
present purposes, however, the text is notable for containing a commitment to
three principles whose subsequent importance within the analytic tradition it
would be hard to overestimate. First, Frege explicitly and self-consciously takes
what has come to be called 'the linguistic turn'. He poses the question 'How,
then, are numbers to be given to us, if we cannot have any [sensory] ideas or

intuitions of them?' (Frege 1884: 73). His answer, however, is formulated not by appeal to epistemic or psychological considerations concerning perception, experience, ideas, belief, and the like, but solely on the basis on an examination of how numerals and number words contribute to the meaning of sentences in which they occur. As Dummett observes, 'an epistemological enquiry (behind which lies an ontological one) is to be answered by a linguistic investigation' (Dummett 1988 [1993: 5]).

In this investigation Frege relies crucially on the second of the principles I shall highlight here, namely the context principle according to which 'it is only in the context of a sentence that a word means anything' (Frege 1884: 73). The shift from word meaning to sentence meaning as the prior and primary target of linguistic analysis was to have profound consequences in many areas of philosophy. The third principle, ultimately no less consequential than the other two, is expressed by Frege thus: 'If we are to use the symbol *a* to signify an object, we must have a criterion for deciding in all cases whether [some arbitrary object] *b* is the same as *a*' (Frege 1884: 73). Under Quine's slogan 'no entity without identity', the search for identity conditions of sets, propositions, thoughts, facts, states of affairs, events, persons, mental states, substances, and natural kinds, has been a central preoccupation of analytically orientated philosophy.

The final (and as it turned out disastrous) step in Frege's prosecution of the logicist programme was to have been embodied in his two-volume work *Grundgesetze der Arithmetik* (Frege 1893, 1903). This work was intended to provide nothing less than a proof that number theory could be reduced to pure logic, by comprising a valid logical derivation of the primitive truths and principles of arithmetic from just six axioms each of which was, supposedly, a truth of logic. Before the second volume could appear, however, Bertrand Russell had already communicated to Frege the news that his axiom-set was inconsistent. Ironically, the culprit was Axiom V, the very axiom that was to have provided identity conditions for the entities to which class names refer.

3. THE ANALYSIS OF FORMAL AND NATURAL LANGUAGES

Like both Russell and Wittgenstein, Frege distinguished between the genuinely logical (or deep) and the merely grammatical (or surface) properties possessed by the sentences of ordinary, everyday language. The form and composition of such sentences are a product of historical, contingent factors which, as often as not, serve to obscure or even distort rather than reveal the underlying logical form. One aim of Frege's conceptual notation, as likewise of Russell's 'symbolic language', was logical transparency: the surface grammar of such a symbolism would exactly reflect its logical form; the syntax of its sentences would perspicuously manifest the logical form of the thoughts they expressed. Frege's conceptual notation is built up out of the following elements: the content-stroke, the assertion-stroke, singular terms, variables, first-level function-names – including sub-sentential function-names, sentential function-names (like predicates and relational expressions), and supra-sentential function-names (like the negation and conditional strokes) – and second-level function-names (like quantifiers). Using these resources Frege could, for example, symbolise the content of the judgement that *every husband is married to someone*, by the complex symbol:

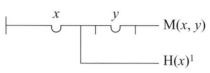

This raises in stark form the question of how exactly the familiar sentences of everyday language, and the thoughts they are used to express, are related to such artificial devices and the contents they are intended to symbolise. Although Frege's primary concerns were esoteric and technical, requiring the formulation of a symbolic notation powerful enough to comprise the medium of proof for the reduction of arithmetic and analysis to pure logic, and although he believed that ordinary language was misleading and hence that 'the main task of the logician consists in *liberation from* language', there were nevertheless two factors which made an investigation of our everyday talk and thought a matter of some urgency.

In the first place, that is, Frege needed to demonstrate that the revolutionary principles, techniques, concepts, and devices that he had introduced belonged, precisely, *to logic*. His entire rationalist, logicist programme would lose all philosophical interest and would become intolerably arbitrary and self-serving if it transpired that the 'new logic' was not really a kind of logic at all, or that its sole justification was, question-beggingly, that the basic laws of arithmetic could be expressed in it. Frege accordingly placed himself under an obligation to show that his new principles and techniques did indeed belong to pure logic, and as such were of strictly universal applicability, governing all coherent and rational thought whatsoever, regardless of its specific content, and irrespective of the particular linguistic means by which it might be expressed. The syntactic and semantic principles governing Frege's conceptual notation, that is, needed to apply to any language capable of expressing a coherent thought. He therefore provided, as an adjunct to his formal work, a single, elegant, and powerful

---

[1]   In modern notation this is equivalent to $(\forall x)(Hx \supset (\exists y)(Mxy))$, or more informally, if anyone, x, is a husband then there exists someone, y, such that x is married to y.

theory of meaning whose range of application was intended to include every sign and complex of signs capable of constituting the expression of an intelligible thought. In the case of a language such as English or German, that theory provided not only the means of identifying, but also an account of the significance of, expressions belonging to such syntactic categories as atomic and molecular sentences, proper names, pronouns, definite descriptions, quantifiers, predicates and verbs, relational expressions, logical constants, and signs within both direct and indirect quotation.

The second source of pressure, making it inevitable that Frege would address non-technical issues concerning the nature of human concepts, thoughts, judgements, and the everyday language in which they are formulated and communicated was as follows. An essential ingredient in the logicist programme was the demonstration that the truths of arithmetic are neither synthetic, contingent claims, nor synthetic a priori ones. As truths of pure logic, they are, in Kantian terminology, knowable a priori because they are *analytic*. As Frege and his readers were well aware, however, to claim that some judgements are analytically true is to risk assigning them the uninteresting status of trivial, uninformative judgements, devoid of substantial content, true by definition, or based merely on 'conceptual identities'. Accordingly Frege recognised the pressing need to provide answers to such questions as, in his words, 'How can the great tree of the science of number as we know it, towering, spreading, and still continually growing, have its roots in bare identities? And how do the empty forms of logic come to disgorge so rich a content?' (Frege 1879: 22). In responding to these questions, he was led to consider, in general terms, what concepts are, how they combine to form thoughts, and how they are related one to another in such a way that a 'bare identity' can yet have a content rich enough to possess 'cognitive value'. The pressure, again, is to extend the investigation from formal, largely syntactic issues in the foundations of arithmetic, so as to address broader questions to do with sense, meaning, information, understanding, and truth – issues, that is, which belong ultimately to ontology, epistemology, the philosophy of mind, and the metaphysics of experience.

In summary outline, Frege's account of how language works is as follows. Syntactically, we can take two types of expression as 'complete', namely whole sentences, in so far as they express a complete thought, and proper names, in so far as they purport to stand for a single individual. Virtually the whole of Frege's philosophy of language can then be generated by repeated applications of just two procedures: syntactic categories are identified on the basis of intersubstitutability *salva congruitate*; and semantic categories are identified via intersubstitutability *salva veritate* within those syntactic categories. With respect to the former Frege writes:

Suppose that a simple or complex symbol occurs in one or more places in an expression (whose content need not be a possible content of judgement). If we imagine this symbol as replaceable by another . . . at one or more of its occurrences, then the part of the expression that shows itself invariant under such replacement is called the function; and the replaceable part, the argument of the function. (Frege 1879: 16)

If a complete expression contains a component complete expression, and if we remove the latter from the former (marking the gap that is left by a Greek letter) the result is an incomplete or functional expression. (The Greek letters merely mark the place or places at which, as Frege says, we are to imagine one symbol as replaceable by another.) From the proper name 'the capital of France' we can remove the component proper name 'France' to leave the function-name 'the capital of ξ'. Likewise, the complete expressions 'France' and/or 'England' can be removed from the complete expression (in this case, sentence) 'France is larger than England', to yield the sentential function-names (i.e., predicates) 'ξ is larger than England' and 'France is larger than ξ' as well as the relational expression 'ξ is larger than ζ'. If, from the sentence 'It is not the case that Berlin is the capital of France', we remove the complete component expression (sentence) 'Berlin is the capital of France', we generate the supra-sentential function-name (i.e., the truth-functional logical constant) 'It is not the case that ξ.' The Greek letters here mark the places at which 'replacement', or 'intersubstitution' of expressions is envisaged; and the restriction on what can be intersubstituted *salva congruitate*, that is, without destroying the grammaticality of the resulting expression, determines the syntactic category of the relevant expression. Thus, for Frege, predicates, relational expressions, and logical constants are first-level function-names which yield a complete expression when the appropriate number of complete expressions are inserted into their argument-places.

This account of the generation of first-level function-names can now, in its turn, be used to generate a variety of second-level function-names – that is, incomplete expressions whose argument-places can only be filled by first-level function-names. For example, the sentence 'Henry has spatial properties' contains the first-level function-name (or predicate) 'ξ has spatial properties', as also does the sentence 'Everything is such that it has spatial properties'. If we now remove the predicate, we are left with an incomplete expression 'Everything is such that it Σ', which cannot be completed *salva congruitate* by any complete expression. 'Everything is such that it France', for example, and 'Everything is such that it Paris is the capital of France' are simply malformed. Quantifiers, it turns out, are second-level function-names, that is, incomplete expressions whose argument-places must be filled by expressions belonging to the category of first-level function-name. In this way, then, Frege formulates a logical syntax or grammar strong enough to incorporate, and perspicuous enough to reveal the structure of, simple and complex proper names, sub-sentential functional expressions, atomic and molecular sentences, predicates, relational expressions, logical connectives, and quantifiers.

Next, Frege's semantic theory assigns to expressions of each syntactic type an appropriate *Bedeutung*, or reference. An expression can possess a reference in virtue of its expressing a *Sinn*, or sense, whose function it is to determine the identity of the reference in some particular way. Informally, we might say that the reference of an expression is just whatever the expression must possess if it is to be capable of participating in the formulation of deductively valid arguments: the expression must in effect be 'truth-valuable', that is, such that it either possesses a determinate truth-value, or is capable of being used (and not merely mentioned) in sentences which have a determinate truth-value. More formally, we can define Frege's notion of reference as follows:

(R). The reference of an expression E is that in virtue of whose identity expressions can be intersubstituted for E, *salva veritate*, throughout any context of the appropriate kind.

There are three kinds of context: direct use, direct quotation, and indirect quotation. We can take contexts of direct use first, and examine the reference assigned by (R) to expressions belonging, respectively, to the syntactic categories of proper name, predicate, and sentence:

(i) Two proper names, 'a' and 'b' are everywhere interchangeable *salva veritate* just in case one and the same object is designated by both of them, that is, just in case '$a = b$' is true. The reference of a proper name, according to (R), is thus the object named, or picked out, or designated by that name.

(ii) The reference of a predicate expression in contexts of direct use is determined by the principle that two predicates '$F(\xi)$' and '$G(\xi)$' have the same reference just in case every object that falls under one also falls under the other, that is, just in case '$(\forall x)$ $(F(x) \equiv G(x))$' is true. So the reference of a predicate expression is the 'incomplete' or 'unsaturated' entity whose identity is determined by the identity conditions of its extension. Frege calls such entities 'concepts', and assigns them the semantic role of mapping objects onto truth-values. So, for example, the predicate '(ξ) is in France' refers to a concept whose value (truth-value) is *true* for Paris, but *false* for Berlin.

(iii) Sentences, in contexts of direct use, are everywhere intersubstitutable *salva veritate* as long as they have the same truth-value: two arbitrary sentences 'P' and 'Q' can be interchanged, without affecting the truth-value of the context in which they occur, just in case 'P $\equiv$ Q' is true. It follows immediately from (R), therefore, that the reference of a sentence is its truth-value.

Expressions of any syntactic type can be intersubstituted *salva veritate* within a context of direct quotation if and only if they are tokens of the same type.

And so, according to (R), a directly quoted token expression refers to its own type. This seems right, given that the constraints on accurate direct quotation are so very stringent: to report truly what someone actually said one must use expressions of exactly the same type as those uttered by that person.

The reference of expressions in indirect quotation or *oratio obliqua* is determined by (R) as follows. The sentence (1) 'Albert thinks that Berlin is in France' contains the component sentence (2) 'Berlin is in France' in *oratio obliqua*. But neither the latter sentence as a whole, nor any of the expressions that occur within it can be assigned the reference they would possess were (2) to appear in a context of direct use. This follows directly from (R), because one manifestly cannot substitute for (2) any other sentence with the same truth-value, and one cannot substitute for 'Berlin' or 'France' any other expressions which refer to the same objects, while guaranteeing that the truth-vale of (1) will not change. For example, from the truth of (1) it does not follow that Albert thinks that London is in Egypt: even though 'Berlin is in France' and 'London is in Egypt' have the same truth-value, those sentences cannot be exchanged *salva veritate* in a context of indirect discourse. Under what circumstances, then, is intersubstitutability allowable within *oratio obliqua*? Intuitively it seems that expressions in such a context can be interchanged as long as they have the same content or meaning: in reporting the content of a remark or thought one is justified in employing any expression which accurately captures the meaning of the original. Here the intuitive notions of 'meaning' and 'content' correspond to Frege's notion of sense. And so, according to (R), because identity of sense is necessary and sufficient to warrant interchange of expressions in *oratio obliqua*, the sense of such expressions is their reference. As it occurs within (1), the name 'Berlin' does not refer to a city but to the sense of the name 'Berlin'; and likewise, the component sentence (2) does not refer to a truth-value but to the sense of the sentence 'Berlin is in France'. Frege's term for the sense expressed by a sentence is a 'thought' (*Gedanke*), and this enables him to say, most plausibly, that what (2) refers to in the context of (1) is a thought (Albert's thought). Clearly at this point we need to know in more detail what, according to Frege, senses and thoughts are.

Although Frege himself nowhere expresses the matter in just this way, it is possible to capture his notion of sense as follows:

(S). The sense of an expression *E* is determined by the condition which anything must satisfy if it is to be the reference of *E*. (This condition may be such that there is nothing which in fact satisfies it.)

This account is meant to capture our intuitions about what it is that one grasps when one understands an expression, and is based on the insight that the things we think about and refer to are never *merely* thought about or referred to, but are always presented, in language or in thought, *in some way*. In Frege's words, 'besides that which a sign designates, which may be called the reference of the sign, [there is] also what I should like to call the sense of the sign, wherein the mode of presentation is contained' (Frege 1892: 26). The two expressions 'the largest city in France' and 'the capital city of France', for instance, have the same reference, but they present that reference in different ways. And an understanding of those expressions requires a grasp of the 'modes of presentation' which they respectively employ. One could not, for example, be said properly to have grasped the respective meanings of those two expressions if one knew about them only that they both stood for Paris.

If we now apply (S) to expressions such as proper names and sentences, we generate the following results. The sense of a proper name '*a*' is determined by the condition that something must meet if it is to be the reference of '*a*'. Such a condition will comprise an answer to the question 'Under what circumstances is it the case, for an arbitrary object, x, that $x = a$?' Quite literally, then, the sense of a proper name is given by the identity condition of the reference of that name.

According to (R), the reference of a sentence is its truth-value. A literal application of (S) thus yields the result that the sense expressed by a sentence is determined by the condition which must obtain in order for it to have the truth-value which it in fact has. But because there are only two truth-values, which are interdefinable with the aid of negation, this result can be simplified. We can say: the sense of a sentence is determined by the condition under which its reference = true. In short, the sense of a sentence is determined by its 'truth-condition': 'Every such name of a truth-value [i.e., declarative sentence] *expresses* a sense, a *thought*. Namely, by our stipulations it is determined under what conditions the [sentence] refers to the True. The sense of this [sentence] – the *thought* – is the thought that these conditions are fulfilled' (Frege 1893: 50). Wittgenstein put this more simply: 'To understand a proposition is to know what is the case if it is true' (Wittgenstein 1921: 4.024). The relation of reference, at least typically, holds between an expression's sense and an extra-linguistic item in the external world. The notion of a thought, likewise, is the notion of a truth-condition which, typically, the external, objective world will either meet or fail to meet.

In this complex of ideas we have the embodiment of a vision whose aim is to explain, in detail, how logic, language, thought, and reality are related one to another, in such a way as to make intelligible the possibility of objectivity, truth, understanding, rationality, the expression of one's thoughts, and the communication of information about the world. These issues comprise, as we noted earlier, the subject matter of the traditional 'theory of judgement'. The resources Frege employs in articulating his radically different vision include, amongst other elements, theories concerning logical syntax, functorial analysis, reference, sense, identity conditions, and truth conditions. None of these theories is, of course, unproblematic, and some are highly contentious; but all are strongly and intentionally anti-psychologistic. We can witness here what Michael Dummett calls 'the extrusion of thoughts from the mind'. In Frege's hands, that is, problems concerning thought, judgement, intentionality, concepts, understanding, and rationality are to be solved wherever possible by using the techniques of logico-linguistic analysis in which subjective, mental phenomena play no role at all.

4. RUSSELL AND LOGICAL ANALYSIS

Bertrand Russell's views underwent considerable development, even during the period (roughly 1900 to 1914) under review here. With only occasional exceptions, however, in what follows I shall concentrate on those elements of his thought which remain constant during that time, and which comprise his distinctive contributions to the matters at hand. Three such contributions are of particular significance. They concern analysis, meaning, and acquaintance.

Fregean logico-linguistic analysis relies almost entirely on the discernment of function-argument structures, and on the isolation of the conditions under which, for any given argument, a particular function yields a certain value. In this way Frege's theory of meaning and thought gives prominence, for instance, to predicative functions, truth functions, truth-values, identity conditions, truth conditions, and the like. Bertrand Russell, by contrast, viewed logical analysis as the discernment of whole-part structures. Following G. E. Moore's lead, Russell meant by 'analysis' simply the process of mereological decomposition by which a complex entity is broken down into the (ultimately simple) elements of which it is composed. Analysis of this kind is applied by Russell to propositions, concepts, facts, concrete and abstract objects, and states of mind. Indeed, the programme to which he gave the title 'Logical Atomism' is in large part a reflection of his commitment to the universal applicability of whole-part analysis.

Russell's theory of meaning is based on the view that, in the last analysis, the role of linguistic signs is to stand for things: a meaningful linguistic expression functions, that is, by standing in a direct, unmediated relation to the entity which it designates. The entity that an expression designates is its meaning; from which it follows that if an expression fails to stand for an entity then it is literally meaningless. In *The Principles of Mathematics* (Russell 1903), Russell concluded that there must 'be'(though there need not 'exist') an entity corresponding to every meaningful word; and as a result his ontology came to include mythical, fictional, abstract, and even impossible objects, like chimeras, Greek gods, sets, extensionless points, and round squares. As he came increasingly to view ordinary language as at best logically opaque, and at worst logically pernicious, however, he began to develop a series of analytic techniques – many of them involving 'incomplete symbols' – which enabled him to escape what he saw as the unacceptable consequences of this earlier theory. In particular his new analytic tools enabled him to resolve the following embarrassing dilemma. Take a phrase like 'the present king of France': either it doesn't stand for anything (France is after all a republic), in which case the phrase is simply meaningless, or the phrase is meaningful, in which case it must stand for something (perhaps a monarch who, without actually existing, nevertheless in some sense 'is'). Russell needed to resolve this dilemma while at the same time continuing to maintain that meaning is an unmediated relation between expressions and items in the world. He could not, however, adopt a Fregean solution – according to which a sign can express an intelligible sense while failing to possess a reference – if for no other reason than that the determination of reference by sense is a functional relation, one that Russell's whole-part analysis is incapable of capturing.

The key to Russell's resolution of this dilemma was, in Wittgenstein's words, to 'show that the apparent logical form of a proposition need not be its real one' (Wittgenstein 1921: 4.0031). The superficial grammatical form of the sentence 'The present king of France is bald' appears to comprise a complex singular term 'the present king of France' as the subject, and a simple predicate 'bald', which is joined to the subject term by the copula 'is'. The overall function of the sentence, it seems, is to predicate baldness of the individual designated by the subject term. Russell's alternative analysis, published in 'On Denoting' (Russell 1905), provides a logical rather than a grammatical account of the underlying form of sentences of this kind. In effect he makes explicit the logical commitments which are tacitly involved in a literal use of sentences containing expressions of the form 'the so-and-so' – expressions, that is, comprising the definite article, 'the', followed by a descriptive or attributive phrase. Such expressions are now universally called 'definite descriptions'. Serious use of a sentence containing a definite description would be inappropriate and misleading, Russell suggests, if one knew either that there is no such thing as 'the so-and-so', or that there is more than one. To assert a sentence of the form 'The Φ is F' is therefore, albeit tacitly, to adopt a commitment to both the existence and the uniqueness of something that is Φ. If, for example, I were seriously and literally to assert that *the man who stole my car is now in prison*, I would be taken to have implied that *someone did indeed steal my car* and, moreover, that *only one person* did this. In which case, Russell argues, the proposition expressed by a sentence whose grammatical form is 'The Φ is F', will logically be analysable into three component propositions: (i) there exists something that is Φ, (ii) there is exactly one thing that is Φ, and

(iii) whatever is Φ is also *F*. And just this is expressed in Russell's logical notation by the formula

$$(\exists x)(\Phi x \;\&\; (\forall y)(\Phi y \equiv x = y) \;\&\; Fx).$$

This analysis reveals, Russell claims, that although a definite description appears to be a singular term – which as such ought to function by standing for a particular object – in fact it is not an integral grammatical unit at all: on analysis it simply disappears; it dissolves into a complex series of quantifiers, predicates, and logical connectives. And with its disappearance as a genuine singular term there also disappears of course any temptation to think that there must be something that the unanalysed phrase stands for. (Russell's theory can be assessed independently of this motivation for it, and indeed independently of the specific epistemology and theory of meaning which gave rise to it: even if Russell is wrong about denotation, analysis, and acquaintance, it may still be the case that certain uses of the English word 'the', like uses of the words 'a', 'some', 'many', and 'three', are essentially quantificational.)

The analysis of sentences containing definite descriptions became the model for the analysis of 'incomplete symbols' of all kinds. 'By an "incomplete symbol" we mean a symbol which is not supposed to have any meaning in isolation, but only as defined in certain contexts' (Whitehead and Russell 1910–13: 66). So the analysis of an incomplete symbol '*S*' does not assign a syntactic category to '*S*' as such, and neither does it assign to '*S*' a unitary meaning (for it has no such meaning in isolation). Rather, the analysis proceeds indirectly, by assigning a meaning to any complete sentence in which '*S*' occurs. The process, called 'contextual definition', consists in the provision of a systematic procedure by which any sentence containing '*S*' can be translated into an equivalent sentence in which that symbol does not appear. We have already examined the case in which '*S*' is any phrase of the form 'the so-and-so'. Russell subsequently applied the same procedure to expressions which purport to name classes and sets, to numerals and number words, to ordinary proper names, and to names of points, instants, other minds, and ultimately, to any expression which purports to name something which is not an object of immediate 'acquaintance'. It is at precisely this point that Russell's account of logical form merges with his account of understanding, thought, and knowledge.

The distinction between complete symbols, which function by directly designating a particular entity, and incomplete symbols, which function descriptively and which disappear on analysis, is exactly mirrored by an epistemological distinction between immediate 'acquaintance' with objects, and descriptive knowledge of them. Russell writes:

The subject of denoting is of very great importance not only in logic and mathematics, but also in theory of knowledge. For example, we know that the centre of mass of the Solar System at a definite instant is some definite point, and we can affirm a number of propositions about it; but we have no immediate acquaintance with this point, which is only known to us by description. The distinction between *acquaintance* and *knowledge about* is the distinction between the things we have presentations of, and the things we only reach by means of [descriptive] . . . phrases. (Russell 1905 [1956: 41])

We have 'knowledge by acquaintance' of an object if we are directly and immediately aware of it, as is most obviously the case, Russell maintains, with a sense-datum. When I am directly conscious of, say, a red patch in my visual field, the object of my awareness is 'there in person', it is directly presented to me. Now such immediately presented objects of direct acquaintance can be given names of a particular kind – Russell calls them 'logically proper names' – which have the following properties: they refer to exactly one determinate object; they have no descriptive content or sense; they are syntactically simple; the object to which they refer is their meaning. Apparently referential expressions which are not logically proper names are, on this view, essentially descriptive, and will therefore disappear on analysis. To understand a logically proper name, that is, to know its meaning, is to be directly acquainted with that meaning, which is to be directly acquainted with the object of which it is the name. As propositions are complex wholes, built up from the simple elements for which logically proper names stand, Russell accordingly subscribes to the principle:

Every proposition we can understand must be composed wholly of constituents with which we are acquainted. (Russell 1912: 91. See also Russell 1948: 512)

Russell's whole-part analysis is applied, symmetrically, to syntactic, semantic, ontological, and epistemological phenomena: propositions are complex wholes made up of ultimately simple elements; the sentences of ordinary language express such propositions, but unperspicuously – when fully analysed, sentences contain a logically proper name corresponding to every simple element in the proposition expressed; thought and understanding are complex phenomena analysable, ultimately, into states of acquaintance, such that there is direct acquaintance with each of the elements comprising the proposition which we understand, or assert, or know to be true.

5. RUSSELL'S THEORY OF JUDGEMENT, AND WITTGENSTEIN'S RESPONSE

Russell's commitment to a form of analysis based exclusively on the discernment of whole-part structures presented him with a problem: there appears to be a

class of phenomena whose members are not only philosophically of the greatest importance, but whose composition is recalcitrant to mereological analysis.
Whole-part analysis, that is, fails to provide a satisfactory account of irreducibly
propositional phenomena – namely complex wholes whose unity is essentially
syntactic, such as sentences, propositions, facts, thoughts, judgements, beliefs,
and the like. The problem, crudely, is that if a propositional unity is decom-
posed into its constituent parts, the result is a list of items, a mere aggregate of
elements, and not the sort of thing that could possibly be believed, or thought,
or true. Russell recognised this as early as 1903:

> The only kind of unity to which I can attach any precise sense . . . is that of a whole
> composed of parts . . . A proposition has a certain indefinable unity, in virtue of which
> it is an assertion; and this is so completely lost by analysis that no enumeration of
> constituents will restore it, even though itself be mentioned as a constituent. There is, it
> must be confessed, a grave logical difficulty in this fact, for it is difficult not to believe that
> a whole must be constituted by its constituents. (Russell 1903: 466–7; see also 48–51)

He nevertheless continued for some time to subscribe to the thesis that a proposition is a complex whole made up of its component parts. Judgements, thoughts,
and other 'propositional attitudes' were construed, correspondingly, as themselves complex wholes: to understand a proposition is to be acquainted with
that proposition, and this is simply a complex state built up out of acquaintance
with each of the proposition's component elements. Russell became increasingly dissatisfied with elements in this account, however, and in May and June
1913 he began to write a work, entitled *Theory of Knowledge*, in which he hoped
to formulate a more sophisticated analysis of 'propositions' and 'propositional
attitudes'. The objections levelled at this project by the young Wittgenstein,
however, caused Russell to abandon it and, indeed, to suffer a crisis of confidence which left him philosophically 'paralysed'.

   How, philosophically, are we to construe the situation in which someone
judges that something is the case? In other words, if a sentence of the form

   (J). *X* judges that *p*

is true, what is the appropriate logical analysis of the situation thereby represented? In the 'Theory of Knowledge' Russell defended a 'multiple relation
theory of judgement', according to which (J) does not express a relation between two entities, the judger *X* and a proposition *p*, but rather a series of
distinct relations between *X* and each of the separate items which comprise *p*.
So in the case in which *X* judges that *Socrates is mortal*, the structure (in part –
see below) can be represented as

In the case in which *X* judges that *Tom and Harry love Mary*, on the other hand, the structure will involve (at least) the following relations:

Each of these relations is a relation of acquaintance. And so, Russell writes, in order to understand or assert a proposition, say '*A* precedes *B*',

> it is obviously necessary that we should know what is meant by the words which occur in it, that is to say, we must be acquainted with *A* and *B* and with the relation 'preceding'. It is also necessary to know how these three terms are meant to be combined; and this . . . requires acquaintance with the general form of a dual complex. (Russell 1913: 111)

Unfortunately the last sentence quoted here raises, again, precisely the problems to which the new theory of judgement was to have been the solution. There are two problems. One is this: the judgement that *A precedes B* is clearly quite distinct from the judgement that *B precedes A*; and yet at this point Russell's analysis gives us no grounds for distinguishing them, for they both are complex wholes made up of precisely the same constituent elements. The other is this: the analysis still suffers from a failing which Russell had originally noted in 1903, namely that a propositional unity has been reduced to a mere list of entities. In his 'Theory of Knowledge' Russell struggled to solve these two problems: at one point he was tempted to say, in response to the first, that in an act of judging, *X* is related by acquaintance not only to the constituents of the proposition, but also to the logical form of the complex which they together comprise: 'It is difficult to see how we could possibly understand how [*A* and *B*] and "precedes" are to be combined unless we had acquaintance with the form of the complex' (1913: 99). At other times he was quite clear that the form of a complex 'cannot be a new constituent, for if it were, there would have to be a new way in which it and the . . . other constituents are put together, and if we take this way as again a constituent, we find ourselves embarked on an endless regress' (1913: 98).

Wittgenstein discussed these matters with Russell in the early months of 1913, and in June of that year he wrote to Russell:

I can now express my objection to your theory of judgement exactly: I believe it is obvious that, from the proposition '*A* judges that (say) *a* is in the relation *R* to *b*', if correctly analysed, the proposition '*aRb*. v. ~*aRb*' must follow directly *without the use of any other premiss*. This condition is not fulfilled by your theory. (Wittgenstein 1974: 23)

Now if we take Wittgenstein's insistence that, in general, '*A* judges that *p*' should entail '*p* or *not-p*', as incorporating the demand that in the context '*A* judges that *p*', '*p*' must itself be a syntactically well-formed, meaningful proposition, then Russell's theory does indeed fail to meet it. A major cause of this failure, I have suggested, is Russell's exclusively mereological approach to analysis, and his reluctance or perhaps inability to acknowledge function–argument analysis as, also, a powerful tool in the solution of philosophical problems concerning the nature of judgement, thought, meaning, reference, and understanding.

The next major contributions to the development of logico-linguistic analysis, and to the formulation of a theory of thought and judgement were to be made by Wittgenstein. It is worth noting, however, that in his first work, the *Tractatus Logico-Philosophicus*, the tensions between mereological (or Russellian) and functional (or Fregean) forms of logical analysis are still present, and unresolved. This is evidenced by his subscribing in that work not only to the Russellian view that 'Every statement about a complex can be resolved into a statement about its constituents' (Wittgenstein 1921: 2.0201), but also to the Fregean view that 'Wherever there is complexity, argument and function are present' (1921: 5.47).

SECTION FOUR

PHILOSOPHY AND THE NEW PHYSICS

THE ATOMISM DEBATE

ELI ZAHAR

1. INTRODUCTION

The Greeks put forward atomism in response to a philosophical problem: that of reconciling the Parmenidean thesis of the immutability of Being with the undeniable existence of phenomenal change. Democritus postulated a void containing a plurality of indivisible and immutable particles called *atoms*. The flux of appearances was to be explained in terms of different configurations of the same particles within the same empty space. Thus the only change admitted by the atomists was that of spatial position with respect to time. Through the work of chemists like Boyle and Dalton, atomism was gradually transformed into a testable theory. It proved to be a remarkably successful explanatory conjecture.

In the nineteenth century, atomism faced a serious challenge posed by a rival programme: *phenomenological thermodynamics*. The latter was based on two principles: those [A] of the conservation and [B] of the degradation of energy. [A] was familiar; [B] novel and challenging. [B] enabled Clausius to define entropy as a function S of the state of a system Ω such that S never decreases over time; intuitively, S is a measure of the disorder within Ω. In all real, as opposed to idealised processes, S actually increases and can therefore be used to explain the unidirectionality of time. The increase of S also entails that no quantity of heat can be converted into an equivalent amount of (useful) mechanical work.

Thermodynamics was empirically successful but its capacity for further development remained limited: it had to rely on unexplained experimental results in order to arrive at the laws enabling it to make verifiable predictions. It accepted, as simply given, the principle of the convertibility of heat into work and the equations of state of certain substances (see Clark 1976: 44). It was natural, therefore, for atomists to seek to accommodate thermodynamics by reducing [A] and [B] to atomist principles. [A] presents no fundamental difficulty: according to mechanism, heat is motion, so the conservation of energy follows from the mechanical and electromagnetic conservation laws, where the latter are consequences of Newton's and Maxwell's theories. [B] however posed seemingly insuperable problems. We should recall that atomism was based not only on the thesis of the particulate nature of matter, but also on the laws of mechanics. Over and above being deterministic, classical mechanics treats prediction and retrodiction on a par. Consider any time-interval $[t_0, t_1]$. The initial conditions at t_0 both determine and are uniquely determined by the final conditions at t_1. Newtonian mechanics is furthermore time-reversible in the following sense. Let an isolated system of particles $P_1, P_2, \ldots, P_n$ describe some trajectory Γ during the time-interval $[t_0, t_1]$; were the velocity of each P_i to be reversed at t_1, then during the interval $[t_1, 2t_1-t_0]$ the system would retrace Γ in the reverse order, with all velocities being reversed at corresponding (mirror-image) points. Let Γ^* denote this inverted path. Thus a mechanistic definition of the entropy S appears impossible; for if S were to be defined in terms say of positions and speeds (as distinct from directed *velocities*), then any increase of S along Γ would be matched by an equal decrease along Γ^*. This problem will be carefully examined when we come to talk about Boltzmann's work.

Let me end this introduction by mentioning some empirical successes and one serious failure of the atomistic programme. Atomism explained the convertibility of heat into work; it also enabled its adherents to derive important equations of state like those of Boyle and van der Waals. In Maxwell's hands, it yielded the unexpected result that viscosity depends, not on density, but solely on temperature. This counter-intuitive consequence was moreover confirmed (Sears and Salinger 1975: 286–91).

Atomism however seemed unable to determine the correct relative specific heats of polyatomic substances. Let $\gamma = c_p/c_v$, where c_p and c_v denote, respectively, the specific heat capacities of a substance at constant pressure and at constant volume. As a result of the equipartition of energy, classical kinetic theories entail $\gamma = (f + 2)/f$, where f denotes the degrees of freedom of one molecule of the substance. In the monoatomic case, $f = 3$; hence $\gamma = 1.66$, which is confirmed. But in the general case, classical mechanics ascribes too large a value to f. For diatomic molecules, $f = 7$; hence $\gamma = 1.29$, which differs from the observed value, namely 1.4. The atomists had consequently to set f equal to 5. This meant ignoring the rotational or the vibrational energy of the molecule, whose existence was however entailed by mechanism (Sears 1953: 246–51). The atomist programme thus threatened to succumb to its internal contradictions. Physicists did not of course realise that the fault lay not with the atomic hypothesis as such, but with classical dynamics. The latter subsequently proved inapplicable to microscopic phenomena and was replaced by quantum physics.

These difficulties (and successes) are mentioned not for their own sake, but in order to bring out an important philosophical point. Towards the end of the nineteenth century, the methodological situation was indecisive. Atomism had a powerful *heuristic*, in that it suggested many avenues for further research. After some initial breakthroughs, however, it faced seemingly intractable problems; while thermodynamics, though superficially faultless, offered only a weak heuristic. Let us recall that the core of every scientific programme is metaphysical: taken in isolation, it cannot be directly pitted against experience; but it can be indirectly either undermined by experimental failures, or else supported by the successes of the theories constituting the programme. (For more details, see Zahar 1989: 13–38.) The situation remains indecisive as long as the each programme can both be credited with some empirical successes and impugned for certain setbacks. Then no methodology alone can explain why an individual scientist opted for one programme rather than another. In order to account for such decisions, the historian has to adduce external, for example, religious, metaphysical and even moral *motives*: the latter influence the way in which a scientist, by weighting the available evidence, extrapolates the successes or, alternatively, the failures of rival programmes.

I shall now examine the appraisals of atomism by Mach, Ostwald, Duhem, and Boltzmann. Briefly, I shall show that, because of the phenomenalism he derived from Kantian philosophy, Mach opposed all realist versions of atomism; that Ostwald adopted a paradoxical attitude born out of an inductivism so naïve as to be baffling; that in view of his fideism, Duhem, while remaining a realist, objected to all forms of reductionist atomism; and that Boltzmann, despite his cautious fallibilism, was at heart a firm believer in reductionist physicalism and continued working on the atomic programme in spite of the latter's shortcomings.

2. MACH

Mach found that although scientists talk about space and time, about forces, point masses, and atoms, whenever they come to test their theories, they make use only of their thoughts and of their sense-impressions. So why posit anything beyond the elements of sensation, that is, the constituents of our sense-data? These consist of colours, smells, sounds, and shapes, together with the observer's feelings, volition, and thoughts.

Mach's idealist position can alternatively be described by invoking a central Kantian thesis; namely that we have knowledge only of appearances; that all we can say about the noumena or things-in-themselves is that they somehow give rise to the phenomena. The way in which the thing-in-itself founds a phenomenon will however always remain hidden from us. Since noumena do very little work in Kant's account of theoretical reason, Mach decided to eliminate them and look upon ontology as consisting of a nexus of interconnected appearances. (Mach 1886 [1959: ch. 1]).

Mach's objections to atomism are a consequence of this overall philosophical position: since they have never been observed, atoms are purely mental constructs; yet some physicists ascribe to them the spatial and tactile properties which have been experienced only as sense-data or as relations between sense-data. Notwithstanding this paradoxical extension of perceived properties to hidden entities, there is the further demand for an 'explanation' of other qualities like colours, sounds and smells in terms of the 'primary' properties of the unobservable particles. This empirically unjustifiable requirement flows from a prejudice; that of forcing the whole of science into the straitjacket of mathematics. Apart from its intrinsic absurdity, this project leads us straight into an insoluble mind-body problem.

Mach also had methodological objections to atomism: the decision to explain all processes in terms of atomic mechanisms reduces the number of parameters available to the physicist; for he is restricted to the following basic quantities: $<xyz>$ (space), t (time), $<v_x v_y v_z>$ (velocity), m (mass), e (charge). Being therefore compelled to regard the temperature T as shorthand for the mean kinetic energy of a system of atoms, he is prevented from using T as an independent parameter. Another example given by Mach is as follows. Suppose we try to reduce all the relations between atoms to their spatial properties within a 3-dimensional continuum. Given any 3 non-collinear particles: Q_1, Q_2, Q_3, the position of an arbitrary point P is (to within reflection in the plane $Q_1 Q_2 Q_3$) uniquely determined by the distances: PQ_1, PQ_2, PQ_3. Thus all relations between P and any other point B are essentially fixed by 6 numbers: PQ_i and BQ_i ($i = 1,2,3$). Hence the decision to account for the behaviour of a gas exclusively in terms of the spatial relations between its atoms strongly constrains the number of available parameters (Mach 1872 [1910: 50–7]).

Against Mach, it should be remarked that such constraints have the merit of limiting the ways in which a theory can be adjusted – *post hoc* – to fit pregiven facts; these restrictions therefore compel the scientist to construct highly testable hypotheses and are thus methodologically desirable. Furthermore, as long as the meanings of all observational terms are kept fixed, no reduction can diminish the empirical content of a hypothesis. On being reduced, the latter may of course be refuted by new results; in which case one can always revert to the unreduced theory.

We should however mention one important concession which Mach made to atomistic language: the latter can be legitimately used as a device for bringing order and economy into our perceptual domain. Unlike absolute space and time, 'atoms' and 'electrons' may thus turn out to be convenient tools in certain areas of knowledge; it being understood that such terms possess no realist import (Mach 1883 [1960: ch. 4]).

3. OSTWALD AND DUHEM

Ostwald's position is worth describing if only because it presents us with the negative image of Duhem's. Ostwald subscribed to determinism, to realism, and to physicalist reductionism. Being a naive inductivist, he took atomism to consist of gratuitous hypotheses while claiming to have directly 'read off' his own *energetics* from the facts. Energetics is the thesis that the universe consists, not of atoms, but of various forms of energy, where the latter are taken to be irreducibly different because they are perceived differently by the senses (Ostwald 1937: chs. 4, 7, 10, 11). We need not dwell on these *non-sequiturs*, which nonetheless show that atomism was opposed from a realist as well as from a phenomenalist angle.

Like Mach, Duhem separated science from metaphysics. But his reasons were very different: unlike Mach he was not inclined to regard metaphysics as meaningless. Instead, being devoutly Catholic, he was committed to one revealed ontology. Thus Duhem introduced fallibilism at all levels of scientific enquiry, thereby 'clipping the wings' of science in order to make room for faith.

Duhem was struck by the cumulative pattern displayed by the growth of mathematical knowledge and wondered whether a similar pattern had been achieved in the natural sciences. The cumulative pattern of mathematics derives from two points: (i) being very simple, all mathematical axioms afford an unmediated insight into their intended domains; (ii) the mathematical rules of inference are moreover deductive, and therefore infallibly transmit truth from premises to conclusions. Mathematical theorems are consequently never revised but simply added to. Are the natural sciences similar? According to Duhem, mathematics is synthetic, so there is no difference in this respect between its propositions and those of physics. The natural sciences are, however, different in respect of points (i) and (ii). Physical hypotheses are complex, hence far from being self-evidently true; so we have no direct access to their domain of discourse. Further, since empirical theories must somehow be based on observation, their rules of inference cannot all be deductive. Nonetheless, according to Duhem, the methods of induction and of crucial experimentation were respectively intended to provide empirical analogues to the mathematical methods of direct proof and of *reductio ad absurdum* (Duhem 1906 [1954: 168–90]). But, he argued, the analogies break down in crucial respects.

(a) Induction and direct proof

In a direct mathematical proof, we postulate 'self-evident' premises from which a sequence of theorems is derived. In the case of physical induction, we allegedly start from indubitable factual statements from which a general hypothesis is inferred. Duhem shows this method to be invalid on at least two counts. Unlike their common-sense counterparts, the empirical results on which induction rests are 'symbolic' and theory-laden, hence fallible. We thus face the vertical transcendence of all scientific factual propositions *vis-à-vis* common-sense statements. We are also confronted with the Humean horizontal transcendence of every universal law with respect to any of its instances.

Even though Duhem's views about the incorrigibility of common-sense reports are dubious, his thesis concerning the fallibility of all objective empirical statements is unchallengeable.

(b) Indirect method and crucial experiments

Duhem also examines the thesis that the scientist can often enumerate a sequence of scientific assumptions: H_1, H_2, . . ., H_n such that at least one (hitherto unidentified) H_j must be true; the disjunction (H_1 or H_2 or . . . H_n) would thus be known to hold. Through refuting all but one of these hypotheses, the scientist could then single out the true theory H_j. This is supposed to be an analogue of a method often used by mathematicians: they prove a theorem H_1 by first establishing (H_1 or H_2); then, by refuting H_2, they validly infer H_1. Duhem counters this claim by maintaining that 'the physicist is never sure he has exhausted all the imaginable assumptions' (Duhem 1906 [1954: 190]).

Duhem's answer is unsatisfactory by itself; for one might suppose that it is a priori that $H_n \equiv$ (not-H_1 & not-H_2 & . . . not-H_{n-1}), in which case (H_1 or H_2 or . . . H_n) would certainly hold. In order to vindicate Duhem's claim, therefore, we need a rigorous definition of 'scientificity' which denies scientific status to statements like (not-H_1 & not-H_2 & . . . not-H_{n-1}), while entailing that propositions of the form (H_1 or H_2 or . . . H_n) can never be ascertained as true. Consider then Popper's demarcation criterion, according to which a theory is scientific iff it is both unverifiable and empirically falsifiable. Let each H_j be scientific in this sense. Then (H_1 or H_2 or . . . H_n) is falsifiable since it will be falsified by any conjunction of potential falsifiers of H_1 . . . H_n. Further, any verification of (H_1 or H_2 or . . . H_n) would entail verifying some H_i, which is incompatible with its scientific status. (H_1 or H_2 or . . . H_n) is therefore scientific itself; so the scientist is never objectively in a position to know that any such disjunction must be true. Further, since each H_j is unverifiable and falsifiable, each not-H_j is verifiable and unfalsifiable, and therefore not scientific. So (not-H_1 & not-H_2 & . . . not-H_{n-1}) is not scientific either, and it cannot therefore be that $H_n \equiv$ (not-H_1 & not-H_2 & . . . not-H_{n-1}).

(c) The Duhem-Quine problem

One question remains unanswered: though unsure of the truth of H_1 or . . . or H_n, could we not at least be certain about the empirical refutation of some isolated theory H_i? Duhem rightly draws our attention to the fact that a falsifying experiment undermines not an isolated theory, but a whole system including the theory in question. This gives rise to the so-called Duhem-Quine problem, which can be partially solved as follows.

Let (H & A) be an empirically falsified conjunction. If successive variants A1, A2, . . . , A_n of A lead to the refutations of (H & A1), (H & A2), . . . and (H & A_n), then according to Duhem, we can reasonably conjecture that the fault lies with H. (Needless to say, such reasonableness rests on an intuitive probability argument. For more details, see Zahar 1997: 33–7.)

The above considerations show that there can be no exact parallel between the linear progress of mathematics on the one hand, and the tortuous development of physics on the other. Yet Duhem maintains that, when viewed in the right perspective, physics displays a quasi-cumulative pattern of growth. But, he held, there is a price to be paid for gaining this new insight: science has to renounce all metaphysical and hence all strictly realist claims.

Realism faces a major problem posed by the frequent occurrence of scientific revolutions. Although the Correspondence Principle, the requirement that new theories should yield old laws as limiting cases in those areas where these laws were strongly confirmed, guarantees a substantial degree of syntactic continuity between consecutive theories, at the semantic level of reference there is often a chaotic sequence of upheavals and eliminations. The referents of the latest hypothesis often oust those of the old one with which they seem to have nothing in common. In the face of such repeated overthrows, how can scientists legitimately claim to be gradually homing in on the real structure of the universe? (See Zahar 1996: 49–55.)

This question led Duhem to distinguish between the representative part of a theory (REP), which he accepted, and an explanatory or interpretative part (EXP) which he totally rejected. REP consists of purely formal relations whose only function is to entail well-tested experimental laws, whereas EXP claims to provide a realist semantic interpretation of the whole system: it purports to anchor REP in a transcendent reality whose existence is warranted by some metaphysical system. Though describing EXP as interpretative, what Duhem really meant was that EXP is intended to be reductive in the sense that REP allegedly follows from EXP. This is, however, impossible: metaphysical conjectures are too weak to imply testable laws, although they are typically strong enough to conflict with some scientific theories. Indeed far from yielding any new predictions, EXP may prove to be incompatible with REP, which does all the empirical work on its own (note how close Duhem came to formulating Popper's criterion).

Because of its semantic pretensions, EXP misrepresents the history of science as a chaotic series of revolutions. Axing EXP will therefore represent a double gain: there is first an increase in the economy of thought without any loss of empirical content; the development of science can secondly be seen as a gradual process during which, thanks to the Correspondence Principle, the mathematical form of confirmed physical laws is largely preserved. This sustains our belief that we could be moving towards a 'natural classification' which mirrors the ontological order without actually signifying it. Such a natural classification possesses two defining characteristics: it displays a high degree of unity, i.e. all its components are tightly interconnected; and it entails hitherto unknown laws, which ought subsequently to be confirmed (Duhem 1906 [1954: 19–39]).

Duhem substantiated his hostility to reductive realism in scientific theory by showing that all attempts at reducing physics to mechanistic atomism had been not merely otiose but were essentially counter-productive. He defined mechanism as the thesis that the ultimate constituents of reality are charged particles subject to the laws governing the motion of macroscopic objects, but pointed out that mechanism need not carry a commitment to realism. Thus, according to Duhem, the 'English physicists' are non-realistic mechanists: they illustrate their theories with dynamical images without regarding the latter as genuinely explanatory; such 'models' are offered only on account of their so-called intelligibility. By contrast, Aristotle was certainly a realist but was not a mechanist.

Having renounced all metaphysical speculation, at least in science, Duhem, as a conventionalist, was bound to accept some form of inductive reasoning. He held that the only legitimate inductive inferences consist in 'generalising' theory-laden empirical results in ways which are also theory-dependent. It follows that empirical induction is doubly fallible; but it remains the only method of gaining new factual knowledge and Duhem argues that it provides no support for mechanistic atomism. Properties like shape, impenetrability, and motion are admittedly revealed by the phenomena; but so are colours, smells, and tastes; and experience in no way tells us that this second group of 'secondary' qualities is reducible to the 'primary' one. So Duhem justifiably holds energetics (the thesis that the universe consists of various forms of energy) rather than atomism to be closely linked to the domain of sense-experience. Though conceding that many great physicists were atomists, he denies that their atomistic metaphysics helped them towards achieving their breakthroughs. In many cases, these scientists actually found it difficult to reconcile their discoveries with their ontological prejudices. Mechanical theories possess only two advantages: they postulate very few basic predicates; and the latter are moreover easy to picture, which accounts for their appeal to the English 'ample but weak' mind.

Although Duhem does not explicitly target realism as such, but only reductive mechanism which, when realistically interpreted as atomism, allegedly threatens Christian dogma, his criticisms are nonetheless so global that they hit all reductive explanations. Hence because of his fideism, Duhem gave greater weight to the (undeniably serious) difficulties facing 'materialist' physics than to its heuristic fruitfulness coupled with its capacity for anticipating novel facts. According to realists like Boltzmann, by contrast, such a capacity points to the truth-likeness of atomism, whose difficulties are shelved as mere 'anomalies' to be ironed out by future research. The case of Duhem thus shows how during periods of scientific uncertainty, philosophy can play a determining role in the development of science. Duhem's antipathy towards all versions of reductive explanation accounts for his negative appraisal of, and for his refusal to contribute to, the hypotheses which were to dominate early twentieth-century natural science: atomism, electromagnetic field theory, relativity, and Darwinism.

4. BOLTZMANN

Boltzmann's philosophy can be consistently set out, provided his ontology is sharply distinguished from both his epistemology and his methodology. Qua metaphysician, Boltzmann subscribed to atomistic realism and to a Darwinian version of reductionism. He held that our aesthetic and moral values, our supposedly a priori principles and even our logic are genetically encoded beliefs. Because of their survival value, the latter are transmitted from one generation to the next. Epistemologically speaking, this hard-headed physicalist position was tempered by Boltzmann's fallibilist hypothetico–deductivism. He recognised that in constructing his laws, the physicist must go beyond the 'facts' which inevitably underdetermine his theories. Boltzmann rightly accused both the idealists and the inductivists of having ignored this basic limitation on the certainty of all scientific hypotheses. Furthermore, phenomenalists such as Mach are not only driven to solipsism; but in setting up relations between their elements of sensation, they have to rely on past and hence on remembered experiences; these are as imperfectly known as any 'external' objects or as any contents of other people's minds; so we might just as well postulate transcendent entities rather than gratuitously limit ourselves to descriptions of sense-impressions (Boltzmann 1869 [1979]: 26–46).

Boltzmann tried to turn most ontological problems into methodological questions. He did not object to phenomenological thermodynamics as such but held it to possess limited *heuristic* value. He consequently advised all researchers, even those who did not believe in atomism, to work on the atomistic programme; for the latter had yielded a host of novel laws, for example, the equations of state for certain substances and the independence of the viscosity of gases from their density.

Thus Boltzmann advocated a pluralist and anti-essentialist methodology. In order to forestall criticisms emanating from his scientific opponents and from the Church, he offered to regard all hypotheses as no more than mental images whose main purpose was to subsume our experiences. His sincerity can be doubted; for he also maintained that if a unified theory successfully predicts unexpected results, it can be taken to simulate the objective order of things. His protestations nevertheless underline an important methodological point: a physical conjecture derives its validity not from its inherent plausibility, but solely from its internal consistency together with its entailment of true observable consequences (Boltzmann 1869 [1979]: 170–98).

It seems to me that Boltzmann's philosophy of science is not only surprisingly modern but also unchallengeable. The problems facing him stemmed, not from his methodology, but from the logical and experimental difficulties confronting atomism. To these we must now turn.

In the Introduction (above), the problems pertaining to the specific heats of polyatomic substances were mentioned. These difficulties were resolved by replacing classical mechanics by quantum physics, whose development postdated Boltzmann's death. However, in the first decade of the twentieth century, the work of Einstein, Smoluchowski, and Perrin had already provided strong empirical support for atomism. Through considering the fluctuations entailed by atomic theory, Einstein explained the irregular movements of Brownian particles: these arise from the successive collisions of the particles with a large number of surrounding molecules. Einstein derived a formula which was later confirmed by Perrin; and this unexpected success eventually led doubters like Ostwald – but not Mach – to accept the atomic hypothesis (Stachel 1989: 206–36).

There remains one outstanding problem which atomism appeared unable to solve: namely that posed by the irreversibility of some observable processes. In section 1, I mentioned the difficulty of mechanically defining the entropy S in such a way that the Second Principle [B] is verified – either exactly or approximately. Boltzmann proposed the equation: $S(q) = k.logW_q$, where k is a constant, q denotes a given macrostate, and W_q is proportional to the number of microstates giving rise to q. To within some constant factor, W_q therefore denotes a *thermodynamic probability*.

Boltzmann initially conjectured that no physical process involves a decrease of W_q. This gives rise to the question whether such a proposition can be derived from the laws of mechanics conjoined with descriptions of boundary conditions. In section 1, a bijection was established between the two sets Δ and Δ^*: where Δ and Δ^* consist respectively of those initial conditions which cause an increase, and those which cause a diminution of the entropy S. This result led Boltzmann to concede that a decrease of S is possible but remains highly improbable. Instead of establishing his claim, however he merely asserted that his critics had failed to prove theirs; namely that the diminution of S is as likely as its increase (Brush 1966: paper 4).

Boltzmann had in effect shifted the burden of proof onto his opponents by challenging them to show that the measure of Δ^* is at least as great as that of Δ. (Note that the bijection between the sets Δ and Δ^* establishes the equality of their cardinals, not that of their *measures*. Since the notion of measure is a generalisation of that of length, area, or volume, probabilities are proportional to measures, not to cardinalities.) In order to derive the Second Principle from atomism, it was however up to Boltzmann himself to prove that Δ^* is smaller than Δ; whereas he merely pointed to his critics' failure to establish the incompatibility of mechanics with thermodynamics. Be that as it may, Zermelo's objections proved even harder to rebut (Zermelo 1966: 229–37). In showing the impossibility of any reduction of the Second Principle to mechanics, Zermelo invoked Poincaré's recurrence theorem (Brush 1966: papers 5 and 7). Poincaré's theorem can be informally stated as follows. Consider a physical system Ω and any closed and bounded region B within the space of all possible initial conditions of Ω. Then B contains a subset B' of zero measure such that: if Ω is started at an arbitrary point of B-B', that is, at practically any point of B, the entropy of Ω cannot steadily increase but might – at best – remain constant.

Boltzmann's response to this paradox was unsatisfactory: he maintained that given improbable initial conditions, it can safely be assumed that for a long time to come, entropy will steadily increase; after which the universe would approximately resume its initial state, with a corresponding diminution of entropy (Brush 1966: paper 8). This *ad hoc* move might have established the compatibility of the Second Principle with, but certainly not its derivability from, the atomic hypothesis. Thus atomism had not (yet?) superseded thermodynamics.

5. CONCLUSION

Because of its undeniable empirical triumphs, atomism is nowadays accepted by most physicists. It can thus be concluded that the internal consistency of a theory plays a minor role when compared with its capacity for yielding novel experimental results.

THEORIES OF SPACE-TIME IN
MODERN PHYSICS

LUCIANO BOI

1. INTRODUCTION

Among the most important events of twentieth-century physics, we must surely count the development of the special and the general theories of relativity by Einstein in 1905 and 1916, and that of quantum mechanics, which was worked out about ten years later by Bohr, Heisenberg, Schrödinger, and de Broglie. Owing to these theories, the physicist's conception of space-time underwent two major upheavals.

Although they apply on different scales, the general theory of relativity and the quantum field theory play a fundamental role in describing the natural world, so a complete description of nature must encompass both of them. The formal attempt to quantise general relativity, however, leads to nonsensical infinite formulas. In the sixties non-Abelian gauge theory emerged as a framework for describing all natural forces except gravity; however, at the same time, the inconsistency between general relativity and quantum field theory emerged clearly as the limitation of twentieth-century physics. The resulting problem is a theorists' problem *par excellence*: experiments provide little help, and the inconsistency illustrates the intermingling of philosophical, mathematical, and physical thought.

It is a fact of great significance that every physical theory of some generality and scope, whether it is a classical or a quantum theory, a particle or a field theory, presupposes a space-time geometry for the formulation of its laws and for its interpretation, and the choice of this geometry predetermines to some extent the laws which are taken to govern the behaviour of matter. Thus Newton's classical mechanics (and especially its law of gravitation) is based on the assumption of an absolute simultaneity relation between events and a Euclidean geometry; similarly, the physical principle of the universal proportionality of inertial and gravitational mass, as recognised by Einstein between 1907 and 1915, requires the assignment of a non-integrable, that is, path-dependent, linear connection with non-vanishing curvature to space-time (the law of parallel displacement).

The fact that space-time geometry cannot adequately be considered in isolation from other parts of physics, and hence that its concepts and laws are inextricably interwoven with those of mechanics, electrodynamics, etc., was first recognised by B. Riemann and W. K. Clifford, thereafter by H. Minkowki and A. Einstein, and was particularly emphasised by H. Weyl (Weyl 1918).

2. THE SPECIAL THEORY OF RELATIVITY

Classical physics is grounded on the assumption that space, time, and physical events are completely independent realities. This assumption was called into question by the special theory of relativity, which affirms 'the principle of relativity' that a frame of reference in uniform translatory motion relative to an inertial frame cannot be distinguished from that inertial frame by any physical experiment. The first point to grasp here is Einstein's analysis of the concept of simultaneity, according to which time is a co-ordinate expressing the relationship of an event to a concrete physical process involving light signals by which this co-ordinate is measured. Given the constancy of the velocity of light for all observers, it follows that observers moving at different speeds will not agree on the time co-ordinate to be ascribed to distant events, and thus will not agree on the length of objects or the rates of clocks. The special theory thus implies that there is no absolute notion of simultaneity to ground a 'universal' time, and thus that simultaneity is a relative notion which depends upon the reference frame from which events are observed; events which are simultaneous for one observer need not be simultaneous for another. Hence the assumptions behind common sense and the classical notions of space and time must be dropped.

In 1908 Minkowski realised that the special theory can be formulated in terms of a four-dimensional spatio-temporal structure which is absolute, and not relative, since it is the same as seen from all reference frames. Hence he proposed the unification of space and time in the single concept: *space-time*. Space-time becomes thus the natural arena where the mathematical description of physical phenomena takes place. In particular, it permits the reformulation of the laws of special relativity in a new, more mathematical, language. Hence, according to Minkowski, the world can be regarded as a four-dimensional non-Euclidean hyperbolic manifold, a 'four-manifold'. Special relativity thus endows the world four-manifold with a geometric structure no less rich than, though distinct from, that of Euclidean four-dimensional space (see Torretti 1996). This geometric structure is at the core of special relativity as well as of other physical theories.

3. IDEAS AND DEVELOPMENTS OF SPACE-TIME
THEORIES IN RELATIVISTIC PHYSICS

Einstein's relativisation of time was the conceptually decisive step which transformed the varied results and suggestions of Lorentz, Poincaré, and others into a
transparent, coherent theory, the special theory of relativity. Einstein eliminated
apparent contradictions from the electrodynamics and optics of moving bodies by substituting an operationally meaningful time concept for a dogmatically
postulated absolute time. This provided the model for a critical, empirically
oriented, re-examination of physical concepts in general which was of great
methodological importance for the evolution of physics, especially quantum
theory. The special theory of relativity succeeded in reconciling the principle of
relativity and the principle of the constant velocity of light in a vacuum (which
asserts that light in a vacuum has a constant velocity of propagation independent of the state of motion of the observer or of the source of the light) by a
modification of kinematics – that is, of the laws relating to space and time. It
became clear that to speak of the simultaneity of two events has no meaning
except in relation to a given co-ordinate system (that is, a geometrical frame),
and that the shape of measuring devices and the speed at which clocks move
depends on their state of motion with respect to the co-ordinate system.

The content of the special theory of relativity is included in the postulate:
the laws of nature are invariant with respect to the Lorentz transformations (see Rindler
1960, and Synge 1964). Furthermore, the heuristic method of the special theory
of relativity is characterised by the following principle: only those equations are
admissible as an expression of natural laws which do not change their form
when the co-ordinates are changed by means of a Lorentz transformation. The
Lorentz transformation equations are:

$$x' = \frac{x - vt}{\left(1 - \frac{v^2}{c^2}\right)^{\frac{1}{2}}} \qquad z' = z,$$

$$y' = y, \qquad t' = \frac{\left(t - \frac{vx}{c^2}\right)}{\left(1 - \frac{v^2}{c^2}\right)^{\frac{1}{2}}}$$

If the principle of relativity is true, then all laws of physics which are valid in
an inertial frame must be invariant under these transformation equations. An
important feature is that Lorentz transformations are non-singular and form a
group, the Lorentz group (see Penrose 1968, and Torretti 1996). The Lorentz

group can be understood as a group of (linear) space-time transformations, leaving a light cone invariant.

The second, even more profound revision of our conception of space-time was Einstein's discovery, between 1912 and 1915, that gravity is not a force field existing in addition to the inertia-determining world-geometry, but should be considered as an aspect of the metrical and affine structure of space-time, indicating in fact the curvature of the space-time continuum and thereby furnishing the physical basis of that structure which Riemann had speculated about at the end of his celebrated inaugural lecture of 1854 (Riemann 1892; for a detailed analysis of Riemann's conceptions, see Boi 1995). With this second step, Einstein transformed the geometrical structure of space-time from a rigidly given, never changing, absolute entity into a variable dynamical field interacting with matter (Ehlers 1973). He thereby removed a disparity between geometry and physics which had been criticised some thirty years earlier by Mach (Mach 1883) in the course of his reflections on Leibniz's criticisms of Newton's absolute space.

4. MINKOWSKI SPACE-TIME

Riemann's generalisation of Gauss's intrinsic geometry of curves and surfaces and the resulting concept of a four-dimensional manifold endowed with a non-Euclidean (or Lorentzian) metric as well as a differentiable structure was the first fundamental step towards the geometrisation of physics. The second step was the construction by Minkowski of a new geometry which for the first time encompassed space and time into the single concept of *space-time*. The Minkowski geometry (called also *the Minkowski world*) is a geometrical characterisation of the kinematics discovered by Einstein in his famous paper of 1905 on the electro-dynamics of moving bodies (Einstein 1905), in which he adopted the principle of relativity for mechanical and electromagnetic processes and assumed the independence of the velocity of light from the velocity of the source. According to Minkowski, space-time is a pseudo-Euclidean, four-dimensional space whose metric tensor $\eta_{\alpha\beta}$ has signature $(+, +, +, -)$. The null cones defined by $\eta_{\alpha\beta}$ describe light propagation, timelike straight lines represent the world lines of free particles, and the arc length

$$\int \sqrt{-\eta_{\alpha\beta}\,dx^\alpha\,dx^\beta} = \int \sqrt{1-v^2}\,dt$$

$(x_4 = t, c = 1)$ of a timelike curve L gives the proper time measured by a standard clock carried by a particle with world line L.

The most important difference between the nonrelativistic space-times and that of special relativity lies in their causal structures. In Minkowski's space-time the causal future (past) of an event E is bounded by the future (past) null cone, and thus there is a four-dimensional region whose events are causally disconnected from E, in contrast to the situation in nonrelativistic space-times. The (co-ordinate) topology of special relativistic space-time can be easily obtained from its chronological order (see Zeeman 1967). Let b be called later than a, for a, $b \in M$, if b is contained in the interior of the future null cone of a, written $a < b$. Then the set $\{x | a < x < b, a, b \in M\}$ generates the topology of (the space-time) M. This way of introducing the topology of M is physically very satisfactory since it says that an event a is 'close' to b if there is a particle P through a and a 'short' time interval on P containing a within which P can 'communicate' with b.

We see thus that the requirements of special relativity are kinematic, or geometric, stipulating a certain space-time structure and demanding any dynamical theory to be in accordance with it. The Minkowski space-time structure consists of two ingredients: an inertial structure governing the motion of force-free bodies or particles (described mathematically by an affine structure), and a geometrical chronometry, or chronogeometry for short, governing the behaviour of (ideal) measuring roods and clocks (described mathematically by a pseudo-Riemannian metric structure). Given the chronogeometry, compatibility conditions between the two fix the inertial structure (see Stachel 1995).

5. GENERAL RELATIVITY THEORY AND THE NEW IDEAS ABOUT SPACE-TIME AND PHYSICS

Next, we return to the consideration of new ideas concerning space-time. In order fully to appreciate the outstanding transformation in our conceptions of space and time achieved by the Einstein's general theory of relativity, we shall consider again Newton's theory. It is characteristic of Newtonian physics that it has to ascribe independent and real existence to space and time as well as to matter. In effect, Newton's space must be thought of as 'at rest', or at least as 'unaccelerated', so that one can consider acceleration, as it appears in the laws of motion, as being a magnitude with any meaning. Much the same holds with respect to time, which of course also enters into the concept of acceleration. In Newtonian classical mechanics, the essential thing is that 'physical reality', thought of as independent of the subjects who experience it, is conceived as consisting (at least in principle) of space and time on one hand, and of material points, moving with respect to space and time, on the other. The idea of the independent existence of space and time can be expressed drastically in this way:

if matter were to disappear, space and time would remain behind – as a kind of stage for physical happenings.

This standpoint is completely rejected in the general theory of relativity. In classical mechanics, and even special relativity, in order to be able to describe that which 'fills up' space, space or the inertial system with its metrical properties must be thought of as existing independently. According to the general theory of relativity, however, no separate existence can be assigned to space as opposed to 'what fills space'. If we imagine the removal of the gravitational field, that is, the functions or metric tensor $g_{\mu\nu}$ (which enters into the quadratic form $\sum_{\mu\nu} g_{\mu\nu}\, dx^\mu dx^\nu$ giving the general form for measuring the distance between neighbouring points of a manifold M), there does not remain an 'empty' space, but absolutely nothing. For the functions $g_{\mu\nu}$ describe not only the gravitational field, but also the topological and metrical structural properties of the manifold. Space-time does not have existence on its own; it exists only as a structural quality of the field (Einstein 1956).

In general relativity, the physically meaningful aspect of a gravitational field is contained only in the 'tidal force' which results from a *nonuniform* gravitational acceleration field. Minkowskian and Einsteinian space-times differ radically from classical space-time in that no additive concept of time difference is defined between events. Instead, a pseudo-Riemannian metric form ds^2, of Lorentzian signature $(+, +, +, -)$, is defined on the space-time. The time difference between two points A, B in the space-time depends on the choice of world line connecting the points and is given by the integral of ds along the world line:

$$t = \int_A^B ds. \tag{5.1}$$

Einstein's field equations then describe how this space-time curvature is to be related to the density of matter – that is, of stress-energy-momentum (see below). Hence the metric of space-time must differ in a gravitational field from the ordinary flat space-time form. In general relativity one is led to look for a theory which agrees locally (approximately) with special relativity, but has, instead of the integrable, affine connection of Minkowski space-time, a nonintegrable linear connection capable of representing the combined inertial-gravitational field.

The central feature of general relativity is therefore that it has furnished, for the first time, an unified description (and explanation) of space, time, and gravitation which is essentially geometrical in nature. Indeed, the gravitational field is represented by a symmetric connection Γ, which is a geometrical object, and the equations relating the gravitational field to matter turn out to be expressible as a relation between the contracted curvature tensor $R_{\alpha\beta}$ of Γ, so that the second law of dynamics can be formulated in terms of a covariant derivative with respect to Γ. A further feature of general relativity is the principle of general covariance, a constraint on the dynamical equations permitted by the theory. The symmetry group acting (locally) on the four-dimensional space-time manifold, on which all physical fields are defined, consists of all diffeomorphisms (sufficiently smooth point transformations of the manifold); this group leaves invariant a general quadratic form (the metric) characterising the manifold.

Einstein's equations form a system of ten second-order non-linear differential equations in the four space-time variables. These equations are to be solved for the ten unknown components of the metric tensor g_{ik}, which we may interpret as gravitational potential. In general relativity, however, we cannot simply speak of the density of matter in space; we must also include the energy density, since, as Einstein has shown, matter and energy are indistinguishable with regard to their inertial properties. One may express the influence of matter and field energy in the form of a tensor $T^{\mu\nu}$ which is called the *energy-momentum tensor*. Thus we arrive at Einstein's gravitational field equation for nonempty space-time, which lies at the core of general relativity,

$$R_{\mu\nu} - (1/2)g_{ik}R = 8\pi\,T^{\mu\nu}, \tag{5.2}$$

where $R_{\mu\nu}$ and R are respectively the Ricci tensor and the scalar curvature of g_{ik}. Hence the equation (5.2) may be expressed as follows: (Tensor representing geometry of space) = (tensor representing mass-energy content of space).

In general relativity one makes the following assumption: by including all significant physical quantities in the complete energy-momentum tensor, that is, matter, fluid pressure, electromagnetic fields, etc., we obtain a *zero-divergence tensor* in flat space. According to this view, physical quantities influence each other by exchanging energy and momentum in such a way as to keep the divergence of $T^{\mu\nu}$ equal to zero; that is, total energy and momentum are conserved. We conclude that $T^{\mu\nu}$ characterises the non-gravitational energy content of space. Thus we assume that the gravitational field equations have the form:

$$R_{\mu\nu} - (1/2)Rg_{\mu\nu} + \lambda\,g_{\mu\nu} = -2KT^{\mu\nu} \tag{5.3}$$

where $R_{\mu\nu}$ is the Ricci curvature tensor, $g_{\mu\nu}$ the metric tensor, λ and K are real constants with $K > 0$, and $T^{\mu\nu}$ is the energy-momentum tensor of matter. In other words, the properties of space geometry are equal to the physical content of space (here matter refers to any field except gravitation itself). In fact, gravitational energy cannot be adequately defined in a *local* way and emerges, instead, as some kind of non-local quantity.

6. CONCEPTUAL DISCUSSION OF SPACE-TIME
GEOMETRICAL STRUCTURE AND ITS PHYSICAL MEANING

In view of the facts discussed above, one can affirm that philosophically the crucial conceptual innovation in general relativity, the one that allowed the possibility of a scientific revolution and a new conceptual synthesis, was the interpretation of magnitudes which had previously been considered physical in terms of geometrical magnitudes; and at the same time, the rejection of the conception of *physical* geometry as something given a priori (despite its being predetermined by the mathematical structures of a certain manifold) and its replacement by a treatment of it as wholly determined by the physical situation (Graves 1971 and Friedman 1983). Physics and geometry became so interwined that any assertion about the one necessarily implied an assertion about the other.

General covariance had restricted physics to the use of tensor quantities, without specifying how they might be derived or what they should signify. The identification of physics with geometry added the new requirement that the tensors in terms of which the fundamental physical laws were to be expressed must be derived from or equated to tensors which have a purely geometric significance. But the fundamental tensor used to characterise a space is the metric tensor g_{ik} (which is assumed by Einstein, following Riemann, to be symmetric) and all other geometrical tensors are derived from this by various mathematical operations. Thus if the metric tensor were given at all points in physical space-time (along with the co-ordinate system in which it was being represented) we would know, at least ideally, not only all the geometrical properties of space-time, but all the (large-scale) physics there as well. The metric tensor thus plays a central role, in that every other piece of information about the geometry of the space can be derived by a purely mathematical development from the metric and the co-ordinates in which its components are expressed. For this reason it has epistemological priority. However, it is less fundamental ontologically: it does not describe a purely geometrical invariant property of the manifold, such as its set of co-ordinates and the basic metric ds^2. But there are other derived tensors, such as the Ricci tensor $R_{\mu\nu}$, which do refer directly to geometrical properties and may thus be taken to have ontological priority.

From a philosophical point of view, if we consider four-dimensional space-time to have any sort of independent existence, we must assume that (i) it has definite properties at its various points, that is, its metrical co-ordinate system can be locally characterised; (ii) these properties must be geometrical or spatial, such as the various curvatures; and (iii) they must be quite independent of any co-ordinate system, since the latter is a human convenience (or, more precisely, a conventional statement stipulated by us upon nature) and cannot affect geometry. General relativity develops the mathematics and geometrical model first, and only later considers the 'second interpretation' of this model in terms of actual physical objects, such as rigid rods and paths of light rays (Penrose 1968, Graves 1971). As Wheeler has pointed out (Wheeler 1962), the requirement that general relativity must have a purely geometrical content goes beyond general covariance in placing an additional physical restriction on the form of the laws allowed. In the broad sense, covariance allows any law that can be written in tensor form. However, the field equations must not determine the g_{ik} uniquely. They must give us information about geometry but not about co-ordinates. In satisfying covariance, they rule out no system of co-ordinates, but many possible geometries.

For these reasons, it is very important to recognise that this identification of space (space-time) with matter and therefore geometry with physics is the central conceptual feature of general relativity. Philosophers such as Reichenbach and Grünbaum have misinterpreted the theory by attempting to keep them separate. They recognise the interdependence of physics and geometry only in that physical laws which involve geometric magnitudes such as lengths must change their mathematical form when the geometry changes, making thereby (at least implicitly) the wrong assumption that the geometry which enters physics has a purely conventional nature. According to them, for example, the 'co-ordinative definitions' relating abstract geometry (or the mathematical structures of the space-time manifold) to physics (or the properties of the physical space model) are arbitrary conventions, and just determine the content and the meaning of the geometry involved in physics. Consequently, they think in terms of adjustments by successive approximations, leading ultimately to the correct geometry and correct physics for that set of co-ordinative definitions. They argue moreover that if geometry were nothing but the articulation of relationships among standard objects, we should expect that somehow physics would be lost if it were reduced to or identified with geometry. But this point of view is somewhat mistaken. In fact, two distinct although related aspects of this issue should be stressed here. It is true that neither the conventional character of the choice of co-ordinative definitions nor the possibility of using a particular stipulation to make an empirical determination of geometry is relevant for general relativity, as the above statement of the mathematical contents of general relativity should have proved. (For an interesting and proper criticism of the Reichenbach and Grünbaum positions, see Petitot 1992, and Torretti 1996.) Nevertheless, Grünbaum proposes to determine ds^2 experimentally; he is thus thinking, in some sense, that the identification of gravity with geometry would not entail any loss of physical content.

To sum up, in general relativity space-time becomes a dynamical variable curving in response to mass and energy, and dynamics becomes an aspect of the geometrical structure of the world. For the first time in the history of physics, the space-time structure is not specified a priori, but becomes a dynamical physical field (Stachel 1995). However, it should be emphasised that in general relativity, the space-time metric plays a dual role. On the one hand, it represents the gravitational potential and is thus a dynamical variable. On the other hand, it determines space-time geometry. In short, general relativity taught us that space-time geometry is dynamical, and thus similar to physical fields; indeed, space-time geometry is the gravitational field. However, the dynamics of the gravitational field is profoundly peculiar, and it cannot be captured, as other physical fields can, by techniques which rely on the existence of a fixed background space-time. Consequently, the background geometry is itself a dynamical object. This 'structural' and 'relational' view of space-time is the basical conceptual idea that general relativity has contributed to our understanding of the natural world.

In view of these facts, the assertion that space-time is 'really' curved, can now, owing to the recent experimental work and further theoretical analyses, be considered as well established (on this important aspect of general relativity, see Penrose 1968, and Damour 1995), and the phenomenological foundation for the assignment of a curved, pseudo-Riemannian structure to space-time is as firm as those of other fundamental theoretical conceptions of physics.

7. CONCLUSION

Einstein's basic contribution to physics lay not so much in proposing new formulas as in introducing fundamental changes to our basic notions of space, time, and matter. Furthermore, the theory of relativity is not just the culmination of earlier developments; on the contrary, the theory takes a radically new line which contradicts Newtonian concepts in the very same step in which it extends physical law in new directions and into hitherto unexpected new domains.

Einstein's fundamental new step was in the adoption of a *relational* approach to physics. Instead of supposing that the task of physics is the study of an absolute underlying *substance* of the universe (such as the ether) he suggested that it lies in the study of relationships between various aspects of this universe, relationships that are in principle observable. In Newtonian physics, space and time were regarded as absolute. Einstein, instead, considered space and time as having essentially 'relativistic' properties; in particular, in his analysis of the concept of simultaneity, he treats time as a 'co-ordinate system' which characterises the relationship of an event to a concrete physical process in which this co-ordinate system is measured. Given the constancy of the velocity of light for all observers, it follows that observers moving at different speeds will not agree on the time co-ordinate to be ascribed to distant events; and equally, therefore, that they will not agree about the lengths of objects.

This is an account of an essential feature of the structure of the physical world rather than an arbitrary relativisation which reflects our causal relationship with it. Indeed, the Lorentz transformations and the more general Poincaré transformations play the important role of characterising the causal structure between events occurring in the physical world in accordance with the intrinsic structure of space-time geometry. For these transformations lead in a natural way to the principle of relativity – that is, the principle that the basic physical laws are the invariant relationships: the same for all observers.

Another important concept of relativity theory is that of a *Minkowski diagram* (see Ellis and Williams 1988). Besides making it possible to illustrate the meaning of the principle of relativity in a graphical and geometrical way, this type of diagram shows the way in which the concepts of *event* and *process* are basic notions in relativistic physics, instead of those of an *object* and its *motion*, which are basic in Newtonian theory. This leads to the (hyperbolic) geometry of Minkowski space-time, with its invariant distinction between events inside the past and future light cones and the events outside. This geometrical picture of relativity serves to illustrate the meaning of 'proper-time', and throws new light on the way in which Einstein's notions of space and time leave room for two observers who separate to have experienced different intervals of 'proper-time' when they meet again.

The philosophical meaning and import of the general theory of relativity is a difficult and rich subject. The general theory is both a theory of gravitation and a theory of space-time geometry (Souriau 1964, Penrose 1968). Whereas in Newtonian physics and in the special theory space-time is considered as given rigidly once and for all, in general relativity it is treated as a physical field interacting with matter. The distinction between gravitational field and space-time geometry had of course already been questioned, in one sense, by Mach. Mach's idea was that the distant matter in the universe determines local inertial effects such as rotation: if someone were somehow to accelerate the distant matter in the universe, our local determinations of non-accelerating and non-rotating systems should be affected. Thus if there were no matter in the rest of the universe, there should be no such thing as inertia or rotation. Hence even before general relativity, space-time geometry, as manifested by the class of inertial reference frames, was a universal external field acted upon by matter, but not acting on it. The crucial point about general relativity is that it recognises that space-time geometry is on an equal footing with other fields and matter, both 'acting' and 'suffering'.

Clifford's famous conjecture that we can assign to variations of the curvature of space the phenomena which we term the motion of matter anticipated Einstein's explanation of gravity in purely geometrical terms as the curvature of space-time (Wheeler 1962, and Boi 1995). This theme of the geometrisation of physics is further exemplified by the Yang-Mills fields, which are based on the concept of local (gauge) invariance obeyed by the dynamical symmetries and governing all fundamental interactions of nature. For these fields are geometrical in essence, since a connection is really just a rule for parallel translation, and the Yang-Mills field, being just the curvature of a connection, measures the dependence of parallel translation on the path taken between two points. Finally, general relativity itself is even more geometrical, since it concerns, not just any old bundle, but the tangent bundle. The basic ingredient of general relativity is the metric on space-time, but this metric defines a connection on the tangent bundle, and its curvature, the Riemannian tensor, is the most important feature of this history (Weyl 1921, Trautman 1973).

General relativity is therefore the physical realisation of Riemannian geometry. From both a philosophical and a scientific point of view, the most important discovery made by Einstein is that the way in which the gravitational field behaves depends on the infinitesimal nature (both metrical and topological) of the geometry characterising space-time. According to general relativity, geometrical concepts cannot be dissociated from physical ones, and space-time geometry shares the dynamical character of the electromagnetic field and the other physical fields. Einstein succeeded in the goal of geometrising the physical world.

As we have shown, the crucial feature of general relativity is that we have to think in terms of the curvature of four-dimensional space-time. In particular, we think of the lines which represent the world-lines of particles and the ways in which these paths are distorted as a measurement of the curvature of space-time. Thus Einstein's theory is essentially a geometric theory of four-dimensional space-time, and the ideas of non-Euclidean geometry are actually the natural language for describing the curvature of space-time and the properties of forces acting on it. Therefore in general relativity we have a mathematical structure which really does underlie the behaviour of the physical world in an extraordinarily precise way.

SECTION FIVE

THE IDEA OF SOCIAL SCIENCE

15

THE DEBATE OVER THE
GEISTESWISSENSCHAFTEN IN
GERMAN PHILOSOPHY

R. LANIER ANDERSON

The decades around 1900 witnessed a lively debate in German philosophy about the nature of knowledge and methodology in the social and cultural sciences, and about the appropriate demarcation criterion distinguishing these *Geisteswissenschaften* (human sciences) from the more established natural sciences. This debate engaged philosophers (W. Dilthey, W. Wundt, G. Simmel, W. Windelband, H. Rickert) and leaders from the empirical *Geisteswissenschaften* (K. Lamprecht, M. Weber).

The problem of humanistic knowledge assumed philosophical importance for many reasons, but the most important was a serious tension within a widely held constellation of views about the human sciences. On the one hand, humanistic learning was prominent in the German intellectual landscape, both because of nineteenth-century scholarly achievements, and because of the central place of classical languages and literatures in gymnasium education. Work in the *Geisteswissenschaften* thus served as an example of intellectual rigour for students and scholars alike, and it was standard to see humanistic learning as exemplary *science*. On the other hand, the older and more established natural sciences were still paradigms of *mature* science, and the progress of the natural and human sciences had carried them far apart, both in their methods, and in the nature of their results. Natural sciences subjected phenomena to relatively simple quantitative laws, which permitted improvements in precision and confirmation of theory by controlled experiment. Because the nineteenth century saw repeated extensions of this broad approach to new areas in physics, chemistry, and fields like physiology and psychology, it could claim to be *the* model for mature scientific knowledge. By contrast, the *Geisteswissenschaften* in Germany were dominated by the 'Historical School', whose highest accomplishments rested on sensitive historical interpretations of unique and valuable cultural achievements. They produced few results that were quantitative or lawlike, in the sense of the natural sciences. Thus arose a tension within the common view: it seemed obvious that the *Geisteswissenschaften* should be treated as sciences, but the natural scientific model for a mature scientific result was a poor fit for their best achievements.

This problem raised a number of difficult philosophical issues which are still alive today. For example, the demarcation issue posed questions about the nature of scientific laws, and their relative absence from the human sciences. Moreover, much debate centred on the appropriate role for psychology in grounding the system of the *Geisteswissenschaften*, and a position on this point had implications for the acrimonious debates over psychologism which arose in the years before 1900. In the context of the *Geisteswissenschaften* debate, psychologism raised a wider question about the relation of norms to the natural world. That general problem is crucial for an account of knowledge in the human sciences, since it often purports to be knowledge about human norms and values.

1. BACKGROUND

The *Geisteswissenschaften* debate was provoked by the emergence of a positivist account, which advocated reforming the human sciences on the model of natural science. The nineteenth century *locus classicus* for this view was Mill 1843. Mill lamented that the contemporary moral sciences were 'still abandoned to the uncertainties of vague and popular discussion', but he thought they could be rescued 'by generalizing the methods successfully followed' in natural science (Mill 1843 [1974: 833–4]). On his view, the fundamental moral science is individual psychology, which provides simple laws of association governing the succession of mental states (Mill 1843 [1974: 853]). Predicting and explaining human actions also involves higher empirical generalisations of ethology (the science of character types), but these are merely 'empirical', and attain the rank of laws only if they are explained by derivation from underlying 'causal laws' of associationistic psychology (Mill 1843 [1974: 864]). Ultimately, all of social life is explicable on the basis of these psychological laws: 'All phenomena of society are phenomena of human nature, generated by the action of outward circumstances upon masses of human beings: and if, therefore, the phenomena of human thought, feeling, and action, are subject to fixed laws, the phenomena of society cannot but conform to fixed laws, the consequences of the preceding' (Mill 1843 [1974: 877]). Thus, the reformed moral sciences should discover universal natural laws, and they should be ordered into a system, in which the explanatory laws of individual psychology play a foundational role similar to that of mechanics in the natural sciences.

Mill's positivism did attract followers writing in German. Ernst Mach remarked in an 1867 lecture that the human and the natural sciences are 'only parts of the same science', so that belief in an essential distinction between them 'will appear as naïve to a matured age as the lack of perspective in [ancient] Egyptian painting does to us' (Mach 1903: 98, trans. mine; cf. Erdmann 1878).

More commonly, however, positivism about the human sciences was rejected in the German-speaking world, because it lacked any natural way to accommodate the practice of the Historical School. Mill's model was a reasonable fit for some sciences of man, like political economy and associationistic psychology – areas prominent in the British context. But a positivist reformation of the German language *Geisteswissenschaften* would have had to jettison as unscientific all or most of the Historical School's results, including groundbreaking work like that of Wilhelm von Humboldt in anthropology and linguistics, the Grimms in comparative mythology and the history of languages, the great historians Ranke, Mommsen, and Droysen, and historians of special areas of culture, like Jhering on Roman law and Burckhardt on intellectual and art history. Little of this work gave a prominent role to laws, and those it did contain often lacked the clear connections to elementary psychological laws envisioned by Mill.

In his 1862 rectoral address, Helmholtz gave voice to the common, antipositivist sentiment, and foreshadowed many themes around which the later debates would revolve. He insisted that the distinction between the natural sciences and the human sciences is 'grounded in the nature of things' (Helmholtz 1865 [1971: 127], translations mine), arising from differences in both subject matter and method. For example, Helmholtz argued that *geisteswissenschaftlich* method rests ultimately on a distinctive form of 'artistic induction', which differs from the 'logical induction' of natural science, because it 'cannot be carried through to the perfect form of logical inference, or to the erection of an exceptionless valid law' (Helmholtz 1865 [1971: 131–2]). Lacking universally valid laws, the human scientist unifies her data into a scientific whole by deploying a refined ability to see the meaningful connections among cultural phenomena. An instinctive feeling for the material – a 'psychological feeling of tact [*Tactgefühl*]' (Helmholtz 1865 [1971: 132]) – is therefore distinctively essential to method in the human sciences. Helmholtz also anticipated the later debate by hinting that one key source of the differences between the groups of sciences rests in the human scientist's attention to *value*, whereas the natural sciences deal only 'with outer, indifferent matter' (Helmholtz 1865 [1971: 127]).

2. BEGINNINGS: THE 1880s

From the 1880s, debate over the status of the *Geisteswissenschaften* was dominated by four main standpoints. One of these was positivism of Mill's type. The non-positivist camp included the remaining three. First, there was a hermeneutic account of the human sciences offered by Dilthey, which emphasised the interpretive methods of the *Geisteswissenschaften*, and their cognitive aim of understanding (*Verstehen*) the meaning of their objects. Second, Wundt argued for the fundamental dependence of the *Geisteswissenschaften* on psychology. Wundt's view was similar to Mill's, but his more complicated conception of psychology included methods not accessible to natural sciences. He therefore denied the core positivist thesis that the human sciences should be reformed on the methodological model of natural science. Third, a Neo-Kantian position emerged in opposition to Dilthey and Wundt, as well as positivism. This view emphasised the *methodological* autonomy of the human sciences from the natural sciences, at the expense of the difference between the subject matters of spirit (*Geist*) and nature. All three non-positivist approaches operate within Helmholtz's general framework: the aim was to identify the special methods and/or subject matters which make it necessary to defend an independent scientific status for the *Geisteswissenschaften*, and to provide a system of these sciences that articulates their interdependence.

The first two major attempts to fill in the details of Helmholtz's outline were Dilthey 1883 and Wundt 1883. While similar in their claim that psychology is the foundational *Geisteswissenschaft*, Dilthey and Wundt are far apart in spirit, especially in their conceptions of psychology. Dilthey emphasised the role of psychology because it provides the fundamental concepts (e.g., thinking, willing, feeling) in terms of which the directly given inner world of lived experience can be understood. Lived experience and its products form the proper subject matter of the *Geisteswissenschaften*, and therefore all higher, special human sciences also depend on specific psychological concepts. These second-order psychological concepts – e.g., concepts of need, thrift, work, and value in political economy, will and responsibility in law, imagination and the ideal in art (Dilthey 1883: 96–108 [1989: 46–59]) – describe fundamental dispositions of human nature *as they express themselves* in the particular socio-cultural context treated by the relevant special science. Their deployment simultaneously establishes a systematic connection between psychology and the special *Geisteswissenschaften*, and affords certainty to the foundations of those special sciences, because the second-order concepts apply to immediately given lived experience. But the psychology envisioned by Dilthey has little in common with the kind of experimental work included in Wundt's account. For Dilthey, the goal is simply to understand inner psychic life in all its forms, not to provide the causal laws to predict and explain it. By contrast, Wundt rejects Dilthey's appeal to inner experience as the distinctive object of psychology (Wundt 1895: 14), and counts prediction and explanation as central aims of psychology. For Wundt, psychology is a bridge science between the natural sciences and the human sciences. Like a natural science, psychology exploits the experimental and comparative methods, as it seeks the causal laws governing the mind. At the same time, its results play a key ancillary role in the human sciences. The use of comparative method in the *Geisteswissenschaften* takes guidance from the development of that method in psychology, and Wundt treats even the distinctive humanistic methods of interpretation and critique as forms of explanation terminating in the discovery of causally efficacious psychological motives. Thus, while the *Geisteswissenschaften* do have distinctive methods that separate them from the natural sciences, they are related to a psychology that shares much in common with natural science. Moreover, Wundt rejects as unscientific any Helmholtz-style appeal to a special form of intuition proper to the human sciences. In these respects, the separation between the sciences advocated in Wundt 1883 is less sharp than Helmholtz and Dilthey had proposed.

3. COMPLICATIONS: 1890–1910

Starting in the 1890s, Dilthey and Wundt were answered by major Neo-Kantian treatments of the problem, including works by Simmel (1892, 1905, 1918), Windelband (1894), and Rickert (1896–1902, 1898). The Neo-Kantians were unified by several commitments. All opposed positivism by advocating a sharp separation in method and theoretical aims between the human and natural sciences, rather than classifying the sciences in terms of their different subject matters. Neo-Kantians were also concerned to defend historical knowledge against perceived threats of naturalism and historicism. In this context, they opposed historical realism, as well as positivism. They emphasised that the human or historical sciences, like all sciences, operate by separating the essential from the inessential in their data, and they claimed that this selection organises historical experience by means of a (Kantian) conceptual *construction* of the object of knowledge, ordering it into a theoretical whole with other knowledge. Therefore, one of the key tasks for a philosophy of the *Geisteswissenschaften* is the identification of the 'historical a priori' (Simmel 1905 [1977: 87–93, *et passim*]), that is, the conceptual resources which must be presupposed if historical knowledge is to be possible. Since such concepts must be presupposed, they elude naturalistic or historical determination themselves. Windelband and Rickert pushed this line further, and raised the spectre of psychologism as a form of naturalistic determination, concluding that psychology should have no role in grounding the human sciences. Simmel (1905) did not follow the Neo-Kantian line on this point, but continued to treat psychology as the basic human science (but cf. Simmel 1918 for qualifications). Thus, Simmel, Windelband, and Rickert shared significant commitments, but the Neo-Kantian camp was also divided about the role of psychology, and some details of the demarcation criterion.

With the addition of the Neo-Kantian school, the debate opened by Dilthey 1883 and Wundt 1883 grew more complicated. Simmel 1892 combined Dilthey's emphasis on the method of understanding through empathetic recreating of historical life, with the general Kantian framework just rehearsed, and a picture of foundational psychology closer to Wundt's (but even more naturalistic; see Wundt 1895: 135). Simmel's primary aim, brought out more fully in Simmel 1905, was to refute historical realism. Windelband turned to the *Geisteswissenschaften* in his 1894 rectoral address. He argued in favour of a strictly logical[1] demarcation of the two kinds of science, offering an influential distinction between nomothetic sciences, which aim to identify universal laws, and idiographic sciences, whose main cognitive aim is not law discovery, but the description of significant individual objects. Windelband 1894 insisted that individuals as such can become legitimate objects of scientific interest (thereby making idiographic science possible) only if they are valuable or significant. This move makes the conceptual distinction between the natural and the normative central to the demarcation criterion for the human sciences, which are idiographic, and therefore treat valuable objects. Both the nomothetic/idiographic demarcation, and the threat to normativity posed by psychologism, led Windelband to reject the view of Dilthey, Wundt, Simmel, and positivism, that psychology is the fundamental *Geisteswissenschaft*. On the contrary, according to Windelband's demarcation, psychology, *qua* science of the general laws of the mind, is a *natural* science, incapable of accounting for the essentially valuable or significant objects of the human sciences.

This point about psychology was particularly telling against Dilthey, since the work of understanding immediately given lived experience, which he envisioned as the basic human science, had little in common with the increasingly naturalistic, experimental work of contemporary psychology. This issue for Dilthey was already apparent from the contrast between his (1883) conception of psychology and Wundt's (1883). Dilthey 1894 attempted to address the issue by arguing for a reform within psychology, which would de-emphasise explanatory psychology – that is, the search for the causal laws of atomic mental states, whose operation

---

[1] Nineteenth-century logic was less centred on the theory of inference than twentieth-century mathematical logic. Logic texts included major treatments of the theory of the concept and the theory of judgement, before reaching a relatively truncated theory of inference. Especially in its first two parts, traditional logic focused on the strategies of conceptualisation necessary for scientific knowledge, and thus included a great deal of work that we would now classify under epistemology, methodology, philosophy of science, and philosophy of language. It is this traditional logic that Windelband and Rickert had in mind when they insisted that the demarcation of the two groups of sciences must be treated as a purely logical (i.e., for us, a purely conceptual, epistemological, methodological) question. Classic works in traditional logic included Mill 1843 and Wundt 1883 and 1893–5, both of which included extensive discussions of the human sciences, and also works like Lotze 1880 [1874] and Sigwart 1889 [1873].

explains more complicated mental processes – in favour of a descriptive and analytic psychology. This new psychology depends on the analysis of mental life to isolate its meaningful aspects, and develops descriptive concepts adequate to understand these aspects, extending ultimately to the whole of lived experience. Dilthey 1894 counts only the reformed descriptive psychology as fundamental to the *Geisteswissenschaften*.

The next year, Wundt published a revised and expanded theory of the *Geisteswissenschaften* (Wundt 1895). This account still treats psychology as the foundational human science, but it enriches the conception of psychology compared to Wundt 1883, allowing Wundt to accommodate many insights of Dilthey and the Neo-Kantians. The key development is a greater emphasis on the role of *Völkerpsychologie* (ethno-psychology). Ethno-psychology investigates general features of human mental nature as they are expressed through and within social phenomena such as language, myth, and ethical life. Because of the social nature of these phenomena, investigators must rely exclusively on comparative and interpretive methods, rather than controlled experiment, so this part of psychology bears the closest relation to the special human sciences. Ethno-psychology must use their specialised results to identify the capacities it investigates, and in turn, its discoveries inform humanistic interpretations. Since Wundt's (1895) conception of psychology includes these essentially interpretive methods, his psychologistic view now has the resources to acknowledge, with Dilthey, the methodological importance in human sciences of understanding the meaning of cultural objects by appeal to the psychological motives of historical actors and creators. Likewise, Wundt can emphasise, with Windelband, that the explanation and evaluation of significant *individual* historical events, personalities, and cultural products count among the central theoretical aims of the human sciences. At the same time, Wundt retains from (1883) his doctrines (i) that the psychological motives posited in interpretive explanations must be genuinely causal, and figure in laws of a naturalistic individual psychology (Wundt 1895: 237, 240–1); and (ii) that, contra some Kantians, the values exemplified in the objects of the *Geisteswissenschaften* must be immanent in the historical products themselves, and cannot have any transcendental status, which would be inexplicable on psychological grounds (Wundt 1895: 119–21).

In 1896, Windelband's student Rickert published the first part of *Die Grenzen der naturwissenschaftlichen Begriffsbildung* (1896–1902), soon followed by Rickert 1898, which defended and qualified Windelband's purely methodological, nomothetic/idiographic demarcation criterion. Rickert also addressed some major outstanding problems with Windelband's approach, including (1) the problem of how the general concepts essential to any scientific representation could capture an individual object, without simply subsuming it under a general law in the fashion of natural scientific concept formation; and (2) how the human sciences could be objective, when the individual objects that attract their scientific interest were identified by reference to values. Rickert insisted, against Dilthey 1883, that the demarcation criterion must be understood in purely logical terms, and not on the basis of the mental, or spiritual, subject matter of the human sciences. In this connection, Rickert advanced anti-psychologistic, anti-naturalistic, considerations against any role for psychology in the foundations of the human sciences. Finally, Rickert introduced the influential concept of value-relevance, which allowed him to follow Windelband's claim that individuals become objects of scientific interest only if they have some connection to value or significance, without concluding that the human sciences themselves are essentially evaluative (and therefore not fully objective). *Geisteswissenschaften* do not *create* values, or *assess* the value of individuals – at least in the first instance. Rather, they appeal to values to pick out their objects, making objective, *factual* judgements about those individuals' *relevance* to some value. Rickert's position became the dominant Neo-Kantian logic of the *Geisteswissenschaften*. It powerfully influenced Weber (1904, 1906, 1913), and to some extent Simmel (1905). By the late 1920s, Rickert could write in a gratified tone about several followers of Dilthey (Spranger 1921; Rothacker 1927) who had largely come over to his camp on key points. Even E. Troeltsch, who famously complained that Rickert's view was overly formal (Troeltsch 1922: 150–8, 227–39, 559–65), still took Rickert's account of the historical individual as a crucial starting point for demarcating the human sciences (Troeltsch 1922: 22–4, 29ff.).

Not everyone was converted to the Neo-Kantian view, of course. Dilthey continued to articulate his position until his death (Dilthey 1910, 1927). In his later writings, he gives central place to hermeneutic interpretive method as the distinctive mark of the human sciences, instead of resting his argument for their autonomy on the role of psychology as the fundamental *Geisteswissenschaft*. This late view emphasises that cultural artefacts carry objective, publicly accessible, cultural meanings which the human sciences attempt to understand, thereby cutting off any interpretation of his earlier work as claiming that the psychological lives of historical actors and creators are the *only* legitimate objects of understanding. The hermeneutic method is especially appropriate to the investigation of such cultural meanings, because of their holistic nature. The meaning of a sentence in a novel depends on the content of the surrounding work. Similarly, the meaning of the Battle of Borodino (e.g., that the Russians failed to stop Napoleon before Moscow, or that Napoleon failed to crush Kutuzov's army) depends on surrounding events; it does not become clear that the latter meaning is the truth of the battle except in the light of later events (e.g., the Grand Armée's disastrous retreat). The hermeneutic method approaches holistic cultural meanings by its famous circular procedure: first, the interpreter projects a hypothesis about the meaning of the whole, which she uses as background for understanding each part in turn; but the initial hypothesis is only tentative, and the interpreter allows her gradual discoveries about the meanings of the parts to influence her hypothesis about the whole, revisions of which, in turn, once again affect the way she sees the parts. Hermeneutic procedure consists in this repeated mutual adjustment, aiming at interpretive equilibrium. This procedure applies to objective meanings, as well as psychological lived experience. Nevertheless, Dilthey maintains his commitment to a role for empathetic 're-experiencing' of historical life in this process of interpretation, and re-experiencing still operates by analogical inference from characteristics of the historian's own psychological life, to that of her historical subject. Thus, Dilthey's later 'hermeneutic' conception of the human sciences remains largely compatible with his earlier views regarding the actual work done by descriptive psychology in *geisteswissenschaftlich* investigation (see Makkreel 1975). It therefore cannot be said that the late Dilthey moved very far in the direction of his anti-psychologistic Neo-Kantian critics.

In clearer opposition to Rickert, the positivist position was forcefully restated in the late 1890s by Barth (1897, 1899, 1915), who argued that the human sciences must aim to discover the exceptionless laws of history and society, conceived on the model of natural laws. In his view, any scholar who followed Dilthey and the Neo-Kantians by insisting on a distinct, *geisteswissenschaftlich* method was simply departing from science altogether, and practising something more like art (Barth 1899: 325). Barth claims that deploying the concept of causality in the human sciences (which is essential to their status as sciences) already commits us to historical and societal laws, and thus to the ' "natural scientific conception" of history', as far as *method* is concerned, although naturally, the *content* of the human sciences is distinctive (Barth 1899: 341, 355). In these claims, Barth echoed the views of the prominent historian of Germany, K. Lamprecht (1896, 1900, 1909 [1904]), who also insisted on the universal applicability of lawlike causation. Lamprecht thereby rejected as unscientific the view he associated with Ranke and a philosopher (doubtless Windelband or Rickert), that the proper object of history was not law discovery but the description of singular individuals (Lamprecht 1900: 24). On the relations between psychology and history, though, Lamprecht is closer to Wundt than to Mill, advocating a partnership of mutual interdependence, rather than a one-sided dependence of history on psychology.

Even though Rickert did not convince such critics, the positivist revolution in the human sciences simply failed to materialise in the decades after 1900. On the contrary, major figures in the *Geisteswissenschaften* – even in areas like political economy where the role of laws is relatively great – went over to an essentially

Neo-Kantian account of their methodology. Weber, for example, in his leading article after taking over the *Archiv für Sozialwissenschaft und Sozialpolitik* (Weber 1904), argues that, while the sciences of society and economy do sometimes discover laws, such laws are not the aim of human science, but only a preliminary result of instrumental value for the real task, which is 'the knowledge of [individual] *reality* with respect to its cultural *significance*' (Weber 1904 [1949: 75]). Even if the human sciences succeeded in connecting laws of society and economics with lower-level psychological laws, Weber argues, this would not contribute to their genuine goal – describing the particular configurations into which law-described social factors are arrayed in special historical circumstances, and explaining the meaning or significance of those configurations (Weber 1904 [1949: 75–6]). This Rickertian approach is the source of Weber's famous doctrine of 'ideal type concepts' in the cultural sciences (Weber 1904 [1949: 90–7]). These concepts (e.g., the concept of the mediaeval city economy, or of the capitalist industrial economy) do not function as general, descriptive concepts; indeed, they are not met with precisely in any actual economy, and can be applied fruitfully to historical cases which depart quite far from the ideal type. They serve as idealised models facilitating the *understanding* of particular developments in concrete cases, and it is always an empirical and historical question how far the ideal type is realised in particular historical circumstances. These idealisations differ from idealisations in natural science, because the underlying scientific aim of the ideal type concept is to illuminate the significance of the individual historical cases, rather than to elicit general laws that govern the behaviour of those cases. Weber's view is essentially in line with Rickert, and directly contrary to Lamprecht's (1896) rejection of any such ideal concepts in favour of strictly descriptive, general concepts like those of the natural sciences (see Oakes 1988).

4. EPILOGUE

The mantle of the Neo-Kantian account of the *Geisteswissenschaften* was inherited by Cassirer, whose monumental *Philosophy of Symbolic Forms* presents itself as a 'universal philosophy of the cultural sciences' (Cassirer 1921–9 [1955: I, 78]), designed to address the problem that 'general epistemology . . . does not provide an adequate methodological basis for the cultural sciences' (Cassirer 1921–9 [1955: I, 69]). Cassirer rejects the particular form of a logic of the human sciences adopted by Windelband and Rickert, because, as Rickert (1898) himself had noted (anticipating many critics), all sciences must make use of both nomothetic and idiographic procedures; both general concepts and statements of particular initial conditions play key roles in both natural and historical sciences.

Rather than remain content with Rickert's observation that the natural and historical sciences place opposing emphasis on the two methods in identifying their fundamental theoretical aims, Cassirer concludes that the Windelband/Rickert criterion is not decisive or fundamental. In later work (1942), Cassirer traces the demarcation of human from natural sciences to two distinctions: (1) at the level of perception, Cassirer marks off ordinary thing-perception from expression-perception, by which we directly *perceive* the meaning expressed by an action, person, utterance, artefact, etc. (Cassirer 1942 [1961: 39–62]); and (2) at the level of conceptualisation, Cassirer distinguishes between the causal concepts which are central to the natural sciences and the concepts of form and style that are central to the human sciences (Cassirer 1942 [1961: 63–112]). Our interest in the *form* of *geisteswissenschaftlich* objects explains both Windelband's insight that the *Geisteswissenschaften* are concerned with individual objects (conceived now as exemplars bearing formal characteristics) in a way the natural sciences are not, and also Dilthey's insight that the human sciences are interested in the meaning of their objects, which, for Cassirer, is carried by their formal, structural, and stylistic features.

Cassirer follows the general Kantian assumptions about the appropriate structure for any account of the human sciences. Like Rickert, Cassirer wants to explain the methodologically distinctive features of work in the human sciences, not mere differences of subject matter among sciences, and he, too, starts from the actual results of these sciences, and attempts to identify the methodological conditions of their possibility as scientific knowledge. Moreover, Cassirer 1921–9 gives this agenda philosophical centrality, proposing that first philosophy itself should consist of the analysis of the forms of human symbolic activity. The empirical materials for such an analysis must come from human sciences like comparative linguistics, comparative mythology, history of art, history of science, etc. Understanding the methods, structure, and validity of such sciences is therefore of fundamental philosophical importance. In Cassirer's hands, 'the critique of reason becomes the critique of culture' (Cassirer 1921–9 [1955: I, 80]).

Cassirer's view represents the last sweeping solution proffered to the problem of the *Geisteswissenschaften* as set out by Helmholtz, the problem of articulating the distinctive structure of the human sciences as opposed to natural science, while maintaining their status as *sciences*. This left the Neo-Kantian account in possession of the field. The positivist approach continued to have some influence in the twentieth century, particularly in the social sciences, but positivism seems less and less able to capture the structure of most work in the humanities. Consider, for example, the different fates of Hempel's deductive-nomological model of natural scientific explanation, and his parallel idea about historical explanation (Hempel 1942, 1962). Both contributions sparked lively debate, but the D-N model for natural science has attained textbook status as an acknowledged classic, whereas the account of historical explanation does not enjoy such standing.

Psychology, which was supposed to become the fundamental human science, is nowadays most often seen in just the way Windelband and Rickert proposed to see it – that is, not as a human science at all, but as the natural science of the mind. Dilthey's general approach also continued to have influence through the work of Heidegger (1957 [1927]) and Gadamer (1960), but they were less concerned to account for the *scientific* status of distinctive human sciences, and more interested in the suggestion that humanistic enquiry might offer a philosophically richer and deeper kind of access to truth or being, than any science (increasingly understood to mean *only* natural science) ever could (Gadamer 1960 [1989: 428–36, 450–6, 475–6, 484]). In this sense, this phenomenological tradition can be seen as encouraging the humanities to leave the fold of science altogether, just as Barth (1899) thought non-positivists were bound to do, though naturally Gadamer would deny Barth's positivist assumption that any non-scientific enquiry must fail to produce serious knowledge.

5. THE DEMARCATION CRITERION

Our story offers an important philosophical lesson about the structure of a demarcation criterion separating the human from the natural sciences. Positivists like Mill and Barth refused to treat the demarcation as fundamental, but they freely agreed that the moral sciences form a separate class, with its own subject matter. For example, while Mill argues that sociological laws must be derived from underlying, simple, and strictly causal laws, there is no suggestion that they must ultimately be rooted in mechanics or physics. On the contrary, they are to be based on laws of associationistic psychology, another moral science. Likewise, Barth acknowledges the difference in *content* between the human and natural sciences, insisting only that the human sciences must follow natural scientific *method*, if they are to be genuine sciences (Barth 1899: 341, 355).

From this standpoint, we can see the dialectical weakness of Dilthey's (1883) version of the demarcation criterion, relative to the later, Neo-Kantian accounts. Dilthey made differences of subject matter fundamental, but this position does not mark a *principled* contrast to Mill's and Barth's positivist line. Such differences in content are also routine within the natural sciences; indeed *every* science is distinguished from others (especially from the closely related fields) by the fact that it addresses a distinct, special domain of phenomena. The question is not whether there are special sciences of art history, political economy, linguistics, etc., each with its field of research, but rather, whether these sciences share some special mode of cognition, some set of methods and pattern of concept formation, which is proper to the human sciences, but not the natural sciences. Thus, the logical/methodological demarcation is more fundamental than the difference in subject matter. It alone can mark a difference among *forms of science*, as opposed to differences of field within science, and this is why the Neo-Kantians insisted so strongly on the logical nature of the demarcation criterion. In one sense, this result confirms the seriousness of the positivist view: either there is some basic difference between alternative forms of scientific thinking and methodology, or positivism about the human sciences is right.

CONCLUSION

The view that the humanities do not belong with the sciences at all has perhaps become the most popular way of understanding the problem of knowledge in the human sciences today. In the conventional scholarly common sense, the social sciences are widely supposed to approximate natural scientific methodology, and the humanities are widely supposed to be simply unscientific. Some lament this state of the humanities, as Barth did; others praise it as a potential source of knowledge outstripping any science, like Gadamer sometimes seems to.

The assumption that humanistic knowledge is simply not science may simplify our attempts to understand science, but only at the cost of complicating (or even shirking the task of developing) any account of a wider class we might call disciplined expert knowledge. In this sense, the problem as posed by the non-positivist side in the *Geisteswissenschaften* debate – the problem of conceiving the human sciences as methodologically distinct from natural science, but nonetheless as sciences – has a great deal to recommend it. Surely work in the humanities produces knowledge, and equally surely, its claims are typically not everyday knowledge, but expert knowledge, complete with methodological standards, disciplinary identities, etc. Our confidence that this knowledge is not science is simply the flip side of a significant embarrassment in our scholarly self-understanding – the embarrassment that we lack any serious account of what is distinctive about humanistic knowledge, what underwrites its claim to be expert knowledge, and what justifies our persistent sense that the humanities belong together as a class, as a kind of system within the larger realm of knowledge.

The *Geisteswissenschaften* debate of a century ago generated a number of important insights about the problem conceived in this way: Dilthey's idea that the human sciences aim at the understanding of cultural meanings, and therefore deploy hermeneutical methods; Wundt's insistence that an adequate account of human nature must include the culturally mediated capacities which he wanted to investigate through ethno-psychology; Windelband's and Rickert's insight that the humanities are distinctively concerned with individual objects; and Cassirer's account of concepts of form and style. The historical debate also produced an important result that sets a condition of adequacy for any improved philosophy of humanistic knowledge: any demarcation criterion that captures the distinctive form of such knowledge will emphasise its *form* as science, as well as its differences from natural scientific knowledge in method and theoretical aims. These contributions provide useful starting points for new investigation. That said, many of the core philosophical difficulties which faced thinkers in the historical debate still await solution; this is especially true of attempts to understand the nature and sources of normativity. Our predecessors a century ago had a clearer grasp of the nature of the problems raised by knowledge in the human sciences than perhaps any generation since. Progress on these problems, however, is still elusive. In this case, therefore, close attention to the historical debate is a crucial first step for philosophical investigation.

FROM POLITICAL ECONOMY TO POSITIVE
ECONOMICS

MARGARET SCHABAS

1. INTRODUCTION

Although discourses on the subject of wealth and money reach back to antiquity, extensive theorising about economic phenomena only emerged in the seventeenth and eighteenth centuries. Adam Smith's *Wealth of Nations* (1776) launched the classical theory of political economy which was developed in the nineteenth century, most notably by Jean-Baptiste Say, Thomas Robert Malthus, David Ricardo, and John Stuart Mill. Despite numerous differences, they were of one mind on the significance of labour in determining value and prices, on the perpetual strife between landowners, capitalists, and labourers, and on the inevitable onset of the 'stationary state' due to a tendency of the profit-rate to decline. Notwithstanding the fact that the British economy had grown at an unprecedented rate since the mid-eighteenth century, nineteenth-century economists were preoccupied with the problems of scarcity of land and capital, coupled with an overabundant population.

By the 1820s, it was commonplace in learned circles to refer to political economy as a science. It had an extensive list of laws and, in the hands of Ricardo, had gained a deductive rigour that was often compared to Euclidean geometry. Nevertheless, political economy was almost entirely a literary pursuit. Ricardo used hypothetical numerical examples to illustrate his principles, but he did not posit algebraic functions or undertake quantitative verifications of his derivations. The basic assumptions about human behaviour were also left rather vague, though it could be argued that, with the immediate ancestry of Hume and Smith, classical political economy was actually founded upon a rich set of insights into human nature.

2. THE MARGINAL REVOLUTION

In the early 1870s, William Stanley Jevons and Léon Walras independently called for a radical transformation of the subject, towards what came to be known as neoclassical economics. This so-called Marginal Revolution constitutes the most important watershed in the history of economics. Building on the insight that price ratios are commensurable with marginal utilities (and not, strictly speaking, with labour inputs), they found the means to insert the calculus into economic theory. Economics, they argued, was necessarily a mathematical science; in the market place our minds calculate and compare infinitesimal quantities of goods and prices with the goal of maximising utility.

Jevons died in 1882, at the relatively young age of forty-six, but he was satisfied that his campaign to mathematise economics had taken hold in the decade since the publication of his *Theory of Political Economy* (1871). Francis Ysidro Edgeworth, John Neville Keynes, Philip Henry Wicksteed, and Alfred Marshall all endorsed the utility theory of value and mathematical methods in a series of books issued in the 1880s and 1890s. Jevons also inspired two American scientists, Simon Newcomb and Irving Fisher, to take up his cause.

Marshall's *Principles of Economics* (1890) served as the authoritative text for the next fifty years and, as a longstanding professor of political economy at Cambridge University, he shaped the minds of the next two generations, notably A. C. Pigou, Arthur Bowley, and John Maynard Keynes. Jevons had proposed that the name economics replace that of political economy, but it was Marshall who consolidated the substitution, accompanied by explicit declarations of political and ethical neutrality on the part of economists. Although in his later years Marshall became more equivocal about the merits of mathematics in economic theory, as a second wrangler his formulations, most of which were delegated to his appendixes, were much more rigorous than those by Jevons.

In addition to the calculus, Jevons had used probability theory in the case of exchange under uncertainty, and statistical techniques in his applied work. Edgeworth developed both of these lines of enquiry, as well as some elementary topology to represent market exchange in the form of indifference and contract curves. Edgeworth is also celebrated for introducing Lagrangian multipliers into economic analysis and thus recognising in full that economic exchange can be treated in terms of constrained maximisation. Marshall favoured the use of geometry and cultivated many of the simple graphs of market exchange that are now the bread and butter of elementary textbooks. He gave us the demand curve as we know it and the graphical illustrations of consumer's and producer's surplus. Economists have since made use of fixed point theorems and set theory, and are proud to point to genuine contributions to applied mathematics (Franklin 1983).

Numerous pre-1870 economists had incorporated mathematics into their analyses, most notably William Whewell and A. A. Cournot. Why the widespread shift to a mathematical theory of economics only transpired in the

1870s and 1880s is difficult to explain, but certainly one key factor was the provision of new conceptual foundations. The early neoclassicals construed everything in terms of utility, even capital, and thus freed economics from its material constraints. The economy was mind-driven through and through, as plastic and expandable as the human imagination. In that respect, economics had become a mental science. As Jevons remarked, 'The theory presumes to investigate the condition of a mind, and bases upon this investigation the whole of Economics' (Jevons 1871 [1957: 14–15]). Scarcity no longer haunted the economist as a fundamental stumbling block, precisely because he traded only in mental states. As Alfred Marshall remarked: 'man cannot create material things. In the mental and moral world indeed he may produce new ideas; but when he is said to produce material things, he really only produces utilities; or in other words, his efforts and sacrifices result in changing the form or arrangement of matter to adapt it better for the satisfaction of wants' (Marshall 1890 [1920: 53]).

Walras demonstrated algebraically that a stable equilibrium set of prices would clear the market, insofar as the number of unknown variables (prices and quantities exchanged) equalled the number of equations (supply and demand). He could not, alas, specify the solution numerically, nor move to the more realistic setting of a dynamic market. The prototypical market was that of an auction, where sale prices were announced sequentially, creating a groping process (*tâtonnement*) towards final prices. To his credit, Walras recognised that his account was an idealisation of actual market conditions, but nonetheless believed that utility calculations (*rareté*) were the foundation for the analysis of market prices.

Despite numerous efforts, Walras was unable to forge close ties with his British contemporaries, and remained in relative obscurity as a Professor at the University of Lausanne until his death in 1910. Nevertheless, it is the Walrasian system of general equilibrium that eventually became the predominant theory by the 1920s, particularly with French, Italian, and American economists. For the sake of greater realism, Marshall had wedded his analysis to the concept of partial equilibrium, but it was Walras's efforts to seek a general equilibrium that carried the day. One can view the Arrow-Debreu formulations of the theory of general equilibrium during the 1950s as the crowning achievement of the neoclassical programme (see Ingrao and Israel 1987; Weintraub 1985).

3. WELFARE ECONOMICS

The problem of distributive justice has been at the centre of economic discourse since Aristotle, but in the 1880s it received a new lease of life with the absorption of utilitarianism and the techniques of marginalism. Henry Sidgwick,

Edgeworth, Marshall, and A. C. Pigou are the most important pre-war contributors. They were also united in the belief that economic wellbeing was highly correlated with welfare overall. Sidgwick laid the foundation with his distinction between the private and the social net product. Marshall's tools of consumer's and producer's surplus paved the way to other graphical representations of welfare economics. Edgeworth developed the principle of 'equal sacrifice' in terms of net utility and demonstrated that the principle of diminishing marginal utility of income entails a system of progressive taxation.

The first authoritative text on the subject was Pigou's *Wealth and Welfare* (1912). His command of mathematical economics, particularly marginal analysis, enabled much more precise terminology. In keeping with the revival of utilitarianism, Pigou defined welfare in mental rather than in material terms. Taking his cue from G. E. Moore, he resisted a definition of the good and thus of welfare, which he made synonymous to the good. Pigou focused on the goal of maximising the national product via technical progress, as the means to increase overall welfare. While apprised of the problem of externalities, he measured welfare exclusively in monetary terms. He also addressed the problem of transferring wealth from the rich to the poor via taxes and subsidies, and he proposed that a wealthy country should insist upon a minimal standard of living for the poor and destitute. In most problems, Pigou envisioned a greater role for the state.

Social welfare functions generally assume that utility can be treated in cardinal terms: only this assumption allows for the addition of individual utility functions and thus meaningful comparisons of aggregates. Paradoxically, most of the early neoclassicals, with the notable exception of Edgeworth, insisted that one could not draw interpersonal comparisons of utility, that each mind is inscrutable, and that there is no universal scale for the measurement of utility. Thus they implicitly assumed that utility could only be treated in ordinal terms. Yet they also assumed, without justification, that market prices were the reflection of subjective calculations and that one could therefore add up utility functions from the individual to the market as a whole. This manoeuvre is further unwarranted if one takes into account the fact that commodities are not independent of one another and that demand is not constant as income increases. To this day, these inconsistencies have never been fully resolved. Economists believe that the only sensible interpretation of utility is the ordinal one (there is no measurable unit such as a 'util'), yet they blithely treat utility in aggregate terms, especially in welfare economics. Edgeworth and Marshall made some headway on the matter by assuming that the marginal utility of income was constant for all persons, but economists are still committed to an unwarranted causal account whereby the utility judgements of individuals result in price movements and aggregate social welfare.

Vilfredo Pareto, who succeeded Walras at Lausanne, developed some important conceptual apparatus for problems in welfare economics, even though, ironically, he heaped scorn on the subject. Pareto's law established the rigidity of income distribution, stating that even under economic growth it was impossible for the poor to appropriate a greater percentage of the pie. Pareto also came increasingly to believe that economics should be merged with sociology and that subjective phenomena such as utility (or in his terminology, ophelimity) should be turned over to the psychologists. He was also increasingly sceptical about the correspondence of neoclassical economic theory to the real world, and he came to see that the mathematical aspirations of Jevons and Walras were at the expense of realism. Nonetheless, the notions of Pareto optimality remain at the centre of welfare economics; they permit one to make meaningful comparisons between alternative distributions of wealth in terms of marginal rates of substitution, without an explicit reference to utility. A Pareto improvement transpires when one person's lot is improved without reducing the lot of others, and a Pareto optimum obtains when no reallocation could bring about such an improvement.

Welfare economics necessarily incorporates ethical judgements, both in determining what counts as socially desirable and in carrying out its policy recommendations given a world of scarcity. Yet its early practitioners often resisted ethical excursions, despite a solid grounding in the subject. Possibly swept away by the powerful new techniques offered by marginal utility analysis, Edgeworth, Marshall, and Pigou maintained that they could reach objective, ethically neutral recommendations. Jevons had laid the cornerstone when he insisted that economists deal only with the lower wants: pushpin, not poetry. But his caveat was forgotten over time, and Pigou believed that one could make tradeoffs between any two goods, however much they might differ in terms of their ethical importance.

4. AUSTRIAN SCHOOL

In Vienna, a very distinctive school of economic theory commenced with Carl Menger's *Grundsätze der Volkswirtschaftslehre* (1871). As Professor of Political Economy at the University of Vienna, Menger spawned a school of thought which counted among its adherents Friedrich von Wieser, Eugen von Böhm-Bawerk, Ludwig von Mises, Friedrich von Hayek, and Joseph Schumpeter. Because the latter three emigrated during the interwar years, the influence of the

Austrian school is also evident in mid-twentieth century British and American economics.

Menger has often been joined with Jevons and Walras as an instigator of the Marginal Revolution, because he too made use of the notion of marginal utility and saw himself as overturning the views of his predecessors. Menger's major text appeared in the same year as Jevons's, suggesting a Mertonian multiple. But if one looks more closely at their respective historical trajectories, this was purely coincidental. Menger's *Principles of Economics* was a reaction to the German historical school of Wilhelm Roscher and Gustav Schmoller, which was itself highly critical of the classical theory of political economy.

Menger was also critical of Bentham's utilitarianism. He portrayed persons not as pleasure seekers but as rational agents. Menger privileged introspection and a priori reasoning. Economic phenomena were essentially the products of individual minds – a logic of choice – in a world in which information is meagre and the satisfaction of needs and wants is a time-consuming process. Menger also repudiated the use of mathematical methods. The main agenda was to set down the essential attributes of economic phenomena – value, profits, etc. – and not to discern functional relationships between them. A strong allegiance to methodological individualism kept the Austrians indifferent to the techniques of aggregation and welfare economics, and focused them more on the heroic efforts of the entrepreneur in driving economic growth. Following Mises, Austrian economics also endorsed a strong liberalism if not libertarianism. Austrian economists evince a complete faith in market mechanisms and an appreciation for cases of unintended beneficial consequences (Smith's invisible hand). For all of the above reasons, it seems better to keep their thinking apart from that of the early neoclassicists.

5. AMERICAN INSTITUTIONALISM

Under the influence of Herbert Spencer and Social Darwinism, several American economists of this period cultivated a very different approach to the science of economics. Thorstein Veblen most notably opposed the methodological individualism and strong assumptions of rationality that were so central to neoclassical economics. Instead, he explored the evolution of economic institutions and emphasised the role of instincts and habits. His *Theory of the Leisure Class* (1899) advanced the concepts of conspicuous consumption, pecuniary emulation, and the division of labour in terms of our species-being. He was uncannily prescient about cultural practices in late twentieth-century America.

John R. Commons and Richard Ely were also prominent voices of American institutionalism. Like Veblen, they opposed the mathematical turn of the neoclassicals. They placed much more emphasis on the broader social and historical context, and highlighted some of the distinctively American problems of underdeveloped capital markets, abundant resources, and imperfect competition (monopolies). While these efforts were eclipsed by the spread of neoclassical theory, certain ideas survived into the 1940s and have recently been revived by the 'new institutionalism' of the 1980s (see Rutherford 1994).

6. SCIENTIFIC STATUS

While political economy had been widely viewed as a science since the eighteenth century, it gained additional standing in the period examined here. We find numerous references to the label 'positive economics' in the Comtean sense. Ironically, Comte did not believe that there could be a separate science of economics. But his aversion to metaphysical notions and admonition to restrict enquiry to the observable were widespread sentiments among *fin-de-siècle* economists. Many took this to mean that one could devise a pure economics in advance of policy applications and that it would be neutral in terms of political and ethical decisions. Applied economics was thus sharply distinguished from pure economic theory.

The early neoclassicists were also keen to strengthen the empirical study of economics; one finds frequent declarations of the possibility of verification and the grounding of economic analysis in the realm of the observable. As Jevons declared in his *Principles of Science*, 'among the most unquestionable rules of scientific method is that first law that *whatever phenomenon is, is*. We must ignore no existence whatever, . . . if a phenomenon does exist, it demands some kind of explanation' (Jevons 1874: 769). Thus, contrary to the classical economists, one no longer theorised about a natural and unobservable price to which market prices gravitated. Rather, every observable price was of equal status and thus to be subsumed under economic theory.

Nevertheless, the early neoclassicals did not always practise what they preached. Jevons, Edgeworth, and Marshall were quite enthusiastic about psychology, despite its truck with the unobservable. True, they favoured recent empirical work, by Alexander Bain and William Carpenter in the case of Jevons and Marshall, and by Theodor Fechner in the case of Edgeworth. But one of the most metaphysical concepts ever to grace economics, namely utility, was the lynchpin of the early neoclassical economists. It was only purged much later with Samuelson's theory of revealed preferences.

The advent of positive economics was part and parcel of a wider movement to enhance the professional standing of the discipline. Political economy had been taught in conjunction with the study of law since the early 1700s, particularly on the continent, but only became widespread as a recognisable field in the latter half of the nineteenth century. In Britain, most classical economists, including Ricardo and Mill, did not hold university positions. Only in the period discussed here did the number of professorships grow considerably. Marshall and Edgeworth also oversaw the establishment, in 1890, of the Royal Economic Society (originally the British Economic Assocation) and the *Economic Journal*. In the United States, the American Economics Assocation was founded in 1885, and the *American Economic Review* in 1891. Both organisations and journals have remained at the forefront of the profession, which now numbers in the tens of thousands in the United States alone.

Links between economics and philosophical ideas were very much in evidence during the period from 1870 to 1914, and a full explanation of the shifts in the methods and content of economic theory must take them into account. J. S. Mill wrote the first extensive essay on economic methodology in 1836, and in many respects his arguments for viewing economics as a separate and inexact science are still meritorious (see Hausman 1992). Mill had also deemed economics a deductive science like physics, and these sentiments were cemented even more by the early neoclassical and Austrian economists. Mill had also insisted that economic man was a hypothetical construct, that no one ever supposed that people are driven solely by the pursuit of wealth. But the 1870s brought a distinct shift toward a conviction that economic man was a flesh and blood creature. Both Menger and Marshall insisted that economists had a realistic image of human agency; subsequent construals of rational economic man have made even greater claims to veracity. And yet the pretensions of universality and use of mathematics suggest that the neoclassical model is much more stylised than the classical one.

Of all the early neoclassicists, Jevons contributed the most to philosophical literature. His *Principles of Science* (1874) was the only major book on the philosophy of science in the fifty-year period between Mill's *System of Logic* (1843) and Karl Pearson's *Grammar of Science* (1892). It popularised the new logic of Boole and De Morgan, and advanced the thesis of logicism. While most inspired by John Herschel's appeals to analogical reasoning, Jevons absorbed the turn towards greater scepticism among the scientists of his day. He underscored the importance of non-Euclidean geometry and the theory of probability and recognised that physics was replete with limitations and uncertainties. Biology and economics were not as far down the epistemological ladder as Comte had once maintained.

Edgeworth had first published on the subject of ethics, and Marshall, who was much more immersed in continental philosophy, had taught logic and ethics in his early days at Cambridge. Benjamin Jowett, who considered Ricardo to have been the greatest mind to come along since Plato, was the one to steer Marshall towards the dismal science. But Marshall downplayed his philosophical allegiances when it came to economics; for him practical considerations always outweighed theoretical ones. However, his most renowned student, John Maynard Keynes, restored philosophical links to the forefront via his close associations with G. E. Moore, Frank Ramsey, Bertrand Russell, and Ludwig Wittgenstein.

Walras was a disciple of Victor Cousin, an idealist, and took socialist ideas very seriously. While less philosophical than Jevons, he articulated some methodological rules for attaining economic realism and grappled with the philosophical dimensions of economic needs. Pareto engaged in lengthy debates on the subject of economic value with Benedetto Croce. Menger was directly inspired by Franz Brentano and, more indirectly, by Aristotle. Through Menger's son Karl and Otto Neurath, the Vienna circle of logical positivism left its mark on economics.

As yet another indication that economics and philosophy were closely linked in the pre-1914 period, it is worth noting that both Charles Sanders Peirce and John Dewey wrote on economics, albeit in a fragmentary fashion. Their pragmatism held sway among American economists for several decades, first with Newcomb, Fisher, and the aforementioned institutionalists, and then with Milton Friedman, who put forth an enduring definition of positive economics in his seminal paper of 1953.

Economists since Smith had looked to physics as the science to emulate, but this mostly took the form of the search for laws and a predilection for deductive reasoning. The early neoclassicals went much further in that they cultivated analogies to mechanics and thermodynamics. Jevons treated exchange as analogous to the law of the lever, and thereby employed the analytical tool of an infinitesimal displacement from equilibrium. He also borrowed imagery from the pendulum and made some groundbreaking insights into the problem of dimensions in economics under the guidance of physical dimensions (space, time, and mass). Edgeworth treated utility as analogous to potential energy and thereby utilised Lagrangian techniques. His *Mathematical Psychics* (1881) is replete with references to physics. Fisher had written his dissertation under the supervision of J. Willard Gibbs, a leading physicist at Yale University, and as a result his books and papers draw frequent comparisons between economics and physics. Fisher's celebrated money equation, for example, mimics the ideal gas law. Walras, who first trained in engineering, made considerable use of idealised conditions and the properties of equilibria in mechanical terms. Even Pareto, despite numerous reservations, allowed his scientific training to seep into his economic formulations.

Most non-economists are suspicious of such efforts to imitate and incorporate physics; they seem to be unfounded steps to dress economics in mathematical garb, with little gained in terms of economic insight. And there is a large grain of truth in this view. But there is nonetheless a path by which one might justify the use of mathematics in economics, at least as much as in physics. As Jevons pointed out, the phenomena of the economy are quantitative. Indeed, it is the only realm that is truly Pythagorean. Prices, interest rates, and the like are numbers to begin with. They do not require a mapping from physical events to mathematical representations, as is the case even for the more exact sciences such as positional astronomy. Furthermore, as Jevons argued under the inspiration of George Boole, our minds are governed by the laws of logic and thus necessarily operate in algebraic terms. It is only a short step to the belief that, insofar as we make rational calculations in the market place, we are necessarily reasoning in a quantitative and hence mathematical fashion. The source of disdain for mathematical economics should not, therefore, be about whether mathematics is warranted; it clearly is. The problem lies in whether it can be used judiciously and advance our understanding of economic patterns. Even mainstream economists often note, albeit with some sarcasm, that the mathematics often drives the economic argument rather than vice versa. And although economists are not renowned for making reliable predictions, Nobel Laureate George Stigler, based on statistical analyses of the leading periodicals in economics during the first half of the twentieth century, established not only that the majority of articles used mathematics by the 1950s, but also that by the year 2003 the subject would be entirely mathematical. Alas, he did not live long enough to see his prediction come true.

SOCIOLOGY AND THE IDEA OF
SOCIAL SCIENCE

GEOFFREY HAWTHORN

INTRODUCTION

For the larger part of its history, those practising what they think of as a 'sociology' have not intended to be doing 'science', and have not been taken by others to be doing so. It is true that Auguste Comte, who coined the neologism in the 1830s, did so to distinguish a kind of social understanding that would be consonant with what he took to be the modern *esprit*, and called it 'positive'. It is also true that nearly two hundred years later 'sociology' is commonly thought of as one of the 'social sciences'. Comte's programme for the reorganisation of all knowledge, however, had no direct intellectual descendants, and to think of 'sociology' in the twenty-first century as a 'science' is to accept a classification that is more institutional, or instrumental, than intellectual. It would nevertheless be wrong to suggest that there has never been any such aspiration. There has, and this was perhaps at its strongest at the turn of the nineteenth and twentieth centuries. Even then, however, it was not pervasive. In Germany, the contemporary contrast was between the *Naturwissenschaften* and the *Geisteswissenschaften*, and although sociology might in practice have descended to empirical enquiry, and ordered the facts it discovered in the manner of what might be described as the administrative sciences, those who considered it in principle put it fairly firmly in the second of these two classes. In England and the United States, where the empirical impulse was stronger, the idiom in the later nineteenth and early twentieth centuries may have been that of 'evolution', but this merely described the conviction, in the one, that there was some sort of progression from the simpler societies to the more complex, in the other, that what drove modernity was the pursuit of interest and the competition between interests, a conviction that soon found it convenient, in a culture that did not think of itself historically, to talk instead of 'pragmatism'. Only in France, and even there, only in one man, Emile Durkheim, was there a clear and deliberate intention to establish 'a science of the social'.

DURKHEIM

Emile Durkheim was a Kantian who, like Kant's more immediate successors in Germany, accepted his starting point but could not accept it as a premise. For Kant's immediate successors, to start with the idea of the rational individual who in virtue of his reason was autonomous, in principle free from natural determination and thereby capable of freely creating the rational law, was to start with something that had itself to be understood, perhaps reflexively, and perhaps also historically. For Durkheim, it was to start with an idea that had to be understood, as he put it, sociologically. But the difference was little more than nominal. Durkheim's philosophy of history was considerably more attenuated than that, say, of Hegel. It could not, indeed, have been more primitive. Once upon a time, there had been individuals who did not act individually, but collectively, and did not think of themselves as individuals, but as members of a group or society. Now, there were individuals who, as a result of the economic division of labour, were individuated, acted as individuals, and thought of themselves as such. The mistake of the philosophical individualists, both the Kantians and the philosophic radicals, like Spencer, was to suppose that these latter-day individuals owed nothing to society. Empirically, Durkheim argued, they owed their origin to its history, or 'evolution'. Morally, they owed a duty to preserve the kind of society that sustained them as the self-conscious individuals they were. This, he said, cleverly turning the conservatives' rhetoric against them in a polemic against the anti-Dreyfusards in 1898, was 'the religion of today'. In Kant's language, which Durkheim himself did not use, the 'phenomenal' self, the seat of desire and interest, was indeed individual, but the 'noumenal', the seat of reason, was social. The 'religion of today' was sociology.

In the 1890s, however, Durkheim did not wish to give the impression that the social was a kind of collective transcendental, accessible to reason but drawing its imaginative force and moral power from something akin to faith. His teachers at the Ecole Normale had left him with the belief that cognitive authority now lay with science, and the belief that each science has its own distinctive ontological realm. The authority of his sociology, therefore, could lie only in his being able to show that it was a science of the distinctively social. This, he characterised as the *conscience collective*. But since science dealt in facts, he had to demonstrate the facticity of this (see Durkheim 1895). That, he saw, he could only do indirectly, by showing what can go wrong when modern man has an imperfect sense of his relation to the social. The plainest indication of such imperfection, he agreed with many of his contemporaries, was taking one's own life. Suicide, indeed, was not just an indication of imperfection, but its direct effect, and from the rates available to him in volumes of official statistics, he wrote a monograph

(Durkheim 1897) to distinguish its kinds, which he classified according to four imputed kinds of fault in the individual's relation to the *conscience collective*. In this way, he used information being gathered by methods useful to the administration of the modern state to make the case for a cognitively and morally authoritative sociology as the science of 'objectively' demonstrable 'subjective' facts.

Yet one of the weaknesses in this argument that Durkheim continued to worry about made his name even as it undermined his claim. If *consciences collectives*, as he had argued, varied with the nature of the collective, if the quality of 'the social' varied accordingly, then there was no one quality for sociology to be the science of. Indeed, in some *consciences collectives*, the Kantian preconditions for science itself could be absent. To practise a science of the social on societies whose conceptions of themselves allowed for no such thing would be to practise a knowing misapprehension. He battled against this inference, most notably in an attempted refutation of William James's essay on pragmatism, but did so vainly. Eventually, he turned instead to what even then was regarded as the anthropological question of how cognitive categories connect to the social forms of those who hold them formed and had the moral force that they did. In preparation for a treatise on *La morale* of his own society, which he did not live to begin, he wrote *The Elementary Forms of the Religious Life* (Durkheim 1912) about what he saw as the simplest society, or set of societies, still in existence, that in native Australia. The 'science' that he thereby bequeathed owed nothing to the conception of science with he had begun.

It is ironic that the philosophically most deliberate case for a 'science' of 'sociology' should have so decisively undermined itself. It is less ironic, but more telling, that the most deliberate case for a 'science' of 'sociology' was undermined in pursuit of what, historically, had always been the subject's central purpose. This had been to overcome the distinction that gained ground in the later eighteenth and early nineteenth centuries between ethics and history in order to ground a naturalistic morality. The elements of such a project were not, of course, Durkheim's own. They had always been to settle on a coherent, defensible and *ab initio* appealing conception of the nature of individual human beings as they were, or could be; to specify the conditions in which this nature could flourish; to show how these conditions could obtain, either by selecting from among those which already exist or working to produce those that were necessary (and perhaps even sufficient) in the future; and to conclude that when realised, these would constitute the best end. What has been peculiar to naturalisms of a distinctively sociological kind was the belief that the morally important characteristics of human nature do not just require certain social conditions, but are themselves, and entirely, a social product, created by 'society'. (Durkheim himself went so far as to suggest in the 1900s that the moral sense itself was contingent on the kind of society in which one lived, rather than something which all individuals have *qua* individuals.) It is a belief which, for the degree of universalism that moral theorists have commonly sought, requires all moral beings to be the product of one kind of society. It is also a belief which, whether moving to a putatively universalist conclusion or to one of a more contingent, relativist kind, casts doubt on the persistence and perhaps even the existence of moral agency. A few, most notably Foucault, were to be prepared by the end of the twentieth century to take the argument that far. But there is no question that in so doing, they were practising what might be described as a moral social science.

THE IDEA OF A SOCIAL SCIENCE

In practice, sociology as a recognisable 'science' has been more mundane. In common with the other social sciences, it has since at least the early nineteenth century been mundane as science in using the methods of descriptive and inductive statistics that were devised for other purposes as methodological conventions with which to specify the generalisations that all science, by convention, should produce. In themselves, these methods have little of philosophical interest that is distinctive to sociology. It has also, at least since the early nineteenth century, been more literally mundane as a social and political practice, in that it has served the purposes of the modern administrative state (or the purposes of those who are critical of what a particular administrative state might be doing and wish on grounds that those who govern it would accept to present a case for doing something different). In themselves, these purposes also are of little philosophical interest. In conjunction, however, they are. To see sociology as a mundane science in pursuit of mundane purposes, what in seventeenth-century England was nicely and precisely described as 'political arithmetic', is to see something of wider importance about the very idea of a social science.

This is in fact several things. The first is substantive. The modern idea of 'society' dates only from the eighteenth century. In its first use, in the thinking of the Scottish political economists, it marked a realm of relations that were independent of the state and derived rather from the similarly new sphere of 'the economy'. Previous ideas, in the earlier use, for instance, of 'civil society', were of entities that would in the nineteenth and twentieth centuries be thought of as instances of the 'political'. The term 'society' came into common use in the nineteenth, and by then, 'a society' was taken to refer to relations, and commonly, relations of all kinds, political, legal, cultural, and economic, as well as what in the vernacular would be thought of as the more narrowly 'social', among the people of a territorially defined nation state. States were coming increasingly to be thought of as the political expression of nations, and 'nations' were more or less idealised and frequently imagined representations of 'the people', or 'the society', that states governed. 'Sociology', as the nineteenth-century science of society, was in fact the science of the qualities, precepts, practices, and institutions of the citizens of modern nation states. In its presumption that 'societies' were distinct, whatever common properties they might share, it accordingly became a convenient instrument of information for the administration of these states.

The second important feature of the idea of a social science followed from this, and was methodological. It suited governments to presume that citizens of the state they governed shared qualities that distinguished them, as the citizens of that particular state, from others. It came therefore to be presumed that one could generalise across them. And in order effectively to govern its citizens, the state needed to know what these qualities were. Sociology served the purpose. As the generalising 'science' of the social, it could conveniently use the new methods of descriptive (and later in the century, inductive) statistics to gather information that the state required and generalise about it. Hence the systematic census of population, the invention of the social survey, the new idea of 'public opinion' (which originated in the United States at the beginning of the twentieth century) and polls to ascertain it, together with the succession of similar instruments that governments and a range of non-governmental organisations since, including those that have wished to press government from outside, have devised to find out what they claim they need to know.

The third feature followed in turn from this, and might, in an extended sense of the word, be thought of as philosophical. States not only need information on which to rest their policies of control, taxation, and, more recently, provision. (And it has not only been the governments of modern states that have had such a need; William I's Domesday survey is one of the earliest instances of what might now be thought of as 'social science' in the service of administration in what is now Britain. States' intelligence services, even if necessarily less systematic, have been another.) States also need information on which they can devise measures with the authority that, as states, they have to exercise to remain the states they are. The intellectual authority of science has accordingly, and conveniently, come to serve the political authority of the government of modern states. Sociology, as one of the new administrative social sciences, had a strong motive, therefore, to acquire such authority. The persistently pressing academic question of whether sociology is, or can be, a science has also been a pressingly political question.

Historically, however, an interesting question of a rather different kind arises from this. Why is it that the question of whether sociology is, or can be, a science has ceased to press as urgently as it once did? The answers, once again, are both political and intellectual. Politically, the instruments of the nineteenth-century 'social science' of administration have since become part of the ordinary business of modern government. It has become usual to make the case for policy, inside government and outside it, with general information that is assembled and presented quantitatively. Offices of the census have almost everywhere widened to become offices of general social statistics. Of course, the validity and reliability of much of this information, the intrusions that gathering it make into citizens' lives, and more recently, the offence that doing so presents to what are taken by some to be their 'rights', have long been derided. 'Thou shalt not', insisted W. H. Auden in a piece of doggerel in the 1930s, 'commit a social science'; 'thou shalt not answer questionnaires'. Nonetheless, although particular 'findings' may still be challenged, the practice itself has ceased to be much remarked upon. In private organisations and others of a non-governmental kind, as well as in government itself, it is taken for granted that comprehensive 'data' are indispensable. Questions about what kind of practice gathering, presenting and working from data amount to have ceased publicly to be asked. Practically, its authority is all but taken for granted.

UNDERSTANDING SOCIAL ACTION

Intellectually, by contrast, the idea of a 'science' of sociology has in the twentieth century been subject to a series of attacks from which, at the start of the twenty-first, it seems unlikely to recover. The objections from those who even in the later nineteenth and early twentieth centuries, regarded social understanding as one of the *Geisteswissenschaften* are described elsewhere in this volume. These in general derived from an idealist metaphysic. The claim was that human actions had their impulse in the workings of mind and imagination that were wholly inaccessible to any technique or instrument of observation, and had rather to be grasped through sympathy with those who performed them. Later objections have come from the very different and purportedly unmetaphysical quarter of the philosophy of language. The argument here starts from much the same point as that of the idealists: action is not mere behaviour, bodily motion that can reliably be observed and sufficiently explained as a physiological response to observable external stimuli. It avoids an imputation of *Geist*, however, and points instead to the fact that action, in being constituted by conscious mental intention, is constituted thereby by language. An action is the action it is as it is described by the actor. Actions, therefore, the subject matter of a sociology, are the actions they are within a particular language. The sociologist may translate back into his or her own language, and in so doing, may not only choose to re-characterise the actor's action but also to put it in a larger class of actions. Whichever language is used, however, the point remains: to grasp a language is to grasp a set of concepts and their meaning, and not any independently observable and more widely generalisable fact. All understanding of actions, that is to say, is relative to a language.

Moves in what in the twentieth century came to be described as 'the philosophy of science' have extended the argument. Not only is it the case, as Max Weber argued in his 'philosophy of social science' at the beginning of the century, that we choose what facts to study according to the 'values' or interests we have in the world (Weber 1904). It is also the case that having chosen what facts to study, we characterise them in terms that are our own, and which derive from a more general set of presuppositions about what the world consists in. These presuppositions may be widely shared. They also may not, and derive instead from a more arcane scheme. Philosophically, this is immaterial. What Durkheim insisted in his study of suicide were 'social facts' are always 'facts relative to a scheme'. This argument presents problems enough for the sciences of what has come to be called 'nature', for the objects of which 'realism', in the philosophical sense, may be thought to be true. It presents crippling arguments for the sciences of the social, or indeed for much of the more generally human, many of the objects of which, such as love, or justice, or the state, can themselves be construed as 'constructions', for which realism cannot be true. It is of course the case that from the many idioms in which we may choose to describe 'the social' and to think about it, we may choose the canonically 'scientific'. But it just as surely follows that this is one idiom amongst others, an idiom that serves our interests and perhaps even that of a wider 'public', and, by the earlier argument, these interests are as relative to a scheme as anything else in our minds and our language.

These arguments from the philosophy of language and its extensions into the philosophy of science, which bear in turn upon older questions about how we may regard 'reality', in turn bear back upon the historically more recent project of sociology. This I described as the project of overcoming the early nineteenth-century distinction between philosophical ethics and empirical history in order to ground a naturalistic morality, and to do so with the methods of 'science'. It was to put the philosophy of history on firm ground. The arguments from the philosophy of language and the new philosophy of science do not undermine the project of a naturalistic morality itself. Indeed, they can be used to support it. The anti-naturalist arguments that were pressed by various empiricists and positivists between the eighteenth and early twentieth centuries rested on a clear and, it was supposed, incontestable distinction between claims of fact and claims of value. The difference that this distinction was held to mark, however, is not a difference that can itself incontestably be claimed to be found in our languages for the human, vernacular, or theoretical. We may still not be able to show beyond all reasonable doubt what it is that we or others should do, or value. But we can persuade them of the qualities of the world, more exactly, of how to see the qualities of the world, in such a way as then to be able to persuade them that it makes better sense to do or to value one kind of thing rather than another.

CONCLUSION

What then remains of the project of a scientific sociology? Just this. Ontologically, there is no reason to suppose that it makes no sense to speak of 'the social', if by that is meant the precepts and practices with which we relate to each other; but there is danger in too readily supposing that there are distinct 'societies' beyond sets of citizens in the world which are the sets they are in virtue of their members being subject to the particular opportunities and constraints of the political authority under which they live. Epistemologically, there is behaviour which it makes sense to think of as being of one kind rather than another, for which we can arrive at mutually intelligible descriptions and mutually convenient measurements, and for which we can provide mutually confirmable (and falsifiable) explanations in the manner of the sciences of nature; but even if we can conveniently do the same for actions and institutions, we should be aware that there are no good grounds for believing that these are of one kind rather than another, independently of the ways in which choose to describe and explain them. Morally, the project of a naturalistic ethics is once again evidently viable; but we should beware of supposing that we can incontrovertibly or even indeed very forcibly demonstrate this beyond the circle of those who assent to the way in which we characterise its grounds and share the sensibilities and intuitions that these characterisations secrete. As an intellectual project, it is no more than this, but also no less. As a practical project, it will doubtless continue to be of use to those who wish to improve the administration of the state.

ETHICS, POLITICS, AND LEGAL THEORY

UTILITARIANS AND IDEALISTS

ROSS HARRISON

1. NEW BEGINNINGS

The 1870s was a decade of new beginnings in British moral philosophy. This was partly in reaction to the work of J. S. Mill, who had dominated the previous decade and whose *Utilitarianism* had appeared in book form in 1863. First, in 1870, John Grote's *Examination of the Utilitarian Philosophy* was posthumously published (Grote had been professor at Cambridge when Mill's work appeared). Then in 1874, also from Cambridge, came what has justly been called the first work of modern professional moral philosophy, Henry Sidgwick's *Methods of Ethics*. Meanwhile an idealist response to Mill (and to empiricist thinking more generally) had been brewing in Oxford, particularly in the lectures of T. H. Green. Its first significant ethical work was F. H. Bradley's *Ethical Studies*, published two years after Sidgwick's in 1876 (whereupon Bradley and Sidgwick promptly fell on each other in critical reviews and pamphlets). At the end of this decade, in 1879, came Herbert Spencer's *Data of Ethics*. Although Spencer was more favourable to empirical methods than Sidgwick, Green, or Bradley, and although like Mill and unlike them he worked outside the established universities, he was nevertheless another critic of Mill.

Mill stood for empirical, observational, methods and held that the central ethical issue was between results based on observation of actual human behaviour (which he thought led to his own utilitarianism) and results based upon supposed direct intuitions of moral truths (as believed in by his Cambridge opponent, Whewell). In 1870 the conflict between empiricist utilitarianism and intuitionism seemed to be the central issue, or problem, in ethics. For example W. Lecky's *History of European Morals* of 1869 frames its study round the 'great controversy, springing from the rival claims of intuition and utility' (Lecky 1869: 1). However, once the 1870s arrived, empirical utilitarianism against intuitionism was not in fact the issue that divided Bradley, Sidgwick, and Spencer. So these thinkers should not be seen merely as continuing Mill's debate, only with new or improved weapons. In fact, different as these new thinkers were from each other, they all thought that they had solved the great problem (or divide) of the previous period. For all of them, although in different ways, thought that they could be both intuitive and observational; as well as being (for Sidgwick and Spencer) utilitarian. We have new beginnings.

For most of these philosophers the very idea of deriving ethical conclusions from empirical observation also came under attack; and Mill's infamous proof, which derived the desirability of utilitarianism from the supposed psychological observation that people desire happiness, was subjected to relentless criticism. First Grote noted that Mill's argument depended upon an ambiguity between 'desired' and 'desirable' (Grote 1870: 65). Then both Sidgwick and Bradley diagnosed Mill's project as a hopeless attempt to move from an *is* to an *ought*. As Sidgwick puts it, 'experience can at most tell us that all men always do seek pleasure as their ultimate end . . . it cannot tell us that any one ought so to seek it' (Sidgwick 1874[1907: 98]). Bradley also worried about desired/desirable confusions and thought that utilitarianism was a 'monster' of which 'we must say that its heart is in the right place but its brain is wanting' (Bradley 1927: 115). It was for him a monster because it attempted to combine a perfectly correct moral belief about the goodness of serving other people (its right 'heart') with a derivation of this from psychological observations about individuals' search for happiness (its deficient 'brain').

Bradley also tore apart the second part of Mill's proof, the part which attempted to move from the observation that each person desires their own happiness to the conclusion that we all desire the general happiness. For Bradley this is rapidly demolished by wondering whether each pig eating at a common trough, in 'desiring his own pleasure, desires also the pleasure of all', noting that 'this scarcely seems conformable to experience' (1927: 113). Sidgwick earlier had combined the two criticisms when he noted that 'from the fact that every one actually does seek his own happiness we cannot conclude, as an immediate and obvious inference, that he ought to seek the happiness of other people' (1874 [1907: 412]).

Of the philosophers discussed here, the most significant to his European contemporaries was Herbert Spencer (when the news of his death arrived, the Italian parliament ended business for the day). However, the two with the greatest surviving reputation are Sidgwick and Bradley, and they form the chief focus of what follows (Green is more important for his political than his strictly ethical thought).

If Sidgwick and Bradley are the central philosophers and their dispute is the central dispute, then, although it is a dispute about utilitarianism, from what has just been said it follows that it is not Mill's dispute continued. For it has just been illustrated how similar their thought is in its criticism of Mill. Of course, with three groups of thinkers being discussed here, it is unsurprising that issues can be found which line any two of the groups up against the third. If, for example, we ask whether the issue was the truth of utilitarianism, or at least a form of it, then we get Sidgwick and Spencer on one side against the Oxford idealists on the other; if we ask whether it was the importance of development then we get Spencer and the (Hegelian-inspired) idealists against Sidgwick. However, the question which distinguishes the thinkers of continuing importance, Sidgwick and Bradley, on the one side from Spencer on the other is whether it is possible to deduce ethical truths from observation of human behaviour. Here Green, Sidgwick, and Bradley stand together (although none of them were hostile to the importance of facts). When tracing the history of his own thought, Sidgwick remarked that he ended as 'a Utilitarian again, but on an Intuitional basis' (1874 [1907: xx]). He was explicitly committed to both sides of Mill's fundamental divide; and with him we have moved into a new theoretical world.

With all these thinkers we have rival attempts to theorise what is already morally known, rather than (as for example with their contemporary Nietzsche) to subvert and transcend it. That is, they were all concerned to explain or justify normal moral beliefs rather than to criticise or change them. Common-sense morality, identified with Sidgwick with intuitive morality, is taken to be a reliable, if not completely perfect, guide to the truth. Sidgwick spends a whole book of the *Methods* on the Aristotelian project of outlining the common sense morality of his day. Both Green and Bradley think that the moral deliverances of the common man should be respected and, indeed, are more likely to be right than the philosophers. For example, Bradley starts his *Ethical Studies* by comparing the 'vulgar' notion of free will with that of the 'philosophers'; and it is clear that for him the vulgar have the better of the disagreement.

2. HENRY SIDGWICK

In his central work, the *Methods of Ethics*, Sidgwick wishes to reveal the 'different methods of ethics . . . implicit in our common sense reasoning' (1874 [1907: 14]). He takes it as a deliverance of common sense that we are aware of practical principles, that is, of imperatives telling us what we ought to do. He does not doubt that there are such imperatives, telling us what it is reasonable for us to do, and his aim is to lay out their nature. Here Sidgwick finds a dispute, a dispute between different 'methods' (where a 'method' for Sidgwick is 'any rational procedure by which we determine what individual human beings "ought" . . . to do' (1874 [1907: 1]). The 'methods' he chiefly considers are partly classified by means of discovery, partly by content. Thinking that people hold that the good consists either in happiness or else in excellence or perfection, he arrives at two methods which promote happiness: 'egoism', which dictates that we should pursue our own individual happiness, and 'utilitarianism', which dictates that we should pursue general happiness. The other method he considers is 'intuitionism'. In the light of his initial classification, it would seem that this should mean perfectionism, but in fact 'intuitionism' has a less stable sense throughout Sidgwick's work, often meaning the morality of common sense itself. In any case he later divides intuition into several sub-species.

It was noted in the last section how Sidgwick criticised Mill's derivation of the desirable from the desired. This fits with Sidgwick's wider claim about the independence of ethics. The deliverances of practical reason which he finds us to possess are not derivable from any other source. Sidgwick not only criticises Mill's derivation of ethics from psychology but also the psychology used in the derivation. So, in terms of Mill's infamous proof of utility, Sidgwick holds that Mill is mistaken in the truth of his premises as well as in the validity of his inferences. For Sidgwick, people do not only pursue pleasure (or happiness). They also seek other objects for their own sakes. Hence psychological hedonism is incorrect; people are not just pleasure-maximising machines.

From this it might be thought that Sidgwick would also hold that egoism is false. But here Sidgwick's distinction between *is* and *ought* again comes into effect. Psychological hedonism is false, but egoism, just like any other moral theory, has to be considered as an independent moral imperative, which is not based upon psychological facts. People do not always pursue their own individual pleasures but this does not show that they should not. In fact, Sidgwick does not think that he can fully refute egoism, holding that individual prudence is a rational requirement. However (in yet another criticism of earlier utilitarianism), since he thinks that we cannot actually calculate possible future pleasures and pains in more than a rough way, he thinks that we do not have access to the information which we would need in order to be successful egoists. It may be right, that is, that my correct goal is to maximise my individual pleasure through the duration of my life; but if I attempt to do it, I am unlikely to succeed. This is only one example of Sidgwick's distinction between the correct criterion for right action and what it is best to aim at. Another example is when he suggests that the convinced utilitarian should not always encourage others to aim at utility or publish the truths of utilitarianism.

After his examination of egoism, Sidgwick considers (under the heading of 'intuitionism') whether common-sense morality could be organised into a con-sistent system of rules. After an extensive examination of the moral views of his day (treating topics like chastity and courage) he does not find that common-sense morality provides precise rules. Some cases it cannot decide; others it disagrees about. The maxims of common sense, he thinks, have a fairly universal acceptance until they are made precise enough to be treated in a properly scientific manner. Then, as soon as this happens, disagreement appears.

This is a criticism of (what Sidgwick calls) intuitions. So he holds that his predecessor Whewell's project of producing a science of ethics from the intuitions of common sense is not tenable. However, this does not mean that Sidgwick abandons the use of intuition as a method of moral discovery. For as well as particular intuitions about the right thing to do in particular cases (which Sidgwick calls 'aesthetical' intuitionism) and as well as the Whewell project of systematising the rules of common sense (which Sidgwick calls 'dogmatical' intuitionism), Sidgwick thinks that there is a third kind of intuitionism, 'philosophical' intuitionism. He thinks, that is, that there are some 'absolute practical principles' whose truth, once it is properly examined, is self-evident. Hence they are moral truths which can be known by intuition (or direct inspection), rather than, for example, being deduced from observation of behaviour.

Sidgwick finds three such intuitively discoverable principles. One is the Kantian claim that 'whatever action any of us judges to be right for himself, he implicitly judges to be right for all similar persons in similar circumstances' (1874 [1907: 379]). Another is that 'the good of any one individual is of no more importance, from the point of view . . . of the Universe, than the good of any other' (1874 [1907: 382]); that is, that all persons are of equal importance. The third self-evident principle is that all times are of equal importance.

These principles, if we accept them, determine the appropriate distribution of the good between people and times. As regards the content of the good, Sidgwick holds that it is composed of desirable states of mind; that is, those things which a person would desire if they were properly informed. Given this, and that one person's good is of equal importance with another's, Sidgwick arrives at a proof of utilitarianism on intuitive grounds. The correct criterion of right action is that it produces the maximum amount of desirable states of mind, distributed without respect of persons.

Granted that the fundamental principle of utilitarianism is intuitive, Sidgwick draws out the consequences. Unlike Mill, there is no point in trying to give it an empirical base, or in trying to derive the genesis of aimed-at objects by association of ideas with desired states. For Sidgwick origin is irrelevant. Also, although universal happiness is the ultimate standard of right action it is not necessarily the thing which we should aim at; we may well maximise happiness by aiming at other things, and here common-sense morality can return as a guide. Indeed for Sidgwick there has to be another guide to assist the ultimate utilitarian principle. This is partly because he holds that the ultimate practical principles are too abstract to be applied to particular cases without the use of intermediate or other assumptions. It is also because our inability to calculate pleasures and pains correctly not only causes difficulties for egoism but also causes difficulties for the direct application of utilitarianism. So we need another guide to help us to apply the abstract utilitarian truth, and Sidgwick finds this in common-sense morality.

Just as Sidgwick took himself to have healed the breach between intuitionism and utilitarianism at a more abstract level by deriving utilitarianism on intuitive principles, he also takes himself to have healed the breach between utilitarianism and common sense (or more low-level intuitions). Disputes inside common sense, he claims, are often resolved by recourse to utilitarianism; common-sense morality therefore shows 'unconscious utilitarianism'.

3. BRADLEY AND GREEN

Bradley's *Ethical Studies* was one of the first works in which the developing idealism of Oxford was displayed to the general public. It has a style something between an academic treatise and contributions to general reviews; its explicit form is as a series of essays. Partly because of this, but also because of its dialectical method (this is the most Hegelian of all Bradley's works), it is difficult to tell how committed Bradley is to his intermediate conclusions. Thus the famous chapter entitled 'My Station and its Duties', which is usually all that anyone knows about Bradley's ethics, is placed right in the middle of the work. It is true that Bradley says there that 'we have found ourselves, when we have found our station and its duties' (1927: 163). Yet in the later chapters he moves beyond this position of rest; and indeed in the chapter itself, one page after making the claim that 'there is nothing better than my station and its duties', he says that there are 'very serious objections' to it (1927: 202). In *Ethical Studies* the conclusions of each chapter are modified by the chapter which follows; and so a complete picture of ethical thought is built up in dialectical manner.

Bradley's first essay displays the contradiction noted above between normal and philosophical thought about free-will. With a contradiction already in his bag, he then starts his main enquiry by asking the question why we should be moral. Holding that such a question can only be answered by providing something which is both an end in itself and also something we desire, he decides that the aim of morality is self-realisation. For Bradley morals arise because I seek to realise myself as a unified whole. In so far as I am real self, I am a unified whole, for which distinctions can be made but not divisions. Given this, he can show the error (or partial truth) in two earlier important theories: utilitarianism and Kantianism. In utilitarianism ('pleasure for pleasure's sake') there is no unified whole, but merely a sequence of sensations. By contrast, in

Kantianism ('duty for duty's sake') morality is merely formal and has no specific content.

After these examinations comes the temporary resting place of 'my station and its duties'. Here I find unity, self-realisation, and objective moral truth by finding my morality in the requirements of my role or position in an organised and unified society. Again utilitarianism is a target: just as utilitarians are mistaken in thinking that the person is a mere collection of sensations, so also are they mistaken in thinking that the state or society is a mere collection of persons. In both cases, at least when the society is properly organised and the individual is properly able to appreciate their position in it, we have a real unity rather than a mere collection. For Bradley individuals become what they are because of what the whole social organism or state already is. It is this whole which gives individuals their language, beliefs, and moral goals.

The general metaphysics underlying this, that is, the equation of the real with the single unified system, is only finally established by Bradley nearly twenty years later in his masterly metaphysical work, *Appearance and Reality*. In his early *Ethical Studies* the idea is only used with respect to people and states to establish a social morality. In doing this he thinks that he is merely pointing out common-sense morality; the morality which the pre-philosophical people know perfectly well before being confused by bad philosophy. As he puts it here, 'what is moral *in any particular given case* is seldom doubtful. Society pronounces beforehand' (1927: 198). T. H. Green later makes a similar claim in his *Prolegomena to Ethics* when he says that 'ordinarily it will be an impertinence for the philosopher to pretend either to supplement or to supersede those practical directions of conduct, which are supplied by the duties of his station to any one who is free from selfish interest in ignoring them' (1883: sect. 313).

Bradley's famous chapter on stations and duties was the first appearance of Hegelian ethics in England. However, as noted above, Bradley himself takes this answer to his original question to be only partial, and his argument in the rest of the work advances beyond Hegel (and T. H. Green). We find ourselves and our morality in an organised society, or state. However, the actual states that there are may be partial, conflicting, or evil; and Bradley holds that there is also a cosmopolitan (or 'ideal') morality which reaches beyond the border of a single state or society. Furthermore Bradley thinks that there are values that are not particularly social in nature. The ends of an artist or scientist have value; they form part of self-realisation, yet are not the fulfilling of given functions in an existing society.

These different bases of moral truth in Bradley pose the problem of how to reconcile their different goals. Green ends his *Prolegomena to Ethics* with an example of a similar problem: how to balance service to society with developing one's skills as a musician. Yet for Green this is not ultimately a problem; social service wins out. Indeed, more generally, Green thinks that the good must be self-consistent. He thinks that it can be identified by identifying the only object which can be consistently willed by everyone. Hence it has to be a non-competitive good, and therefore (he thinks) a public good.

In contrast to Green, Bradley both finds inconsistency in ethics to be inevitable and is also correspondingly more relaxed about it. As he puts it in his later work, contradiction is merely a sign that we are dealing with appearance, not reality. So in *Appearance and Reality* he says specifically that the good is an appearance. Indeed, even in *Ethical Studies*, Bradley ends by saying that morality is intrinsically contradictory (it tries to make the *ought* into an *is* when the whole point of *is* and *ought* is that they be distinguished); hence we have to pass beyond morality into religion.

Quite apart from these problems of inconsistency, Bradley runs into the problem that bad actions also involve a certain kind of self-realisation (the realisation of what he calls the 'bad self'). Furthermore, we may have to sacrifice ourselves for the sake of others or our country, therefore the goodness of self-realisation may actually involve self-annihilation. In *Appearance and Reality* he explicitly distinguishes between the self-realisation which consists in self-assertion and the self-realisation which consists in self-denial; and finds that it is the combination of these contradictory tendencies which underwrites his claim that the good is mere appearance.

So although Bradley has shown that morals aims at a single, systematic, self-realised individual, he also holds that as long as we restrict ourselves to morals we have only partial, or mutually contradictory, views of this individual. For an impression of the whole we have to pass beyond morality. Therefore, in spite of the confident assertions about 'my station and its duties', and in contrast with Green's hopeful developments, Bradley ends by displaying his deep-rooted scepticism.

Two years before Bradley's *Ethical Studies* Sidgwick had also ended the very different (utilitarian, individualistic) thought of his *Methods of Ethics* with a problem arising from inconsistency. Sidgwick holds there that there is a 'dualism of practical reason' so that we have an ultimate rational requirement both to care for ourselves and also to care for the general welfare (to be both egoistic and also utilitarian). Since Sidgwick thinks that ultimate ethical intuitions must be consistent, this provides him with a serious problem. Lacking any Hegelian escape hatch, he cannot afford to be as relaxed about contradiction as Bradley seems to have been; nor was he temperamentally as prepared as Bradley to live with scepticism.

4. EVOLUTION AND ETHICS

For Herbert Spencer, philosophy differs from science only in its generality, and he gives a would-be scientific account of moral thought. Similarly Leslie Stephen, influenced by Spencer but an independent and a more elegant writer, called his main work the *Science of Ethics*. In both cases the science involved is evolutionary theory; morals is explained in terms of its contribution to the 'survival of the fittest'. (Both the term 'evolution' and the explanatory expression 'the survival of the fittest' were put into circulation by Spencer even though, like many of the other leading evolutionary thinkers, he was himself highly unfit.)

Spencer's general theory of evolution is of a change from homogeneity to heterogeneity: he claims that things become progressively more differentiated and specialised. Spencer thinks that this holds for both inanimate and animate objects, but only works it out in detail for the latter. He does this in a line of massive books, each with the title '*Principles of . . .*' (successively: *Biology*, *Psychology*, and *Sociology*), only reaching the *Principles of Ethics* in 1893 (although the first half of this had previously been published as the *Data of Ethics*). Ethics is in fact Spencer's first and chief interest, even though (as his intellectual opponents happily pointed out) he declared that he was disappointed by his final results. In his psychological work Spencer shows that the experience of the species is responsible for the innate knowledge by particular individuals of logical and mathematical truths. (Here, as elsewhere, Spencer is helped by his belief that acquired characteristics are inherited.) Hence he takes himself to have solved the dispute between Mill and his opponents about whether such truths are empirical or intuitive. (The answer, that is, is both: empirical for the species; a priori for the individual.) In his ethical work he reaches a similar resolution of the analogous dispute between Mill and his opponents about whether moral beliefs were founded on experience or intuition. The analogous answer is that the race (or group) acquired beliefs in the struggle for survival leading to its evolutionary progression, but for any individual member of these groups these moral beliefs are innate or intuitive. The principles which are essential for individual, group, and species survival and development come from the cumulative experience of the species; and these are the things which individuals intuitively hold to be good.

Spencer gives these beliefs a utilitarian content. Good things are those which produce happiness, so there is a coincidence between evolutionary and utilitarian ethics. This argument is more elegantly laid out in Leslie Stephen's *Science of Ethics* in terms of only possible explanation. For Stephen people are such that they have to pursue happiness; they are also such that they have to be explained in evolutionary terms; hence it has to be the case that evolutionary ends can be secured by the pursuit of happiness (or, as Stephen puts it, 'the "useful", in the sense of pleasure-giving, must approximately coincide with the "useful" in the sense of life-preserving' (1882: 83)). In this way both Spencer and Stephen explain particular values such as veracity, chastity, or justice. Thus Stephen shows that veracity is necessary for the use of language, and that language is necessary for the survival of society; hence trustworthiness is shown to be a quality the development of which is essential to social growth; hence we instinctively think that it is wrong to lie.

Spencer aims to show in his *Ethics* both why a particular society has the moral precepts it does and also to show what moral precepts all societies ought ultimately to have. Both are explained by evolution. The precepts that a society actually has are explained by finding the ideas which enabled that particular society to survive. The precepts a society ought ultimately to have are those which would enable a perfectly evolved society to survive. The distinction, in his terms, is between relative and absolute ethics.

Spencer's sociological thought gives him a guide to what the most evolved state will be, and hence to absolute ethics. He thinks that there has been a continuing transition from military to commercial values. Eventually we will get to what he calls his 'law of equal freedom' which is that 'every man is free to do that which he wills, providing he infringes not the equal freedom of any other man' (1893: sect. 272). This is Spencer's central principle of justice, which he thinks would hold in the most highly evolved societies, and would guarantee the survival of such societies. In this most highly evolved state, as described in absolute ethics, everything fits together. The state withers away into something that does no more than enforce contract; and individual desires and external obligations coincide so perfectly that individuals no longer feel the constraints of duty. Spencer's views here reveal his suspicions of the state, a constant feature of his position ever since his first writings. The old-style liberal suspicion is in tension with the sociological dynamic. Stephen, by contrast, more consistently takes the evolutionary dynamic to operate at the level of the group. Unlike Spencer, he refuses to discuss ideal ethics, or possible futures, restricting himself to an account of how things are and have been (helped here by his good historical sense). Like the idealists discussed in the last section, he holds that individuals are the products of society, culture, and language; and that such things have been variable through time. For Stephen, we get our logic, as well as our morals, from our language.

Both Stephen and Spencer take it that evolutionary theory works in support of ethics, explaining and clarifying common moral thought. However, the distinguished evolutionary biologist T. H. Huxley, who fought trenchant battles in defence of Darwin and evolutionary theory, took a different course when he came to ethics. In two late articles Huxley holds that ethics is in conflict with evolution. Rather, he says, than promoting the survival of the fittest, we should be fitting as many as possible to survive. The forces which help evolution are not those supported by our moral thought. Huxley's analogy is that of a gardener, who tries to prevent, restrain, and redirect the forces of nature rather than giving them free scope. Evolutionary theory deals only with the wild woods of nature; ethics by contrast polices the gardens of civilisation.

19

NIETZSCHE

EDGAR SLEINIS

Nietzsche went virtually unnoticed during his productive life, but after his mental collapse in early 1889 his influence increased dramatically although unevenly. He has been a major figure in Europe for virtually the whole of the twentieth century with philosophers and intellectuals such as Vaihinger, Spengler, Jaspers, Heidegger, and later Foucault, Deleuze, and Derrida regarding him as one of the most important philosophers of modern times. His influence on artists and writers has been remarkable. But until the middle of the twentieth century, philosophers in the English-speaking world tended to regard him with hostility or indifference (Bertrand Russell's unsympathetic attitude is typical, see Russell 1946). Perceptions of Nietzsche as a thinker worth exploring have risen steadily in the English-speaking world since then, and he is increasingly seen as important in the formation of twentieth-century consciousness. But this is not the emergence of an unruffled consensus, and Nietzsche continues to produce ardent worshippers and vehement revilers in a way unimaginable for the other major philosophers in the Western tradition. Nietzsche passionately wants to influence our approach to life, and no other philosopher places such importance on the affirmation of this world. In part this is a reaction to his early pessimistic philosophical hero, Schopenhauer. The task Nietzsche undertook as his philosophy matured was the revaluation of all values (Nietzsche 1882: §269).

THE REASSESSMENT OF REASON

Nietzsche's reassessment of reason is fundamental to his critique of values. Although at times Nietzsche appears to be an outright enemy of reason and a proponent of irrationalism, this is misleading. He is certainly a fierce critic of standard conceptions of reason, but he is basically concerned to furnish what he regards as a more realistic and more modest account of reason and its scope. Fundamental here is the rejection of the idea of a pure knowing subject able to become aware of things just as they are in themselves, and the rejection of the

266

closely connected idea of absolute truth. Knowers can never completely evade their biological, individual, social, linguistic, and historical position: 'There is *only* a perspective seeing, there is *only* a perspective "knowing"; the *more* affects we allow to speak about one thing, the *more* eyes, different eyes, we can use to observe one thing, the more complete will our concept of this thing, our "objectivity" be' (Nietzsche 1887: III §12 [1969: 119]).

The only road to better understanding is through the comparison, contrast, and assessment of different perspectives. For Nietzsche, there are no absolute truths: hence, there are no absolute value judgements, and no absolute moral truths. Moralities are never more than just human products (this position is adopted in the relatively early Nietzsche 1878–80 and consistently maintained thereafter). Assessing a morality always requires taking into account its effects, and the nature of its proponents. He accepts that there are many moralities and that a science of morality needs to deal with them all, but his own thinking is dominated by several types that he regards as basic.

THE MASTER, SLAVE, AND HERD MORALITIES

The master morality emerges from the top of the group whom Nietzsche assumes are more powerful, more dynamic, more daring, more life-affirming, healthier, and harder. It is produced autonomously in conditions of abundance. Its function is to enhance the life of the masters and promote their qualities. It centres on enrichment and self-fulfilment; it does not seek to change everyone to fit one mould. The slave morality is generated by those at the bottom of the group whom Nietzsche assumes are weak, lacking vitality, timid, and ease-seeking. It is the product of resentment, fear, powerlessness, and hatred. It is a reaction to the unfavourable position of the slaves. Its function is to advance the interests of the slaves. The powerful who constitute a threat to the slaves need to be neutralised. It is essentially reactive, defensive, and negative. Its object is the control of others and warding off threats rather than enrichment or self-fulfilment (Nietzsche 1886: §260; Nietzsche 1887: I, §10).

The herd morality emerges from the dynamics of groups independently of hierarchy. Most members of a natural group cluster around an average, and this is what the herd morality seeks to promote and preserve. The herd morality is not essentially reactive, and is produced in conditions of contentment. Its function is to maintain the life of the herd by the production of herd animals as close to the herd average as possible (Nietzsche 1886: §268). While the slaves want to change their situation, the herd animals want to preserve theirs. It seeks to eliminate whatever disturbs herd life, and is directed towards such fulfilment as is available in subordination to the herd. Its dominating ideal is mediocrity.

Whereas the slave morality is a morality of discontent, the herd morality is a morality of contentment.

Nietzsche regards the master morality as superior to both the slave morality and the herd morality, but it is not the case that the master morality is espoused and every other morality criticised from its standpoint. Rather the superiority of the master morality itself follows from Nietzsche's higher-order values of life enhancement. Nietzsche nowhere suggests that the value crisis he sees Western civilisation as facing can be resolved by returning to a pre-existing master morality. He repeatedly maintains that there is a vital need for a 'new table of values', and for the creators of new values (Nietzsche 1886: §211). Nietzsche sees the slave morality as having an unhealthy grip on Western civilisation, even though its metaphysical underpinnings have collapsed. The slave morality has dominated Western civilisation co-extensively with, and as an integral part of, the domination of Christianity. The danger is that the slave morality will continue its dominance in spite of the collapse of its metaphysical underpinnings, epitomised in his well-known saying 'God is dead' (this occurs first in Nietzsche 1882 and then again in Nietzsche 1883–5 where it plays a more significant role). His attitude towards the herd morality is more ambiguous. Its effects are disastrous if permitted total sway (Nietzsche 1887: I, §9). But if it is not accorded total sway, it may have a positive role to play. Ultimately the slave morality is vitiated by corrosive discontent, and herd morality by mediocrity and bovine complacency.

THE ASSAULT ON MORALITY

Universality

Universality is central to the Kantian approach to morality, and has independently been widely accepted as an essential feature of morality. Nietzsche takes universality to be a key feature of the slave morality, but a successful attack on universality would be of major significance even if the slave, master, and herd morality conceptions were entirely untenable. Nietzsche has numerous objections to universality. For one, human reason is incapable of furnishing universally valid moral prescriptions. For another, universality is anti-nature. Nature contains such a rich diversity of types that it is absurd and counterproductive to require conformity to one set of rules (Nietzsche 1889: V, §6).

Further, a universalising morality advocates as valuable what everybody is expected to attain. Nietzsche's problem is how anything that is attainable by all could be valuable (Nietzsche 1886, §43). For him, a crucial component of value is rarity and difficulty of attainment. This is characteristic of aesthetic valuation.

In the arts, the unique achievement, the attainment of standards not attainable by everyone is valued most. In morals, everybody is expected to do the same. Nietzsche maintains we ought to assess persons and lives on an aesthetic value model rather than a moral value model (Nietzsche 1878-80: §107).

He has an important argument against the universality-based moral value model and in favour of the uniqueness-based aesthetic value model. According to Nietzsche, moral values have been taken to be the highest values. But the highest values have a special role in human life. The issue is whether moral values can fulfil that role. For Nietzsche, one's life having value or meaning is of fundamental importance (Nietzsche 1889: I, §12). Evidently the highest values must give value or meaning to one's life. If the highest values cannot do this, nothing else can. The riddle is how universal moral rules could fulfil this role. Suppose I have adhered to universal moral rules all of my life. Of what value is my life to me? Where is the value or meaning for me? Surely my life has no more value or meaning for me than that of another person who has also adhered to the moral rules in exactly the same way I have. For all who adhere to the universal moral rules, given that moral rules constitute the highest values, there are no further value considerations that can lend special value to their individual lives. My own life is no more valuable, no more meaningful than the life of any other person who has conformed equally to the same moral rules.

But I want to know what is different about my life, what my life is or can be that no other life is or can be. Uniqueness seems to be an essential element of this individual sense of worth. If the individual sense of value or meaning is essentially something unique, something that differentiates one from others, then of necessity this cannot be supplied by mere conformity to universal rules. Individual value requires uniqueness, and uniqueness cannot arise from universal rules. Universal moral rules are supposed to embody the highest values, and as the highest values they must ultimately lend value to life, but it is specifically their very universality that precludes them from giving individuals any unique sense of their own worth. '"This – is now *my* way: where is yours?" Thus I answered those who asked me "the way". For *the* way – does not exist!' (Nietzsche 1883-5: III, §11 [1961: 213]). Universal moral rules cannot fulfil the key role required of the highest values, and this role can only be fulfilled by a uniqueness based aesthetic mode of valuation.

However, Nietzsche's opposition to universal moral rules is not a blanket opposition to all moral rules. Typically, depending on circumstances, some system of rules will be justified, and these will constitute the framework within which the highest values can be attained (Nietzsche 1886: §188). Nietzsche's principal attack is against certain kinds of morality, and against the placement of morality at the peak of a value system; it is not principally an attack against morality conceived in the broadest sense. Indeed, for him, the enhancement of life is inconceivable without protracted constraint at both a group and individual level.

Altruism

Nietzsche was a persistent critic of altruism, and takes it to be the dominant value in the slave morality. It is important to understand why altruism is a significant feature in it. Altruism is a transfer of resources from haves to have–nots, and it is the have–nots who are the generators of the slave morality. If the slaves can get altruism espoused by the whole community, the slaves will benefit. The self-interest of the slaves drives the advocacy of altruism. Nietzsche has a range of objections to altruism, and regards the egoistical drives as valuationally more fundamental.

The concept of an altruistic act is essentially the concept of an act that is the means to a good. As a means, its value is entirely dependent upon the values it seeks to attain. The point is graphically illustrated in the case of extreme self-sacrifice. Suppose that someone sacrifices his life to save the life of another, who immediately sacrifices his life to save the life of another, who immediately sacrifices his life to save the life of another, and this is repeated without end. The whole process is absurd and pointless. Self-sacrifice has no value as an act in its own right; it only has value if it attains its end, and it is from this end that value accrues to it. To rank altruism as the highest value is to be guilty of a valuational absurdity. Altruism cannot be the highest value, and it is not even a value capable of standing on its own. A value system containing only altruism as a value would contain no value at all. If everyone sacrifices him or herself for everyone else, then no one benefits.

Nietzsche has other objections to altruism. By an altruistic act one secures for another a benefit that could have been secured for oneself; this reveals that one is valuing the other person more highly than oneself. If one is prepared to give up one's life for the life of another, the obvious way to make sense of this is to suppose that the sacrificer believes his or her life to be of less value than the life being saved. For Nietzsche, this can only arise where the self-sacrificer has an impoverished self-conception, and this can only arise in devitalised and declining life forms. Dynamic and ascending life forms have a robust self-conception and take their own worth for granted. Ascending life forms insist on the right to endure, expand, and increase. Only declining life forms voluntarily surrender what they have, and diminish themselves. Nietzsche thinks that acting altruistically is both an expression of life in decline and contributes to its decline.

Nietzsche regularly thinks in terms of types. As a type, the altruist is oriented exclusively towards the interests of others; this is not the conception of one who merely occasionally or even frequently performs altruistic acts. This casts the issue in a new light. The altruist is a type with no independent projects and interests of his or her own. Resources are spent on furthering the projects and interests of others. But the altruist is simply making a slave of himself to others. However active he may be in the aid of others, it is essentially the activity of a servant or a slave. For Nietzsche, such an exclusive orientation towards the interests of others presupposes a lower valuation of oneself, and expresses declining life.

But Nietzsche is not worried by the anaemic and declining spending their meagre resources on others, just as he is not concerned about the superabundantly endowed directing some of their resources to others. His basic fear is that the advocacy of this ideal will induce the capable to sacrifice themselves for the incapable. 'The sick represent the greatest danger for the healthy; it is *not* the strongest but the weakest who spell disaster for the strong. Is this known?' (Nietzsche 1887: III, §14 [1969: 121–2]). There is no problem about a 'nobody' sacrificing himself to save a threatened genius. There is everything wrong with a genius sacrificing himself for a threatened 'nobody'. What concerns Nietzsche most about the embrace of the altruistic ideal is that he sees it as having a deleterious influence on life as a whole (Nietzsche 1889: IX, §35). In addition, Nietzsche maintains that the advocacy of altruism has been self-undermining. Essentially the case is that altruism has been advocated on selfish grounds; the slaves seek their own benefit in advocating altruism. Nietzsche sees such selfish advocacy as undermining altruism as a value.

Utilitarianism

Nietzsche was a resolute critic of utilitarianism regarding it as part of the slave morality. The slaves have limited resources, be they mental or physical. Unlike those with boundless resources, those with limited resources must calculate their expenditure carefully. Utilitarianism belongs to the slaves because it favours the preservation of the slaves, while it is at best a hindrance to the masters (Nietzsche 1886: §260). For Nietzsche, a major difficulty in hedonistic utilitarianism arises from considering the biological role of pleasure and pain. There is no doubt that pain is a functional state whose purpose is to limit or avoid organic damage. Similarly, though less obviously, pleasure is a functional state, the purpose of which is to maintain organic wellbeing. Pain is only a means to avoiding a more important disvalue than the pain itself, namely organic damage. Similarly, pleasure is only a means to a more important value than the pleasure itself, namely organic well-being.

From a biological standpoint, to judge pain as a greater disvalue than bodily damage and pleasure as a greater value than bodily health is an absurd valuation.

Perhaps there are aspects of pain which contribute to its disvalue independently of its being a means, and there are aspects of pleasure which contribute to its value independently of its being a means. But it does not follow that pleasure and pain are of greater value and disvalue than those bodily states which they are a means to producing or preventing. Utilitarians need an account of what warrants the transformation of pleasure and pain from mere means for the organism to ultimate values for the person. For Nietzsche, the health and vitality of the body take precedence over feelings of pleasure and pain. Furthermore, once their nature as a mere means is understood, then other important goals can come into play and override both pleasure and pain: 'all these modes of thought which assess the value of things according to *pleasure* and *pain*, that is to say according to attendant and secondary phenomena, are foreground modes of thought and naïveties which anyone conscious of *creative* powers and an artist's conscience will look down on with derision, though not without pity' (Nietzsche 1886: §225 [1973: 135–6]).

Further, for hedonistic utilitarianism, autonomy cannot constitute an independent value: if there is greater pleasure in a non-autonomous life, then it ought to be preferred. Nietzsche is totally opposed to such a valuation. For him, self-initiated and self-controlled activity is the essence of healthy life forms. To permit or not be able to prevent one's life from being controlled by others is a manifestation of diminished life capacity and value. For Nietzsche, not only is autonomy an independent value, it is an independent value higher than happiness or pleasure. It is better to be in charge of one's life and unhappy than to have one's life controlled by others and be happy (Nietzsche 1889: IX, §38).

Nietzsche's concern with the origins of value systems leads to a characteristic question here. What kind of being has pain as its ultimate negative value and pleasure as its ultimate positive value? What kind of being needs such a value system? According to Nietzsche, it is the exhausted and decadent. To explain the connection some remarks are in order about Nietzsche's theory of value. The inner power that draws one to something is the principal determinant of its value for oneself. This implies that, other things being equal, if person A is drawn twice as strongly to something than person B is, then there is twice as much value in it for A than there is for B. It immediately follows that the value available for the exhausted is less than that available to those with robust health and dynamism.

The robustly healthy and dynamic set their own goals and pursue them. Indeed it takes robust health and dynamism to set and pursue your own goals. The exhausted are incapable of setting or pursuing their own goals. As a result, pain becomes the ultimate negative value and pleasure the ultimate positive value for the exhausted. They do not have the energy to posit or pursue their own goals, and they have insufficient power to resist the natural repulsion of pain or the natural attraction of pleasure. Pain and pleasure control those who do not have the power to be in control. For Nietzsche, the more exhausted you are, the less autonomous you are, and the more values are set *for you* rather than *by you,* and the more you will be controlled by pain and pleasure. Nietzsche does not maintain that the exhausted and decadent should abandon this value system; indeed for them it may be the best system to adopt. But it is an inappropriate value system for the robustly healthy and dynamic. It is a trap for them, yielding a value system that delivers less value overall than is otherwise attainable. Nietzsche is not opposed to the exhausted operating with such a value system, as long as they do not seek to impose it on others. Different values are appropriate for different groups.

THE PLACE OF SUFFERING

Suffering appears as an objection to life, and seeking to defeat the objection while accepting the unavoidability of suffering was a constant preoccupation for Nietzsche. Here, an outline of Nietzsche's theory of value and ultimate values is in order. For Nietzsche, life is the will to power, the drive to master. Doing rather than undergoing, acting rather than reacting, setting goals rather than having goals set for one are the prerequisites of positive value. Value arises when goals are set and pursued. The value of something depends principally on the strength of the inner power that draws one to that thing. Value depends on an active, positive orientation towards what is valued. The ultimate value is itself the increase of power – which essentially means active mastery (the coherence of this position is examined in Sleinis 1994: 8–10).

The will to power, the drive to master cannot express itself where there is no resistance. Active mastery requires the expenditure of effort, overcoming resistance, enduring pain and hardship. To want to actively master is to want to experience resistance and to overcome it; it is to want hard tasks that require surmounting pain and suffering (1886: §225). Typically the worth of an achievement is proportional to the difficulty of attaining it. This means that many worthwhile achievements require struggle and suffering. If, for Nietzsche, the relation between the suffering and the achievement were merely one of means and ends, then this would not constitute any novel or remarkable revaluation of struggle and suffering. In common modes of valuation, we take whatever negative value attaches to the means and subtract it from the positive value of the attained goal. Suffering and struggle are justified if we have a net positive value at the end. It is crucial to this way of viewing the matter that the value of the means and the value of the end are capable of independent assessment and are capable of being added and subtracted. But for Nietzsche, the relation is not simply one of means and ends. The struggle and the suffering are not independent steps on the way to achievement; they are parts of its very fabric.

To illustrate Nietzsche's point, suppose that you genuinely want to win a marathon race. Exerting yourself against the other runners over the distance is not merely a means which has crossing the line first as an end. To want to win is to want to exert yourself against the other runners over the full distance and to cross the finishing line first. There is no coherent way of splitting the activity into a means that is of negative value, and an end that is of positive value. To want to win a marathon is to want the inevitable pain and strain, and to want to master them. For Nietzsche, one cannot value achievement without also valuing the suffering that is inseparable from it. This does not imply a positive valuation of all suffering. But it does imply that there are cases in which the pain and suffering act as measures of positive value. In some cases, the more of yourself you have paid for it, the more valuable it is (Nietzsche 1889: IX, §38). Contrast this with utilitarian valuation, where every pain invested detracts from the ultimate value of the attainment. For Nietzsche, suffering is often an integral part of our desire when we desire to attain positive goals. Once the role of suffering in positive achievement is understood, suffering is no longer something to be automatically avoided or deplored. It is a recurrent theme with Nietzsche that many of the goods we now enjoy are simply unattainable without suffering.

But this does not exhaust Nietzsche's revaluation of pain and suffering. Pain and suffering can be the source of a firmer and more purified view of life. They test comfortable illusions, complacent assumptions, and the quality of one's positive orientation towards life (Nietzsche 1881: II, §114). But the perspective from the standpoint of pain and suffering is not a mere means to a better perspective when not undergoing pain and suffering. Rather, one's view is more soundly based because it incorporates the view *from* the position of pain and suffering. Further, pain and suffering can be strengtheners (Nietzsche 1908: I, §2). This is not something that could be replaced by pills or training. A strengthening through pain and suffering is not attainable in any other way. This unique relation between suffering and strengthening resists analysis in simple utilitarian, means and ends, terms.

In addition, pain and suffering can be life-experience intensifiers. It is better to have a large pain and a large joy than to have a little pain and a little joy, or indeed no pain and no joy (Nietzsche 1881: IV, §354, §402). For the utilitarian, these situations are equivalent; for Nietzsche they are not. The presence of the positive value is of greater importance than the presence of the negative value. Furthermore, pain and suffering often have a private meaning. Your pain and suffering are part of what makes you unique. Nobody can really understand your pain and suffering (Nietzsche 1882: §338). This point grounds one of Nietzsche's objections to pity: there is something sham about pity because it cannot be based on a genuine understanding of the pain and suffering involved for the person undergoing the suffering. Collectively these points imply that pain and suffering can be accepted and integrated with positive elements in experience to yield a valuable and meaningful life. They do not make pain and suffering desirable for its own sake nor do they make pain and suffering positively desirable for its consequences. But they do imply that pain and suffering are not inevitably life diminishing, that their place in the fabric of life is not to be unconditionally deplored, and that it is not always, and perhaps not even often, our highest task to eliminate them. (This is not the insensitive indifference of a stranger to suffering; Nietzsche had to put up with an inordinate amount of suffering in his own life, see Hayman 1980.)

For Nietzsche, there is an ultimate positive value but there is no ultimate negative value. The increase of power is the top value (Nietzsche 1886: §13), but there are no fixed ultimate bottom values. Most importantly, positive values have priority over negative values. 'If we possess our *why* of life we can put up with almost any *how*' (Nietzsche 1889: I, §12 [1968: 23]). It is only where the negatives dominate to the point of threatening the production of positive values that the negatives merit attention. For Nietzsche, it is better to have one victory and two defeats rather than no victory and no defeats. The point is to get something positive out of life. In general, pain and suffering do not have a fixed value, and, apart from extreme cases, their value is dependent on the positive values present. 'Man, the bravest of animals and the most accustomed to suffering, does *not* repudiate suffering as such; he *desires* it, he even seeks it out, provided he is shown a *meaning* for it, a *purpose* of suffering. The meaninglessness of suffering, *not* suffering itself, was the curse that lay over mankind so far' (Nietzsche 1887: III, §28 [1969: 162]).

NIETZSCHE'S PATH FORWARD

The *Übermensch* (superman) ideal is fundamentally a response to what Nietzsche sees as the value crisis arising from the realisation that 'God is dead' (the *Übermensch* figures prominently in Nietzsche 1883–5 but virtually disappears from his thought thereafter). The *Übermensch* can be characterised as the optimal human expression of the will to power, and will be a more powerful, more dynamic, more creative, more disciplined, and harder type with boundless love and enthusiasm for life and this world. Indeed the *Übermensch* will exemplify the Dionysian affirmation of life. The crucial ambiguity here is whether the *Übermensch* already completely embodies the requisite new values or whether it is the function of the *Übermensch* to create new values. The latter appears to be vital, but it entails an essential and problematic indeterminacy in the conception.

The doctrine of eternal recurrence was of more importance to Nietzsche. The underlying conception is of the world repeating itself endlessly in identical cycles (the idea is first introduced in Nietzsche 1882 but it is exploited more fully in the immediately following Nietzsche 1883–5). On the most plausible interpretation, the function of this notion is to graphically depict the maximally affirmative attitude to this world and oneself. The maximally affirmative attitude incorporates a love of life extending not only to its joys and good fortune, but also to its pains and misfortunes. It embraces a love of all the aspects of life to the extent of eagerly welcoming their eternal recurrence in their entirety. This is the Dionysian affirmation of life and constitutes Nietzsche's principal ideal. His popular audience has largely been drawn by such positive conceptions, whereas his academic audience has typically been more impressed with his destructive critiques.

THE NEW REALISM IN ETHICS

CHRISTIAN PILLER

In the period from 1870 to 1914 there was a shift within moral philosophy towards meta-ethical concerns. Metaethics and its guiding idea that the first task in moral philosophy is an enquiry into the semantics of moral discourse and into its ontological foundations, though by no means an invention of twentieth-century philosophy, has become its most characteristic feature.

The history of twentieth-century ethics starts in Cambridge, where in 1903 G. E. Moore published *Principia Ethica*. It rarely happens, as it did with *Principia Ethica*, that one book accounts for so many of the later developments in a field. It was Moore's declared intention to break sharply with the philosophical tradition. According to him, even the most prominent figures in the history of moral philosophy, for example, Aristotle, Kant, and Mill, have misunderstood the foundations of ethics. Too late to be of any influence on *Principia Ethica*, Moore thinks he has discovered a soul-mate. In the Preface to the first edition of *Principia Ethica* Moore writes: 'When this book had been completed, I found, in Brentano's *Origins of the Knowledge of Right and Wrong* opinions far more resembling my own, than those of any other ethical writer with whom I am acquainted' (Moore 1903 [1993a: 36]).

Brentano and Moore both try to provide a philosophical foundation of ethical knowledge that can withstand the undermining efforts of relativism and subjectivism. In this sense they are both realists. They also share the methodological conviction that only meta-ethical investigations can provide solid foundations for morality. Brentano and Moore agree in their philosophical aims; their arguments, however, lead them through quite different territories: ontology and the nature of moral properties in Moore's case, psychology and the nature of moral thinking in Brentano's case.

1. G. E. MOORE

According to Moore, moral philosophy has to answer three questions: which actions ought we to perform? Which things are good in themselves? And, what is it to be good? The answers to these questions depend on each other. First, we can only find out what we ought to do once we know which things are good. And, secondly, our knowledge of what is good can only be secured by knowing what it is to be good. The first statement expresses Moore's commitment to a consequentialist moral theory, which holds that whether some action is morally right or wrong depends on the value of the consequences this action brings about. The second statement expresses Moore's view about the priority of meta-ethics. In order to have a philosophically sound view of what things are good, we need to know what it is to be good, or – what Moore regarded as equivalent – we need to know how 'good' is to be defined.

What then is it to be good? Moore's answer is brief. 'If I am asked "What is good?" my answer is that good is good, and that is the end of the matter. Or, if I am asked "How is good to be defined?" my answer is that it cannot be defined, and that is all I have to say about it' (1903a [1993: 58]).

In *Principia Ethica* Moore's first argumentative aim is to establish the inde-finability of goodness. If 'good' is indefinable, then goodness will have to be a simple property, because, if it were complex, it could be defined by giving its constituents. Simplicity, however, is not a sufficient ontological match for indefinability. The same simple property could, in principle, be picked out by two different expressions, and Moore adds a further claim: the property of being good is unique. This idea we find already in Moore's motto for *Principia Ethica*: 'Everything is what it is and not another thing.'

With his famous open-question argument Moore tries to establish the inde-finability of goodness. Considering the idea that being good is nothing but being pleasant, Moore writes: 'Whoever will attentively consider with himself what is actually before his mind when he asks the question "Is pleasure (or whatever it may be) after all good?" can easily satisfy himself that he is not merely wonder-ing whether pleasure is pleasant' (1903a [1993: 68]). The question 'Is something that is pleasant, thereby good?' is an open question; the question 'Is something that is pleasant, thereby pleasant?' is not open, its answer is trivial. Therefore, Moore reasons, being good can neither be defined nor identified with being pleasant.

Could not someone who endorses an identification of goodness in some other way simply deny that the relevant question really is open? Although no one will deny that to some people it seems to be an open question, this fact could only establish that it is an open question if the identity of properties or notions is revealed to a thinker by simply thinking them. This assumption – an assumption which Moore thinks can rightly be made – is an important premise in the open-question argument. If Moore is right, a coherent doubt concerning the correctness of any analysis will by itself be sufficient for refuting it. Consequently, only trivial analyses could be correct. This problem has become known as 'the paradox of analysis'.

Moore became unhappy with the way in which he developed his ideas in *Principia Ethica*. In his draft for a preface to the second edition, written in 1921/2, he says that 'the book as it stands, is full of mistakes and confusions'; nevertheless, it aims to express 'a proposition of cardinal importance' which he still regards as true (1903a [1993: 2ff.]). Moore came to realise that he had chosen the wrong starting point. His concern was always ontological. He concentrated on the indefinability of goodness to say something about the nature of what it is to be good. The indefinability thesis, however, fails to establish the intended conclusion, which is that goodness is a unique property. We can think of goodness in different ways. One can find the recognition of this point already in *Principia Ethica*: 'Whenever he thinks of "intrinsic value", or "intrinsic worth", or says that a thing "ought to exist", he has before his mind the unique object – the unique property of things – which I mean by "good"' (1903a [1993: 68]). Moore regards ethics as autonomous, a view shared by Sidgwick and Kant among others. What distinguishes Moore from Sidgwick and Kant is that Moore tries to secure the autonomy of ethics ontologically: its most fundamental object, the property of being good, is unique. 'What I think I really meant is that it [the property of being good] is very different from all natural and metaphysical properties; and this I still think is true' (1903a [1993: 15]).

All things that are good might also have other properties in common. They might, for example, be all objects of a supersensible will or, if they are experiences, they might all be pleasant. Still, it would be a mistake to identify goodness with any of these properties, a mistake Moore sees being committed by, amongst others, Aristotle, Bentham, Kant, and Mill: 'far too many philosophers have thought that when they named those other properties they were actually defining good; that these properties, in fact, were simply not 'other', but absolutely and entirely the same with goodness. This view I propose to call the "naturalistic fallacy"' (1903a [1993: 62]).

Moore's claim that there is naturalistic fallacy is not an argument for but rather an expression of his idea that goodness is unique. The problem with the uniqueness thesis – a problem Moore is well aware of in his later writings – is how to distinguish it from a tautology, like 'everything is what it is' or 'good is good and that is the end of the matter'. What Moore tells us about goodness is that it is neither a natural nor a metaphysical property, 'Non-naturalism' has become the standard label for Moore's position. A substantial account of the non-natural would give substance to Moore's uniqueness thesis.

In his writings we can distinguish four attempts to characterise the non-natural. (1) A non-natural property is not detachable. 'It is immediately obvious that when we see a thing to be good, its goodness is not a property which we can take up in our hands, or separate from it even by the most delicate scientific instruments, and transfer to something else' (1903a [1993: 175]). The idea that, in contrast to non-natural properties, natural properties could exist in time by themselves is part of Moore's early metaphysics, which he rejected later on. (2) True ascriptions of a non-natural property do not entail any ontological commitment to that which has these properties. ' . . . all truths of the form "This is good in itself" are logically independent of any truth about what exists' (Moore 1903b: 116.) (3) A non-natural property is a derivative or, in terms of contemporary philosophy, a supervenient property. 'It is *impossible*', Moore writes, 'that of two exactly similar things one should possess it [intrinsic value] and the other not, or that one should possess it in one degree, and the other in a different one' (Moore 1922 [1993a: 287]). This attempt to capture the non-natural is most prominent in Moore's writings (and within the framework of his rejected early metaphysics the suggestion made in (1) also points in this direction). Moore's struggle to give a clear account of supervenience is evident in the draft of the Preface (Moore 1903a [1993: 1–27]), in 'The Conception of Intrinsic Value' (1922), as well as in his 'Replies to My Critics' (1942) where he says: 'It is true, indeed, that I should have never thought of suggesting that goodness was "non-natural", unless I had supposed it was "derivative" in the sense that, whenever a thing is good (in the sense in question) its goodness (in Mr. Broad's words) "depends on the presence of certain non-ethical characteristics" possessed by the thing in question' (Moore 1942: 588). If it is indeed Moore's considered view that the mark of the evaluative is its supervenience on the natural, then his project to distinguish the evaluative from the natural domain via supervenience alone must look doubtful, because why should what supervenes on the natural be itself non-natural? (4) A non-natural property is intrinsically normative. We have seen that in *Principia Ethica* Moore treats 'ought to exist' as a synonym for 'being good', and so it has been suggested that one should analyse Moore's non-natural goodness in terms of what we ought or have reason to do. Moore, however, rejects such a proposal. Even if goodness gives us, provided that we are in the appropriate circumstances, a reason to act and even if, furthermore, all reasons for acting are grounded in goodness, the evaluative, Moore insists, cannot be reduced to the deontic: 'Is it not possible to *think* that a thing is intrinsically good without thinking that the fact that an action within our power would produce it would be a reason for supposing that we ought to do that action? It certainly seems as if we can; and this seems to me to be a *good*, even if not *conclusive*, reason for supposing that the two functions ['x is good' and 'the fact that we can produce x is a reason for doing so'], even though logically equivalent, are *not* identical' (Moore 1942: 599). Moore's rejection of an account of goodness in terms of reasons could also be seen as an expression of his commitment to a consequentialist moral theory, a view that requires an independent notion of goodness.

Trying to explain the non-natural was Moore's way of giving substance to his thesis that goodness is unique. But the fact that a property is unique doesn't seem to require any specific ontological placement. Surely some properties that are unique and simple, yellow for example, will belong to the natural properties. Thus, goodness need not be non-natural in order to be unique and simple. Moore agrees: 'Even if it [being good] were a natural object, that would not alter the nature of the [naturalistic] fallacy nor diminish its importance a whit' (Moore 1903a [1993: 65]). If we left accounts of the non-natural behind, uniqueness would simply amount to non-reducibility.

Once we know what it is to be good, how can we find out which things are good? Moore thinks that here we need to rely on our intuitions. No commitment to any strange faculty that would infallibly put us in touch with the evaluative domain is thereby implied. By talking about intuitions, Moore says, 'I mean *merely* to assert that they are incapable of proof' (Moore 1903a [1993: 36]). The attempt to distinguish between things good in themselves on the one hand and instrumental goods on the other leads Moore to the test of absolute isolation when considering whether something is good in itself: 'In order to arrive at a correct decision on ... this question [what things have intrinsic value], it is necessary to consider what things are such that, if they existed *by themselves*, in absolute isolation, we should yet judge their existence to be good (Moore 1903a [1993: 236]). This account not only excludes instrumental goods from those things good in themselves, it also falsifies any relational account of goodness, like the suggestion that something is good if it is what most agents most deeply want. Thus, it has to be seen as an account of intrinsic goodness that works under the assumption that being good is the simple property as Moore conceived it. His view that ethical egoism, the view that for everyone one's own well being is one's highest good, is inconsistent, also arises from this view about what it is to be good. For Moore, the egoist's central notion goodness-for-someone has to be explained, contrary to the egoist's intentions, by Moore's notion of simple or absolute goodness.

Applying the isolation test, Moore claims that 'by far the most valuable things, which we know or can imagine, are certain states of consciousness, which may roughly be described as the pleasures of human intercourse and the enjoyment of beautiful objects' (Moore 1903a [1993: 237]). Beautiful objects are good by themselves, even if never experienced, but when they are, the unity of experience and beauty is far more valuable than its parts, thereby illustrating Moore's doctrine of organic unities, according to which the value of a whole is not simply the sum of the value of its parts.

Our reasons for doing something are grounded in the value of what will be brought about by our actions. 'The only possible reason that can justify any action is that by it the greatest possible amount of what is good absolutely should be realized' (Moore 1903a [1993: 153]). Moore is not an intuitionist about what we ought to do. Uncertainty concerning the consequences of our actions, as well as the fact that value attaches to organic unities, makes it difficult to know what our duties are. Thus, Moore did not develop a catalogue of duties and, strictly speaking, his practical ethics cannot go beyond the simple advice to do whatever is best.

2. FRANZ BRENTANO (1838–1917)

Brentano was appointed professor of philosophy in Vienna in 1874 where he taught for twenty years. His main works in moral philosophy are *The Origin of Our Knowledge of Right and Wrong* (1889) and *The Foundation and Construction of Ethics* (1952), which is based on lecture notes Brentano used for his course on practical philosophy given at the University of Vienna between 1876 and 1879. His moral philosophy, though, is not confined to these writings because it arises from views developed in his major work *Psychology from an Empirical Standpoint* (1874).

Brentano shares Moore's view that ethics is both autonomous and objective. 'Is there such a thing as moral truth taught by nature itself and independent of ecclesiastical, political, and every kind of social authority? Is there a moral law that is natural in the sense of being universally and incontestably valid – valid for men at all places and all times – and are we capable of knowing that there is such a law? My answer is emphatically affirmative' (Brentano 1889 [1969: 6]). Whereas Moore tried to secure the autonomy and objectivity of ethics on an ontological level, Brentano's approach is psychological. But psychological in the special sense of belonging to what Brentano calls 'descriptive psychology', the aim of which is an analysis of the conceptual framework of the mental. 'To understand the true source of our ethical knowledge, we must consider the results of recent investigations in the area of descriptive psychology' (1889 [1969: 11]).

In opposition to Kant, who distinguishes between thinking, feeling, and willing as the three fundamental classes of mental phenomena, Brentano's three-fold distinction separates the intellectual phenomena into the class of presentations and the class of judgements and subsumes feeling and willing under the phenomena of love and hate. Presentations are the fundamental category of all mental phenomena. Their characteristic feature is their *intentionality*. In every mental activity the mind is related to an object: every thinking is a thinking of something (see Brentano 1874 [1995: 88–91]). Judgements are not simply combinations of presentations. In judging we take a stand in regard to the existence of the object of our presentation. A judgement is a genuine mental act in which what we think of is either accepted as existing or rejected (and not both).

This 'polarity' of judgements allows us to introduce a notion of correctness. If one person accepts something that another rejects only one of them can be correct. Mainly for epistemological reasons, Brentano came to reject a correspondence theory of correctness. We could not find out whether a judgement is correct if, in order to do so, we had to compare our beliefs with facts in themselves and see whether they correspond to each other. But Brentano did not embrace a coherence theory of truth either. He thinks that as an empiricist he has to provide an account of correctness that is based on our experiences. In some cases, he holds, we can experience the correctness of our own judgement. If I am thinking of something, I know with certainty that I am thinking of something. In this sense, judgements of inner perception are immediately 'evident'. If I judge with evidence, Brentano argues, then I experience myself as judging correctly. On the basis of this notion of evidence, Brentano introduces the wider notion of truth. A judgement concerning some object O is true if an evident judger of O – God, for example – would accept O.

The third class of mental phenomena, the phenomena of love and hate, share with judgements the feature that in loving or hating something we take a stand in regard to something we think about. Because the phenomena of love and hate exhibit polarity, we can introduce a notion of correct and incorrect love and hate, and the notion of correctness as it applies to love and hate is introduced in an analogous way to the notion of a correct judgement. In some cases of loving or hating our love or hate is experienced as being correct. 'We know with immediate evidence that certain of our attitudes are correct. And so we are able to compare the objects of these various attitudes and thus to arrive at the general concept of a correct emotion' (Brentano 1966: 294).

Moore and Brentano share the philosophical aim of showing that morality is an objective matter. They also agree on the structure of ethics. Both are consequentialists and both think that meta-ethics is fundamental: 'How are we to go about establishing the concept of the good? This is the first and most urgent question, and everything depends on its being answered' (Brentano 1952 [1973: 122]). But on the very central issue, the issue of what it is to be good, Brentano departs from Moore. It is a general feature of Brentano's philosophy to explain apparently ontological distinctions in psychological terms. For example, because rejecting something is a different mental act from accepting something, one will not need negative correlates to whatever is part of one's ontology. Similarly, modal notions are explained in terms of distinct kinds of judgements. When thinking of an object alone gives rise to our rejection of it, we reject it apodictically, and that explains, according to Brentano, its impossibility. To be true, for Brentano, is to be accepted by an evident judger, and a similar move explains what it is to be good. Whereas Moore would say that something is rightly loved because it is good, Brentano reverses the order of explanation. Something is good because it can be loved with a love that is correct. 'We have arrived at the source of our concepts of the good and the bad, along with that of our concepts of the true and the false. We call a thing true when the affirmation relating to it is correct. We call a thing good when the love relating to it is correct' (Brentano 1889 [1969: 18]). There is no property of being good that some things have and others do not and whose unique ontological status would give ethics its genuine subject matter. The basic subject matter of ethics is the correctness of a genuine intentional relation, the relation of loving or hating something. This account solves a problem any objectivist has to face. If Brentano is right and to be good is to be loved correctly, then the motivational aspect of being good is built into its analysis: the good moves us because what is good is loved. Whereas if goodness is a non-natural property, more needs to be said as to why we should we care about it.

Which things are loved correctly? Brentano mentions the love of knowledge and insight, the preference of joy over sadness (unless it is joy in the bad), and the love of the correctness of our emotional attitudes, i.e. correctly loving something is itself an object of correct love. Like Moore, Brentano argues against classical hedonism, allowing for a multiplicity of goods. Right action is determined by the value that these actions promise to bring about. 'Thus one must consider not only oneself, but also one's family, the city, the state, every living thing upon the earth, and one must consider not only the immediate present but also the distant future. All this follows from the principle of the summation of good. To further the good throughout this great whole as far as possible – this is clearly the correct end in life, and all our actions should be centred around it' (Brentano 1889 [1969: 32]).

Brentano's moral philosophy is built on his analogy between judgements and the phenomena of love and hate. But judgements are not strictly parallel to love and hate. Whereas truth, arguably, does not admit of degrees, goodness definitely does. Brentano argues that the act of preferring is the psychological basis of the being-better-than relation. As our knowledge of what is good comes from our experience of correct love, so does our knowledge of what is better come from our experience of correct preference. But the fact that goodness comes in degrees is not the only disanalogy. The crucial step, the step from the polarity of mental phenomena to a notion of correctness, seems to exhibit a further divergence. Polarity implies that what we accept we cannot, at the same time, reject; that what we love we cannot, at the same time, hate. This point alone is not sufficient for a notion of correctness, which requires also that if one person accepts (loves) something and another rejects (hates) it, only one of them will have judged (loved) correctly. It is generally agreed that in the case of judgements a general notion of correctness applies, though Brentano, understanding truth in psychological terms, cannot explain why it does by any appeal to a correspondence between what is judged and what is the case. In the case of love and hate a general notion of correctness seems more dubious. If our attitudes toward some food diverge, why should my love of it be correct? Brentano did indeed make room for such cases: 'So far as the feelings about sense qualities are concerned, we might say that these things are a matter of taste, and "De gustibus non est disputandum"' (Brentano 1889 [1969: 22]). But then Brentano has also to admit that the polarity of the phenomena of love and hate does not in all cases give rise to a notion of correctness. This finds no parallel in the case of judgements and thus puts some pressure on Brentano's analogy between judgements and the phenomena of love and hate.

3. FURTHER DEVELOPMENTS

Moore and Brentano advance different versions of an objective view of morality. The following decades see the emergence of new forms of subjectivism (Ralph Barton Perry) and relativism (Edvard Westermarck) as well as the rise of non-cognitivism (Axel Hagerström, A. J. Ayer). We also see the development of a distinctive moral philosophy within American pragmatism which is naturalistic and which sees ethics, by analogy with the natural sciences, as an on-going process of experiment and adjustment. The roots of this pragmatist position go back to William James, who starts his programmatic essay 'The Moral Philosopher and the Moral Life' (1891) with the claim 'that there is no such thing possible as an ethical philosophy dogmatically made up in advance' (p. 184). Moral concepts have their source in the interests, needs, and desires of living beings. The only reason why something ought to be the case is that someone wants it to be the case. Moral problems arise because interests and needs can come into conflict. As a solution to conflict James suggests that one 'invent some manner of realizing your own ideals which will also satisfy the alien demands' (p. 205). John Dewey, another leading pragmatist, agrees that such a harmonisation of interests is what the morally educated person will aim for. Also in agreement with James, Dewey emphasises the exclusive means-end character of all practical deliberation. There is no metaphysical justification of something as an ultimate standard; everything, even our evaluations themselves, Dewey thinks, has to be judged empirically by the consequences it has in regard to our interests and needs. What is regarded as a final standard in one situation can be put into question in another. Dewey's instrumentalism leads to an anti-foundationalist and holistic picture of practical justification.

Returning to the legacy of Moore and Brentano, the most important development in England is the emergence of the 'intuitionist' school based in Oxford, of which Harold Prichard and Sir David Ross were the most prominent members. While broadly agreeing with Moore on meta-ethics, these philosophers differed sharply from him on ethical theory (see chapter 58 for an account of their work). Much more similar to Moore's ethical theory is the position advanced by Hastings Rashdall in *The Theory of Good and Evil* (1905). Rashdall had been a student of Sidgwick, and, like Moore, rejected Sidgwick's hedonism while preserving his consequentialist account of morality in the context of a plurality of goods. Rashdall coined the term 'ideal utilitarianism' to describe the resulting position and the term has been subsequently applied to Moore.

Among Brentano's students, Alexius Meinong and Christian von Ehrenfels made substantial contributions to value theory. Alexius Meinong's (1853–1920) views on the nature of value developed and changed substantially over his lifetime. He left the psychologistic views of *Psychologisch-Ethische Untersuchungen zur Werttheorie* (*Psychological-Ethical Investigations in the Theory of Value*, 1894) behind and emphasised the objectivity of values in his later works 'Über emotionale Präsentation' ('On Emotional Presentations', 1917) and *Zur Grundlegung der allgemeinen Werttheorie* (*The Foundation of a General Theory of Value*, 1923). His writings on value theory are unified by the same methodological approach that we have found in Brentano. In order to understand what values are we have to look at how values are manifested in our experience. The basis of value theory is an analysis of value experience which itself has to be fitted into a general conceptual framework of mental phenomena. Following Kazimir Twardowski's *Zur Lehre vom Inhalt und Gegenstand der Vorstellungen* (*On the Content and Object of Presentations*, 1894 [1977]), Meinong distinguishes between the act, content, and object of mental phenomena. The object of a thought need not be real – we can think of golden mountains without there being such things – but the content as part of our presentation is always real. The distinction between the mental act, its content, and its object is not limited to the class of presentations. We also find it in judgements, and, Meinong suggests, in feelings and desires.

Feelings are the primary location at which values manifest themselves. Suppose someone expresses a feeling by saying that the sky is especially beautiful today. This feeling presupposes the judgement that the sky with its natural qualities, like its blueness and brightness, exists. But the feeling also makes us aware of its beauty. The feeling, Meinong would say, has a content by which it refers to an object which in this case is the sky's beauty. We need the category of content to describe mental phenomena and because content is by its nature representational, the assumption that feelings have content leads to the acceptance of values as their referential objects. 'When I say, "The sky is blue," and then say, "The sky is beautiful," a property is attributed to the sky in either case. In the second case a feeling participates in the apprehension of the property, as, in the first case, an idea does. And it is natural to let the feeling be the presentative factor in the second case, as an idea is always taken to be in the first case' (1917 [1972: 28f.]).

If we think of a golden mountain we think of something physical that is not real; the object of our thought is a physical mountain that is not real, it is not a real mental image of a golden mountain. This leads Meinong to the view, famously criticised by Russell, that there are things, like golden mountains and round squares, that do not, or even cannot, exist. The relevance of this point for moral philosophy is the following: to show that there is an object of feeling, a 'dignitative', does not establish their existence. Although Meinong has provided a place for objective values as what our feelings refer to, he recognises that he has not yet shown that these objects exist or are real. He is sceptical about Brentano's view that immediate evidence can secure the objectivity of value statements. In the end, Meinong appeals to common sense. 'For anyone who considers the facts, and is not merely making deductions from ready-made theories, cannot well deny that justice, gratitude, and benevolence carry the guarantee of their worth in themselves in a way in which their opposites not only lack such a guarantee but also carry a guarantee to the contrary' (1917 [1972: 109]).

Christian von Ehrenfels (1859–1932), who today is best remembered for inaugurating Gestalt psychology with his essay 'Über "Gestaltqualitäten"' ('On "Gestalt qualities"', 1890), was a student of both Brentano and Meinong. The relationship with Meinong was one of acknowledged mutual influence, illustrated in their extensive debate about the analysis of feelings and desires and the relations that hold between them. The underlying view that a theory of value will be based on an analysis of psychological phenomena is, as we have seen, central to all philosophers of the Brentano school. For Meinong, feelings acquaint us with values, whereas Ehrenfels thought that desires are the phenomena most closely connected with value. In contrast to Meinong's later philosophy, Ehrenfels remained sceptical of any objective account of values. Desiring, according to Ehrenfels, is not based on the recognition of some essence of things called 'value', rather we take things to be valuable because we desire them. 'Value is a relation between an object and a subject which expresses that the subject either actually desires the object or would desire it if the subject were not already convinced of its existence' (Ehrenfels 1897 [1982: 261]).

Ehrenfels rejected Brentano's idea that some of our emotional attitudes are experienced as correct. The agreement in our evaluation of knowledge, for example, can be explained, without recourse to evident emotions, simply by the general usefulness of knowledge for anyone, whatever one's aims are. The ideas of the Austrian school of economics (Menger, Böhm–Bawerk, von Wieser) were another source of inspirations for Ehrenfels. The law of marginal utility, Ehrenfels argues, applies beyond the domain of economic goods. Take for example the different attitudes to motivational dispositions like being altruistic and being mainly concerned about one's own good. Without self-interest, Ehrenfels argues, the human race could not exist. Thus, the effects of altruism and self-interest on the common good alone cannot explain why we hold the one in much higher esteem than the other. The true explanation has to focus on a comparison of the rarity of the two dispositions. Altruism is valued higher because the demand for it exceeds its supply. If values are subjective, they change with our concerns and interests. Ehrenfels's analysis of the mechanisms of these changes, from which intrinsic values, things desired for their own sake, are of course not exempted, is influenced by Darwinian ideas. He talks about the struggle for existence among values and sees the changes of values as an aspect of general evolutionary processes.

INDIVIDUALISM VS. COLLECTIVISM

PETER NICHOLSON

INTRODUCTION

In Britain, the period from 1870 to 1914 was one of a general movement, both in politics and in philosophical reflection on it, from individualism to collectivism (Collini 1979: ch. 1; Gaus 1983: ch. 1; Greenleaf 1983; Bellamy 1992: ch. 1). These are loose and disputed terms (M. Taylor 1996). Roughly, individualism meant leaving the individual as free as possible to pursue his own interests as he saw fit, society being simply a collection of individuals and a means to their ends. Collectivism was more or less the opposite, holding that individuals are not isolated atoms but social beings with shared interests, and that society may act through the state to promote them. Collectivism ranged in degree from occasional government action to effect particular social reforms, to state socialism's control of the means of production and restructuring of society.

The dominant political theory, Liberalism, adapted itself to the new political conditions. Earlier in the nineteenth century, Liberalism had sought to maximise individual freedom and assumed that this entailed minimising state action. It restricted state action to what was unavoidable because all state action was by its very nature an interference with individual liberty and therefore intrinsically bad, and also bad in its effects, especially by reducing individuals' self-reliance. But later many Liberals accepted state action. They realised that for most individuals freedom from interference was worthless because they lacked the means to utilise it. State action could secure those means, and thus was not necessarily opposed to individual liberty.

J. S. Mill was an important background figure. He had begun the shift from individualism by focusing on a rich idea of 'individuality' instead of self-interest understood in bare material and hedonist terms, though he did not sufficiently emphasise its social nature (Mill 1859). He had already allowed that there should be exceptions to the general rule of *laissez-faire*, giving the state an interventionist role on a small scale and within strict limits set by an inviolable sphere of individual liberty (Mill 1848: Bk V, ch. xi). Mill came to envisage a larger role for the state, and in his *Autobiography* called himself a 'socialist' (Mill 1873: 239, 241). In the period considered here, a succession of British thinkers, all in the broad Liberal tradition, continued to move towards recommending greater state action, in response to circumstances and always within limits set by moral criteria and especially by a fundamental concern for individual autonomy. Mill is now usually seen as himself a significant contributor to collectivism (Bellamy 1992; Wolfe 1975: ch. 2); but the idealist thinkers reacting to him were more exercised by the negative features of his thought – his emphasis on liberty as absence of restraint, on its restriction only to prevent harm to others, and on the apparent equation of law with restraint (Ritchie 1891: ch. III; Bosanquet 1899: ch. III).

The philosophers discussed here were part of the movement towards collectivism, responding to it and adding considerable impetus. They attacked individualism, both the popular attitude of the individual's absolute right to 'do as he liked with his own' and its theoretical defence, notably by Herbert Spencer (Spencer 1884; M. W. Taylor 1992), as politically retrograde and intellectually confused. They sympathised with Matthew Arnold's complaint that 'we have not the notion, so familiar on the continent and to antiquity, of *the State*, – the nation in its collective and corporate character, entrusted with stringent powers for the general advantage, and controlling individual wills in the name of an interest wider than that of individuals' (Arnold 1869: 83). The British idealists advocated greater state action, and to this extent were collectivists. However, they were strongly opposed to state socialism. Their own position, a kind of collectivist liberalism, is rooted in their moral and political philosophy, which may be classed as perfectionist (Hurka 1993). This is clearly visible in the work of T. H. Green, and is replicated in all essentials, as well as developed, by a series of thinkers influenced by him, D. G. Ritchie, Bernard Bosanquet, and L. T. Hobhouse.

GREEN

In his *Prolegomena to Ethics* (1883) Green holds that men act to gain self-satisfaction on some idea of their own good. But because they are social beings their interests are bound up with the interests of other members of the community; hence their idea of their own good includes the good of others, for example, a mother's includes her children's. The idea that men always have opposed interests, and must choose between good for others (Benevolence) and good for self (Self-Love), is 'a fiction of philosophers' (Green 1883: sect. 232), due to abstracting men from the facts of their social context. There must be some idea of *a* common good among its members for any community to exist, and for moral duty and authoritative law to be intelligible (Green 1883:

sects. 190, 199–205; Green 1886: sects. 25–6, 113–39). Individuals draw their conceptions of their own and the common good from their society, sometimes amending them (the social dimension of individuality is strikingly presented by another British idealist, F. H. Bradley who supplements it by exploring individuals' contributions to their society – see Bradley 1876: Essays V and VI). What has been judged the common good has developed historically. Modern European societies recognise that all human beings are equal and form a single moral community, and that the moral good is virtuous action for its own sake (Green 1883: sects. 206–45). These are 'complementary': only moral goodness can be *the* common good for all humanity, because only that could be achieved simultaneously by every human being (Green 1883: sect. 244). The content of this universalisable life of moral perfection, which is the true good whose achievement would provide permanent self-satisfaction, is still being worked out as mankind gradually refines and extends its moral ideas. Furthermore, the ideals which have been acquired as abstract principles are not always put into practice (Green 1883: sects. 213, 245; Green 1886: sects. 154–5, 220).

Everyone has a duty not to seek their own good at anyone else's expense. In addition, 'the responsive conscience' acknowledges 'a claim on the part of all men to such positive help from all men as is needed to make their freedom real' (Green 1883: sect. 270). Green considers this principally in relation to one's own society. One can help others as an individual, or by voluntarily associating with others, or collectively through the state. In all cases there is a fundamental difficulty. The aim is to help others to be good, but: 'No one can convey a good character to another. Every one must make his character for himself' (Green 1883: sect. 332). The problem is greatest with state action. On the one hand, the state works through compulsion or the threat of compulsion and therefore it cannot promote morality directly, since to be moral one must do what is right because it is right, not because one is compelled to do it; moreover, enforcement may weaken moral motivation. On the other hand, Green holds that it is the function of the state to maintain the conditions for individuals to act morally, for example, by ensuring people receive education (Green 1881: 202; Green 1886: sect. 18). He tries to balance the two considerations. He rejects the individualists' confinement of the state to protecting individuals' rights of person and property. He allows the state to act positively to promote for everyone conditions favourable to moral life. This may interfere with the liberty of the individual to do as he likes, so valuable to the individualist, but the interference is permissible. The individual has no right prior to society guaranteeing him absolutely from interference by the state: rather, rights are recognised by society to protect the powers it judges individuals need to exercise in order to live morally. However, the state 'must take care not to defeat its true end by narrowing the region within which the spontaneity and disinterestedness of true morality can have play', and to limit itself to maintaining conditions for the performance of self-imposed duties (Green 1886: sect. 18). Ideally, people would help themselves, or others would help them spontaneously (hence his support for cooperatives, friendly societies, and trades unions). But Green qualifies the traditional Liberal doctrine of self-help by explicitly acknowledging that people may be in such desperate circumstances that they cannot help themselves, and that voluntary action may be absent or inadequate – then, as in Britain in his day, the society should act collectively through the state (Green 1881: 203–4; Nicholson 1990: Study V; Bellamy 1992: 35–47). With popular government, state action is simply the society acting through law (after the 1867 Reform Act, though only a minority of adults had the vote, the majority of them were working class).

Obviously, this is an open-ended approach requiring practical judgement. Green himself supported legislation to regulate conditions of work in mines and factories, higher standards of housing, compulsory free unsectarian elementary education, improved opportunities for women (especially in education), reform of the land law to encourage wider ownership, and stricter control of the sale of liquor. All are described as 'removing obstacles' to living the moral life (Green 1886: sects. 209–10). There are also definite limits. Green can endorse some socialistic measures, that is, measures restricting individuals' actions for the sake of the social good, but his fundamental acceptance of capitalism rules out any systematic and widespread socialism. Full state control of the economy 'would imply a complete regulation of life' incompatible with moral freedom (Green 1886: sect. 223). He favours capitalism for the opportunities it allows individuals: it is a necessary condition of the development of individuals as moral agents that 'free play should be given to every man's powers of appropriation' (Green 1886: sect. 219). However he subjects capitalism, like everything else, to moral criteria, and recommends limitation of the power of landlords, and protection for workers, in order to ensure a fair chance for all to acquire (through labour) sufficient means for an independent life (Green 1886: sects. 210–31; Muirhead 1908: xi–xiii, 91–103; Greengarten 1981: ch. 5; Nicholson 1990: Study III).

After Green, it was fully explicit that Liberalism had a new option. He provided a moral justification for the 'constructive' Liberalism emerging in the 1870s. This was collectivist to the extent that it assigned a larger and more positive role to the state, using it as society's agent to create the conditions necessary for everyone to have a fair chance to develop their moral capacities. Green reconceived the individual from an isolated atom to an active member of his society, and redefined his freedom from absence of restraint to the achievement of morality – freedom is 'a positive power or capacity of doing or enjoying something worth doing or enjoying . . . in common with others' (Green 1881: 199).

Thus he simultaneously undermined the older individualism which minimised state action, and offered a powerful justification for expanding state action in the service of the moral ideal. But the emphasis on collective political action is balanced by a continuing moral individualism: moral development can occur only in and through the lives of persons, who are morally valuable as states and nations are not (Green 1883: sects. 180–91). Individuals remain responsible for critically appraising and revising the moral standards of their society, and for implementing their ideals. Green's is, as Bellamy neatly expresses it, 'an individualist collectivism' (Bellamy 1992: 35), where collectivism is limited through subordination to a moral goal whose achievement requires that individual self-reliance is safeguarded from excessive state action.

RITCHIE, BOSANQUET, AND HOBHOUSE

Green's position is intrinsically open-ended and flexible and demands constant adjustment as circumstances change, and as social investigation reveals more about poverty and the success or failure of measures to deal with it. Did Green provide principles which were a definite guide to the amount of state action which was morally justified, or were they too general and ambivalent? Some have stressed the vagueness of Green's position and claimed that as a result his idealist followers diverged widely, splitting into a more collectivist and radical 'left' and a more individualist and conservative 'right', exemplified by Ritchie and Bosanquet respectively (Richter 1964: chs. 9, 10; Collini 1976: 107–9). An alternative view, followed here, is that there are underlying similarities and continuities which count for more than any differences.

Ritchie was very close to Green theoretically. He understood Green as repudiating the presumption in favour of *laissez-faire*, and assigning the state 'the duty of providing such an environment for individual men and women as to give *all*, as far as possible, an equal chance of realising what is best in their intellectual and moral natures' (Ritchie 1891: 149–50). Ritchie repeats that some things can only be done by individual effort (Ritchie 1902: 77). He was perhaps more explicit that the extent of state action is a matter of expediency, and suggested that idealists should borrow from Utilitarian methods and always pose 'the Utilitarian question: "Is this particular measure expedient in this case?"' as a means of avoiding misleading appeals to abstract justice or natural rights (Ritchie 1891: 105–23; Ritchie 1902: 33–8; Otter 1996: 109–11). But Ritchie accepted Green's strictures against Utilitarianism's hedonism (Green 1883: *passim*) and accordingly his criterion of expediency was social well-being defined in idealist terms instead of the greatest happiness (Ritchie 1891: 142–5, 167–72). But none of the actual examples he discussed suggests that he would have supported more extensive state action than Green had supported. Ritchie was also more explicit about the social nature of wealth, which is the product of the labour of many individuals working as members of an organised society (Ritchie 1893: 191–2). This seems to justify taxing owners of the means of production to finance measures to promote social well-being – something Green had thought would be fair but counter-productive (Green 1886: sect. 232). Like Green, however, Ritchie proposed the regulation of capitalism for the common good, not its abolition.

In his main philosophical treatment of politics, *The Philosophical Theory of the State* (1899), Bosanquet wrote that he followed Green 'very closely' on many points (Bosanquet 1899 [1924: iii]), and the chapter on 'Nature of the End of the State and Consequent Limit of State Action' repeated Green's central ideas with only minor variations (Bosanquet 1899: ch. VIII). For Bosanquet too 'the ultimate end of Society and the State as of the individual is the realisation of the best life' (Bosanquet 1899 [1923: 169]), and the function of the state was to maintain the necessary rights (Bosanquet 1899 [1923: 188–9]). Since the state acted through coercion it could not promote the good life directly, but it could and should 'remove obstructions' or 'hinder hindrances' to the moral life (Bosanquet 1899 [1923: 177–8]). There was little 'with which the State must not in some sense busy itself' (Bosanquet 1899 [1923: xii]). But such action was hard to perform successfully because it employed coercive law to 'elicit' the moral activity which by definition it could not produce (Bosanquet 1899 [1923: xxxix]). Bosanquet frequently stressed the dangers. For instance, to provide free school meals for the children of the poor would damage the self-reliance of the parents and set the wrong examples, showing the feckless that if they did not do their duty the public would do it for them and failing to reward the thrifty poor who did feed their children. This kind of approach to poverty was too mechanical and did not treat the parents as individual moral agents, some of whom might be persuaded to pay for the food (Bosanquet 1893: 346–8). Nonetheless, he argued his case on the merits of each particular instance. He did not rule out all social legislation. Whilst he rejected full state socialism, he allowed that socialist methods might be appropriate on occasion, as the most efficient (Bosanquet 1899 [1923: 296]; Bosanquet 1893: ch. X). The critical issue always was whether or not state action developed, or crushed, the moral character indispensable to the moral life which the state was intended to promote. It was the self-reliance side of Green's position, and the use of voluntary organisations to deliver help with discrimination and minimal risk of moral and material damage, which Bosanquet pressed, possibly in reaction against increasing calls for legislative solutions to poverty.

Hobhouse, on the other hand, one of the intellectual leaders of the New Liberals, energetically attacked the minimal state of the old Liberalism and advocated a positive and much more active state. He was not an idealist in philosophy, but in his political thought he was often very near to Green and he acknowledged that he and Green belonged to the same progressive stream of Liberalism. Precisely how near Hobhouse was to Green is controversial (compare Freeden 1978: 66–70 with Collini 1979: 125–30). Certainly Hobhouse also drew considerably on J. S. Mill (Freeden 1996: 195–203), but he described Green as Mill's 'true successor in the line of political thinkers' (Hobhouse 1904: 226 n.). In setting out his own account of Liberalism he adopted Green's idealist reformulations of the key concepts: the old freedom to do as one likes is curbed for the sake of positive freedom for all; rights (including property rights) are social and subject to control in the common interest; and the state is the widest association at the disposal of a people for the pursuit of common moral ends, though of limited use because it employs coercion (Hobhouse 1911a; Hobhouse 1911b: ch. IX; Hobhouse 1913b). He used these ideas, however, to support more state action than did Bosanquet, for example the introduction of old age pensions, health insurance, and a minimum wage (Hobhouse 1911a: ch. VIII). Addressing the self-reliance issue, Hobhouse contended that it was unjust to leave people to fend for themselves in the market and earn enough for a civilised life, when experience had proved that it was not possible for everyone to do so. The state must step in and 'secure conditions upon which its citizens are able to win by their own efforts all that is necessary to a full civic efficiency'. That was not the individual's responsibility (it was beyond his power) but society's. Securing economic rights (a right to work, a right to a living wage) might involve far-reaching economic reconstruction, and socialistic organisation of industry, but it would be a 'Liberal Socialism' (Hobhouse 1911a: 74–80). For Hobhouse, like Bosanquet and the other idealists, sought to moralise the market, and deployed socialism simply as a principle to guide reform not as a wholesale replacement for capitalism (Hobhouse 1911a: ch. VIII; Bellamy 1992: 54).

Undoubtedly, Hobhouse wanted more state action, especially in the economy, than did Bosanquet. Hobhouse was passionate about what needed to be done: Bosanquet was more cautious about whether legislation and government intervention would do it. Thus they often had different diagnoses of the facts of the situation, and different estimates of the likely outcome of proposed policies (in areas where agreement has still to be reached). Yet these were tactical disagreements over the practical application of shared principles. Notwithstanding Hobhouse's later onslaught on Bosanquet for illiberal Hegelianism, the fairness of which is disputable, it is legitimate to put them in the same category because both work with so many of Green's assumptions (Hobhouse 1918; Gaus 1983; Meadowcroft 1995: ch. 3).

CONCLUSION

These writers possessed a moral philosophy which enabled them to revise the earlier individualism and make room for greater state intervention in the interest of giving all members of society – and ultimately all mankind – the opportunity to develop their moral capacities completely. The individual, truly conceived, could develop completely only in a society and with its aid, including aid from its state. In that sense, individualism and a measure of collectivism were complementary. The same philosophy led them to reject full-scale collectivism because it would not allow individuals sufficient freedom to become moral agents, and everything depended upon the ability of agents to formulate moral ideals critically and to act upon them. Instead these philosophers supported a moralised capitalism which would be an arena for the exercise of freedom. Their restricted collectivism, therefore, was not some political compromise between individualism and collectivism, and their assertion of self-reliance was not merely a reflection of Victorian values. Both derived from a position independently grounded in philosophical principles.

Those principles were decisive between capitalism and state socialism, but not fully determinate at the level of particular policies. Such questions as whether the right to bequeath land should be limited, or whether the state should provide old-age pensions, could not be answered on any absolute principle but depended on circumstances (Green 1886: sect. 231; Bosanquet 1899 [1923: 179]; Ritchie 1902: 58–65; Muirhead 1908: 99; Hobhouse 1911b: 154–5). That unavoidably left much to individual interpretation, different estimates of the facts and their significance being possible. Specific policy questions could only be dealt with 'in the light of a true social ideal and of the best available experience' (Muirhead 1908: 99). These writers sometimes differed in their experience, and reached different policy conclusions. What is important is that they had the same social ideal.

MARXISM AND ANARCHISM

ALEX CALLINICOS

The years between 1870 and 1914 saw the emergence of international socialism as a force in European and, to a lesser extent, North American politics. Most notably in Germany, socialist parties began to attract significant blocs of votes. Their broader aspiration to become the agency of a global social transformation was reflected in the formation of the Second International in 1889. Plainly such aspirations required theoretical articulation, and thanks to the influence in particular of the German Social Democratic Party (SPD), Marxism became the most important socialist ideology (though its position never went unchallenged). Indeed, Marxism's transformation from the doctrine of a handful of German exiles in London into the ideology of a mass movement was largely the work of the SPD. Engels's key work of popularisation, *Anti-Dühring* (Marx and Engels 1975–98: XXV), was originally serialised in the SPD paper *Vorwärts* in 1877–8. The task of simplifying the complexities of Marx's concepts was later taken on by Kautsky as editor of the Social Democratic weekly *Neue Zeit*. His voluminous writings provided the way into Marxism for a generation of socialist militants, not merely in Germany but elsewhere in Europe.

MARX VS. BAKUNIN

The Marxism that was thus popularised itself gained sharper definition thanks to the emerging contrast between it and a rival radical ideology, anarchism. The contest between the followers of Marx and Bakunin helped to destroy the First International in the early 1870s. The respective movements which arose from this dispute – social democracy (as, following the example of the SPD, Marxists tended to call their parties) and anarchism – competed for influence in many countries, with Bakunin's followers often gaining the upper hand in Southern Europe.

The thought of both the founding figures had been formed in the same intellectual context – the disintegration of Hegelian idealism in the 1840s. Bakunin had, along with the critic Vissarion Belinsky, originally embraced an extravagantly quietist version of the Hegelian dialectic, according to which the rational understanding of reality required reconciliation with it. Perhaps because reconciliation with the specific social reality which confronted them – Romanov absolutism – was so unpalatable, this proved an impossible position to sustain. By the early 1840s Bakunin had moved from Right to Left Hegelianism.

In a celebrated article, 'The Reaction in Germany' (1842), he taxed Hegelian orthodoxy for its 'positive' treatment of existing social reality. This critique developed in some respects in parallel with Marx's later attempt to extract the 'rational kernel' of the Hegelian dialectic from its 'mystical shell'. Both seized on Hegel's concept of determinate negation, the flaw intrinsic to every concept, form of consciousness, and social institution necessitating its replacement by a more inclusive version. Marx gave the concept a straightforwardly social and historical reference – to the contradictions internal to every social formation which would doom it, after a phase in which it permitted the further development of the productive forces, to revolution, stagnation, or collapse. Bakunin, by contrast, treated negation as a abstract force, subverting and destroying every determinate social form. His essay ends with the famous announcement: 'Let us therefore trust the eternal Spirit which destroys and annihilates only because it is the unfathomable and eternally creative source of all life. The passion for destruction is a creative passion, too' (1842 [1965: 406]).

The conflict between these rival appropriations of Hegel reached its climax after the defeat of the Paris Commune in May 1871. Both Marx and Bakunin championed the Commune and claimed it as an instance of their version of social revolution. In the aftermath of the Commune Bakunin wrote *Statism and Anarchy*. Here he does not repudiate Marx's materialist conception of history. Conflicts between classes rooted in production are indeed the driving force of history. But the domination of the exploiters over the exploited reaches its most developed, concentrated, and malevolent form in the shape of what Bakunin calls 'statism' – the bureaucratic rule of the modern centralised state. He does not, as Max Weber would a little later, see this state as representing a source of social power distinct from and independent of class, but rather understands class exploitation and political domination as a single complex which it is the task of social revolution to destroy.

This revolution Bakunin saw at work within the Europe of his day. It would be carried out by a proletariat which he conceived much more broadly than did Marx. Whereas the latter identified the working class with wage-labourers, especially those employed in modern large-scale industry, Bakunin regarded the generality of the lower classes – peasants and unemployed, artisans and factory workers – as the agent of revolutionary transformation. Self-organised in small-scale communes, they would dismantle the centralised structures of economic and political power and replace them, not with a new form of state, but with a federation of self-governing collectives. The goal of the revolution was thus anarchy, the abolition of the state. Preparations for this transformation were already well advanced in Southern Europe and in Russia, where the innate collectivism of the peasantry predisposed them to anarchy. Counterposed to them as the embodiment of the rival principle of statism was Germany. The bureaucratic structures of the new Bismarckian Reich corresponded to the inborn servility of the German people – a servility displayed even by democrats and socialists. Thus Marx and his followers represented little more than the attempt to impose a new form of statist domination in the guise of social liberation.

As a theoretical critique of Marxism, Bakunin's arguments are fairly inept. The experience of the Commune encouraged Marx to clarify and extend his intuition, already expressed after the defeat of the Revolutions of 1848, that socialist revolution, at least on the continent, would have to direct itself against the modern bureaucratic state. In *The Civil War in France* (Marx and Engels 1871), Marx praised the Commune particularly for the steps it had taken to dismantle the centralised apparatuses of state power and replace them with structures much more directly accountable to the working people of Paris (themselves, in the shape of popular militias, forming the armed basis of political power). In his drafts, he went even further, calling the Commune 'a Revolution against the *State* itself, this supernaturalist abortion of society, a resumption by the people for the people, of its own social life' (Marx and Engels 1975–98: XXII, 486). That this was no temporary enthusiasm is suggested by the later 'Critique of the Gotha Programme' (1875), where Marx criticised the concessions which his German followers had made to Ferdinand Lassalle's state socialism when forming the SPD, affirming: 'Freedom consists in converting the state from an organ superimposed upon society into one completely subordinate to it' (Marx and Engels 1975–98: XXIV, 94).

The critical disagreement between Marx and Bakunin was therefore not over the objective of abolishing the state. Both regarded it as an inherently oppressive institution. Engels in *The Origin of the Family, Private Property, and the State* (Marx and Engels 1975–98, XXVI), sought to show how the state – conceived as a specialised coercive apparatus separate from the rest of society – emerged as part of the same process in which class antagonisms first crystallised. The point at issue was rather whether the state could be abolished instantaneously, in the act of revolutionary overthrow, or rather would gradually be dismantled in the course of a much larger process of transformation. Marx argued that this period of transition required a distinctive form of political rule, the dictatorship of the proletariat. Like any state, this would be a form of class domination, but in this instance the ruling class would be the majority, the proletariat, using radically democratic forms in order to eradicate their exploitation.

In the 'Critique of the Gotha Programme', Marx suggested that the transition period would require a different principle of distribution from that prevailing in what he called the 'higher phase of communist society'. Under the dictatorship of the proletariat, income would be distributed according the productive contribution made by individuals. What seemed to him the manifest defects of this principle – namely that it took no account of differences in individual needs and abilities – would be overcome only once further productive development and a transformation of motivations made possible the full flowering of a communist society in which neither classes nor the state any longer existed. Here the communist principle first formulated by Louis Blanc would apply: 'From each according to his abilities, to each according to his needs!'(Marx and Engels 1975–98: XXIV, 87).

Marx's differences with Bakunin therefore arose from his attempt to specify realistically the historical circumstances in which egalitarian principles could become operative. '*Willpower*, not economic conditions, is the basis of his revolution', he wrote of Bakunin (Marx and Engels 1975–98: XXIV, 519). Yet, if the latter's critique did not begin to engage with the complexity of Marx's views, one might still argue that it possesses a prophetic quality. Bakunin's claim to have detected a will to dominate concealed beneath German socialists' talk of emancipation could be taken as an anticipation of the way in which Russian revolutionaries after 1917 erected new structures of bureaucratic domination (though, given Bakunin's tendency to reduce social and political differences to ethno-racial categories, he would have been baffled by the fact that this was the outcome of a *Russian* revolution).

Thus Bakunin homes in on the supposedly temporary nature of the dictatorship of the proletariat: 'There is a flagrant contradiction here. If their [i.e. the Marxists'] state is to be truly a people's state, then why abolish it? But if its abolition is essential to the real liberation of the people, then how do they dare to call it a people's state' (1873 [1990: 179]). In his notes on *Statism and Anarchy*, Marx comments: 'as the proletariat in the period of struggle leading to the overthrow of the old society still acts on the basis of the old society and hence still moves within political forms which more or less correspond to it, it has at that stage not yet arrived at its final organization, and hence to achieve its liberation has recourse to methods which will be discarded once that liberation has been obtained' (Marx and Engels 1975–98: XXIV, 521). But, what if these methods turn out to be rather difficult to discard, perhaps because those adept in them have an interest in their preservation? Or, as Bakunin put it, 'no dictatorship can have any other objective than to perpetuate itself' (1873 [1990: 179]).

In any case, the radicalism of Marx's own critique of the state was initially concealed. The SPD leadership prevented the publication of the 'Critique of the Gotha Programme' till 1891. By then an association of socialism with the expansion of state power had become well entrenched in the parties of the Second International. Since various historical factors were promoting the state's greater involvement in social and economic life, it was natural for socialist parties' practical demands to require different kinds of state action. It was only during the First World War, which revealed a very different face of the state, that Lenin rediscovered the anti-statist thrust of Marx's political thought and made it the central theme of *The State and Revolution*.

NATURALISM AND MARXISM

The Marxism that was popularised under the Second International presupposed a particular interpretation (or, rather, a range of interpretations) of Marx's main concepts and theses. It was largely agreed that Marx's theory of history was one specification of a much broader conception of nature. In this sense, late nineteenth-century Marxism participated in the more general tendency of post-Darwinian intellectual culture to treat the social world naturalistically, as continuous with, and subject to the same laws as the physical world. Engels, who represented the link between the founders of historical materialism and the new mass socialist parties, played a critical role in articulating this understanding of Marxism. Thus, in his speech at Marx's graveside in March 1883, he compared Marx to Darwin.

Such a naturalistic interpretation of Marxism raised the question of what place within it could be found for Marx's Hegelian philosophical heritage. Engels's solution, most fully developed in the posthumously published *Dialectics of Nature*, was to extract from Hegel's logic certain general 'laws of the dialectic'. These – he usually listed three: the unity and interpenetration of opposites, the transformation of quantity into quality, and the negation of the negation – were universal laws of nature, operative everywhere. Nature as a whole was therefore subject to the same processes of historical transformation generated by internal conflicts which Hegel and Marx had detected in human society.

Though Engels's dialectics of nature is sometimes counterposed to Marx's philosophical views, various *obiter dicta* indicate that it had the latter's approval. As a philosophical strategy, it had two particular advantages. In the first place, the thought that the fundamental laws of nature were dialectical served to differentiate this version of naturalism from the fairly reductive physicalistic materialism which the writings of Büchner, Moleschott, and Vogt had made popular among liberals and radicals in mid-nineteenth-century Germany. Marx had contrasted his approach with earlier versions of this kind of materialism in the 1840s by arguing that humans interact and shape their environment through social labour rather than passively depend on it. This theme is continued by Engels, notably in the celebrated fragment, 'The Role of Labour in the Transition from Ape to Man'.

Secondly, conceiving nature as a complex of processes of historical transformation allowed Engels to connect Marx's theory of history with contemporary developments in the physical sciences, notably Darwin's theory of evolution by natural selection and the laws of thermodynamics. Insofar as these theories, like historical materialism, deal with time-oriented, irreversible processes, Marxism could be presented as going with the flow of scientific discovery. But, since the developments in the physical sciences on which Engels concentrated had taken place without the help of the Hegelian dialectic, in what sense could his dialectical 'laws' be said to direct or guide scientific research? The insistence by Stalinist ideologists in the Soviet Union that they should do so in a very strong sense has helped to discredit the very idea of dialectical materialism. Engels's own approach, however, seems to have been a much more relaxed one. His discussions of specific cases imply some sort of concept of emergence, in which particular domains of being have their own distinctive laws. Thus he argues that the mechanisms of natural selection discovered by Darwin do not govern the social world, and that Social Darwinist claims that they do are little more than capitalist apologetics. Where this relatively pluralistic naturalism leaves the three great 'laws' of the dialectic is an open question.

Of more immediate interest to the Marxists of the Second International were the implications of dialectical materialism for their understanding of history and politics. They had a very different intellectual formation from the founders of Marxism. As the most important among them, Kautsky, put it: 'They [Marx and Engels] started out with *Hegel*, I started out with *Darwin*. The latter occupied my thoughts earlier than Marx, the development of organisms earlier than the economy, the struggle for existence of species and races earlier than the class struggle' (1927 [1988: 7]). Kautsky indeed came to Marxism with an already formed evolutionary theory which reflected the very common contemporary tendency to accept Lamarck's view of evolution as the inheritance of adaptive features acquired by organisms through the impress of their environment on them.

His 'materialist Lamarckianism', as Kautsky called it, led him to conceive evolution, both biological and social, as a matter of the interaction between organism and environment. In this relationship, the requirements of the environment would invariably prevail over whatever initiatives the organism might make. The chief peculiarity of social evolution arose from the capacity of humans to construct 'artificial organs' – material means of production – to supplement their natural ones in meeting their needs. The unequal distribution of the means of production gave rise to exploitation and to class struggle, which Kautsky treated as occupying a relatively brief episode in the history of the human species, bracketed between the 'primitive communism' of early societies and the advanced communism which would follow socialist revolution.

This broad conception of social evolution led Kautsky to view the historical process as governed by what he liked to call 'irresistible' forces driving towards the progressive transformation of society. He brushed off the efforts of his friend Eduard Bernstein to argue that contemporary capitalist society was gradually ameliorating itself in ways that were making both Marxist social theory and revolutionary politics obsolete. The conflict between the increasingly concentrated and organised forces of capital and labour remained, according to Kautsky, the dominant fact about modern society. Yet the electoral growth of the SPD in the pre-war era encouraged him to believe that an organised working class would be able to conquer political power by electoral means, and subsequently to socialise the economy. While this process might suffer temporary reverses and delays, it would sooner or later lead to the replacement of capitalism by socialism: 'The capitalist social system has run its course; its dissolution is now only a question of time. Irresistible economic forces lead with the certainty of doom to the shipwreck of capitalist production. The substitution of a new social order for the existing one is no longer simply desirable, it has become inevitable' (1892 [1971: 117]).

Kautsky, therefore, while refusing formally to endorse historical determinism, regarded progressive social transformation as effectively inevitable. Other leading Marxists of the Second International took a similar stance. Plekhanov, for example, was much better read philosophically than Kautsky; his own version of historical materialism was, like Marx's and Engels's, shaped by his interpretation of Hegel. But, whereas Marx had taken from Hegel the idea of human subjectivity defining itself by acting on and transforming its environment, Plekhanov's was a reading which highlighted Hegel's teleology: '*The irresistible striving to the great historical goal, a striving which nothing can stop – such is the legacy of the great German idealist philosophy*' (1977: I, 483).

The 'irresistible' historical tendency that mattered most for him was not, as it was for Kautsky, the triumph of socialism in the Western industrial countries, but the transformation of Tsarist Russia by capitalism. At the roots of Plekhanov's Marxism lay his break, in the early 1880s, with the Populism dominant in the Russian revolutionary movement. The Populists believed that a conspiratorial putsch against the absolutist regime was necessary if Russia was avoid the kind of suffering which, according to Marx, the English working class had suffered during the Industrial Revolution. Russian society – and in particular, the peasant commune – contained within it all that was required to construct socialism. But revolution – to be achieved through the assassination of the Tsar and his leading officials – would have to happen quickly if Western capitalism were not to entrench itself in Russian society.

Plekhanov came to view this ideology (on which Bakunin's influence is manifest) as a form of voluntarism which sought to impose social revolution in the absence of the economic conditions required to sustain it. Socialism presupposed a development of the productive forces that only capitalism could bring. And capitalist social forms had already penetrated deep into Russia's soil. The commune was disintegrating as a result of commodification and social differentiation. The revolutionary movement would have to wait until capitalism had triumphed in Russia. Only then could there emerge the industrial working class which alone could carry through a socialist revolution. In the meantime, Russian Social Democracy should ally itself to the liberal bourgeoisie, the chief contemporary agent of historical progress and the potential leader of a revolution which, as in 1789 in France, would sweep away the absolutist order and create the bourgeois-democratic political framework required if capitalism were fully to attain its potential.

As Andrzy Walicki points out, Plekhanov's Hegel bore a remarkable resemblance to that of Belinsky and the young Bakunin in their right-Hegelian phase: 'The Marxism of Plekhanov and his comrades could also be called a specific variant of reconciliation with reality (the reality of Russian capitalism) in the name of historical necessity' (1995: 237). The political setting in which it developed drew Plekhanov into an unremitting polemic against the voluntarism of the Populists. He was particularly stringent in his denial of any creative historical role to individual actors. If, for example, a falling roof-tile had removed Robespierre from the French political scene in January 1793, someone else would have stepped forward to take his place. The influence of Hegel's conception of the world-historical individual, who expresses rather than creates the forces he appears to master, is evident here.

Plekhanov thus provided a particularly forceful statement of the understanding of historical materialism common to the Marxists of the Second International. It does not follow, of course, that this shared understanding ruled out disagreements among them. One such disagreement is worth discussing for what it reveals about the difficulties involved in the naturalistic interpretation of Marxism which prevailed in this period. It arose from Antonio Labriola's *Essays on the Materialistic Conception of History* (1896). This book constituted the first sophisticated account of Marx's theory of history, which is perhaps chiefly remembered for its critique of the idea that society can be understood as an aggregate of discrete independently constituted 'factors'. Labriola's insistence that such factors are in fact abstractions from a single, integrated social '*complexus*' greatly influenced Trotsky and anticipated Lukács's identification of the Marxist method with the category of totality.

Labriola says that this method 'makes history objective and in a certain sense naturalises it', by tracing the underlying causes of social action in the process of production. But he immediately distinguishes naturalising history in this way from what he calls 'Darwinism, social and political'. It is easy to see why he should, since the prevailing Social Darwinist appropriations of the theory of evolution by natural selection portrayed *laissez-faire* capitalism as a case of the survival of the fittest. His solution is to offer natural selection its own domain within history, namely the very first stage of human existence, 'that of simple nature not modified by work, and from thence are derived the imperious and inevitable conditions of the struggle for existence, with the consequent forms of adaptation'. Among these forms are 'races in the true and authentic sense', as opposed to 'secondary historico-formations, that is to say, peoples and nations'. Subsequent to this very early phase, humans came to rely on 'artificial means' – fire, tools, and the like – for their survival, unleashing a historical process which could no longer be understood in Darwinian terms (although the influence of race is one complicating factor when it comes to establishing the material causes of ideology) (Labriola 1896 [1908: 113, 114, 116, 221]).

Plekhanov takes Labriola to task for giving race even this limited explanatory role. He points out the difficulty of imagining a form of human existence which did not involve the use of artificial – in the sense of more or less consciously invented – devices of some kind in order to act on and thereby to change their environment, and dismisses the concept of race as an obstacle to scientific enquiry (1969: 113–15, 118–23). In taking this stance, he was expressing, in all probability, the position of most of his Marxist contemporaries. Kautsky, for example, was scathing about the racial theories of history fashionable among the German intelligentsia of his day. Yet if Plekhanov sought to exclude one supposedly 'natural' factor from history – namely race – he championed the cause of another, geography. Indeed, in his own account of historical materialism, he expounded what amounts to a version of geographical determinism: 'the properties of the geographical environment determine the development of the productive forces, which, in its turn determines the development of the economic forces, and of all other social relations' (1977: III, 144).

ANTI-NATURALIST CHALLENGES

Thus, where the idea of the dialectic of nature had provided Engels with a broad metaphysical doctrine of the dynamic unity of physical and social processes and with an affirmation of the identity of the scientific method (rather flexibly conceived) in all natural domains, the theorists of the Second International tended rather to formulate a theory of history which isolated some 'natural' element relatively untouched by or unamenable to human intervention, whether it be the environment in Kautsky, geography in Plekhanov, or race in Labriola. Race in fact plays a secondary and residual role in Labriola's relatively dialectical version of historical materialism, but in Kautsky's and Plekhanov's cases the impulses deriving from this underlying substratum of history seem to be the source of the ultimate guarantee that events will proceed in the required fashion. The resulting stress on historical necessity leaves, as we have seen, little scope for creative political intervention.

Inevitably this version of Marxism generated a series of reactions. Politically these were usually motivated by the refusal to wait patiently on the long-term evolution of historical forces counselled by Kautsky and Plekhanov. Inasmuch as this political critique required theoretical elaboration, it could draw on the increasingly wide range of philosophical anti-naturalisms which became available as the nineteenth century drew towards a close. Denying the kind of continuity posited by Engels and the Marxists of the Second International between the physical and human worlds could serve as a way of insisting that individual and collective agents played an ineliminable role in making and remaking social structures. The most important case of this reaction came after the First World War and the Russian Revolution, in Lukács's *History and Class Consciousness* (1923). There were, however, many earlier instances of this kind of rebellion against the historical determinism and political *attentisme* of Second International Marxism.

It was Bergson's philosophy which helped to provided Sorel with his way out of orthodox Marxism. Bergson, of course, was not in any simple sense an anti-naturalist, expressing as he does as strong a sense of the unity of the physical and the human as did, say, Spencer. But Bergson's vitalism and his critique of rationalism helped to provide Sorel with an image of history governed not by the gradual development of the productive forces but by heroic assertions of will. His readings of contemporary philosophy (James and Poincaré as well as Bergson) convinced Sorel that a primarily scientific understanding could not provide the required motivation for revolutionary action. Only a myth of some kind could do so: thus the Enlightenment conception of historical progress, though largely Utopian, had given the French Revolution its necessary ideological stimulus.

Contemporary capitalist society was sinking into decadence and mediocrity, Sorel argued. The development of parliamentary democracy, far from being (as Kautsky and Plekhanov believed) a welcome step in the direction of social-ism, was serving to sap the working class of its revolutionary energy, and to integrate it into the state, thereby providing once-progressive intellectuals with power and office. The anarcho-syndicalist myth of the proletarian general strike, directed against the state rather than to secure limited reforms, was the necessary means of revitalising both the labour movement and society more generally. The violence that was an unavoidable accompaniment of class confrontation should be welcomed for the stimulus it offered to social renewal: 'Proletarian violence, carried out as a pure and simple manifestation of the sentiment of the class war, appears thus as a very fine and very heroic thing; it is in the service of the immemorial interests of civilization; it is not perhaps the most appropriate method of obtaining immediate material advantages, but it may save the world from barbarism' (1908 [1950: 113]).

While Sorel developed a quasi-Nietzschean version of anarcho-syndicalism, theoretical challenges to orthodoxy also developed within the Second International. Perhaps the most intellectually creative challenge was provided by the Austro-Marxists, an extremely talented group of theoreticians headed by Otto Bauer, Max Adler, and Rudolf Hilferding, and associated with the Austrian Social Democratic Party. Influenced both by the various German schools of Neo-Kantianism and by Mach's phenomenalist philosophy of science, they sought to remedy what Bauer called the 'bastardisation of Marx's doctrine' by Kautsky and other popularisers. More particularly, Adler tried to show that Kant's transcendental deduction of the categories in the first *Critique* demonstrates not simply the necessity of these categories in constituting our experience of an objective world, but also the inherently social character of consciousness. Thus 'an Ego-consciousness is only possible where there is an immanent relation to an indeterminate multiplicity of knowing subjects, with which every individual consciousness sees itself connected' (Bottomore and Goode 1978: 75).

In thus discovering in individual consciousness 'a supra-individual, transcendental-social, a priori socialized character', Kant had provided Marx with his starting point, 'socialized man', or what Adler calls 'sociation' (*Vergesellschaftung*). Marx in turn, by formulating the concept of sociation, provided a transcendental justification of the causal explanation of social life, just as Kant had done for that of the physical world. So, unlike some versions of Neo-Kantianism, Austro-Marxism did not seek to treat the human and the physical as requiring fundamentally different forms of enquiry. Nevertheless, Adler agreed that the dividing line between the two domains was provided by the presence of mental activity: 'In general, therefore, the materialist conception of history is concerned with the activities of the human mind by which it establishes and develops the conditions of life through social life' (Bottomore and Goode 1978: 65, 67). This stress on social consciousness leaves its traces on the more substantive works of Austro-Marxism. For example, in *The National Question and Social Democracy* (1907) Bauer tends to conceive national identity as deriving more or less exclusively from the possession of a shared culture, a surprisingly 'idealist' approach for a Marxist.

More generally, however, in their content these works did not stray far from the mainstream of the Second International. Indeed, in his book *Finance Capital* (1910) Hilferding provide the movement with its most important economic treatise. In the preface to that work he famously denies that 'Marxism is simply identical with socialism.' A Marxist causal account of the tendencies driving capitalism towards socialism is logically independent of the value-judgement that such an outcome would be desirable: 'it is one thing to acknowledge a necessity, and quite another thing to work for that necessity' (1910 [1978: 23]).

Such an affirmation of the autonomy of morality was, of course, a standard Neo-Kantian position. But it went against the drift of Marx's and Engels's scattered remarks on the subject, which followed Hegel in rejecting any such separation of ethical and causal judgements, and, in some moods at least, seemed to require the reduction of the former to the latter. Beyond any considerations of orthodoxy, or indeed of what might be the right way of viewing the question, Hilferding's remarks highlighted the tension running through socialist thought in the era of the Second International, between the scientific understanding of the tendencies which would, by historical necessity, bring about the overthrow of capitalism at some time in the future, and the subjective will to achieve that outcome quickly through insurrectionary action. Sometimes this tension was expressed in the confrontation between orthodox Marxism and its opponents on the left, chiefly the anarchists and anarcho-syndicalists. Sometimes it took the form of political debates and theoretical aporias within Marxism itself. Before 1914, while the parliamentary strategy of the SPD and its allies seemed to offer the prospect of success, the tension was more or less manageable. With the outbreak of war, and the upheavals it brought in its wake, this ceased to be the case.

23

LEGAL THEORY

STANLEY L. PAULSON

1. LEGAL POSITIVISM IN ENGLAND, THE CONSTRUCTIVIST COUNTERPART IN GERMANY, AND THE BEGINNINGS OF THE INTEREST THEORY

Although Thomas Hobbes can be read as arguing that the obligations of the citizen are to be understood normatively, that is to say, in terms of an initial agreement to create and then to obey the sovereign, a later doctrine of sovereignty and obligation, grounded solely in matters of fact, carried the day in Britain. The paradigm of that doctrine, in both form and influence, is found in the legal philosophy of John Austin.

In his *Lectures on Jurisprudence* (1861–3), Austin refers more frequently to German treatises on pandect law[1] than to the English case law. Still, it would be a mistake to cast him as a Romanist or pandectist rather than as the philosophically inclined English jurist he was. On his central doctrines of command and sovereignty in particular, the greatest influence stems from Jeremy Bentham. And this is hardly surprising. Austin, in Sarah Austin's words, 'looked up to [Bentham] with profound veneration' as 'the most original and inventive of all writers on Law' (Ross 1893: 382).

Austin's command doctrine captures the idea that directives or laws exist '*by position*' (Austin 1861–3 [1885: 87, 171]), reflecting a power relation, that is, a relation between superior and inferior. The factual underpinnings of the power relation are clear: '[T]he term *superiority* signifies *might*: the power of affecting others with evil or pain, and of forcing them, through fear of that evil, to fashion their conduct to one's wishes' (1861–3 [1885: 96]). Applied to positive laws, Austin's doctrine has it that commands are general, speaking to a class of acts or forbearances, and that the superior in the power relation is a political superior – most obviously the sovereign itself. '[I]ncapable of *legal*

---

[1] 'Pandect law' refers to the law stemming from the piecemeal reception of Roman law that took place on the European continent prior to codification. 'Pandect', from the Greek, is familiar as a name for Justinian's Digests or 'Pandects'.

limitation', the sovereign cannot be the inferior member of any power relation of legal import (1861–3 [1885: 263]). Like the command doctrine, the doctrine of sovereignty is grounded in fact, namely, the habitual obedience of subjects. Since the factual base of the doctrines of command and sovereignty is sufficient for law, then – a leitmotif of legal positivism – morality cannot be necessary: 'The existence of law is one thing; its merit or demerit is another' (1861–3 [1885: 214]).

Well into the twentieth century, jurisprudence in Britain and the Commonwealth countries was Austinian through and through. To be sure, Austin's extraordinary influence stems in no small part from Bentham's failure to publish his own remarkable work in the field, work that was conceptually far richer and more expansive than Austin's.[2] As J. S. Mill put it, speaking of Bentham's achievement, 'He found the philosophy of law a chaos, he left it a science' (Mill 1838 [1875: 368]).

In Germany, a counterpart to legal positivism, far-reaching and extravagant in its pretensions, was well entrenched by the middle of the nineteenth century. Familiar under the rubric of legal constructivism, pandectism, or, as its critics termed it, *Begriffsjurisprudenz* ('jurisprudence of concepts'), it supplanted in some circles Friedrich Carl von Savigny's historical school and remained, thanks to the work of Georg Friedrich Puchta, Rudolf von Jhering, and Bernhard Windscheid, the dominant view in private law right up to the adoption of the German Civil Code in 1900. The machinery of legal constructivism was transferred to public law by Carl Friedrich von Gerber in the middle of the nineteenth century, a development which brought about a sea change in the conceptualisation of public law and which held sway well into the twentieth century. No less a figure than Hans Kelsen, in his early years, was its last major spokesman.

It was Jhering above all, in the earlier volumes of *Geist des römischen Rechts*, who worked out the details of legal constructivism. The law appears in two forms, both 'as the legal *institute*' and 'as legal *norms*' (Jhering 1858: II.2, §41 [1898: 359]). The latter form, which Jhering also describes as 'the *imperatival*, the *directly practical* form of the command or prohibition', provides the raw material that is then re-formed or 'constructed' as the elements and qualities of legal institutes. Far from being mere collections of individual legal norms, legal institutes are 'juridical bodies' (*Rechtskörper*) with their own distinct properties (1898: 358, 360). Construction lends a modicum of clarity to the law, both

---

[2] Bentham developed four 'aspects' of law (command, prohibition, permission to act, permission to forbear from acting) and rudiments of a deontic logic to depict their relations, as well as a doctrine of the individuation of laws, a unitary concept of obligation (common to the law and morality), and a great deal more (see Bentham 1970; Hart 1982).

quantitatively by reducing the bulk of material and qualitatively by simplifying the law's internal structure. It also has a 'productive' dimension, for the legal scientist's derivations, based on the appropriate juridical body, fill gaps in the law.

In its heyday, legal constructivism reflected all too plainly the decidedly negative side of formalism in the law – abstract definitions and categories in legal reasoning, for example, that notoriously led to neglect of the exigencies giving rise to the disputed legal issue at hand. Constructivism became a *cause célèbre* in later nineteenth-century German legal science, and Jhering himself, thoroughly disillusioned with the constructivist project, led the movement against it. 'Constructing' the law, he wrote in 1865, had simply been an attempt to demonstrate its '*logical* necessity', and 'at one time there was something utterly seductive about this effort, stemming from a temptation deeply rooted in the essence of legal theorizing itself'. In fact, however, 'this pseudo-justification, this logical self-deception, diverts us from . . . a true understanding of the law' (Jhering 1865: III, §59 [1906: 318]).

Jhering began anew, turning to a teleologico-naturalistic theory, which he first adumbrates in a short work, *Der Kampf um's Recht* (1872). His mature work in the field, the unfinished two-volume treatise *Der Zweck des Rechts* (1877, 1884), represents a celebration of purpose. 'It is not the sense of what is right that has produced law; rather, law has produced the sense of what is right. And the law knows but one source – the practical source, purpose' (Jhering 1877: xiii). Jhering moves the idea of purpose to stage centre in the law. Where the protection of interests is understood as a means of achieving the individual's ends or purposes, the question (familiar from the interest or benefit theory of rights) arises: which interests, with an eye to creating rights to secure them, ought society to recognise? (see Jhering 1865: III, §§60–1 [1906: 327–68], 1877: v). Jhering's new approach, promising a social theory of law, led over time to a transformation in juridical thought, away from legal constructivism. The pulling and hauling on this front is evident in a sustained debate over the merits of the interest theory, which was defended, above all, by Philipp Heck (see Heck 1932).

2. HISTORICISM: OTTO VON GIERKE AND HENRY SUMNER MAINE

When 'Savigny, [Karl Friedrich] Eichhorn, and [Jacob] Grimm made the discovery that the law was historical, they did not thereby offer the world a new speculative system; rather, they unveiled a truth' (Gierke 1883a: 7). So declaimed Otto von Gierke, who went his own way, criticising in the name of a hugely expansive 'theory of associations' (*Genossenschaftstheorie*) not only legal constructivism and natural law theory but, indeed, the earlier nineteenth-century historical school celebrated in the present quotation.

Where legal constructivism is concerned, Gierke shows no mercy. Its fundamental mistake, manifest not least of all in the work of public law writers of a constructivist bent, consists 'in overestimating the capabilities of formal logic', a misconception of the role of logic that led, in the case of Paul Laband, to egregious conflations: 'the logical definition coincides with the comprehension of content, the logical derivation with the causal explanation, the logical classification with the conceptual synthesis' (Gierke 1883b: 1110, and see Gierke 1874: 153–69, but compare, on Laband, Stolleis 1992: 456). By contrast, Gierke strikes a positive note where natural law theory is concerned. No notion of the law is possible at all without the concept of justice, and it is natural law theory that explicates and develops that concept (see Gierke 1880: 318). Still, natural law theory cannot be said to have the last word, failing as it does to distinguish justice from the law itself (Gierke 1916–17: 245, and see Gurwitsch 1922–3: 95). Finally, Gierke addresses critically the earlier nineteenth-century historical school, in particular its revivification of the Roman law doctrine of *persona ficta*, a doctrine that Savigny had placed alongside that of legal subject *qua* human being. The result was a bifurcated notion of the legal subject, some being fictitious, others flesh and blood. And this, in turn, generated anomalies. Where a legal subject is a fictitious legal person, there can be no attribution of human will or human acts to it. But if not, how can this legal person lay claim, say, to property rights? Savigny's own effort to resolve the anomaly in terms of representation gave rise to further anomalies.

Gierke rejects the Roman law doctrine *in toto*, arguing that legal personality exists only as real personality, a notion that encompasses the state, corporations, and other associations, all of them understood as social organisms. Not only do these social organisms exist, they manifest a reality 'higher' than that of the individual organisms or human beings that they comprise (Gierke 1902: 31–2). And not only do they have legal capacity, they are 'also *capable of willing and acting*' (Gierke 1887: 603). In no sense the product of lawmaking activity, these collective or social organisms are living forces, a reflection of 'historical or social action' (Gierke 1902: 24).

Not surprisingly, these 'supra-personal realities' were seen by many as a flight of fancy. Gierke, however, defends his position with great tenacity and resourcefulness. He contends, for example, that the puzzles arising from the existence of social organisms *qua* 'real corporeal and ideal unities' do not count as an argument against his view, for comparable puzzles arise in considering the human being. 'Do social unities actually exist? Direct proof of their existence cannot be given, to be sure, but there is no direct proof of the unity of the individual either' (1902: 19).

Even if this analogy is unconvincing, and even if, more generally, Gierke was unable to win very many others to his view, his extraordinary recasting of legal concepts and social facts, coupled with his brilliant criticism of the tradition, throws new light on the field. In addition, Gierke's penetrating and richly detailed scholarly work on the natural law theorists of the Middle Ages and the Renaissance is unrivalled to this day (see Gierke 1868–1913).

Gierke and Sir Henry Sumner Maine, both seen as historicists of the later nineteenth century, present a study in contrasts – where Gierke champions bold, even audacious theory, Maine is deeply suspicious of high theory in all its forms. Critical of Austin, Maine points out that sovereignty and command have not always been compelling doctrines, drawing for his illustration on the Punjab region of India before its incorporation into the British Indian Empire. The Punjab had come to be governed by a single chieftain, Runjeet Singh, who seemed on first glance the paradigm of the Austinian sovereign. 'He was absolutely despotic [and] kept the most perfect order.' Closer examination revealed, however, that the chieftain made no laws, issued no commands. 'The rules which regulated the life of his subjects were derived from their immemorial usages, and these rules were administered by domestic tribunals, in families or village-communities' (Maine 1875 [1888: 380–1]). Maine is contending not that Austin's doctrines are false, but that their application is limited, presupposing legislation as the predominant form of law (see 1875 [1888: 385]). Law may take other forms, and when it does, Austin's doctrines are without application.

Maine's criticism of natural law theory is less successful. His aversion to high theory and his complete neglect of developments in the Middle Ages portend an arid discussion. 'Logically', the law of nature 'implie[s] a state of Nature', and Maine argues in effect that since the latter never existed, the former cannot be said to exist either (Maine 1861 [1963: 70, and see 84–8]; Pollock 1906 [1963: 396–401]). This, however, is simply to confuse historical fact with theoretical precept, as if the existence of a 'state of nature' *qua* historical fact were somehow essential to the validity of arguments drawing on natural law theory.

Maine's keenest interests were in the evolution of law and society, and in the explanation of legal change. The initial stage of social life is *stricto sensu* pre-legal. '[P]atriarchal despotism' (Maine 1861 [1963: 8]), reflecting the agnatic origins of society and counting as the source of both judgement and punishment, does not reflect the application of any species of law. That comes later, in an 'epoch of Customary Law, and of its custody by a privileged order' (1861 [1963: 12]). A related development is the embodiment of customary law in a code, and at this point 'the distinction between stationary and progressive societies begins to make itself felt' (1861 [1963: 21]). Whereas the law in progressive societies is responsive to social needs, the law in stationary societies acts as a constraint and so must be 'brought into harmony with society'. The instrumentalities for carrying out this task are 'Legal Fictions, Equity and Legislation' (1861 [1963: 24]). Maine understands the legal fiction broadly, as 'any assumption [concealing], or affect[ing] to conceal, the fact that a rule of law has undergone an alteration'. Thus, '[t]he *fact* is . . . that the law has been wholly changed; the *fiction* is that it remains what it always was' (1861 [1963: 25]). It is by means of these instrumentalities, as Calvin Woodard puts it, that the law develops its 'own internal means of propagating innovation, flexibility and the capacity to respond to changing social circumstances' (Woodard 1991: 233).

Much that had been understood under the rubric of historicism and – Paul Vinogradoff's expression – 'historical jurisprudence' (Vinogradoff 1920) is today a subject of enquiry for legal anthropology, a lively field over the past fifty years. Maine, a forerunner in the field, continues to enjoy attention here.

3. PRECURSORS OF LEGAL REALISM IN AMERICA: OLIVER WENDELL HOLMES AND ROSCOE POUND

In *The Common Law* (1881), in his essays, most prominently 'The Path of the Law' (1896–7), and in a host of judicial opinions, Oliver Wendell Holmes anticipates central themes in what would emerge, in the later 1920s and the 1930s, as American Legal Realism. First, as underscored in his aphorism that '[t]he life of the law has not been logic: it has been experience' (Holmes 1881: 1), there is a hard-hitting polemic against formalism. Second, arguably the flip side of the anti-formalist polemic, Holmes insists that judges' decisions – like those of other lawmakers – are based on policy. Third, he emphasises prediction in place of the 'axioms' or 'deductions' of the tradition, writing that 'the prophecies of what the courts will do in fact, and nothing more pretentious, are what I mean by the law' (Holmes 1896–7: 461).

Holmes's anti-formalist polemic is nowhere more evident than in his analysis of rights and duties, for these, too, are 'nothing but prophecies' (1896–7: 458). To incur a contractual duty by making a promise means simply that 'you are liable to pay a compensatory sum unless the promised event comes to pass' (1896–7: 462, and see Holmes 1881: 299–300). Thus, you have a choice – performance or the payment of compensation. The 'choice' theory, however, is hard to square with the import of 'duty', for, once incurred, a duty is supposed to preclude all options other than performance. As W. W. Buckland puts it, '[y]ou don't buy a right to damages, you buy a horse' (Buckland 1945: 98). What is more, as

Frederick Pollock objects, it is 'wrong to procure a man to break his contract' (Pollock 1941: I, 80), but this could not be wrong if the 'choice' theory were right. To be sure, Buckland and Pollock are assuming precisely what Holmes rejects – an objective standard for the determination of rights.

In his arguments against formalism in *The Common Law*, Holmes addresses nineteenth-century German legal theory. And his critique of formalism is evident, too, in his judicial opinions. In *Lochner v New York* (1905), the Supreme Court held unconstitutional a New York State statute that had limited the length of the workweek in bakeries. The Court contended that the statute violated 'liberty of contract' between employer and employee, a concept purportedly drawn from language in the Fourteenth Amendment on liberty. The decision, it can be argued, is formalistic. As the means for realising the Court's chosen end, the preservation of the *status quo*, the Court uses 'liberty of contract' – a contrivance where even a rough equality of bargaining power between employer and employee is conspicuously lacking – and thereby ignores the issue that gave rise to the challenged legislation in the first place, the plight of overworked bakers' helpers in the State of New York. Justice Holmes, in a stinging dissent, writes that '[t]he Fourteenth Amendment does not enact Mr. Herbert Spencer's *Social Statics*'. A majority of the people, Holmes adds, had rejected *laissez-faire* economics, and 'my agreement or disagreement has nothing to do with the right of a majority to embody their opinions in law' (Holmes 1905 [1992: 306]).

Roscoe Pound's early work was in some respects comparable. Extraordinarily well read in nineteenth-century German legal theory – neither Holmes nor anyone else was a match for him – Pound, too, was sceptical of what he saw as formalism on the European continent. Like Holmes, he took aim at formalism as he found it in the case law. In *Lochner*, the 'conception of freedom of contract is made the basis of a logical deduction', and the result, paradoxically, is a decision that, 'tested by [its] practical operation, defeat[s] liberty' (Pound 1908: 616; Pound 1908–9, and see Hull 1997: 64–74).

Pound pleads for a 'sociological' view of the law (Pound 1907: 609). The law 'is not scientific for the sake of science. Being scientific as a means toward an end, it must be judged by the results it achieves, not by the niceties of its internal structure' (Pound 1908: 605). These lines might have been written by the later Jhering, and Pound in fact draws on Jhering's example with an eye to developing a theory of social interests. Empirical research, required in order to assess 'the results' that Pound favoured over the conceptual niceties of the formalist tradition, was not, however, his forte. The pretence of empirical research, with decidedly mixed results, would await the full-blown Realist movement of the later 1920s and the 1930s (see Schlegel 1995).

4. PRECURSOR OF LEGAL REALISM IN SCANDINAVIA: AXEL ANDERS HÄGERSTRÖM

Influenced in his early years by, above all, Kant, and reacting sharply to the idealistic metaphysics of C. J. Boström, which was then in favour in Uppsala ('Boströmianism'), the Swedish philosopher Axel Anders Hägerström concentrated initially on problems in Kant's philosophy (see Hägerström 1902). A shift toward empiricism is marked by a major early work in epistemology (see Hägerström 1908). Hägerström then turned to value theory, and later to legal philosophy and Roman law.

On value judgements, Hägerström writes that 'value itself means nothing' apart from the pleasure or displeasure of the judging party (Hägerström 1910, 1929: 152 [1964: 68]), a stance representative of his decidedly sceptical view. Despite this uncompromising emotivism, Hägerström offers in his jurisprudential work not only a penetrating critical study of the 'will theory' of law but also the rudiments of a strikingly original theory of the uses of legal language.

Rejecting all reductive accounts of legal rights, legal obligations, and the like as without foundation, Hägerström depicts – a leitmotif of his Roman law treatise – legal obligation as nothing other than 'one person's being mystically bound to another' (see Hägerström 1927). This bewildering idiom of the 'mystical' and 'magical' led most of the critics to dismiss Hägerström's treatise out of hand, Wolfgang Kunkel contending, for example, that Hägerström's thesis was 'anachronistic' (Kunkel 1929: 485) and Julius Binder invoking the spectre of Hägerström's 'legal nihilism' (Binder 1931: 280). In fact, Hägerström had been misunderstood. In order to explain the origins of fundamental concepts of the *jus civile*, it was instructive to trace them, as Hägerström did, back to ancient beliefs in mysterious powers. At the same time, his explication of these concepts anticipates what is familiar today as performatory uses of legal language (see Olivecrona 1953: xiii–xviii, Olivecrona 1971: 240, 245–6). Among Hägerström's contemporaries – apart from his younger colleagues in Uppsala – only Ernst Cassirer, writing from Göteborg in 1939, appears to have recognised this contribution (see Cassirer 1939: 89). Hägerström argues, *inter alia*, that the import of the operative language in, say, the transfer of ownership – 'I hereby grant unto you the estate Blackacre' – cannot be understood as a description of the speaker's intention. Rather, the speaker's intention 'has as its content the act of declaring' or giving voice to the operative language, which, once declared, brings about the desired change in legal relations (Hägerström 1935 [1953: 301], and see Hart 1955: 370).

Thanks to his philosophical gifts and a radical departure from the tradition, and thanks as well to the force of his personality, Hägerström profoundly influenced a generation of 'Scandinavian Legal Realists', among them Vilhelm Lundstedt, Karl Olivecrona, and the remarkable Alf Ross, whom Hägerström took under his wing in Uppsala after Ross's doctoral dissertation had been rejected in Copenhagen. The contributions of the Scandinavian Legal Realists to European legal philosophy in the middle of the century have proved to be fundamental and far-reaching.

PHILOSOPHY OF RELIGION AND ART

SCEPTICAL CHALLENGES TO FAITH

JAMES LIVINGSTON

The 1870s were the high noon of nineteenth-century scientific rationalism in Europe. In the succeeding years to 1914 several important critiques of religion were advanced by philosophers and influential men of letters in France, England, and Germany.

THE CRITIQUE OF RELIGION IN FRANCE

In France, August Comte (1798–1857) was the leading proponent of mid- and late nineteenth-century scientific positivism. He also proved a formative critic of the European religious tradition. He declared it no longer credible and sought to replace Christianity with a religion that he baptised the Religion of Humanity. His writings on religion continued to have influence in Europe and North America in the latter decades of the nineteenth century.

While Comte disavowed Christianity, he undertook to establish a religion on the scientific principles enunciated in the six volumes of his *Cours de philosophie positive* (1830–42) (*The Positive Philosophy of August Comte*, 1853). In later writings, such as the four-volume *Système de politique positive* (1851–4) (*The System of Positive Polity*, 1875–7) and the *Catéchisme positiviste*, 1852 (*The Catechism of Positive Religion*, 1858), Comte brings together his positive philosophy (see chs. 1 and 18) and his vision of the Religion of Humanity. Some of his disciples repudiated the latter as a wholly foreign and superfluous addition to Comte's positivism. It is clear from his earliest writings, however, that the creation of a new humanistic religion was integral to Comte's positive programme. He was impressed by Catholicism's proven social efficacy, and the Religion of Humanity can be viewed as an effort to simulate but secularise Catholic cult and organisation. T. H. Huxley dubbed Comte's new religion 'Catholicism *minus* Christianity'. The details of Comte's religious cult need not be enumerated. Suffice it to say that the worship of humanity (the 'Great Being') replaces the worship of God. Comte's effort proved precarious from the outset. The ridicule it often received was, perhaps, predictable, for by positing the 'Great Being' Comte appeared to 'regress' to the metaphysics that he had denounced.

What is important about Comte, however, is the radicalness of his humanistic religious reconstruction. While other philosophers of the period – the Hegelians, Neo-Kantians, and British idealists – attempted philosophical reconceptions, or various forms of 'demythologisation' of the Jewish and Christian historical revelation, Comte sought a more thoroughgoing religious revolution by rejecting any appeal to either historical revelation or metaphysical theism.

The scientific critique of religion in France in the second half of the century was further advanced by the two eminent and influential writers, Ernest Renan (1832–92) and Hippolyte-Adolfe Taine (1828–93). Neither was a professional philosopher, but both were learned scholars whose sensibilities were more subtle and complex than Comte's. Both, however, placed their final hope in the advance of scientific rationalism. Renan illustrates this mode of critique.

In *L'Avenir de la science* (*The Future of Science*), written in 1848–9 but published in 1890, Renan envisions the goal of science as the progressive knowledge of human consciousness. He calls this progress the immanent Deity that is increasingly manifest in history. Renan rejects the idea of a transcendent personal God who intervenes supernaturally. His Deity is a universal divine striving towards the realisation, through human consciousness, of an ideal end. One cannot be certain, however, whether Renan thinks of God as the world process itself in a state of deification or as an eternal ideal order to be realised in the evolutionary future. In any case, one notes a tension, if not a conflict, between Renan's scientific naturalism and his romantic idealism.

The same tension is present in Renan's vast writings on religion that include his seven-volume *Histoire des origines du christianisme* (1863–81) and his five-volume *Histoire du peuple d'Israël* (1887–93). The first volume of the *Origines* is the *Vie de Jésus* (*The Life of Jesus*, 1863), an extraordinary book that sold close to half a million copies in many languages. Its popularity is, in part, explained by its thoroughly naturalistic treatment of Jesus as a moral teacher shaped by the religious and social climate and events of his time. Working with limited New Testament data, Renan was required to exercise his subtle imagination to supply the enormous gaps in his biography. As a result, the rigorous German and British New Testament scholars dismissed the biography as largely worthless. But Renan intuitively recognised that his humanistic portrait of Jesus as a moral genius and man of deep sanctity – once stripped of a theology of the supernatural God-man and the miraculous – would touch a deep religious feeling. *The Life of Jesus* remains important, then, as the first detailed effort to understand Jesus in terms of the forces in the natural-historical environment of his time. Thus, paradoxically, Renan's largely pseudo-historical portrait placed the future study of Jesus squarely *in* history.

Comte's disciple, Emile Durkheim (1858–1917), suffered none of Renan's or Taine's ambiguities about religion, but he shared their scientific naturalism. For Durkheim, religion is unquestionably *the* critical foundation of society and its moral life. In his *Les formes élémentaires de la vie religieuse*, 1912 (*The Elementary Forms of the Religious Life*, 1915) he suggests that religion's universality points to its enduring social functions in the natural life of societies. It is, he asserts, a 'social fact' open to a purely scientific investigation. The distinctive and crucial role of religion is found in its ability to represent the collective consciousness of a group that imposes upon its members certain attitudes, values, and prohibitions which serve to bind these individuals to the society. He offered a classic definition of religion as 'a system of beliefs and practices associated with the sacred . . . which unite individuals into a moral community or church'. Religion need not take on all the *accoutrements* that Comte created for his Religion of Humanity, for every society will develop its own natural, though non-rational, sacred symbols and institutions as a bulwark against social and moral chaos. An important change is taking place here. Religion is a purely natural social phenomenon that requires no supernatural explanation or special revelations. At the same time, religion is not a mere 'survival'; it is an indispensable 'social fact' in any society.

THE CRITIQUE OF RELIGIOUS BELIEF IN BRITAIN

The decade of the 1870s was the acme of Victorian rationalism. During these years a number of English writers published powerful criticisms of the religious tradition. Most of these critics shared the same intellectual inheritance of British empiricism from Locke and Hume to John Stuart Mill. They looked to Mill's *A System of Logic* (1843; 8th edn, 1872) as their principal guide. It was, in the words of Leslie Stephen (1832–1904), 'a kind of sacred book'.

Mill's *Logic* was a thorough setting-out of the inductive, scientific empiricist epistemology. The fundamental question to be asked of any received belief was, is it true? Does it stand up to the test of scientific induction? For these agnostic freethinkers, the enemy of scientific empiricism was any appeal to authority, revelation, or 'intuitionism', for example, as defended at the time by John Henry Newman in his *Essay in Aid of a Grammar of Assent* (1870) (see ch. 25).

The most prominent of the empiricist critics of traditional religion, particularly orthodox Christianity, were W. K. Clifford (1845–79), T. H. Huxley (1825–95), Fitzjames Stephen (1829–94), Leslie Stephen, Herbert Spencer (1820–1903), and John Tyndall (1820–93). None of these men were professional philosophers.

They were scientists or men of letters. Yet all of them wrote philosophical essays and engaged in vigorous philosophical debate, frequently at the meetings of the Metaphysical Society. Here special attention is given to the writings of Clifford, Huxley, Leslie Stephen, and Herbert Spencer.

Closely allied with the philosophical criticisms of these men was a powerful ethical indictment of both religious belief and practice. It took two forms. First, certain theological doctrines – original sin, substitutionary atonement, and eternal damnation – were judged to be morally abhorrent. By the 1870s, a growing agnostic temper of mind looked upon clerical pronouncements on these and other deep questions of life as pretentious and immoral. Not only the declared immorality of the doctrines themselves was at issue, however. Believing on false or insufficient evidence was considered an even graver matter. If the church's creeds are subscribed to and recited, and yet are looked upon indifferently by priests and theologians as hardly credible, was it not immoral to continue to subscribe to and recite them?

The empiricist disciples of J. S. Mill relentlessly challenged churchmen and theologians, for example, J. H. Newman (see ch. 25) to justify morally their assent to and their teaching of certain doctrinal beliefs. The most provocative statement of this moral critique of religious belief was W. K. Clifford's essay 'The Ethics of Belief' (1877). It became the classic statement of the empiricists' position on belief. Clifford argued that there is a moral duty of enquiry into belief no matter how trivial the matter, for assent to beliefs prepares the individual to receive more of the same kind, and this weakens the habit of testing things. 'The credulous man', Clifford warns, 'is father to the liar and the cheat.' The moral issue has to do with whether a person has the right to believe on the evidence before him or her – whether a belief, for example, in the sea-worthiness of a ship, is held by honest, patient investigation, or by a desire to believe it to be true and a slothful stifling of doubt. Whether the ship's voyage ends without disaster is irrelevant to the moral question. Furthermore, assent to religious belief often is warranted on the grounds of the moral excellence of the proposer. But, Clifford argues, assent on such grounds is unjustified unless there are reasons for supposing that the proposer knows the truth of what he is saying, and that 'the verification is within the reach of human appliances and powers'.

The moral critique of religious belief often was joined with the epistemological enquiry into the limits of religious knowledge. And the latter dominates what came to be called the 'Agnostic Controversy'. It occupied the attention of philosophers, theologians, and scientists alike in the last three decades of the century in Britain. T. H. Huxley coined the term 'agnostic' at a meeting of the Metaphysical Society in 1869. Being 'without a rag of a label to cover himself with', Huxley was called a number of things by both opponents and friends – positivist, atheist, pantheist, and materialist. None appropriately described his position, since all of these labels implied that he had attained some 'gnosis' or certain knowledge. Huxley was confident that he had not and, with Hume and Kant on his side, he thought the term agnostic best described his real position. Huxley's agnosticism included two basic principles: (1) the doctrine that metaphysical, and thus Christian theological *knowledge* is impossible in light of the inherent limits of the human mind; and (2) that the scientific method be applied to the study of all experience, including the Bible's historical claims. Characteristic of the writing of Huxley and his fellow agnostics is their certainty that supernatural explanations of nature and history were fading under the remorseless pressure of scientific fact. Now 'an outbreak of pestilence', Huxley happily reported, 'sends men not to the churches, but to the drains'.

The real force of Huxley's critique did not lie in his rather too literalist biblical-historical criticism but, rather, in his analysis of the linguistic confusions present in the theological arguments of contemporary theistic apologists. Here Huxley can be seen as a precursor of twentieth-century analytical philosophy and its critique of theological discourse. A telling example is Huxley's critique of A. J. Balfour's popular defence of theism, *The Foundations of Belief* (1894). Huxley demonstrates how confused and illogical is Balfour's use of language when, for example, the latter proposes that theists believe that 'Creative reason is interfused with infinite love.' Huxley subjects such airy metaphysical claims to a devastating logical analysis.

Herbert Spencer (1820–1903) shared Huxley's and Stephen's confidence in scientific progress and their agnostic temper of mind – at least up to a point. Huxley and his agnostic friends were suspicious, however, of the quasi-religious tone and shape of Spencer's philosophy. It included what, for them, was a rather illogical transcendental doctrine that posited an eternal power that Spencer called the Unknowable. Spencer was not a professionally trained philosopher. He was an omnivorous reader who was able to cobble together, with remarkable synthetic acuity, the ideas of others into his own ten-volume *System of Synthetic Philosophy* (1862–96).

The initial volume of Spencer's *Synthetic Philosophy*, *First Principles* (1862), was published before Huxley coined the term, but *First Principles* is considered the first comprehensive treatment of the principles of agnosticism. It came to be referred to as 'the agnostic's Bible'. In *First Principles* Spencer attempts to show that both ultimate religious concepts (atheism, pantheism, theism) and ultimate scientific ideas (space, time, matter) represent realities that lie beyond rational comprehension. At the same time, we cannot rid ourselves of the consciousness of these realities. That is, our intellectual limits do imply 'the existence of something of which we do not and cannot think'. Yet, for Spencer, our consciousness of the Absolute is not simply a negation of our knowledge; it is something positive that persists in consciousness. While Comte's positivism ends in an 'Everlasting No' with regard to metaphysics and the transcendent, Spencer insists that his agnosticism, despite its nescience, emphatically utters an 'Everlasting Yes'. It is neither a materialism nor an atheism. Herein lies his reconciliation of science and religion – a religion devoid, of course, of any appeal to revelation, a personal God, or other 'impious' anthropomorphisms.

Spencer's effort to purify the theistic tradition, and to justify the evolutionary process, was not well received by his philosophical compatriots. F. H. Bradley remarked that the Unknowable seemed to be 'a proposal to take something for God simply because we do not know what the devil it is'. It appeared to many astute critics that Spencer's logical confusions were simply the result of his pious attempt to put a bit of spiritual unction into Ignorance. Nonetheless, Spencer's significance lies in the fact that he offered the educated middle class what was, for them, an attractive philosophy: the joining of science and religion within a progressive Lamarckian evolutionary world-view. By the 1890s, the agnostic *doctrines* of Spencer, Stephen, and Huxley were, however, largely discredited and on the wane; they were not, ironically, agnostic enough. The more enduring legacy of their writings is, perhaps, their contribution to a more inchoate agnostic sensibility that challenges all presumptive dogmatisms, be they religious or scientific.

THE CRITIQUE OF RELIGION IN GERMANY

Between 1870 and 1914 German criticism of religion took two notable forms. The first was a component of the defence of scientific and philosophical materialism. That movement began in the 1850s, but many of the popular writings of its leaders – including the scientists Karl Vogt (1817–95), Jacob Moleschott (1822–93), and Ludwig Büchner (1824–99) – went through numerous later editions and translations. As a result, the materialist critique of religion persisted through the latter decades of the century, and it was furthered by the popular writings of the young scientist and philosopher Ernst Haeckel (1834–1919).

Ernst Haeckel saw Darwin's laws of evolution as the key to his own monistic philosophy. He predicted that they would unlock 'the riddle of the universe', the English title of his immensely popular book, *Die Welträtsel* (1899). Haeckel was especially critical of all forms of theological dualism, and he saw his monism as negating belief in God, teleology, freedom, and immortality. He did not, however, regard himself as simply a materialist. Like Spinoza, Haeckel perceived the one Substance as an eternally living, animated matter. In his later years he embraced a thorough pantheism and panpsychism that appeared to lapse into a form of romantic *Naturphilosphie* that he had censured earlier. By 1914 the materialists' metaphysical claims and their doctrinaire reductionism were widely criticised and had lost their appeal.

The second form of religious critique in Germany is found in the writings of the philosopher Friedrich Nietzsche (1844–1900) (see ch. 19). It is a powerful psychological, epistemological, and moral criticism of Christianity. Despite its overstated rhetoric, it remains suggestive a century later.

Nietzsche judged the modern world to be in a state of cultural decline that he called nihilism. He associated this nihilism with the 'death of God', a notion often misrepresented. Nietzsche did not see God's death as a result of modern philosophical analysis. Rather, it was a cultural fact on its way to realisation, but one not yet fully grasped by humanity. For the 'death of God' is the obliteration of the ultimate ground and support of our most cherished values. For two millennia Western civilisation has derived its 'thou shalts' and its 'thou shalt nots' from God, but when humanity awakens to the fact of God's death madness will erupt, for 'there is no one to command, no one to obey, no one to transgress'. Humanity will be caught in a terrible dilemma: to proclaim the death of God is to deny everything its ultimate meaning and value; but to believe in God is to live in a world of fictions. Nietzsche explores the interesting idea that it is the truth-seeking encouraged by Christianity itself that has led to its own death.

A second theme in Nietzsche's critique is his crucial idea of the 'will to power' as he applies it to the origins and growth of the Christian religion. Nietzsche was deeply influenced by the evolutionary biology of his time. He saw humanity as a species of animal that must be understood naturalistically, and he traces human 'moralities' back to their *extra-moral* naturalistic origins. Here, however, Nietzsche parts with Darwin and develops his key notion of the protean 'will to power'. The 'will to power' is not the same thing as Darwin's adaptive fitness and preservation of type in the struggle for existence. For Nietzsche, self-enhancement is not a question of superior species but of superior individuals who risk existence itself to achieve a mastery of life. This 'will to power' is the most elemental fact of nature: 'not self-preservation, but the will to appropriate, dominate, increase, grow stronger'. The 'will to power' is independent of conscious intention, and Nietzsche sees knowledge itself as a form of 'will to power', and the act of interpretation as a means of mastering.

Nietzsche applies his concept of the 'will to power' to his critique of Christianity. What Christianity reveres as 'godlike', Nietzsche perceives as 'a declaration of war against life . . . against the will to live'. And at the root of this decadent and other-worldly consciousness is a disguised *ressentiment* – a resentment of the Jews and the early Christians directed at their aristocratic Roman superiors. This resentment is, in fact, an expression of the 'will to power', the Christians

avenging themselves by inverting the cultural values of their Roman superiors –
nobility, power, and beauty – for the values of impotence: poverty, world-
denying sorrow and suffering. Nietzsche calls this the 'slave revolt' in morals
which is the root of Western decadence. Slave morality is a herd morality since,
in the herd, 'love of one another' is born of a fear of one's superiors. All the
values of the life-affirming 'master morality' are condemned as evil.

Nietzsche's judgement of Jesus is ambivalent. He respects Jesus's integrity
(there was 'only *one* Christian and he died on the cross'). But he also sees in
Jesus the prototype of the Eastern achievement of an other-worldly serenity – a
life of unconditional love and nonresistance, a kind of spiritual childishness or
infantilism – as an instinctive 'will to nothingness'. His passionate critique of
Christianity is, however, principally directed at the Apostle Paul who, Nietzsche
believes, completely distorted Jesus's teaching and invented his own history of
Christianity. Nietzsche sees Paul's doctrine of justification by faith as a shrewd
rationalisation for his own failure to live up to the extraordinary ethical demands
of Jesus. It also allows Christians to adopt a double standard of truth. Some
things are known by reason and others known by faith alone. 'Faith', Nietzsche
asserts, 'is the *veto* against science.' No one has the 'right' simply to believe
something; rather, one should have the courage to *attack* one's convictions.
Nietzsche looked for the coming of a radical 'revaluation of values' and a new
type of human existence. These values would be embodied in a new individual
he called the *Übermensch* or superior person. The *Übermensch* will be 'God's
successor', but he will also supersede nihilistic humanity for it, too, needs to be
overcome. The *Übermensch* will channel the will to power towards self-mastery
through self-discipline. He will overcome his passions and sublimate his instincts.
The *Übermensch* will treat others more tenderly than himself; he will have claws
but will not use them. He will live the Dionysian life, loving fate (*amor fati*) and
possessed of the yea-saying instinct, though without any belief in an ultimate
purpose or *telos*. Nietzsche offered, to what he considered a resentful humanity,
a new naturalistic religious vision. In place of God he proposes the *Übermensch*
and in place of divine grace he offers a form of self-mastery.

THE DEFENCE OF FAITH

JAMES LIVINGSTON

In the period 1870 to 1914 there emerged new philosophical defences of religious experience and belief and new philosophies of faith. These programmes
undertake a critique of the then dominant scientific positivism and its materialist
and behaviourist doctrines. They can best be set out in the work of representative thinkers in four different contexts: in France, in Britain and the United
States, and in Germany.

THE DEFENCE OF RELIGIOUS FAITH IN FRANCE

In France these new spiritualist philosophies trace their beginnings to a number
of influential philosophers earlier in the century, such as François-Pierre Maine
de Biran (1766–1824). He had argued that the study of human consciousness
must begin with the distinctive experience of the human will and its efforts,
without which perception, memory, habit, and judgement remain inexplicable.
A true philosophy insists on free will and deliberative action, and points to an
exigency or need for faith and religion. These interests are later pursued in
the work of Emile Boutroux (1845–1921) and Henri Bergson (1859–1941). In
his *De la contingence des lois de la nature* (1874), Boutroux attacks all forms of
monistic materialism and determinism. He argues that natural laws alone are,
finally, inadequate explanations, as is shown when one moves from the laws of
one science to another, for example, from physics to biology to sociology and
history. In *Ideé de la loi naturelle* (1895), Boutroux further argues that the activity
of the human mind is holistic, necessarily engaging the entire person, and this
activity portends certain spiritual needs that issue in such creative activities as
art, morality, and religion.

The most influential critique of scientific behaviourism in France is the
'Vitalist' philosophy of Henri Bergson who was Boutroux's student (see ch. 5).
Bergson explored human psychic experience as a way of countering the claims
of mechanistic doctrine and behaviourist psychology. Key to his critique, and
to his defence of metaphysics and the spiritual life, are his studies of time, that

is, of duration, memory, and the human ego. He argues that the consciousness that we humans have of our own selves in flux is a truer model of reality than is scientific abstraction. Experience teaches us that we are interdependent beings and that reality is better understood as an interdependent community of durations. Scientific abstraction cannot do justice to this unique concreteness and fluidity. Bergson's contribution to a spiritual metaphysics is best revealed in a letter written to an enquirer in 1911:

> In my *Essai sur les données immédiates de la Conscience* (1889), I stressed the existence of freedom. In *Matière et mémoire* (1896), I succeeded, I hope, in demonstrating the reality of the soul. In *L'Evolution créatrice* (1907), I presented creation as a fact. From this the existence should stand out clearly of a God freely responsible for creation and the generator of both matter and life, through the evolution of the species and the constitution of human personalities. (*Études*, 20 February 1911 cited in Dansette 1961: 317)

While not a traditional theist – Bergson's God is creative evolution itself – his popular success in favouring a theistic world-view and in opening up a way to truth that lies beyond scientific knowledge alone was important in advancing other forms of theistic apologetic.

Contemporary with Bergson was a group of thinkers who, building on the tradition of the French 'spiritualist' philosophy, developed a distinctive 'philosophy of action' which was applied to the cause of Christian apologetic. The chief representative of the 'philosophy of action' is Maurice Blondel (1861–1941). In *L'Action* (1893) Blondel sets forth what he calls an authentic *Christian* philosophy, one that will demonstrate both the limitations of philosophy itself and the failure of human self-sufficiency. He argues that the human self naturally aspires to what transcends nature, that is, it possesses a need for the transcendent or the supernatural.

Blondel's philosophy purports to be entirely autonomous and modern, by which he means it pursues the *method of immanence*, or a type of phenomenology of human experience, that points to humanity's spiritual need and quest. Blondel insists that the modern method of immanence requires a philosophy of *action*, a word often misunderstood by Blondel's critics. For Blondel, action is not an exercise of the will only, for thought itself is a form of activity. Nothing in our conscious life is not an individual initiative. Thus, it is false to isolate abstractly thought, instinct, will, and trust or faith. Action is the term that Blondel uses to describe their convergence. Experience shows that humans possess an aspiration to achieve goals – and that this willing or continuous striving of the self always ends in a falling short or failure. Blondel speaks of the latent, actuating will (*la volonté voulante*) as life's continuous effort to fulfil itself through its manifest or actuated will (*la volonté voulve*), the latter never being fully satisfied. Some individuals seek the infinite itself through some finite object or cause, such as a political ideology.

It is the gap between our potential and our achievement that opens up the way to the transcendent that, we discover, is *in* but not *of* us. The transcendent is more than we can fully conceptualise or objectify. Thus we have a choice: we can make some finite end our source of security and repose or, by an act of 'mortification' and self-surrender, give our will over to the infinitely transcendent, or God. Blondel concludes that philosophy can only point to the need for God or the transcendent as a hypothesis; genuine belief demands a personal choice, an act of self-surrender. Therefore, only in practice will knowledge of God be an existential reality. The method of immanence cannot give *positive knowledge* of the transcendent, it can only reveal our human need and point to this 'undetermined supernatural'.

THE DEFENCE OF RELIGIOUS FAITH IN GREAT BRITAIN AND THE UNITED STATES

The year 1870 also represents an intellectual turning-point in Great Britain. The tradition of British empiricism – from John Locke through David Hume to John Stuart Mill's *System of Logic* (1843) – began to be challenged on two fronts. One was the new movement of British idealism. The second was represented by a varied group of radical empiricists and philosophical realists who concluded that the heirs of John Stuart Mill's scientific induction and of T. H. Huxley's creed of agnosticism (see chapter 24) were neither empirical enough nor truly agnostic. This latter form of critique is marked by the publication of John Henry Newman's (1801–90) *An Essay in Aid of a Grammar of Assent* in 1870.

Newman directed his *Essay* in defence of belief at the evidentialism characteristic of British empiricism since John Locke. Locke had advanced an influential standard or ethic of belief (see chapter 24). Newman considered Locke's demand that all assent be proportioned to the evidence to be a counsel unrelated to the real practices of humankind. There are many truths which cannot be demonstrated, yet that everyone unconditionally accepts, such as the existence of a free will. Newman proceeds to argue that it is perfectly honest and rational to 'believe what you cannot absolutely prove'. It is wrong, then, to concentrate exclusively on evidential proof as employed in the natural sciences when examining human believing. Newman contends that enquiry regarding belief should begin by contrasting assent and inference. According to Locke and his later disciples, inference and assent are the same mental activity, and since there only can be conditional degrees of assent, probabilities should never lead to certitude.

Newman disagrees. He argues that inference and assent are not the same thing, since one can be present when the other is absent. Furthermore, inference and assent do not vary proportionately. For example, good arguments often do not command assent. Most individuals assent and reach certitude by a process that Newman calls 'implicit reasoning', an informal inferential process. It involves the accumulation and convergence of probabilities whereby individual conditional inferences can and do move to an unconditional assent, that is, to a willingness to believe and to act on these convergent probabilities, none of which, taken separately, would admit of demonstration. The whole process of informal reasoning is greater than, and not reducible to, the sum of its parts. Moreover, such an informal inferential process is an individual activity, and what is a proof to one person often is not so for another. So we find that an authority in one field, for example, the art connoisseur, may prove to be a worthless judge of politics. Newman calls this special power of informal, concrete reasoning the *illative sense*. In the last analysis, everyone brings to their reasoning processes certain 'prepossessions' or 'antecedent considerations'.

Newman proposes his philosophy of belief explicitly as a defence of religious belief in which assent and certitude are reached by a different mode of reasoning than is the case in the sciences. Newman reveals his modernity, moreover, in his awareness of the varieties of human reasoning and knowing appropriate to, for example, the artist, the chemist, and the religious believer. The scientific empiricists, nevertheless, criticised Newman for producing a brilliant psychology of belief that wholly failed to address the laws of right or true belief. Newman's understanding of belief is, however, frequently misunderstood. He did not propose a blind, wilful 'leap of faith', any more than he suggested an agnostic suspension of belief. Newman considered religious belief an intellectual act. A person does not 'leap' to an assent or conviction but, rather, grows into it. Newman alludes to the metaphor of boiling water that reaches a threshold. The water gets hotter and hotter but does not come to the boil until it reaches a critical threshold whence it undergoes a decisive, qualitative change. The personal process of reasoning that Newman calls the 'illative sense' operates similarly. In the act of believing there are both precedent, measurable degrees of evidence ('probabilities') but also a qualitative change in the act of assent.

The assumptions of mid- and late-nineteenth-century scientific positivism and reductive materialism were also challenged by the American psychologist and philosopher William James (1841–1910), whose purpose was a defence of the spiritual life and its ideals. In his classic *Principles of Psychology* (1890), James defends the active, autonomous, goal-directed function of human consciousness. Consciousness is, James wrote, 'a fighter for ends'. He perceived the knower as an actor and thought as a complex of perception, conception, and *action*. Interests, expectations, and faith are essential components of human thought.

James recognised that his insight into the psychological role of the will in belief offered little help itself in determining when a belief is *right* and morally responsible. He addressed this question in his important essay 'The Will to Believe' (1896), a defence of the *right* to believe. James calls anything proposed for our belief an hypothesis. He noted that when a person is faced with competing hypotheses these alternatives possess certain affective qualities for that person. They can be live or dead, forced or avoidable, momentous or trivial. To be alive, an hypothesis must be among the mind's real possibilities; to be forced 'there must be no standing place outside of the alternatives'; to be momentous the option involves 'a one and only chance when the stakes are high'. In many cases, of course, our options may neither be live, forced, nor momentous. In such instances, scientific dispassion should be the ideal. But moral and religious questions, for example, abortion, may present a person with options that are live, forced, and momentous – and where one is required to act without complete or compelling evidence.

James further points out that whether an hypothesis is live or dead depends on our previous experience, that is, on certain preconditions, predispositions, and beliefs, on 'doctrines assumed as facts'. James not only finds W. K. Clifford's ethic of belief too sweeping, he also recognises that Clifford's scientific empiricism is loaded with foundational preconceptions about knowledge and truth (see ch. 24). James insists that there is no knock-down test for such conflicting foundational claims about, for example, determinism or freedom, purpose or no purpose. When considering many truly urgent moral and religious questions, which are not susceptible of proof, a person cannot simply 'wait and see'. For in such cases scepticism is not, James insists, the avoidance of an option; it is an option or risk of a particular kind: 'Better loss of truth than chance of error.' Both options are, in any case, based on our passions and not on reason alone. For Clifford, it is not intellect against all passions; it is intellect with a passion laying down its law.

James further insists that there are occasions when a belief can be tested only *through* an initial trust or expectation. Moreover, there are cases 'where faith in a fact can help create the fact', such as in personal relations where the bond of friendship requires such prior trust and expectation. On this point, it is clear that James does not mean, for example, that belief in God can make God exist. Yet, a responsiveness in regard to belief in God might allow for an attention to factors that are necessary for one to come to experience the reality of God, just as a scientist's attention to certain facts might make possible the scientist's discovery of a new reality. Evidence will be withheld until one's attention and action are engaged.

James's claims in 'The Will to Believe' sparked a lively debate that has continued. The general criticism is that James legitimates 'wishful thinking' or credulity. These criticisms sometimes ignore the careful qualifications that James placed on the *right* to believe. For example, the 'liveness' of an hypothesis, for James, assumes certain socially shared agreements on what experiences are in accord with reality as a control against emotional anarchy. Furthermore, some critics fail to recognise the limited scope that James intended for the application of his proposal, namely, situations where a person feels absolutely compelled to decide between two disjunctive beliefs when the evidence for either is ambiguous and/or does not allow for a purely scientific or rational settlement.

The second, distinctive movement in Great Britain and the United States that sought an alternative to both scientific positivism and a mechanistic evolutionism were various forms of philosophical idealism. Hegelian idealism entered Britain in the 1870s, and one of its principal tasks was the reconstruction and defence of the religious tradition and its values. Among those British idealists who especially carried out this task were the philosophers Thomas Hill Green (1836–82) and Edward Caird (1835–1908), and the latter's brother, the theologian John Caird (1820–98). These men had great influence on a generation of students in Oxford and in the Scottish universities.

In the United States, the Harvard philosopher and Absolute idealist, Josiah Royce (1855–1916), played a similar role. It is said that in the 1890s Royce taught the students at Harvard how to sublimate their Calvinism into a religious idealism and thereby to save their faith. At the centre of Royce's work is his interest in the 'problem of Christianity', which involved reinterpreting the Christian tradition and its central ideas in such a way as to make them compelling to modern minds by displaying these ideas as being consonant with experience and philosophical thought.

Crucial to this task was Royce's conception of the social character of selfhood and community. It is in *The Problem of Christianity* (1913) that Royce fully develops his understanding of religion, not as an individual experience, but as essentially a communal reality. For the human self cannot be known either by itself or by another as a datum; self-knowledge is forthcoming only through an ongoing comparison with other selves which implies a community of interpretation. Royce insisted that the individual can be 'saved' only through ceasing to be a *mere* individual, that is, through loyalty to a community that involves practical devotion to a goal or an ideal of humanity. Only through such loyalty can the self find true self-realisation beyond the arbitrariness and constraints of a purely subjective individual life.

For Royce, the special role of the church, the Beloved Community, is to redeem and free human beings from self-centred sin and disloyalty which endanger genuine community. The Beloved Community is, for Royce, the first of three truths of Christianity that are especially in accord with a deep human need for a living spiritual unity and an ideal challenge. The second essential idea of Christianity is what Royce calls 'the moral burden of the individual'. As social beings, humans sense a disturbing conflict between their individual will and the social will and authority, the latter seen both as an enemy and as what is right. Here lies the source of moral guilt which, Royce sees, is beyond the individual's capacity to redeem. In recognising responsibility for one's moral disloyalty, persons are also aware that they cannot forgive themselves, or undo what is done. Royce also perceived the enduring truth embodied in a third idea, the atonement, namely that wilful sin and disloyalty can be forgiven only beyond the self through the mediation of the Community whose spirit, paradoxically, conjoins divine judgement and redeeming love. Furthermore, the Spirit is the power that unites distinct individuals into the one Beloved Community that shares a common memory and hope. So understood, Royce believed that the ancient Christian symbols could once again live and would assist in the coming of the future universal community.

THE DEFENCE OF RELIGIOUS BELIEF IN GERMANY

In the latter decades of the nineteenth century in Germany there was a considerable reaction against idealist metaphysics. At the same time, scientific materialism was gaining support in Germany, although its popularisers were often dismissed for failing to take account of Kant's strictures concerning the limits of science and its metaphysical pretensions. The result was a cry of 'Back to Kant!', whose upshot was the development of new philosophical movements that claimed to be faithful to Kant's legacy. Together, these 'schools' comprised what is called Neo-Kantianism, which dominated German philosophy between roughly 1870 and 1920 (see ch. 2).

One of these schools, called Marburg Neo-Kantianism, was especially interested in developing a philosophy of culture that would include a defence of religion within the limits of human reason. It was concerned with what appeared to be a breakdown of the unity of science, moral values, and religion. The two leaders of this movement, Hermann Cohen (1842–1918) and Paul Natorp (1854–1924), defended religion or the idea of God, either as a unifying ideal of truth and guarantor of the accord of our knowledge of nature – that is, theoretical causality – with morality or ethical teleology (Cohen), or as the feeling and power that engenders *Bildung* or humane cultural formation (Natorp).

Marburg Neo-Kantianism proved to have little impact on later twentieth-century philosophy of religion. It did, however, have an important influence on twentieth-century Neo-Orthodox theology and theological Existentialism that warrants mention. The theologian Wilhelm Herrmann (1846–1922) was a colleague of Cohen and Natorp in Marburg between 1879 and 1917. Herrmann, too, was concerned about the hegemony of a positivistic science, agreed with his colleagues that freedom and the ethical will were central issues, and accepted the Neo-Kantian critique of metaphysics as it bore on both theology and the limits of science. Herrmann, however, went further than his colleagues in his use of the Kantian critique, not only to separate religion from the realm of science but also from the pure, deductive philosophical speculations of Marburg Neo-Kantianism, which he saw as the last vestige of rationalism.

In two works, *Die Metaphysik in der Theologie* (*Metaphysics in Theology*, 1876) and *Die Religion im Verhältnis zum Welterkennen und zur Sittlichkeit* (*Religion in Relation to Knowledge of the World and Morality*, 1879), Hermann argued that neither scientists nor philosophers appear to understand the true limits of human knowledge. He then proceeded to show that beyond the drive for a scientific mastery of nature, and beyond philosophy's search for the universal grounds of knowledge, there lies a deeper human concern which is to answer the question of how the world is to be judged if, as Cohen believed, there really is to be a highest Good – a guarantee of the meaning and purpose of existence. In contrast to science and philosophy, Herrmann argued that religious faith recognises that both nature and the human spirit are under the teleological guidance of a personal God, but that this faith is not capable of objective demonstrable proof. It is, rather, an unconditional trust that issues in a sense of moral freedom in the face of nature's necessities. For Herrmann, there is no conflict between scientific knowledge and religion – that is, moral faith and freedom – for the two spheres have wholly different foundations. Here one can see the opening for twentieth-century Neo-Orthodox theology under the leadership of Karl Barth (1886–1968) and for the Christian Existentialism of the theologian Rudolf Bultmann (1884–1976). Both Barth and Bultmann came to Marburg to study with Herrmann in the first decade of the twentieth century. One significant result was the almost complete separation of German theology from the concerns of science and the natural world for at least the next half-century.

ART AND MORALITY: AESTHETICS AT 1870

PAUL GUYER

During the eighteenth century, the field of aesthetics (first so called by Alexander Baumgarten in Baumgarten [1735: cxvi]) flourished in Britain, France, and Germany, pursued not only by men of letters such as the third Earl of Shaftesbury, Edmund Burke, Denis Diderot, Jean-Jacques Rousseau, Moses Mendelssohn, and Friedrich Schiller, but also by prominent philosophers such as Francis Hutcheson, David Hume, and Immanuel Kant. In Germany, the subject remained central to the metaphysical projects of philosophers such as Friedrich Schelling, Georg Hegel, and Arthur Schopenhauer through the first third of the nineteenth century. In the middle part of the century the subject largely disappeared from the agenda of British philosophers, although it remained a standard subject of philosophical treatises by both Hegelians and their opponents in Germany. By the end of the century, however, aesthetics was once again lively in Britain, Germany, Italy, and the United States, and since then it has continued to be central to the concerns of many major philosophers throughout the twentieth century. This chapter and the next will describe some of the highlights in the revival of aesthetics in the last third of the nineteenth century and around the turn of the twentieth century. This chapter will focus on influential views of art at the beginning of the period, which largely came not from philosophy professors but from more popular writers such as John Ruskin and Friedrich Nietzsche.

On a standard view of the history of modern aesthetics, its central fact has been the development of the idea of the disinterestedness both of the experience of natural and artistic beauty and of the production of art, the idea, that is, that our response to aesthetic properties and our motives for the production of artistic works are autonomous, independent of all our other practical and cognitive interests, a special dimension in which we can enjoy the play of our senses and imagination free of all our usual worries and constraints (see Stolnitz 1961a, 1961b). This idea of disinterestedness is supposed to have been introduced at the beginning of the eighteenth century by Shaftesbury and Hutcheson, and then to have been refined in Kant's great *Critique of Judgment* (1790), whence it made its way into Schopenhauer's *The World as Will and Representation* (1819), from where it was passed on to the late nineteenth century, in the shape of 'formalism' and the ideology of 'art for art's sake', and thence to the twentieth century. This picture is radically misleading (Guyer 1993: chs. 2 and 3).

Shaftesbury had made a narrow point, namely the independence of aesthetic response from considerations of personal need and possession, within the context of an otherwise Neo-Platonic identification of the true, the good, and the beautiful, and, with the sole exception of Hutcheson, eighteenth-century philosophers writing on beauty took their challenge to be to show how our pleasures in beauty and other aesthetic phenomena such as the sublime are rooted in our most fundamental sources of value in spite of Shaftesbury's indisputable point. Only with Kant was anything like Hutcheson's more general idea of disinterestedness revived, but even then only as part of a complex dialectic in which the ultimately moral value of aesthetic experience was argued to rest precisely on the freedom of the imagination in aesthetic experience from inappropriate cognitive and practical constraints. This delicate relationship between aesthetic disinterestedness and moral interest was expressed in their different ways by Schiller and Schopenhauer, each of whom saw profound moral benefits, although quite different ones, in the freedom of the imagination manifested in aesthetic experience. And through most of the rest of the nineteenth century, the assumption of virtually all previous aesthetic theory prevailed, namely that the task of aesthetics is not to establish the independence of artistic production and aesthetic experience from moral concerns but rather to show how this peculiarly free region of human experience nevertheless complements our deepest moral concerns: in their different ways, writers such as Ruskin and Nietzsche aimed not to deny the moral significance of the aesthetic but to interpret it. Even at the *fin de siècle*, popularly associated with the slogan 'art for art's sake,' few thinkers attempted to revive anything like Hutcheson's extreme conception of disinterestedness; most writers built upon the tradition of Kant, Schiller, and Ruskin.

1. JOHN RUSKIN (1819–1900)

The most influential writer on art in mid-nineteenth-century Britain was not a philosopher at all, but the art critic, art historian, and artist John Ruskin. Ruskin's career was long and prolific; some of his most influential work was done well before 1870, but retained its influence past this date; and other important work was done in the 1870s and even in the 1880s, before the breakdown that incapacitated Ruskin for much of the rest of his life (for a useful description of Ruskin's career, see Landow 1985). We can focus here on three main stages in his thought, all of which reveal the deep connection between art and morality which Ruskin always assumed: a first period, in which he emphasised the moral and ultimately religious base of our response to the beauty of nature and its artistic representation; a second stage, in which he famously emphasised the moral value of freedom in artistic production; and finally, a third, political stage, in which he expanded his admiration for free artistic production into a general advocacy of socialism.

Ruskin began his career with an apologia for the painter J. M. W. Turner, which in turn became the basis for the first two volumes of his series *Modern Painters* (1843, 1846). He argued that Turner's paintings, which seemed to many critics so unrealistic, were in fact deeply true to nature, once nature is understood not superficially but in terms of its infinity and unity, which are in turn expressions of the glory of God as the creator of nature (Ruskin 1995: 53, 61). The young Ruskin thus argued that the primary use of art is to set the glory of God before us (Ruskin 1995: 49), a glory which it requires the full use of what he distinguished as both our theoretic and imaginative faculties to grasp (Ruskin 1995: 52). In this early work, Ruskin focused on artistic genius as the power to grasp the divine attributes of infinity and unity in nature (Ruskin 1995: 71), or, more loosely, as the power to grasp truth (Ruskin 1995: 96). The ability to grasp 'truth' led in turn to a focus on sincerity as the genuineness or truthfulness of the artist (Ruskin 1995: 86–7, 104), and thus, for example, Ruskin catalogued the indispensable qualities of artistic genius as nobility of subject, love of beauty, and sincerity (Ruskin 1995: 98–104). The requirement of sincerity, even when severed from Ruskin's connection of it with the artist's religious attitude towards nature, has ever since remained a central expectation in art criticism.

Ruskin came to stress the necessity for greatness of soul and breadth of imagination on the part of the audience for art as well as in the artist. In the conclusion to *The Stones of Venice* (1851–53), Ruskin stressed first what is required of the artist and then what is required of the beholder of art. First, 'the great principle, to which all that has hitherto been stated is subservient', is 'that art is valuable or otherwise, only as it expresses the personality, activity, and living perception of a good and great human soul . . . and that if it have not this, if it show not the vigour, perception and invention of a mighty human spirit, it is worthless' (Ruskin 1995: 249–50). Then, addressing the artist on his duty to the audience:

All your faculties, all that is in you of greatest and best, must be awake in you, or I have no reward. The painter is not to cast the entire treasure of his human nature into his labour merely to please a part of the beholder: not merely to delight his senses, not merely to amuse his fancy, not merely to beguile him into emotion, not merely to lead him into thought: but to do *all* of this. Senses, fancy, feeling, reason, the whole of the beholding spirit, must be stilled in attention or stirred with delight: else the labouring spirit has not done its work well. (Ruskin 1995: 252–3)

From Ruskin's point of view, a conception of aesthetics as the theory of either artistic creativity alone or audience reception alone would be too narrow, just as would be any theory that restricts what is significant in art either to the purely intellectual and cognitive or to the pleasures of the senses.

What is most famous about *The Stones of Venice*, however, is Ruskin's encomium to the freedom of those involved in the creation and production of medieval art. This argument, although cast in the art-historical form of a contrast between classical, Renaissance, and nineteenth-century neo-classical art and architecture on the one hand and medieval and medieval revival art and architecture on the other, is in the tradition of the critique of the alienated condition of modern labour pioneered in Schiller's *Letters on the Aesthetic Education of Mankind* (1795) and of course in the work of Karl Marx. In the division of labour, Ruskin writes, 'It is not, truly speaking, the labour that is divided; but the men: – Divided into mere segments of men – broken into small segments and crumbs of life; so that all the little piece of intelligence that is left in a man is not enough to make a pin' (Ruskin 1995: 198–9; Ruskin's reference to the intelligence needed to make a pin is surely an allusion to Adam Smith's famous illustration of what he saw as the benefits of the division of labour by the example of pin-making; see *The Wealth of Nations* (1776), book I, ch. 1). Ruskin then bases his preference for medieval over classical art and architecture on his opposition to the division of labour: the regularity and perfection called for by Greek architecture and by its subsequent revivals may allow for some freedom of imagination on the part of the designer, but can only be realised by the labour of workers functioning like slaves or machines, who must reproduce innumerable components each of which is completely specified by the designer without any exercise of their own imaginations. In Gothic architecture, however, every mason and stonecarver gets to exercise his own imagination within the organic and evolving whole of an edifice. Thus Ruskin exhorts his reader to 'go forth again to gaze upon the old cathedral front . . . examine once more those ugly goblins, and formless monsters, and stern statues, anatomiless and rigid: but do not mock them, for they are signs of the life and liberty of every workman who struck the stone' (Ruskin 1995: 197).

This line of thought led Ruskin to a full-barrelled advocacy of socialism, and much of his work from the 1860s on, beginning with *Unto this Last: Four Essays on the First Principles of Political Economy* of 1862 and continuing with many other volumes and series of articles (see Ruskin 1985), was devoted to this purpose with very little further discussion of art at all. In his advocacy of a medievally inspired socialism Ruskin was followed by the gifted designer, decorator, poet, and political organiser William Morris (1834–96), whose Utopian novel *News from Nowhere* (1890) was as striking if ultimately not as influential as his marvellous floral patterns for fabrics, wallpapers, and carpets (see Morris 1910–15, Morris 1995, and Stansky 1983).

However, Ruskin did not completely give up writing about art after *Unto this Last*. In 1870 he was appointed as the first Slade Professor of Fine Art at Oxford, and in this capacity he lectured on fundamental issues about the nature of art as well as on the more concrete principles of drawing and design. These lectures are notable for the secularisation of Ruskin's view of the connection between art and morality, a consequence of his 'deconversion' from evangelical Protestanism in 1858. In these lectures, Ruskin no longer sees the beauty captured by the imaginative grasp of both artist and audience as a glorification of God, but simply as the expression of 'the two essential instincts of humanity: the love of Order and the love of Kindness' (Ruskin 1996: 129). The love of these qualities, which is the basis of morality, is also the basis of artistic beauty: 'All the virtues of language', Ruskin writes, but he could just as easily have written this of all the virtues of the arts in general, 'are, in their roots, moral: it becomes accurate if the speaker desires to be true; clear, if he speaks with sympathy and a desire to be intelligible; powerful, if he has earnestness; pleasant, if he has a sense of rhythm and order. There are no other virtues of . . . art than these' (Ruskin 1996: 116–17). And Ruskin accompanies this view with two notable thoughts. First, he insists that art itself cannot make people moral, but can at best enhance the moral condition of the individual: 'You must have the right moral state first, or you cannot have the art. But when the art is once obtained, its reflected action enhances and completes the moral state out of which it arose' (Ruskin 1996: 115). Second, the mature Ruskin strictly limits the dependence of art on religion, because he strictly limits the dependence of morality on religion: in a remarkably Kantian vein, Ruskin writes that the fundamental human instinct for morality 'receives from religion neither law, nor place; but only hope, and felicity' (Ruskin 1996: 85).

Thus, while throughout the evolution of Ruskin's thought it remains clear that the human capability to produce and appreciate art is an expression of the most fundamental cognitive and moral capacities of human beings, in his final position this exhausts the significance of art: artistic beauty need not be conceived of as a grasp or celebration of the glory of God, but is an expression of the love of order, truth, and kindness which is the basis of human morality quite independently of any divine law or divine reward.

2. FRIEDRICH NIETZSCHE (1844–1900)

At virtually the same time as Ruskin was delivering his lectures on art at Oxford, Friedrich Nietzsche, the young Basle professor of classical philology, was preparing his first book, *The Birth of Tragedy* (1872). On the surface, nothing could seem further from the confident moralism of Ruskin, whether in its earlier religious or later secular form, than Nietzsche's radical association of the consummate art form of the ancients with the terrifying, Dionysian forces beneath the placid, Apollonian surface of life. But Nietzsche's work does not break with the tradition of finding art's deepest justification in its significance for human morality; Nietzsche just has a very different conception of morality than his predecessors. Or, to be more precise, than most of his predecessors: for this still youthful work of Nietzsche is deeply indebted to Schopenhauer's earlier account of the connection between art and morality. Both what is radical and what is traditional in the views of both Schopenhauer and Nietzsche might be best appreciated, however, against the background of more standard German academic aesthetics in our period, and so our discussion of Schopenhauer and Nietzsche will itself be prefaced with a look at the leading German academic aesthetician of the mid-nineteenth century, Hermann Lotze (1817–81), professor of philosophy at Göttingen.

There were two main streams of academic aesthetics in mid-nineteenth-century German universities: a formalist and scientific strain, begun by Johann Friedrich Herbart (1776–1841) and developed by Gustav Theodor Fechner (1801–87), Hermann Helmholtz (1821–94), and Robert Zimmerman (1824–98), who attempted to give psychophysical explanations of our pleasure in the perception of particular aspects of external objects; and an idealist strand, influenced by Georg Wilhelm Friedrich Hegel's (1770–1831) posthumously published lectures on aesthetics (1844), and developed by writers such as the father and son Friedrich Theodor Vischer (1807–87) and Robert Vischer (1847–1933), who stressed the significance of art as a symbolic stage in the emergence of human cognition and self-consciousness. But it was Lotze who had the broadest influence, especially on the development of neo-idealism in both Britain and North America, through Bernard Bosanquet's 1884 translations of his *Logic* and *Metaphysics* and the 1885 translation of his whole system of philosophy, the *Microcosmos* (see Lotze 1856–64 [1885]). Of his works in aesthetics – the early *Begriff der Schönheit* ('Concept of Beauty', 1845), the mid-career *Geschichte der Ästhetik in Deutschland* (*History of Aesthetics in Germany*, 1868), or the posthumous lectures on the outlines of aesthetics, *Die Grundzüge der Ästhetik* (1884) – only the last and briefest was translated into English, but they were all certainly influential in Germany. Lotze is often thought to belong among the neo-Hegelians, but in aesthetics, at least, his views were more deeply rooted in the fundamentally Leibnizian tradition of German philosophy. His basic ideas were that the cosmos is a scene of ultimate unity amidst infinite variety, that the perception of beauty is a perception of both the variety and the unity of things (Lotze 1884: 7 [1990: 11]), and that the various arts are alike in making beauty so understood available to us, but differ in the particular aspects of the unity and variety of existence that their media allow them to represent to us: music arouses our feeling by its formal representation of the structure of existence (Lotze 1884: 39–47 [1990: 38–43]), genre painting by exhibiting common features of humanity in different historical, economic, and cultural circumstances (Lotze 1884: 66 [1990: 57–8]), and so on. Lotze's emphasis on beauty as the reflection of unity and order amidst the infinite variety of the world was thus similar to Ruskin's conception of beauty, and though he was not as explicitly moralistic as Ruskin, in the Leibnizian tradition he did not need to be: the value of order could be taken for granted, as could the value of art as revealing that order.

Schopenhauer and Nietzsche certainly broke with the Leibnizian assumption that the value of artistic beauty lies in its representation of the essential orderliness of existence. At the same time, both Schopenhauer and at least the young Nietzsche worked within a dualistic framework that they derived from Kant. In *The World as Will and Representation*, first published in 1819 but much more influential throughout the second half of the nineteenth century in its much expanded second edition of 1844, Schopenhauer divided existence into the realm of appearances, subject to the various forms of the law of sufficient reason deriving from the human cognitive subject, and its arational underlying reality, painfully manifest to us in the irrelevance of reason to our own willing. The third book of *The World as Will and Representation* presented Schopenhauer's aesthetics within this framework. The beauty and sublimity of the arts, Schopenhauer argued, free us from our ordinary and inevitably unsatisfying self-interested willing by presenting to us the universal essences of things, in comparison with which our individual desires and strivings are insignificant, and thus inducing in us a painless state of pure, contemplative, and will-less cognition (Schopenhauer 1844: 36 [1958: 184–94]). All the arts except music do this, Schopenhauer argues, by presenting us with 'Platonic ideas' that are universal forms of appearance, and which thus suppress our ordinary desires for the particulars of the world of appearance; music, however, is nothing less than 'a copy of the will itself' (Schopenhauer 1844: 52 [1958: 257]). It might seem paradoxical that a representation of the will itself is supposed to set us into a painless state of will-less cognition, but Schopenhauer's idea was that by focusing our attention on the general nature of reality, even or perhaps especially in the case of the will itself, the experience of music distracts us from the frustrating particularities of our own individual wills (for discussion of Schopenhauer's aesthetics, see Magee 1983: ch. 7, and Guyer 1996, as well as other essays in Jacquette 1996).

In *The Birth of Tragedy*, Nietzsche adapted much of this, but particularly Schopenhauer's contrast between music and the other arts, to give an account of the power of Greek tragedy in the classical works of Aeschylus and Sophocles (see Young 1992; Nietzsche thought that the tragedies of Euripides represented a decline in the art form under the influence of the rationalism of Socrates). The arts which on Schopenhauer's account produce 'Platonic ideas' as representations of the characteristic forms of appearance become for Nietzsche 'Apollonian', named after the sun-god Apollo: arts by means of which 'the incompletely intelligible everyday world' is given a kind of perfection like that which things may have in (pleasant) dreams; this tendency is characteristic 'of all plastic arts', Nietzsche maintains, and 'of an important part of poetry also' (Nietzsche 1872: 1 [1967: 34–5]). For the Greeks, the Apollonian tendency was also represented by the Olympian gods, perfected but still recognisable versions of the different and differentiable forms of human existence (Nietzsche 1872: 3 [1967: 41–2]). All of this is contrasted to the 'Dionysian', the recognition, 'brought home to us most intimately by the analogy of intoxication' (Nietzsche 1872: 1 [1967: 36), of the 'truly existent primal unity, eternally suffering and contradictory' (Nietzsche 1872: 4 [1967: 45]), the recognition of which is both terrifying, for it implies the loss of all sense of individuality and thus ordinary human existence, but yet also blissful, because 'Under the charm of the Dionysian not only is the union between man and man reaffirmed, but nature which has become alienated, hostile, or subjugated, celebrates once more her reconciliation with her lost son, man' (Nietzsche 1872: 1 [1967: 37]; see also 10 [1967: 74], and 17 [1967: 104–5]). The Dionysian is paradigmatically expressed in music, and it is Nietzsche's historical thesis that tragedy was originally Dionysian because it originated with the dithyrambs of the tragic chorus. 'The metaphysical comfort – with which . . . every true tragedy leaves us – that life is at the bottom of things, despite all the changes of appearances, indestructably powerful and pleasurable – this comfort appears in incarnate clarity in the chorus of satyrs' (Nietzsche 1872: 7 [1967: 59]). In Nietzsche's view, the Apollonian addition of roles for one then two individual actors by Aeschylus and Sophocles did not overwhelm the Dionysian essence of tragedy; that happened only by the addition of yet further individual roles by Euripides.

In the original edition of *The Birth of Tragedy*, Nietzsche seems to conceive of his theory of the Apollonian and Dionysian elements in tragedy as a straightforward application of Schopenhauer's distinction between the arts of representation and music, the art of the will itself, and he presents his view of the initially terrifying but ultimately consoling recognition of the primal unity of all things behind the appearances of individuality as consistent with Schopenhauer's view (Nietzsche 1872: 1 [1967: 36]). In the 'Attempt at a Self-Criticism' added as a preface to the work in 1886, Nietzsche distances himself from Schopenhauer, quoting Schopenhauer's remark that 'the tragic spirit . . . leads to *resignation*' while insisting that his own life-affirming conception of the Dionysian is 'far removed . . . from all this resignationism!' (Nietzsche 1872 [1967: 24]). Since on Schopenhauer's view, however, the indifference to one's own desires that can be achieved through art and above all through music and the ensuing recognition of the essential unity of all existence can lead to the sympathy with the suffering of *others* that is the basis of morality, it would seem as if on Schopenhauer's view, too, art can ultimately lead to an affirmation of life and not to mere resignation to suffering. Schopenhauer's sympathy-based ethics may have been more conventional than Nietzsche's view of the necessity to assert life precisely through the Dionysian, which seems like anathema to ordinary conceptions of ethics, but it is a misrepresentation to present his ethics as one of resignation alone.

However he should have understood his relation to Schopenhauer, it is clear that Nietzsche's conception of art in *The Birth of Tragedy* is fundamentally life-affirming, and that it is therefore appropriate to intepret him as having a moral conception of art. It may seem strange to say this of the thinker who later boasted to have gone 'beyond good and evil', and who is most famous precisely for his critique of morality. But Nietzsche's critique of morality is a critique of what he saw as the peculiarly ascetic and self-denying morality of Christianity, not necessarily a critique of any possible morality, and Nietzsche's early characterisation of the life-affirming morality of art seems like a first step in his own 'transvaluation of values', not a rejection of the possibility of moral value itself.

It has been argued that Nietzsche's mature philosophy is also based on aesthetics throughout: in his perspectivism, the world is conceived of like a work of art, unavoidably subject to a multiplicity of interpretations; and in his critique of traditional notions of the unity and substantiality of the self, the self is understood as a work of art – instead of discovering ourselves, we actually construct our selves like literary characters (see Nehamas 1985, especially chs. 3 and 6). But in the period covered by this history, it was *The Birth of Tragedy* which was most influential on both academic aesthetics and artistic practice, so our account of Nietzsche must end here (for further discussion of *The Birth of Tragedy*, see Silk and Stern 1981).

3. WALTER PATER (1839–94)

A close contemporary of Nietzsche who has also been considered as an advocate for an aesthetic view of human experience as a whole is the Oxford classicist, critic, and novelist Walter Pater, whose 1873 *Studies in the History of the Renaissance* (later retitled *The Renaissance: Studies in Art and Poetry*) was published just a year after *The Birth of Tragedy* and whose novel *Marius the Epicurean* (1885) was published one year before Nietzsche's *Beyond Good and Evil*. Pater has often been counted as an adherent of 'art for art's sake', and such statements as the closing words of *The Renaissance* – 'For art comes to you proposing frankly to give nothing but the highest quality to your moments as they pass, and simply for those moments' sake' (Pater 1873 [1986: 153]) – make it easy to see why. But it would be as much of a mistake to think of Pater as an amoralist who prizes artistic as well as natural beauty for its sensuous pleasures heedless of any moral requirements as it would be to think of Nietzsche that way; rather, like Nietzsche, Pater is better thought of as an unconventional moralist for whom an intense focus upon the quality of our experience, of a kind paradigmatically afforded by art, is itself an indispensable part of and condition for the best way of life available to human beings. Sometimes Pater expresses this view by proposing an Aristotelian morality in which contemplation is the highest good; thus in an 1874 essay on Wordsworth, he writes: 'That the end of life is not action but contemplation – *being* as distinct from *doing* – a certain disposition of the mind: is, in some shape or other, the principle of all the higher morality. In poetry, in art, if you enter into their true spirit at all, you touch this principle, in a measure: these, by their very sterility, are a type of beholding for the mere joy of beholding' (Pater 1973: 131; as we will see in the next chapter, this line of thought leads to the ethics of G. E. Moore and its application by the Bloomsbury art critic Clive Bell). Sometimes Pater suggests a more conventional moral underpinning for a devotion to the experience of art by suggesting that greatness of 'matter' is a *sine qua non* of great art, thus that what makes the experience of art important is not the sheer importance of contemplation as such but the importance of an intensive awareness of something important: thus in a later (1889) essay on 'Style' he writes: 'the distinction between great art and good art depend[s] immediately, as regards literature at all events, not on its form, but on the matter . . . on the quality of the matter it informs or controls, its compass, its variety, its alliance to great ends, or the depth of the note of revolt, or the largeness of hope in it' (Pater 1973: 88). And sometimes he suggests that the significance of our experience of art lies in its stimulation of our ability to imagine alternatives to the reality we ordinarily observe, which is at least a necessary condition of any moral development: 'The basis of all artistic genius lies in the power of conceiving humanity in a new and striking way, of putting a happy world of its own creation in place of the meaner world of our common days . . . according to the choice of the imaginative intellect' (Pater 1873 [1986: 137]). Pater was not a philosophy professor, and it would be a mistake to look to him for a rigorous moral theory to serve as the basis of a rigorous aesthetic theory. But equally clearly it would be a mistake to think of him as someone who advocates devotion to aesthetic experience independently of any other human values; on the contrary, he clearly held that the value of aesthetic experience is tied up with the most fundamental sources of value in human life, whatever exactly those might be and however close or distant his conception of them may have been to conventional Victorian morality. Pater's defence of the moral value of aesthetic experience as such would find echoes in the writings of the Bloomsbury group, above all Clive Bell, influenced by the early moral philosophy of G. E. Moore; but this approach, we will see, is very much a minority view in a period still under the spell of Ruskin.

FORM AND FEELING: AESTHETICS AT
THE TURN OF THE CENTURY

PAUL GUYER

1. 'ART FOR ART'S SAKE'

The popular conception of the development of the arts at the turn of the twentieth century is dominated by the transition from naturalism to abstraction in painting and from realism to modernism in literature. The popular conception of art theory and aesthetics in this period is likewise dominated by formalism and the ideology of 'art for art's sake'. The painter James MacNeill Whistler (1834–1903) gave expression to both of these themes. In 1878, in his libel suit against John Ruskin, who had described him as 'flinging a pot of paint in the public's face', Whistler stated that he had meant to divest the offending picture 'from any outside sort of interest which might have been otherwise attached to it. It is an arrangement of line, form and colour first' (Harrison, Wood, and Geiger 1998: 834–5). Such an emphasis on the sensible properties of artworks and on the formal relations among them, coupled with de-emphasis on the content of such works and their moral, political, and religious associations, is the doctrine of formalism in its most general sense.

The ideology of 'art for art's sake' is the view that a special pleasure afforded by art is a necessary and sufficient condition of its value, and that art is to be neither valued nor criticised for moral, political, or religious reasons. The view is often said to have been introduced by Théophile Gautier (1811–72) in the preface to his 1835 novel *Mademoiselle de Maupin*, where he asserted that a novel should have no moral, political, or economic use at all, other than that of perhaps putting a few thousand francs into its author's pocket, and that instead 'the useless alone is truly beautiful' (Harrison, Wood, and Geiger 1998: 98–9). Half a century later, Whistler gave voice to the same sentiment in his 'Ten O'Clock Lecture' of 1885, claiming that art 'is a goddess of dainty thought – reticent of habit, abjuring all obtrusiveness, purposing in no way to better others. She is, withal, selfishly occupied with her own perfection only – having no desire to teach – seeking and finding the beautiful in all conditions and in all times' (Harrison, Wood, and Geiger 1998: 839, 846). Whistler's thesis was that art exists only for the pleasure it brings, making no contribution to the moral, political, and economic well-being of peoples and states, and that its value is therefore independent of all utility and thus immune to the decline and fall of the states and economies in which it may have been produced.

2. TOLSTOY

The radical separation of aesthetic pleasure from all other forms of value drew a violent response from the great Russian novelist Leo Tolstoy (1828–1910) in his 1898 polemic *What is Art?* Although the younger author of *War and Peace* (1869) and *Anna Karenina* (1877) may have been the most humane and empathetic of the great nineteenth-century novelists, the cranky old man who wrote *What is Art?* produced a work that was deeply hostile to virtually all of the art that had been produced in modern Europe.

Tolstoy starts his work by setting a high normative bar for any theory of art: he describes the economic costs of the production of art (without comment on the benefits of the employment it creates) and the personal costs to many involved in their production, whom he describes as forced labour, practically slaves, without reference to the personal satisfaction that many seem to derive from devoting their lives to the creation or performance of art in spite of the pain or poverty that may involve (Tolstoy 1898: chs. I–II [1995: 3–16]). The only thing, he argues, that can justify these extraordinary costs is the communication of morally beneficial feeling from artist to audience: 'Art is that human activity which consists in one man's consciously conveying to others, by certain external signs, the feelings he has experienced, and in others being infected by those feelings and also experiencing them' (Tolstoy 1898: ch. V [1995: 40]). Initially, it might seem as if any noble and religious feeling could be valuably communicated by art. But Tolstoy concludes that while 'all art has in itself the property of unifying people' by means of the communication of some common feeling, 'non-Christian art, by uniting certain people with each other, thereby separates them from other people', so that the only truly valuable art is that which communicates a feeling of 'the Christian union of people, contrary to the partial, exclusive union of some people, one that unites all people without exception' (Tolstoy 1898: ch. XVI [1995: 129]). Thus Tolstoy rejects as worthless a great deal of art produced throughout history, and accepts as valuable only art which he perceives as communicating the supposed Christian feeling of the union of all people as children of God.

Tolstoy is not entirely dead to the formal merits of artworks, and indeed requires properties such as clarity and lucidity as necessary conditions of successful communication. But it is clear that the moral benefit of the attitudes induced by the feelings communicated by a work of art is not just a necessary but also the central condition for its value. Tolstoy holds it to be a causal condition of the successful communication of feeling to an audience that an artist should actually have felt the feeling he is trying to induce in his audience and that he should communicate this feeling truthfully, and thereby makes the artist's sincerity the foremost criterion for the critical evaluation of art (Tolstoy 1898: ch. XV [1995: 122]). This has probably been the most influential idea in his work. But it must be noted that the value of sincerity for Tolstoy rests on the positive value of the feeling that is to be communicated. Perhaps the most questionable feature of Tolstoy's account is his repeated characterisation of the effect of a work of art on its audience as 'infection': a completely passive response, in other words, in which an audience automatically responds to the work by replicating and further transmitting whatever feeling the artist has communicated to them. This seems deeply problematic from both a theoretical and a practical point of view: it completely eliminates the active role of the imagination of the audience in response to a work of art, and it equally eliminates the critical judgement of the audience, their responsibility for deciding on their own moral or political response to what is presented to them.

3. BOSANQUET

Most philosophical aestheticians, however, drew on Ruskin rather than Tolstoy to counter the ideology of art for art's sake. In Britain, the Ruskinian tradition was represented by Bernard Bosanquet (1848–1923). Bosanquet was the only one of the British idealists to publish major work in aesthetics. Indeed, although the history of aesthetics was already a well-established genre in Germany by the time that Bosanquet published his stout *A History of Aesthetic* in 1892, Bosanquet's book appears to have been the first and for many years the only work of its kind in Britain. Late in his career, Bosanquet also published *Three Lectures on Aesthetic* (1915), a brief and accessible statement of the conception of art underlying his earlier *History*.

Bosanquet begins with a polemic against the Greeks: Plato criticised the arts because he took works of art merely as defective imitations of reality, failing to see them as products of the kind of free imagination that is necessary to get past mere appearances. Aristotle recognised the cognitive and emotional benefits of art, but still failed to see the vital role of imagination in elevating art past the level of mere imitation. Only with Plotinus's conception of emanation did the ancient world break the grip of the model of imitation and glimpse that in the work of art nature is not merely imitated but rather infused with both form and meaning by a higher power – though, to be sure, divine reason, not yet human imagination (Bosanquet 1892: 114). Not until modern times does it come to be understood that both the form and content of art are free products of human imagination, which can be set in tension as well as in harmony with each other, and thus that art must make room for ugliness as well as beauty. This last claim is a central theme throughout Bosanquet's work and is emphasised again in his lectures of 1915. It seems safe to venture that this thesis was meant to clear the philosophical way for the radical departures from classical conceptions of beauty that characterised so many art forms in the late nineteenth century and that would characterise so much art throughout the twentieth century.

For Bosanquet, modern aesthetic theory began when Kant, responding to the empiricism of Hutcheson and Hume on one side and the rationalism of Leibniz and Baumgarten on the other, grasped that the key question of aesthetics is, 'in its general form, "How can the sensuous and the ideal world be reconciled?" and in its special aesthetic form, "How can a pleasurable feeling partake of the character of reason?"' (Bosanquet 1892: 187). Kant earns Bosanquet's unstinting praise for his recognition that beauty cannot be merely subservient to morality, but is nevertheless linked to morality by the central fact that both are expressions of human freedom:

Now if beauty is regarded as subservient to morality, or is judged by the standard of specifically moral ideas, it is beyond a doubt unfree or dependent. But if the content of life and reason is taken into beauty and perceived not as the expression of morality, but as the utterance in another form of that reasonableness which is also to be found in morality, then we first destroy the restriction of ideal beauty to man – for there is reasonableness in all nature – and we secondly break down the extraordinary paradox that the highest beauty is the least free. That beauty which is the largest and deepest revelation of spiritual power is not the most dependent but the freest beauty. (Bosanquet 1892: 272)

According to Bosanquet, Kant's hint at the fundamental significance of the freedom of the imagination was then taken up by Schiller and especially Schelling, who recognised that 'The ideal world of art and the real one of objects are . . . products of one and the same activity' (Bosanquet 1892: 321), but also that art gives expression to the constant tension between necessity and contingency, nature and freedom, that is the essence of the human condition. The work of art cannot always be an effortless reconciliation of nature and freedom: sometimes it 'is also racked and burdened to the uttermost, so that it may take on something of the character of the infinite which has to be expressed' (Bosanquet 1892: 327). It is thus Schelling who first makes room for the artistic expression of the sublime, the difficult, and even the ugly which is characteristic of modern art (see Bosanquet 1892: 424, 434.)

The argument of *A History of Aesthetic* reaches its conclusion with an appreciation of Ruskin's famous chapter 'On the nature of Gothic' and of William Morris. Ruskin and Morris are praised because they recognise that artistic beauty is not the mere imitation of anything given in nature, but the product of the freedom of the imagination in the labour of the artist, the artisan, and even the audience, by means of which nature is infused with meaning. The root of the relation between form and content that is the essence of beauty, whether easy or difficult, 'is not a causal process of nature assigned a meaning by analogy, but it is the life of a self-conscious being' (Bosanquet 1892: 451); hence 'The work reveals the man, and the man is the incarnation (in sense and feeling) of ideas' (Bosanquet 1892: 453). Through their emphasis on the human being as the agent who freely connects sense and feeling with ideas, Ruskin and Morris brought the metaphysical insights of Schelling and Hegel down to earth.

In the *Three Lectures on Aesthetic* Bosanquet himself brought the abstract ideas of his earlier work down to earth. What makes the later work so much more direct than the earlier is the replacement of the vague specification of the content of art in that earlier work with the simple statement that art is that in which human 'Feeling becomes "organized," "plastic" or "incarnate"'' (Bosanquet 1915: 7). While in ordinary life feelings of all kinds may be fleeting and vague, affecting our conduct but without being open to reflection and understanding, art has 'the power to draw out or give imaginative shape to the object and material of . . . experience.' In art, 'The feeling is submitted to the laws of an object. It must take on permanence, order, harmony, meaning, in short value. It ceases to be mere self-absorption' (Bosanquet 1915: 8). Aesthetic feeling is ordinary feeling transformed into something enduring, comprehensible, and valuable by its embodiment in something concrete, the work of art, and whatever the affective value of the original feeling, it is compatible with the pleasure of aesthetic feeling because of the pleasure that we can take in the embodiment and grasp of that feeling.

As in his earlier work, Bosanquet's aim is to make philosophical room for modern art's need to go beyond the boundaries of conventional beauty in order to allow for the expression of feeling, without losing sight of the fact that there are expectations of pleasure connected with the objective embodiment of feeling. To this end, Bosanquet argues that there must be two kinds of beauty. In the narrower sense, beauty is that which is 'prima facie aesthetically pleasant' (Bosanquet 1915: 84), or simply that with which it is easy to be pleased; in the broader sense, however, beauty is whatever we can consider 'aesthetically excellent' (Bosanquet 1915: 83), whether doing so is easy or difficult. What makes some beauty difficult is characteristics like 'intricacy', 'tension', and 'width', or a breadth of conception that undermines all sorts of normal expectations. Difficult beauty includes the sublime and even the ugly, as long as those can be found in 'a creation, a new individual expression in which a new feeling comes to exist' (Bosanquet 1915: 109). Whether the relation between the feeling and its embodiment is harmonious or tense, if the object can ultimately be perceived as the embodiment of a feeling and the feeling understood through its embodiment, then the purpose of art has been realised.

4. SANTAYANA

The conclusion that Bosanquet reached with the help of Kant and later German idealists is not very different from that reached by the American philosopher George Santayana (1863–1952) with the help of the empiricist tradition, especially the empiricist psychology of William James (1842–1910).

The Sense of Beauty (1896) was Santayana's first book. In this work, Santayana famously held that beauty is pleasure objectified, 'pleasure regarded as the quality of a thing'; it is 'a value, that is, not a perception of a matter of fact or of a relation: it is an emotion, an affection of our volitional and appreciative nature' (Santayana 1896: 31), but one that we treat as if it were a property of an external object because the perception of it is typically immediate, like the perception of a genuine property of an external object, and typically shared, like the perception of an external object's more ordinary properties.

There is nothing original in this claim; it is already to be found in Hutcheson and Hume. Nor is there anything original in Santayana's account of pleasure itself, according to which 'it is in the spontaneous play of his faculties that man finds himself and his happiness' (Santayana 1896: 19). This goes back directly to Kant's conception of the free play of imagination and understanding. Rather, what earned *The Sense of Beauty* its audience is the richness of Santayana's account of the materials with which our faculties can pleasurably play. The heart of the work is Santayana's argument that we can play with the materials of perception, such as colour and texture, with formal relations among our perceptions, such as balance and symmetry, and with the expressions of emotions associated with objects: thus the pleasure that is objectified into beauty is pleasure produced by our free play with the matter and form of perceptions as well as with the emotions associated with the objects of our perception, and with the relations among all these factors. Santayana's insights on each of these make *The Sense of Beauty* still rewarding. Under the 'Materials of Beauty' (Part II), he refers to the influence of sexual and social feelings on perception, but also draws attention to our enjoyment of the sensuous materials of art: 'Form cannot be the form of nothing. If, then, in finding or creating beauty, we attend only to their form, we miss an ever-present opportunity to heighten our effects'

(Santayana 1896: 49). This is a completely reasonable observation to make in
an era marked by the rich sonorities of Wagner and Brahms or the luscious
surfaces of Monet or Klimt, but hardly one emphasised in previous aesthetic
theory. Under the rubric of 'Form' (Part III), Santayana cites not just traditional
notions like symmetry and uniformity in variety, but also treats our pleasure in
images that strike us as typical and characteristic of objects of a kind – without
succumbing to the idealist insistence that only universal and hence a priori ideal
types can be relevant to aesthetics: 'Relativity to our partial nature is . . . essential
to our definite thoughts, judgements and feelings' (Santayana 1896: 80). Concerning 'Expression' (Part IV), Santayana argues that the associations of objects
with emotions not original to them is a twofold source of pleasure, invest-
ing perceptual objects with an interest they might not immediately have but
also transforming emotions that may be unlovely into a lovely form. This section concludes with thoughtful reflections on the relation between beauty and
morality: on the one hand, Santayana argues, 'the aesthetic world is limited in
its scope' and 'must submit to the control of the organizing reason, and not
trespass upon more useful and holy ground' (Santayana 1896: 136); on the other
hand, morality has no call to impose any rigid standards of taste upon our individual senses of beauty: 'All that morality can require is the inward harmony of
each life' (Santayana 1896: 134). Beauty is a reminder that all our experience,
even our experience of moral agency, takes place within nature; the naturalist
Santayana concludes with the Kantian thought that 'Beauty is a pledge of the
possible conformity between the soul and nature, and consequently a ground
of faith in the supremacy of the good' (Santayana 1896: 164).

Santayana's sense of aesthetic experience as a fundamental reflection of humanity's place in nature led him to attack the possibility of aesthetics as a special
discipline of philosophy in a 1904 article but also to make art the subject of
Reason in Art, the fourth volume of *The Life of Reason*, his five-volume phenomenology of the natural history of human reason published in 1905–6. As
the earlier work had argued that our sense of beauty is our experience of our
fundamental harmony with nature, so Santayana now argues that art is the means
by which we literally add to that harmony. By means of our sense of beauty, we
can find beauty virtually anywhere in nature; by means of art, we can produce
beauty out of virtually anything in nature. Santayana shows how the various arts
have all arisen from the ordinary and natural activities of human beings, from
making containers to talking to each other, rather than from any special impulse
or emotion. The implication that aesthetic interest might be found in almost
anything is often taken to be an objection to descriptive aesthetic theories that
propose to define a special realm of art by the criterion of aesthetic experience;
for Santayana, the implication that beauty may be found and/or created virtually

anywhere in nature is clearly a virtue of his theory, intended as a normative and by no means merely descriptive aesthetics.

5. CROCE

Although inspired by different sources, Bosanquet and Santayana reached similar views about the interpenetration of perceptual form and emotional expression in any successful art and the interpenetration of imagination and action in any successful life. In 1905, the Italian philosopher and historian Benedetto Croce (1866–1952) opened his ambitiously entitled *The Aesthetic as the Science of Expression and of the Linguistic in General* with what appears to be a similar account of the work of art as a synthesis by means of which form is given to and for the expression of feeling, but his general philosophy of mind led him to insist upon a rigid separation between imagination and action even though so many of his contemporaries grounded the value of art on the interplay between them.

Croce describes the work of art as intuition given form and thus transformed into expression. In the *Aesthetic* Croce is vague about what he means by 'intuition', although in a later work he suggests that art typically gives expression to 'intense feelings', and thus he seems to have in mind, like his contemporaries, that art is the means by which we give public and enduring form to our otherwise obscure and often ephemeral emotions. However, Croce's general philosophical framework forces him to reject this straightforward position. Croce draws a rigid distinction between the human capacities for intuition, conceptualisation, and action, and thus draws strict boundaries between the disciplines of aesthetics, science, economics, and ethics (action gives rise to two disciplines rather than one because action can be self- or other-regarding). Because giving physical expression to intuition is a form of action, Croce is led to the remarkable conclusion that what we would ordinarily consider the locus of artistic expression, namely the creation of a form in a publicly accessible medium such as paint, stone, printed or spoken words, is not properly a part of the work of art at all, but at most an aid to the memory of the artist for the repetition of an intuition he has once clarified in some purer realm of thought or an aid to an audience for the recreation in its own mind of what the artist had in his: 'The aesthetic stage is completely over and done with when impressions have been worked up into impressions. When we have captured the internal word, formed an apt and lively idea of a figure or a statue . . . expression has begun and ended. That we then open, or want to open, our mouths in order to speak, or our throats in order to sing . . . all this is something additional', because 'the latter activity is something practical or voluntary' (Croce 1905: 56–7). This may express a striking recognition of the physicality of the act of artistic production, but only at the cost of any recognition of the physicality and therefore public accessibility of the work of art itself.

Croce's conception of the aesthetic leads him to some striking conclusions. His equation of the aesthetic with expression leads him to deny that there can be any rigid distinction between art and non-art, since any form of expression has the potential to rise to the clarity of expression demanded of art; it leads him to deny that there can be rigid divisions among the arts, since the physical media on which the customary classifications of the arts are based are not essential to the real work of art; and it leads him to deny that any traditional kind of beauty is essential to art, since any intense feeling, no matter how ugly or distasteful, can become a subject of the expressive activity of art – the only thing that can be ugly is flawed expression itself. These conclusions are clearly meant to make philosophical room for the experimentation in the arts at the turn of the century. Croce's underlying premises also lead him to a subtle position on the issue of the autonomy of art, or the relation between art and morality: on the one hand, he claims, that art takes place in the sphere of intuition rather than action means that it need have no immediate connections to the ordinary purposes of economics and morality; on the other, since the externalisation of the inner work of art by means of physical media is an entry not only into the public space but also into the sphere of practice, there is no reason for the artist to think that the presentation of his inner work in any publicly accessible medium can remain immune from the laws of economics or morality.

These are genuine insights, but they are bought at a high price, namely that of denying that much of the fascination of art lies precisely in the interaction between our thoughts and emotions on the one hand and the potentials and limits of the physical media for their expression on the other. Although they are less widely read today than Croce, writers like Bosanquet and Santayana seem to have been wiser on this score.

6. BLOOMSBURY

Apart from Croce, resistance to the mainstream synthesis of form and content, and through that of art and morality, is also often thought to be characteristic of the writers and artists of the 'Bloomsbury' group. The writer on art most often cited as the apostle of strict formalism in this circle is Clive Bell (1881–1964).

Bell begins his famous manifesto *Art* (1914) with what he calls 'the aesthetic hypothesis', which he argues can be based only on 'the personal experience of a peculiar emotion'. His claim is that aesthetic emotion is a distinct genus of emotion, 'provoked by every kind of visual art, by pictures, sculptures, buildings, pots, carvings, textiles, &c., &c.', and by no other objects. That it arouses this emotion is 'the essential quality in a work of art, the quality that distinguishes works of art from all other classes of objects'. And that in the work of art, Bell continues, which arouses this distinctive kind of emotion is 'significant form': 'lines and colours combined in a particular way, certain forms and relations of forms' (Bell 1914: 17). Bell then asserts that since it is significant form alone that produces aesthetic emotion, it is to the form of a work of art alone that a viewer who would have the proper aesthetic response to it must attend: there is no need to worry about 'the state of mind of him who made' the object (Bell 1914: 19) because the only thing that can be aesthetically significant in that state of mind is the intention to produce the significant form that the observer sees in the work itself; and there is no need for the viewer to worry about the content or representational significance of the work, because although 'The representative element in a work of art may or may not be harmful always it is irrelevant' (Bell 1914: 27).

Bell worries that by placing the value of art in our experience of a special aesthetic emotion, unrelated to any of the ordinary human emotions – love, hate, fear, pride, and so on – that might seem to be the province of morality, he has stripped art of all moral significance. In order to block such an objection, Bell appeals to G. E. Moore's *Principia Ethica* (1903). Moore had argued that any moral theory must recognise some things as ends that are good in themselves, to which other good things, including the norms and obligations of morality, could be prescribed as means; he had then argued that 'the enjoyment of beautiful objects' is one of the greatest goods. Following Moore, Bell argues that aesthetic emotion is a state of mind that is good in itself, and indeed that 'Art is not only a means to good states of mind, but, perhaps, the most direct and potent that we possess' (Bell 1914: 83). This is not an argument that would have appealed to eighteenth-century moralists such as Kant and Schiller, nor would it seem an adequate account of the value of art to many twentieth-century theorists, especially in the wake of the First World War that was about to shatter the Victorian-Edwardian peace in which Moore and Bell had formed their views.

The name of Roger Fry is invariably linked with that of Bell, and indeed the two men collaborated on important exhibitions of the 'post-Impressionists' (notably, Cézanne) presented in London in 1910 and 1912. But Fry, a painter as well as a critic, was a subtler thinker than Bell. Indeed, Fry protested at his constant association with Bell, because his view of the emotions expressed in art was not the same as Bell's. In the 'Retrospect' to his 1920 essay collection, *Vision and Design*, Fry argued that Bell had gone too far in connecting significant form with a special aesthetic emotion; in his view, a work of art uses its formal properties to communicate 'some emotion of actual life' apprehended by the artist. He claims that artists possess a special 'detachment' that allows them to focus on emotion and communicate it, but he does not suppose that there is any special emotion that is communicated by all art and only by art. In one of the earlier essays in this book, 'An Essay in Aesthetics' (1909), Fry had linked art with 'the imaginative life' rather than ordinary life, meaning by this that what he would later call the special detachment of the artist is the ability to suspend our normal concerns about the consequences of objects and the actions they ordinarily call for in order to focus instead on the appearance of things themselves; but what he meant by this was not that through detachment art discovers some special kind of emotions, but rather that by suspending our normal concern with actions and consequences it allows us to focus on the nature of our emotions themselves. Fry summed up this position by stating that 'Morality . . . appreciates emotion by the standard of resultant action. Art appreciates emotion in and for itself' (Fry 1920: 19).

Although he did not recognise a distinct aesthetic emotion, Fry did believe that there are certain emotions that works of art are uniquely well qualified to express. In a lecture on 'Expression and Representation in the Graphic Arts' (1908), Fry held that while art has the aim of expressing and communicating emotion in general precisely by its special focus on perceptual forms, whether naturalistic or more abstract, there is a certain group of emotions of which we typically become aware only through art, namely, emotions connected with the very conditions of our existence in the physical world:

The artist's attitude to nature, then, is that he uses it for communicating emotions. And, moreover, in doing this he draws upon the conditions of our situation in the universe, upon the condition of our physical being, to arouse emotions which are normally dormant. We have in ordinary life but little emotion about the force of gravity or about mass. The artist continually evokes our latent perception of these things, and enables us to grasp their imaginative significance. Similarly he evokes emotions about spacial relations [*crossed out*: sex instincts,] and social instincts. (Fry 1996: 69)

Art expresses and gets us to focus on the whole range of our emotions, those connected by the most fundamental forces of the physical, which we ordinarily ignore altogether, as well as those, like sexual and social instincts, which we perhaps rarely appreciate in themselves because we are too focused on the actions they may suggest. To be sure, perhaps most artists, like the rest of us, have been typically concerned with the latter rather than the former sort of emotions; however, Fry's special admiration for Cézanne is based on Cézanne's powerful focus on the former.

Fry also distinguished his view from Bell's by making room for ugliness as well as beauty in art. In linking significant form with a special aesthetic emotion, Bell inevitably suggested that all art must be beautiful. But Fry recognised that if art expresses only ordinary human emotions, but the entire range of such emotions, then it must express emotions that strain at the confines of beautiful sensuous form as well as emotions that fit within such bounds. In his 1908 lecture he wrote that his definition:

> has also the advantage . . . that it freely admits ugliness as a part of aesthetic beauty . . . Ugliness . . . will not be admitted for its own sake, but only as allowing of the expression of an emotion so intense and pleasurable that we accept without demur the painfulness inherent in the ugly image . . . inasmuch as our most poignant emotions are connected with the struggle of life, the cruelty and indifference of fate, and the contrasting warmth and consolation of human sympathy, and inasmuch as all these forces of life tend to produce distortions from formal regularity, ugliness is a method of appeal to the emotions which is likely to be used by the artists who penetrate deepest into the human heart. (Fry 1996: 67)

Significant form does not arouse a special aesthetic emotion detached from all other emotions of life; on the contrary, form is significant just in so far as it expresses and even arouses emotions from real life.

Fry's recognition that there is pleasure in the perception of both sensory beauty and deep emotion, and that these distinct sources of pleasure may be in tension as well as harmony with each other, brings him much closer than Bell to the idea that art must make room for the ugly as well as for the conventionally beautiful that was central for both Bosanquet and Croce. Another figure who is often associated with Bell, the Cambridge lecturer on modern languages and ultimately Professor of Italian Literature, Edward Bullough, also turns out to be far closer to the mainstream of pre-war aesthetic theory than he initially appears.

Bullough is famous for a 1912 essay in which he argued for something like Fry's concept of 'detachment', namely the concept of 'psychical distance' as a 'factor in art and an aesthetic principle' (Bullough 1912 [1957]). Bullough introduced his concept of psychical distance by means of an example that has become inescapable. 'Imagine a fog at sea', he writes; ordinarily, someone sailing on a ship trapped in fog will be too worried about possible delays and dangers to pay much attention to the sensuous properties and fascinating associations of the fog itself. But if one can abstract from such concerns, then 'a fog at sea can be a source of intense relish and enjoyment': this enjoyment arises from 'direct[ing] the attention to the features "objectively" constituting the phenomenon', such as 'the veil surrounding you with an opaqueness as of transparent milk', 'the curious creamy smoothness of the water, hypocritically denying as it were any suggestion of danger; and, above all, the strange solitude and remoteness of the world' (Bullough 1957: 93–4). The ordinary reading of this example is that by means of distance we allow ourselves to attend strictly to the perceptual features of an object, natural or artistic, and to take pleasure in the formal relations among those features, such as pure colour and shape, that give themselves to immediate sensory perception. But Bullough's example makes it clear that psychical distance does not restrict our attention solely to perceptual form; rather, it shows how by abstracting from self-regarding emotions, such as annoyance at delay or fear of danger, we open ourselves up to all sorts of other thoughts and emotions, such as thoughts of solitude and the remoteness of the world, and the quite intense emotions that can be induced by such thoughts. Such emotions are clearly not any special aesthetic emotion engendered by purely formal features of perceptual objects, and can instead be among our most fundamental emotions; they are just not self-regarding, and may be accessed only if we can put some distance between ourselves and our more self-regarding emotions.

As Bullough's conception of emotion is richer than Bell's, his metaphor of 'psychical distance' is also richer than Fry's concept of detachment. His idea is that one has to put a certain distance between oneself and some of one's personal concerns and interests in order to be able to put the right distance between oneself and an object of aesthetic interest; in a sense, putting more distance between oneself and some of one's self-regarding interests can allow one to put less distance between oneself and an aesthetic object, and thereby focus on the latter all the better. Thus, whereas we may have to *increase* our distance from our ordinary concerns in order to appreciate the aesthetic object, 'what is desirable' with regard to the distance between such an object and ourselves 'is the *utmost decrease of Distance without its disappearance*' (Bullough 1957: 100). Yet the aesthetic attitude as Bullough conceives it is by no means simply impersonal, but rather requires setting aside some feelings so that other feelings may be more fully explored and enjoyed. 'Distance does not imply an impersonal, purely intellectually interested relation . . . On the contrary, it describes a *personal* relation, often highly emotionally coloured, but *of a peculiar character* . . . It has been cleared of the practical, concrete nature of its appeal, without, however, thereby losing its original constitution' (Bullough 1957: 97).

Prior to publishing his article on 'Psychical Distance', Bullough had given Cambridge's first lecture course on aesthetics. In these lectures, privately printed in 1907, he did not use the concept of distance at all, but instead emphasised that aesthetic experience of an object 'implies *eo ipso* the recognition of its uniqueness, of those distinctive qualities, which are its exclusive property, and make it different from, and incommensurable with, any other work, however similar in subject, conception or technique . . . The more we appreciate it, the more we let ourselves be imbued with its spirit and enveloped by its peculiar atmosphere, the stronger do we realise its uniqueness and its solitary perfection'

(Bullough 1957: 46). There is no hint here that in focusing on the object we respond to its perceptual form alone; on the contrary, to appreciate fully an object is to enter into the whole sphere of thoughts and emotions that surround it.

Bosanquet concluded his *History* with an appeal to Ruskin; Bullough closed his lectures with words which were not but could have been written by Schiller:

The contemplative immanence of aesthetic consciousness is par excellence the medium for extending the limited range of our personal experience and of forcing those experiences which do fall within it into the highest relief of which they are susceptible . . . What we are, the sum total of our most personal being, we undoubtedly owe in a much larger degree to experiences made through the medium of aesthetic impressions, than to the extension of our personality by contact with the real world. (Bullough 1957: 88)

This expansion of our experience through the medium of art would not be possible if art aimed to induce only a special emotion detached or distanced from all other human emotions; on the contrary, art aims to give expression to the full range of human emotions, a range much wider than any of us individually experience in our own lives, although it takes a certain amount of distance from the details and demands of our own lives to open ourselves up to this full range.

INTERLUDE

PHILOSOPHY AND THE FIRST WORLD WAR

THOMAS BALDWIN

The division of this volume at the 1914–18 war raises the question of whether the war induced a significant shift in philosophical thought and writing. This is a question which is addressed in English surprisingly rarely (the only extended discussion occurs in Wallace 1988, and this deals only with British philosophers). We are familiar with the thought that the First World War gave rise to a distinctive literature, poetry, art, and so on, and that it at least accentuated subsequent changes in these cultural forms. But the question of whether philosophy was similarly changed is not much discussed, as if philosophy's status as an abstract, a priori, discipline sets it apart from the messy world of war and politics. But this presumption has only to be stated to be seen to be questionable, since the concepts with which philosophers operate, especially in the areas of ethics and political philosophy, are necessarily grounded in that ordinary social and political world which, at least in Europe, was shaken to its foundations by the First World War.

Yet it is equally important to oppose the view that philosophy is just a cultural superstructure whose development can be explained by changes in underlying social and political conditions – as if one were to propose that the loss of interest in idealism outside Germany after 1918 is to be explained by reference to the First World War. In truth, of course, several chapters in the first part of this book have already demonstrated that challenges to idealism were well under way before the war; similarly in the second part of the book the continuing idealist tradition, outside as well as inside Germany, will be discussed. More generally, however, the chapters in this volume demonstrate that philosophy has an intrinsic argumentative, or dialectical, history; so if there is a connection between this history and the First World War, it will not be a simple one.

This essay is an attempt to characterise some of its features, drawing primarily, though not exclusively, on sources in English. In writing it I have become increasingly aware of the limitations this constraint imposes; a full account would need to draw on a much wider range of sources than I have been able to access. Nonetheless a partial account is better than none at all.

'THE NEW BARBARISM'?

On 21 September 1914 *The Times* printed a letter entitled 'The New Barbarism'. The author (who is identified only as 'Continuity') begins with a quotation from Heine:

Christianity – and this is its highest merit – has in some degree softened, but it could not destroy, that brutal German joy of battle. When once the taming talisman, the Cross, breaks in two, the savagery of the old fighters, the senseless, Berserker fury of which the northern poets sing and say so much, will come anew.

The letter then continues:

So wrote Heine 80 years ago, and he foretold that at the head of the new barbarians would be found the disciples of Kant, of Fichte, and of Hegel, who, by a regular logical and historical process, which he traces back to the beginnings of German thought, had shorn the 'talisman' of its power.

This letter exemplifies one side of a vigorous debate that took place at the start of the war among British and American philosophers concerning the connections, or lack of them, between German idealist philosophy and German 'militarism' (as it was often called). Those who agreed with the letter could point to a remarkable essay by General Friedrich von Bernhardi, *Germany and the Next War* (1912), in which Kant's *Critique of Pure Reason* was invoked to justify a call for military preparations:

Two great movements were born from German intellectual life, on which, henceforth, all the intellectual and moral progress of mankind must rest – the Reformation and the critical philosophy. The Reformation that broke the intellectual yoke imposed by the Church which checked all free progress; and the Critique of Pure Reason which put a stop to the caprice of philosophic speculation . . . On this substructure was developed the intellectual life of our time . . . The German nation not only laid the foundations of this great struggle for a harmonious development of humanity but took the lead in it. We are thus incurring an obligation for the future from which we cannot shrink . . . To no nation except the German has it been given to enjoy in its inner self 'that which is given to mankind as a whole' . . . It is this quality which especially fits us for leadership in the intellectual domain and imposes on us the obligation to maintain that position. (Bernhardi 1912: 73–4)

More commonly, however, it was Hegel, rather than Kant, who was held to have legitimated the kind of aggressive violence that Germany's critics attributed to its military tactics. In a famous passage at the start of his critique of Hegelian political philosophy, *The Metaphysical Theory of the State* (1918), L. T. Hobhouse describes how, while he was writing the book, he witnessed a German Zeppelin attack on London:

Presently three white specks could be seen dimly through the light haze overhead, and we watched their course from the field. The raid was soon over . . .

As I went back to my Hegel my first mood was one of self-satire. Was this a time for theorizing or destroying theories, when the world was tumbling about our ears? My second thoughts ran otherwise. To each man the tools and weapons he can best use. In the bombing of London I had just witnessed the visible and tangible outcome of a false and wicked doctrine, the foundations of which lay, as I believe, in the book before me. (Hobhouse 1918: 6)

This kind of rhetoric was, of course, deeply antithetical to the British idealist philosophers and their disciples, who included such establishment figures as Lord Haldane (Secretary of State for War (1905–12) and Lord Chancellor (1912–15)). While not uncritical of Hegel, these philosophers held that his philosophy was an essential resource for philosophical argument and insight. Pre-eminent among them were F. H. Bradley and B. Bosanquet, whose *The Philosophical Theory of the State* (1899) was in fact Hobhouse's main target. Bradley and Bosanquet, however, chose to remain silent, in public at least, on this issue and the task of defending German idealist philosophy against the imputation of 'militarism' was undertaken by another philosopher closely associated with them, J. H. Muirhead, in *German Philosophy in Relation to the War* (1915). Muirhead here stresses that, as far as Kant is concerned, this accusation fails to acknowledge his commitment to the ideal of a 'Perpetual Peace' which is to be upheld by a confederation of states which collectively affirm their respect for the 'Laws of Nations' – the fundamental principles of international law. Equally, Muirhead argues, Hegel's political philosophy is founded upon a conception of the profound intrinsic ethical significance of the state; hence, Muirhead argues:

there is no ground to ally his political teaching with militarism as we are learning to know it today. The keynote of militarism is the doctrine that the State rests upon force. But this is precisely the view against which Hegel contends in the *Philosophy of Right*. (Muirhead 1915: 35–6)

The truth of the matter, according to Muirhead, is that in the latter part of the nineteenth century German philosophers became seduced by anti-idealist, materialist doctrines, and it is these doctrines which provide the intellectual origins for what he calls Treitschke's 'philosophy of militarism' – he cites Haeckel's Social Darwinism and Nietzsche's doctrine of the Superman in particular. So although Muirhead accepts that German 'militarism' has philosophical roots, he seeks to exonerate the idealist tradition from any involvement in this philosophy.

Among those who accepted the presumption that philosophy had played some part in German 'militarism', Muirhead's argument was not widely accepted (see, e.g., Dewey 1915), and it has to be said that his argument is not, on the face of it, persuasive. For example, he does not address the fact that Hegel explicitly rejects Kant's conception of an ideal of perpetual peace and advances instead a defence of the ethical value of war – 'War has the higher significance that by its agency . . . the ethical health of people is preserved . . . ; just as the blowing of the winds preserves the sea from the foulness of a prolonged calm, so also corruption in nations would be the product of prolonged, let alone "perpetual", peace' (*Philosophy of Right*, §324). Furthermore, Muirhead will have known well that the dominant trend in German philosophy at this time was the Neo-Kantian idealist movement and not the assorted group of materialist Darwinians and Nietzscheans whom he sought to blame.

Indeed, it was well known in Britain that almost the whole German academic community had come out explicitly in support of the war in the notorious 'Manifesto of the Intellectuals of Germany' of October 1914. This document, signed by four thousand academics – virtually all the German professors – protested that Germany had acted only in self-defence against France in send- ing its army through Belgium, that no acts of violence had been committed in Belgium, and that, quite generally, Germany sought only to defend German civilisation against attacks from its enemies. Since the German destruction of Louvain had been reliably witnessed, and the operation of the Schlieffen plan for the conquest of France by its invasion through Belgium could not reasonably be regarded as an act of self-defence, this manifesto did great damage to the reputation of the German academic community. It destroyed the grounds for faith in the existence of 'Two Germanys' – the Bismarckian military-political nexus and a separate academic community willing and able to challenge the state. It certainly does not follow from this that the German military and politi- cal strategy which led up to German actions in August 1914 did in fact have any philosophical roots. It seems in fact likely that the German government acted from a combination of fear, aggression, and covetousness. But the manifesto, together with other statements and writings of major philosophers such as Paul Natorp, Max Scheler, and Alfred Weber, does show unequivocally that this was a strategy which, for one reason or another, commanded the support of almost all German philosophers in 1914 (the only exception, to my knowledge, being Hans Vaihinger, who supported a pacifist line).

The British academic community responded to the German manifesto with a somewhat similar document, expressing support for the Allied cause, though more in sorrow than in anger. It was not, however, signed by all the major British philosophers (for example, neither Bradley nor Bosanquet signed it), and the attitudes of British philosophers to the war were rather more varied than those of German philosophers. The majority (especially those at Oxford) were supporters; but others (including many Cambridge philosophers) had doubts, especially those who joined the Union of Democratic Control, such as Moore, Ogden, Dickinson, and Russell, to whom I return below.

PHILOSOPHERS AND THE WAR

It is common, when writing about the First World War, to write of 'the lost generation', and to mourn especially the loss of so many young men whose early work seemed full of promise. How far is this true of philosophy?

The only philosophers with established reputations to have died, so far as I know, were Emil Lask, the Neo-Kantian philosopher from Heidelberg who was an associate of Rickert, Adolf Reinach, the Austrian philosopher who discovered performative speech-acts fifty years before they were rediscovered by J. L. Austin, and T. E. Hulme, the chief exponent in English of Bergson's philosophy. No doubt there were others; there were certainly also many deaths among younger men who were just at the start of a possible career, such as A. G. Heath, a young Fellow in philosophy at New College Oxford. In all armies, much the highest percentage of fatalities fell upon the junior officers who were expected to lead their men from the front, and these junior officers were often young university graduates. Some of them were of course sons of distinguished philosophers, such as Husserl's elder son Wolfgang and Whitehead's younger son Eric.

What of those who survived? For many who went on to have important careers as philosophers, their involvement in the war was primarily an attachment to the Civil Service. In Britain there was a large group of philosophers in Admiralty intelligence (presumably on account of their knowledge of German): J. Baillie (translator of Hegel), H. J. Paton (translator of Kant), N. Kemp Smith (another translator of Kant), R. G. Collingwood and H. Rashdall. In addition Francis Cornford worked in the ministry of munitions, Maynard Keynes was in the Treasury, and A. D. Lindsay was 'Deputy Controller of Labour in France'. Paton later advised the Foreign Office at the Paris Peace conference and my old philosophy tutor, Casimir Lewy, once told me that the 'Curzon line' which fixed, temporarily, the Eastern frontier of Poland at the 1920 Spa conference should have been called the 'Paton line'. There were similar attachments of philosophers in other countries: Bergson, for example, worked for the French embassy in the United States for much of the war.

In the case of these philosophers, war work does not seem to have affected their subsequent philosophy (except that in the case of Keynes it helped to steer him away from philosophy towards economics). But in other cases involvement in one way or another with the war did make a difference: I shall discuss briefly

Teilhard de Chardin and Martin Heidegger, before discussing in more detail the significance of the war for Bertrand Russell and Ludwig Wittgenstein.

The French philosopher Teilhard de Chardin served at the front in the French army throughout the war, and his *Writings in Time of War* record his reflections from the trenches. Most of these writings are religious reflections, and in them de Chardin emphasises his faith that the experience of the war was a way of showing the potential inherent in human life:

> It seems to me that one could show that the Front is not simply a line of fire, the interface of people attacking each other, but that it is also in some way the 'crest of the wave' that bears the world of humans towards its new destiny. (de Chardin 1965, 201)

de Chardin expresses his faith in this 'new destiny' in terms of a progressive evolutionary faith which looks forward to the evolutionary philosophy he later set out in *The Phenomenon of Man*:

> *When it came to the test*, abundant resources were found in the storehouse of our being. *In a practical experiment*, short but conclusive, we were able to measure the evolutionary reserves, the potential, of our species. (de Chardin 1965 [1968: 284])

The substance of the 'new destiny' is the recognition of a common humanity which transcends all boundaries, what one might regard as a cosmopolitan ideal:

> Here we come to the heart of the lesson taught us by the war: *the condition of human progress* is that men must at last cease to live in isolation; they must learn to recognize *a common goal for their lives* . . . not in an individual, nor in a national, nor in a social, but in *a human effort*. (de Chardin 1965 [1968: 285])

The importance of de Chardin, therefore, is that he shows one way in which 'the idea of progress' survived first-hand experience of the trenches, and I shall return at the end to his ideal. But I want now to take the more complex case of Heidegger.

Heidegger's direct experience of the war was minimal. Although there was military conscription in Germany at the start of the war, for reasons of health Heidegger was not conscripted, and for much of the war his only involvement was his work as a postal censor in Freiburg, which did not substantially impede his studies of philosophy (he received his habilitation in July 1915). From late 1917 onwards, however, when the German High Command's need for men had become more urgent, Heidegger was called up and, after training, joined a meteorological observation unit on the Western front whose main job was to provide weather information in support of poison-gas attacks. He actually served for two months until the end of the war (Ott 1993: 103).

This was a minimal experience of the war. Nonetheless it seems to me that an indirect experience of the war enters deeply into Heidegger's philosophy. In the second 'division' of *Being and Time*, Heidegger takes it that there is an 'authentic' attitude to death ('anticipation' – *Vorlaufen*) which reveals us to ourselves as beings whose lives are to be informed by the 'freedom' which comes from grasping the impossibility of escaping our own death:

We may now summarize our characterization of authentic Being-towards-death as we have projected it existentially: *anticipation reveals to Dasein its lostness in the they-self, and brings it face to face with the possibility of being itself in an impassioned* **freedom towards death**. (Heidegger 1927: 266 [1962: 311])

The possibility of this attitude becomes a central theme of the later chapters of *Being and Time*, especially when 'anticipation' is enriched to become 'anticipatory resoluteness' (*vorlaufende Entschlossenheit*), which is for Heidegger our most profound form of authenticity: it is that understanding which 'frees for death the possibility of acquiring *power* over Dasein's *existence*', thereby bringing us an 'unshakeable joy' (Heidegger 1927: 310 [1962: 357–8]).

In developing this theme Heidegger makes no reference to the German experience of the war; but it seems to me inconceivable that someone writing in this way, in Germany, about attitudes to one's own death during the 1920s could not have expected, and indeed intended, to be read with some such reference. The attitude to death which Heidegger here characterises is manifest in Ernst Jünger's famous descriptions of the war, in passages such as these:

And so, strange as it may sound, I learned from this year's schooling in force and in all the fantastic extravagence of material warfare that life has no depth of meaning except when it is pledged for an ideal. (Jünger 1920 [1994: 316])

It was made plain to us that it was all or nothing. How could we have found the strength for an achievement whose meaning was not plain to us? Hence the war is more to us than a proud and gallant memory. It is a spiritual experience too; and a realization of a strength of soul of which otherwise we should have had no knowledge. It is the point of focus in our lives. It decided our whole further development. (Jünger 1928 [1988: x])

In citing these passages, I do not claim that Heidegger was implicitly alluding to *The Storm of Steel* (Junger 1920) in *Being and Time* (he later drew explicitly on Junger's later writings when discussing Nietzsche). He did not need to, since, as the popularity of Junger's works shows, the attitude was widely shared. All I do claim is that the second division of *Being and Time* includes an attempt at a philosophical response to the experience of the war, and that the military associations of 'anticipatory resoluteness' are not far below the surface of Heidegger's conception of authenticity as 'freedom towards death'.

As earlier chapters in this volume indicate, Bertrand Russell had long been one of the fiercest critics of German idealist philosophy. Hence it would have been easy for him to go along with Germany's critics. But in fact Russell became the most famous critic of the war; he was one of the small group of intellectuals of the period who were not guilty of 'the treason of the clerks' of which Julien Benda was famously to accuse his generation (in *La Trahison des Clercs* 1927).

Russell's opposition to the war was not motivated by any wish that Germany should win or by the kind of absolute opposition to war affirmed by the Quakers. Instead he judged, surely rightly, that in this case war had been avoidable; and also, more questionably, that even after the German invasion of Belgium and France Britain should have stayed out in order to facilitate a negotiated peace. It is not easy to evaluate this judgement: it is hard to envisage how the British Government could have prudently, and honourably, stood aside while the German army overran Belgium and France (the most likely outcome without the presence of the BEF), thereby enabling the German government to take control of the Belgian Channel ports and dictate terms for peace to a humiliated France. On the other hand, the main theme of Niall Ferguson's book *The Pity of War* (1998) is, in effect, that Russell was right, that the war (and, in particular, British involvement in the war) was 'nothing less than the greatest *error* of modern history' (p. 462).

Initially Russell took up the cause of opposition to the war as a welcome distraction, for his capacity for original work in philosophy had largely come to a halt following Wittgenstein's criticisms in 1913 of his theory of judgement. So when the war started, Russell largely stopped working at philosophy, or, at any rate, at the kind of logico-analytic metaphysics which had inspired him since 1900. Instead, while expressing disgust at conventional ethical theories which seek to persuade people to sacrifice themselves for a 'just' cause that simply expresses the interests of one group in a situation of conflict (Russell 1914 [1986: 63]), he turned to political writings, such as his *Principles of Social Reconstruction* (1916). When military conscription was introduced in Britain in 1916 (all the other European states at war had had some form of conscription from the start), Russell threw himself into active opposition to it and, as a result of his public support for this cause, he was convicted in July 1916 of 'impeding recruiting and discipline', contrary to the Defence of the Realm Act and fined £110. Because he refused to pay the fine Russell was nearly imprisoned, but in the end the fine was paid by his friend Philip Morrell (Monk 1996: 464). The conviction did, nonetheless, have an important consequence: Russell was deprived of his lectureship at Trinity College Cambridge. The College's reason for this act was that Russell's criminal conviction was incompatible with his position as a college lecturer; but this rationale was disingenuous, and it was clear that in fact the act was just a reaction against Russell's political activities by the 'bloodthirsty old men' (as Russell called them) who ran Trinity College council while the younger Fellows were away at the Front.

Some of these young Fellows wrote to protest at Russell's expulsion, as did many philosophers (e.g. A. N. Whitehead) and others (e.g. Gilbert Murray) who disagreed with Russell's anti-war stance. Russell himself, however, was not much bothered by the loss of his lectureship and continued his work for the No-Conscription Fellowship, of which he became Chairman in 1917. For a time he was much excited by the (first) 'February' Russian Revolution and the possibility of similar changes in Britain; but by the end of the year he was weary of all his political activities and ready to start work in philosophy again, committing himself to giving a course of lectures on 'The Philosophy of Logical Atomism' early in 1918. At the start of 1918, however, he published an intemperate attack on the newly arriving soldiers of the American Army, accusing them of being just a 'garrison' sent to Britain to be used to intimidate strikers. For this he was again prosecuted and tried in February 1918, at a time when he was also delivering some of his lectures on 'The Philosophy of Logical Atomism' – a remarkable interweaving of the political and philosophical sides to his life. This time Russell was sentenced to six months' imprisonment.

This period of imprisonment, in the comfortable conditions permitted to him following the intervention of influential friends, was in fact just what Russell needed in order to get back to some new work in philosophy, and it was while he was in prison that he completed the bulk of his work on *The Analysis of Mind* (1920), in which he worked out a new conception of judgement which was intended to circumvent Wittgenstein's objections to his earlier position and which he continued to refine for the rest of his long life. Thus although there is little direct connection between the war and the content of Russell's philosophy, the disruption in Russell's academic career brought about by his anti-war activities and their consequences is matched by a deep change in his philosophy. After 1918 Russell was no longer much interested in his earlier logico-analytic programme; instead, insofar as he worked at philosophy, it was in the context of developing the naturalistic, externalist, scientific programme that he had commenced in *The Analysis of Mind*.

In a letter to Ottoline Morrell in October 1914 Russell wrote:

It seems strange that of all the people in the war the one I care for much the most should be Wittgenstein who is an 'enemy'. (Monk 1996: 374)

Wittgenstein was on holiday in Austria in July 1914 and enlisted as soon as war was declared. His sister Hermine wrote later that his motive was not simply a desire to defend Austro-Hungary from Russia; instead he 'also had an intense desire to take something difficult upon himself and to do something other than purely intellectual work' (Rhees 1984: 3), in particular to serve at the front and show himself capable of facing up to the threat of death. In his diary for 1914 he wrote, 'Now I have the chance to be a decent human being for I am standing eye to eye with death' (Monk 1996: 112). This passage should be set alongside a piece of advice Wittgenstein gave to Drury in 1944, about which Drury comments that he felt that this was advice Wittgenstein had given to himself in First World War: 'If it ever happens that you get mixed up in hand-to-hand fighting, you must just stand aside and let yourself be massacred' (Rhees 1984: 149). It is not clear how far Wittgenstein felt that anyone who was fit to fight had a duty to fight; but he certainly rejected the principles behind Paul Engelmann's pacifism (Engelmann 1967: 71–2) and Engelmann describes him as also rejecting Russell's position:

When he heard that his friend Bertrand Russell was in prison as an opponent of the war, he did not withhold his respect for Russell's personal courage in living up to his convictions, but he felt that this was heroism in the wrong place. (Engelmann 1967: 73)

The record of Wittgenstein's war service is a complicated matter. He was initially placed on board a gun boat on the river Vistula, the *Goplana*, and thus took part in the confused fighting between the Austro-Hungarian and the Russian armies at the start of the war which ended with an Austrian withdrawal deep into Poland. He was then transferred in 1915 to an artillery workshop, which was located first in Cracow and then, following Austrian advances, moved to near Lvov. In March 1916 he was transferred, as he had long wished, to an artillery regiment fighting on the Russian front, and, at his request, used as an observer, which was the most dangerous position in the artillery since it was exposed to enemy fire. For the next year he moved backwards and then forwards across Poland with the front, ending up in the Ukraine following the Bolshevik revolution. He was decorated several times for bravery. In February 1918 he was transferred to the Southern front, facing the Italians. After some periods of very tough fighting in the mountains he was taken prisoner by the Italians in November 1918, and not released by them until August 1919.

The remarkable fact is that during this experience one of the greatest works of twentieth-century philosophy was composed – the *Tractatus Logico-Philosophicus*. The starting point for this work is the notes Wittgenstein dictated to Moore when they were in Norway together in April 1914. These notes deal exclusively with logic and cover some of the ground covered in the early parts of the *Tractatus*. By the end of 1915 Wittgenstein had worked up these notes into a treatise which, he told Russell in a letter at the time, he was prepared to publish after the war. The treatise does not survive but one can surmise from his surviving notebooks for 1915 that this would still have been almost entirely concerned with logic. The 1916 notebook, however, introduces new themes, concerning fate, death, God, happiness, the will, and the self – some of which recur in the later parts of the *Tractatus*. This notebook belongs to the period when Wittgenstein became friends with Paul Engelmann while on leave at Olmütz (Olomouc), and Engelmann is emphatic that from this time onwards Wittgenstein attached at least as much importance to these ethical themes as to his earlier treatment of logic. In July 1918 Wittgenstein stayed with his brother Paul near Salzburg while on leave, and it was here that he finally completed the book, before taking it back with him to the front.

It is, then, reasonably certain that it was the experience of the war that led Wittgenstein to extend his work 'from the foundations of logic to the nature of the world' (1961: 79e), and to treat ethics precisely as 'a condition of the world, like logic' (1961: 77e). This is not the place for a detailed study of this comparison between logic and ethics, which holds that both are 'transcendental' (*Tractatus*: 6.13, 6.421) and, as such, not theories which describe facts within the world but, somehow, theories which display conditions under which a world is possible. But, very briefly, Wittgenstein's claim is that where logic indicates the limits of any language within which sense is possible, ethics sets out the limits of any life that makes sense as lived, the limits of the life-world. But in both cases, in the end, the attempt to characterise directly the limits of sense leads only to nonsense – so both logic and, especially, ethics concern what can only be shown, and not said. Wittgenstein picked out this last point as 'the point of the book' (when trying, unsuccessfully, in 1919 to persuade Ludwig von Ficker to publish the *Tractatus* in his journal *Der Brenner*):

. . . the point of the book is ethical. I once wanted to give a few words in the foreword which now actually are not in it, which, however, I'll write to you now because they might be a key for you: I wanted to write that my work consists of two parts: of the one which is here, and everything which I have *not* written. And precisely this second part is the important one. For the Ethical is delimited from within, as it were, by my book; and I'm convinced that, *strictly* speaking, it can ONLY be delimited in this way. (Monk 1996: 178)

When the *Tractatus* was eventually published, it came, not with this foreword, but with an introduction by Russell, which Wittgenstein notoriously hated. But it seems to me a great pity that Wittgenstein did not write to Russell about the book in the way in which he wrote here to Ficker. For in truth Russell, also under the influence of the war, had adopted a similar position about ethics:

The ethical work of Spinoza, for example, appears to me of the very highest significance, but what is valuable in such work is not any metaphysical theory as to the nature of the world to which it may give rise, nor indeed anything which can be proved or disproved by argument. What is valuable is the indication of some new way of feeling towards life and the world, some way of feeling by which our own existence can acquire more of the characteristics which we deeply desire. The value of such work, however immeasurable it is, belongs with practice and not with theory. (Russell 1914 [1986: 64])

THE CONSEQUENCES OF THE WAR

The previous section set out some of the ways, complex and sometimes indirect, in which the war affected the lives and work of the three greatest European philosophers of the twentieth century – Heidegger, Russell, and Wittgenstein. But their involvements with the war were unusual: by and large 'normal philosophy' continued much as before. Samuel Alexander, for example, delivered his Gifford lectures on *Space, Time and Deity* between 1916 and 1918 without any reference, explicit or implicit, to the war (Alexander 1920). So if one sets aside the individuals discussed above, it is sensible to ask whether the war made any significant difference to the general course of subsequent philosophy.

Some of the political consequences of the war certainly did make a difference – most notably the Bolshevik revolution of 1917 and the re-creation of states such as Poland. Without the Bolshevik revolution, Marxist thought would surely not have had the role it has had in twentieth-century philosophy; equally the tradition of Russian philosophy that flourished at the start of the twentieth century would not have been killed off as it was by Lenin in 1922. Again, although Twardowski's revival of Polish philosophy in Lvov belongs within the Austro-Hungarian period, the amazing renaissance of Polish logic and philosophy after 1920 was dependent upon the reconstitution of a Polish state.

No doubt there were further similar consequences. But these are primarily external to the internal dialectic of philosophy; and the interesting, and important, question is whether philosophy in any way internalised the experience of the war. If one thinks of developments in metaphysics, logic, and epistemology, it is not easy to point to any general changes which were dependent upon the war – both the phenomenological and analytical movements were well under way before the war and continued after it. Furthermore, the great changes in the understanding of the physical world induced by Einstein's General Theory and by the rise of Quantum Theory would have happened anyway. Hence, if there are any significant changes, they should lie in the areas of ethics, aesthetics, and political philosophy, at the points where philosophical reflection might be supposed to start from new understandings, somehow induced by the war, of the meaning of life, of art, and the state.

There certainly are philosophical writings in these areas which continue earlier debates and traditions, such as the works of Collingwood (e.g. Collingwood 1924). But if we now look back to the post-1918 period for major new contributions in these areas, it is hard not to feel that these were areas of philosophy in which, for a time, not much was written that is of enduring value. In ethics, in particular, apart from Ross's refinements of the intuitionist position (Ross 1930), most attention was directed to the emotivist position advanced by the logical empiricists, which precisely affirmed that nothing of importance could be established by ethical enquiry, since ethical judgement is no more than a way in which people express their emotions with a view to encouraging others to come to share their feelings.

Thus the impact of the war was, I think, primarily negative. It was not that people took from the war new understandings of life, art, and the state which were then fed into new philosophical reflections; rather, the war called into question older ways of thinking about these matters, without providing replacements. In particular, the war did seem to show that the nexus of dialectical-cum-evolutionary ideas which can be summarised as 'the idea of progress' was illusory. As a result, younger philosophers who wanted to make their mark on the subject turned to the new questions thrown up by advances in logic, mathematics, and the sciences, social as well as natural; and insofar as they attended at all to ethics, aesthetics, and political philosophy, it was often to argue that there is no a priori knowledge to be gained here, and thus that these are not sensible areas for sustained philosophical enquiry.

THE LEAGUE OF NATIONS

There is, however, one respect, which connects with de Chardin's faith that the war pointed the way to a 'new destiny', in which this negative conclusion needs to be qualified, though it concerns not so much the war's impact upon philosophy as an influence of philosophy upon the aftermath of the war. Early in 1915 the Cambridge philosopher Goldsworthy Lowes Dickinson revived Kant's conception of a confederation of states committed to upholding peace. He called this the idea of a 'League of Nations', and after it had been taken up by Woodrow Wilson the establishment of a League of Nations became a central aim of the Allied powers. It also became a popular aspiration – through the establishment of a League, the First World War was to be 'a war to end war'. This faith that something good could yet be created out of the ruins of war is movingly attested by the inscription on the memorial constructed by the Quaker (and thus pacifist) Rowntree family for the citizens of York who fought in the war:

Many were inspired by the faith that this war might be an end of war – that victory would lead to an enduring peace and to a greater happiness for the peoples of the world. The creation of a League of Nations will be a fitting crown to the faith and hope of the men who have fought and a true memorial to their endurance, heroism, comradeship and sacrifice.

Sadly, this memorial is now accompanied by a further memorial to those who fought in the Second World War. This second memorial offers no similar testament of faith.

Part II

1914–1945

SECTION EIGHT

LOGIC AND PHILOSOPHY: THE ANALYTIC PROGRAMME

28

LOGICAL ATOMISM

PETER SIMONS

Logical atomism is a complex doctrine comprising logical, linguistic, onto-logical, and epistemological elements, associated with Russell and Wittgenstein early in the twentieth century. The first appearance of a form of logical atomism (though not explicitly identified as such) is in Russell's philosophical introduc-tion to *Principia Mathematica* (1910a; see esp. 43–5). Russell had acquired elements of this position from his earlier studies of Leibniz (who is a clear precursor of logical atomism), from his reaction against absolute idealism (where the influ-ence of G. E. Moore's early atomism, as in Moore 1899, was important), and from his analysis of knowledge. A year later Russell used the term 'logical atom-ism' for the first time (though in French) in his lecture 'Le réalisme analytique', where he says of his analytic realism 'this philosophy is the philosophy of logical atomism' (1911 [1984– : VI, 135]).

Russell's conception of logical atomism developed further in the course of his discussions and correspondence with Wittgenstein during the period from 1912 to 1914. These were primarily concerned with the foundations of logic, but the lessons learnt there were applied by Russell and Wittgenstein to other areas. The term 'logical atomism' then became known in English through Russell's 1918 lectures 'The Philosophy of Logical Atomism' which provide the fullest presentation of his position (1918 [1984– : VIII]). Though Russell there de-scribes his views as 'very largely concerned with explaining ideas which I learnt from my friend and former pupil Ludwig Wittgenstein' (1918 [1984– : VIII, 160]), there are significant differences between their versions of logical atom-ism. Wittgenstein's logical atomism is set out in his *Tractatus Logico-Philosophicus* (1921). It had been developed in the notebooks leading up to this (Wittgenstein 1961), and was modified in his 1929 paper 'Some Remarks on Logical Form' (Wittgenstein 1929). He thereafter clearly abandoned the doctrine, whereas Russell did not.

1. BASIC STATEMENT

In the Introduction to the second edition of *Principia Mathematica* in 1927 Russell gives a concise formulation of logical atomism:

> Given all true atomic propositions, together with the fact that they are all, every other true proposition can theoretically be deduced by logical methods. (1927: xv)

Logical atomism holds that the world consists of elements which combine to form complex entities. It differs both from the physical atomism of Democritus or Dalton and from the psychological atomism of Hume in holding that the reasons we have for believing in the atoms come not from physics or psychology but from logic. Logical analysis is to convince us of the truth of logical atomism as a doctrine and to reveal to us the general nature of the atoms and the way they combine. Russell says in 1911: 'the philosophy I espouse is *analytic*, because it claims that one must discover the simple elements of which complexes are composed, and that complexes presuppose simples, whereas simples do not presuppose complexes' (1911 [1984– : VI, 134]), and in 1918, 'The reason that I call my doctrine logical atomism is because the atoms that I wish to arrive at as the last residue in analysis are logical atoms and not physical atoms' (1918 [1984– : VIII, 161]).

2. THE TWO LEVELS OF ATOMISM

Logical atomism applies at two levels: the propositional and the sub-propositional. At the propositional level it proposes an analysis revealing simple or 'atomic' propositions (Russell 1918: 199), which Wittgenstein called *Elementarsäzte* (1921: 4. 21) and which express what Russell in the introduction to *Principia Mathematica* had called 'elementary judgements' (1910a: 44). True atomic propositions correspond to special entities in the world, called variously 'complexes' (Russell 1910a), 'atomic facts' (Russell 1918), and *Sachverhalte* (states of affairs) (Wittgenstein 1921). The second level of analysis reveals elements within these atomic facts. Wittgenstein calls them simply *Gegenstände* ('objects') whereas Russell differentiates them into particulars and universals, universals dividing further into qualities, dyadic relations, triadic relations, and so on. Russell integrates his Platonism of universals and his theory of particulars as sense data into his logical atomism, since he contends we must be acquainted with the parts of a proposition (particulars and universals) in order to be able to understand it: this is his principle of acquaintance. Wittgenstein on the other hand embraces no such epistemological accessibility thesis concerning elements:

his atomism remains throughout a wholly logical doctrine concerning language and the world, leaving epistemology aside.

3. TRUTH FOR ATOMIC PROPOSITIONS, AND THEIR COMPONENTS

The account of truth for atomic propositions as set out in *Principia Mathematica* (1910a: 44) is that an elementary judgement is true if there exists a complex (atomic fact) corresponding to it, and false otherwise. This 'elementary truth' (1910a: 45) is correspondence, which involves a correlation between the terms of which an atomic proposition (which expresses an elementary judgement) is composed and the elements in the world denoted by such terms. Russell takes atomic propositions to consist of one predicate, denoting a universal, and an appropriate number of proper names, denoting particulars related by the universal in an atomic fact. Wittgenstein on the other hand calls all the simple components of an atomic proposition 'names' and the entities they stand for 'objects'. He does not pronounce on whether some of these names are for universals, others for particulars, so his atomism as stated is compatible with Russell's dualism of particulars and universals but also with a nominalism of particulars alone. Unlike Russell, Wittgenstein is unconcerned whether we have acquaintance with the elements of atomic facts. All we need to know is that an analysis of propositions into atomic ones and an analysis of atomic propositions into objects is a priori possible and, indeed, that in principle such an analysis always exists. During his discussions with the Vienna Circle in the late 1920s Wittgenstein for a while allowed the objects to be sense-data, but this is not mandated by his analysis in the *Tractatus*, which is neutral on the metaphysical nature of the objects, and in his earlier *Notebooks* he frequently compares objects with the point-particles of classical mechanics (e.g. Wittgenstein 1961: 35).

Wittgenstein contends that all atomic propositions are logically independent of one another: from the truth or falsity of some nothing follows about the truth or falsity of others. Russell does not demand such independence, since the universals in his atomic propositions come in families of contraries: if *a* is *F* and *F* excludes *G* then *a* cannot be *G*, though *F* and *G* both be elementary universals such as exact colour shades. Wittgenstein's attempt to sidestep such incompatibility in the *Tractatus* is unconvincing (1921: 6.3751) and in 1929 he abandoned the independence doctrine shortly before giving up logical atomism altogether.

Wittgenstein argues for a more thoroughgoing atomism than Russell, contending that all objects are simple or lacking in parts. The argument, tersely outlined in the *Tractatus Logico-Philosophicus* (1921: 3.24), is that a proposition about a complex depends on propositions about related simpler objects. The proposition that the complex exists is equivalent to the proposition that the parts are so related. So if [aRb] is the complex of a and b standing in the relation R, then '[aRb] exists' is equivalent to 'aRb' (1961: 93) and this and any other proposition about [aRb] will not be nonsensical but merely false if a and b are not so related. Wittgenstein supposed this process of analysis to be similar to Russell's theory of definite descriptions, but it is quite different. Whereas Russell's theory takes apparent complex names and distributes their semantic weight to the predicates in logically complex statements, Wittgenstein's analysis replaces complex names by simpler names (Griffin 1964: 48). Russell's and Wittgenstein's early use of 'complex' tends to obscure the categorial distinction between a complex thing and a fact or state of affairs which this argument exploits. Wittgenstein later made the distinction much clearer: complexes are things whose names disappear on analysis; states of affairs correspond to true atomic propositions but are not nameable.

Since for Wittgenstein, for a proposition to have sense is for it to be possible for it to be true or false, he cannot run the risk that a lack of denotation for a name in a proposition leads to a truth-value gap, for then all propositions containing that name would be senseless. We must always be able in principle to analyse complex names so that we end up with only names of non-complex things which cannot fail to exist and whose existence can therefore be meaningfully neither stated nor denied. Without such bedrock, simple objects forming what Wittgenstein called the substance of the world (1921: 2.021), discourse about the world would hang loose and propositions about the world would lack determinate truth-conditions, that is, sense. Russell by contrast is committed to no such stern thesis. Sense-data, Russell's particulars, may contain other sense-data as parts, and reference terminates with objects of our immediate acquaintance, not remote simples discernible by an obscure kind of mereological analysis for which Wittgenstein offers no worked-out example.

Wittgenstein's terminology is in a related way more complex than Russell's. He distinguishes between a state of affairs (*Sachverhalt*), the fact that a state of affairs exists (a positive fact, 1921: 2.06), and the fact that it does not exist (a negative fact). Strictly it is not the state of affairs but its existing or obtaining (*bestehen*) or its not existing that determines whether a proposition is true or false, and in general the truth or falsity of other propositions depends on the combination of states of affairs existing and not existing. Russell's version lacks this distinction and Wittgenstein also does not observe it scrupulously, for example in his correspondence with Russell and in his acceptance of the Ogden-Ramsey translation 'atomic fact' for '*Sachverhalt*'.

4. OTHER PROPOSITIONS AND FACTS

The logical complexity of propositions arises through the introduction of logical connectives such as negation and conjunction which form molecular propositions and the quantifiers which form general propositions. Russell and Wittgenstein agree that molecular and general propositions logically presuppose atomic ones, but disagree on what this involves. The truth-conditions of standard molecular propositions are unproblematic: they are given by the truth-tabular analysis of connectives, the perspicuous graphics for which were invented by Wittgenstein. But there is a difficulty about the analysis of propositions which appear complex but not truth-functional, such as propositions about beliefs. Russell and Wittgenstein take different ways out of this. Because of Russell's changing views about the nature of propositions at this time, it is difficult to state his view about this matter concisely. But after 1907 Russell rejected his early analysis of propositions of the form *A believes that p* which treats belief as a relationship between a subject, *A*, and a complex object, the 'proposition' *p* (where propositions are not linguistic, but are more like possible states of affairs); instead he now held that belief is a 'multiple' relation connecting *A* and the simple objects (universals and particulars) which he had previously thought of only as constituents of *p* (see Russell 1910b). Wittgenstein rejected both of Russell's positions (in the latter case giving rise to a crisis in Russell's work – Russell 1968: 57). He advanced instead an elusive account which extends Russell's multiple relation theory by dispensing with the apparent subject of belief *A* as well as with propositions conceived as complex objects of thought; instead belief, thought, and other similar psychological states are conceived on the model of a semantic correlation between a complex sign and the world, as in ' "*p*" says *p*' (1921: 5.542).

Russell and Wittgenstein also differ on whether there are special molecular facts corresponding to true molecular propositions. Both agree that there are no disjunctive facts, but Russell admits negative and conjunctive facts. If *p* is a false atomic proposition then while for Wittgenstein the lack of an existing state of affairs corresponding to *p* suffices for the falsity, for Russell there has to be a negative fact that not-*p* making the negative proposition true. Russell readily admits that his view 'nearly caused a riot' when he advanced it in lectures in Harvard in 1914 (1918 [1984: VIII, 187]). This difference takes us to the heart of the distinction between Russell's and Wittgenstein's versions of logical atomism.

For Wittgenstein a proposition and its negation do not correspond to two different realities. However the world is, only one of them is true, the other is false. These are not two independent facts but two sides of the same coin. Using

Frege's distinction between meaning (*Bedeutung*) and sense (*Sinn*) Wittgenstein says in *Notes on Logic* that the propositions *p* and not-*p* have the same meaning but opposite sense; the meaning is whichever fact happens to be the case (1961: 94). Later, in the *Tractatus*, however, propositions are denied meaning (*Bedeutung*) altogether on the grounds that this treatment of them assimilates them to names, whereas in fact propositions, contra Frege, are completely unlike names because of their true/ false polarity: 'A name is like a point, a proposition like an arrow, it has sense' (1921: 3.144). Wittgenstein develops a notation for logical truth-functions, the a–b-notation, which stresses this bipolarity: this was later replaced by the clearer truth-table notation. Russell never got the hang of Wittgenstein's true-false polarity doctrine: he thought it amounted simply to bivalence. Russell thinks of a pair of opposed propositions as both corresponding to whatever fact is the case, corresponding truly for one and corresponding falsely for the other. He is thus led to postulate negative facts as corresponding (falsely) to false atomic propositions:

When, e.g., you have a false positive proposition, say, 'Socrates is alive', it is false because of a fact in the real world. A thing cannot be false except because of a fact, so that you find it extremely difficult to say what exactly happens when you make a positive assertion that is false, unless you are going to admit negative facts. (1918 [1984– : VIII, 190])

Wittgenstein on the other hand does not need negative facts as items in the world: if a certain state of affairs does not exist, its atomic proposition is thereby false, and its negation by default automatically true. Hence for Wittgenstein but not Russell it is self-evident that any atomic proposition is positive.

Likewise for Wittgenstein if *p*, *q*, *r* are atomic propositions which are all true, then the existence of their respective states of affairs jointly suffices for the truth of the conjunction *p & q & r*, whereas Russell looks for an additional, single, conjunctive fact which makes it true. Similarly, according to Russell, but not Wittgenstein, true general propositions require general facts to make them true. If *a*, . . ., *z* are all the *F*s, and every one is a *G*, then the atomic facts *that a is G*, . . ., *that z is G* fail to suffice for the truth that *All Fs are G* for Russell, because we need to conjoin the fact *that a*, . . ., *z are all the F*s, which is itself general. Hence we cannot avoid general facts. Wittgenstein by contrast denies general facts. The facts *that a is G*, . . ., *that z is G* together, jointly, suffice for the truth that *All Fs are G*, even though that conjunction is not logically equivalent to the general proposition. Thus Wittgenstein, unlike Russell, does not expect the analysis of a proposition to reveal a proposition logically equivalent to it (Russell clearly affirms his position in the passage about logical atomism quoted earlier from the introduction to the second edition of *Principia Mathematica* (1927: xv)).

5. TRUTH-FUNCTIONALITY

The logical analysis of propositions put forward in *Principia Mathematica* is intensional, in that distinct propositional functions can be extensionally equivalent. Wittgenstein contends by contrast that all propositions are truth–functional compounds of atomic propositions (1921: 5), which implies a thesis of extensionality, and in the second edition of *Principia Mathematica* Russell swings in favour of this view. Wittgenstein is immediately confronted with the apparent counterexamples of propositions about attitudes like belief; as explained earlier he proposes that these be construed on the model of a correlation between sign and the world which dissolves the apparent non–truth–functional context. But he also faces an objection concerning general propositions, since these are not, on the face of it, truth–functions of atomic propositions. His response in this case is to allow truth–functions to take not just finitely many but arbitrary sets of atomic propositions as their basis: the multigrade negation operator N with which Wittgenstein attempts to cover all truth–functions (1921: 5.502) can do this provided a notation is provided (at which Wittgenstein merely hints) for all propositions of a certain form. If $[x: Fx]$ stands for the propositions Fa, Fb, etc. for all objects, and N as applied to a finite set is given by a list as, for example, $N(p, q, r)$, then a complex sentence such as

$$\forall x(Fx \rightarrow \exists y(Gy \ \& \ xRy)$$

can be formulated using N and variables alone as

$$N[x : N(N(Fx), N(N[y : N(N(Gy), N(xRy))]))]$$

Wittgenstein's idea here, which like many of his views in logic he merely sketches, can be made to work. On the other hand his assumption that deciding what is a logical truth and what follows logically from what will turn out to be a matter of merely inspecting propositions (1921: 4.461, 5.132) is wrong: generalising imprudently from the decidability of the truth–functional calculus, he does not anticipate that theoremhood and logical consequence for predicate logic will turn out to be undecidable. Wittgenstein's deflationary terminology of *tautologies* for the truths of logic has thus been generally adopted only for truth–functional logic.

6. OTHER ASPECTS OF LOGIC AND MATHEMATICS

Russell spent much time and effort finding a way around the paradoxes in the foundations of mathematics. The result was the theory of types, which attained its most complex form, ramified but with the Axiom of Reducibility, in

Principia Mathematica. Wittgenstein dismissed the theory of types in a few words as being unnecessary, the inadmissibility of paradoxes arising from the syntactic incongruity of attempting to make a function its own argument. The scorn is ill directed: the paradoxes are substantive matters concerning the non-existence of posited abstract entities such as numbers and sets. When Wittgenstein returned to consider mathematics later, he remained deflationary in outlook but had abandoned atomism.

7. OUTSIDE LOGIC

From the start Russell crafted his version of logical atomism to suit his episte-mology of sense-data and universals, and despite being impressed by many of Wittgenstein's positions, he failed to understand fully some and did not adopt many. Being less stringent in his atomism over non-atomic facts and independence, he was less compelled to modify the position, and as a result he remained happy with the general outline of the position well into the 1930s. The doc-trine of logical constructions, which arose out of the rejection of his own earlier exuberant realism, and was influenced by Whitehead's method of extensive ab-straction, is prominent in Russell's version of logical atomism. According to it, '*Wherever possible logical constructions are to be substituted for inferred entities*' (1914 [1984– : VIII, 11]). It is the primary tool of Russell's analyses of mind, matter, and much else, going on to influence Carnap, Goodman, Quine, and others. This positive, constructive element has no counterpart in Wittgenstein. Other-wise, Russell's philosophical positions well away from logic, in epistemology, ethics and politics, are largely unconnected with logical atomism. Wittgenstein by contrast drew sweeping and radical but wholly negative conclusions from his analyses of the foundations of logic. According to his doctrine of saying and showing the only things that can be said are those expressed by proposi-tions with a sense (contingent propositions): anything else, including semantics and metalogic, ethical, aesthetic, and religious language, and all metaphysics, is unsayable. Thus according to Wittgenstein there is no truth-apt discourse in ethics, aesthetics, religion, or philosophy. This view not only determined Wittgenstein personally to quit philosophy, it heavily influenced the negative pronouncements of the Vienna Circle. But the inconsistency of Wittgenstein's stance, in particular stamping the *Tractatus* itself as nonsense, was apparent to Russell and Ramsey, and observation of the similarly self-refuting status of the Vienna Circle's verifiability criterion for meaning drew the teeth of that attack on metaphysics and other nonsense.

THE SCIENTIFIC WORLD CONCEPTION:
LOGICAL POSITIVISM

ALAN RICHARDSON

Logical positivism had almost as many names as it had roots. Among the terms used by its promoters were: logical positivism, logical empiricism, scientific empiricism, consistent empiricism, and other, similar names. All these names came fairly late in the day, stemming from around 1930, when the work of the logical positivists was first being brought before the English-speaking philosophical community. The initial public statement by the Vienna Circle, the *Wissenschaftliche Weltauffassung: Der Wiener Kreis* (*Scientific World Conception: The Vienna Circle*; Neurath *et al.* 1929 [1973]), eschews all of these terms, adopting instead the general term 'scientific world conception'. This term was chosen in self-conscious opposition to the then dominant idealist, conservative, Catholic Austrian *Weltanschauung* philosophy. The Vienna Circle offered a scientific way of conceiving the world, not an intuitive grasp of the world's ineffable essence and meaning.

The more general term is useful. It warns us away from expecting to find a short-list of doctrines about which the logical positivists agreed. It reminds us, also, that logical positivism grew up in an Austro-Germanic context. This context provided much of the philosophical training of the logical positivists; it also supplied the arationalist philosophical perspectives, *Weltanschauungslehre* and *Lebensphilosophie* (philosophy of life), against which the Vienna Circle publicly situated itself. Thus, while I will here, for ease of reference, employ the term 'logical positivism', the reader should bear in mind that this term suggests a greater commonality of project than one actually finds among the logical positivists (for attempts to situate the development of logical positivism within its broader intellectual context, see the essays in Uebel 1991 and Giere and Richardson 1996, as well as Galison 1990; the essential reference work on the career of logical positivism is Stadler 1997).

1. THE VIENNA CIRCLE AND OTHER GROUPS

Who were the logical positivists? This is a surprisingly difficult question. The perplexity is due to the way in which the internationalist leanings of the core members led them to stress affinities between their points of view and those of a wide range of philosophers and scientists around the world. The 1929 pamphlet already cited, for example, found Austrian antecedents in the positivism and empirio-criticism of Ernst Mach, the phenomenology of Franz Brentano, the rational economics of Josef Popper-Lynkeus, and the Marxism of Otto Bauer and Max Adler. Similarly, it maintained that 'the spirit of the scientific world conception' was being promulgated not only in the Vienna Circle, but also by Bertrand Russell and Alfred North Whitehead in England, in Berlin in the work of Hans Reichenbach, Kurt Grelling, Walter Dubislav, and Albert Einstein, and also in Russia and the United States. For ease of discussion, the core logical positivists will be taken here to be those listed at the end of the 1929 pamphlet as members of the Vienna Circle or as sympathetic to the Circle, as well as some of the leading students of those groups (Neurath *et al.* 1929 [1973: 318]). None of those listed there as 'leading representatives of the scientific world conception' – Albert Einstein, Bertrand Russell, and Ludwig Wittgenstein – are thus counted as logical positivists; they serve more as influences (sometimes reluctant ones) than as comrades.

The most famous group of logical positivists was the Vienna Circle. The Circle was organised by Moritz Schlick, who held the Chair in Philosophy of the Inductive Sciences at the University of Vienna from 1922 until his death by gunshot on the steps of the university in 1936. The Circle met in Schlick's home and in the mathematical seminar at the University of Vienna from 1924 until Schlick's death. The group had a fluid membership, but by its glory days around 1930 the core members included Schlick, Gustav Bergmann, Rudolf Carnap, Herbert Feigl, Philipp Frank, Kurt Gödel, Hans Hahn, Karl Menger, Otto Neurath, Friedrich Waismann, and Edgar Zilsel. Schlick also was the chairman of the Verein Ernst Mach, a wider group of philosophers, scientists, and others who sponsored public talks and discussions. The group had substantial contact with many other Viennese intellectuals, especially Ludwig Wittgenstein, whose influence on many members of the group was enormous, and Karl Popper, who fancied himself the official opposition to the group in Vienna.

The Circle had enormous organisational energy. It was a prime mover, together with the Berlin Society (see below), of the conferences on the philosophy of the exact sciences held in Prague in 1929 and Königsberg in 1930. It began publishing a journal, *Erkenntnis*, under the editorship of Carnap and Reichenbach, in 1930. It released a series of monographs, edited by Schlick and Frank, under the title *Schriften zur wissenschaftlichen Weltauffassung* (*Writings towards the scientific world conception*). Under the leadership of Otto Neurath, and the editorship of Neurath, Carnap, and Charles Morris, the group began its most massive publishing project, *The International Encyclopedia of Unified Science*, in the late 1930s. The Encyclopedia, after Neurath's death wholly based at the University of Chicago, where Morris and Carnap were then on faculty, published over twenty monographs by the time it ceased publication in the 1960s.

While the Vienna Circle is the crucial group of true logical positivists in the Austrian context, the institutional path to that group was greatly aided by the work of what has been called 'the first Vienna Circle' (Uebel 1991). The first Circle met in the first decade of the twentieth century and counted Richard von Mises, Neurath, Hahn, and Frank as its core members. Hahn, a professor of mathematics at the University of Vienna, was the main catalyst and supporter of Schlick's candidacy for the chair in the philosophy of the inductive sciences. Given the state of Austrian philosophy throughout the early part of the twentieth century, it is not surprising that the proto-Circle members were all trained in scientific disciplines: Neurath in economics, von Mises in engineering, Hahn in mathematics, Frank in theoretical physics.

The Berlin Society for Empirical/Scientific Philosophy, founded in 1927, was the main home of the scientific world conception within the context of German philosophy. It included in its membership Reichenbach, then in the Physics Department at the University of Berlin, as well as Grelling, Dubislav, Josef Petzoldt, Carl Hempel, and others. Activity in Berlin was centred around the work of work of Einstein, who was professor of physics there at the time. This group, too, had roots going back to before the First World War; Petzoldt had founded the Berlin Society for Positivistic Philosophy in 1912, the founding document for which had been signed by, among others, David Hilbert, Albert Einstein, Felix Klein, and Sigmund Freud (Stadler 1997: 81). After the war, the group joined with the local Kant Society, then under the direction of Hans Vaihinger – an indication that Neo-Kantianism and positivism had common scientific goals and common anti-scientific enemies. The journal for this group was the journal that became *Erkenntnis* in 1930.

Further afield, the logical positivists found important fellow travellers in the Polish logicians working in Lemberg (Lvov) and Warsaw. Alfred Tarski's work on the semantics of formal languages, in particular, was seen as a crucial contribution by certain of the logical positivists (while being decried as metaphysics by others). Earlier, the work of Russell, Whitehead, and Wittgenstein at Cambridge had provided the key element to the Circle's sense of how logic could be considered the essence of philosophy. In the 1930s, A. J. Ayer visited the Circle from Oxford, where he returned to pen his influential *Language, Truth, and Logic*, perhaps the most widely read account of logical positivism in the English language (Ayer 1936). By the early 1930s, work in the United States was also seen as importantly connected with the general vision of philosophy promulgated by the Vienna Circle. Whitehead was by then at Harvard, where his former student, W. V. Quine, after visiting Vienna and Prague, became a vocal, though critical, supporter of the logical and philosophical work of Carnap (Quine 1936 [1976]). At the University of Chicago, Charles Morris became the main link between logical positivism and American pragmatism (Morris 1937). Under Morris's influence, a somewhat reluctant John Dewey wrote two pieces for the *Encyclopedia* in the 1930s (Dewey 1938, 1939).

2. LOGICAL POSITIVISM: SOME CENTRAL THEMES

Logical positivism, as we have noted, was not a movement that proceeded along strict doctrinal lines. Any set of theses put forward as definitive of logical positivism would be subject to clear counter examples. There are some main themes, however, in the thought of the logical positivists. Many of these themes are suggested in the various names adopted by the movement.

The logical positivists in the 1930s frequently pointed to their affinity to earlier versions of positivism. positivism was understood by the logical positivists to be primarily an anti-metaphysical movement. The logical positivists were vehemently anti-metaphysical thinkers. Anti-metaphysical thought was, for them, empirical, scientific thought. This meant, in particular, the rejection of any claim to the effect that philosophy had its own special methods for acquiring knowledge of the world or that philosophy had a distinctive, extra-scientific domain of enquiry. Strict adherence to nonmetaphysical ways of thinking meant, therefore, the rejection of intuition as a source of knowledge. It also meant the denial of the quasi-mysticism that frequently went with intuitionist views; the logical positivists had no time for philosophical claims to knowledge of facts that could not be represented in language or be subjected to rational enquiry.

This nonmetaphysical way of thinking shows clear affinities to hard-headed empiricism of a traditional sort. This is reflected in the term that many of them, especially those like Reichenbach who were happy to take sides on metaphysical issues such as realism and anti-realism, preferred – 'logical empiricism'. Indeed, logical positivism is frequently taken to be the apex (or nadir) of the empiricist tradition. In Carnap's (1928a) *Der logischer Aufbau der Welt*, for example, it seems that the anti-metaphysical drive stemmed from a virulent empiricism; the metaphysical was that which could not be spoken about in a language of pure experience. The verification principle that Schlick and others gleaned from their reading of Wittgenstein was emblematic of this reading of logical positivism. Schlick (1934 [1979]) demanded that the meaning of a sentence was the means by which it would be verified in experience. If no such verification conditions could be given, the sentence was meaningless.

On such a view, the new logic of Russell and Whitehead was, for the logical positivists, simply a new tool employed in order to complete some old empiricist projects. The new logic provided the definitional and derivational equipment needed to fulfil centuries-old promissory notes issued by Locke and Hume about the extent to which all theoretical discourse could be captured in a language of sensation. Moreover, the logicist reduction of mathematics to logic blocked a possible objection to empiricism. The certainty of mathematics was shown by logicism to stem from the emptiness of mathematical claims; mathematics and logic made no claims about the world. The certainty of mathematics and logic is, therefore, of a linguistic, not epistemological, sort: it is the certainty that accrues to conventions for the usage of signs.

There is another main theme of logical positivism that appears to follow from these considerations. If the metaphysical is recognisable as such through not being reducible to experience, then all theoretical claims in science must be reducible to experience. This strict reductionism with respect to science has the unity of science as an immediate consequence. If every scientific claim has experiential truth conditions, there can be no principled distinctions between the subject matters of the various sciences. Moreover, since this verificationist semantics is also an empiricist epistemology, there can be no differences in the methods by which the various sciences come to be known. Logical positivism thus resisted, through these philosophical moves, the cleavage that some philosophers at the time found between the natural and the social sciences.

This is a tidy account, one suggested by many of the documents written by the logical positivists themselves (including Carnap 1950 [1963] and Neurath *et al.* 1929 [1973]). It is, however, too tidy an account to be adequate to the complexities of the movement. The account suggests strongly that a rather traditional empiricist point of view was the fundamental commitment of the logical positivists – on this standard view the empiricism drives the anti-metaphysical stance, the adoption of logicism and the tools of the new logic, and the commitment to the unity of science. This order of philosophical explanation may fit the work of some of the logical positivists, but it certainly does not fit all of them.

Recent scholarship has supported the claim that a more complex story must be told by stressing at least four related aspects of the development of logical positivism that are either ignored or under-valued in the standard story. First, it has become clear that the philosophical and scientific training of the nascent logical positivists included many philosophical perspectives beyond positivism and empiricism that can be shown to play positive and long-lasting roles in their thought. Second, the sheer diversity of opinion on fundamental matters such as the place of logic in philosophy, the nature of empiricism, and the possibility of naturalism renders any tidy general account suspect. Third, a detailed look at the development of the philosophies of some of the core logical positivists reveals that empiricism was not an original core commitment; rather empiricism was itself a problematic notion of traditional philosophy that had to be clarified before it could be endorsed. Fourth, the stress on the continuity of logical positivism with traditional empiricism misses the sense in which the logical positivists were united in their claim that their work was philosophically revolutionary.

These four interrelated themes can be briefly illustrated by considering certain aspects of the philosophical view points of four of the leading logical positivists: Reichenbach, Carnap, Schlick, and Neurath. Schlick and Neurath were nine years older than Carnap and Reichenbach, the former being born in 1882, the latter in 1891. Schlick was a student of Planck in physics; Carnap and Reichenbach trained in physics but took degrees in philosophy. Neurath, on the other hand, combined an interest in history of science and in economics by doing a dissertation with Eduard Meyer on ancient views of economics. The role of Einsteinian physics on the early thought of Schlick, Reichenbach, and Carnap is well known. Neurath's engagement with methodological issues in the social sciences, especially his own attempt to dissolve the Mach-or-Marx debate in the foundation of social science, has only recently received significant attention (Cartwright *et al.* 1996; Uebel 1996b). Neurath's engagement with Marxist problems is a key to understanding his strong commitments to physicalism and naturalism and served to underpin to his anti-methodological stance. Among the others, Reichenbach and Carnap grew up within a more clearly Neo-Kantian atmosphere, which was reflected in the Kantian and conventionalist approaches they took to issues in the methodology of relativistic physics early in their careers (Carnap 1922; Reichenbach 1920 [1965]). Carnap's early engagement with a variety of traditions is reflected in the self-proclaimed epistemological neutrality of the *Aufbau*, which stands at odds with the strict empiricist reading of the work that was briefly mentioned above.

The second point can be illustrated by considering the sharp disagreement within the Circle about the foundations of empirical knowledge, which was the topic of the so-called protocol-sentence debate of the early 1930s (Oberdan 1993; Uebel 1992). Schlick was a conservative figure in the debate, insisting on a directly experiential foundation to empirical knowledge and claiming to find Carnap's and Neurath's view both obscure and decidedly nonempiricist. Neurath combined a linguistic understanding of the foundation of knowledge – knowledge begins with protocol *sentences* – with a thoroughgoing fallibilism (even the protocol sentences could be revised). Carnap, finally, took a conventionalist line about which sentences were the protocol sentences but maintained a stricter methodology within the language of science so construed (for Carnap, protocol sentences could not be rejected on epistemic grounds, there being no more fundamental epistemic grounds to which to appeal).

As to the third point, the case of Carnap is instructive. We have already mentioned his self-proclaimed epistemological neutrality in the *Aufbau*. Recent commentators on that work have found in it significant influences from a variety of epistemological points of view, including positivism and empiricism, certainly, but also phenomenology and, especially, Neo-Kantianism (Coffa 1991; Friedman 1987, 1992; Moulines 1991; Richardson 1998; Sauer 1989). Carnap's main stance throughout his career was a neutralism with respect to traditional philosophical issues combined with attempts to make sense of those issues through the tool of logical analysis. This tool did not express a prior commitment to empiricism, however, since empiricism itself was clarified in the same way. Only in the mid-1930s did Carnap feel that he had adequately explicated a notion of empiricism that he could himself support (Carnap 1936/7). The whole business of explication, however, was done from a generally formalist point of view that neither raised nor answered any epistemological questions about logic. Thus, Carnap did not find logic 'certain' in any philosophically interesting sense at all – no logic-independent epistemological vocabulary could explain how logic played the methodological role that it did play (Richardson 1997b, 1998; Ricketts 1994).

The final point is, perhaps, the most crucial one. The easy assimilation of logical positivism to long-standing historical traditions such as positivism and empiricism drew philosophical attention away from the revolutionary rhetoric that was ubiquitous in the early years of the movement (Galison 1990, 1996; Richardson 1997a; Uebel 1996a, 1996b). This rhetoric, however overstated it may seem in retrospect, was serious. Even Schlick, who was in every way a more conservative thinker than Neurath or Carnap, thought that a decisive turning point in philosophy had been reached (Schlick 1930 [1979]). The collectivist, modernist, technocratic framing of the project was central to the social and political point of scientific philosophy among the logical positivists. Far from removing philosophy from social engagement, the technical, scientific form it was to take in logical positivism first gave to philosophy such an engagement. In the view of Neurath and Carnap, philosophy was a sort of conceptual engineering to be employed in the aid of rational solutions to social problems. The practical nature of logical positivism was the main cause of the mutual attraction between it and American pragmatism in the 1930s (Morris 1937).

3. THE SIGNIFICANCE OF LOGICAL POSITIVISM, 1930–1945

If the logical positivist revolution was meant finally to terminate theretofore 'pseudoproblems and wearisome controversies' (Carnap 1934 [1937: xiv–xv]) in philosophy, then on its own terms it must be convicted of failure. Nevertheless, the revolutionary ambitions of logical positivism do point us to the significance of the movement within the context of philosophy in the first half of the twentieth century. The most important aspects of logical positivism are not to be found in technically sophisticated but philosophically derivative attempts to institute strict empiricism. They are rather to be found in the role that logical postivism played in developing the methods of analytic philosophy and in helping to create the disciplines of philosophy of science, metalogic, and philosophy of language.

The decade of the 1930s was the time during which logical positivism found its positive agenda. During this decade, Otto Neurath instituted his project of unifying the sciences on the basis of a physicalist language. This project, as carried forward in the *Encyclopedia*, became the leading large-scale project in philosophy of science for the logical positivists in the late 1930s (Reisch 1994). Neurath, Carnap, Hempel, Zilsel, and Frank all made early contributions to the project. They were joined by leading members of the international philosophical and scientific communities such as Morris, Dewey, Leonard Bloomfield, Ernest Nagel, and Giorgio de Santillana. Also, during this decade, Reichenbach was doing much to create the disciplines of technical philosophy of physics and philosophy of probability theory (Reichenbach 1928 [1958], 1935).

Carnap, meanwhile, was providing the philosophical framework that led from a general concern with the theory of knowledge to technical work in philosophy of science. In the mid-1930s, Carnap argued that scientific philosophy had entered a new phase in which epistemology was to be set aside in favour of 'the logic of science' (Carnap 1934 [1937], 1936). This was because epistemological problems had shown themselves to be pseudoproblems. Epistemologists had never become clear as to whether they were working on empirical issues regarding the structure and content of human experience and the causes of change in beliefs or on logical issues about the justification of some scientific knowledge claims on the basis of others. Adopting a metalogical approach adapted from David Hilbert and Gödel that allowed him to see scientific theories on the model of formal systems, Carnap argued that the role of the philosopher was only to deal with the latter sort of issue, and even then only in close collaboration with the scientific expert. Philosophical issues were, therefore, formal, technical questions about the structure of scientific theories, the logic of confirmation, and so forth. This logic-based philosophy of science was offered as the scientifically acceptable successor project to the confused and obscure project of epistemology. Although perhaps not fully understood, Carnap's point of view and proffered methods in philosophy of science were adopted by most working logical positivists from the mid-1930s onwards.

This creative philosophical work went forward in the context of an increasingly hostile political environment in Germany and Austria in the 1930s. Feigl, sure that there was no future for him as a young Jewish philosopher in Vienna, had already emigrated to the United States in 1931, and had joined the Philosophy Department at the University of Iowa. Reichenbach was forced out of his position in Berlin with the institution of the race laws in Germany in 1933, going first to Turkey (with, among others, von Mises) and then, in 1938, to the University of California at Los Angeles. Carnap had first gone to the German University of Prague in 1931 and then to the University of Chicago in 1936. Frank had gone to Harvard University in 1938, where he remained for the rest of his academic career. Neurath was in Russia at the time of the *Anschluss* in 1938. He never returned to Austria, going first to Holland and, following the Nazi invasion there, to England, where he died in 1945.

Indeed, all the major figures listed in the 1929 pamphlet who were living in Austria or Germany at the time of its publication were, by the start of the war in 1939, either dead or in exile. Most tragic of all, was, of course, the murder of Schlick by a deranged former student, who was in essence released to freedom within two years of the event by the government that came into power with the *Anschluss* (Stadler 1997: 920–61). The death of Schlick was the end of the official existence of the Vienna Circle, the end of the existence of the Chair in the Philosophy of the Inductive Sciences at the University of Vienna, and, in effect, the end of the era of scientific philosophy in Austria (Stadler 1991: 65–7).

This tragic scenario may, nonetheless, have helped the philosophical agenda of logical positivism. Logical positivism became a central movement in philosophy only when it moved to the United States. The reasons why this small, technical movement in philosophy became so important in the United States are not clear. It is, however, undeniable that logical positivism was a major force in shaping American philosophy almost from the first moment that the practitioners began to arrive. Part of the success is surely due to the prestige of science and technology in America in the war and immediate post-war periods – and the distinction of logical positivism's scientific friends in the States (e.g., Einstein, Hermann Weyl, Percy Bridgman). Part of it is due to the welcoming attitude of some of the finest American universities (Harvard, Chicago, Berkeley), as well as some up-and-coming public universities (UCLA, Iowa, Minnesota) and some institutions that worked very hard for exiled academics in general (the New School for Social Research, City College, Queen's College).

Whatever the occasioning causes of the success of logical positivism may have been, it was in the United States that the projects of the logical positivists were taken up with vigour. Logic and formal semantics went forward under the influence of Tarski, Gödel, Quine, and Carnap (Carnap 1942; Quine 1942). Philosophy of science took shape as the logical analysis of scientific and metascientific concepts. Here, Reichenbach took the lead in philosophy of physics, while Carnap, Feigl, and Hempel joined Reichenbach in pointing the way in general issues such as realism, confirmation, and explanation (Carnap 1936/7; Feigl 1934, 1945; Hempel 1942, 1945; Reichenbach 1938, 1944). The *Encyclopedia* began publication in 1938 and continued, though with delays and ultimately in severely scaled-back form, into the 1960s. It was in the American context that logical positivism had its most important interactions with social scientists, also. It was influential in behaviourism and operationism in psychology, in helping to prepare the ground for mathematical techniques in economics and econometrics, and in shaping the science of linguistics.

The scientific philosophy that the logical positivists promoted in North America in the late 1930s and early 1940s was less frequently and less stridently announced as having socio-political motivations than it had been in Europe. While Carnap and Neurath joined Morris and Dewey in maintaining that there were political and social benefits to a project of unified science and scientific philosophy, other logical positivists had a more detached view. The attitude that came to be associated with mature logical positivism is more the one that Reichenbach recommended at the end of his essay on Dewey (Reichenbach 1939: 192):

The early period of empiricism in which an all-round philosopher could dominate at the same time the fields of scientific method, of history of philosophy, of education and social philosophy, has passed. We enter into the second phase in which highly technical investigations form the indispensable instruments of research, splitting the philosophical campus into specialists of its various branches. We should not regret this unavoidable specialization which repeats on philosophical grounds a phenomenon well known from all other fields of scientific enquiry.

Logical positivism was criticised already in the 1930s and 1940s for replacing philosophy with a naïve scientism. For a logical positivist of Reichenbach's frame of mind, this sounded very much like criticising logical positivism for both its success and its promise.

THE ACHIEVEMENTS OF THE POLISH
SCHOOL OF LOGIC

JAN WOLEŃSKI

1. INTRODUCTION

In the most narrow sense, the Polish school of logic may be understood, as the Warsaw school of mathematical logic with Jan Łukasiewicz, Stanisław Leśniewski, and Alfred Tarski as the leading figures. However, valuable contributions to mathematical logic were also made outside Warsaw, in particular by Leon Chwistek. Thus, the Polish school of logic *sensu largo* also comprises logicians not belonging to the Warsaw school of logic. The third interpretation is still broader. If logic is not restricted only to mathematical logic, several Polish philosophers who were strongly influenced by formal logical results, for example Kazimierz Ajdukiewicz and Tadeusz Kotarbiński, can be included in the Polish school of logic *sensu largissimo*. Polish work on logic can therefore encompass a variety of topics, from the 'hard' foundations of mathematics (e.g. inaccessible cardinals, the structure of the real line, or equivalents of the axiom of choice) through formal logic, semantics, and philosophy of science to ideas in ontology and epistemology motivated by logic or analysed by its tools. Since the development of logic in Poland is a remarkable historical phenomenon, I shall first discuss its social history, especially the rise of the Warsaw school. Then I shall describe the philosophical views in question, the most important and characteristic formal results of Polish logicians, their research in the history of logic, and applications of logic to philosophy. My discussion will be selective: in particular I will omit most results in the 'hard' foundations of mathematics.

2. A BRIEF HISTORY OF LOGIC IN POLAND

Mathematical logic was introduced into Polish academic circles in the academic year 1899–1900, when Kazimierz Twardowski delivered a course in Lvov on the algebra of logic. Thirty years later, which is to say in the lifetime of one generation, Warsaw was commonly regarded as one of the world capitals of mathematical logic. How did it happen that a country without any special tradition in logic so soon reached pre-eminence in this field? What happened to bring about the following statement: 'There is probably no country which has contributed, relative to the size of its population, so much to mathematical logic and set theory as Poland' (Hillel and Fraenkel 1958, p. 200)? The answer is that the success of logic in Poland was a result of exceptionally good cooperation between philosophers and mathematicians.

Twardowski, the father of analytic philosophy in Poland, was a student of Brentano and inherited some general metaphilosophical views from his teacher, in particular rationalism, the search for clarity of language and thought, hostility to speculation, and the belief that philosophy is a science. He wanted to introduce these ideas into Polish philosophy and to establish a school of scientific philosophy. He succeeded in this and established the analytic movement, commonly known as the Lvov-Warsaw School. Twardowski himself was not a logician, but he stressed the importance of logical culture for philosophy. Moreover, his metaphilosophical views were a natural environment for doing semiotics, formal logic and methodology of science. In fact, most Polish logicians were direct or indirect students of Twardowski.

It was Łukasiewicz who became the first Polish specialist in mathematical logic. He studied the works of Frege and Russell and lectured in Lvov on mathematical logic from 1906. His courses attracted many young philosophers, including Ajdukiewicz, Tadeusz Czeżowski, Kotarbiński, and Zygmunt Zawirski. In 1911, Leśniewski came to Lvov to complete his doctoral dissertation under Twardowski's supervision and joined the Lvov group. It was also important that Wacław Sierpiński was a professor of mathematics in Lvov at that time, and young philosophers interested in logic participated in his classes on set theory. In particular, Sierpiński trained Zygmunt Janiszewski, who played an important role in the subsequent development of logic and the foundations of mathematics in Poland.

In 1915, the German war authorities allowed Warsaw University to be reopened (it had been closed by the Tsarist government in 1869), and Łukasiewicz was appointed as professor of philosophy. He began to give lectures on logic, which were welcomed by young mathematicians and philosophers, but the decisive point for the rise and development of the Warsaw logic group was the place of logic in the programme for the development of mathematics elaborated by Janiszewski and implemented in Warsaw. According to this programme, mathematicians were to concentrate their work in set theory and topology as well as in applications of the classical parts of mathematics, such as algebra, geometry, and analysis. This project also gave an important role to mathematical logic and the foundations of mathematics; both were placed in the very centre of mathematics.

The Janiszewski programme also led to some important developments in the organisation of the University of Warsaw. A department of philosophy of mathematics in the Faculty of Mathematics and Natural Sciences was soon founded, and Leśniewski was appointed as the professor on the recommendation of Sierpiński. Why Leśniewski, not Łukasiewicz? Because the latter had left the university for a position in the new government under Paderewski, as the Minister of Religion and Education. But he came back to the university in 1920 as professor of philosophy in the Faculty of Mathematics and Natural Sciences, though it was a position in mathematical logic. The University of Warsaw thus had two professors of logic. It also had a journal: *Fundamenta Mathematicae*. The first idea had been to publish it in two series, of which one should be entirely devoted to logic and the foundations of mathematics. In the end, the journal was organised without a division into series, but logic was widely present in it. Mazurkiewicz, Sierpiński, Leśniewski, and Łukasiewicz constituted the editorial commitee: two mathematicians and two logicians.

These facts are remarkable from a sociological point of view. The appointment of two non-mathematicians as professors of logic at the Faculty of Mathematics and Natural Sciences was a brave experiment, with very beneficial results. It explains why mathematical logic developed much more strongly in Warsaw than in any other place in Poland – in particular in Cracow and Lvov, where mathematicians were not as sympathetic to logic as in Warsaw. Jan Sleszyński was the most important logician in Cracow, and Leon Chwistek (who began his academic career in Cracow) held the main position as a logician in the Mathematics Faculty in Lvov, where Ajdukiewicz taught logic to philosophers.

Leśniewski and Łukasiewicz had to change their scientific profile in this new environment: they could not be mathematicians in the normal sense. However, it was accepted by Sierpiński and other professional mathematicians in Warsaw that doing logic was a proper mathematical activity, so it was quite normal that gifted students of mathematics would decide to concentrate on mathematical logic. Łukasiewicz and Leśniewski consciously aimed to establish a school of logic, and succeeded because of their great teaching skills, which attracted good students. The first of them, Alfred Tarski, rapidly became the third leader of the school. Other students included Stanisław Jaśkowski, Adolf Lindenbaum, Andrzej Mostowski, Moses Presburger, Jerzy Słupecki, Bolesław Sobociński, and Mordechaj Wajsberg. Jaśkowski, Lindenbaum, Presburger, Sobociński, and Wajsberg graduated in the 1920s, and Mostowski and Słupecki in the 1930s (Sobociński in philosophy, the rest in mathematics); Czeław Lejewski, later a professor in Manchester, graduated just before 1939. Was this a large group? Judging by today's standards, a group of a dozen or so people working together on logic is perhaps not all that large. However, if we look at the Warsaw group from the perspective of the interwar period, we must remember that at that time no other place at which logic was studied had even a third of this number. Nor was the Warsaw logical community limited to the school of logic. It was also propagated in Warsaw by Kotarbiński, who was professor of philosophy. There were also some instances of luck: for example, it was a lucky event that Alfred Tarski arrived as a student about 1920 and that he decided to work in logic, and that Adolf Lindenbaum moved from topology to logic. However, any important achievement in science is connected with some lucky opportunities.

Łukasiewicz, the moving spirit of the Warsaw school of logic, was also a very effective organiser. In his view, logic was an autonomous subject which is subordinate neither to philosophy nor to mathematics. It therefore requires special journals and societies, because not all of its needs can be fulfilled by institutions connected with other fields, even those very close to logic. Łukasiewicz inaugurated the Polish Logical Society (1936) and a special journal, *Collectanea Logica*. Logic in Poland, and in particular the Warsaw school, was thus well equipped with human and institutional resources, and it is clear that this was the result of a quite conscious and systematically realised enterprise. In contrast to the five professorships in mathematical logic in Poland in 1939 (two in Warsaw, one in Cracow, one in Lvov, and one in Poznan), outside Poland there was only one, in Münster in Germany, held by Heinrich Scholz. In addition, the subject was extensively taught in universities and secondary schools, and textbooks show that the level of training was high. Polish students were trained also in propositional calculus and predicate logic. At universities, advanced logic was included in courses of philosophy for students of various specialities.

3. THE PHILOSOPHICAL FOUNDATIONS OF LOGIC AND MATHEMATICS

Mathematical logic, from its beginnings, was closely connected with the great schools in the foundations of mathematics, namely logicism, formalism, and intuitionism. Logicians belonging to particular schools, especially in the early stage of the development of mathematical logic (1900–30), were often interested in different logical problems and even systems; the Hilbertians, the Russellians, and the Brouwerians stressed different points of logical investigations. What was the situation like in Poland?

We can divide Polish logicians into two groups. Leśniewski and Chwistek based their research on explicit philosophical presuppositions, and in this respect, they aimed to develop foundational schemes (systems of *logica magna*) similar to logicism (see section 7 below for more details). However, the rest of the Warsaw school of logic was not bound by any philosophical ideology. Łukasiewicz and Tarski were typical examples here. Both were ready to investigate any logical problem, independently of whether it originated in logicism, intuitionism, or formalism. Tarski stressed several times that his formal research did not assume any general foundational view. This attitude was connected with the ideology of the Polish mathematical school, and perhaps its clearest expression can be found in Sierpiński:

Still, apart from our personal inclination to accept the axiom of choice, we must take into consideration, in any case, its role in the Set Theory and in the Calculus. On the other hand, since the axiom of choice has been questioned by some mathematicians, it is important to know which theorems are proved with its aid, and to realize the exact point at which the proof has been based on the axiom of choice; for it has frequently happened that various authors have made use of the axiom of choice in their proofs without being aware of it. And after all, even if no one questioned the axiom of choice, it would not be without interest to investigate which proofs are based on it and which theorems can be proved without its aid – this, as we know, is also done with regard to other axioms. (Sierpiński 1964: 95)

Tarski himself summarised very clearly the prevailing philosophical position of the Warsaw school:

As an essential contribution of the Polish school to the development of metamathematics one can regard the fact that from the very beginning it admitted into metamathematical research all fruitful methods, whether finitary or not. (Tarski 1986: IV, 713)

On the other hand, this general 'aphilosophical' position does not mean that particular logicians had no philosophical views of their own connected with logic. They had, and sometimes it led to a sort of a cognitive tension, for example in the case of Tarski:

Tarski, in oral discussions, has often indicated his sympathies with nominalism. While he never accepted the 'reism' of Tadeusz Kotarbiński, he was certainly attracted to it in the early phase of his work. However, the set-theoretical methods that form the basis of his logical and mathematical studies compel him constantly to use the abstract and general notions that a nominalist seeks to avoid. In the absence of more extensive publications by Tarski on philosophical subjects, the conflict appears to have remained unresolved. (Mostowski 1967: 81)

Mostowski himself was close to constructivism. However, writing of the difficulties of producing a textbook on mathematical logic, he says:

As far as the matter concerns the third difficulty connected with acceptance of a definite philosophical standpoint in the foundations of mathematics, I intentionally avoided touching on those questions in the text, because they obviously exceed the scope of formal logic. I treat a logical system as a language in which one speaks about set and relations. I adopted the axiom of extensionality for these entities and I recognised that they obey the principles of the simple theory of types. This standpoint is a convenient base for developing formal problems and concurs with the more or less conscious views of most mathematicians, which does not mean at all that it would have to be accepted by philosophers without any reservation . . . I am inclined to think that a satisfactory solution of the problem of the foundations of mathematics will follow the route pointed out by constructivism or a direction close to it. However, it would be impossible to write a textbook of logic on this base at the moment. (Mostowski 1948: vi)

This is a very instructive passage. Firstly, it makes a clear distinction between the 'official' science, in this case mathematical logic, and a 'private' philosophy. Secondly, it shows an equally clear preference for the needs of 'official' science. Thirdly, we have here a good summary of the set-theoretical ideology for doing mathematical logic and the foundations of mathematics which perhaps could be regarded as a continuation of logicism, although without its principal claim that mathematics is reducible to logic. In fact the set-theoretical programme in the foundations of mathematics arose as the project of the mathematical foundations of mathematics, which corresponds to contemporary views.

All logicians in the Warsaw school (and indeed in Poland) agreed that logic is extensional. Thus there is no logic of intensional contexts. This explains why Polish logicians were not particularly interested in modal logic as an extension of classical logic, because it leads to intensional modal logic (as in the case of the Lewis systems). Although Łukasiewicz's discovery of many-valued logic is certainly one of the most remarkable achievements of Polish logicians, most of them recognised the priority of the two-valued pattern. Only Łukasiewicz and Zawirski voted for the superiority of many-valuedness for philosophical reasons; the rest regarded many-valued logic as purely formal constructions, deserving attention, for example, for algebraic reasons, but not as rivals of classical logic. Leśniewski was perhaps the most radical advocate of classical logic.

Traditionally, the problems of how logic is related to reality and what the epistemological status of logical theorems might be are among the most important ones in the philosophy of logic. Łukasiewicz discussed these questions in connection with the choice between two-valued and many-valued logic. At first he believed that experience would decide this question, as in the case of geometry. However, he later accepted a more conventionalist position, holding that the usefulness and richness of logical systems are decisive factors in their value for science. Most other Polish logicians, though, did not subscribe to this conventionalism and pragmatism. They rather thought that logic refers to very general features of reality. Kotarbiński gives the following characterisation of Leśniewski's calculus of names:

We will add that Leśniewski calls his system 'ontology' . . . It must, however, be admitted that if the Aristotelian definition of the supreme theory . . . be interpreted in the spirit of a 'general theory of objects', then both the word and its meaning are applicable to the calculus of terms as expounded by Leśniewski. (Kotarbiński 1966: 210–11)

This interpretation was fully confirmed by Leśniewski himself:

taking into consideration the relation existing between the single characteristic primitive term of my theory and the Greek participle [i.e. *on*-J. W.] explained by Kotarbiński, I used the name 'ontology' . . . to characterize the theory I was developing, without offence to my 'linguistic instincts' because I was formulating in that theory a certain view of 'general principles of existence'. (Leśniewski 1992: 374)

This realistic view of logic resulted in the rejection of the view that logical theorems are tautologies which are devoid of empirical content. Thus Tarski considered empiricism a correct view of logic: experience can force rejection of logical axioms in the same way as happens with empirical hypotheses, for example, in physics; the difference between logic and empirical science consists in the degree of generality, which is much greater in the case of logical principles. Thus, the prevailing view of Polish logicians was that formal sciences are basically empirical, although they are further from experience than other elements of our knowledge.

Leśniewski summarised his view of the nature of logic, which he called 'the intuitionistic [better 'intuitive'] formalism', in the following way:

Having no predilection for various 'mathematical games' that consist in writing out according to one or another conventional rule various more or less picturesque formulas which need not be meaningful, or even – as some of the 'mathematical gamers' might prefer – which should necessarily be meaningless, I would not have taken the trouble to systematize and to check often quite scrupulously the directives of my system, had I not imputed to its theses a certain specific and completely determined sense, in virtue of which its axioms, definitions, and final directives . . . have for me an irresistible intuitive validity. I see no contradiction, therefore, in saying that I advocate a rather radical 'formalism' in the construction of my system even though I am an obdurate 'intuitionist'. Having endeavoured to express my thoughts on various particular topics by representing them as a series of propositions meaningful in various deductive theories, and to derive one proposition from others in a way that would harmonize with the way I finally considered intuitively binding, I know no method more effective for acquainting the reader with my logical intuitions than the method of formalizing any deductive theory to be set forth. (Leśniewski 1992: 487–8)

This passage is of the utmost importance for an understanding of the spirit of logical research in the Warsaw school. It gives a very good indication of the general attitude towards logic, as something that is not a meaningless activity but essentially deals with sense. Leśniewski once said (personal communication of H. Hiż): 'logic is a formal exposition of intuition'. It is perhaps the best short summary of the philosophy of logic proposed by most Polish logicians.

Finally, let me mention some conditions governing the 'quality' of good formal systems. Apart from the obvious demand for consistency, Polish logicians demanded that logical systems should be as simple and economic as possible, based on the minimal number of primitive notions, axioms, and rules of inference. Many formal investigations undertaken in Poland were driven by this general task of finding the most economical and elegant formal systems of logic, independently of their possible applicability outside logic. Clearly, if one assumes that logic is autonomous, its applicability is not a primary criterion of the quality of logical investigations.

4. THE CLASSICAL PROPOSITIONAL CALCULUS

Propositional calculus became the speciality of the Warsaw School and a laboratory of its logical research. A special form of notation (variously called bracket-free notation, Polish notation, Łukasiewicz's notation) under which logical operations are always written before their arguments without any need to use typical punctuation signs (dots, brackets) was often used in investigations in this system. Thus, the symbols *Np*, *Cpq*, *Kpq*, *Apq*, *Epq*, and *Dpq* stand respectively for negation (with 'p' as the argument), implication (with 'p' and 'q' as the arguments), conjunction, disjunction, equivalence, and the Sheffer stroke. This symbolism was very convenient for investigations that aimed at the most economical systems.

Investigations in the field of propositional calculus concerned, above all, systems of functionally complete propositional calculus (i.e. with all sixteen propositional functors), based on various conceptual bases: on negation and implication (or disjunction or conjunction) and on the Sheffer function as the sole functor. The most popular system with negation and implication as primitives (the *C-N* system) was formulated by Łukasiewicz. It has three axioms: *CpCpq*, *CCpCqrCCpqCpr*, *CCNpNqCqp*, and two rules of inference: substitution and *modus ponens*. The criteria of good logical systems required a search for the shortest sole axiom for the *N-C*-calculus. Finally, the following formula (23 letters) was proved to be such an axiom: *CCCpqCCCNrNstrCuCCrpCsp*. Similar results were achieved for partial propositional calculi, that is, a system with just one functor as sole primitive. For example, Łukasiewicz showed that the shortest axiom of the equivalential calculus cannot have less than ten letters; in fact the eleven-letter formula *EEpqEErqEpr* may be taken as its sole axiom.

In 1926, Łukasiewicz posed the following problem: since mathematical proofs do not use logical theorems, but refer to assumptions and rules of inference, it is important to construct logic as a system of rules; how can this be done? The problem was solved by Jaśkowski in 1927 and finally published in Jaśkowski 1934; in fact, Jaśkowski's system was formulated also for predicate calculus. Thus, one form of natural deduction emerged in Poland (the other is the calculus of sequents developed by Gerhardt Gentzen).

Intensive research into the metatheory of propositional calculus was conducted in Warsaw in the interwar period. The first results achieved by Łukasiewicz concerned the independence of axiom systems of PC. In particular, Łukasiewicz proved that some earlier axiomatics of Frege and Hilbert contained redundant axioms. This particular research served as a logical laboratory for more general results, which were summarised in Łukasiewicz and Tarski 1930. This paper also contains results concerning metalogic of many-valued systems, and develops the concept of the logical matrix as the main tool of semantic investigations into propositional calculi. Among the many ideas and results outlined in this important paper, it is worth mentioning the concept of the Lindenbaum algebra and the theorem: every propositional calculus has a characteristic matrix which is finite or infinite. Polish logicians also invented several methods of proving the completeness theorem for PC.

5. MANY-VALUED AND OTHER NON-CLASSICAL SYSTEMS

There is no doubt that the invention of many-valued logic was one of the most important logical achievements in Poland. Łukasiewicz discovered three-valued logic in 1918; then it was generalised to finitely many-valued logic and infinitely-valued logics. Łukasiewicz's discovery of many-valued logic was strongly motivated by philosophical reasons, primarily as a weapon against determinism, which he regarded as inconsistent with freedom. For Łukasiewicz, determinism is closely connected with the principle of bivalence that every statement is either true or false. His discussion treats the question of the truth-value of so-called future contingents – statements about the future whose truth or falsity is not determined at present. Łukasiewicz pointed out that Aristotle already had doubts about whether we could ascribe truth or falsity to future contingents. He concluded that many-valued logic was not non-Aristotelian, but rather non-Chrysippean, because the Stoics strongly defended the principle of bivalence. For Łukasiewicz, many-valued logic does not consist in the rejection of a particular logical theorem, but rather appeals to a fundamental revision of metalogic based on the rejection of bivalence.

Formal construction of many-valued logic begins with the adoption of more than two truth values. In the simplest case, namely three-valued logic ($Ł_3$), we admit that the valuation of propositional variables is a function from the set $1, \frac{1}{2}, 0$

of truth values to variables. In particular, the function Np is governed by an additional rule, namely $N\frac{1}{2} = \frac{1}{2}$ (the negation of the third value yields the same value), and the rule for disjunction prescribes that $A\frac{1}{2}\frac{1}{2} = \frac{1}{2}$. This means that the rule of excluded middle ($ApNp$) fails in three-valued logic. There is not room to give further formal details here: let me simply note that Łukasiewicz, Wajsberg, and Słupecki axiomatised various systems of many-valued logic.

In his early writings about many-valued logic Łukasiewicz interpreted the truth value $\frac{1}{2}$ as possibility. Hence he thought of his three-valued system as a form of modal logic. However he was also guided by the principle that any logic should be extensional, so he demanded truth-functionality of the expression 'it is possible that p (Mp)'. Moreover, according to his view, modal logic must formalise the following traditional theses as theorems: *ab oportere ad esse valet consequentia* (necessity implies actuality), *ab esse ad posse valet consequentia* (actuality implies possibility), *ab non posse ad non esse valet consequentia* (impossibility implies non-actuality), and *unumquodque, quanda est, oportet est* (assumed actuality implies necessity). Now, Łukasiewicz demonstrated that no truth-functional extension of two-valued logic preserves these principles, and this for him was the motivation for grounding modal logic on three-valued logic. Tarski suggested that Mp could be defined as $CNpp$ in three-valued logic, and this route satisfied most substantial intuitions. However, Łukasiewicz did not complete his construction of modal logic until after 1945, when he proposed four-valued logic as the base for modal logic (the so-called Ł-systems of modalities). Lewis's systems were in fact investigated by logicians from the Warsaw school, despite their hostility to non-extensional system of logic. Wajsberg proved that the system $S5$ is complete with respect to algebraic semantics, and Tarski (together with J. C. C. MacKinsey) constructed topological semantics for modal logic.

Polish logicians were responsible for important achievements in intuitionistic logic. I will mention three metalogical results: the separation theorem, that each consequence deducible from the axioms of propositional calculus is deducible from such axioms which apart from implication include only the propositional connectives that occur in consequence (Wajsberg); the construction of the infinite adequate matrix for intuitionistic propositional logic (Jaśkowski); and the topological interpretation of intuitionistic logic (Tarski). Jaśkowski's matrix construction is a very impressive illustration of the inter-connections between various results. As was mentioned above, Lindenbaum proved that every propositional calculus has an adequate matrix. In 1932, Kurt Gödel showed that no finite matrix is adequate for intuitionistic propositional calculus. This suggested that such a matrix had to be infinite. Jaśkowski's construction consisted in defining an infinite sequence of matrices replaceable by a single infinite matrix. It is interesting that intuitionistic logic was highly appreciated in Poland not for its philosophical basis, but rather for its logical beauty. Indeed, Łukasiewicz said that intuitionistic logic was perhaps the most elegant of all non-classical systems.

6. METAMATHEMATICS AND FORMAL SEMANTICS

In the 1920s, under Hilbert's influence, metalogic and metamathematics were reduced to the syntax of formal systems. However, model theory was later also taken into consideration. Polish logicians studied metamathematics very extensively, and their studies concerned topics including the following: the axiomatisation of the consequence operation (Tarski), the axiomatisation of calculus of systems (Tarski), the systematisation of various metamathematical concepts: completeness, independence, consistency, etc. (Tarski), the rules of definitions in formal systems (Leśniewski), definability (Tarski), decidability (Józef Pepis – a logician from the Chwistek circle in Lvov), the theory of syntactic categories (Leśniewski, Ajdukiewicz), and the method of elimination of quantifiers (Tarski). Several more concrete results were of the utmost importance, for example, the Lindenbaum theorem on maximalisation (every consistent set of sentences has its maximal consistent extension), which is the foundation of modern proofs of the semantic completeness (the Henkin-style proofs), the deduction theorem (Tarski, also Jacques Herbrand), the upward Löwenheim-Skolem-Tarski theorem (if a system has a model, then it also has a model of an arbitary infinity), the completeness of arithmetic with addition as the sole operation (Presburger), and the completeness and decidability of the arithmetic of real numbers (Tarski).

Tarski's semantic definition of truth is perhaps the most important logical idea to have emerged in Poland. It is a good example of a formal result stemming from various sources, both philosophical and mathematical. Philosophically, Tarski was influenced by the Aristotelian tradition in the theory of truth which was very popular in the Lvov-Warsaw school, particularly with Twardowski, Kotarbiński, and Leśniewski. This point is worth emphasising because ignorance of Tarski's philosophical pedigree can lead to misinterpretation of the semantic truth-definition. Looking at it from the mathematical side, Tarski's construction is given in set-theory; it was originally formulated for languages stratified into logical types, and it can be considered as a contribution to the theory of types. However, the most important point is that it requires infinitistic methods. Since Tarski's definition and his solution to the Liar Paradox are easily accessible from any serious textbook on mathematical logic, I will not give details of them here. It is very important to see that the infinitary character of Tarski's truth-definition contrasts with the finitary shape of syntax. Thus, there is an essential gap between syntax and semantics. Semantics, as outlined by Tarski in the 1930s, was later extended by him and his students in Berkeley to model theory, one of the basic parts of mathematical logic. The proposition that model theory cannot be fully reduced to finitary syntax became perhaps the most important feature of logical ideology of the second half of the twentieth century. To be fair, this semantic revolution is owed also to Gödel, who used the concept of truth essentially as a heuristic device in his celebrated incompleteness theorems. Tarski himself proved another limitative theorem: the set of truths of a theory which contains arithmetic is not definable in that theory (the Tarski limitative theorem). This theorem fits well with the infinitistic character of truth. In general, the results of Gödel and Tarski show that truth and proof are not equivalent (the first is more comprehensive), at least in the case of classical logic.

7. LEŚNIEWSKI AND CHWISTEK

I group Leśniewski and Chwistek together in this section, because their systems were in a sense unorthodox and did not belong to the mainstream of logic. Moreover, as I have already mentioned, both Leśniewski and Chwistek, unlike most Polish logicians, were guided by some general philosophical assumptions. In particular, they tried to establish nominalistic foundations of mathematics; note, however, that their proposals for doing so were completely different.

Leśniewski constructed three logical systems intended to be the foundations of mathematics: prototethic, ontology, and mereology. Prototethic is a generalised propositional calculus: it contains quantifiers which bind propositional variables and variables which refer to objects of arbitrary syntactic categories defined from the basic category of propositions. Prototethic is a very rich system which can express both the principle of bivalence and the principle of extensionality; this was the reason why Leśniewski rejected non-classical logics. Ontology is a calculus of names or a theory of the copula 'is', taken as synonymous with Latin *est*. It plays the same role in Leśniewski's scheme as predicate logic in the usual one. Ontology is a free logic – it does not require any existential assumption. An interesting feature is that identity can be defined in elementary ontology, contrary to the first-order predicate calculus in which the identity predicate must be added as a new symbol. Ontology provides philosophically interesting definitions of existence and objecthood. Mereology is a theory of classes understood as collective wholes. In fact, mereology is a theory of parts and wholes; Leśniewski considered it as a substitute of the usual set theory, but it was proved that the former is weaker than the latter. Leśniewski's radical nominalism is clear when we look at details of his systems. In particular, these systems are concrete physical objects, finite at any stage but always freely extensible.

It became clear that Leśniewski's systems were too weak to constitute the foundations of mathematics, partly because of the limited power of mereology, which is weaker than the usual set theory. On the other hand, these systems were always regarded as interesting in themselves and they attracted many logicians and philosophers; in fact, Leśniewski's ideas are perhaps the strongest realisation of traditional nominalistic claims. In Warsaw, Tarski, Wajsberg, and Sobociński contributed considerably to Leśniewski's systems, and since 1945, these systems have been investigated in many other countries as well. It should also be noted that Leśniewski's influence in Warsaw was enormous, comparable only to that of Łukasiewicz. In fact, most criteria of good logical systems go back to Leśniewski.

Chwistek, in the early stage of his career (before he moved to Lvov), tried to improve Russell's ramified theory of types by deleting existence axioms, in particular the axiom of reducibility; he developed a version of the simple theory of types. This effort was very highly regarded by Russell himself:

Dr. Leon Chwistek . . . took a heroic course of dispensing with the axiom [of reducibility] without adopting any substitute . . . (Russell and Whitehead 1925: I, xiii)

After moving to Lvov, Chwistek abandoned his work on reforming Russell's systems and passed on to the construction of his own logical system, proposing another nominalistic basis for logic. It was rational semantics, a theory of systems of expressions that was intended to provide a uniform scheme for logic and mathematics. It starts with a list of primitive signs which is as economical as possible, then gives the rules of proof, and finally gives the rules of interpretation. Unfortunately, Chwistek was not able to complete his investigations, so many details are provisional or even unclear. However his semantics is sufficiently strong to be used for the arithmetic of natural numbers. In particular, Chwistek used his system to prove the Gödel incompleteness theorem.

8. THE HISTORY OF LOGIC

Łukasiewicz initiated a special programme of looking at the history of logic through the lens of modern logic. In particular, he regarded the old systems as predecessors of modern mathematical logic, and felt that it was unjust to denigrate them; he had in mind the attitude widely held by the originators of modern logic, including Frege and Russell, who maintained that modern logic completely broke with the past. Łukasiewicz argued that it was in fact Descartes who was responsible for the degeneration of logic and its slide towards psychologism. Even Leibniz, who deserves to be considered a predecessor of modern mathematical logic, could not stop this process.

9. THE APPLICATIONS OF LOGIC TO PHILOSOPHY

Logic exerted a great influence upon Polish philosophy. Above all, it became a pattern of precision and good scientific method, but in addition it was applied to many philosophical problems. The applications of logic to philosophy of science were straightforward. Polish philosophers of science did not propose any uniform doctrine: they were instead interested in concrete questions. Some results were quite remarkable.

Łukasiewicz, before concentrating on mathematical logic, had worked extensively on the theory of induction and the foundations of probability. He quickly gave up hope of a satisfactory theory of induction, and developed instead a deductivist methodology of theoretical science, anticipating the essential points of Popperism. In particular, according to Łukasiewicz: (a) induction has no real application in theoretical science; (b) the initial probability of any universal hypothesis is close to zero and cannot be increased by any further empirical research; (c) deduction is the only method in science; (d) deduction leads to falsification, not verification; (e) theories are human constructions, not mirrors of reality. Another important criticism of logical probability came from Tarski, who observed that it is not extensional.

Most Polish philosophers of science, however, believed in induction. Janina Hosiasson (who was married to Lindenbaum) did pioneering work in the axiomatic construction of inductive logic. The axioms are as follows (c is the confirmation function in Carnap's sense): (a) if h follows logically from W, then $c(h, W) = 1$; (b) if $\neg (h_1 \wedge h_2)$ follows logically from W, then $c(h_1 \vee h_2, W) = c(h_1, W) + c(h_2, W)$; (c) $c(h_1 \wedge h_2, W) = c(h_1, W) \times c(h_2, W \wedge h_1)$; (d) if sets of sentences W_1 and W_2 are equivalent, then $c(h, W_1) = c(h_2, W_2)$. Zawirski and Czeżowski followed Reichenbach in their attempts to base induction on the theory of probability; Zawirski tried to combine the many-valued logics of Łukasiewicz and Post in order to formulate a satisfactory logical theory of probability, and was also a pioneer in the application of many-valued logic to physics.

Ajdukiewicz and Kotarbiński formulated general epistemologies or ontologies based on logical ideas. At first, Ajdukiewicz radicalised the French conventionalism of Henri Poincaré and Pierre Duhem. Radical conventionalism is based on a theory of language modelled by logical formalism. A good language is connected (it has no isolated parts) and closed (no new expression can be introduced without changing the meanings of old items). A conceptual apparatus is a set of concepts occurring in a connected and closed language. According to Ajdukiewicz, conceptual apparatuses completely determine world-views. Thus, if we have an inconsistency between a theory and empirical data we can solve the problem by changing the language. The radicalisation of conventionalism consists in the status of empirical statements. In French conventionalism, we have freedom in manipulating principles, but in Ajdukiewicz's version, experiential reports are also subjected to rejection by changing language. Later Ajdukiewicz abandoned conventionalism in favour of semantic epistemology. In particular, he defended realism (that reality is independent of the subject) by applying metamathematical arguments. Roughly speaking, the concept of existence is semantic-like, contrary to the concept of knowledge which is syntactic-like. Since semantics is essentially richer than syntax, we are not able to reduce existence to sense data. Hence *esse = percipi* is false.

Kotarbiński's reism is a radically nominalistic ontology. For Kotarbiński, only material concrete things exist; there are no properties, relations, or events. Every meaningful sentence contains, apart from logical constants, only names of things, or is reducible to such sentences. Names of *abstracta* are called apparent names. There is an interesting connection between reism and Leśniewski's calculus of names. In Leśniewski's ontology a sentence of the form '*a* is *b*' is true, if the *a* is a non-empty singular name. Thus, Leśniewski's logic fits nominalistic needs much better than the first-order predicate logic. Abstract terms can be used, but this must be done very carefully, and only if related utterances are reducible to genuine reistic sentences – that is, sentences without apparent names – otherwise hypostases arise. A hypostasis consists in the assumption that something exists as a *denotatum* of an apparent name. Hypostases are responsible for pseudo-problems in philosophy. Although there are some affinities between reism and logical empiricism, the former is less radical than the latter, as is generally true of the relationship between the Vienna Circle and the Lvov-Warsaw school.

10. CONCLUSION

Leśniewski died in May 1939. Hosiasson, Lindenbaum, Pepis, Presburger, and Wajsberg, who were Jewish, were killed by the Nazis; Salamucha was also killed. Chwistek died in 1944. During the period from 1939 to 1945 or just after the war, Łukasiewicz, Tarski, Bocheński, Sobociński, Mehlberg, and Lejewski left Poland. Thus the war interrupted normal scientific work and education, although not completely. The Poles organised a remarkable system of clandestine teaching, and several logicians, including Andrzej, Grzegorczyk, H. Hiż, Jan Kalicki, Jerzy Łoś, and Helena Rasiowa, studied and graduated during these years. The losses of the Second World War were enormous, but they did not stop the development of logic in Poland. In addition, logicians who had emigrated also achieved many results of the first importance. Some of the most notable work done by Polish logicians up to approximately the mid-1950s includes paraconsistent logic (Jaśkowski), propositional logic (classical and intuitionistic) with variable functors (Łukasiewicz), Ł-modal systems (Łukasiewicz), Lewis's modal systems (Sobociński), model theory (Tarski, Łoś), the Kleene-Mostowski arithmetical hierarchy (Mostowski), and the Grzegorczyk hierarchy (Grzegorczyk).

LOGIC AND PHILOSOPHICAL ANALYSIS

THOMAS BALDWIN

As we look back to the philosophy of the period from 1914 to 1945, we tend to think of this as a time when 'analytic philosophy' flourished, though of course many other types of philosophy also flourished at this time (idealism, phenomenology, pragmatism, etc.). But what was this 'analytic philosophy' of which John Wisdom wrote when he opened his book *Problems of Mind and Matter* (1934) by saying 'It is to analytic philosophy that this book is intended to be introduction' (1934: 1)? Wisdom makes a start at answering this question by contrasting analytic philosophy with 'speculative' philosophy: the contrast is that speculative philosophy aims to provide new information (for example, by proving the existence of God), whereas analytic philosophy aims only to provide clearer knowledge of facts already known. Much the same contrast is to be found in the 'statement of policy' which opens the first issue of the journal *Analysis* in 1933: papers to be published will be concerned 'with the elucidation or explanation of facts . . . the general nature of which is, by common consent, already known; rather than with attempts to establish new kinds of fact about the world' (Vol. I: 1). As we shall see, the thesis that philosophy does not aim to provide new knowledge is indeed a central theme of many 'analytic' philosophers of this period. But first we need to investigate the relevant conception of analysis – 'philosophical' analysis.

The thesis that analysis of some kind has a contribution to make to philosophy is an old one. Typically, it rests on the thought that it helps one to understand complex phenomena if one can identify their constituent elements and method of combination. This thought is clear in the theories of ideas characteristic of much seventeenth- and eighteenth-century philosophy: 'complex' ideas are to be understood by analysing them into their constituent 'simple' ideas. One of Kant's insights was to subvert this tradition by affirming the priority of judgement over its constituents, and this led him to affirm the priority of synthesis over analysis (1787(B): 130). But Kant did not dispute the possibility of the analysis of concepts, and indeed contributed the distinction between analytic and synthetic truths. His initial account of this is that an analytic truth, such as that all bachelors are unmarried, is one whose truth depends only on the analysis of concepts (1781(A): 7). Notoriously, he then maintained that analytic truths include all those whose denial leads to contradiction (1781(A): 150); since trivial logical truths such as that all bachelors are bachelors do not depend in any obvious way on the analysis of a concept, this is not an obvious implication of his first account. Nonetheless, Kant was right to develop his account in this way, since it is only by assuming the truth of the judgement that all bachelors are bachelors that the analysis of the concept bachelor implies the truth of the judgement that all bachelors are unmarried. So if this latter judgement is to be an analytic truth, the assumed logical truth must also be an analytic truth; and if this is so, then logic in general must be, in some sense, analytic. This conclusion was reaffirmed by Frege at the end of the nineteenth century; but its significance was not really grasped until, as I shall explain below, Wittgenstein made it a central theme of his early philosophy.

Kant's immediate successors did not pursue this theme, however; instead they developed and extended the holistic aspects of his conception of the priority of judgement into a general thesis concerning the priority of wholes over their constituent parts, elements or 'moments'. Nor surprisingly, therefore, within their work analysis has only a provisional significance, as a method of identifying elements which, it is held, can only be properly understood when they are considered in the broader context of the synthetic wholes from which they have been abstracted. A crucial episode in the development of 'analytic philosophy' as we know it was the reaction of the young G. E. Moore against this holistic philosophy in his paper on 'The Nature of Judgment' (1899). For central to Moore's position was his belief that all complex phenomena, including judgements, are to be understood in terms of their constituent concepts, which are also the constituent elements of the world, so that 'A thing becomes intelligible first when it is analysed into its constituent concepts' (1899 [1993: 8]).

It is not easy to make sense of this position, but in Moore's ethical treatise *Principia Ethica* (1903) we find a more straightforward claim: 'good' is a 'simple notion' insofar as it is 'one of those innumerable objects of thought which are themselves incapable of definition, because they are the ultimate terms by reference to which whatever *is* capable of definition is to be defined' (1903 [1993: 61]). Moore writes here of 'definition', but he explains that the relevant conception of definition is not a 'verbal' definition through which one clarifies the use of words such as 'good', but an analysis of goodness itself, the meaning of the word. Since he holds that meanings are objects and properties, an analysis of meaning, so conceived, is equally an analysis of structure of the world. There is no sense/reference distinction to keep these projects apart.

Russell 'followed closely in Moore's footsteps' (as he put it later, 1959 [1995: 42]) in turning against the holism of the idealist philosophy he had initially supported; but he then transformed the prospects for a serious analytic philosophy by introducing new conceptions of *logical* analysis in the light of his work in logic during the first decade of the twentieth century. For this development implied that *philosophical* analysis was to be guided, in part at least, by logical considerations. A famously influential case in point was Russell's theory of descriptions (see 1905), which was taken to provide an analysis of the meaning of sentences involving definite descriptions such as 'The Queen of England is wise' by characterising this meaning as the 'proposition' that there is at least and at most one Queen of England, and she is wise.

There are several points here. (i) Russell provides substantial arguments for his theory, intended to show that his analysis is 'imperative'. Although the arguments are disputed, they show how questions about the merits of a logical analysis are closely tied to questions about the validity of various arguments. (ii) Although the analysis does not challenge the existence of the Queen of England, there is a sense in which the Queen is not a 'constituent' of the analysis since in specifying the proposition which gives the analysis one does not use a phrase which functions as a name of her. Thus although the analysis does not provide any reason for changing our beliefs about what things there are (e.g. a Queen of England), Russell took it that there is a sense in which things which we only describe are not fundamental; somewhat tendentiously, he took it that they can be regarded as 'logical constructions' or even 'logical fictions'. (iii) The analysis is described as an analysis of the 'proposition' expressed by the sentence 'The Queen of England is wise.' During most of the first decade of the twentieth century Russell, following Moore, took it that propositions, the meanings of indicative sentences, are complex objects, with constituents such as people and their properties. But the conception of false propositions of this kind is problematic; and it is easy to see how the analysis can be characterised without reference to propositions at all, as an analysis of what is meant by our use of sentences with definite descriptions, namely that their meaning is clarified when it is analysed in terms of our use of the corresponding sentence which lacks a definite description (i.e. 'There is at least and at most one Queen of England, and she is wise'). Thus the logical analysis of meaning can easily be represented as a logical analysis of the use of language.

By 1914 Russell had developed this conception of logical analysis into what he called 'the logical-analytic method' of philosophy (1914: v). A central presumption of this was the hypothesis of 'logical atomism', that is, that logical analysis of language can be used to identify the basic objects and properties which combine together in 'atomic' facts. These facts constitute the world and are represented by the true 'atomic' propositions (now conceived of as meaningful sentences) of an ideal language which is the result of subjecting our ordinary language to logical analysis. Russell's confidence in this approach was now such that he regarded it as the only fruitful way to conduct philosophical enquiry – 'every philosophical problem, when it is subjected to the necessary analysis and purification is found either to be not really philosophical at all, or else to be, in the sense in which we are using the word, logical' (1914: 33).

One might well wonder how Russell could affirm this in a book about knowledge (his title is *Our Knowledge of the External World*). It seems to be implied, somewhat implausibly, that logic alone is to provide solutions to the questions of epistemology. In fact it turns out that epistemology is built into the project via the conception of an atomic proposition; for in order that such a proposition be meaningful, Russell held that the names and predicates which occur within it must be such that we are 'acquainted' with the objects and properties referred to, where acquaintance is a cognitive relationship which provides an adequate basis for knowledge (see 1918–19 [1986: 173] for a clear statement of this point). So atomic propositions are such that if we can understand them at all, then we can find out whether they are true; and knowledge of truths of other kinds can, Russell thinks, be guaranteed by using logical techniques of abstraction to show how these truths (e.g. truths about the external world and other minds, with neither of which have we acquaintance) depend upon the truth of simple atomic propositions. So logic provides the structure of this account of the world and our knowledge of it; but its foundations are dictated more by epistemology than by logic. Thus Russell's analytic philosophy was in fact a hybrid, involving both logical and epistemological analysis.

As Russell acknowledged, in developing this position during the period from 1913 to 1914 he was much indebted to his 'pupil' Wittgenstein. But the differences between them became apparent when Wittgenstein published his *Tractatus Logico-Philosophicus* (1921). Wittgenstein here affirmed that 'Philosophy aims at the logical clarification of thoughts. Philosophy is not a body of doctrine but an activity' (4.112). This sounds at first like Russell's logical-analytic method; but there was an important difference in their implementation of their methods. Russell used his method to propound 'logical constructions' of the external world and other minds which are legitimately regarded as 'doctrines' whose merits and defects are proper objects for debate. Wittgenstein, by contrast, offers no such substantive theses, except concerning logic itself. This difference connects with a disagreement concerning ordinary language: for Wittgenstein, although ordinary language requires logical clarification, this clarification does not consist in providing a replacement for it by means of an ideal language involving logical constructions, as Russell supposed; instead, it just consists in making explicit all that is only implicit in our use of ordinary language, which is in fact in perfect logical order just as it is (5.5563).

Wittgenstein also rejects the epistemological dimension of Russell's method. There is no requirement that the 'elementary' propositions revealed by analysis be epistemologically basic; instead, it is the logical inferences we make, the 'application of logic' (5.557), which determines what propositions are elementary. For the basic condition on an elementary proposition is just that its truth be logically independent of that of all other propositions (5.134). According to Wittgenstein, in fact, epistemology is scarcely part of philosophy at all: the 'theory of knowledge' is just the 'philosophy of psychology', that is, it just involves logical analysis of our talk of knowledge, certainty, doubt, and the like; and this will show us that scepticism is 'obviously nonsensical' since it tries to raise a doubt where there is nothing at all that can be said.

A central aspect of Wittgenstein's position is his thesis that analytic propositions are propositions of logic, which are tautologies that say nothing (6.11). Wittgenstein here harks back to Kant and Frege. But whereas Frege held that the mark of logic was its universality, Wittgenstein denies that this accounts for the special status of logic. Equally, he denies that the truths of logic depend on the analysis of concepts, as in Kant's explicit account of analyticity; instead logic has to be antecedent to any such analysis. What then gives logic its special status? It is that it constitutes the a priori condition of the possibility of representation of truths. Wittgenstein holds that a language can be used to say something (to represent truths) only where its use satisfies the logical conditions that can be elaborated in the truth-tables. These truth-tables then generate, as a by-product, certain propositions as tautologies, and these are the propositions of logic. Since they are true come what may, they say nothing: but they show the way in which it is possible for a language to represent a world.

This transfer of Kant's general conception of the synthetic a priori to logic is ingenious. Wittgenstein extends his account to arithmetic and suggests that Kant's insistence on a role in this context for intuition, such that for Kant arithmetic is synthetic a priori, can be accommodated since 'in this case language itself provides the necessary intuition' (6.233). One way to characterise the resulting position would be to say that in the case of logic and arithmetic the analytic/synthetic distinction turns out not to apply. But that was not the way Wittgenstein was read in the 1920s and 1930s. Instead he was taken to have held that the truths of logic and arithmetic are analytic in the sense that they just represent the meaning of the logical connectives and number words. Since it was often also held that the meaning of language is a matter of convention, it was inferred that the special status of logic and arithmetic is due to the fact that 'they simply record our determination to use words in a certain fashion', as Ayer put it in *Language, Truth and Logic* (1936 [1971: 112]).

Ayer's book provided the classic statement in English of the 'logical empiricist' (or 'logical positivist') position developed in Vienna in the late 1920s and early 1930s by the philosopher-scientists of the Vienna Circle, especially Moritz Schlick and Rudolph Carnap. Schlick and Carnap were both greatly influenced by Wittgenstein (who was himself in Austria for some of this time), and they both accepted his thesis that philosophy could be only a method of logical analysis, a method for characterising 'the logic of science' which was to inform the new scientific world-conception which they sought to shape. There can be no distinctively philosophical knowledge, they held, for all genuine knowledge is scientific; hence 'as soon as one exactly formulates some question of philosophy as logic of science, one notes that it is a question of the logical analysis of the language of science' (Carnap 1934 [1967: 61]).

Despite the influence of Wittgenstein, it is clear from the very name – 'logical empiricism' – that this analytic programme in philosophy was like Russell's in having a strong epistemological content: the elementary propositions were to be foundations of knowledge. This, however, provided a straightforward route back into genuine philosophical debate: for the disagreements concerning the proper justification of claims to knowledge between foundationalists such as Schlick and Ayer and coherentists such as Carnap and Neurath could not be represented as debates concerning 'the logical analysis of the language of science'. So in this tradition it was clear by the end of the 1930s that philosophy could not be just the logical analysis of language.

I have concentrated so far on Russell, Wittgenstein, and the logical empiricists because it is their work which provided the core models of analytic philosophy. It should be noted, however, that many other philosophers of the period stressed the importance of philosophical analysis, but without committing themselves to a single conception of it or to supposing that philosophy is just analysis. Moore's later work is a clear case of this: he famously devoted much of his attention to the analysis of judgements of perception, committing himself to a sense-datum analysis which seems to be primarily motivated by epistemological considerations; but he also discussed such topics as the analysis of free-will and of the use of names in fictional discourse, where epistemological considerations have no place. Moore's later uses of philosophical analysis were, therefore, eclectic and unprogrammatic (in this respect it resembles the work of most contemporary analytic philosophers).

Moore's later work does not manifest any commitment to the 'simples', 'atoms', or 'elements' of his own early work and that of Russell, Wittgenstein, and others. It raises, therefore, the question as to how far one can undertake philosophical analysis without such a commitment. The thesis that this commitment is neither necessary nor desirable was advanced by C. I. Lewis in *Mind and World-Order* (1929). Lewis here combines an analytical conception of the a priori which draws on his work in logic with a holistic conception of meaning. So although he affirms that 'the a priori is not a material truth, . . . but is definitive or analytic in its nature' (1929: 231), he denies that logical analysis is 'dissection' into elements, and affirms instead that it is a way of marking the inferential relationships between propositions. Just as a spatial map shows spatial relationships without picking out any points as basic, a logical 'map' similarly shows logical relationships without any need for elementary propositions (1929: 81–2). Indeed, he remarks, once we think about the circularity inherent in logical theories, whereby we use logic to systematise logical inferences, we must see that in logic there is no such thing as 'intrinsic simplicity or indefinability' (1929: 107).

As a holist, therefore, Lewis rejects all conceptions of logical atomism; but, equally, he is insistent that logical analysis has a proper place in clarifying the a priori conditions which, he says, constitute our 'criteria for reality' (1929: 262–3). Lewis adds, however, the further claim that there is a plurality of logical systems, each internally consistent and generating its own set of analytic truths. This claim is substantiated by reference to the existence of alternative systems of logic which Lewis discussed in his important books of logic (see Lewis and Langford 1932: 222–3). It is not entirely clear whether he thinks of these different systems of logic as genuine rivals or as simply dealing with different subject matters. But he certainly ends up endorsing the thesis that the selection of a logical system must in the end be determined on pragmatic grounds (1929: 248).

Lewis's combination of holism and pragmatism is far removed from the atomism and rationalism of Russell and Wittgenstein. Yet he remained committed to the theses that a priori truth is analytic, and that logic should provide the basis of the requisite analysis. Carnap, independently, worked towards an essentially similar position which he articulated in terms of his famous distinction between 'internal' questions which assume the analytic rules of a language and 'external' questions which rely on pragmatic criteria to assess these analytic rules (Carnap 1950). There is then a direct route from the pragmatist positions of Lewis and Carnap into the post-1945 debates concerning the analytic/synthetic distinction between Quine and Carnap. But there are many other links forward in the evolution of analytic philosophy; most obviously from Wittgenstein's *Tractatus* to his later *Philosophical Investigations*, but also from Moore's later work to the conception of philosophical analysis informed by a concern with 'ordinary language' which was characteristic of post-war Oxford philosophy. The development of analytic philosophy post-1945 is a complex story, and one which is still evolving. But the foundations were laid in the works discussed here.

SECTION NINE

THE DIVERSITY OF PHILOSOPHY

32

THE CONTINUING IDEALIST TRADITION

LESLIE ARMOUR

In the thirty years after 1914, idealist philosophers found themselves divided and uncertain. Many left boxes of unpublished material which record their struggles. Much that remains will prove to be of interest as philosophers return to some of the traditional questions, but much of it is as yet unexplored.

Despite the fact that a concern with language was prominent in the British idealist movement, by the end of this period the movement, along with its realist rival, was eclipsed by a 'linguistic philosophy' which was stridently anti-metaphysical in tone. In France the near-idealist *philosophie de l'esprit* was similarly eased out by existentialism, though Jean Guitton (1939) thought a logical idealist development of Malebranche remained one of the two great philosophical possibilities. In Austria and Germany the idealist tradition continued in the work of the phenomenological movement which flourished alongside the brief flowering of logical positivism; by the end of the period, however, phenomenology itself gave way to Heidegger's philosophy of being which rejects idealism by affirming the priority of being over thought. Only in Italy did idealism remain the dominant mode of thought, and the conflicting idealist philosophies of Giovanni Gentile and Benedetto Croce were the dominant strands, fascist and liberal, of Italian political thought (idealism also held its own in Canada; see Armour and Trott (1981)).

May Sinclair said (1917: v) that, if you were an idealist philosopher, 'you [could] not be quite sure whether you [were] putting in an appearance too late or much too early'. Widely circulated arguments had been raised by Bertrand Russell, G. E. Moore, and the American realists against idealism. The idealism they criticised affirmed that mind and its objects form a very close unity, such that the material world cannot be the ultimate reality because its parts are separable and therefore lack the requisite unity. Moore's counter argument (Moore 1903) was that thinking and perceiving must be separate from their objects. Russell similarly urged the impossibility of a seamless system encompassing the world, on the ground that the implied system of internal relations falsified the facts of individuality. These arguments were cogent against the doctrines objected to, but they assumed that the idealists held positions more extreme than most of them would have accepted. Moore could quote A. E. Taylor, but few philosophers confused perceiving with perceptions, and all twentieth-century idealists agreed that the Absolute must exhibit itself in a variety of forms. Considerably later, A. J. Ayer (1936 [1946: 36]), quoting a sentence from F. H. Bradley, argued that idealism gives rise to nonsense, the kind of nonsense that logical positivism would eradicate. But Ayer's alleged 'nonsense' sentence, 'the Absolute enters into evolution but does not itself evolve' (Bradley 1893: 499), is not necessarily devoid of sense. A similar sentence, 'Gravity enters into evolution but is itself incapable of evolution and progress', is quite sensible.

It was popular currents of thought as much as specific arguments which undermined idealism. The bloody disaster that was the First World War made it hard to believe in the universe as an expression of a rational order that embraced human life and civilisation; it called into question the belief that philosophers as well as scientists were well fitted to discover the nature of 'reality'. At the same time the definition of 'idealism' became increasingly difficult. Idealism asserts the primacy of ideas. But the notion is slippery. Platonic idealism – never far from the surface of the work of many English-speaking idealists, as Bernard Bosanquet often hinted and J. H. Muirhead (1931) insisted – centres on the view that the explanation of the world is ultimately to be found in a transcendent rational order, so that high order values pervade the universe and the good and the true must come together. Yet while idealist theologians like William Temple and physicists like Eddington and Jeans still believed that science and religion could support one another, enthusiasm for the notion that reason pervaded the universe was hard to arouse after a world war.

At the opposite extreme of the idealist spectrum is the notion that reality is to be found in immediate experience whose atomic components are 'ideas' in a sense derived from Descartes and Locke. Giovanni Gentile associated this doctrine with Berkeley, and was attacked by Bosanquet for holding it himself. Despite G. E. Moore's view that this was the basic form of idealism, few philosophers have ever held it. A. A. Luce (1954) defended it, but he was almost alone. Even Berkeley who gave it circulation mentioned the more Platonic view that the world is 'the natural language of God' in his early work, and later adopted a still more Platonic view.

There were valiant defences and some new foundations, but in 1945 philosophers returning to Oxford, once the heart of the English-speaking idealist movement, found only H. J. Paton and G. R. G. Mure, the one immersed mainly in Kant studies and the other soon to be happily ensconced as the Warden of Merton College (Bradley's old college) but rather isolated philosophically.

Mure's own ideas appeared later (1958, 1978); Paton (1955) eventually expressed his own views.

PHYSICS, BIOLOGY, AND METAPHYSICS

The success of science supported the view that philosophy was a 'second-order' discipline which analysed ordinary and scientific views of the world, but did not add anything new. But idealist philosophers did think they had something to add.

Bosanquet (1923) talked about relativity theory and its tendency to make the universe seem observer-centred, but he had his doubts about philosophers like Samuel Alexander who used current notions of evolution and cosmological development to support their metaphysics (Alexander 1920). Sir Arthur Eddington's (1920, 1928, 1929, 1939) thesis was that science had disposed of the materialist notion that the world consists of little lumps of matter scattered through an absolute space. He favoured instead a conception of the universe as an expression of mathematical intelligence; Sir James Jeans stated the position most clearly. 'The final truth about a phenomenon resides in the mathematical description of it . . . The making of models or pictures to explain mathematical formulas, and the phenomena they describe is not a step towards, but a step away from reality; it is like making graven images of a spirit' (1930 [1937: 176–7]). This universe of 'pure thought', he conceded, poses problems about time. His solution – which he saw as related to Berkeley's – was to see reality as unrolling in our minds and in the mind of an eternal spirit: 'If the universe is a universe of thought, then it [the universe] must be an act of thought.' He was still, however, physicist enough to warn his readers to be cautious of such generalisations.

A more subtle view was suggested by Viscount Haldane (1921) and further developed in a long correspondence with Gustavus Watts Cunningham (1916–24). The thesis – perhaps the developed form of it really belongs to Watts Cunningham – is that our knowledge shapes our consciousness in a way which makes the two inseparable. John Elof Boodin tried hard to integrate his philosophy with the scientific cosmologies of his time, but there was a constant tension between his notions of a universe which exhibited progress and the physics of his time. The tension was sometimes downplayed, but a hand-written note (1921) exposes the pith of his position more clearly than his main books (1925, 1934). In the note he argued that science has so far proved itself good at analysis and at charting the dispersion of energy and the running-down of systems, but its only explanation for the apparent 'upward movement' of evolution is 'chance', and this, he says, cannot be a sufficient explanation.

METAPHYSICS AND THE QUESTIONS OF PHILOSOPHERS

Susan Stebbing (1937) questioned the positions of Jeans and Eddington. As the development of analytic philosophy focused attention on problems of meaning, the charge that idealist philosophers 'misused language' gained currency. If a philosopher maintains that material objects, or time, are 'unreal', the claim implies that everything that moves and meets the ordinary criteria of materiality – elephants, trains, and stars, for instance – has been judged to have some important deficiency. This deficiency is not noticed by ordinary people or by scientific investigators. Either, then, idealist philosophers have additional knowledge or they are using words in an unusual way. It seemed obvious to many philosophers that the language problem was central, though questions of the legitimatisation of language often proved harder to settle even than metaphysical questions.

J. M. E. McTaggart (1921–7) thought that much of the deficiency in scientific and common sense accounts of the world stemmed from unacceptable concepts of time. Although McTaggart's thesis that time is 'unreal' looked at first like a standard case of a philosopher misusing language, behind his arguments there were in fact serious questions about language. He believed that the 'fixed' earlier-later series in which Cromwell's rule always comes before Charles II's is incompatible with the past-present-future series which is always changing and is incoherent in itself. And yet without change there is no time. The argument almost certainly depends on the fact that one cannot define 'past', 'present', and 'future' except in terms of other temporal expressions like 'what was', 'what is', and 'what will be', and that one cannot identify the 'past' or the 'future' as one identifies yellow things by pointing at them.

There is, anyway, a reason for philosophers to say something of their own about reality. Physicists and philosophers ask different questions. R. G. Collingwood (1938a, 1940) thought truth depended (in part) on relations of questions and answers; and philosophers do ask questions that physicists, chemists, and biologists do not ask: one does not find articles in *Nature* about whether the world consists of substances or events or both. Some philosophers used the fact that physics was developing in a way which made fields seem more fundamental than particles as a reason for believing that the evidence favours the abolition of substances other than the Absolute. If reality is a field, and thus a unity without really discrete parts, they thought, it must be spiritual rather than material, since matter requires spatial discreteness. McTaggart, by contrast, insisted on keeping the notion of substance. He produced a simple argument for the existence of substance defined as 'something [which] exists, has qualities and is related without itself being either a quality or a relation' (1921: 68). A man can be happy; he may also be wise and good. But wisdom and goodness (or any aggregate of them) cannot be happy. Qualities then must be predicated of something other than other qualities.

This again looks like an argument which depends on the way we talk. Still, substance is central to McTaggart's metaphysical system. He added that such 'substances', being discrete, must be describable in ways which distinguish each from everything else. He associated the necessary conditions for absolute discreteness with being a centre of perception. Perceivers were thus the ultimately real entities and they got their individuality from their interrelations (many thought McTaggart's basic intuition about this was better than his technical arguments).

H. W. B. Joseph – who himself never really wavered from idealism, though he worried about how to express it – noticed the need for a 'metaphysical subject' and tried to clarify these issues. He urged (1916: 166–8) that propositions have grammatical, logical, and metaphysical subjects. He took an example: 'Belladonna dilates the pupil.' There is a grammatical subject – 'belladonna'. But if the proposition answers the question 'What dilates the pupil?', the *logical* subject is 'dilating the pupil' whereas if the proposition answers the question 'What do you know about belladonna?' the *logical* subject is 'belladonna'. But neither of these need be the 'metaphysical' subject.

If the proposition is true and about the world, it must be 'about something' that is determinate enough to be, as Joseph puts it, 'what we are thinking about'. It can be vague, as with 'It is raining', but not indeterminate beyond what is needed for reference. Joseph says the subject thought about is most often considered 'in ordinary thinking' to be 'a concrete object'. But the metaphysical subject – what the referred to thing really is – might be the Absolute if the Absolute is the only thing which can be really independent and a final referent. The issue is really about what counts as a genuine particular. In other unpublished writings (1931) Joseph struggled to put precision on the idea of a genuine particular, but the concept proved resistant. His problems about 'real particulars' had something to do with his itch to retain ordinary ways of talking which, like John Cook Wilson (1926), he thought reflected an accumulation of human experience.

These arguments suggest the existence of different starting points, originating either in experience or in basic choices about language. Collingwood urged that these are 'absolute presuppositions' (1940), which we can explore in their historical contexts; we should see philosophy as the interplay between them. Collingwood is probably here developing a notion suggested by J. A. Smith. In the surviving fragments of his unpublished Gifford Lectures of 1929–30, Smith had emphasised the importance of 'suppositions' in philosophy, and the context for this can be reconstructed from Smith's (also unpublished) Hibbert Lectures of 1914–16. Smith begins here with an account of ultimate reality as pure spirit in the sense of Giovanni Gentile, but he quickly argues that reality requires the introduction of plurality. Pure spirit must manifest itself as a series of discrete states, none of which reveals its full nature. Hence although there remains the objective truth that reality is the set of manifestations of spirit, reality manifests itself in a way which admits of a variety of interpretations, that is, as a variety of 'suppositions' (or, in Collingwood's term, 'absolute presuppositions'). This position had the effect of associating time with the most fundamental nature of the Absolute, a position attacked by Bosanquet in *The Meeting of Extremes in Contemporary Philosophy* (1923). Smith wrote to Alexander (1926) that 'the universe is essentially a history'. He added 'I admit Bosanquet has shaken me' and 'I have alarmed [H. W. B.] Joseph.' Moved by Bosanquet, perhaps, he allowed that not everything is within time. There is a timeless good behind the successive appearances of the Absolute.

IDEALISM AND THE PROBLEM OF KNOWLEDGE

Platonic idealism had its origins in the notion that knowledge consists of a grasp of ideas which transcend the immediacies of sense, and that knowledge of or about the world consists in an understanding of the ways in which these ideas form that world through participation. Bosanquet's *Meeting of Extremes* shows one of the forms in which that idea persisted into the 1920s. Bosanquet saw the world as the expression of the absolute idea, and spoke of the Absolute as being beyond space and time. 'Time is in the Absolute, not the Absolute in time' is a slogan which runs through the book. The argument is that the bits of science and other knowledge fit together like the answers to a crossword puzzle (a metaphor recently revived by Susan Haack, 1993). Just as we believe we have the right answer when the intersecting lines of the puzzle all make sense, so it is with our picture of the world. Yet we believe the picture represents a real unity which was there before we filled in the blanks. This unity is Bosanquet's Absolute.

Bosanquet had successors, such as R. F. Alfred Hoernlé (see Hoernlé 1927). Rupert Lodge was another, though of a very different sort. Using Bosanquet's test of rational unity, he conceded (1937) that there is more than one such rational system. Following one line in *The Meeting of Extremes*, he suggested that a reasonable understanding of idealism, realism, and pragmatism would see them as three complementary visions with different, but rational, starting points. There were also echoes of ideas not far from Bosanquet's in France in the work of Leon Brunschvicg, whose work had a Kantian slant and in that of René Le Senne (see Brunschvicg 1939; Le Senne 1930). Emile Meyerson (1931) associated idealism with an idea of a universal intelligibility which was close to

Bosanquet's as a way of satisfying what he took to be the logical presuppositions of the sciences.

Bosanquet (1920, 1923) did not believe that the truth could be deduced from self-evident first principles (see also Gustavus Watts Cunningham 1933). These two simply believed that the puzzle-bits of experience must fit together. Croce gave a historical slant to this task: he returned to Vico's critique of the Cartesian emphasis on self-evident principles and insisted on the importance of history as a way of unifying knowledge since all our knowledge itself has a history. Equally, for Croce, history is a way of restoring the values of the humanities to the centre of epistemological concern: since history is something we make it is something we know from the inside and there is a role for art in the process of coming to know it.

Collingwood (1938a, 1946) developed these ideas in the context of a theory of historical knowledge: the past is gone, but thoughts can be rethought and the past can be reenacted in the mind of the historian. Since history includes the parade of absolute presuppositions which have been influential in the past, there is a sense in which history can overcome these limitations. Was this a development of the theory of overlapping forms which begins in *Speculum Mentis* (1924) and a way of ordering the kinds of knowledge mentioned there – art, religion, science, history, and philosophy? Or was it a new departure? Collingwood scholars remain divided. In *Speculum Mentis*, history is an advance on science in the sense that science can be represented within history; philosophy is not another subject matter, but the perspective from which the others can be seen as united.

Collingwood's epistemology is in fact best seen in the context of his almost life-long concern with the ontological argument. He insisted (1935) on the reality of an ultimate 'universal' which provides intelligible order to the world. Acceptance of this doctrine, he said (1919), was the alternative to scepticism and dogmatism. His guiding notion seems to have been that this intelligibility took many forms which exhibited themselves throughout history as a variety of systems, each of which rests, in our minds, on 'absolute presuppositions'. As suggested above, in this doctrine Collingwood may have been influenced by his friend J. A. Smith who had been the first to suggest that all systems which we can actually construct rest on 'suppositions'.

Ernst Cassirer's work has some affinity with the works of Collingwood and Smith. *The Philosophy of Symbolic Forms* (1923–96) began with Kant and addressed the central puzzle: how are we to understand Kant's three critiques? His answer was that they represent different aspects of the human 'spirit', pulling together the perspectives of pure reason, practical reason, and aesthetic and religious sensibility. The world is invariably understood through 'symbolic forms', but that tells us something of its nature: the one world has a variety of aspects. Cassirer's system is Kantian in that it focuses on the structures of thought and the ways in which thoughts are expressed, but it has links with later idealism in that it suggests that reality is a unity whose nature it is to have a variety of expressions.

IDEALISM AND RELIGION

Idealism gives mind (sometimes 'spirit') a central role. So it is natural to suppose that it admits of a religious interpretation. But the idealists themselves took a variety of positions. Collingwood continued to see Christianity as a central force in civilisation, but he played no part in organised religion, though he was quite close to B. H. Streeter (see Streeter 1927). McTaggart, by contrast, was an avowed atheist, and Bosanquet said he hoped to live to see the churches turned into museums. Yet Bosanquet hoped for human progress, and McTaggart believed in immortality. Indeed if orthodoxy were to allow many persons in the Godhead, McTaggart's theology would be Christianity democratised: the persons remain separate, but they are so closely intertwined that love between them is inevitable.

One could be acceptably orthodox within the Anglican community and be Hegelian in the spirit of the brothers John and Edward Caird (see Metz 1936 and Jones and Muirhead 1921). William Temple, who began as a philosophy don at Oxford, rose through the church to occupy his father's old post as Archbishop of Canterbury. He used revelation (1934) to avoid the vagueness of the accounts of the universal mind provided by the later idealists. Temple's God – a benign and personalised Absolute – was close to the world, and Temple himself was a democratic socialist. Canon Bernard Streeter also accepted the idealist arguments as far as they went but argued (1927) that Christianity demanded something more than Bosanquet's intelligibility.

After the death of Josiah Royce in 1916 the personalist movement begun by Borden Parker Bowne (1908) played an increasing role in American philosophy. Its interwar leaders, Edgar Sheffield Brightman and Ralph Tyler Flewelling, the founding editor of *The Personalist*, were philosophers of religion and culture. Brightman, who began his career as a biblical scholar, had his personal faith shaken by the death of his young wife. He analysed (1930, 1940) the problem of God and evil and concluded that because the traditonal conception of God could not account for 'dysteleological surds' – the type of evil which is 'inherently and irreducibly evil and contains within itself no principle of development or im-provement' (1940: 245–6) theists should withdraw to a more modest conception of God as a finite being (Bruce Marshall's novel *The Month of the Falling Leaves*, which chronicles the adventures of a young man who writes a thesis on the dysteleological surd and finds that it is a best-seller in Poland, is one of the spoofs Brightman provoked). Flewelling taught at the University of Southern California, one of the many American universities with Methodist associations. Like its sister institutions, Boston University and Ohio Wesleyan, USC played a major part in the development of personal idealism, a philosophy which blended well with historical Methodist enthusiasm. The association of personal idealism with powerful Methodist institutions is almost the only case of a close association of American philosophy with a religious denomination other than the traditional alliance between Catholics and Thomists.

Flewelling (1935) said he was 'more or less in sympathy' with Royce, Bosanquet, and Hoernlé. But he added that these people 'despise us' because 'personalism is not monistic but pluralistic. It stresses the independence of particular selves.' He saw his own philosophy as 'sharply contradictory to that of Hegel'. Flewelling had strong connections with Pierre Lecomte du Noüy and associated himself with George Holmes Howison as well as with Brightman. Like McTaggart, Flewelling rejected the notion of an all-encompassing Absolute as something which was logically empty, but unlike McTaggart he insisted that experience demanded an acceptance of the reality of time. He comes close (1935) to the position developed by Howison and John Watson (1897) that God is a community, but there remains in his philosophy a more traditional 'Intelligence' whose reality is expressed through the human community.

William Ernest Hocking was closer to Hegel, though he claimed to have replaced Hegel's logical dialectic with a 'dialectic of experience'. He was often critical of orthodoxy, but his metaphysical and religious theories (1912, 1940) remained consistent with his view that Christianity was ultimately a superior religion, despite his attempts at a religious synthesis, which in many ways strongly resembled those of the Indian idealist Sarvepalli Radhakrishnan (1932). In the same vein, K. C. Bhattacharyya (1976) continued to explore the relations between idealism and Hinduism, and M. M. Sharif, a Moslem philosopher, adopted (1966) a Leibnizian ontology (with Hegelian modifications) as a philosophical underpinning for an Islamic view of reality (Bhattacharyya 1976 and Sharif 1966 are both compilations from earlier works, mainly within the period covered by this chapter).

Boodin (1934) took a Platonic view, frequently citing Henry More and associating God with the source of the multiplicity of forms which descend from the original unity of things. Boodin's philosophy resembles Whitehead's but provides more challenge to the claims of science while Whitehead (1929) gives his Platonic eternal objects less work to do.

MORALS AND POLITICS

Idealists have favoured ethical theories which emphasise self-realisation and po-litical theories which emphasise community. There is a paradox here. One way of resolving this, exemplified in Bosanquet's later work, is to question the ultimate metaphysical reality of the self. He acknowledged no necessarily continuing self which might survive death and be 'perfected', though 'perfection' was always his term for the highest value. In knowledge, in action, and in sharpening our awareness, we come closer to the Absolute. But if we came too close we would disappear, for the Absolute was said to be more real than us earthlings. Thus idealists such as Bosanquet sought to overcome the paradox by holding that the Absolute could only be fully expressed as a plurality. It was too rich to be exhausted by any one person or even any one culture. John Watson (1919) used this argument to defend political federalism.

Some idealists, like A. E. Taylor (1932), made moral theory the basis of their metaphysics. They tended to found their theories not on the logical analysis of the concepts of goodness and duty – though Taylor analysed concepts, too – but on experiences like love, as well as the necessity of reconciling happiness and duty. They often saw mind and reason as directed towards the transcendence of the immediate and the particular. The tradition on which these idealists drew had it that evil is always a negation, a lack of something, so that goodness and being are therefore ultimately equatable, culminating in the goodness or being of God, or the perfection of the Absolute as what lacks nothing. This explains something of the fascination of thinkers like Collingwood and even Bosanquet for a kind of Hegelian ontological argument.

Such arguments support communitarianism, though Collingwood and McTaggart both balanced this with a strong emphasis on the importance of the individual. Though Bosanquet's metaphysical theory seemed to give the community priority and *The Philosophical Theory of the State* (1889) attacked ex-treme individualism, he was in practice a liberal. Croce's liberalism had its roots in his belief that history unfolds in the life of the individual who is the source of creativity. Although Gentile's association with Mussolini was more than acci-dental, he himself did not originally see fascism as oppressive and on some issues he was more liberal than the 'official' liberal Croce.

In England, France, and North America, idealists clustered near the political centre. Bosanquet admired the Labour Party aloofly. R. B. Haldane was first a Liberal and then a Labour Lord Chancellor. Jacob Gould Schurman, a Canadian president of Cornell University, also became president of the then middle-of-the-road New York State Republican Party (Schurman was also a serious philosopher in his own right; see Armour and Trott 1981). R. F. A. Hoernlé who taught at Harvard went to South Africa where he battled the growing apartheid movement in the name of an ethical universalism (see Hoernlé 1939). The personalists generally stood on the left-liberal side of national politics, striving, again, to balance the demands of individual and community. In France, Brunschvicg, though regarded as the archetypical bourgeois philosopher, was in fact constantly engaged in projects for social reform, and René Le Senne stood on the same side. Gentile, on the far right, was a rare exception.

ART AND KNOWLEDGE

Bosanquet was always interested in aesthetics and eventually wrote a massive history of the subject (1934), but Collingwood wrote to Samuel Alexander (1928) saying 'Bosanquet knows nothing about art'; he added 'Bradley knows something, but won't say.' Clearly, there was no single view. Nonetheless all the idealists sought to integrate art into the basic structures of human experience. Thus although 'aesthetic experience' calls to mind the high arts – especially poetry, music, drama, and the serious novel – Croce (1920) and Collingwood (1938b), who were the most significant idealist philosophers of art, located art at the roots of human experience. Art comes from the way in which we put order on the data of experience; hence it plays a role in everyone's life. Croce and Collingwood disagreed (at least in Collingwood's view) about the way in which art works. Croce thought of art as a first step in the organisation of knowledge and then as a means of communication. Collingwood saw it as something which feeds the imagination and thus contributes to conscious awareness. But they agreed that art is a free activity which is both an end in itself and something leading on to higher modes of thought.

TRANSFORMATIONS IN SPECULATIVE PHILOSOPHY

JAMES BRADLEY

EXISTENCE

Existence, like tea, can be taken strong or weak. Speculative philosophy charac-teristically defends a strong theory of existence, while other kinds of philosophy strenuously defend a weak theory. So fundamental is the difference between strong and weak theories of existence to any account we give of the nature of things that the debate between them lies at the very heart of philosophy.

Admittedly, weak theorists would regard such a claim as contentious, for weak theorists characteristically understand existence in terms of the analysis which Frege developed in the 1880s: statements of the type 'horses exist' are interpreted as quantificational statements to the effect that 'for some x, x is a horse'. On this view, existence amounts to no more than the satisfaction or instantiation of a predicate, such as '. . . is a horse'. To exist is to answer a description. Whether one is talking about prime numbers, stones, or people, existence statements are defined in the same way, as saying that something satisfies a description. The weak theory of existence is thus not properly a theory of existence at all. Existence is simply removed from the realm of reflection and replaced by an account of the logical structure of language. Yet such claims do not impress strong theorists, the speculative philosophers, for speculative philosophy holds that existence is more than the silent, featureless pendant of the 'existential' quantifier ('for some x'). The 'is' of existence is not to be reduced to the 'is' of instantiation.

Both strong and weak theories of existence are concerned with the nature of the real understood as that which is incapable of further demonstration, that which is not further derivable, that which is ultimate in the order of analysis. However, speculative philosophy maintains that the so-called ultimates of other kinds of philosophy are in fact open to further enquiry and derivation. It pushes philosophy's commitment to intellectual enquiry to its limits by asking whether or not whatever is claimed to be ultimate can be understood to be *self-explanatory*. The self-explanatory, if there be such, is that which is not further demonstrable or derivable in that it provides all the reasons required to explain the nature of existence. Modern accounts do not identify it with a special kind of entity which contains all the reasons for its existence in itself, nor do they depend on any a priori appeal to the principle that nothing is without a reason. Rather, the self-explanatory is usually understood as a set of interdependent relations that only together and by way of their descriptive adequacy to experience satisfy the speculative enquiry. The search for such an ultimate is the basis of the critique of the quantificational treatment of existence which, as will emerge, is so marked a feature of speculative philosophy after 1900. Speculative philosophy can be conceived as putting to logical analysis what may be called the speculative question of existence: 'What is it for something to be instantiated?'

This question is an expression of the traditional speculative attempt to establish a strong theory of existence as a theory of what may be termed 'actual existence' or 'actualisation' on account of the *activity* which, in one form or another, speculative philosophy characteristically maintains to constitute the self-explanatory ultimate. Yet those terms are not to be taken as implying that actualisation is to be understood as a matter of causal activity, efficient or final. Self-explanatory activity, if there be such, is what defines the nature of reasons, causes, and their relation.

SERIES

The concept of series is a fundamental motif of modern as of traditional speculative philosophies. It is the driving and distinctive concern of most modern speculative thinkers, even if often elaborated in critical engagement with the absolute idealisms of Hegel, Royce, and Bradley. The focus of this chapter will be the different theories of serial actualisation developed by four of the most original and influential philosophers of seriality – Bergson and Heidegger in the continental tradition, Peirce and Whitehead in the Anglo-American tradition. Nevertheless, the general serial orientation of modern speculative philosophy is evident in Nietzsche's stoic doctrine of eternal recurrence, in the dialectical materialism of the Marxist tradition, in the later James's growing buds or drops of experience, in the order of Alexander's space-time matrix, in McTaggart's account of the eternal community of loving spirits in terms of the 'C-series', in Collingwood's historical series of absolute presuppositions, and in Cassirer's Neo-Kantian functional rules of serial synthesis. Cassirer subjects the status of the proposition to systematic criticism, arguing that it requires a reference to the synthetic activity of a cognitive subject, even though that activity is not something over and above the operation of a functional order, as it is in Kant (Cassirer 1910 [1923: 16–26], 1923–9 [1957: III, 279–480]).

It should not be surprising that speculative philosophy views actualisation in terms of serial relations. Because anything that is intelligible is ordered, and order is minimally a matter of a two terms and their relation, a speculative or actualising order must be composed of at least two terms and their relation. Thus a speculative or actualising order characteristically has three elements, as in the late Plato's triad of the Unlimited, Limit, and their Mixture. To overcome the dualism inherent in the platonic account of actualisation as a struggle between form and matter, the Neo-Platonists generally define the constituents of their triadic schemes as an hierarchical order or procession of determinations out of the first term of the series. The processions are rendered intelligible to the extent that they stand to one another in serial relations which are asymmetrical, transitive, connected, irreflexive, and intransitive. Neo-Platonic accounts of actualisation as a threefold causal emanation from the transcendent One are taken up and revised in terms of eminent cause in the complex medieval doctrine of the Trinity as the procession from the Father of the Son in the unity of the Spirit. Here the two terms and their relation are regarded as coequal in that they are the dynamical grounds of their own mutual configuration. While it is held that God's transcendent nature is the eternally active and irreducible or 'subsistent' relations of the persons, the relations of Son and Spirit to human nature and its history are defined in terms of the 'mission' (*missio*) and 'gift' (*donum, datio*) of grace. Creation in general is understood as standing in a cycle-serial relation to the Creator (*exitus et reditus*). More recently, there are the immanently causal and monistic-serial accounts of actualisation elaborated in Spinoza's doctrine of infinite substance, with its attributes and modes, in the trinitarian dynamic of Hegel's absolute subject, and in the later Schelling's self-evolving threefold God.

Although in some modern speculative philosophers, notably Bergson, intransitive triadic structure is primarily a matter of the relations of tensed time, it plays a wider role in Peirce, the later Heidegger, and to some extent Whitehead. In Bergson, the instances of the serial structure of actualisation are unique, intransitively related, and stand in a cumulative relation to their predecessors, but they are not analysed as having a complex, internal order. In Peirce and Whitehead, the instances of the series are unique, intransitively related, and cumulative, but they are endowed with complex, internally intransitive, triadic structures. In the later Heidegger, serial actualisation is intransitive and non-cumulative; its three basic terms operate indivisibly, though without any cyclical loop-back to the first term of the series. Both cumulative and non-cumulative theories of serial actualisation can be divided into two types, which, for want of better words, can be termed 'subjective' and 'objective' theories. Subjective theories define actualisation anthropocentrically, by reference to some distinctive feature of human experience. Objective theories define actualisation in terms of structures which are mind-independent and primordial in the sense that human experience, however significant, is held to be only one instance of their operation. The history of some of the most important modern speculative thinkers is the history of their move from subjective to objective theories of serial actualisation (Bergson, Heidegger).

While, as will emerge, modern serial theory is a self-conscious development of the speculative tradition (both Peirce and Heidegger, for example, are experts in medieval philosophy), its main distinctive features are its explicit opposition to the idea of a completely realised reality of any kind, and its concomitant preoccupation with the nature and status of temporal existence. All notions of an independently existing substance are abandoned and replaced by definitions of entities as intrinsically immanent and relational. Thus the notion of a directing or totalising meta-subject as a *tertium quid* over and above its component structures is rejected, and the subject is redefined either in terms of, or as an effect of, differentiating series.

AESTHETIC SERIES: BERGSON AND HEIDEGGER

The most influential modern serial theories in recent times have been those of Bergson and Heidegger. They are best understood in the context of Kant's treatment of time as a matter of 'aesthetic intuition', which means three things. First, time is underivable or irreducible in that it cannot be analysed by reference to anything which is nontemporal. Secondly, time is nonconceptual in that it is not a relation of concept to instance, for there is no general time of which particular times are instances: times are always parts of the whole of time. Thirdly, time is a matter of 'aesthetic' intuition in that it is not the product of cognitive synthesis on the part of the subject and is thus given not made.

By applying this Kantian analysis to tensed time, Bergson and Heidegger attempt from within the limits of experience to show that existence is not exhausted by existential quantification and is more than a matter of cognition or language. Bergson argues against what he takes to be Aristotle's view of time, that only the limited, segmented parts of time are real. He reverses this analysis, claiming that the real nature of time resides not in its segmented parts but in its given, experiential character as duration (*durée réelle*): the irreducible, purely qualitative, cumulative flow of a multiplicity of states which forms an indivisible, heterogenous continuum. For Bergson, actual existence is nothing else than the serial indivisibility of durational becoming, and all attempts to partition it into quantifiable items are no more than derivative and distorting 'spatialising' abstractions. In Bergson's later writings, duration develops from being a subjective, into an objective principle of actualisation which he terms *élan vital* and which has strong Neo-Platonic overtones.

Heidegger challenges Bergson's reading of Aristotle (Crocker 1997: 405–23), and criticises both as mirror-images of one another (Heidegger 1975 [1982: 239–57]; 1978 [1984: 203–11]). Temporality is a matter neither of limited times nor an indivisible continuum, but of the activity of actualisation which makes such distinctions possible. This activity Heidegger calls 'temporalisation' (*Zeitigung*); it is defined in *Being and Time* (1927) and other writings of that period as a matter of the self-unfolding, 'ekstatic' (literally, 'standing outside of itself') order of the tenses that, in contrast to Husserl's analysis (1928 [1964]), constitute a differential structure of which human subjectivity is a consequence.

Even in the late 1920s, however, Heidegger turns his attention to what he calls the 'ontological difference' between temporalisation as tense-order and the activity of temporalisation itself, which he characterises as the 'There is' or 'It gives' (*Es gibt*) and which he comes to term 'the event' (*das Ereignis*; Heidegger, 1978 [1984: 210] and 1989). The notion of 'the event' is developed into a fully objective theory of actualisation, and in his late writings Heidegger finally endows it with a trinitarian structure (see Harris 1997: 54–65) as a matter of the 'It gives', the 'sending' (*die Sendung*; Latin, *missio*) and the 'gift' (*die Gabe*; Latin, *donum, datio*): loosely, the unfolding of the structure of tensed time is the sending of finite situatedness, which offers to human nature the gift of the openness of time ((Heidegger 1969 [1972: 1–24]). Heidegger's threefold is thus defined in immanentist fashion: it is strictly an intransitive, aesthetic serial structure constituted by its differential, finitising, activity and yet it is ever in ekstatic movement beyond any given finite situation. It is always more than, and so 'held back' (Greek: *epoche*) and 'concealed' in, any given finite situation. As such, Heidegger's non-productive, radically immanent 'event' is a finitising of the infinite and an infinitising of the finite. His is a world of pure surface in which – as always in modern serial theory – difference is prior to sameness.

Despite their evident roots in the speculative tradition, the radical immanentism of Bergson and Heidegger leads them to elaborate striking critiques of traditional speculative philosophy, which are prosecuted in three main areas: the critique of the synthesising subject, of philosophical representation, and of philosophical method. Heidegger is the more influential figure here.

First, the critique of the subject is best expressed in Heidegger's triadic account of the artist, artwork, and audience as an internally related complex of terms such that none could be what it is without the others and none is privileged over the others (Heidegger 1960 [1971: 15–88]). It follows that the subject (artist or audience) is not a synthetic principle of actualisation but is constituted by its relations to other components of the complex as their effect. It is no accident that Heidegger's critique of the synthetic subject goes hand-in-hand with an orientation to the work of art, for he takes the work of art as a model and instance of finite actualisation. More precisely, Heidegger appropriates Kant's account of the aesthetic judgement of the work of art as a matter of 'purposiveness without purpose' (i.e. the spontaneous adaptive play of the cognitive faculties without pre-established purpose); detached from Kant's theory of cognition, this analysis is employed to define actualisation as a complex, adaptive structure without any pre-given end or purpose. Intransitive serial actualisation is thus an *aesthetic* series in a double sense: it is a given structure that is nothing else than the active interplay of its elements.

Heidegger's account of finite actualisation in terms of aesthetic adaptiveness means that human actions are not primarily understood as directed by the rational exercise of free-will on the part of reflective agent-subjects. Rather, freedom for Heidegger, as for Nietzsche and Bergson, is the freedom of aesthetic spontaneity: human actions are seen as the underived irruption of complexes of factors that, like great works of art, themselves create the principles by which they are to be assessed. It is not too much to say that Heidegger drew what he took to be the appropriate conclusions for the Germany of the 1930s.

Secondly, the aesthetic serialists have rejected the modes of representation traditionally employed in philosophical and particularly speculative enquiry: categorial and analogical analysis. The speculative description of the real in terms of a scheme of categories is repudiated because categorial principles are held to be, not aesthetic operations, but productive or synthetic principles and are thus seen as abandoning the principle of immanence and referring things away from themselves to an originating ground, cognitive or otherwise. Similarly, the speculative method of analogy is repudiated on account of its connection with philosophical notions of production: the resembling series is regarded as representing in varying degrees an eminent term or perfection which is understood as the productive principle and complete reality behind the series. Working always in terms of production or synthesis, speculative philosophy since Plato is thus revealed as caught within the sway of technological thinking. Its discourse is the discourse of power, of control and manipulation, reification and domination, in contrast to which aesthetic-serial thinking opens up new possibilities of thought and action.

Thirdly, the critique of representation raises the question of the status of the aesthetic-serial descriptions in the name of which that critique is prosecuted. To avoid entanglement in the question of self-referential consistency here, Bergson constantly negates his metaphorical accounts of duration, while Heidegger casts his discourse in an interrogative and ostensive mode, explicitly invoking the tradition of negative theology (Heidegger 1969 [1972: 47]). Their language thus enacts the evacuation of its own predicative content by gesturing away from itself. The task of thinking is to deconstruct the conceptualising impulse from within so that the unsayable nature of pure difference, which is the unique, unrepeatable duration or event, can manifest itself.

THE LOGIC OF SERIES: PEIRCE AND WHITEHEAD

Although the speculative serial theories of Peirce and Whitehead are generally less well known than those of Bergson and Heidegger, and Whitehead in particular is often regarded as a marginal figure, their originality and importance as speculative philosophers cannot be overemphasised. Their work is quite distinct from that of their continental counterparts in that it is elaborated in close relation to modern developments in mathematics and the logic of relations (to which they themselves signally contributed), and it is marked by an insistence on the rationality of actualisation and of freedom. They see themselves as the inheritors of the speculative tradition and as bringing about a renaissance of speculative philosophy: their work has the empiricist intent of rescuing rational structure from the absolute necessities of Mind or pure Reason, characteristic of European rationalism and idealism, and the rationalist intent of restoring intelligible order to those structures of experience which speculative and anti-speculative philosophers alike have often consigned to the realm of the nonrational, typically under the rubrics of 'ineffability', 'feeling', or 'action'.

Despite the constantly developing character and astonishing range of Peirce's work, the most direct way of characterising the overall import of his speculative thought is as a self-conscious reworking and transformation of the trinitarian-serial theory of actualisation. In line with his emphatic declarations of indebtedness to Augustine, Aquinas, Hegel, and, above all, Duns Scotus, actualisation is understood by Peirce as a threefold serial structure, which he defines in terms of the categories of Firstness or Spontaneity, Secondness or Existence, and Thirdness, which is Community or Continuity.

Firstness, like the Father in traditional trinitarianism, is the *principium non de principio*, the principle without origin or ground. It is interpreted by Peirce as free, spontaneous activity, which is intelligible in that it is intrinsically self-differentiating (Peirce 1931–68, VI, 214–20). Spontaneity is the primordial origin of all things, that in their nature which cannot be exhaustively traced back to antecedents and for which no doctrine of mechanical necessity or lawlike regularity can account. As the primordial origin, spontaneity is the ground of Secondness, which, like the Son, is the principle of existence, the individuality or *haecceitas* of an entity. Individuality or *haecceitas* is secondness because it is a dyadic relation: it is the positive, nonqualitative difference between one thing and another without reference to any other kind of relation. This is Peirce's reinterpretation of the Scotist doctrine of the primacy of will over intellect: the individual is not the product of necessity but of freedom, and so in this sense always involves chance or contingent variation, however slight. It is the *haecceitas* of an entity which for Peirce makes possible the operation of the universal and the existential quantifier. Having discovered quantification in the early 1880s, independently of Frege, he argues that the generality of logical structure does not allow descriptions to specify their objects and that reference can be explained only by postulating a characteristic of objects in virtue of which they can be named by the nonqualitative term 'this' (Peirce 1931–68: III, 393, VIII, 41). For Peirce, the theory of *haecceitas* provides that characteristic, without which logical analysis is incomplete.

Thirdness, like the Spirit, is the principle of community: it is the systematic order of relations in which any two things stand and as such is the realm of mediation, law, and meaning. (Peirce's favourite example is, unsurprisingly, the triadic structure of gift-giving.) In an attempt to redevelop the Augustinian project of the *vestigia trinitatis* ('the traces of the Trinity') in which the structures of all things are analysed as having the threefold structure of the divine, Peirce prosecutes what he calls his 'triadomania' with great originality (and some procrustean contortions) across the entire field of philosophy. Thus, for example, his 'phenomenology' of experience reworks the triadic faculty-psychology of Augustine's *De Trinitate* in nineteenth-century terms: firstness is interpreted as the intensity of pure quality and defined in terms of J. S. Mill's 'pure possibilities of sensation'; secondness is 'struggle', the resistance or force of 'fact'; and thirdness is the activity of interpretation, understood in Kantian terms as synthesis. (For a brilliant elaboration of Peirce's theory of interpretation by one of the few philosophers who have understood his trinitarianism, see Royce 1913: II).

That Peirce's speculative Trinity is not to be confused with the medieval Creator God, the post-Kantian absolute, or Heidegger's threefold 'event', is best seen by considering it in the context of the tension within traditional trinitarian analysis between the 'economic' and the 'essential' Trinity. The economic Trinity refers to the history or economy of creation and salvation (sometimes interpreted as the biblical order in which the ages of the Father, Son, and Spirit follow one another). The essential Trinity refers to the interpretation of the divine nature, under the influence of Greek philosophy, as the completely realised unity of three co-inherent activities or persons. Peirce resolves the tension between the two by abandoning the idea of a threefold which (as in Schelling) resolves its own basic nature independently of finite order. The first speculative metaphysician ever to do so, he defines the evolution of the threefold as subject to its finite determinations: the threefold grows with its own spontaneous differentiation. Thus Peirce's threefold is both an intransitive structure which characterises all things, and it is also, in each of its instances, a cumulative serial principle which has no actuality apart from its particular, intrinsically situated activity of realisation. Peirce's 'pragmaticism' (as he preferred to call it) is properly to be understood as the analysis of that activity. It constitutes an 'evolutionary cosmology' which applies, not only to human nature, but to all things, and which is radically immanent in character, allowing him to develop a striking theory of universals as 'generals', or real, ontologically vague structures of possibility, which, as in the case of the threefold itself, grow with the movement of actualisation.

However, Peirce's trinitarian series is not only intransitive and cumulative; it is also cyclic-serial or teleological, as is indicated by his account of thirdness as the 'final opinion' or, more widely, the 'final community'. As a matter of the evolution of cosmic order, which 'must reach, however vaguely, beyond this geological epoch, beyond all bounds' (Peirce 1931–68: II, 654), the final community is essentially a re-thinking of the doctrine of the Spirit. It is the infinite movement of the entire cosmos towards the completeness of the kingdom of God, which is only partially realised in any order and thus always remains to be fulfilled. So understood, the notion of final opinion or community is in Peirce at once both real and regulative (not, as is usually thought, either one or the other). Some of the wider implications of Peirce's serialism are best considered in the context of Whitehead's writings.

As the revision and culmination of his work in *Principia Mathematica* (1910–13), Whitehead calls his speculative philosophy a 'generalized mathematics' (Whitehead 1947: 109). In *Process and Reality* (1929a) he builds on the brilliant success of the Frege-Russell generalisation of the mathematical function as the concept or propositional function. He takes functional structure as primitive and generalises it in two distinguishable senses.

First, Whitehead generalises the *meaning* of the function. That is, he seeks the most general description of the nature of the function in order to provide a meta-functional description of the nature and conditions of any function at all. Secondly, Whitehead generalises the *range* of the function over any identifiable entity, including concrete objects such as stones and people, so that his description of the function is intended to provide an account of the nature of all that is. He thus gives functional structure what he calls 'ultimate' status. This means in part that he regards functional structure as primitive (as not further definable or derivable from any higher principle) and as transcendental (as universal in range or application). However, Whitehead's functional analysis is a transcendental theory, not of cognition, but of the constitution of all order. Moreover, his ontology of functional structure provides a self-explanatory description of the nature of things which he terms 'process' or 'creative process'. Process is composed of three main interdependent elements, each of which are intransitively threefold in nature (1929 [1978: 21, 87–8]).

Starting out from the set-theoretical definition of the function as the class of many-to-one relations, Whitehead makes two basic moves. He interprets the general nature of the function constructively, as a matter of mapping activity or the establishment of many-to-one correspondences between a domain and a codomain; and he defines the speculative concept of the activity of actualisation wholly in terms of mapping. Many-to-one mapping activity or 'creativity' is not any specific ordered relation, but the activity of ordering relations. It is not a self-differentiating origin, but is intrinsically relative to, and determined by, its instances. Its primary instance is God, who maps from indeterminacy to structure itself (the realm of 'eternal objects'). Finite instances or 'occasions' of mapping are defined as iterative in the sense that they take for their bases the results of antecedent mappings, both divine and finite. As a matter of finite iteration, there is here no totality to generate reflexive paradoxes. Further, defined in terms of iterative succession, every finite occasion of mapping requires an 'initial value' or predecessor; every occasion cumulatively 'contains' its predecessor in its domain (which Whitehead analyses in terms of a complex theory of immediacy or 'feeling'); and the values of any given occasion are not knowable in advance but are defined by context. Because any occasion of the rule-constructing activity of mapping is not exhaustively traceable to its antecedents, it is held to be the principle of its own activity in that it (and nothing else) determines how it constructs or synthesises itself out of its predecessors. Thus the extent to which any new term added to the series derives from the determinacy of the antecedent terms always involves some element of free construction. In Whitehead as in Peirce, there is no opposition between metaphysical realism and constructivism, for the real is itself a finite, immanent activity of construction.

THE DEFENCE OF SPECULATIVE REASON

The significance of Peirce and Whitehead resides in their defence of speculative reason against its critique by continental and analytical thinkers alike. First, serial actualisation is for both the condition of quantification and is a concrete unity of whole and part, a nonconceptual ultimate which, as in Kant's analysis of time, has a structure which is perfectly rational and intelligible. Thus everything can be said, without denying the irreducibility of the gap between thought and existence. There is no need here to abandon speculative reflection, either for the unsayability of pure difference or for naturalism. (John Dewey's *Experience and Nature* (1929) offers a naturalist philosophy of series, of which Whitehead remarked that it was a good description but not a theory (Lowe 1966: 67). That is, it takes seriality as ultimate, but does not give an account of what it is about seriality that makes it ultimate: namely, its self-explanatory structure.) Secondly, the *mathesis universalis* of Peirce and Whitehead's serial analysis is not a matter of mathematical equalisation but a non-manipulative logic of freedom. For they do not define power as domination; rather, using a key word in the Anglo-American speculative tradition (remarkable in its absence from Heideggerian writings), they define power as love. Theirs is a *mathesis amoris*: as Peirce puts it, serial actualisation is *agape*, the unconditional bestowal of love on that which is, whether good or evil. Thirdly, therefore, they have no hesitation in elaborating and constantly reconstructing complex categorial schemes as theories of power or activity, which are non-dogmatic and self-referentially consistent in that they are defined as experimental hypotheses that have the finite, revisable status of 'claims' in constructivist mathematics: they are neither true nor false, but rules for philosophical construction (Bradley 1996: 233–45).

Perhaps, however, the most unusual feature of the serial analyses of Peirce and Whitehead is their different ways of preserving one of the central concerns of speculative philosophy since Descartes: the concept of the subject. In Peirce, the subject is any kind of mediating activity, individual or communal. In Whitehead, the subject or occasion is a matter of synthesising activity, of which there is no higher finite instance than human consciousness. For both, functional structure and activity are not fundamentally different in kind. The subject is not merely an effect of the differential structures (as in Heidegger and many logical analysts), but a constitutive element of them. Serial order is not a relational activity without an actor, but is realised only through the activities of the subjects of which it is the condition. Furthermore, the teleology of subjective activity is defined aesthetically: the self-actualisation of serially situated subjects is a matter of the achievement of qualitative intensity or adaptiveness. The upshot is that the opposition between aesthetic and productive analysis is dissolved in an immanentist analysis which allows the rational freedom of self-conscious agent-subjects to be defined as a complex instance of the universal freedom of serial activity, thereby preserving, in marked contrast to Bergson and Heidegger, the possibility of a rational politics. (Dorothy Emmet told me that she heard Whitehead say of *Process and Reality*, 'It's a defence of liberalism!') In the context of the work of Peirce and Whitehead, perhaps it is not too much to say that speculative reason will, as always, attend the funeral of its gravediggers.

REALISM, NATURALISM, AND PRAGMATISM

CORNELIUS DELANEY

The reaction to nineteenth-century idealism took many forms. On the epistemological front several species of realism reasserted themselves while on the metaphysical stage a variety of naturalistic tempers made their appearances. In addition, pragmatism, in a guise that purported to transcend the terms of the traditional polemic, came into the ascendancy. While there clearly were major European versions of these various reactions to idealism, and more specifically British versions (Moore, Russell, and F. C. S. Schiller), the concerted reaction to idealism in terms of realism, naturalism, and pragmatism was a decidedly American phenomenon.

1. REALISMS

The most powerful American spokesperson for the philosophical perspective of idealism was Josiah Royce. From his position at Harvard his version of absolute idealism exerted considerable influence on American thought. The initial realist reaction to this idealist hegemony took a cooperative form when six philosophers (Ralph Barton Perry, Edwin Holt, William Pepperell Montague, Walter Pitkin, Edward Spaulding, and Walter Marvin) published in 1910 'A Program and First Platform of Six Realists' followed in 1912 by a cooperative volume entitled *The New Realism* (Holt *et al.* 1912) for which each provided an essay. This volume gave rise to the designation 'The New Realists' for this group of six.

Although these six differed on many particulars, they did concur on several matters of philosophical style and epistemological substance that characterised their reaction to absolute idealism. Procedurally, they endorsed a cooperative and piecemeal approach to philosophical problems and they were constitutionally inclined to a closeness of analysis that would prepare the way for later philosophical tendencies. Substantively, they were in agreement on several epistemological stances that constituted the centrepieces of their 'refutation of idealism'.

This New Realism was a form of 'direct realism' that viewed the notions of mediation and representation in knowledge as disastrous gambits on the slippery slope to idealism and saw knowledge rather as a matter of being directly presented with external independent objects. Downplaying 'subjectivity' and 'the privacy of consciousness' they rejected the fundamentality of epistemology and denied that the entities under investigation in logic, mathematics, or science were 'mental' in any ordinary sense of that word. Mathematical and physical objects were taken to be directly confronted as features of the external world. The metaphysical views underlying this presentational realism varied considerably among the six. Perry and Holt espoused a version of the 'neutral monist' view of William James (their mentor at Harvard) while the other four differed metaphysically both from the Harvard pair and among themselves.

The core view of cognition was that the objects of knowledge were immediately and directly present to awareness while existing and having their essential characteristics independent of that relation. The things known were not the products of the knowing relation nor even conditioned in any fundamental way by their being known. This 'refutation of idealism' focused on pointing out the fallacy involved in moving from the truism that 'every object of knowledge is known' to the extremely contentious claim that 'its being consists in its being known'. The fact that we are obviously at the centre of what we know need tell us nothing about the nature of what we know. Perry dubbed this fact about us as knowers 'the Egocentric predicament' and supplemented this basic observation with independent arguments to the effect that the objects of knowledge were in fact independent of the knowing relation.

This New Realism as a version of direct realism had as its primary conceptual obstacle 'the facts of relativity', that is, error, illusion, perceptual variation, and valuation. Various ingenious moves were made to accommodate the distinction between veridical and non-veridical cognitive states with the 'left wing' of the New Realists (Perry and Holt) arguing for the objective existence of all objects of cognition including illusions and errors while the 'right wing' backed off this claim in favour of some weaker status for illusions and errors such as 'subsistence'. However, the attempt to deal with these obvious phenomena without the introduction of 'mental intermediaries' between the knower and the known foundered. This monistic tour de force gave way to a second cooperative venture by another group of American philosophers, the Critical Realists, who would acknowledge the mediation of the mental in our cognitive grasp of the independently real world.

Critical Realism reasserted the fundamentality of epistemology and saw itself as a mean between the speculative excess of idealism and the epistemological naiveté of the New Realists. The term 'Critical Realism' was the title of a book on epistemology by Roy Wood Sellars published in 1916 but its more general use to designate the broader movement derives from the 1920 cooperative volume *Essays in Critical Realism: A Cooperative Study of the Problem of Knowledge* containing position papers by Durant Drake, A. O. Lovejoy, J. B. Pratt, A. K. Rogers, C. A. Strong, George Santayana, and Roy Wood Sellars. At the highest level of generality Critical Realism purports to integrate the positive insights of both the new realism and the earlier idealism. With the former it maintains that the primary object of perceptual knowledge is the independent physical world, and with the latter it acknowledges that it is not the physical object as such that is immediately present to consciousness but rather some intermediate mental state broadly construed. Whereas both New Realism and idealism shared the conviction that no such mediated account of independent objects could be maintained, the Critical Realists felt that only if our knowledge of the independent world was explained in terms of a process involving 'mental' mediation could error, illusion, and perceptual variation be rendered intelligible. The project was to fashion account cognition involving mental mediation that avoided the pitfalls of Lockean representationalism by carefully distinguishing between the object known and the mental state through which it was known. Only by acknowledging this dimension of cognitive complexity could one account for knowledge of a genuinely independent world and at the same time have an explanation of the non-vertical cognitive states of error and illusion.

The Critical Realists took perception as the paradigmatic case of knowing and distinguished three ingredients in the act of perception, namely, (1) the perceiver, (2) the datum or character-complex present to the perceiver, and (3) the independent object perceived. To avoid the slippery slope to Lockean representationalism and then idealism, they underscored the fact that this datum or character-complex was not itself directly known but was rather the means by which the independent physical object was known. The 'vehicle of knowledge' was distinct from the object of knowledge without being an impediment to the latter's being directly known.

With regard to the precise nature of this datum, this intermediary in cognition, the critical realists divided into two quite different camps. Santayana, Drake, Strong, and Rogers construed this datum or character complex to be an 'essence' which both informs the cognitive state and is (or is not) exemplified by the concrete object of knowledge. These essences were not particular existents but intuited characteristics that the particular object may be taken to have. If it does have it, the cognitive state is veridical; if it does not, we have error or illusion. Lovejoy, Pratt, and Sellars shied away from this essence doctrine and maintained that the intermediary datum was indeed a mental existent but one that had the property of pointing beyond itself to the independent object known. These internal mental states were intrinsically intentional enabling the knower to transcend his own mental states and ascribe to independent objects certain characteristics that these objects may or may not possess. Whatever the differences between these two camps of critical realists, they agreed that this intermediary in knowledge was not something we directly knew and from which we then inferred to the characteristics of independent objects. Thus they avoided Lockean representationalism while providing logical space for illusion and error.

Other than this united epistemological front against both idealism and New Realism, the Critical Realists did not have much in common. Some were dualists, some were panpsychists and some were materialists, so the direction in which their broader philosophical projects developed had no real unity. So, like the New Realists before them, the co-operative dimension of their project dissipated and the 'realist movements' faded away. But they left their mark: idealism continued to recede from view as the baton of criticism was passed on to naturalism.

2. NATURALISM

There was a naturalistic temper in American philosophy in the 1920s that was not only opposed to idealism *per se* but to all forms of dualism such as mind/nature or supernatural/natural that were seen as residues of the Platonic-Cartesian picture that eventually led to idealism. These dualisms were to be overcome by the reassertion of a unified natural order of which man was an integral part.

This naturalistic temper took two quite different forms. A tradition which might be called 'New York Naturalism' was methodological in nature and took great pains to distinguish itself from 'materialism' which it viewed as reductive. The emphasis was on the unity of nature and its multi-level strata rather than on the 'stuff' of which it was composed. The traditional dualities of mind/body, natural/supernatural, individual/social, and fact/value were to be overcome by an appeal to dynamic natural processes rather than reduced to a material substrate. The unifying factor was a universal empirical methodology rather than a reductive metaphysics. This empirical tradition was in sharp contrast to a form of naturalism that was more substantive in nature and did not shy away from the designation 'materialism', while being careful to insist that it was a non-reductive variety of materialism.

There were several strains of this empirical naturalism. One strain grew out of a new appreciation of a naturalised Aristotle under the guidance of F. J. E. Woodbridge at Columbia (Woodbridge 1926, 1937). His Aristotle was not that of the Middle Ages but rather an Aristotle as proto-scientist who understood human cognition as a thoroughly natural process involving different levels of structure within a unified natural order. Spinoza was seen as the authentic heir of Aristotle and the metaphysical vision was that of a unified natural order that could be described on different but compatible levels. The world we saw, the world that we acted in, and the world science described comprised the one natural order revealing itself in different ways. J. H. Randall continued this strain of naturalism into the next generation.

A second strain of this methodological naturalism was the more thorough-going scientific naturalism of Morris R. Cohen (Cohen 1931, 1933; Cohen and Nagel 1934). For Cohen, science was most fundamentally scientific method and scientific method was for him (following Peirce) the only reliable way of grasping the structure of the natural world. Cohen's scientific naturalism emphasised the interconnectedness of all things and proposed scientific method as providing access to the structure of connectedness. He was concerned to argue against a reductively empiricist concept of science which construed the natural order as an order of experiences and in favour of a more rationalistic conception of science that enabled the enquirer to get at the real structures of the natural world in which we live. Science was reason concretised and gave us access to the rational structure of the unified natural order. Ernest Nagel continued this strain of naturalism into the next generation.

The third strain of this methodological naturalism (and by far the most influential), was the experimental naturalism of John Dewey (Dewey 1925, 1938). Whereas Cohen stressed the rational dimension of scientific method Dewey stressed the empirical dimension with the resulting views being markedly different. Like Cohen, Dewey defined his naturalism in terms of the primacy of scientific method as providing our cognitive access to the structure of reality but his focus on the pragmatically empirical dimension of science led his speculation in a different direction.

For Dewey this unity of method mirrored a unity of nature not marked by any discontinuities that would require the introduction of non-natural categories. The sharp dualisms of mind/body, individual/social, secular/religious, and, most importantly, fact/value he viewed as conceptual constructs that had long out-lived their usefulness. The inherited dualisms had to be overcome, particularly the one involving fact and value inasmuch as it functioned to block the use of reason as the guide for human action. On Dewey's view man naturally has values as well as beliefs. Given human nature there are certain activities and states of affairs that man naturally prizes, enjoys, and values. The human problem is that these are not always easy to come by nor are they always compatible. We are forced to deal with the problem of what we really want and what we ought to pursue.

Dewey advocated the extension of scientific method to these domains. The deliberative process culminating in a practical judgement, is not radically unlike the deliberative process culminating in a factual belief. Both kinds of judgement can be responsible or irresponsible, right or wrong. This deliberative sense of evaluation as a process presupposed the more basic sense of evaluation having to do with those dimensions of human experience we prize and find fulfilling. Here too there is a dimension of appropriateness, one grounded in the kinds of beings we are where the 'we' includes our social history and development. On these matters Dewey had a very Greek view, albeit one transposed into a modern evolutionary perspective. Fundamental questions of value and human fulfilment ultimately involve our conception of the human community, and this in turn led Dewey to the issues of democracy and education. Sidney Hook continued this strain of naturalism into the next generation.

A contemporary of Dewey in his Michigan and Chicago years, George Herbert Mead, was a seminal mind of the highest order who worked out the details of a Deweyan-like naturalism (Dewey 1925, 1938). A founding father of what became the tradition of symbolic interactionism in psychology and sociology, Mead developed an impressive and quite detailed account of the 'emergence' of mind, consciousness, and self-consciousness in a thoroughly evolutionary setting. Language in a sense that included significant gestures was the mechanism of the social evolution that resulted in individuals with minds who then bootstrapped themselves into the modern human world. Mead's detailed account of social emergence provided the fine-grained structure of the naturalistic account of value and society that Dewey made publicly available.

Woodbridge's classical naturalism, Cohen's scientific naturalism, and Dewey's experiential naturalism all agreed that nature was a unified, ordered system in which we lived and moved and had our being. They were opposed to any and all bifurcations of nature. However, they were equally opposed to a reductive materialism that would render unintelligible or illusory the distinctive features of the world revealed to us in human experience. Dewey in particular saw his naturalism as a kind of empiricism and invoked a pragmatic view of scientific theories to render compatible the primacy of scientific method with the irreducibility of the salient features of our experienced world. Scientific theories are construed as tools for predicting and controlling experience. The salient features of our experienced world are the beginnings and endings of complex natural affairs with science revealing the ways in which natural events are ordered in history. This understanding gives us a handle on those natural processes so that we can secure or avoid the desirable or undesirable of them. Dewey called his view about scientific theories 'instrumentalism' because it construed theories not as pictures of the world in conflict with experience but as tools for guiding us through our experienced world.

This multi-faceted picture of methodological naturalism contrasts sharply with another more substantive tradition in American naturalism in this same period. Not all who thought of themselves as naturalists were so reluctant to embrace the implications of an ontologically more robust 'materialism'. The *locus classicus* for the articulation of the deep difference between 'methodological naturalism' and 'materialistic naturalism' was the 1925–7 exchange between Dewey and Santayana on the differences between what Santayana saw as Dewey's 'half-hearted' naturalism and what Dewey saw as Santayana's 'broken-backed' version of naturalism (Santayana 1925, Dewey 1927).

Santayana acknowledged what he and Dewey had in common, that is, the rejection of dualism, the recognition as basic the interactions of physical objects, and taking science seriously as our fundamental way of understanding these interactions. He saw the differences between them, however, as even greater. Santayana saw the fundamental difference as traceable to 'the dominance of the foreground' in Dewey's naturalism, a foreground 'whose name is experience'. He saw Dewey as an empiricist first, not an individual empiricist but a social empiricist, and a naturalist secondarily and only because those experiences happened to be a function of physical processes and thereby the objects of science. Santayana charged Dewey with anthropocentrism in his reduction of nature to the sum of those 'situations' and 'histories' that are related to human life and serve as the background to our projects.

For Santayana nature was just the total system of material processes that began long before the advent of any experience and which will persist long after its demise. Nature had neither foreground nor background, neither centre nor periphery; it has its ontological standing in and of itself quite independently of our projects. He viewed those naturalisms that were filtered through empiricism as 'half-hearted and short-winded' and as such presenting a skewed perspective on nature and our place in it. Old-fashioned materialism was the honest view warranted by science.

Dewey responded with some name-calling of his own, maintaining that Santayana's non-perspectival materialism was a 'broken-backed' version of naturalism that was scientifically passé. It called for a sharp divide between nature as it really is and nature as it appears to humans. Santayana's picture of nature as a material system would be cognitively accessible from our experienced world only by a mysterious 'animal faith' which Dewey saw as opening the door to the dual spectres of dualism and supernaturalism again. Dewey acknowledged that his naturalism drew its fundamental categories from experience, from the foreground, but insisted that it was the foreground 'of nature' and therefore not a screen that concealed the background but was rather nature's own point of access to her deepest structures.

Roy Wood Sellars joined the fray on Santayana's side (Sellars 1943). He viewed Dewey's empirical naturalism as epistemologically impoverished and ontologically shallow. Scientific theories should not be viewed merely instrumentally but realistically, as providing our best account of the fundamental entities and structures of our world. Whereas Dewey construed scientific 'entities' (and hence the scientific picture of the world) as mere constructs that enable us to deal effectively with our lived world, Sellars construed scientific entities realistically according existential status to the microscopic objects of the scientific picture, maybe not as presently described but in their ultimately adequate scientific characterisation. Sidney Hook joined the fray on Dewey's side arguing that this metaphysical materialism was cut from the same cloth as idealism and that neither did justice to the controlled empirical enquiry that was natural science (Hook 1944). What was fundamental to scientific naturalism was not a theory of 'stuff' but a view of 'method', a view that Dewey's empirical naturalism provided. Sellars replied that this methodological naturalism was not enough; it needed a reformed materialism for its conceptual completion (Sellars 1944). Clearly this debate between the naturalisms hinged on the issue of a pragmatic versus a straightforwardly realistic interpretation of scientific objects. Sellars saw this and thought pragmatism had to be transcended; Dewey, of course, being the third of the great Trinity of American pragmatists, viewed pragmatism as sufficient.

3. PRAGMATISM

'Pragmatism' has always been a multivalent term. In the 1870s C. S. Peirce initially articulated it as a general theory of meaning modelled on the social dimension of science; at the turn of the century William James developed it into a theory of truth modelled on individual psychology; in the 1920s John Dewey expanded it under the rubric 'instrumentalism' to a general theory of value and interrelated knowledge, action and value at both the individual and the social levels. It was through Dewey that pragmatism permeated American culture, both moral and political, and became 'the' American contribution to philosophy (Dewey 1922, 1938).

Dewey's pragmatism (which he called 'instrumentalism') was a general theory of rational enquiry modelled on science but applicable to all spheres of human life. It was basically a theory about how thinking functions to solve problems and thus guide action in all domains from science to morals. Thinking was a matter of confronting problematic situations with new conceptualisations which enable us to overcome the problem and thus restore our experienced world to some kind of equilibrium. The structure of reflective thought is thus future oriented and involves the movement from the recognition and articulation of a felt difficulty to the elaboration of 'hypotheses' as possible resolutions of the difficulty, and thence to the verification or falsification of the proposed resolutions.

On this view knowing is a kind of doing and the criterion of knowledge is 'warranted assertibility'. On the first point, Dewey felt that one of the cardinal errors of philosophy from Plato to the modern period was what he termed 'the spectator theory of knowledge'. Knowledge had been viewed as a kind of passive recording of facts and its success seen as a matter of the correspondence of our beliefs to these acknowledged facts. To the contrary, Dewey viewed knowing as a constructive conceptual activity, which involved the anticipation and guidance of our adjustment to future experiential interactions with our environment. For him concepts were seen to be instruments or tools for dealing with our experienced world. Furthermore, the purpose of thinking was to effect some alteration in the problematic experiential situation, and for this purpose some concatenations of concepts were more effective than others in resolving the problem. This would be the context in which 'truth' is normally invoked but Dewey proposed in its stead 'warranted assertibility'. He eschewed the notion of truth because he saw it as too suggestive of a static and finalised correspondence between two separate orders. He saw successful cognition, on the contrary, as a more dynamic matter of a present resolution of a problematic situation resulting in a satisfactory reconstruction of our experience, which he termed a 'consummation'. 'Warranted assertibility' was the success characterisation, having an appropriately normative connotation without the excess metaphysical baggage.

This theory about the structure of cognition applied to evaluation as well as description, values as well as facts. Ideas are seen as validated by their usefulness in guiding conduct both in the speculative realm and in the practical realm. The deliberative process culminating in a practical judgement is not unlike the deliberative process culminating in a factual belief. Both kinds of judgement can be responsible or irresponsible, right or wrong, and both kinds of judgement presume certain goals to be attained. While theoretical enquiry has its own evaluative setting, our practical deliberations as to how to comport ourselves presuppose a basic evaluative grasp of those dimensions of human experience which we prize and find fulfilling. Here too is a dimension of appropriateness, one grounded in the kinds of beings we are where the 'we' include our social history and development. On this issue, Dewey was an Aristotelian, but a modern evolutionary Aristotelian. We are developing, organic systems with natures that are intrinsically social, and these natures circumscribe possible models of human fulfillment.

Grounded intelligence should be our ultimate guide for action but given our social natures the proximate guides for action would be socially instilled habits. This moved Dewey to situate his moral philosophy in a general conception of a developing human community involving an elaborate theory of democracy, including a specification of the role that education played therein. In this way his commitment to the ideal of scientific reason as a guide to a fulfilling human life led him to devote a considerable percentage of his energy to social philosophy and to educational theory. In fact, the most pervasive and persistent influence of Dewey's pragmatism was in these domains.

This broad vision of scientific social reconstruction that was Dewey's pragmatism was grounded in a detailed social behaviourism with symbolic interactionism at its core. The details of this social behaviourism that legitimate this pragmatic vision were not worked out by Dewey himself but by his Chicago colleague, George Herbert Mead. The conceptual work necessary to naturalise mind and consciousness was also instrumental in enabling pragmatism to flower into a pervasive social theory.

Like Dewey, Mead was profoundly impressed by the broader philosophical implications of Darwin's theory of evolution (Mead 1934). This scientific landmark signalled the turning point away from all forms of dualism and idealism and charted the course for evolutionary naturalistic accounts of mind and all the dimensions of the social world. What Mead rejected in Darwin was the residual individualism and subjectivism that remained in his characterisation of the mental, a defect Mead set out to overcome. Mead starts from a model of an organism in its environment attempting to lead a satisfactory and fulfilling life but encountering obstacles, which it attempts to overcome through action. Mead's point of emphasis is that it is not the solitary organism that is so acting but a group of organisms whose confrontation with the environment is intrinsically social and essentially involves co-ordinated social action which in turn essentially involves communication.

At the core of Mead's account of the human world, then, is an evolutionary account of communication moving from cries, through gestures, through controlled signals to language proper, and this communicative activity is embedded in cooperative social activities ranging from fighting, through hunting to playing. Moreover, rather than being the products of private minds, this rudimentary communicative activity accounts for the emergence of minds, selves, consciousness, and self-consciousness until the organisms in question attain a capacity for a kind of purposive behaviour and self-control that characterises a community of persons. Mead articulates the details of this emergence of a human community from co-ordinated animal behaviour in impressive detail and this articulation gave an inner texture to his naturalistic pragmatism that complemented Dewey's more expansive presentation.

At the centre of Mead's generalised pragmatism was the notion of the social act (Mead 1938). This notion is continuous with, but broader than, Dewey's notion of enquiry. In the basic phases of the act thinking is depicted as instrumental in a process by which problematic features of our experienced situation become reconstructed and consummated. Moreover, for Mead there is no sharp line between organism and environment such that the surrounding organisms and physical objects are as much parts of the social act as the groups primarily engaged in them. In contrast to a view of 'objects' as fixed and given to us, Mead saw the realm of objects as at least partially constituted by the attitudes, habits, and structured responses of the organisms to them. On his account, cognitive agents certainly do not create their world, but what objects there are is conditioned by our responses to the world. He sketched a relativistic world of contexts and perspectives that were socially constructed by responses to the world by social groups, a pragmatic cosmology in which his pragmatism more narrowly construed was situated. However, this broader vision did not have much impact on the philosophical community, in no small part because of the fragmentary and somewhat opaque character of his writings (class notes edited and published by his students). On the positive side, Mead's pragmatism was profoundly influential in the development of social psychology and was a formative influence also in sociology and anthropology.

A third, and very different kind of pragmatic strain at this time was that developed by C. I. Lewis. Lewis was, of course, intimately familiar with the pragmatisms of James and Dewey (and to a lesser extent, Mead) but his natural affinity was for the original pragmatism of Charles Sanders Peirce, and this for several reasons: like Peirce, Lewis took logic proper to be a central pillar of his philosophy and, unlike the Deweyan tradition, he was not a naturalist. He called his (and Peirce's) pragmatism 'conceptual pragmatism' so as to avoid any unwanted assimilation.

Like the pragmatists before him (and like Kant) Lewis articulated a theory of knowledge that transcended the old dilemmas of rationalism and empiricism, was responsive to new developments in science and logic, and avoided various sorts of simplistic reductionisms. The centrepiece of this theory of knowledge was what he termed 'a pragmatic conception of the a priori'. Like Kant and Peirce before him, he construed perceptual knowledge as the interpretation of the sensuously given by categories and principles supplied by the mind. Both a posteriori and a priori elements are required but for Lewis there was nothing 'transcendental' about the a priori element. Any particular a priori scheme had alternatives, and the acceptance of a given a priori scheme was subject to pragmatic considerations. While no bit of experience could force revisions in our categorical scheme, it could not be a matter of mere private preference as to what categorical scheme would best serve our collective interests. The social dimension of our making sense out of experience functioned as a constraint on any conceptual scheme that would be deemed acceptable. Any range of phenomena would not strictly 'falsify' a categorical scheme but could render it useless for dealing with our world (Lewis 1929). Hence, it was the a priori element in knowledge that was pragmatic, not the empirical element.

Lewis held that evaluations too are a form of empirical knowledge and are subject to the same general kind of pragmatic assessment. To assert that something is valuable (good, beautiful, etc.) involves predictions as to how knowledgeable and properly functioning individuals would experience this thing. The objective value of things is tied to how these things would manifest themselves in experience. Moreover, since a priori principles are partially constitutive of how things present themselves to us, there are definitive criteria of value that are a priori in an analogous sense ('only pleasure is good'; 'only the good will is good') which cannot be falsified by a particular set of experiences but may ultimately be rejected for failure to make sense out of the myriad of our evaluative experiences (Lewis 1950).

What distinguished Lewis from Dewey and Mead was Lewis's life-long concern with fundamental issues in logic proper (Lewis 1918). He was an early appreciator and critic of Russell and Whitehead's monumental *Principia Mathematica*. His particular difficulty with the *Principia* had to do with its construal of 'implication'. In contrast to its notion of 'material implication' he developed the notion of 'strict implication', partly motivated by the central role of counterfactuals in his conceptual pragmatism but also by his more general concern that the Russell/Whitehead system could not do justice to the important realm of modalities.

Pragmatism as a pervasive philosophical temper began to fade from the American scene under the influence of the influx of a group of powerful philosophers who were fleeing Europe because of the persecutions in Germany and Austria. This vibrant group of Logical Positivists (e.g., Carnap, Bergmann, Feigl, Neurath, Schlick) found fertile soil in pragmatism, and through the catalytic efforts of facilitators like C. W. Morris they grew together in the America of the 1930s–1940s. Initially, the more austere scientism of the logical positivists had the upper hand but under the pressure primarily from within (Quine, Goodman, Putnam) a more classical form of pragmatism seems to have emerged on top in the end.

35

FRENCH CATHOLIC PHILOSOPHY

DANIEL LEDUC-FAYETTE

I. 'CATHOLIC PHILOSOPHY'?

The words 'Catholic' and 'philosophy' form an uneasy combination which arguably should not exist at all, since it seems to carry the misleading implication that all the authors to whom it refers had an allegiance to Rome, and reduces to a questionable common denominator a number of thinkers whose views were sometimes conflicting. It is therefore preferable to speak of 'Catholic philosophers' in the plural, or, if we still insist on using the expression, to put the epithet between cautious quotation marks: 'Catholic philosophy'.

One thinker to whom the term 'Catholic philosophy' could, in a sense, be applied was Maurice Blondel (1861–1949), despite the fact that, in his anxiety to avoid the accusation that his philosophy was an apologetics, he was careful to point out in a revealingly entitled book *Le problème de la Philosophie Catholique* (1932) that he had not used this problematical expression 'one single time' in his earlier classic work *L'Action* (1893). Even so he wanted to restore it to its original, etymological, meaning of universality, the full significance of which was indissociable from the ecclesiastical dimension. Thus, in the third part of the work, he endeavoured in twenty pages to demonstrate 'in what sense, with what reservations, and at what price "Catholic" . . . philosophy is conceivable and achievable'. This was logically in keeping with his Pan-Christianism, which was stated with supreme self-assurance in *La philosophie et l'Esprit chrétien* (1944), the fourth part of a 'tetralogy' of works written with a common purpose, the other parts being *La Pensée* (1934), *L'Etre et les Etres* (1935), and a new volume again entitled *L'Action* (1936–7). In these works modernist ideas were very far from his thinking and he revived several of his own earlier themes, as when in the second *Action* he expressly singled out the central theme of 'agnition', understood as 'the acknowledgement that as it advances through the process of mental growth, the spirit will come across all the truths that are the light, the food and the purpose of intelligence'; thus it will acknowledge the Word Incarnate which 'recapitulates total order' as the light and the bread of life, and, as Pascal had said, as 'the object of everything and the centre towards which everything tends'. Blondel here remained faithful to one of his earliest doctrines: in the first *Action*, he had written, of the Word Incarnate: 'It is this that is the measure of all things'; and in his Latin thesis, *Le lien substantiel et la substance composée d'après Leibniz* (1893), he had taken care to observe that it was in connection with the mystery of the Eucharist that Leibniz had introduced the hypothesis of the 'universal binder', the 'link of links', the famous *Vinculum substantiale*.

For Blondel, therefore, 'Catholic' philosophy was just the true Christian philosophy. He claimed that the expression 'Christian philosophy' had in fact first appeared in the title of Leo XIII's encyclical *Aeterni patris* (1879), which had heralded the renaissance of the philosophy of St Thomas Aquinas and prompted the future Cardinal Mercier to inaugurate a chair of Thomist philosophy in Louvain in 1882. This Thomist revival was marked by the appearance of works by a number of writers, including Antonin-Dalmace Sertillanges (1863–1948), the Belgian Jesuit Père Joseph Maréchal (1878–1944), who opposed Kant's critical philosophy in a highly original manner, Jacques Maritain (1882–1973; see below), and Etienne Gilson (1884–1978), the great scholar who was founder of the *Archives d'histoire doctrinal et littéraire du Moyen-Age* and author of *Le thomisme – Introduction à l'étude de St Thomas d'Aquin* (1919), *L'Esprit de la philosophie médiévale* (1932), and *Réalisme thomiste et critique de la connaissance* (1939).

Despite this connection between Thomism and 'Christian' philosophy, Blondel's conception of a 'Christian philosophy' provoked an important debate following a lecture he gave on this theme in 1931 to the Société française de philosophie (see especially Blondel's *Lettre* which was published as an appendix to the 1931 bulletin of the Société). Responding to Blondel, in *De la philosophie chrétienne* (1933) Maritain questioned the very existence of 'Christian philosophy'. He was supported by a large number of 'neo-Thomists' (although it should also be noted that Maritain stated: 'There is a Thomist philosophy; but there is no neo-Thomist philosophy'!). They demonstrated their mistrust of a fused entity in which the noun 'philosophy' was in danger of being consumed in the flames of the qualifier 'Christian'. Thus it seemed that there was no end to the differing shades of opinion in this dispute between those in favour of uniting the two words and those against it.

2. THE 'SANCTIFICATION OF REASON'

Rather than becoming lost in the subtleties of complex distinctions, it is more fruitful to emphasise the concerns that these Catholic religious thinkers had in common. All of them, for different reasons, wanted to make manifest the relationship (in the fullest sense of the word) which, in their eyes, existed between philosophy and Christ. Blondel was the classic representative of a '*philosophia Christi*', to use one of Tilliette's now standard typological categories. As Tilliette (1993) shows, Christ was the focal point of his outlooks, 'the secret code and ultimately the open sesame' of Blondelian philosophy. The author of *L'Action* structured 'the philosophical exposition from within so that it might receive the gift of God' (Tilliette 1990). Whilst always defending the rights of reason, Blondel revealed its fundamental inadequacy. The realisation of this inadequacy was a source of progress, since it obliged philosophy (by immanent necessity) to open itself to the dimension of divine transcendence. In particular, action, when carefully analysed in the dual register of phenomenological description and reflective reappraisal, was found to be endowed with a metaphysical status. In this preoccupation with the purpose of human action, Blondel saw the disproportion between our 'willing will' (*volonté voulante*) and our 'willed wills' (*volontés voulues*) as the constant moving force of all transcendence and all progress. Thus an innate dynamism which testifies to the presence of God made man works profoundly on our will, and is at the root of the decisions to which we commit ourselves (here, as with Malebranche and the Scotist and Franciscan traditions, Blondel reaffirms the Incarnation as the purpose of creation). This underlying supernatural force, to which we tend to remain blind, transforms our biological destiny into one that is truly human, in the full sense of a condition that combines thought, action, and Being.

There can be no question of equating Blondel and Maritain and forgetting the differences between them. Nonetheless, each of them in his own way was a believer in the true 'sanctification of reason'. This was Blondel's phrase (but let us not forget that Maritain also acknowledged that 'there is a Christian condition for philosophy itself') and in philosophical terms it is equivalent to 'going over to Christ' (to use Saint Justin's famous expression). Thus according to this way of thinking, reason must be converted, and we can therefore attribute a symbolic value to the 'conversions' in the broad sense, whether by a return to the faith of childhood or by adult baptism, which were a common phenomenon of the years following the 1914–18 war. One example of this was Gabriel Marcel (1889–1973), who had himself baptised in 1929 and regarded this as the most important event of his life, despite the fact that he himself was given to saying, 'We must not say "we Catholics", it is dreadful!', and in 1951 would write to Père Fessard (1897–1978; see below): 'What is wonderful is to come within sight of Catholicism, but to be inside it, to settle into it – in order to judge and condemn, no, I cannot possibly do that.' Such a 'threshold philosophy' certainly had very little in common with that of Blondel or indeed Maritain (who had also been converted under the influence of Léon Bloy, and was baptised in 1906).

3. MARITAIN: 'DISTINGUISH TO UNITE'

Jacques Maritain enjoyed friendships with many of the famous intellectuals and artists of his time (see *Les grandes amitiés* (1949) by his wife Raïssa). But his philosophy of art (as in *Art et scolastique*, 1920) is inseparable from his fervent, austere metaphysics. This was the product of lengthy research which took him from Bergson to Thomas Aquinas (*De Bergson à Thomas d'Aquin* (1944)), and for which the expression 'Distinguish to unite', sub-title of his famous work *Les Degrés du savoir* (1932), will serve as an emblem.

Maritain studied under Bergson at the Collège de France, and devoted his first work, *La philosophie bergsonienne* (1914), to Bergson's philosophy, before accusing him of 'anti-intellectualism'. Unlike Bergson, Maritain was anxious to reconcile intelligence and intuition. The famous expression 'Intelligence sees' is significant here; according to Maritain, seeing, that is, intuition, shapes conceptualisation itself: 'Intelligence sees by conceiving and conceives only in order to see.' Eventually Maritain went on to invent the concept of 'abstractive intuition' to characterise the relationship between intelligence and intuition. He was also, he said, devoted to the idea of introducing into philosophy a spirit of 'sangfroid and reflection', and wanted to keep alive and carry to the heart of the twentieth century the philosophy that underpins the work of Aquinas (as in Maritain 1930). For Maritain, this philosophy was the true 'existentialism', as opposed to Sartre's atheistic, 'apocryphal', existentialism which rejects any conception of intelligible nature and essence (see Maritain 1947).

Since 1912 Maritain had contributed to the *Revue thomiste* and he was one of those actively involved in its revival between 1936 and 1940. In *Quatre essais sur l'esprit dans sa condition charnelle* (1939), he endeavoured to lay the foundations of a Christian way of thinking and acting. He framed here the notion of '*une philosophie adéquatement prise*' ('a properly constructed philosophy') for a moral philosophy which respects the primacy of spiritual values while not undervaluing the virtue of prudence. He had earlier defined the conditions for moral knowledge in *Science et sagesse* (1935): it is only a philosophy which does justice to the true nature of man as revealed by a theology 'which has its roots in heaven' that is capable of providing a properly scientific basis for moral knowledge. He therefore rejected Aristotelian and subsequent naturalistic ethics as inadequate: a philosophy 'which has its roots in the earth' should be subordinate to theology; but far from being, as in the Middle Ages, the 'maidservant' of theology, naturalistic philosophy has now been promoted to the position of 'Secretary of State'. In *L'Humanisme intégral* (1936) he took this position further, attempting to provide a theological basis for this concrete historical ideal of a new Christianity, while opening up a way to 'secularisation'. It was Pope Pius XI's condemnation of the right-wing Action française in 1926 which had provided the impetus for this moral philosophy and the political philosophy which is its application, as can be seen in the long correspondence between Maritain and Journet, which reflects the painful debates that have so often racked the Catholic conscience (see also the correspondence with Gilson; Gilson and Maritain 1991).

4. HISTORICAL ACTUALITY

Two pairs of dates – 1914–18 and 1939–45 – have a sinister ring indeed. In the period between, while the wounds of the First World War were still open, the second was brewing, as Europe fell prey to the resistible rise of totalitarian regimes. It was inevitable that philosophers on all sides, Marxists, atheist existentialists, and, with even stronger reason, those who proclaimed themselves Christians, should take up a position. The manifesto *Pour le bien commun: la responsabilité du chrétien et le moment présent*, launched in 1934 by Maritain and Gandillac, bore the signatures of Gilson, Marcel, etc., all of whom rose above their differences to unite in defence of the same living tradition of charity. This was the time of 'commitment'. In 1932 Emmanuel Mounier (1905–50) joined with Izarel and Deléage to found the review *Esprit*; then in 1935, in *La révolution personnaliste et communautaire*, he resumed the attacks that Péguy had made at the time of the Dreyfus affair on any form of nationalism or clericalism. He was equally vigorous in his opposition to Marxist atheism and to capitalist liberalism, which he denounced for its bourgeois hedonism. Christians could most certainly not remain deaf to the monstrous cacophony of this 'broken world', as it was called in the title of one of Marcel's most famous plays.

This sensitivity to history, and in an even more pointed fashion to 'historical actuality', can also be found in the work of the Jesuit Gaston Fessard, a privileged witness of the period in question. At the age of twenty he was at the Chemin des Dames at the Great Battle of Rheims in 1917, and at forty-seven found himself running from the Gestapo. In *Pax nostra: examen de conscience international*, his first work, written between 1935 and 1936, he opposed all forms of exaggerated nationalism by introducing the famous theme 'Christ is our peace'. This work aroused the intense admiration of Marcel, who wrote to him: 'Your book . . . makes clear the truth about Christianity . . . which is the only thing that counts . . . It is a book which would change something in the world if it were understood.' In 1941 Fessard edited the first issue of the clandestine journal *Témoignage chrétien, France, prends garde de perdre ton âme*, while in 1946, in *France, prends garde de perdre ta liberté*, he emphasised the parallels between the two conflicting ideologies, Nazism and communism. Springing from the urgency of the historical situation, his thinking hinged on logic, history, and existence. He pondered at length on the works of Marx and Kierkegaard; as for Hegel, he had discovered him in 1926–7, although it was not until much later that he wrote *Hegel, le christianisme et l'histoire*. From 1933 to 1939 he took an active part in Alexandre Kojève's famous seminar on Hegel, taking issue with its atheist stance. In *La dialectique des Exercices spirituels de saint Ignace de Loyola*, largely written in 1931, but published in 1956 after circulating in manuscript, Fessard identified a philosophy of freedom as the starting point for all human reality. A large amount of his unpublished material has been brought together by Père Sales in *Le mystère de la Société: recherches sur le sens de l'histoire* (1997). This general survey is in a sense the crowning achievement of a 'Christian social philosophy' which has made its mark on a number of thinkers.

5. A PHILOSOPHY OF ANXIETY: GABRIEL MARCEL

The peculiar feature of the soul, said Marcel in 1944, 'is that it is on a journey'. As the author of *Homo viator* (1945a) he had a sense of man's 'itinerant condition', and brought the journey into its truly philosophical dimension. In the context of a lofty 'metaphysics of hope' whose constitutive categories were ethical and theological, Marcel posited the essential, 'intimate' link between the soul and hope. Placing the latter in its proper register, the world of Being as opposed to that of having, he preserved its status as a theological virtue along with its sisters, faith and charity, and refused to disfigure it by reducing it to profane hope which was merely the reverse of fear. Deprived of hope, he said, the soul becomes 'extenuated' in the etymological sense of the term; it 'dries out'. 'Hope', wrote Marcel, 'is to the soul what breathing is to the living organism.'

But the odyssey of the consciousness is a perilous voyage, however immovable the entirely spiritual quest of Being may be. It is a search that is full of piercing anxiety; and one, moreover, which is doomed to remain incomplete. One of the themes of the *Journal métaphysique*, begun in 1914 and continued in *Etre et avoir* (1935), was the impossibility of apprehending total reality: 'this harrowing, exhausting experience of drilling down, supposedly in search of . . .' The suspension points here are revealing. Marcel was given to saying: 'When we *talk* about God, it is not *God* we are talking about.' The experience of transcendence, which admittedly moves into the speculative dimension (since it is reflected upon by the philosopher), is real and intense. The analysis of the consciousness becomes meaningful only 'through the deeply felt tension between the self and the depths of Being'. This is achieved by reflective interiority (which in this case is not immanent, however). Experience and reflection are the two sources of this concrete philosophy which weaves a web studded with concepts, and sets up a harmonic resonance between these notions, as when the key dipoles mystery/problem and *disponibilité/indisponibilité* ('availability/unavailability') echo the Being/having dipole. Thus the requirement that authentic philosophising be inherently systematic is met, without the idea of system becoming dominant.

This search may be described as 'existential', and stands in contrast to any form of 'essentialism' or indeed 'existentialism'. In *Le Mystère de l'Etre* (1951), Marcel condemned 'the dreadful term "existentialist"'. 'Superior empiricism' was the expression that came naturally to his pen as he revealed the point where his thinking coincided with that of Kierkegaard: there was a similarity between their approaches, for both of which the moving force was religious: 'I belong to the same family as the author of *Philosophical Fragments*.' It is through music, he said, that we experience the faith that transcends all knowledge. In the face of existential anguish, this major art acts as an antidote and gives us, without the help of concepts, the mysterious self-assurance that anticipates the feeling of confidence we shall experience in our eternal dwelling-place (which we hope for by right, since it has been promised to us: 'this' world is endured only insofar as another world, invisible but present, does exist).

Marcel sought to reveal 'the structurally dramatic character of human experience'. Any examination of his philosophy must include a study of his works for the theatre, which cannot be considered solely from the point of view of their effect on stage. Much more important, they represent a real 'communion' between the 'self', the philosopher-dramatist, and the 'other', the audience. Indeed, this dimension of intersubjectivity is implied by the need for an attitude of openness to transcendence which characterises Marcel's way of thinking. This relationship between the ontological and the existential is the ethical link itself. Ethics overlaps with ontology insofar as the gift, a fundamental ontological category which precedes us, is to be given. In fact it is up to our *disponibilité*, our 'availability' to Being, an ethical force *par excellence* which is quite the opposite of '*disposer de*' – 'disposing of Being', to accept or refuse this gift, to be faithful to it or to betray it.

The metaphysics of hope thus includes the idea of an entirely ideal moral world, but Marcel criticises the Kantian ethic, which he condemns as 'a speculative aberration'. For Marcel, true 'universality' does not come within the order of the conceptual, and as for 'autonomy', it refers to the worldly realm of having! Human society is viewed ideally as a 'Church', in the evangelical dimension of the ecclesiastical, as a communion with the body of Christ. Marcelian thought on 'holiness', of which Christ was the archetype, showed the extent to which Christianity underlay the development of this philosophy. The 'human dignity' of which Marcel established the existential bases became the ethical principle for the evaluation of technical progress, whose negative side he condemned as a monstrous alienation of Being to the advantage of having: when man allows himself to be possessed by his possessions. In 1948 Marcel contributed to a collection of essays edited by Claudel, *Le Mal est parmi nous: un problème actuel*, with a piece which he called 'Les techniques d'avilissement dans le monde et la pensée d'aujourd'hui' ('Methods of Debasement in the World and Thought of Today'). It would seem from this title that he had a great deal of foresight into the future.

SPANISH PHILOSOPHY

MANUEL GARRIDO

From 1870 to 1945 Spanish philosophy lived moments of splendour which, in contrast with the spiritual stagnation of the two preceding centuries, have earned it the epithet 'The Silver Age' of Spanish culture and thought. The great thinkers Unamuno and Ortega can be seen as its culmination. But it would be oversimplifying matters to reduce that splendour to only these two figures. In this chapter I shall consider five major moments: (1) Krausism; (2) Unamuno and the 'Generation of '98'; (3) Ortega and the 'Generation of '14'; (4) the Catalan philosopher Eugeni d'Ors; and (5) Zubiri and the 'Generation of '27'.

1. KRAUSISM

For political and religious reasons Spanish culture has long kept itself apart from the rest of Europe. This explains why, especially since the Enlightenment, Spanish intellectual circles have raised again and again, with angry protest by traditionalists, the question of the *europeización* of Spain. Initially, people understood by this an opening up to French influence. But in the middle of the nineteenth century this term acquired a new meaning. The young Spaniard Julián Sanz del Río, who was interested in reforming the thought of his country, travelled to Germany in 1843, contacted there the philosophical circle of the Kantian/Schellingian Christian Krause, and returned home a converted apostle of Krausism, which spread like wildfire along university circles.

The Spanish Krausists embraced enthusiastically the Kantian moral idealism which was so characteristic of Krause himself. In time, nevertheless, this idealism entered into an alliance with the positivist materialism which was also in fashion: the common denominator of the idealist Krausists and materialist positivists was their passion for liberalism and progress. The result of this alliance, the philosophical centaur known as *krausopositivism*, turned out to be one of the most powerful trends of Spanish thought at the end of the nineteenth century. The moral integrity of a large number of krausopositivist academics who defended the freedom of speech and teaching gave rise both to the dismissal of several of them and to spectacular crises in the governments of the period. One of the most notable achievements of krausopositivism was the construction of a teaching institution independent of the state, whose cultural, social, and political impact made it a pedagogic experiment unique in the Europe of that time. This was the *Institución Libre de Enseñanza*, founded in 1876 by the krausopositivist Francisco Giner de los Ríos (1839–1915), called by Unamuno 'the Spanish Socrates'.

2. MIGUEL DE UNAMUNO AND THE 'GENERATION OF '98'

The Spanish colonial disaster in 1898 – the loss of Cuba – was the catalyst of a will to reform involving many Spanish intellectuals of very different tendencies. The date gave its name to the so-called *Generación del 98*, which included a handful of angry young writers. Miguel de Unamuno belonged to this group; he was philosophically influenced by Schopenhauer's pessimism and Nietzsche's spirit of revolt but also much concerned with the question of Spain's identity and with the regeneration of Spanish culture. The philosopher Angel Ganivet (1865–98) was also a precursor of this movement, though he committed suicide in 1898. In his best-known essay, *Idearium español* (1897), he regretfully proposed the spiritual isolation of his country (on Ganivet, see Olmedo 1965). The desire for change was also felt, but with more pro-European aspirations, by krausists, by the political *regeneracionism* led by Joaquín Costa, and by the *98 científico* ('scientific 98'), a label which can be applied to the biologist Santiago Ramón y Cajal, the founder of the neuronal theory of the brain, and to Leopoldo Torres Quevedo, forerunner of cybernetics, whose theory of automata anticipates Turing's project of artificial intelligence.

It is usual to describe Miguel de Unamuno (1864–1936) as a philosopher of life and as a Christian existentialist. But his deepest affinities were not with the existentialists, but with their great precursors, Pascal and Kierkegaard, and like them he was primarily a dissident Christian thinker. Unamuno was a dialectical and paradoxical writer, able to combine philosophy with literary and poetic creation. Together with Ortega, he led the Silver Age of the Spanish culture, at least in the philosophical realm.

Unamuno's philosophy is mainly contained in *Del sentimiento trágico de la vida* (*The Tragic Sense of Life*) (1913), the most important of his works. Extrapolating from Spinoza's famous thesis of the will (*conatus*) to persist in existence, Unamuno maintains that the deepest aspiration of man considered as 'the man of flesh and blood', not merely as the abstract subject of knowledge, is not to die. But the inescapable fact of death, combined with the fact that scientific reason supports only a sceptical attitude to the immortality of the soul or any similar hypothesis which might satisfy our radical will to live, leaves the human condition in a situation of tragedy. Schopenhauer had already pictured, in Kantian terms, a deep conflict between the world as will and the world as object of rational representation. In a similar vein, Unamuno maintains that the conflict which converts human life into tragedy is the fight between reason and will, or, as he says, remembering Pascal, between reason and the heart. Reason directs us to an attitude of scientific empiricism when seeking to understand the physical world and to an attitude of religious scepticism when seeking to understand the soul; but the heart asks us to believe in the sense of the universe, in the immortality of the soul, and in God's presence. This conflict has no rational solution; it is a contradiction which does not admit any rational synthesis and gives rise to the tragic sense of life. The solution suggested by Unamuno is to accept the resulting uncertainty, the abyss in which we remain condemned by this conflict, but to have faith that, without falling prey to illusion, the dictates of the heart will save us from tragedy.

The faith postulated by Unamuno is, in more than one sense, a religious faith, but it is not the traditional faith of Christianity nor that of any other positive religion. In his opinion, the traditional arguments in favour of God's existence – the famous *preambula fidei* which Aquinas developed – are not unchallengeable and have been undermined by modern science. In a later work, *La agonía del cristianismo (The Agony of Christianity)* (1925), which continues this line of thought concerning the tragic sense of life, Unamuno speculates sympathetically on the Pascalian faith, which is not based, as traditional faith is, on supposedly demonstrative arguments, but appeals instead to a gamble, a wager, that is backed up by the probability calculus.

As an imaginative illustration of this wager, though it is only distantly similar to Pascal's, Unamuno appeals to his vision of the literary figure of Don Quixote, something he had dealt with before in *Vida de don Quijote y Sancho (The Life of Don Quixote and Sancho)* (1905). Quixote is conceived as a hero who combines reason with madness in order to will belief, creating thereby a fiction for whose immortality he can fight. This kind of 'spiritual quixotism' is for Unamuno his vital experience of religious faith and it finds a new literary embodiment in his philosophical novel *San Manuel Bueno, mártir* ('Saint Emmanuel the Good, Martyr') (1933), a remarkable Spanish remake by Unamuno of Rousseau's story in *Emile* of the creed of the vicar from Savoy. Manuel Bueno is a humble parish priest of a small village who has lost, or who believes himself to have lost, his faith, but nonetheless struggles desperately until his death to retain it so that he can preserve it in the heart of his parishioners.

The thinker who signed with the name of Georges Santayana such books as *Dialogues in Limbo* (1925) or *Realms of Being* (1942), and who years before had been a colleague of Royce and James in the golden years of Harvard University, was born in Spain (1863) from Spanish parents and kept his real name, Jorge Ruiz de Santayana, and his Spanish nationality and passport until the day of his death in Rome (1952). This would be merely anecdotal if Santayana's work did not betray, notwithstanding that it was written in English, an unmistakable Spanish family resemblance, so much so that the novelist and literary critic Ramón Sender maintained that Santayana was the doyen of the Generation of '98. Bertrand Russell wrote that 'to understand Santayana, it is necessary to bear in mind some general features of his circumstances and temperament. While his environment has been mainly American, his tastes and preferences have remained predominantly Spanish' (Russell 1940 [1971: 454]). And Santayana himself, after admitting the limits to his Americanism, acknowledged that 'I might be said to have been guilty, quite unintentionally, of a little stratagem, as if I had set out to say plausibly in English as many unenglish things as possible' (Santayana 1940a [1971: 7]; for the Spanish side of Santayana's philosophy, see especially J. Mª Alonso Gamo 1966).

3. JOSÉ ORTEGA Y GASSET AND THE 'GENERATION OF '14'

José Ortega y Gasset (1883–1955) was the most influential Spanish thinker of the twentieth century. Brilliant essayist in all realms of intellectual creation, his genius for language has dignified the literary style of Spanish philosophical production. He is for many people the *epónimo* (leading figure) of the *Generación del 14*, whose cultural hegemony in Spain followed that acquired by the previous 'generation of '98', demanding the *europeización* of the country, the professionalisation of the intellectuals and an effective political reform (Manuel Azaña, president of the last Spanish republic, belonged to this 'generation').

The formula 'I am I and my circumstance', which appears already in *Las meditaciones del Quijote* (*Meditations on Quixote*) (1914), his first important book, encapsulates the fundamental thesis of Ortega's philosophy, for which he coined the label *raciovitalismo* (ratiovitalism). In his posthumous essay *Prólogo para alemanes* (*Prologue for Germans*) (1958) Ortega recounts the vicissitudes of his discovery of the idea of *razón vital* (vital reason). Educated in the Marburg of the Neo-Kantian Cohen, from whom he inherited a passion for strict method and for the idealist notion of culture, Ortega became a skilled admirer of the new method of phenomenology. Nevertheless, his philosophical vocation could find full satisfaction only after the discovery of something more substantial and radical than a method. This was his discovery of the radical reality of life, which Ortega arrived at with the help of von Üxküll's biology and the philosophy of life and culture of Georg Simmel and Max Scheler.

In his first works, such as *Las Meditaciones del Quijote* (1914) and *El tema de nuestro tiempo* (*The Modern Theme*) (1923), Ortega claims that it is necessary to construct a rational theory of human life. But he adds that since the theoretical reason of Aristotle and the physicomathematical reason of Descartes are unable to accomplish this task, one must invoke a new kind of reason, which he calls *razón vital* (vital reason). Initially he expounded his theory as a philosophy of culture, an extrapolation from a philosophical biology. But later, after the appearance of Heidegger's *Sein und Zeit* (*Being and Time*) (1927), through the influence of Heidegger and (via Heidegger) of Dilthey's historicism, Ortega formulates his ratiovitalism as an ontology of human life, appealing now in his explanations not only to vital reason, but also to *razón histórica* (historical reason). This may be appreciated in works such as *En torno a Galileo* (*Man and Crisis*) (lectures of 1933; published in 1959), or *Historia como sistema* (*History as a System*) (1935 [1941]) and also in his posthumous works.

Living a life, which is in each case 'one's own life', is for Ortega the unavoidable task which every human being must undertake from within their situation in the world. More than just a fact, a *factum*, this task is a *faciendum*, something which we must do using our reason and our liberty, in accordance with Goethe's profound injunction: *werde, wer du bist* ('become who you are'). One fundamental ontological datum captured by Ortega's formula 'I am I and my circumstance' is that the union of man with the world is not, contrary to the thought of traditional philosophers, like the union of a substance with its accidents, but, instead, like the co-substantial union which those traditional philosophers saw between the soul and the body. In order to illustrate symbolically this structural nexus between man and world, Ortega used to evoke the mythical image of Castor and Pollux, the inseparable pair of pagan gods. In his more mature thought the famous formula is explained as follows: the initial 'I' is to be understood as replaceable by expressions such as 'human life', 'what there is', 'the radical reality', or 'my life'; whereas the final phrase ('I and my circumstance') is to be understood as the interaction of my innate vocation or call to be (my 'I'), with my world, situation or 'circumstance', which comprises many parameters – the geographical *here* and the historical *now*, but also the repertoire of social customs and beliefs which operate in us behind or below the ideas we defend.

Ortega remarks insistently that these parameters are contextual or situational features whose role can be characterised through symbols which are like the variables in the mathematical language of physics which acquire a value only in concrete cases. He deduces from this that, unlike tigers or stones, man has no 'nature' but does have a history. This conclusion accounts for the incredible plasticity of human life and explains the need for historical reason to complete the task of vital reason. Furthermore, just as rational mechanics and dynamics characterise in the abstract, through a system of formal equations, the processes which physics will study by applying the equations to concrete cases, *razón vital* characterises in abstract formulas the laws of the general theory of life, while the *razón histórica* implements or gives concrete content to these formulas, developing in that way the science of biography. Ortega sometimes defined his project as a 'cartesianism of life'; equally, the project could be described from a complementary perspective as a 'galileism of history'.

Liberalism, pro-europeanism, aristocratic intellectualism, and antidemocratic elitism are the keywords of Ortega's thought concerning cultural, social, and political matters. His support for the *europeización* of Spain led to a confrontation between the young Ortega and the older Unamuno, who, following a line already initiated by Ganivet, had proposed in *En torno al casticismo* (*On Authentic Tradition*) (1895) the cultural introversion of his country. But the main feature of the cultural and political philosophy of Ortega was the defence of the elitist thesis of select minorities, in the style of Pareto and Mosca, which he developed first in *España invertebrada* (*Invertebrate Spain*) (1921) and later in the best known of his books, *La rebelión de las masas* (*The Revolt of the Masses*) (1929). It should be remarked, however, that in the *Prologue* and the *Epilogue* which he added to later editions of this work Ortega clarified and moderated his antidemocratic elitism, his aristocratic challenge to the social irruption of the masses.

From the *Meditaciones del Quijote* (1914) until his death in 1955, Ortega's thought spanned four decades. The spectacular triumph of the first two decades was followed by nine hard years of self-exile after 1936 and eleven years of harassment by the powers of the dictatorship following his return to Spain in 1945. Until recently, this period of Ortega's life has been strangely neglected (but see Gregorio Morán (1998) for a recent discussion); nevertheless, in these last years Ortega regained his international fame and prepared two of his most ambitious works, which were published posthumously: *El hombre y la gente* (*Man and People*) (1957) and *La idea de principio en Leibniz* (*The Idea of Principle in Leibniz*) (1958). The first is an extensive ratiovitalist vision of social reality which combines Ortega's ideas with a Husserlian methodology. The second, written on the occasion of Leibniz's centenary, combines a critical confrontation with Heidegger, an attack on his scholastic adversaries in which Ortega criticises the empiricism of the Aristotelian tradition, and a defence of his own system of thought, which he assimilates to the rationalist tradition of Plato, Descartes, and Leibniz.

4. THE CATALAN PHILOSOPHY: EUGENI D'ORS

Spain is a country of several languages and cultures. The names of Ramon Lull, Luis Vives, and Jaume Balmes exemplify earlier contributions of Catalan culture to philosophy; and at the start of the twentieth century the movement known as *novecentisme* brought about a new flourishing of Catalan culture. The leader of this movement was the Catalan philosopher Eugeni d'Ors (1881–1954) (though in the 1920s d'Ors moved to Madrid and wrote thereafter in the Castilian language). D'Ors's thought can be characterised as a 'humanist intellectualism': he explains his intellectualism both as the will to transcend the dilemma of the philosophy of his time, which was the dilemma between rationalism (from Descartes to Hegel) and irrationalism (from Kierkegaard to Bergson), and as the will to continue the *heliomaquia*, the fight for the sunny light and clarity which is the inheritance of Mediterranean classicism. His humanism is explained by his '*integral*' (complete) consideration of man in the triple dimension of *faber* (the man who works), *sapiens* (the man of knowledge and wisdom), and *ludens* (the man who plays and evaluates). His systematic work, *El secreto de la filosofía* (*The Secret of Philosophy*) (1947), contains a doctrine of dialectics, a philosophy of science influenced by his French master Boutroux, and an original philosophy of history and culture.

5. XAVIER ZUBIRI AND THE 'GENERATION OF '27'

The civil war of 1936–39 interrupted the Silver Age of Spanish culture and, consequently, the flourishing of the schools of Madrid and Barcelona, whose members, many of them representative of the third intellectual generation of this period, the *generación del 27*, took refuge in exile. A typical case was David García Bacca (1901–92), a member of the School of Barcelona and a pioneer in mathematical logic (see García Bacca 1934); as a result of the civil war he left Spain for Latin America.

Another case was Xavier Zubiri (1898–1983). A disciple of Ortega and influenced also by Heidegger, Xavier Zubiri has described the evolution of his thought as a progress from phenomenology to ontology and from ontology to metaphysics. As a seminarian, he studied philosophy in Louvain and theology in Rome, becoming a deacon in 1920. He obtained his PhD under Ortega's direction in 1921 at the University of Madrid, and became a Professor of Philosophy there in 1926. During the civil war he lived in Rome and Paris, but in 1939 he returned to Spain and accepted a chair of philosophy in the University of Barcelona; but he taught there from 1940 only until 1942, when he resigned as a consequence of political pressures, and thereafter he lectured only privately. In his book *Naturaleza, Historia, Dios* (*Nature, History, God*) (1944), he assembled a collection of essays on the philosophy of science, on the ontology of history, and on religion. A notable feature of this is his extrapolation of Heidegger's philosophy of existence to provide an account of the religious dimension of man. His later, metaphysical, writings fall outside the scope of this volume.

THE PHENOMENOLOGICAL MOVEMENT

HERMAN PHILIPSE

The Phenomenological Movement was one of the dominant philosophical fashions on the continent of Europe from the early 1920s until the late 1970s. Hundreds of philosophy professors in Europe, Japan, and in the United States conceived of themselves as phenomenologists in at least some stage of their careers, and countless articles and books have been published under the phenomenological flag. Among the many causes that explain the popularity of phenomenology, three may be mentioned. First, whereas the scientific revolutions of the beginning of the twentieth century threatened the traditional position of philosophy as a separate and foundational discipline, seminal phenomenologists such as Husserl and Heidegger, at least in his early works, reasserted the foundational role of philosophy, claiming that they had discovered a philosophical method distinct from the methods of empirical science. Second, this method seemed to enable phenomenologists to widen the scope of philosophical research in unprecedented ways, thereby attracting those who felt suffocated by philosophy as a limited academic discipline. Finally, phenomenology allowed philosophers to discuss problems of life which became pressing during and after the world wars, in particular because of the way in which Heidegger had integrated the existential philosophy of Kierkegaard and the philosophy of life of Wilhelm Dilthey into his phenomenological masterpiece *Sein und Zeit* (*Being and Time*, 1927). The popularity of phenomenology cannot be understood without taking such cultural factors into account.

The very attractions of phenomenology also constituted its weakness. The term 'phenomenology' had been used, both outside and within philosophy, before phenomenologists picked it up. Natural scientists employed the word for classificatory and descriptive branches of science. Within philosophy, Lambert called his theory of illusions 'phenomenology' in 1764 and in his *Phänomenologie des Geistes* (*Phenomenology of the Spirit*, 1807), Hegel used the word for stages of human knowledge in a philosophical ascent, culminating in the philosophical insight that individual human minds are part of Absolute Spirit. Phenomenologists claimed that they used the term 'phenomenology' with a different meaning; indeed, according to Husserl's philosophical teacher Franz Brentano, Hegel was a case of 'extreme degeneration of human thought'. They agreed that the label had a methodological meaning, but, unfortunately, this was virtually the only thing phenomenologists could agree upon. In particular, they never endorsed a common methodological doctrine and, when the movement progressed, methodological reflection became ever more sporadic and elusive. Since the phenomenological pretension to possess a special philosophical method was never substantiated, the movement was always liable to degenerate into a proliferation of subjective opinions without much epistemic value.

This degeneracy may be read off from the phenomenologists' own ruminations on method. In Husserl's writings – both the works published during his lifetime and the 40,000 pages of manuscript which Van Breda rescued from Nazi destruction and stored in the Husserl Archives in Leuven, Belgium – considerations of method play a large part. Husserl claimed that the phenomenological method is both intuitive and descriptive, and that it aims at conceptualising essences or 'essential structures' of phenomena. Description of essences would be possible in all fields thanks to an 'eidetic reduction' (*Wesensschau*) and, being cast in synthetic a priori propositions about sectors or 'regions' of reality, phenomenological descriptions would be more fundamental than the empirical disciplines studying these sectors. Apart from these 'regional ontologies' there allegedly was an even more fundamental philosophical discipline, transcendental phenomenology, which investigates a domain of phenomena that is hidden to our normal view and had to be made accessible by a series of 'transcendental reductions': the field of transcendental consciousness, its mental acts, and the intentional correlates of these acts that are constituted by transcendental consciousness.

Husserl's pupil Heidegger devoted only twelve pages to phenomenological method in *Sein und Zeit*, section 7, while the method seems to be abandoned altogether in most of his later works. Although Heidegger still pretended that the descriptions of human existence or *Dasein* in that book have essential generality, he also claimed that phenomenology is 'hermeneutics', an interpretation of phenomena that is inescapably historical. Heidegger did not attempt to explain how the Husserlian claim that phenomenology describes timeless essences or necessary structures can be reconciled with Dilthey's historical hermeneutics. Furthermore, whereas the phenomenology of *Sein und Zeit* is still a transcendental philosophy of some kind, Heidegger rejected Husserl's conception of transcendental consciousness as a last offspring of the Cartesian tradition. For Heidegger, the transcendental phenomena which phenomenology purports to describe are not mental acts of transcendental consciousness and their intentional correlates. Heidegger characterises a phenomenon in general as 'that which shows itself', but, paradoxically, the phenomenological phenomenon *par excellence* does not show up. 'Manifestly, it is something that proximally and for the most part does not show itself at all: it is something that lies hidden . . . the Being of entities' (Heidegger 1927: 35 [1962: 59]). What Heidegger meant by 'the Being of entities' never became unambiguously clear: was it a Kantian transcendental structure, an essential ontological constitution of the kind sought by Husserl, or rather the level at which entities belong to Being in the sense of the God of Eckhart and the Scholastics?

At the very end of the historical period described in this volume, Maurice Merleau-Ponty published his main phenomenological book, *Phénoménologie de la perception* (1945, *Phenomenology of Perception*). In a foreword that became famous at the time, he summarised the contradictions in phenomenological methodology. Phenomenologists purported to describe essences and yet claimed that existence has priority over essence. On the one hand they wanted to suspend our belief in the existence of the world (Husserl's transcendental reduction) and on the other hand they held, with Heidegger, that the world is always already 'there'. However, instead of showing that these and other contradictions were merely apparent and in lieu of elaborating a methodological doctrine of his own, Merleau-Ponty concluded that phenomenology had to exist as a philosophical movement before it developed a determinate method: it could be practised and recognised as a certain 'style' of doing philosophy. If this style is purely descriptive and not explanatory, Merleau-Ponty says, this must be seen primarily as a refusal of the scientific view of the world (*désaveu de la science*). Indeed, according to Husserl, Heidegger, Sartre, and Merleau-Ponty, the human subject is not a product of multiple causal factors but rather a free creator of meaning, living in a meaningful world. This anti-naturalist thesis is yet another reason why the phenomenological movement became popular in a time of great scientific advancements. But, clearly, it is a philosophical thesis and not a methodology. The claim that phenomenology is characterised by a proper philosophical method had evaporated by 1945, although a great many minor figures echoed it long after.

Analytical philosophers typically complain that phenomenologists do not give arguments for the truth of what they are saying. From the phenomenologists' point of view this is not a defect but an advantage. Husserl's slogan *Zu den Sachen selbst* ('back to the things themselves') meant that philosophers had to stop arguing and constructing theories: the argumentative battle of theories had gone on too long without a winning party. Instead, they should gain access to a domain of properly philosophical phenomena (essences, transcendental consciousness) and restrict themselves to a meticulous description of these phenomena. But this descriptivist creed, which phenomenologists shared with philosophers of language such as Wittgenstein, had at least two possible drawbacks.

First, it might be argued that the phenomena which the phenomenologist purported to describe do not exist. According to Wittgenstein, essences are illusory; they are 'shadows which grammar casts upon reality', whereas Husserl's idea that we might describe mental phenomena that are accessible only to the person to whom they belong has perhaps been refuted by Wittgenstein's private language argument. Similarly, Heidegger's thesis that there is a phenomenon of 'Being' that 'proximally and for the most part does not show itself at all' might be the product of a linguistic illusion: the illusion that the verb 'to be' is used as a referring expression. The second drawback is at least as serious as this first one. The descriptivist bias prevented phenomenologists from stating the philosophical problems they were implicitly dealing with, and from critically assessing the various possible solutions to these problems. Very often, their 'theory-neutral' descriptions turn out to be attempts at solving traditional philosophical problems that remain naïve and unreflected because they are not recognised for what they are.

In the following synopsis of the phenomenological movement we focus on its two most influential protagonists, Husserl and Heidegger, and on the two main phases of the movement, the German phase before the Second World War (1900–39) and the French phase, which started in the late 1920s with books such as *Phénoménologie et philosophie religieuse* (1925, *Phenomenology and religious philosophy*) by Jean Héring and *La Théorie de l'intuition dans la phénoménologie de Husserl* (1930, *The Theory of Intuition in Husserl's Phenomenology*) by Emmanuel Levinas, and which culminated with Sartre's *L'être et le néant* (1943, *Being and Nothingness*) and *Phénoménologie de la perception* by Merleau-Ponty (1945). As far as possible, we try to reconstruct the philosophical problems and solutions underlying the descriptions that the phenomenologists tried to provide. The phenomenological movement has also been influential after the Second World War and in many disciplines apart from philosophy, such as psychology, the social sciences, law, and theology, but these influences cannot be discussed here.

1. THE PHENOMENOLOGY OF EDMUND HUSSERL (1859–1938)

Edmund Husserl, born into a Jewish bourgeois family in Prossnitz, Moravia, studied physics, astronomy, and philosophy at the University of Leipzig and moved to Berlin in order to specialise in mathematics under supervision of the well-known mathematicians Kronecker and Weierstrass. He wrote a doctorate on calculus in Vienna in 1882, where he met his philosophical teacher Franz

Brentano (1838–1917) and converted to Protestantism in 1886. One might say that the phenomenological movement began when Brentano convinced the young Husserl that philosophy could be practised as a 'rigorous science'.

Trained in scholastic philosophy and an expert on Aristotle, Brentano was an all-round philosopher who had been deeply influenced by British empiricism. Despising the speculative outbursts of German idealism and impressed by the successes of natural science, he tried to reconstruct philosophy as a scientific discipline by adopting the empirical methods of the sciences. Like Hume, Brentano identified philosophy with psychology. He held that explanation in psychology is premature unless it is preceded by a careful description of the phenomena to be explained: explanatory psychology had to be preceded by descriptive psychology. The first task of descriptive psychology was to distinguish mental from physical phenomena, all phenomena being either mental or physical. Like Descartes, Brentano assumed that our own mental phenomena are indubitable for us whereas the existence of physical objects may be doubted. According to Brentano the most important characteristic of mental phenomena is that they are 'intentional': they are directed at something or have an 'objective content', even though they need not be directed at an object which exists or is real or true (note that 'intentional' is a technical term and does not just mean 'intended', or, indeed, the technical logical term 'intensional'). For example, whenever we perceive, we perceive something; whenever we think, we think of something, and whenever we hate or love, we hate or love someone (Brentano 1874 [1924: 124–5]). According to Brentano, mental acts that represent objects or states of affairs other than themselves in this 'intentional' manner (*Vorstellungen*) are at the basis of all other mental phenomena.

This notion of intentionality, which Brentano found in scholastic writings, turned out to be a fruitful concept. It played a central role in the phenomenological movement and has been absorbed and further clarified by the analytical tradition. In order to understand Brentano's importance for a young mathematician such as Husserl, however, we have to mention a more Humean element in Brentano's philosophy. Following Hume, Brentano assumed that mathematics is about relations of ideas and can be developed a priori by symbolical methods. Yet in order to verify the axioms of a mathematical discipline such as the calculus, we have to clarify its fundamental concepts or ideas by tracing them back to the phenomena from which these ideas are 'abstracted'. According to Brentano and the young Husserl, the concepts of algebra and the calculus cannot be abstracted from physical phenomena, because these branches of mathematics may be applied to everything. Like Locke and Hume, they concluded that fundamental concepts of mathematics such as 'natural number' must have been abstracted from mental phenomena, since all phenomena supposedly are either mental or physical. Hence descriptive psychology or 'phenomenology' must be the foundational discipline for mathematics, geometry excepted.

In accordance with this Humean programme, Husserl set out to find the 'origins' of the concept of number in his *Habilitationsschrift* (Halle 1887), an enlarged version of which was published in 1891 as *Philosophie der Arithmetik* (*Philosophy of Arithmetic*). Like Frege, Husserl understood natural numbers as determinations of sets or 'collections'. Because in mathematics anything whatsoever may be considered as a member of a set – we can form a set consisting of God, an angel, a human being, and a movement – Husserl concluded that the 'collecting link' which makes entities into members of a specific set cannot be some physical or other given relation between the members: it must be a mental act of collecting. Hence an individual set consists of its members plus the mental act of collecting, and it is by abstracting from the members and by concentrating on such mental acts of collecting in a second, reflective mental act, that the concept of a set is formed.

Clearly, Husserl preferred enumeration as a set-forming operation to definitions of sets as the extensions of general concepts, but this is only one of the differences between his approach and Frege's in *Die Grundlagen der Arithmetik* of 1884. Husserl radically rejected Frege's view that we might provide the foundations of arithmetic by definitions of numbers in terms of sets and the notion of equinumerousness. His reason is derived from the traditional theory of definitions: one can define only what is logically complex. In the case of logically simple concepts such as set or number, the only thing one can do is to show the concrete phenomena from which these concepts are abstracted, and to elucidate the process of abstraction. Bertrand Russell still advocated a similar procedure in the first edition of his *Principles of Mathematics* of 1903. As he said in its preface: 'The discussion of indefinables . . . is the endeavour to see clearly, and to make others see clearly, the entities concerned, in order that the mind may have that kind of acquaintance with them which it has with redness or the taste of a pineapple.' According to Husserl, natural number words are general names for individual collections of objects. If these collections are small, they may be 'given' in psychological reflection or 'inner perception', that is, by reflecting upon the collecting act and, through it, upon the entities collected. However, if collections are larger, such an 'intuitive' conception of numbers is impossible. In the second part of *Philosophie der Arithmetik*, Husserl tried to justify the symbolical methods of arithmetic by showing that the system of symbolical concepts runs parallel with the intuitive concepts of numbers which we have only where numbers are small.

Frege wrote a devastating review of *Philosophie der Arithmetik* in 1894, arguing that numbers are objective entities in a third realm and not mental representations. Although Frege largely misunderstood Husserl because he overlooked the subtleties of Husserl's descriptive psychology, he touched a weak spot in Husserl's philosophy of arithmetic: how can one guarantee the objectivity of mathematical knowledge, if the collecting links that make items into members of a concrete set are mental acts of an individual mathematician, which are accessible only in the psychological reflection of that mathematician? In *Logische Untersuchungen* (1900/1, *Logical Investigations*), Husserl embarked upon his first major philosophical project: to rescue the objectivity of logic and mathematics without, however, abandoning the idea that the ultimate foundations of these formal disciplines are provided by descriptive psychology or phenomenology.

In the *Prolegomena* of this book, Husserl argued that empiricist or 'psychologistic' conceptions of logic, such as those of Mill or Sigwart, lead to scepticism, for if one interprets the laws of logic as empirical laws about mental acts, one actual violation of a logical law would refute it. Yet Husserl conceived of logic and mathematics as consisting of theories about a domain of objects. If this domain was neither that of physical nor that of mental phenomena, what could it be? Inspired by Herbart and Lotze, Husserl resorted to the solution of enlarging his ontology with a third domain, the domain of Platonic objects outside time and space. In the case of logic, these objects are propositions and their parts; in the case of formal ontologies, such as set theory or the theory of wholes and parts, the objects are formal types of entities. Because such objects exist outside of time and space and are not subjected to change, laws about them can be objective, necessarily true, and a priori. Yet the foundations of mathematics and logic had to be provided by descriptive psychology or phenomenology, and Husserl's first, fifth, and sixth investigation were exclusively concerned with this discipline. The reason was that Husserl conceived of the Platonic objects of logic and mathematics as types or 'ideal species' of tokens belonging to the mental realm. For instance, the proposition or 'ideal meaning' that Caesar crossed the Rubicon would be an ideal type, the tokens of which are all the mental acts of judging that Caesar crossed the Rubicon. In order to grasp the objective and ideal meaning of signs (types), one would have to reflect on these mental acts (tokens) and intuit their type or meaning-essence by 'eidetic abstraction' (*Wesensschau*). Therefore, the description and analysis of mental acts was the first step in providing the foundations of logic and mathematics.

This conception ran into difficulties when Husserl came to think more carefully about numbers and logical constants in his sixth logical investigation. For surely the concept of counting is different from the concept of number, and this difference must be explained by supposing that the concrete basis for the eidetic abstraction of these concepts is a different one in each case. Similarly, the concept of conjoining is different from the concept of a conjunction, and the concept of implying is not identical with the concept of an implication. In sections 40 to 52, Husserl argued that the basis for abstracting concepts of numbers and logical constants such as 'and' or 'being' does not consist in mental acts but rather in the intentional objective correlates of mental acts, and he held that these correlates may be perceived in 'categorial intuition'. For instance, in verifying the proposition 'This paper is white' we would not only perceive the paper and its whiteness with our senses; we would also perceive by categorial intuition the *is*, which allegedly is a dependent formal part of an objective state of affairs. These notions of objective correlates of mental acts and of categorial intuition not only later encouraged Heidegger in believing that *Being* might be a phenomenon that we may perceive; they also exploded Husserl's initial conceptions of the mental, of phenomenology as descriptive psychology, and of epistemology.

Initially, Husserl shared Brentano's Cartesian conviction that only our own mental acts and our other mental phenomena may be indubitably present to us. Descriptive psychology was defined accordingly, as a reflective study of one's own mental life. Descriptive psychology or phenomenology had to be the foundation of all sciences, not only because it provides the basis of abstraction for mathematical, logical, and moral concepts, but also because the objects of physics are known to us only to the extent that they are represented by mental contents. But now Husserl had discovered that it was not mental acts but their intentional correlates that were the basis for the abstraction of the concepts of mathematics and of logical constants. Since he considered logic and mathematics as paradigm cases of intellectual certainty, Husserl concluded that the intentional correlates of mental acts are as indubitable as these acts themselves, and he re-defined phenomenology as a descriptive analysis of the 'intentional correlation' between mental acts and their objects. His mature conception of phenomenology, published in the first book of *Ideen zu einer reinen Phänomenologie und phänomenologischen Philosophie* of 1913 (*Ideas pertaining to a Pure Phenomenology and Phenomenological Philosophy*) resulted from a series of reflections on the paradigm case of this intentional correlation, the case of sense perception. Traces of these reflections may be found already in the second volume of *Logische Untersuchungen* (1901).

In *Logische Untersuchungen*, Husserl defended a sophisticated sense–datum theory of perception, which he presented, misleadingly, as a theory-free description of the perceptual phenomenon. Although Husserl endorsed the view that the perceptual act contains non-intentional sensations (*Empfindungen, hyletische*

Daten), he rejected phenomenalism à la Berkeley or Mach, which identifies the external world with series of sensations. According to Husserl, sensations are 'objectively interpreted' in the perceptual act and by this objectivating interpretation the intentional correlate of the perceptual act is 'constituted'. This correlate is not an image or a sign of external reality, as Locke thought; it is the external object itself. However, because the external object is constituted by consciousness, it remains dependent upon consciousness for its existence. In Kantian terms, one might be tempted to say that it is the phenomenal object and not the thing in itself. However, Husserl rejected the Kantian notion of a thing-in-itself for Humean reasons: as this notion cannot be abstracted from phenomena, it is a pseudo-concept. The only meaningful concept of a thing in itself, Husserl argued in the wake of some Neo-Kantians, is the concept of a complete series of 'adumbrations' of the phenomenal object.

The upshot of Husserl's argument was psychological idealism: the view that the external world is ontologically dependent upon human consciousness. But this view is absurd and it implies a paradox which Husserl later called 'the paradox of human subjectivity'. Since human bodies are parts of the external world, and because human minds depend causally upon human bodies, psychological idealism implies that the entire external world depends ontologically upon an insignificant and recent part of it: my body. In the first book of his *Ideas*, Husserl solved this paradox not by rethinking his theory of perception and its implications, but by postulating a temporally infinite transcendental consciousness upon which the world, including my mind and my body, depends ontologically. Each of us would be able to discover such a transcendental consciousness in him- or herself by a series of methodological operations, the transcendental reductions, and ultimately, all reality would depend upon a community of spiritual 'monads', which are substances in the Cartesian sense that they need nothing else in order to exist. Husserl called this Leibnizian view 'transcendental idealism', and he never gave it up.

We now see that Husserl's method of the transcendental reductions and of 'theory-free' description of the 'field' of transcendental consciousness and its intentional correlates was itself not free of theoretical presuppositions. On the contrary, it was based upon substantial assumptions, borrowed from the Cartesian and empiricist tradition in epistemology. According to Husserl, however, the method was presuppositionless and allowed him to develop a universal philosophy. Since mundane entities are transcendentally constituted by transcendental consciousness, we should be able to solve all ontological problems, that is, to articulate the ontological 'sense' of each type of existent, by a descriptive analysis of their intentional constitution. For instance, mathematical objects such as numbers or geometrical types 'exist' in a sense different from tables or other minds, and one might elucidate these different senses of being by a transcendental analysis of how these entities are 'given to' or 'constituted by' consciousness. Such regional ontologies were the foundations of the respective scientific disciplines, and they were themselves founded by transcendental phenomenology.

Husserl soon realised that this new and fundamental 'science' of transcendental phenomenology could not be developed by one philosophical explorer alone. Hence he sought to engage pupils and colleagues as collaborators in a joint enterprise, who had to specialise in phenomenology of mathematics (Oskar Becker), of beauty (Moritz Geiger), of religion (Martin Heidegger), or in ethics and art (Roman Ingarden). But alas, none of Husserl's pupils could be convinced of the value of Husserl's new 'first philosophy'. Husserl therefore spent the remainder of his days in writing ever new introductions to transcendental phenomenology, which took different 'paths' to the promised land of transcendental consciousness: the Cartesian path of *Méditations cartésiennes* (1931, *Cartesian Meditations*), the path via a reflection on logic described in 'Formale und transcendentale Logik' (1929, 'Formal and Transcendental Logic'), or the path via the life world sketched in 'Die Krisis der europäischen Wissenschaften' (1936, 'The Crisis of the European Sciences'). Although Husserl argued in this latter work that the theoretical entities of the physical sciences since Galileo are constituted on the basis of the 'life-world' (*Lebenswelt*), which is the meaningful world in which we humans live, he remained a transcendental idealist: the life-world itself is constituted by transcendental consciousness and ontologically dependent on it. For this reason, Husserl's notion of a *Lebenswelt* was different from the conceptions of the daily world of Heidegger and Merleau-Ponty, in spite of many superficial resemblances.

Once Husserl had reached his mature position of transcendental idealism, he started to make ever more extravagant claims on behalf of transcendental phenomenology. Transcendental phenomenology was not only the 'first philosophy' that philosophers had sought since Antiquity. It could also overcome the crisis of the European sciences, that is, their loss of significance for human life, and it was the only remaining bulwark against scepticism and cultural relativism. Moreover, although Husserl treated the theme discreetly, phenomenology was a way to personal salvation. Each transcendental stream of consciousness is infinite in time, he argued, and the fact that we find a coherent series of sensations in our transcendental ego, which allows us to constitute an external world, points to a transcendent and benevolent God. Like Berkeley, Husserl used an idealist ontology as a springboard to faith, and his later philosophical style sometimes acquires a messianic ardour.

Perhaps events in Husserl's life prompted this religious stance: in 1916, his younger son Wolfgang was killed during a battle at Vaux, and in 1917 his elder son

Gerhart was seriously wounded. In the same year Husserl's friend and pupil Adolf Reinach was killed and his mother, with whom he had a close relationship, died. During the First World War, like many converted Jews, he was a loyal German patriot, but he was never affected by the kind of pro-war frenzy exemplified by Max Scheler, who extolled 'the genius of war'. After Germany's defeat in 1918, Husserl's works were increasingly inspired by a humane and rationalist ethos that he held to be the hidden motive of the development of philosophy from Plato to transcendental phenomenology.

In 1916 Husserl had been appointed to a chair at the University of Freiburg im Breisgau. He gradually acquired an international reputation and lectured in London (1922), Amsterdam (1928), Paris (1929), Berlin (1932), Vienna, and Prague (1935). When he discovered in 1928 that Heidegger, who succeeded him at the Freiburg chair in that year, rejected phenomenology as Husserl understood it, his life took a tragic turn. He felt more and more isolated from his pupils. After the Nazis seized power in February 1933 and Heidegger had become an ardent supporter of this movement, Husserl retired into the intellectual bastion of his philosophy. Feeling too old for emigration, he died in Freiburg on 27 April 1938.

2. THE GERMAN PHASE OF THE MOVEMENT

Having been *Privatdozent* in Halle from 1887 onwards, Husserl was appointed as an extraordinary professor at the University of Göttingen in 1901. There he started to attract students who, inspired by his *Logische Untersuchungen*, wanted to practise phenomenology for themselves, such as Adolf Reinach, Johannes Daubert, Moritz Geiger, Theodor Conrad, Hedwig Conrad-Martius, Alexander Koyré, Roman Ingarden, Fritz Kaufmann, and Edith Stein. About 1907 a special circle was formed which met once a week for philosophical discussions and became a philosophical society in 1910, when Max Scheler also became a member. In 1913, Husserl started the *Jahrbuch für Philosophie und phänomenologische Forschung*, in which the first volume of his *Ideas* appeared in 1913 and Heidegger's *Sein und Zeit* in 1927. Apart from Husserl, the editorial committee consisted of Geiger, Alexander Pfänder, Reinach, and Scheler.

None of these pupils could follow the master on his way towards transcendental idealism. What attracted them in phenomenology was rather the method of eidetic reduction. Husserl had defended the existence of essences or 'ideal species' in his second *Logical Investigation*, because he held that one cannot avoid scepticism regarding logic, mathematics, and knowledge in general except by assuming that logic is about essences which exist beyond space and time, and which are the ideal types of meaning-bestowing mental acts. The laws of logic and mathematics could be verified by intuition of essences, Husserl thought. Husserl's pupils were not primarily interested in mathematics, however, except Geiger and Becker. Taking for granted that there are essences which can be 'intuited', they set out to explore a great many phenomena by means of 'eidetic reduction' or *Wesensschau*, phenomena such as the will, human personality, and religious belief (Pfänder), civil law (Reinach), empathy and the psychological function of art (Geiger), the nation and one's homeland (Kurt Stavenhagen), time, space, colours, and sounds (Conrad-Martius), or values and value-blindness (Dietrich von Hildebrand). After 1933, Nazism scattered the phenomenological movement. Some members fled to the United States (Geiger, Hildebrand, Schutz), others became Nazis (Heidegger, Becker), whereas Edith Stein and Paul-Ludwig Landsberg opposed Nazism and were murdered in concentration camps. Apart from Pfänder and Reinach, and before Heidegger appeared on the scene, the most important phenomenological associate of Husserl was Max Scheler (1874–1928).

Scheler was certainly more than a phenomenologist: he was a dazzling star whose brilliant ideas and boundless energy impressed his contemporaries. Whereas Husserl claimed to be the founder of a new scientific philosophy, Scheler was preoccupied with the moral crisis he perceived in his epoch, in which the values of a calculating and egotistic bourgeois capitalism replaced those of Christianity. Being of Jewish descent but converted to Catholicism, he wanted to reconstruct Christian ethics after Nietzsche's attacks as an ethics free of the *ressentiment* which Nietzsche had discovered at the heart of Christian morality. Phenomenology was a means for doing so, and Scheler published a phenomenological study of sympathy, love, and hate in 1913, the second edition of which was called *Wesen und Formen der Sympathie* (1923, *The Nature of Sympathy*). Scheler's ethics was not formal, like Kant's. It aimed at a phenomenology of 'material' values, as Scheler explained in *Der Formalismus in der Ethik und die materiale Wertethik* (1913, 1916, *Formalism in Ethics and Non-Formal Ethics of Values*). These values are neither individuals nor universals. Like Moore in *Principia Ethica*, Scheler held that they may be intuited or 'felt' in moral experience, being the 'pure whatness' of valuable goods or aims. Scheler made a complicated classification of values and seemed to have special liking for values such as nobility and holiness. Anticipating Maslow, he sketched a hierarchical ordering of values and discussed the different criteria for doing so.

Scheler's ethics was narrowly connected to his philosophical anthropology. He thought that the problem of the external world can be solved by pointing out that the world is what resists to our will, hence the reality of the external world is experienced in our pragmatic involvement in it. Science is part and parcel with this pragmatic involvement, Scheler claimed, echoing American pragmatism, but the human individual is able to say 'no' to the involvement in the world. The possibility of such a spiritual act of negation is what characterises man in his essence, and relates him to the personal Deity. The crowning achievement of Scheler's philosophy was a phenomenology of the essence of religion, in which he described both the essential attributes of the Deity and the receptive acts in which the human being intuits the Divine. The essential attributes of the Divine are absoluteness, superiority, holiness, spirituality, and personality, whereas the individual experiences the Deity in an experience of his own nullity and of being God's creature. As Scheler apparently thought that Christian monotheism is closer to the essence of religion than polytheism, one might conclude that his subjective opinions were masquerading as specimens of phenomenological *Wesensschau*. Indeed, there are convincing arguments for the view that the idea of intuitable essences is an illusion. But this does not imply that all phenomenological writings are worthless. Many of them contain valuable insights and may be re-interpreted as essays in conceptual analysis.

3. MARTIN HEIDEGGER (1889–1976)

Heidegger was Husserl's most promising pupil and after the end of the twentieth century Heidegger's popularity is greater than ever. Next to Plato, Aristotle, and Kant, Heidegger inspires the largest output of secondary literature concerned with an individual thinker; indeed many philosophers on the European continent and elsewhere regard him as the greatest philosopher of the twentieth century. No contemporary philosopher except Wittgenstein managed to change the philosophical agenda so drastically and to impress so deep a mark on posterity. However, reception of Heidegger's philosophy is complicated by several factors: his political engagement as a Nazi in 1933, the uncritical nature and size of the edition of his collected works (*Gesamtausgabe*), and Heidegger's language, which is often obscure and idiosyncratic.

Like Scheler, Heidegger held that there is a type of knowledge or thought (*Denken*) more profound than science, and although Heidegger emancipated himself gradually from his Catholic upbringing, his works retain a distinct religious flavour without being overtly religious. Born as a son of the sexton to the Catholic church in Messkirch, Baden, Heidegger was initially heading for a career as a priest. Disappointments with the church, studies of Luther, and a mixed marriage drove him away from Catholicism, and he became Husserl's assistant for the phenomenology of religion at the University of Freiburg in 1918. After an intermezzo in Marburg, he succeeded Husserl to the chair at Freiburg in 1928, where he lectured until the senate of the university forbade him to teach in 1946 by way of denazification, partly because of a report written by his former friend Karl Jaspers. The ban lasted until 1950, when Heidegger resumed lecturing until retirement.

In *Sein und Zeit* (1927), the first major publication after his *Habilitation*, Heidegger wanted to raise anew 'the question of Being', which had inspired the philosophical investigations of Plato, Aristotle, and the Scholastics. However, only one third of the book was published, and in the published part Heidegger argued that the question of Being cannot be raised properly without a preparatory analysis of the human being that we are (*Dasein*). *Sein und Zeit* is a revolutionary book. According to Heidegger, the concepts with which traditional philosophers and scientists analysed the human mode of being are inadequate, because they were originally derived from other ontological domains, such as that of artefacts. The primary task of philosophy is to develop new ontological concepts which are more adequate for interpreting daily human life, the so-called *existentialia*. In a series of brilliant but often unclear analyses, Heidegger developed the themes that *Dasein* is essentially being-in-the-world, that the world in which *Dasein* lives is a meaningful world of tools, roads, farmland, and work, and that each *Dasein* projects freely its future life and is concerned with itself, others, and the world. *Dasein* faces a fundamental choice between attaining 'authenticity' (*Eigentlichkeit*) by finding itself or losing itself in inauthenticity by doing what 'one' (*das Man*) normally does. The only way to become authentic, Heidegger said, is to face our own death in *Angst*, and to grasp the time of our life as a finite whole. The 'existential' analysis of *Sein und Zeit* drew its inspiration from St Paul, St Augustine, Luther, Kierkegaard, Aristotle, and Dilthey, and it inspired in its turn Karl Jaspers, Sartre, Merleau-Ponty, Levinas, and many others, including theologians such as Tillich and Bultmann. It is the seminal book of the later existentialist movement, although Heidegger emphatically denied in 1946 that he had ever been an existentialist.

Apart from being the seminal text of existentialism, *Sein und Zeit* is both a treatise in transcendental philosophy and the starting point of the post-war hermeneutic movement. Radically transforming Husserl's transcendental doctrine, Heidegger argued that the ultimate source of meaning or being is not an eternal transcendental ego but rather a finite ecstatic time structure or 'clearing' (*Lichtung*) in human beings in-the-world (*Dasein*). The objects of natural science are constituted on the basis of an a priori framework, which, Heidegger claimed, is projected by *Dasein*. The real world *an sich* is the meaningful world of daily life, and not a meaningless multiplicity of particles and other theoretical entities of physics. Although Heidegger rejected transcendental idealism, the outcome of his transcendental turn was similar to that of Kant and Husserl: the world of physics is thought to be secondary and superficial, whereas the meaningful world of daily life and morality is fundamental.

Like Carnap, Heidegger held that the traditional problem of the external world is a pseudo-problem. In opposition to Carnap, however, he thought that the problem is caused by the assumption that the scientific view of the world is fundamental: it would disappear as soon as one realises that *Dasein* exists primarily in the daily meaningful world. Yet one wonders whether Heidegger's transcendental philosophy is not a *solution* to the problem of the external world, and hence whether the various strands in *Sein und Zeit* are mutually compatible. The latter question also arises with regard to Heidegger's conviction that *Dasein* is fundamentally interpretative. Our human identity allegedly depends on how we understand ourselves, and because understanding is historically situated, human beings are historical. As the ontology of *Dasein* is an auto-interpretation of *Dasein*, this ontology is hermeneutic. But if our view of the world is the product of an interpretation, as Heidegger asserts, how can the meaningful world of daily life be a world *an sich*?

While *Sein und Zeit* was a phenomenological interpretation of human existence, Heidegger's later writings from the lecture course *Einführung in die Metaphysik* (1953; based on lectures delivered in 1935) onwards had a very different nature. Heidegger now developed a grandiose historical narrative, according to which Being had shown itself to man in the writings of pre-Socratics such as Anaximander or Parmenides, but had withdrawn since then in the history of Western metaphysics. Heidegger interpreted major philosophers such as Aristotle, Plato, Descartes, Leibniz, Hegel, Schelling, and Nietzsche as thinkers who did not succeed in asking the question of Being in Heidegger's sense, even though Being sent hints to man in their writings. The task of the post-metaphysical philosopher was to 'think', that is, to prepare a future advent of Being by diagnosing the fundamental nature of our epoch, the epoch of technology, as a result of the history of metaphysics and as a 'fate' (*Geschick*) sent (*geschickt*) by Being. Heidegger's later thought resembles Hegel's philosophical history of salvation (*Heilsgeschichte*) and it should not be seen primarily as a contribution to historical scholarship in philosophy. In contrast to Hegel, however, Heidegger interpreted his own epoch not as the culmination point of history, but as a deep fall or crisis, which his thought (*Denken*) purported to overcome, taking Hölderlin's poetry as a lead.

From the *Brief über den 'Humanismus'* (1947, *Letter on Humanism*) onwards, Heidegger claimed that his later thought was connected to *Sein und Zeit* by a *Kehre* (turn). What is the nature of this connection, which allegedly unifies Heidegger's oeuvre? Pupils such as Karl Löwith and Jürgen Habermas have argued that the link between the book of 1927 and the publications that appeared after the Second World War is more or less contingent. The radical change in Heidegger's thought had to be explained by external factors, such as the advent of Nazism, and when Heidegger reintroduced the *existentialia* of *Sein und Zeit* into his later writings, they acquired meanings opposite to those in the earlier book. However, there is a more charitable interpretation of the *Kehre* and Heidegger's reinterpretation of the existentialia, which is based on his Lutheran conception of faith in *Sein und Zeit*. According to Luther and Heidegger, faith is a gift from God, and theology cannot be anything but an analysis of human existence as it is radically transformed by the grace of faith. In a lecture on 'Phenomenology and Theology' of 1927, Heidegger explained the relation between the fundamental ontology of *Dasein* in *Sein und Zeit* and theology as follows. *Sein und Zeit* had to be a purely secular ontology of *Dasein*, whereas theology, as an ontology of *Dasein* as transformed by faith, would have to re-interpret the *existentialia*.

Could it be that the ontological interpretation of *Dasein* in *Sein und Zeit* was written as a preparation of man for the grace of faith, and that Heidegger was convinced that he had received faith when he later re-interpreted the existentialia? This would explain the gloomy view of human existence-in-the-world which Heidegger sketched in the book of 1927: such a view might prepare man for the leap to faith. And it would also explain the overtly mystical nature of Heidegger's inaugural lecture *Was ist Metaphysik?* (*What is Metaphysics?*) of 1929. In any case, Heidegger's later faith was not Christian faith any more, for in 1933 Heidegger agreed with Nietzsche that the Christian God is dead. It remains an urgent task for historical scholarship to determine the precise meaning of Heidegger's later works and, indeed, of his oeuvre as a whole. Was Heidegger's later philosophy an attempt to rescue religion after the death of God? Or did Heidegger rather want to replace actively the Christian religion with a post-Christian and more German creed, in accord with the urges of many Nazis? These questions are rarely raised by modern Anglo-American Heidegger scholarship, which tends to play down the religious aspect of Heidegger's thought and to concentrate on its allegedly pragmatist or Wittgensteinian side. However this may be, Heidegger held the opinion that Being sends hints to mankind. The thinker or the poet pays heed to these hints, and the natural language for thought is German.

Heidegger has been a source of inspiration for, but also a rival of, contemporaries such as Helmuth Pleßner, Nicolai Hartmann, and Karl Jaspers. Unfortunately, there is no space to discuss their works here, which were important at the time, but none of them deeply influenced later thought nor clearly belong to phenomenology.

4. THE FRENCH PHASE OF THE MOVEMENT

Whereas in Germany an existentialist such as Karl Jaspers was not considered to be a phenomenologist, because he held that the philosopher should elucidate the meaning of individual human life (*Existenzerhellung*) instead of intuiting essences, in France existentialism and phenomenology became nearly equivalent. The reason is that instead of Husserl's phenomenology Heidegger's analysis of human existence was a main source of inspiration. However, since Heidegger's phenomenology of *Sein und Zeit* was seen as a logical continuation of Husserl's works, French phenomenologists underestimated the revolutionary import of Heidegger's book. In 1927, Heidegger had rejected the tradition of Descartes, Hegel, and Husserl, but Jean-Paul Sartre formulated his phenomenological ontology of the human subject in Cartesian and Hegelian terms. Most French phenomenologists and existentialists were also influenced by Hegel, who became popular in France after the lectures on his *Phänomenologie des Geistes* by Jean Hyppolite and the Russian Marxist Alexandre Kojève at the *Ecole des Hautes Etudes*. As Kojève had argued that Hegel's phenomenology was not very different from Husserl's, French phenomenologists often did not bother to distinguish between these two conceptions. The existentialist analyses of human life were suitable for illustrations by literature, and major French existentialists such as Gabriel Marcel (1889–1973), Jean Wahl (1888–1974), Simone de Beauvoir (1908–86), and Jean-Paul Sartre (1905–80) wrote novels, poetry, or plays. Many of them were also engaged in left-wing politics, and Sartre argued that existentialism should replace dialectical materialism as a philosophical basis of Marxism.

Sartre had spent the winter semester of 1933–4 in Berlin, studying Husserl's works. His early phenomenological writings include two studies of the imagination, *L'imagination* (1936a) and *L'imaginaire* (1940), a study of emotion (*Esquisse d'une théorie des émotions*, 1939), and a criticism of Husserl in which Sartre argued that the human ego is a construct of consciousness instead of being an independent 'transcendental' substance ('La Transcendance de l'ego', 1936b). Indeed, in his phenomenological masterpiece *L'Etre et le néant* (*Being and Nothingness*, 1943), Sartre held that the human subject is nothing at all, a contingent 'gap' in the causal structure of being, that is, absolute freedom. Consciousness, whose being is being-for-itself (*pour soi*) is radically distinct from matter, whose being is being-in-itself (*en soi*), for consciousness is negation, the negation of being-in-itself. Because the human subject or consciousness is nothing, it has no essence and it has to choose its course in life and its values in total freedom. Our existence precedes our essence, that is, what we do with our lives. Sartre thought that freedom inspires *angoisse*, because it implies universal responsibility, and that people therefore deny their freedom, pretending that they are determined by external factors, and holding that values are pre-existent instead of being the product of free choice.

With uncompromising zeal, Sartre combated this 'bad faith' in his philosophical and political opponents, especially Catholics. He held that the Christian concept of God is an inner contradiction, because it is the concept of a being-for-itself that is also in-itself. Furthermore, Sartre thought that human love is impossible, for human subjects cannot really communicate. As soon as they try to reach each other's being-for-itself, this being will appear as something whose being is being-in-itself, a being-for-the-other. In a psychological adaptation of Hegel's dialectics of master and slave, Sartre argued that whenever we look at each other, we reify the other person and thereby deny his or her freedom. Since we do not want to be reified by someone else, the others are 'hell' for me and the death of the others is my final victory over them. There is an intimate relation between Sartre's existentialist philosophy of freedom and his political commitment. Indeed, the only thing necessitated by freedom is commitment (*engagement*), and Sartre argued, unconvincingly, that the individual choice of a particular commitment such as communism implies the view that everyone should have made this same choice. Hence individual choices imply universal responsibility for everyone, the very responsibility people of bad faith try to escape from.

After 1945, Sartre became the best-known intellectual in France. He started the periodical *Les Temps modernes*, which would dominate French literary and leftist political culture until the 1960s. He also wrote at length about Marxism and other topics; but these writings fall outside the scope of this volume. Sartre's fame at this time is best illustrated by an anecdote according to which a minister proposed to De Gaulle that he imprison him because he was inciting young people to protest during the Algerian war. Allegedly, De Gaulle replied: 'One does not incarcerate Voltaire.' But whereas De Gaulle did not want to imprison Sartre, his existentialism was condemned by the Roman Catholic Church in the Encyclical 'Humani generis'.

Next to Sartre, the greatest French phenomenologist has been Maurice Merleau-Ponty (1908–61). Like Sartre, he was educated at the Ecole Normale Supérieure in Paris. They became friends and edited *Les Temps Modernes* together until Merleau-Ponty published an undisguised critique of Sartre's philosophy – the chapter on 'Sartre's Ultra-bolshevism' in his book *Aventures de la dialectique* (1955, *Adventures of Dialectics*). Simone de Beauvoir replied in *Les Temps Modernes* by a paper called 'Merleau-Ponty et le Pseudo-Sartrisme', after which Merleau-Ponty's name disappeared from the list of editors. In contrast to Sartre, Merleau-Ponty pursued an academic career. Having been professor of child psychology and education at the Sorbonne, he was appointed to a chair at the Collège de France in 1952. In his first book, *La structure du comportement* (1942, *The Structure of Behaviour*), he argued that neither perception nor behaviour can be understood in terms of linear causality à la Watson and Pavlov. From Wolfgang Köhler and others he borrowed the notion of *Gestalt*, and held that both behaviour and perception have to be seen as *Gestalten*. However, the notion of *Gestalt* had not been defined adequately by *Gestalt* psychology, because it never overcame traditional philosophical dilemmas such as physicalism versus mentalism. For this reason, a new foundational study of perception was needed, in which the intentional correlation between the perceiving organism and the perceived world was described from within, as it is experienced by the perceiving subject.

This conclusion of *La structure du comportement* contained the philosophical programme for Merleau-Ponty's next book, *Phénoménologie de la perception* (1945). Whereas Sartre's existentialism was closer to conceptual speculation in the manner of Hegel than to Husserl's careful phenomenological descriptions, Merleau-Ponty started from Husserl's later analysis of the life world (*Lebenswelt*) and from Heidegger's analysis of human existence as being-in-the-world. In *Phénoménologie de la perception*, Merleau-Ponty tried to describe the perceived world and our bodily commitment in it as it is really experienced and not as it is analysed by psycho-physics and other sciences. The phenomenological field, the object of this description, allegedly is the basic stratum of all knowledge, which is overlooked by the scientific view of the world. Merleau-Ponty rejected Sartre's Cartesian conception of the subject, according to which consciousness and the material world are opposites that exclude each other, because in reality our body is the vehicle of our being-in-the-world. Perception is not a passive reception of sensations or sense-data which are interpreted by consciousness, but an active bodily exploration of the human environment. Likewise, human behaviour is not a series of meaningless physical movements of the body, caused by mental processes in the brain, but an intrinsically meaningful dynamic structure, which is inseparable from the meaningful world in which the human being is situated. Indeed, the world is full of 'meaning' (*sens*), a word which Merleau-Ponty uses for everything that refers to something else. The phenomenon of language is but one meaningful phenomenon among others, and when we hear or read a language which we know, the perception of meaning is indistinguishable from the perception of the physical aspect of the words.

With a literary talent rare among philosophers, Merleau-Ponty provided descriptions of phenomena such as our own body, the experience of space and bodily movement, the sexual nature of the human body, language, and gestures. The phenomenon of bodily exploration of the world is correlative with the phenomenon of the world-as-perceived, as Merleau-Ponty showed, taking space, perceived things, and our experience of other persons as examples. His phenomenological descriptions were meant to refute traditional philosophical dichotomies such as intellectualism versus sensationalism and realism versus idealism. In the third part of the book, Merleau-Ponty sketched a philosophy of the human subject, of time, freedom, and history, which stresses the many-sided nature of these phenomena and resists any attempt at an absolute and final knowledge. If the phenomenology of Merleau-Ponty was a refusal of the scientific view of the world (*désaveu de la science*), as he wrote in the preface, this does not mean that Merleau-Ponty neglected the sciences. On the contrary, his descriptions were interlarded with results of the sciences of man, which functioned as pointers to concrete phenomena. What he meant is that the phenomenological description of the intentional correlation between the perceiving subject and the world-as-perceived is more fundamental than the sciences: it is the transcendental discipline upon which the sciences are ultimately founded. Moreover, the world-as-perceived is the fundamental phenomenon, which is overlooked by the scientific view of the world.

In 1945, both Sartre and Merleau-Ponty were at the beginning of their intellectual career. Other French phenomenologists and existentialists, such as Simone de Beauvoir (1908–86), Paul Ricoeur (1913–), or Emmanuel Levinas (1906–95) wrote their main works well after the Second World War. Indeed, it was only after the war that existentialism became a popular movement, which inspired many generations of students and intellectuals, drawing its inspiration from the dilemmas that citizens of countries involved in war had to face.

HEIDEGGER

RAYMOND GEUSS

The German philosopher Martin Heidegger (1889–1976) is by a wide margin the single most influential philosopher of the twentieth century. His original motivation for doing philosophy arose out of religious concerns (he was raised as a Roman Catholic and studied for the priesthood, before converting to a radical form of Lutheranism just after the First World War), and one of the easiest ways to try to make sense of much of his philosophy is to trace in it the shadow of various traditional religious beliefs and doctrines. Thus philosophically in parallel to Heidegger's own conversion from Catholicism to Protestantism, his early interest in scholastic metaphysics was increasingly placed in the service of a project that had its origins in a certain radical Protestant tradition of 'negative theology'. The negative theologian holds that God is so different from anything else, so 'transcendent', that it is utterly impossible to grasp him in conceptual terms; he is accessible only through faith. Since human reason cannot know him, any form of theology (of rational, conceptually articulated doctrine) can be no more than a perverting distortion of the vital reality of religious belief. The only task left for philosophy in this construction is to destroy theology totally, to undermine from within the pretensions of human reason. Heidegger's philosophy, like the National Socialism he espoused in the 1930s, was intended to initiate a conservative revolution, which would consign the whole of traditional philosophy, especially Neo-Kantianism, to the rubbish-bin, and also in some not easily definable way transform human life. His religious commitments after the National Socialist period seem to have remained strong until the very end of his life, although they became difficult to categorise in any conventional terms. Thus in an interview given in old age and published by his own request only after his death, he famously remarked that the modern world was so debased that 'only a God could save us'.

I. HEIDEGGER'S BASIC PROJECT

The central portion of Heidegger's philosophy is a certain view about history and metaphysics. The biblical story of the Fall from Grace and original sin provides a convenient image for Heidegger's basic view of Western history. Adam and Eve had a relatively direct unproblematic relation to God in Eden, which was a state of such innocence and happiness that post-lapsarian humanity cannot recapture it even in thought and imagination. Similarly, for Heidegger, the Greeks of the pre-Socratic period had a primordial experience of Being that was direct, meaningful, and satisfactory in a way that modern humans can hardly conceive. This raises the first question that confronts any serious study of Heidegger. 'Being' is the central object of his philosphical reflection, but what exactly does he mean by 'Being'? Since it is obviously some kind of successor concept to God, it should come as no surprise that 'Being' for Heidegger, given his background as a negative theologian, was of tremendous, indeed overwhelming importance, but also was not amenable to clear, direct conceptual definition, analysis, or even description. 'Being' designates a numinous primordial experience in which subject and object are not yet distinguished, nor are particular and universal, experience and thing-experienced, etc. Being is around us all the time; it is everywhere and nowhere; we understand it, as Augustine says of 'time', without being able to say what it is. It is that through which alone we are human and are able to encounter anything in our world. Humans, in fact, are defined, according to Heidegger, by their need to ask the question of Being – the question what Being is. This is his analogue of the traditional Christian view that all humans are defined by their ineluctable seeking to know the true God. In both cases – that of traditional Christianity and that of Heidegger's thought – the 'asking' and 'answering' need not take an explicitly verbal or conceptual form. I can seek God without knowing exactly that that is what I am doing, just as I can 'question authority' simply by living in a certain way without saying anything. Similarly, 'finding an answer' is not a question of having a verbal formula or a correct theory, but of having found an appropriate way of living.

To return to the biblical story, just as Adam and Eve became estranged from God and lost paradise through their sin, so Western humanity destroyed this blessed, unitary pre-Socratic form of experience by inventing conceptual thought. This destruction occurs because conceptual thought splits Being, driving a wedge between subject and object, and by this means gives rise to the possibility of, and indeed the need for, metaphysics, as the attempt to think conceptually about the relation between subject and object, word and thing, thought and world. Metaphysical thinking, however, distorts the original question about Being and reconstrues it in one of two ways, both of which are pernicious. Either the metaphysician asks about the nature of the highest entity there is (God), or about the properties possessed by everything that is. In the first case metaphysics becomes theology and in the second it becomes ontology (which in Heidegger's view is the matrix from which all Western science emerged and on which it remains dependent).

Heidegger thinks that all traditional metaphysics is essentially a form of either theology or ontology. In either case metaphysics overlooks and tacitly denies what he calls the 'ontological difference', the radical difference between Being and beings, reducing, in one way or another, the former to the latter. Theology construes 'Being' as something like an individual entity (God); ontology as an abstract property common to all that which is, in the way in which traditionally 'cathood' designates the property all cats have in common. To respect the 'ontological difference' and find a way of speaking about Being without reducing it to the status of a being or a common property of beings is the central philosophical task Heidegger set himself.

Western metaphysics as a whole, then, is the story of a downward spiral, an increasing falling away from primordial Being. The more conceptual thought develops, the more estranged we become from Being, and the more desperate, then, our attempts become to get back into contact. In our frantic despair we are then tempted to use the major resource we have, metaphysical thinking (and its off-shoots, theology and science), but further elaboration of metaphysics merely means creating a further layer of distorting conceptual structures that move us yet further from the immediate relation to Being to which we aspire. Thus we end in a modern world in which our basic relation to Being is through a form of technology in which all that is is reduced to a set of mere objects to be controlled by humans for our own accidental purposes. Our situation, then, is one in which in one sense we cannot stop asking the question of Being (because this is what constitutes us as human), but in another sense we have now fallen so far away from the primordial experience of Being that even the question is to some extent lost from our explicit sight and covered over.

The conclusion Heidegger draws from this is that we need to try to ask the question of Being again, while breaking completely with the whole metaphysical tradition, in particular with its whole conceptual apparatus and its language, because by asking the question through the conceptual vocabulary of the tradition, one is distanced from a correct relation to Being. Since, however, he also holds the view that we are to some extent constituted by our history, we seem to be trapped. It is difficult to see what possible position we might occupy from which we could strip off our history and 'begin again', get back into contact with Being. Indeed I have told the story of Western metaphysics above as if it were one concerning human agents and their doings, but if Heidegger's own view is right this is not the full or correct story. If he is right, to be sure, it should also be virtually impossible for me as a descendant of over two thousand years of metaphysics to tell the story in any other way. I have spoken as if 'human subjects' stood over on one side, spontaneously initiating various actions directed at a 'Being' which stood over on the other side and was the detached, inert object of their concerns, ministrations, and manipulations. This is precisely to accept the standpoint of metaphysics, to treat Being as if it were a mere thing, like an ashtray, that could be used and abused in this way. To be able to tell the story in any *other* way would be to have broken exactly the spell of metaphysics which it is part of the point of Heidegger's philosophy to analyse, and from which he thinks we cannot extract ourselves except (at best) by dint of the most rigorous existential-philosophical exertions.

Although, then, for reasons Heidegger thinks he can specify, one cannot really tell the story except by invoking the whole metaphysical apparatus of subjective human agents and their actions, which is radically inappropriate for describing what is going on, it is at least possible to gesture at what is left out. The other side of the story, then, is that the initial philosophical fall from grace is not just something individual philosophers do by inventing conceptual thought, but it is also something Being does, or solicits, or invites, or calls us forth to do. Particularly in his later writings, Heidegger emphasised the need to get away from all forms of anthropocentrism and construe our relation with Being as a cooperative dialogue. The later works propound a paradoxical view that has some similarities with Buddhism: disciplined ontological questioning is to lead to an attitude of letting-be (*Gelassenheit*), a giving up of the active attempt to control the world.

Heidegger's views on how one can try to break out of and 'overcome' the tradition of metaphysics underwent a change during his long career. In the early period (roughly pre-1936), he envisaged the possibility that by analysis of certain existential phenomena of human life (such as *angst*) we could find a starting point that would allow us to 'work our way back' through the historical tradition, and by doing so we could undermine it from the roots, thereby freeing ourselves from the fixed and frozen conceptual distinctions which constitute it and which it has imposed on us. The second half of his first major published work *Being and Time* (1927), as originally conceived, was to carry through this 'destruction of the tradition' (as he calls it). This second half was never completed in publishable form. Heidegger's own later interpretation of this fact was that the original project was a failure because it was not radical enough. It underestimated the hold which traditional metaphysics and its conceptual language has on us. Because it retained the form of an academic treatise and the method of conceptual thinking, *Being and Time* had been unable to break out of metaphysics. In the later period

Heidegger attempted to to approach Being by giving a series of philosophical interpretations of poetry (by Trakl, Mörike, Rilke, George, Benn, C. F. Meyer, and, most notably, the early German Romantic poet Hölderlin), hoping to find in this a way of non-conceptual 'saying' that would put the metaphysical tradition and its conceptual vocabulary out of action.

2. *BEING AND TIME*

Although *Being and Time* was considered by Heidegger to be a failure and was never completed, at the same time he thought it a necessary failure and one which presented a certain path of thought that needed to be followed through to the end by anyone who wished to go beyond it. Part I of *Being and Time* was supposed to reopen in a preliminary way the question of Being. To ask about the meaning of Being, Heidegger argues, one needs first a theory of how this meaning could be understood, that is, a theory of human understanding as the mode of access to Being. A theory of human understanding, though, is possible only in the context of a general theory of what it is to be human. Given Heidegger's view about the way in which traditional language and concepts distort the question of Being, he believed he needed to invent a whole new vocabulary for describing human life and our forms of understanding. He uses the term *Dasein* ('being-there') to designate what we humans are. *Dasein* is thus to replace such previous terms as 'rational animal', 'thinking thing', 'consciousness', and 'spirit'. The analysis of human life and of our forms of understanding is, therefore, for Heidegger 'analysis of *Dasein*'.

In *Being and Time* Heidegger discusses six features of *Dasein*, each of which refers to a way in which a human being is different from the ways in which something (e.g. a chair, an animal, a stone) which is not a human being is. First, the essential features of *Dasein* are answers to the question 'who?' rather than (as is the case with non-human things) 'what?' Second, *Dasein* is a kind of being for whom Being is at issue, or is a concern. This means both that *Dasein* is defined by its concern for Being (part of this being its concern with asking and answering the question 'What is Being?'), and that *Dasein* is essentially concerned with its own Being, that is, with who (or what kind of person) it is. Third, *Dasein* is in each case irreducibly individual, is 'in each case my own'. Fourth, *Dasein* is its possibilities. Whereas a stone has certain real properties, and these are what it is important for us to know about if we want to know what the stone is, what it is important for us to know about a human being is that human being's possible ways of being or acting. Just as it is central to this stone, let us say, that it weighs one kilo, it is central to being John Jones that he can speak French, can control himself in certain ways, can be generous, etc. Fifth, *Dasein* is always characterised by a complex kind of 'understanding' of Being, of itself, its own possibilities, the world it lives in, things in its world, other people, etc. The 'understanding' in question is not a matter of having the correct set of beliefs, but of being able to deal with the thing in question, whatever it is (myself, the world, other things), in a certain way. To be a person of a certain kind is to be an entity with certain possible ways of existing, and correspondingly certain ways of understanding. Finally, *Dasein* is always being–in–a–world: this means that a human always exists as a person who is thrust into a set of already existing objects, projects, and arrangements and one who is always already engaged in complicated dealings with the entities in such a world.

To be a human, Heidegger claims, is to be a 'thrown project', by which he means what is important in specifying who *Dasein* is is the set of projects it has. To have projects means always to be running ahead of oneself to a future in which the next step of the project exists. It means understanding oneself and one's world in a certain way and having (or rather being) certain possibilities. To be me means to have the project of eating lunch soon, finishing this chapter, going to the cinema this evening. What I am now cannot be understood except by reference to these ways in which I am oriented towards an inherently uncompleted future. On the other hand these projects are not the free creation of *Dasein*, but are taken over from the world into which it is thrown. I can only have the project of writing a book if the institution 'book' exists, and it is not an institution I brought into existence.

The central portion of the published version of *Being and Time* is devoted to the contrast between two specific ways in which *Dasein* can exist, which Heidegger calls 'authentic' (*eigentlich*) and 'inauthentic' (*uneigentlich*) forms of existence. To exist 'inauthentically' is to understand oneself in categories drawn from (non-human) things we encounter in the world, to understand oneself therefore as one thing among others, that is, to fail in some sense to register the fundamental difference that exists between the way in which human beings are and the way in which other things are. To the extent to which in inauthentic existence I am 'absorbed' in my everyday concerns, I give the present a kind of priority in my existence, and see the future as a potentially orderly uni-form sequence of moments in time, each of which will in due course become present. The comfortable life of absorption in everyday tasks, however, cannot be the whole truth about human life. It is, Heidegger believes, an essential truth about human life that *angst* can break in at any time and destroy all our cosy constructions. The experience of *angst* has, Heidegger thinks, overwhelming metaphysical significance, because in *angst* I am taken out of my absorption in the world and confronted with my own death as my 'ownmost possibility'. This means that I am in some sense forced to ask the question of Being, both my own and that of the world, given that with me my world will end. Furthermore *angst* reveals to me the possibility of an 'authentic' mode of existence and an authentic temporality. Because of the way in which as a human I am essentially always ahead of myself, for me to be brought vividly to confront my death is to be confronted with a loss of present which is also equally loss of future. If I can grasp this truth and live with it – that my present is always a possible loss of the very possibility of my having a future – I am existing authentically, and, Heidegger claims, in such authentic existence the future has a priority over the present which is in some sense the reverse of the priority of the present over the future which he finds in inauthentic existence.

Despite the unfinished state of *Being and Time*, the text that was actually published, plus fragments and drafts of the remaining unpublished portion which have since come to light, make it possible to tell fairly reliably how the work was to have continued. The basic theme is that historically metaphysics has used time, and in particular a certain conception and experience of time, as the criterion for defining being. What is real has been construed as that which is forever present, present at all times. This means that time has had a kind of priority over being, although characteristically Heidegger also claims that traditional philosophy has been unaware of this priority or has even in some sense suppressed awareness of it. If this is right, one might go on to ask *what kind of (experience of) time* it is that gives rise to the concept of time which is used as the criterion for Being in traditional metaphysics. Heidegger's answer to this is that it is the 'inauthentic' time of everyday experience – time as a single linear succession of present instants – which has traditionally functioned as a criterion. This leaves open the possibility that a different form of life, an authentic mode of existence, might have associated with it or even be constituted by a different form of temporality, and that asking the question of Being through the lens of this authentic temporality would give one a completely different kind of metaphysics. If traditional metaphysics was 'a metaphysics of presence' – what really existed was what was present – the new Heideggerian metaphysics will be different, because in it that which pre-eminently *is*, namely our death (because to live authentically is to live with death as our most real possibility and hence our fundamental reality), is something which by its very nature is not present (as long as we are). From the novel point of view provided by the experience of authentic temporality, the second part of *Being and Time* was to have completed the destruction of the history of metaphysics, and the reopening of the question of Being in its full richness. In principle this philosophy could have not just an existential, but also an eschatological dimension.

3. HEIDEGGER'S POLITICS AND HIS INFLUENCE

In 1933, just after Hitler came to power, Heidegger, who was at the height of his philosophical reputation, joined the Nazi Party and became Rector of the University of Freiburg, the much-celebrated first National Socialist Rector of any German university. During an initial period he was a very visible and outspoken partisan of the regime, issuing public appeals to support Hitler (for instance, in the plebiscite to legitimise withdrawal from the League of Nations), organising forms of espionage and denunciations of politically suspect colleagues, etc. He seems to have been motivated by the belief that he could 'lead the *Führer*' (*den Führer zu führen*), and he threw himself into academic politics with a will. After about a year, however, he lost a struggle within the Party for control over the universities and resigned the Rectorship. During the war he became increasingly disaffected with the Party leadership and criticised some aspects of the official ideology in his lectures, retreating into what one Party source called a 'private National Socialism'. Although he lived on until 1976, he seems never to have seriously questioned or revised this private National Socialism.

After the war he was banned (until 1951) from teaching or publishing, but continued to dominate the German academic world until well into the mid-1960s. In this connection it is important to recall that Germany in the immediate post-war period was an intellectual and cultural vacuum. Virtually all intellectual figures of any standing had been exiled, killed, or forced to spend years in military service and/or captivity. Despite the ban, Heidegger, along with one or two extremely aged Neo-Kantians, was the only game in town. Already in the 1930s Heidegger had had a profound effect on some younger French philosophers, and after the war he was also able to maintain and even extend excellent relations with a number of leading French intellectuals. Eventually, however, the Heideggerian intellectual hegemony in Germany was undermined by two developments. First, in the early 1950s two of the members of the so-called Frankfurt School (Horkheimer and Adorno) returned from exile in the United States and began gradually to try to build up a progressivist intellectual culture in the German Federal Republic, and this eventually provided a kind of counterweight to Heidegger's philosophy (which they interpreted as being of a piece with his politics). Adorno's first public attack on Heidegger, *Jargon der Eigentlichkeit*, appeared in 1964, and in 1966 he published a philosophically more substantive criticism of Heidegger in his *Negative Dialektik*. In parallel to these rather mandarin forms of rejection, the German student movement, which was committed to effecting a break with the academic-rightist past, was gaining momentum in the 1960s, making it difficult for Heideggerian forms of thought to retain their hold on university students. The second development was the rise of 'analytic' philosophy, which began in the mid-1960s under the auspices of Günther Patzig at Göttingen and Ernst Tugendhat at Heidelberg. Tugendhat was a former Heideggerian who described himself as having been 'converted' (*bekehrt*) during a sabbatical he spent at the University of Michigan. Heidegger turned out eventually to have put down deeper roots in France than in Germany, perhaps precisely because it was possible for French thinkers, given their greater distance, to read Heidegger in abstraction from his immediate political context. In the 1930s Heidegger had also had some students from China and Japan, most notably perhaps Shuzo Kuki of Kyoto University. Several of his works were translated into Chinese, and his philosophical views have continued to be extremely influential throughout East Asia ever since.

Heidegger's combination of high, if idiosyncratic, philosophical gifts, substantial historical erudition, a wilfully rebarbative and cryptic style, and extreme right-wing politics has made it extremely difficult to get him into focus, and even more difficult to assimilate his philosophy into any of the usual philosophic categories – which, of course, was precisely part of his intention. His influence on the philosophy of the second two-thirds of the twentieth century can hardly be overestimated, and was by no means confined to figures on the political Right. No other philosopher has had anything approaching his impact on the philosophical life of continental Europe, Asia, or South America. Sartre, Merleau-Ponty, Marcuse, Derrida, Foucault, Rorty, and Levinas are only some of the philosophers who have been deeply influenced by his work. His influence on the general cultural life of Europe in the latter part of the century was equally profound, most notably on certain forms of psychology, anthropology, environmental studies, and theology, on the academic study of literature, architecture, and the visual arts, and on individual creative artists like Beckett, Blanchot, Celan, Godard, and Kundera, to name but a few of the more distinguished.

In contrast Heidegger has had relatively little effect on the philosophy of the English-speaking world. Despite the existence of a community of Heidegger scholars in North America, his philosophy is still not part of the common universe of discourse in that part of the world. The radical right-wing political philosopher Leo Strauss kept the memory of Heidegger alive in the United States among his coterie of followers, and Hannah Arendt, who made a name for herself in the 1960s as a political journalist, had written her doctoral dissertation under Heidegger, and publicised some of his views, but much of the interest in Heidegger which this generated was biographical and prurient – Arendt, who was Jewish, had been Heidegger's mistress during the late 1920s. None of this contributed to any philosophical appropriation of Heidegger's thought. Perhaps not surprisingly, the part of the US academy that has been most hospitable to Heidegger is the large community of Roman Catholic philosophers and their institutions. The reason for Heidegger's neglect in the world of analytic philosophy derives from his complete lack of interest in natural science or logic as models for human knowledge and in everyday ethics, and his basic orientation towards religious and historical questions. This reason has combined with a reaction to his obscure, pretentious style and repellent politics to produce a very powerful exclusionary effect. In the context of the world as a whole, however, this Anglo-American reaction is a local phenomenon, and must be viewed as such by anyone interested in trying to come to a judicious assessment of the significance of Heidegger's philosophy and its place in history.

LATIN AMERICAN PHILOSOPHY

EDUARDO RABOSSI

1. TWO SENSES OF 'LATIN AMERICA'

'Latin America' is used as a collective noun to denote a number of states (nineteen in 1945) in North, Central, and South America. Each has idiosyncratic geographic, ethnic, cultural, social, political, and economic features. But in spite of their differences, Latin American countries share a common political origin (Spanish/Portuguese conquest), a similar linguistic heritage (Spanish/ Portuguese), a dominant religion (Catholicism), and comparable predicaments *vis-à-vis* local, regional, and international affairs. It is no surprise, then, that Latin American countries show, by and large, similar patterns of development and evolution, and that the term 'Latin America' is also used to signify these shared traditions and relationships. Philosophical thinking is no exception to the rule. It has evolved in analogous periods, with similar influences and traditions, and produced comparable outputs. In referring to Latin American philosophy, therefore, I am presupposing this intensional sense of 'Latin America' and in what follows, I will ignore the national peculiarities associated with its extensional sense.

2. POSITIVISM VS. ANTIPOSITIVISM AND THE RISE OF ACADEMIC PHILOSOPHY

Positivism ruled the Latin American philosophical scene from 1870 to 1910. But from 1910 to 1920 onwards a wave of antipositivistic philosophies wiped out positivism and took over the stage. The antipositivist turn was influenced by a parallel and overlapping change in the institutional setting of philosophy. It was a turn from a non-academic to an academic practice, from a non-professional to a professional conception of the role of philosophy and philosophers. Philosophy departments and faculties, flourishing 'athenea' and 'colleges', became the proper places to learn and to do philosophy. The transition from

positivism to antipositivism was mostly envisaged, promoted, and accomplished
in them.

The philosophical arguments advanced by the antipositivists against the dogmatic strictures, presuppositions, and generalisations of the positivists were generally cogent but were mixed up with *ad hominem* stratagems. Typically, the
antipositivists identified their views with 'serious' philosophy and criticised
positivism as an amateurish, second-rate, philosophy. In 1940, the Argentine
philosopher Francisco Romero famously heralded the entrance of Latin American philosophical thinking into 'normality'. By this he meant the widespread
adoption of European professional standards. But he also implied that there
are 'normal' philosophical problems, methodologies, and outcomes – precisely
those which antipositivist philosophies were disclosing and elaborating. This
identification of normal professional standards with normal philosophical contents and methods (provided, mostly, by German philosophers and philosophies)
is still operative in many Latin American philosophical quarters.

Thus from 1910 to 1920 onwards philosophical thinking in Latin America
was transformed into an activity undertaken in university cloisters. This was
not an unprecedented phenomenon. What was going on in Latin America at
that time could be equated to what had happened in British universities forty
years earlier when the professionalisation of philosophy came together with
an upsurge of admiration for German philosophy and sustained criticism of
positivism.

3. POSITIVISM

There was no such thing as a *standard* version of Latin American positivism. The
number of Latin American positivist thinkers was large, and their extraction and
importance were diverse; but it is agreed that the Venezuelan-Chilean Andrés
Bello (1781–1865), the Argentinian José Ingenieros (1877–1925) and the Cuban
José Varona (1849–1933) were among the most original and influential.

'Positivism' was a philosophical stance comprising antimetaphysical, scientific,
empiricist, deterministic, psychological, evolutionary, biological, and sociological topics. Positivists admired Charles Darwin and prized Comte and Spencer
as their philosophical heroes. Preference for one or the other gave rise to social or evolutionary positivist accounts. In essence, positivism was a naturalistic
philosophical endeavour. Positivists rejected a priori and intuitive methodologies, execrated abstract metaphysical speculations, praised science as providing
the most reliable knowledge about man and the universe, and tried to produce
syntheses of scientific findings in which they elucidated the nature of physical,
biological, psychological, and social phenomena.

But positivists did not conceive of themselves as playing a mere intellectual game: most of them were personally concerned with the institutional, moral, educational, and social problems of their countries and were influential in the design and implementation of governmental policies (some held relevant political positions). They were truly engaged intellectuals and positivist tenets were incorporated in the working ideology of the leading classes, progressive or conservative alike. Some outcomes were eccentric. For instance, in Mexico, there was for a time, a positivist political party, the 'Científicos' (the 'Scientists'); the Brazilian flag reproduces the positivist motto 'Ordem e Progresso' ('Orden and Progress'); as late as 1925–35, a 'Comité Positivista Argentino' (Argentine Positivist Commitee) was very active and published a periodical named *El positivismo* (*positivism*). This list could be extended.

4. ANTIPOSITIVISM

The antipositivist reaction was based on a sharp criticism of positivist tenets. Antipositivists stressed the autonomy of philosophy, argued for the legitimacy of metaphysical speculation and the reliability of intuition, expressed contempt for logical strictures, thought of themselves as opening philosophical paths arbitrarily precluded or ignored by positivists, and were unimpressed by scientific achievements. The French philosophers Emile Boutroux, Emile Meyerson and Henri Bergson were important allies. But German philosophy was the dominant tradition: Karl Krause, Hermann Cohen, Paul Natorp, Wilhelm Dilthey, Edmund Husserl, Max Scheler, Nicolai Hartmann, Martin Heidegger, among others, were influential at different times and in different degrees.

A host of local figures took up an active role under the canopy provided by the new heroes. Most of them had been trained in positivist strictures and shared a strong reaction against positivism. They have been described as the 'Founding Fathers': the standard list includes: Argentinians Alejandro Korn (1860–1936) and Francisco Romero (1891–1962), Brazilian Raimundo de Farias Brito (1862–1917), Chilean Enrique Molina (1871–1964), Mexicans José Vasconcelos (1882–1959), Samuel Ramos (1897–1959) and Antonio Caso (1883–1946), Peruvian Alejandro Octavio Deustúa (1849–1945), and Uruguayan Carlos Vaz Ferreira (1872–1958).

Marxism also made its entrance at this time. For instance, in Argentina, Juan B. Justo (1865–1928), one of the founders of the Socialist Party, translated *Das Kapital* into Spanish. He was influenced by Eduard Bernstein, and also wrote on the philosophy of history. In Perú, José Carlos Mariátegui (1895–1930), the most original Latin American Marxist thinker, 'read' Peruvian reality through a fresh interpretation of Marxist tenets. Thomist and Neo-Thomist philosophers were also active in confessional centres, universities, and schools; the French philosoher Jacques Maritain was most popular among them.

The influence of 'travellers', like the Estonian Hermann Keysserling and the Spaniard José Ortega y Gassett, was also important. Ortega's criticisms of positivism and his attractive presentation of contemporary German philosophy were crucial in Mexico and Argentina for the success of the antiposivist turn. The activity and influence of emigrés fleeing from Spanish Francoism and Italian Fascism, were also relevant, such as the Spaniard José Gaos (1900–69) and the Italian Rodolfo Mondolfo (1877–1976), who settled in Mexico and Argentina respectively. There were many others.

Antipositivism set the mood of Latin American philosophical thinking for years to come. The lack of strong philosophical traditions and the recurrent attitude of ignoring or despising their own philosophical ancestors and contemporaries favoured the systematic 'importation' of philosophies from some preferred country or tradition. The philosophical *status quo* thus created was a pluralistic co-existence of competing views. It was not a successful experience. Instead of inspiring fresh theoretical blendings and synthesis, it gave rise to an eclecticism that tended to reproduce the quarrels of its European counterparts. Consequently, the standard way of doing philosophy consisted mainly in mimicking the styles, problems and arguments of the imported philosophers and philosophies.

However, mimicry did not necessarily produce second-rate or plainly repetitive outputs. Both during the positivist and the antipositivist periods, some Latin American philosophers produced interesting and, at times, original pieces. A tentative list, no doubt controversial, includes Andrés Bello's (1781–1865) *Filosofía del entendimiento* (*Philosophy of Understanding*) (1880), José Ingenieros's *Principios de Psicología* (*Principles of Psychology*) (1919), Juan Carlos Mariátegui's *Siete ensayos sobre la realidad peruana* (*Seven Essays on Peruvian Reality*) (1928), Carlos Vaz Ferreira's *Lógica viva* (*Live Logic*) (1910), Carlos Astrada's (1894–1970) *El juego existencial* (*The Existential Game*) (1933), and Antonio Caso's (1943) *La existencia como economía, como desinterés y como caridad* (*Existence as Economy, Unselfishness and Charity*) (see bibliography pp. 886–7).

5. PHILOSOPHY AND LITERATURE

Normally, there are boundaries, albeit vague, between philosophy and other disciplines or genres, but Latin American philosophical thinking does not respect any such boundaries. I have mentioned thinkers and works that fit a standard philosophical pattern. But this leaves out a number of Latin American essayists who gave a philosophical tone to their works and reached, at times, high levels of philosophical reflection – such as Argentinian Domingo F. Sarmiento (1811–88), Bolivian Alcides Arguedas (1879–1946), Cuban José Martí (1853–95), Mexicans Justo Sierra (1848–1912) and Alfonso Reyes (1889–1959), Peruvian Manuel Gonzalez Prada (1848–1918), Uruguayan José Enrique Rodó (1871–1917).

There are also important literary works, since the strategy of relating stories with the intention of disclosing philosophical presuppositions and implications has permeated Latin American literature from its very beginning. Novels are great instruments to that effect and it is agreed that Rómulo Gallegos's (1884–1969) *Doña Bárbara* (1929) is a representative example of that genre.

6. LATIN AMERICAN PHILOSOPHY AND THE QUEST FOR IDENTITY

By 1925–30 a most interesting controversy began to unfold. It involved some of the most renowned Latin American philosophers and lasted for almost four decades. The controversy was about the identity and aims of Latin American philosophising. A large number of issues were involved: the unrestricted universality attributed to philosophical statements, problems, and theories versus a restricted, 'located', universality or, even, sheer particularism; the cosmopolitan airs of philosophy versus a regional or national élan; the possibility of an original and authentic philosophical thinking versus a dependent, importative, or imitative one; the seemingly economic, political, and ideological neutrality of philosophy versus the assumption of its real, earthly, commitments; the impact of philosophy in everyday affairs versus its abstract and detached condition.

The controversy turned on the description and evaluation of the practice of philosophy in Latin America: how to *assess* the value of the professional practice of philosophy; what sort of *diagnosis* its shortcomings, deficiencies, and frailties merited; what a proper *prognosis* of its course of development would be; what philosophy *ought* to do and achieve in Latin America. These different topics, obviously related, were very often mixed up.

Questions about the identity and proper aims of philosophising in Latin America were not problematic for the positivists. They held that evolving countries needed a philosophical ideology to ground institutional, educational, and cultural policies. Therefore importing suitable philosophies and elaborating them domestically with an eye on local problems was a proper course for intellectual action. Things changed, however, when antipositivism, with its professional claims and abstract proposals, took over the stage; and the debates were accentuated in the aftermath of the First World War, in the light of new political movements from Europe such as fascism, nazism, and francoism, the economic crisis of the 1930s, and the paramount role that the United States started to play in Latin American affairs. All these changes instituted a new context in which questions about the role of philosophy and the part that philosophers were supposed to play were obviously relevant.

As one would expect, there were voices in favour of practising academic philosophy according to universal standards. They claimed that there was nothing peculiar about the practice of philosophy *in* Latin America. Like doing philosophy *in* France, Germany, or Britain, it had to be serious, technical, and original. Our shortcomings were due to contextual problems that could be overcome by creating adequate conditions. Other voices gave a very different answer. They ran from messianic appeals to the peculiar historical role of the Latin American 'man', to more balanced views that stressed the peculiarity of our history, the predicaments of our situation, and the necessity of elaborating a philosophy that might help to undersand and to deal with them.

This way of setting the problem gave rise to the quest for a proper object of study and an adequate methodology. Was *Latin America* itself such an object? What of more specific entities, such as *México* or *Mexicans*, *Perú* or *Peruvians*? Were the regional or national cultures or problems possible objects of philosophical study? And what was the appropriate philosophical methodology? Was it acceptable to rely on imported ones? Did the whole quest mean leaving the universal claims of philosophy aside, or was it a way, perhaps *the* way, to redraw them in a refreshing way? Were these claims capable of producing an authentic Latin American philosophy? Those were the questions that worried Latin American philosophers for a while. (For a useful overview of the controversy and its protagonists, see Salazar Bondy (1968).)

After 1945, the discussion went off along different paths. But the question concerning the identity and aims of Latin American philosophising is (and should be) still with us. Philosophical Euro/North American centrism is a fact. For self-conscious Latin American philosophers, the search for a point of equilibrium between professional practice and philosophical authenticity is still an unsolved riddle.

Two final points. First, whatever the technical merits of the controversy, as early as the 1930s and 1940s Latin American philosophers were discussing a set of basic questions concerning the universal and neutral claims of philosophy that only years afterward were raised by Feminist and African philosophies. Second, from 1870 until 1945 (indeed until the 1960s) English-language philosophy was almost completely ignored. Only Hebert Spencer, William James (mostly on religious experience), and John Dewey (on education) were taken into serious consideration.

JAPANESE PHILOSOPHY

THOMAS KASULIS

The year 1868 marks the formal beginning of Japan's modern period and by the late nineteenth century we find distinctively modern modes of philosophising. In the Japanese context 'modern philosophy' suggests significant knowledge of, and response to, the Western philosophical tradition. In 1854 US gunboats ended two and a half centuries of self-imposed Japanese national isolation. Aware that they had fallen behind the West technologically, the Japanese overthrew the shogun in 1868 and reinstated imperial rule with hopes of rapid modernisation. Real power, however, lay in the hands of an elite class of intellectuals, many of whom at a formative age were sent to the West to study any number of subjects, including philosophy. Upon returning home they immediately applied their knowledge to restructuring Japanese society and to translating or analysing a wide variety of Western intellectual works.

The Japanese philosophers' reading of the Western situation was that it was mired in a series of apparently irresolvable polarities: Kant's or Hegel's idealism versus Comte's positivism or Locke's empiricism; deontological versus utilitarian ethics; the imperial system versus democracy; individualism versus collectivism; Marxism versus capitalism. Furthermore, there was the new Japanese conflict between Western and traditional Asian values. There were two common approaches to this polarised situation: either to argue for one pole over the other or to seek for a dialectical reconciliation between the opposites. Increasingly, especially from around the second decade of the twentieth century, the reconciliationists tended to dominate.

I. NISHIDA KITARŌ

Most scholars, both Japanese and Western, consider Nishida Kitarō (1870–1945) to have made a breakthrough with his *Zen no kenkyū (An Inquiry into the Good)* in 1911, which is still one of the most widely read books in modern Japanese philosophy. What most excited readers was Nishida's innovation of writing in a Western philosophical style of argument while incorporating and developing ideas borrowed from the Asian as well as the Western tradition. The book's central purpose was its attempt to overcome major bipolarities, especially that between positivism and idealism, fact and value.

Nishida's practice of Zen Buddhist meditation has a bearing here. Zen maintains that through meditation one can have access to reality 'as it is', without the interference of human conceptualisation. In itself, that reality is completely meaningless ('empty'): meaning requires concepts. Yet, that immediacy is the raw material out of which one may construct meaning conceptually and affectively, with either delusion or insight. In the book Nishida hardly referred to meditation at all, but instead built upon William James's notion of 'pure experience'. With his Zen-nuanced sense of the term, Nishida argued that thought arises out of the immediacy of pure experience to address disunities and once thought has accomplished its task, there is a return to pure experience. In effect, Nishida had hoped to develop not a religious philosophy based on Zen, but instead to apply certain general Zen insights to a philosophical psychology or epistemology built on Western terms. There were problems with this approach. For example, how does one know when to shift from immediacy into thought? Does not that decision itself require thought? Enamoured of Western voluntarism, Nishida thought of pure experience as having a will towards unity that connected the immediacy with thought. Later, he saw this position as overly 'psychologistic' and 'mystical'.

In time, Nishida abandoned his old philosophical formulations for new ones. A most striking innovation was his 'logic of *basho*', developed in 1920s and 1930s (see, for example, Nishida 1927, 1929, and 1934). The Japanese word *basho* is an ordinary word for 'place', but it also had at the time some technical meanings as well, for example, as 'field' in physics or as a translation for the ancient Greek term '*topos*'. The important move in Nishida's use of this term was that he wanted to shift his focus from a psychologistic voluntarism to something more 'logical', namely, an analysis of conceptualisation and judgement as formed within context or *basho*. For example, he believed empirical judgement operates in one *basho* and idealist judgement in another. Yet there is a hierarchy among such *basho*. For one to make an empirical judgement such as 'the cup is on the table', one must first be in the idealist *basho* of judging, for example, 'I visually experience the cup on the table.' Empirical judgement, therefore, cannot occur without a preceding idealist judgement as part of its larger context. Within its own *basho* empiricism ignores this dependency, dissolving its experientially idealist or subjectivist roots into an unarticulated 'nothingness' *vis-à-vis* its own judgements. For idealism, on the other hand, empiricism's *basho* is nothing more than the 'being' constructed by the self.

That is not the end of Nishida's analysis, however. Both empiricism and idealism operate within a self-world polarity, each emphasising one pole. There is a third even more foundational *basho,* sometimes referred to as the *basho* of 'absolutely nothing' *(zettai mu).* This *basho,* defying anything but the most crude articulation, is not a 'place' for philosophising but is the ground out of which philosophies (such as idealism and empiricism) arise. For Nishida, the acting of self on the world (the idealist moment) and the world's being intuited by the self (the empiricist moment) are in fact inseparable parts of one event, the so-called 'acting-intuiting'. A corollary is that what is fundamental is no longer the Aristotelian substance (found in the sentential subject) with its qualifying attributes (found in the sentential predicate). Instead, by making the acting-intuiting event the foundation for all judgements, Nishida argued for a 'logic of the predicate' in which the substance qualifies an event, just as the sentential subject modifies the predicate. Through this analysis, Nishida hoped to show that empiricism and idealism are distinct but logically interdependent and both depend on a 'place' of infinite, boundless scope.

Throughout his career Nishida applied his current epistemology to ethics, philosophical psychology, logic, aesthetics, philosophy of religion, and politics. Given both his prominence as one of Japan's leading intellectuals and the ultranationalism rampant in the 1930s through 1945, Nishida found himself called upon (in a way he could not easily refuse) to make public addresses on topics related to 'the Japanese spirit'. Within the severe restrictions on freedom of thought and expression at the time, Nishida tried to rework some ideas of Japanese nationalist ideology to fit into a less ethnocentric and jingoistic context more to his personal liking. Depending on one's own perspective, this could be interpreted as either collaborating with, or undermining, the ultranationalist ideology and those two interpretations continue to be debated today (see Heisig and Maraldo, 1994). Even in Nishida's own lifetime, some prominent members of the Kyoto School such as Tosaka Jun (1900–1945) and Miki Kiyoshi (1897–1945) criticised their mentor's philosophy for its possible application to right-wing ideology. Both died in prison for their own leftist philosophical leanings.

2. TANABE HAJIME

When a name besides Nishida's is associated with the early Kyoto School, it is usually that of Nishida's younger colleague at Kyoto University, Tanabe Hajime (1885–1962). Although sympathetic to the questions Nishida raised, Tanabe was dissatisfied with Nishida's answers. With a strong background in logic, mathematics, philosophy of science, and epistemology, in 1922–3 Tanabe studied in

Germany with Edmund Husserl and Alois Riehl. Not surprisingly, his criticism
of Nishida focused on the logic of *basho*. Tanabe's fundamental objection was
that Nishida's logic essentially moved directly from the level of the universal
(for example, 'all men are mortal') to the particular ('Socrates is mortal'), or as
Tanabe often described it, from the genus to the individual. Tanabe maintained
that in so doing Nishida had overlooked the critical middle component, the
level of the 'species' where the specification of Socrates' being a man serves to
connect the major premise in the syllogism to the conclusion. Tanabe suggested
this level of 'species' *(shu)* is not only logically necessary, but also in some ways
experientially primary as well. We experience Socrates first as a man, then abstract out from that his membership in the genus of mortal human beings, and
finally logically deduce his individual mortality. Tanabe dubbed this a 'logic of
species' to contrast it with Nishida's position.

   In his social thought, Tanabe saw species as the crucial domain of cultural,
ethnic, social, and national identification: our experience is formulated in the
language, concepts, and values of our social context. Of course, some ultra-
nationalists happily embraced such a theory that people are first concretely and
experientially Japanese, only by abstraction human beings, and only by deduction individuals. Tanabe himself had generally accepted that interpretation, a
position causing him anguish in the last years of the war, leading to his philosophy of 'metanoia' which maintained that every adequate philosophy must
contain a basis for self-criticism to prevent its absolutising itself.

3. WATSUJI TETSURŌ

Watsuji Tetsurō (1889–1960) was a third major philosophical figure from this period. He is only loosely associated with the Kyoto School, spending most of his
career teaching at Tokyo University. As a young man he was deeply interested in
nineteenth-century European thought, focusing on Schopenhauer, Nietzsche,
and Kierkegaard. Following those interests, he studied philosophy in Germany
from 1927–8 and was deeply impressed with Heidegger's thought. Upon returning to Japan, however, Watsuji realised that the traditional thought and
values of Japanese culture did not mesh well with Western, including Heideggerian, assumptions. So he immersed himself in analysing culture's relationship
to history, thought, and value. Appointed professor of ethics first at Kyoto and
later Tokyo University, Watsuji worked on his *magnum opus* in ethical theory,
his three-volume *Rinrigaku* (*Ethics*, 1937–49). Drawing on his general understanding of culture, his previous studies of Japanese culture, and his insights into
Western philosophical thinking, Watsuji provoked a new way of understanding
the human situation and its relation to ethical values and behaviour.

Watsuji claimed that being fully human and being fully ethical were both realised in what he called 'betweenness', the space between the social and the individual. We are born into that betweenness and then the social pole takes over by educating us in the basic values of human relatedness (a 'Confucian' paradigm). For ethics to flourish, one must eventually negate that pole to move towards the individuality wherein values arise from autonomy and personal freedom (a 'Western' paradigm). To achieve fully one's deepest humanity and ethical nature, however, one must also negate that pole as well and move again towards a betweenness that accepts socially instilled values, not this time as part of socialisation, but instead as a freely chosen option. Such a dialectical betweenness negates the poles of both the simply social and the simply individual. During the nationalistic period Watsuji emphasised Japan's distinctive geographical and intellectual position between a Confucian East Asia and an individualist West. He believed Confucianism was ultimately unviable because it denied human freedom and he believed Western (especially American) culture would eventually fail because of individualism's denial of social connectedness.

In examining those three major Japanese philosophers of the period, we find they all tried to establish a third position that would be the logical or experiential ground for the binary oppositions. Unlike Hegel, these Japanese dialectical thinkers did not see the third position as sublating the logically prior opposites. Instead they analysed the opposites as emerging out of the abstraction from the third position. Because of the politics of the time, however, those theoretical and logical analyses were sometimes given (by the philosophers themselves or by their interpreters) a politicised reading. Ironically, that situation only confirmed the thrust of their own philosophical systems, namely, that philosophers' ideas cannot be excised from their experiential context in culture and history.

KNOWLEDGE, LANGUAGE, AND THE END OF METAPHYSICS

SENSIBLE APPEARANCES

MICHAEL MARTIN

The problems of perception feature centrally in work within what we now think of as different traditions of philosophy in the early part of the twentieth century, most notably in the sense-datum theories of early analytic philosophy together with the vigorous responses to them over the next forty years, but equally in the discussions of pre-reflective consciousness of the world characteristic of German and French phenomenologists. In the English-speaking world one might mark the beginning of the period with Russell's *The Problems of Philosophy* (Russell 1912) and its nemesis in Austin's *Sense and Sensibilia* (Austin 1962 – published posthumously, but given originally as lectures at the end of our period in 1947). On the continent, a corresponding route takes us from Husserl's *Logical Investigations* (Husserl 1900/1) to Merleau-Ponty's *Phenomenology of Perception* (Merleau-Ponty 1945).

While the structure of the problems is recognisably the same in both traditions, over this chapter I elaborate and comment on some of the differences in these treatments. It is easy to feel at home with the alleged attachment to common sense and obvious truths that the analytic tradition from the outset avows. But when one looks at the topic of perception, a concern as central to the development of early analytic philosophy as is the study of logic and analysis of meanings, early analytic theories look strange and idiosyncratic. Much of what the phenomenologists have to say, on the other hand, strikes more of a chord with contemporary English-speaking philosophers than their analytic forebears. But the development of early-twentieth-century discussions shows that the parallels and differences among these thinkers, and the echoes with the way that we now conceive of these problems, are somewhat more elusive than one might expect.

1. THE SENSE-DATUM THEORY

The question of realism is intertwined with the discussion of sense perception in much early-twentieth-century English-speaking philosophy. Different varieties of realist insist that we have cognition of a world independent of this cognition at the same time as worrying about how sense perception can put us, at least in part, in contact with this world. For example, some philosophers who dubbed themselves *critical* realists emphasise both the reality of a world apart from us, and also the problematic nature of our sensory contact with it (see Drake *et al.* 1920). In Oxford, at the turn of the century Harold Prichard follows his teacher John Cook Wilson in throwing off idealism (Prichard 1909). From then on, his work on the theory of knowledge is dominated by discussion of perception and the topic of perception remains a favourite one among Oxford philosophers of succeeding generations – H. H. Price, Gilbert Ryle, A. J. Ayer, G. A. Paul and J. L. Austin. Nonetheless, the dominant strand within the English-speaking tradition is a peculiarly Cambridge development: sense-datum theories of appearance and perception.

The term 'sense-datum' was coined for use in this discussion by G. E. Moore in 1909 (see Moore 1909) but put first into the public sphere by Bertrand Russell in *The Problems of Philosophy* (Russell 1912), though the term was in fact first used in relation to perception in the late nineteenth century in Royce and James. Along with Moore and Russell we can count two other figures as important in developing this tradition: C. D. Broad, one of Russell's pupils (his preferred term, though, is 'sensum' – see Broad 1914) and H. H. Price (see Price 1932). Price was an Oxford philosopher who studied with Moore before returning to Oxford, where in due course he taught Wilfrid Sellars, son of the Critical Realist Roy Wood Sellars and a fierce and influential critic of the 'myth' of the given (i.e. the sense-datum) that Price had helped to promulgate.

Sense-data are much discussed by many philosophers in the first half of the twentieth century, though few actually advocated the theory. Later in the century, in discussions of sense-datum theories, we find A. J. Ayer's name added to the list. Ayer certainly uses the term 'sense-datum' in outlining his views (see Ayer 1940), and J. L. Austin (with an obvious Oxford bias) identifies Ayer along with Price as a representative of the sense-datum tradition. As we shall see below, though, Ayer has a rather different view of these matters and should not be included among the sense-datum theorists simply because he also employs the term they used.

Sense-datum theorists claim that when someone senses, he or she is 'given' a sense-datum in their experience. Within these terms, the problem of perception then becomes that of determining what the relation is between the sense-datum and any material object of perception. Note that the term 'sense-datum' is introduced as standing for *whatever* is given to the mind in sense perception. As introduced, the term is not intended to be prejudicial between physical objects, parts of physical objects, or non-physical objects. Nonetheless, in using the term the sense-datum theorists implicitly make two further assumptions which are hardly commented on in their presentations, but which we should now view as highly controversial. First, Moore, Russell, Broad, and Price all assume that whenever one has a sensory experience – when one perceives an object or when at least it appears to one as if something is there – then there must actually be something which one stands in the relation of sensing to; indeed they assume there must be something which actually has the qualities which it seems to one the object sensed has. So if it now looks to me as if there is a brown expanse before me as I stare at the table, then an actual brown expanse must exist and be sensed by me. This is so even if we consider a case in which I am misperceiving a white object as brown, or even suffering an hallucination or delusion of the presence of brown tables when none are in the vicinity.

If one made a similar proposal about the objects of psychological states such as belief or desire, few would find the idea compelling. If James wants Santa Claus to visit, we do not assume that there is an actual being, Saint Nicholas, of whom James has the desire that he should visit. We all accept that such psychological states can have merely 'intentional' objects, that they are seemingly relations to objects, but no such appropriate object need actually exist for us to be in such psychological states. One popular diagnosis of the key error made by sense-datum theorists is therefore that they have become confused about this point: they ignore the intentionality of perception and fail to note that the objects of sensing may be merely intentional objects, not actually existing (see, for example, Anscombe 1965 and Searle 1983: ch. 2). This is also one aspect in which the early analytic tradition seems strikingly different from the phenomenological school, which precisely emphasises the intentionality of perception. However, as we shall see, the relation between sense-datum theories and intentionality, and consequently the contrast between the sense-datum tradition and phenomenology, is more complex than this suggests.

The second questionable assumption at play is that there is a theoretically interesting unity to the category of things which can be given to us in sensing. Only given this assumption would we suppose that there is any point in talking about sense-data and having a sense-datum theory. One could introduce the term 'stomachum-datum' for whatever is placed in one's stomach, but it does not follow that stomacha-data constitute a theoretically useful kind of thing to debate about. That the sense-datum theorists suppose that we can debate in general about sense-data reflects the further assumption not only that things are given to us, but that an important species of thing is so given.

This said, sense-datum theorists do not immediately assume that what is given must be something other than a physical object. Although they almost invariably believe that sense-data are non-physical, this is normally a conclusion that they argue for. In Russell's *The Problems of Philosophy*, the argument is swift and its brevity unsatisfactory – he merely appeals to the fact that we can have conflicting appearances of one stable object, namely a table, as we view it from different perspectives (Russell 1912: ch. 1). Russell's discussion is almost definitely intended to echo the (equally brief and unsatisfactory) argument to similar conclusions in Hume's *Enquiry concerning Human Understanding*. Moore, on the other hand, tends to agonise protractedly over the matter, repeatedly so in paper after paper (see Moore 1914, 1925). On the whole, he sets out to establish the conclusion through some variant of the argument from illusion (that is, appealing to the fact that an object can appear to be other than it really is) and the same is true in Broad and Price.

For these authors, we first identify a case which we would agree is one of something looking brown to one, even if no physical candidate for perception is brown. Following the assumption highlighted above, the sense-datum theorist concludes that in this case one senses some non-physical brown object of sense. Then, they employ some generalising move to show that even in cases in which we thought there could be no illusion there must still be some such non-physical entity present to the senses. The grounds for this generalising move are not always made explicit, though in general it seems to be taken as offering us the best explanation of the data, even though the philosophical theories on offer are not intended to replace a psychological or neurophysiological study of perceiving.

On the whole, these authors propose non-physical sense-data as the direct objects of sense without denying that we also sense physical objects. In Moore's case, throughout his writings, the sense-datum theory is combined with a robust and common-sense realism about the ordinary world (see especially Moore 1925). Russell at different times flirts with phenomenalism, according to which the physical world is a construction out of sensory elements and facts (see Russell 1914), and with neutral monism, according to which both the world, and then the mind, are constructions out of a common basis in sensory acts (see Russell 1921). While Price's account of the perceptual act echoes Moore in many of its details, when it comes to metaphysics he is much more drawn to phenomenalism, though his eventual final position is not quite phenomenalistic in form.

In both England and the United States, these original sense-datum theorists were greatly influential, but principally as a target of criticism. What is of interest in them is how the problems as they conceive them form a framework for discussion, rather than the ways in which others adopted their approach and elaborated on it. Before tracing out the various lines of criticism, though, I want first to contrast this theoretical framework with a seemingly radically different one from the same period within the German-speaking world.

2. PHENOMENOLOGY AND PERCEPTION

In the late nineteenth century, Franz Brentano reintroduced into philosophical usage the term 'intentionality' from scholastic philosophy, in order to designate the problem of how the mind can be related to objects in thought (see Brentano 1874 [1973: 84]). Edmund Husserl, a student of Brentanian psychology, founded Phenomenology as a philosophical discipline which has the task of describing how the various phenomena of the world can be given to the mind and be the objects of psychological states. Husserl placed as much emphasis on the problems of perception as on those surrounding the case of thought. In this he parallels the concerns of the sense-datum theorists. Much of the second part of Husserl's *Logical Investigations* is given over to an account of perceptual consciousness. This focus is continued in later works as well, for example *Ideas*, his major treatise elaborated after the key turn in phenomenology where he introduced the idea of the 'phenomenological reduction' according to which the phenomenologist needs to bracket his or her ontological presuppositions in theorising and simply focus on an exact description of consciousness and its objects (Husserl 1913).

In the terms of *Ideas*, Husserl distinguishes the psychological act of perceiving, the *noesis*, from its content, the *noema*, which directs itself onto an object as presented in the act of perceiving. An act with this content can occur in the absence of its object. In this way Husserl affirms the intentionality of perception – the possibility that perceptual acts, no less than thoughts, can be seemingly directed on objects where no actual object exists to be perceived (Husserl 1913 [1982: 213–14]). At the same time, though, Husserl does not suppose that only intentional objects are involved in sense perception. He also affirms the presence of sensational aspects, or in the terms of *Ideas*, *hule*, the matter of an act of sensing (Husserl 1913 [1982: 203ff.]).

Husserl's thought is developed and radically criticised in Heidegger (Heidegger 1927) and in the works of Sartre and Merleau-Ponty; his views on perception are particularly addressed and elaborated by the latter two. Sartre's most Husserlian text is *The Psychology of Imagination* (Sartre 1940) and here one finds an emphasis also present in Husserl's lectures – the contrast within consciousness between sensing objects and imagining them. The thought that this introduces a difference within consciousness rather than a difference in the kinds of objects of consciousness contrasts strikingly with Moore's and Price's affirmations that any variation in consciousness is just a variation in the objects of consciousness. In Sartre's later *Being and Nothingness* (Sartre 1943), the focus is rather on the idea that pre-reflective consciousness is empty in itself, a vessel for the presentation of the world to the subject. Here Sartre joins Merleau-Ponty in being critical of Husserl's commitment to a passive aspect of experience in the form of *hule* (Sartre 1943 [1956: xxxv]).

One problematic question within both the phenomenological tradition and later interpretations is whether the phenomenologists can, or do, embrace realism about the perceived world. Raised as a question purely of phenomenology, the question of the reality of the object of sense is focused on how an object is given in sensation as real rather than imaginary. It is a matter of further and delicate debate whether these philosophers allow one to raise the external question whether the subject genuinely is related to an object independent of them in perception of the real. One line of interpretation sees Husserl, from *Ideas* on, as endorsing a transcendental idealism which avoids one raising this external question. Sartre's discussion of the objects of sensory consciousness in *Being and Nothingness* also has an idealistic flavour – as if the existence of a world for me is a matter of actual and potential course of sensory encounters. But for both authors there is a vocal line of interpretation which seeks to reconstruct a realist reading of their discussion of perceptual intentionality.

Merleau-Ponty's views indicate how delicate some of these questions are. First in *The Structure of Behaviour* (Merleau-Ponty 1942) Merleau-Ponty develops a phenomenology of perception which both exploits and is critical of Gestalt psychology. In part IV of that work he emphasises the thought that there is a conflict between 'naïve realism' as reflected in the phenomenology of perception – that we are given objects whose nature extends beyond what is given in perceptual consciousness – and the thought that our experiences are an upshot of causal processes in the natural world. This is a familiar theme within the analytic tradition as well. But it is notable that the early analytic tradition did not rely on this form of argument to any great extent. One reason for this is that much of the analytic discussion is done as a form of 'first philosophy', entirely prior to any empirical knowledge and hence scientific knowledge of the working of the senses.

Merleau-Ponty's attitude to empirical work on perception contrasts strikingly with this attitude. In his later *Phenomenology of Perception* (Merleau-Ponty 1945) Merleau-Ponty discusses the critical status of the body as phenomenally given in experience, partly appealing to neurological evidence in support of the claims he makes. Nonetheless, transcendental idealism is not rejected: experience is still a transcendental condition of empirical science. The key move here is rather that the transcendental ego is replaced as a precondition of experience by the phenomenal body acting as a condition of experience, so that nothing stands outside of consciousness as a condition of it.

Within both the analytic tradition and the phenomenological school there is the recognition that the objects of sense can present different, and even conflicting, appearances. Both allow for a contrast between mere momentary appearance and reality. Both recognise that the causal underpinnings of perception are open to empirical study, and both contrast such empirical work with philosophical reflection on the status of experience. Still the resulting philosophical discussion of these common problems is markedly different. And, strikingly here, the sense-datum tradition seems much, much further from us than the detailed phenomenological observations of Husserl, Sartre, and Merleau-Ponty, despite its claims to rest philosophical method on common-sense truths and analysis. Wherein lies the difference?

3. COMPARISONS AND CONTRASTS

Where Husserl emphasises the intentional object of perception and affirms that the ordinary world is given to us in sensory consciousness, Moore worries whether only the surfaces of objects or even something entirely distinct from the objects of the ordinary world can be present to us in vision. If Moore's anxieties seem to be at odds with naïve reflection on our experience, it may be tempting to follow recent analytic critiques of sense-datum theories and to suppose that their key mistake is to deny or ignore the intentionality of perception. And it is tempting to see this as the fundamental contrast between the development of the two discussions.

Yet the contrast is more elusive than this, and echoes down the analytic tradition beyond the limited and idiosyncratic commitments of the early sense-datum theorists. It is best to see them not as ignoring the phenomenon of intentionality, but rather questioning its centrality when one's concern is perception. Moore and Russell discussed the nature of judgement as they did the nature of sensing. In developing theories of judgement they did not suppose that when one makes a mistaken judgement there must be an entity which appropriately corresponds to what one judges about. When they treat sensing differently from judging, as they go on to do, this is presumably because they suppose that there is something distinctive about sensing which requires that an object be present to the mind.

Even if Moore seems to deny any intentionality to sense perception, the same is not true of all sense-datum theorists. Broad employs a distinction between the ontological and epistemological objects of sense which may be interpreted as admitting intentionality to sense perception (Broad 1937: 141–2). Price more clearly affirms this, and in doing so explicitly alludes to Husserl, in his account of perceptual acceptance; according to which, in being conscious of a non-physical sense-datum one is also under the impression of being presented by some aspect of a physical object (Price 1932: 151ff.).

Even in the context in which sense-datum theories were initially proposed, alternative approaches were offered which insisted that objects can appear other than they are. Critical Realists insisted that we are sensorily related to the world itself, but to account for appearances we need to recognise that objects have properties of appearing bent, or appearing red, as well as the more familiar intrinsic properties of actual shape and colour (see, for example, Dawes Hicks 1917). It is sometimes suggested that sense-datum theorists fail to note that there is no logical route from a claim about how things appear to how anything actually is. But if one looks at Broad's careful discussion of the critical realists, under the heading of the 'multiple relation theory of appearing', one can see that he is keenly aware of this alternative to his view, but thinks it explanatorily inadequate (Broad 1937: 178ff.). Sense-datum theorists do not assume that the truth of their view follows as a matter of logic. Nor do they need to insist that all aspects of how things appear to us need correspond to some property a sensed object actually has. The key assumption – undefended but constantly asserted – is that sensing involves the presentation of observable properties which must be instantiated for one to be appeared to as one is. This is consistent with supposing that there are other aspects of appearance which are to be explained differently. Again, this helps to underline that the sense-datum tradition could allow for intentional aspects to sense perception. So the explanation of why they emphasise what they do needs to look elsewhere.

These theorists are not subject to a general confusion about the phenomenon of intentionality. Rather, they seem to think that there is something distinctive about the case of sensing. However they seem ill prepared to offer any argument in support of this differential treatment. When Price comes to justify the assumption of the necessary existence of an object of sense, he claims it to be an indubitable principle that is just self-evident to us (Price 1932: 3ff.). On the whole, then, these various theorists suppose that there is an important difference between sensing proper and mere thinking, treating the two very differently.

At the same time, as we noted above, Husserl does not deny a role for sensation in perceptual consciousness and he emphasises the role of sensory matter, *hule*, in consciousness as well as *noema*. It cannot be said that the phenomenological tradition need insist that all that there is to sensory consciousness is the intentional object as given – although, Sartre did go on to affirm this, and Merleau-Ponty resisted any role for sensation in the phenomenology of perception. The contrast, therefore, seems to be more muted: the phenomenological tradition emphasises the intentionality of perception, while in some cases allowing for sensational aspects as well; with the sense-datum tradition the emphasis is on non-intentional aspects of sensing, and the contrast between it and thought, yet not all sense-datum theorists deny intentionality a role in perception.

To get at the essence of the opposition here, we need really to look to the aspects of the sense-datum theory which contemporaries reacted against. The essential contrasts stand out once we look at two further criticisms of the sense-datum theories, objections focused on elements of the approach which we now tend to play down. Recall that Moore insists that despite being non-physical sense-data are also mind-independent (Moore 1914). Broad is more cautious, carefully considering the various arguments for and against supposing mind-dependence, before settling on the same conclusion: that all sensa are (probably) mind-independent (Broad 1923 ch: XIII). Now, in claiming that non-physical sense-data are mind-independent, these theorists make their positions much more problematic than if they conceived as sense-data as akin to something sensational, subjective, or mind-dependent as many now conceive of mental images.

As Austin complains, in his scathing attack on the sense-datum tradition in *Sense and Sensibilia*, neither term of the sense-datum/material object dichotomy takes in the other's washing. Public objects of perception are not without exception material or physical: tables and trees may be composed of matter, but what of rainbows or shadows, sounds or smells? All of these belong among the shared objects of perception (Austin 1962: lect. VII). But if one can find no property in common among the material objects of sense, sense-datum theorists rule out finding an easy candidate for what sense-data are to have in common. For the only plausible such candidate would be that sense-data universally are dependent on our awareness of them in contrast to material objects; and this claim the sense-datum theorists denied. Of course, they still claimed that sense-data were 'private': a given sense-datum can be an object of awareness for one subject only. But this cannot operate as a definition of what a sense-datum is, since something's being private in this sense needs an explanation and the simple explanation of this in terms of mind-dependency is ruled out. Instead it must be claimed that the laws of nature are such that when a subject is in a position to have a sense experience, there must be some suitably placed sense-datum available, and that such a sense-datum would not thereby be available to anyone else. One gets no account of the intrinsic nature of sense-data from being told that they have the function of acting as the immediate objects of awareness. So the sense-datum theorists appear to commit themselves to there being a science of sense-data, dedicated to both the manner in which sense-data are correlated perfectly with our states of awareness and the underlying nature they have to allow for this.

When one looks to the early reactions to sense-datum theories, it is this picture of the nature of sense-data, the idea that there really is a substantive matter of disagreement about them and the nature of sense perception which needs to be settled by investigation, albeit one beyond any natural science, which provokes the most disagreement. C. I. Lewis, for example, who otherwise defends a notion of the given, criticises sense-datum theories for supposing that something substantial and independent of the subject can be given in a simple, single act of sensing. His preferred account of sensing (in terms of the instantiation of qualia, qualities as sensed) gives a role to our conceptual powers in bundling up qualia in different ways: one way as substantial objects to be perceived, the other way as acts of a perceiver apprehending such objects (Lewis 1929: appendix D). Similarly, the core of the disagreement between Ducasse and Moore is that Ducasse denies that it is obvious to us that the objects of sense must be substantial mind-independent objects (Ducasse 1942; Moore 1942). Again, G. A. Paul's puzzlement about the individuation and persistence conditions for sense-data is a matter of keen interest (in a way that the parallel question about mental acts would not be), precisely because it presses the question how substantial are we to suppose the realm of appearances to be (Paul 1936).

In fact it is here that one should also locate Ayer's theory of perception, which Austin lumps together with Price as an example of a sense-datum theory. Ayer takes over from Carnap and the logical positivists the thought that there can be no genuine metaphysical disputes – so what is at issue in debate about perception must surely be a disagreement about the choice of scheme to depict the facts which are agreed in common through empirical investigation. Sense-datum theorists cannot be concerned with the existence of controversial entities. Instead, Ayer suggests that we should see talk of sense-data as just offering us an alternative way of talking about facts that all parties already agree – that appearances can conflict and that illusions are possible (Ayer 1940: 55–7). Few philosophers at the time thought Ayer's reconstruction adequate. W. H. Barnes, for example, dismisses Ayer's suggestion as inaccurate to the debates he discusses, and his complaint seems to prefigure Wilfrid Sellars's later objections in 'Empiricism and the Philosophy of Mind' about Ayer's proposal that we simply have a novel language of sense-data (Barnes 1945, Sellars 1956 [1963: 135–9]).

Yet, if Ayer is not faithful to the debate and problems which preceded him, he does offer us a significant move in the development of this debate. For with the rejection of a substantive metaphysics of the non-physical objects of perception, the focus of the debate comes to both the argument from illusion and the need for an incorrigible basis for empirical knowledge. In turn, it is these elements that become the target for Austin's critique, even though incorrigibility is not central to the early sense-datum theorists.

Leaving these later developments aside for a moment, why should sense-datum theorists have insisted on the mind-independence of sense-data, given that this claim left them open to such attack? The answer is simple: they were concerned with realism. Moore's earliest forays into the area take place in his would-be refutation of absolute idealism. In his 'Refutation of idealism' he claims that in sensing we are aware of something independent of the mind, and hence through sensing we have a clear example of the falsity of idealism (Moore 1903). From then on we have the assumption that sensing is a form of knowing – for Russell it is the prime, but not sole, example of knowledge by acquaintance (Russell 1912: 72ff.). With this, we have the endorsement of the doctrine that knowledge is only of things independent of the knowing of them. The thought is echoed in Price too. Nor is this central element of the tradition overlooked by critics. In an early reaction to Russell, Harold Prichard accuses him of a 'sense-datum fallacy' (Prichard 1950: 200ff.). This is not, as one might expect from later criticisms, a focus on the invalidity of the argument from illusion. Rather, Prichard complains that the sense-datum theorists suppose that we know the objects of sense but that this is patently not so, since these objects cannot be mind-independent, as revealed by the argument from illusion.

And it is here that we get the hint of how the early analytic school developed so differently from the phenomenological tradition. When C. I. Lewis affirms the existence of an *ineffable* given, his target is in part the sense-datum approach (Lewis 1929: 53). He is critical of the idea that one can know anything without the mediation of concepts to bind together different instances into a common kind. That is to reject a key element of the sense-datum tradition: sensing as an example of a simple, primitive, or unanalysable state of knowing which relates the knower to something independent of the mind, where the subject's grasp of what is known is pre-conceptual.

This aspect of the sense-datum approach does contrast fundamentally with the phenomenological tradition. Although Husserl allows a role for the matter of episodes of perceiving, such aspects are not given to a subject as objects of awareness – they are not candidates for knowledge in the way that sense-data are supposed to be. In taking the most basic element of sensing to be knowledge of something preconceptual, the sense-datum tradition downplays any intentional aspect of experience, as if the intentionality of experience would result from the conceptual capacities of the thinker and so would not be a clear example of knowledge of a mind-independent realm.

Given the dominance of Moore's and Russell's work, discussion of perception within the analytic tradition tended to treat sensible appearances as predominantly a non-intentional phenomenon. But as Moore's and Russell's idiosyncratic preoccupations fell away, the motivation for such theories of perception shifted. As suggested above, Ayer is motivated more clearly by epistemological concerns, an interest in finding a proper foundation for empirical knowledge. Later in the century, the sense-datum approach is presented as combining suspect epistemological preoccupations with a controversial response to the argument from illusion. In fact, the common element in both the analytic and phenomenological tradition is a respect for the argument from illusion and problems of conflicting appearances – sense-data and the intentionality of perception are appealed to in different ways to solve these concerns. The peculiar development of the analytic tradition led to critiques in the works of Wilfrid Sellars and J. L. Austin at the mid-point of the century in the former's attack on the myth of the given and the latter's mocking rejection of the terms of the debate, which question even the force of the argument from illusion.

From the second half of the twentieth century, the analytic tradition is dominated by physicalism. Consequently the ontology of non-physical sense-data becomes increasingly unfashionable. Austin's attacks, begun at just the end of the period which concerns us here, mark the high point of interest within the English speaking world with perception. By the time the subject is of general interest again, the concern with illusion makes the idea of the intentionality of perception more attractive. Yet before one takes this to show a common concern with the phenomenological tradition, one should reflect that that tradition has a strikingly different, and more circumspect, attitude towards the natural sciences than does contemporary analytic work.

42

THE RENAISSANCE OF EPISTEMOLOGY

LUCIANO FLORIDI

The renaissance of epistemology between the two world wars forms a bridge between early modern and contemporary philosophy of knowledge. At the turn of the century there had been a resurgence of interest in epistemology through an anti-metaphysical, naturalist, reaction against the nineteenth-century development of Neo-Kantian and Neo-Hegelian idealism. Within German-speaking philosophy, this reaction had its roots in Helmholtz's scientific reinterpretation of Kant, in Brentano's phenomenology, and in Mach's neutral monism. In British philosophy, it had acquired the specific nature of a rebuttal of Hegelianism by G. E. Moore and Bertrand Russell. And in America, the new pragmatist epistemology of William James and C. S. Peirce had directed attention away from the traditional a priori to the natural sciences. The interwar renaissance of epistemology, however, was not just a continuation of this emancipation from idealism. It was also prompted by major advances in mathematics, logic, and physics which engendered new methodological concerns (as in the influential tradition of French philosophers of science: Duhem, Poincaré, Bachelard). Hence among the traits that became prominent as a result of this renaissance, one may list an interest in mathematical, natural, and social sciences; criticism of the possibility of synthetic a priori truth; logical and semantic investigations which transformed epistemology from a theory of ideas and judgement into a theory of propositional attitudes, sentences, and meanings; a realist and naturalist orientation that tended to accommodate, if not to privilege, commonsensical and empiricist demands; a reconsideration of the role of philosophy as a critical exercise of analysis rather than as an autonomous and superior form of knowledge; and, finally, a disregard for the philosophy of history and the temporal dialectic of conceptual developments.

Of course, these perspectives never formed a unified programme of research. Philosophers between the wars took very different positions when developing their epistemological investigations, and the full reconstruction and analysis of these cannot be the task of this brief chapter. Its more limited aim will be to outline the discussions, within different traditions, of one central theme – scepticism and the foundations of knowledge.

THE TWO FACES OF SCEPTICISM

Two questions set the issues for sceptical debates:

(K) Is knowledge possible?
(KK) Is epistemology possible?
    (i.e. is an epistemology that answers (K) possible?)

(K) proceeds bottom-up whereas (KK) works top-down in dealing with issues concerning the legitimacy of epistemic claims. At the beginning of our period, Edmund Husserl and the Neo-Thomistic philosopher Desiré Mercier clarified further the normative character of these issues.

According to Husserl (1950), the justificatory ground of a theory of knowledge cannot be provided by other instances of knowledge. Following a Cartesian strategy, we can analyse potential instances of knowledge by affixing to them an 'index of questionability'. The sceptic questions the possibility of ever removing the index permanently, and Husserl argued that any supposed solution of the sceptical challenge simply by some extension of knowledge would be fallacious. The infringement of Husserl's principle can be considered of a piece with the 'naturalistic fallacy' in ethics: (K) is not a question of natural science; by positing it, one asks whether what is considered to be knowledge *justifiably deserves* to be so described. Husserl formulated his principle by reacting against his previous psychologism and this explains why it can easily be formulated as an anti-naturalist dilemma: if a naturalised epistemology differentiates itself from a philosophical theory of knowledge by being empirically testable it raises the question of its own justification. Yet if it claims to be able to solve this foundational problem, it must provide a solution which cannot be in itself an instance of empirical knowledge, and with respect to which it must abandon its aspiration to gain the status of empirical science. The acceptance of this anti-naturalist stand was one of the reasons why Husserl argued for a purely conceptual approach to epistemology. Thus he held that the only correct way of dealing with (K) is by means of principled and convincing arguments, by 'placing it in the logical space of reasons of justifying and being able to justify what one says' as Sellars was later to say (Sellars 1963: 169).

But one can never be in a position to establish an answer to (K) if no satisfactory reply to (KK) can be provided. Questioning the possibility of epistemology rests on *the problem of the criterion* (Sextus Empiricus 1976: II.2) which Mercier relaunched as 'le cheval du bataille du scepticisme' (Mercier 1923; for a recent discussion, see Chisholm 1973, 1989). To know whether things really are as they seem to be, one needs a criterion for distinguishing between true and false appearances. But to know whether the criterion is reliable, one needs to know whether it succeeds in distinguishing between true and false appearances. And one cannot know this unless one already knows which appearances are true and which are false. So it seems that an epistemology cannot establish what, if anything, deserves to be called knowledge.

ANTI-NATURALISM AND THE FOUNDATIONAL PROBLEM IN GERMAN-SPEAKING PHILOSOPHY

Owing to his limited concern with scepticism, Kant had not considered (KK). The transcendental method of his first *Critique* was supposed to yield a justification for scientific knowledge, but what type of knowledge is exemplified by the *Critique* itself? How can it be justified without incurring a vicious circle? In 1807, the Kantian philosopher Jakob Friedrich Fries addressed this issue in his *Neue oder anthropologische Kritik der Vernunft*. Fries summarised the (KK) problem in terms of a trilemma: the premises of an epistemology can be dogmatically assumed, or justified by an endless chain of statements, or anchored to a psychological basis which is justificatory but not in need of a justification. During the 1910s and the 1920s there was a 'Fries-Renaissance', particularly in the work of Leonard Nelson (Haller 1974; Nelson 1971). Drawing on Fries's analysis, Nelson came to object to the entire project of an epistemology in the Cartesian, anti-sceptical, and justificatory sense, and to favour a more descriptive and psychologistic approach (Nelson 1930, 1965). Despite his criticism of foundational debates, Nelson's 'naturalised epistemology' contributed greatly to reawakening philosophers' interest in the foundational issue in the late 1920s and early 1930s. One philosopher especially influenced by his work was Moritz Schlick.

Schlick endorsed the Cartesian requirement that there be an absolutely certain foundation of knowledge. He also accepted that it was 'self-evident that the problem of the foundation of all knowledge is nothing else but the question of the criterion of truth' (Schlick 1979: II, 374) and supported a correspondence theory of truth. However, in his view 'anyone who holds that the Cartesian thesis [i.e. the direct perception of a fact of consciousness] constitutes knowledge will inevitably be drawn into a similar circle [i.e. Fries's trilemma]' (Schlick 1925 [1974: 86]). So he came to defend a foundationalism according to which there are objective facts, external to the knower's doxastic states, that are accessible by the knower and capable of justifying the knower's beliefs in a way that is sufficient for knowledge.

According to Schlick, *protocol propositions*, that is, basic statements, 'in absolute simplicity, without any forming, change or addition, set forth the facts, whose elaboration constitutes the substance of all science' (Schlick 1979: II, 370, see also 400–13). But although they are logically prior to other factual propositions, they are themselves grounded on a prior layer of indubitable, empirically contentful, 'affirmations' (*Konstatierungen*). These affirmations, for example, 'there is red here now', are expressions of immediate, simple, existential experiences which provide a genuine acquaintance with reality even though they are wholly subjective, fleeting, and ineffable. They are indubitable because to understand their meaning is to understand their truth; hence they constitute the basic form of evidence for protocol propositions, which are constantly tested against them. These 'affirmations' are, therefore, the foundation of science, not in a fixed, static, sense, but only in the sense that they form the constantly renewed ground necessary and sufficient for its open-ended development.

Schlick's foundationalism requires a verificationist semantics, an ostensive theory of meaning of elementary propositions, and a conception of ineffable experience of the world which is immediately 'given' to the subject. As a result it appeared to critics such as Otto Neurath similar to a philosophy of intuition; they argued that it was beset with solipsistic difficulties and contained unacceptable metaphysical theses.

Neurath's view was that only a nominalist and constructivist interpretation of the nature of protocol propositions – as actual statements, expressed in a physicalistic language, recording empirical observations – is metaphysically acceptable. Scientific theories could be grounded, empirically, on these basic protocol sentences, but no position 'external' to language is achievable. Sentences could be compared only with other sentences. Direct reference to external reality or internal experience is to be avoided as empty metaphysics. Since protocol sentences are intrinsically fallible and hence always corrigible in principle, any Cartesian demand for absolute certainty is unrealistic and misleading. For Neurath, the epistemic justification of science was not to be achieved by means of an appeal to external facts or alleged intuitions, but internally, through logical coherence (which did not necessarily exclude some ordering relations), instrumental economy, pragmatic considerations of social and scientific ends, a rational use of conventions by the scientific community, and a constantly open and public debate. Following Duhem, Neurath argued that, given an apparently successful theory, rival explanations can be made to fit the same evidence that supports it, and that in replacing or revising a theory, hypotheses and observation statements come under scrutiny as whole networks, not individually. Practical expedience rather than absolute truth was determinant.

Neurath summarised his position in a famous analogy: 'We are like sailors who have to rebuild their ship [the system of knowledge] on the open sea, without ever being able to dismantle it in dry-dock and reconstruct it from its best components' (Neurath 1983: 92). Hegel had stressed a similar point: 'the examination of knowledge can only be carried out by an act of knowledge. To examine this so-called instrument is the same thing as to know it. But to seek to know before we know [i.e. Kant's critical project] is as absurd as the wise resolution of Scholasticus, not to venture into the water until he had learned to swim' (Hegel 1830 [1975: 14]). This was not the only similarity between Neurath's and Hegel's coherentism. A direct consequence of the former's holistic and non-subjectivist 'pan-internalism' was a strong tendency towards a unified and synoptic approach to the entire domain of human knowledge. This 'epistemological totalitarianism' was a feature shared by other approaches to the foundational problem, such as Hilbert's and Cassirer's, which were similarly suspicious of the Cartesian subjective turn, though favourable to Kantian constructionism rather than pure coherentism. In Neurath, this tendency was reflected in his project for an *International Encyclopedia of Unified Science* (1938–70). The programme of the *Encyclopedia* was presented as an explicit development of the ideas of the French Enlightenment, of Diderot's famous *Encyclopédie*. But the latter had a Cartesian basis, so the comparison should rather be with Hegel's *Encyclopaedia of the Philosophical Sciences*, although Neurath's project had a methodological justification in place of Hegel's ontological one.

Schlick was firmly hostile to Neurath's coherentism. If epistemic statements are not based on a specific set of more basic protocol propositions ultimately rooted in sense-experience of the world, all propositions may be regarded as in principle corrigible and their truth can only consist in their mutual agreement within the system of knowledge. Schick argued that such coherence provides too little – truth can be equated to logical consistency only in a formal system but not in an empirical science, since a coherent tale may otherwise become as acceptable as a scientific fact. Moreover, the absence of coherence leaves it utterly unclear what propositions may need to be revised, eliminated, or adjusted, and how. But despite Schlick's criticisms, Neurath's coherentism found an ally in the pragmatist movement, which was equally anti-Cartesian. Quine's fallibilist and holistic, naturalised epistemology can be interpreted as its latest development (Quine 1969, 1992).

Another philosopher deeply influenced by the 'Fries Renaissance' was Popper (Popper 1962, 1979). His discussion of the problem of the nature of basic statements in scientific theory and his dynamic solution – we can simply leave the presuppositions of a specific science open to the possibility of further testing – became the source of some later important works on the foundational problem (Albert 1978, 1985; Apel 1975; Lakatos 1978). It was also the origin of a signif- icant modification in the interpretation of (KK), now understood no longer as a meta-epistemological problem, but as a problem concerning the foundation of scientific knowledge.

COHERENTISM, NATURALISM, AND THE REFUTATION OF SCEPTICISM IN BRITISH PHILOSOPHY

Coherentism in epistemology is a natural ally of anti-realism in ontology, and both find a fertile environment in idealistic philosophies, whose claims about the contradictory nature of appearances in defence of a monistic supra-naturalism may easily make use of the sceptic's dualist anti-naturalism (Hegel 1802). Neurath had charged Schlick with metaphysical inclinations but found himself sharing a coherentist epistemology not entirely different from that of some idealists.

During the post-First World War period the most interesting and influen- tial idealist epistemology remained that of F. H. Bradley (Bradley 1914, 1922, 1930). Bradley held that the Absolute remains unknowable because knowledge is necessarily discursive and relational, and hence always inadequate with respect to the continuously unified nature of reality. Ideally, reality, its true description and its complete knowledge are identical. In practice, knowledge remains frag- mentary and truth can only be more or less adequate. Knowledge, including science, is like the biography of a person: no matter how accurately written, it is still only partly true and conspicuously unsatisfactory when compared to actual life. Justification, understood as the process through which possible instances of partial knowledge may or may not be included in the epistemic system, is inter- preted in terms of coherence. There is only one, ultimate, complete, accurate description of reality and every limited truth, insofar as it is true, concurs with every other limited truth in realising it.

The kind of holistic coherence involved here that Bradley and his friend Bernard Bosanquet (1920) seemed to have in mind, and that was further refined by J. J. Joachim (1939) and Brand Blanshard (1939), is richer than Neurath's mere logical consistency. It can be compared to the web of internal, reciprocal relations linking a set of words in a complex crossword, or a set of pieces in a puzzle: each truth is meant to interlock, meaningfully and uniquely, with the other components to constitute the whole, final system. It was justified by ontological considerations and some of the problems affecting later coherentist epistemologies, such as Neurath's, can be interpreted as stemming from the lack of a similar metaphysical commitment.

The reaction against idealism amongst British philosophers had been motivated in part by scepticism concerning these metaphysical commitments (e.g. internal relations and organic wholes). Amongst these realist critics, G. E. Moore's positive approach to epistemology was distinctive and influential. Against the sceptical position, Moore held that there are many commonsensical beliefs that everyone is naturally inclined to hold and that are endorsed upon reflection by all. These beliefs have the highest (a) *presumptive* and (b) *pervasive* credibility. Their presumptive credibility means that it is virtually impossible to doubt them or dissent from them. We are perfectly entitled to start by accepting them as being *prima facie* epistemically justified, leaving to the sceptic the hard task of showing that, on the whole, there are better reasons to believe that not-p rather than p. Their pervasive credibility means that the sceptic's claims are incoherent. The denial of p's credibility presupposes p itself or a system of credible ps.

Moore based his defence of common sense on (a) and (b) (Moore 1925, 1939). Re-evaluating Reid's philosophy, he concluded that there is an objective and mind-independent, physical reality, which we can come to know through our sense-data. However, how our immediate awareness of these sense-data is related to our knowledge of the world remained a constant problem for Moore and led to Ducasse's adverbial realism: sensations are ways of perceiving an object, not entities, so in looking at a tomato we are not directly aware of red sense-data but 'we are being appeared to redly by an object' (Ducasse 1942).

Moore's antisceptical strategy rested on an inadequate, if influential, assessment of scepticism. Ancient sceptics themselves had already disposed of (b) (Sextus Empiricus 1976: II, 144–203). Scepticism is not a doctrine but a process of immanent criticism that gradually rots away Neurath's ship from within. As for (a), it could not be employed against the sceptic without presupposing an antisceptical answer to (K) and hence begging the question. Moore's reliance on common sense suggests an appeal to naturalised epistemology to provide an answer to (K). But since (K) involves a *de jure* epistemological problem this would have meant committing in epistemology that naturalistic fallacy which Moore himself had helped to clarify in ethics. Moore's anti-Cartesian naturalism could thus only be defended convincingly by conceding something to the sceptic, as Gassendi and Hume had done before, and Wittgenstein, in effect, did later (Wittgenstein 1969).

The problem of our 'knowledge of the external world' was also a central theme in Russell's writings. In response to this traditional problem, he developed the famous distinction between 'knowledge by acquaintance and knowledge by description' which is grounded upon his theory of descriptions and his 'fundamental epistemological principle' that 'any proposition which we can understand must be composed of constituents with which we are acquainted'

(Russell 1912: 91). In *The Problems of Philosophy* (1912) Russell had argued that the sense-data, concerning colour, shape, texture, etc., with which we are acquainted in sense-experience give rise to self-evident, intuitive, truths which provide a foundation for our knowledge of the external world. This sounds like familiar empiricist foundationalism; but there remain questions concerning the ontological status of these sense-data and how truths concerning them relate to truths concerning physical objects such as a table, and Russell's answers to these questions were unusual. In his 1913 'Theory of Knowledge' (in Russell 1984) he took it that sense-data are physical but located in private spaces, though once he adopted neutral monism in 1921 he regarded them as neutral, antecedent to the mental/physical distinction (Russell 1921: lect. VIII). Physical objects themselves can only be 'known by description', and from 1913 he held that this knowledge rests upon a complex 'logical construction' whereby the different private spaces (or 'perspectives') in which sense-data are located are somehow combined into a public space so that truths about physical objects can be interpreted in terms of the contents of the perspectives which make them up.

This complex constructionism never gained much support and in later writings (e.g. Russell 1927) Russell developed alternatives to it. But what is more interesting about his writings from 1921 onwards is the way in which he began to develop an 'externalist' conception of knowledge. In *The Problems of Philosophy* (1912: ch. 13) Russell set out the classic analysis of knowledge as 'true, justified, belief' while observing in passing the difficulty that there are cases in which, because of some unfortunate circumstances, S may be fully justified in believing that p, p may be true and yet S may still not really know that p because S has in fact merely hit on the truth by chance. Russell did not linger with this observation, which he thought he could handle by raising the standards for justification (when the point was famously revived by Edmund Gettier it gave rise to a branch of modern epistemology – see Gettier 1963). But what happened from 1921 onwards, when Russell became converted to neutral monism and was profoundly influenced by behaviourist psychology, was that he began to develop and defend a conception of knowledge as an inner state which accurately, or reliably, represents some feature of the world (he sets out the now famous 'thermometer-analogy' for knowledge in Russell 1921: 181). Russell applied this first to memory; in later writings he extends its application further – in particular using it to develop a sophisticated externalist account of induction in his last major work (1948). It should be added, however, that on this last matter Russell had been anticipated by F. P. Ramsey (1931: 197), who had also generalised Russell's tentative presentation of an externalist conception of knowledge into the bold statement that 'a belief [is] knowledge if it is (i) true, (ii) certain, (iii) obtained by a reliable process . . . [that is, one that] must be caused by what are not beliefs in a way or with accompaniments that can be more or less relied on to give true beliefs' (Ramsey 1931: 258). The merits of this position are now widely appreciated, partly indeed because it is thought to provide a better solution to Russell's 'Gettier problem' than Russell had offered. Hence in this respect Russell and Ramsey together set the stage for a central dimension of contemporary epistemology.

PRAGMATIST EPISTEMOLOGIES IN AMERICAN PHILOSOPHY

The philosophers who best represent the epistemological renaissance during the interwar period in the United States are John Dewey and C. I. Lewis.

In Dewey, the influence of Darwinism, psychology, and Hegel's dialectics is reflected in an anti-Cartesian, naturalistic epistemology (Dewey 1925, 1929, 1938). He contended that traditional epistemology has been beset by four main errors:

1. foundationalism;
2. the assumed primacy of knowledge in our access to reality;
3. the artificial distinction between the known reality, the knowing process and knowledge as its outcome;
4. the spectator theory of knowledge – the conception of the object of knowledge as a detached reality, passively contemplated by an external and uninvolved spectator.

Consequently, he attempted to rectify these errors by arguing that:

1. knowledge is a non-hierarchical and relational phenomenon that emerges from natural and fallible interactions between two dependent *relata*, mind and nature ('contextualism');
2. non-reflective and non-cognitive experiences provide direct access to the world;
3. the epistemic continuum includes both the process of enquiry, as a series of self-corrective, organising acts, and knowledge, defined as the attainment of 'warranted assertibility' and interpreted as its appropriate completion;
4. the object of knowledge is just the observable outcome of experimental procedures.

For Dewey, then, the elaboration of knowledge is the semiotic means – the process of inferential signification – through which we can facilitate the experimental determination of future consequences, by bridging the gap between the known and the unknown. Cognition is an always-contextualised way of dealing with a problem situation ('epistemological immanentism'). Rather than speaking of some static correspondence with reality, satisfactory theories or concepts are those that turn out to be usefully reliable in all the practical and theoretical endeavours for which they are developed. Dewey's critique of Cartesian epistemology has been more influential (as in the work of Quine, Putnam, and

Rorty) than his instrumentalism has been. Russell and Reichenbach, for example, immediately objected that the latter failed to account for mathematical sciences.

C. I. Lewis stands in a similar relation to Kant as Dewey does to Hegel. Following Kant, he analysed knowledge in terms of judgements whose correctness depends on their relations to their references, and whose justification requires supportive reasons. Knowledge, he held, has a hierarchical structure, based on the infallibility of sensory states. The sensory given – the immediate apprehension of what is presented to the senses – is devoid of a conceptual structure and is not yet a form of knowledge, for there can be no possibility of error, since the apprehension of what is sensibly presented and the latter's existence *qua* appearance are indistinguishable, and, contrary to Descartes, Lewis held that we can speak of knowledge only if error is possible. But the epistemically infallible given supports 'terminating judgements', which are certain and have a predictive value. Their logical form is: 'Given the sensory cue S, if the possible action A is performed then the expected experiential appearance E will occur.' The certainty of terminating judgements is established by their being verified by practical tests concerning the predicted consequence. All other empirical judgements which concern objective facts different from the sensory given (e.g. physical objects) are non-terminating. Non-terminating judgements are at most probable and increasingly verifiable, never absolutely certain. Their logical form is 'If O is a physical object, then if S and A occur, then in all probability E will occur.' They entail terminating judgements, on which they are based. Lewis argued that probability ultimately requires and is based on certainty, for if no judgement could count as certain even probable judgements would be impossible (they would be merely 'probably probable'). The grounding relation between terminating and non-terminating judgements grants that the former, if verified, confer on the latter their degree of probability and hence their meaningfulness.

Although for Lewis the a priori was coextensive with the analytic, a priori concepts, categories, logical relations and truths were not empirically irrelevant linguistic conventions. They provide the indispensable ordering, taxonomic, and interpretative criteria without which the given could not rise to the level of knowledge but would remain unintelligible. Thus they have the crucial role of conceptualising and giving sense to the unlimited and undetermined continuum of the sensory given. Contrary to Kant's view, a priori structures are creative constructions that do not constrain but need to be adequate to experience and hence are not fixed. Having a hermeneutic function, they represent stable semantic commitments which are modifiable or replaceable in the light of pragmatic requirements: intelligibility, order, simplicity, economy, comprehensiveness, resilience and, in the long run, intellectual and practical satisfaction.

Lewis tried to reconcile his 'phenomenalist' foundationalism with a realist theory of perception of physical objects (terms in non-terminating judgements denote genuine physical objects, not just phenomena or subjective appearances), without resorting to Kant's doctrine of the synthetic a priori, but his original 'pragmatic apriorism' remained a rather isolated attempt to develop a transcendental epistemology between the wars.

THE SOLIPSISM DEBATES

DAVID BELL

The term 'solipsism' derives from the Latin *solus ipse*, meaning *oneself alone*. Broadly speaking a method, or doctrine, or point of view is solipsistic to the extent that it assigns a fundamental, irreducible, and asymmetrical role to subjective phenomena of the kind that are normally indicated by use of the singular form of the first person pronoun. Solipsistic theories, that is, stress what is both unique and irreducible about, say, the 'I', me, myself, my ego, my subjectivity, or my experience.

Explanatory reliance on such essentially first-personal phenomena is a necessary condition of adoption of a form of solipsism, but it is not sufficient. The use made by Descartes of the principle '*Cogito, ergo sum*', for example, requires that the principle be formulated in the first person singular. The Cartesian *cogito* is not, however, intrinsically or inescapably solipsistic, if only because it fails to imply the necessary asymmetry between what is the case for *me*, as against what is the case for *others*. On the contrary, as indeed Descartes himself explicitly points out, the *cogito* is a principle that *anyone at all* can apply to himself or herself. Solipsism, I shall take it, requires commitment to a stronger view, namely that there are basic metaphysical and epistemological truths of the form 'I *alone* −', or '*Only* I −'. Ontologically, for example, a solipsist might claim 'I alone exist', 'Only I am conscious', or, in Wittgenstein's words, 'Mine is the first and only world'. Epistemologically, on the other hand, solipsism might take the form of a theory committed to the conclusion that 'For all it is possible to know, only I exist', or 'There can be no justification for denying that I alone am conscious.'

It will be useful to distinguish at this point two further types of theory which I shall call respectively *partial* and *global* versions of solipsism. To a first approximation, a theory will be a form of partial solipsism to the extent that it provides an affirmative answer to questions such as 'Am I alone in the world?' or 'Is mine the only consciousness that there is?' The scope of a such a theory is restricted to the ontological and/or epistemological asymmetries between the existence, the nature, or the knowability of my mental states, in contrast to the existence, the nature, or the knowability of the mental states of others. A familiar instance of partial solipsism is the form of scepticism which concludes, roughly speaking, 'I am warranted in asserting the existence of one and only one conscious being, namely myself; the claim that there exist other such beings is at best groundless, and at worst false or downright incoherent.' Partial solipsism, in other words, is a theory about *minds* (mental phenomena, psychological states, sentient beings, conscious subjects, and the like), and as such it can remain neutral about the existence, the nature, or the knowability of non-mental phenomena. Global solipsism, by contrast, involves a considerably more radical series of commitments, according to which it is nothing less than *the world*, reality as a whole, that must be accounted for in essentially solipsistic terms. Commitments of this sort can perhaps be found in the thought underlying Wittgenstein's startling assertion that 'The world is *my* world' (Wittgenstein 1922: 5.62) and, again, that 'at death the world does not alter, but comes to an end' (6.431).

During the period under review here, questions concerning the possibility of a coherent ontological or epistemological solipsism, in either a partial or a global form, exercised a number of philosophers working within a variety of quite different philosophical traditions. The purpose of this chapter is to chart the most significant of the resulting debates, so as to bring out not only their idiosyncratic features, but also the shared assumptions and common procedures on which they sometimes rely.

1. COMMON SENSE

The claim is often made that the philosophical importance of solipsism can hardly arise from the fact that some philosopher has actually adopted or advocated it, 'for none has done so' (Craig 1998: 25). '*Nobody*', Sartre declared, 'is truly solipsistic' (Sartre 1943 [1958: 250]). The belief is widespread, moreover, that solipsism *can* have no advocates because it is psychologically impossible to believe that it is true – or, more precisely, because it is impossible for a sane person to believe sincerely that it is true. Schopenhauer was the first to object to solipsism in these terms. As a doctrine, he wrote,

it can never, of course, be demonstrably refuted. Yet in philosophy it has never been used other than as a sceptical sophism, i.e., as a pretence. As a serious conviction, on the other hand, it could only be found in a madhouse, and as such stands in need, not of a refutation, but of a cure. Therefore we need go into it no further. (Schopenhauer 1844 [1969: I, 104])

Bertrand Russell's attitude, though more urbanely expressed, was no different:

Solipsism is the view that I alone exist. This is a view which is hard to refute, but even harder to believe. I once received a letter from a philosopher who professed to be a solipsist, but who was surprised that there were no others. Yet this philosopher was by way of believing that no one else existed. This shows that solipsism is not really believed even by those convinced of its truth. (Russell 1927: 302; see also Russell 1948: 195–6)

As a form of scepticism solipsism may be 'logically impeccable', Russell maintained, but it is nevertheless 'psychologically impossible, and there is an element of frivolous insincerity in any philosophy which pretends to accept it' (Russell 1948: 9).

The grounds on which a sane advocacy of solipsism is judged to be insincere typically invoke the common-sense principle that actions speak louder than words: there will inevitably be, it is claimed, a discrepancy between, on the one hand, what solipsists say or profess to believe, and on the other hand, what they actually do – especially, that is, if they dine, play backgammon, and are merry with their friends. And this discrepancy is also the basis of the familiar gibes about solipsists having no one to talk to, and no reason to express, or to try and communicate their views (see Moore 1925: 203; Stebbing 1933: 27).

Mere common sense is, however, a blunt instrument with which to attack solipsism: it fails to differentiate the various forms that the latter doctrine can take, and it fails to reveal the philosophical motives which can underlie its adoption, the insights it can embody, and the reasons, if any, for finding it mistaken (see Braithwaite 1993: 14–15). Russellian common sense provides no grounds for concluding that solipsism is false; at best it provides a weak excuse for taking no notice of whatever an imaginary character called 'the solipsist' might say.

2. ANTI-CARTESIANISM

There exists a set of plausible, interconnected, and mutually supporting doctrines which together make up a picture of how my mind, my body, the minds of others, and the physical objects which populate the external world stand related one to another. The picture can justifiably be called Cartesian, and intrinsic to it is a commitment to the following theses. (i) My mind (and its contents) is merely externally, contingently related to my body (and its behaviour). (ii) My knowledge of the mind of another person is merely contingently related to my knowledge of his or her body and behaviour. (iii) The mind, in Descartes's words, 'is better known than the body' (Descartes 1954: 66). 'Nothing is more easily or manifestly perceptible to me than my own mind' (Descartes 1954: 75). (iv) Knowledge of my own mind is merely externally related both to my knowledge of other minds, and to my knowledge of material objects. Finally and more generally, (v) the prior, philosophically most fundamental phenomena here are *cognitive*: in coming to understand oneself, one's relations with others, and one's place in the world, the issues to be addressed concern, first and foremost, self-knowledge, knowledge of others, and knowledge of the external world.

Although none of these commitments is, as yet, inescapably solipsistic, they are clearly capable of further development and interpretation in ways that would generate a variety of solipsistic theories, both ontological and epistemological, partial and global. On both sides of the Channel, a recurring theme in twentieth-century debates about solipsism has been the need for a radical critique of Cartesianism, aimed at articulating a quite different vision of oneself, others, and the world, from which all solipsistic tendencies and temptations have been removed.

3. EXISTENTIALISM AND ONE'S EXPERIENCE OF OTHERS

From within the Cartesian framework, the priority assigned to cognitive phenomena (thesis (v)) yields an account of my relations with others according to which 'the Other's soul is separated from mine by all the distance which separates first my soul from my body, then my body from the Other's body, and finally the Other's body from his soul' (Sartre 1943 [1969: 223]). In the section of *Being and Nothingness* entitled 'The Reef of Solipsism', Sartre mounts an attack on the assumption, implicit in this view, that 'my fundamental connection with the Other is realised through *knowledge*' (233). He provides a series of vivid phenomenological descriptions designed to bring to the fore 'a fundamental connection' between myself and another, 'in which the Other is manifested in some way other than in the knowledge I have of him' (253) – a connection which, it turns out, is immediate, irreducible, and ultimately emotional, rather than dispassionately cognitive. The presence of another person – and especially the presence of someone who confronts me, subjects me to scrutiny, and for whom I could become an object of prurient curiosity, say, or physical repugnance – is something I experience directly as threatening, and to which I spontaneously respond with anxiety and shame. There is here, Sartre claims, a primitive, given, and inescapable bond between myself and another, but it is 'a bond not of knowing, but of being'. 'Beyond any knowledge I can have, I *am* this self which another knows' (261). As this last remark suggests, Sartre provides an account of human existence, of what it is to *be* a human being, in which not only one's awareness of others, but also one's spontaneous response to their awareness of oneself, are alike constitutive of one's very identity as a conscious being. This comprises a direct attack on theses (iv) and (v) above.

This existentialist strategy – within which cognitive relations involving reasons, justifications, inference, evidence, belief, and knowledge are displaced by an appeal to a putatively more primitive species of non-cognitive phenomena involving spontaneous attitudes, emotions, and commitments – this strategy has its prototype in Kierkegaard's account of religious faith and the nature of one's relations to God. In a secularised form, the general strategy is adopted also by Heidegger, for whom the existential analysis of *Dasein* (human existence) reveals a spontaneous, primitive social dimension which he called *Mitsein* ('being-with' or 'being-with-Others'): '*Dasein* is itself essentially *Mitsein* . . . *Mitsein* is an existential characteristic of *Dasein*' (Heidegger 1927 [1967: 156]).

Mitsein belongs to the being of *Dasein*, which is an issue for *Dasein* in its very being. Thus as *Mitsein*, *Dasein* 'is' essentially for the sake of Others. This must be understood as an existential statement as to the essence of *Dasein* . . . Because *Dasein's* being is *Mitsein*, its understanding of being already implies the understanding of Others. This understanding . . . is not an acquaintance derived from knowledge about them, but a primordially existential kind of being, which, more than anything else, makes such knowledge and acquaintance possible. (Heidegger 1927: 161)

In Heidegger's footsteps, both Sartre and Merleau-Ponty conclude that *L'être-pour-soi* (being-for-itself, or self-conscious being) essentially involves *L'être-pour-autrui* (being-for-others, or intersubjective, social being). 'The social world', in Merleau-Ponty's words, must be construed as 'a permanent field or dimension of [human] existence' (Merleau-Ponty 1945 [1962: 362]). The common element present in these existentialist responses to the threat of solipsism is summarised by Sartre: 'If we are to refute solipsism', he claims, 'then my relation to the Other [must be] first and fundamentally a relation of being to being, not of knowledge to knowledge' (Sartre 1943 [1958: 244]).

4. PHENOMENOLOGY AND ONE'S EXPERIENCE OF OBJECTS

In the late works of Edmund Husserl, and in the thought of those influenced by them, the possibility of a coherent global solipsism of a broadly Cartesian kind is undermined by the use of phenomenological methods and insights. In particular, phenomenology is used to attack the assumption that self-awareness and self-knowledge are merely externally related to one's awareness of material objects (compare thesis (iv) above). If it can be shown that even my most intimate subjective experience, my most primitive forms of self-awareness, are by their very nature shot through with references to and assumptions about objects in the external world, then at least one familiar route to sceptical solipsism will have been closed off. The aim, then, is to show, in Merleau-Ponty's words, that as conscious beings 'we are through and through compounded of relationships with the world' (Merleau-Ponty 1945 [1962: xiii]).

Perhaps the single most influential contribution in this regard is Husserl's doctrine of 'the horizontal structure of the intentional object' – his *theory of horizons* for short. In the course of providing a painstaking analysis of the complex intrinsic structure possessed by our immediate awareness of everyday objects (whether in perception, memory, thought, or imagination), Husserl distinguishes between two kinds of aspect that every such intentional object exhibits. On the one hand, that is, there are those aspects of the object which are present in a given experience as *actual* or as *explicit*, and on the other there are those aspects which, though also discernible within the experience, are present only as *possible* or as *tacit*. In a straightforward visual perception of the book which is sitting in front of me on my desk, for example, the front cover, the spine, and the bottom edges of the pages are turned towards me: I have a direct, explicit, actual perception of them. Husserl stresses, however, that my experience would be utterly mis-described if its content were taken to comprise no more than, say, three contiguous, plane, coloured surfaces standing to one another in certain geometrical relations. On the contrary, what I see is *a book* – it is given to me as a three-dimensional, material, solid artefact; something that has sides, properties, aspects, and possibilities which are not explicitly present in my perception. It is something which has a history; something that has a weight; something that I could reach for, pick up, open, and explore.

Although intrinsically indeterminate, these 'aspects of potentiality' inform my perceptual experience and make it what it is. Husserl characterises the situation metaphorically: every intentional experience, he claims, possesses a kernel comprising those aspects of the object which are present 'in person' in the experience, and this kernel is surrounded by a horizon of indeterminate possibilities, comprising a tacit awareness of, say, what the object would look like from over there, what it would look like if I turned it round, what it would feel like if I were to touch it or pick it up, and so on. 'The *horizon structure* belonging to every intentionality thus prescribes for phenomenological analysis and description methods of a totally new kind' (Husserl 1931 [1973: 48]). The most salient of these methods, and one employed not only by Husserl but also by such other phenomenologists as Heidegger, Sartre, and Merleau-Ponty, is the making explicit of the structural elements tacitly present *as a horizon* in our experience.

In the hands of these philosophers this method has yielded results of a strongly holistic kind. As an inseparable part of an everyday experience of some common or garden object, they claim to discover, for instance, a complex structure of internal relations linking that experience to an indefinitely large number of other experiences, both actual and possible. The importance of these findings for the

debate about solipsism stems from the fact that the class of relevant experiences
is not restricted to those which are given to me *as my own*: intrinsic to my
perception of this book, for instance, is not primarily an awareness (albeit tacit
and indeterminate) of what it would look like *to me*, if *I* were viewing it from
over there, but quite simply of *what it would look like from over there* – what it would
look like, that is, to *anyone* who viewed it from that position. The holism here
is sufficiently strong to incorporate a reference to other conscious beings and
their experiences as an integral and ineluctable component of my experience
of physical objects. And if this is right, then the partial solipsist's attempt to
construe my commitment to the existence of other minds as independent of
my commitment to the existence of the material world is straightforwardly
incoherent. Merleau-Ponty writes: 'Solipsism would be strictly true only of
someone who managed to be tacitly aware of his existence, without being or
doing anything, which is impossible . . . [For] transcendental subjectivity is
revealed subjectivity, revealed to itself and to others, and is for that reason an
intersubjectivity' (Merleau-Ponty 1945 [1962: 361]).

The holism which characterises this approach receives its most uncompromising expression in Husserl's late writings, in the doctrine according to which
my intentional experience takes place only within the horizon of an entire
Lebenswelt, or 'life-world'. My experience, on this view, is not a mere aggregate
of self-contained atoms, each of which possesses its own content and meaning
independently of all the rest. On the contrary, the existence, the identity, and
the nature of any particular experience depend essentially on its place within
the whole of which it is a part; and far from being given *as mine*, that whole is
given, immediately and inescapably, as possessing social, cultural, and historical
dimensions within which the reference to other conscious beings is constitutive,
and hence ineradicable (compare Wittgenstein on 'forms of life' – Wittgenstein
1953: 226). This is a vision which Husserl attempts to communicate, though
none too perspicuously, as follows:

Every natural object experienced or experienceable by me . . . receives an appresenta-
tional [i.e., intersubjective] stratum (though by no means one that becomes explicitly
intuited), . . . viz: the same natural object in its modes of givenness to the other Ego.
This is repeated, *mutatis mutandis*, in the case of subsequently constituted mundanities
of the concrete objective world as it always exists for us: namely as a world of men and
culture. (Husserl 1931 [1973: 125])

5. SOLIPSISM AND LANGUAGE

Within the analytic tradition, largely as a result of the influence of Wittgenstein
and Russell, debates about the possibility of a coherent solipsism have tended
to emphasise issues of a broadly linguistic nature and, in particular, the question

whether solipsism is in principle expressible, whether, that is, it can even be put into words. Russell, for example, argued that a global solipsist must say 'I alone exist', or 'I myself am the whole universe', or must use some equivalent form of words containing one or more first person pronouns such as 'I', 'myself', 'mine', and the like. Russell then objects to the doctrine as follows:

> We must not state it in the words 'I alone exist', for these words have no clear meaning unless the doctrine is false. If the world is really the common-sense world of people and things, we can pick out one person and suppose him to think that he is the whole universe . . . But if other people and things do not exist, the word 'myself' loses its meaning, for this is an exclusive and delimiting word. Instead of saying 'myself is the whole universe', we must say 'data are the whole universe'. Here 'data' may be defined by enumeration . . . In this form the doctrine does not require a prior definition of the Self. (Russell 1948: 191)

Russell's challenge to the would-be global solipsist is to provide a formulation of the theory which neither inconsistently employs the terms 'I', 'myself', 'mine', and the like in their normal sense – a usage which presupposes a contrast between me myself, on the one hand, and all the rest of creation on the other – nor employs those terms in an incomprehensible solipsistic sense, that is, in a way which serves to mark no intelligible distinction or contrast of any kind whatsoever. To accept this strategy as a cogent refutation of global solipsism requires commitment to two further assumptions: (1) that in everyday usage the terms 'I', 'myself', and the like function always to 'pick out one person' and are thus what Russell calls 'exclusive and delimiting words'. (2) That if solipsism can be shown to be inexpressible in everyday language then it stands, *ipso facto*, refuted. In a variety of works spanning his lifetime as a philosopher, Wittgenstein engaged in a continuous, sympathetic series of investigations into the possibility of solipsism (in approximate order of composition, the most notable passages occur in Wittgenstein 1961: 72–91; Wittgenstein 1922: V, 6–5.641 and VI, 4–6.522; Wittgenstein 1975: 88–96; Wittgenstein 1979: 17–27; Wittgenstein 1958: 57–72; Wittgenstein 1968: *passim*; and Wittgenstein 1953: §§256–317 and 398–429). And throughout these investigations his hostility to both of the above-mentioned Russellian assumptions was implacable. Antipathy to (1) is signalled, for instance, as follows:

> 'When I say "I have a pain", I do not indicate a person, the one who has the pain; for in a certain sense I simply don't know *who* has it.' And this can be justified. Above all, the point is this: I simply didn't say such-and-such a person has a pain, but on the contrary, 'I have . . .' Now in saying this I don't name some person – anymore than I name a person when I *groan* with pain. (Wittgenstein 1953: §404)

The Russellian assumption (2), that the inexpressibility of a thesis renders it worthless, is flatly contradicted by Wittgenstein's assertion that 'There are,

indeed, things that cannot be put into words. They make themselves manifest' (Wittgenstein 1922: VI, 522). And, it transpires, 'the truth of solipsism' is
indeed one such thing.

A typical and revealing passage in which Wittgenstein argues for the falsity
of both (1) and (2) occurs in his posthumously published work, *Philosophical
Remarks* (1975), in which he presents the parable of the solipsistic despot. We
are asked to imagine a despotic oriental state whose ruler is a solipsist and who
imposes on his subjects his own preferred solipsistic way of talking. The ruler, let
us suppose, believes that he is the universe, no less. Accordingly he has no need
for any terms or linguistic devices which would function by picking him out,
or distinguishing him from other items in the world. He therefore simply expels
from his language any terms that might be thought to perform any such role.
When he has a toothache he says 'There is toothache'; when he thinks that *p*, he
says 'It is thought that *p*', and so on. The philosophically less fortunate subjects,
on the other hand, are to adopt a quite different way of speaking. When one of
them is in pain (or thinks that *p*), the others say: 'So-and-so is behaving as the
Ruler does when there is pain (or when it is thought that *p*).' Unlike the despot
at the centre of this language, the subjects need to use the first person pronoun:
one of them might cry out 'I behave as the Ruler does, when there is pain' –
when, say, he hits his thumb with a hammer. 'It is evident', Wittgenstein writes,
'that this way of speaking is equivalent to ours', in that it comprises a language
with the same expressive powers as ours: anything that can be said in the one
can be said in the other. The relevance of these considerations is spelled out by
Wittgenstein as follows:

One of the most misleading representational techniques in our language is the use of
the word 'I', particularly when it is used in representing immediate experience. . . . It
would be instructive to replace this way of speaking by another in which immediate
experience would be represented without using the personal pronoun; for then we'd be
able to see that the previous representation wasn't essential to the facts. (Wittgenstein
1975: 88; compare Wittgenstein 1979: 22: 'What the solipsist wants is not a notation in
which the ego has monopoly, but one from which the ego vanishes.')

Now the solipsistic representation, Wittgenstein claims, has a privileged status –
though only, of course, for the person who is its centre:

This language is particularly adequate. How am I to express that? That is, how can I
rightly represent its special advantage in words? This can't be done. For if I do it in
the language with me as its centre, then the exceptional status of the description of
this language in its own terms is nothing very remarkable; and in the terms of another
language my language occupies no privileged status whatever. (Wittgenstein 1975: 89)

The conclusion to which Wittgenstein is drawn is that there is a form of solipsism, of the kind exemplified by the oriental despot, which is internally coherent, materially adequate, and philosophically attractive, but which requires neither use of the first person pronoun, nor reference to any entity such as the self or subject of experience. Although this form of global, metaphysical solipsism cannot be put into words, its adoption is nevertheless something that can be expressed: it can show itself, it can make itself manifest for example in my adoption of a language with a certain form. The form of that language will be recognisably solipsistic, but the language itself will lack, just as does our everyday way of talking, any means for explicitly *stating* the truth of solipsism: 'What the solipsist *means* is entirely correct', Wittgenstein claims in the *Tractatus*, 'only it cannot be *said*. It makes itself manifest' (Wittgenstein 1922: 5.62).

44

LANGUAGE

DAVID HOLDCROFT

Language became a major concern during this period. Moreover, theories of language suggested methodologies for the study of philosophy itself, so that the two topics often became intertwined. A number of main tendencies can be distinguished: whereas at the beginning of the period models suggested by logic and other formal disciplines predominated, by the end there was a growing interest in psychological and sociological approaches, and increasing scepticism about the value of formal models.

I. LOGICAL ATOMISM

Russell coined this term in a series of lectures given in 1918 (Russell 1918 [1956: 177]). Non-logical expressions are, he argued, either complex or simple. To understand the former one has to understand the simple expressions contained in their analyses. Since complex expressions can be analysed only in the context of analyses of sentences in which they occur, the apparent form of such sentences may be a poor guide to the logical form revealed by analysis (for Russell an important example of this situation arises from his theory of descriptions). Analysis terminates when all the complex non-logical items have been eliminated, and only simple ones remain. To understand these it is necessary to be cognitively acquainted with the items they stand for, which are literally their meanings. So, to understand (S1) 'This is blue' one has to be acquainted both with the sense-datum identified by 'this', and with the universal blue. A sentence such as (S1) that cannot be further analysed corresponds to what Russell called an atomic fact. The fact to which it corresponds, if true, is of the simplest kind and consists in the possession by a particular of a property. The next simplest atomic fact involves a relation between two particulars, and so on. A molecular sentence is one that contains another sentence, for example, 'This is blue and that is red', which contains both (S1) and (S2) 'That is red'. The truth of this sentence does not require the existence of facts other than atomic ones since it is true if and only if both (S1) and (S2) are true. Russell argues, however, that there are facts other than atomic facts, including negative facts (a claim that produced a riot when he made it at Harvard) and general facts, since no set of atomic propositions implies a general one.

The admission of facts other than atomic ones detracts from the simplicity of Russell's theory, whilst the empiricist elements were also uncongenial to some. Wittgenstein (Wittgenstein 1922) addressed these concerns and argued that one can dispense with both of them. His starting point was an account of the possibility of pictorial representation. He knew that in Parisian law courts accidents were reconstructed by using model dolls and vehicles. How was this possible? First, there must be a correlation between the toys and the vehicles and people involved, so that, for example, the doll stands for the person injured and the toy van for the van (Wittgenstein 1922: 2.131). Second, the fact that the elements of the reconstruction, the 'picture', have a certain structure is significant; the spatial relationship between the doll and the toy van displays the spatial relationship between the person and the van (1922: 2.15). The possibility that the toys could enter into this relationship Wittgenstein calls the picture's 'form of representation' (1922: 2.15). In this case it is the three-dimensional nature of the toys which enables them to enter into the same spatial relationships as the people and vehicles involved. The form of representation is thus common both to the picture and what it pictures. Once the toys have been correlated with the things involved, then in virtue of its form of representation the picture depicts the existence of a state of affairs without further intervention. However, because its form of representation is shared with what it represents, the picture cannot represent its own form; this is something shown but not said (1922: 2.171). And since a picture only represents a possibility, it cannot determine its own truth; to ascertain this it has to be compared with reality (1922: 2.223).

What enables Wittgenstein to generalise these claims to natural language and to assign a central role to logic in doing so is the contention that every representation must have in common with reality a 'logical form' which is also 'the form of the reality' (1922: 2.18) it represents. It is because an elementary sentence of the form '*aRb*' has a relational logical form, which is also the form of relational facts, that the theory applies to it; and it can have this form because it too is a fact (1922: 3.14). Its names '*a*' and '*b*' stand for simple objects, and it is the fact that they do, together with the fact that they stand in a determinate relationship to each other, that enables the sentence to represent a relational possibility. It is because '*a*' in '*aRb*' stands in a certain relation to '*b*' that it says *that aRb* (1922: 3.1432). Wittgenstein then claims that all other sentences are truth functions of elementary sentences, or equivalent to them. The latter qualification is needed to account for sentences of the form '($\forall$x)(Fx)' (e.g. 'Everybody smokes'). These are not truth functions; but the function 'Fx' specifies a set of sentences ('Fa', 'Fb', 'Fc' . . .) whose logical product (Fa & Fb & Fc . . .) is a truth function whose truth guarantees that of '(∀x)(Fx)'. Thus the need for general facts is eliminated at a stroke; whilst the need for Russell's riot-inducing, irreducibly negative, facts is removed by distinguishing facts from states of affairs and holding that a putative negative atomic fact is simply the non-existence of an atomic state of affairs (1922: 2.06).

However, an appeal to metaphysics is needed to underpin Wittgenstein's claim that elementary sentences picture atomic facts, the existence or non-existence of possible atomic states of affairs. An atomic state of affairs is a combination of simple objects that fit together like links in a chain (1922: 2.03); and to represent the existence of such a state of affairs the names in an elementary sentence have to be correlated with the objects. But why must the objects be simple? And what kind of things could they be, if atomic facts are independent of each other (1922: 2.061)? Indeed what would be an example of a simple object? Disconcertingly, whilst convinced that they must exist, Wittgenstein was unable to give a simple example! Moreover, though the claim that all non-elementary sentences are truth functions of elementary sentences is ontologically simplifying, it is difficult to embrace Wittgenstein's conclusion that the totality of true propositions is co-extensive with natural science (4.11); for ethics and philosophy itself are thereby excluded from that totality. Hence just as Russell's theory was entangled with a metaphysics, so is Wittgenstein's discussion, albeit of a very different kind. This is one reason why Logical Atomism slowly lost favour. But the ideas of logical form and of reductive analysis, together with the powerful analytical tools forged, are among the enduring achievements of twentieth-century philosophy.

2. LOGICAL POSITIVISM

The Vienna Circle was a group of philosophers with a keen interest in science who had been influenced by Mach's positivism. They learned much about the new analytical techniques from reading Russell and Wittgenstein, and also from meetings with the latter. The fusion of the two influences led to many of their more characteristic doctrines. These were first popularised for English-speaking readers in Ayer 1936. But although Ayer's discussion of the criterion of verifiability – the thesis that a meaningful statement is either analytic or else verifiable – is valuable, it is not a theory of meaning (Hempel 1950 [1952]). We shall therefore concentrate on attempts to formulate a verificationist theory of meaning – sometimes called 'the Verification Principle' (Hanfling 1981a: 33).

A concerted attempt to do this is to be found in the work of Schlick. Schlick was much impressed with Einstein's achievement in telling us how '*X* and *Y* are simultaneous' is to be verified and thereby understood (Schlick 1979: II, 266 [1981b: 91]). Generalising from this, Schlick maintained that to understand a statement it is necessary to understand its rule-given connections with other statements including those descriptive of our experience ('protocols'). Quine's influential criticism that positivists such as Schlick assumed that each statement could be verified in isolation (Quine 1951 [1961: 41]) is, therefore, beside the point. Schlick explicitly denied that verification is presuppositionless, insisting that an extraordinary number of factual judgements enter into an actual verification (Schlick 1979: II, 268 [Hanfling 1981b: 93]). The real criticism of Schlick is that there are two very different elements in his theory between which he fails to make a convincing connection.

The first accords a crucial role to ostensive definition; non-logical terms must, he argues, be ostensively definable either directly or indirectly. The second insists that the truth conditions of statements cannot transcend logically possible experiences, hence the requirement of verifiability. Schlick tried to connect the two points by insisting that the meaning of a sentence should be given compositionally, so that our understanding of its truth conditions is linked ultimately to the experiences involved in the ostensive definitions of its non-logical terms (Schlick 1979: II, 464). One reason Schlick may have had for invoking ostensive definitions in this way was a belief that they need not have presuppositions, unlike an act of verification. But this is surely mistaken (Hanfling 1981a: 21). Further, it is rather implausible to suppose that it is possible to define theoretical terms – such as those of a species and a genus – using only terms that are ostensively definable. But if not all theoretical terms are ostensively definable, then the requirement that meaning be given compositionally does not guarantee a link with experience. Paradoxically, Schlick seems to have come close to defending a truth-conditions theory of meaning which involves potentially verification-transcendent truth-conditions. This is the main issue that he grapples with, and whilst his discussion of many standard objections to the theory – for example, that statements about the past/future are meaningless – is incomparably better than most, he never resolved it.

Though Carnap, another member of the Vienna Circle, greatly admired Schlick, his views evolved very differently. At first sight his claim that verification rests on protocol sentences is simply a different way of saying that it rests on experience. Not so according to him: the latter claim is in the material mode, which talks about objects, things, states of affairs, etc., whilst the former is in the formal mode which speaks only of linguistic forms. Further, it is only by adopting the latter that we free ourselves from confused discussions leading to nonsensical conclusions (Carnap 1932a [1981a: 157]). Though the formal mode is restricted to syntax, it can nevertheless be used to define key terms in the theory of meaning. Entailment, for instance, can be defined purely formally (Carnap 1934a [1967: 57]); and having done this we can say that a sentence is verifiable if it entails a protocol sentence. Moreover, the adoption of the formal mode does not prevent us from explaining the 'meaning' of a word. This is given either by a translation or by a definition, each of which can be formulated syntactically (Carnap 1932a [1981a: 151]). Translations are rules for transforming a word from one language into another, for example, 'cheval' = 'horse'; whilst definitions are rules for transforming words within the same language, for example, 'vixen' = female fox. Carnap adds that this includes ostensive definitions, since they are of the form '*X* is a *Y* of the same kind as that at such and such a position in space-time'. If correct, this undermines at a stroke a central plank of Schlick's theory. Further, the definition of verifiability as the entailment of a protocol sentence enabled Carnap to argue that a meaningful sentence need not be *equivalent* to a set of protocol sentences. So he proposed a looser connection between meaningful sentences and 'experience' (Carnap 1938 [Hanfling 1981b: 118]), which is immune to Quine's strictures (Quine 1951 [1961: 41]).

The detailed implementation of these ideas is to be found in Carnap's *Logische Syntax der Sprache* (1934b). A novel and important proposal here is that because philosophical problems concern language not the world, they should be formulated in a rigorously constructed meta-language (Carnap 1963: 55). If a putative claim can be reformulated syntactically within such a language then it is meaningful, otherwise it has to be rejected. Since this approach involves the construction of a formal language, it has been thought to favour the conception of an 'ideal language' for the expression of all genuine knowledge (Rorty 1967, introd.). However, Carnap argued for a principle of tolerance of a variety of languages because he took it that conflicting approaches often involve different linguistic proposals (Carnap 1963: 54); so the uniqueness implied by the phrase 'ideal language' is misleading.

Whilst to some the programme of Carnap 1934b is a defining moment of twentieth-century philosophy, to many it seems to rest on implausible claims about translations into the formal mode. At this point one can discern the emergence of two wings of analytic philosophy, one taking formal models seriously, and one strongly inclined to deny their relevance (Carnap 1963: 68).

3. FORMAL THEORIES

If, as Wittgenstein claimed, a language cannot represent itself, then a formal theory of language is impossible. However, the positivists never accepted this (Carnap 1963: 29). We saw that Carnap himself argued that a language can be described by specifying its vocabulary and the rules for the construction of sentences and for their transformation into other sentences. Further, he believed that key terms in the theory of meaning could be defined syntactically; and the only defensible theory of truth seemed to him to be a coherence theory since in Carnap 1934b he rejected any attempt to define the meaning of terms semantically.

One reason for adopting this position was the existence of the semantic paradoxes, and in particular the liar paradox. It seems reasonable to maintain that for any arbitrary sentence of a language there is a 'T-sentence':

S is true if and only if p,

in which 'p' is replaced by that sentence, and 'S' by a name of it (Tarski 1936 [1952: 16]). For example: 'Snow is white' is true if and only if snow is white. It seems moreover that all T-sentences must be true. But the T-sentence for 'This sentence is false'

'This sentence is false' is true if and only if this sentence is false

is paradoxical, because it follows that if the sentence is false it is true, and *vice-versa*. Thus the apparently reasonable requirement that a semantic theory should imply all T-sentences of a language – which Tarski calls Convention T – leads to paradox.

Tarski, however, showed that this can be avoided by rejecting the assumption, implicit in the construction of the paradoxical T-sentence, that the truth of the sentences of a given language *L* is definable in *L* itself. It is necessary rather to define it in a formal meta-language which is richer than *L* (Tarski 1936 [1952: 21]). Tarski went on to show how to do this using the semantic notion of satisfaction, so that he showed not only how to avoid the paradox but also how to define 'is true-in-*L*' semantically, at least in a formal language. It seemed to some, including Carnap who went on to publish an introductory book on semantics (Carnap 1942), that Tarski's work made formal semantics philosophically respectable. But that was by no means a universal reaction. Many doubted its applicability to natural languages, arguing, for example, that these contain predicates which cannot be included in a semantic definition because they are inherently vague.

It should be added that during this period in linguistics there had also been an increasing emphasis on formal analyses. The most influential of these was that of Saussure, who argued that the proper object of study for linguistics is not the individual act of speaking (*la parole*), but the system of signs (*la langue*) internalised by speakers of the same language which makes communication possible (Saussure 1916). The job of the linguist is then to describe that system in terms of the relationships between its signs. Saussure's ideas revolutionised linguistics, but had little or no effect on philosophy during our period, even though they were to become the starting point of many structuralist and post-modernist discussions after the Second World War.

4. BEHAVIOUR, SIGNS AND ATTITUDES

As well as logic, psychology was a leading source of ideas about language. Russell, who was always alert to new ideas, drew on both. In Russell 1921 he argues that all aspects of the mental are either explicable in behavioural terms, or else can be reduced to sensations or images. In Russell 1918 he did not discuss the analysis of '*S* understands the meaning of *Y*', because he thought that language was 'transparent' (Russell 1959: 145). But in Russell 1921 this becomes a central issue. He argues for a behaviourist account of demonstrative uses of language, i.e., ones that point out a feature of the environment. Such uses involve using a word appropriately; reacting to it appropriately; associating it with another word (e.g., in French) with an appropriate effect; and associating it with the object that it 'means' (Russell 1921: 199). However, to account for narrative and imaginative uses of language it is necessary to recognise the use of a word to describe or recall a memory-image, and to describe or create an imagination-image (Russell 1921: 202). Since Russell concedes that in many cases the image is theoretically dispensable, this is puzzling. But the real problem lies elsewhere in his philosophy of mind, where he concedes that a behaviourist account of memory and belief is not possible. His appeal to images is thus an attempt to deal with areas in which behaviourism is, on his own account, inadequate. Nevertheless his achievement was to show how a behaviouristic theory might be developed, whilst remaining candid about the difficulties.

Such caution is less evident in Ogden and Richards 1923. They thought little of the philosophical literature on meaning, and championed the contribution of psychology, arguing that the proper way to proceed is to understand what is involved in our interpretation of a sign. Central to this is 'our psychological reaction to it, as determined by our past experience in similar situations, and by our present experience' (Ogden and Richards 1923: 244). Such a causal account may indeed be adequate in principle to explain why we interpret smoke as a sign of fire, since past experiences of contexts which have included both smoke and fire, together with a present experience of smoke, may lead us to expect fire. But can the meaning of 'smoke' be explained in this way? There would seem to be a far from uniform reaction to its past uses, presumably because its use does not make the occurrence of smoke, or indeed fire or 'fire', probable. Nevertheless, such objections did not lessen the attraction of behaviourist approaches, and consideration of the wide variety of responses that language both evokes and is used to evoke, led to a recognition that there are many different uses of language, of which assertive uses are but one. One of the more interesting approaches is that of Morris, who introduced a distinction between three broad areas of the study of language (Morris 1938): syntax, semantics, and pragmatics, the latter being defined as the study of 'the relation of signs to interpreters' (Morris 1938: 6), which included, for example, indexical uses of language, that is, the use of such pronouns as 'I' and 'you'.

Ogden and Richards had also introduced an important distinction between symbolic and emotive uses of language. The former is typified by *statement*, whilst the latter 'is the use of words to express or excite feelings and attitudes' (Ogden and Richards 1923: 149). They argued boldly that the ethical use of 'good' is emotive (Ogden and Richards 1923: 125); an idea that is further developed in Ayer's analysis of ethical sentences (Ayer 1936, ch. 6). In the context of a verification theory of meaning an attraction of this approach is that it enables one to account for the meaning of ethical sentences even though they are not verifiable. However, Stevenson proposed the most influential version of the emotive theory of ethics. In an important paper he defended an interest theory of ethics with a difference in that, according to him, the function of ethical sentences is to *create* an interest. Arguing that meaning is a causal or dispositional property of a word, he claims that an approximate analysis of 'This is good' is given by 'I *do* like this; do so as well' (Stevenson 1937 [Ayer 1959: 275]). This is approximate, because the command in the former is implicit, but explicit in the latter. So Stevenson explains both why 'good' has the force it has, and why it is indefinable in the last resort. Non-cognitivist theories of this sort were to cast a long shadow over ethical discussions in the following decades (Warnock 1960: 98).

5. NEW DIRECTIONS

(a) Phenomenology

Heidegger's view of language is a radical alternative to those we have considered, for all that it is not a direct critique of them. It is instead a critique of some very general assumptions that many of these approaches share, broadly characterisable as 'Cartesian', which he thought were profoundly mistaken (Dreyfus 1995: 108). To begin with, the critique was motivated by Heidegger's efforts to understand Husserl's phenomenology. Though for a long time captivated by Husserl, he was also perplexed. Husserlian phenomenology studies the essence of conscious experience and the structure of mental acts. Concentrating on what is essential in experience, it needs no further justification, and provides a secure

foundation for the other branches of philosophy (Smith and Smith 1995: 12). In
Husserl's early theory of meaning (Husserl 1900–1) the meaning of expressions
is explained in terms of features of mental acts of a special kind – ones in which
objects are intended (Simons 1995: 110). This does not mean that meanings are
mental entities. Nor does it imply that they can be identified with the things
intended; the descriptions (D1) 'the victor at Jena' and (D2) 'the vanquished
at Waterloo' stand for the same person, but have different meanings. Instead
meanings are the abstract species of these mental acts. If I think that something
is red, then my mental act has a feature, which Husserl calls its matter, which
a thought that it is green, blue, etc., does not have and the meaning of 'red'
is then the abstract species of that feature (Simons 1995: 113). Thus Husserl's
early theory tries with some success to explain meaning without lapsing into
psychologism.

However there were significant changes in Husserl 1913. These come about
not because of changes internal to the theory of meaning, but because of a
major methodological change (Simons 1995: 124). Concerned that his earlier
phenomenology might contain empirical elements, Husserl adopted a methodological tool, the phenomenological reduction, which would guarantee that
it did not. This brackets out whatever we believe or assume about the natural world, thereby making the study of consciousness presuppositionless. The
intentional content of an act is now called a *noema*, which is described as the
'object as intended', so that the descriptions (D1) and (D2) have different objects. However, there are many conflicting views about the nature of a *noema*
and its relation to a species meaning (Smith and Smith 1995: 23). Moreover, if
the theory is presuppositionless, how can we explain truth and reference? But
if we cannot, can we give any account of ordinary thought?

Heidegger thought that to resolve his perplexity with Husserl's phenomenology a new concept of experience was needed. To develop this it is necessary to
understand the kind of being which human beings ('*Dasein*') have. This calls for
a description of the structure of *Dasein*'s mode of 'being-in-the-world', which
reveals a primordial level of experience that does not have the subject-object
structure taken as basic by Husserl in his conception of consciousness. Indeed,
the latter kind of experience can be understood only in terms of the former
(Dreyfus 1995: 62). Hence, at this level we are not dealing with Cartesian
subjects and their consciousness. Insight into the structure of *Dasein*'s being-
in-the-world is to be obtained by examining its everyday activity, which reveals
that the sense in which *Dasein* is in-the-world is not spatial. Instead it implies
familiarity and engagement with things as in 'I'm in the middle of doing this.'
Moreover, the basic kind of experience that *Dasein* has, which Heidegger calls
'circumspection', does not involve a relation between an inner sphere and an

outer one (Heidegger 1927 [1962: 89]). Nor is it the product of theoretical knowledge; on the contrary the latter depends on it. Its nature is revealed rather by a description of *Dasein's* engagement with the immediate environment, exemplified in the use of tools and utensils. *Dasein's* basic understanding of a hammer is not in terms of its size, shape, etc., but in terms of what can be done with it, which can be grasped only by using it. This use has a referential character: the hammer is used *in order to* make something, *from* something, *for* someone. Moreover, the tool's use arises in the context of a set of uses of other tools, each of which has its own referential character.

Signs too are tools, which unlike other tools have the function of indicating an aspect of an interdependent set of practices, which their use presupposes. The stop sign, for instance, doesn't make sense on its own, and 'is available within-the-world in the whole equipment-nexus of vehicles and traffic regulations' (Heidegger 1927 [1962: 109]). Since signs presuppose shared practices, of which our basic understanding, circumspection, is not theoretical, then we can neither bracket these as Husserl tried to do, nor rest our account of what makes a sign significant on its relation to a prior idea. Heidegger went on to deepen his account of being-in-the-world before turning to the topic of language as such. But in the light of the discussion of signs his conclusions are unsurprising. Language does not create the interdependent set of practices and tools of which *Dasein* is aware at the most basic level. Words are tools used in a shared context of practices that is already structured and articulated in a way that makes them meaningful (Aler 1972: 55). Language is yet another practice the meaning of the elements of which arise from their place in other practices. From this perspective, the idea that there is a problem about the way in which language relates to the world is hardly intelligible. At the same time the practice of analysis becomes questionable. If *Dasein* is embedded in a totality of practices, the proper methodology is hermeneutic not analytic. A methodological gulf opens up at this point between Heidegger and those of an analytic persuasion.

(b) The Later Wittgenstein

Wittgenstein abandoned philosophy after publishing the *Tractations Logico-Philosophicus* in 1922, and did not return to it for seven years. Though he wrote prolifically throughout the remainder of our period, only one item was published (Wittgenstein 1929). In this, though still broadly committed to the views of Wittgenstein 1922, he ceases to maintain that elementary sentences are independent of each other, a change the implications of which he went on to discuss at length with Schlick and other colleagues (Waissman 1967). Moreover, he expresses reservations about the a priori methodology of his earlier work, and argues that there is a need to look at the phenomena themselves when describing the structure of elementary propositions (Wittgenstein 1929: 163). This was a pointer to one of the major changes in his thought, the concentration on detailed examples and the use of expressions for specific purposes in concrete contexts, in short what he calls 'language games' (Wittgenstein 1953: §7). This leads to the conclusion that there is not just one way in which expressions have meaning, but a variety of ways that do not share an essential feature but have a family likeness. In another analogy (strikingly comparable to Heidegger's account) he compares the uses of language with the tools in a toolbox (Wittgenstein 1953: §11). The concentration on specific uses of language brings into question the assumption that every sentence must have a perfectly definite sense, and also leads to the conclusion that the notions of complexity and simplicity are themselves relative. But if this is so, then the kind of philosophical analysis practised by logical atomists has to be rejected.

When published after the Second World War, these ideas had a major impact on the development of philosophy, especially in Great Britain. But it is not easy to describe the impact they had during our period. Many able philosophers who attended Wittgenstein's lectures were deeply impressed, and notes taken were circulated and discussed. But it is difficult to trace that influence during our period, since it is not easy to comment on or allude to the unpublished view of another without their permission. Waissman's attempt to produce an 'authorised' account of Wittgenstein's views failed to win his approval, and so only appeared after our period (Waissman 1965). But there were anyway increasing reservations about Logical Atomism and Logical Positivism, as well as a growing awareness of the diverse uses of language, so there was fertile ground for Wittgenstein's ideas to fall on. Nevertheless, just as the emotive theory influenced ethical thought after the Second World War, so Logical Atomism and Logical Positivism profoundly affected philosophical thought in general. Though unhappy with their metaphysics, many philosophers made extensive use of the methodological tools bequeathed. Philosophy of language with minimal metaphysical assumptions was to become quite common; but that emphatically was not the approach taken within our period.

45

THE END OF PHILOSOPHY AS METAPHYSICS

SIMON GLENDINNING

The discussion in this chapter aims at clarifying the views of Heidegger and the later Wittgenstein on the idea of the end of philosophy. The chapter begins with a sketch of the conception of philosophy at issue in their work. There follows an examination of the idea of its end as it is developed first in the work of Heidegger and then in the work of Wittgenstein.

PHILOSOPHY AS METAPHYSICS

What both Heidegger and Wittgenstein mean by 'philosophy' when they broach the possibility of its ending is the understanding of non-empirical enquiry which is more usually characterised simply as 'metaphysics' (see Heidegger 1969 [1977: 432] and Wittgenstein 1968: §116). However, although both authors are engaged with questions concerning the end of philosophy *qua* metaphysics there is a *prima facie* difference in the way they approach this topic. For Heidegger the 'end of philosophy' is discussed primarily in terms of its *terminus*, and in particular in terms of the idea of its *dissolution into empirical science*. By contrast, for Wittgenstein the 'end of philosophy' is discussed primarily in terms of its *telos* or goal, and in particular in terms of the idea of its *achievement of complete clarity* concerning the foundations of the empirical sciences. I want to leave that contrast in the air for the moment in order first to highlight a significant confluence in their views, namely in their conception of what precisely the 'metaphysical' understanding of non-empirical enquiry is.

At the start of the so-called 'Chapter on Philosophy' in the *Philosophical Investigations* (1953: §89–§133), having just called into question the determinacy and precision of linguistic rules, Wittgenstein specifies the ultimate motivation for his reflections on language in terms of its relation to just such an understanding:

These considerations bring us up to the problem: In what sense is logic something sublime?

For there seemed to pertain to logic a peculiar depth – a universal significance. Logic lay, it seemed, at the bottom of all the sciences. – For logical investigations explore the nature of all things. It seeks to see to the bottom of things and is not meant to concern itself whether what actually happens is this or that. — It takes its rise, not from an interest in the facts of nature, nor from a need to grasp causal connexions: but from an urge to understand the basis, or essence, of everything empirical. Not, however, as if to this end we had to hunt out new facts; it is, rather, of the essence of our investigation that we do not seek to learn anything *new* by it. We want to *understand* something that is already in plain view. For this is what we seem in some sense not to understand. (Wittgenstein 1968: §89)

This interpretation of the nature and aim of non-empirical enquiry is that which specifies philosophy as metaphysics. In Heidegger's work this enquiry into 'the essence of everything empirical' is generally characterised as the 'enquiry into the Being of entities' (the enquiry into 'what it is to be' an entity) but where 'Being' is interpreted as the 'ground' or 'foundation' of the presence of entities. Thus, as with Wittgenstein's presentation, the emphasis is on the idea of metaphysics as a non-empirical enquiry into the foundations of everything empirical. This conception has its origins in ancient Greek thought, but it is perhaps best summarised by Kant:

All pure a priori knowledge . . . has in itself a peculiar unity; and metaphysics is the philosophy which has as its task the statement of that knowledge in this systematic unity. Its speculative part, which has especially appropriated this name, namely, what we entitle *metaphysics of nature*, and which considers everything in so far as *it is* (not that which ought to be) by means of a priori concepts, is divided in the following manner. (Kant 1787 [1933]: A845 B873)

That philosophy which Kant here calls 'metaphysics of nature' is what is at issue in the discourses on philosophy and the end of philosophy in Heidegger and Wittgenstein. This is 'philosophy' as a non-empirical enquiry into everything in so far as *it is*; it is an enquiry into the *whole* universe ('The first and most important problem of philosophy is: To give a general description of the *whole* universe' – Moore, 1953: 1–2), an enquiry which tries to grasp the essence (as ground or foundation) of everything empirical, an enquiry which is concerned with the Being (as ground or foundation) of entities: an enquiry which thus reaches '*over* beings'. In short, *meta*-physics.

It is not difficult to see how this determination of philosophy will lead to a view of such enquiry as that which finds its final 'completion' when it has opened up *every* region of entities for empirical investigation (Heidegger's view); nor is it difficult to see how this determination of philosophy will have 'completeness' as its goal, in the sense that the full understanding of 'everything in so far as it is' which it aims for is achieved only when one grasps in a *single* account the *whole* of reality with which science deals (Wittgenstein's view). With these observations, however, it becomes less than clear whether Heidegger and Wittgenstein are really as far apart on the question of the end of philosophy as the initial contrast suggested. For both conceive of philosophy as metaphysics and both conceive metaphysics in what is essentially the same way. Moreover, as we shall see, whether it is conceived as having run its course (Heidegger) or as requiring elimination (Wittgenstein), neither see the end of philosophy as metaphysics 'positivistically', that is, as a victory for or validation of empirical science as the only legitimate mode of enquiry. On the contrary, both still see a 'real need' for a distinctively non-empirical style of thinking (Wittgenstein 1968: §§108–9); a style which now would be 'neither metaphysics nor science' but which would still have 'its own necessity' (Heidegger 1969 [1977a: 436, 449]). In what follows these ideas of philosophy and the end of philosophy as metaphysics will be explored first in the work of Heidegger and then in the work of Wittgenstein.

HEIDEGGER ON METAPHYSICS AND SCIENCE

Writing influenced by either Heidegger or Wittgenstein is likely to stress the distinction between philosophical and scientific investigations. However, familiarity with this position can readily cover over the fact that the traditional view of philosophy as metaphysics also acknowledges a distinction between philosophical (a priori, logical, formal, conceptual) investigations and scientific (*a posteriori*, empirical, material, factual) investigations. The crucial difference here is not between those who assimilate philosophical to scientific enquiries and those who do not, but *within those who do not*, between those who position philosophy as having a distinctive, foundational role with respect to positive sciences and those who do not. In terms of the latter contrast, occupying the first position is distinctive of metaphysics, and (an attempt at) occupying the second is what is distinctive in the work of (but not only the work of) Heidegger and Wittgenstein.

Gilbert Ryle infamously chided Husserl for supposing that philosophy could or should occupy the first position (see Ryle 1971: 181–2), but at least one British philosopher of Ryle's generation, J. L. Austin, also held this view, and it is worth noting how plausible a view it is:

In the history of human enquiry, philosophy has the place of the initial sun, seminal and tumultuous: from time to time it throws off some portion of itself to take station as a science, a planet cool and well regulated, progressing steadily towards a distant final state. This happened long ago at the birth of mathematics, and again at the birth of physics: only in the last century we have witnessed the same process once again, slow and at the same time almost imperceptible, in the birth of the science of mathematical logic . . . Is it not possible that the next century may see the birth . . . of a true and comprehensive *science of language*? Then we shall have rid ourselves of one more part of philosophy (there will be plenty left) in the only way we ever can get rid of philosophy, by kicking it upstairs. (Austin 1979: 232)

The idea that Austin so vividly captures here, that philosophy has its end in a kind of *aufheben* into science, is precisely what Heidegger envisages as the end, the 'dissolution' which is also the 'legitimate completion', of philosophy as metaphysics (Heidegger 1969 [1977: 434]). The notable contrast between Austin and Heidegger on this point is that while Austin seems to think that there is a long way to go before the philosophical sun is exhausted, Heidegger believes that the end is nigh: 'Philosophy is', he states, 'ending in the present age' (1969 [1977]). In order to see why Heidegger is convinced that philosophy as metaphysics is facing imminent demise, it is worth looking at some of the details of his conception. For, unlike Austin, the question of the relationship between philosophy and science is not only investigated explicitly but, from *Being and Time* onwards, was 'the point of departure' for his thinking in general (Heidegger 1969 [1977: 431]).

I touched on the point that Ryle had criticised Husserl for 'puffing philosophy up' into a 'Mistress Science' (Ryle 1971: 181). It is, in fact, extremely misleading to suggest, as Ryle did, that Husserl *assimilated* philosophy and science. However, Husserl does affirm a tripartite division of human enquiry which draws philosophy into a relationship with science of the kind that Austin proposes, and which had a decisive influence on the development of Heidegger's views. According to Husserl (at least after 1913), the empirical sciences are founded by what he calls 'regional ontologies', ontologies which, as Heidegger puts it, 'lay the foundations' for the sciences by 'leaping ahead, as it were, into some area of Being' (Heidegger 1927 [1962: 30]). This running ahead of science involves the 'disclosure' *in advance of empirical investigation* of a specific area of 'subject-matter', thus opening up the possibility for a science which examines entities 'as entities of such and such a type' (1927 [1962: 30]). On this view, every positive science of entities, what Heidegger calls 'ontical enquiry', presumes, as its founding condition of possibility, 'ontology in its widest sense': the articulation of 'basic concepts' which prepare for empirical investigation some definite 'area' within the domain of entities as a whole. This is the enquiry into the Being of entities: the enquiry into *what it is to be*, for example, a mathematical, physical, biological, chemical, social, psychological, etc., entity. And the basic thought is, to use Austin's image, that 'in the history of human enquiry, *philosophy* has the place of the initial sun' which opens up a field or subject matter for science and which, in the first instance, supplies its basic concepts. Moreover, with the *complete* achievement of that task, the work of philosophy would be *completely* over. In Austin's terms, we would have then 'got rid of philosophy'.

I noted, however, that Husserl, unlike Austin, draws a threefold division: for Husserl the regress from positive science to regional ontology does not reach bedrock. There is, for Husserl, a further stage: from the 'regional ontologies' to what he calls 'transcendental phenomenology'. The latter enquiry would have as its concern the disclosure of the foundations of all regional ontology. Now, for Husserl, following in the tradition of philosophy at least since Descartes, this emerges as a regress to that enquiry which brings to full presence the presence of a *subject*. That is, transcendental phenomenology is conceived as the 'universal science', identifying the constitution of the objectivity of all objects (the Being of *all* entities) as having its ultimate ground in the structures of 'absolute subjectivity' (Husserl 1913 [1931], cited in Heidegger 1969 [1977: 440]).

Significantly, it is precisely characteristic of Heidegger's work to call into question the traditional regress to the subject, to question the interpretation of the Being of entities in terms of the abiding presence of subjectivity. However, it needs to be stressed that he does retain *something* of the regress outlined by Husserl. For, according to Heidegger, 'ontology in its widest sense' (i.e., regional ontology) 'requires a further clue':

> Ontological enquiry is indeed more primordial, as over against the ontical enquiry of the positive sciences. But it remains naïve and opaque if in its researches into the Being of entities it fails to discuss the meaning of Being in general . . . The question of Being aims therefore at ascertaining the a priori conditions not only for the possibility of the sciences . . . but also for the possibility of those ontologies themselves which are prior to the ontical sciences and provide their foundations. (Heidegger 1927 [1962: 31])

Paradoxically, Heidegger's attempt to develop 'fundamental' and not merely 'regional' ontology (i.e. an enquiry into 'Being as such' rather than an enquiry into 'the Being of entities') is carried out as an enquiry into the Being of an entity, namely, that entity which *we*, the enquirers, are. However, according to Heidegger, this is not just another regress to the 'subject'. That the disclosure of Being as Being is sought in the 'existential analytic' of the entity that we are is due, according to Heidegger, to our being the entity which already 'is' as such only in so far as it possesses a 'preontological' (in the widest sense) 'understanding of Being'. Crucially, it is the conceptual clarification, the bringing to concepts, of *what is understood* in this understanding (namely, the meaning of Being as such) which is the ultimate and radical end (*telos*) of non-empirical enquiry for Heidegger. It is the question of Being as such and not a question concerning the Being of an entity (even the entity that we are) which stands, for Heidegger, as *the* fundamental, *the* pre-eminent question for the entity that we are. Moreover, it is the question which *metaphysics*, the enquiry into the Being of entities, constantly opens on to and yet, since ancient Greek times, has consistently failed to address explicitly.

HEIDEGGER AND THE TASK OF THINKING AT THE END OF PHILOSOPHY

Heidegger's basic view then is that metaphysics is that enquiry which aims to reveal entities with respect to their Being, and as such it lays the foundations for the development of positive sciences in various domains. He further claims that metaphysics in the present age is nearing completion. When Austin forecast the possibility of the development of a science of language, and hence the dissolution 'of one more part of philosophy' he confidently added that 'there will be plenty left'. Austin does not give any indication of what gets left over here, but one might suppose that problems in areas where the subject matter involves an irreducible reference to subjectivity and value will remain, will perhaps always remain, outside the reach of positive science. But it is precisely here that Heidegger sees the claims of science becoming ever more confident: 'it suffices to refer to the independence of psychology, sociology, anthropology as cultural anthropology, or to the role of logic as symbolic logic and semantics' (Heidegger 1969 [1977: 434]). It is indeed plausible to suppose that for *every* area of enquiry which continues to be investigated in philosophy today there is some scientist (or some 'philosopher' who *does* wish to assimilate philosophical to scientific enquiries) who believes that the proper way to settle the questions will be through the development of a 'scientific theory', and who believes that the philosophers who are still going on in their old non-empirical ways are dinosaurs soon to disappear.

As far as philosophy as metaphysics is concerned, perhaps Heidegger might agree. However, Heidegger's appropriation of Husserl's tripartite analysis leaves open the question whether the *aufheben* of philosophy as metaphysics into science amounts to 'the complete actualisation of *all* the possibilities in which the thinking of philosophy was posited?' (1969 [1977]: 435). And of course he thinks that it does not. There is, he suggests, 'a *first* possibility . . . from which the thinking of philosophy would have to start, but which *as* philosophy [i.e. *as* metaphysics, the enquiry into the Being of entities] it could nevertheless not expressly experience and adopt' (435). For Heidegger, in the enquiry into the Being of entities there lies unasked the nevertheless always available possibility of an enquiry into Being as Being, Being as such. The openness of our existence to Being is called by Heidegger 'the clearing of Being' (the 'of' here being both the genitive and the possessive). It is an 'unconcealment' or original 'truth' (*aletheia*) which lets 'what is' show itself. The clearing of Being will thus constitute that which philosophy as metaphysics depends on yet which cannot appear as such within it: 'only what *aletheia* as clearing grants is experienced and thought, not what it is as such' (Heidegger 1969 [1977: 448]). That is, since we are more or less constantly 'turned only to what is present [everyday life and science] and the presentation of what is present [philosophy as metaphysics]' the clearing which grants it 'remains unheeded', 'this remains *concealed*' (448). The point is that, in order for entities to appear as such the clearing must not appear as such: the clearing of Being, 'unconcealment', must be 'self-concealing' if 'what is' is to be present as such. Or again, 'self-concealing, *lethe*, belongs to *a-letheia* . . . at the heart of *aletheia*' (448).

How then is thinking to take up the task of 'thinking Being without entities'? At first sight, this looks like a task requiring a pure turning away from philosophy as metaphysics. But this is not in the least the movement of Heidegger's thought. First, Heidegger insists that what is required is an 'explicit restating' of the question of Being (Heidegger 1927 [1962: 21]). The question has already been posed, most notably by Plato and Aristotle. Second, the understanding of Being cannot leave no traces in the enquiry which aims to grasp the Being of entities. Thus Heidegger's attempt 'to think Being as such' cannot develop as a simple movement *away* from attempts 'to think the Being of entities'. On the contrary, if it is not to be wholly free-floating and rootless, it can take place *only* as a *return* to something which has, in a certain way, always been heard within philosophy as metaphysics: its radical yet concealed opening, its 'first possibility'. Thus, from his earliest to his last writings, reanimating the question of Being is always and at once involved in what he calls a 'destruction' of philosophy (a hunting out of its positive achievements with regard to the question of Being): 'The task of thinking would then be the surrender of previous thinking to the determination of the matter for thinking' (Heidegger 1969 [1977: 449]). This task, the bringing to concepts of the clearing of Being, is 'not accessible' to philosophy as metaphysics, still 'less' to the sciences stemming from it (436). However, it is, Heidegger suggests, the incomparable task 'reserved for thinking' at the end of philosophy (436).

WITTGENSTEIN *CONTRA* HEIDEGGER?

This task might be thought fundamentally at odds with anything proposed by the later Wittgenstein. Heidegger, it seems, conceives of fundamental ontology as the first and most basic level of human enquiry, the enquiry which thus provides the ultimate foundations of science. Against this Wittgensteinian 'grammatical investigations' disclaim all pretensions at giving the foundations for anything. I think this misunderstands Heidegger's appropriation of Husserl's threefold division, and probably simplifies Wittgenstein's position too.

First, it should be emphasised that Heidegger does not represent fundamental ontology as basic or pre-eminent in a foundational sense. True, he conceives it as aiming to 'bring to concepts' that 'understanding of Being' which is presupposed by regional ontologies and makes them possible, and he does conceive of regional ontology as a laying of the foundations for science. However, he does not conceive of fundamental ontology as a laying of the foundations for regional ontology in the way in which Husserl had conceived transcendental phenomenology. The 'priority' of fundamental ontology is simply that it has the character of what can be done *first*. And that is a character that Wittgenstein also attributes to the subject he calls 'philosophy' and whose title he arrogates for his own work: 'One might also give the name "philosophy" to what is possible *before* all new discoveries and inventions' (Wittgenstein 1968: §126). Prior to all science and technology there can be 'philosophy'. Of course, that priority is conceived by philosophy as metaphysics in foundational terms. And the founding character of philosophy as metaphysics is completely rejected by Wittgenstein. But this is true of Heidegger too. Fundamental ontology is pre-eminent without being foundational. It is thus, Heidegger states, 'less than philosophy . . . because its task is . . . not of a founding character' (Heidegger 1969 [1977: 436]).

For all the analogies and similarities between them, however, there is one aspect of Heidegger's thought which looks completely at odds with Wittgenstein's. And that is nothing other than his (Heidegger's) basic aim to restate the question of Being. The very idea of identifying something, anything, as the 'primal matter' [*Ursache*] for thinking (Heidegger 1969 [1977: 442]), or as '*the* fundamental question' for philosophy (Heidegger 1927 [1962: 24]) would seem to be itself a distinctively *metaphysical* movement, and a movement that is ripe for Wittgensteinian critique. For Wittgenstein, philosophical difficulties arise not when we fail to grasp *the* sense of a concept-word like 'being' but when we fail to realise that 'the sense' of our expressions display no such formal unity (see Wittgenstein 1968: §116 and Hacker 1986: 153).

As we shall see it is his challenge to the assumption that there *must* be an underlying *formal unity* to our experience of things, and so his challenge to the assumption that we *must* be able to attest that 'everyday existence . . . deals with beings in a unity of the "whole"' (Heidegger 1967 [1977: 99]), which stands as Wittgenstein's most fundamental break from previous philosophy. This break announces a completely new kind of end for philosophy, one which, as we shall see, could go equally by the slogans: 'Never an end to philosophy!' or 'Stop when you like!'

WITTGENSTEIN AND THE SEARCH FOR
COMPLETE CLARITY

In a revealing remark Heidegger describes the work of fundamental ontology inaugurated in *Being and Time* as representing 'the latent goal' of 'the whole development of Western philosophy' (Heidegger 1975 [1982: 106]). This self-conception ties in very directly to the conception of philosophy which Wittgenstein seeks to 'end' in his later works. It is a conception of philosophy which sees itself as 'moving towards a particular state', a state which once achieved would bring philosophy to an end: Done! So while Heidegger typically writes of 'the end of philosophy' as the *completion* of metaphysics, he also (if somewhat less explicitly) works with a conception of 'the end of philosophy' as the *accomplishment* of a basic (if, until the end, latent) goal: the coming to concepts of the meaning of Being as such.

This kind of conception of a final and ultimate end of philosophy, and the sense in which reaching that end finally discloses what philosophy really *is*, in short what one might call an *apocalyptic* conception of philosophy, is at the centre of Wittgenstein's criticism in the 'Chapter on Philosophy' in the *Philosophical Investigations*. As we shall see, in his critique of this conception, Wittgenstein aims to wean us from the urge to pursue apocalyptic philosophy, and thus teaches us how to bring it to an end.

For reasons which will become clearer shortly Wittgenstein insisted that the important thing about his work was that 'a new method had been found' (cited in Hacker 1986: 147), and he compared this with the kind of shift that occurred when chemistry was developed out of alchemy. The new methodological discovery effects 'a "kink" in the evolution of philosophy' (cited in Hacker 1986: 146) so radical that it is no longer clear that the new subject should still go by the old name: 'If . . . we call our investigations "philosophy", this title, on the one hand seems appropriate, on the other hand it certainly has misled people. (One might say that the subject we are dealing with is one of the heirs of the subject which used to be called philosophy)' (Wittgenstein 1969: 28–9).

Of course, it is not in the least peculiar to Wittgenstein to write of, and so in some sense beyond, a tradition they are willing to call simply 'philosophy'. However, it is at least arguable that previous 'new' modes of thought (Aristotelian, Cartesian, Humean, Kantian, Hegelian, Fregean, Heideggerian, etc.) are characteristically of the form of 'a going-one-better in eschatological eloquence, each newcomer more lucid than the other' (Derrida 1993: 146). That is, with each new stage in the history of philosophy a new claim is made to have found a way of achieving the kind of completeness which brings philosophy to an end.

It is precisely in this respect that the approach pursued by Wittgenstein constitutes a new 'kink' in the history of philosophy which separates his writing from previous Western thought. For Wittgenstein's later method is precisely characterised by its abandoning the aim of completeness which would bring philosophy to an apocalyptic end. Thus, if Wittgenstein's work constitutes an end of philosophy as metaphysics that is because it rejects the assumption that philosophy can ever end apocalyptically:

> Disquiet in philosophy might be said to arise from looking at philosophy wrongly, seeing it wrong, namely as if it were divided into (infinite) longitudinal strips instead of into (finite) cross strips. This inversion in our conception produces the *greatest* difficulty. So we try as it were to grasp the unlimited strips and complain that it cannot be done piecemeal. To be sure it cannot, if by a piece one means an infinite longitudinal strip. But it may well be done, if one means a cross-strip. – But in that case we never get to the end of our work! – Of course not, for it has no end. (Wittgenstein 1981: §447)

As I read it, a central claim of Wittgenstein's later philosophy is that the apocalyptic conception of philosophy is sustained by a misunderstanding of what achieving conceptual clarity is. Perhaps paradoxically, this misunderstanding is derived from the way in which we 'eliminate misunderstandings' in ordinary linguistic exchanges, namely, 'by making our expressions more exact' (Wittgenstein 1968: §91). In Wittgenstein's view, apocalyptic philosophy is characterised by an urge to sublimate or idealise the logic of this procedure: 'All at once it strikes us' (§88) that when every possible ambiguity has been removed *the* sense of an expression will be *completely clear*. The precise identity of a thought or an idea or a concept will be perfectly captured. The 'discursive intelligibility' or *logos* of the phenomenon that is *meant* will then be *perfectly delimited*. The desire for 'complete clarity' in this sense thus has the form of a desire to accomplish complete conceptual exactness or of providing 'a *single* completely resolved form of every expression' (Wittgenstein 1968: §91). This conception of conceptual clarity as exactness is, I want to suggest, the basic target of Wittgenstein's later philosophy. That is, for the later Wittgenstein, it is our attachment to this conception which leaves us in the dark: the traditional aim of philosophy, the 'urge to understand' the essence of the world, (§89) is, *at once*, an 'urge to misunderstand' the actual structure and functioning, the essence, of language (§109, §92).

WITTGENSTEIN'S APOCALYPTIC LIBRARIAN

This claim can be illustrated by seeing a connection between an analogy Wittgenstein develops in the *Blue Book* and a notoriously difficult remark on philosophy in the *Philosophical Investigations*. The *Blue Book* analogy is of someone sorting books in a library. It appears shortly after the text turns from the topic of the objects of thought and experience to the topic of personal experience. As the turn is made Wittgenstein indicates that he held the latter topic in abeyance because it had features which would tend to disrupt our thinking on the former. The disruption one can envisage here is that we might suddenly be inclined to subjectivise the 'objects' which had figured as unproblematically objective in the former topic. The disruption would thus be of a kind such that 'it might seem that all we have said . . . may have to go into the melting pot' (Wittgenstein 1969: 44). Wittgenstein identifies this situation as typical in philosophy, 'and one sometimes has described it by saying that no philosophical problem can be solved until all philosophical problems are solved; which means that as long as they aren't all solved every new difficulty renders all previous results questionable' (44). Defending the possibility of a more piecemeal approach he offers the following analogy:

Imagine we had to arrange the books of a library. When we begin the books lie higgledy-piggledy on the floor. Now there would be many ways of sorting them and putting them in their places. One would be to take the books one by one and put each on the shelf in its right place. On the other hand we might take up several books from the floor and put them in a row on a shelf, merely in order to indicate that these books ought to go together in this order. In the course of arranging the library this whole row of books will have to change its place. But it would be wrong to say that therefore putting them together on a shelf was no step towards the final result. In this case in fact it is pretty obvious that having put together books which belong together was a definite achievement, even though the whole row of them had to be shifted. (Wittgenstein 1969: 44)

By contrast, the apocalyptic librarian would be the one who supposed that we cannot be *certain* that we have achieved anything until *every* book is in its proper place. On this view, one cannot be really satisfied just by placing this or that book or row of books on a shelf because further work may always render their location questionable. So the apocalyptic librarian will find herself constantly tormented by the questionable status of all her previous work. For her a 'real discovery' would be finding *the* governing principle of the library's order, as it were *the* essence of the library. She will, therefore, yearn for a method of grasping *all* the books *at once and as a whole*. That would be *the* sorting method because it would answer *the* sorting problem.

Drawing the analogy takes us to the heart of Wittgenstein's remarks on philosophy in the *Investigations*. For the equivalent aim in apocalyptic philosophy would also be a discovery of method, and it would be *the* philosophical method because it would answer *the* fundamental problem, namely, *how to grasp all the problems of philosophy, and so of philosophy itself, at once and as a whole*. Such a discovery would be 'the one that gives philosophy peace, so that it is no longer tormented by questions which bring *itself* in question' (Wittgenstein 1968: §133).

The *Blue Book* discussion can thus be seen to segue perfectly with Wittgenstein's final enigmatic remark in the so-called 'Chapter on Philosophy'. This remark is of particular significance since it is also in this remark that Wittgenstein seems to declare *his* 'real discovery' that will end apocalyptic philosophy. Watch the movement of thought. Wittgenstein has already indicated that his enquiry will focus on the essence of language (§92), but in anticipation of what we might now call an apocalyptic reading of that task, he warns that the order in our knowledge of the use of language that he seeks does not have the status of '*the* order' (§132). Section 133 continues and develops the point:

It is not our aim to refine or complete the system of rules for the use of our words in unheard-of ways.

For the clarity that we are aiming at is indeed *complete* clarity. But this simply means that the philosophical problems will *completely* disappear.

The real discovery is the one that makes me capable of stopping doing philosophy when I want to. – The one that gives philosophy peace, so that it is no longer tormented by questions which bring *itself* in question. – Instead, we now demonstrate a method, by examples; and the series of examples can be broken off. – Problems are solved (difficulties eliminated), not a *single* problem.

There is not *a* philosophical method, though there are indeed methods, like different therapies.

The difficulty of this remark is that it says as much about Wittgenstein's view of apocalyptic philosophy as it does about his own non-apocalyptic alternative, and it does so at the same time. 'The real discovery', for example, is one which Wittgenstein claims to have made. He's saying: if you want to talk about real discoveries (as the apocalyptic philosopher addressee is wont to) look at *this*, *this* is something to shout about. However, this 'real discovery' is precisely the one which allows us to stop looking for the all-embracing solution to *the* problem of philosophy that talk of a 'real discovery' invokes for apocalyptic philosophers. Here we can see why Wittgenstein was inclined to stress that what was distinctive about his new work was a discovery of method. For what he is offering us is a way of doing philosophy that avoids the interminable torment of apocalyptic philosophising. A method is demonstrated, by examples 'and the series of examples can be broken off'. Stop when you like! (See McManus 1995: 360).

Wittgenstein's 'examples' stand, of course, as examples of the application of a method of *eliminating* problems from 'the subject that used to be called "philosophy"'. But if this is the case why does he also assert that philosophy as he practises it will *never* come to an end? Won't we eventually run out of problems? Space precludes a full discussion of this point, but Wittgenstein's basic idea here seems to be that interminability is unavoidable because as soon as we begin to think conceptually we are inclined to think metaphysically (see Glendinning 1998: ch. 5). Thus, for each of us, being-in-need-of-more-therapy will tend to be, as it were, our normal state (see Wittgenstein 1981: §568). *Plus de philosophie.* (No) More philosophy. Eternally.

CONCLUSION

What is distinctive about Heidegger and Wittgenstein is the challenge they pose to the metaphysical conception of non-empirical investigation. In virtue of this challenge Wittgenstein says that calling his own work 'philosophy' could be misleading. However, he also saw crucial analogies of his own work to metaphysics, analogies which make the use of the old title appropriate. Because of the disanalogies, Heidegger called what comes after the end of philosophy as metaphysics 'thinking'. Yet he considers that activity to be taking up the 'first possibility' of philosophy as metaphysics. So he too is not really abandoning philosophy. What really prevents Wittgenstein or Heidegger from identifying their work unproblematically as 'philosophy' is that their work does not have a 'founding character', and that idea was central to philosophy as metaphysics. But neither writer would, I submit, suppose that their kind of work should, for that reason, be conceived as being 'on an equal footing with science' (Rorty 1982: xlii). They would reject such a view not because science is actually higher or lower than philosophy, but because philosophy alone is, historically, *the* subject which attempts to respond to what Wittgenstein called 'our real need': the need for clarity on what we *already* know, a bringing to concepts of what is in some sense *already* in view, and yet which, for some reason, remains hidden from us (Wittgenstein 1968: §§89, 108, and 129). Thus the end of philosophy as metaphysics is by no means the end of philosophy as such.

PHILOSOPHY AND THE EXACT SCIENCES

FIRST-ORDER LOGIC AND ITS RIVALS

MICHAEL SCANLAN

1. INTRODUCTION

The first-order logic that is commonly taught and used today did not exist at the beginning of the twentieth century. A series of investigations in 'foundations of mathematics' by a variety of researchers led to its treatment as the core element of 'mathematical logic'. These investigations searched for a detailed account of how our finite reasoning capacity could lead to knowledge of the infinite quantities involved in mathematics. This issue took on an acute form in the late 1800s when Georg Cantor (1845–1918) showed that mathematics could not be understood without accepting the existence of infinite sets of entities, in particular the complete set of counting (or natural) numbers. He also showed that the existence of such a denumerably infinite set entails the existence of ever larger infinite sets, each having a larger infinite 'cardinal number'. The methods developed in the studies of mathematical logic were taken over to formulate alternatives to first-order logic. The most important of these were modal logic and intuitionistic logic. This chapter tells the story of these changes.

2. FIRST-ORDER LOGIC

A first-order logic is a set of logical axioms and formal inference rules for a first-order language. Such a language will contain one-place predicate symbols and multiple-place relation symbols. The language may also have symbols for individual objects and functions. For logical symbols, it typically has the sentential connectives $\sim$, $\&$, $\rightarrow$, $\vee$, $\leftrightarrow$, and the two quantifiers, $\forall$, $\exists$. The language is 'first-order' because quantifiers apply only to variables which range over the individual objects of the domain. Second-order or higher-order languages have variables that range over sets of objects or of n-tuples drawn from the domain.

A first-order language for the positive integers might contain the following symbols: the predicate symbol, Px, for 'x is a positive integer', the two–place relation symbol, $x < y$, to indicate the 'less than' relation, the individual constant, 1, to designate one, and the two-place function symbol, $x + y$, for the addition function. This language will also include the identity symbol, $=$, as an additional logical symbol. Not all first-order languages have the identity symbol. It cannot be defined in first-order logic and so must be introduced, with additional axioms, if needed.

In this language we can make such statements as the following:

P1	(1 is a positive integer)
$\forall x \, (Px \rightarrow P(x + 1))$	(the successor of a positive integer is a positive integer)
$\sim\exists x \, (x + 1 = 1)$	(1 is not the successor of any positive integer)
$\forall x \, (x + 1 = y + 1 \rightarrow x = y)$	(each positive integer has a unique predecessor)

These are the first four of what are known as the 'Peano axioms'. In a first-order formulation, the fifth Peano axiom, the axiom of mathematical induction, has a special character. It is not properly a sentence of the first-order language. It is instead a *schema* representing an infinity of first-order sentences in which Φ is replaced by a formula containing one free variable. This schema is,

$$(\Phi 1 \, \& \, \forall x(\Phi x \rightarrow \Phi(x + 1)) \rightarrow \forall y \Phi y$$

This can be read as saying 'Whatever formula with one free variable holds for 1 and also, if it holds for a positive integer then holds for its successor, holds for every positive integer.' An instance is the following,

$$((1 + 1 = 1 + 1) \, \& \, \forall x((1 + x = x + 1) \rightarrow (1 + (x + 1)$$
$$= ((x + 1) + 1))) \rightarrow \forall y(1 + y = y + 1),$$
$$\text{where } \Phi \text{ is '}(1 + x = x + 1)\text{'}.$$

In contrast to a first-order language, in a second-order language, the induction axiom is not written as a schema, but is instead a sentence of the language,

$$\forall A((A1 \, \& \, \forall x(Ax \rightarrow A(x + 1)) \rightarrow \forall y Ay)$$

Here the letter A is a second-order variable which ranges over all *subsets* of the domain. So, the second-order variable A ranges over the set of all subsets of positive integers. This has the cardinality of the set of real numbers that form the continuum. The set of formulas that can be substituted for Φ in the first-order schema has only the smaller cardinality of the positive integers. This means that the inductive character of every property of positive integers, represented by the set of integers it applies to, is not fully expressed by the first-order schema.

First-order logic has a set of 'nice' metamathematical properties. These include completeness and compactness, as well as the Löwenheim-Skolem theorem that any countable set of first-order sentences which has a model of some infinite cardinality also has a model that is denumerably infinite. These properties do not hold for second-order and higher-order theories. On the other hand, one consequence of the Löwenheim-Skolem theorem is that there is no categorical first-order theory of the natural numbers, or of any theory which has an infinite domain for its intended interpretation. (For categorical theories all models are isomorphic, that is, 'structurally' similar.) To those who are interested primarily in providing a careful formulation and analysis of theories of mathematics, this is an obvious defect of first-order theories (see Shapiro 1985).

3. THE ORIGINS OF FIRST-ORDER LOGIC

In 1914, neither the distinctions between set theory and logic nor that between first-order and higher-order logic were clearly marked. The just-completed *Principia Mathematica*, by Whitehead and Russell, exemplified this. The central logical concept there, 'propositional function', was not clearly defined. It often corresponds to the traditional logical notion of objective properties and relations. A propositional function with a single variable, ϕx, delineates the set of objects for which the property ϕ holds (represented as $\hat{x}(\phi x)$). A propositional function with two variables, $\psi(x, y)$, has associated with it the set of ordered pairs of objects for which the binary relation ψ holds (represented as $\hat{x}, \hat{y} \ \psi(x, y)$). *Principia* shows how more complicated relations can be built up on the basis of binary relations. Using the concept of propositional function, the notions of set theory can be defined and the cardinal numbers (the natural numbers, plus the infinite numbers discovered by Cantor) can then be defined. On this definition, a number is a set of sets which each have a one-one relation to each other. Intuitively, this means that each member of the set that is the number n contains n elements. Whitehead and Russell were able to show that the sets defined in this way as 'numbers' have the properties described in the Peano axioms. Since previous authors had shown how to develop all other known mathematical theories on the basis of the theory of natural numbers, Whitehead and Russell took themselves to have shown how to develop all of mathematical theory starting from only logical concepts.

The logic of *Principia Mathematica* is not first-order. It is sometimes described as ω-order logic. This means that the variables in the language of *Principia* can be thought of as ranging over an infinite hierarchy of objects. This includes a base group of individuals, properties of these individuals, relations of properties, properties of relations of properties, etc. The hierarchy can also be thought of in terms of sets. The set of finite numbers in *Principia* is fourth-order. It is a set of sets of sets of individuals. The language is sometimes said to be a 'universal language', that is, it aspires to include statements about any possible object.

But already in 1902, Russell had discovered that the concept of the set of all sets which are not members of themselves, that is $\hat{x}\ (x \notin x)$, is contradictory. Russell's analysis of this problem was that it arose from allowing the variable x in the propositional function $(x \notin x)$ to take as values all objects in the universe. This led Russell to develop his 'type-theory' in which the range of variables in different propositional functions was limited to specific 'types' of objects. The separate types, roughly, correspond to the different orders of objects sketched earlier. Thus '$x \notin x$' is not well-formed, since the membership relation requires variables of different types.

The most influential alternative approach to developing a foundational theory for mathematics, while avoiding paradoxes, is axiomatic set theory, inaugurated in 1908 by Ernst Zermelo (1871–1953). The critical axiom in Zermelo's presentation was the axiom of separation (*Aussonderung*): 'Whenever the propositional function $\mathfrak{C}(x)$ is definite for all elements of a set M, M possesses a subset $M_{\mathfrak{C}}$ containing as elements precisely those elements x of M for which $\mathfrak{C}(x)$ is true' (Zermelo 1908 [1967: 202]). This axiom restricts the way in which a set is determined by a propositional function; it can only be separated out from a set that is already allowed by the axioms. Zermelo was rather vague about what made a propositional function 'definite'. He also was not explicit about what he took to be the logic underlying his system of axioms and his axioms were not presented in a formal language.

The treatment of axiomatic set theory as a first-order theory is due to Thoralf Skolem (1887–1963). He proved in 1920 an extended version of Löwenheim's theorem by showing that every set of first-order sentences satisfiable in some infinite domain is satisfiable in a domain that is at most denumerably infinite. This theorem took on great significance for him when he proposed that Zermelo's restriction of the separation axiom to 'definite' set-theoretic properties should be interpreted as meaning that a 'definite' property is one expressible by a formula with one free variable in a first-order language containing '$\in$' as its only non–logical symbol (Skolem 1923). In making this proposal he did not give an account of why the interpretation should be in terms of formulas of a language or why that language should be first-order. Skolem thought his formulation of the separation axiom was a very 'natural' approach. In favour of this approach, he says it is a 'completely clear concept' and that it is adequate to develop all of the usual set theoretic concepts. In Skolem 1930, he suggests that if Zermelo's proposal is understood as allowing second-order formulations in the language of set theory ('functions of propositional functions'), then the concept of function involved is unclear.

Despite this, Skolem thought that any axiomatised first-order theory is inadequate as a secure foundation for mathematics. He pointed out that given the

Löwenheim-Skolem Theorem his first-order axiomatised set theory must have a denumerably infinite model, despite the fact that within the theory it is possible to prove Cantor's classic theorems about the existence of nondenumerable sets. Skolem explained that this conclusion is only apparently paradoxical and stems from the inability, within the theory, to prove the existence of one-one correspondences between sets which, when viewed from outside the theory, are denumerable. He thought one important conclusion to be drawn from this state of affairs was what he called the 'relativity' of all set-theoretic notions. By this he meant that even the existence of models of the axioms is not enough to ensure the existence of nondenumerable sets, except 'relative' to the theory itself.

Skolem seems to have been more comfortable with number theory as a secure foundational basis for mathematics in general. But even here he did not take an axiomatic approach, since this assumes the existence of models that are adequately specified by the axioms. Rather, he showed that the first-order Peano axioms are not categorical (Skolem 1934). That is, they have many non-isomorphic (now called 'non-standard') models. Thus the first-order Peano axioms fail to characterise uniquely the sequence of positive whole numbers, their intended interpretation. For him this meant that we cannot characterise our fundamental mathematical concepts by such means. Skolem's own preferred foundational theory uses only a base set of arithmetical functions and their combinations to build up a set of specific arithmetic equational truths, such as $2 + (3 + 5) = (2 + 3) + 5$, along with what are, in effect, schematic generalities containing only free variables and no quantification. The development of such an arithmetic, including proof by induction as a basic rule of reasoning, is what he called the 'recursive mode of thought'. Skolem took this to be the only epistemically secure approach to mathematical foundations since it did not presuppose infinite totalities. This is now called 'primitive recursive arithmetic' and is not adequate to develop full number theory.

Similarly to Skolem, Hilbert (1862–1943) sought to confirm the epistemic soundness of mathematical theories on the basis of a 'finitistic' number theory that did not incorporate assumptions about infinite totalities. This finitistic number theory would then be used to provide a metatheory for the language of other mathematical theories ('metamathematics'). This metatheory would be adequate to show that a formal deduction system for the axioms of the theory does not allow both a formula and its negation to be derived ('consistency'). This 'formalism' pushed Hilbert and his co-workers to more precise formulations of theories and their underlying languages and deductive systems. The publication in 1928 of *Grundzüge der theoretischen Logik* (*Principles of Mathematical Logic*) by Hilbert and Ackermann was a landmark in the development of first-order logic.

They explicitly distinguished in that text between first-order logic (*der engere Functionenkalkül*) and second-order logic (*der erweiterte Functionenkalkül*). They also gave the first precise recursive definition of the languages of those logics (ch. 3, sect. 4). In these languages they took the capital predicate letters, for example, F(*x*) or G(*x*, *y*), to be variables. A first-order logical formula (i.e. with no nonvariable symbols) was 'universally valid' (*allgemeingültig*) when any interpretation of the individual and predicate variables produces a true statement. Somewhat in passing, Hilbert and Ackermann formulated for the first time the completeness question for first-order logic: 'Whether the axiom system is at least complete in the sense that all logical formulas that are true for every individual domain can be derived [from the axioms]' (Hilbert and Ackermann 1928: 68). This is the question that Gödel would answer affirmatively in his dissertation of 1929. A more prominent discussion was given to the decision problem (*Entscheidungsproblem*) for the first-order logical formulas. In terms of universal validity the problem is described as follows: 'how can one determine for an arbitrarily given logical expression, which contains no individual symbols, whether the expression represents a true assertion or not, for an arbitrary assignment for the variables occurring in it.' (Hilbert and Ackermann 1928: 72–3). Church showed in 1936 that there is no such general decision procedure for the first-order logical formulas.

Hilbert and Ackermann go on in their final chapter to add quantifiers for the function variables of the first-order system. They say that this approach is necessary if one is to develop a logic adequate for the development of mathematics. For instance, they point out that numbers are best understood as 'a property of that concept under which the selected individuals are combined' (Hilbert and Ackermann 1928: 86). They then show how various concepts of number theory can be expressed by second-order formulas. They also sketch how the concepts of set theory can be developed in a second-order language. But paradoxes, especially Russell's paradox, can be developed in this unrestricted second-order logic. This leads them to conclude the book by describing type theory (*Stufenkalkül*) as the appropriate logic in which to develop mathematics while avoiding the paradoxes.

4. MODAL LOGIC

Modern development of modal logic had its origin largely in the work of C. I. Lewis (1883–1964). As early as 1912, he expressed concern that the 'material implication' of *Principia Mathematica*, with its truth-functional meaning, did not reflect the normal meaning of 'implication'. In particular, he found inappropriate the 'paradoxes of material implication' by which any actually false proposition materially implies any other proposition, while any actually true proposition is materially implied by any other proposition. Thus, on the standard truth-functional treatment of the propositional connective →,

(Julius Caesar was US President → Washington DC is the US capital)

is true. In contrast, reading '→' here as 'implies' produces a false statement. Lewis's proposal was that 'P implies Q' should be understood as meaning 'it is not possible for both P and ∼Q ', symbolised as ∼◊(P . ∼Q). He represented this relation by a symbol for 'strict implication', 'P ≺ Q', commonly read 'P hook Q'.

In his *Survey of Symbolic Logic* (1918) Lewis presented a set of postulates for his first system of strict implication. This system contains the propositional logic of material implication as a subsystem, along with theorems for strict implication. It was subsequently shown (by E. L. Post) that matching theorems hold for both → and ≺ in this system, thus failing to provide a distinction between them. Work by Lewis and others led to revised postulate sets. Lewis's most complete development of his system of strict implication was presented in *Symbolic Logic* (1932, with C. H. Langford). In Appendix II of that work he outlines a set of progressively stronger postulate sets for systems of strict implication, labelled S1–S5. This means that, for example, the theorems of S1 are a proper subset of the theorems of S2. In a different sense, S1 is the most 'strict' of the systems and S5 the least 'strict'. This is because S5 comes closer to having a matching theorem stated in terms of ≺ for every theorem stated in terms of →.

Today postulates for these systems of modal logic (and others) are often given in terms of the operators ◊, 'it is possible that', and □, 'it is necessary that', instead of Lewis's strict implication. Although combining quantification with the modal operator ◊ is discussed in *Symbolic Logic*, there is no systematic development of a derivational logic involving quantification and modal operators. This was first done by Ruth Barcan (later Marcus) in a series of papers in 1946–7. These developed systems based on S2 and S4. They included as an axiom what came to be known as the 'Barcan formula', ◊(∃α)A ≺ (∃α)◊A (where α is an arbitrary variable and A is an arbitrary formula). An equivalent form of this is (∀α)□A → □(∀α)A. There have been various controversies about this formula. All of them centre around the interpretation of *de re* modalities, which seem an inherent feature of quantified modal logics.

Where a modal operator occurs before a quantified formula, as in □(∀α)A, one has an interpretative situation similar to that in propositional modal logic, except that the domain of propositions is enlarged. This sort of modal statement is said to be *de dicto*, since the modality seems to affect the proposition (or sentence) in the scope of the operator. In case the modal operator occurs between the quantifier and the formula containing its bound variable, as in (∀α)□A, the modality seems to affect the individuals that form the domain of quantification and is thus said to be *de re*. This is perhaps clearer in the example, $(\forall x)\Box(x$ is human $\rightarrow x$ is mortal). Such statements seem to ascribe necessary, that is, essential, properties to individuals and open a vast field of philosophic controversy.

An independent development of modal propositional logic by Jan Łukasiewicz (1878–1956) had its origins about 1920. This arose out of his concern with the ancient problem of determinism of the future by predictive statements that are true today. Łukasiewicz proposed a three-valued logic containing, besides truth and falsity, a third value that could be thought of as 'possibility'. For propositional logics, he explicated this in terms of a three-valued 'matrix' for the truth-functional connectives of his propositional logic, analogous to the familiar truth-table definitions of the two-valued connectives. Using a definition provided by Tarski, a possibility operator can be defined in a three-valued propositional logic using the equivalence $\Diamond p \leftrightarrow (\sim p \rightarrow p)$. In the three-valued interpretation the right-hand side of this equivalence is only false when p is false, in the other cases, p is true or has the 'possible' value. The notion of possibility defined in this way is not equivalent to that in the Lewis systems. In subsequent researches in modal logic, Łukasiewicz replaced a three-valued system with a four-valued system (see Łukasiewicz 1953).

The modal systems of Lewis, Barcan Marcus, and others are often described as 'intensional' logics, since their intended interpretation concerns the meaning of propositions and not the 'extension' of a proposition, that is, whether it is simply true or false. Despite the use of Łukasiewicz-style many-valued propositional interpretations in independence and consistency proofs by Lewis's students, these extensional interpretations were not viewed as legitimate interpretations of the real meaning of the modal systems. The issues of the proper interpretation of modal systems were exacerbated in 1959 when Kripke provided the first workable model theory for quantified modal logic. His approach was extensional in that it specified interpretations in set theory. Instead of the single domain and set of relations on the domain used in first-order model theory, multiple copies of the domain with varying relations on that domain are used. One of these is the actual world. The others are (somewhat fancifully) described as possible worlds reflecting how things could have been.

5. INTUITIONISTIC LOGIC

Intuitionistic logic has its origins in the ideas of L. E. J. Brouwer (1881–1966). Brouwer saw mathematics as based on the human desire to ascribe order to basic experience. The source of the mathematical conception of a sequence is the human ability to abstract 'two-oneness' from the intuition of objects in time. Roughly, Brouwer seems to mean by this the ability to see two objects of experience as having a sequential relation in time; they are two, but united in their relation. Once this occurs for two, then they can be united with a third, and so on.

The concept of 'and so on' is taken by Brouwer to be mathematical induction. This principle is inherent in our understanding of sequences and hence of the natural numbers. Brouwer rejected the attempt by Frege and Russell to define mathematical induction as a logical property of the natural numbers. For Brouwer, this is because logic is something that comes *after* mathematics. Mathematics is a 'free' activity of constructing order in the material of experience. Logic, on the other hand, deals only with language. Language is an imperfect mechanism to get others to carry out the same mental constructions that we have. Logic detects some patterns in these linguistic communications, but it is the activity of mathematical construction which justifies these patterns, not the other way round.

This viewpoint meant that Brouwer did not take logical principles to be a priori and immune from criticism. In particular, he identified the principle of excluded middle (that either a proposition or its negation is true) as a source of paradoxes when applied to some infinite domains. Brouwer's rejection of excluded middle as a generally applicable principle of reasoning is based on his view of mathematical existence. As an idealist, being and being known amount to the same thing for him. As he expressed it, '*truth* is only in *reality*, that is, in the present and past experiences of consciousness' (Brouwer 1948 [1975: 488]). This creates a situation where a mathematical object is true/real only when we experience it, i.e. construct it. From this point of view there is, besides the two possibilities that we have experienced that the object has a given property or that we have experienced that the object does not have the given property, a third possibility, that we have experienced neither of these.

In the intuitionistic propositional logic published by A. Heyting (1898–1980) in 1930, the negation symbol, $\neg$, corresponds to Brouwer's notion of an 'absurd' statement. This is a statement for which it is possible to prove that it leads contradiction. Asserting a statement, on the other hand, is saying that the statement can be proven. In this logic, the classical principle $p \rightarrow \neg\neg p$ holds. This is because, if we can prove p, then we cannot also prove $\neg p$ without inconsistency. On the other hand, the classical theorem $\neg\neg p \rightarrow p$ fails to hold in the intuitionistic propositional calculus. On the intuitionistic view of this theorem, if I have shown that it is absurd for p to lead to inconsistency, this does not mean that I have constructed/know p.

Heyting's propositional calculus does contain the formula $(p \vee \neg p) \rightarrow (\neg\neg p \rightarrow p)$. The intuitionistic view is that while the principle of excluded middle is not a general principle, it does hold for many domains. In these, the classical logic applies and that is what is warranted by this formula. For Brouwer, the principle of excluded middle holds in any finite domain. It also holds in any domain in which we have a general principle for constructing proofs, such as the principle of mathematical induction provides for the natural numbers. In infinite domains in which there is no general constructive method for proving statements or solving problems, such as the classical real numbers, the principle of excluded middle does not apply and the special character of intuitionistic logic comes into effect.

In his development of an intuitionistic quantificational calculus in 1930b, Heyting points out that '$(\exists x)$ can neither be defined from $(\forall x)$, nor can $(\forall x)$ be defined from $(\exists x)$' (1930b: 58). That is because of the intuitionistic failure of the classical equivalences

$$(\exists x)\phi x \leftrightarrow \neg(\forall x)\neg\phi x$$

and

$$(\forall x)\phi x \leftrightarrow \neg(\exists x)\neg\phi x$$

Intuitionistically, $(\exists x)\phi x$ means that we can construct an object for which ϕ holds. $(\forall x)\phi x$ means that there is a general constructive method to show for each object that ϕ holds. In this situation $\neg(\forall x)\neg\phi x \rightarrow (\exists x)\phi x$ fails, since the lack of a general method for showing $\neg \phi x$ does not mean that we have a specific construction for some x to show that ϕ holds for it. The converse does however hold intuitionistically. Similarly, $\neg(\exists x)\neg\phi x \rightarrow (\forall x)\phi x$ fails to hold, because even if we do not have a specific construction of a counterexample to ϕ, this does not mean that we have a general construction for showing that ϕ holds for each x. Once more, the converse does hold in intuitionistic as in classical predicate calculus.

One might expect that we can interpret the Heyting propositional calculus in a domain of three values, true, false, and undecided. But, in fact, Gödel showed (Gödel 1932) that the Heyting propositional calculus does not have an interpretation with finitely many values. This is not so surprising since Heyting did not intend to represent the logic of statements with independent truth-values. In the intuitionistic context, rejecting $p \vee \neg p$ is saying that there are statements which can neither be proven nor disproven. This is not a comment about the truth-value of the statement, but about our method of proof.

Indeed, Gödel gave a system of translation in 1933 in which the Heyting propositional calculus can be understood as a theory of proof added to a classical logic. For this he added an additional predicate symbol for the language, B (for '*beweisbar*', i.e. 'provable'), plus axioms and a rule of inference. 'Provable' here means 'provable in some way'; if it is limited to 'provable in a specific formal system', a conflict with Gödel's second incompleteness theorem arises. Gödel also gives a translation scheme to translate the formulas of the intuitionistic propositional calculus into a formula about provability. For instance, a formula $\neg p$ is translated into $\sim Bp$. A formula is in the Heyting intuitionistic calculus if and only if its translation is in the Gödel provability calculus. This 'provability interpretation' was later extended to quantified intuitionistic logic and to intuitionistic arithmetic. Somewhat surprisingly, Gödel's provability logic is the Lewis modal system S4, if 'B' is replaced by '$\Box$'. An extensive 'logic of provability' has been developed on this basis.

6. ENVOI

The efforts of researchers in this period to formulate in a precise fashion the underlying logic of mathematical proof led to a situation in which the logics and formalised theories themselves became objects of mathematical study. Over the course of the 1930s, Tarski developed a mathematical treatment of 'the methodology of deductive sciences'. This made fundamental logical concepts (e.g. truth, logical consequence, decidability) themselves the subject of formal deductive theories. In the period after the war, Tarski, his students, and others would develop this framework into model theory. Also in the 1930s, the work of Church, Turing, Post, Gödel, and others turned the theory of recursive functions into a vehicle for the study of effective mathematical calculation and proof.

Formal studies of the new logics became a vehicle for philosophic explorations and controversies. By 1939, W. V. Quine was suggesting that examining the use of quantification in formalised mathematical and scientific theories reveals the ontological requirements of those theories, particularly the commitment to universal as opposed to individual entities. Less than a year after Marcus's treatment of quantified modal logic, Quine was questioning the possibility of a coherent interpretation of it (Quine 1947). An ongoing debate ensued on the metaphysics of essential properties, buttressed by formal studies. Intuitionistic logic became a vehicle for the study of the concept of constructive procedures in mathematics. An early example is Kleene's proposal to use the recursive functions as an analogue of intuitionistic constructions in number theory (Kleene 1945). In the rebirth of academic life after the Second World War, particularly in the US, the formal systems that had originated in the study of mathematical foundations would give an entirely new cast to the 'logical-analytic method of philosophy' that Russell had outlined at the beginning of the period (Russell 1914: v).

47

THE GOLDEN AGE OF MATHEMATICAL LOGIC

JOHN DAWSON

OVERVIEW

Modern symbolic logic, including axiomatic set theory, developed out of the works of Boole, Peirce, Cantor, and Frege in the nineteenth century. The contours of the subject as it is known today, however, were largely established in the decade between 1928 and 1938. During those years the scope of the discipline was expanded, both through clarification of the distinction between syntax and semantics and through recognition of different logical systems, in contrast to the conception of logic as a universal system within which all reasoning must be carried out. At the same time the primary focus of logical investigation was narrowed to the study of first-order logic (then called the 'restricted functional calculus'), in which quantification is allowed only over the elements of an underlying structure, not over subsets thereof. The former development made possible the formulation and resolution of metasystematic questions, such as the consistency or completeness of axiomatic theories, while the latter, by isolating a more tractable logical framework, facilitated the derivation of theorems. Both developments led to the study of model-theoretic issues, such as the compactness of logical systems and the existence of non-isomorphic models of arithmetic and set theory.

In addition, questions concerning definability and decidability by axiomatic or algorithmic means were given precise mathematical formulations through the definition of the class of recursive functions and the enunciation of Church's Thesis (that the recursive functions are exactly those intuitively characterised as being effectively computable). Formal proofs of indefinability and undecidability theorems thereby became possible, with profound implications for Hilbert's proof theory and for the subsequent development of computer science. Definability considerations also gave rise to the definition of the class of constructible sets, the principal conceptual tool in Gödel's proof that the axiom of choice and the generalised continuum hypothesis are consistent relative to the axioms of Zermelo-Fraenkel set theory.

1. DERIVABILITY, VALIDITY, AND THE *ENTSCHEIDUNGSPROBLEM*

The deduction from specified axioms of truths concerning the objects of particular mathematical domains has been the exemplar of mathematical method since the time of Euclid. In practice, though, deductions are generally carried out informally, without precise specification of the rules of inference employed or explicit mention of the underlying axioms. In the late nineteenth century logicians such as C. S. Peirce, Gottlob Frege and Giuseppe Peano and geometers such as Moritz Pasch and David Hilbert did much to restore the Euclidean ideal in number theory and geometry. Yet they failed to achieve a synthesis between syntactic and semantic points of view. The fundamental distinction and interrelation between a statement's derivability from axioms and its validity within a particular interpretation of those axioms remained murky until well into the twentieth century.

Distinctions between language and metalanguage were likewise ignored or blurred until the appearance of paradoxes, especially those of Bertrand Russell (1903) and Jules Richard (1905), forced their consideration. The theory of types, expounded by Russell and A. N. Whitehead in their *Principia Mathematica* (1910–13), provided one way of resolving those paradoxes, but it was compromised by the axiom of reducibility, a makeshift principle introduced out of necessity that, in effect, rendered the hierarchy of types superfluous. Moreover, despite the stratification of type levels, the theory of types was formulated within a single object language, which Russell and others of the logicist school regarded as all-embracing. Consequently, metalinguistic questions, such as whether the axioms for number theory are consistent or whether they suffice to yield proofs of all true statements about the natural numbers, could not be posed within the theory – and hence, from the logicist perspective, not at all (see van Heijenoort 1967 and Goldfarb 1979). The utility and reliability of axioms could only be established empirically, by deriving a multitude of facts from them without encountering contradiction.

In contrast, logicians following in the algebraic tradition of George Boole and Ernst Schröder employed naïve set theory, without reference to axioms and rules of inference, to study the satisfiability of statements within particular structures. A particularly striking result was the theorem of Leopold Löwenheim, first published (though with a faulty proof) in Löwenheim 1915: If a first-order statement in a denumerable language is satisfiable in a structure S, it is satisfiable in a denumerable structure D.

The gap in Löwenheim's proof was repaired by the Norwegian logician Thoralf Skolem, who also extended Löwenheim's result to denumerable sets of statements. In the first of two papers (Skolem 1920) he used choice functions (now called Skolem functions) to associate with each first-order formula containing existential quantifiers a purely universal one (its Skolem normal form) in an expanded language containing new function symbols. (The formula $\forall w \exists x \forall y \exists z\, A(w,x,y,z)$, for example, has the normal form $\forall w \forall y F(w,f(w),y,g(w,y))$.) A formula of the original language is satisfiable in a structure therefor if and only if its Skolem normal form is satisfiable in the corresponding structure for the expanded language. From that Skolem went on to prove that the denumerable structure D in Löwenheim's theorem could be taken to be a substructure of S. In the second paper (Skolem 1923b) he showed that Löwenheim's original theorem, without the substructure condition, could also be established without appeal to the axiom of choice, and by applying the result of the first paper to set theory he obtained the Skolem paradox (that the axioms of set theory, within which the existence of indenumerable sets is provable, must be satisfiable within a denumerable structure).

Closely related to the question of a statement's satisfiability (whether there is *any* structure in which it is satisfiable) is the question of its validity (whether it is satisfiable in *all* structures for the underlying language). More generally, the decision problem (*Entscheidungsproblem*) is the question whether there is an effective procedure for determining the status of an *arbitrary* statement of a given logical system with regard either to its satisfiability, its validity, or its derivability from axioms.

For the logic of connectives (the propositional calculus) affirmative answers to all three decision problems were obtained in the doctoral dissertations of Emil Post and Paul Bernays (published as Post 1921 and Bernays 1926) using the devices of truth tables and conjunctive normal forms, respectively. During the 1920s affirmative answers to the decision problem for satisfiability were also obtained for various prefix classes of quantificational formulas (surveyed in Ackermann 1954 and Dreben and Goldfarb 1979), by exhibiting intuitively effective decision procedures for them. In addition, the satisfiability of an arbitrary first-order formula was shown to be reducible to that of certain other prefix classes of formulas. But, in the absence of a precise characterisation of the intuitive notion of effective procedure, no undecidability results could be established.

2. COMPLETENESS, INCOMPLETENESS, AND CONSISTENCY PROOFS

The appearance of the book *Grundzüge der theoretischen Logik (Fundamentals of Theoretical Logic)* (Hilbert and Ackermann 1928) heralded the beginning of a decade of path-breaking advances in mathematical logic. In that text Hilbert and Wilhelm Ackermann drew attention to first-order logic and to three unsolved problems concerning it: the decision problems for satisfiability and validity (p. 72), and the question (p. 68) 'whether . . . all logical formulas that are correct for each domain of individuals can be derived' from the axioms of the system (semantic completeness). A positive answer to the latter question was expected, and was obtained the following year in the doctoral dissertation of Kurt Gödel (published, in somewhat revised form, as Gödel 1930). Most of the steps in the proof were implicit in Skolem 1923b, but Gödel was the first to link syntax with semantics: whereas Skolem had concluded that a first-order formula that is not satisfiable in a denumerable structure must not be satisfiable at all, Gödel showed that it must in fact be formally refutable. In addition, he proved the (denumerable) compactness theorem (that a denumerably infinite set of sentences is satisfiable if and only if every finite subset is), a result later extended to arbitrary sets of sentences by A. I. Maltsev and Leon Henkin. Regarded today as a central result in model theory, the compactness theorem was long overlooked (see Dawson 1993), while some of its now familiar applications were obtained by other methods. In particular, the existence of non-isomorphic models of the set of all statements true of the natural numbers was established in Skolem 1934, using techniques that foreshadowed the later notion of ultraproducts.

In the introduction to his dissertation (Gödel 1929), Gödel noted that the completeness theorem may be recast as the statement that every consistent first-order axiom system has a model, and so it justifies the expectation that the consistency of a theory can be demonstrated by finding a structure in which its axioms are satisfied. At the same time, however, he criticised the view, advanced especially by Hilbert, that the existence of notions introduced through an axiom system is synonymous with the system's consistency. Such a belief, he stressed, 'manifestly presupposes' that every closed formula A of the theory must either be provable or refutable, since otherwise, by adjoining one or the other of A or $\sim A$ to the axioms, two consistent but incompatible theories would result.

For his formalisation of the propositional calculus, Post had shown that the adjunction of any unprovable formula to the axioms would produce inconsistency. But Gödel foresaw that such syntactic completeness might not always hold for quantificational theories, and in his epochal paper 'On Formally Undecidable Propositions of *Principia Mathematica* and Related Systems I' (Gödel 1931) he proved that whenever the axioms and rules of inference for formal number theory are specified in a primitive recursive fashion and satisfy either the semantic criterion of *soundness* (that every provable formula be true when interpreted in the natural numbers) or the syntactic one of *ω-consistency* (that whenever every numerical instance $A(n)$ of a formula $A(x)$ is provable, the formula $\exists x \sim A(x)$

is not provable), some closed formula must be undecidable (neither provable nor refutable). That the hypothesis of ω-consistency can be weakened to that of simple consistency was shown five years later (Rosser 1936).

In proving that first incompleteness theorem Gödel encoded formulas of number theory into natural numbers, so that statements about the formal system could be expressed as statements about numbers. He then showed that a large stock of number-theoretic relations – in particular, all those now called *primitive recursive*, including the relation 'm is the code number of a proof of the formula with code number n' – are formally representable within the theory, in the sense that for each such relation R there is a formula F of the language such that $R(n_1, n_2, \ldots, n_k)$ holds of natural numbers $n_1, n_2, \ldots, n_k$ if and only if $F(\mathbf{n_1}, \mathbf{n_2}, \ldots, \mathbf{n_k})$ is provable, where $\mathbf{n_1}, \mathbf{n_2}, \ldots, \mathbf{n_k}$ are the corresponding symbols for numerals. Thence, using a diagonalisation device, he constructed an undecidable number-theoretic formula that, if decoded as a metamathematical statement, affirmed its own unprovability.

The notion of consistency can also be expressed within formal number theory, by a formula F that encodes the statement 'No natural number is the code number of a proof of the statement $0 = 1$'; but Gödel sketched a proof that no primitive-recursively specifiable schema of axioms for number theory (or any stronger theory, such as set theory) can yield the formula F as a theorem, unless the axioms are in fact *in*consistent (the second incompleteness theorem, first proved in full detail in Hilbert and Bernays 1939). Consistency proofs are not precluded altogether, but for all but very weak theories some principle not formalisable within the theory itself must be invoked in any such proof. Consequently, the principal aim of Hilbert's proof theory, that of establishing the consistency of strong theories by reducing their consistency to that of weaker ones, cannot be achieved.

For number theory, a consistency proof based on an ordinal-theoretic analysis of proof structures (sequents) was given by Gerhard Gentzen five years after Gödel's work (Gentzen 1936); it employed the principle of transfinite induction up to the first fixed-point of the ordinal exponentiation function. Another proof, based on the notion of functionals of finite type, was given by Gödel himself in 1938 and 1941.

3. UNDEFINABILITY AND UNDECIDABILITY THEOREMS

The notion of truth or, more generally, that of a formula being satisfiable in a structure for a formal language, is central to the papers of Skolem and Löwenheim cited above, as well as to Gödel's completeness theorem. In none of those works, however, were the underlying semantic concepts precisely defined:

the proofs relied instead on an informal understanding of the meaning of satisfiability. A definitive analysis of the concept of truth in formalised languages was ultimately provided by Alfred Tarski, who (in Tarski 1933) both gave an inductive second-order definition of satisfaction and proved that in number theory the notion of truth, unlike that of provability, can not be expressed in any first-order formalisation (Tarski's undefinability theorem), a fact that Gödel had recognised independently at an early stage in his work on the first incompleteness theorem.

The formal study of inductive definitions had been initiated by Richard Dedekind, who in his famous monograph *Was sind und was sollen die Zahlen? (What are the Numbers and What Should They be?)* (Dedekind 1888) proved the basic theorem justifying the definition of functions by primitive recursion and gave the now well-known inductive definitions for addition, multiplication, and exponentiation of natural numbers (often attributed to Peano). Skolem and Hilbert subsequently employed such definitions in their foundational studies (Skolem 1923a and Hilbert 1926), and in his incompleteness paper Gödel formally defined the class of (primitive) recursive functions as those that are built up from the constant functions and the successor function by repeated use of recursion and substitution. But in his 1926 paper Hilbert also gave an example, due to Ackermann, of an effectively computable function that is not primitive recursive (as demonstrated in Ackermann 1928).

A general formalism (the λ-calculus) for defining number-theoretic functions and distinguishing them from their values was developed by Alonzo Church in the early 1930s. At first it was not clear that even the predecessor function could be defined within the λ-calculus, but Church's student Stephen Kleene eventually established the λ-definability of that and a wide range of other effectively calculable number-theoretic functions (Kleene 1935) – evidence that impelled Church in 1934 to posit that *all* such functions must in fact be λ-definable (the original form of Church's Thesis). Gödel, however, remained unconvinced, even after Kleene in his paper 'λ-definability and Recursiveness' (1936a) established the equivalence of λ-definability with the notion of general recursiveness Gödel had himself introduced (Gödel 1934: 26–7, a notion based on a suggestion of Jacques Herbrand, involving the derivability of equations of the form $\phi(k_1, k_2, \ldots, k_l) = m$ from certain systems of equations between terms built up by functional substitution). Church's Thesis, stated in terms of Gödel's notion rather than λ-definability (cf. Sieg 1997), first appeared in print in Church 1935, the abstract of a talk that Church delivered to the American Mathematical Society on 19 April 1935. Details appeared the following year in Church's 'An Unsolvable Problem of Elementary Number Theory' (1936a), one of a series of fundamental papers in recursion theory (surveyed in Kleene 1981) that appeared in quick succession during the next two years. On the basis of his Thesis, Church demonstrated the undecidability of the *Entscheidungsproblem* (Church 1936b), as did Alan Turing, independently and at almost the same time (Turing 1937). Kleene, in his 1936b, proved that the general recursive functions are generated from the primitive recursive ones by application of the least-number operator (the Normal Form Theorem), and in his 1936a formulated the Recursion Theorem or fixed-point theorem of recursion theory, a special case of which asserts that if the partial recursive functions – those defined on a (possibly proper) subset of the natural numbers – are enumerated in a sequence ϕ_k, and if f is any recursive function, then there is an integer n for which $\phi_n = \phi_{f(n)}$. Turing, in the aforementioned paper, gave another, especially perspicuous, analysis of computability in terms of abstract finite-state machines (Turing machines) that are capable of reading, writing, and acting upon symbols on an unbounded tape. The naturalness of Turing's approach, together with its equivalence with λ-definability, general recursiveness, and other notions of computability introduced by Post and A. A. Markov finally secured the widespread acceptance of Church's Thesis. (See Gandy 1988 for an extended analysis of this remarkable confluence of equivalent notions.)

4. THE AXIOM OF CHOICE AND THE GENERALISED CONTINUUM HYPOTHESIS

The theory of transfinite cardinal and ordinal numbers, developed by Georg Cantor as an outgrowth of his studies of sets of points at which Fourier series may fail to converge, was one of the most original and controversial creations of nineteenth-century mathematics. The idea of different orders of infinity and the paradoxes, such as the 'set' of all ordinals, to which the naïve theory of sets gave rise, provoked heated controversy. Cantor's work was attacked by many, but was championed by Hilbert, who in his address 'On the infinite' (Hilbert 1926) declared (p. 376), 'No one shall drive us from the paradise that Cantor created for us.' Earlier, in his turn-of-the-century address to the International Congress of Mathematicians (Hilbert 1900), Hilbert had listed as the first of the problems he posed as challenges to mathematicians of the twentieth century two questions arising from Cantor's theory: whether any infinite collection of real numbers must be equinumerous either with the set of integers or the set of all real numbers (Cantor's continuum hypothesis), and whether the set of all real numbers can be well-ordered. Since the reals are equinumerous with the set of all subsets of the integers, and since Cantor had proved that every set has a cardinality strictly less than its power set (the set of all its subsets), the continuum hypothesis may be restated as the assertion that no set of reals has a cardinality intermediate between that of the integers and the power set thereof. By extension, the generalised continuum hypothesis asserts that for no infinite set A is there a set B whose cardinality is intermediate between that of A and its power set.

Just four years after Hilbert's address Ernst Zermelo (Zermelo 1904) proved that the well-orderability of the reals, and indeed, of any set whatever, follows from the axiom of choice – a principle that had been invoked unconsciously in various proofs in analysis, but that, once called to mathematicians' attention, generated much dispute. Four years after that, in response to the continuing controversy, Zermelo formulated his axioms for set theory (Zermelo 1908) – axioms which, as revised later following suggestions of Abraham Fraenkel (Zermelo 1930), were eventually adopted as the standard formalisation of Cantor's ideas. The status of the continuum hypothesis relative to the other axioms remained unresolved, however, save for the observation that (when formulated as above) the generalised continuum hypothesis implies the axiom of choice (Lindenbaum and Tarski 1926).

The consistency of both the axiom of choice and the generalised continuum hypothesis with the other axioms of Zermelo-Fraenkel set theory was finally established by Gödel in 1938. In his proof Gödel singled out the syntactically definable class L of constructible sets, generated inductively by analogy with the usual *rank hierarchy* of set theory by iterating the power-set operation but restricting it to *definable* subsets. The class L possesses a definable well-ordering, and so satisfies the axiom of choice. In addition, the notion of constructibility is *absolute* (invariant when restricted to the class L), so that within L, every set is constructible. Likewise, the axioms of Zermelo-Fraenkel set theory hold within the class L if they hold of sets in general, so that, from a semantic point of view, the constructible sets form an inner model within any given model of set theory. By a difficult proof involving the *non*-absoluteness of cardinalities, Gödel showed that the generalised continuum hypothesis holds in L as well.

Gödel's consistency proofs (published in the monograph Gödel 1940) mark the culmination of the golden decade of research in logic surveyed in this chapter. By 1940 almost all the concepts and results covered today in introductory logic courses had been formulated. The principal exception is the method of constants, introduced by Leon Henkin in his doctoral dissertation (1947), which has since become the standard method for proving Gödel's completeness theorem and extending it to uncountable languages (Henkin 1949).

GENERAL RELATIVITY

THOMAS RYCKMAN

The initial empirical corroboration of the General Theory of Relativity (GTR) was announced to the world at a packed joint meeting of the Royal Society of London and the Royal Astronomical Society on 6 November 1919. Lengthy data analysis of solar eclipse observations, made the previous May by a joint British expedition to Brazil and to an island off the coast of West Africa, confirmed that the GTR-predicted amount of 'bending' of light rays in the solar gravitational field had indeed been found. Under a portrait of Isaac Newton, J. J. Thompson, president of the Royal Society, pronounced this 'the most important result obtained in connection with the theory of gravitation since Newton's day, and . . . one of the highest achievements of human thought' (quoted from Pais 1982: 305). There followed the 'relativity-rumpus' (Sommerfeld 1949: 101), a public clamour that, regarding a purely scientific theory without apparent military or technological application, was completely unprecedented, and is, as yet, unmatched. Almost overnight, Albert Einstein, hitherto largely unknown outside the rarefied (and by present standards, miniscule) circle of theoretical physicists, became world famous and a favoured target of anti-Semitism.

A plausible explanation of this astonishing spectacle points to the exhausted state of European culture, eager for diversion after the ravages of four years of world war, political revolution, and an influenza pandemic in which millions perished. Diversion the theory certainly provided, with the novelty of claims made on its behalf and its aura of incomprehensibility. But even among the scientifically literate, there was considerable controversy and misunderstanding concerning the theory's physical content as well as its philosophical implications. To a considerable extent this was due to unfamiliarity with the differential geometric basis of the theory. In part, however, responsibility for certain of these disagreements rests upon several rash formulations of Einstein himself. Even the very name of the theory designated a philosophical ambition rather than a physical achievement. For in an endeavour to eliminate references to 'absolute space' in the way in which the earlier Special (or, as it was then known,

Restricted) Theory of Relativity (STR) had eliminated reference to 'absolute time', Einstein promoted his theory of gravitation as a Machian-inspired generalisation of the relativity principle of STR and he misleadingly baptised it a theory of 'general relativity', seemingly permitting only relative motions between physical objects ('matter' in the strict sense). This the theory does not actually require and may not even condone. In Einstein's defence, it must be noted that early on, he preferred the name *Invariantentheorie* to 'Relativity theory' (which is due to Max Planck) and used the locution, 'the so-called "relativity theory"' in his own publications up to 1911. After that time, he presumably thought it too late to make the change (see Holton 1986: 69, 110).

1. CONTROVERSY OVER GENERAL COVARIANCE

One incautiously elliptical passage alone in Einstein's canonical presentation of the theory (in April 1916) has resulted in 'eight decades of dispute' (Norton 1993). Einstein here presented reasons why his gravitational theory must satisfy the purely formal requirement of general covariance, that is, that the laws of nature must be expressed by equations having the same form in all systems of coordinates:

In the general theory of relativity, space and time cannot be defined in such a way that differences of the spatial coordinates can be directly measured by the unit measuring-rod, or differences in the time coordinate by a standard clock . . . This comes to requiring that: – The general laws of nature are to be expressed by equations which are valid for all coordinate systems, that is, are covariant with respect to arbitrary substitutions (generally covariant). It is clear that a physics which satisfies this postulate will be suitable for the postulate of general relativity . . . That this requirement of general covariance, which takes away from space and time the last remnant of physical objectivity (*den letzten Rest physikalischer Gegenständlichkeit*), is a natural requirement, will be seen from the following reflection. All our spacetime verifications (*Konstatierungen*) invariably amount to a determination of spacetime coincidences. If, for example, events consisted merely in the motion of material points, then ultimately nothing would be observable but the meetings of two or more of these points. Also, the results of our measurements are nothing other than verifications of such meetings of the material points of our measuring rods with other material points (respectively, observed coincidences between the hands of a clock and points on the clock dial) – point-events happening at the same place and at the same time. The introduction of a reference system serves no other purpose than to facilitate the description of the totality of such coincidences . . . Since all our physical experience can be ultimately reduced to such coincidences, there is no immediate reason for preferring certain coordinate systems to others, that is to say, we arrive at the requirement of general covariance. (Einstein 1916: 117–18)

This 'requirement of general covariance' is puzzling, for it appears to conflate a principle of relativity, postulating the relativity of all motions, with freedom to make arbitrary transformations of the coordinates. Even more mysteriously, this requirement somehow 'takes away from space and time the last remnant of physical objectivity' while reducing the content of physical experience to 'point coincidences'. It is not surprising that these extremely confusing remarks were seized upon as evidence for rival philosophical interpretations by Machian positivists, Neo-Kantians, and even logical empiricists (see Ryckman 1992). To be sure, part of Einstein's reasoning can be reconstructed from the context. That his gravitational theory must satisfy the requirement of general covariance is a straightforward implication of what Einstein termed the principle of equivalence, which in effect postulates that inertial effects (such as Coriolis and centrifugal forces) in allegedly gravity-free regions of space-time, the domain of validity of the STR, are physically indistinguishable from the effects of weak uniform gravitational fields. For Einstein, this meant that his gravitational theory must be a generally covariant theory because, according to the equivalence principle, an inertial frame of a body may be locally transformed to a non-inertial frame in which the body is freely falling in a rather artificial gravitational field. Global inertial reference frames cannot exist. But the implication does not go the other way round: general covariance does not necessarily manifest a principle of relativity of motion.

Already in 1917 a young mathematician in Königsberg, Erich Kretschmann, observed that general covariance was merely the formal requirement of mutually consistent descriptions of the same object from different viewpoints and so had nothing to do *per se* with a 'principle of general relativity' or indeed with the theory of gravitation. In response, Einstein admitted that the requirement of general covariance could have only a 'significant heuristic force', a reply widely viewed as fundamentally backpedalling from his earlier claim. Thus Einstein has been seen as committing the logical fallacy of 'affirming the consequent' in the inference: if the general principle of relativity – 'no inertial coordinate systems', that is, no privileged reference frames – is to obtain then generally covariant formulations are required; generally covariant formulations are required by the occurrence in the GTR of generic non-flat space-times in which no global inertial coordinate systems can exist; therefore, the general principle of relativity obtains. The fallacious inference is accounted for by pointing to Einstein's enthusiasm to carry out a Machian agenda of completely relativising inertia. In so doing, it is said, even by some of Einstein's close collaborators (Hoffmann 1972: 127), he inadvertently conflated mathematical technique and physical content, the unravelling of which continues into the present.

Recent scholarship which makes essential use of Einstein's correspondence with P. Ehrenfest, H. Lorentz, and others, has, however, made a persuasive case that Einstein's 1916 claim for the physical significance of general covariance, as taking away 'the last remnant of physical objectivity from space and time', is, in fact, the conclusion of an argument whose premises have been here suppressed (Einstein himself dubbed this the 'Hole Argument' – *Lochbetrachtung*; uncovering the hidden context of the Hole Argument was initiated by John Stachel; see Stachel 1989, Norton 1989). These remarks of Einstein were but elliptical references for a different, and considerably more intricate conclusion, that the points of the four-dimensional manifold, intended as a representation of the space-time continuum, have no inherent physical individuality (derived, say, from the underlying topology), and hence no physical objectivity independently of the presence of the gravitational field defined on the manifold. In the absence of such a field, the points are not points of *space-time*, that is, they have mathematical, but no physical, meaning. Once the largely hidden context of the Hole Argument is restored, it becomes clear that in locating what is physically objective in 'point coincidences' Einstein is just giving rhetorical force to the fact that co-ordinates have (should have!) no direct physical, that is, space-time meaning.

Late in his life, Einstein made several attempts to elucidate his position regarding general covariance (e.g. Einstein 1952: 155). These efforts occur within the context of Einstein's futile unified field theory programme. For Einstein, the fundamental meaning of general covariance may be expressed thus: there can be no such thing as motion with respect to a fixed space-time background. In this broadened sense, then, the meaning of general covariance encompasses the purely formal requirement of the freedom to make 'arbitrary' transformations of co-ordinates, while the field-theoretic programme within which the distasteful notion of an inertial system can finally be dismantled has this formal requirement as an implication. So any theory in which there is no principled distinction between space-time structure and the 'contents' of space-time must be given a generally covariant formulation. That Einstein was not actually able to completely remove the concept of an inertial system within the framework of the GTR (a point famously illustrated by Gödel's 'rotating universe' solution of the gravitational field equations – see Friedman 1983) should not detract from the programmatic commitment which motivated its development: the *ambition* to remove from physical theory, once and for all, the notion of a privileged frame of reference – 'I see the most essential thing in overcoming of the inertial system, a thing that acts upon all processes, but undergoes no reaction. This concept is in principle no better than that of the center of the universe in Aristotelian physics' (Einstein letter to Georg Jaffe, 19 January 1954; cited by Stachel 1986: 1858).

2. MACH'S PRINCIPLE AND RELATIVISTIC COSMOLOGY

In the 1918 paper containing his response to criticism of his understanding of the principle of general covariance, Einstein coined the term 'Mach's Principle' for the requirement for a dynamic realisation of the relativity of inertia which he placed at the foundation of the GTR: 'in a consistent relativity theory there can be no inertia relatively to "space" but only an inertia of masses relatively to one other' (Einstein 1917: 180). It was recognised that whether or not GTR (or any other theory) satisfied this principle could only be answered by cosmological considerations which, as yet, scarcely belonged to physical science (Barbour 1999). Already in 1917, in an attempt to avoid the un-Machian requirement of boundary conditions at spatial infinity for solutions of his gravitational field equations, Einstein proposed the model of a closed (spherical) universe whose guiding assumption was that the universe is static. However, the implementation of a static solution of his field equations proved impossible without addition of a supplementary term, the so-called 'cosmological constant'. But the Dutch astronomer de Sitter almost immediately found a solution of the thus-amended Einstein field equations giving another apparently static cosmological model containing no matter at all, and so concluded that Einstein's theory still appeared to be not in harmony with the requirement of relativity of inertia. Some five years afterwards, the Russian mathematical physicist A. Friedmann showed that the original equations had solutions corresponding to expanding and contracting universes. Meanwhile, observations of the red-shift of distant stars by Slipher since 1910 and Hubble beginning in the mid-1920s, led to general agreement by 1930 or so, that the universe, as viewed from Earth, appeared to be linearly expanding in all directions, with the most distant objects receding the most rapidly. The end of Einstein's static universe came with proof by Eddington, following upon earlier work of Lemaître, that it was actually unstable. Faced with the inevitable, Einstein accepted the expanding universe in 1930, reportedly remarking that the cosmological constant was 'the biggest blunder of my life'.

3. 'GEOMETRISATION' OF PHYSICS?

It is often said that gravity has been 'geometrised' by the GTR; indeed, in the first years of triumph of the new theory, before the advent of quantum mechanics in the mid-1920s, the claim was frequently made that physics had been 'geometrised'. What precisely is meant by these claims? Within the GTR, there is an obvious sense in which gravity has been geometrised: the expression for the metric of the (pseudo-)Riemannian geometry of space-time, which determines not only length and angle measurements but also the path and velocity of light propagation, is formed from terms which are the 'potentials' of the gravitational field, functions of the space-time co-ordinates and from which other terms arise representing 'forces' comprising the phenomena of inertia and gravity. In thus holding that these forces have been 'geometrised', what is meant is simply that they can be mathematically expressed in terms deriving from the metrical description of space-time. More fundamentally, unlike in the Euclidean space of Newtonian gravity or in the Minskowski space-time of special relativistic electrodynamics, the metric of GTR is dynamical, not globally fixed: metrical determinations in a given region of space-time are causally conditioned by local matter-energy densities and in turn provide a measure of these densities. In the somewhat provocative formulation of Weyl, space is no longer the *Schauplatz* or arena, in which physical processes occur but, as is epitomised by the gravitational field equations, is an inseparable component of a common causally interrelated structure of space-time and matter (Weyl 1918).

That, it might be said, is the party line of Einstein's theory. But strict adherence to this line has proven difficult, both in application and in empiricist conception. Regarding application, a fully dynamical conception of metric prohibits reference to non-dynamical background structures such as boundary or initial conditions, but without these, it is almost impossible to extract predictions from observational cosmology, the primary domain of application of GTR (Smolin 1992: 232). Regarding empiricist conception: in developing his theory, Einstein had, as a practical expedient, followed Helmholtz in postulating the existence of *de facto* rigid bodies and ideal clocks as physical indicators of the metric interval ds of space-time geometry, thus making this concept the fundamental 'observable' of his theory. To be sure, he was well aware that acute thinkers, notably Poincaré, had convincingly argued that the use of physical objects and processes as correlates for geometrical concepts was not at all innocent, and that one could thus only with some latitude assign measurable physical properties to space (or space-time) itself on their basis. But to Einstein the empirical confirmation of GTR rested for the moment entirely upon 'norming' ds to 'infinitesimal rigid rods' and to 'atomic clocks' with perfectly constant frequencies. This is a supposition which, if not theoretically satisfying, was nonetheless a provisional and even necessary stratagem (Einstein 1921).

Einstein's cautiously *pro tem* view of measurement in GTR was subsequently transformed by Reichenbach into a methodological postulate that empirical results could be extracted from a physical theory only following stipulation of conventions governing the behaviour of measuring rods and clocks. However, in the generic case of variably curved space-times permitted by GTR, the notion of a rigid body (or a perfectly regular process) is suspect for just the reason suggested by Riemann some six decades earlier: there are no congruences (or durations) corresponding to the supposed invariant length (period) of a rigid body (perfect clock). For this reason, the most consistent theoretical procedure, as Weyl pointed out, is to renounce the postulate of transportable measuring devices (and so, standard lengths and perfect clocks) at the foundation of the geometry of physical space and instead to assume that units of length and of duration may be independently chosen at each space-time point. In 1918, reformulating the GTR in accordance with this demand, Weyl discovered a broader geometry which, in addition to gravitation, also brought electromagnetism within the metric of space-time geometry and so 'geometrised' it. This was the first 'unified field theory', but the basis of unification was purely formal and geometrical: two separate fields were clothed within a common geometry (Weyl 1918 [1923 fifth edn]). Weyl's theory was premature, and he withdrew his support for it with the advent of quantum mechanics. But it had considerable impact, in two ironically contrasting ways. First, it appears to have inspired Einstein with the thought that unification in physics would come through development of a comprehensive space-time geometry from which all manifestations of physical forces, including quantum phenomena, could be derived. This became the programme of Einstein's long and unsuccessful search for a unified field theory. On the other hand, Weyl's theory introduced the concept of arbitrariness of gauge (or scale) and the associated requirement of local gauge invariance of the fundamental laws of nature. These ideas have become the core of a contemporary programme of geometric unification of gauge quantum field theories of three of the four (excluding gravity) basic forces known in nature (Ryckman 2004).

4. CONTINUING REVOLUTION

The unmistakable distinguishing characteristic of revolution is that it outstrips its own vanguard; such was also the case with General Relativity and Albert Einstein. The conceptual resources of the theory proved so rich with unsuspected physical and philosophical implications that even Einstein required years to digest conclusions he found philosophically unacceptable (for example, un-Machian solutions to his field equations, the expanding universe). Some were so unpalatable that he never endorsed them at all. Foremost among these are the existence of singularities and what would, much later, be termed 'black holes'. Already in 1916, the astrophysicist Karl Schwarzschild gave an exact calculation from Einstein's field equations of the space-time geometry within a star from which the prediction followed that every star has a critical circumference, depending on its mass, beyond which, because of gravitational red-shift due to space-time warpage, no light from the star's surface would escape. That Newtonian gravity made similar predictions of the non-escape of light from sufficiently massive heavenly bodies had long been known. But to Einstein, given his deep-seated belief in the supremacy of classical field laws, the so-called 'Schwarzschild singularity' was intolerable because any singularity, where the field quantities can in principle take on infinite values, represented a breakdown of the postulated laws of nature. If the GTR predicted the existence of singularities, then 'it carries within itself the seeds of its own destruction' (Einstein as reported by Bergmann – see Bergmann 1980: 156): that this is nonetheless so was further confirmed by the celebrated Hawking-Penrose theorems of the late 1960s which proved the existence of singularities in a wide class of solutions to the Einstein field equations (Earman 1995).

In another significant respect, Einstein began as a reluctant convert and then became a fervent revolutionary, embracing the novel method of physical research through mathematical speculation inspired by the theory of general relativity only after Weyl, Eddington, Kaluza, and several other of his contemporaries had done so. But once he had taken it up, he tenaciously clung to it, steering an unwavering course towards what Hans Reichenbach lamented, already in 1928, as the 'sirens' magic' of a Unified Field Theory. Einstein, of course, was not ultimately successful in this pursuit, which sought to derive quantum phenomena from a theoretical basis of continuous functions defined on a space-time continuum. But his heuristic viewpoint, that position or motion with respect to a background space-time is a meaningless concept, continues to guide theorists in quantum gravity; and the construction of physical theory through mathematical speculation, seeking unification through geometry, found a new generation of adherents again in the 1970s and continues into the present.

49

SCIENTIFIC EXPLANATION

GEORGE GALE

1. INTRODUCTION

The great French philosopher-historian of science Emile Meyerson (1859–1933) began his 1929 *Encyclopedia Britannica* article 'Explanation' with the following words:

What is meant by explaining a phenomenon? There is no need to insist on the importance of this question. It is obvious that the entire structure of science will necessarily depend upon the reply given. (Meyerson 1929: 984)

Meyerson's conclusion would be difficult to overstate: the structure of any given science – indeed, of science itself – is developed around the ideal of explanation peculiar to it. Explanations in physics differ formally and materially from those in biology; and both differ from explanations provided by geologists and sociologists; even more generally, explanations in science differ widely from those given in, say, law or religion.

2. MEYERSON ON THE TWO MODES OF EXPLANATION

From the publication of the 1908 first edition (of three) of his monumental *Identité et Realité* (*Identity and Reality*) until his death in 1933, Emile Meyerson was not only France's dominant philosopher of science, he was one of the most important philosophers of science throughout the Western world. In the opening chapter of *Identity and Reality*, Meyerson speaks of two sharply opposed modes of explanation: the 'mode of law', and the 'mode of cause'. Each mode has ancient philosophical roots. Law-explanations may with some justice be traced to Heraclitus's dictum that everything changes except the law of change itself. Cause-explanations, according to Meyerson, trace back through atomic theory all the way to Parmenides's notion of the unchanging self-identity of being. In his own era, Meyerson identified himself with the philosophical lineage that espoused cause-explanations; as his opposition he identified most especially

608

Comte, Mach, and their followers in positivism, among whom he numbered his contemporary Pierre Duhem and the members of the Vienna Circle.

To speak very roughly, the two forms of explanation may be characterised as follows. Law-explanations show that phenomena are related in dependable patterns. Meyerson quotes Berkeley's view as paradigmatic:

> For the laws of nature being once ascertained, it remains for the philosopher to show that each thing necessarily follows in conformity with these laws; that is, that every phenomenon necessarily results from these principles. (Berkeley 1901: §37)

Taine puts it even more simply: 'A stone tends to fall because all objects tend to fall' (Taine 1897: 403–4). An adequate law-explanation, then, is produced by showing that some target phenomenon is a consequence of an accepted rule, or, best, of a well-established law of nature. For the most part, French philosophers of our period – with the exception of Duhem and also Poincaré – were not *légalistes* (supporters of law-explanations). It was among the Anglo-Saxons, including Russell, Bridgeman, Carnap, and others of the Vienna Circle, that the law-explanation was brought to its highest perfection, as we will see below.

Meyerson links modern cause-explanation to Leibniz's principle of sufficient reason, most especially its dynamical statement that 'the whole effect can reproduce the entire cause or its like' (Leibniz 1860: 439). Underlying this, Meyerson notes, 'we see that the principle of Leibniz comes back to the well-known formula of the scholastics, *causa aequat effectum*' (Meyerson 1908 [1930]: 29). Thus, 'the principle of causality is none other than the principle of identity applied to the existence of objects in time' (Meyerson 1908 [1930]: 43). Although murky as here stated, when cashed out in practice the principle is clear enough: 'according to the causal principle', in an adequate explanation 'the original properties plus the change of conditions must equal the transformed properties' (Meyerson 1908 [1930]: 41). In other words, an adequate cause-explanation necessarily entrains an object or objects, and describes how these objects preserve relevant aspects of their identity throughout the change. Prototypical examples of this type of explanation would include chemical equations which exhibit the conservation of mass and energy at the level of the atom, ion, or molecule. Since Meyerson was a trained chemist, his choice of prototype is not in the least odd.

Underlying Meyerson's distinction between the two forms of explanation is his analysis of the goals of science. Science, he says, has two separate and distinct goals. The first is a utilitarian one, namely, science serves to make our lives easier, or better, or, in some cases, possible at all. This it does through prediction: 'foresight is indispensable for action' and 'action for any organism of the animal kingdom is an absolute necessity' (Meyerson 1962: 22). Thus, the dog, when pursuing the rabbit, is able to foresee – to predict – the path of his quarry. Humanity's science, according to proponents of law-explanation, is nothing less than an exquisite means to satisfy this necessity. Meyerson quotes Poincaré with satisfaction: ' "Science" as H. Poincaré has so well said, "is a rule of action which succeeds" ' (Meyerson 1908 [1930]: 20; Poincaré 1902a: 265). Proponents of law-explanation justify their choice by arguing that science's goal is prediction alone.

On the other hand, underlying cause-explanation is the deeply human need to understand: Meyerson again cites Poincaré, who 'says: "In my view knowledge is the end, and action is the means [and] Aristotle had already said: 'All men by nature are actuated by the desire for knowledge' " ' (Meyerson 1908 [1930]: 42; Poincaré 1902a: 266). Referring again to Leibniz's version of the principle of cause-explanation, Meyerson remarks: 'wherever we establish it, the phenomenon becomes rational, adequate to our reason: we understand it and we can explain it. This thirst for knowledge, for understanding, is felt by each one of us' (Meyerson 1908 [1930]: 42).

Scientific reasoning, indeed, scientific rationality, is not in principle different from ordinary, common sense, human reasoning and rationality. In ordinary reasoning, a phenomenon is made understandable, 'rational', when it has been linked to an object, its properties, and its behaviour. Science, according to Meyerson, is nothing more than the extension of 'common sense' into new domains: in this role, science creates, invents, discovers new sorts of objects which can act as the causes of phenomena which are beyond ordinary experience. Thus, the ordinary concept of 'boiling' and an object's 'boiling point' is linked to the disappearance of a spot of a new substance, gasoline (Meyerson 1908 [1930]: 45).

3. OTHER *EPISTEMOLOGISTES*

Léon Brunschvicg (1869–1944) was not a philosopher of science in the same measure as Meyerson: although Brunschvicg based his thought in the history of science (as well as in the history of Western philosophy), his focus upon science was as means, and not as end. Brunschvicg's goal was to understand how reason contributed to human experience, and, in so doing, became ever more conscious of itself over time. Since, like Meyerson, Brunschvicg believed that the history of science captured some of the finest examples of the powers and behaviours of human reason at work, analysis of the history of science would serve his goal of understanding reason and its works. Brunschvicg, again like Meyerson, believed that the mind itself made a significant contribution to the world as it was finally known: 'Positive science goes from the mind to matter, and not from matter to the mind' (Brunschvicg 1931: 144). Yet, his idealism was not unalloyed; in the end knowledge was a product both of the mind and of matter, working together, in an essentially dialectical interaction. Most importantly, Brunschvicg viewed science as a dynamic process, an open-ended creative action, that not only exhibited the speculative freedom of the mind, but also assured humanity's practical liberty.

Brunschvicg's ideas about scientific theorising and explanation were less dramatic. A hypothesis or explanation was true just in case it was intelligible. Over time, the dialectic between scientific reasoning and matter 'gives to thought an increasing approximation to reality' (Brunschvicg 1905: 12). It is evident that both the spirit of Brunschvicg's thought, as well as some of its particular doctrines, were influential during the period between the wars. After all, he occupied the chair of general philosophy at the Sorbonne for thirty years: 1909–39. One philosopher of science who came especially under his influence was Gaston Bachelard.

Bachelard (1884–1962) was a late bloomer: he started his work life as a postman; later, in 1913, he got a teaching certificate and taught secondary-school science for fourteen years. Then, in 1927, he got his doctorate and in 1930 became professor of philosophy in Dijon. His experiences as a science teacher directly affected his philosophy of science. At the time when he was teaching, the ministry of education kept extremely tight reins on what would be taught in science, and how. In particular, the strictures forced an ontology-free positivism: 'One was directed not to speak the word "atom". One always thought about it; but one could never speak about it. Some authors . . . gave a short history of atomist doctrines, but always after a totally positivist exposition' (Bachelard 1933: 93). As far as Bachelard was concerned, this was all wrong: 'In actual fact, as Meyerson has proved, science usually postulates a reality' (Bachelard 1969: 13; Jones 1991: 24). But, except for the usual focus upon the knower, and agreement about foundations in history of science, this was one of the few points where Bachelard's philosophy agreed with that of his older colleague, Meyerson.

From Brunschvicg, Bachelard got the idea of the open-endedness of the task of scientific reasoning. He communicates this notion in a particularly evocative way: 'The scientist leaves his laboratory in the evening with a program of work in mind, and he ends the working day with this expression of faith, which is daily repeated: "Tomorrow, I shall know"' (Bachelard 1973: 177; Jones 1991: 59). Bachelard's doctoral thesis was entitled *Essai sur la connaissance approchée (Essay on the Approach on Knowledge)* (1969); this connotes (at least in French) the notion of knowledge as approximate, 'being approached only as a limit', perhaps even, 'under construction'. Again, the root of the idea is found in Brunschvicg: knowledge is a product, a synthesis produced by the mutual interaction between the mind and the world. Although Bachelard himself does not use the term 'dialectic' to refer to this interaction, Brunschvicg would not have so hesitated; neither should we: knowledge is produced by two compelling, albeit contradictory, impulses: 'rationalism' and 'realism'. In practice, these two metaphysics play out simply enough: '*if scientific activity is experimental, then reasoning will be necessary; if it is rational, then experiment will be necessary*' (Bachelard 1973: 7; Jones 1991: 48). Obviously, what is involved here is mutual interaction between mind and matter in producing knowledge. But mutuality is not equality: in the end, at least in post-Einsteinian science, it is the rationality of mathematics which will prove most significant over against the matter of experimental reality:

Mathematical realism, in some shape, form, or function, will sooner or later come along and *give body* to thought, making it psychologically permanent, . . . revealing, here as everywhere else, the dualism of the subjective and the objective. (Bachelard 1973: 8; Jones 1991: 49; italics in original)

This remark shows two important ways in which Bachelard differs from Meyerson. In the first place, Bachelard believed that Einstein's relativity theory represented so great a divergence from earlier theories – mostly because it raised to an unprecedented level the ontological creative power of mathematicisation – that it required a 'break' (= *rupture*) in philosophy of science, a rupture of the classical from the modern. Meyerson argued, in opposition, that relativity theory in fact represented the triumph of classical mechanics. The two thinkers fought it out in book-length form: Meyerson's *La Déduction relativiste* (1925) versus Bachelard's *La Valeur inductive de la relativité* (1929). The opposition between Meyerson's 'deduction' and Bachelard's 'induction' in their respective book-titles is especially salient: after Einstein, Bachelard believed, all attempts to use deductive logic in scientific explanations are fruitless. Meyerson believed precisely the opposite.

The second issue dividing the two men follows directly on the first. According to Meyerson, scientific reasoning – most particularly, scientific explanation – is not different in kind from reasoning in ordinary common affairs. Reason's activities were then, are now, and will always be the same. Bachelard denied this flat out. Because post-relativity scientific thinking mathematicises the world in an entirely new way, the world as newly mathematicised reaches back into the thinking apparatus and re-shapes it; thus the new explanatory achievements produce a psychologically 'permanent' change, an epistemological rupture in the manner of thinking itself (Bachelard 1973: 59). It follows from this that scientific thinking in general, and scientific explaining in particular, is different from what it once was; most especially, it is and can no longer be, deductive.

It is obvious from even this short discussion that these French thinkers have had enormous influence throughout the twentieth century. Meyerson's historical approach, plus his conclusion that scientific theories and explanations necessarily include ontologies, were taken up intact by Kuhn, as he himself admitted. Brunschvicg and Bachelard adopted historical approaches as well, and added to Meyerson's thinker-centred idealism the notion of the open-ended 'project' of constructing scientific knowledge. This latter view is now, sixty years later, one of the major themes in end-of-the-century science studies. Clearly, the French *causalistes* held significance far beyond their own times. But France did not hold a monoply on cause-explanation proponents.

4. NORMAN CAMPBELL

Norman Campbell (1880–1949) was an English physicist who, after reflecting deeply upon his practice, developed and propounded an influential philosophy of science. Like Meyerson, he believed that explanation in science was contiguous with explanation in ordinary life; moreover, again similarly to Meyerson, he held that explanations necessarily entrained causes: objects, their properties, and interactions. Finally, writing of the positivists, and most certainly Mach in particular, he wrote: 'I cannot understand how anybody can find any interest in science, who thinks that its task is completed with the discovery of laws' (Campbell 1921: 89).

Laws, of course, are part of a scientific theory. But, thought Campbell, they are not the important part; indeed, almost invariably, discoverers of laws 'have no claim to rank among the geniuses of science' (Campbell 1921: 92). On the other hand, every important explanatory theory 'is associated with some man whose scientific work was notable apart from that theory' either because of other important discoveries or because of their 'greatly above average work' (Campbell 1921: 92). Explanations do their work by reducing the unfamiliar to the 'familiar' (Campbell 1921: 77). The reduction takes place when the objects, properties, or interactions in the unfamiliar system are placed in analogy with objects, properties, or interactions in a familiar system:

The explanation offered by a theory . . . is always based on an analogy and the system with which an analogy is traced is always one of which the laws are known. (Campbell 1921: 96)

Moreover, the familiar system 'is always one of those systems which form part of that external world' which science studies (Campbell 1921: 96). Analogies, therefore, inevitably make claims about what exists in the external world.

Campbell's prototypical case involves gases. The laws of the behaviour of gases – Boyle's Law and Gay-Lussac's Law are his examples – are well known. But what makes these laws intelligible, what provides an explanation, is the Dynamical Theory of Gases: 'a gas consists of an immense number of very small particles, called molecules, flying about in all directions, colliding with each other and with the wall of the containing vessel . . . etc.' (Campbell 1921: 81). The phenomena described by the two laws – pressure, for example – are explained by the movements and interactions of the molecules. But the reason this explanation succeeds is simply the fact that the movements of the molecules are analogous to motions in the ordinary world:

the behaviour of moving solid bodies is familiar to every one; every one knows roughly what will happen when such bodies collide with each other or with a solid wall . . . Movement is just the most familiar thing in the world . . . And so by tracing a relation between the unfamiliar changes which gases undergo when their temperature or volume is altered, and the extremely familiar changes which accompany the motions and mutual reactions of solid bodies, we are rendering the former more intelligible; we are explaining them. (Campbell 1921: 84)

With Campbell we reach the last cause-explanation advocate of the period from 1915 to 1945. We now turn to an examination of the other side of the controversy and examine the views of those who argued that scientific explanations are provided by applications of laws, those philosophers called positivists.

5. POSITIVISM

Positivism began as a reform movement, an attempt to bring philosophical salvation to wayward science (Gale 1984: 491). Two names are especially associated with the origins of positivism, those of the French mathematician and social scientist Auguste Comte (1798–1857), and the German physicist Ernst Mach (1838–1916). As all reform movements must, positivism contained both an attack upon a perceived evil, and a manifesto proclaiming the correct way forward. The attack focused upon the metaphysical proclivities of then-contemporary science. Explanatory hypotheses such as atomic theory and, for Mach especially, energy, and absolute space and time, were taken to be speculative excesses, unverifiable postulates about forever-hidden structures of Reality. The problem with causal explanations, according to positivism, is that they tend to be wrong, and, once new theories are proposed, old hypotheses must be discarded along with the commitments of the scientists who believe them. A major case in point was Lavoisier's revolution in chemistry, during which the substance 'phlogiston' went out of existence, only to be replaced by the substance 'oxygen'. Science, according to the positivists, simply had no need to become involved with such illusory entities.

What behoved science was to stick to its 'positive' (hence the name) contributions: the well-verified laws which tended to remain constant even through a drastic revolution, such as Lavoisier's. Moreover, according to the positivists, laws satisfied the most important goal of science, its utilitarian promise to provide prevision, prediction, of the future course of events. Although elimination of cause-explanation would leave unattained humankind's desire for intellectual satisfaction – the goal of science according to Meyerson, Bachelard, *et al.* – law-explanation and its attendant prediction was a safe and eminently satisfiable goal.

Underlying the safety of law-explanation and prediction was a thoroughgoing empiricism, a commitment to exclude from science all notions, concepts, and words which could not, one way or another, be tied to entities apparent to the senses. Thus, following Hume, in order for a term to have any meaning at all, it must be tied to some observable entity. For example, 'pressure of a gas' could be tied to the felt elasticity of a balloon, or, perhaps, the visible reading of a manometer. But since 'an atom' provided no such empirically observable concomitant, the term had no meaning at all; hence the concept, and its verbal expression, must be discarded from science. The ultimate sought-for goal was the reformulation of all scientific theories in meaningful terms, terms with direct ties to empirical observation. This would be accompanied by the elimination of all meaningless terms, that is, all those terms such as 'atom', 'energy', and 'absolute space and time', which referred to entities hidden or otherwise unavailable to empirical observation.

Two French thinkers added significant elements to the positivist tradition. These are the physicists Henri Poincaré (1854–1912) and Pierre Duhem (1861–1916). For both men the only acceptable theory is one which is strictly mathematical; this because, as Poincaré notes, the sole end of theory 'is to co-ordinate the physical laws which experience makes known to us, but which, without the help of mathematics, we could not even state' (Poincaré 1889: 1). Duhem, Meyerson remarks, 'affirms in the same way that the mathematical theory is not an explanation, but a system of mathematical propositions; it classifies laws' (Meyerson 1962: 52). Duhem was a genuinely talented historian of physics; he knew full well that 'several of the geniuses to whom we owe modern physics have constructed their theories in the hope of giving an explanation of natural phenomena' (Duhem 1906: 46). Yet, as Meyerson remarks, Duhem's 'own ideas are diametrically opposed to this manner of thinking' (Meyerson 1908 [1930]:

53). Duhem's heroically steadfast rejection of metaphysics, directly in the face of his own thorough grounding in the history of his subject, served as an inspiration to later positivists.

Poincaré's contribution was more direct. Although both he and Duhem were strictly committed to mathematicised theories in physics, just as Mach before them, this commitment, when carefully examined, represented a sharp challenge to their equally strict empiricist beliefs. Although 'pressure of a gas' and 'volume of a gas' are concepts which can be cashed in via empirical observations, what can be made of the mathematical operations contained in, say, Boyle's law that the pressure multiplied by the volume of a given container of gas has a constant product throughout changes in either? That is, what is one to make of the '×' and the '=' in the law $p_1 \times v_1 = p_2 \times v_2$? At least prima facie, multiplication signs and equal signs do not signify anything genuinely empirical.

Poincaré made a very sensible response to this difficulty. He proposed that mathematical operations referred to the behaviour of physicists; that is, through convention, physicists had come to agree to use multiplication and equality as procedures during instances of Boyle's Law applications. Thus, if one were to observe a physicist doing a Boyle's Law application, one would observe the physicist measuring the pressure of the gas, then measuring the volume of the gas and then multiplying the measurements. The physicists' 'multiplying the measurements' is just as empirically observable as their 'measuring the volume'. This conventionalist analysis extended to all mathematical operations; indeed, as we shall see, it applied to all formal manipulations, including those of formal logic.

Poincaré's solution became a permanent part of the positivist view. At about the same time, however, a development of equal significance to the development of positivism was taking place in England. I refer, of course, to Russell and Whitehead's development of symbolic logic (Whitehead and Russell 1910–13).

6. ADDING LOGIC TO POSITIVISM

Philosophical concern to impose logical methods on scientific thinking is an ancient and honorable endeavour. It was Aristotle himself who laid it down that deductive logical structure is a necessary condition for any discipline to call itself 'scientific'. Descartes and Leibniz reaffirmed this demand during the early stages of modern science. But none of these projects fully succeeded. What was missing was a sufficiently rich, powerful, and precise logical apparatus. Deductive syllogisms produced from the syntax and semantics of everyday speech just could not do the job capturing the richness of scientific language. Whitehead and Russell's axiomatic system for symbolic logic, the logic of quantifiers and predicates with identity, made available for the first time a language which seemed to offer the potential to allow the empiricist re-formulation so desired by the positivists. Thus did the positivists become the 'logical' positivists (or, in some camps, and for obvious reasons, the 'logical' empiricists).

Rudolf Carnap (1891–1970) presented the first mature interpretation of logical positivism in his 1928 *Der logische Aufbau der Welt*. Carnap, true to Mach's empiricism, employs as his central concept *Zurückführbarkeit*, or 'reducibility', a process through which one concept is reformulated in terms of other(s). A concept *x* is said to be *reducible* to a set of concepts *Y* if every sentence concerning *x* can be reformulated in sentences concerning concepts belonging to *Y*, with no loss of truth. The reformulation is carried out according to a 'constitutional definition', one side of which is ultimately – perhaps through more reformulations – linked to a 'basis', a set of basic objects. For Carnap, at this stage of development staying close and true to Mach's sensationalism, the basic objects were mental objects: a certain kind of experience. During the re-formulation process, the number of, and number of kinds of, concepts was sizeably reduced, with the result that the final product, the concepts of the basis, would be both simplest and minimum in number.

Carnap's basic concepts got their meaning by being cashed into statements about mental experiences. Although this procedure certainly satisfies most empiricist criteria of meaning (including the very one Carnap used, which he called 'Wittgenstein's principle of verifiability'), it did not satisfy Carnap's Vienna Circle colleagues, in particular, Otto Neurath, who was a thoroughgoing physicalist. After some argument, Neurath convinced Carnap that basic concepts should be defined in physicalist terms, that is, by reference to quantitative descriptions of events occurring at definite spatio-temporal locations. Neurath preferred this physicalist language because it allowed for agreement among observers about the occurrence or non-occurrence of the event referred to (Neurath 1932). Moreover, since the language symbolised the events of physics, it would serve to capture all other sciences which, presumably, would be reducible to physics. Thus, for example, theories in chemistry or biology would be formulatable in terms of the physicalist basis concepts. When fully implemented, the physicalist basis would accomplish once and for all that long-sought Holy Grail of all empiricist proponents of law-explanation, the elimination from science of the metaphysical excesses hypothesised by the cause-explainers. This achievement was duly announced by Carnap in his article 'Überwindung der Metaphysik durch logische Analyse der Sprache' ('The Elimination of Metaphysics through the Logical Analysis of Language') (Carnap 1932).

A final fillip was added to physicalist empiricism by the Nobel-prize-winning American physicist: W. Bridgman (1882–1961). Bridgman held that Einstein's brilliant achievement in discovering relativity theory did not come through a disclosure of facts or by showing something new about nature. Rather, Einstein's discovery dramatically highlighted the value of sound conceptual analysis: after an analysis of then-current notions of time, and the operations used in measuring it, Einstein, according to Bridgman, saw that the concept of time, as generally understood, was severely flawed (Bridgman 1936).

For example, Einstein saw that there was no possible way to measure whether two spatially separated events were simultaneous or not. Hence 'simultaneity of occurrence' was a temporal concept that could not be given a meaning in terms of a measuring operation. But since this very concept was fundamental in Newtonian theory, Einstein's analysis suggested that Newtonian theory was fundamentally flawed, and needed to be replaced. Based upon this case, Bridgman argued forcefully for elimination from physics of all concepts which could not be defined in terms of operations, actual measurements, carried out by actual physicists.

The empiricist bent of this, not to mention its positivist reformational spirit, will not go unnoticed. Although not all logical positivists adopted Bridgman's emendation, many did. Moreover, scientists in psychology (e.g., Skinner) and linguistics (e.g., Bloomfield) called for operationalist reform. With Bridgman's contribution, logical positivism was finally in a position to provide a canonical formulation of its view on scientific theories. This is what it looked like:

A *theory* is an axiomatised deductive system formulated in a symbolic language having the following elements:

1. The theory is formulated in a first-order mathematical logic with equality, L
2. The nonlogical terms or constants of L are divided into three disjoint classes called *vocabularies*:
   a. The *logical vocabulary* consisting of logical and mathematical constants.
   b. The *observation vocabulary*, V_o containing observation terms.
   c. The *theoretical vocabulary*, V_T containing theoretical terms.
3. The terms in V_o are interpreted as referring to directly observable physical objects or directly observable attributes of physical objects.
4. There is a set of theoretical postulates T whose only nonlogical terms are from V_T.
5. The terms in V_T are given an *explicit definition* in terms of V_o by *correspondence rules* C – that is, for every term 'F' in V_T, there must be a definition for it of the form '$(\forall x)(Fx \equiv Ox)$' where 'Ox' is an expression of L containing symbols only from V_o and possibly the logical vocabulary.

(But it must be kept in mind that various aspects of the positivist view on theories were in nearly constant change from the first moment of their publication in 1928; most of the changes concerned clauses 2 and 5, particularly where their content involved the logic of the conditional.)

An example of this approach applied to the theory of metals might look something like this:

> *Observation vocabulary*, V_o:
>> conducts electricity, is ductile, expands, is heated
>
> *Theoretical vocabulary*, V_T:
>> is a metal

In accordance with clause 5, the predicate 'is a metal' would thus be introduced by a correspondence rule, in this case:

$$(\forall x)[x \text{ is a metal} \equiv (x \text{ is ductile \& } x \text{ conducts electricity})]$$

that is, metals are things which are ductile and conduct electricity. Laws of Nature presumably would be postulates (or, in some cases, axioms or theorems) of the theory. The following might be taken to be a plausible example of a Law of Nature:

$$(\forall x)[(x \text{ is a metal \& } x \text{ is heated}) \rightarrow x \text{ expands}]$$

i.e. metals expand when heated.

7. PREDICTION, EXPLANATION AND THE COVERING-LAW MODEL

As noted earlier, law-explainers typically take prediction to be science's goal. For the most part, the logical positivists agree with this position, but with a very interesting twist. The logical positivist account of explanation is embedded in the view of theories and laws given just now, and one of its features is the symmetry of explanation and prediction. According to this view, an explanation and a prediction have exactly the same logical form, but with reversed time-signatures. Thus, an explanation is a 'prediction' of the past (sometimes called a 'retrodiction'), and a prediction is an 'explanation' of the future! What lies at the centre of the doctrine is the single logical form which serves both explanations and predictions; let us therefore examine the logical form of explanations.

In this account, L stands for a suitable Law; and C stands for an initial (factual) condition. The form of an explanation is:

$$\frac{L_1, \ldots, L_n, C_1, \ldots, C_n}{E} \quad \begin{matrix}\text{(Explanans)}\\[1em]\text{(Explanandum)}\end{matrix}$$

Thus the Law(s) in conjunction with the initial conditions – the 'explanans' – are sufficient to imply logically the explanandum, that is, the phenomenon needing to be explained. The name 'covering law model' of explanation comes from the fact that laws are used to 'cover' all the cases needing explanation. Here is a simple example:

Phenomenon / Query: 'Why did the copper penny (p) expand when heated?'
Explanans:
  Law: $(\forall x)$ [(x is a metal & x is heated) $\rightarrow$ x expands]
  Conditions: p is a metal & p was heated
Explanandum:
  p expands

It is clear that such explanations function as deductive arguments. In justifying a prediction exactly the same form would obtain, but the initial query and the verb tense would be different:

Query: What would happen if I heated this copper penny?
Prediction: Given that this copper penny is metal, if it were heated it would expand.

It should be noted that the account presented here was never given as such by any particular logical positivist thinker, especially as regards its rendering in logical symbols. However, given what many of these thinkers stated, remarked, and argued at various time during the 25-year history of this model, they would be hard put to provide an account materially different from that presented here.

8. CONCLUSION

After a brief hiatus during the Second World War, philosophers of science resumed work on the problems of scientific explanation. For the most part, the Anglophone community counted itself among the *legalistes*, more particularly, especially in America, as logico-empirico-positivists. Yet opposition from the *causalistes* never entirely disappeared. By the 1960s, the legalist model of explanation was under serious attack, from both within and without. Harré and Hesse, for example, continued the Meyersonian-Campbellian tradition of emphasis upon the role of analogies and models, with their attendant causal ontologies. Indeed, Hesse's (1966) dialogue featured a legalist called 'The Duhemist' pitted against a causalist called, naturally enough, 'The Campbellian'. Kuhn, with explicit reference to Meyerson, opposed an historical methodology to the logical perspective of the positivists, with devastating results.

In the end, what is perhaps surprising is that the entire century's agenda for philosophical controversy about scientific explanation was effectively set, in France, by the argument in 1908 between Poincaré and Duhem – the legalists – and Meyerson – the causalist. In a very real sense, much of the following ninety-two years of philosophical controversy are footnotes to that argument.

THE RISE OF PROBABILISTIC THINKING

JAN VON PLATO

1. PROBABILITY IN NINETEENTH-CENTURY SCIENCE

Variation was considered, well into the second half of the nineteenth century, to be deviation from an ideal value. This is clear in the 'social physics' of Adolphe Quetelet, where the ideal was represented by the notion of 'average man'. In astronomical observation, the model behind this line of thought, there is supposed to be a true value in an observation, from which the actual value deviates through the presence of small erratic causes. In mathematical error theory, one could show that numerous small and mutually independent errors produce the familiar bell-shaped normal curve around a true value. But if observations contain a systematic error, this can be identified and its effect eliminated. All sorts of data regarding society were collected into public state records (whence comes the term statistics), showing remarkable statistical stability from year to year. Such stability, as in criminal records, was explained as the very nearly deterministic result of the sum of a great number of free individual acts (see Krüger *et al.* 1987 for studies of these developments).

Around 1860, the physicist James Clerk Maxwell theoretically determined a normal Gaussian distribution law for the velocities of gas molecules. This discovery later led to statistical mechanics in the work of Ludwig Boltzmann and Josiah Willard Gibbs. Here there was no true unknown value, but genuine variation not reducible to effects of external errors. The world view of classical physics held that all motions of matter follow the deterministic laws of Newtonian mechanics. It was therefore argued, throughout the second half of the nineteenth century, and well into the twentieth, that there is an inherent contradiction in the foundations of statistical physics. In particular, classical mechanics is *time reversible*, symmetric in time, but processes in statistical physics display a unidirectional approach to energetic equilibrium, the state of maximum entropy. Maxwell's well-known 'demon' was a popular illustration of the new statistical interpretation of the second law of thermodynamics: approach to equilibrium is overwhelmingly *probable*, but not strictly necessary.

The radical thought that the atomic world might not obey mechanical laws, was barely hinted at by Maxwell in his lecture on the freedom of the will (1873). Boltzmann had a view of scientific theories as useful models, hence, he was less committed to mechanics as a metaphysical doctrine, and already by the early 1870s viewed the state of a physical system as *completely described* by a probability distribution. But such positions were exceptions. Generally probabilistic concepts and methods were just used to obtain practical results, with less concern for their philosophical implications. One field where probabilistic ideas clearly were present was Darwinian evolution, enthusiastically welcomed by Boltzmann for this reason. The changes over time in biological features in a population are statistical phenomena where the random fate of an individual usually has very little effect.

2. CLASSICAL AND STATISTICAL PROBABILITY

The *classical interpretation* of probability is based on the idea of a finite number n of 'equally likely' alternatives, each receiving the numerical probability $1/n$. This is a very natural concept in games of chance, the very origin of the classical calculus of probability. Given the probabilities of symmetric simple alternatives, the task of this calculus is to compute the probabilities of more complicated results, such as getting at least once a double-six in ten tosses of two dice.

It was found very hard to state in a general way a principle of symmetric elementary alternatives. Instead, symmetry seemed to be a property relative to a *description* of a situation. Further, there is little reason to think that gambling devices and the like are absolutely symmetric: as macroscopic objects, they would contain imperfections, and perfect symmetry would perhaps only be found in the world of microphysics where one particle of a given kind is just like another of that kind (in fact, this is the scientific application of classical probability today). Actual data from society showed that perfect symmetry is never found. Boys and girls are born at different rates, actual dice produce unequal frequencies of the six numbers, and so on. (One Wolff performed some twenty thousand tosses in the 1890s, to find out that there were significant differences, presumably due to material inhomogeneities in the dice.)

There thus emerged slowly an idea of a new concept of probability, *statistical probability*. As a concept it is less immediate than classical probability, for it is a theoretical concept, an ideal limit of observed relative frequency as the number of repetitions in constant circumstances grows to infinity. In symbolic notation, let $n(A)$ stand for the number of occurrences of event A in n repetitions. Then the relative frequency is $n(A)/n$, a number between 0 and 1. Relative frequency is also *additive* in the same way that probability is additive: If two events A and

B cannot occur simultaneously, the probability that either *A* or *B* occurs, is the sum of the individual probabilities. For example, one cannot get 5 and 6 in one toss of a dice, so the probability of getting 5 or 6 is such a sum. Relative frequency has the same additivity property. But probability is thought to be a constant, even if its exact value remains unknown, and relative frequency instead varies when the repetitions grow.

Ever since Bernoulli around 1700, proofs of *laws of large numbers* have been presented that purport to bridge the gap between a probability value and the value of observed relative frequency. Bernoulli's result states that the probability of observing a difference greater than any small prescribed number between probability and relative frequency can be made as small as desired if the number of repetitions is made sufficiently great. Thus, loosely speaking, in a long series, it is overwhelmingly probable that one will find a relative frequency very close to the theoretical probability value.

The main representatives of statistical or *frequentist* probability, in the period under discussion, were Richard von Mises and Hans Reichenbach. Von Mises was an applied mathematician and a logical positivist close to the Vienna Circle and the Unity of Science movement. A scientific theory must lead to empirically verifiable consequences, but in systems of statistical physics, with an enormous number of particles, the assumption that individual particles follow the deterministic laws of motion of mechanics, lacks such empirical meaning. Von Mises formulated a purely probabilistic conception of statistical physics around 1920, with no underlying deterministic mechanics. Thus, it is an indeterminism stemming from a methodology of science, rather than a metaphysical outlook. At the same time, von Mises had developed a mathematical approach to statistical probability, and wrote also a philosophical exposition of it (1928), published as the third volume of the book series *Schriften zur wissenschaftlichen Weltauffassung* (*Texts for a Scientific World Conception*) of the Vienna Circle.

Von Mises's position represents a *limiting relative frequency* interpretation, where probability is identified as the theoretical limit of an ever-growing series of repetitions, with unknown exact value. As an empiricist, he needs to explain what the empirical, finite meaning of probability statements is. Von Mises compares them with other theoretical idealisations in science, such as mass as an exact real number. The theory of probability as a whole he sees as a branch of natural science, dealing with 'mass phenomena'. The philosopher Hans Reichenbach was more explicit about the limitations on theoretical concepts set by logical empiricist criteria of verificational and operational content. He suggested that the observed relative frequency is a well-behaved *estimate* of probability (theories of statistical estimation and testing were actively developed at that time).

Jan von Plato

Reichenbach's main work in the field of foundations of probability is the book *Wahrscheinlichkeitslehre* of 1935. He had started his philosophical career with a doctoral dissertation in 1915, reviewing most of the existing philosophical literature on probability of the preceding decades. Perhaps the most influential contribution of that period is the book by Johannes von Kries (1886). Other philosophers of the time with probabilistic ideas of note were Gustav Theodor Fechner, 'the first indeterminist' (see Heidelberger 1987), and, in the Anglophone world, C. S. Peirce. But for the development of probability theory, and in foundational and philosophical work of substantial effect, these remained rather marginal thinkers. Around the turn of the century, the dominant idea still was that probability relates to knowledge, or rather, lack of knowledge, of the true course of a deterministic world. This is the old interpretation of Laplace, of probability in a mechanical clockwork universe. The writings of influential thinkers such as Poincaré (1912) contain a mixture of this *epistemic* conception of probability, relating to knowledge, and an *objective* conception of probability, relating to objectively ascertainable statistical frequencies or some theoretical account that could explain the form and appearance of probabilistic laws.

3. MAIN FEATURES OF MODERN MATHEMATICAL PROBABILITY

In the early years of this century, probabilistic problems and results gradually started making their appearance in pure mathematics. The first such result of note is Borel's *strong* law of large numbers. Bernoulli's law only stated the vicinity of relative frequency and probability, Borel's instead was a strongly infinitistic result about the actual limit in infinite series. Using modern measure theory, developed by himself and Henri Lebesgue, he showed that in the space of infinite repetitions those series that do not display the same limit of relative frequency are of 'measure zero'. Measure is a theoretical generalisation of relative number and relative proportion (e.g. length, area, volume). The rational numbers, for example, have measure zero since they can be covered by a denumerably infinite set of intervals the sum of lengths of which can be made arbitrarily small. The strong law was applied to problems in arithmetic sequences, such as decimal expansions, for example, but its true nature was at first not clear to everyone. It was thought paradoxical to obtain a probabilistic conclusion, for how can chance find a place in sequences 'determined by mathematical laws'. Borel himself saw that probability theory can only transform one kind of probability into another, and that there is a hidden probabilistic assumption behind his result.

Following the example of David Hilbert's axiomatisation of elementary geometry (1899), Andrei Kolmogorov (1933) gave an abstract mathematical formulation of probability. It is based on two mathematical theories: first, the events probability theory talks about are represented as *sets* and the combination of events as operations on these sets. Thus, the combined event expressed by 'event A or event B occurs', is represented as the set-theoretical union of the sets representing A and B. The set-theoretical conceptualisation of mathematical theories has become so commonplace that this crucial feature of Kolmogorov's axiomatisation goes unnoticed in most accounts, though not in Kolmogorov's own work. The second mathematical theory is measure theory. Probability is, as the saying goes, 'a normalized denumerably additive measure'. In plain terms, it means that probabilities are numbers between 0 and 1 and that probability is additive, and that this additivity extends to denumerable infinity. In a finitary situation, the measure-theoretic characterisation, often given by probability theorists as a purported answer to the question, 'What is probability?', adds the set-theoretical vocabulary to the classical theory and nothing more. In particular, such an answer does not address the *application problem* of probability.

Thus, use of measure theory by no means avoids the problem of interpretation of probability, it just hides it behind mathematical detail. Measure-theoretic probability very carefully embeds the notion of *chance* or *randomness* in a notion of 'random variables'. These are numerical functions on the space of all possible results. The idea is that chance determines the arguments of these functions, but for the probability mathematics, only the mathematical form of the functions need be considered. Kolmogorov considered his representation of random variables to be the essential novelty in his treatment. Indeed, there had been earlier attempts at formalising probability in terms of set theory and measure theory. On a more technical level, the two main novelties of Kolmogorov's book, and the reason why measure-theoretic probability turned into such a powerful tool, are the treatment of *conditional* probability and of *random processes*. Both have profound connections to the mathematical treatment of problems in statistical physics, and were actually motivated by such problems in Kolmogorov.

After Kolmogorov's decisive contribution, probability theorists have paid little attention to foundational and philosophical questions, so that from the point of view of these questions, we can consider Kolmogorov's axiomatisation the *end* of an era rather than a beginning. In his book, Kolmogorov states that in questions of interpretation he follows the frequentist views of von Mises. Much later, he wrote that questions of interpretation were not prominent in the book because he could not figure out an answer to the application problem of the theory. But it can also be presumed that his reluctance to philosophical commitment was a guard against official Soviet-Marxist philosophy of the thirties, a remnant of German mechanical materialism of the nineteenth century that would not have tolerated any metaphysical commitment to chance in nature. On a more general level, Kolmogorov thought that the new infinitistic probability mathematics would have the same significance as infinitistic concepts elsewhere in mathematics. According to Hilbert, the infinite in mathematics is just a powerful tool for making conclusions about the finite. This idea, however, has been seriously undermined by the well-known incompleteness theorems of Gödel.

4. THE ROLE OF QUANTUM PHENOMENA

Contemporary ideas about probability and chance are permeated by quantum mechanical indeterminism. It has been suggested (see van Brakel 1985) that quantum phenomena, known since Planck's discovery in 1900, played no role in the acceptance of probabilistic methods in science before the advent of quantum mechanics in 1925, the discovery of the Heisenberg uncertainty relations in 1927, and the explanation of that prime quantum-mechanical chance phenomenon, radioactivity, in 1928. It is, indeed, remarkable that the most intensive period in the development towards modern mathematical probability can be very precisely dated to between 1925 and 1933, parallel to the development of quantum mechanics from 1925 on. Pre-quantum mechanical indeterminists among prominent scientist-philosophers were few: von Mises, Hermann Weyl who did not believe in exact point-like real numbers as the basic building blocks of natural description, and Erwin Schrödinger. The last-mentioned is somewhat of a paradox: the Viennese tradition of statistical physics, from Boltzmann to Exner (1919), had made him an outspoken indeterminist. The simultaneous discovery of the two basic formulations of quantum mechanics, Heisenberg's matrix mechanics and Schrödinger's own wave mechanics, turned him back into a *determinist* in a dramatic development of ideas.

There is evidence that ultimate randomness in nature, as manifested in radioactivity, was recognised or at least contemplated even before quantum mechanics (see von Plato 1994). But the mathematical form of modern probability theory runs against the basic tenet of quantum physics, the discretisation of nature's phenomena. Indeed, the essential novelty of measure-theoretic probability is its treatment of conditional probability in a continuous space of alternatives and the treatment of random processes in continuous time. But on a more philosophical level, the indeterminism of quantum mechanics served to legitimate interest in probability theory, not as a chapter of applied science, but as a theoretical representation of some of the basic features of the scientific description of nature.

5. PROBABILITY AND KNOWLEDGE

In a single-minded pursuit of one idea, the Italian probability theorist Bruno de Finetti developed the philosophically strongest approach to probability in the twentieth century. He was influenced by Italian variants of pragmatist philosophy early in the century, and by the operationalism of Bridgman and its manifestation in Einstein's relativity principle. De Finetti's approach did not receive much attention at first, but has since the 1950s become extremely important in many parts of probability theory and its applications, and in foundational and philosophical work. De Finetti's basic idea of *subjective* probability, from the late 1920s, is that probability statements are like reports of perceptual data: once made, they are correct by definition, and probability is a subjectively felt *degree of belief* of a person, in the occurrence of an event that person is uncertain about. This approach wipes all metaphysical speculation about chance versus determinism under the carpet, as meaningless. At times, de Finetti sees even subjective probability as a theoretical construct, a latent disposition of a person in situations of uncertainty, that can be rendered operationally measurable in situations such as betting. Corresponding to this interpretation, de Finetti (1931) was able to justify the formal properties of probability by a theorem stating the following: Probability numbers calculated from betting ratios chosen by a person obey the laws of probability if and only if the system of bets never leads to sure loss. This *Dutch book* argument was also sketched by Frank Ramsey in 1926, and appeared posthumously in Ramsey (1931). Another discovery of de Finetti's was the concept of *exchangeability*: he was dissatisfied with the objectivist idea of a constant but unknown statistical probability behind an experimental arrangement. Through exchangeability, a symmetry condition with immediate intuitive content, he was able to show that talk about 'objective unknown probability' can be reduced to a subjectively meaningful probability assessment, thus performing through a mathematical result a remarkable act of epistemological reductionism (de Finetti 1937).

De Finetti's importance is twofold: he is the representative *par exemple* of a positivistic way of thinking about probability, brought close to the extreme of idealism. He is also the thinker whose ideas best fit such applications of probability as game theory and decision theory, fields that have grown to maturity in the 1950s and 1960s. Further, a whole field of 'Bayesian' philosophy and methodology of science has evolved from the conviction that scientific reasoning is essentially of a probabilistic character. An early pioneer of this idea was Harold Jeffreys with his book, *Theory of Probability* (1939; a comprehensive discussion is found in Howson and Urbach (1989)).

Last, it is well to keep in mind that probabilistic thinking is not only, and not even primarily, the following of a philosophical idea, but an art practised every day by probability theorists and those who apply probability and statistical methods in their work. The best reading from this point of view is Feller's classic *An Introduction to Probability Theory and Its Applications* (1968).

MIND AND ITS PLACE IN NATURE

VITALISM AND EMERGENCE

BRIAN McLAUGHLIN

While vitalism can be traced to ancient Greece (Aristotle's *On the Soul* is a vitalist work), modern vitalism arose as a rejection of Descartes's mechanistic view that plants, animals, and even living human bodies are kinds of machines. Early modern vitalists such Georg Ernest Stahl maintained that what distinguishes living things from nonliving things is that the former contain an irreducible component that is responsible for animating the body. By the start of the nineteenth century, however, a number of researchers had followed Antoine Laurent Lavoisier's lead in applying the new chemical theory to physiology. And the debate between vitalists and mechanists became focused on whether it is possible to give chemical accounts of vital behaviour such as metabolisation, respiration, and fermentation (Asimov 1964). Many vitalists argued that an account of these vital behaviours would require the discovery of fundamental, vital forces, while mechanists argued that there are no fundamental vital forces, and that organic and inorganic processes differ only in complexity (see Bechtel and Richardson 1993 and 1998). By the close of the nineteenth century, mechanism appeared to be winning on the battlefronts of metabolisation, respiration, and fermentation. Nevertheless, vitalism had begun a powerful resurgence. In the last two decades of the century, biologists began to study the underlying mechanisms of developmental and regulative processes in organisms. And the work of Hans Driesch (1867–1941), one of the founders of this new field of experimental embryology, played a major role in igniting a new period of intense interest in vitalism that lasted well into the 1930s.

1. HANS DRIESCH

A mechanist in his early writings, Driesch eventually came to believe that his experimental findings concerning the processes of organic regulation could be marshalled as a refutation of mechanism. He observed that, unlike machines and inorganic matter generally, an organism often repairs or restores itself on its own in response to injuries and disruptions of function. And he argued that some of his experimental findings about organic regulation escape mechanistic explanation in principle, in the sense that attempting a mechanistic explanation of them would be obviously absurd.

The empirical findings to which he appealed were the results of his experiments with sea-urchin eggs. He discovered that if, when a sea-urchin egg first divides into two cells, the cells are separated, each cell will develop normally through all of the stages of division, resulting ultimately in a sea-urchin, albeit one with smaller dimensions than a normal sea-urchin. He also discovered that if one of the four blastomeres (dividing cells) of a four-celled sea-urchin embryo is separated from the other three, it will develop into a complete organism (of smaller than normal dimensions), as will the clump of three cells from which it is separated. In sea-urchin embryos, cell division ceases when the embryo is composed of about 800 cells, at which stage it is called a blastule. Then, a new period of development begins in which embryonic layers are formed from which separate organs grow. Driesch discovered that if, at this stage, the blastule is cut in half in a certain way, each of the halves will nevertheless develop into a sea-urchin. On the basis of these results, he claimed that each blastomere has the same potential for development, and so each can fulfil the function of any other. He therefore called the entire organism 'an harmonious equipotential system'. What potential a blastomere realises depends, he noted, on two mechanistic factors: the spatial location of the blastomere and the size of the whole system. But these mechanical factors, he pointed out, are insufficient to explain the developmental process. Mechanism, he claimed, is false of harmonious equipotential systems, and that fact illustrates the autonomy of biology from physics and chemistry. Instead, he maintained that the best explanation of these results is that there is a vital component that directs the process of development by selectively 'suspending' and 'relaxing the suspension' of the various potentialities of the elements of the embryo. Borrowing a term from Aristotle, he called this component an entelechy, though his use of 'entelechy' differed from Aristotle's use. Entelechies, he claimed, are nonspatial components of organisms that control organic processes and without which an organism will cease to live and eventually break down in chemical compounds.

Coming from an eminent scientist who purported to defend it with experimental results, Driesch's vitalist theory was received with great respect, especially by the philosophical community. He eventually left the field of embryology and took a Chair in Philosophy at the University of Leipzig, where he espoused his 'philosophy of organicism'; in 1907 he delivered the Gifford Lectures at the University of Aberdeen on 'The Science and Philosophy of the Organism' (Driesch 1908). By 1914, his views were a topic of intense international discussion, and they continued to have enormous impact for two more decades, inspiring, for example, J. S. Haldane's *Mechanism, Life and Personality* (1923) and C. E. M. Joad's *The Future of Life* (1928). Indeed, when Haldane, who had attended Driesch's 1907 Gifford Lectures, delivered his own Gifford Lectures, he endorsed Driesch's philosophy of organicism. In the United States, Arthur O. Lovejoy criticised the American Bergsonians for misreading Driesch's work. And in the 1930s, the Swiss philosopher of biology and psychoanalyst Adolf Meyer defended a Drieschian brand of vitalism (Rousseau 1992: 57–8).

Driesch was of course not without his critics. Labelling Driesch's brand of vitalism, 'Substantial Vitalism,' C. D. Broad (1887–1971), in his 1923 Tarner lectures (Broad 1925) remarked: 'Driesch's arguments do not seem to me to be in the least conclusive, even against Biological Mechanism . . . and, even if it be held that Driesch has conclusively *dis*proved Biological Mechanism, I cannot see that his arguments have the least tendency to *prove* Substantial Vitalism' (1925: 58). In 1926, J. C. Smuts rejected Driesch's postulation of an entelechy on the grounds that 'the action of this non-mechanical agent on the mechanical physical body remains entirely unexplained' (Smuts 1926: 172). In that same year, in a truly masterful critique of Driesch's work, the Russian philosopher Mikhail Bahktin explained in detail why Driesch's arguments fail to refute mechanism: while Driesch was correct that the spatial location of the blastomere and size of the whole system are insufficient to explain the developmental process, his inference that no purely chemical explanation was possible was a *non sequitur*. Indeed, in the early 1930s, a chemical explanation of Driesch's experimental results was found. The Stockholm School of experimental embryology, headed by John Runnstrom, discovered a chemical mechanism in the sea-urchin egg that peaks at the upper pole and the lower pole of the egg. The balance between the chemical mechanisms at the two poles explains the regulative development of blastomeres. When the poles of the egg are separated from each other, the regulative process breaks down completely (M. I. Wolsky and A. A. Wolsky 1992: 157–8).

As a result, by the time of his death in 1941, Driesch's Substantial Vitalism (to use Broad's term) had ceased to have any impact either in science or in philosophy. When, in 1951, Ernest Nagel remarked: 'Vitalism of the substantive type advocated by Driesch . . . is now almost entirely a dead issue in the philosophy of biology', he was simply stating what was by then the received view.

2. HENRI BERGSON

There is a second figure whose responsibility for the resurgence of vitalism in the early twentieth century was as great as that of Driesch, the French philosopher Henri Bergson (1859–1941). Born in the same year as the publication of

Charles Darwin's *Origin of Species*, Bergson's 1907 *L'Evolution créatrice* (*Creative Evolution*) speculated that there is a an *élan vital*, a vital impulse, at work in the process of evolution. Until about 1882, Bergson had embraced the mechanistic theory espoused by Herbert Spencer. He reports that his change of heart with respect to mechanism was due to his realisation that physics does not capture time as it is experienced in consciousness, which he called *durée* (duration) (Burwick and Douglass 1992, p. 3). But it is clear that he also came to reject Herbert Spencer's view of us as conscious automata because of its accompanying epiphenomenalism; in its place he stressed the fundamental causal influence of the *élan vital* and of consciousness.

In *L'Evolution créatrice* Bergson rejected both the traditional conception of evolution as a process with a predetermined goal, and the mechanistic conception of evolution as simply the elimination of the unfit. Although he acknowledged a central role for adaptation, he rejected the mechanist view that 'knowledge of the elements and of the elementary causes would have made it possible to foretell the living form which is their sum and their resultant' (1907 [1911]: 35); hence while 'analysis will undoubtedly resolve the process of organic creation into an ever-growing number of physico-chemical phenomena, and chemists and physicists will have to do, of course, with nothing but these', nonetheless 'it does not follow that chemistry and physics will ever give us the key to life' (1907 [1911]: 36), which is, instead, the *élan vital*.

Bergson mentions Driesch only once in *L'Evolution créatrice*, in a footnote, in which he speaks of Driesch's 'admirable studies' (1907 [1911]: 48). In the text that immediately follows the footnote, however, Bergson rejects the view that each living organism has its own vital principle, and thus, by implication, Driesch's view that each living organism has its own entelechy. Bergson maintained that 'the individual itself is not sufficiently independent, not sufficiently cut off from other things, for us to allow it a "vital principle" of its own' (1907 [1911]: 48). There is, rather, a single *élan vital* that is manifested in many and diverse ways throughout the life world and that drives the process of evolution.

The *élan vital*, Bergson maintained, works to overcome the resistance of inert matter in the formation of living bodies; indeed, he sometimes describes it as a 'tendency to act on inert matter' (1907 [1911]: 107). But the *élan vital* does not work towards a predetermined end, as finalists might claim; rather, it creatively explores possibilities working within the confines of matter. Some of its creations are adaptive, and so persist, and some are not, and so perish. 'The impetus of life', Bergson proclaimed, 'consists in a need of creation. It cannot create absolutely, because it is confronted with matter, that is to say with the movement that is the inverse of its own. But it seizes upon this matter, which is necessity itself, and strives to introduce into it the largest possible amount of indetermination and liberty' (1907 [1911]: 274). Of the *élan vital's* interactions with matter he says: 'The movement it starts is sometimes turned aside, sometimes divided, always opposed; and the evolution of the organized world is the unrolling of this conflict' (1907 [1911]: 277). Moreover, linking the evolution of consciousness to the struggles of the *élan vital* in its confrontations with matter, he says: 'The whole history of life until man has been that of the effort of consciousness to raise matter, and of the more or less complete overwhelming of consciousness by the matter which has fallen back on it' (1907 [1911]: 288). Thus the creative impulse of the *élan vital* receives its highest expression in self-conscious human beings.

The impact of *L'Evolution créatrice* was enormous. Burwick and Douglass (1992: 3) report that: 'between 1909 and 1911, over two hundred articles about Bergson appeared in the British Press alone'. They go on to note that: 'in America . . . the reaction was even more enthusiastic. There, Bergson's popularity and influence outstripped that of William James' (1992: 3). James himself was a famous admirer of Bergson: shortly after the publication of *L'Evolution créatrice*, James wrote to him saying: 'Oh, my Bergson, you are a magician and your book is a marvel, a real wonder . . . if your next book proves to be as great an advance on this one as this is on its two predecessors, your name will surely go down as one of the great creative names in philosophy' (quoted in Burwick and Douglass 1992). Bergson's views influence extended beyond philosophy to religion and literature, and Bergson was himself awarded the Nobel Prize in Literature in 1927.

Bergson's work never had much impact in the science of biology, however, and with the rise of analytical philosophy his popularity in philosophical circles suffered a precipitous decline. When he died in Paris in 1941 (the same year as Driesch's death) at the age of eighty-one, after having caught pneumonia while waiting in a queue to register as a Jew, his views on life and evolution were widely regarded among scientists and philosophers as poetic mysticism, not to be taken seriously as a description of reality.

3. C. LLOYD MORGAN

In *Instinct and Experience* (1912), the British biologist C. Lloyd Morgan (1852–1936) remarked:

With all due respect, for M. Bergson's poetic genius – for his doctrine of Life is more akin to poetry than to science – his facile criticism of Darwin's magnificent and truly scientific generalizations only serve to show to how large a degree the intermingling of problems involving the metaphysics of Source with those of scientific interpretation may darken counsel and serve seriously to hinder the progress of biology. (Quoted in Passmore 1957: 270)

In this work and then in his 1923 Gifford Lectures, published as *Emergent Evolution*, Lloyd Morgan set forth his own 'scientific interpretation' of evolution. He explicitly rejected any kind of substance dualism, eschewing Cartesian minds and entelechies, but maintaining instead that through the course of evolution driven by adaptation genuinely novel qualities arises when matter becomes configured in certain ways, and that these novel qualities then affect the future course of events in ways unpredictable before their emergence. Morgan's *Emergent Evolution* (1923) is one of the major works in a tradition of British emergentism that began with J. S. Mill's *A System of Logic* (1843), and includes George Henry Lewes's *Problems of Life and Mind* (1875), Samuel Alexander's two-volumed *Space, Time, and Deity* (1920), and C. D. Broad's *The Mind and Its Place in Nature* (1925).

In his *System of Logic*, Mill introduced a distinction between 'two modes of the conjoint action of causes, the mechanical and the chemical' (p. xviii). According to Mill, two or more causal agents combine to produce an effect in the mechanical mode when but only when the effect of the agents acting jointly is the sum of what would have been the effects of each of them acting alone. He gave 'the name of the Composition of Causes to the principle which is exemplified in all cases in which the joint effect of several causes is identical with the sum of their separate effects' (1843: 243). The 'chemical' mode of the conjoint action of causes is simply joint causation that is not in the mechanical mode: two or more causes combine in the chemical mode (so-called because chemical processes exhibit it) when the effect of the causal agents acting jointly is not the sum of what would have been the effects of each agent acting alone. Combining methane and oxygen, for example, produces carbon dioxide + water, a product that is not in any sense the sum of what would have been the effects of methane and oxygen acting in isolation. Mill called the effects of two or more causes combining in the mechanical mode, homopathic effects, those of two or more causes combining in the chemical mode, heteropathic effects, and called the laws governing these transactions, respectively, homopathic laws and heteropathic laws. It is, on Mill's view, breaches of the Composition of Causes as matter reaches various levels of complexity that account for why there are special sciences. A special science may contain homeopathic laws, but the laws linking its special kinds of objects and their special properties with the properties of substances of lower or higher levels of complexity are heteropathic. On this view, physics is not the most fundamental science; it is just the broadest science, the science concerned with the properties that all or most matter possesses and the way matter behaves in virtue of those properties.

George Henry Lewes introduced the term 'emergence' and cognate terms to describe the resulting hierarchy of special sciences. Lewes called Mill's heteropathic effects 'emergents' and Mill's homopathic effects 'resultants'. Hence chemical phenomena are emergents of mechanical physical phenomena, vital phenomena are emergents of chemical phenomena, and mental phenomena are emergents of vital phenomena. Lloyd Morgan adopted Lewes's terminology, and, in the first section of *Emergent Evolution* (entitled 'Emergents and Resultants') he contrasts his emergent evolutionary cosmology with mechanistic cosmology saying:

> The essential feature of a mechanical – or, if it be preferred, a mechanistic – interpretation [of evolution] is that it is in terms of resultant effects only, calculable by algebraic summation. It ignores the something more that must be accepted as emergent . . . Against such a mechanical interpretation – such a mechanistic dogma – emergent evolution rises in protest. The gist of its contention is that such an interpretation is inadequate. Resultants there are; but there is emergence also. Under naturalistic treatment, however, the emergence, in all its ascending grades, is loyally accepted, on the evidence, with natural piety. That it cannot be mechanically interpreted in terms of resultants only, is just that for which it is our aim to contend with reiterated emphasis. (1923: 8)

According to Morgan, the various emergent levels in the ascending grades of complexity of matter are governed by their own laws. The wholes governed by these laws effect 'the go of events' at lower levels of complexity in ways unanticipated by laws governing matter at lower levels of complexity. Thus, the course of events at lower levels of complexity depends, in part, on the novel emergent properties of higher-level wholes. We thus find in Morgan a notion of downward causation: fundamental causation from higher to lower levels.

4. C. D. BROAD

In *The Mind and Its Place in Nature* (1925), Broad distinguishes Substantial Vitalism from Emergent Vitalism. Driesch's view is Substantial Vitalism, whereas Alexander and Morgan advocate Emergent Vitalism (1925: 58). Broad tells us that both Emergent Vitalism and Biological Mechanism deny that there is a special component (an entelechy) that is present in all living things and absent in nonliving things. Moreover, he says, both try to explain the differences in vital and nonvital behaviour 'wholly in terms of difference of structure'(1925: 59). But the views differ on 'the laws which connect the properties of the components with the characteristic behaviour of the complex wholes which they make up' (1925: 59). According to Biological Mechanism, 'the characteristic behaviour of the whole could, in theory at least, be deduced from a sufficient knowledge of how the components behave in isolation or in other wholes of simpler kinds' (1925: 59). In contrast, according to Emergent Vitalism, no such deduction can be carried out. Broad held that while it is logically possible that

Substantial Vitalism is correct, 'there seems to be nothing to be said for Substantial Vitalism, and a great deal to be said against it' (1925: 91). He maintained, however, that Emergent Vitalism escaped all of Driech's criticisms of Biological Mechanism and that the teleological features of living organisms tend to support Emergent Vitalism over Biological Mechanism.

Broad usefully contrasts the ideal of 'Pure Mechanism' with the Emergentist view of reality:

On a purely mechanical theory all the apparently different kinds of matter would be made of the same stuff. They would differ only in the number, arrangement and movements of their constituent particles. And their apparently different kinds of behaviour would not be ultimately different. For they would all be deducible by a single simple principle of composition from the mutual influences of the particles taken by pairs; and these mutual influences would all obey a single law which is quite independent of the configuration and surroundings in which the particles happen to find themselves. The ideal which we have been describing may be called 'Pure Mechanism'. (1925: 45–6)

On the Emergentist view, in contrast: 'we have to reconcile ourselves to much less unity in the external world and a much less intimate connection between the various sciences. At best the external world and the various sciences that deal with it will form a hierarchy' (1925: 77). For, if Emergentism is true, then

we should have to recognize aggregates of various orders. And there would be two fundamentally different types of laws, which might be called 'intra-ordinal' and 'trans-ordinal' respectively. A trans-ordinal law would be one which connects the properties of aggregates of adjacent orders. A and B would be adjacent, and in ascending order, if every aggregate of order B is composed of aggregates of order A, and if it has certain properties which no aggregate of order A possesses and which cannot be deduced from the A-properties and the structure of the B-complex by any law of composition which has manifested itself at lower levels. An intra-ordinal law would be one which connects the properties of aggregates of the same order. A trans-ordinal law would be a statement of irreducible fact that an aggregate composed of aggregates of the next lower order in such and such proportions and arrangements has such and such characteristic and non-deducible properties. (1925: 77–8)

Broad held that it is a priori that secondary qualities (such as colour and smell) are emergent, and thus the laws connecting them to primary physical qualities are 'trans-ordinal'; but he also held that it is an empirical issue whether any chemical and biological properties are emergent.

5. DEVELOPMENTS ELSEWHERE

While emergentism arose in Britain, it was by no means confined there. There was a large emergentist movement in America that included William

James, Arthur Lovejoy, and Roy Wood Sellars (who claimed that consciousness emerges from brain processes). In 1926, the Sixth International Congress of Philosophy devoted a section to emergentism, with Hans Driesch lecturing on 'Emergent Evolution', Lovejoy lecturing on 'The Meanings of "Emergence" and its "Modes" ', and W. M. Wheeler lecturing on 'Emergent Evolution and the Social'. Meanwhile, there was a raging debate in the former Soviet Union between mechanists and the emergentists of the Deborin School, headed by A. M. Deborin. The Deborin School spoke of the emergence of new forms in nature, and maintained that the mechanists 'neglected the specific character of the definite levels or stages of the development of matter' (Kamenka 1972: 164).

6. EPILOGUE

While the product of a chemical process is indeed not in any sense the sum of what would have been the effects of the chemical agents acting in isolation or in other combinations, physical chemistry as it developed in the 1920s yielded a reductionist explanation of chemical bonding in the early 1930s. This resulted in the complete rejection of emergent chemistry. Advances in molecular biology, such as the 1944 discovery that genes are made of DNA and the 1953 Crick-Watson model of the structure of DNA, more than any other factor, have similarly led to the demise of vital emergentism in biology. Today, it is only the question whether consciousness is an irreducible, emergent phenomenon that remains a topic of debate.

52

BEHAVIOURISM AND PSYCHOLOGY

GARY HATFIELD

1. BEHAVIOURISM AND NATURALISM

Behaviourism was a peculiarly American phenomenon. As a school of psychology it was founded by John B. Watson (1878–1958) in 1913, and grew into the neobehaviourisms of the 1920s, 1930s and 1940s. Philosophers were involved from the start, prefiguring the movement and endeavouring to define or redefine its tenets. Behaviourism expressed the naturalistic bent in American thought, which came in response to the prevailing philosophical idealism and was inspired by developments in natural science itself.

There were several versions of naturalism in American philosophy, and also several behaviourisms (Williams 1931; O'Neil 1995). Most behaviourists paid homage to Darwinian functionalism; all forswore introspection and made learned changes in behaviour the primary subject matter and explanatory domain of psychology. Most behaviourists acknowledged that scientists begin from their own conscious experience, but denied that such experience could be an object of science or a source of evidence in psychology. They differed in their descriptions of behaviour, modes of explanation, and attitudes towards mentalistic concepts. Watson was a strict materialist who wanted to eliminate all mentalistic talk from psychology. Edward Chace Tolman (1886–1959) regarded mind as a biological function of the organism. He permitted mentalistic terms such as 'purpose' in behavioural description, and posited intervening processes that included 'representations' of the environment, while requiring such processes be studied only as expressed in behaviour. Clark L. Hull (1884–1952) developed a hypothetical-deductive version of behaviourism, akin to Tolman's functionalism in positing intervening variables but without his cognitivist constructs. B. F. Skinner (1904–90) rejected intervening variables and developed his own account of the behaviour of the whole organism, based on the laws of operant conditioning.

The naturalism in American philosophy of the early twentieth century showed respect for the natural sciences, especially biology and psychology. John Dewey

(1896, 1911), George Santayana (1905, 1920), and F. J. E. Woodbridge (1909, 1913) expressed this attitude. It animated the neorealism of E. B. Holt and Ralph Barton Perry (Holt *et al.* 1912), who gave special attention to psychology, and the evolutionary naturalism and critical realism of Roy Wood Sellars (1916, 1922). This naturalism differed from Watson's in regarding mind as part of nature from a Darwinian and functionalist perspective, and treating behaviour as the product of the mental functioning. It fed Tolman's version of behaviourism. It was not materialistic or physical-reductionist. Only later, with Quine and logical empiricism, was behaviourism seen as essentially physicalistic.

2. BIRTH OF BEHAVIOURISM IN PSYCHOLOGY

After the turn of the century there was increasing interest in behaviour as a subject matter and form of evidence in psychology, and as an objective expression of mind. Both philosophers and psychologists were growing sceptical of introspection as a method for knowing mind. They believed traditional introspection had to rely on a shaky inference from analogy to extend its first-person results to other humans and to animals. Among philosophers, Perry (1909) and E. A. Singer (1911) promoted behaviour as a means of perceiving mental functioning in humans that allegedly would not depend on introspection and analogy. Psychologists (e.g., Warren 1914), partly prompted by biological study of animal behaviour (e.g., Jennings 1906), called for greater attention to 'objective' factors in human psychology. Behavioural evidence was touted by the comparative psychologists Thorndike (1898), Washburn (1908), and Yerkes (1907), but despite Yerkes's claim to the contrary (1917, p. 155), that did not make them behaviourists, for they used such evidence to frame theories of the traditional subject matter of psychology, consciousness or mind regarded as an object of introspection.

Other psychologists argued that the very subject matter of psychology should be changed, from consciousness to behaviour. William McDougall (1905, 1912), then at Oxford, and Walter Pillsbury (1911) at Michigan proposed to define psychology as the science of 'conduct' or 'behaviour'. But they did not ban introspective methods for finding the mental causes of behaviour (McDougall 1905: 2; Pillsbury 1911: 5), and McDougall was an avowed dualist (1911: ch. 26). Behaviourism did not arise from making behaviour the primary evidence or subject matter of psychology. It arose from a strict repudiation of introspective methods and a proposed change in the theoretical vocabulary of psychology.

Behaviourism as a self-conscious movement was initiated by Watson in two articles (1913a and b) and two books (1914, 1919). He proposed changing psychology's subject matter, evidence, and theoretical vocabulary. The subject matter would now be behaviour, described as muscle movements and glandular secretions; the evidence would be this same behaviour, along with a physical description of the stimulus setting; the theoretical vocabulary of reflex arcs and Pavlovian conditioned learning would be used to explain stimulus–response relations. Animals were to be regarded as complex machines whose current behavioural propensities are a function of innate structure and previous stimulus exposure. Instinct was to be minimised, and could perhaps be explained through Lamarckian inheritance of acquired characteristics (1914: 174). What a complex animal does is primarily a function of its reactional or conditioning biography, that is, its history of observable pairings of stimulus and response. While Watson believed that the chain of events from stimulus to response would eventually be accounted for in purely physical-chemical terms, he offered behaviourism as the science that would presently lead to the prediction and control of animal behaviour. Behaviourism differs from physiology in studying the responses of the whole organism, but Watson permitted postulation of unobserved physiological states (glandular or muscular). Nonetheless, everything of importance is in principle available at the periphery of the organism; 'there are no centrally initiated processes' (1913a: 423).

Behaviourist principles apply to humans and other animals alike. If one must account for the processes previously labelled 'thought' in humans, they should be seen as laryngeal subvocalisations (again, in principle detectable at the surface of the throat). Emotions are to be equated with glandular secretions and genital tumescence. Perception is a matter of sensory discrimination as manifested through differential behavioural response, including, for humans, verbal response. As Heidbreder observed, Watson wanted to extend 'the methods and point of view of animal psychology into human psychology' (1933: 236). It was not just any animal psychology, but the mechanistic version propounded by Jacques Loeb, who taught Watson at Chicago (where he took his PhD after studying philosophy and psychology at Furman University in Greenville, South Carolina). Loeb (1900) considered himself a biologist and an opponent of 'comparative psychology', which drew analogies between human and animal cognition based upon introspection. Even the animal biologist H. S. Jennings (1906), at Johns Hopkins when Watson arrived in 1908, permitted attribution of consciousness down the phylogenetic scale to amoeba and paramecium. But Watson's comparative psychology, and his general psychology of humans, were to be of the Loeb style – mechanistic, materialist, and deterministic – and for that reason presumably objective and scientific. Watson left Hopkins in 1920 and went into advertising, where he flourished. When after 1930 he withdrew from psychology, behaviourism was on the way up: the young Skinner (1976: 299) and W. V. O. Quine (1985: 110) had already been drawn to Watson's variety.

3. PHILOSOPHICAL AND CRITICAL RESPONSES

Watson's articles drew immediate response from both psychologists and philosophers. Sustained discussion occurred in the *Psychological Review* and the *Journal of Philosophy, Psychology and Scientific Methods* (which published psychological articles and results even after abbreviating its name in 1921). Titchener (1914) argued that Watson's new movement was not really new. Its criticisms of introspection could be found in Comte and Maudsley. Its positive teaching should be seen as a continuation of the biological study of animal behaviour, something Titchener welcomed, including its extension to humans, but which he believed neither could nor should replace mentalistic psychology. Angell 1913 was more favourably disposed to the new movement, though he refused to forgo introspection.

Among philosophers, Dewey (1914), Holt (1915), and De Laguna (1916, 1918) praised the new movement. An enthusiastic Holt was all but prepared to do away with introspective methods. Dewey believed mind is best studied as it functions purposively to adjust organism to environment. De Laguna developed this functionalist outlook but she was unwilling to preclude introspection. But all agreed in seeing behaviour as the expression of mind and no one was prepared to reject mentalistic descriptions of behaviour. Holt and Dewey argued that behavioural acts are unified as expressions of purpose. The behaviour of an animal that moves about and then eats when it finds food expresses the fact that the animal was looking for food. Holt argued that such 'objective reference' of behaviour is too often neglected. Such reference may be to things that do not exist, that existed only in the past, or that will exist in the future (Holt 1915 [1915: 172–3]).

The notions of purpose and objective reference in behaviour were developed by Perry (1918, 1921a and b). Perry approvingly saw behaviourism as a return to the Aristotelian view that 'mind and body are related as activity and organ' (1921a: 85). According to the usual introspectivist, who adopts psychophysical parallelism, the mind simply 'supervenes' on physiological events; but for the behaviourist the mind 'intervenes' between stimulus and response (1921a, p. 87). Behaviourism closes the gap between mind and body.

Perry did not rule out introspection, and he claimed the behaviourist did not either (citing De Laguna 1916). He believed that behavioural evidence enlarged the data of psychology, and that behaviourism would yield improved psychological explanations. Consider his discussion of psychological dispositions, whether 'instincts' or Freudian 'complexes'. He regarded such dispositions as nonconscious and considered three types of explanation for them. They could be mental and not physiological, a possibility he found nonsensical for unconscious states;

they could be physiological and nonmental; or, 'accepting the behaviouristic version of mind, one may regard dispositions as both physical and mental: phys- ical because consisting in certain physiological structures, mental because of the peculiar type of function or activity in which these structures are engaged' (1921a: 94). Perry used the same notion of disposition to analyse purposive action, which he found to consist of a 'set' or 'determining tendency' to pur- sue a course of action in appropriate environmental circumstances, bringing in 'auxiliary responses' as needed to achieve the desired end. Such dispositions towards purposive action are linked conditionally to cognitive states such as be- liefs, which are 'suppositions' about environmental circumstances ascribed to organisms in virtue of their dispositions to behave (1921b).

Bertrand Russell adopted the view that behaviour is an expression of mind in Russell 1921, a work that attempted to solve the mind–body problem through the neutral monism of James and the neorealism of Holt and Perry, hence one that did not preclude introspection. He spoke approvingly of Watsonian be- haviourism throughout Russell 1927, though again retaining introspection as the means of knowing the ontologically neutral 'data' of both physics and psy- chology. Woodbridge (1921, 1925) argued that behaviour is inherently teleolog- ical and so must be understood in relation to ends. His position was consonant with earlier functionalism and with Perry's recent work. Psychological critics of behaviourism cited these and other philosophical discussions (see Roback 1923: chs. 3–7). Such critics charged Watson with using a double standard in denying theoretical posits to the mentalists while invoking unseen physiological states. They argued that behaviourist descriptions tacitly rely on the psycholo- gist's own introspective knowledge, predicted that Watson's account of learning would be shown factually inadequate, and questioned whether his talk of muscle twitches and glandular secretions could effectively describe behaviour without Holt's notion of 'objective reference'.

4. NEOBEHAVIOURISM AND PHILOSOPHY: TOLMAN, HULL, SKINNER

Behaviourism became the leading school of scientific psychology through the research and theorising of the neobehaviourists, notably Tolman, Hull, and Skin- ner. None were simple stimulus–response reflexologists; all considered behaviour to be a function of variables beyond previous and current stimulation. All were methodologically reflective and philosophically engaged. Tolman and Hull were strongly influenced by American neorealism and pragmatist functionalism. Hull took theoretical and methodological inspiration from philosophical and scien- tific classics, especially Hume's associationism and the deductive exposition of

Newton's *Principia*. Skinner came to behaviourism through Russell 1927, his philosophical outlook being further shaped by Mach (1912 [1919]), Poincaré (1902), and the operationism of P. W. Bridgman (1927). Just when neobehaviourism was coming to maturity, the logical empiricists alleged that all psychological statements can be translated into physical statements referring to physical states of a person's body (Carnap 1932, affirming epistemological solidarity with American behaviourism; Carnap 1935; Hempel 1935). The neobehaviourists took note of the scientific philosophy of the Vienna Circle and its Berlin allies, but it was not formative of or influential on their positions (see Smith 1986).

Tolman studied psychology at Harvard, with instruction from Holt and Perry. He converted to behaviourism after going to Berkeley, where he spent his career, producing laboratory studies of maze-learning in rats, theoretical and methodological papers (collected in Tolman 1951a), and a major book (1932). He adopted an avowedly nonmetaphysical, pragmatist stance in metaphysics and epistemology (1932: ch. 25), and did not deny the existence of 'raw feels' or qualia accessible to individuals. From early on he characterised Watson's brand of behaviourism as a 'muscle twitchism' directed at the 'molecular' behaviour of muscle contractions and glandular secretions. Tolman (1932: ch. 1) argued that even molecular behaviourism must rely on 'molar' descriptions of what animals do as whole organisms interacting with their environments (something Watson had acknowledged in other terms, 1919: 13). Believing that effective behaviour classification requires consideration of the animal's purpose or end, Tolman advocated a 'purposive behaviourism' (with credit to Holt and Perry).

He regarded the inherent teleology of behaviour as a biological and psychological fact. His work with rats in mazes, including their running into walls when a shortened path was substituted for a previously longer one, led him to attribute 'cognitive postulations', 'expectations', and 'representations' to rats (1926, 1927 [1951a: 60, 65]). These representations might be of objects that no longer exist, thereby exhibiting intentionality (see Amundson 1983). In response to Gestalt psychology, Tolman came to attribute 'sign-Gestalt expectations' to his animals, consisting of a sign-object perceived as standing in a means-end relation to a signified object or state of affairs. Inspired by Bridgman 1927, he developed the notion of 'intervening variables' as operationally defined internal states of animals (listed in Tolman 1938 [1951a] as demand, appetite, sensory differentiation, motor skill, hypotheses, and biases), which, together with stimulation, heredity, maturity, physiological drive, and previous training, combine to yield a response. For Tolman such intervening variables were realistically interpreted and not reducible to a purely physical or (positivistic) observational language. Intervening variables are defined in relation to observable features of the animal's environment and behaviour, described (as he thought they must be) in the functionalist language of purpose. When MacCorquodale and Meehl (1948) proposed that 'intervening variables' be viewed as merely empirical correlations and that 'hypothetical construct' be used when internal entities or processes are posited, Tolman (1951b) explained that his intervening variables were hypothesised processes and states of the organism proper to psychology, not requiring physiological interpretation to be classed as hypothetical constructs (though he was newly tolerant of neurophysiological hypotheses, Tolman 1949).

Although Tolman's self-classification as a behaviourist was questioned (Harrell and Harrison 1938), it became widely accepted (Williams 1931; Woodworth 1948; O'Neil 1995). In the 1920s many saw behaviourism as rendering study of mental activity objective, by substituting behavioural for introspective evidence. Hull and Skinner insisted on more austere vocabularies for describing such evidence than Tolman, though without returning to Watsonian twitchism. Unlike Tolman, Hull was an avowed materialist, adopting the working hypothesis that the organism can be wholly described within a 'physical or mechanistic' view (1930, 1937 [1984: 140, 319]). He was not an eliminativist regarding conscious phenomena, but his vision of behavioural science excluded introspective methods. He allowed mentalistic language such as 'goal response' into his system, but unlike Tolman demanded it be rigorously defined in pure stimulus-response language containing no mentalistic terms (and no intentional notions).

Hull earned his PhD at Wisconsin in 1918 and taught there until moving to Yale in 1929. At first interested in hypnosis and mental testing, he converted to behaviourism while teaching it in seminars during the mid-1920s (using Watson 1924 and Roback 1923 as texts). At Yale he produced a series of important papers (collected in Hull 1984) and two major books (1943, 1952). He conceived the organism in a functionalist and Darwinian framework; he took Newtonian physics as his model of theory structure, with definitions, postulates, and theorems. He is best known for his highly formalised theory of learning or 'habit strength'. He identified himself as a 'molar' behaviourist, arguing that behaviour theory could progress despite the lack of knowledge in neurophysiology, and granting behavioural science its own observational and theoretical vocabulary. At the same time, he treated intervening variables such as 'drive' (e.g., hunger) or 'need reduction' as referring to as-yet-unknown neural states. Hull was familiar with Carnap 1935, but did not interpret his theoretical apparatus using the analyses of theory and observation proposed by the Vienna Circle. Later interpreters retrospectively characterised his position in that light (e.g., Bergmann and Spence 1941; Feigl 1951; Koch 1954; Spence 1944), thereby eliding his materialistic realism (see Amundson and Smith 1984).

Like Tolman and Hull, Skinner wanted to produce a science of behaviour together with an account (or 'philosophy') of that science. He absorbed Machian positivism before and after arriving at Harvard in 1928 to study psychology, adopting Mach's anti-metaphysical inductivism, his focus on biological adjustment, and his suspicion of posited theoretical entities. For a time Skinner wanted to marry this Machian bent with Bridgman's operationism. Then he came to see operationism in psychology as allied with logical positivism, and so as overly formal and physicalistic (1938, 1945). Skinner rejected mind and any mentalistic talk that could not be translated into neutral behavioural descriptions. But he did not think behaviourist psychology should be reduced to physiology or that its descriptions should be restated in physical language, and he was unenthusiastic about the unity of science. He avoided materialism because it led to prejudice against the behavioural level of analysis and in favour of concrete physical states of the organism (1938: chs. 12–13). He was a molar behaviourist who sought to discover the laws of behavioural change. He rejected intervening variables of any kind (causing his behaviourism to be dubbed that of an 'empty' or 'hollow' organism), looking instead for empirical correlations among empirically determined factors such as stimulus, response, reinforcer, and hours of deprivation (of food, water, etc.). He emphasised Thorndikian conditioning, that is, behavioural changes occurring when reinforcement (getting food or another reinforcer) is contingent upon a particular type of response 'emitted' by the organism (such as pressing a bar or pecking a target). His most noted results related the speed and permanence of learning to schedules of reinforcement (Ferster and Skinner 1957).

Skinner spent the mid-1930s in the Society of Fellows at Harvard, then held positions at Minnesota and Indiana before returning to Harvard in 1947. He extended his behaviouristic analysis to perception and language, where his efforts were superseded by perceptual psychologists and linguists. He lived to see the behaviouristic revolution replaced by new cognitive approaches inspired by work on perception, memory, and attention, and influenced by communication theory and the rise of computer science, linguistics, and artificial intelligence.

5. BEHAVIOURISM AND AMERICAN NATURALISM

The main movements in American philosophy during the first third of the century, pragmatism, neorealism, and critical realism, were naturalistic (Perry 1912; Sellars 1916). They foresaw extending the cognitive practices of the sciences to all enquiry. These philosophies were not physicalistic or materialistic. They numbered biology and psychology among the sciences, and included biological and psychological phenomena, imbued with teleology and known through introspection, within the sphere of the natural. This was naturalism without materialism (Dewey, Hook, and Nagel 1945); it was critical of Watsonian behaviourism as narrow-mindedly denying plain facts of nature (Pepper 1923; Woodbridge 1925). Mind was to be integrated into nature, not excluded from it (Dewey 1925: chs. 6–8). This sort of naturalism was embraced by Tolman, but Hull and Skinner agreed only with its general biological orientation. Their neobehaviourisms shaped the perception of American behaviourism in later decades, while Tolman came to be seen as a predecessor of the newer cognitive approaches.

After the 1940s the character of philosophical naturalism in America changed. The physicalism of some logical empiricists and Quine became prominent. Behaviourism was philosophically reinterpreted in physicalist terms. The biological bent of earlier American naturalism and the functionalism of neobehaviourism were thereby masked. These developments conditioned retrospective interpretations of the philosophical context of behaviourism in the first half of the century, though these interpretations themselves belong to the history of philosophy after the middle of the century.

GESTALT PSYCHOLOGY

THOMAS LEAHEY

Gestalt psychology was a movement related to phenomenology, especially that of Husserl, a contemporary of the founding Gestalt theorists. Gestalt psychology and phenomenology arose from the philosophy of Brentano, which emphasised the description of consciousness, rather than its analysis. However, Gestalt psychologists were scientists, not philosophers, wanting to put psychology on sound experimental footings and seeking physiological explanations of consciousness. Their work extended beyond investigating consciousness to include memory, problem solving, creativity, group dynamics, child development, and animal behaviour, although their theories in these areas were informed by their original theorising about perception. Moreover, the movement's changing historical circumstances took Gestalt psychology ever farther from philosophy. The Gestalt psychologists were second-generation German psychologists, struggling against philosophers to win autonomy in the German university system. Like phenomenology, Gestalt psychology arose in a country already deeply troubled by modernity which then experienced the vicissitudes of the First World War, the Weimar period, and the rise of Hitler and Nazism (the best general account of the development of Gestalt psychology is Ash 1995). The major Gestalt theorists joined the diaspora of German intellectuals to the United States. There, the Gestalt movement was shaped by a culture very different from Germany's, and by their encounter with behaviourism.

1. BACKGROUND

The science of psychology was born in the late nineteenth century of a marriage between philosophy and physiology. The goal of the founding psychologists was providing scientific answers to philosophical questions. They deployed experimental techniques developed by physiologists and formulated physiological theories of consciousness, the initial focus of their science. The leading concerns of philosophy being epistemological, psychology was dominated by the study of cognition, primarily sensation and perception, but encompassing research into thinking and memory. Early German cognitive psychology was different from American. In America, psychology from the outset was influenced by evolution, and American psychologists looked at the mind from a pragmatic, functional, perspective, inquiring into the adaptive utility of consciousness. German psychologists were concerned more with issues of mental ontology than mental function. Nevertheless, in Germany experimental psychologists were outside the philosophical mainstream. At a time when post-Kantian idealism dominated German philosophy, psychologists' theorising was heavily influenced by empiricist and positivist orientations imported from physiology. Especially influential were Hermann von Helmholtz (1821–94), and Ernst Mach (1838–1916), who did important work in sensory and perceptual physiology and psychology.

Psychology as the Gestalt psychologists found it investigated consciousness within the representational framework established by Descartes and epitomised by Hume, reinforced by the analytic spirit of post-Newtonian natural science. Psychologists took it for granted that the objects of consciousness were complex combinations of sensory elements just as material objects were complex combinations of atomic elements. Thus, the psychologist's task was to use experimentally controlled introspection to analyse conscious complexes into constituent parts and discover how association assembled them into the meaningful objects of experience. They then tried to match the objects and processes of the mind with underlying physiological events and functions.

However, some thinkers opposed the reigning atomistic-representational framework. In America, William James (1842–1910) took a descriptive – that is, phenomenological – look at experience in his *Principles of Psychology* (1890). He rejected the claim that consciousness was assembled out of bits of 'mind-stuff' in an unconscious mental 'machine-shop'. James offered instead an evolutionary vision of consciousness as a continuously flowing stream shaping experience and striving for survival, setting in motion American psychology's concern with mind as an instrument of evolutionary adaptation. Moreover, Scottish realism had long survived in America, and at the time when Gestalt psychology began in Germany neorealism arose in the United States led by James's follower and biographer, Ralph Barton Perry (1876–1957). Neorealism said that there was no private realm of consciousness for introspection to interrogate, pushing American psychology towards behaviourism.

In Germany, however, the revolt against the atomistic view of consciousness was led by Franz Brentano (1838–1917), who viewed mental phenomena as acts inherently directed at meaningful objects, rather than as meaningless sensations assembled into meaningful objects by association. Brentano's philosophy gave rise to Husserl's phenomenology and indirectly to Gestalt psychology. Brentano's student, psychologist Carl Stumpf (1848–1946), taught or trained all of the founders of Gestalt psychology, inspiring them to describe consciousness as it was, not as empiricist atomism said it must be.

2. GESTALT PSYCHOLOGY

The leading Gestalt psychologists were Max Wertheimer (1880–1943), Wolf-gang Köhler (1887–1967), and Kurt Koffka (1887–1941). Wertheimer was the founder and inspirational leader of the movement. Köhler headed the prestigious Berlin Psychological Institute, and was the primary theorist and researcher of the group, having been trained in physics as well as philosophy and psychology. Koffka was the first to write up Wertheimer's ideas, and spread the message of Gestalt psychology worldwide through books and articles. Of their many students and associates, the most important was Kurt Lewin (1890–1947), who devised practical applications of Gestalt theories.

Gestalt psychology arose out of the problem of object perception. By the end of the nineteenth century it was becoming clear that the empiricist-associative theory faced formidable difficulties in explaining how meaningful, organised, objects of perception are created out of meaningless sensory atoms. Christian von Ehrenfels (1859–1932), with whom Wertheimer studied, had begun to for-mulate a rival viewpoint, introducing the term *Gestalt* to psychology. A melody, Ehrenfels said, is more than a sequence of notes. A melody may be transposed into a different key such that none of the notes – the sensory elements of which the melody is supposedly composed – remains the same, without altering our perception of it. Ehrenfels proposed that in addition to sensory elements there were form-elements – *Gestaltqualitäten* – composing the objects of conscious-ness. When Ehrenfels advanced this hypothesis in 1890, he left the ontological status of Gestalt qualities ambiguous. Were they imposed on sensory atoms by the mind, as Ehrenfels's own teacher, Alexius Meinong (1853–1920), proposed? Or were they something more, objective *structures* (not elements) that existed in the world and were picked up by consciousness, as philosophical realists and phenomenologists thought? Gestalt psychology forcefully pursued the latter possibility.

3. GESTALT REJECTION OF EXISTING PSYCHOLOGY

Gestalt psychologists repudiated atomistic theories of consciousness and offered Gestalt psychology as a liberating revolution against psychology's *ancien régime*. As Köhler said to the American Psychological Association:

We were excited by what we found, and even more by the prospect of finding further revealing facts. Moreover, it was not only the stimulating newness of our enterprise which inspired us. There was also a great wave of relief – as though we were escaping from a prison. The prison was psychology as taught at the universities when we still were students. At the time, we had been shocked by the thesis that all psychological facts (not only those in perception) consist of unrelated inert atoms and that almost the only factors which combine these atoms and thus introduce action are associations formed under the influence of mere contiguity. What had disturbed us was the utter senselessness of this picture, and the implication that human life, apparently so colorful and so intensely dynamic, is actually a frightful bore. This was not true of our new picture, and we felt that further discoveries were bound to destroy what was left of the old picture. (Köhler 1959 [1978: 253–4])

Gestalt theorists held that the old picture rested upon two flawed and un-examined assumptions. The first was the 'bundle hypothesis', identified by Wertheimer, which held that like chemical compounds, the objects of consciousness were made up of fixed and unchanging atomic elements. The bundle hypothesis was a theoretical presupposition imposed on experience, not a natural description of consciousness as we find it. Wertheimer wrote:

I stand at the window and see a house, trees, sky.

Theoretically I might say there were 327 brightnesses and nuances of colour. Do I have '327'? No. I have sky, house, and trees. It is impossible to achieve '327' as such. And yet even though such droll calculation were possible and implied, say, for the house 120, the trees 90, the sky 117 – I should at least have this arrangement and division of the total, and not, say, 127 and 100 and 100; or 150 and 177. (1923 [1928: 71])

The second flawed presupposition imposed on experience by the old picture was the 'constancy hypothesis', identified by Köhler (1913 [1971]). The constancy hypothesis held that every sensory element in consciousness corresponded to a specific physical stimulus registered by a sense organ.

That the bundle hypothesis and the constancy hypothesis were not straw men is demonstrated by this diagram from Descartes's *Treatise on Man*. Atomism about consciousness began when Descartes severed the world of experience (ideas) from the world of physical objects. Perception became a matter of point-for-point projection of physical stimuli onto the screen of consciousness, as in a *camera obscura*. In figure 1, we see how the physical stimulus points *A*, *B*, and *C* on the arrow stimulate points *1*, *3*, and *5* on each retina, and how these points of stimulation are carried by specific nerves 2, 4, 6 to the pineal gland, projected as points *a*, *b*, and *c* for perception in consciousness.

This diagram also shows the physiological side to psychologists' treatment of consciousness that was not present in philosophy. Unlike philosophers,

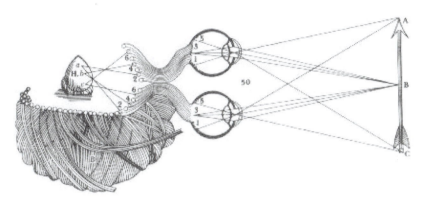

Figure 1

psychologists wanted to link conscious experiences to the physiological processes causing them. While Descartes's treatment of sensation and perception was crude compared to nineteenth-century theories, his framework of point-for-point projection of stimulus elements onto perceptual elements remained. While the Gestalt theorists shared the phenomenological orientation of philosophers such as Husserl, as psychologists they laboured to replace atomism with holism in neuroscience.

4. GESTALT THEORY

As a research programme, Gestalt psychology began in 1910 with investigations into 'apparent motion', led by Wertheimer aided by Köhler and Koffka. Apparent motion is familiar through movies, which are a series of rapidly presented still pictures that are experienced as objects in continuous smooth motion. In Wertheimer's (1912 [1961]) experiments, subjects viewed successive stroboscopic presentations of two vertical black bars in two different, fixed, locations on a white background. Wertheimer varied the interval between the offset of the presentation of the first stimulus and the onset of the presentation of the second stimulus. When the interval between presentations of the bars was 30 milliseconds, the subject saw two bars appearing simultaneously; when the interval was 60 milliseconds, the subject reported seeing a single bar moving from point to point.

To give this experience a name free from presuppositions, Wertheimer dubbed it the *phi* phenomenon. The term 'apparent motion' reflected the reigning interpretation when Wertheimer did his experiments. In the grip of the bundle and constancy hypotheses, psychologists explained apparent motion as an

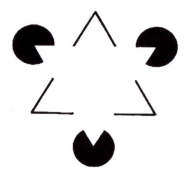

Figure 2

illusion, a cognitive error, in which the subject sees two identical objects in two places and then falsely infers that a single object moved from the first to the second point. Such an explanation holds that there is no experience of motion given in consciousness – the motion is merely 'apparent,' and the experience is explained away. Wertheimer and his followers insisted, on the contrary, that the experience of motion was real, genuinely given in consciousness, although it did not correspond to any physical stimulus, contrary to the bundle and constancy hypotheses.

This Gestalt idea may be illustrated by the perception of illusory contours. In figure 2, one clearly perceives a triangle that is not, strictly speaking, there. Moreover, observers typically see the area enclosed by the phantom triangle as being lighter in colour than the space outside. They thus experience a contour, a difference of light and dark, to which there is no corresponding physical stimulus.

Illusory contours also show how Gestalt study of the *phi* phenomenon could be brought to bear on the problem of object perception. In this figure, as in the perception of melodic form and in the *phi* phenomenon, we perceive a form – a Gestalt – to which no local physical stimulation corresponds. Objects – Wertheimer's house, trees, and sky – are immediately given in consciousness as meaningful wholes, not as collections of atomic sensations. 'When we are presented with a number of stimuli we do not as a rule experience "a number" of individual things, this one and that', Wertheimer (1923 [1938: 78]) wrote. 'Instead larger wholes separated from and related to one another are given in experience . . . Do such arrangements and divisions follow definite principles?' Wertheimer said they did, and laid down a set of 'organizing principles' still cited in textbooks today. For example, following the Law of Similarity we tend to see figure 3 as alternating columns of squares and circles rather than as five rows of alternating squares and circles.

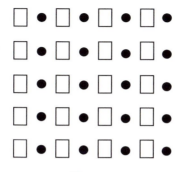

Figure 3

Later, Köhler formulated an overarching organising law, the Law of *Prägnanz*, the tendency of experiences to assume the simplest shapes possible (Hochberg 1974 provides a brief but rigorous overview of the Gestalt theory of perception).

It is important to understand that, according to Gestalt psychology, Gestalts were not imposed *on* experience by the mind, but were discovered *in* experience. Gestalts were objective, not subjective (Ash 1995). Especially as formulated by Köhler, Gestalts were physically real, natural self-organisations in nature, in the brain, and in experience, all of them isomorphic to one another. In physics we find that dynamic forces spontaneously organise material particles into simple elegant forms. The brain, Köhler said, is likewise a dynamic field of self-organising force-fields reflecting the physical Gestalts and giving rise to the Gestalts of experienced objects. 'In a sense, Gestalt psychology has since become a kind of application of field physics to essential parts of psychology and brain physiology' (Köhler 1967 [1971: 115]).

The conflict between atomism and Gestalt self-organisation extended to the study of behaviour, including animal behaviour. The leading student of animal behaviour at the turn of the century was Edward Lee Thorndike (1874–1949), who turned the atomistic theory of consciousness inside out into an atomistic theory of behaviour. He studied cats learning to work a manipulandum in order to escape from a 'puzzle box.' From watching their apparently trial-and-error behaviour, Thorndike concluded that animals do not form associations between ideas, but between the stimuli in the box and the response needed to escape it. A little later, Köhler studied the intelligence of apes and drew different conclusions. His apes showed insight, as problems suddenly resolved themselves into simple solutions, just as Gestalts emerge spontaneously in consciousness. Because the construction of Thorndike's puzzle boxes hid their workings from the animal, it was reduced to trial and error by its situation, not because it was limited to forming stimulus–response associations. As the old atomistic picture of consciousness imposed its presuppositions on psychologists' understanding of perception, Thorndike imposed random, atomistic stimulus-response learning on his subjects. Köhler sought a phenomenology of behaviour no less than a phenomenology of consciousness. Later, the Gestalt concept of insight as self-organisation of behaviour was applied to human thinking by Wertheimer, and the Gestalt concept of the dynamic field was applied to social behaviour by Kurt Lewin.

In the late nineteenth century, educated Germans feared atomistic conceptions of the universe. For them atomism was linked to the twin evils of The Machine – an object made of separable parts – and Chaos – a formless void of atoms. Believing in real wholes – Gestalts – offered a third way in which order and meaning were inherent in nature. However, the term Gestalt was also linked to conservative and racist strains of German thought that tended to reject modern science. For example, Houston Stewart Chamberlin (1855–1927) said that Life is Gestalt, and that with the exception of the atomised Jews, each race was a Gestalt, the highest race-Gestalt being the Teutonic. While not anti-Semitic, von Ehrenfels voiced similar opinions, setting Gestalt (good) against Chaos (evil), and finding hope of salvation in German music. It was therefore a bold move when Wertheimer, a Jew, appropriated the term Gestalt for a scientific, democratic, urban, movement. Rather than blaming science for the modern predicament, he hoped to use good tough-minded science to demonstrate that the world of experience was not a lie, but corresponded to a structured, organised, meaningful physical reality (Ash 1995; Harrington 1996).

5. RECEPTION AND FATE

By the mid-1930s, Gestalt psychology was well known around the world, a fact that briefly shielded Köhler from Nazi persecution. Nevertheless, there were significant German criticisms of Gestalt theory. The most important came from the Leipzig school of *Ganzheit* (roughly, 'holistic') psychology. They found Gestalt psychology's theory that Gestalts are physically objective to be insufficiently psychological. Their motto was 'No Gestalts without a Gestalter', adhering to the view that Gestalts are imposed by the mind rather than discovered. Gestalt psychology had little initial influence on philosophy since philosophers such as Husserl were then trying to expel from their midst what they saw as an alien body of science. Gestalt psychology did briefly attract the interest of the Frankfurt school, who would later turn to psychoanalysis for a psychology to support their Marxist critique of society. Moreover, after the noisy rejection of 'psychologism' by Husserl, later philosophers in the phenomenological tradition, most notably Merleau-Ponty and Sartre, became much friendlier to Gestalt ideas.

From 1927 onwards, the leading Gestalt psychologists left Germany for the United States. There, they confronted behaviourism in a society for which the concept of Gestalt had no cultural resonance. Although American psychologists respected the experimental findings of Gestalt psychology, and even elected Köhler President of the American Psychological Association, they found Gestalt theory strange and bewildering. In addition, the Gestalt theorists tended not to shed their German ways and found few opportunities to train graduate students (Sokal 1984). The exception was Kurt Lewin, who re-made his personality on American lines, made sure he could train PhDs, and took up American topics such as group dynamics. After the Second World War, American theories came to dominate German psychology, marginalising the remaining Gestalt psychologists.

The legacy of Gestalt psychology in psychology is hard to measure. Their demonstrations and principles of organisation are still found in psychology text-books. Their greatest contribution lay in reformulating the study of perception to 'carve nature at the joints'. They objected not to analysing experience into parts, but to analysing it into arbitrary parts. Perhaps because of Gestalt in-fluence, psychologists remain wary of imposing pretheoretical assumptions on their data, and Köhler's view of the brain as a self-organising system is return-ing, unacknowledged, in connectionist psychology and neuroscience. Never-theless,the Gestalt concern with wholeness and unity seems a faint voice from the dusty past.

WITTGENSTEIN'S CONCEPTION OF MIND

MARIE McGINN

1. INTRODUCTION

In looking at Wittgenstein's philosophy of mind up to 1945 we are attempting to survey a period that covers virtually the whole of Wittgenstein's philosophical development, from the *Notebooks, 1914–1916* to the end of Part 1 of the *Philosophical Investigations*. One of the central interpretative questions raised by the large body of work that is produced in this period is whether we should see it as the more or less continuous development of a reasonably unified philosophical vision, or view it as containing one or more important discontinuities or radical breaks. It is a question on which interpreters of Wittgenstein fundamentally disagree. There can be no question of doing justice to this dispute in this brief introduction to Wittgenstein's thought. I shall therefore limit myself to attempting to develop one clear line of interpretation, in which I side with those who see Wittgenstein's later philosophy as a development, rather than a rejection, of his early work.

From the very beginning, Wittgenstein characterises philosophy as a 'critique of language' (1921 [1922] *Tractatus Logico-Philosophicus (TLP)* 4.0031) and associates philosophical problems with 'our failure to understand the logic of our language' (*TLP*: 4.003). We should, therefore, expect his view of the mind to be grounded in his conception of language and how it functions. Similarly, we should expect any development in his view of the mind to be traceable ultimately to developments in his view of language and of how the task of achieving a clarified understanding of it is to be accomplished. Equally, the suggestion that we can trace a continuous development in Wittgenstein's philosophy of mind from the early to the later work commits us to the claim that there is an important, underlying continuity between his early and his late philosophy of language. One natural place to start this account of Wittgenstein's philosophy of mind is in a statement of what I take this latter continuity to consist in.

The *Tractatus* uses the comparison between pictures and propositions to bring a certain order to our perception of the phenomena of language. This order involves our applying the following distinctions to the propositions which constitute our language: the content (the simple or non-articulate parts – names – into which the proposition can be analysed), the structure (the determinate arrangement of these simple parts into a complex or articulate proposition), and form (the limit of the possible arrangement of content of a proposition into determinate structures which express thoughts). One consequence of this order is that we come to see names as representing particular objects in virtue of their place in a system of propositions that describes all the possible states of affairs in which that object might be a constituent. For it is only in virtue of its form – possibilities for occurring in propositions – that an expression comes to have the content it does.

This conception of language allows Wittgenstein to dispense with the idea that a sign comes to have a meaning in virtue of some sort of immediate connection, between the sign and an object, that is made by a mind, for example, through an act of pointing. Instead, the meaning of a sign is determined by its place in a language, or system of propositions, and is completely independent of any pyschological occurrence that accompanies its utterance. This conception, in modified form, remains fundamental throughout Wittgenstein's philosophical development; it is a central element in his overall attempt to present a vision of language in which meaning belongs entirely to the public domain and is fully communicated between speakers. It is essential to this anti-psychologistic vision of language that psychological statements should not introduce any private meanings.

What Wittgenstein sees, right from the beginning, is that we avoid this only if we avoid thinking of the psychological on mistaken analogy with the physical: the distinction between the psychological and the physical must not be thought of as a distinction between kinds of object (public and private). It is characteristic of Wittgenstein's idea of philosophy as a 'critique of language' that he believes that the failure of this analogy, and the emptiness of the idea of a private object, is something that language itself reveals. Thus, when we examine language carefully, we see that psychological language is different in its logic, or grammar, from physical language. What I want to do now is show how this idea is expressed in the *Tractatus*, and how it develops in the later philosophy in tandem with the evolution in Wittgenstein's conception of the logic of language and his approach to clarifying it.

2. THE EARLY VIEW

The psychological enters into the discussion twice in the *Tractatus*: first, in connection with the analysis of sentences of the form 'A believes that p' (*TLP*:

5.541–5.542), second, in connection with the question how much truth there is in solipsism (*TLP:* 5.6–5.641). I begin with the first analysis.

In the *Tractatus*, Wittgenstein's thought is governed by a number of preconceptions which have their root in a primitive idea of language. These preconceptions underlie Wittgenstein's claim that the propositions of our everyday language can be analysed in a way which shows them all to be truth-functions of logically independent elementary propositions which consist of absolutely simple names. He introduces the discussion of psychological language by observing that 'it looks as if it were possible for one proposition to occur in another in a different way', for in 'A believes that p', 'it looks as if the proposition p stood in some kind of relation to an object A' (*TLP:* 5.541). The surface form of the proposition tempts us to treat the proposition by analogy with ordinary relational propositions, although in this case the relation is not between objects, but between a subject and a proposition. The result of this failure to observe a difference in the logical form between psychological statements and statements that belong to physical language is that we hypostatise an ego: the subject of psychological ascription, the subject who thinks or entertains ideas.

Wittgenstein's response to this is not to try to show that the idea of the thinking subject is problematic, but to point out that the way pyschological propositions function shows that they are not relational propositions at all, for we don't determine the truth of these statements by means of correlating a fact with an object. Psychological propositions do not belong to the same system of propositions as elementary propositions and propositions built from these by means of the truth-operations; they are propositions of a quite different kind:

5.542   It is clear, however, that 'A believes that p', 'A has the thought that p', and 'A says p' are of the form ' "p" says p': and this does not involve a correlation of a fact with an object, but rather the correlation of facts by means of the correlation of their objects.

Thus, Wittgenstein draws our attention to the way in which the ascription of belief depends upon our recognition of the sense of someone's words. We can see how far this diverges from a fact-stating proposition when we recall that the correlation of objects, by means of which one fact (a propositional sign) comes to represent another (a possible state of affairs) depends upon the latter's sharing a form with the former. That is to say, the possible state of affairs which a proposition represents depends upon the horizon of possibilities for combining its elements in ways that represent possible states of affairs in which the objects for which the elements stand might figure. This is not something that can be determined in the way that a fact is, that is, by means of an inspection of what is actually present or occurring here and now, but depends upon a grasp of the possibilities that the elements of a proposition have for combining in further propositions. Thus, ' "p" says p' does not state a fact in the way that the proposition p itself states a fact, but attempts to put into words something which can only be shown by the symbolism as a whole. In the same way, 'A believes that p' does not state a fact (an intrinsic state of affairs which might be established by inspection), but gives expression to something which depends upon the relation between the sounds A utters or otherwise affirms and the symbolism of which they are a part, that is, upon what surrounds A's utterance and not what is intrinsic to it.

Careful attention to the way these psychological propositions function reveals that their use is grounded in a recognition of the meaning or significance of what is presented to us, that is, in something that is exhibited over time. Recognising another as a subject of psychological ascription is not like identifying an object, but closer to perceiving a pattern that has implications for what comes before and after. For Wittgenstein this is equivalent to saying 'that there is no such thing as . . . the subject' (*TLP*: 5.5421): there is nothing lying behind the expression of thoughts in language – nothing over and above the use of language – which turns propositional signs into thoughts. Thus, Wittgenstein's critique of language uncovers, or clarifies, the distinction between the psychological and the realm of facts, and thereby frees us from a psychologistic conception of the subject and of psychology as a domain of facts.

The second discussion of the psychological takes the form of a series of remarks on solipsism. In the remarks we have just been looking at, we might see Wittgenstein as concerned with the logic of 3rd-person psychological ascription; the remarks on solipsism now take up the investigation of the psychological from the perspective of the 1st-person use of language. Wittgenstein describes the purpose of these remarks as one of showing that 'what the solipsist *means* is quite correct; only it cannot be *said*, but makes itself manifest' (*TLP*: 5.62). Let us look first at the claim that what the solipsist means cannot be said. What the solipsist *says* is that '[t]he world is *my* world' (*TLP*: 5.62). Wittgenstein points out that the statement necessarily fails to express what the solipsist means, for, by referring to the subject in an apparent statement of fact, the solipsist is essentially presupposing that the subject is a part of the world, something that can be talked about or described in fact-stating language. Thus the solipsist's statement leads him to hypostatise the subject or treat it as one object among others. But this means that his attempt to give this object the sort of special status expressed in the claim that the world is my world becomes obviously absurd. In this way, Wittgenstein leads us, by a different route, to the same realisation that he expressed earlier, namely that '[t]here is no such thing as the subject that thinks or entertains ideas' (*TLP*: 5.631). The solipsist, like the philosopher who treats

'A believes that p' as a relational statement, makes the error of supposing that the subject for whom the world exists, or who represents the world in thought, can be spoken of in the same way as the objects which, combined into facts, make up the world.

What now of the claim that what the solipsist means is quite correct 'but makes itself manifest'? What the solipsist means is clearly connected with the distinctive status of his own 1st-person perspective. The idea that what he means 'makes itself manifest' suggests that Wittgenstein believes that the solipsists's attempt to put the distinctive status of his own 1st-person perspective into words is to be seen as a failed attempt to articulate something that is already shown, in some way, by language itself, and which can be brought out by the sort of critical reflection that Wittgenstein's idea of a critique of language recommends. Thus, if we are to understand what the solipsist (rather than his words) means, then we must not take what he says as a statement of fact, but must see him as trying to elucidate, or draw our attention to, something that is already manifest in language *prior* to his attempt to articulate it, and which we necessarily already grasp in understanding language. Wittgenstein offers his own elucidation of what it is about language that the solipsist is attempting to articulate as follows:

5.6   *The limits of my language* mean the limits of my world.
5.61   . . .
        We cannot think what we cannot think; so what we cannot think we cannot *say* either.
5.62   This remark provides the key to the problem, how much truth there is in solipsism.
        For what the solipsist *means* is quite correct; only it cannot be *said*, but makes itself manifest.
        The world is *my* world: this is manifest in the fact that the limits of *language* (of that language which alone I understand) mean the limits of *my* world.

One of the few points on which interpreters are generally agreed is that the expressions 'my language' and 'that language which alone I understand' do not refer to my own private language, but to my understanding of the ordinary, public language which, up to *TLP*: 5.6, Wittgenstein has been discussing. This public language is *my* language insofar as it is the language that I understand and in which I express my thoughts, beliefs, etc. Thus, we can see that both the world and the subject come into language, but in quite different ways. The world is mirrored in language, or laid down in it through the possibilities for description of the world that it makes available. The subject is not a part of the world that is mirrored in language, but is revealed in the use that a speaker makes of language to describe the world as he finds it. The distinctive status of the 1st-person, which Wittgenstein suggests the solipsist is attempting to articulate, is something that is shown, or manifest, in the application that I make of language in expressing my thoughts and perceptions of the world.

It immediately follows from this account of the way in which the distinctive status of the 1st-person shows itself that there is no 1st-person perspective whose distinctive status is absolute. The distinctive status of the 1st-person is shared across all speakers of the language, and is revealed in the general asymmetry of 1st-person and 3rd-person use that characterises language as a whole. What these reflections on solipsism lead us to, therefore, is a realisation that there is no private subject and no private world. There is the world that is laid down in our public language, about which all who use this language speak. The subject and his experiences are not parts of this world, but are revealed entirely through the application that the subject makes of public language in expressing his thoughts or describing the world as he finds it. It is the fact that the subject who thinks and for whom the world exists is not in this sense part of the world, but is shown in the application – the 1st-person use – that he makes of language, that prompts Wittgenstein to assert that philosophy has something essential to contribute to our understanding of the nature of subjectivity. For it is by seeing this aspect of our language – viz. the asymmetry of 1st-person and 3rd-person use – more clearly that we grasp what is distinctive about the psychological and what makes it impossible to treat it as part of the realm of physical nature.

3. LATER DEVELOPMENTS

Wittgenstein's way of expressing these points about subjectivity, in the *Tractatus*, is characteristically abstract and schematic. There is virtually no attempt either to address the details of our language of psychological description, or to explore the nature of the 1st-person/3rd-person asymmetry in any depth. His thoughts here seem like germs from which his later investigation of our psychological language-game grows. The significant turning point comes in the immediate post-Tractarian period, in which Wittgenstein comes to realise that his early conception of the logic of our language, which is based on the notations of Frege and Russell, is inadequate and his idea of analysis mistaken. By the time of the *Philosophical Remarks* (1975), Wittgenstein has rejected the idea that our language can be described or analysed in terms of the restrictive set of categories – name, predicate, relational expression, truth-function – that the logic of Frege and Russell provides, and has come to see that the notion of a tautology is irrelevant to the more fundamental idea that the propositions of logic are an articulation of inference rules that are already laid down in the formal connections that exist between the propositions of our language. This fundamental idea concerning logic remains, shorn of its connection with tautologies, more or less unaltered in Wittgenstein's later philosophy. So too does the idea that philosophy is a critique of language. But having abandoned his primitive picture of the essence of fact stating language, Wittgenstein now believes that all the logical distinctions between kinds of expression, and between different regions of our language, are only fully revealed in their actual use or application by speakers. There is still the same concern with elucidating the essence of language, but there is a fundamental switch from thinking that this can be grasped by thinking about language as a symbolism in abstraction from its concrete employment by speakers. Wittgenstein gradually comes to realise that understanding the essence of language – and the differences between the language-games that make it up – is something that depends upon our achieving a clarified view of the intricate details of what he calls 'the spatial and temporal phenomenon of language' (1984: §108), that is, of the different patterns of employment that characterise our use of language within our everyday, practical lives.

One result of this switch is that Wittgenstein's eyes are opened to the extraordinary complexity, the subtlety, and the ambiguity of our ordinary language, and hence to the difficulties in articulating, or clarifying, its essence. His investigation must attempt to capture the complexity and indeterminateness of our language, without either falsification or distortion. What he is trying to achieve, Wittgenstein believes, is an overview of one of the most complex phenomena in existence, and it is a struggle to attend properly to this complexity and the distinctions it reveals. Thus, the schematic thoughts of the *Tractatus* are now replaced by a meticulous articulation, not only of a general grammatical distinction between psychological and physical language, but of the grammatical differences – the differences in use – that distinguish one kind of psychological concept from another. However, underlying this profound shift in Wittgenstein's conception of the essence of language, and in his approach to capturing it, there remains a firm and continuous commitment to both the anti-psychologism of the *Tractatus* and to the following, associated, ideas: first, that there is an absolute distinction between the logic of psychological language and the logic of the language in which we describe the physical world; and second, that it is the distinctive logic (use, application) of psychological language that reveals the essence of subjectivity and the nature of the distinction between the subject and the world of nature that confronts him.

Wittgenstein's later investigation of the distinctive logic, or grammar, of our psychological language is thus firmly focused on distinctions that are revealed in the ways in which we operate with words, that is, in the variety of circumstances in which we use them, in the way in which we teach them to a child, in the ways we verify assertions employing them, in the role of disagreement and the degree of certainty that is possible in connection with these assertions, and so on. What we see, from the *Philosophical Remarks* onwards, is the way in which Wittgenstein's attention to how we actually operate with words leads him to an increasingly subtle conception of our psychological language – and of the phenomena it describes – as he becomes more and more open to its distinctions, its nuances, and its indeterminacies. Yet within this development, we can clearly discern the two basic strands of the Tractarian investigation: namely, the concern with the grammar of 3rd-person psychological description and with the asymmetry that is revealed in the contrast between 1st-person and 3rd-person employment of language. The switch of Wittgenstein's attention to the vast spectacle that the spatial and temporal phenomenon of language presents means that these themes are now developed in connection with the expression not only of thoughts and beliefs, but also of our sensations, emotions, intentions, images, etc. Although the picture of the psychological that he lays before us becomes inevitably more and more complex, there is the same underlying unity of purpose which we saw in the *Tractatus*: to show that the ideas of an ego inhabiting a body and of a private realm of consciousness arise only insofar as we are misled by a false analogy with physical language; these ideas make no connection with the way our psychological concepts actually function.

Thus, Wittgenstein uses the distinctive grammatical investigations that char-acterise his later method to show, on the one hand, that the idea of a private object within a psychological realm emerges as a result of a mistaken sense of analogy between psychological and physical concepts, and on the other, that the distinction, which we are mistakenly tempted to characterise as one be-tween kinds of objects, is already fully revealed in the distinctive grammar of 3rd-person and 1st-person uses of psychological language. As in the *Tractatus*, Wittgenstein's concern is, first of all, to diagnose and resist the very idea of the pyschological as a realm of intrinsic states or processes conceived on analogy with physical states or processes. 3rd-person psychological statements have an utterly distinctive use, which is sensitive, in complex and indefinable ways, to patterns of behaviour and context that are extended in both space and time. In their 3rd-person application, psychological concepts do not refer to intrinsic states, but, as in the *Tractatus*, relate to the meaning of what we see and hear. In this way their use implicitly connects with what surrounds, or forms the back-ground to, our psychological ascription. Secondly, Wittgenstein's concern is to show that the distinctive status of the 1st-person is not something that can be captured by appeal to my having something that is unique, but is expressed in the application of language, that is, in the asymmetry of 1st-person and 3rd-person use that is the defining characteristic of our use of psychological concepts.

SECTION THIRTEEN

PHILOSOPHY AND SOCIAL SCIENCE

55

THE METHODOLOGY OF THE SOCIAL SCIENCES

JAMES BOHMAN

As the social sciences began to come into their own in the early part of the twentieth century, the utility of the Neo-Kantian dualism between the human (*Geisteswissenschaften*) and the natural sciences (*Naturwissenschaften*) once again became controversial. Previously philosophers who were in favour of this distinction saw it as the only way to save the human sciences from the encroachment of the natural sciences, especially from positivism's denial of the status of 'science' to enquiries that did not issue in prediction and control. Such dualism demanded strict separation, marked by ontological differences involving distinctive features of the objects of study, such as their particularity rather than generality, or epistemological differences between understanding and empirical observation. After 1915 the participants in the debate changed as it shifted away from a conception of human sciences modelled on history or textual interpretation towards a debate about the social sciences themselves, specifically sociology and its theories of social action. Even those philosophers who maintained weakened versions of dualism did so for a different purpose. Distinctions were now formulated in *methodological* terms and the issue became how to understand distinct explanatory and interpretive tasks within the social sciences themselves.

Once formulated in methodological rather than ontological or transcendental terms, the divide between the sciences no longer seemed to be an unbridgeable gap. The issue now became not whether or not there are different legitimate methodologies, but whether they can be brought together in some methodological unity or should be left as a heterogeneous plurality of unrelated approaches. Once the discussion of the social sciences included well-developed disciplines as diverse as economics, sociology, and history, the task of distinguishing the human from the natural sciences became less important than that of figuring out how such disciplines and the diverse approaches within each of them might be brought 'under one roof', as Max Weber demanded for sociology.

1. MAX WEBER

Influenced by his research in historical sociology, Max Weber stands as one of the first to put the issue of the methodology of the social sciences in this surprisingly contemporary form. Rather than think about the status of social science in either/or terms, Weber sought to combine features of both the empirical and interpretative sciences in a conception of sociology as a science of social action. As opposed to other sciences, the sciences of social action are to combine the methodological principles and goals of the previously opposed types of science: because social actions have a hybrid status, an adequate scientific account of social action must have *both* explanatory and interpretive adequacy (Weber 1922b [1978: 4–8]). Thus while general theories can discover and explain regularities of behaviour, these general regularities must also be made intelligible as the product of intentional actions according to agent's purposes and normative self-understandings. This requirement of intelligibility, or interpretive adequacy, is made more complex by the reflexive status of the investigator as social actor, whose enquiry has an evaluative significance in a specific cultural situation.

This evaluative significance might be thought to engender scepticism about the rationality of the enterprise, on the grounds that it makes it dependent upon 'given' cultural values or 'gods and demons' (Weber 1922a [1949: 129–56]). Weber answered this question with scepticism about rationality in deciding ultimate values; but he anticipated the direction of debate in the following decades by arguing that the normative presuppositions of the social sciences were fundamentally practical and link social scientists to their cultural situation in much the way that knowledgeable social actors are themselves situated. The problem for the philosophy of the social sciences is thus not merely to leave the tensions among the various and heterogeneous methods and aims of social science in place but to show the possible interrelationships among them in a fruitful research practice that is reflexively situated in and guided by its own specific historical and social setting.

2. POSITIVISM

In its attempt to defeat interpretive dualism about the human sciences, positivism seems at first to contradict Weberian practical pluralism. Positivism sought the universal and necessary conditions for those empirical methods that unify enquiry in all domains of scientific enquiry. However, even positivism could not sustain this argument, as the development of Neurath's work shows (N. Cartwright, J. Cat, L. Fleck, and T. Uebel 1995). As the philosopher of the Vienna Circle most concerned with the social sciences and the practical implications of the unity of science as a social movement towards a rational society, Neurath consistently argued against the distinction between the natural and the human sciences (Neurath 1910 [1981: 23–46]). Although a metatheory, or 'Universal Science', would order all the sciences, it would not do so in a Comtean hierarchy, leading from the most fundamental (physics) to the least determined disciplines (the social sciences). Instead it develops methodological and theoretical connections inductively through an investigation of individual sciences, based on shared methodological principles (Neurath 1910). This form of the unity of science required a 'theory of scientific theories' whose normative prescriptions could not be developed separately from the actual sciences themselves, but which could be unified in a meta-theory or science of the sciences; and this basic conception of methodologically unified science continues informally in some naturalised epistemologies of today.

Even given the complex commitments and social interests that motivated his version of the unity of science thesis (which included non-reductive naturalism, the unity of science as a practical project, and Marx as a model for social enquiry), Neurath's own mounting criticisms of positivist epistemologies in the debate about protocol sentences seemed to tell against his own programme of a universal science unified around basic abstract methodological principles (Neurath 1932 [1983: 48–51]). The well-known image of science as a boat that must be rebuilt plank by plank while at sea rejects the epistemological foundations necessary for a clear separation of first-order science and second-order methodological unification. As the debates about protocol sentences and the demarcation problem were to show, the unity of the sciences was just as much dependent on foundationalist empiricism (to provide a basis for demarcating science and non-science) as the dualism of the sciences rejected by Neurath was dependent on transcendental arguments from Kantian epistemology. Without protocol sentences or reductive naturalism about law-like regularities at a fundamental level, it is hard to see how a single set of methodological prescriptions could be generated from the practices and results of the actual sciences themselves. Instead, the pragmatism that follows from 'Neurath's boat' suggests something similar to Weberian methodological pluralism whereby interconnections among the sciences are created according to various practical aims and social projects. Indeed, the anti-reductionism which led Neurath to leave room for the social sciences in the first place also led him to distinguish (as did Weber) between the abstract character of scientific concepts and the complexities of everyday historical reality (Neurath 1944). Thus, what is left of the project without universal methodological norms is a practical rather than a theoretical unity: the project of social reform. Science is then unified primarily as a discursive and social practice, much as pragmatists such as Dewey or Mead sought to unify science practically as the form of enquiry characteristic of democratic societies. The practical and political project of science is not, as Dewey notes, to apply science 'to human affairs', but rather 'in them' as the aspect of enquiry in cooperative practice (Dewey 1927).

3. HISTORIOGRAPHY, PHENOMENOLOGY, AND HERMENEUTICS

Idealist historiography, phenomenology, and hermeneutics emerged as the primary reactions to the positivist naturalism and unity-of-science thesis in their dominant and less subtle forms. By opposing the prevailing account of empiricist methodology and explanations, Collingwood argued against the unity thesis with a sharp idealist distinction between history on the one hand and behaviourist and nomological science on the other. While nomological sciences merely account for external relationships and behavioural regularities, historical sciences attempt (as Dilthey thought as well) to capture 'the inner side of events' and thus to develop internal relations among them (Collingwood 1946). Historical enquiry engages not only particular, unique, and nonrepeatable events, but employs explanations that require reliving the actor's experience and the holistic and practical context in which he or she lived rather than constructing generalisations among contingent events. As in hermeneutics, Collingwood saw the intelligibility of history as exhibiting a circular structure of interpretation: when the historian 'knows what has happened he already knows why it has happened' (Collingwood 1944). While this is because Collingwood thought that the intelligibility of intentions reveals the same underlying normativity of all thought, phenomenology and hermeneutics attempt to do without such normative assumptions about rationality or beliefs. Indeed it is the human sciences that provide the larger perspective in which to situate and judge the significance of the specific achievements of the empirical sciences. This anti-naturalist version of the distinction between the human and the natural sciences was offered in various forms by Edmund Husserl, Alfred Schütz, and Martin Heidegger.

As Husserl gradually abandoned his early focus on constitutive consciousness in favour of the social 'lifeworld' in which to situate meanings and concepts, his phenomenology becomes more socially concerned. He argues in his late writings that, while the sciences are universal in their aim, they are a specific historical project of European culture, which is now in crisis. The crisis arises from the lack of awareness of the status of 'Galilean' scientific concepts which are not justified by epistemic certainty or metaphysical correspondence. Instead, they are idealisations and abstractions from the social lifeworld, the presupposed background understanding operative 'behind the backs' of investigators that cannot be made fully explicit by them (Husserl 1936 [1970: 23ff.]). Following Husserl, Schütz broadened the focus of the phenomenological analysis of the lifeworld presuppositions to the social sciences as well, which he took to be grounded in the typifications of various kinds of social institutions, such as the way markets typify individuals as bundles of preferences. The social sciences presuppose these typifications or systems of relevance which enter into their analyses as Weberian ideal types (Schütz 1932 [1967: 167ff.]). Similarly, Heidegger analysed the natural sciences in terms of just one sort of orientation to the world, in which things are regarded as simply 'present to hand' and thus independent of the human significance of any active orientation to the world which encounters things as 'ready to hand' (Heidegger 1927 [1962: 114]). All these phenomenological analyses aim to show the presuppositions of scientific abstractions; and from this they infer the limited legitimacy of these sciences and their inability to clarify reflexively their own presuppositions and commitments. This reflective task requires concepts of meaning and intentionality as they operate in the everyday lifeworld.

Husserl still understood this lifeworld in theoretical rather than practical terms. Heidegger's analysis of human 'being-in-world' rejected this approach and in so doing provided the basis for a hermeneutics or the interpretative approach to the human sciences that is later exemplified in the 'thick descriptions' of cultural anthropologists such as Clifford Geertz. Whereas the natural sciences start with conceptions defined by their own research practices, the human sciences start with interpretations and thus from within 'the hermeneutic circle' of interpretations. The point of such a science is not to escape the hermeneutic circle via idealisations but to 'enter into it right way' (Heidegger 1927 [1962: 195]). This circularity entails that interpretation is inherently explication (*Auslegung*), the interpretation of interpretations. Heidegger does not, however, adopt the model of textual interpretation typical of earlier historical and hermeneutic approaches of the late nineteenth century, but rather seeks to explicate significance in terms of intersubjective practices and their holistic and practical 'referential context'.

Rather than focus on the way in which the background of practices creates a hermeneutic circle, Schütz analyses the 'genuine understanding' in terms of the lived experience of intersubjectivity (Schutz 1932 [1970: 113]). Such close descriptive analyses of everyday practices of intelligibility in dialogue and interaction influenced later ethnomethodological approaches articulated best by Harold Garfinkel. Here we see a significant methodological shift in terms of the position of the interpreter even in comparison with Heidegger's hermeneutic approach. The interpreter is not merely explicating practices or providing interpretations of interpretations. Rather, he or she occupies a particular perspective

on the activities in which meaning is constituted: the perspective of the participant in interaction and dialogue. The interpreter is, however, not merely one
more participant; he or she is a 'reflective participant' who analyses the structure
of intersubjectivity and shared significance that is at one and the same time the
basis and outcome of interpretation. Thus, Schütz's phenomenological approach
goes beyond merely criticising the presuppositions of positivism and develops a
distinctive methodology for the social sciences as reflective participation as the
practical engagement with others under the conditions of dialogue. This new
methodology has the consequence that Schütz accepts methodological and theoretical pluralism. He clearly recognises a variety of perspectives and approaches
in the social sciences, including the 3rd-person perspective of general theories
and nomological generalisations (Schütz 1932 [1970: 229ff.]). The validity
of each approach is not established empirically, but philosophically from the
reflective perspective of the transcendental phenomenology of the lifeworld.

4. CRITICAL THEORY AND PRAGMATISM

An alternative approach would not only analyse the interconnections of various
approaches and aspects of social world as a complex and practical whole, but
would also see philosophy and empirical social science as cooperating in the
enterprise of understanding the social world in which the researcher is involved
as a participant. The idea that empirical social science could cooperate with and
contribute to philosophical and normative analysis was the programme of the
Critical Theory of the Frankfurt School in the 1930s that Max Horkheimer
called 'interdisciplinary materialism'. As a programme for social science that is
at once empirical, normative, and practical, such a materialism is inherently
pluralistic: it must seek to combine not only the best social theories but also the
'most varied methods of investigation' (Horkheimer 1931 [1993: 13]). Given
that its theoretical and empirical work attempts to analyse modern society as a
whole, no one distinctive method, approach, or theory can capture it in all of
its dimensions and aspects. Moreover, pluralism is also suggested by the reflexive
and practical character of critical social science. A critical social scientist is not
only Schütz's reflective participant, but also a social actor engaged in a project
of practical change for the sake of emancipation, for the goal of 'liberating
human beings from all the circumstances that enslave them' (Horkheimer 1937
[1982: 188]). Methodological pluralism here reflects commitments to theoretical
holism and to practical reflexivity about the normative orientation of critical
enquiry itself. Philosophy provides a strong conception of rationality with which
to ground the resolution of the potential conflicts among often competing
explanatory perspectives.

Critical Theory's form of pluralism reveals distinct similarities with American pragmatism's view of the social sciences as engaged in the project of promoting the reform of a democratic society. While Horkheimer and other Critical Theorists had nothing but contempt for pragmatism's idea of a practical orientation (which they thought of as mere orientation to 'cash value' success), their attempt to combine normative and empirical components in a practical enterprise of social change reveals methodological and political commitments shared with the pragmatists (Habermas 1968 [1971]). In particular, the pragmatists articulated a more specific practical and social basis for reflexive social science: linguistic intersubjectivity and the role of science in democratic deliberation. Both of these ideals of enquiry gave the idea of public reason a communicative form, seeing the sciences as democratic and democracy as a form of enquiry. By shifting the debates in methodology towards particular reflexive and communicative abilities at work in everyday communication and problem solving, pragmatism located social sciences within the context of contemporary practices. Two pragmatists stand out in this regard.

George Herbert Mead provided an analysis of what is distinctive about human communication by reference to 'significant symbols' that create the space for reciprocity of perspective and role taking as well as intersubjectively shared experience; all human thought is 'inherently socialized' and science is a 'logical community' (Mead 1934: 379). The abilities of human communication employed in linguistic interaction are the same ones that the social scientist refines in enquiry into social norms of thought and action. These same abilities are required for participation in cooperative practices and democratic institutions. John Dewey spelled out why democracy seeks to institutionalise those practices and also why cooperative and pluralist methodology is the only possible practical model of social enquiry. Seen in this light, the social sciences have a political role to play: as enquiry into the basis for on-going cooperation, they provide the necessary evidence for judging various practical solutions and resolving social conflicts. The social scientist does not therefore offer solutions to problems, but enables normative reflection on our practices and participates in the public testing of various democratic reforms and experiments (Dewey 1935). Rather than providing instrumental knowledge for independently arrived at or given ends, they provide reflective knowledge about the ongoing basis of cooperation and the democratic self-regulation and public problem solving.

Both Pragmatism and Critical Theory thought of the practical orientation towards public self-reflection as an integral part of such social practices of enquiry, especially in so far as their success depends on making the terms of cooperation open to democratic testing and revision. Both are concerned with a peculiarly self-reflective activity: they make the political and social organisation of cooperative practices an object of enquiry, including the social organisation of enquiry itself. Critical Theory did so in the context of organised and co-operative interdisciplinary enquiry within the context of its Institute for Social Research; pragmatism conceived of the problem more generally in terms of the democratic organisation of society in which the plurality of different social per-spectives and roles make such enquiry more likely to be fruitful. Indeed, Dewey notes that social enquiry (as opposed to physical enquiry) is characterised by controversies concerning 'the efficacy of different methods of procedure', mak-ing it unlikely that only one of various alternative hypotheses will be accepted or rejected. Rather, 'the plurality of alternatives is the effective means for rendering inquiry more extensive (sufficient) and more flexible, more capable of taking cognizance of all the facts that are discovered' (Dewey 1938 [1986: 500]). Such pluralism suggests that we ought not to view social enquiry from the 'standpoint of theory', so that 'one theory must be accepted and the other rejected in toto' (Dewey 1938 [1986: 500]). As in Critical Theory, for Dewey 'full publicity' and 'uninhibited communication' are the strict conditions for self-reflective and democratic social enquiry (Dewey 1927 [1988: 339]).

These reflections show the common attempt to connect second-order re-flection and critical social enquiry to on-going transformations in the nature of democracy and the public sphere. Rather than simply testing particular poli-cies for their practical value or their actual consequences (Dewey 1938 [1986: 493]), some social enquiry examines the extent to which practices themselves are responsible for the problems that they are supposed to solve. At a certain point, first-order problem-solving breaks down for a lack of genuinely shared ends. Like Kuhn's distinction between normal and revolutionary science, second-order critical reflection considers whether or not the framework for cooperation itself needs to be changed. Such criticism is directed at current institutions as well as towards formulating new terms of cooperation under which problems are solved. Hence critical social theory contributes to democracy its method of enquiry into its own organisation and goals: the role of philosophically moti-vated social enquiry is to be 'the critical method of developing critical methods' (Dewey 1938 [1986: 437]). Such second-order reflection is part of a pluralist social enquiry, where reflection works out the terms of cooperation among the various disciplines and participants.

Much as in Neurath's understanding of the unity of science as a programme for reform, however, Dewey too often seems to assume that the ends of enquiry are already agreed upon simply by virtue of our social existence and thus need only to be specified by moral reflection and made efficacious by enquiry into the proper means to achieve already given 'consensual ends' or 'common interests in controlling consequences' (Dewey 1927 [1988: 314]). But introducing this distinction between the technical and moral aspects of reflection gives us no basis for thinking of second-order reflection precisely in those situations in which it is needed: we cannot assume consensus about the interests and ends that shape our practices when the continued cooperation itself is at stake. For this reason, Habermas found Peirce's forward-looking account of the role of consensus in enquiry as more appropriate to its critical role as a regulative ideal for, rather than a constitutive feature of, social life (Habermas 1968 [1971: 139]). Here the debates about methodological pluralism in the social science suggest not only a practical criterion for verification in the social sciences, but also for all social reforms and criticism. Adjudication among conflicting interpretations, criticisms, and explanations is ultimately practical and procedural. The issue is not to develop a general theory of rationality, but to show the social and communicative conditions of free and equal dialogue such that all could agree. Such a practical criterion further suggests that moral and epistemic features of social science cannot be distinguished, indeed that the social sciences are inherently normative or 'moral sciences'.

5. CONCLUSION

The debates about the methodology of the social sciences in this period began with great divergence but ended in a surprising convergence among the major and conflicting philosophical approaches. They converge because the shift to methodology and to the practical situation and goals of the social scientists made the ontological and epistemic demarcation problems that guided both sides of the previous debates more or less irrelevant. On the one side, the mounting arguments against the idea of protocol sentences led to the abandonment of pure observation as the basis of science. Positivism itself could not provide a clear and distinct demarcation between science and non-science in methodological terms. Faced with no opposition, proponents of understanding no longer needed to embrace dualism. On the other side, the idealist (ontological) and Neo-Kantian (epistemological) attempts to establish a clear distinction between the natural and the human sciences were abandoned for a methodological approach that sought possible interrelationships between interpretation and explanation in the social sciences. Formerly in the domain of transcendental analysis of presuppositions, interpretation was now used empirically to analyse linguistic interaction and grounded practically in everyday practical abilities of dialogue and participation in social practices. In both cases, the abandonment of the empiricist and Kantian demarcation problems led not only to methodological pluralism, but also to an increasing emphasis on the practical character of the social sciences.

Given a broad acceptance of pluralism, the practical character of social sciences becomes paramount. Social scientists are not only reflective participants in practices and in social communication, but also engaging in projects whose validity will be subject to practical forms of verification such as agreement or consensus. Neurath's non-reductive unity-of-science programme attempted to make social life better through rational reforms of practices and social organisation; Critical Theory sought to initiate reflection among actors so that they could change their practices and make consensus the basis of social life; and Pragmatism saw the role of enquiry as a cooperative practice that could lead to the democratisation of complex modern societies. Rejecting any strict methodological distinction between the human and natural sciences does not have the consequences it had prior to Weber, Neurath, Critical Theory, and Pragmatism. Their common pluralism permits as many different methodological and theoretical approaches as there are practical projects and goals. The task of both the social scientist and the participant is to reconcile these diverse methods and goals both practically and politically. This practical possibility demands not only a normative and politically involved social science; it also establishes a basis for the practical verification of explanations and interpretations in pluralistic social sciences.

THE RISE OF SOCIAL ANTHROPOLOGY

MERRILEE H. SALMON

1. INTRODUCTION: A SCIENCE OF ANTHROPOLOGY?

Social anthropology studies the construction and mechanisms of social systems, as well as the interactions among these systems, their members, and the larger environment. Social anthropology embraces a spectrum of theoretical approaches, including but not limited to evolutionism, diffusionism, and functionalism. The evolutionary approach of early social anthropologists differs from the evolutionary theory that today's biologists espouse. Contemporary biologists reject the view that evolution is progressive, whereas nineteenth-century evolutionists believed that human societies evolve from 'primitive' forms to those represented in their own 'advanced' European civilisations. Diffusionists, in contrast to evolutionists, see new social forms arising, either spontaneously or in response to internal or external pressure, in the context of a particular social and environmental setting. Once a new form takes hold, it may spread to other groups. The diffusionist research programme emphasises locating the original source of an idea and tracing its spread. Functionalism eschews the historical (or pseudo-historical) character of the other two approaches, and focuses on the functions served by various social institutions or the functional interrelationships among the constituent parts of a larger social system.

Social anthropology as understood in this chapter is one of the four main fields of anthropology, and includes what is often called 'cultural anthropology'. The other fields are physical anthropology, which studies how modern humans came to assume their present physical form and how their biological characteristics determine their relationships to the rest of their environment; archaeology, which studies humans by examining the remains of their material culture; and linguistic anthropology, which studies human development and diversity by investigating the history and structure of languages.

In this chapter, I discuss the philosophical themes that informed the work of social anthropologists from 1870 to 1945. During this period, a pervasive and even overriding concern was the attempt to establish social anthropology as a science. Preliterate societies seemed to constitute ideal laboratories for natural experiments that could further the discovery of laws of human behaviour. The diversity of physical, cultural, and social environments that anthropologists encountered in their research offered the opportunity to investigate which qualities of humans belonged to their fundamental nature, and which were inessential. The anthropologist, moreover, could judge which sets of social arrangements worked poorly or well. Social anthropologists believed that their work in the service of pure science had important practical applications; the beginnings of social anthropology are permeated with the vision of social reform. A darker aspect of the practical applications of social anthropology also emerges, however. Since social anthropologists carried out most of their fieldwork in the colonies of the dominant Western nations, and with the support of colonial governments, the anthropologists have been accused of formulating theories that helped to oppress and control indigenous peoples.

Although social anthropologists were trying to discover social laws, they were not the first to do so. Sir Edward Evans Pritchard (1964: 21), for example, identifies C. de Montesquieu as 'the founder of the lineage of social anthropology' because in *The Spirit of Laws* (1748), Montesquieu analysed functional interrelationships among social institutions and regarded them as candidates for laws (Malefijt 1974: 80). The issue of laws of social behaviour is intimately related to the possibility of social controls, and thus to philosophical questions of what constitute good social arrangements and the degree to which individual humans can or should be moulded to meet the needs of society.

2. THE BEGINNINGS OF MODERN SOCIAL ANTHROPOLOGY: MORGAN AND TYLOR

Two influential works by evolutionists, *Systems of Consanguinity and Affinity in the Human Family*(Morgan 1870) and *Primitive Culture* (Tylor 1871), mark a useful starting point to discuss the rise of social anthropology. Morgan's work on systems of kinship and social organisation was grounded in his lifelong study of the Iroquois, as well as on data gathered from questionnaires mailed to missionaries and diplomatic representatives around the world. His comparative work on kinship invoked a common-cause principle to account for the evolution of structural similarities in systems of kinship terminology among widely separated groups. Karl Marx was so impressed with Morgan's analyses of social organisation that he urged Friedrich Engels to make Morgan's work known to a wider audience (Engels 1884). Tylor, who held the first British university post in anthropology, gathered data on hundreds of societies. He used the comparative method to try to understand the development of social institutions (Tylor 1889). His work inspired

James Frazer, author of the widely read and extremely influential *The Golden Bough* (1890), to turn from classics to anthropological studies. Both Morgan and Tylor assume the psychic unity of humans, and regard cultural evolution as a progression through stages of social development (savagery, barbarism, and civilisation). Depending on the circumstances in which a group finds itself, its members might spend a longer or shorter time in any of the stages. Although progression to the next stage is the norm, circumstances can hasten or retard evolution. In some cases a group might even pass out of existence before advancing to the next stage. Anthropologists in their worldwide studies can catch glimpses of various stages,and thus see the laws of progressive evolution at work.

Although Morgan lived and worked closely with his Iroquois informants, and Tylor participated in a brief ethnological expedition to Mexico, their studies, like Frazer's, depend more on library research than on fieldwork. The following generation of social anthropologists, however, made fieldwork the *sine qua non* of professional respectability. Not surprisingly, two of the most influential, Franz Boas and Bronislaw Malinowski, were both trained in the physical sciences. These pioneers shared a commitment to the possibility of scientific anthropology and clearly understood the importance of direct observation, hypothesis formation and testing.

3. CULTURAL RELATIVISM AND THE REJECTION OF PROGRESSIVE EVOLUTION

Boas, as a result of his fieldwork with indigenous peoples of the American Northwest, gradually abandoned the evolutionary perspective and its accompanying racism. He also criticised the simplistic use of the comparative method, which assumes that similar effects always result from similar causes, and urged anthropologists to pay greater attention to the historical development of individual cultures in the context of their own particular physical and social environments (1940). Because Boas focuses on gathering data about the details of a culture in its historical context, he has been accused of naïve inductivism in his attempts to establish general laws of human behaviour. Boas never abandoned his hope for discovering universal laws. By the end of his career, however, he increasingly turned his attention to recording information about societies whose survival in their traditional form was threatened.

Among Boas's chief contributions to anthropology were his recognition and demonstration that the languages, artworks, religious beliefs, practices, and values of indigenous peoples were not mere stages on the way to a more civilised way of life. The view that the culture of each group must be understood and valued in the context of its own setting is known as *cultural relativism*. Boas's respect for the many diverse and exquisite ways of constructing satisfactory sets of social institutions inspired much important anthropological research, including the innovative linguistic studies of Benjamin Lee Whorf (1956) and Edward Sapir (1921). Cultural relativism is now considered a hallmark of anthropological wisdom. Although some anthropologists, drawing on the work of Boas's famous students Margaret Mead (1928) and Ruth Benedict (1934) assume that *ethical relativism*, which denies any extracultural standards for ethics, is a consequence of cultural relativism, such a view cannot be supported in Boas's work (Salmon 1997).

4. BRITISH SOCIAL ANTHROPOLOGY AND THE RISE OF FUNCTIONALISM

Relatively late in Boas's long career, the functionalist approaches that are so closely identified with British social anthropology began to dominate the field. Malinowski and Radcliffe-Brown deserve particular attention. Malinowski earned a PhD from Cracow in philosophy of Science before going to the London School of Economics, and was clearly influenced by Ernst Mach's (1886) phenomenalism and functionalist interpretation of laws of science. Malinowski's extensive and meticulous field studies in the Australian territories were the basis for his anthropological writings, which sold millions of copies and continue to be read by the general public as well as students (1929, 1944, 1954). Malinowski regarded cultural institutions as society's way of satisfying the various biological, psychological, and social needs of individual members of the society. Whereas all humans need food, shelter, a means to reproduce, and the like, the manner of satisfying these needs depends on environmental and historical factors particular to a given society. Malinowski held that to understand any cultural form, however, one need not know how it arose, but must instead grasp the function it serves in terms of a complex set of primary and derived requirements for human survival.

Malinowski's focus on individual biological and psychological needs in his adaptive account of culture poses theoretical difficulties for understanding and explaining societies as integrated units. In part because of this problem, Alfred Radcliffe-Brown dissociated himself from the individualism and functionalism of Malinowski, and offered an alternative holistic theory of *structural functionalism* that addresses directly the issue of social integration (1952). Radcliffe-Brown was a true disciple of Emile Durkheim (1895) both in his functional explanations and in his commitment to the primacy of social over individual facts. Radcliffe-Brown treated social systems analogously to biological systems, and tried to understand each feature and each subsystem of a social system in terms of its contribution to the functioning of the whole. Thus, for example, one subsystem of social systems, the kinship nomenclature system, helps to maintain the social system by classifying kin into relevant categories with respect to duties owed, expectations of assistance of various kinds, and suitability as marriage partners. Radcliffe-Brown hoped that by investigating kinship nomenclatures in various social systems, and noting structural similarities, one would eventually be able to state functional laws relating, for example, particular types of nomenclature systems to other features of social systems. Such laws lack the requisite temporal order of traditional causal laws, but in this respect they resembled the sort of laws that Mach and Bertrand Russell (1914) believed were truly scientific. Like Boas, Radcliffe-Brown eventually conceded his lack of progress in discovering nontrivial laws of anthropology. Some of his distinguished students, such as Meyer Fortes (1953) continued to insist on the scientific nature of anthropology, and to link this view with the search for laws. Others though, including Evans-Pritchard, disagreed. They, along with Boas's students, took the position that anthropology was a historical discipline rather than a scientific one. The disagreement about whether anthropology is 'science' or 'history' continues to divide contemporary anthropologists.

5. SOCIAL ANTHROPOLOGY AND COLONIALISM

The complex relationships between social anthropology and colonial governments are explored in Kuklick (1991). She argues that although anthropological research depended on the support of colonial administrators and private agencies with an interest in supporting government policy, the anthropologists were not mere instruments used to oppress indigenous peoples. Most colonial powers saw themselves as benevolent rulers, whose attempts to preserve the peaceful relationships necessary to foster trade were advantageous to the people whom they governed. The British, moreover, were committed to a policy of 'indirect rule', governing their colonies by engaging the support of indigenous political structures. To govern in this way, they needed to understand both how indigenous structures worked and how to maintain their stability. At the upper levels of government, those responsible for colonial affairs turned to anthropologists for advice. Anthropologists of different theoretical persuasions, however, disagreed about what sort of advice to give. Evolutionists, diffusionists, and functionalists competed for funds that would allow them to conduct field research and respond to government queries. Functionalists were most successful in obtaining funds, but their recommendations were not always followed. While Malinowski's

arguments might persuade the funding agency, they would not necessarily overcome the evolutionist commitments of field officers who were responsible for
implementing government programmes. Functionalism thrived in part because
of the support of the British colonial government; it is not so clear that colo-
nialism's fortunes depended on the advice given by anthropologists.

WESTERN MARXISM AND
IDEOLOGY CRITIQUE

ALEX CALLINICOS

The Russian Revolution of October 1917 and the subsequent formation of the communist International encouraged a philosophical recasting of Marxism. This involved crucially the rejection of the naturalistic interpretation of historical materialism which had prevailed in the Second International. Thus Antonio Gramsci hailed the October Revolution as a 'revolution against *Capital*', that is, against the conception elaborated by Kautsky and Plekhanov of history as an evolutionary process governed by natural laws which operated by 'irresistible' necessity. The thought was that the Bolsheviks' attempt to carry through a socialist revolution in an economically backward country and their stress on the indispensable role of a vanguard party in the class struggle required a version of Marxism in which the driving force of change was, not the development of the productive forces, but the constitution of classes as revolutionary subjects.

1. GEORG LUKÁCS

Various theorists – for example, Karl Korsch and Gramsci himself – participated in this projected philosophical revolution. But its key work was undoubtedly Georg Lukács's *History and Class Consciousness* (1923). Lukács brought to Marxism an already formed and sophisticated philosophical sensibility shaped by Neo-Kantianism. A pupil of Simmel and Weber, he took from them chiefly a sense of the extreme fragmentation of modern society. Whatever formal coherence might arise from the use of instrumental rationality to discover the most efficacious means to attain arbitrarily chosen goals, capitalism was unable to integrate its different aspects into a self-equilibrating whole. Individual actors confronted a social world which together they had created, but whose overall workings they were unable either to understand or to control. Developing Marx's analysis of commodity fetishism in *Capital*, Vol. I, Lukács argued that the structure of capitalism was one of *reification*, in which social relations were transformed into things, treated as natural phenomena that could not be changed by consciously directed human action.

The significance of Marxism in this context was precisely that it provided an understanding of capitalist society as a totality. Indeed, Lukács argues that the treatment of social institutions and practices as different aspects of a integrated totality is definitive of the Marxist method: '*The primacy of the category of totality is the bearer of the principle of revolution in science*' (1923 [1971: 27]). At the very least this assertion represented a significant shift of emphasis from the versions of Marxism dominant in the Second International. Not that Lukács ignores economic processes. On the contrary, he argues that it is the process of commodification – the transformation under capitalism not only of goods and services but also of every aspect of social life into commodities bought and sold on the market – that underlies the structure of reification.

The question naturally arises of how it is possible to arrive at the kind of comprehension of the social totality which Lukács claims Marxism offers if experience is as thoroughly reified and fragmented as he claims. The answer is provided by one of the most distinctive themes of the book, namely the account it offers of class consciousness. Lukács has what one might call a perspective theory of ideology. The concept of ideology as developed by Marx implies that beliefs are socially caused. But there are various ways in which this causal influence on our beliefs might operate. Perhaps the the most obvious is that various social institutions directly shape either the beliefs themselves or the processes through which beliefs are formed. Thus Marxists often depict the education system, churches, and the mass media as both directly inculcating certain beliefs and inhibiting the development of the critical powers of those subject to them.

While Lukács does not explicitly reject this view of the social causation of beliefs, his own emphasis lies elsewhere. He suggests that an actor's beliefs are to a large extent a consequence of the place he or she occupies in the social structure. More specifically, a person's position in the relations of production, and the class identity and interests which arise from this position, form the perspective from which he or she views the world. It follows that one can impute the kind of consciousness appropriate to a particular class location:

By relating consciousness to the whole of society it becomes possible to infer the thoughts and feelings which men would have in a particular situation if they were *able* to assess both it and the interests arising from it in their impact on immediate action and on the whole structure of society. That is to say, it would be possible to infer the thoughts and feelings appropriate to their objective situation . . . Now class consciousness consists in fact of the appropriate and rational reactions 'imputed' (*zugerechnet*) to a particular typical position in the process of production. (1923 [1971, p. 51])

Lukács stresses that this imputed class-consciousness does not necessarily correspond to the actual beliefs of individual members of the particular class in question. Nevertheless, it is sufficiently effective, particularly at moments of major historical crisis, to provide the basis of the analysis of the actual consciousness of the two main classes in capitalist society, the proletariat and the bourgeoisie. The bourgeoisie's dependence on the exploitation of the working class sets limits to its ability to arrive at an understanding of capitalist society as a whole. Its major theorists may achieve profound partial insights, but a grasp of the totality eludes them. For since that totality depends on the extortion of surplus-value from the proletariat, the bourgeoisie would not be able to maintain either its ideological dominance over other classes or indeed a sense of its own moral right to rule if it were to acknowledge this reality.

Similarly, during economic crises the bourgeoisie is forced to confront in a confused way the fact that capitalism is an a historically transitory social system inherently liable to move through a destructive cycle of boom and slump:

But equally it is something the bourgeoisie can never fully understand. For the recognizable background to this situation is the fact that 'the *real barrier* of capitalist production is *capital itself*' [Marx]. And if this insight were to become conscious it would indeed entail the self-negation of the capitalist class.

In this way the objective limits of capitalist production become the limits of the class consciousness of the bourgeoisie . . . *The fact that it must necessarily remain in ignorance of the objective economic limitations of its own system expresses itself as an internal, dialectical contradiction in its class consciousness.* (1923 [1971: 63–4])

In the central essay of *History and Class Consciousness*, 'Reification and the Consciousness of the Proletariat', Lukács explores this 'tragic dialectics of the bourgeoisie' further (1923 [1971: 65]). Analysing what he calls the 'Antinomies of Bourgeois Thought', he argues that Western philosophy from Descartes to Dilthey and Rickert has been unable to develop a rational conception of the social whole, either denying the possibility of arriving at such a conception, or producing a mystified version (Hegel's Absolute is the prime example of the latter). This failure corresponds to the position of the bourgeoisie, able to rationalise specific institutions or practices, but not to provide any coherent overall order.

It is the proletariat, by contrast, that is able to develop the comprehensive understanding denied bourgeois thought. The extraction of surplus-value on which the capitalist economy depends arises from the transformation of labour-power into a commodity purchased and sold on the labour-market. The worker thus represents the most extreme form of the commodification and reification pervasive in capitalist society, the reduction of persons to things. Precisely because of this, it is from the worker's standpoint that it is possible to arrive at a real insight into the nature of this society:

his immediate existence integrates him as a pure, naked object into the production process. Once this immediacy turns out to be the consequence of a multiplicity of mediations, once it becomes evident how much it presupposes, then the fetishistic forms of the commodity system begin to dissolve: in the commodity the worker recognizes himself and his own relations with capital. Inasmuch as he is capable of raising himself above the role of object his consciousness is the *self-consciousness of the commodity*; or in other words it is the self-knowledge, the self-revelation of the capitalist society founded on the production and exchange of commodities. (1923 [1971: 168])

Lukács does not argue that every worker actually attains an understanding of the social totality. It is rather that the class-consciousness appropriate to the position occupied by the proletariat in capitalist relations of production involves such an understanding. Since workers' exploitation is the basis of bourgeois society, articulating their interests requires a recognition of this fact, and, beyond this, of the historically transitory character of capitalism and of the dynamic and internally contradictory nature of the historical process itself. Thus Marxism, formulated on the basis of a political identification with the proletariat and its interests, represents a conceptual articulation of the kind of understanding implied by this class's location within capitalist society. Since it is only from a working-class perspective that this society can be fully made sense of, '[h]istorical materialism in its classical form . . . means the *self-knowledge of capitalist society*' (1923 [1971: 229]).

Behind this recasting of Marxism lies a left-Hegelian reading of the dialectic in which 'thought can only grasp what it has itself created'. The proletariat is 'the identical subject-object of history', capable of understanding capitalism because it is created by its labour (1923 [1971: 121–2]). On this basis Lukács could vehemently repudiate the determinism of Second International Marxism, and insist that socialism would arise, not from the automatic workings of impersonal economic mechanisms, but through the political constitution of the working class as a self-conscious revolutionary subject. Though it proved too unorthodox for a Third International in the process of being subordinated to Soviet foreign policy during the mid-1920s, *History and Class Consciousness* had a major impact on theoretical debates in Weimar Germany; it helped to provide the starting point for the development of a Western Marxist tradition located in the academy rather than in the labour movement, and preoccupied with ideology and consciousness rather than with capitalist economic structures.

2. KARL MANNHEIM

The idea that beliefs reflected the perspective on the world entailed by a particular social location found a ready audience in an intellectual climate where it seemed increasingly implausible to treat ideas as essentially detached from the historical context of their formulation. The sticking point came, however, with the epistemologically privileged position which Lukács accorded the proletariat. On the one hand, a conception of subjectivity as somehow self-constituting and self-justifying was coming under increasing challenge, for example, from Heidegger in *Being and Time*. On the other hand, even intellectuals sympathetic to Marxism found the idea of the working class as 'the identical subject-object of history' hard to swallow in an era when the left was suffering catastrophic defeats at the hands of fascism.

But if no position offered a privileged insight into the nature of the total-ity, surely the social causation of beliefs implied some sort of relativism, in which the world-views of rival classes clashed without there being any ra-tional means of adjudicating between them? This problem forms one of the main themes of Karl Mannheim's attempt to develop a sociology of knowledge (*Wissensoziologie*). At the basis of this sociology lies Lukács's perspective theory of ideology: 'A position in the social structure carries with it . . . the probability that he who occupies it will think in a certain way. It signifies with existence oriented with reference to certain meanings (*Sinnangerichtessein*)' (1929 [1936: 264]). In specific studies, for example, his 1925 *Habilitationsschrift* on German romantic conservatism, Mannheim sought to develop a method of 'sociological imputation' which would establish the connection between particular 'styles of thinking' and social strata (1984 [1986: 36ff.]).

Yet despite the influence which Lukács's version of Marxism manifestly ex-ercised on his thought, Mannheim sought to go beyond *History and Class Con-sciousness*. He distinguishes between partial and total conceptions of ideology. The first is present when one of the parties to a debate or conflict seeks to expose the interests which the other's position seeks to conceal. The latter refers to 'the ideology of an age or of a concrete historico-social group, e.g. of a class, when we are concerned with the characteristics and composition of the total structure of the mind of this epoch or of this group'. Marxism deserves the credit for hav-ing formulated the total conception of ideology. But: 'Nothing was to prevent the opponents of Marxism from availing themselves and applying it to Marx-ism itself' (1929 [1936: 49–50, 67]). Ideology-critique and counter-critique, the exposure of each side's 'false consciousness', of the social roots of rival belief-systems, thus transforms the socio-political conflicts which, for example, destroyed the Weimar Republic into 'the crisis of scientific thought'. For 'in the measure that the various groups sought to destroy their adversaries' confidence in their thinking by the most modern intellectual method of radical unmask-ing, they also destroyed, as all positions gradually came to be subjected to analysis, man's confidence in human thought in general' (1929 [1936: 34, 37]).

Mannheim believes that the sociology of knowledge can offer a way out of this crisis. It can do so because it renders explicit one of the main implications of the total conception of ideology, namely that an absolute conception of knowledge, according to which thought exists essentially without historical and social determinations, is untenable. Thought is situationally determined, reflecting its specific social setting. Mannheim therefore distinguishes relativism, which presupposes an absolute conception of knowledge and accordingly treats any evidence of situational determination as implying that objective knowledge is unattainable, from what he calls *relationism*: 'Relating individual ideas to the total structure of a given historico-social subject should not be confused with a philosophical relativism which denies the validity of any standards and of the existence of order in the world' (1929 [1936: 254]).

'Relationism' forms the epistemological basis of the sociology of knowledge. Rather than, as Lukács does, argue that the class position of the proletariat allows it to arrive at an objective understanding of the social totality, Mannheim believes that the theoretical distortions produced by rival sectional interests tend to cancel each other out: 'It seems inherent in the historical process itself that the narrowness and the limitations which restrict one point of view tend to be corrected by clashing with the opposite points of view.' By demonstrating to the contending parties the genesis of their views in social locations which limit their ability to understand the issues, the sociology of knowledge thus makes possible 'a broad, dynamic mediation [*dynamische Vermittlung*] of conflicting points of view' (1929 [1936: 72, 144]).

Though Mannheim denies any class a priviliged insight into the whole, he nevertheless argues that this function of providing a provisional synthesis of the rival perspectives has a definite social location. The 'experimental outlook' required to play such a role can only be developed by 'a relatively classless stratum which is not too firmly situated in the social order', namely what he calls (after Alfred Weber) the 'free-floating intelligentsia' (*freischewebende Intelligentz*) (1929 [1936: 137–8]). The decline of class consciousness in the increasingly bureaucratised mass societies of the West may well, Mannheim believes, facilitate the assumption of this mediating function by intellectuals.

3. THE FRANKFURT SCHOOL

In advancing 'the ideal of an essentially human point of view' through which, 'by juxtaposing the various points of view, each perspective may be recognized as such and a new level of objectivity attained' Mannheim was offering a relatively optimistic take on the possibility of reconciliation in contemporary society (1929 [1936: 266]). The Frankfurt School, like him, adopted elements of Lukács's analytical framework while rejecting the idea of the proletariat as the identical subject-object of history, but, unlike Mannheim, they took absolutely no comfort from contemporary social and political developments. Thus, on the one hand, starting from Lukács's critique of reification, they portrayed social experience in liberal capitalism as systematically fragmented by the penetration of every aspect of life by commodity relationships and its subordination to them. On the other hand, they denied the possibility of arriving at the kind of total understanding to which Lukács had counterposed reified everyday experience.

Thus in his celebrated essay 'Traditional and Critical Theory' (1937), Max Horkheimer argues that 'traditional theory', by which he means the various schools of academic philosophy and social science, is fatally disabled by its intellectual fragmentation, which in turn reflects the process of relentlessly increasing specialisation that is one of the main consequences of capitalist economic domination. 'Critical theory', by contrast, seeks to understand the world in the way recommended by Marx and Lukács, historically and dynamically. But Horkheimer disjoins this understanding from the working class, arguing that '[e]ven the situation of the proletariat is, in this society, no guarantee of correct knowledge' (1972, p. 213). The very processes of reification which Lukács had analysed were blocking the development of the revolutionary class-consciousness that he had imputed to the proletariat.

This diagnosis raised, in even more acute form than Mannheim's sociology of knowledge, the question of the epistemological basis on which ideology-critique could pursued. The Frankfurt School rejected his solution. Thus Theodor Adorno wrote: 'the very intelligentsia that pretends to float freely is fundamentally rooted in the being that must be changed and which it merely pretends to criticise. For it the rational is the optimal functioning of the system, which postpones the catastrophe without asking whether the system in its totality is not in fact the optimum in irrationality' (1955 [1967: 48]). But according to what criteria can 'the system' be judged irrational? This problem was radicalised when in *Dialectic of Enlightenment* (written in 1944) Horkheimer and Adorno implicated reason itself in the process of social domination; it would continue to be a major source of difficulty in the subsequent history of Western Marxism.

SECTION FOURTEEN

ETHICS, RELIGION, AND THE ARTS

FROM INTUITIONISM TO EMOTIVISM

JONATHAN DANCY

Moral philosophy during the period under review was marked by the dominance in England of a form of ethical intuitionism that arose in response to G. E. Moore's *Principia Ethica* (1903). By the mid-1930s this began to be challenged, both in England and in the United States, by various forms of emotivism. In some isolation from this debate, Dewey continued to write extensively on ethics.

1. INTUITIONISM

The intuitionist school consisted of H. A. Prichard, W. D. Ross, H. W. B. Joseph, and E. F. Carritt in Oxford and C. D. Broad and A. C. Ewing in Cambridge. Prichard should probably be considered the leader of the school, though he published the least; Broad called Prichard 'a man of immense ability whom I have always regarded as the Oxford Moore' (1971: 14).

The intuitionists believed that rightness and goodness were distinct qualities, qualities that such things as people, actions, emotions, motives, intentions, and consequences could have. They were interested in the nature of and relation between these two qualities and in the distinction between intrinsic and extrinsic forms of them, and in which things in fact have these properties. Ross, for instance, argued that there was no such thing as instrumental goodness, that is, value as a means (1930: 133, 1939: 257); but he insisted that there was such a thing as intrinsic value, and that it was distinct from intrinsic rightness. Further, nothing was capable of being both intrinsically good and intrinsically right (Prichard 1912: 5–6).

The view that rightness and goodness are distinct qualities was held in conscious opposition to Moore's (1903) attempt to define the right as that which promotes the most good, and also to his weaker (1912) view that though we are dealing here with distinct properties, the only way for an action to be right is for it to promote the most good. In refusing to take this line, the intuitionists saw themselves as rejecting all forms of Utilitarianism. Like Ewing (1929), Ross (1930: ch. 2) argued that there are many other ways in which actions can get to be right. He contrasted the general duty of beneficence with special duties such as that of gratitude and those deriving from acts of promising, taking the latter not to be concerned with the promotion of valuable consequences, and suggesting that the special duties are more important than the general duty.

In other respects, however, the intuitionists found much to agree with in Moore's position. They accepted Moore's doctrine of organic unities, they agreed that we have a general duty to maximise value, they saw no prospect of identifying either goodness or rightness with any natural property (though they allowed that the evaluative supervenes on the natural, and that moral properties are consequential, that is, obtain *because of* the natural properties of their bearers), they accepted that no action is intrinsically good, and they offered accounts of the bearers of intrinsic value that were very similar to the one that emerges at the end of *Principia Ethica*. In reading them, one is clear that Moore set the agenda for discussion for the next fifty years. In many respects, indeed, it is not wrong to classify Moore as an intuitionist. It depends what one takes intuitionism to be. Paul Edwards (1955: ch. 4) takes intuitionism to be the claim that goodness and rightness are unanalysable non-natural qualities. On this count, the Moore of 1903 is half an intuitionist and the Moore of 1912 is a whole one. J. O. Urmson (1975) takes twentieth-century intuitionism to be a form of pluralism; but one must be careful to distinguish pluralism about values from pluralism about duties. Moore was a value-pluralist, but held that we have really only one duty, to maximise value. The intuitionists took it, by contrast, that we have many irreducibly different duties. Rashdall (1907: xiv) defines intuitionism as the view that actions are pronounced right or wrong without reference to consequences; but Ross calls this view 'out and out intuitionism' (1939: 79) and says that it is plainly false.

The view that rightness and goodness are distinct instantiable qualities, and the doctrines of Moore's that I have cited, were far from being the only ones common to the intuitionists, however. They were remarkably unanimous on a wide range of issues. They agreed first and foremost on Ross's conception of prima facie duties (1930: ch. 2). There was some internal debate about how best to express this doctrine, and perhaps the term 'pro tanto' used by Broad (1930: 282) would have been a better choice than 'prima facie'. (Prichard suggested 'claims'; Carritt offered 'responsibilities'.) But the general idea was agreed; indeed Ewing called it 'one of the most important discoveries of the century in moral philosophy' (1959: 126). Ross held that what we first notice is that certain features make a difference to how we should act in the case before us. We infer from this, by a process called intuitive induction, that these features make the same difference wherever they occur; one that counts in favour of action here counts generally in favour. There is a wide variety of such features, and any action that has one of them is called by Ross 'prima facie right' or a 'prima facie duty'. What is more, there is no prospect of reducing our varied prima facie duties to anything less than a list of three or four general types. Some of the relevant features concern the consequences of our action, but a significant number do not, and this is why consequentialism is false. These prima-facie duties combine to determine our 'duty proper', that is, what we actually ought to do in the present case. The action we should do is the one favoured by the balance of prima-facie duty. Which action that is, however, is something we can never be certain about. We can be certain that a feature is one that makes any action that has it a prima-facie duty, but we cannot be certain about duty proper. This theory is challengeable in various respects, but it still seems to me to be a lasting contribution to moral theory, one that is of value whatever one thinks of intuitionism as a whole.

The intuitionists also agreed on a conception of rightness as a sort of fittingness between action and situation which derived from Broad 1928: 79–80 (Ross 1939: 52ff.; Ewing 1947: 132), and originally of course from Richard Price, the founding father of intuitionism (Selby-Bigge 1897: 154–5, para. 670). They all accepted a broadly 'Humean' conception of motivation as the product of a combination of belief and desire, and accepted the possibility of moral judgement (the recognition of a duty) failing entirely to motivate the judger, in the absence of appropriate desire (Prichard 1928: 225; Ross 1939: 226–8; Broad 1930: 107, 274 – but see Prichard 1912: 11 for a different view under which the sense of obligation can move one in the absence of desire). They also agreed that acts are never good in themselves, but can only be called good in respect of their motives or of their consequences (Ross 1930: 43; Broad 1928: 78–9; Joseph 1931: 28 – but see Ewing 1947: 143–4). The only potential bearers of intrinsic value, therefore, are things like motives and other states of mind, the people who have those states of mind, and certain features of the world. None of these things can be called intrinsically right; only actions can be right or wrong. So the things that are intrinsically good are never the things that are intrinsically right. There are traces of this conclusion in Mill and his utilitarian predecessors, but the argument for it seems to stem from Prichard (1912: 6–7). It is that we can only have a duty to do what we can choose to do or not to do; but we cannot choose our motives, and so nothing that includes a motive can be a duty.

Finally, the intuitionists agreed on a view about the relation between moral judgement and what they called 'affect', that is, emotion or other sense of approval, liking, attitude, or interest. They took it that even though it was unlikely that there could be moral judgement without affect, this fact should not be allowed to infect our account of the state of affairs which, in making the moral judgement, we are judging to obtain. Ross wrote:

what we *express* when we call an object good is our attitude towards it, but what we *mean* is something about the object itself and not about our attitude towards it. When we call an object good we are commending it, but to commend it is not to say that we are commending it, but to say that it has a certain character. (1939: 255: see also Ross 1930: 90–1; Broad 1930: 109; Ewing 1929: 194 and 1947: 24)

This last matter becomes important when we turn to consider the intuitionists' fairly dismissive response to emotivist attack.

Though the intuitionists agreed on so much, there remained plenty of internal disagreement to keep them occupied, and much of their work consists of arguments against each other. Three constant themes of disagreement stand out. The first concerned the question whether it could ever be our duty to do less good than we might. Ross and Prichard thought that this could and indeed did often happen. Joseph and Ewing argued to the contrary. Joseph asked: 'Why ought I to do that, the doing which has no value . . . and which being done causes nothing to be which has value? Is not duty in such a case irrational?' (1931: 26; Ewing 1959: 105, 188). In taking this line, Joseph and Ewing of course weaken their defences against consequentialist conceptions of rightness.

The second topic of debate concerned the ground for duties. Ewing 1929, Broad 1930, and Ross 1930 set the standard by taking it that duties are grounded in the nature of the situation, rightness being a sort of fittingness between the action done and the situation that 'demands' it. But Prichard 1932 argued that duty is grounded in the agent's beliefs about the situation rather than in its objective nature, and Ross 1939 adopted this view wholesale (though not fully consistently). Carritt 1947 and Ewing 1947 argue broadly against Prichard's 'subjectivist' position, however, and Broad stuck to his original objective view.

The third topic of debate was the exact relation between goodness and rightness. Ross maintained to the end that these two qualities were entirely distinct. Broad (1930: 283) did however consider favourably the possibility of defining a good object as one which is a fitting object of desire, that is, one that it would be right to desire. And Ewing (1947: 148–9) offered an unapologetic definition of 'good' as 'what ought to be the object of a pro-attitude', where the pro-attitudes include choice, desire, liking, pursuit, approval, and admiration. These attempts to define goodness in terms of rightness had the advantage of halving the number of irreducible normative qualities, and offered an explanation of the fact that value seems to be intrinsically reason-giving. But they were resisted by Ross (1939: 278–9), where he argued that since admiration involves thinking good, the notion of a fitting object of admiration does not offer us a reduction of the good to the right. This argument seems ineffective against Ewing's later position, which takes admiration to be only one of the pro-attitudes appropriate to a valuable object; the others cannot be shown to include the notion of goodness in the same circular way.

2. THE EMOTIVIST CHALLENGE

In the 1930s there arose a specific form of challenge to intuitionism – or rather two forms, often in the service of the same thing. The first form is in fact mooted in Broad 1934, and ascribed there to Austin Duncan-Jones. It amounts to asking whether the intuitionists were right in their basic assumption that there were moral qualities of rightness and goodness. The sentence 'this is good' is no doubt of the same syntactical form as the sentence 'this is square'. But a sentence may be in the indicative mood but be quite different from normal sentences of that type. It might merely express an emotion of the speaker's, or call on the hearer to act in some way. If I say, for instance, 'that is a relief' when you tell me that expected bad news has not materialised, I am surely expressing relief rather than doing the sort of thing normally associated with the indicative mood. If moral utterances were like this, there would be no need, indeed, it would probably be a mistake to suppose that 'good' and 'right' were names of qualities in the way that 'square' and 'old' are. So this first challenge amounts to asking what reason the mere form of moral assertions gives us to suppose that the qualities that the intuitionists took themselves to be investigating exist to be investigated.

The second, allied challenge derived from a doubt whether the intuitionists had succeeded in capturing the practical nature of moral thought and judgement. They took moral enquiry as an attempt to establish which objects had the special qualities of rightness and goodness. But they also admitted that one could, if one lacked any relevant desire, perfectly well discern the presence of these supposed qualities and be entirely unmoved. But this seems to undermine the very nature of moral enquiry, which seems to be about what to do; by thinking of it as the attempt to find out some peculiar facts about the world we have turned moral enquiry theoretical when it is in fact intrinsically practical.

This second challenge is aimed at the intuitionists' conception of motivation. In our own terms, it amounts to saying that it is impossible to marry a cognitivist account of moral judgement to a 'Humean' conception of motivation. It supports the first challenge, because if an alternative, non-cognitive account of moral thought and judgement can be produced, one that will restore the practical nature of the thought that this action is wrong and that possible outcome the best, the result is that by abandoning the intuitionists' supposed moral qualities we recover the practical purport of moral thought. And there was available an alternative account of moral language, as a system for the expression of feeling (or more generally pro-attitude) in the speaker and for the production of similar affects in the hearer.

There were other considerations at work as well as these. Ayer's 1936 version of emotivism was driven by a positivistic theory of meaning. Russell's 1935 position was driven more by a sense of the complete impossibility of finding any defensible answer to the question what is of intrinsic value (1936: 238), though he also appealed to the impossibility of being motivated by moral judgement as the intuitionists conceived of it (240). Most notably, however, nobody seems to have been very much influenced by naturalist metaphysics. The dominant idea seems not to be that non-natural moral properties are metaphysically impossible, but that they are metaphysically awkward, and that since they are luckily redundant abandoning them simply relieves one of certain artificial philosophical questions.

Before turning to some of the details of the forms of emotivism that were offered, it is worth looking back at the intuitionist response to these various arguments. This was in many ways very disappointing. Ross (1939: 35) addresses Ayer's position, and seems to suppose that all he has to do is to refute the positivistic theory of meaning that underlies it. Broad 1934 is the first intuitionistic mention of the new expressivism (which he later calls the interjectional theory), but having outlined its nature, and detailed what seem to be quite impressive arguments in its favour, he fails to offer anything by way of criticism. Later he does respond, but only with a typical Broad lampoon. He wrote, in a discussion of the views of Richard Price:

As is well known, there is a theory that such sentences do not really express judgements at all. It has been held that they express only certain emotions felt by the speaker, or certain desires of his, or certain commands . . . Price does not consider this extreme view. If it had been put to him, he would probably have regarded it as too fantastically absurd to be taken seriously. It is, indeed, a kind of theory which can be swallowed only after one has undergone a long and elaborate process of 'conditioning' which was not available in the eighteenth century. (1945: 190)

Ewing was more circumspect, and more respectful, and in the Note to chapter 7 of the 1964 edition of his *Ethics* he accepts that he had been wrong to think 'that the distinctive function of ethical . . . judgements is to ascribe properties to anything . . . I should not now admit an objective non-natural quality of goodness or an objective non-natural relation of obligation as belonging to reality . . . If . . . moral judgements do not describe the real, what do they do? It seems to me now . . . that they must have reference primarily to some kind of practical attitude which they express' (181–2). Ewing does continue his intuitionist devotion to objective truth in ethics, however, suggesting that moral judgements 'do not merely express this attitude but claim that it is objectively justified or required'. It is this complex change of heart that led to his *Second Thoughts*.

The reason why Ross and Broad felt that they did not need to take emotivism seriously seems to me to be that they thought they had already drawn attention to a mistake committed, in their view, by all versions of emotivism, namely that of supposing that just because there must be affect where there is moral judgement, this is some reason for denying the existence of a genuine claim to truth made by such judgements. As Ross wrote in 1939 (quoted above): 'what we *express* when we call an object good is our attitude towards it, but what we *mean* is something about the object itself and not about our attitude towards it' (255). Like Broad, he thought that emotivism derived from ignoring this distinction, which he, Broad, and Ewing had all drawn by 1930, and that it should be sufficient just to point this out. More generally, however, I suspect that the intuitionists felt that what emotivism was doing was to attempt (fallaciously) to solve the problems of metaethics by appeal merely to the philosophy of language, in tune with the 'linguistic turn' that philosophy was taking at the time.

3. EMOTIVISM

The most sophisticated form of emotivism is found in C. L. Stevenson's *Ethics and Language* (1944), though it is prefigured in the various papers he published in the late 1930s. Stevenson starts by distinguishing between belief and attitude. He does not offer an account of this distinction, which can be thought of as a psychological mirror of the distinction between fact and value; he appeals rather to the intuitive claim that it makes good sense to suppose that two people may agree in belief but disagree in attitude or vice versa. In the examples he gives, however, we learn that by 'attitude' he includes desire (7), feeling (60), wish (60), and emotion (59) as well as what we would more naturally think of as an attitude. He does however distinguish attitude proper, which he calls 'a complicated conjunction of dispositional properties . . . marked by stimuli and responses which relate to hindering or assisting whatever it is that is called the "object" of the attitude' (60).

With this contrast between belief and attitude, Stevenson is in a position to make his distinctive claim about the meaning of an ethical or evaluative utterance. Such utterances serve to express the attitudes of the speaker and to evoke a similar attitude in the hearer. The ability they have to do this, which can be thought of as their 'emotive meaning', is a causal matter; indeed, for Stevenson the meaning of *any* term was to be understood causally, differences between styles of meaning (evaluative or descriptive) emerging as differences in effects. He wrote later: 'The emotive meaning of a word or a phrase is a strong and persistent tendency, built up in the course of linguistic history, to give direct expression (quasi-interjectionally) to certain of the speaker's feelings or emotions or attitudes; and it is also a tendency to evoke (quasi-imperatively) corresponding feelings, emotions or attitudes in those to whom the speaker's remarks are addressed' (1963: 21–2).

The practical nature of moral thought and judgement is now easy to explain. By 'practical nature' we mean that moral thought and judgement is about what to do; this is so whether we are thinking about what would be the right action for us or for someone else. We can see that this is so because of the inconceivability of someone saying that this course of action would indeed be wrong but that they don't see that as relevant to the question whether to do it or not. Equally, when we tell someone that what they propose to do is wrong, we are not informing them about some matter of fact to which they may be indifferent, but trying to get them not to do it. The emotive theory of the meaning of ethical terms is in a good position to explain these things. If I say 'that would be wrong' I am using language that tends to cause in my audience the attitudes that I express – disapproval, dislike, disgust, or whatever. This sort of language has what Stevenson called 'a dynamic use'. Equally, when I say to myself 'that would be wrong', I am not expressing some non-natural matter of fact, but an attitude that I now take to acting in that way. The emotive theory of the meaning of ethical terms thus captures well our sense that moral thought and judgement is practical – the very thing that it was held that intuitionism could not do. As Stevenson said, 'the distinguishing features of an ethical judgement can be preserved by a recognition of emotive meaning and disagreement in attitude, rather than by some non-natural quality – and with far greater intelligibility' (1963: 9).

Stevenson was well aware, however, that many evaluative utterances had what he called 'descriptive meaning' as well as 'emotive meaning'. When I say that you did wrong to take a second slice of cake, there is a mixture of description and evaluation going on. It is also true that, even if I just say 'you were wrong to do that' I represent myself as disapproving of your action, in a way that is close to describing myself as disapproving. Stevenson is keen to avoid any understanding of emotive language purely as description of the speaker's attitudes. The intuitionists had succeeded in refuting accounts of 'this is wrong' as identical in meaning to 'I disapprove of this', understood as a self-description. But he wants to allow the presence of description in an utterance that is mainly emotive. He offers us therefore two 'patterns of analysis' of an utterance of 'this is good'. On the first pattern, it is synonymous with 'I approve of this; do so as well.' In this pattern, the description present is self-description. But on the second pattern, ' "This is good" has the meaning of "This has qualities or relations X, Y, Z . . . ," except that "good" has as well a laudatory emotive meaning which permits it to express the speaker's approval, and tends to evoke the approval of the hearer' (1944: 207). Here the description is not of the speaker but of the object of the attitude. Stevenson thinks it possible to offer two patterns of analysis of the 'same' utterance because, as he puts it, ethical terms are vague, and 'whenever a term is vague there is no sharp distinction between its strict descriptive *meaning* and what it *suggests*' (206). The first pattern understands the speaker's approval as part of the descriptive meaning, while the second understands it more as a suggestion; by contrast, the relevant features of the object are no more than suggested in the first pattern, but supposedly part of the descriptive meaning of the utterance on the second pattern.

Stevenson's form of emotivism was not the only form available, for the emotive theory of meaning is only one way of awarding a distinct semantic role to evaluative terms and utterances. It would be possible to take ethical utterances to be simply equivalent to commands, as Carnap did (1935: 24), without any reference to causal tendencies that words have acquired over decades of use. It would also be possible to take it that ethical utterances purport to make assertions, but that no such assertions are true. This 'error theory', under which we think we mean something by our ethical utterances, and are right about what they mean (they are assertions and not commands, for instance), but wrong in thinking that things could be the way we assert them to be, was first propounded by J. L. Mackie (1946; see also Robinson 1948, who propounds this view as a form of emotivism); and it is reported by Derek Parfit that when Ayer first heard this theory, he exclaimed: 'That is what I ought to have said!'

Perhaps the most general expression of emotivism was the claim that there are no ethical propositions. There is no proposition that courage is good that can be believed, asserted, denied, or disproved. (On Stevenson's first pattern of analysis, this 'proposition' becomes 'I approve of courage; do so as well', of which only the first half expresses a proposition.) Interestingly, the claim that there are no ethical propositions was defended by Wittgenstein in his Lecture on Ethics, given in Cambridge probably in 1930 but only published in 1965. Wittgenstein claimed that moral utterances are of the highest possible importance, but senseless. They are senseless because there can be no moral facts. Judgements that express propositions describe facts, and 'no statement of fact can ever be, or imply, a judgement of absolute value' (6). This claim needs to be understood in the light of the final sections of Wittgenstein's *Tractatus* (1921).

4. DEWEY

Dewey had already published several books on ethics by 1914. But after the war there was *Human Nature and Conduct* (1922), the important chapter 10 of *The Quest for Certainty* (1929), a revised edition of *Ethics* (1932) and *The Theory of Valuation* (1939). Dewey is perhaps best known for his insistence on the application of scientific method to practical problems. This in itself would have been of little theoretical interest. It would, and did, lead to charges that he was a rather naïve consequentialist, and that he took the ends of enquiry as given, only insisting rather trivially on a sophisticated investigation of appropriate means. Both of these charges are probably misconceived, as we can see by looking at the background to Dewey's views.

First, Dewey saw his theoretical position as an alternative to the two main theories of value, which he called empiricism and rationalism. Empiricism was the view that value is generated by desire. Something becomes of value by being wanted. Desires determine ends in this way, and it remains for reason to determine appropriate means to those ends. Rationalism was the view that the ends determined by desire could be criticised by reason, and in fact that reason could impose the 'correct' ends for desire. Against empiricism Dewey argued that when we are interested in what is of value we are interested not in what we (or others) do desire, but in what is *to be desired*, the desir*able*. Against rationalism he argued that reason can only suggest very vague and indeterminate ends, and that it is incapable of affecting desire. Rationalism borrows its notion of desire from empiricism, and desire, so conceived, is a natural impulse that is immune to the promptings of reason. What is necessary, then, in order to get away from these tired old theories, is a new conception of desire, one that stresses the way in which desire involves a conception of how things are to be. With this in hand, we can understand how desire can be prompted and corrected by reason.

If neither desire nor reason are capable of determining appropriate ends, what is the criterion we should use? In answer, Dewey appeals to the notion of self-realisation and (later) to that of growth. A practical problem is one in which our search for personal growth is threatened, and a resolution is found when we find the best means of ensuring that growth. This sounds both instrumentalist and consequentialist, but in fact it is probably neither despite Dewey's constant rhetoric of outcomes and consequences. First, Dewey attempts to replace the normal conception of a means–end relation with a relation between constitutive means and 'ends in view'. An end in view is not a determinate end to which we are seeking the most effective means, and the attempt to promote an end in view would not necessarily be helped by achieving a more determinate conception of that end. Rather, Dewey seems to be suggesting that we think of growth as partly constituted by the means that we take with that end in view, if we indeed take the right means. We act with that end in view, and our so acting, if successful, is part of our achieving that end. This is not an instrumentalist conception, and it is probably not consequentialist either.

Of course we would like to know more about the nature of growth; we must have some understanding of what it is if we are to act in such a way as to promote it, and it is not clear where such an understanding is to come from. What Dewey calls 'operational thinking' (i.e. means/end deliberation as he understands it) is not capable of determining appropriate ends. Dewey sometimes suggests that the end is to be justified metaphysically, but there remains the suspicion that his conception of growth hovers unstably between an explanatory psychological notion (the fostering of those traits and dispositions that lie deepest in the agent's psychology, and a search for psychological health) and a normative one according to which we only grow if we become the people we should become (Stratton 1903).

PHILOSOPHY OF RELIGION

RICHARD H. ROBERTS

The philosophy of religion in the period from 1914 to 1945 is considered in terms of five major factors, that inform each section of this chapter. First, as regards context, in an era of progressive secularisation and cultural crisis the philosophy of religion and philosophical theology are seen to have held relatively marginal positions as interlinked sub-disciplines within the institutional academy. Second, mainstream philosophy of religion and philosophical theology were practised under the declining influence of philosophical idealism and in reaction to the challenge of positivism. Third, as dialectical theology and the theology of encounter moved from Europe to Britain and North America, they indirectly mediated a more innovative response within theology and philosophy of religion (and the socio-scientific study of religion) to the *Zeitgeist* of societal crisis, one which drew upon phenomenology and existential thought. Fourth, Roman Catholic philosophy of religion was largely conducted within the framework of Scholasticism which was maintained as a bulwark against philosophical modernity, but new developments were also present that presage the renewal associated with the Second Vatican Council (1962–5). Fifth, in conclusion, towards the end of the period from 1910 to 1945, there is the appearance, alongside other options, of the post-war development of an Anglo-American philosophy of religion strongly connected with the central concerns of analytical and linguistic philosophy.

1. THE MARGINALITY OF THE PHILOSOPHY OF RELIGION

Nineteenth-century German theology and philosophy long held a central position in post-Enlightenment Western religious thought, and their impact is evident across Europe and North America. Yet within the German universities, the academic isolation of theology and its adjunct sub-disciplines can be traced back to Wilhelm von Humboldt's separation of theology (and *Religionsphilosophie*) from the humanities in the faculty of theology in the newly founded University of Berlin in the early nineteenth century. This institutional strategy, formulated in response to the Kantian critique of speculative knowledge, formalised an intellectual and cultural marginalisation which was later to be endorsed by Wilhelm Dilthey's exclusion (see Dilthey 1883) of theology from the manifold of the 'human sciences' (*Geisteswissenschaften*). The policy of separate development for theology provides an important key to understanding the background to the period 1910 to 1945. During this time entrenched religious traditions wrestled with the legacy of the nineteenth century, above all with historicism and the Enlightenment critique of all theologically grounded ontology and epistemology. More distantly, theology and the philosophy of religion were also to be confronted by the emergence of sociology and psychology as scientific disciplines that incorporated the implications of evolutionary theory and a positivistic world-view.

The immediate historical context of the philosophy of religion in the period 1910 to 1945 is one characterised by multiple 'crises'. Yet the First World War, the Russian October Revolution of 1917, the Weimar Republic in a defeated Germany, the Great Depression in Europe and North America, the rise of fascism, the Third Reich and the Holocaust, the Second World War, and the detonation of the first nuclear weapons in 1945 had minimal immediate impact upon the main-line theology and institutional philosophy of religion of the period. Whilst the eclipse of an optimistic philosophical idealism within British philosophy was certainly confirmed by the First World War, Anglo-American philosophy lacked that ingestion of experience and frontal encounter with nihilism characteristic of *fin-de-siècle* Vienna and the cultural explorations of the Weimar Republic, and also remained detached from the developments associated with the reception of the thought of Kierkegaard and Nietzsche.

In general terms, the secularisation of intellectual and cultural life was accelerated in the aftermath of the First World War and in the Depression. Whilst philosophical reflection upon religion continued within institutions sustained by Western denominational traditions (and notably in university faculties of theology and seminaries), this protected status tended to consolidate the isolation of such reflection from what amounted to a persisting crisis of civilisation. Thus, for example, even the 'crisis of the human sciences' outlined by Husserl in his 1936 lectures (Husserl 1936) remained largely external to the relatively sheltered world of mainstream discourse in theology and the philosophy of religion. It was only from and through the intellectual margins that an indirect mediation of this crisis took place, in what was, in the fullness of time, to become a conquest of the core by the periphery. Thus of critical importance in understanding the inter-war period is the growth and subsequent history of the reception (*Rezeptionsgeschichte*) not only of uncompromising positivism, but also of the new, often imperfectly understood, intrusions of continental thought which were to migrate from Europe into British and American traditions. In effect, the full implications both of central questions in mainstream modern philosophy concerned with meaning, language, and the status of the material world, and of world events subversive of all facile theodicy, were only fully absorbed into the philosophy of religion in the period following 1945.

2. THE DECLINE OF ABSOLUTE IDEALISM AND THE CHALLENGE OF POSITIVISM

Narrowly defined, the 'philosophy of religion' has been construed by Alan Sell (Sell 1988) and David Pailin (Pailin 1986) as a sub-discipline of philosophy incorporating the relationship between secular philosophy and philosophical theology. Alternatively, the history of twentieth-century philosophy of religion has been represented by Ingolf Dalferth in terms of the evolution of analytical philosophy, in relation to which the question, 'What does it mean to speak of God?' is constantly reiterated (see Dalferth 1981). Thus Dalferth provides a comprehensive account of the successive phases of logical atomism (G. E. Moore, Bertrand Russell, Ludwig Wittgenstein, F. P. Ramsey, and others), logical empiricism (above all A. J. Ayer), and then post-Second World War linguistic analysis and ordinary language philosophy. Both approaches stress the integrity and continuity of traditions of argument, rather than exploring the contextualised interconnection of contrasting philosophical and religious cultures which is here the main concern.

At the outset of the period from 1910 to 1945, both English and Scottish empiricist, utilitarian, and common sense philosophies, and the philosophy of religion, had already been strongly challenged by successive waves of German thought, above all by absolute idealism. In late nineteenth-century England, the Anglican *Lux Mundi* school had mediated the influence of German immanentism and evolutionary thought in terms of a Christological *via media*. This non-dialectical mode of synthesis based upon a moderate idealism attempted to create a religious episteme in the face of wider intellectual and societal developments, above all those associated with Darwinism. This tendency continued in the theological symposium *Foundations* published in 1912 (Streeter 1912), to which (*inter alia*) the idealist William Temple and the personalist W. H. Moberly contributed. The most respected British comprehensive philosophy of religion of the period was F. R. Tennant's *Philosophical Theology* (1928) which dealt, in two volumes, with 'The Soul and Its Faculties' and 'The World, the Soul and God', respectively. This rigorous treatise was dependent upon the psychology of James Ward and prevenient strands of British and European philosophical discussion. In the first volume Tennant argued on the basis of a non-metaphysical, empirical philosophical psychology and then proceeded with an examination of consciousness and the senses which culminated in a conception of the 'pure ego' or 'abiding soul'. Tennant's survey of philosophy served as the foundation for the second volume in which he engaged with Kant, Karl Pearson, Sir Arthur Eddington, and Newtonian mechanics. Tennant attempted to rebuild a bridge between contemporary philosophy and the Incarnation-centred liberal Anglican theology of his time. Now, however, this endeavour seems to inhabit a different world from that of other contemporaries, be they Freud, the Marburg Neo-Kantians, Marxists, or, indeed, Einstein.

Further distinguished examples of main-line philosophy of religion are associated, above all, with the Gifford Lectures (delivered from 1888 onwards) on 'natural theology, in the widest sense of that term'. Thus, for example, Alan Seth Pringle-Pattison (1912–13), Samuel Alexander (1916–18), W. R. Inge (1917–18), Clement C. J. Webb (1918–20), Friedrich von Hügel (1924–26), Etienne Gilson (1931–2), William Temple (1932–4), F. H. Brabant (1936), Karl Barth (1937–8), and Reinhold Niebuhr (1939) were all contributors during the period from 1910 to 1945. More radical in orientation were the Hibbert Lectures (delivered from 1878 onwards) which provided an early forum for the interaction of Western religious thought with other religious traditions. The publication of A. J. Ayer's *Language, Truth and Logic* in 1936 brought the positivist reductionism of the Vienna Circle into British philosophy. The application of the principle of verification to all utterances belatedly provided the iconoclastic means for a final attack upon residual idealism and for subverting the significance of all theological and ethical locutions. Qualified reaction to logical empiricism was to become a key element in the analytical philosophy of religion in the period after 1945.

3. DIALECTICAL THEOLOGY AND EXISTENTIALISM

The psychological and cultural impact of the First World War was immense; in Britain and France the price of victory was exhaustion. In Britain (and in North America), there was near silence as regards the intellectual and religious implications of the War: the experience was inexpressible. Lacking both the uninhibited release of Dada and Surrealism in France and the raw power of German Expressionism exploited by early dialectical theology, British philosophy of religion remained for the most part fixed in its pre-war postures; it was unable to confront the enormity of the war and largely automatic in its return to traditional tasks. After a decade of silence, the autobiographical writings of those involved, for example, Robert Graves, Siegfried Sassoon, Vera Brittain, and others began to raise trauma into conscious awareness. British academic theology and philosophy of religion achieved little to counter the impression that they lacked the capacity to address the questions that afflicted serious minds. Paradoxically, however, European theology and philosophy in the inter-war period were still to be dominated by ideas flowing from germanophone Europe, a process accelerated by Jewish emigration following Hitler's coming to power in 1933.

Also characteristic of the period is the activity of a number of individuals and groups, often institutionally marginalised, for whom present events had an immediate significance. These included such explicitly religious thinkers as the Jews Franz Rosenzweig and Martin Buber (see Buber 1923, Guttman 1964), the Swiss-German Reformed theologians Karl Barth (and Emil Brunner and the wider circle associated with 'dialectical theology'), the Lutheran philosopher-theologian Paul Tillich, the biblical scholar Rudolf Bultmann, the French Jewish (but Catholic-tending) Simone Weil, the Roman Catholic theologians Erich Przywara, Karl Rahner, and Hans Urs von Balthasar, the apocalyptic-Marxist revisionist Ernst Bloch, and the philosophers Martin Heidegger and Ludwig Wittgenstein. Many of these figures struggled to re-ground thought and action, ontology and epistemology in their respective fields of endeavour, and to proceed by means of contextually relevant 'deductions' from sources to which they ascribed transcendental status. Of crucial importance for understanding this period is the role of South German Neo-Kantianism which facilitated responses to the nihilistic implications of the First World War. As regards the socio-scientific study of religion undertaken across traditions, the application of phenomenology by G. van der Leeuw is of central importance (see van der Leeuw 1933). For the most part, however, the full impact of these thinkers upon mainstream philosophy of religion, theology, and religious thought took place in the period following 1945, not least because of the delay associated with the translation of texts.

As regards theology in Britain and the Anglophone world, such figures as the Cambridge theologians Charles Raven and Sir Edwin Hoskyns, both chaplains in the trenches, responded in different ways to the impact of the war. Raven became acutely sensitive to evolutionary theory and to the struggle of nature, yet, at the same time, he resisted theological reflection that appeared to depend in any direct or unseemly way upon the war. Raven was hostile towards the theology of Karl Barth and the other dialectical theologians who drew into theology something of the violence of war in their exploitation of extreme images and relentless paradox. It is significant to note that there was no British or North American equivalent of the existential war mysticism – conflict as spiritual experience (*Kampf als innere Erlebnis*) – of Ernst Junger's *In Stahlgewittern* (*Storm of Steel*). By contrast, Sir Edwin Hoskyns translated (1933) the second edition (1922) of Karl Barth's *Römerbrief* (Epistle to the Romans), and found in the latter's dialectical or 'crisis' theology a pointed challenge to a shallow English incarnationalism informed by idealism.

Barth's second *Römerbrief* (1922) is one of the most important theological texts of the twentieth century. As a student before the First World War, Barth had absorbed the main theological and philosophical currents of his time. On the outbreak of hostilities as a Swiss-German he had returned home, and served as pastor of a church in Safenwil in the Aargau. Acutely aware of the war, yet a non-combatant and a socialist, Barth underwent a conversion experience from the Liberal Protestantism of Marburg to an intense existential commitment to Pauline theology. In the second edition of the *Römerbrief*, Barth incorporated in an extreme way the radical eschatological account of Jesus Christ's life and death developed by Johannes Weiss and Albert Schweitzer, the paradoxical identity crisis of the rediscovered 'young Luther', and Kierkegaard's 'infinite qualitative difference' between man and God. The result was a text of life-changing potential which inverted the immanent perspective of Liberal Protestantism. The reader is confronted with dialectical either/or, an existential decision: God speaks; man listens and obeys. The 'theology of crisis' posed the possibility of dialectical re-engagement with a 'wholly other' transcendent God paradoxically present in what Kierkegaard had depicted as the 'absolute Paradox' of Jesus Christ, God and man. Barth's text had a powerful resonance and became the main inspiration for a movement within and well beyond Reformed theology. Barth's utter lack of compromise alienated many in Anglo-America for whom the more accommodating Emil Brunner provided a mediating position more akin to traditional liberal thinking in both theology and the philosophy of religion. Barth himself reverted from dialectic to ontology in his great *Church Dogmatics* (1932–67 [1936-69]) and redescribed philosophical questions within the ambit of Christology.

The later post-war development of Anglo-American philosophy of religion is strongly connected with the central concerns of analytical and linguistic philosophy. This central preoccupation should not, however, be allowed to exclude mention of the dominant influence of the émigré philosopher-theologian Paul Tillich (Tillich 1988–), the politically important role of the theologian and ethicist Reinhold Niebuhr, the inspirational impact of A. N. Whitehead's metaphysics upon process thought (Whitehead 1926, 1929), and the early work of the American philosopher Charles Hartshorne (Hartshorne 1941, 1948), all of whom were active during the period from 1910 to 1945 in the United States. In Britain, Donald MacKinnon, a pupil of both the philosopher A. E. Taylor and the theologian Edwin Hoskyns, mediated between the extremities of Barth's dialectical theology and the tradition of analogy (MacKinnon 1940). Unique in his generation, MacKinnon's concerns as both philosopher and theologian prefigured the later renewal of Anglo-American analytical philosophy of religion through continental philosophy in the final decades of the twentieth century. Similarly, Austin Farrer's treatise, *Finite and Infinite*, published in 1943, was a distinguished British work that also engaged with the doctrine of analogy.

4. CATHOLIC PHILOSOPHY OF RELIGION

Throughout the period from 1910 to 1945, the philosophy of religion practised in countries with Protestant theological cultures beyond Germany responded more quickly and with less resistance to innovation than in those countries where the Catholic ethos was dominant. Following the formal condemnation of the Modernists by Pius X in 1907 in the decree *Lamentabili*, Roman Catholic theology and philosophy was confined to Thomism until well after the Second World War. German immanentism represented by Kant and Hegel and their successors was regarded by papal authority as the heretical core of Modernism. Catholic Thomism (and its later Anglican variant propounded by Eric L. Mascall) provided an epistemological and ontological bulwark against the attrition of modernity. Despite this, the influence of a Catholic Modernist thinker of the stature of, for example, Maurice Blondel (1861–1949) was widely felt in the period from 1914 to 1945, although his most important work, *L'Action*, had been published as early as 1893. It was not, however, until Karl Rahner's doctoral thesis, *Geist im Welt* (1939), written under the influence of Joseph Maréchal's *Le Point de départ de la métaphysique* (1923–49) and Martin Heidegger (under whom Rahner had studied at Freiburg), that the Thomist theory of knowledge was directly confronted with Kant's transcendental critique. Subsequently, Rahner's transcendental Thomism has held an important position within Catholic philosophy of religion in continuing the process of philosophical *aggorniomento*, a process later to be countered by the conservative phenomenological theology of Pope John-Paul II.

5. SIGNS OF RENEWAL

Presented in the broad terms employed in this chapter, the 'philosophy of religion' of the period from 1910 to 1945 is not easy to summarise, not least because of the dislocation of traditions caused by catastrophic wars, revolution, and totalitarian politics. In sociological terms, the philosophers and theologians of this period stand 'between the times' (echoing the title of the journal of the dialectical theology, *Zwischen den Zeiten*): on the one hand they inherited the self-confidence of nineteenth-century philosophy, on the other they were confronted by what Max Weber described as the 'iron cage' of modernity. Thus whilst the philosophy of religion, narrowly understood, continued to address its traditional questions, major innovations emerged indicative of a growing pluralism. Whereas in the 'first postmodernity' of Weimar culture the multifarious quests for an episteme capable of confronting nihilism were essentially conducted as a marginal and elite activity, although eventually absorbed into the mainstream, it has only been in the 'second postmodernity' of the final decades of the twentieth century that resurgent nihilism has once more allowed the ideas of the innovative thinkers of the period from 1910 to 1945 to enter the mainstream of mass cultures unified by globalised capitalism, yet simultaneously beset by uncertainty and fragmentation.

LITERATURE AS PHILOSOPHY

RHIANNON GOLDTHORPE

A survey of the themes which preoccupied writers and philosophers in parallel between 1914 and 1945, some perennial, some of more recent urgency, would doubtless include the following: relativism; the subjectivity of perception; the paradoxes of temporality; the instability of the self; vitalism and the limits of reason; the validity of intuition as a basis for knowledge; the mind–body relationship; the inadequacy, in expression or representation, of conceptual language; the problem of meaning; the relation between art and life. In the rich creativity of the period three paradigm texts stand out in that they do not simply mirror but actively renew reflection on these issues: Marcel Proust's *A la recherche du temps perdu* (*In Search of Lost Time*) (1913–27), Thomas Mann's *Der Zauberberg* (*The Magic Mountain*) (1924), and Jean-Paul Sartre's *La Nausée* (*Nausea*) (1938). Proust's emphasis on discontinuity and contingency complicates his supposed affinity with Bergson; Mann's dialogue with the ongoing legacy of Nietzsche evolves throughout his career; Sartre's pre-war novel is a phenomenological and heuristic fiction which clears the ground for his future theory.

1. PROUST: *A LA RECHERCHE DU TEMPS PERDU*

Proust's 'search for lost time' was also a search for truth – a search which would entail a portrayal of our errors. And, indeed, in the experience of his hero, Marcel, and in the often disabused voice of his narrator (Marcel's older self), errors proliferate, whether they be perceptual errors, errors of self-knowledge, errors of recollection, or errors in Marcel's judgement of others. Perception yields no sense of a stable world; vivid flights of imagination or expectation find no correspondence or fulfilment in an elusive reality. Marcel, anxiously seeking for external sources of truth, is forced to acknowledge the impossibility of knowing anything of the world outside himself. The shifting images of others created and projected by desire, whether in erotic fantasy or in the compulsive *libido sciendi* provoked by jealousy, frustrate the search for knowledge. We cannot share our individual perspective, nor move beyond it towards a consensual 'truth'.

The vagaries of desire in turn confirm the discontinuity of the self, while the futility of self-analysis in the search for an 'inner' truth leads Marcel to doubt the very existence of the self. In describing the void encountered by introspection he calls into question the source itself of the subjectivity which imprisons us. The desire for a stable identity is further frustrated by memory which, dulled by habit and by practical concerns, retains only a travesty of the personal past; but the time even more crucially 'lost' is the present. Marcel, waiting for his mother's goodnight kiss, learns that between the fever of anticipation and the pain that will follow fulfilment, the moment of fulfilment itself is lost.

This reductive inventory of philosophical problems could be continued. But Marcel's pessimism is not the whole story. It is belied, in part, by his delight in the comic idiosyncrasies and foibles of those whom, he claims, he cannot know; by his intoxicated sensuous absorption in the natural world; by his grow-ing conviction that art, if not love, may enable us to apprehend another person's vision and experience. Indeed, one of the major ironies of the novel is that Marcel's eventually positive discoveries have their source in the errors and lim-itations he has denounced, and reveal themselves when they are least expected, independently, at first, of any act of will. The body, with its fickle perceptions, bcomes the bearer of enlightenment through memories which imply a prior forgetting: the chance repetition of a trivial sensation – the taste of a *madeleine*, later, the unevenness of paving stones, or the texture of a napkin – not only unlocks the past but imbues the present with intense well-being and intellectual joy. In the novel's final volume, as Marcel makes his way to the Guermantes *matinée* after many years of reclusion, these paradoxically transient intuitions of the extra-temporal suggest to him the unifying power of metaphor, analogous in its identification of apparently disparate terms to the superimposing of present and past in a moment outside time – a moment in which the discontinuity of the self is transcended. However, this resolution, with its implication of stasis, is no sooner asserted than questioned, and it has in practice already been overtaken by a more dynamic vision of the power of language to decipher, signify, and, above all, transform.

Ironically, again, transformation may seem at odds with the security which Marcel craves, and transformation, too, may spring from error. Yet Marcel has learned from one of the tutelary artists who guide him on his way that meta-morphosis – transposed, for the writer, into metaphor – may spring from or create a truer vision. The painter Elstir celebrates the unique optical illusions of which his first sight is composed, thereby freeing the world, Marcel believes, of the conventional categories and denominations which supposedly ground our knowledge. Elstir transforms the stasis of paint into a mobile re-description, abolishing the limits between sea, land, and air, dislocating planes and perspectives. Whereas, for Marcel, involuntary memory seems to abolish time, Elstir's painting reinstates it, deferring recognition and identification, introducing movement and indeterminacy into the act of vision. For Marcel, returning to Balbec, the once inaccessible, immobile, eternal ocean is transformed into an element permeable to human consciousness and activity. His own exuberantly metaphoric redescriptions, even when inspired by affective memory, do not in practice reveal the identity of two terms, but the mobile relations between successive second terms. They mark not the stability of the self but its growth through time, with the possibility of both self-recognition and self-creation; they renew the experience of, and reflection upon, the time of the world and of consciousness, the interdependence of knowing, imagining and feeling, of language, representation, and action. The barriers between subject and object dissolve even while their persistence is deplored.

The reinstatement of time in the final volume is ambivalent. The euphoria of the discovery of metaphor as the expression of the extra-temporal essence revealed by chance involuntary memories is dispelled when Marcel finally meets his fellow guests at the Guermantes reception. Time has reduced them to grotesquely decrepit travesties of their younger selves. Death, perhaps imminent, threatens Marcel's newly discovered vocation as a writer. And yet he learns that time must be both the medium and the matter of his future work. The book he proposes to write, the book of his life, is not, he tells us, the one we have just read (but to which, we find, it bears a strange resemblance): it would offer a more precise transcription of reality in recording the errors of our perceptions, in leaving faces blank for the projection of the features we desire. *A la recherche du temps perdu* ends not with nostalgia for transcendental truth or for a pre-existent essence of the self, but with a celebration of the contingent, the unstable, the provisional, the indeterminate, and with a tentative promise of continued self-creation.

2. MANN: *DER ZAUBERBERG*

Proust did not believe that he had relativised time in the manner of Einstein (his algebra, he thought, was inadequate). Thomas Mann, however, having read an account of Einstein's Special Theory in 1920, commented on his own parallel insight in making the relativity of time a major theme of *Der Zauberberg*, then in the process of composition. The theme is certainly foregrounded by the setting of the novel in an Alpine sanatorium far removed from the practical preoccupations of the 'flat-land'. There the young and only slightly tubercular hero, Hans Castorp, an engaging and unexceptional product of the North-German bourgeoisie, finds during his seven-year stay (extended from three weeks) that time is no longer structured by familiar co-ordinates: the tempo and rhythm of experience, even the confusion of the seasons, are at first disturbingly strange. Yet this is only one of many relativities. Among the cosmopolitan 'guests' of the Berghof, all with their own sharply distinguished customs and idiosyncrasies, disease creates its own values (the 'good' patient is the patient for whom disease is a vocation), its own hierarchies, rituals, and taboos, its own feverish eroticism. Castorp's passion for the enigmatic, elusive, 'slack' Madame Chauchat obsessively allies physical love with a fascination for corruption and decay; it, too, dilates and compresses time.

It also gives direction to Castorp's life – a life in which, hitherto, his unconscious search for meaning had met only with a 'hollow silence'. It stimulates an ambivalent thirst for knowledge and for speculation on such topics as matter, form, and the origins of life and consciousness. Castorp's curiosity also implies an urge to self-discovery. None the less, Settembrini, Castorp's self-appointed humanist mentor, deplores this morbid attachment. Mann, writing in 1924, had used the phrase 'magic mountain' to describe a decadent Romantic aesthetic which had once tempted him but which he had increasingly come to see during the twelve-year-long writing of *Der Zauberberg* as a threat to rationality, and as allied to a suspect ideology. Settembrini, the Italian man of letters, may therefore speak for Mann. He certainly speaks, at length, for the values of the Enlightenment: for reason, freedom and tolerance, for international democracy, liberal individualism, progress, and peace. He is a bourgeois, free-thinking, monist reformist who stands out against quietism, but for whom action is limited to writing.

The threat of didacticism is disarmed by the often affectionate irony of the narrator. We are also led to see that philosophical or ideological positions are all too often inhabited by their contraries, relativised by the personality of the thinker, or by historical circumstance. We infer that truth may be, in Nietzschean fashion, a matter of perspective. Settembrini's commitment to reason is fanatically passionate; his pacifist internationalism is infected by his hatred, as an Italian patriot, for Austria. Self-contradiction is even more vividly embodied in Naphta, the Jewish Jesuit sceptic and dualist, authoritarian communist and reactionary revolutionary, reader of Hegel and Marx, sybarite proponent of asceticism, who vies with Settembrini for control over Castorp's mind. Pedagogy, it seems, is a form of the will-to-power. Linguistic definition collapses: words like 'democracy' or 'individualism' acquire the meanings which opposed ideologies dictate.

The contradictions which prevail between and within the two extremists are beyond intellectual reconciliation. The task of resolving them in a dream of human wholeness is left to the understandably perplexed Castorp, whose own enlightenment is a matter more of vision than of cerebration. Lost in a life-threatening snowstorm, he overcomes his longstanding feeling for death in a dream of order and serenity, in which mortality, even at its most horrific, is recognised as a part of life but allowed no mastery over man's thoughts. Rather, Man himself is master of these antitheses.

The effect of Castorp's apparently positive insight does not last. Equilibrium is undermined, ironically, by the arrival at the Berghof of a patriarchal colonialist who is also an extreme manifestation of the life-force. Mynheer Peeperkorn, a man of overwhelming physical presence and mesmerising intellectual vacuity, exudes a Dionysiac and literally intoxicated appetite for life, beyond or beneath the purchase of language and argument, which paradoxically undermines his own vitality: he kills himself, preferring death to impotence. Further, Naphta's death during his duel with Settembrini reinforces not vitalism but nihilism (Settembrini, ever the humanist, shoots into the air; Naphta shoots himself).

It is soon evident that the duel between civilisation and Terror, bourgeois culture and anarchy, Enlightenment and Romanticism, life and death is more than a local debate. As the 'thunderclap' of the outbreak of war scatters the increasingly fractious guests of the Berghof we realise that the destruction or the survival and transformation of European culture and of German tradition have been at stake. The novel ends as Hans Castorp stumbles through the shell-strewn mud of the battlefield. He is unconsciously singing Schubert's 'Der Lindenbaum', the song which expresses a world he had, with misgiving, desperately loved, an enchanted world of 'sympathy with death'.

3. SARTRE: *LA NAUSÉE*

As we have seen, Castorp's curiosity stemmed from the failure of his time to meet his search for meaning. In Sartre's *La Nausée* the solitary hero, Roquentin, finds that a growing sense of meaninglessness generates a more acute existential panic. Roquentin's diary records the breakdown of the distinctions and the categories – perceptual, functional, linguistic, social, temporal, causal, scientific – which enable the mind to make sense of the world. Unlike Descartes's voluntary project of systematic doubt, Roquentin's experiential intuitions are passively undergone, although they, too, may ultimately reveal an irreducible truth, and Roquentin's *cogito* is more (or less) than a matter of intellectual process: it is that of a reluctantly embodied consciousness. He finds that inanimate things, however trivial or banal, resist his projects and his control: he can no longer play ducks and drakes with a pebble. They are no longer limited by the functions they are expected to perform: his hand has a new way of grasping, or of being uncannily grasped by, hitherto domesticated objects: his pipe, a fork, a doorhandle. (The sense of sight holds things at a distance in an already conceptualised perception; the sense of touch does not.) The normally instantaneous transition from perception to apperception – the active process of identification and recognition, the basis of knowledge – fails him: when an acquaintance greets him Roquentin finds a hand like a fat maggot placed in his. As he discovers when he contemplates a bristling tram-seat, disquieting metamorphoses escape the stabilising control of language. Climactically, as he sits in the municipal park, mesmerised by the indeterminate blackishness of a tree-root (existing objects cannot embody the essence of blackness, which is a secondary abstraction), Roquentin is assailed by a 'horrible ecstasy'; a revelation, later rationalised, of contingency; a sense of undifferentiated, proliferating existence which is there without reason, without cause, without necessity: the Absurd.

Is Roquentin mad? Has the world changed, or has he? Roquentin realises that to answer his own questions he must scrutinise not only objects but his own ways of being aware of them, the activity of his consciousness, or its 'intentionality'. In other words, he becomes an increasingly queasy phenomenologist – queasy because he discovers that embodiment, itself a matter of contingency, compromises what he (and Sartre) would prefer to think of as the autonomy and transparency of our consciousness of the world, its power to confer meaning. It compromises, too, the power of consciousness to reflect on its own activity. Crises of intentionality and reflection then begin to exacerbate his existential crisis. Awareness of his body assails Roquentin particularly when it is no longer the instrument of a project: instead of going unnoticed it begins to draw attention to itself, to its secretions, its involuntary movements, its materiality. In its collusion with the body, reflection is under threat and, with it, the power to sustain a sense of self. For Sartre, the Ego is a secondary construct created by reflection in an attempt to confer upon consciousness the identity which it lacks: Roquentin, invaded by physical sensations, can no longer say 'I'. And since the diary form is *par excellence* a medium of reflection, designed to stabilise and shape the self, it too collapses into a panic-stricken 'stream of consciousness', into halting syllables and broken syntax: language can no longer identify, differentiate or signify.

A similar crisis occurs when Roquentin finds himself finally alone: his imperious lover, Anny, has left him, and his acquaintance, the Autodidact, ejected from the public library after making tentative advances to two less than innocent boys, has refused his help. Both had tried to dominate contingency. Anny, the actress, had tried and failed to reconcile life and art, the real and the imaginary, time and stasis by attempting wilfully to orchestrate those perfect moments which Proust's Marcel had known to be a matter of chance. The Autodidact had sought meaning in a naïve humanism and in the order of knowledge: he had been working his way through the library from A to Z, and had reached L. Roquentin, abandoned, loses even more radically his sense of identity; the first person lapses into the third. However, the self now lost is no longer the self as Ego. Here Sartre anticipates his later definition of the self as *ipse*, as person: consciousness is reflected back to itself by its involvement in the world and with other people. But when these circuits break, consciousness is revealed as an impersonal or pre-personal activity; Roquentin's is now an empty, anonymous transparency, marginally and unreflectively aware of itself, scattered over the walls and lampposts, diluted in the evening mists. Thus Sartre dramatises his interpretation of Husserl's dictum that all consciousness is consciousness *of* something. He also challenges the limits of narrative.

Roquentin and the diary form are provisionally rescued when he takes refuge in a café and hears a little jazz tune. As a leitmotif throughout his experience it has stood for purity, rigour, and necessity of form against messiness and contingency: it is its own essence. Now he realises that it had been brought into 'being' by the existing bodies of its Jewish composer and its Black singer; it brings together hazard and necessity. Might the writing of a novel do the same for him? We shall never know. He leaves behind only a diary, which, like any diary, is neither a true transcription of life nor its pure transposition into art; like existence, which is neither brute matter nor pure form, it inhabits the world of the in-between.

4. CONCLUSION

Thematically, all three novels question the expressive and signifying power of language and writing. In practice, all three renew that power. In *A la recherche du temps perdu* the vagaries of tense, the uniquely sinuous syntax, and the mingled voices of the younger and older Marcel all help to dissolve the structures of time and memory, while sustained metaphors dramatise the interaction of sensation, affectivity, imagination, and reflection. Mann's tale is told by a strongly characterised but superficially traditional omniscient narrator; however, he questions tradition both thematically and by subverting, through Hans Castorp's uncertain progress, the conventions of the *Bildungsroman*. His use of the leitmotif reinforces the tension between development and stasis. Sartre's virtuoso exploitation and violation of the diary form measures the disproportion between calibrated time and lived time, and registers the instability of our acts of consciousness while exposing the inadequacy of the conventions whereby we seek to capture and represent them. All three novels renew narrative form; all three, like philosophy itself, are open-ended.

AESTHETICS BETWEEN THE WARS: ART
AND LIBERATION

PAUL GUYER

The arts after the First World War, especially in the 1920s, were a scene of tremendous innovation and experimentation: in the visual arts, there was Dada, Surrealism, Constructivism, Futurism, Neue Sachlichkeit, and more, while a previously radical artist like Picasso at least seemed to be taking a step backwards with neo-classicism; in literature, John Dos Passos experimented with visual techniques like collage and newsreel while James Joyce experimented with stream-of-consciousness; in music, the atonal principles of the Vienna school (Schönberg, Berg, and Webern) clashed with the neo-classicism of Stravinsky (another former radical who seemed to be returning to the past), Bartok turned to folk music for inspiration, and in America the influence of jazz blurred the boundaries between popular and high art; in architecture, mysticism and industrialism battled for the soul of the Bauhaus, while Frank Lloyd Wright reinvented himself, transforming his earlier naturalism of wood, brick, and stone into a dazzling new geometry of glass and concrete; and much of this ferment was inspired by political upheaval in Germany and Russia and scientific upheaval in the form of Einstein's theory of relativity, quantum physics, and above all Sigmund Freud's discovery of the subconscious and the all-pervasive sexuality of the human psyche.

At one level, much of this seems to have passed academic aesthetics by. Although prewar aestheticians had seemed bent on making room for modern art with their de-emphasis of beauty and insistence on the possibility of the difficult and ugly, many of the leading aestheticians of the interwar period seemed to have little to say about artistic experimentation. For instance, the invention of conceptual art by Marcel Duchamp in the 'teens didn't seem to make much of an impression on aestheticians until Arthur Danto's famous paper on 'The Artworld' in 1964 (Danto 1964) although since then much in aesthetics has concerned little else but the definition of art supposedly thrown into question by such work as Duchamp's. At another level, however, the very continuity of interwar aesthetics with what went before did make the writers of this period responsive to their times, for as we have seen in chapters 26 and 27 aestheticians from the time of Ruskin – and behind him Kant and Schiller – to the out-break of the First World War had seen art, beautiful or otherwise, as an ex-pression of human freedom; and aestheticians in the 1920s and 1930s continued to argue that the production and reception of art have their ultimate value in their potential for human self-liberation from the constraints of ignorance, con-vention, and even straightforward political and economic domination. This is obvious in the case of some Marxists but is also evident in the work of such leading academic aestheticians as John Dewey in the United States and R. G. Collingwood in Britain, and even in less obviously political thinkers such as Ernst Cassirer and Suzanne Langer. Exceptions to this rule seem to occur only in rad-ically conservative thinkers such as Martin Heidegger or in philosophers who would quarantine philosophy from all controversial values, such as the logical positivists.

1. MARXIST AESTHETICS

In this period, Marxist attitudes to art form a spectrum. At one end there was the perception characteristic of political leaders such as Lenin of art mainly as an instrument for arousing and maintaining revolutionary fervour. In the middle there was the position of those such as Lukács who saw the arts, especially literature, as a locus for the depiction and analysis of the contradictions and costs of capitalism. And at the other end artists and writers such as Brecht and Benjamin looked to the arts for expressions of the alienation in modern life that Marxism was supposed to cure but did not see the arts in a straightforwardly instrumental way as tools for the diagnosis and cure of social ills.

Like many later analytic philosophers, although for very different reasons, Lenin refused to recognise art or the aesthetic as a distinct sphere of human experience and activity, and instead subsumed art under the general category of 'intellectual work', to be employed on behalf of the revolution like any other form of work. Because art was simply to serve as part of the political education of the proletariat, artists were expected to work in well-established conventional forms that would be accessible to its target audience – even if those forms had originally been invented by and for the bourgeoisie. But Lev Bronstein, alias 'Leon Trotsky', struck a more independent path. He too thought that art could serve as a 'hammer' for the building of the new society, but also thought that traditional art needed to serve as a 'mirror' of existing society so that the revolutionaries could learn how to wield the hammer. He also kept in clear view what the ultimate point of a socialist revolution was, namely to extend the benefits of freedom to those whose work had previously provided those benefits only to the owners of the means of production, and reminded his colleagues that art must not only contribute to the revolution but also enjoy the freedom which was the point of the revolution.

Trotsky's plea for even traditional forms of art as a mirror of society was picked up by the Hungarian communist György (Georg) Lukács (1885–1971), even though Lukács suppressed the emphasis on individual self-expression in the precarious conditions of his refuge in Stalin's Moscow through much of the 1920s and 1930s. His first book, *The Soul and the Forms* (1910) was a Neo-Kantian work that he quickly repudiated; his second book, *The Theory of the Novel* (1916) was a more Hegelian work, analysing the historical development of literary forms and treating novels by Goethe, Stendhal, and Tolstoy. During the First World War, Lukács became actively involved in party politics and served in the short-lived Hungarian Soviet Republic in 1919. His writing for the next decade was political, epitomised by *History and Class Consciousness* (1923). Much of his time in the 1930s was taken up with polemics about the proper role of art under communism, as well as with literary studies that prepared the way for an enormous flood of publications after the Second World War. Lukács's constant argument was that every society must be understood as a complex but integrated whole, in which all aspects of life reflect the underlying economic and political realities of the society; that the psychology of individual types reflects the possibilities of the society as a whole; and that the value of art, above all literature, and in literature above all the novel, especially in its classical nineteenth-century form, is its representation of the complex reality of a society and of the psychological types characteristic of it. While not advocating a stylistic naturalism in any narrow sense, Lukács espoused 'realism', that is, a conception of art as essentially representing the society around it and valuable only insofar as it does so, rather than having any value as self-expression of the individual. Thus, he stayed closer to the line of Lenin than to the more lenient line of Trotsky, and was deeply hostile to what he identified as 'modernist' literature, such as that of Kafka or Joyce. All of this can quickly be seen in Lukács's 1938 polemic against Ernst Bloch, which was in turn to be attacked by Bertolt Brecht. Here Lukács wrote:

It goes without saying that without abstraction there can be no art – for otherwise how could anything in art have representative value? But like every movement, abstraction must have a direction . . . Every major realist fashions the material given in his own experience, and in so doing makes use of techniques of abstraction, among others. But his goal is to penetrate the laws governing objective reality and to uncover the deeper, hidden, mediated not immediately perceptible network of relationships that go to make up society . . . In the works of such writers we observe the whole surface of life in all its essential determinants, and not just a subjectively perceived moment isolated from the totality in an abstract and over-intense manner . . .

In contrast to this, what does it mean to talk of an abstraction away from reality? When the surface of life is only experienced immediately, it remains opaque, fragmentary, chaotic and uncomprehended. ('Realism in the Balance', *Das Wort* (1938); quoted from Taylor 1977: 38–9)

Lukács's vast output in both aesthetic theory and literary criticism all serves this simple position.

Within the far more fluid scene of Germany prior to 1933 and among the German-speaking emigration after Hitler's triumph, writers could identify themselves as Marxists but defend a more adventuresome conception of art than this. The playwright Bertolt Brecht (1898–1956) and the critic Walter Benjamin (1892–1940) certainly illustrate this: the furthest away from the party line among self-avowed Marxists in the 1920s and 1930s, they are also those whose literary practice and literary theory continue to be most influential today.

Brecht made his mark as a playwright and librettist in Weimar Germany and then in exile from 1933 to 1948 with plays such as *Baal*, *Mother Courage*, *The Good Woman of Szechwan*, and (with Kurt Weill) operas such as *The Threepenny Opera* and *The Rise and Fall of the City of Mahagonny*. His greatest influence was undoubtedly through these works, which permanently transformed their genres. In particular, Brecht aimed to break the conventions of naturalism and illusion in traditional theatre through what he called *Verfremdungseffekten* ('alienating effects'), beginning by breaking down the barrier between actors and audience imposed by the proscenium arch, and including all sorts of interruptions of and additions to the traditional flow of action in the theatre – placards, background projections, bursts of song, and actors breaking from their rôles to address the audience. As a Marxist, however, Brecht still had to conceive of his work as a form of 'realism', so he reconceived realism, shifting its concern away from the form and content of the work to its effect on the audience. In other words, realistic art does not need to recreate reality within the theatre, but to open or reopen the eyes of the audience to reality outside the theatre. As Brecht put it in his reply to Lukács, realism is not a matter of style but of effect:

Realistic means: discovering the causal complexes of society / unmasking the prevailing view of things as the view of those who are in power / writing from the standpoint of the class which offers the broadest solutions for the pressing difficulties in which human society is caught up / emphasizing the elements of development / making possible the concrete, and making possible abstraction from it.

But the revolutionary effects of art were not to be achieved by transforming the artist into a cog in a party machine:

Moreover we shall allow the artist to employ his fantasy, his originality, his humour, his invention, in following them. We shall not stick to too detailed literary models; we shall not bind the artist to too rigidly defined modes of narrative. (Brecht, 'Against Georg Lukács', Essay IV, 'Popularity and Realism', written in 1938, but not published until his posthumous *Schriften zur Kunst und Literatur* 1967; quoted from Taylor 1977: 62)

While Brecht's influence on drama and other literary forms after the Second World War was inescapable, the influence of his friend Walter Benjamin on contemporary literary theory and especially the field recently known as 'cultural studies', which looks far beyond conventional literature to all sorts of areas of manufacture, advertisement, and material culture for its subjects, is even stronger today. Benjamin defended the kind of modernism scorned by Lukács: while still alive, he was known for his writing on Baudelaire, Proust, Kafka, and many other archetypical modernists, and he spent much of the last decade of his life working on the so-called *Passagenwerk*, which was to describe the characteristics of modern life starting off from reflections on the commercial arcades of mid-nineteenth-century Paris. But his primary influence on aesthetic and literary theory came through several essays published in the 1930s. The most famous of these is 'The Work of Art in the Age of its Mechanical Reproducibility', first published in 1936 and included in the first influential collection of Benjamin's work in English in 1968 (Benjamin 1968: 219–53). In this essay, Benjamin famously argues that the 'aura' of the traditional work of art, above all a piece of sculpture or painting, came not just from its uniqueness but also from its function as 'cult' art, for example, its use in religious practice, which was itself an expression of domination and manipulation; by contrast what he called 'exhibition' art, beginning with painting produced for public exhibitions in the nineteenth century but reaching its full power in the mechanically reproducible media of still photography and cinema in the twentieth century, is not meant for use in a cult, escapes the mystification of 'aura', and instead allows its audience to take an active role like that of a critic or even a cinematographer. Traditional art forms with their aura are thus held to be an instrument for the manipulation of the masses, while modern, mechanically reproducible forms of art are held to be a progressive force that will lead the masses to develop their critical faculties. In a lecture given in 1934, Benjamin had clearly recognised that modern mass media such as newspapers, owned by capitalists, could succeed in co-opting even revolutionary writers; but he seems to have forgotten that lesson in the breathtaking naïveté of his better-known essay of two years later. Here a profoundly romantic conception of the masses and of their revolutionary inclinations seems to have taken over. One can only think that Benjamin could hardly have written this essay as he did if he had been able to remain in Nazi Germany and see the manipulative cinematography of the likes of Leni Riefenstahl. Perhaps this essay explains why it is Benjamin's criticism which so influences contemporary literary and cultural theory and not his theoretical writing, which impresses philosophical aestheticians.

2. DEWEY

While Marxist aestheticians in Europe were trying to figure out how art could help produce a new order out of chaos, aestheticians in the established democracies were reflecting upon the role of the arts in free societies. In the United States, the leading philosopher between the death of William James in 1910 until at least a decade after the Second World War was John Dewey (1859–1952). Dewey hardly mentioned aesthetics during his long career devoted to developing a naturalistic theory of enquiry and conduct, and did not write a systematic work in aesthetics until he was well past a normal retirement age: *Art as Experience* was first delivered as William James lectures at Harvard in 1930–31 and published in book form in 1934, when Dewey was already seventy-five years old. But the book was immediately and widely read.

Like much of Dewey's work, *Art as Experience* begins with an attack upon dualism. In this case, the form of dualism that Dewey has in his sights is the classical separation of aesthetic experience from all other forms of experience, the kind of view epitomised in Clive Bell's *Art* (1914) (see chapter 27). For Dewey, the 'primary task imposed upon one who undertakes to write upon the philosophy of the fine arts . . . is to restore continuity between the refined and intensified forms of experience that are works of art and the everyday events, doings, and sufferings that are universally recognized to constitute experience' (Dewey 1934: 3). The obvious thrust of Dewey's argument is that the experience of art can be the paradigmatic form of experience in general, which it is the point of human life to have and enjoy. Underrepresented, at least in the title of Dewey's work, is the parallel argument that *making* art is the paradigmatic form of activity in general, which also pervades human life. But perhaps the title of the work is justified by the fact that the ultimate point of life is what he calls 'consummatory' experience, experience in which we achieve stability and resolution in our interactions with the rest of nature, know that we do so, and enjoy the fact that we do so, and that activity and practice are means to this end.

The two key notions underlying Dewey's account are that existence is a constant process of interaction between an organism and its environment, in which the organism seeks equilibrium in the exchange of energy with the environment, an equilibrium that is achievable but never permanent; and that experience is the awareness and enjoyment of this effort at equilibrium and its realisation. Conscious living creatures are aware of the search for equilibrium and take pleasure in 'consummation', the experience of a temporary equilibrium. Experience as such, or what Dewey also calls 'an experience', is the distinct realisation of a moment of equilibrium in the flow of existence, and it is through art that such distinct moments of experience are most clearly captured: 'Because experience is the fulfillment of an organism in its struggles and achievements in a world of things, it is art in germ' (Dewey 1934: 19).

Having erected the framework for his account of art within his general theory of experience, Dewey joins the mainstream of aesthetic theory by arguing that art has a special role in the expression of emotion. The connection is effected by the assumption that the attempt to express their own experience to others is a normal part of their ongoing interaction with their environment for human beings. But a work of art is not to be understood as simply a refined sigh or cry; rather, Dewey supposes, art works by objectifying emotion, presenting its content, its object, its context. On the basis of this claim, Dewey then distinguishes his view from that of someone like Clive Bell, to whom he must be alluding when he says that 'emotion as thus "objectified" is esthetic', but then adds 'Esthetic emotion is thus something distinctive and yet not cut off by a chasm from other and natural emotional experiences, as some theorists in contending for its existence have made it to be' (Dewey 1934: 78).

Dewey's general theory of experience seems to focus on the consumer of art, while his theory of art as the expression or objectification of emotion might appear to emphasise the rôle of the producer. But true to his general picture of experience as a constant give-and-take between an organism and its environment, and thus between one human being and others, Dewey's aesthetic theory stresses more clearly than many the place for both producer and consumer and interaction between them in the experience of art. He notes that the term art 'denotes a process of doing or making . . . molding of clay, chipping of marble, laying on of pigments, construction of buildings, singing of songs', and so on, while 'The word "esthetic" refers . . . to experience as appreciative, perceiving, and enjoying. It denotes the consumer's rather than the producer's standpoint.' But, he goes on, 'the distinction between esthetic and artistic cannot be pressed so far as to become a separation' (Dewey 1934: 47). Clearly the artist must also play the role of the consumer, standing back from the work to gauge its potential effect on others and using that perspective to refine his original intention and its objectification in the work on the way to its completion. But, perhaps less obviously, the experience of the consumer also involves activity as well as receptivity. The experience of taking in a work of art is also a flow in which an appreciator takes in external stimulation, forms conjectures about its meaning and coming experiences, refines those in light of further observation of the object, and so on, until some satisfying equilibrium is reached. Appreciating a work of art might not require all of the imaginative invention and manual or technical skills that are required for making one, but it is still a progress which actively involves the mind and imagination as well as the senses of the audience, and requires an interaction between the audience and its environment that is not entirely dissimilar to that which occurs between the artist and his. Perhaps no one since Ruskin had made this point as clearly and emphatically as Dewey does.

How does Dewey's theory of art fit in with his larger project of providing a philosophy suitable for the citizens of an ever-improving democracy? Two points can be made. First, Dewey ultimately values democracy as the system within which individual liberty can flourish, where individual liberty in turn is ultimately valued because it is the condition for the achievement of the kind of consummatory experience exemplified by art. Second, Dewey emphasises that art contributes to the success of communication between people which is necessary for the successful functioning of democracy. The heart of Dewey's account of art thus concludes with these words:

Expression strikes below the barriers that separate human beings from one another. Since art is the most universal form of language, since it is constituted, even apart from literature, by the common qualities of the public world, it is the most universal and freest form of communication . . . That art weds man and nature is a familiar fact. Art also renders men aware of their union with one another in origin and destiny. (Dewey 1934: 270–1)

Like many in the generation before him, Dewey too stands in the tradition of Kant, Schiller, and Ruskin.

3. R. G. COLLINGWOOD

The most memorable work on aesthetics produced in Britain during the interwar period is Collingwood's *The Principles of Art* (1938). Collingwood (1889–1942) in fact addressed aesthetics three times. In his most Hegelian work, *Speculum Mentis* (Collingwood 1924) Collingwood portrayed art as a form of knowledge, but as the most rudimentary form on a scale ascending from art through religion, science, history and philosophy. In *Outlines of a Philosophy of Art* (Collingwood 1925) Collingwood emphasised that art is a form of imaginative activity rather than the mere production of physical objects. In *The Principles of Art*, Collingwood used the clue given in his second work to transcend the position of the first, arguing that by means of the imaginative activity of art both artist and audience can achieve self-knowledge, especially of emotions, that is not to be had in any other way.

The argument of *The Principles of Art* begins in Book I with Collingwood's famous distinction between art and craft. Craft is productive activity characterised by firm distinctions between means and end, planning and execution, raw material and finished product, matter and form, and a hierarchical organisation, in which the finished product of one sort of craftsworker can be the raw material for another, as when the miner supplies coal to the blacksmith and the blacksmith horseshoes to the farmer. Conversely, art proper, as Collingwood calls it, allows for none of these distinctions: a work of art does not serve some end external to it, planning and execution must constantly be intertwined, the distinction between raw material and finished product is typically inapplicable (neither words nor emotions are raw materials for a poem or a song), and there is no obvious hierarchy among the arts – the librettist is not a craftsman who supplies a finished product for the next, the composer, but both 'collaborate to produce a work of art that owes something to each of them' (Collingwood 1938: 25). This set of contrasts leads both to what is most implausible as well as to what is most powerful in Collingwood's views.

The confusion of art proper with mere craft is what Collingwood calls 'the technical theory of art', and he rejects this: 'we must disabuse ourselves of the notion that the business of an artist consists in producing a special kind of artifacts, so-called "works of art" or objets d'art, which are bodily and perceptible things (painted canvases, carved stones, and so forth). This notion is nothing more nor less than the technical theory of art itself.' Rather, the artist produces two different things:

Primarily, it is an 'internal' or 'mental' thing, something (as we commonly say) 'existing in his head' and there only: something of the kind which we commonly call an experience. Secondarily, it is a bodily or perceptible thing (a picture, statue, &c.) . . . Of these two things, the first is obviously not anything that can be called a work of art, if work means something made in the sense in which a weaver makes cloth. But since it is the thing which the artist as such primarily produces, I shall argue that we are entitled to call it 'the work of art' proper. The second thing, the bodily and perceptible thing, I shall show to be only incidental to the first. (Collingwood 1938: 36–7)

This conclusion may follow from Collingwood's premise, the strict distinction between art and craft, but it is so contrary to any common usage – to which Collingwood always professes allegiance – that one might have thought it should only have cast doubt upon that premise itself.

Collingwood's claim that there cannot be a rigid distinction between means and end in the case of art leads to an altogether more attractive part of his view, his argument that art should not be confused with either 'amusement' or 'magic'. Both amusement and magic have as their end the arousal of emotion;

under the rubric of magic, in particular, Collingwood includes the use of art for purposes of religious and political propaganda, and his visceral dislike for these clearly underlies his insistence that art cannot have an end outside itself. This is perhaps overstated, because in fact his view is that art does have a describable end, although this end, unlike the ends of amusement and magic, could not be achieved by anything other than art (and here is where the standpoint of *The Principles of Art* transcends that of *Speculum Mentis*). This end, further, does have something to do with emotion: not with the arousal of emotion, however, but rather with the clarification and understanding of emotion. The primary task of art is the expression of emotion for the sake of understanding it: 'The characteristic mark of expression proper is lucidity or intelligibility' (Collingwood 1938: 122). Without mentioning the name of Tolstoy, Collingwood takes this occasion to dismiss his 'infection' theory of art (see chapter 27). The verses of even sincere 'young men who, learning in the torment of their own bodies and minds what war is like, have stammered their indignation in verses, and published them in the hope of infecting others and causing them to abolish it . . . have nothing to do with poetry', and 'it is not her ability to weep real tears that would mark out a good actress; it is her ability to make it clear to herself and her audience what the tears are about' (Collingwood 1938: 122–3). If Tolstoy's infection theory of art must be rejected even when it is used by sincere people who would arouse emotions for ends that are clearly good, it hardly needs to be stated how dangerous it is if it can be taken to license the propaganda of those, whether fascists or communists, who would destroy the liberty of others in the name of what they conceive of as a greater good.

Collingwood's theory that it is by means of art that we understand emotions puts his view that the work of art is internal to the artist in a better light: the work – that is, the activity rather than the product – of art must certainly begin within the artist, because the artist cannot make clear to others what he has not made clear to himself; yet what the artist does succeed in making clear to himself he can also make clear to others, and while making the character of emotions clear to others is not the whole end for which the creation of a work of art is the mere means, it is part of the end of which self-understanding is also part. This argument is further clarified in Book III of *The Principles of Art*. Collingwood argues here that the creation of art is the creation of a language for the expression of truth, and that in attempting to create such a language the artist must constantly be checking the success of his intentions against the medium he can employ to communicate with his audience and with the responses of his audience. In terms that could quite easily have been taken from Dewey, the supposed pragmatist, Collingwood, the supposed idealist, argues that, for example, the experiences of seeing and painting cannot rigidly be separated, but that the painter is constantly learning how to see in seeing what he paints, and thus that 'production is somehow necessarily connected with the aesthetic activity' after all (Collingwood 1938: 204–5). Likewise, Collingwood stresses that the process of understanding is something that the artist does not for an audience, but with an audience:

In so far as the artist feels himself at one with his audience . . . he takes it as his business to express not his own private emotions, irrespectively of whether any one else feels them or not, but the emotions he shares with his audience. Instead of conceiving himself as a mystagogue, leading his audience as far as it can follow along the dark and difficult paths of his own mind . . . he will be a humbler person, imposing upon himself the task of understanding his world, and thus enabling it to understand itself (Collingwood 1938: 312).

For Collingwood the achievement of this understanding is essential to the possibility of freedom:

Art is not a luxury, and bad art is not a thing we can afford to tolerate . . . In so far as consciousness is corrupted, the very wells of truth are poisoned. Intellect can build nothing firm. Moral ideals are castles in the air. Political and economic systems are mere cobwebs. Even common sanity and bodily health are no longer secure. But corruption of consciousness is the same thing as bad art. (Collingwood 1938: 284–5)

The Principles of Art is *The Stones of Venice* for a time of crisis.

4. THE NEO-KANTIAN AESTHETICS OF CASSIRER AND LANGER

Aesthetics did not loom large among the subjects of the Neo-Kantians who dominated German academic philosophy before the First World War, although Hermann Cohen (1842–1918), one of the founders of the Marburg school of Neo-Kantianism, wrote a commentary on each of Kant's three critiques and also included a treatise on aesthetics in his own tripartite system of philosophy. Aesthetics figured more prominently in the work of Cohen's student, Ernst Cassirer (1874–1945), especially in his own summary of his philosophical standpoint for Anglophone readers, the *Essay on Man* (1944).

As a follower of the Marburg Neo-Kantian tradition, Cassirer held that human beings organise their experience with a variety of symbolic systems, such as those of language and mathematics, and from a number of standpoints, such as those of myth, natural science, and art; unlike latter-day Hegelians, however, Cassirer did not arrange the different symbolic forms or modes of understanding and interpretation in any hierarchy. But he did hold that there is a fundamental difference between such symbolic forms as ordinary language and natural science on the

one hand and the artistic use of language and other media on the other: language
and science depend upon abstraction to identify and organise our recognition of
what is universal and repeatable in the flux of experience, whereas art is aimed at
capturing the form of particular experiences in their individuality. For example,
a landscape painter 'does not portray or copy a certain empirical object – a landscape with its hills and mountains', as he might if he were illustrating a scientific
work on geology or topography; rather, 'What he gives us is the individual and
momentary physiognomy of the landscape' (Cassirer 1944: 144). Having made
this general statement, however, Cassirer goes on to argue that art has the special
task of clearly fixing the form and physiognomy of human passion and emotion:
in art, he claims, 'Our passions are no longer dark and impenetrable powers;
they become, as it were, transparent' (Cassirer 1944: 147). Thus, starting from
neither the Hegelianism of Bosanquet or Collingwood nor the naturalism of
Santayana, but from Neo-Kantianism, Cassirer nevertheless comes to the same
conclusion as so many in the mainstream of aesthetic theory since the turn of
the century, that the special function of art, regardless of medium and style, is
to capture and clarify the subjective aspect of human experience in a way that
none of our other forms of cognition can.

    Cassirer was also a political thinker, and like Dewey and Collingwood he too
thought that aesthetic experience could make a fundamental contribution to
human freedom by transforming passions which might rule us into 'formative
powers' that we can rule. Whereas Collingwood seems to think of the self-
understanding art accomplishes as perhaps first and foremost a defence against
manipulation through propaganda from without, Cassirer – in this certainly
more of a Kantian – considers the primary function of the transubstantiation of
emotion through art to be that of a defence against self-corruption by our own
emotional excesses. But clearly both see art and aesthetic experience not just as
one of the distinctive forms of human cognition but also as a unique support
for morality in human conduct.

    The American Susanne K. Langer (1895–1985) was hardly as political a
thinker as Collingwood or even Cassirer, who was one of the main influences
on her work, but even so the connection between aesthetic experience and
self-liberation is not entirely absent from her work. Langer's main work in aesthetics, especially the 1953 book *Feeling and Form*, falls outside the scope of
this survey; but the germ of her thought about art was already present in her
1942 book *Philosophy in a New Key*. Appealing to contemporary philosophers of
language such as Russell, Wittgenstein, and Carnap as well as to Cassirer, Langer
holds that human thought is essentially symbolic rather than representational,
that it uses a variety of devices to structure our experience rather than simply
copying structures it finds in experience. But unlike some of those mentioned,

she argues that not all forms of human symbolism should be assimilated to the models of natural language or the artificial languages of science and mathematics; in particular, she holds, in a tradition that reaches back not only to Cassirer but long before him to Alexander Baumgarten, that the arts typically do not aim to employ 'discursive' symbol-systems to analyse experience but rather use non-discursive symbols to capture the quality of experience itself. Taking music as her primary example of an art-form that should not be simply assimilated to natural or artificial language, she argues that

The analogy between music and language breaks down if we carry it beyond the mere semantic function in general, which they are supposed to share. Logically, music has not the characteristic properties of language – separable terms with fixed connotations, and syntactical rules for deriving complex connotations without any loss to the constituent elements . . . Yet it may be a presentational symbol, and present emotive experience through global forms that are as indivisible as the elements of chiaroscuro. (Langer 1942: 232)

Like most of her contemporaries, then, Langer supposes that the arts have the special function of capturing and clarifying the nature of human emotions, but adds that the symbolic systems that the arts employ often have distinctive logical properties (it is hard to read a passage like that quoted without suspecting that Langer's work was not a major influence on such a later work as Nelson Goodman's *Languages of Art* (Goodman 1968)).

Langer argues at length that it is by means of these symbol-systems that we exercise our freedom, which is what gives value to our lives, and that the abuse and misuse of symbol-systems is a threat to freedom itself. Hence, although she does not argue that art and aesthetic experience can directly promote the development of human freedom, she certainly seems to assume that freedom for artistic self-expression is an obvious target for those who would attack human freedom more generally and thus at least an index of the health of freedom in a society. One way or another, the issue of human freedom never seems far from the minds of aestheticians in the period leading from the First World War into the Second.

5. EXCEPTIONS

To be sure, not all of the philosophers of the interwar period who touched upon aesthetics incorporated the production and experience of art into a larger theory of human freedom; but often a lack of interest in the moral and political significance of art was part of a metaphilosophical view that excluded much of traditional moral and political theory itself from the proper purview of philosophy, and sometimes indifference to aesthetic experience as a form of human freedom was even connected to a political philosophy hostile to the liberal tradition itself. The first is the case in the dismissal of the possibility of aesthetics by the logical positivists, while the second is certainly true in the case of the Nazi sympathiser Martin Heidegger.

Aesthetics was not directly addressed by the Viennese founders of logical positivism; but A. J. Ayer (1910–89) did address the question of the possibility of aesthetics briefly in his widely read *Language, Truth and Logic* (Ayer 1946). Ayer's comments upon aesthetics come in the course of his more extensive treatment of ethics, in which he argues that apparent value statements in general can be divided into two kinds, verifiable statements of facts and merely hortatory expressions of emotion (see chapter 58). Ayer then went on to apply the same analysis to aesthetic terms and statements: 'Aesthetic terms are used in exactly the same way as ethical terms. Such aesthetic words as "beautiful" and "hideous" are employed, as ethical words are employed, not to make statements of fact, but simply to express certain feelings and evoke a certain response' (Ayer 1946: 113). Thus Ayer thought there could be no aesthetics, as a philosophy of criticism, because critical statements are not cognitive statements at all. This was in opposition to the view of writers in the Hegelian and Neo-Kantian traditions, such as Collingwood and Cassirer, who held that art itself is a form of cognition, although of a distinctive kind.

In the same year (1938) that Collingwood published *The Principles of Art* Ludwig Wittgenstein was lecturing on aesthetics at Cambridge (Wittgenstein 1966). Although Wittgenstein's early writings had been the inspiration for the logical positivists, his views were typically more subtle than theirs, and this was true in aesthetics as well. On the one hand, he was even more extreme than Ayer in rejecting the possibility of any science of aesthetics. This may have been because he had in mind the scientific aesthetics of nineteenth-century Germany, the sort of thing attempted by Fechner and Helmholtz, who sought to discover by psychological experimentation certain forms that would be universally pleasing. This Wittgenstein scorned: 'You might think Aesthetics is a science telling us what's beautiful – almost too ridiculous for words. I suppose it ought include also what sort of coffee tastes well' (Wittgenstein 1966: 11). Unlike Ayer, however, who simply categorised all forms of normative discourse that could not be taken as statements of fact as expressions of emotion instead, Wittgenstein was more concerned to attack the meaningfulness of abstract terms and general statements in aesthetic discourse, arguing instead that critical discourse is successful when it works by using particular terms to focus attention on the interesting features of the objects actually before us:

It is remarkable that in real life, when aesthetic judgments are made, aesthetic adjectives such as 'beautiful', 'fine', etc., play hardly any role at all. Are aesthetic adjectives used in a musical criticism? You say: 'Look at this transition', or 'The passage here is incoherent'. Or you say, in a poetical criticism: 'His use of images is precise'. The words you use are more akin to 'right' and 'correct' (as these words are used in ordinary speech) than to 'beautiful' and 'lovely'. (Wittgenstein 1966: 3)

Wittgenstein then went on to link the particularity of aesthetic terms to the particularity of what he here calls 'ways of living' (what would later become a central concept in his philosophy under the name of 'forms of life'). These must themselves be understood as the context within which particular language games are played, and if they are to be described at all they too must be described in the particular terms that they make available. So there is no place for the generalisations of a 'scientific' aesthetics, or indeed of a sociology or psychology of art.

Politics played little role in Wittgenstein's philosophy, including his comments on aesthetics. The same could be said of the first significant writer on aesthetics in the phenomenological tradition established by Edmund Husserl (1859–1938). Husserl himself said nothing about aesthetics, but the Polish phenomenologist Roman Ingarden (1893–1970) devoted most of his career to the subject. Ingarden's major work was *The Literary Work of Art* (Ingarden 1931). Unfortunately, Ingarden was tied up in the sterile debate about idealism that dominated argument in the phenomenological school after about 1909, and his main argument that a work of art does not fall neatly into either the category of external object or subjective state, displaying rather features of each, would seem obvious to most Western readers. The same might be said for the 'reception aesthetics' of postwar Germany, the school on which Ingarden seems to have had his major influence.

A more interesting but troubling figure in the phenomenological tradition is Martin Heidegger (1889–1976). Heidegger did not deal with art in *Being and Time* (1927), but gave lectures on aesthetics in 1931 and 1934 which in 1935–6 he wrote up as the famous essay 'The Origin of the Work of Art', although it was not published until 1950.

Heidegger attacked traditional aesthetics, thinking of it as a paradigmatic example of the subjectivist tradition in Western thought that he detested. In Heidegger's terms, traditional aesthetics did not adequately recognise the 'thingliness of the thing', nor recognise that in the experience of art 'we yield ourselves to the undisguised presence [*Anwesen*] of the thing', as a form of yielding ourselves to the presence of Being itself (Heidegger 1950 [Hofstader and Kuhns 1964: 656]). While philosophers in the tradition of Kant and Schiller through to

Heidegger's frequent opponent Ernst Cassirer had glorified aesthetic experience as a paradigmatic form of the activity of free human beings, Heidegger's description of aesthetic experience as one of 'yielding' reveals the fundamental passivity of his conception of human nature. But the essay had even more of a political message than that: much of it is a veiled glorification of the attempt of the German soul to break away from the dominance of the rationalist element in the Greek: while the form of the Greek temple reflects the struggle of the Greek soul to break away from the bonds of the earth, Van Gogh's painting of peasant shoes is praised as revealing 'the reliability' of the uncomplaining 'peasant woman' who by wearing and working in them 'is admitted into the silent call of the earth'. Heidegger could not become the official philosophical spokesman of Nazism that he at least briefly hoped to be, but his philosophy nevertheless reflected the political passivism and disvaluation of freedom on which the Nazi triumph actually depended.

LAW AND POLITICS

HANS KELSEN AND NORMATIVE
LEGAL POSITIVISM

STANLEY L. PAULSON

Hans Kelsen's fundamental contributions to legal philosophy are accompanied by seminal work in political theory and on problems of constitutional law and public international law. There are also forays into anthropological speculation, important studies of classical philosophers, most notably Plato, and much more of interest along the way. It is in legal philosophy, however, that Kelsen made his mark. As early as 1934, the erudite Roscoe Pound wrote that Kelsen was 'unquestionably the leading jurist of the time' (Pound 1933–4: 532), and to this day many in jurisprudential circles endorse Pound's assessment.

Three phases of development in Kelsen's theory can be distinguished: an early phase, 'critical constructivism' (1911–21); then the long, 'classical' or 'Neo-Kantian' phase (1921–60), including in the 1920s the formation, around Kelsen, of the Vienna School of Legal Theory; and, finally, the late, 'sceptical' phase (1960–73). The early phase is seen most clearly in Kelsen's first major treatise, *Hauptprobleme der Staatsrechtslehre* (Kelsen 1911). One of Kelsen's central aims in the early phase – but not just there – is to establish legal science as a 'normative' discipline, by which he understands a discipline that is addressed to normative material and whose statements are formulated in normative language. Toward this end, he attempts to 'construct' the fundamental concepts of the law, for, as he argues, to understand these concepts correctly is to understand them as peculiarly normative – and not, then, as amenable to expression in factual terms.

Kelsen's classical or Neo-Kantian phase is commonly known as the Pure Theory of Law. Lasting four decades, it is ushered in by two major developments. First, going well beyond the work of his early phase, Kelsen begins in the 1920s to attempt to set out the rudiments of a Neo-Kantian argument, not only for some of the constructions of the *Hauptprobleme* and other early writings, but also, and more fundamentally, as a means of resolving the normativity problematic (to which I return below). Second, no later than 1923, Kelsen adopts lock, stock, and barrel Adolf Julius Merkl's doctrine of hierarchical structure (*Stufenbaulehre*) (see Kelsen 1923–4: 377–408), which offers a dynamic characterisation of the law 'in motion, in the constantly regenerating process of its self-creation' (Kelsen 1934: §43 [1992: 91]; Merkl 1917 is an early statement of the *Stufenbaulehre*; the most complete statement is Merkl 1931). Kelsen aside, Merkl was far and away the most significant figure in the Vienna School of Legal Theory. Kelsen's adoption of Merkl's *Stufenbaulehre* is also the genesis of Kelsen's fruitful interest in questions on the character of the legal system. Finally, Kelsen's late, sceptical phase emerges in the period 1959–62, marking his abandonment of the Kantian doctrines familiar from the classical phase. Now he defends a voluntaristic or 'will' theory of law instead, the very type of theory he criticised so vehemently in both earlier phases.

1. THE NORMATIVITY THESIS

The aspect of Kelsen's theory that has enjoyed the most attention is the normative dimension of his legal positivism. Kelsen recasts the terms of the traditional debate, and it is well to begin there, lest the force of his own arguments be missed. When Kant, in a well-known passage in the *Rechtslehre*, poses the classical philosophical question 'What is law?' (Kant 1797: §B [1991: 55, trans. altered]), he is following a juridico-philosophical tradition that extends over two millennia. Couched in terms of reason or, alternatively, in terms of will, the leading answers are familiar – natural law theory on the one hand, legal positivism or legal voluntarism on the other. Indeed, the tradition in legal philosophy is often said to consist of variations of these two types of legal theory (see e.g. Alexy 1992 [2002]).

Going a step further, many writers assume that natural law theory and traditional, fact-based legal positivism are together exhaustive of the possibilities on the 'nature of law' problematic: *tertium non datur*, there is no third possibility (see e.g. the papers in Maihofer 1962). Pretenders, theories that purport to be distinct from both traditional types of theory, turn out to be disguised versions of one or the other. The argument on behalf of *tertium non datur* is straightforward: since natural law theory is characterised in terms of the *morality thesis*, namely, the idea that there is a conceptually necessary connection between the law and morality at some juncture or another, and since legal positivism is characterised in terms of the *separation thesis*, the contradictory of the morality thesis, the theories exhaust the possibilities.

This is Kelsen's point of departure. But far from endorsing the idea that natural law theory and traditional, fact-based legal positivism together exhaust the possibilities, Kelsen challenges it. So long as the competing types of theory are characterised in terms of a single pair of theses (the separation and morality theses), they will indeed appear to be together exhaustive of the possibilities. Kelsen insists, however, that a second pair of theses, the facticity and normativity theses, plays every bit as fundamental a role in the 'nature of law' problematic as the traditional pair, the separation and morality theses.

Seen historically, Kelsen is drawing this second pair of theses, facticity and normativity, from the Baden or Heidelberg Neo-Kantians, who in the name of 'methodological dualism' insisted on a hard and fast distinction between *Sein* and *Sollen*, 'is' and 'ought' (Kelsen 1911: 7–11 *et passim*, and see Paulson 1996 [1998: 27–32]). Seen, however, from the standpoint of Kelsen's juridico-philosophical reconstruction of the traditional theories, the *facticity thesis* has it that the law is ultimately explicable in terms of a concatenation of fact, and precisely this position is denied by the *normativity thesis*, the contradictory of the facticity thesis. Appealing to both pairs of theses to show that the two traditional types of theory are not together exhaustive of the possibilities after all, Kelsen places his own theory within this framework as a new type of theory, representing a 'middle way' (Kelsen 1960: §34(g) [1967: 211], see generally Paulson 1992; Raz 1981 [1998]). His theory is new in bringing together the separation and normativity theses, and it counts as a middle way between the traditional theories in taking from each of them what is defensible (the separation thesis from legal positivism and the normativity thesis from natural law theory) (see, on the latter, Kelsen 1911: 7; Raz 1974 [1998: 67]; Ross 1961 [1998: 159–61]), while leaving behind what is not defensible (the facticity thesis from legal positivism and the morality thesis from natural law theory).

In defending a version of the separation thesis, which in later formulations resembles its British counterpart (see Hart 1957–8 [1983]), Kelsen is speaking as the legal positivist. In replying to a host of European predecessors and colleagues in the field, however, he takes a tack that distinguishes his position sharply from the legal positivism of the continental tradition. Whereas proponents of traditional legal positivism defend the facticity thesis, Kelsen, defending the normativity thesis, calls for an explication of the law – and of legal obligation in particular – altogether independently of fact. The ensuing theory – the Pure Theory of Law – has given rise to a great variety of interpretations. Kelsen's own persuasion is Neo-Kantian. A number of doctrinal themes of Kantian import are evident in Kelsen's texts, among them – sketched below – the juridico-transcendental question, the constitutive function of legal science, and peripheral imputation as intellectual category. In addition, there is the inevitable question of how Kelsen's basic norm is to be understood.

2. THE PURE THEORY OF LAW

Kant writes in the *Critique of Pure Reason* that he will call 'all cognition *transcendental* that is occupied not so much with objects but with our manner of cognition of objects insofar as this is to be possible a priori' (Kant 1787: B25 [1998: 133 and 133 note a]). This distinctive reading of 'transcendental' flags the conditions for the possibility of *Erkenntnis* or cognition. Kelsen, following the lead of other *fin de siècle* Neo-Kantians who sought to apply elements of Kant's transcendental philosophy to the standing disciplines, looks to the conditions for the possibility of *Rechtserkenntnis* or legal cognition. In 'Rechtswissenschaft und Recht', he alludes to a formulation of the juridico-transcendental question proffered by his younger colleague Fritz Sander (Kelsen 1922b: 128), and then, in *Philosophical Foundations of Natural Law Theory and Legal Positivism*, he poses the juridico-transcendental question himself: 'How is positive law *qua* object of cognition, *qua* object of cognitive legal science, possible?' (Kelsen 1928 [1945: 437, trans. altered]). In effect, Kelsen is asking for an argument in support of the constitutive function of cognitive legal science.

This constitutive function of cognitive legal science remains prominent throughout Kelsen's classical phase. Cognitive legal science has the task of creating a 'unified legal system' from the 'chaotic material' of the law, from its 'statutes, regulations, judicial decisions, administrative acts, and the like' (Kelsen 1922b: 181–2). Just as natural science 'creates' its object, namely, nature *qua* system of synthetic a priori judgements, so likewise cognitive legal science 'creates' its object, the law *qua* materially unified system of legal norms (1922b: 181). That which is constituted by cognitive legal science manifests the structure of the hypothetically formulated or 'reconstructed' legal norm (see e.g. Kelsen 1925: §10(e), pp. 54–5, and see Kelsen 1934 [1992: Appendix I, at Suppl. Note 5, 132–4]). The key to its distinctive structure lies with the intellectual category of cognitive legal science.

Imputation *qua* category of cognitive legal science, Kelsen argues, can be compared directly to causality *qua* category in the natural sciences (see Kelsen 1934: §11(b) [1992: 23–4]). Specifically, Kelsen understands the category as making possible the attribution of a material fact (say, the elements of a delict) to a subject, thereby establishing the subject's legal liability. When Kelsen writes that the legal 'ought' designates 'a relative *a priori* category for comprehending empirical legal data' (§11(b) [24–5]), he has the category of imputation in mind. It is 'cognitively and theoretically transcendental in terms of the Kantian philosophy, not metaphysically transcendent' (§11(b) [25]).

The basic norm, too, is a concept profoundly informed by Kantian doctrines. 'In formulating the basic norm, the Pure Theory of Law is not aiming to inaugurate a new method for jurisprudence.' Rather, it 'aims simply to raise to the level of consciousness what all jurists are doing (for the most part unwittingly) when, in conceptualizing their object of enquiry, they . . . understand the positive law as a valid system, that is, as norm, and not merely as factual contingencies of motivation' (§29 [p. 58]). A more exacting description of the basic norm presupposes, however, a reconstruction of Kelsen's theory from within the framework of this or that Neo-Kantian persuasion. Though Kelsen himself refers at several points in his writings to Hermann Cohen, the leading figure of Marburg Neo-Kantianism, the textual evidence suggests that here, too, Kelsen's primary debt is to the Baden or Heidelberg Neo-Kantians.

Kelsen's programme is not in the end workable. Unlike Kant's own enterprise, it shares a flaw fatal to various species of Neo-Kantianism. In Kant's theory, failure to satisfy the conditions for cognition that are set by the categories of the understanding undermines cognition altogether; there is no alternative basis for cognition. The various species of quasi-Kantian category, however, adduced by the Neo-Kantians for application to one or another of the standing disciplines, have no comparable force; an alternative explanation of the data in question is always at hand. Be that as it may, Kelsen succeeds in singlehandedly recasting the terms of the juridico-philosophical debate – itself an achievement of fundamental significance.

In lending a new perspective to the problem of normativity in the law and in introducing useful analytical devices, among them the legal sentence or proposition (*Rechtssatz*) as a propositional counterpart to the legal norm (see Kelsen 1941–2 [1957: 268–9], Kelsen 1960 [1967]: §16 [pp. 71–5], cf. von Wright 1963: 104–5), Kelsen's Pure Theory of Law is forward looking. But his fascination with the idea, adapting Kant's phrase, of putting the study of the law on the sure path of science – unmistakable in the Pure Theory from beginning to end – harks back to nineteenth-century constructivism in the law (see chapter 23 in this volume, 'Legal theory'). From this standpoint, the Pure Theory is anachronistic. Its survival in an environment increasingly hostile to nineteenth-century constructivism is a tribute to Kelsen's genius generally and to the appeal of his approach to the problem of normativity in particular.

THE LIBERAL DEMOCRATIC STATE:
DEFENCES AND DEVELOPMENTS

RICHARD BELLAMY

The allies portrayed their defeat of Germany in 1918 as the triumph of liberal democracy over authoritarianism, a victory marked by the establishment of the League of Nations and the creation of the Weimar Republic. However, the Russian Revolution, the rise of fascism and the economic depression of the 1930s almost immediately placed liberal democrats on the defensive. Critics argued that mass democracy and the spread of bureaucracy within both the private and public sectors had rendered the liberal ethic of the autonomous individual an anachronism. The corporate manager had replaced the entrepreneur within the economy, and the manipulation of popular opinion by the media and party machines had supplanted rational debate between disinterested individuals in politics. Individual identity and will were shaped by functional, ethnic and cultural group membership rather than innate preferences and capabilities, the exercise of reason, or effort. New social and economic conditions required novel forms of political and industrial organisation that combined decisive and expert leadership with efficient administration, thereby harnessing popular support and energy to the collective good in a manner supposedly unavailable to liberals. The economic crisis was taken as confirming this diagnosis of liberal democracy's malaise.

The challenge to liberal democracy was threefold, therefore, involving an attack on the contemporary relevance of the market, representative democracy, and the values underlying them. In their various defences against such criticisms, the divisions amongst liberals were often as sharp as (and frequently mirrored) those between them and their opponents. Like the pre-war debates, disagreement centred on the role and nature of the state, the legitimacy and efficacy of its interventions in social life, and the parts played by democracy and leadership within its operations. Progressive liberals continued the attempt to find a *via media* between individualism and collectivism in economics, democracy and expertise in politics, and between both religion and scientific humanism, on the one hand, and universalism and a progressive and pragmatic historicism, on the other, in ethics and epistemology (Kloppenberg 1986). They conceded certain of their critics' objections but argued the liberal ethos could be preserved and rethought in ways suited to the new circumstances of the mass, corporate age. However, others counter-attacked with a robust defence of *laissez-faire* and individual rights, many simply equivocated, combining elements of both these strategies in occasionally inconsistent ways, whilst an appropriately small camp adopted a somewhat elegiac and often elitist tone, whereby liberalism became the creed of a happy few. Finally, a number of liberals, with varying degrees of enthusiasm, changed their allegiance to either fascism or communism. Which position predominated was as much a reflection of the political and social environment as the predilections of individual thinkers. We shall first examine the established liberal democracies of Britain and the United States, therefore, where a more social democratic liberalism prevailed, and then turn to countries such as Germany, Austria, and Italy, where liberal democracy was under threat and a sharper division between liberalism, on the one hand, and socialism and democracy, on the other, appeared appropriate.

1. TOWARDS SOCIAL DEMOCRACY: BRITAIN AND THE UNITED STATES

The liberal grounds for state regulation and welfare had been largely laid out at the turn of the century by British new liberals, such as L. T. Hobhouse, the French Solidaristes, such as Leon Bourgeois, and American progressives, such as John Dewey (Bellamy 1992; Kloppenberg 1986). Though the war led some of these thinkers to distance themselves from any possible charge of neo-Hegelian state worship and to stress their differences with non-liberal versions of collectivism (Hobhouse 1918), they remained remarkably settled in their views.

The following summary of their case from Dewey's 1935 tract *Liberalism and Social Action* could easily have come from Hobhouse's *Liberalism* of 1911, for example. Dewey argued that:

Since liberation of the capacities of individuals for free, self-initiated expression is an essential part of the creed of liberalism, liberalism that is sincere must will the means that condition the achieving of its ends. Regimentation of material and mechanical forces is the only way by which the mass of individuals can be released from regimentation and consequent suppression of their cultural possibilities . . . The notion that organised social control of economic forces lies outside the historic path of liberalism shows that liberalism is still impeded by remnants of its laissez-faire phase, with its opposition of society and the individual. The thing which now dampens liberal ardour and paralyzes its efforts is the conception that liberty and the development of individuality as ends exclude the use of organised social effort as means. Earlier liberalism regarded the separate and competing economic action of individuals as the means to social well-being as the end. We must reverse the perspective and see that socialised economy is the means of free individual development as the end. (Dewey 1935 [1987: 63])

Like the pre-war new liberals, Dewey's argument (and those of similarly minded contemporaries) elaborated a line of reasoning with its origins in T. H. Green but adapted it to a world of organised labour, mass industrial production and bureaucratic management (Ryan 1995: 89–97). The crux of their case was to counter criticism of the egoism and atomism of liberal individualism via a more holistic and positive view of individual liberty (Bellamy 1992: ch. 1, 2000: ch. 2). According to this analysis, an individual's freedom resulted not only from the absence of intentionally imposed, coercive constraints resulting from particular individual actions, such as physical assault, but also required the elimination of social and economic constraints that were the cumulative effect of numerous, and otherwise innocuous, individual decisions. Though these consequences were unintended by the individuals themselves, they were entirely predictable outcomes of a certain kind of social system. We were morally responsible, therefore, to take what Dewey called 'intelligent action' to avoid them.

At one level, this argument neatly placed welfare and especially unemployment insurance on a par with a police force and a regular legal system. Both involved the removal of humanly imposed limitations on liberty. This stratagem allowed its proponents to stress the continuity of the new with the old liberalism. However, the thesis that freedom had a social dimension cut deeper. It was not just disadvantages that were produced by social forces; so were most of the advantages people had hitherto ascribed to their own efforts. To cite Hobhouse's notorious example: 'the value of a site in London is something essentially due to London, not to the landlord' (Hobhouse 1911 [1964: 100]). Two important corollaries were held to follow from this supposed fact. First, the opportunities and even the capacity for autonomous choice on which individual freedom depended were now portrayed as social products. As the representative of the collectivity, the state had a responsibility not only to ensure equal protection from such socially created bads as crime, unemployment, and poverty, therefore, but also to ensure access to the social goods necessary for the exercise of freedom, such as schooling and libraries. To omit to open the requisite doors by denying access to social resources hindered an individual's liberty as much as deliberately closing them by coercive action. Second, progressive taxation to pay for public education and welfare was not so much a tax on individual effort as a reclaiming of the social contribution to that person's success.

Liberal state intervention was distinguished from socialist planning and redistribution on the grounds that the former merely aimed at securing the conditions for individual freedom. It did not seek to substitute for or to take away from the individual's own attempts to make the best of him or herself. A progressive teleology underlay this argument, whereby the self-development of each was deemed to be ultimately compatible with and supportive of the freedom of others.

New liberals, however, divided over the role of the state in promoting this goal. The radicals argued that the very nature of the state had to be changed if some of the authoritarian aspects of collectivism were to be avoided. Moderates maintained it was sufficient simply to change the goals of state policy (Freeden 1986).

Radical progressive liberals advocated a system of industrial democracy. They believed patterns of ownership and class struggle were not the source of the oppression of workers and the poor, so that state control of industry *per se* could not resolve it. The problem lay in the prevailing type of economic government, which allowed certain interests to be ignored. Self-determination in the economic sphere fostered and preserved liberty in much the same way as it did in politics. Political discussion and the need to reach agreement made all aware of their mutual dependence and ensured each contributed to the common goods on which their respective liberties depended. This system was claimed to be essentially open, allowing individuals to innovate whilst at the same time accommodating the evolving needs and changing choices of others (e.g. Dewey 1927; Hetherington and Muirhead 1918).

This scheme had certain similarities with fascist corporatism and communist 'workers' councils', even if these were never more than paper realities. Progressive liberals were nonetheless keen to stress their distance from such arguments. Thus Dewey argued that 'an immense difference' existed between the fascist and communist notion of a 'plann*ed* society' and the 'democratic liberal' ideal of 'a *continuously* plann*ing* society':

The former requires fixed blue-prints imposed from above and therefore involving reliance upon physical and psychological force to secure conformity to them. The latter means the release of intelligence through the widest form of cooperative give-and-take. The attempt to *plan* social organisation and association without the freest possible play of intelligence contradicts the very idea in *social* plann*ing*. For the latter is an operative method of activity, not a predetermined set of final 'truths'. (Dewey 1939 [1988: 321])

This 'democratic liberalism' had much in common with the Guild Socialism of G. D. H. Cole and Harold Laski as well as the theories of certain syndicalist writers (Ryan 1995: 179, 309–10). They too were motivated by a desire to find a middle way between state collectivism and market individualism (Hirst 1989). As Bertrand Russell approvingly remarked, their ideas had a strong appeal for 'all those who still care for the ideals which inspired liberalism, namely the problem of combining liberty and personal initiative with organisation' (Russell 1916). Like them, Dewey saw the extension of democracy throughout society as a way of remedying the apparent impotence of both the state and the individual to control the numerous private as well as public bodies influencing people's lives (Dewey 1927 [1984: 295–7]). Though sympathetic to such ideas, which in Britain influenced the setting up of the Whitley Councils, most new and progressive liberals were nonetheless unwilling to embrace them fully. They feared that it was unworkable since planning required expertise, and gave too much power to producers. Only the state had the capacity to act in the general interest (Freeden 1986: 66–77; Hobson 1934: 89–92). Much as before the war, more moderate new liberals sought to influence policy without greatly changing the character of the political system.

J. M. Keynes and William Beveridge are often taken as emblematic figures of this centrist liberal position, with Roosevelt's New Deal in the United States and the British Liberal Party's 'Yellow Book' and the Beveridge Report the chief fruits of the moderate progressive programme (Freeden 1986: 154–73, 366–72). Certainly both thinkers stressed their liberal as opposed to socialist sympathies and Keynes in particular had some intellectual influence within the British Liberal Party between the wars, notably via the Liberal Summer Schools (e.g. Keynes 1925; Beveridge 1945). Their relationship to liberalism is ambivalent nonetheless and highlights certain problems within the progressive position when moving from theory to practice.

Keynes, a Treasury representative at the Paris Peace Conference, had, in *The Economic Consequences of Peace* (1919), offered a prescient analysis of the dilemmas confronting liberal capitalism in the aftermath of the war. He identified a chief cause of war in the 'competitive struggle for markets', the origins of which he traced to the inadequacy of traditional liberal economic policies in tackling unemployment by stimulating growth. His remedy, however, was an extension of the old liberalism more than a move towards the new. Keynes regarded the 'main political problem of today' as 'the establishment of an economically efficient and economically just society in the changed conditions' arising from 'the new organisation of the wage-earning classes' and the 'arrival of a new industrial revolution' (Keynes 1927 [1981: 639]). However, his concern was principally with efficiency rather than social justice. Indeed, he believed the removal of unemployment via an efficient economy was all workers were entitled to demand. Moreover, his arguments for strategic state intervention were classical rather than new liberal. His famous essay 'The End of Laissez-Faire', for example, raised not moral but technical objections to a totally free market that echoed public goods arguments familiar to Smith, Bentham, and J. S. Mill. He stressed the state's function was 'not to do those things which individuals are doing already, and to do them a little better or a little worse; but to do those things which at present are not done at all' (Keynes 1926 [1972: 291]).

Where traditional economic liberals went wrong was in their 'hopelessly out of date' view of the economic world, since 'the picture of numerous small capitalists, each staking his fortune on his judgement, and the most judicious surviving, bears increasingly little relation to the facts' (Keynes 1927 [1981: 641]). For reasons familiar to students of social choice, individuals had little or no incentive to implement the measures Keynes deemed necessary to ensure the optimal output needed to secure as full employment as practicable – namely currency and credit controls and encouragements to save and invest. On the contrary, many had good self-interested reasons to aggravate the very problems these mechanisms sought to overcome. Though he thought the volume of output was 'determined by forces outside the classical scheme', he raised 'no objection . . . against the classical analysis of the manner in which private self-interest will determine what in particular is produced, in what proportions the factors of production will be combined to produce it, and how the value of the final product will be distributed between them' (Keynes 1936 [1973: 378–9]). 'Intelligent control' of the economy was some distance, therefore, from 'State Socialism' and did not entail either the direction or ownership of the means of production (Keynes 1936 [1973: 378]).

Such control was a matter for experts, however, rather than democracy. Keynes was not an advocate of Deweyean democratic 'social planning'. Rather, he shared the traditional liberal concerns about the newly enfranchised masses, fearing that 'in the ignorant blind striving after justice Labour may destroy what is at least as important and is a necessary condition of any social progress at all – namely, efficiency' (Keynes 1927, 1981: 639]). Nothing could be further from the progressive's credo than Keynes's suspicion 'that some measure of social injustice has often been the necessary condition of social progress' (Keynes 1927 [1981: 639]). Not surprisingly, his view of liberty remained narrowly negative, its purpose largely to preserve the dynamism of society. The new liberals had also abhorred the contemporary authoritarian state systems and stressed the need for personal liberty and choice. But their understanding of freedom embraced a concern for social issues absent from Keynes's analysis. Far from sharing their desire for an ethical liberalism that would unite individuality and solidarity, he worried that 'the reaction against the appeal to self-interest may have gone too far' (Keynes 1936 [1973: 380]).

If Keynes departed from progressive liberals in ignoring their social agenda, Beveridge was distinctive in remaining outside the debates over economic planning that had preoccupied the inter-war generation. Instead, he explicitly linked his Report to the pre-war Social Insurance policies of Lloyd George. His defence of the liberal character of his proposals echoed the characteristic new liberal tactic of justifying social justice in terms of an extended view of liberty as 'more than freedom from the arbitrary power of governments. It means freedom from economic servitude to Want and Squalor and other social evils; it means freedom from arbitrary power in any form' (Beveridge 1945: 10). Similarly conventional arguments led him to distinguish his position from that of socialists. Making liberty rather than equality the basis of greater state intervention meant that his policy was not a matter of levelling to benefit certain sectional interests, but aimed at offering all citizens the opportunities 'of service and earning in accordance with their powers' (Beveridge 1945: 38).

Beveridge claimed to avoid the authoritarianism of socialist planning by allowing individuals the liberty to contribute in a manner most conformable to their own talents. However, he did insist that a duty to cooperate with others for the common good was an entailment of a claim to social rights. Moreover, he shared Keynes's belief that such a system favoured efficiency. This association of freedom with social duty and efficiency raises many of the traditional worries concerning positive accounts of freedom: namely, that individuals are only deemed genuinely free if they pursue ends of a socially useful and morally approved kind. Before the war this aspect of new liberalism had surfaced in debates about eugenics. The insistence by radical liberals on the democratic negotiation and setting of society's goals was intended to counter these sorts of dangers. Of course, Keynes and Beveridge assumed that the state was democratic in the sense of holding regular elections and having certain standard constitutional safeguards for individual civil liberties. But where such liberal mechanisms could not be taken for granted, liberals were unsurprisingly more sceptical about the likelihood of state action fostering rather than hindering freedom.

2. LIBERALISM UNDER THREAT: CONTINENTAL EUROPE

Though a few diehards in Britain and the United States bemoaned the way progressive and centre liberal measures 'day by day, in the well-meaning effort to ease somebody's little trouble, . . . take away a little bit of discretion or liberty from the rest of the 40 millions of us' (Ernest Benn, quoted in Freeden 1986: 267), such complaints were in a minority. In the relatively recent liberal democracies of continental Europe, by contrast, liberals found themselves ousted from power by mass socialist parties and confronted by a growing communist and fascist threat. Here democracy appeared a danger to liberalism and the surest rationale for liberty lay with the market. Indeed the most powerful criticisms of social liberalism came from political economists and social theorists such as Ludwig von Mises and F. A. Hayek in Austria, Luigi Einaudi and Vilfredo Pareto in Italy, and Max Weber in Germany.

These thinkers contended that notions of a common good or general will were meaningless. Individuals pursued a plurality of goods and held very different evaluative standpoints and moral codes. There were no social goals or public purposes, only the diverse ideals and interests of a society's individual members. The market's genius – indeed its very functioning – lay in its harnessing of people's capacity to choose autonomously and pursue a plurality of goods. Any attempt to constrain that capacity via central planning would prove both economically less efficient than the market and entail coercion on a totalitarian scale.

The development of this argument by the Austrians in particular was highly original. Their case was essentially epistemic. Its basic elements were first developed by von Mises in the context of the socialist calculation debate of the 1920s (Hayek 1935; Lavoie 1985). He argued that rational economic planning required an efficient allocation of resources and that this in turn depended upon a knowledge of prices, which provide information on the relative scarcities of capital goods. In a market of any size and complexity, these prices are determined by the innumerable interactions between buyers and sellers and are in constant flux. He believed it would be impossible for socialist planners to solve millions of simultaneous equations in order to determine the relative value of productive resources. Such information could only be provided by a market based on private property in the means of production.

In fact, economists now believe that in principle the relevant equations could be solved. However, Mises's writings also contain a more profound thesis that suggests that monetary prices act as necessary 'aids to the human mind' that could only be generated within the context of a market-exchange system based on private property. According to this view, the requisite knowledge needed by planners would not exist outside of a free market economy. Hayek and later Austrian theorists picked up on this aspect of his work but gave it a somewhat different epistemological basis (Hayek 1935). Hayek pointed out that the difficulty confronting planners is not computational but practical. It relates to the problem of how one central agency could gather the huge amount of information necessary for accurate pricing, much of it of a concrete and contextual nature, such as the capacity of the available machines and workforce in a given locale, which is hard to represent in statistical form and which is in any case constantly changing. Moreover, much of this knowledge is tacit, embodied in practices, dispositions, and intuitions that are unformulatable and often not fully conscious to the individuals concerned. Central planning not only cannot employ such knowledge, it would also probably destroy it by attempting to articulate it in an explicit manner. The achievement of the market was its ability to collect and transmit this dispersed, local, and largely transient knowledge in an intelligible and undistorted form through price signals. By contrast, a planned economy severed the connection between rewards and services essential to the market's efficiency, replacing it with a set of inevitably distorted incentives that have more to do with the whims of bureaucrats than with what people wanted or might have desired in a world where entrepreneurs can invent new products.

Planning by socialist or social democratic states was not only inefficient, however, but also tyrannical (Mises 1932; Hayek 1944). For it involved substituting the free choices of individuals for those of the planner. Indeed, the plan would only have a chance of success if the innovations and changing preferences of producers and consumers were deliberately suppressed. Invoking social justice to justify such interventions did not change their arbitrariness for the plurality of opinions meant that there could be no settled criteria. The chief candidates, need and desert, not only clashed themselves but each could be interpreted in a variety of ways that produced rival outcomes when applied to particular cases. However well-intentioned, appeals to the collective welfare always reflected the partial perspective of their proponents and so inevitably entailed imposing their vision on others. Moreover, redistributive taxation and public social services reproduced all the distorted incentives of planning and involved a similarly coercive interference with people's own choices.

Democracy did not enhance either the legitimacy or effectiveness of planning and welfare. It merely increased the risk of such mistaken policies being pursued. Pareto in particular devoted considerable energy to investigating how political elites wooed the voters with illusory appeals to social justice and the common good (Pareto 1902–3, 1916, 1921; Bellamy 1992: ch. 3). In fact, the only beneficiaries of these policies were the politicians themselves and the various special-interest groups which surrounded them. The taxation required to fund this expanded state sector was in effect a rent imposed on the efforts of others. Unrestrained, democracy replaced economic with political incentives, encouraging groups to organise and influence the machinery of government towards their ends with ultimately devastating effects for freedom and prosperity.

These thinkers attributed the electoral success of socialist parties to an atavistic herd instinct and yearning for organic community that was totally at odds with modern societies (Pareto 1902–3). Whereas the new liberals accepted that the trend within modern societies was towards big government, corporate business, and mass organisations, these neo-classical liberals held on to the notion that entrepreneurship and individual initiative remained crucial and that these developments must and could be resisted (Mises 1927). They advocated a minimal constitutional framework to uphold civil and especially property rights within which individuals could freely contract with each other. Hayek, the chief elaborator of this doctrine, went so far as to castigate all departures from fixed, known, and general laws as arbitrary acts at variance with the Rule of Law that disturbed and distorted the spontaneous order emerging from numerous individual interactions (Hayek 1944). He believed these criteria rendered planning and redistributive taxation illegimate, since both entailed formulating ever more special regulations aimed at particular groups of people. Government, on his account, was to be limited to policing infractions of the Rule of Law not breaking it itself, with democracy serving the purely protective function of allowing the peaceful removal of tyrannical or incompetent governments. An exile to Britain and an admirer of the British liberal tradition, Hayek saw the New Liberalism as but a step along the road to serfdom, with little differentiating it from socialism or fascism – themselves equated with each other in this view.

Not all continental liberal theorists were so pessimistic or economistic in their views. Debating the nature of liberalism with Luigi Einaudi in Italy, for example, Benedetto Croce argued that his compatriot had confused the market mechanism with the liberal ethic that animated *laissez-faire* accounts of it (Einaudi 1928; Croce 1928; Bellamy 1992: ch. 3). The liberal ethic endorsed the free market only to the extent that it offered the best means of preserving the liberal values of human inventiveness and autonomy. He believed it simple dogmatism to exclude a priori the possibility of a 'liberal socialism' such as Hobhouse's. Nonetheless, Croce objected equally strongly to those fellow Italians, such as Guido de Ruggiero, who advocated a social liberalism involving the reconciliation of liberty and justice (De Ruggiero 1925 and 1946; Bellamy 2000: ch. 3; Calogero 1940–4). Once again, he argued that this confused the practical need to accommodate the demands of the working classes with the liberal ideal motivating such policies (Croce 1943). Democracy was similarly a contingent means, of value only to the extent that it furthered liberal ends. Croce followed the youthful Pareto and Gaetano Mosca in rejecting the democratic principle of equality as a socialist denial of the importance of individuality whilst seeing democratic procedures as potentially useful for ensuring a circulation of ideals and elites. Ultimately, Croce conceived liberalism as a 'metapolitical' philosophy, to be identified with his historicist view of history as the product of autonomous individual thought and action, rather than a specific set of policies (Croce 1928).

In Germany, Weber similarly believed that the classic liberalism invoked by the Austrians and others was unrealistic in modern societies (Beetham 1985; Bellamy 1992: ch. 4). Weber contended that the liberal faith in legal formalism implied by notions of the Rule of Law, such as Hayek's, was as impossible within today's complex societies as the bureaucratic proceduralism advocated by socialist planners (Weber 1918a and b, 1919). Just as entrepreneurs remained important in the economic sphere to innovate and direct commercial activity, so leadership was vital within the political sphere. Pluralism rendered coherent collective choice impossible and meant that general norms covering all spheres of activity could not be formulated. Even a regulative as opposed to a planning state would need to make special and particular directives to meet the peculiar circumstances of different functions, communities, and locations. Meanwhile, events were always likely to throw up exceptional cases calling for decisive executive action. With the mass of the population locked into the organisational 'iron cage' of modernity, only charismatic leaders could make the requisite existential decisions capable of giving an organisation and its members a sense of purpose. He reconceived competitive elections as an electoral market aimed at producing such individuals. He believed such mechanisms explained why the liberal democratic Allies had defeated authoritarian Germany's more efficient military machine, which had failed to prevail due to an absence of leadership and an over-reliance on formal rules and procedures (Weber 1918a). Weber was nonetheless all too aware that even such a realist view of liberal democracy would only prove beneficial within a culturally liberal environment that modernity tended to undermine rather than foster. Though the Austrian economist Joseph Schumpeter (1943; Bellamy 2000: ch. 5) later developed his model into an influential characterisation of post war liberal democratic politics, the immediate social and political reality proved rather different from the ideal. The leader thrown up in Weber's native Germany lacked almost all the qualities he had hoped for and plunged both liberalism and democracy into a deeper crisis than ever before.

3. CONCLUSION

If declarations of the death of liberalism by socialists and fascists were premature in intellectual terms, they proved all too accurate a description of its status as a political force. The inter-war years saw the dramatic decline if not the demise of liberal political parties across Europe and on the continent the brief eclipse of all liberal democratic regimes. By 1945, most liberal intellectuals and politicians together with the bulk of their electoral following had deserted to either social democratic or conservative parties. However, their arguments shaped ideological debates within Western democracies for the rest of the century. If centrist liberal economic and welfare policies dominated until the mid-1970s, the challenge of the New Right in the 1980s and 1990s was largely inspired by the ideas of economic liberals such as Hayek. Meanwhile, the contemporary search for a 'third way' between these two positions has frequently involved exploring the various alternatives of fifty years ago, with Dewey and Hobhouse amongst others becoming fashionable once again.

64

THE LIBERAL DEMOCRATIC STATE: CRITICS

WALTER ADAMSON

The crisis consists precisely in the fact that the old is dying and the new cannot be born; in this interregnum a great variety of morbid symptoms appear. Antonio Gramsci (1975 [1971: 276])

Following the catastrophe of the First World War, philosophical critics on both left and right posed their challenges to liberal-democratic politics in terms of a crisis of civilisation. The First World War had ushered out the last vestiges of Europe's old regime; no one imagined a new Metternich-legitimist restoration. But what might be the 'new regime' of modernity that could resolve the crisis? The answer depended in part upon one's national vantage-point. The focus here will be on the central and southern European contexts where communist revolutions were launched in 1919–20 only to be supplanted by fascist reactions thereafter. In France, the political outcomes were different but the intellectual environment, similar. Only in Britain and the United States did bourgeois institutions appear largely unchallenged.

While even partisans of liberal democracy understood that 'rescuing bourgeois Europe meant recasting bourgeois Europe' (Maier 1975: 594), its critics sought to sweep it aside in a bold revolutionary stroke. For them, *fin-de-siècle* fears that a looming mass society would become a quantitative, materialist nightmare had been borne out, necessitating a turn to radical solutions. A radical conservatism demanding new institutions to restore old values came into full flower, particularly in Germany, where the fears had run deepest, while Marxists, emboldened by the Bolshevik triumph in 1917, sought to theorise the nature of, and preconditions for, a new basis of Western civilisation. Both extremes appreciated the raw power of 'Americanism' as a principle of social organisation, but despite occasional admirers (like Gramsci), most detested it as an alien invasion. Likewise, they viewed European forms of democracy as either *sui generis* (Britain), weak (France, Italy), or imposed (Germany). For the right, liberal democracy would simply encourage further chaos because of its alleged tendency towards leaderlessness, mechanicity, and an inability to deal decisively with crises. The left hoped that the new global mode of production might provide the foundation for a dialectical synthesis of objective and subjective experience (Georg Lukács) or a new 'regulated society' (Gramsci). Yet their 'Western Marxist' emancipatory hopes were dashed by defeats in Germany (1919), Hungary (1919), and Italy (1920), unleashing the bitterly polarised politics of the Third International that ultimately turned Gramsci against Stalin and Lukács despairingly towards him. With the worldwide depression, the rise of Hitler, Franco's victory in Spain, the Soviet purges, and the Hitler–Stalin pact, the stage was set for the black turn of Western Marxism made by Theodor Adorno and Max Horkheimer in the *Dialektik der Aufklärung* (*Dialectic of Enlightenment*) written during the war.

Despite obvious differences of policy and principle, there were many convergences in the analyses offered by left and right of the present historical crisis and, even more importantly, in the intellectual sources on which they relied. In both the Germanic world and Italy, critics of liberal democracy drew upon the categories and conceptual strategies of Kant, Hegel, Marx, and above all Nietzsche, though in the former case the philosophical tradition was enriched by the sociological theory of Ferdinand Tönnies, Georg Simmel, and especially Max Weber, all of whom were then largely unknown in Italy. The common reliance upon grand theories meant that while the sense of crisis made for politicised philosophy, few turned to political theory *per se*. Of the thinkers to be considered here, only two – Gramsci and Carl Schmitt – might be considered political theorists, and even they cast their intellectual nets very widely.

1. THE ITALY OF GENTILE AND GRAMSCI

The great problem of early twentieth-century Italian political intellectuals was the legacy of the Risorgimento: the political unification of Italy had not involved the masses either directly in a mass-based political movement or indirectly by morally engaging their hearts and souls. As Gaetano De Sanctis had famously lamented in the 1870s, 'political unification is in vain without intellectual and moral redemption' (Prezzolini 1909: 1). For Gramsci it was the political failure that mattered most, for Giovanni Gentile the moral one; but they were united in their assessment that the roots of the postwar Italian crisis lay here.

Gentile had never written on politics until 1915, but he then developed the argument that the Italian moral crisis could only be resolved through a new conception of the 'ethical state', which he conceived as the realisation of Mazzinian 'liberalism' and a break with the positivistic and 'materialistic' liberalism that was institutionalised in Italy after 1870 (Gentile 1927: 295). For Gentile, true liberalism conceived liberty from the point of view of the state and not from that of the atomised individual. The state, in turn, was a spiritual, ethical entity, more like a secular church than a narrowly juridical or economic-managerial instrument. Here he followed Hegel. Yet unlike Hegel, Gentile saw the state not as part of objective Spirit (a category he rejected) but rather as the 'act' of a subject who thereby creates and continually recreates the political world. 'Every individual acts politically, is a statesman, and holds the state in his heart; he is the state . . . The state for that reason is not *inter homines* but *in interiore homine*' (Gentile 1937: 129). Unlike Hegel's state, which is articulated in relation to family and civil society and subordinated ultimately to absolute Spirit, Gentile's ethical state is unlimited. For him the greater the strength of the state, the fuller the potential realisation of liberty.

Gentile was very much the enthusiast of an abstract logic in which, once premises are accepted, conclusions inexorably follow. His adhesion to fascism was of this sort. In a 1923 letter to Mussolini, he declared: 'Liberal by deep and sound conviction . . . , I have been persuaded that liberalism . . . is today represented in Italy not by liberals who are more or less openly against you, but precisely, by you' (Calandra 1987: 8). Unlike Italy's other famous idealist, Benedetto Croce, with whom Gentile had frequently collaborated, he was not attracted to fascism as a temporary fix for the Italian liberal state or for any other instrumental reason. Rather he believed that his ethical state was in the historical cards, desperately wanted to see it realised, and convinced himself that fascism was its incarnation.

Unlike Croce, whose respect for empirical history was too great to allow him to fall into any Hegelian panlogism even as he borrowed greatly from Hegel's dialectical method, Gentile rejected the method but adopted the panlogism. Yet Hegel, he thought, in holding fast to transcendental idealism by underwriting his epistemology with an ontological argument about the development of *Geist* or Spirit, failed to appreciate the nature of human freedom. Gentile insisted upon a standpoint of 'absolute immanence' in which subjective thought takes on the faculties Kant had located in the transcendental subject and Hegel in Spirit. In this sense thought is a presuppositionless 'pure act', and there is no reality beyond thought. Truth therefore lies within the thought of the historical agent, and philosophy and history must ultimately coincide. Yet by grounding history exclusively in the creative activity of the agent, Gentile had no basis for understanding the coordination of actions among individuals and, thus, the intersubjective nature of community, a problem he resolved in practice by simply identifying the Italian ethical state he anticipated with Mussolini.

The young Gramsci of 1916–17 was strongly drawn to Gentile's philosophy of the pure act, as he was to other voluntarist viewpoints such as those of Henri Bergson, Georges Sorel, and the interventionist Mussolini. Though his

Marxism, which he also came to early, made him appreciate objective conditions as a constraint upon action and as the context in which acts are historically framed, he rejected Marxist positivisms aiming at laws of social action. Theory, for Gramsci, was an account people used in understanding and acting, in this sense inherently unified with practice and immanent in a Gentilian way. 'Objective', he argued, 'always means "humanly objective" which can be held to correspond exactly to "historically subjective"; in other words, objective would mean "universal subjective"' (Gramsci 1975 [1971: 445]).

Gramsci was awestruck by the Bolshevik victory in 1917, which he characterised as 'the living out of Marxist thought' as a 'revolution against *Capital*' rather than a result of 'the canons of historical materialism' (Gramsci 1982 [1994: 39–40]). After Italy's 'mutilated victory' in the war reopened the revolutionary door, he sought to extend Lenin's creativity to Italy by leading a factory-council movement in Turin. The movement failed, and its quasi-syndicalist ideal of direct democracy through the workplace soon appeared to him naïve, but it established his independence from any dogmatic Marxism or Leninism.

Gramsci understood his political activism as an effort to create the 'effective Jacobin force' that had been missing in the Risorgimento and that 'in other nations [had] awakened and organised the national-popular collective will' (Gramsci 1975 [1971: 131]). Political change in modern Italy (not least the advent of fascism) had always come in the form of 'passive revolutions' from above, which meant that urban–rural and North–South cleavages were not only not faced but even exacerbated. The current 'crisis of authority' would persist until an 'organic' solution based on a Jacobin-led 'national-popular' movement could be created. Such a solution would put rulership in the hands of those who had organised a 'hegemony' of active consent among the class or classes central to the mode of production.

If the current crisis was particularly acute in Italy, there were reasons to believe that Europe generally would find it difficult to develop such new 'organic' forms of politics. Unlike in America, where 'there do not exist numerous classes with no essential function in the world of production, in other words classes which are purely parasitic', Europe is 'characterised precisely by the existence of such classes' (Gramsci 1975 [1971: 281]). Moreover, they play an essential role in its parliaments and effectively prevent even the non-parasitic bourgeoisie from developing an organic solution to the current crisis. That is why even far-sighted liberals, such as Piero Gobetti, had come to see that parties representing the industrial proletariat were the key to Europe's future. Yet, since such parties were now currently stymied, the only hope was a long-range strategy of 'war of position' through which 'national-popular' cultural forces might create the potential for a future organic politics.

2. THE GERMANY OF SCHMITT AND HEIDEGGER

The abruptness of Germany's transformation from a newly formed nation-state in 1871 to the leading power in Europe on the eve of the First World War, its defeat in the war, the postwar political and economic instability that followed, and the formation of the ill-conceived and ill-fated Weimar Republic in 1919, all helped make its sense of crisis the deepest of any European country. Attacks on parliamentary democracy, the market, and the pluralism of value systems in the name of a 'conservative revolution' were consequently widespread among the German intellectual mandarinate.

No single figure better exemplifies this reaction than Carl Schmitt. Shaken by Max Weber's analysis of modernity as an 'iron cage' of instrumental rationality, Schmitt aimed to comprehend the current European crisis through an historical analysis of the interconnected rise of Protestantism and technical progress, an analysis inspired by Weber but very much his own (on the connection between Schmitt and Weber, see McCormick 1997: 32–42 and Mommsen 1959 [1984: 382–9]). Since the sixteenth-century wars of religion, he argued, Europe had sought to escape conflict by 'striving for a neutral sphere'. From theological conflict it turned for respite to seventeenth-century metaphysics, and thence to eighteenth-century moralism, nineteenth-century economics, and twentieth-century technology. Yet the history has been dialectical: 'Europeans always have wandered from a conflictual to a neutral sphere, and always the newly won neutral sphere has become immediately another arena of struggle, once again necessitating the search for a new neutral sphere' (Schmitt 1963 [1993: 137–8]).

The nineteenth-century neutral sphere, *pace* Weber, involved 'an apparently hybrid and impossible combination of aesthetic-romantic and economic-technical tendencies' (Schmitt 1963 [1993: 133]). While the latter disenchanted, the former re-enchanted, hence the peculiarly fused character of modernity as the triumph both of instrumental rationality and of a romantic mythology, whether as 'new Soviet man' or as 'Marlboro man'. Thus, although the economic-technical thinking that capitalism and communism share is shockingly indifferent to qualitative considerations – a 'silk blouse' and a 'poison gas' are both treated simply as products (Schmitt 1925 [1996: 14–15]) – the systems do retain a connection to the qualitative, albeit as irrational forms of life.

Yet the effort to retain a neutral sphere of liberal universalism and democracy becomes politically untenable in the new conditions of modern mass societies. Liberalism assumes that state and civil society are separate, such that the former can rationally adjudicate among competing social interests. It assumes that parliaments are capable of deliberating expediently and arriving at rational solutions to political issues. It assumes that the Rule of Law can operate as the impartial application of universally binding, already promulgated rules. Such assumptions are unrealistic in a complex system that necessarily breaks down the divide between state and civil society, burdening the state with social and economic regulation, overwhelming parliaments with a floodtide of conflicting interests, and transforming the legal system into a mechanism for compromise among equally rational, competing claims on resources. Here lie the roots of the contemporary crisis. To overcome it, modern politics must define an aggressive role for executive leadership, do away with parliaments, and reconceive the legal system on a 'decisionist' model of efficient compromise. Most fundamentally, we must abandon the notion of a neutral sphere and restore the true concept of the political, which rests on the firm distinction between 'friends' and 'enemies'.

As a prominent conservative jurist during Weimar, and an adherent of Nazism beginning in 1933, Schmitt sought to foster a politics of radical intervention by elites to actualise fully and rationally modernity's qualitative moment, to assert the rights of a particular people (he referred variously to Europe, Central Europe, and Germany) against the universalism of his leftist enemies, and to overcome the paralysis of the modern, liberal-democratic state. His answer to the crisis of modernity was to re-empower states to decide the question of friend and enemy and to deal effectively with emergencies, which he termed 'the exception'. In a well-institutionalised modern politics, 'sovereign is he who decides on the exception' (Schmitt 1934 [1985: 5]).

Unlike Schmitt and other German conservative revolutionaries, Martin Heidegger did not elaborate a political philosophy, and his concerns were rather different from the human problems (freedom, happiness, justice) that have concerned most political philosophers. For him, philosophy's basic attitude should always be one of questioning, and to assemble such theses as would be necessary for a political theory or ethics would be to miss the essential point of the activity. Moreover, philosophy's fundamental question, that of 'Being', can only be properly pursued when one breaks with the humanist metaphysics that has dominated the Western tradition from Plato's eternal *eidos* to Nietzsche's will to power. In this tradition's failure to pursue the question of Being lie the deepest roots of the current crisis.

Heidegger saw his own philosophy, then, as a way out of a crisis of nihilism produced by the search for truth in a wilful mode rather than according to pre-Socratic *aletheia* whereby phenomena themselves unveil truth. In this sense, his philosophy was always politically engaged. Moreover, his understanding of the crisis of nihilism grew out of his perception of the First World War – as one of the senseless self-destruction of Europe – and of the struggle for world dominion that had followed in its wake. Philosophy was crucial to the hope that this struggle might be settled in a broadly cultural rather than a narrowly military way.

So strong was Heidegger's sense of the historical role of philosophy that he allowed it to justify his adherence to Nazism in 1933 despite the apparent contradiction between this adherence and his conception of philosophy as questioning. Like Gentile before him, Heidegger succumbed to the delusion that what philosophy required of the actual political world the latter had miraculously produced. For a few months at least, he even believed, in the words of his friend Karl Jaspers, that he could 'lead the Führer' (*den Führer führen*) to a spiritual alternative to capitalist and communist materialisms (Dallmayr 1993: 25). Though that confidence would wane after 1934, Heidegger remained a member of the Nazi party until the end of the Second World War and, even after the war, continued to believe in the 'inner truth' of Nazism.

Such a desperate gamble was partly a failure of practical judgement, but it also reflected Heidegger's sense of what was at stake. Though the theme of technology and its connection with nihilism is commonly thought of in relation to the late Heidegger, he had already perceived its significance in his lectures at Freiburg in the early 1920s. By the 1930s, influenced by Ernst Jünger's provocative analysis of the present age as a 'total mobilisation' to decide world-historical supremacy, Heidegger saw that 'Europe, in its ruinous blindness forever on the point of cutting its own throat, lies today in a great pincers, squeezed between Russia on one side and America on the other [which] from a metaphysical point of view . . . are the same; the same dreary technological frenzy' (Heidegger 1953 [1961: 31]).

For Heidegger the essence of technology is not technical but a way of being in the world. Technological societies force entities to reveal themselves in terms consistent with human goals; nature becomes 'enframed' as a 'standing-reserve' for human use (Heidegger 1954 [1977: 298, 301]). Technology, then, is the logical outgrowth of Western philosophy, and the only antidote to it is the openness towards being represented by *aletheia*. Heidegger believed that such openness can be attained through a 'world-disclosing' work of art (*Kunstwerk*) but also through a work of thought (*Denkwerk*) or a work of state (*Staatwerk*) (Wolin 1990: 100).

3. WESTERN MARXISM IN EXILE

If the perception of world crisis led Heidegger to gamble on Nazism, it led Georg Lukács to an equally desperate gamble on Bolshevism. Reared in a wealthy Jewish family in Budapest, Lukács wrote passionate early essays inspired by Kierkegaard. Their essential problem concerned the inability of works of art, committed as they must be to 'form', to express the 'soul' of the artist (Lukács 1910 [1974]). Thus, in a world in which spiritual life has become impoverished, works of art are tragically unable to restore value. During the war, Lukács extended this conclusion in a social and historical direction, portraying the 'abstract systematisation' of the modern world against the backdrop of the organic, 'integrated civilisation' of ancient Greece to which, however, all possibility of return was foreclosed (Lukács 1920 [1971]: 29, 70).

Despite such intimations, however, Lukács stunned everyone in Budapest's intellectual circles when, in December 1918, he suddenly converted to Marxism and joined the Communist Party. Concurrently, his analysis of modernity shifted to a sociological register: the suppression of life's qualitative dimension that Marx had located in commodity fetishism and Weber in rationalisation, he now located in an amalgam of the two called 'reification' (Lukács's debt to Weber reflected his participation in the latter's Heidelberg circle from 1913 to 1915). This triumph of cold abstraction would be historically transcended however by the 'proletariat', which he cast as history's 'identical subject-object', that in which 'the contradictions of history that have become conscious' (Lukács 1923 [1971: 147, 178]).

In his major work of 1923, *Geschichte und Klassenbewusstsein* (*History and Class Consciousness*), Lukács sought to redefine Marxist 'orthodoxy' in terms of a dialectical method of investigation rather than as any closed body of received truths. To establish the method, he set forth a relentless critique of 'bourgeois thought' from Kant through Hegel, arguing that it necessarily ended in 'antimonies' of phenomena and 'things-in-themselves', object and subject, fact and value, and form and content, antimonies it was unable to transcend except in a purely formal way. A true resolution of this philosophical crisis, which was also modernity's crisis, necessarily implied the dialectical transcendence of bourgeois life, a movement that only a properly constituted Marxist theory could grasp.

This solution, set forth with formidable rigour, made sense so long as the reader accepted the characterisation of the proletariat. The trouble arose with a question that lurked just below the text's surface: how can we know that the historical role assigned to the proletariat by philosophy corresponds to its actual consciousness and practice in the world? Efforts to face up to this question led Lukács down a precipitous slope to Stalinism. Initially, he tried to circumvent the problem theoretically with the notion of 'imputed' class consciousness (Lukács 1923 [1971: 325]). By 1924, the year of his book on Lenin and of Lenin's death, he had clearly accepted the latter's solution of the vanguard party, though this hardly saved him from the excoriating criticism of Soviet leaders at the Fifth Comintern Congress that July. From that Congress until the last days of the Stalin era, Lukács lived mostly in exile in the Soviet Union and his public answer to questions of politics was invariably the simple dogma that the party is always right.

The problem of the historical role of the proletariat was bequeathed by Lukács to a group of German theorists, led by Theodor Adorno and Max Horkheimer, who would come to be known as the Frankfurt School, though many of their best years were spent in exile in the United States. They accepted Lukács's *History and Class Consciousness* as a magnum opus and regarded its view of 'orthodoxy' as a paradigm for their project of a Western-oriented Marxist 'critical theory' adequate to the present, but they were increasingly troubled by the painful gap between the proletariats of theory and history. Moreover, even as they redoubled their efforts to deal with the gap by studying contemporary political and familial structures, the problems of alienation and mystification resulting from modern cultural life seemed to redouble as well. Coupled with the catastrophic political developments of the 1930s, the emancipatory hopes that they still held at the beginning of the decade retreated and then plummeted during the war to the nadir represented by *Dialectic of Enlightenment*.

In this book, Adorno and Horkheimer effectively shifted the paradigm of critical theory from class-conflict within capitalism to the bourgeois domination of nature, a story they traced back to the Homeric world. In a breathtaking reading of the *Odyssey*, they sought to show how the enlightenment project was bound up with mythic fear and instinctual renunciation, as when Odysseus has himself tied to the mast of his ship to avoid seduction by the song of the Sirens. Primitive magic, they argued, is untrue, yet it does not seek to dominate nature; enlightenment purchases truth at the price of dominating the 'other' of nature. The two processes were in fact entwined: 'Just as the myths already realise enlightenment, so enlightenment with every step becomes more deeply engulfed in mythology' (Adorno and Horkheimer 1944 [1972: 11–12]).

The inescapable conclusion was that reason itself was responsible for the historical crisis of modernity. Enlightenment 'excises the incommensurable. Not only are qualities dissolved in thought, but men are brought to actual conformity' (12). Fascism and anti-semitism were enlightenment's children. Yet the reason at issue was the instrumental variety that had so preoccupied Weber, the reason that had eliminated the dialectical negative, replaced concepts with formulas, and voiced the demands of the powerful while silencing the oppressed. Heroically, they declared their '*petitio principii* – that social freedom is inseparable from enlightened thought' and held out the prospect of 'a positive notion of enlightenment which will release it from blind domination' (xvi). Yet unlike Gentile, Gramsci, Schmitt, Heidegger, and Lukács, they no longer had any sense of how to attach their hopes to an historical actor. Thus, while saved from the delusions of the former, they also appeared impotent in the face of the future.

BIOBIBLIOGRAPHICAL APPENDIX

ADORNO, THEODOR (1903–69). Born in Frankfurt, Adorno was precocious intellectually and musically, writing a dissertation on Edmund Husserl at twenty-one and then studying with the Arnold Schoenberg circle in Vienna. Returning to Frankfurt in 1927, he began his lifelong collaboration with Max Horkheimer's Institute and, in 1931, began teaching at the university. After the Nazi seizure of power, he first lived in London, then joined Horkheimer in New York in 1938. Throughout the 1930s and 1940s, he did important studies in social psychology and in the sociology of music and culture. With Horkheimer, he wrote the *Dialectic of Enlightenment* (1947) and then, after returning to Frankfurt in 1949, composed his own major works, *Negative Dialectics* (1966) and *Aesthetic Theory* (1970). Important studies of him include Buck-Morss, S. (1977), *The Origin of Negative Dialectics: Theodor W. Adorno Walter Benjamin, and the Frankfurt Institute* (New York: Free Press); Jay, M. (1984), *Adorno* (Cambridge, MA: Harvard University Press); and Rose, G. (1978). *The Melancholy Science: An Introduction to the Thought of W. Adorno* (New York: Columbia Press).

AJDUKIEWICZ, KAZIMIERZ (1890–1963). Ajdukiewicz studied in Lvov with Twardowski, gaining his PhD in 1913 and his Habilitation in 1920. He was an associate professor in Lvov from 1921 to 1926, a professor in Warsaw from 1926 to 1928, in Lvov from 1928 to 1939, in Poznan from 1945 to 1952, and finally once more in Warsaw from 1952 to 1963. His main writings (available in English) are *Pragmatic Logic* (Warsaw: Polish Scientific Publishers and Dordrecht: Reidel, 1974) and *The Scientific World-Perspective and Other Essays, 1931–1963*, ed. J. Giedymin (Dordrecht: Reidel).

Secondary literature: Coniglione, F., Poli, R., and Woleński, J. (eds.) (1993), *Polish Scientific Philosophy: The Lvov-Warsaw School*, Amsterdam: Rodopi; Sinisi, V. and Woleński, J. (1995), *The Heritage of Kazimierz Ajdukiewicz*, Amsterdam: Rodopi; Skolimowski, H. (1967), *Polish Analytical Philosophy*, London: Routledge; Woleński, J. (1989), *Logic and Philosophy in the Lvov-Warsaw School*, Dordrecht: Kluwer and Boston: Lancaster.

ALEXANDER, SAMUEL (1859–1938). Alexander is now primarily remembered for espousing an 'emergentist' position in biology. He was born in Sydney, but studied at Oxford and then spent his career at Manchester. Alexander's most famous work is *Space, Time and Deity* (London: Macmillan, 1920), based on his Gifford lectures. In this work of systematic metaphysics he adopts a realist position, basing his position on 'motions' – space-time units. There are then various levels of complexity, involving matter, life, mind, and (perhaps) deity, each of which 'emerges' from the preceding one, in the sense that its complexity sustains distinctive new properties not reducible to those of lower levels.

AUSTIN, JOHN (1790–1859). Born in Creeting Mill near Ipswich, Suffolk, on 3 March 1790, Austin practised law as an equity draftsman in Lincoln's Inn before being appointed in 1826 as professor of jurisprudence at the newly founded University of London. To prepare for his lectures, Austin spent two years in Bonn studying pandect law and German legal science. Although his early lectures were attended by J. S. Mill and others from Bentham's circle, Austin regarded his efforts as unsuccessful and resigned his chair in 1832. He died in Weybridge on 17 December 1859. But for the efforts of his remarkable wife, Sarah Austin (*née* Taylor), he would not have published at all. Main works: *The Province of Jurisprudence Determined* (1832); *Lectures on Jurisprudence*, 2 vols. (1863).

Secondary literature: Moles, R. N. (1987). *Definition and Rule in Legal Theory*, Oxford: Blackwell; Rumble, W. E. (1985). *The Thought of John Austin*, London: Athlone Press.

AYER, SIR ALFRED JULES (1910–89). Ayer was the most influential British member of the logical empiricist movement. In 1933 he became a lecturer at Christ Church Oxford; after war service he was appointed Grote Professor of Philosophy in London (1946–59) and then Wykeham Professor of Logic at Oxford (1959–78). Ayer's early work was much influenced by the work of the logical empiricists in Vienna, and his first book *Language, Truth and Logic* (London: Gollancz, 1936) is the classic statement in English of the logical empiricist position. In subsequent works, such as *The Foundations of Empirical Knowledge* (London: Macmillan, 1940), he progressively refined his empiricist account of knowledge. Although in later writings he moved away from the reductive empiricism of his earlier work, he remained committed to a philosophy which combines the rigour of logical reasoning with empiricist methods of enquiry. In 1973 he published *The Central Questions of Philosophy* (London: Weidenfeld and Nicholson, 1973).

Secondary literature: Foster, J. (1985). *A. J. Ayer*, London: Routledge.

BACHELARD, GASTON (1884–1962). Bachelard began his work life with the Postes et Telegraphes and taught high-school science from the end of the First World War until 1930, after receiving his doctorate in 1927. After ten years as professor of philosophy at Dijon, he went to the Sorbonne in 1940, where he remained as professor of history and philosophy of science until his retirement in 1954. It is plausible to speak of Bachelard's philosophy as a constructive rationalism, since he believed that reason actively builds scientific knowledge through the rationalisation of the empirical world via experiment and mathematics. Science (and art no less) is a *project*. His main works were: *Valeur inductive de la relativité* (Paris: Vrin, 1929); *Les intuitions atomistiques: essai de classification* (Paris: Vrin, 1933); *Essai sur la connaissance approchée* (Paris: Vrin, 1969); *Le Nouvel Esprit scientifique* (Paris: Presses Universitaires de France, 1973).

Secondary literature: McAllester, M. (ed.) (1989), *The Philosophy and Poetics of Gaston Bachelard*, Washington, DC: University Press of America; Tiles, M. (1985), *Bachelard: Science and Objectivity*, Cambridge: Cambridge University Press.

BAKUNIN, MIKHAIL ALEKSANDROVICH (1814–76). Born in Tver province to a gentry family, Bakunin studied at the Artillery School in St Petersburg from 1828 to 34; from 1836 to 1840 he studied philosophy in Moscow, where he became part of the Stankevich Hegelian circle. In 1840 he moved to Berlin, where he became involved in the Hegelian left. He moved to Zurich in 1843, to Paris in 1845, and to Brussels in 1847. He was active during the revolutions of 1848 in Bohemia and Germany; took part in 1849 Dresden insurrection, and was sentenced to death in both Saxony and Austria, but eventually extradited to Russia in 1851. Having been released from prison and exiled to Siberia in 1857, he escaped from Siberia and made his way to London 1861. In 1864 he moved to Italy and joined the First International. He moved to

Switzerland in 1867 and his factional struggle with Marx culminated in his expulsion from the International in 1872.

His main works were: 'Die Reaktion in Deutschland', *Deutsche Jahrbücher für Wissenschaft und Kunst*, 1842, trans. and ed. 1965 J. M. Edie, J. P. Scanlon, and M.-B. Zeldina, 'The Reaction in Germany', *Russian Philosophy* (3 vols., Chicago: Quadrangle Books), vol. I, 384–406; *Gosudarstvennost' I anarkhiia* (Geneva, 1873, trans. 1900 M. S. Shats, *Statism and Anarchy*, Cambridge: Cambridge University Press).

Secondary literature: Carr, E. H. (1975), *Michael Bakunin*, London: Macmillan; Kelly, A. (1982), *Michael Bakunin. A Study in Psychology and Politics of Utopianism*, Oxford: Clarendon Press.

BARTH, KARL (1886–1946). Barth was the most important theologian of the twentieth century. He was a German-speaking Swiss and trained in Switzerland and Germany. In 1922 he was called to the chair of Reformed theology in Göttingen; in 1925 he moved to Munster, and then in 1930 to Bonn; but he was dismissed in 1935 for refusing to take an oath of loyalty to Hitler. He returned to Switzerland and held a chair of theology at Basle until 1961. Barth's first major work was his discussion of *The Epistle to the Romans* (Zurich, 1922) in which he affirmed the absolute 'otherness' of God. This work initiated the 'theology of crisis' but gave rise to the question: how can we then have any understanding of God? Barth's response to this was that there is no other source than the Word of God, and he worked this out in his monumental *Church Dogmatics* (Munich, 1932–67) to which he devoted the rest of his life.

Secondary literature: Ford, D. (1981), *Barth and God's Story*, Frankfurt: Verlag Peter Lang; Sykes, S. (ed.) (1989), *Karl Barth: Centenary Essays*, Cambridge: Cambridge University Press.

BERDIAEV, NIKOLAI ALEKSANDROVICH (1874–1948). Born near Kiev into an aristocratic family, Berdiaev was brought up in the French manner. He became a student radical, which led to his expulsion from Kiev University in 1898. In 1900, he was banished to Vologda Province. There he wrote *Sub" ektivizm i individualizm v obshchestvennoi filosofii (Subjectivism and Individualism in Social Philosophy)* (St Petersburg: Popova, 1901), a critique of Mikhailovskii which sought to reconcile Marxism and transcendental idealism. In 1908, he moved to Moscow and became prominent in the spiritual searching of the 'silver age', contributing to *Vekhi (Signposts)* (1909). His influences included German idealism, Schopenhauer, Nietzsche, Soloviev, Rozanov, Dostoevsky, and Tolstoi. He adopted a form of religious personalism influenced by the mysticism of Jakob Boehme, which he set out in *Smysl tvorchestva (The Meaning of Creativity)* (Moscow: Leman and Saklavov, 1916). He was briefly a professor at Moscow University, but was expelled from Russia in 1922. He settled in Paris in 1924, where he became the best known of the Russian émigré philosophers. He continued to develop his blend of Christian existentialism and personalistic socialism in many subsequent books (e.g. *Sonysl istorii*, Berlin: Obolisk, 1923; *O rabstve i Svobode cheloveka*, Paris: YMCA Press, 1939), and wrote perceptively about Russian communism. F. Nucho, *Berdyaev's Philosophy* (London: Gollancz, 1966), is the best monograph on his work. N. Lossky, *History of Russian Philosophy* (New York: International University Press, 1951), ch. 16, is a good short account.

BERGSON, HENRI (1859–1941). Bergson entered the École Normale Supérieure in 1878, received his *agrégation* in 1881, and his doctorate in 1889. After some years of teaching in *lycées*, he was named professor at the Collège de France in 1900. He became a member of the Académie des sciences morales et politiques in 1901, became *officier de la Légion d'honneur* in 1902, received an honorary doctorate from the University of Oxford in 1909, and became a member of the Académie française in 1914. From 1916 he was sent on high-level diplomatic missions by the

French government to Spain, and the United States, where he received a great welcome. He received the Nobel prize for literature in 1928. Works which appeared during his lifetime were: *Quid Aristoteles de loco senserit* (doctoral thesis, 1889); *Essai sur les données immédiates de la conscience* (Paris: Alcan, 1889); *Matière et Mémoire: essai sur la relation du corps à l'esprit* (Paris: Presses Universitaires de France, 1896); *Le Rire: essai sur la signification du comique* (Paris: Presses Universitaires de France, 1900); *L'Evolution créatrice* (Paris: Presses Universitaires de France, 1907); *L'Energie spirituelle* (Paris: Alcan, 1919); *Durée et simultanéité: propos de la théorie d'Einstein* (Paris: Alcan, 1922); *Les Deux Sources de la morale et de la religion* (Paris: Alcan, 1932); *La Pensée et le Mouvant: essais et conférences* (Paris: Alcan, 1938). Other texts were later gathered and published as *Mélanges* (Presses Universitaires de France, 1972). Despite the prohibition in Bergson's will, his *lycée* courses have also now been published: as *Cours I, II, III* (1990–4).

Of the massive secondary literature, the following may be mentioned: Deleuze, G. (1966), *Le Bergsonisme*, Paris: Presses Universitaires de France; Gouhier, H. (1964), *Bergson et le Christ des Evangiles*, Paris: Fayard; Hude, H. (1989–1900), *Bergson*, Paris: Editions Universitaires; Lacey, A. R. (1989), *Bergson*, *The Arguments of the Philosophers*, London: Routledge; Moore, F. C. T. (1996), *Bergson: Thinking Backwards*. Modern European Philosophy, Cambridge: Cambridge University Press; Russell, B. A. W. (1914), *The Philosophy of Bergson*, Cambridge: Bowes and Bowes; Soulez, P. (1997), *Bergson*, Paris: Flammarion; Worms, F. (1992), *Introduction à Bergson: l'âme et le corps*, Paris: Hatier.

BLONDEL, MAURICE (1861–1949). Born in Dijon and educated at the local *lycée*, he entered the Ecole Normale Supérieure in Paris in 1881, where he studied with Emile Boutroux and Léon Ollé Laprune. In 1893 Blondel submitted his thesis, *L'Action*, to the Sorbonne. He taught briefly at lycées and the University of Lille, and then was appointed professor at Aix-en-Provence where he taught from 1894 until his retirement in 1927. Blondel's writings influenced several Catholic Modernists; his works, however, were critical of both Neo-Thomism on the right and the Modernists on the left. His *Letter on Apologetics* (1896, trans. 1964 A. Dru and I. Trethowan, London: Harvill Press) was sent to the Holy Office in Rome, but he was never condemned. Blondel also influenced the transcendental Thomists, Pierre Rousselot and Joseph Maréchal. Later in the 1930s and 1940s, Blondel's writings were again influential, for example, on the Nouvelle Théologie and the French Existentialists Gabriel Marcel and Maurice Merleau-Ponty. Among Blondel's other writings are his trilogy: *La pensée*, 2 vols. (Paris: Alcan, 1934), *L'Etre et les êtres* (Paris: Alcan, 1935), and *Action*, 2 vols. (Paris: Alcan, 1936–7). The latter work is not to be confused with *L'Action* (Paris: Alcan, 1893). Also, *La philosophie et l'esprit chrétien*, 2 vols. (Paris: Alcan, 1944–6), and *Exigences philosophiques du christianisme* (1950).

Helpful guides to Blondel's philosophy include: Henri Bouillard, *Blondel and Christianity* (Washington, DC: Corpus Books, 1969); Gabriel Daly, *Transcendence and Immanence: A Study in Catholic Modernism and Integralism*, Oxford: Oxford University Press, 1980, chs. 2 and 4; Alexander Dru and Illtyd Trethowan (eds.), *Maurice Blondel: The Letter on Apologetics and History and Dogma*, London: Harvill Press, 1964 which includes an important 124-page Introduction; Henri Duméry, *La philosophie de l'action* (Paris: Aubier, 1948); Jean Lacroix, *Maurice Blondel: An Introduction to the Man and His Philosophy* (New York: Sheed and Ward, 1968); James M. Somerville, *Total Commitment. Blondel's L'Action* (Washington, DC: Corpus Books, 1968); Claude Tresmontant, *Introduction à la métaphysique de Maurice Blondel* (Paris: Editions du Seuil, 1963).

BOLTZMANN, LUDWIG (1844–1906). Austrian physicist-philosopher; born in Vienna, educated in Linz and Vienna, Boltzmann taught physics and epistemology in Graz, Munich, and Vienna. He recognised the importance of Maxwell's electromagnetic and atomic theories; to the latter he made seminal contributions: he proved the equipartition theorem (in a molecule, every degree of freedom contributes the same quantity of energy); he moreover identified the statistical character of the notion of entropy by linking it to that of thermodynamic probability (see *Vorlesungen über Gastheorie*, Leipzig: J. Barth, 1896). In philosophy (see *Populäre Schriften*, Braunschweig Wiesbaden: Vieweg 1979), he defended materialism and a Darwinian reduction of biology and psychology to physics.

Secondary literature: Blackmore, J. (ed.) (1995), *Ludwig Boltzmann: His Later Life and Philosophy, 1900–1906*, 2 vols. Boston Studies in the Philosophy of Science 168, 174, Dordrecht: Kluwer.

BOSANQUET, BERNARD (1848–1923). As a student at Balliol College, Oxford (1866–70), Bosanquet was much influenced by T. H. Green's idealism and by his example of active citizenship. In 1871 he was elected a fellow of University College, Oxford (beating F. H. Bradley), and taught philosophy and Greek history. Becoming financially independent on his father's death, Bosanquet moved to London in 1881, to have time to write, and to engage in social work and adult education. Besides publishing prolifically in philosophy, he was prominent in the Charity Organisation Society, which aimed to put private philanthropy on a systematic and scientific footing. From 1903 to 1908 he was professor of moral philosophy at St Andrews University. He gave the Gifford lectures in 1911 and 1912. He was President of the Aristotelian Society from 1894 to 1898. His main works were: *Knowledge and Reality: A Criticism of Mr. F. H. Bradley's 'Principles of Logic'* (London: Kegan Paul, 1885); *Logic, or the Morphology of Knowledge* (Oxford: Clarendon Press, 1888); *Essays and Addresses* (London: Swan Sonnenschein, 1889); *A History of Aesthetic* (London: George Allen and Unwin, 1892); *The Civilization of Christendom and Other Studies* (London: Swan Sonnenschein, 1893); *The Essentials of Logic* (London and New York: Macmillan, 1895); *A Companion to Plato's Republic for English Readers* (London: Rivingtons, 1895); *Psychology of the Moral Self* (London and New York: Macmillan, 1897); *The Philosophical Theory of the State* (London: Macmillan, 1899); *The Principle of Individuality and Value* (London: Macmillan, 1912); *The Value and Destiny of the Individual* (London: Macmillan, 1913); *Three Lectures on Aesthetic* (London: Macmillan, 1915); *Social and International Ideals, Being Studies in Patriotism* (London, 1917); *Some Suggestions in Ethics* (London: Macmillan, 1918); *Implication and Linear Inference* (London: Macmillan, 1920); *What Religion Is* (London: Macmillan, 1920); *The Meeting of Extremes in Contemporary Philosophy* (London: Macmillan, 1921); *Science and Philosophy and Other Essays*, ed. J. H. Muirhead and R. C. Bosanquet (London: Allen and Unwin, 1927); *Selected Essays*, ed. W. Sweet (Bristol, 1999); *Essays on 'Aspects of the Social Problem' and Essays on Social Policy*, ed. W. Sweet (Bristol: Thoemmes Press, 1999).

Secondary literature: Bosanquet, H. (1924), *Bernard Bosanquet: A Short Account of his Life*, London: Macmillan; Gaus, G. F. (1994), 'Green, Bosanquet and the Philosophy of Coherence' in C. L. Ten (ed.), *The Routledge History of Philosophy*, vol. VII: *The Nineteenth Century*, London: Routledge, 408–36; Houang, F. (1954), *Le Néo-hégélianisme en Angleterre: la philosophie de Bernard Bosanquet*, Paris, Vrin; Milne, A. J. M. (1962), *The Social Philosophy of English Idealism*, London: George Allen and Unwin; Muirhead, J. H. (1935), *Bernard Bosanquet and His Friends: Letters Illustrating the Sources and the Development of His Philosophical Opinions*, London: Allen and Unwin; Otter, S. den (1996), *British Idealism and Social Explanation: A Study in Late Victorian Thought*, Oxford: Clarendon Press; Randall, J. H., Jr. (1996), 'Idealist Social Philosophy and Bernard Bosanquet', *Philosophy and Phenomenological Research*, 24: 473–502; Sweet, W. (1997), *Idealism and Rights: The Social Ontology of Human Rights in the Political Thought of Bernard Bosanquet*, Lanham, MD: University Press of America; Sweet, W. (1998), 'Bernard Bosanquet' in E. N. Zetla (ed.), *The Stanford Encyclopaedia of Philosophy*, Stanford, CA: CSLI; Vincent, A. and Plant, R. (1984), *Philosophy, Politics and Citizenship: The Life and Thought of the British Idealists*, Oxford: Blackwell.

BRADLEY, FRANCIS HERBERT (1846–1924). Born in London on 30 January 1846, the son of a famous evangelical vicar and brother of A. C. Bradley, the Shakespearian critic. Educated at University College Oxford, he became a fellow of Merton College Oxford in 1870, one year after his degree. The next year he was struck with a severe kidney disease and was for the rest of his life a retired semi-invalid who kept his own company or the company of a few friends. He never lectured and never had any students (the later idealist philosopher, R. G. Collingwood remarked that although he had lived near him in Oxford for sixteen years, he had never to his knowledge set eyes on him). Illness did not prevent Bradley from travelling fairly extensively and he often wintered abroad for the sake of his health, managing to keep himself alive until 18 September 1924. He was awarded the Order of Merit in 1924. His chief works are *Ethical Studies* (Oxford: Clarendon Press, 1876) and *Appearance and Reality* (London: Swan Sonnenschein, 1906).

Secondary literature: Manser, A. and Stock, G. (eds.) (1984), *The Philosophy of F. H. Bradley*, Oxford: Clarendon Press; and Nicholson, P. P. (1990) *The Political Philosophy of the British Idealists*, Cambridge: Cambridge University Press.

BRENTANO, FRANZ (1838–1917). Born in Marienberg (Germany) into a distinguished Italian-German family, Brentano studied in Berlin under Adolf Trendelenburg and in Würzburg, where he also took holy orders. After his rejection of the dogma of Papal infallibility he withdrew from the priesthood in 1873; one year later he became professor of philosophy in Vienna, where for twenty years he taught, among others, Edmund Husserl, Anton Marty, Christian von Ehrenfels, Kazimierz Twardowski, Carl Stumpf, Alexius Meinong, and Sigmund Freud. He moved to Florence in 1896 and to Zurich in 1915. His work, much of it published posthumously, extends across all areas of philosophy: *Von der mannigfachen Bedeutung des Seineden nach Aristotle* (Freiburg: Herder, 1862); *Psychologie vom empirischen Standpunkt* (Leipzig: Duncker and Humboldt, 1874); *Vom sinnlichem und noetischen Bewusstsein* (Leipzig: Meiner, 1928); *Wahrheit und Evidenz* (Leipzig: Meiner, 1930); *Kategorienlehre* (Leipzig: Meiner, 1933), *Philosophische Untersuchungen zu Raum, Zeit, und Kontinuum* (Hamburg: Meiner, 1976); *Deskriptive Psychologie* (Hamburg: Meiner, 1982).

Secondary literature: McAlister, L. L. (ed.) (1976), *The Philosophy of Brentano*, London: Duckworth; Smith, B. (1986), 'Austrian Economics and Austrian Philosophy' in W. Grassl and B. Smith (eds.), *Austrian Economics; Historical and Philosophical Background*, London: Croom Helm.

BRIDGMAN, PERCY W. (1882–1962). Bridgman received his PhD from Harvard University in 1908 and joined the faculty the same year. He became Hollis Professor of Mathematics and Natural Philosophy in 1926. Bridgman's empirical work was in materials under extremely high pressure, for which he received a Nobel Prize in 1946. Yet it is as a philosopher of physics, in such books as *The Logic of Modern Physics* (New York: Macmillan, 1927), *The Nature of Physical Theory* (Princeton, NJ: Princeton University Press, 1936), and *Reflections of a Physicist* (New York: Philosophical Library, 1955), that Bridgman made his greatest impact. Ever an operationalist, Bridgman forcefully defended the principle that it is meaningless to interpret physical concepts except as they are capable of observation, particularly through experimental operations. A whole generation of physicists, and several generations of psychologists, were brought up in Bridgman's philosophical tradition.

Secondary literature: Walter, M. L. (1990), *Science and Cultural Crisis*, Stanford, CA: Stanford University Press.

BROAD, C. D. (1887–1971). Charles (Charlie) Broad was educated at Cambridge University, where he read Natural Sciences Part I and Moral Sciences Part II. He was elected to a prize fellowship at Trinity College in 1911, and was lecturer at St Andrews University from 1911 to 1914 and then professor at Bristol until returning to a fellowship at Trinity College, Cambridge, in 1923. He was elected to the Knightbridge Chair of Moral Philosophy at Cambridge in 1933, and held the chair until his retirement in 1953. His major works (not just on moral philosophy) were: *Scientific Thought* (London: Kegan Paul, 1923); *The Mind and its Place in Nature* (London: Kegan Paul, 1925); 'Analysis of some Ethical Concepts', *Journal of Philosophical Studies*, 3 (1928); *Five Types of Ethical Theory* (London: Kegan Paul, 1930); 'Is "Goodness" a Name of a Simple Non-Natural Quality?', *Proceedings of the Aristotelian Society* 34 (1934); 'Some Reflections on Moral-Sense Theories in Ethics', *Proceedings of the Aristotelian Society*, 45 (1945).

Secondary literature: Schilpp, P. A. (ed.) (1959), *The Philosophy of C. D. Broad*, New York: Tudor.

BROUWER, LUITZGEN EGBERTUS JAN (1881–1966). The founder of the 'intuitionist' movement in logic and the philosophy of mathematics. Brouwer spent his career in Amsterdam, where he was a professor from 1912 until 1955. Brouwer rejected the view that there is a mind-independent mathematical reality which may, or may not, be discovered by mathematicians. Instead he held that mathematical truth depends on the possibility of constructing proofs, and this led him to reject non-constructive methods of argument in mathematics. Although he rejected the logicist thesis that logic is the foundation of mathematics, his approach to mathematical reasoning can be generalised to logic, where it constitutes 'intuitionist logic' which departs from classical logic by rejecting the law of excluded middle. His main works were 'De onbetrouwbaarheid der logische principes' (*Tijdsschrift voor wijsbegeerte* 1: 152–8; trans. 1975 by A. Heyting, 'The Unreliability of the Logical Principles' in A. Heyting (ed.), L. E. J. Brouwer, *Collected Works*, vol. I, Amsterdam: North-Holland, 107–11); and 'Consciousness, Philosophy and Mathematics' (*Proceedings of the 10th International Congress of Philosophy, Amsterdam, 1948*, 1235–49. Repr. 1975 in A. Heyting (ed.), L. E. J. Brower, *Collected Works*, vol. I, Amsterdam: North-Holland, 480–94).

Secondary literature: Dummett, M. A. E. (1973), 'The Philosophical Basis of Intuitionistic Logic' in H. E. Rose and J. C. Shepherdson (eds.), *Logic Colloqium 1973*, 5–40. Repr. 1978 in *Truth and Other Enigmas*, London: Duckworth, 215–47; Dummett, M. A. E. (1977), *Elements of Intuitionism*, Oxford: Clarendon Press.

BRUNSCHVICG, LÉON. (1869–1944). Brunschvicg received his *licence ès lettres* and *licence ès sciences* from the Ecole Normale Supérieure in 1891 and his Sorbonne doctorate in 1897 for his thesis, *La Modalité du jugement*. After teaching in several lycées, he returned in 1909 to the Sorbonne, where he held various chairs until the Nazis occupied Paris in 1940. He was a founder of the *Revue de métaphysique et de morale* and of the Société française de Philosophie. Brunschvicg's general position combined an epistemological and a metaphysical idealism, based mostly upon Kant, but with an historical methodology. During his time he was the leading spokesman of general French philosophy. His main works were: *La modalité du jugement* (*The Modality of Judgment*) (Paris: Alcan, 1897); *L'Expérience humaine et la causalité physique* (*Human Experience and Physical Causality*) (Paris: Alcan, 1922); and *Le Progrès de la conscience dans la philosophie occidentale* (*The Progress of Consciousness in Western Philosophy*) (Paris: Alcan, 1927).

Secondary literature: Boirel, R. (1964), *Brunschvicg*, Paris: Presses Universitaires de France.

CAMPBELL, NORMAN R. (1880–1949). A fellow of Trinity College, Cambridge; he worked under J. J. Thomson in Cambridge from 1904 to 1910 and then became honorary fellow for research in physics at Leeds. After the First World War, he became a researcher for General

Electric until retirement in 1944. Because of his rich physics experience, Campbell brought real, practical knowledge to his philosophical thought – hence his emphasis upon analogy and measurement. Campbell's depth is well indicated by the fact that his highly regarded *Physics: The Elements* (Cambridge: Cambridge University Press, 1920) was later reprinted as *Foundations of Science* (New York: Dover, 1957). Probably his best-known work, however, remains the short, extremely accessible *What is Science?* (Cambridge: Cambridge University Press, 1921).

Secondary literature: Nagel, E. (1961), *The Structure of Science*, New York: Harcourt Brace.

CANTOR, GEORG (1845–1918). Cantor was the founder of set theory and the modern theory of infinite numbers. He secured a teaching position at Halle in 1869, and remained there for the rest of his life. He developed his theory of sets in parallel with his investigations into the size of sets. In 1874 he developed the famous 'diagonal argument' by which he was able to show that the size (cardinal number) of the set of real numbers is greater than that of the natural numbers. 'Cantor's theorem' is the generalisation of this result, and states that the cardinal number of the power set of a set S is always greater than the cardinal number of S itself. This sets up a hierarchy of infinite cardinal numbers ('Cantor's heaven'). Cantor postulated that there is no infinite cardinal between the number of the natural numbers and that of the real numbers (Cantor's 'continuum hypothesis'). Cantor also developed a theory of transfinite ordinal numbers alongside his theory of infinite cardinals, and showed that these have a distinctive arithmetic. His main works were 'Über unendliche lineare Punctmannigfaltigkeiten, 5' ('On Infinite Linear Manifolds of Points') (*Mathematischen Annalen* 1883); 'Beiträge zur Begründung der transfiniten mengenlehre' (*Mathematischen Annalen* 1895, 1897. Trans. *Contributions to the Founding of the Theory of Transfinite Numbers* (New York: Dover, 1955)).

Secondary literature: Dauben, J. W. (1979), *George Cantor: His Mathematics and Philosophy of the Infinite*, Cambridge, MA: Harvard University Press; Hallett, M. (1984), *Cantorian Set Theory and Limitation of Size*, Oxford: Clarendon Press.

CARNAP, RUDOLPH (1891–1970). Carnap was one of the leading figures in the Vienna Circle and had a decisive influence in the United States after he had moved there. He studied under Frege at Jena and wrote his doctoral thesis there on the philosophy of physics. In 1926 he began teaching at Vienna, where he joined the Vienna Circle; in 1931 he moved to a chair at the German University in Prague. But in 1935 he moved to Chicago and began a new career in the United States. In 1956 he moved to UCLA, where he ended his career. Carnap's first major work was *Der logische Aufbau der Welt* (Berlin: Weltkreis Verlag, 1928. Trans. 1967 *The Logical Structure of the World* (Berkeley, CA: University of Californià Press)), in which he sought to show how the structure of the world can be constituted on the basis of experience. In the 1930s Carnap turned to enquiries into the logical structure of language in order to clarify the structure of scientific knowledge and developed a pragmatic, conventionalist, conception of the role of logic. In accordance with this account, he held that all philosophical questions are best regarded as questions about language. In his later writings in the United States Carnap turned to questions of semantics and to the clarification of logical probability; he also defended his pragmatically based analytic/synthetic distinction against Quine's criticism that the distinction itself was misconceived. Carnap's other main works were *Scheinproblems in der Philosophic* (*Pseudoproblems in Philosophy*) (Berlin: Weltkreis, 1928); 'Uberwindung der Metaphysik durch logische Analyse der Sprache' (*Erkenntnis* 2, 1932: 219–41. Trans. 1959 'The Elimination of Metaphysics through the Logical Analysis of Language', in A. J. Ayer, ed., *Logical Positivism* (Glencoe, IL: Free Press)); *Logische Syntax der Sprache* (Vienna: Verlag Julius Springer, 1934. Trans. 1937 *The Logical Syntax of Language* (London: Kegan Paul)); *Logical Foundations of Probability* (Chicago: University of Chicago Press, 1950); 'Empiricism, Semantics and Ontology' (*Revue internationale de philosophie* 4, 1950: 20–40).

Secondary literature: Coffa, J. A. (1991), *The Semantic Tradition from Kant to Carnap: To the Vienna Station*, Cambridge: Cambridge University Press; Friedman, M. (1987), 'Carnap's *Aufbau* Reconsidered', *Noûs* 21: 521–45 and (1992), 'Epistemology in the *Aufbau*', *Synthèse* 93: 15–57.

CASSIRER, ERNST (1874–1945). Cassirer continued the Neo-Kantian tradition of philosophy into the first half of the twentieth century, showing how Kant's conception of the categories could be modified and extended to apply as 'symbolic forms'. He studied in Marburg with Hermann Cohen, and lectured at Berlin from 1906 until 1919 when he accepted a chair at Hamburg. Cassirer left Germany in 1933, and after brief spells in Oxford and Sweden settled at Yale in 1941. Cassirer's main work is *Philosophie der Symbolischen Formen* (*The Philosophy of Symbolic Forms*) (Berlin: B. Cassirer and Darmstadt: Wissenschaftliche Buchgesellschaft, 1923–9) in which he offers a unified account of symbolic representations, including myth, religion, language, art, and science. Cassirer gives a Hegelian phenomenology of these symbolic forms, arguing that they exemplify the different relations between symbols and the symbolised. Cassirer also wrote a series of works on the history of philosophy, which include important studies of the Renaissance and Enlightenment. Other important works include *An Essay on Man* (New Haven, CT: Yale University Press, 1944); and *Die Philosophie der Aufklärung* (Tübingen: Mohr, 1932. Trans. 1961 *The Philosophy of the Enlightenment*, Princeton, NJ: Princeton University Press).

Secondary literature: Krois, J. H. (1987), *Cassirer: Symbolic Forms and History*, New Haven, CT: Yale University Press.

CHURCH, ALONZO (1903–1995). Church is best known as the creator of the λ-calculus, a formalism for defining functions that is of great importance in computer science, and for his Thesis (1934) that all effectively computable functions are λ-definable. In 1936 Church showed that the valid sentences of Peano arithmetic do not form a recursive set. One of the founders of the Association for Symbolic Logic, Church served as editor of its *Journal* from 1936 to 1979. He was a member of the faculty at Princeton from 1929 to 1967 and at UCLA from 1967 to 1991. His principal works were: 'An Unsolvable Problem of Elementary Number Theory', *American Journal of Mathematics* 58, 345–63; 'A Note on the Entscheidungsproblem', *Journal of Symbolic Logic* I (1936): 40–1 and 101–2; 'A bibliography of symbolic logic', *Journal of Symbolic Logic* I (1936): 121–216 (additions and corrections 3: 178–92); and *The Calculi of Lambda Conversion* (Princeton, NJ: Princeton University Press, 1941).

Secondary literature: Anderson, C. A. (1998), 'Alonzo Church's Contributions to Philosophy and Intensional Logic', *The Bulletin of Symbolic Logic* 4: 129–71; Barendregt, H. (1997), 'The Impact of the Lambda Calculus in Logic and Computer Science', *The Bulletin of Symbolic Logic* 3: 181–215; Enderton, H. B. (1998), 'Alonzo Church and the Reviews', *The Bulletin of Symbolic Logic* 4: 181–203; Sieg, W. (1988), 'Step by Recursive Step: Church's Analysis of Effective Calculability', *The Bulletin of Symbolic Logic* 3: 154–80.

CHWISTEK, LEON (1884–1944). Chwistek studied in Cracow, gaining his PhD in 1906 and his habilitation in 1928. He was a professor in Lvov from 1930 to 1939. His main work was his *Outline of Logic and of the Methodology of the Exact Sciences*, London: Kegan Paul, 1948.

Secondary literature: Jordan, Z. (1945), *The Development of Mathematical Logic and of Logical positivism in Poland Between Two Wars*, Oxford: Oxford University Press.

CLIFFORD, WILLIAM KINGDON (1845–1879). English mathematician and philosopher, born and educated in Exeter and, at the age of fifteen, at King's College, London. In 1863 he entered Trinity College, Cambridge, where his mathematical genius was recognised and where he began, as an undergraduate, to publish mathematical papers. At Cambridge he was a member of the elite club, the Apostles, and was a spirited supporter of High Church Anglo-Catholicism. Through his study of Darwin and Herbert Spencer, who were dominant influences on him, Clifford became an agnostic and was one of the leading Victorian unbelievers, through his highly effective and popular lectures and essays.

In 1868 Clifford was elected a fellow of Trinity College, where he remained until his appointment in 1871 as professor of applied mathematics at University College, London. In 1874 he was elected to the Royal Society and became a valuable member and contributor to the discussions of the famous Metaphysical Society. In the last four years of his life he suffered from advancing tuberculosis; he died in Madeira on 3 March 1879. Some of Clifford's mathematical papers remain classics in the field. His philosophical position set forth in numerous papers on epistemology and metaphysics has been referred to as idealistic monism. He defended freedom and rejected purely mechanistic explanations of matter and mind and pure phenomenalism. All entities in nature have elementary feelings or mind-stuff that have mental or psychic characteristics. Hence the physical and mental are two modes of apprehending the same world.

Main works: all of Clifford's important papers on philosophy and ethics were published together posthumously by F. Pollock and L. Stephen (eds.), *Lectures and Essays*, 2 vols. (London: Macmillan, 1879). Volume 1 includes a life of Clifford by Pollock. Clifford's Mathematical Papers (London: Macmillan, 1882) are edited by R. Tucker, with an introduction by H. J. S. Smith. Clifford's fragmentary *Common Sense of the Exact Sciences* (London: Kegan Paul, 1885) was edited and partly written by Karl Pearson and has been reissued with a preface by Bertrand Russell and a new introduction by James R. Newman (New York, 1955).

Secondary sources: For Clifford's contribution to the debate on the ethics of belief, see McCarthy, Gerald D. (1986), *The Ethics of Belief Debate*, Atlanta: Scholars Press; Livingston, James C. (1974), *The Ethics of Belief: An Essay on the Victorian Religious Conscience*, Tallahassee, FL: Scholars Press.

COHEN, HERMANN (1842–1918). German philosopher and one of the founders of the Marburg school of Neo-Kantianism. He was born in 1842 in Coswig. His early university interest centred on the Greeks but shifted to Kant. As a student of F. A. Trendelenburg, he defended him against Kuno Fischer but modified that position in *Kants Theorie der Erfahrung* (Berlin: Dämmler, 1871), a commentary on the *The Critique of Pure Reason*. He also wrote commentaries on Kant's second and third *Critiques* (Berlin: Dämmler, 1877, 1889). He went to Marburg in 1873, befriending Lange, and after Lange's death took over the chair in philosophy. In 1880 Paul Natorp joined him, beginning a productive relationship. Cohen retired in 1912 and moved to Berlin where he worked on religious questions. He died in 1918.

Secondary literature: Poma, A. (1988), *Filosofia Critica di Hermann Cohen*, Milan: Ugo Mursia editore. Trans. 1997 J. Denton, *The Critical Philosophy of Hermann Cohen*, Albany, NY: State University of New York.

COLLINGWOOD, ROBIN GEORGE (1889–1943). Trained as an historian who worked on the Roman period of British history, Collingwood become the foremost philosopher of history in England in this period. Not only did he distinguish first-person historical knowledge from positivist conceptions of scientific enquiry in his *Idea of History* (Oxford: Oxford University Press, 1946), he also attempted to provide the metaphysical foundations of his antireductionist view in *An Essay on Metaphysics* (Oxford: Clarendon Press, 1940). On Collingwood's philosophy of history, see W. J. van der Dussen, *History as a Science* (Oxford: Oxford University Press, 1981) and Lewis Mink, *Mind, History and Dialectic* (Bloomington, IN: Indiana University Press, 1969).

CROCE, BENEDETTO (1866–1952). Croce was the leading Italian philosopher of the twentieth century and gave a distinctive new form to the Hegelian tradition, especially as it concerned the philosophy of art and of history. He studied at Rome and began writing as a private scholar; his first important works on aesthetics, logic, practical philosophy, and philosophy of history were conceived as a four-part 'Philosophy of Spirit' (1902, 1907, 1909, 1917). His views in all these areas developed during the next decades, as Croce defended the value of art as a distinctive way of giving content to our emotions, argued that 'all history is contemporary history' (because, as distinct from a mere chronicle, it involves interpretation), and opposed utilitarian reductions of ethical value. Croce also wrote a large number of historical studies, especially concerning the Baroque period and the kingdom of Naples.

His main works are *Estetica come scienza dell'espressione e linguistica generale* (Milan, Palermo and Naples: Sandron, 1902; trans. 1909 D. Ainslie, *Aesthetic*, London: Macmillan); *Logica come scienza del concetto puro* (Bari: Laterza, 1905; trans. 1917 D. Ainslie, *Logic*, London: Macmillan); *Filosofia della practica, economia ed etica* (Bari: Laterza, 1909; trans. 1917 D. Ainslie, *Philosophy of the Practical*, London: Macmillan); *Teoria e storia della storiografia* (Bari: Laterza, 1917; trans. 1921 D. Ainslie, *Theory and History of Historiography*, London: Harrap).

Secondary literature: Orsini, G. N. G. (1961), *Benedetto Croce, Philosopher of Art and Literary Critic*, Carbondale IL: Southern Illinois University Press; Roberts, D. D. (1987), *Benedetto Croce and the Uses of Historcism*, Berkeley, CA: University of California Press.

DE FINETTI, BRUNO (1906–1985). Italian mathmatician and probabilistic thinker. He developed a distinctive positivist philosophy of probability on the basis of ideas found in Italian pragmatist philosophy early in the twentieth century, and was also influenced by Bridgman's operationalism. Probability was interpreted as a degree of belief, not determined by external facts. Degree of belief manifests itself in the subject's behaviour in situations of uncertainty. Probability statements gain operational numerical meaning in situations such as betting, but only if all events meet strict criteria of empirical verifiability. His main works were: 'Sul significato soggettivo dell probabilità' ('On the Subjective Significance of Probability', *Fundamenta Mathematicae* 17 (1931) 298–329) and 'La prévision: ses lois logiques, ses sources subjectives' (*Annales de l'Institut Henri Poincaré* 7 (1937), 1–6; trans. 1964 'Foresight: Its Logical Laws, Its Subjective Sources' in H. Kyburg and H. Smokler (eds.), *Studies in Subjective Probability*, New York: Wiley).

Secondary literature: von Plato, J. (1994), *Creating Modern Probability*, Cambridge: Cambridge University Press.

DEWEY, JOHN (1859–1952). Dewey was the most important philosopher in the United States during the first half of the twentieth century, as well as an influential public intellectual. His philosophical corpus is vast and wide ranging, systematically expressed in works such as his *Logic: The Theory of Inquiry* (New York: Henry Holt, 1938). Motivated by a non-reductive naturalism and a broad understanding of democracy, Dewey saw the political importance of science in complex societies as a matter of making it a democratic form of social enquiry and problem-solving in *Liberalism and Social Action* (Carbondale: Southern Illinois University Press, 1935) and *The Public and Its Problems* (New York: Henry Holt, 1927). Recent literature on Dewey is vast, including comprehensive works by Robert Westbrook, *John Dewey and American Democracy* (Ithaca: Cornell University Press, 1991) and Alan Ryan, *John Dewey and the High Tide of American Liberalism* (New York: Norton, 1995).

DILTHEY, WILHELM (1833–1911). Dilthey devoted himself to providing a 'Critique of Historical Reason' which would do for the human sciences what Kant's *Critique of Pure Reason* had achieved for the natural sciences. He was appointed in 1882 to Hegel's chair at Berlin. In his first work, his 1883 *Einleitung in die Geisteswissenschaften* (Leipzig), Dilthey argued that neither metaphysics nor the natural sciences provides a methodology that is appropriate to the human sciences. In order to develop such a methodology he first argued that psychology needs to be reconceived, not as a natural science, but as a description of lived experience which aims at providing an 'understanding' of human life. He later came to think that a descriptive psychology of this kind needed to be enriched by a 'hermeneutic' approach which looks to levels of meaning that are not manifest in experience. This approach led him back to Hegel's conception of 'Objective Spirit' as the general framework for his self-reflexive critique of historical reason. His other main works are: 'Ideen über eine beschreibende und zergliedernde Psychologie' (1894; trans. 1977 R. Zaner and K. Heiges, 'Ideas Concerning a Descriptive and Analytic Psychology' in R. A. Makkreel (ed.), *Descriptive Psychology and Historical Understanding* (The Hague: Nijhoff), and 'Enstehung der Hermeneutik' (1900; trans. 1966 R. A. Makkreel and K. Rodi, 'The Rise of Hermeneutics' in R. A. Makkreel (ed.), *Hermeneutics and the Study of History*, Princeton, NJ: Princeton University Press).

Secondary literature: Makkreel, R. A. (1992), *Dilthey: Philosopher of the Human Studies*, 2nd edn Princeton, NJ: Princeton University Press.

DUHEM, PIERRE M. (1861–1916). Duhem studied physics in Paris, and, after publishing a major book on thermodynamics, moved to the faculties of science at, successively, Lille (1887), Rennes (1893), and Bordeaux (1895–1916). His interest in the systematic and formal aspects of scientific theories led to his most important philosophical work, the anti-metaphysical account of scientific theory in *La Théorie physique: son objet et sa structure* (Paris: Chevalier and Rivière, 1906). Duhem's belief that a subject's history formed an essential part of its nature led to his important *Les Origines de la statique* (Paris: A. Hermann, 1905–6) and the monumental ten-volume history of astronomy *Le Système du morde* (Paris: A. Hermann, 1913–59). Today's Duhem Problem is an offshoot of Duhem's view that there are no crucial experiments in science because no scientific hypothesis can be independently tested.

Secondary literature: Ariew, R. and Banker, P. (eds.) (1990), *Pierre Duhem: Historian and Philosopher of Science*, special issue of *Synthèse* 85; Martin, R. N. D. (1991), *Pierre Duhem*, La Salle, IL: Open Court.

DURKHEIM, EMILE (1858–1917). Durkheim was one of the founders of sociology. Although he is famous for insisting on the distinctiveness of 'social facts', his sociology was informed by a social philosophy which relied on an evaluative distinction between 'normal' and 'pathological' social phenomena. He began his academic career in 1887 in Bordeaux; in 1902 he moved to the Sorbonne in Paris, where he taught until his death in 1917.

In his first work, *De la division du travail social* (*The Division of Labour in Society*) (Paris: Alcan, 1893, trans. 1933 G. Simpson, New York: Macmillan), Durkheim contrasted the structure of modern and traditional societies, arguing that the introduction of the division of labour is not just an economic phenomenon, but brings with it a profound reorganisation of social structure and the values of social solidarity (see *The Rules of Sociological Method*, Paris: Alcan, 1895). In pathological situations, these values are threatened, leading to 'anomie' and the collapse of social solidarity. Durkheim then used this analysis to argue (in *Le Suicide* (Paris: Alcan, 1897, trans. 1951 A. Spaulding and G. Simpson, Glencoe, IL, Free Press)) that suicide, which looks on the face of it a distinctively individual phenomenon, is in fact a social phenomenon. For suicide is typically a product of social pathologies such as anomie. In his last work, *Les Formes élémentaires de la vie religiense* (*The Elementary Forms of Religious Life*) (Paris: Alcan, 1912, trans. 1915 J. W. Swain, New York: Macmillan), Durkheim extended much further his emphasis on the priority of social life, arguing that society is the source of all that makes us human.

Secondary literature: Lukes, Steven (1973), *Emile Durkheim: His Life and Work*, New York: Harper and Row.

EINSTEIN, ALBERT (1879–1955). Einstein was the most famous scientist of the twentieth century. He was born in Ulm in Germany, but in 1901 acquired Swiss citizenship and worked as a patent examiner in Berne until 1909. After holding academic positions in Zurich and Prague he moved to a research professorship Berlin in 1914. He became a celebrity in 1919 after confirmation of his General Theory of Relativity and was awarded a Nobel Prize in 1922. In 1933 he left Germany and worked at Princeton until his death.

In 1905 Einstein published his Special Theory of Relativity, in which he reconciled the observed constancy of the speed of light with the thesis that all inertial states of motion are equivalent. During the next ten years he developed his General Theory of Relativity to show that gravitation is inseparable from space-time geometry. At the same time he worked on the foundations of quantum theory, and in his later years he sought to develop a unified field theory which would bring together electromagnetic and gravitational fields in a new physics. During this period he criticised standard quantum theory for its acceptance of a statistical, non-deterministic, framework which he held to be incompatible with our experience of macroscopic phenomena. His main works were 'Zur Elektrodynamik bewegter Körper' (*Annalen der Physik* 17 (1905): 891–921); 'Die Grundlagen der allgemeinen Relativitätstheorie' (*Annalen der Physik* 14 (1916): 769–822); 'Kosmologische Betrachtungen zur allgemeinen Relativitätstheorie' (*Sitzungsberichte der Preußischen Akademie der Wissenschaften. Math.-Phys. Kl.* (1917), trans. 1923 W. Perrett and G. B. Jeffrey in H. A. Lorentz, A. Einstein, H. Minkowski, and H. Weyl, *The Principle of Relativity* (repr. New York: Dover, 1952), 175–88); 'Geometrie und Erfahrung' (*Sitzungsberichte der Preußischen Akademie der Wissenschaften. Math.-Phys. Kl.* (1917), separately issued 1923 by W. Perrett and G. B. Jeffrey in expanded form and trans. as 'Geometry and Experience' in *Sidelights on Relativity*, New York: E. P. Dutton, 27–56).

Secondary literature: Earman, J., Glymour, C., and Stachel, J. (eds.) (1977), *Foundations of Space-Time Theories*, Minneapolis: University of Minnesota Press; Pais, A. (1982), '*Subtle is the Lord*', *The Life and Science of Albert Einstein*, New York: Oxford University Press.

ENGELS, FRIEDRICH (1820–95). Born in Barmen to a family of Protestant mill-owners; worked in Manchester for the family firm Ermen and Engels, obtaining the materials for *The Condition of the Working Class in England* (1845) (*Die Lage der arbeitende Klasse in England*, Leipzig: no publisher. Trans. in K. Marx and F. Engels, *Collected Works* (1975–98), London: Lawrence and Wishart). He was Marx's closest friend and collaborator from 1844 onwards; took part in armed struggles in Elberfeld and the Palatinate during the death-agony of the 1848 Revolution; worked at Ermen and Engels in Manchester 1850–69, providing the Marx family with indispensable family support; edited the second and third volumes of *Capital* after Marx's death. During the last twenty-five years of his life, his home in London became one of the main centres of the British and international labour movement.

Secondary literature: Arthur, C. J. (ed.) (1996), *Engels Today: A Contenary Appreciation*, London: Macmillan; Canven, T. (1989), *Friedrich Engels: His Life and Thought*, Basingstoke: Macmillan.

EWING, A. C. (1899–1973). Alfred Ewing was born in 1899. He studied at University College, Oxford, and then taught at the University of Michigan and University College, Swansea, before moving to Cambridge in 1931 as lecturer in moral science. He was elected to a readership in 1954 and retired in 1966. He wrote mainly on idealism and on moral philosophy. His major works were *Kant's Treatment of Causality* (London: Kegan Paul, 1924); *The Morality of Punishment* (London: Kegan Paul, 1929); *Idealism: A Critical Survey* (London: Methuen, 1934); *The Definition of Good* (London: Routledge 1947); *Second Thoughts in Moral Philosophy* (London: Routledge, 1959).

FISCHER, KUNO (1824–1907). German philosopher and historian, Kuno was born in 1824 in Silesia. He studied at Leipzig and Halle. He became *Privatdozent* at Heidelberg in 1850 but was dismissed three years later because of his pantheistic views. He returned to teaching at Jena in 1856 and then in 1872 moved to Heidelberg where he remained until retiring in 1903. He is remembered for his fight with F. A. Trendelenburg over Kant's notion of space and for his multi-volume *Geschichte der neuern Philosophie* (1852–93 (Heidelberg: Carl Winters Universitätsbuchhandlung)) which was popular because of his sympathetic understanding and clarity. His other major work is *Kants Leben und Grundlagen seine Lehre* (Heidelberg: Carl Winters Universitätsbuchhandlung, 1860). He died in 1907.

Secondary literature: Köhnke, K. C. (1986), *Entstehung und Aufstieg des Neu-Kantianismus*, Frankfurt: Suhrkamp, trans. 1991 R. J. Hollingdale as *The Rise of Neo-Kantianism*, Cambridge: Cambridge University Press.

FREGE, GOTTLOB (1848–1925). Friedrich Ludwig Gottlob Frege was born in Wismar, and studied mathematics at the Universities of Jena and Göttingen. In 1879 he published the *Begriffsschrift*, which inaugurated the modern era in logic with the introduction of quantifiers, relations with any number of terms, truth-functional connectives, and an axiomatised version of the predicate calculus. His professional life was spent as a mathematician at the University of Jena, where he devoted himself to implementing his 'logicist' programme, according to which arithmetic and analysis can be shown to be reducible to pure logic. In the process he articulated a theory of meaning for formal and natural languages based on the twin distinctions between function and object, and between sense and reference. In 1902 he learned from Bertrand Russell that his logicism was fatally flawed. He died, bitter and unacknowledged, in 1925. Since then his genius has come to be recognised, and his thought has had a formative influence on the development of twentieth-century philosophy. His main works were: *Begriffsschrift, eine der arith-metischen nachgebildete Formelsprache des reinen Denkens* (*Conceptual Notation: A Formula-Language of Pure Thought, Modelled on the Language of Arithmetic*) (Halle: L. Nebert, 1879, trans. 1972 T. W. Bynum, *Conceptual Notation and Other Articles*, Oxford: Oxford University Press); *Die Grundlagen der Arithmetik, eine logisch-mathematische Untersuchung über den Begriff der Zahl* (*The Foundations of Arithmetic. A Logico-Mathematical Investigation of the Concept of Number*). (Breslau: W. Koebner, trans. with German text 1953 J. L. Austin, *The Foundations of Arithmetic*, Oxford: Blackwell); 'Über Sinn und Bedeutung', *Zeitschrift für Philosophie und philosophische Kritik* 100 (1892): 25–50, trans. 1984 M. Black, 'On Sense and Meaning', in G. Frege (ed. B. McGuinness) *Collected Papers on Mathematics, Logic, and Philosophy* (Oxford: Blackwell), 157–77; *Grundgesetze der Arithmetik* (volume I) (Jena: H. Pohle, 1893, partial trans. M. Furth 1964, *The Basic Laws of Arithmetic: Exposition of the System*, Berkeley, CA: University of California Press); *Grundge-setze der Arithmetik* (vol. II) (Jena: H. Pohle, 1903, partial trans. M. Furth 1964, *The Basic Laws of Arithmetic: Exposition of the System*, Berkeley: University of California Press); 'Der Gedanke. Eine Logische Untersuchung' ('Thoughts. A Logical Investigation'), *Beiträge zur Philosophie des deutschen Idealismus* I (1918): 58–77 (trans. 1984 P. Geach and R. Stoothoff, 'Thoughts' in G. Frege (ed. B. McGuinness), *Collected Papers on Mathematics, Logic, and Philosophy* Oxford: Blackwell, 351–72).

Secondary literature: Dummett, M. A. E. (1973), *Frege, Philosophy of Language*, London: Duckworth, also (1981), *The Interpretation of Frege's Philosophy*, London: Duckworth, and (1991), *Frege: Philosophy of Mathematics*, London: Duckworth; Kneale, W. C. and Kneale, M. (1962), *The Development of Logic*, Oxford: Oxford University Press; Resnik, M. (1980), *Frege and the Philoso-phy of Mathematics*, Ithaca: Cornell University Press; Wright, C. (ed.) (1983), *Frege: Tradition and Influence*, Oxford: Blackwell.

FREUD, SIGMUND (1856–1939). Freud was born in Moravia, of Jewish parentage. He completed a medical training at Vienna, specialised in neurology and then psychopathology, and studied in Paris under J. M. Charcot. Until forced by the Gestapo in September 1939 to flee to London, where he died, Freud worked in Vienna. The Vienna Psychoanalytical Society, founded by Freud in 1908, inaugurated the psychoanalytic movement. *Die Traumdeutung* (Frankfurt on Main: Fischer Verlag, 1900) is Freud's first properly psychoanalytic publication; important later works include *Zur Psychopathologie des Alltagslebens* (1904), *Drei Abhandlungen zur Sexualtheorie* (1905), *Jenseits des Lustprinzips* (1920), and *Das Ich und das Es* (1923).

Secondary Literature: Jones, E. (1953–7), *Sigmund Freud: Life and Work* 3 vols., London: Hogarth Press; Gay, P. (1988), *Freud: A Life for Our Time*, London: Dent; Hook, S. (ed.) (1964), *Psychoanalysis, Scientific Method and Philosophy*, New York: New York University Press; Lear, J. (1990), *Love and its Place in Nature: A Philosophical Reconstruction of Psychoanalysis*, London: Faber; Ricoeur, P. (1965) *De l'interprétation: essai sur Freud*, Paris: Editions du Seuil, trans. 1970 D. Savage, *Freud and Philosophy: An Essay in Interpretation*, New Haven: Yale University Press; Wollheim, R. (1974), *Freud: A Collection of Critical Essays* New York: Anchor Doubleday, and (1991) *Freud*, 2nd edn, London: Fontana Collins; Wollheim, R. and Hopkins, J. (eds.) (1982), *Philosophical Essays on Freud*, Cambridge: Cambridge University Press.

GENTILE, GIOVANNI (1875–1944). Born in Castelvetrano, Sicily, Gentile studied philosophy in Pisa, then began teaching in Naples and collaborating with Benedetto Croce on *La Critica* in 1903. The collaboration continued for two decades, but they increasingly disagreed philosophically (Gentile's actualist idealism was more radical than Croce's idealism) and politically (Gentile was an interventionist in the First World War, Croce a neutralist). In 1922 Gentile joined Mussolini's cabinet as minister of public instruction and sought to restructure the education system with the reforms known as *La riforma Gentile* (1923). He remained a fascist stalwart until the day he was murdered by communist partisans in 1944. His major works are *Teoria generale dello spirito come atto puro* (Bari: Laterza, 1915, trans. H. W. Carr, *The Theory of Mind as Pure Act*, London: Macmillan) and *Fondamenti della filosofia del diritto* (Pisa: Mariotti, 1916).

Important studies of him include G. Calandra (1987), *Gentile e fascismo*, Rome and Bari: Laterza; S. Romano (1984), *Giovanni Gentile: La filosofia al potere*, Milan: Bompiani; D. Veneruso (1984), *Gentile e il primato della tradizione culturale italiana: Il dibattito all'interno del fascismo*, Rome: Edizioni Studiuin.

GIERKE, OTTO VON (1841–1921). Born in Stettin (in Prussia) on 11 January 1841 and educated in Berlin, Gierke held professorial posts in Berlin, Breslau, and Heidelberg. He served in Bismarck's wars of 1866 against Austria and 1870–1 against France. Gierke died in Berlin on 10 October 1921. Major works of juridico-philosophical interest include: *Das deutsche Genossenschaftsrecht*, 4 vols. (Berlin: Weidmann, 1868–1913); 'Die Grundbegriffe des Staatsrechts und die neueren Staatsrechtstheorien', *Zeitschrift für die gesamte Staatsrechtswissenschaft*, 30 (1874); *Johannes Althusius und die Entwicklung der naturrechtlichen Staatstheorien* (Breslan: Marcus, 1880); 'Labands Staatsrecht und die deutsche Rechtswissenschaft', *Schmollers Jahrbuch für Gesetzgebung, Verwaltung und Volkswirtschaft im Deutschen Reiche*, 7 (1883); *Naturrecht und Deutsches Recht* (Frankfurt: Rütter und Loening 1883); *Die Genossenschaftstheorie und die deutsche Rechtsprechung* (Berlin: Weidmann, 1887); *Das Wesen der menschlichen Verbände* (Berlin: Gustar Schade 1902); *Die historische Rechtsschule und die Germanisten* (Berlin, 1903); 'Recht und Sittlichkeit', *Logos*, 6 (1916–17).

Secondary literature: Mogi, S. (1932), *Otto von Gierke: His Political Teaching and Jurisprudence*, London: P. S. King.

GÖDEL, KURT (1906–1978). Considered the greatest logician of the twentieth century, Gödel was born in Brno, Moravia, and educated at the University of Vienna, where, in his doctoral dissertation (1930), he established the semantic completeness of first-order logic. The following year, in his epochal incompleteness paper, he showed that no consistent, recursive axiomatisation of number theory can prove all statements true in the natural numbers and that, in particular, no such theory can prove its own consistency. Consequently, the goals of Hilbert's proof theoretic programme could not be fully realised. In 1938 Gödel demonstrated the consistency of the axiom of choice and of Cantor's continuum hypothesis relative to Zermelo-Fraenkel set theory, and in 1949 he exhibited solutions of Einstein's equations of gravitation that permitted time travel into the past. Gödel emigrated to the United States in 1940, where he accepted an appointment at the Institute for Advanced Study in Princeton, New Jersey. His main works were: 'Die Vollständigkeit der Axiome der logischen Funktionenkalküls', *Monatshefte für Mathematik und Physik* 37 (1930): 349–60; 'Über formal unentscheidbare Sätze der Principia Mathematica und verwandter Systeme I', *Monatshefte zür Mathematik and Physik* 38 (1931): 173–98; *The Consistency of the Axiom of Choice and of the Generalized Continuum Hypothesis with the Axioms of Set Theory*, Princeton, NJ: Princeton University Press (1940); 'An example of a new type of cosmological solutions of Einstein's field equations of gravitation', *Reviews of Modern Physics* 21 (1949): 447–50; *Collected Works* (New York and Oxford: Oxford University Press).

Secondary literature: Dawson, J. W., Jr. (1997), *Logical Dilemmas: The Life and Work of Karl Gödel*, Wellesley, MA: A. K. Petens, Ltd; Shanker, S. G. (ed.) (1988), *Gödel's Theorem in Focus*, London: Croom Helm.

GRAMSCI, ANTONIO (1891–1937). Born in Ales, Sardinia, he studied linguistics in Turin and became a socialist in 1913, but supported Italian intervention in the First World War. After the war, he led a factory-council movement in Turin and, after its defeat, helped to found the Italian Communist Party (1921). In the early 1920s he represented the Party in the Comintern, was elected a parliamentary deputy, and then served as Party leader until his arrest in October 1926. Sentenced to twenty years in prison, he took up a scholarly life but died before he could complete his most important work, the *Prison Notebooks*, which was first published in 1947.

Important studies of him include R. Bellamy and D. Schecter (1993), *Gramsci and the Italian State*, Manchester: Manchester University Press; Femia, J. (1981), *Gramsci's Political Thought: Hegemany, Consciousness and the Revolutionary Process*, Oxford: Oxford University Press; and W. L. Adamson (1980), *Hegemony and Revolution: Antonio Gramsci's Political and Cultural Theory*, Berkeley and Los Angeles: University of California Press.

GREEN, THOMAS HILL (1836–82). Born at Birkin in Yorkshire, Green was the youngest of the four children of Valentin Green, an evangelical rector, and Anna Barbara Vaughn Green. He was educated at Rugby and at Balliol College, Oxford, where he became a fellow in 1860 and probably the first layman ever appointed as a tutor in 1866. Greatly admired for his personal qualities, Green rose to prominence in the university as the most inspiring teacher of his generation. He was elected Whyte's Professor in 1878, a few years before his untimely death. A radical in politics, Green was active in university reform, in the temperance movement, and as an Oxford town councillor. He married Charlotte Symonds in 1870. His main writings were: 'General Introduction to Vol. I' and 'Introduction to Moral Part of the Treatise' in D. Hume, *Treatise of Human Nature* (ed. T. H. Green and T. H. Grose) (London: 1874); *Prolegomena to Ethics* (Oxford: Clarendon Press, 1883), *Lectures on the Principles of Political Obligation* (1886).

Secondary literature: Greengarten, I. M. (1981), *Thomas Hill Green and the Development of Liberal-Democratic Thought*, Toronto: Toronto University Press; Nettleship, R. L. (1888), *Works of Thomas*

Hill Green, London: Longmans, Green; Nicholson, P. P. (1990), *The Political Philosophy of the British Idealists*, Cambridge: Cambridge University Press; Richter, M. (1964), *The Politics of Conscience: T. H. Green and His Age*, London: Weidenfeld and Nicholson and Cambridge, MA: Harvard University Press; Thomas, G. (1987), *The Moral Philosophy of T. H. Green*, Oxford: Clarendon Press; Vincent, A. (1986), *The Philosophy of T. H. Green*, Aldershot: Gower.

HÄGERSTRÖM, AXEL ANDERS (1868–1939). Born at the parsonage of Vireda, near Jönköping, in the Swedish province of Småland, on 6 September 1868, Hägerström showed great promise at a young age, doing outstanding work in school in ancient languages and mathematics. Influenced by deeply religious parents and, for a time, by the evangelical revivalism of his day, Hägerström enrolled in Uppsala University with the intention of studying theology. He quickly turned to philosophy, however, taking his doctorate in 1893. He was thereupon named *Privatdozent* or unsalaried lecturer at Uppsala, where, in 1911, he won a professorship, which he held until his retirement in 1933. Hägerström died in Uppsala on 7 July 1939. His main works were: *Kants Ethik im Verhältnis zu seinem erkenntnistheoretischen Grundgedanken* (Uppsala: Alqvist and Wiksell, 1902); *Das Prinzip der Wissenschaft, I. Die Realität* (Uppsala: Alqvist and Wiksell, 1908); *Till frågan om den gällande rättens begrepp* (Uppsala; Alqvist and Wiksell, 1917); *Der römische Obligationsbegriff im Lichte der allgemeinen römischen Rechtsanschauung*, vol. I (Uppsala: Alqvist and Wiksell, 1927), vol. II (1941). Some of Hägerström's papers, and selections from his treatises, translated from Swedish and German, are brought together in two volumes: *Inquiries into the Nature of Law and Morals*, trans. C. D. Broad (Uppsala: Alqvist and Wiksell, 1953); *Philosophy and Religion*, trans. R. T. Sandin (London: George Allen and Unwin, 1964).

Secondary literature: Passmore, J. (1961), 'Hägerström's Philosophy of Law', *Philosophy* 36: 143–60.

HARTMANN, EDUARD VON (1842–1906). Born in Berlin, he served for several years as an artillery officer, before in 1867 settling in Berlin to pursue the development of his philosophical system. His principal work, *Philosophie des Unbewußten* (Berlin: C. Duncker, 1869), was spectacularly successful, ran to several editions, and remained influential past the turn of the century. Hartmann's numerous later writings included further metaphysical studies (*Kategorienlehre* (*Doctrine of Categories*) Leipzig: Haacks, 1896), studies in the history of philosophy (*Geschichte der Metaphysik*, Leipzig: Haacks, 1899–1900), and works on ethics and aesthetics (*Phänomenologie des sittlichen Betwußtseins*, Berlin: C. Duncker, 1879, *Philosophie des Schönen*, Leipzig: W. Friedrich, 1887).

Secondary literature: Darnoi, D. (1967), *The Unconscious and Edward von von Hartmaan: A Historico-Critical Monograph*, The Hague: Nijhoff; Windelband, W. (1892), *Geschichte der Philosophie* Freiburg, §§44, 46.

HEIDEGGER, MARTIN (1889–1976). Born in Messkirch in southwestern Germany, Heidegger is generally regarded as the leading Western philosopher of the twentieth century, though his reputation has been damaged by posthumous revelations about the depth of his commitment to Nazism. Catholic by background, he broke with the faith in 1919 and, as a student of Edmund Husserl's phenomenology, wrote his masterwork, *Sein und Zeit* (Tübingen: Niemeger, 1927, trans. J. Macquarrie and E. Robinson, *Being and Time*, Oxford: Blackwell, 1962), which greatly influenced subsequent existentialism. After the Nazi takeover, he became rector at Freiburg for two years. His later, 'antihumanist' philosophical essays, such as *The Question Concerning Technology* (1953), were similarly pathbreaking for hermeneutics (H. G. Gadamer) and post-structuralism (Jacques Derrida).

Important studies of him include Dallmayr, F. (1993), *The Other Heidegger*, Ithaca, NY: Cornell University Press; Safranski, R. (1994), *Ein Meister aus Deutschland: Heidegger und Seine Zeit*, Munich: Carl Hanser Verlag, trans. 1998 E. Osers, *Martin Heidegger: Between Good and Evil*, Cambridge, MA: Harvard University Press; Wolin, R. (1990), *The Politics of Being: The Political Thought of Martin Heidegger*, New York: Columbia University Press; Zimmerman, M. (1990), *Heidegger's Confrontation with Modernity: Technology, Politics, and Art*, Bloomington, IN: Indiana University Press.

HELMHOLTZ, HERMANN VON (1821–94). Helmholtz was born in Potsdam in 1821. His father was a man of great enthusiasms, especially for the arts and for philosophy. As a child Helmholtz was surrounded by passionate debates. Training as a doctor, he managed to attend science courses at the university. He served as an army surgeon but was released to take up a post in physiology at Konigsberg, and then to Bonn. He married in 1849. His research interests covered all the senses including the kinaesthetic. He moved back to Berlin in 1891, and began the study of electromagnetism, having Hertz as his assistant. His return marked his steady elevation into the most powerful and influential person in German science, despite a marked personal diffidence. In later life he suffered periods of intense depression, relieved only by music and walking in the hills. He died in Berlin in 1894.

Main works: Kahl, R. (ed.) (1971), *Selected Writings of H. von Helmholtz*, Middleton, CT: Wesleyan University Press.

Secondary literature: Cahan, D. (ed.) (1993), *Hermann von Helmholtz and the Foundation of XIX Century Science*, Berkeley, CA: University of California Press.

HERTZ, HEINRICH RUDOLPH (1857–94). Born in 1857, Hertz came from a distinguished Protestant family. He had a very strict schooling, and showed a marked talent not only for languages, but also for practical hobbies. His higher education took him towards a career as a professional engineer, but by 1877 he decided to prepare himself for scientific research. At the University of Munich he showed the combination of mathematical skill and laboratory technique that was characteristic of his whole career. In 1880 he became research assistant to Helmholtz as the great man turned more and more to studies in electromagnetism and gas physics. Following the usual German career pattern, Hertz moved to Kiel as a Privatdozent in mathematical physics, reading a great deal of philosophy, but soon moved to a general physics appointment at Karlsruhe from 1885 to 1889, where he could be back at the laboratory bench. Here he began the work on 'electric waves' that gave him international fame. Soon he was at work on the foundations of physics again. From about 1888 he suffered a series of painful operations on his jaw, and contracting an infection in the course of the last of these he died of septicaemia in 1894. His main works were: *Die Prinzipien der Mechanik* (Leipzig: Barth, 1894, trans. 1899 D. E. Jones and J. T. Walley, *The Principles of Mechanics*, London: Macmillan); Mulligan, J. (ed.), *Heinrich Rudolf Hertz (1857–94): A Collection of Articles and Addresses* (New York: Garland, 1994).

Secondary literature: Buchwald, J. Z. (1994), *The Creation of Scientific Effects: Heinrich Hertz and Electric Waves*, Chicago, IL: University of Chicago Press.

HILBERT, DAVID (1862–1943) was born in Königsberg, where he also received his doctorate and began his professorial career. One of the most preeminent mathematicians of his age (rivalled only by Henri Poincaré), his breadth of mathematical achievements spanned the fields of invariant theory, algebraic number theory, integral equations, axiomatics of geometry and logic, and mathematical physics. In 1895 Hilbert accepted a call to Göttingen and there carried on the mathematical tradition established a century earlier by Carl Friedrich Gauss. In 1900, in his address to the International Congress of Mathematicians, he posed twenty-three problems as challenges for the century ahead, and in 1917 he initiated the study of *proof theory*, whose development he hoped would secure the foundations of mathematics. His main works were: *Grundlagen der Geometrie* (Leipzig: Teubner, 1899); 'Mathematische Probleme' (*Nachrichten von der königlichen Gesellschaft der Wissenschaften zu Göttingen*, 1900: 253–96); *Grundzüge der theoretischen Logik* (Berlin, 1928) (with W. Ackermann); *Grundlagen der Mathematik* (Berlin: Springer Verlag, 1934) (with P. Bernays); *Gesammelte Abhandlungen* (Berlin: Springer Verlag, 1935).

Secondary literature: Bernays, P. (1967), 'Hilbert, David (1862–1943)' in P. Edwards (ed.), *The Encyclopedia of Philosophy*, vol. III, 496–504, New York: Macmillan and Free Press; Browder, F. E. (ed.) (1976), 'Mathematical Developments Arising from Hilbert Problems', *Proceedings of Symposia in Pure Mathematics*, XXVIII, Providence: American Mathematical Society; Reid, C. (1970), *Hilbert*, New York: Springer Verlag; Sieg, W. (1997), 'Step by Recursive Step: Church's Analysis of Effective Calculability', *The Bulletin of Symbolic Logic* 2: 338–48.

HOBHOUSE, LEONARD TRELAWNY (1864–1929). An undergraduate at Corpus Christi College, Oxford (1883–7), Hobhouse became a prize fellow of Merton College, then returned to Corpus in 1890 as tutor and later fellow. He taught philosophy, but also studied psychology, sociology, and the labour movement. From 1897 to 1902 he worked on the staff of the great Liberal newspaper, the *Manchester Guardian*, then moved to London where he continued his journalism but also developed his interest in sociology. In 1907 he was appointed (jointly with E. A. Westermarck) to the Martin White Professor of Sociology at the London School of Economics and Political Science, the first chair of sociology in Britain. His main works were: *The Theory of Knowledge* (London: Methuen, 1896); *Mind in Evolution* (London: Macmillan, 1901); *Democracy and Reaction* (London: Fisher Unwin, 1904); *Morals in Evolution* (London: Chapman and Hall, 1906); *Liberalism* (London: Williams and Norgate, 1911); *Social Evolution and Political Theory* (New York: Columbia University Press 1911); *Development and Purpose* (London: Macmillan, 1913); *The Metaphysical Theory of the State* (London: George Allan and Unwin, 1918); *The Rational Good* (London: George Allen and Unwin, 1921); *The Elements of Social Justice* (London: George Allen and Unwin, 1922); *Social Development* (London: George Allen and Unwin, 1924).

Secondary literature: Clarke, P. (1978), *Liberals and Social Democrats*, Cambridge: Cambridge University Press; Collini, S. (1979), *Liberalism and Sociology: L. T. Hobhouse and Political Argument in England 1880–1914*, Cambridge: Cambridge University Press; Freeden, M. (1978), *The New Liberalism: An Ideology of Social Reform*, Oxford: Clarendon Press; Hobson, J. A. and Ginsberg, M. (1931), *L. T. Hobhouse: His Life and Work*, London: George Allen and Unwin.

HOLMES, OLIVER WENDELL (1841–1935). Born in Boston on 8 March 1841, Holmes studied at Harvard College and then volunteered for service in the Civil War. After the war, he enrolled at the Harvard Law School. Appointed to the law faculty at Harvard a year after the publication of *The Common Law*, Holmes left the academy for an appointment as associate justice of the Massachusetts Supreme Judicial Court, where he served for twenty years, followed by another twenty-five years on the United States. Supreme Court. He died in Washington, DC, on 6 March 1935. Holmes's main book-length work is *The Common Law* (Boston, MA: Little Brown, 1881). In addition, there are important collections: *The Formative Essays of Justice Holmes*, ed. Frederic Rogers Kellogg (Westport, CT: Greenwood Press, 1984) (Holmes's essays from the period 1870–80); *Collected Legal Papers* (New York: Harcourt, Brace, and Co. 1920) (essays from the period 1885–1918, including the celebrated paper, 'The Path of the Law'); *Holmes–Pollock Letters. The Correspondence of Mr Justice Holmes and Sir Frederick Pollock 1874–1932*, ed. Mark DeWolfe Howe, 2 vols. (Cambridge, MA: Harvard University Press, 1941); *Holmes–Laski*

Letters. The Correspondence of Mr Justice Holmes and Harold J. Laski 1916–1935, ed. Mark DeWolfe Howe, 2 vols. (London: Oxford University Press, 1953); *The Essential Holmes*, ed. Richard A. Posner (Chicago, IL: University of Chicago Press, 1992) (selections from letters, speeches, judicial opinions).

SIDNEY HOOK (1902–89). An American naturalist and pragmatist whose lectures and writings on politics, morality, law, and education gave him the status of a 'public philosopher'. At first a Marxist, he became a staunch advocate of democratic socialism. Among his major works were *The Metaphysics of Pragmatism* (Chicago: Open Court, 1927), *From Hegel to Marx* (Ann Arbor, MI: University of Michigan Press, 1936) and *Pragmatism and the Tragic Sense of Life* (New York: Basic Books, 1975).

Secondary literature: Hook, S. (1987), *Out of Step: An Unquiet Life in the 20th Century*, New York: Harper and Row; Phelps, C. (1997), *Young Sidney Hook: Marxist and Pragmatist*, Ithaca, NY: Cornell University Press.

HORKHEIMER, MAX (1895–1973). One of the founding members of the Frankfurt School of Western European Marxism (or Critical Theory), Horkheimer was its leading philosopher and lifelong director. After becoming Director of the Frankfurt-based Institute for Social Research in 1929, Horkheimer elaborated the philosophical basis for its programme of a critical social science in his methodological writings from the 1930s, published in the Institute's *Zeitschrift für Sozialforschung*. Besides his work in the Institute and his special role in its empirical analyses of fascism, Horkheimer's more philosophical works include analyses of the paradoxical character of Enlightenment rationality written in the dark days of the Second World War in *Dialektik der Aufklärung* (*Dialectic of the Enlightenment*) (Amsterdam: Quierdo, 1944, with T. W. Adorno).

The most comprehensive works on Horkheimer and the Frankfurt School are Held, D. (1980), *Introduction to Critical Theory*, Berkeley, CA: University of California Press; Wiggershaus, R. (1994), *The History of the Frankfurt School*, Cambridge, MA: Cambridge University Press.

HUSSERL, EDMUND (1859–1938). Born in Prossnitz (then within the borders of the Austro-Hungarian Empire, now in the Czech Republic) to a German-speaking Jewish family. He studied in Leipzig with W. Wundt, and attended lectures given by Weierstrass and Kronecker in Berlin, before moving to Vienna in 1881 where he studied with F. Brentano. In 1887 he become *Privatdozent* in Halle where he met C. Stumpf and G. Cantor and completed his habilitation, which was published as *Philosophie der Arithmetik* (Halle: Pfeffer, 1891). After the publication of volume 1 of his *Logische Untersuchungen* (*Logical Investigations*) in 1900 (Halle: Niemayer), which was especially influential through its critique of all forms of psychologism, Husserl joined the faculty at Göttingen in 1901. During this period he developed his 'phenomenological' method of enquiry which led to the development of the phenomenological movement. His most influential work in this respect was *Ideen zu einer reinen Phänomenologie und phänomenologischen Philosophie* I (1913; *Husserliana* III, The Hague: Nijhoff, 1950). From 1916 until 1928 he was professor in Freiburg where his students included A. Reinach, R. Ingarden, E. Stein, M. Heidegger, E. Levinas, and G. Marcel. After his retirement he continued to write prolifically and his later books include: 'Formale und transzendentale Logik' (1929; Husserliana XVII, The Hague: Nijhoff, 1974), *Méditations cartésiennes* (Paris: Colin, 1931), and *Die Krisis der europäischen Wissenschaften und die transzendentale Phänomenologie* (1936; Husserliana VI, The Hague: Nijhoff, 1954), which is often now regarded as his most interesting book.

Secondary literature: Smith, B. and Smith, D. W. (eds.) (1995), *The Cambridge Companion to Husserl*, Cambridge and New York: Cambridge University Press.

HUXLEY, THOMAS HENRY (1825–95). English biologist, influential educator in the field of science, and eminent Victorian intellectual. Born at Ealing, near London, he was essentially self-educated, studying history, geology, logic, and languages as an adolescent. At fifteen he was apprenticed to a medical practitioner but soon received a scholarship to Charing Cross Hospital Medical School in London, where he won many prizes and published his first research paper. From 1846 to 1850 he served as assistant physician on HMS *Rattlesnake*, which surveyed the Australian waters. During these voyages, Huxley studied marine specimens and sent home his researches, which were published in eminent journals. This established his reputation as a leading biologist and, on his return in 1851 he was elected Fellow of the Royal Society at the age of twenty-six.

Huxley secured a part-time lectureship at the government School of Mines in London, where he remained, helping to transform it into the great Royal College of Science. He was an early and tenacious defender of Darwin after the appearance of the latter's *Origin of Species* in 1859. He became known as Darwin's bulldog. Huxley carried out valuable research in paleontology, taxonomy, and ethnology while expanding his influence on educational reform in the sciences and as a popular, provocative lecturer and essayist on a wide range of philosophical, political, and religious questions. Though Huxley was not a professional philosopher, his essays and his books on Descartes and Hume were influential. He coined the word 'agnostic' to define his own position, and he was looked to as the leader of the agnostic movement. He was highly critical of supernaturalism and traditional Christian claims, but he accepted a somewhat Spinozistic form of theism. Huxley's final position on ethics set forth in *Evolution and Ethics* in 1894 (London: Macmillan) opposes Herbert Spencer's evolutionary ethics and sees nature in conflict with human morality. His main works were: *Evidence as to Man's Place in Nature* (London: Williams and Norgate, 1863); *Hume* (London: Macmillan, 1879); *Collected Essays*, 9 vols. (London: Macmillan, 1893–4); *Scientific Memoirs*, ed. M. Foster and E. R. Lankester, 5 vols. (London: Macmillan, 1898–1902).

Secondary sources: Bibby, C. (1960), *Scientist, Humanist and Educator*, New York and London: Horizon Press; Desmond, A. (1997), *Huxley: From Devil's Disciple to Evolution's High Priest*, Reading, MA: Addison Wesley: Huxley, L. (ed.) (1900), *Life and Letters of Thomas Henry Huxley*, 2 vols., London: Macmillan.

JAMES, WILLIAM (1842–1910). Born in 1842, William James was professor of psychology and of philosophy at Harvard University. His *Principles of Psychology* was an important spur to the development of scientific psychology, and he achieved prominence through his writings on pragmatism and philosophical issues concerning religious belief. He died in 1910. His main publications were: *The Principles of Psychology* (New York: Henry Holt, 1890); *The Will to Believe and other Essays in Popular Philosophy* (New York and London: Longmans, Green, 1897); *The Varieties of Religious Experience* (New York and London: Longmans, Green, 1902); *Pragmatism: A New Name for some Old Ways of Thinking* (New York and London: Longmans, Green, 1907); *The Meaning of Truth* (New York and London: Longmans, Green, 1909); *A Pluralistic Universe* (New York and London: Longmans, Green, 1909); *Essays in Radical Empiricism* (New York and London: Longmans, Green, 1912).

Secondary literature: Bird, G. (1986), *William James*, London: Routledge; Ford, M. (1982), *William James's Philosophy: A New Perspective*, Amherst, MA: University of Massachusetts Press; Myers, G. E. (1986), *William James: His Life and Thought*, New Haven, CT: Yale University Press; Putnam, R. A. (ed.) (1997), *The Cambridge Companion to William James*, Cambridge: Cambridge University Press.

JEVONS, WILLIAM STANLEY (1835–82). Born in Liverpool, Jevons taught logic and economics, first at Owens College, Manchester, and then, in 1876, at University College London.

Although he drowned at the age of forty-six, Jevons had already left his mark on numerous disciplines, notably economics, statistics, philosophy, logic, meteorology, and physics. He was one of the first to advance the logicist view and to popularise, thanks to a clear system of notation, the sentential logic set out by Augustus De Morgan and George Boole. His *Principles of Science* (London: Macmillan, 1874) emphasised a fallibilist and inductivist approach to scientific knowledge, and was the leading text in the period between J. S. Mill and Karl Pearson. His main works were: *Pure Logic* (London: E. Stanford, 1864); *Theory of Political Economy* (London: Macmillan, 1871); *Principles of Science* (London: Macmillan, 1874); *Studies in Deductive Logic* (London: Macmillan, 1880).

Secondary literature: Schabas, M. (1990), *A World Ruled by Number: William Stanley Jevons and the Rise of Mathematical Economics*, Princeton, NJ: Princeton University Press.

JHERING, RUDOLF VON (1818–92). Born in Aurich on 22 August 1818, Jhering studied in Heidelberg, Göttingen, Munich, and Berlin, and held professorial posts in Basle, Rostock, Kiel, Giessen, Vienna, and Göttingen, where he died on 17 September 1892. Precocious and witty, Jhering, once he began dismantling his own constructivist system, took to twitting his former allies, the constructivists. As a civil lawyer, legal historian, and legal theorist, Jhering counts as one of the leading figures in nineteenth-century German legal science; only Savigny is comparable in influence. Main works: *Geist des römischen Rechts* (in three parts, the second of which is divided into two volumes) (Leipzig: Breitkopf and Härtel, 1852–65); *Der Kampf um's Recht* (Vienna: G. J. Manz, 1872); *Der Zweck des Rechts*, 2 vols. (Leipzig: Breitkopf and Härtel, 1877–83); *Scherz und Ernst in der Jurisprudenz* (Leipzig: Breitkopf and Härtel, 1884). Jhering's correspondence with Carl Friedrich von Gerber is collected in *Der Briefwechsel zwischen Jhering und Gerber*, ed. Mario G. Losano (Ebalsbach: Gremer, 1984).

KAUTSKY, KARL JOHANN (1854–1938). Born in Prague to a theatrical family, and raised in Vienna, but spent most of his life in Germany. Editor of *Die Neue Zeit*, the SPD weekly, 1883–1917; author of numerous books and pamphlets, and editor of various of Marx's works, notably *Theories of Surplus-Value*. Dismissed from the editorship of *Neue Zeit* for his opposition to the First World War; returned to Vienna in 1924. The Nazi *Anschluss* of March 1938 forced him to flee to Amsterdam, where he died.

Secondary literature: Geary, D. (1987), *Karl Kautsky*, Manchester: Manchester University Press.

KELSEN, HANS (1881–1973). Born in Prague on 11 October 1881, Hans Kelsen was educated in Vienna. After playing a key role in the drafting of the Austrian Federal Constitution of 1920, he served throughout the 1920s as a judge on the Constitutional Court and as professor of law at the University of Vienna. His dismissal from the Court, early in 1930 (for failing to do the bidding of the ruling Christian-Social Party), prompted him to accept a professorship in Cologne. Dismissed from that post by the Nazis in the spring of 1933, Kelsen held a professorship in Geneva until he left Europe, in 1940, for America. After several uncertain years on the East Coast, he accepted a professorship at the University of California in Berkeley, where he spent thirty years. Kelsen died in Berkeley on 19 April 1973. His major jurisprudential works were: *Hauptprobleme der Staatsrechtslehre* (Tubingen: J. C. B. Mohr, 1911), *Das Problem der Souveränität* (Tubingen: J. C. B. Mohr, 1920), *Der soziologische und der juristische Staatsbegriff* (Tubingen: J. C. B. Mohr, 1922), *Allgemeine Staatslehre* (Berlin: Springer, 1925), *Die philosophischen Grundlagen der Naturrechtslehre und des Rechtspositivismus* (Charlottenburg: Rolf Heise, 1928), *Reine Rechtslehre*, 1st edn (Leipzig: Deuticke, 1934), *General Theory of Law and State* (Cambridge, MA: Harvard University Press, 1945), *Reine Rechtslehre*, 2nd edn (Vienna: Denticke, 1960), *Allgemeine Theorie der Normen* (Vienna: Manz, 1979).

Secondary literature is collected in Paulson, S. L. and Paulson, B. L. (eds.) (1998), *Normativity and Norms*, Oxford: Clarendon Press.

KOFFKA, KURT (1886–1941). Koffka obtained a PhD in psychology in 1908 in Berlin under Carl Stumpf, and served as second subject in Wertheimer's experiments on apparent motion, the starting point of the Gestalt movement. Shortly before the Nazi seizure of power, Koffka emigrated to the United States, taking a professorship at Smith College. Koffka was noted for his numerous articles on Gestalt psychology and for applying it to developmental psychology. His major work was a general psychology text written from the Gestalt perspective, *Principles of Gestalt Psychology* (New York: Harcourt, Brace and World, 1935).

KÖHLER, WOLFGANG (1887–1967). Köhler obtained a PhD in psychology in 1909 in Berlin under Carl Stumpf, and served as first subject in Wertheimer's experiments on apparent motion, the starting point of the Gestalt movement. After futilely resisting the Nazis, Köhler emigrated to the United States, teaching at Dartmouth and Swarthmore Colleges, and was President of the American Psychological Association (1959). The leading theorist of the group, Köhler also extended Gestalt psychology to behaviour in *Intelligenzprüfen an Menschenaffen* (*The Mentality of Apes*, New York: Liveright, 1927). Of his several books, the most important was *Gestalt Psychology* (New York: Liveright, 1947).

KOLMOGOROV, ANDREI (1903–87). A Russian mathematician who became the leading probability theorist of the twentieth century. His main work was *Grundbegriffe der Wahrscheinlichkeitsrechnung* (Berlin: Springer Verlag, 1933). He developed the axiomatisation of probability as part of mathematical measure theory. In the interpretation of probability he followed the frequentist ideas of Richard von Mises; but he was very careful not to express philosophical commitments in his work, possibly because of the incompatibility of probabilistic ideas with the official Soviet philosophy of the 1930s. In logic and foundations of mathematics he followed the Dutch intuitionist L. Brouwer. In 1925 he invented a way of interpreting classical logic in intuitionistic logic, and in 1932 a way of interpreting the latter as a calculus of problems.

Secondary literature: von Plato, J. (1994), *Creating Modern Probability: Its Mathematics, Physics and Philosophy in Historical Perspective*, Cambridge: Cambridge University Press.

KOTARBIŃSKI, TADEUSZ (1886–1981). Born in Warsaw, he studied architecture in Darmstadt and classical languages and philosophy at the University of Lvov under Twardowski. From 1918 until 1957 he taught at Warsaw University. Kotarbiński is known primarily as a defender of reism and as the founding father of the science of praxiology. His works include 'Zagadnienie istnienia przyszłości' (1913), 'Sprawa istnienia przedmiotów idealnych' (1920), *Elementy teorii poznania, logiki formalnej i metodologii nauk* (Lvov: Ossolineum, 1929), *Traktat o dobrej robocie* (Warsaw: PWN, 1955), 'Fazy rozwoju konkretyzmu' (*Studia Filozoficzne* 4, 11 (7) (1958), 3–13).

Secondary literature: Woleński (ed.) 1990, Smith, B. (1994), *Austrian Philosophy*, Chicago: Open Court; Woleński, J. (1989), *Logic and Philosophy in the Lvov-Warsaw School*, Dordrecht: Kluwer; Woleński, J. (ed.) (1990), *Kotarbiński: Logic, Semantics and Ontology*, Dordrecht: Kluwer.

LANGE, FRIEDRICH ALBERT (1828–75). German philosopher and writer, born in 1828 near Solingen. His father became a well-known professor at Zurich. Lange began studies at Zurich but graduated from Bonn in 1851. He began his main work *Geschichte des Materialismus* in 1857 but it was not published until 1866 (Iserlohn and Leipzig: von Baedeker). In the meantime he published newspapers and was active in political and social questions. Seriously ill with cancer, he worked on a much revised second edition (1873–75). He moved to Marburg in 1872 and died in 1875.

Secondary literature: Stack, G. J. (1983), *Lange and Nietzsche*, Berlin and New York: De Gruyter.

LASK, EMIL (1875–1915). Born in Poland in 1875 he moved to Germany to study law and then philosophy. In the middle 1890s he attended lectures by both Rickert and Weber. He did his doctorate under Rickert's direction at Freiburg but Windelband was the nominal director of his *Habilitationsschrift* (Weber's influence is also clear). Lask taught at Heidelberg for a number of years but left to join the army and was killed in battle in 1915. During his Heidelberg years he was a member of the Max Weber Circle but he always respected what he had learned from Windelband and Rickert. Rickert provides an introduction to Lask's *Gesammelte Schriften* (Tübingen: J. C. B. Mohr, 1924).

Secondary literature: Wilk, K. (1950), *The Legal Philosophies of Lask, Radbruch, and Dabin*, Cambridge, MA: Harvard University Press.

LAVROV, PËTR LAVROVICH (1823–1900). Lavrov was born the son of a rich landowner and educated in St Petersburg. He embarked upon a successful military career, becoming a colonel at only thirty-five. In 1860, he published *Ocherki voprosov prakticheskogo filosofii (Essays on Questions of Practical Philosophy)* (St Petersburg: Glazunov), which advanced a form of anthropologism that drew sympathtic criticism from Nikolai Chernyshevsky. Associated with the first 'Land and Freedom' organisation, Lavrov was exiled in 1866. His *Istoricheskie pis'ma (Historical Letters)* (Geneva: 1891) was enormously influential, becoming the definitive voice of Russian populism. In 1870 Lavrov escaped abroad, joining the International Workingmen's Association and participating in the Paris Commune. He became friends with Marx and Engels. From 1873 to 1876, Lavrov published the journal *Vpered (Forward)* from Zurich and London, attacking 'Jacobinism' within the populist movement and defending his agrarian socialism. When populism lost momentum, Lavrov devoted himself to scholarship. He died in Paris in 1900. A two-volume edition of Lavrov's selected works, *Filosofiia i sotsiologiia: izbrannye proizvedeniia*, was published in Russian in 1965.

Secondary literature: Walicki, A. (1980), *A History of Russian Thought from Enlightement to Marxism*, trans. H. Andrews-Rusiecka, Oxford: Oxford University Press, ch. 12, is a fine short treatment of Lavrov's life and thought. The best history of Russian populism is Venturi, F. (1960), *Roots of Russian Populism: A History of the Populist and Socialist Movements in Nineteenth-century Russia*, trans. F. Haskell, New York: Knopf.

ŁEŚNIEWSKI, STANISLAW (1886–1939). Born in Serpukhovo (near Moscow) into a Polish family, he studied philosophy in Munich under Hans Cornelius and in Lvov under Twardowski. While in Lvov he also studied mathematics under Sierpinski and Puzyna. His early philosophical works criticise theories of universals and the Whitehead-Russell theory of types proposing instead a Husserl-inspired doctrine of semantic categories. During the First World War Łeśniewski taught mathematics in a Polish grammar school in Moscow, where he prepared his first outline of mereology published as *Podstawy ogólnej teorii mnogości* (Moscow: Drakarnia Poplawskiego 1916). From 1919 until 1939 he was professor of mathematics at the University of Warsaw. His writings include: 'Czy prawda jest tylko wieczna, czy teżwieczna i odwieczna?' (1913), 'Krytyka logicznej zasady wylaczonego srodka' (1913), *Podstawy ogólnej teorii mnogości* (1916), 'O podstawach matematyki' (1927). His major writings are translated in his *Gollected Works* (Dordrecht: Kluwer, 1992).

Secondary literature: Srzednicki, J. T. J., Rickey, V. F., and Czelakowski, J. (eds.) (1984), *Leśniewski's Systems: Ontology and Mereology*, The Hague: Nijhoff and Wrocław: Ossolinenm; Woleński, J. (1989), *Logic and Philosophy in the Lvov-Warsaw School*, Dordrecht: Kluwer.

LEWES, GEORGE HENRY (1817–78). Born in London, Lewes was a literary critic and independent scholar who worked on topics in philosophy, psychology, physiology, and biology. He tried his hand at acting, but from 1840 to 1850 earned his living as a literary critic, and published two novels. In 1850 he co-founded the *Leader*, serving as literary editor. From 1854 he lived with George Eliot (Marian Evans). His major works include *Biographical History of Philosophy* (London: Parker and Son, 1857, originally published in 1845–6) and the five volumes of *Problems of Life and Mind* (Boston: Osgood, 1874, 1877, 1879, 1880).

Secondary literature: Tjoa, H. G. (1977), *George Henry Lewes: A Victorian Mind*, Cambridge, MA: Harvard University Press; Rylance, R. (2000), *Victorian Psychology and British Culture*, Oxford: Oxford University Press.

LEWIN, KURT (1890–1947). Lewin received a PhD in psychology in Berlin under Carl Stumpf. Under Stumpf's successor, Wolfgang Köhler, Lewin developed applications of Gestalt ideas. He emigrated to the United States in 1932, teaching at the State University of Iowa, MIT, and the University of Michigan. Lewin proposed a topological psychology (*Principles of Topological Psychology*, New York: McGraw Hill, 1936), applying Gestalt field-concepts to the explanation of behaviour, and conducted research in personality, child development, and group dynamics. By re-orienting his psychology away from consciousness and towards group and individual behaviour, Lewin became the most influential Gestalt psychologist in the United States.

Secondary literature: Marrow, A. J. (1969), *The Practical Theorist: The Life and Work of Kurt Lewin*, New York: Basic Books.

LEWIS, CLARENCE IRVING (1883–1964). Lewis is now largely remembered for his work in logic, but he was an important philosopher in his own right, combining American pragmatism with elements of Kant's philosophy and the logico-analytic programme. He studied at Harvard and taught in California (1911–20) and Harvard (1920–53). Lewis's first book, *A Survey of Symbolic Logic* (Berkeley, CA: University of California Press, 1918), provides a lucid account of the field, notable for its emphasis on the algebraic tradition. In his second logic book, *Symbolic Logic* (New York: The Century Co., 1932), Lewis develops his criticisms of Russell's extensional conception of 'implication' and sets out his systems of 'strict implication' and modal logic. In *Mind and World Order* (New York: C. Scribner's, 1929) Lewis set out his conception of the 'pragmatic a priori' which is articulated in the context of an original analytical programme and a Neo-Kantian epistemology. In his later writings Lewis turned increasingly to moral philosophy.

Secondary literature: Kucklick, B. (1977), *The Rise of American Philosophy, Cambridge, Massachusetts 1860–1930*, New Haven, CT: Yale University Press.

LOTZE, RUDOLPH HERMANN (1817–81). Lotze was an important figure in the development of German philosophy, helping to connect the Hegelian tradition to later Neo-Kantians. He was much admired in Britain at the end of the nineteenth century. His academic career was based at Göttingen, where he became a professor in 1844.

Lotze's early work is, in part, a philosophy of biology: he argues that although organisms provide a distinctive domain for teleological explanations, this does not imply that distinct 'vital' forces are required to explain biological phenomena. His main work builds around two further themes: (i) the is/ought distinction, which he applies to epistemology, arguing that psychological enquiries cannot provide epistemological justifications; (ii) the distinction between 'validity' and metaphysical realism, which leads Lotze to hold that the validity of a priori truths does not bring with it a commitment to a Platonist metaphysics. His main works were: *Medzinische Psychologie, oder Physiologie der Seele* (Leipzig: Weidmann, 1852); *Mikrokosmus: Ideen zur Naturgeschichte und Geschichte der Menschen* (3 vols., Leipzig; trans. 1885 E. Hamilton and E. Jones, *Microcosmus: An*

Essay Concerning Man and his Relation to the World, 2 vols., Edinburgh: T. & T. Clark); *Logik* (2 vols., Leipzig: S. Hirzel, 1874, trans. 1884–8 B. Bosanquet, Oxford: Clarendon Press).

Secondary literature: Woodward, W. R. (1999), *From Mechanism to Value. Hermann Lotze: Physician, Philosopher, Psychologist 1817–1881*, Cambridge: Cambridge University Press.

LUKÁCS, GEORG (1885–1971). Born in Budapest, the son of a leading Hungarian Jewish banker, Lukács was educated in Germany and was influenced by Kierkegaard, Max Weber, and the novels of Dostoyevsky before turning suddenly to Marxism in December 1918. For a few months in 1919 he was commissar for education in Béla Kun's government, then fled to Vienna, Berlin, and Moscow; he was briefly arrested as a Trotskyist agent, in 1941. He was loyal to Lenin and Stalin until the latter's death, but returned to Hungary in 1945 and became Minister of Culture in Imre Nagy's short-lived government (1956). He wrote a major work on Hegel and polemicised against literary modernism, but his best works remain his early ones: *Soul and Form* (1910), *Theory of the Novel* (1920), and *History and Class Consciousness* (1923).

Secondary literature: Arato, A. and Breines, P. (1979), *The Young Lukács and the Origins of Western Marxism*, London: Pluto; Gluck, M. (1985), *George Lukács and his Generation 1900–1918*, Cambridge, MA: Harvard University Press; Jay, M. (1973), *The Dialectical Imagination*, London: Heinemann; Kadarkay, A. (1991), *George Lukács: Life, Thought and Politics*, Oxford, Blackwell; Löwy, M. (1979), *George Lukács – From Romanticism to Bolshevism*, London: Verso; Stedman Jones, G. (1972), 'The Marxism of the Early Lukács', *New Left Review* 70: 27–64.

ŁUKASIEWICZ, JAN (1879–1956). Born in Lvov, he studied law and philosophy under Twardowski at the University of Lvov. From 1911 to 1915 he was a professor in Lvov, and between 1915 and 1944 professor of philosophy in Warsaw. From 1946 he was professor of logic in Dublin. His students included Kazimierz Ajdukiewicz and Alfred Tarski. Łukasiewicz is renowned for his studies of Aristotle and for his discovery of many-valued logic and of the so-called Polish notation for propositional calculi. His writings include: 'Logika a psychologia' (1907), 'O prawdopodobieństwie wniosków indukcyjnych' (1909), *O zasadzie sprzeczności u Arystotelesa* (Cracow: PAU, 1910), *Die logischen Grundlagen der Wahrscheinlichkeitsrechnung* (Cracow: PAU, 1913), 'O logice trówartościowej' (1920), 'O determiniśmie' (1922), 'Interpretacja liczbowa teorii zdas' (1923), 'Untersuchungen ber den Aussagenkalkül' (1930, with Alfred Tarski), *Aristotle's Syllogistic from the Standpoint of Modern Formal Logic* (Oxford: Clarendon Press, 1951). Many of his papers are translated in his *Selected Works* (Amsterdam: North-Holland, 1970).

Secondary literature: Woleński, J. (1989). *Logic and Philosophy in the Lvov-Warsaw School*, Dordrecht: Kluwer.

MACH, ERNST (1838–1916). Mach was born at Chirlitz-Tura in Moravia. His father was a gentleman farmer of wide interests, both literary and scientific. His mother was artistically inclined. Young Ernst was educated at home by his father until he was fourteen. By 1855 he was at the University of Vienna studying mathematics, physics, and philosophy. From 1860 he was *Privatdozent* giving very popular lectures and researching into the propagation of energy. He turned to research in physiology and the psychology of perception, and gradually abandoned the molecular point of view for a sensationalist metaphysics. From 1864 he was at Graz, moving to Prague in 1867, the year he married. In 1895 he took up the chair of philosophy in Vienna. Despite a stroke in 1897 he continued active work all his life. He died at Vaterstatten in Germany in 1916. His main works were: *Die Mechanik in ihrer Entwicklung historisch-critisch dargestellt* (Prague, 1883, trans. 1893 T. McCormack, *The Science of Mechanics*, Chicago: Open Court). *Populärwissenschaftliche Vorlesungen* (Leipzig, 1894, trans. 1894 T. J. McCormack, *Popular Scientific Lectures*, Chicago: Open Court). *Die Ananlyse der Empfindungen* (Jena, 1906, trans. 1914 C. Williams, *Contributions to the Analysis of Sensations*, Chicago: Open Court).

Secondary literature: Cohen, R. and Seeger, R. (eds.) (1970), 'Ernst Mach, Physicist and Philosopher', *Boston Studies in the Philosophy of Science* 6, Dordrecht: Reidel.

McTaggart, John McTaggart Ellis (1866–1925). McTaggart was one of the last of the 'British idealists', now remembered primarily for his arguments for the unreality of time. He studied at Trinity College, Cambridge, and made his academic career there. His first works were critical studies of Hegel's philosophy, but in 1908 he published his famous argument for the unreality of time ('The Unreality of Time', *Mind* 1908). He devoted the later part of his life to writing *The Nature of Existence* (Cambridge: Cambridge University Press, 1921, 1927), in which he argues that there are three a priori conditions which substances have to satisfy, and that the only things which satisfy them are the loving perceptions of a community of selves.

Secondary literature: Geach, P. T. (1979), *Truth, Love and Immorality*, London: Hutchinson.

Maine, Henry Sumner (1822–88). Born in Kelso, Roxburghshire, Scotland, on 15 August 1822, Maine was sent to Christ's Hospital School and from there to Pembroke College, Cambridge, where he excelled in classics. His academic career began with a tutorship at Trinity Hall, where he commenced his study of early law and legal systems. As a lad of twenty-five he was appointed to the Regius Professorship of Civil Law. He was called to the bar in 1850 and became in 1852 the first reader on Roman law at the Inns of Court. From 1862 to 1869 he served as legal member of the Viceroy's council in India and as Vice-Chancellor of Calcutta University, thereby acquiring the knowledge of India that he used to such good advantage in his writings. Upon his return to England, he held a professorship first at Oxford and then at Cambridge. Maine died in Cannes on 3 February 1888. His main works were: *Ancient Law* (London: J. Murray, 1861); *Village Communities in East and West* (London: J. Murray, 1871); *Lectures on the Early History of Institutions* (London: J. Murray, 1875); *Dissertations on Early Law and Custom* (London: J. Murray, 1883); *Popular Government* (London: J. Murray, 1885).

Secondary literature: Stein, P. (1980), *Legal Evolution: The Story of an Idea*, Cambridge: Cambridge University Press.

Malinowski, B. (1884–1942). Malinowski gained his PhD from Cracow in 1908 and his DSc from the London School of Economics in 1913 and was especially famous for his fieldwork among the Trobriand Islanders (*Argonauts of the Western Pacific*, 1922). He attained the rank of professor of social anthropology at the University of London in 1927. As a leading exponent of one version of functionalism, he trained many students in Great Britain, and in the United States, where he was visiting professor of anthropology at Yale from 1939 until his death.

Secondary literature: Firth, R. (ed.) (1957), *Man and Culture: An Evaluation of the Work of Bromislaw Malinowski*, London: Routledge.

Mannheim, Karl (1893–1947). Born in Budapest, of Jewish parents, Mannheim studied at Budapest, Berlin, and Freiburg universities. From 1915 to 1918 he was involved in the Lukács circle in Budapest. He taught at Budapest University under the Soviet Republic, and was therefore forced to flee to Germany in 1920 from the counterrevolutionary reaction under Admiral

Horthy. From 1921 to 1926 he was a private scholar in Heidelberg and in 1926 was licensed as *Privatdozent* (university teacher) at Heidelberg. From 1930 to 1933 he was professor of sociology at Frankfurt University, and from 1933 to 1945 lecturer in sociology at the London School of Economics. In the period 1945 to 1947 he was professor of the sociology and philosophy of education at the Institute of Education, University of London. His main works were *Ideologie und Utopie* (Bonn: Friedrich Cohen, trans. 1936 L. Wirth and E. Shils, *Ideology and Utopia*, London: Routledge); and *Konservatismus* (Frankfurt: Suhrkamp, 1984, trans. 1986 D. Kettler, V. Meja, and E. R. King: *Conservatism*, London: Routledge).

Secondary literature: Kettler, D., Meja, V., and Stehr, N. (1984), *Karl Mannheim*, London: Tavistock.

MARCEL, GABRIEL (1889–1973). Marcel was born in Paris on 7 December 1889. In 1929, at Mauriac's urging, he converted to Catholicism. After his *agrégation* in 1910, he taught at secondary level until 1923, then devoted himself to a career as a playwright and essayist which was inseparable from his vocation as a philosopher. He edited the 'Feux Croisés' collection for Plon. In 1934, he met Père Fessard. From 1936 onwards he held his famous 'vendredis' at 21 rue de Tournon in Paris; these 'Friday meetings' brought together a number of philosophers and students. His influence continued to grow after 1944. He gave lectures in Aberdeen and Harvard. By the time he died, on 8 October 1973, he had won numerous honours, including the Grand Prix de littérature de l'Académie française in 1948 and his election to the Académie des sciences morales et politiques in 1973. His main works were: *Journal métaphysique* (Paris: Gallimard, 1927); *Etre et avoir* (Paris: Aubier, 1935); *Du Refus à l'invocation* (Paris: Gallimard, 1940); *Homo viator* (Paris: Aubier, 1945); *La métaphysique de Royce* (Paris: Aubier, 1945).

Secondary literature: Fessard, G. (1938), *Théâtre et mystère: introduction à Gabriel Marcel*, Paris: Tequi; Hersch, J., Levinas, E., Ricoeur, P., and Tilliette, X. (1976), *Jean Wahl et Gabriel Marcel*, Paris: Beauchesne; Lapointe, F. H. and C. (1977), *Gabriel Marcel and His Critics, International Bibliography* (1928–76), New York and London; Lubac, H. de, Rougier, M., and Sales, M. (1985), *Gabriel Marcel et Gaston Fessard, Correspondence*, Paris: Beauchesne; Plourde, S. (1985), *Vocabulaire philosophique de Gabriel Marcel*, Paris: Cerf; Ricoeur, P. (1948), *Gabriel Marcel et Karl Jaspers, deux maitres de l'existentialisme*, Paris: Temps present; Sacquin, M. (ed.) (1988), *Colloque Gabriel Marcel*, Paris: Bibliothèque nationale; and Schilp, P. A. and Hahn, L. E. (eds.) (1984), *The Philosophy of Gabriel Marcel,* La Salle, IL: Library of living philosophers.

MARITAIN, JACQUES (1882–1973). Maritain was born in Paris on 18 November 1882. He was brought up in an atmosphere of liberal Protestantism. While a student at the Sorbonne he followed Péguy's advice and attended courses given by Bergson at the Collège de France. After an initial period as Bergson's disciple, he converted to Catholicism in 1906, as did his wife Raïssa. From 1906 to 1908 he lived in Germany, where he studied biology with Hans Driesch, and discovered Thomas Aquinas. In 1923 he became a founder member of the Société thomiste. In 1933 he started Plon's 'Roseau d'or' collection. From 1933 to 1944 he taught at the Institut catholique in Paris, at the Pontifical Institute for Medieval Studies in Toronto, at Princeton, and at Columbia; he also presided over the Institut des hautes études françaises in New York. He died in 1973 after a brilliant career as a diplomat, during which he continued to publish. His main works were: *La philosophie bergsonienne: études critiques* (Paris: Marcel Rivière, 1914); *Art et scolastique* (Paris: Art Catholique, 1920); *Le Docteur angélique* (Paris: Desclée de Brouwer, 1930); *De la philosophie chrétienne* (Milan: Rivista de Neo-scolastica, 1932); *Les degrès du savoir: distinguer pour unir* (Paris: Desclée de Brouwer, 1932); *Sept leçons sur l'Etre et les premiers principes de la raison spéculative* (Paris: Téqui, 1934); *L'Humanisme intégral* (Paris: Aubier, 1936); *Quatre essais sur l'esprit dans sa condition charnelle* (Paris: Desclée de Brouwer, 1939); *Saint Thomas and the Problem of Evil* (Milwaukee: Marquette University Press, 1942); *De Bergson à Thomas d'Aquin* (New York: Editions de le Maison Française, 1944).

Secondary literature: Bars, H. (1959), *Maritain en notre temps*, Paris: Grasset and (1962), *La Politique selon Jacques Maritain*, Paris: Editions ouvrières; Doering, B. E. (1983), *J. Maritain and the French Catholic Intellectuals*, Notre Dame; Fecher, C. A. (1953), *The Philosophy of J. Maritain*, Westminster: Newman Press; Maritain, R. (1949), *Les Grandes amitiés*, Paris: Desclée de Brouwer; Smith, B. W. (1976), *J. Maritain: Anti-modern or Ultramodern? An Historical Analysis of His Critics, His Thought and His Life*, New York and Amsterdam.

MARTY, ANTON (1847–1914). Born in Schwyz (Switzerland), Marty studied in Würzburg with Brentano. He was a professor in Czernowitz and Prague. His works include: 'Über subjektlose Sätze und das Verhältnis der Grammatik zu Logik und Psychologie' (1884), *Untersuchungen zur Grundlegung der allgemeinen Grammatik und Sprachphilosophie* (Halle: Max Niemayr, 1908); *Zur Sprache. Die 'logische', 'lokalistische', und andere Kasustheorien* (Halle: Max Niemayr, 1910); *Raum und Zeit* (Halle: Max Niemayr, 1916).

Secondary literature: Mulligan (ed.) 1990, *Mind, Meaning and Metaphysics: The Philosophy and Theory of Language of Anton Marty*, Dordrecht: Kluwer, 1990.

MARX, KARL HEINRICH (1818–83). Born in Trier to a secularised Jewish family, Marx studied law and then philosophy at Bonn and Berlin universities. He was editor-in-chief of the liberal *Rheinische Zeitung* from 1842 to 1843, moved to Paris in 1843 and to Brussels in 1845. From 1847 to 1850 he was leader of the communist League and editor-in-chief of the *Neue Rheinische Zeitung* during the revolutions of 1848. In 1849, after the revolutions' defeat, he went into exile in London, where he spent the rest of his life, often in great poverty. During that time he composed his great work, *Capital* (only the first volume of which was published during his lifetime, in 1867). He was the founder and leader of the International Working Men's Association (the First International) from 1864 to 1872.

Secondary literature: Callinicos, A. (1985), *Marxism and Philosophy*, Oxford: Oxford University Press; Cohen, G. A. (1978), *Karl Marx's Theory of History: A Defence*, Oxford: Oxford University Press; Wood, A. (1981), *Karl Marx*, London: Routledge.

MEAD, GEORGE HERBERT (1863–1931). Mead is in many respects one of the founders of social psychology, focusing his work on the role of communication and the emergence of the self as a social agent. Like Dewey he was also a leading public intellectual, especially in his participation in the Progressive Movement. His account of the sociality of thought and the role of communication led him to orient his form of pragmatism towards the emerging social sciences, which he thought would have direct social consequences in the emergence of a more rational and democratic form of society. His major works were all published posthumously, the most important of which is *Mind, Self, and Society* (Chicago: Chicago University Press, 1934) with its discussion of linguistic symbols and communication. His essays and lectures on morality emphasise an intersubjective and dialogical form of Kantian ethics, with a test procedure for maxims in dialogue of all those affected. H. Joas's *G. H. Mead: A Contemporary Reexamination of his Thought* (1985) and G. A. Cook's *George Herbert Mead: The Making of a Social Pragmatist*

(Urbana, IL: University of Illinois Press, 1993) provide comprehensive treatments of all aspects of Mead's pragmatism.

MEINONG, ALEXIUS (1853–1920). Meinong was born in Lvov, at this time capital of the Austro-Hungarian province of Galicia. Between 1870 and 1874 he studied history in Vienna. For the next two years he studied philosophy under Brentano. From 1878 to 1882 he taught philosophy at the University of Vienna. In 1882 he was appointed to the University of Graz (Austria), where he founded the first laboratory of experimental psychology in Austria and established the so-called Graz School of philosophy. He is the author of, among other writings, *Psychologisch- ethische Untersuchungen zur Werttheorie* (Graz: Leuschner and Lubensky, 1894), 'Über Gegenstände höherer Ordnung und deren Verhältnis zur inneren Wahrnehmung' (*Zeitschrift für Psychologie und Physiologie der Sinnesorgane*, 21 (1899), 182–72), *Über Annahmen* (Leipzig: Barth, 1902), 'Über Gegenstandstheorie' (1904), *Uber Möglichkeit und Wahrscheinlichkeit* (Leipzig: Barth, 1915), 'Über emotionale Präsentationen' (1917).

Secondary literature: Findlay, J. N. (1963), *Meinong's Theory of Objects and Values*, Oxford: Clarendon Press; Grossmann, R. (1974), *Meinong*, London: Routledge; Routley, R. (1980), *Exploring Meinong's Jungle and Beyond*, Canberra: Australian National University.

MERLEAU-PONTY, MAURICE (1908–1961). Educated at the Ecole normale supérieure, he took his *agrégation de philosophie* in 1930. He was a member of the resistance during the Second World War. He was a professor at the University of Lyon from 1948 to 1949; a professor for child psychology and pedagogy at the Sorbonne, Paris, from 1949 to 1952. He was professor of philosophy at the Collège de France from 1952 to 1961. Merleau-Ponty's main philosophical works are *La Structure du comportement* (Paris: Presses Universitaires de France, 1942); *Phénoménologie de la perception* (Paris: Gallimard, 1945), and *Les Aventures de la dialectique* (Paris: Gallimard, 1955).

Secondary literature: Matthews, E. (2002), *The Philosophy of Merleau-Ponty*, Chesham: Acumen.

MEYERSON, EMILE (1859–1933). Born in Russia, trained and educated in Germany, with advanced work in chemistry under Bunsen, Meyerson emigrated to Paris in 1882. After a brief exposure to industrial chemistry, he spent the rest of his life working as an editor and administrator. Meyerson never held a university position. However, his erudition, especially in the history and philosophy of the sciences, was enormous, well known, and universally respected. It led both to his being surrounded by a circle of protégés (including, e.g., Koyré and Metzger) and to the writing of his metaphysically anti-positivist, epistemologically Neo-Kantian historico-philosophical masterpieces: *Identité et réalité* (Paris: Alcan, 1908), *De l'Explication dans les sciences* (Paris: Payot, 1921), *La Deduction rélativiste* (Paris: Payot, 1925), and *Du Cheminement de la pensée* (Paris: Alcan, 1931).

Secondary literature: Boas, G. (1930), *A Critical Analysis of the Philosophy of Emile Meyerson*, Baltimore, MD: Johns Hopkins University Press.

MIKHAILOVSKII, NIKOLAI KONSTANTINOVICH (1842–1904). One of the principal theorists of Russian populism, Mikhailovskii was born in Kaluga into the family of an impoverished landowner. After the death of his parents in 1855 he was educated at the St Petersburg Mining Institute. He became a student activist and was expelled in 1861. In 1869, he took over the journal *Otchestvennye zapiski (Annals of the Fatherland)*, in which he published all his major works. Influenced by Mill, Proudhon, and Lavrov, Mikhailovskii was a champion of radical causes, including the rights of women. A tireless critic of scientism, Mikhailovskii stressed how the

Russian word for truth, *pravda*, refers not just to objective representation, but to moral truth and justice. He attacked the positivism of Comte and Spencer, defended 'subjective' methods in history and sociology, and upheld the supreme value of the individual. Towards the end of his life, Mikhailovskii was a critic of Russian Marxism. Unlike many of his contemporaries, he remained in Russia for his entire career, somehow managing to escape serious persecution.

An edition of Mikhailovskii's complete works was published in Russia (1906–15). Translation of extracts from his works, including part of his famous article 'Chto takoe progress?' (1869) (reprinted in *Sochineniya N. K. Mikhailovskovo*, vol. I, St Petersburg), appeared in J. M. Edie, J. P. Scanlan, and M.-B. Zeldin (1965), *Russian Philosophy*, vol. II, Chicago, IL: Quadrangle Books. J. H. Billington (1958), *Mikhailovkii and Russian Populism*, Oxford: Clarendon Press, is the sole monograph in English on Mikhailovskii. A. Walicki, *A History of Russian Thought from the Enlightenment to Marxism*, trans. Hilda Andrews-Rusiecka, Oxford: Oxford University Press, is a fine short account.

MOORE, GEORGE EDWARD (1873–1958). Moore was one of the most important British philosophers of the twentieth century, an early critic of both idealism and psychologism and a defender of the irreducibility of ethical values and of the irreplaceability of common-sense belief. He studied at Cambridge and, having obtained a position there in 1911, remained there for most of his academic career.

Moore's early writings, especially his book *Principia Ethica* (1903), are a sustained critique of idealism and reductive empiricism ('naturalism'), especially in ethics. He then turned his attention to questions concerning perception and knowledge. He developed a 'sense-datum' theory of perception and elaborated a defence of 'common sense' against scepticism. In these writings he paid careful attention to insights gained from Russell's work in logic and he was an early supporter of 'philosophical analysis' as a method of applying logic to philosophy; in his later writings the emphasis on logic is combined with careful attention to ordinary language. His main works were 'The Refutation of Idealism' (*Mind* 12 (1903), 433–53); *Principia Ethica* (Cambridge: Cambridge University Press, 1903; revised ed. 1993); 'A Defence of Common Sense' (in J. H. Muirhead, *Contemporary British Philosophy*, London: George Allen and Unwin); and 'Proof of an External World' (*Proceedings of the British Academy* 25 (1939), 273–300). His main non-ethical writings are collected in his *Selected Writings* (ed. T. Baldwin, London: Routledge, 1993).

Secondary literature: Baldwin, T. (1990), *G. E. Moore*, London: Routledge.

MORGAN, L. H. (1818–81). Morgan practised law in Rochester, New York, and saw the need to record changing Indian cultures before they disappeared. His *League of the Ho-dé-no-sau-nee, or Iroquois* (1851) offered a very early scientific account of a native American tribe. His *Systems of Consanguinity and Affinity of the Human Family* (Washington, DC: The Smithsonian Institution, 1870) inspired Engels's *The Origin of the Family, Private Property and the State* (1884). His *Ancient Society* (1877) elaborated Tylor's evolutionary scheme of savagery, barbarism, and civilisation, and offered diagnostic characteristics for each stage.

Secondary literature: Fortes, M. (1969), *Kinship and the Social Order*, Chicago: Archae.

MORRIS, C. W. (1901–79). An American pragmatist who facilitated the constructive interaction of pragmatism with logical positivism at the University of Chicago. He was instrumental in founding *The Encyclopedia of Unified Science*. Among his major works were *Logical Positivism, Pragmatism and Scientific Empiricism* (Paris: Hermann, 1937) and *Signs, Language and Behavior* (New York: Prentice Hall, 1946).

NATORP, PAUL (1854–1924). A German philosopher born in 1854 in Düsseldorf, his early interests were in mathematics and music; he went to Strasburg in 1874 to pursue studies in music, but he turned to philosophy. He moved to Marburg to continue work on Kant, but his *Habilitationsschrift* was on Descartes. He became close friends with Cohen, his interests ranging from pedagogy to Plato. His most important work was *Platons Ideenlehre* (1903). He died in 1924.

Secondary literature: Holzhey, H. (1986), *Cohen und Natorp*, Basle: Schwabe; Köhnke, K. C. (1986), *Entstehung und Aufstieg des Neu-Kantianismus*, Frankfurt: Suhrkamp, trans. R. J. Hollingdale as *The Rise of Neo-Kantianism*, Cambridge: Cambridge University Press.

NEURATH, OTTO (1882–1945). Trained as an economic historian and a committed socialist, who participated in the 1918 Bavarian Revolution as its Economic Minister, Neurath was a founding member of the Vienna Circle and a leading member of the Unity of Science Movement. His public and political activities included an emphasis on the dissemination of knowledge in museums and organising the project of an *Encyclopedia for Unified Science*. In his early work Neurath argued for a politically engaged empirical social science. His later work moves in the direction of methodological pluralism, seeing the unity of science as a social project rather than an abstract unification based on methodological proscriptions. His main works were *Philosophical Papers 1913–1946*, trans. and ed. 1983 R. Cohen and M. Neurath (Dordrecht: Reidel, 1913–46) and *Foundations of the Social Sciences* (Chicago: University of Chicago University Press, 1944). Current research significantly revises older one-sided interpretations of his positivism, as in *Philosophy Between Science and Politics* (Cambridge: Cambridge University Press, 1996) by N. Cartwright, J. Cat, B. Fleck, and T. Uebel, and T. Uebel, *Overcoming Logical Positivism From Within* (Amsterdam: Rodopi, 1992).

NEWMAN, JOHN HENRY (1801–90). Newman was born in London and entered Trinity College, Oxford in 1817. He became a Fellow of Oriel College in 1822 and vicar of St Mary's, Oxford in 1828. As a leader of the Oxford Movement, Newman had a profound influence on the Church of England. He later came to have doubts about Anglicanism's claim to be the *via media* between Protestantism and Roman Catholicism, and in 1845 he was received into the Roman Catholic Church. His influential work on religious belief, *An Essay in Aid of a Grammar of Assent*, appeared in 1870 (London: Burns, Oates). In 1879 Newman was made a Cardinal by Pope Leo XIII.

Among his other influential works are J. H. Newman (1843), *Sermons, Chiefly on the Theory of Religious Belief Preached before the University of Oxford* (London and Oxford: Rivington and Park); *Apologia Pro Vita Sua* (Oxford: Clarendon Press, 1864), and *The Idea of a University* (London: Pickering, 1873).

Secondary literature: Ian Ker, *John Henry Newman: A Biography* (Oxford: Clarendon Press, 1988); A. J. Boekraad, *The Personal Conquest of Truth* (Louvain: Editions Nauwelaerts, 1955); M. Jaime Ferreira, *Doubt and Religious Commitment: The Role of the Will in Newman's Thought* (Oxford: Clarendon Press, 1990); H. H. Price, *Belief* (London: George Allen and Unwin, 1969); E. J. Sillem (ed.), *The Philosophical Notebook of John Henry Newman*, 2 vols., Introduction (Louvain: Nauwelaerts, 1969); and Thomas Vargish, *The Contemplation of Mind* (Oxford: Oxford University Press, 1970).

NIETZSCHE, FRIEDRICH (1844–1900). A brilliant scholar, Nietzsche was appointed Professor of Classical Languages at Basle in Switzerland at the age of twenty-four. Initially he was strongly influenced by the philosophy of Schopenhauer. He was a friend and great admirer of Richard Wagner until they had a falling out. He taught for about ten years, and then retired because of ill health in 1879. He never married. His philosophically most productive period came after his retirement from Basle and before his final mental collapse in 1889. Thereafter he lingered in a vegetative state until his death. His main works were: *Die fröhliche Wissenschaft* (Chemnitz: E. Schmeitzner, 1882, trans. 1974 W. Kaufmann, *The Gay Science*, New York: Vintage); *Also sprach Zarathustra* (Chemnitz: E. Schmeitzner, 1883–5, trans. 1961 R. J. Hollingdale, Harmondsworth: Penguin); *Jenseits von Gut und Böse* (Leipzig: C. G. Naumann, 1886, trans. 1973 R. J. Hollingdale, *Beyond Good and Evil*, Harmondsworth: Penguin); *Zur Genealogie der Moral* (Leipzig: C. G. Naumann, trans. 1968 W. Kaufmann and R. J. Hollingdale, *On the Genealogy of Morals*, New York: Random House); *Götzen-Dämmerung* (Leipzig: C. G. Naumann, 1889, trans. 1968 R. J. Hollingdale, *Twilight of the Idols*, Harmondsworth: Penguin).

Secondary literature: Clark, M. (1990), *Nietzsche on Truth and Philosophy*, Cambridge: Cambridge University Press; Danto, A. C. (1965), *Nietzsche as Philosopher*, New York: Macmillan; Heidegger, M. (1961), *Nietzsche*, Pfullingen: Verlag Gunter Neske, trans. 1979–82 D. Krell and others, San Franciso, CA: Harper and Row; Jaspers, K. (1936), *Nietzsche: Einführung in das Verständnis seines Philosophierens*, Berlin and Leipzig: de Gruyter, trans. 1965 C. F. Wallraff and F. J. Schmitz, *Nietzsche: An Introduction to the Understanding of His Philosophical Activity*, Tucson: University of Arizona Press; Kaufmann, W. (1974), *Nietzsche: Philosopher, Psychologist, Antichrist*, Princeton, NJ: Princeton University Press; Magnus, B. (1978), *Nietzsche's Existential Imperative*, Bloomington: Indiana University Press; Nehamas, A. (1985), *Nietzsche: Life as Literature*, Cambridge, MA: Harvard University Press; Schacht, R. (1983), *Nietzsche*, London: Routledge; Sleinis, E. E. (1994), *Nietzsche's Revaluation of Values*, Urbana and Chicago: University of Illinois Press; Tanner, M. (1994), *Nietzsche*, Oxford: Oxford University Press; Young, J. (1992), *Nietzsche's Philosophy of Art*, Cambridge: Cambridge University Press.

NISHIDA, KITARŌ (1870–1945). The founder of the Kyoto School, Nishida was Japan's most influential philosopher of the twentieth century. Nishida was the first philosopher to synthesise Western and traditionally East Asian ideas in a comprehensive manner. With a special student degree from Tokyo University, Nishida's fame did not begin until the publication of his pioneering book *Zen no kenkyū (An Inquiry into the Good)* in 1911. Appointed to Kyoto University in 1910, he became the mentor to a number of outstanding philosophical students. He is most noted for his theories of 'pure experience' (giving William James's notion a Zen Buddhist nuance) in *Zen no kenkyū* and his 'logic of place' *(basho)* as developed in such important books as *Hataraku mono kara miru mono e (From the Acting to the Seeing*, Tokyo: Iwarami shoten, 1927), *Ippansha no jikakuteki taikei (The Self-Conscious System of the Universal*, Tokyo: Iwarami shoten, 1929), and *Tetsugaku no kompon mondai (Fundamental Problems of Philosophy*, Tokyo: Sophia University Press, 1934).

Secondary literature: Abe, Masao (1988), 'Nishida's Philosophy of Place', *International Philosophical Quarterly* 28: 355–71; Nishitani Keiji (1991), *Nishida Kitavo*, Barkeley CA: University of California Press.

ORTEGA Y GASSET, JOS (1883–1955). Born in Madrid after studies at a Jesuit college at Málaga and at the University of Madrid, a government grant in 1905 gave Ortega the opportunity to broaden his philosophical training in Germany. In 1910 he became professor of metaphysics in the University of Madrid. This was the beginning of twenty-five years of intellectual and political activity which was crowned with unparalleled success. He created his own system of thought, ratiovitalism, which he expounded in a series of books of increasing rigour and depth; meanwhile his political activity culminated in 1931 with the foundation of the Agrupación al Servicio de la República (Group for the Service of Republic), which contributed to the fall of monarchy and the arrival of the republic in Spain. The Spanish civil war of 1936 changed Ortega's fate: he spent the next nine years in exile in Europe and South America, and remained isolated after his return to Spain in 1945. Nevertheless he devoted these years to writing his most ambitious works. Ortega died of cancer in Madrid in 1955.

His main works were *Meditaciones del Quijote* (Madrid: Edicions de la Residencia de Estudiantes, 1914, trans. 1961 *Meditations on Quixote*, New York: Norton); *El tema de nuestro tiempo* (Madrid: Espasa Calpe, 1923, trans. 1931 and 1933 *The Modern Theme*, London: C. W. Daniel and New York: Norton); and *La rebelión de las masas* (Madrid: Revista de Occidente, 1929, trans. 1932 *The Revolt of the Masses*, London: George Allen and Unwin and New York, Norton).

Secondary literature: Ferrater Mora, J. (1957), *Ortega y Gasset: An Outline of His Philosophy*, Cambridge: Bowes and Bowes and New Haven, CT: Yale University Press; Morán, G. (1998), *El maestro en el erial: Ortega y Gasset y la cultura del franquismo (The Master in the Uncultivated Land: Ortega y Gasset and the Culture of Franquism)*, Barcelona: Tusquets; and Orringer, N. (1979), *Ortega y sus fuentes germánicas (Ortega and his German Sources)*, Madrid: Gredos.

OSTWALD, WILHELM (1853–1932). A German chemist, born in Riga, educated in Estonia; Ostwald taught in Riga, then in Leipzig. He founded physical chemistry. His work on catalysis and on reaction velocities earned him the Nobel Prize in 1909. Ostwald defended a form of realism according to which scientists can directly induce laws from observed facts. He opposed atomism (atoms are unobservable) and espoused *energetics:* the universe consists of forms of energy which, though irreducibly different, can be converted into one another. After the experimental confirmation of the atomic hypothesis, Ostwald accepted atomism. His philosophical views are set out in his *Grundriß der Naturphilosophie (Outline of Natural Philosophy*, Leipzig: Reclam, 1908).

PEARSON, KARL (1857–1936). Pearson was born in London in 1857. His father was a lawyer. At Cambridge, Pearson did well in mathematics, but began a legal career. He was persuaded to return to mathematics and became professor of applied mathematics at University College, London, in 1884. His early interests in social matters led to his pioneering work in mathematical statistics, which in turn led to an interest in the management of populations. He was the first occupant of the chair of eugenics in 1911, and at the same time held the professorship of geometry at Gresham College, a post he used as a platform for popular science lectures. He married twice. His department became the world centre of statistical studies, and his influence therefrom was immense. He was a formidable character, admired, feared, and even hated by those who knew him. He died in 1936 at Coldharbour. His main work was *The Grammer of Science* (London: Walter Scott, 1892).

PERRY, RALPH BARTON (1876–1957). Perry was one of the leaders of the American 'new realist' movement and later developed an influential naturalist theory of value. Throughout his career he was based at Harvard. In the 'new realist' manifesto, *Present Philosophical Tendencies* (London: Longmans, Green, 1912), Perry gathered together a series of essays in which young American philosophers argued that the characteristic mistake of idealists and many other philosophers had been to interpose 'ideas' or some other representation between the mind and the world; and in place of this they argued for a 'direct realist' account of perception and knowledge. Perry combined this with a version of James's neutral monism. Later Perry turned to ethics and in his *General Theory of Value* (New York: Longmans, Green, 1926) he argued that value attaches to any object that is of interest to anyone; moral value requires the harmonising of all interests.

Secondary literature: Kucklick, B. (1977), *The Rise of American Philosophy, Cambridge Massachusetts 1860–1930*, New Haven, CT: Yale University Press.

PEIRCE, CHARLES SANDERS (1839–1914). Born in 1839, Peirce studied at Harvard and taught there briefly before becoming lecturer in logic at Johns Hopkins University in 1879 and working for the United States Coast Survey. A founder of pragmatism, he worked in formal logic and semiotic as well as developing an ambitious philosophical system. After 1885, he worked in isolation, giving occasional lectures around Harvard. Peirce died in 1914. His main works were: 'On a New List of Categories' (*Proceedings of the American Academy of Arts and Sciences* 7 (1867): 287–98); The *Journal of Speculative Philosophy* series (1868–9); 'Illustrations of the Logic of Science' (Popular Science Monthly (1877–8); 12 and 13; The *Monist* series on Metaphysics (1891–3); *Reasoning and the Logic of Things* (ed. K. L. Katner, Cambridge, MA: Harvard University Press, 1992, written in 1898) Harvard Lectures on Pragmatism (1934, delivered in 1903). *Monist* papers on Pragmaticism (*The Monist* 15: 161–81; 481–99, 1905–6).

Secondary literature: Brent, J. (1993), *Charles Sanders Peirce: A Life*, Bloomington and Indianapolis Indiana University Press; Fisch, M. (1986), *Peirce, Semiotic and Pragmatism: Essays by Max Fisch*, ed. K. L. Ketner and C. J. W. Kloesel, Bloomington and Indianapolis: Indiana University Press; Hookway, C. J. (1985), *Peirce*, London: Routledge; Ketner, K. L. (1995), *Peirce and Contemporary Thought*, New York: Fordham University Press; Murphey, M. (1961), *The Development of Peirce's Philosophy*, Cambridge, MA: Harvard University Press.

PLEKHANOV, GEORGI VALENTINOVICH (1856–1918). Plekhanov trained as a mining engineer. Initially active in the Populist movement, he spent most of his life in exile in Switzerland where he formed the first Russian Marxist group, Emancipation of Labour, in 1883. He wrote extensively on philosophy, aesthetics, and Russian history; broke with Lenin after the Russian Social-Democratic Party split between the Bolsheviks and Mensheviks in 1903; supported the First World War; and opposed the October 1917 Revolution. His main works are collected in G. V. Plekhanov, *Selected Philosophical Works* (5 vols., Moscow: Progress, 1977).

Secondary literature: Walicki, A. (1979), *A History of Russian Thought from the Enlightenment to Marxism*, Stanford: Stanford University Press and *Marx and the Leap to the Kingdom of Freedom*, Stanford: Stanford University Press.

POINCARÉ, JULES HENRI (1854–1912). Although trained as a mining engineer, Poincaré's autodidactic successes in mathematics led him first to the faculty of science at Caen (1879) and two years later to the Sorbonne. His philosophy of science deeply exhibits his formal propensities: theories form around differential equations themselves founded upon inductive generalisations from observations; differences between theories may result from different interpretations of the equations; theories change because their observational bases originate in selective choices made by the physicists. Prediction and not explanation is the goal of science. Among Poincaré's voluminous list of publications, the most philosophically relevant are *La Science et l'hypothèse* (Paris: Flammarion, 1902), *La Valeur de la science* (Paris: Flammarion, 1905), and *Science et méthode* (Paris: Flammarion, 1908).

Secondary literature: Giedymin, J. (1982), *Science and Convention*, Oxford: Pergamon Press; Holton, G. (1974), *The Thematic Origins of Scientific Thought: Kepler to Einstein*, Cambridge, MA: Harvard University Press; Torretti, R. (1984), *Philosophy of Geometry from Riemann to Poincaré*, Dordrecht: Reidel.

POUND, ROSCOE (1870–1964). Born in Lincoln, Nebraska, on 27 October 1870, Pound first specialised in botany, earning a doctorate in that field at the University of Nebraska. After studying law at Harvard, he was admitted to the bar in Nebraska. He practised law briefly and then served as a commissioner (auxiliary judge) of Nebraska's Supreme Court. Beginning in

1903, he served on faculties of midwestern law schools before moving, in 1910, to Harvard Law School, where he served as Dean from 1916 to 1936. Pound died in Cambridge, Massachusetts, on 1 July 1964. His main works were: 'The Need of a Sociological Jurisprudence' (*The Green Bag*, 19 (1907)); 'Mechanical Jurisprudence' (*Columbia Law Review*, 8 (1908)); 'Liberty of Contract' (*Yale Law Journal*, 18 (1908–9)); 'The Scope and Purpose of Sociological Jurisprudence' (*Harvard Law Review*, 24–5 (1910–12)); 'Law in Books and Law in Action' (*American Law Review*, 44 (1910)); *An Introduction to the Philosophy of Law* (New Haven, CT: Yale University Press, 1922); *Social Control through Law* (New Haven, CT: Yale University Press, 1942); and *Jurisprudence* (5 vols., 1959, St Paul, MN: West Publishing Co.)

Secondary literature: Summers, R. S. (1982), *Instrumentalism and American Legal Theory*, Ithaca, NY and London: Cornell University Press.

PRICHARD, H. A. (1871–1947). Born in 1871, Harold Prichard studied at Oxford and taught there all his working life. He was Fellow of Hertford College (1894–8) and then Trinity College (1898–1924). He was elected to the White's Professorship of Moral Philosophy in 1928, and retired in 1937. He published little during his lifetime but had an enormous influence on the development of moral philosophy between the wars. He died in 1947. His main works were: 'Does Moral Philosophy Rest on a Mistake?' (*Mind* 21 (1912) 21–37); 'Duty and Interest' (inaugural lecture, 1928, repr: in Prichard, *Moral Obligation*, Oxford: Clarendon Press, 1968); 'Duty and Ignorance of Fact' (*Proceedings of the British Academy* (1932), 67–92). His writings have recently been collected in *Moral Writings* (ed. J. MacAdam, Oxford: Clarendon Press, 2003).

RADCLIFFE-BROWN, A. R. (1881–1955). Educated at Trinity College, Cambridge. Radcliffe-Brown's field work on the close-knit and isolated societies in the Andaman Islands provided material that supported his theory of structural-functionalism. During his long career, he held professorships at major universities in South Africa, Australia, North America, South America, Egypt, and China. He was professor of social anthropology at Oxford University from 1937 to 1946, and was succeeded in that chair by his student E. E. Evans-Pritchard (1902–73). His main works were: *Structure and Function in Primitive Society* (Glencoe, IL: The Free Press, 1952).

Secondary literature: KuKlick, H. (1991), *The Savage Within: The Social History of British Anthropology* (Cambridge: Cambridge University Press).

RAMSEY, FRANK PLUMPTON (1903–30). Ramsey was the most gifted British philosopher of the 1920s, making important contributions in many areas of philosophy, despite his early death. He studied at Cambridge and his brief career was based there. His first work lay in the field of mathematical logic: he produced a simplified and much improved version of the logicist position of Whitehead and Russell. He then turned to probability, and developed a way of measuring both the strength of desire and the strength of belief, of which he took (subjective) probability to be a measure. This work connected with new positions concerning truth, belief, and knowledge: he developed a 'deflationary' conception of truth, which he combined with a pragmatist account of the content of belief and a reliabilist account of knowledge. In other papers he sketched out important new accounts of scientific theories, laws of nature, and causation. His main papers were collected in *The Foundations of Mathematics* (ed. R. B. Braithwaite, London: Kegan Paul, 1931).

Secondary literature: Sahlin, N.-E. (1990), *The Philosophy of F. P. Ramsey*, Cambridge: Cambridge University Press.

REINACH, ADOLF (1883–1917). Reinach born in Mainz (Germany). He entered the University of Munich in 1901 where, with some interruptions, he remained until 1909, studying law and philosophy under Theodor Lipps. In 1905 he spent some time in Göttingen, where he came into contact with Husserl. From 1909 until 1912 he was back in Göttingen, where he worked with Husserl as *Privatdozent* and served as mentor of many early phenomenologists including Roman Ingarden, Edith Stein, and Dietrich von Hildebrand. He died in battle in Flanders. His works include: 'Zur Theorie des negativen Urteils' (1911; reprinted in Reinach, *Sämtliche Werke: Kritische Ausgabe mit Kammertar* vol. I, Munich, 1989) and 'Die apriorischen Grundlagen des bürgerlichen Rechts' in *Jahrbuch für Philosophie und phänomenologische Forschung*, 1 (1913), 685–847.

Secondary literature: Mulligan, K. (ed.) (1987), *Speech Act and Sachervalt. Reinach and the Foundations of Realist Phenomenology*, Dordrecht/Boston/Lancaster: M. Nijhoff.

REICHENBACH, HANS (1891–1953). Reichenbach made important contributions to the philosophy of physics and to the philosophy of science generally. He studied physics and in 1920 attended Einstein's seminar on relativity in Berlin. With Einstein's help he became professor of the philosophy of physics in Berlin in 1926; but in 1933 he left Germany for Turkey. In 1938 he moved to the United States and taught at UCLA until his death in 1953. Reichenbach's main early work (*Philosophic der Raum-Zeit-Lehre*, Berlin: de Gruyter, 1928) concerns space and time; against Kant and Kantians, he argued that theories of space and time are fundamentally empirical. In his next major work (*Wahrscheinlichkeitslehre*, Leiden: Sijthoff, 1935) he developed and defended a frequentist account of probability. Both these works brought him into close contact with the work of the members of the Vienna Circle; but in *Experience and Prediction* (Chicago: University of Chicago Press, 1938) he argued from a fallibilist realist position against the standard 'logical positivist' account of scientist knowledge.

Secondary literature: Salmon, W. C. (1979), *Hans Reichenbach: Logical Empiricist*, Dordrecht: Reidel.

RICKERT, HEINRICH (1863–1936). A German philosopher born in 1863 at Danzig, he spent his early years in Berlin. He rejected an early interest in materialism and his emphasis on value is already apparent in his *Habilitationsschrift*. His most important work is *Die Grenzen der naturwissenschaftlichen Begriffsbildung* (part one 1896, part two 1901, and whole 1902; abridged and trans. Guy Oakes from 5th edn 1929 as *The Limits of Concept Formation in Natural Science*, Cambridge: Cambridge University Press, 1986). He was Alois Riehl's successor at Freiburg in 1896 and then Windelband's successor at Heidelberg in 1926. He retired in 1934 and died two years later. He exerted considerable influence on, among others, Lask and Weber.

Secondary literature: Oakes, G. (1988), *Weber and Rickert*, Cambridge, MA: MIT Press.

RITCHIE, DAVID GEORGE (1853–1903). After graduating at Edinburgh University in 1875, Ritchie proceeded to Balliol College, Oxford, where his tutor was T. H. Green (1875–8). He was a fellow of Jesus College, Oxford, from 1878, and tutor from 1881, until 1894, when he became professor of logic and metaphysics at St Andrews University. He was President of the Aristotelian Society in 1898–9. His main works were: *Darwinism and Politics* (London: Swan Sonnenschein, 1889); *The Principles of State Interference* (London: Swan Sonnenschein, 1891); *Darwin and Hegel* (London: Swan Sonnenschein, 1893); *Natural Rights* (London: Swan, Sonnenschein and New York: Macmillan, 1894); *Studies in Political and Social Ethics* (London: Swan Sonnenschein and New York: Macmillan, 1902); *Philosophical Studies* (ed. R. Latta, London and New York, 1905);

Miscellaneous Writings (*Collected Works of D. G. Ritchie*, ed. P. P. Nicholson, Bristol: Thoemmer Press, 1998).

Secondary literature: Harris, F. P. (1944), *The Neo-Idealist Political Theory: Its Continuity with the British Tradition*, New York: King's Crown Press; Latta, R. (ed.) (1905), 'Memoir' in *Philosophical Studies by David George Ritchie*, London and New York: Macmillan; Otter, S. den (1996), *British Idealism and Social Explanation: A Study in Late Victorian Thought*, Oxford: Clarendon Press.

ROSS, W. D. (1877–1971). Sir David Ross was born in 1877. He studied at Edinburgh University, and then held a fellowship at Merton College, Oxford, before moving to Oriel College, Oxford, where he spent the rest of his working life as fellow (1902–29) and then as Provost (1929–47). He was Deputy White's Professor from 1923 to 1928, but did not stand for election on Stewart's retirement in the hope that Prichard would be elected. He was knighted in 1928. Towards the end of his career he served a term as Vice-Chancellor of Oxford, and was also President of the British Academy. In addition to his work on moral philosophy, he was the greatest Aristotelian scholar of his day and an active public servant. He died in 1971. His main works (on moral philosophy) were: *The Right and The Good* (Oxford: Clarendon Press, 1930); *Foundations of Ethics* (Oxford: Clarendon Press, 1939).

Secondary literature: McNaughton, D. (1996), 'An Unconnected Heap of Duties?' *Philosophical Quarterly* 46: 433–47; Urmson, J. (1975), 'A Defence of Intuitionism', *Proceedings of the Aristotelian Society* 75: 111–19.

ROYCE, JOSIAH (1855–1916). The youngest of four children of pioneer parents, Royce was born in Grass Valley, California, a mining camp. After his graduation at the University of California at Berkeley, financial support from local businessmen enabled Royce to study in Germany for two years. Royce then returned to the United States and earned his PhD from Johns Hopkins University in 1878. After teaching English for four years at the University of California at Berkeley, and spending three years teaching at Harvard on a temporary basis, Royce was appointed an assistant professor of philosophy at Harvard in 1885. He remained at Harvard for the rest of his career where along with William James he was the mainstay of the philosophy department and a central figure in what has come to be called 'the Golden Age in American Philosophy'. Royce married Katherine Head in 1880. His main works were: *The Religious Aspect of Philosophy* (Boston: Houghton Mifflin, 1885); *The Spirit of Modern Philosophy* (Boston: Houghton Mifflin, 1892); *The World and the Individual, First Series* (1899); *The World and the Individual, Second Series* (New York: Macmillan, 1901); *The Philosophy of Loyalty* (New York: Macmillan, 1908); *The Problem of Christianity* (New York: Macmillan 1913).

Secondary literature: Clendinning, J. (1985), *The Life and Thought of Josiah Royce*, Madison: University of Wisconsin Press; Fuss, P. (1965), *The Morality of Josiah Royce*, Cambridge, MA: Harvard University Press; Kuklick, B. (1972), *Josiah Royce: An Intellectual Biography*, Indianapolis: Bobbs-Merrill; Muirhead, J. H. (1931), *The Platonic Tradition in Anglo-Saxon Philosophy*, New York: Macmillan.

ROZANOV, VASILII VASIL'EVICH (1856–1919). Born into a poor provincial family in Vetluga, Rozanov had a difficult childhood. His father died when he was five, his mother eight years later. He studied history and philology at Moscow University, and afterwards taught history in provincial schools. He entered a disastrous marriage with Dostoevsky's former mistress, Apollinariia Suslova. She refused him a divorce when they separated in 1888 and in 1889 Rozanov secretly (and bigamously) married Varvara Rudneva. His first book, *O ponimanii (On Understanding)* appeared in 1886 but was largely ignored. In 1891, he produced a significant work on Dostoevsky, serialised in *Russkii vestnik*. Thereafter Rozanov became a journalist, developing his characteristically brilliant and impressionistic style, and publishing numerous influential articles, usually in the right-wing press. His writing was sarcastic, outrageous, and iconoclastic. He was sometimes guilty of anti-semitism. Many collections of his articles were published, including his two volumes on the metaphysics of Christianity, *Tëmnyi lik (Dark Face)* and *Liudi lunnogo sveta (People of the Moonlight)* (St Petersburg: Merkushev 1911), *Uedinënnoe (In Solitude)* (St Petersburg: Suvorin, 1912), and *Opavshie list'ia (Fallen Leaves)*, published in two bundles (St Petersburg: Surovin, 1913, 1915). These works have been recently republished in a two-volume edition of Rozanov's works (Moscow: Nauka, 1990). The principal theme of Rozanov's work is the affirmation of life, which informs his metaphysics of sex, and his critique of the church, which in its preoccupation with death, and its denial of the flesh, had robbed Christianity of joy. He died in poverty in 1919.

RUSSELL, BERTRAND (1872–1970). Bertrand Arthur William Russell studied mathematics at Trinity College, Cambridge. Although his earliest works were devoted to technical problems in logic and the philosophy of mathematics, he later wrote extensively and passionately on a vast range of subjects, including education, sex, morals, politics, economics, religion, literature, and history, in addition to works on philosophy. In 1916 he lost his post as lecturer in philosophy at Trinity College, and in 1918 he was imprisoned, because of his pacifist activities. He subsequently held academic posts in Chicago and California, visited China and Russia, founded a progressive school, and was active in such organisations as Pugwash, the Campaign for Nuclear Disarmament, and the International War Crimes Tribunal. In 1950 he was awarded the Order of Merit and the Nobel Prize for Literature. He died at the age of ninety-eight, having devoted his last years to establishing the Bertrand Russell Peace Foundation, and to protesting against the foreign policy of the United States, especially in Vietnam. His main works were: *The Principles of Mathematics* (Cambridge: Cambridge University Press, 1903, repr. 1937, London: George Allen and Unwin); 'On Denoting' (*Mind* 14 (1905): 479–93, reprinted 1956 in B. A. W. Russell (ed. R. C. Marsh), *Logic and Knowledge*, London: George Allen and Unwin, 41–56); with A. N. Whitehead, *Principia Mathematica* (3 vols., Cambridge: Cambridge University Press, 1910–1913); 'Knowledge by Acquaintance and Knowledge by Description' (*Proceedings of the Aristotelian Society* 11 (1911): 108–28); *Theory of Knowledge* (1913, posthumously published 1984 in B. A. W. Russell (ed. E. R. Eames), *The Collected Papers of Bertrand Russell*, vol. VII, *Theory of Knowledge: The 1913 Manuscript*, London: George Allen and Unwin); 'On the Nature of Acquaintance' *Monist* 24 (1914): repr. 1956 in B. A. W. Russell (ed. R. C. Marsh) *Logic and Knowledge* (London: George Allen and Unwin, 127–74); *Our Knowledge of the External World as a Field for Scientific Method in Philosophy* (London: George Allen and Unwin, 1914); 'The Philosophy of Logical Atomism', *Monist* 28 (1918); repr. 1956 in B. A. W. Russell (ed. R. C. Marsh), *Logic and Knowledge*, London: George Allen and Unwin, 177–281); *The Analysis of Mind* (London: George Allen and Unwin, 1921); *The Analysis of Matter* (New York: Harcourt Brace and London: Kegan Paul, 1927); *An Enquiry into Meaning and Truth* (New York: Norton and London: George Allen and Unwin, 1940); *Human Knowledge, its Scope and Limits* (London: George Allen and Unwin, 1958).

Secondary literature: Ayer, A. J. (1971), *Russell and Moore: The Analytical Heritage*, London: Macmillan and (1972), *Russell*, London: Fontana/Collins; Clark, R. W. (1975), *The Life of Bertrand Russell*, London: Jonathan Cape and Weidenfeld and Nicolson; Evans, G. (1982), *The Varieties of Reference*, Oxford: Oxford University Press; Hylton, P. (1990), *Russell, Idealism, and the Emergence of Analytic Philosophy*, Oxford: Clarendon Press; Kneale, W. C. and Kneale, M. (1962), *The Development of Logic*, Oxford: Oxford University Press; Orstertag, G. (ed.) (1998), *Definite Descriptions. A Reader*, Cambridge, MA: MIT Press; Pears, D. F. (1967), *Bertrand Russell and the*

British Tradition in Philosophy, New York: Random House; Sainsbury, R. M. (1979), *Russell*, London: Routledge.

SANTAYANA, GEORGE (1863–1952). Santayana combined the aspiration to a systematic metaphysics characteristic of nineteenth-century idealism with a twentieth-century affirmation of realism and naturalism. He was born in Spain, but moved to the United States as a child. He studied at Harvard and became a professor of philosophy there; but he retired in 1912 and spent the rest of his life in Europe, mostly in Rome. In his first work, *The Sense of Beauty* (New York: C. Scribner's, 1896), he criticised idealist aesthetic theories and argued for a naturalist account of aesthetic appreciation. In the five volumes of *The Life of Reason* (New York: C. Scribner's, 1905–6) he gives a naturalist account of the place of reason and value in human life. His later writings, such as *The Realms of Being* (New York: C. Scribner's, 1927–40), start from a 'critical realist' epistemology and then set out an ambitious ontology, based around a theory of essences and absolute truth.

Secondary literature: Sprigge, T. L. S. (1995), *Santayana*, London: Routledge.

SARTRE, JEAN-PAUL (1905–80). Sartre was educated at the Ecole normale supérieure and took first place at the *agrégation de philosophie* in 1929. His first novel was *La Nausée* (Paris: Gallimard, 1938). A philosopher, novelist, playwright, political commentator, activist, biographer, in short, the 'complete intellectual' Sartre's main philosophical works were *L'être et le néant* (Paris: Gallimard, 1943), *Critique de la raison dialectique* (Paris: Gallimard, 1958–1960) and his autobiography: *Les Mots* (Paris: Gallimard, 1964).

Secondary literature: see *The Cambridge Companion to Sartre* (Cambridge: Cambridge University Press, 1992).

SCHELER, MAX (1874–1928). Scheler gained his doctorate on logical and moral principles at Jena in 1899 and his *Habilitation* on transcendental and psychological method in 1900. He was *Privatdozent* at Jena from 1899 to 1906 and at Munich from 1906 to 1910, professor in Cologne from 1919 to 1928 and was appointed professor of philosophy and sociology at Frankfurt on Main, 1928. Scheler's works are re-issued in the edition of the *Gesammelte Werke* (Berne: Francke, 1954–).

Secondary literature: For a bibliography, see Frings, M. S. (ed.) (1974), *Max Scheler (1874–1928) Centennial Essays*, The Hague: Nijhoff.

SCHILLER, F. C. S. (1864–1937). Born in 1864, Schiller studied at Cornell University and was a fellow of Corpus Christi College, Oxford. He defended pragmatic humanism and was the most distinguished pragmatist outside the United States. He finished his career at the University of Southern California and died in 1937. His main works were *Riddles of the Sphinx: A Study of the Philosophy of Evolution* (London: Swan Sonnenschein, 1891); *Humanism* (London: Macmillan, 1903); *Logic for Use* (London: G. Bell, 1929); *Must Philosophers Disagree?* (London: Macmillan, 1934).

Secondary literature: Abel, R. (1955), *The Pragmatic Humanism of F. C. S. Schiller*, New York: King's Crown Press; and Thayer, H. S. (1968), *Meaning and Action: A Critical History of Pragmatism*, Indianapolis: Bobbs-Merrill.

SCHLICK, FRIEDRICH ALBERT MORITZ (1882–1936). Schlick was an important contributor to logical empiricism and the convenor of the Vienna Circle. He began his academic career as a physicist, but his work became increasingly philosophical and in 1922 he was appointed to the chair of 'natural philosophy' at Vienna, where he was assassinated in 1936. His first works were inspired by Einstein's new theories of space and time. He then turned to the epistemology of natural science in his *Allgemeine Erkenntnislehre* (Berlin: Springer Verlag, 1918, trans. 1974 A. Blumberg and H. Feigl as *General Theory of Knowledge*), where he used the notion of 'implicit definition' to refine a conventionalist position. In his later writings Schlick turned increasingly to the relationship between language, experience, and knowledge. He endorsed the verification principle and used it to denounce traditional metaphysics; but he argued strongly for a conception of ineffable private experience as the basis for verification and for a correspondence theory of truth grounded upon these experiences. Other main works were *Raum und Zeit in der gegenwärtigen Physik* (Berlin: Springer, 1917, trans. 1979 P. Heath, 'Space and Time in Contemporary Physics' in M. Schlick, *Philosophical Papers*, vol. I, Dordrecht: Reidel, 207–69); *Allgemeine Erkenntnislehre* (Berlin: Springer, 1925, trans. of 2nd edn 1974 A. Blumberg and H. Feigl, *General Theory of Knowledge*, La Salle, IL: Open Court); 'Die Wende der Philosophie' (*Erkenntnis* I (1930): 4–11, trans. 1979 P. Heath, 'The Turning-Point in Philosophy' in M. Schlick, *Philosophical Papers*, vol. II, Dordrecht: Reidel, 154–60); 'Über das fundament der Erkenntnis' (*Erkenntnis* 4 (1934): 79–99, trans. 1979 P. Heath 'On the Foundation of Knowledge' in M. Schlick, *Philosophical Papers*, vol. II, Dordrecht: Reidel, 370–87).

Secondary literature: Oberdan, T. (1993), *Protocols, Truth and Convention*, Amsterdam: Rodopi.

SCHMITT, CARL (1888–1985). Born at Plettenberg in the Sauerland, Schmitt was raised as a Catholic, involved himself in Munich expressionist circles in his youth, studied law, and served as a legal counsellor to the German Army in the First World War. After the war he became a professor of law first at Bonn, then Berlin, and also worked in government, though he was privately critical of the evolution of the Weimar Republic and joined the Nazis in 1933. He wrote influential political and historical studies. Among the former are *Politische Theologie* (Munich: Duncker and Humboldt, 1922, 2nd edn 1934; trans. 1985 G. Schwab as *Political Theology*, Cambridge, MA: MIT Press). Among the latter are *Politische Romantik* (Munich: Dunker and Humboldt, 1919, 2nd edn 1925; trans. 1986 G. Oates as *Political Romanticism*, Cambridge, MA: MIT Press); *Römischer Katholizmus und Politische Forme* (Munich: Theatiner, 1925, trans. 1996 G. Ulmen as *Roman Catholicism and Political Form*, Westport, CT: Greenwood Press); *Der Begriff der Politische* (Berlin: Duncker and Humboldt, 1928, 2nd edn 1932, trans. 1976 G. Schwab, *The Concept of the Political*, New Brunswick, NJ: Rutgers University Press).

Important studies of him include J. Bendersky (1983), *Carl Schmitt: Theorist for the Reich*, Princeton: Princeton University Press; P. E. Gottfried (1990), *Carl Schmitt: Politics and Theory*, New York: Greenwood Press; and J. McCormick (1997), *Carl Schmitt's Critique of Liberalism: Against Politics as Technology*, Cambridge: Cambridge University Press.

SCHÜTZ, ALFRED (1899–1959). Like the methodological work of Max Weber, by whom he was greatly influenced, Schütz provided a systematic phenomenological approach to the methodological integration of the social sciences. His major work, *Der sinnhafte Aufbau der sozialen Welt* (Vienna: Springer Verlag 1932), provided a phenomenological analysis of the structures of the everyday life-world of the social actor from his or her mundane perspective. After emigrating to the United States in 1938, Schütz also wrote phenomenological studies of various sorts, such as the analysis of 'The Stranger' and of democracy and scientific expertise in 'The Well-Informed Citizen' (*Social Research*, 3, 1952; repr. 1964 in *Collected Papers*, vol. II, 120–34, The Hague: Nijhoff).

Secondary literature: Helmut Wagner's *Alfred Schütz: An Intellectual Biography* (Chicago: Chicago University Press. 1983) offers an overview of his work, while Maurice Natanson, *Anonymity: A Study in the Philosophy of Alfred Schütz* (Bloomington, IN: Indiana University Press, 1986) examines his social phenomenology.

SELLARS, ROY WOOD (1880–1973). An American critical realist and materialist who spent most of his life at the University of Michigan. He defended a version of scientific realism through the period when this was unfashionable and eventually passed the torch on to his son, Wilfrid, who was a very influential philosopher in his own right. Among his major works were *Critical Realism* (Chicago: Rand McNally, 1916), *Evolutionary Naturalism* (Chicago: Open Court, 1922), and *The Philosophy of Physical Realism* (New York: Macmillan, 1932).

Secondary literature: Delaney, C. F. (1969), *Mind and Nature: A Study of the Naturalistic Philosophies of Cohen, Woodbridge and Sellars*, Notre Dame, IN: University of Notre Dame Press.

SIDGWICK, HENRY (1838–1900). Born in Skipton, Yorkshire, on 31 May 1838. He was educated at Cambridge University, where he took all the top prizes in classics. In 1859 he was elected a fellow of Trinity College and retained a close association with Cambridge for the rest of his life, although he resigned his fellowship of Trinity on conscientious grounds in 1869. He was elected professor of moral philosophy in 1889 and was active in promoting university reform and the admission of women to Cambridge. He died on 28 August 1900. His chief ethical work is *The Methods of Ethics*, first published in 1874 (London: Macmillan, 7th edn 1907).

Secondary literature: Schneewind, J. B. (1977), *Sidgwick's Ethics and Victorian Moral Philosophy*, Oxford: Clarendon Press; Schultz, B. (1992), *Essays on Henry Sidgwick*, Cambridge: Cambridge University Press.

SKOLEM, THORALF (1887–1963). Skolem contributed to several areas of mathematics, particularly logic and number theory. His career was spent almost entirely at the University of Oslo, from which he received his doctorate in 1926. His name is attached to numerous theorems and concepts in logic, including the Löwenheim–Skolem theorem, the Skolem paradox, Skolem functions, and the Skolem normal form for satisfiability. Skolem came close to proving the completeness of first-order logic and was the first to establish the existence of non-isomorphic models of Peano arithmetic. His main works were: 'Einige Bemerkungen zur axiomatischen Begründung der Mengenlehre' (*Matematikerkongressen I Helsingfors 4–7 Juli 1922, Den femte skandinaviska matematikerkongressen, Redogorelse*, Helsinki: Akademiska Bokhandlen, 217–32, trans. S. Bauer-Mengelberg, 'Some Remarks on Axiomatized Set Theory', in van Heijenoort, *From Frege to Gödel*, Cambridge, MA: Harvard University Press); 'Über die Unmöglichkeit einer vollständigen Charakterisierung der Zahlenreihe mittels eines endlichen Axiomensystems' (*Norsk matematisk forenings skrifter* 247 (1933): 730–82), reprinted in *Selected Works in Logic* (ed. J. Fenstad, Oslo: Universitetsforlaget, 1970).

Secondary literature: van Heijenoort, J. (1967), *From Frege to Gödel, A Source Book in Mathematical Logic, 1879–1931*, Cambridge, MA: Harvard University Press.

SOLOVIEV, VLADIMIR SERGEEVICH (1853–1900). Soloviev's father was a prominent liberal historian, his mother came from an aristocratic Polish family, and his paternal grandfather was an Orthodox priest, a circumstance that helps explain his commitments to ecumenicalism and liberalism. A materialist in his youth, Soloviev studied science at Moscow University, but by

1872 his Christian faith had returned. After defending his candidate's thesis, *Krizis zapadnoi filosofii: protiv pozitivistov* (1874) (trans. 1996 B. Jakim *The Crisis of Western Philosophy: Against the Positivists*) (West Stockbridge, MA: Lindisfarne Press), he travelled to England and Egypt, where he experienced visions of Sophia. In 1878, he lectured on Godmanhood in St Petersburg and defended his doctoral dissertation in 1880. He was then briefly an academic, but resigned after he gave a public lecture appealing to Alexander III to spare the lives of his father's assassins. Thereafter, as an independent scholar, he wrote on the unity of the churches, on moral, legal, and political themes, on the nature of love, and on eschatology. He was an accomplished poet. Soloviev lived as a wandering scholar of no fixed abode. He is reputed to have had an otherworldly demeanour and was often taken for a priest. He had frequent visions and mystical experiences. Dostoevsky reputedly modelled Alyosha Karamazov on Soloviev. A twelve-volume Russian edition of Soloviev's works was reprinted in 1966–70, and a two-volume selection in 1988. English sources include *Lectures on Godmanhood* (London: Dennis Dobson, 1948), *The Meaning of Love* (West Stockbridge, MA: Lindisfarne Press, 1985), *The Crisis of Western Philosophy: Against the Positivists* (West Stockbridge, MA: Lindisfarne Press, 1996), and the excellent *A Solovyov Anthology* (London: SCM Press, 1950), which includes 'A Short Story of Antichrist'.

E. N. Trubetskoi, *Mirosozertsanie VI. S. Solov'ëva* (*Soloviev's Worldview*), Moscow: Medium, 1995 is the fullest account of Soloviev's life and thought. S. L. Frank ('Introduction', *A Solovyov Anthology*, ed. S. Rank, trans. N. Duddington, London: SCM Press, 1950, 9–31), N. O. Lossky (*History of Philosophy*, New York: International Universities Press, 1951, 81–133), and A. Walicki (*A History of Russian Thought from the Enlightenment to Marxism*, trans. Hilda Andrews-Rusiecka, Oxford: Oxford University Press, 1980, ch. 12 and *Legal Philosophies of Russian Liberalism*, Oxford: Clarendon Press, 1987, ch. 3) offer fascinating short accounts.

SPENCER, HERBERT (1820–1903). Spencer was born in Derby on 27 April 1820. After leaving school he worked as an engineer building the London-to-Birmingham railway; the fossils he found while doing so first interested him in what he later called 'evolution'. In 1848 he moved to London and was a sub-editor on *The Economist*. In 1860 he set out the prospectus of his *System of Synthetic Philosophy*, and after this the rest of his life is mainly the story of his struggle to bring this enormous project to completion. Racked by ill-health and nervous troubles which prevented him from working, Spencer lived as a semi-recluse, dictating parts of the system between bouts of the violent activity he engaged in to circumvent his nervous troubles. The system was finally completed in 1896 and Spencer died on 8 December 1903, having consistently refused honours and academic appointments. Spencer's chief ethical works are *The Data of Ethics* of 1879 and *The Principles of Ethics* (London: Williams and Norgate, 1897), a two-volume work, of which vol. I is a reissue of *The Data of Ethics* (1879). But his main achievement is his *System of Synthetic Philosophy* (6 vols., London: Williams and Norgate, 1862–96).

Secondary literature: Peal, J. D. Y. (1971), *Herbert Spencer, The Evolution of a Sociologist*, London: Heinemann.

STEPHEN, LESLIE (1832–1904). Born in London on 28 November 1832. Stephen's university education was at Trinity Hall in Cambridge, where he became a fellow in 1854 as well as an Anglican clergyman. Both these positions he resigned from for conscientious reasons and after 1864 earned his living as a journalist and writer in London. He was editor of the *Dictionary of National Biography*. A keen walker and climber, who made several first ascents in the Alps, Stephen died on 22 February 1904. His chief ethical work is *The Science of Ethics* (London: Smith, Elder, 1882).

Secondary literature: Annan, N. (1984), *Leslie Stephen: The Godless Victorian*, London: Weidenfeld and Nicolson.

STEVENSON, C. L. (1908–79). Born in 1908, Stevenson studied at Yale University, majoring in English literature. He went on to Cambridge to continue in English, but was attracted to philosophy by Moore and Wittgenstein. He took a BA in philosophy at Cambridge before moving to Harvard for his doctoral work. He then taught at Harvard for a short while before moving to Yale in 1939 and then in 1946 to the University of Michigan at Ann Arbor, where he spent the rest of his working life. His main works were: *Ethics and Language* (New Haven, CT: Yale University Press, 1944); *Facts and Values* (New Haven, CT: Yale University Press, 1963).

Secondary literature: Goldman, A. and Kim, J. (eds.) (1978), *Values and Morals: Essays in Honor of William Frankena, Charles Stevenson, and Richard Brandt*, Dordrecht: Reidel.

STOUT, GEORGE FREDERICK (1860–1944). Born in South Shields, Stout studied in Cambridge from 1879 onwards. In 1884 he was appointed University Lecturer in the Moral Sciences at Cambridge, where he remained until 1896. Among his students were G. E. Moore and Bertrand Russell. Between 1891 and 1920 he was editor of *Mind*. From 1896 to 1899 he taught in Aberdeen, and between 1903 and 1936 he was a professor in St Andrews. The last period of his life he spent in Sydney as professor in moral and political philosophy. His works include *Analytic Psychology* (London: Swan Sonnenschein, 1896), *A Manual of Psychology* (London and New York: University Correspondence College Press, 1899), *Studies in Philosophy and Psychology* (London: Macmillan, 1930), *Mind and Matter* (Cambridge: Cambridge University Press, 1931).

Secondary literature: Passmore, J. (1957), *A Hundred Years of Philosophy*, London: Duckworth; van der Schaar, M. (1991), *G. F. Stout's Theory of judgement and proposition*, Leiden (no publisher).

STUMPF, CARL (1848–1936). Born in Wiesentheid (Germany), Stumpf studied in Würzburg under Brentano. From 1873 he was professor in Würzburg and later, between 1879 and 1884 a professor in Prague. From 1884 to 1894 he was a professor in Halle (where his students included Husserl) and in Munich. From 1894 he was a professor in Berlin, where he established the renowned Institute of Psychology, and where his students Wolfgang Köhler, Kurt Koffka, and Max Wertheimer founded the so-called Berlin school of Gestalt psychology. His writings include: *Über den psychologischen Ursprung der Raumvorstellung* (Leipzig: Hirzel, 1873), *Tonpsychologie* (Leipzig, 1883), 'Zur Einteilung der Wissenschaften' (in *Abhandlungen der Königlichen Preussischen Akademie der Wissenschaften*, Phil.-hist. Kl., 4, 1907) and *Erkenntnistheorie* (Leipzig: Barth 1939/40).

Secondary literature: Smith, B. (ed.) (1988), *Foundations of Gestalt Theory*, Munich: Philosophia.

TAINE, HIPPOLYTE-ADOLPHE (1828–93). He was born in Vouziers in 1828, into a provincial middle-class family. His father was a solicitor. His talents took him to Paris, where he attended the Ecole Normale Supérieure, but despite his brilliance, failed the *agrégé* examination because of his radical opinions. For several years he taught in provincial schools, travelling in Italy and especially England. His outspoken criticisms of both the revolutionaries and of the conservatives did not endear him to the authorities of the Second Empire. He left teaching for a life of private tutoring and journalism from 1852 to 1863. In 1864 he became professor of aesthetics at the Ecole des Beaux Arts. But his clashes with the establishment continued and he was elected a member of the Académie Française only in 1878. His writings were influential both on psychologists such as Pierre Janet, while his criticisms of the revolutionaries were admired by Catholic traditionalists.

He died in Paris in 1893. His main works were: *Le Positivism Anglais* (Paris: Balliere, trans. 1896 J. Durand, *Lectures on Art*, New York: Holt); *Philosophie de l'Art* (21st edn, Paris: Hachette, 1865).

Secondary literature: Charlton, D. G. (1959), *Positivist Thought in France during the Second Empire: 1852–1870*, Oxford: Clarendon Press.

TANABE, HAJIME (1885–1962). A member of the Kyoto School, Tanabe was trained in Western logic, epistemology, and the philosophy of science. Appointed to Kyoto University in 1919, Tanabe spent 1922–3 studying with Alois Riehl and then Edmund Husserl in Germany. Critical of Nishida's logic of place, Tanabe constructed his own logic of species. When applied to social thought, that philosophy gave special priority to cultural and ethnic identity. Tanabe later regretted the political implications of his theory and wrote a new philosophy in 1946, his *Zangedō to shite no tetsugaku* (Tokyo: Iwanani Shoten, trans. 1988 Takauchi Yoshinori *et al.*, *Philosophy as Metanoetics*, Berkeley, CA: University of California Press), in which he argued that philosophies should contain their own critical apparatus to prevent themselves from being absolutised.

TARSKI, ALFRED (1901–83). Tarski was primarily a logician and developed the basic framework for model theory; his main importance for philosophy lies in his definition of truth. He was born in Warsaw, and studied mathematics at the University of Warsaw, where he was appointed a lecturer in 1926. In 1939 he visited the United States, and stayed there for the rest of his life, holding a chair at Berkeley from 1942 until 1968.

His definitions of truth (1933) and logical consequence (1936) provide the basis for contemporary model theory. Although philosophers at the time regarded these papers as primarily of technical interest, they are now recognised as raising critical issues – for example, can truth be defined? What, if anything, is special about logical truth? His main works were: *Pojęcie prawdy w językach nauk dedukcyjnych* (Prace Towarzystwa Naukowego Warszawskiego, 1933, wydial III, no. 34, trans. 1956 J. H. Woodger, 'The Concept of Truth in Formalized Languages', in A. Tarski, *Logic, Semantics, Metamathematics. Papers from 1923–1938*, Oxford: Clarendon Press); 'über den Begriff der logischen Folgerung' (1936; trans. 1956 J. H. Woodger, 'On the Concept of Logical Consequence', in *Logic, Semantics, Metamathematics*); 'The Semantic Conception of Truth', *Philosophy and Phenomenological Research*, 4: 341–75, 1944).

Secondary literature: Field, H. (1972), 'Tarski's Theory of Truth', *Journal of Philosophy* 69, 347–75.

TURING, ALAN (1912–54). Turing was a seminal figure in the development of recursion theory and computer science, as well as a brilliant cryptanalyst who led the successful British assault on the German 'Enigma' cipher during the Second World War. His abstract model of a universal computing machine and his demonstration of the unsolvability of the halting problem provided a new and remarkably perspicuous perspective on the undecidability results of Gödel and Church, and led to the general acceptance of Church's Thesis. Turing also contributed to the practical design and construction of the two of the earliest general-purpose digital computers. His main work was: 'On Computable Numbers, with an Application to the Entscheidungsproblem' (Proceedings of the London Mathematical Society 42 (1937): 230–65; Correction 43: 544–6).

Secondary literature: Herken, R. (1988), *The Universal Turing Machine*, Oxford: Oxford University Press; Hodges, A. (1983), *Alan Turing: The Enigma*, New York: Simon and Schuster.

TWARDOWSKI, KAZIMIERZ (1866–1938) was born in Vienna into a Polish family. Between 1885 and 1889 he studied at the University of Vienna under Franz Brentano. Six years later, after his habilitation degree, he was appointed a professor in Lvov, where he remained until 1930 and where he established the Polish school of philosophy known as the Lvov-Warsaw School. His students, including Stanislaw Leśniewski, Jan Łukasiewicz, Tadeusz Kotarbiński, and Roman Ingarden, became professors of philosophy in almost all the Polish universities. Twardowski also founded the first Polish laboratory of experimental psychology (in 1907) and stimulated the development of scientific psychology in Poland. His main works include: *Idee und Perzeption: eine Erkenntnis-theoretische Untersuchung aus Descartes* (Dissertation, Vienna: W. Konogen, 1891), *Zur Lehre vom Inhalt und Gegenstand der Vorstellungen: Eine Psychologische Untersuchung* (Vienna: Hölder, 1894), 'O tak zwanych prawdach względnych' (1900) and 'O czynnościach i wytworach' (Lvov: Uniwersytat Lwowski, 1912).

Secondary literature: Woleński, J. (1989), *Logic and Philosophy in the Lvov-Warsaw School*, Dordrecht/Boston/Lancaster: Kluwer; Smith, B. (1994), *Austrian Philosophy*, Chicago: Open Court.

TYLOR, E. B. (1832–1917). Tylor's definition of 'culture' as 'the complex whole which includes knowledge, belief, art, morals, law, custom, and any other capabilities and habits acquired by man as a member of society' (*Primitive Culture*, London: Murray, 1871, 1) helped to earn him the title of 'founder of modern anthropology'. He worked to establish anthropology as an academic discipline, serving as Keeper of Oxford's university museum and later as a professor of anthropology in Oxford. His other main work was *Researches into the Early History of Mankind and the Development of Civilization* (London, 1865).

UNAMUNO (Y JUGO), MIGUEL DE (1864–1936). Unamuno was born in Bilbao and studied there and at the University of Madrid. In 1891 he became professor of Greek at the University of Salamanca; he was Rector of the University, first during the period from 1901 to 1914 and then after 1934. Because of his criticisms of both Primo de Rivera's and Franco's dictatorships, he was exiled to the Canary Islands in 1924 and then brutally humiliated by Franco a few months before his death in 1936. Unamuno mastered fourteen languages and published novels, plays, journalism, and poems as well as philosophy. His main works were: *Vida de Don Quijote y Sancho* (1905 trans.: *Our Lord Don Quixote and Sancho with Related Essays*, Princeton, NJ: Princeton University Press, 1967); *Del sentimiento trágico de la vida en los hombres y en los pueblos* (Madrid: Renacimiento, 1913, trans. 1921 J. E. Crawford-Flitch, *The Tragic Sense of Life*, London); *La agonía del cristianismo* (Madrid: Compania Ibero Americana de Publicaciones, 1925; trans. 1974 A. Kerrigan, *The Agony of Christianity and Essays of Faith*, Princeton, NJ: Princeton University Press); *San Manuel Bueno, mártir* (Madrid: Espasa Calpe, 1933, trans. 1956 A. Kerrigan, 'Saint Emmanuel the Good Martyr', in *Abel Sánchez and Other Histories*, Chicago: Regnery).

Secondary literature: Nozick, M. (1971), *Miguel de Unamuno*, New York: Twayne.

VAIHINGER, HANS. (1852–1933). Hans Vaihinger was born near Tübingen in 1852. He began his original work *Die Philosophie des Als-Ob* in 1876 but it was not published until 1911 (Aalen: Scientia Verlag). He published his massive and still useful *Kommentar zur Kants Kritik der reinen Vernunft* (Aalen: Scientia Verlag) in 1881 and 1892; however, it covers only the first seventy-five pages of *The Critique of Pure Reason*. Vaihinger is also important for beginning *Kant-Studien* in 1897 and the *Kant Gesellschaft* in 1904. He suffered from a number of illnesses and had bad eyesight, but continued to work. He died in 1933.

VON MISES, RICHARD (1883–1953). A German-American applied mathematician and positivist philosopher, von Mises's philosophical career began around 1920 with the denial of the universal validity of classical mechanics on the ground that it lacks empirical content on the microscopic level. To accommodate the ensuing indeterminism in a scientific world view he developed a statistical theory of probability. His main work was *Wahrscheinlichkeit, Statistik und Wahrheit* (Vienna: Springer, 1928, trans. 1957 as *Probability, Statistics and Truth*, New York: Dover).

Secondary source: von Plato, J. (1994), *Creating Modern Probability. Its Mathematics, Physics and Philosophy in Historical Perspective*, Cambridge: Cambridge University Press.

WATSUJI, TETSURŌ (1889–1960). After graduating from Tokyo University in 1912, Watsuji published books on Nietzsche, Kierkegaard, and Schopenhauer and then studied in Germany from 1927 to 1928. Critical of Heidegger for ignoring the cultural, social, and geographical aspects of philosophy, Watsuji turned his attention to the interface of culture and thought in both East and West, with such representative works as *Fudo* (*Climate*, Tokyo: Iwanami Shoten, 1935) and his two-volume 1952 work *Nihon rinri shisōshi* (*A History of Japanese Ethical Thought*, Tokyo: Iwanami Shoten). Moving to Tokyo University from his position at Kyoto University in 1934, Watsuji focused his energies on developing a new theoretical model of ethics published in his three-volume *Rinrigaku* (*Ethics*, Tokyo: Iwanami Shoten) published in 1937, 1942, and 1949. He argued for an understanding of human existence as a 'betweenness' between inherited social values and individual human autonomy.

Secondary literature: Dilworth, D. A. (1974), 'Watsuji Tetsurō: Cultural Phenomenologist and Ethician', *Philosophy East and West* 24.

WEBER, MAX (1864–1920). Weber was the leading German sociologist of the pre-First World War era, with diverse writings on economics, law, methodology, religion, and morality. His most systematic work is *Wirtschaft und Gesellschaft* (Tübingen: Mohr) (*Economy and Society*), published posthumously in 1922, in which he provides a macro-sociological explanation of the development of modern societies as a process of rationalisation. His methodological writings sought to unify interpretive and explanatory approaches and to develop causal and meaning adequacy as twin criteria of good social science. Weber was also a leading political figure of his age, defending a form of liberal nationalism that emerges not only in his political essays but in his understanding of science and politics as professions or vocations in modern societies (*Gesammelte Aufsätze zur Wissenschaftslehre*, Tübingin: Mohr, 1922). His other main works include *Gesammelte Politische Schriften*, Münich: Drei' Masken Verlag, 1921.

Secondary literature: In *On the Logic of the Social Sciences* (1967) Habermas shows the central importance of Weber's pluralism in the later discussions of social science methodology. Regis Factor and Stephen Turner provide the context for Weber's view of reason and the role of values in social science in *Max Weber and the Dispute over Reason and Value* (London: Routledge, 1984).

WERTHEIMER, MAX (1880–1943). Wertheimer was the founder and spiritual leader of the Gestalt psychology school. Gestalt psychology began with studies of apparent motion carried out by Wertheimer, with Wolfgang Köhler and Kurt Koffka as subjects. He studied with Carl Stumpf in Berlin, but took his PhD with Oswald Kölpe at Würzburg. He taught at various German universities, but left Germany in 1933 as the Nazis came to power, emigrating to the United States, taking a position at the New School for Social Research in New York. Though productive in ideas, Wertheimer published little, his major work being the posthumous *Productive Thinking* (New York: Harper and Row, 1945), a study of creativity and problem solving.

WHITEHEAD, ALFRED NORTH (1861–1947). Whitehead began his career in England. In 1884 he was appointed to Trinity College, Cambridge, to teach mathematics and in 1910 he moved to London as a professor of applied mathematics. But in 1924 (aged sixty-three) he moved again, this time to the United States to take up a position at Harvard as professor of philosophy. He retired in 1937.

Whitehead's first work (*A Treatise on Universal Algebra*, Cambridge: Cambridge University Press, 1898) was in the field of abstract algebra; logic was at this time closely allied to algebra, so it was no surprise that Russell turned to Whitehead as a collaborator for his logicist project *Principia Mathematica* (Cambridge: Cambridge University Press, 1910–13). Whitehead then turned to philosophy of science, applying mathematical logic to the construction of space and time in *The Concept of Nature* (Cambridge: Cambridge University Press, 1920). His later work is dominated by *Process and Reality* (Cambridge: Cambridge University Press, 1929, corrected edn, New York: The Free Press, 1978) in which Whitehead sets out an idiosyncratic quasi-mathematical metaphysics of serial processes through which actual occasions are unified as apparent objects in accordance with various categories.

Secondary literature: Lowe, V. (1966). *Understanding Whitehead*, Baltimore, MD: Johns Hopkins University Press.

WINDELBAND, WILHELM (1848–1915). A German philosopher and historian, Windelband was born in Potsdam in 1848. He was an important student of Kuno Fischer and was considered, along with Dilthey, the most important historian of philosophy in the nineteenth century. He taught at Zurich, Freiburg, Strasburg, and finally in 1903 he took Fischer's chair of philosophy at Heidelberg. He is best remembered for his history of philosophy, written not in chronological order but by problems (1892, *Geschichte der Philosophie*, Friesburg and successive editions) and his Rector's speech in Strasburg in 1894: *Geschichte und Naturwissenschaft* (in *Präludien*, Tübingen: J. C. B. Mohr, 1924). He died in 1915.

Secondary literature: Köhnke, K. C. (1986). *Entstehung und Aufstieg des Neu-Kantianismus*, Frankfurt: Suhrkamp, trans. 1991 by R. J. Hollingdale as *The Rise of Neo-Kantianism*, Cambridge: Cambridge University Press.

WITTGENSTEIN, LUDWIG JOSEF JOHANN (1889–1951). By common consent the greatest philosopher of the twentieth century, Wittgenstein was born in Vienna; he studied with Russell in Cambridge from 1911 until 1914. After fighting with the Austro-Hungarian army, he became a school-teacher. In 1927 he returned to Cambridge, where he became professor of philosophy in 1939. He withdrew and did hospital work during the Second World War. He returned to Cambridge in 1945 but retired in 1947. He then lived mainly in Ireland before returning finally to Cambridge, where he died in 1951. Wittgenstein's first main work, written during the First World War while he was a soldier, is the *Tractatus Logico-Philosophicus* (1921). It is an enquiry into the limits of sense, based in logic but supposedly also indicating a role for ethics, as that which cannot be 'said' but can only be 'shown' by the course of one's life. His writings from the 1930s are distilled into his *Philosophical Investigations* (1953), in which he again explores the limits of language and seeks to show that philosophical problems characteristically arise from a failure to grasp the structure of our ordinary language-games. His main works were: 'Logische-philosophische Abhundlung' (*Annalen der Naturphilosophie* 1921, trans. 1922 C. K. Ogden as *Tractatus Logico-Philosophicus*, London: Routledge; rev. trans. 1961 D. F. Pears and B. F. McGuiness, London: Routledge); *Philosophische Untersuchungen* (1953, ed. G. E. M. Anscombe and R. Rhees, trans. G. E. M. Anscombe as *Philosophical Investigations*, Oxford: Blackwell).

Secondary literature: Anscombe, G. E. M. (1971), *An Introduction to Wittgenstein's Tractatus*, London: Hutchinson; Pears, D. F. (1987), *The False Prison*, 2 vols., Oxford: Oxford University Press.

WOODBRIDGE, F. J. E. (1867–1940). An American naturalist metaphysician in the tradition of Aristotle and Spinoza, who spent most of his academic years at Columbia. He was one of the founders of *The Journal of Philosophy* and among his works were *The Realm of Mind* (New York: Columbia University Press, 1926), *Nature and Mind* (New York: Columbia University Press, 1937), and *An Essay on Nature* (New York: Columbia University Press, 1940).

Secondary literature: Delaney, C. F. (1969), *Mind and Nature: A Study of the Naturalistic Philosophies of Cohen, Woodbridge and Sellars*, Notre Dame, IN: University of Notre Dame Press.

WUNDT, WILHELM (1832–1920). Wundt studied physiology at Heidelberg (1852–56), with a semester in Berlin under Johannes Müller and Emil Du Bois-Reymond. From 1858 to 1865 he was Helmholtz's assistant in teaching laboratory physiology; he also taught courses in anthropology and 'psychology as a natural science', and published his *Beiträge zur Theorie der Sinneswahrnehmung* (Leipzig: C. F. Winter'sche Verlagshandlung, 1862) and *Vorlesungen ber Menschen- und Thierseele* (Leipzig: Voss, 1863). Appointed extraordinary professor at Heidelberg in 1872, in 1874 he assumed the Zurich chair of 'inductive philosophy' and published *Grundzüge der physiologischen Psychologie* (Leipzig: Engelmann, 1874). In 1875 he moved to Leipzig, where he taught as a psychologist and philosopher, retiring in 1917 at the age of eighty-five. He published many works in both fields.

Secondary literature: Hatfield, G. (1997), 'Wundt and Psychology as science: Disciplinary Transformations', *Perspectives on Science* 5: 349–82.

ZERMELO, ERNST (1871–1953). Zermelo is best known for his recognition of the role of the axiom of choice in mathematical arguments, for his use of that axiom to prove that every set can be well ordered, and for his axiomatisation of set theory (later modified by Abraham Fraenkel). Zermelo earned his doctorate at the University of Berlin in 1894 and later taught in Zurich and Freiburg im Breisgau. Zermelo's conception of quantifiers as infinitary connectives led him to criticise the works of Skolem and Gödel. His main works were: 'Beweis, dass jede Menge wohlgeordnet werden kann' (*Mathematische Annalen* 59 (1904): 514–16); 'Untersuchungen über die Grundlagen der Mengenlehre I' (*Mathematische Annalen* 65 (1908): 261–81).

Secondary literature: Moore, G. (1982), *Zermelo's Axiom of Choice: Its Origins, Development and Influence*, New York/Heidelberg/Berlin: Springer Verlag.

BIBLIOGRAPHY

CHAPTER 1 POSITIVIST THOUGHT IN THE NINETEENTH CENTURY

Austeda, F. (1967). 'Avenarius', trans. A. E. Blumberg. In P. Edwards (ed.), *The Encyclopedia of Philosophy*, New York: Macmillan.

Avenarius, R. (1888–90). *Kritik der reinen Erfahrung (Critique of Pure Experience)*, Leipzig: O.R. Reisland.

Blackmore, J. T. (1995). *Ludwig Boltzmann; his Later Life and Philosophy*, Dordrecht and London: Kluwer.

Cahan, D. (1993). *Herman von Helmholtz and the Foundations of Nineteenth Century Science*, Berkeley and London: University of California Press.

Charlton, D. G. (1959). *Positivist Thought in France during the Second Empire: 1852–1870*, Oxford: Clarendon Press.

Comte, A. (1830–42). *Cours de Philosophie Positive*, Paris: Baillière. Trans. (in part) 1853 H. Martineau, *The Positive Philosophy of Auguste Comte*, London: Chapman.

Comte, A. (1852). *Catéchisme Posìtiviste*, Paris. Trans. 1858 R. Congreve, *The Catechism of Positive Religion*, London: Chapman.

Haeckel, E. H. P. A. (1874). *Anthropogenie oder Entwicklungsgeschichte des Menschen*, Leipzig: W. Engelmann. Trans. 1905 J. McCabe, *The Evolution of Man*, London: Watts.

Haeckel, E. H. P. A. (1899). *Die Weltrathsel*, Bonn: Strauss. Trans. 1900 J. McCabe, *The Riddle of the Universe*, London: Watts.

Hegel, G. W. F. (1830). *Enzyklopädie der philosophischen Wissenschaften im Grundrisse*, II: *Naturphilosophie*, Heidelberg: Winter. Trans. 1970 A. V. Miller, *The Philosophy of Nature*, Oxford: Clarendon Press.

Hertz, H. R. (1894). *Die Prinzipien der Mechanik*. Trans. 1899 D. E. Jones and J. T. Whalley, *The Principles of Mechanics*, London: Macmillan.

Huxley, T. H. (1863). *Evidence as to Man's Place in Nature*, London: Williams and Norgate.

Lenin, V. I. (1920). *Materialism and Empirio-criticism*, London: Martin Lawrence.

Mach, E. (1883). *Die Mechanik in ihrer Entwicklung historisch-critisch dergestellt*, Prague. Trans. 1893 T. J. McCormack, *The Science of Mechanics*, Chicago: Open Court.

Mach, E. (1886 [1906]). *Die Analyse der Empfindungen*, 5th edn, Jena. Trans. 1914 C. M. Williams and J. Waterlow, *The Analysis of Sensations*, Chicago: Open Court.

Mach, E. (1894). *Populärwissenschaftliche Vorlesungen*, Leipzig: J. A. Borth. Trans. 1894 T. J. McCormack, *Popular Scientific Lectures*, Chicago: Open Court.

Mill, J. S. (1843). *A System of Logic, Ratiocinative and Inductive*, 5th edn 1862, London: John Parker.

Passmore, J. (1957). *A Hundred Years of Philosophy*, London: Duckworth.

Paulsen, F. (1893). 'Wesen und geschichtliche entwicklung der deutschen universitaten' in W. Lexis (ed.), *Die deutschen universitaten*, Berlin: A. Asher. Trans. 1895 E. D. Perry, *The German Universities: Their Character and Historical Development*.

Pearson, K. (1892). *The Grammar of Science*, London: Walter Scott.

Peirce, C. S. (1892). Review of 'The Grammar of Science', *Nation* 55: 15.

Spencer, H. (1862–96). *System of Synthetic Philosophy* vols. I–VI, London: Williams and Norgate.

Spencer, H. (1862). *First Principles*, vol I of Spencer (1862–96). Repr. 1996, London: Routledge and Thoemmes.

Taine, H. (1864). *Le Positivisme Anglais*, Paris: Baillière. Trans. 1870 T. D. Haye, *English Positivism*, London: Simpkin, Marshall and Co.

Taine, H. (1865). *Philosophie de l'Art* Paris: Baillière. Trans. 1865, Taine, *The Philosophy of Art*, London: Baillière.

Turner, R. S. (1980). 'Helmholtz', *Dictionary of Scientific Biography*, vol. V, New York: Scribners, pp. 241–53.

Whewell, W. (1847). *The Philosophy of the Inductive Sciences*, 2nd edn, London: J. W. Parker. Repr. 1967, ed. J. Herival, New York and London: Johnson Reprint Corporation.

CHAPTER 2 NEO-KANTIANISM: THE GERMAN IDEALISM MOVEMENT

Adair-Toteff, C. S. (1994). 'The Neo-Kantian *Raum* Controversy', *The British Journal of the History of Philosophy* 2, no. 2: 131–48.

Adair-Toteff, C. S. (1996). 'Hans Vaihinger's *Kant-Studien*', *Kant-Studien* 87: 390–5.

Arnoldt, E. (1870). *Kants Transzendental Idealität des Raumes und der Zeit (Kant's Transcendental Ideality of Space and Time)*, Königsberg: Albert Rosbach.

Beck, L. W. (1967). 'Neo-Kantianism', *Encyclopedia of Philosophy*, ed. P. Edwards, vol. V, 468–73.

Cohen, H. (1870). 'Zur Controverse zwischen Trendelenburg und Kuno Fischer' ('On the Controversy between Trendelenburg and Kuno Fischer'), *Zeitschrift für Völkerpsychologie und Sprachwissenschaft* 7: 249–96.

Cohen, H. (1871). *Kants Theorie der Erfahrung (Kant's Theory of Experience)*, Berlin: Dümmler, 2nd edn 1885, 3rd edn 1918.

Cohen, H. (1877). *Kants Begründung der Ethik (Kant's Foundations of Ethics)*, Berlin: Dümmler.

Cohen, H. (1889). *Kants Begründung der Aesthetik (Kant's Foundations of Aesthetics)*, Berlin: Dümmler.

Cohen, H. (1902). *Logik der reinen Erkenntnis (Logic of Pure Knowledge)*, Berlin: Bruno Cassirer.

Cohen, H. (1904). *Ethik des reinen Willens (Ethics of Pure Will)*, Berlin: Bruno Cassirer.

Cohen, H. (1912). *Ästhetik des reinen Gefühls (Aesthetic of Pure Feeling)*, Berlin: Bruno Cassirer.

Fischer, K. (1860a). *Kants Leben und die Grundlagen seiner Lehre (Kant's Life and the Foundations of his Teaching)*, Heidelberg: Carl Winter's Universitätsbuchhandlung.

Fischer, K. (1860b). *Geschichte der neuern Philosophie (History of Modern Philosophy)*, Heidelberg: Carl Winter's Universitätsbuchhandlung.

Fischer, K. (1865). *System der Logik und Metaphysik oder Wissenschaftslehre (System of Logic and Metaphysics or the Doctrine of Science)*, 2nd edn, Heidelberg: Verlagsbuchhandlung von Friedrich Bassermann.

Fischer, K. (1870). *Anti-Trendelenburg*, Jena: Hermann Dabis.

Grappengiesser, C. (1870). *Kants Lehre von Raum und Zeit (Kant's Doctrine of Space and Time)*, Jena: Friedrich Mauke.

Holzhey, H. (1986). *Cohen und Natorp*, Basle and Stuttgart: Schwabe and Co. Ag. Verlag.

Kant, Immanuel (1781, 1787). *Critique of Pure Reason*. Trans. 1998 P. Guyer and A. Wood. Cambridge: Cambridge University Press.

Köhnke, K. C. (1986). *Entstehung und Aufstieg des Neu-Kantianismus*, trans. 1991 R. J. Hollingdale as *The Rise of Neo-Kantianism*, Cambridge: Cambridge University Press.

Lange, F. A. (1865). *Die Arbeiterfrage (The Question of the Worker)*, Winterthur: Bleuer-Hausheer, 3rd edn 1875.

Lange, F. A. (1866 [1887]). *Geschichte des Materialismus*. Iserlohn und Leipzig: Verlag von J. Baedeker. Trans. 1925 E. C. Thomas, *History of Materialism*, Boston, MA: Osgood.

Lask, E. (1924). *Fichtes Idealismus und die Geschichte (Fichte's Idealism and History)*. In *Gesammelte Schriften*, vol. I, ed. Eugen Herrigel, Tübingen: Verlag von J. C. B. Mohr (Paul Siebeck).

Liebmann, O. (1865). *Kant und die Epigonen (Kant and the Epigones)*, Stuttgart: Carl Schoben. Repr. 1965, Erlangen: Fischer.

Natorp, P. (1902). *Platons Ideenlehre (Plato's Doctrine of Ideas)*. Leipzig: Felix Meiner.

Natorp, P. (1912). 'Kant und die Marburger Schule' ('Kant and the Marburg School'), *Kant-Studien* 17: 193–221.

Oakes, G. (1988). *Weber and Rickert*, Cambridge, MA: MIT Press.

Ollig, H.-L. (1979). *Der neu-Kantianismus (Neo-Kantianism)*, Stuttgart: J. B. Metzlersche Verlags-buchhandlung.

Orth, E. W. and Holzhey, H. (1994). *Neu-Kantianismus (Neo-Kantianism)*, Würzburg: Könighausen and Neumann.

Rickert, H. (1902). *Die Grenzen der Wissenschaftlichen Begriffsbildung*, 1st edn 1902. Abridged and translated 1986 by Guy Oakes from the 5th edn (1929), *The Limits of Concept Formation in Natural Science*, Cambridge: Cambridge University Press.

Simmel, G. (1904). *Kant*, Leipzig: S. Hirzel.

Trendelenburg, F. A. (1840). *Logische Untersuchungen (Logical Investigations)*, Berlin: Gustav Bethge.

Trendelenburg, F. A. (1867). 'Über eine Lücke in Kants Beweis der ausschliessenden Subjectivität des Raumes und der Zeit *Ein kritisehes und anti-kritisches Blatt*' ('On a Gap in Kant's Proof of the Exclusive Subjectivity of Space and Time. A Critical and Anti-critical Page'), *Historische Beitrag zur Philosophie* 3: 214–76.

Trendelenburg, F. A. (1869). *Kuno Fischer und sein Kant (Kuno Fischer and his Kant)*, Leipzig: S. Hirzel.

Troeltsch, E. (1922). *Der Historismus und seine Probleme: Das logische Problem der Geschichtsphilosophie (Historicism and its Problems: The Logical Problem of the Philosophy of History)*, Tübingen: J. C. B. Mohr.

Vaihinger, H. (1882–92). *Kommentar zur Kants Kritik der reinen Vernunft (Commentary on Kant's Critique of Pure Reason)*, 2 vols. Stuttgart. Repr. 1970 Aalen: Scientia Verlag.

Vaihinger, H. (1902a). *Die Deduktion der Kategorien (The Deduction of the Categories)*, Halle a.S.: Max Niemeyer.

Vaihinger, H. (1902b). *Nietzsche als Philosophe (Nietzsche as Philosopher)*, Halle a.S.: Max Niemeyer.

Vaihinger, H. (1911). *Die Philosophie des Als Ob. System der theoretischen, praktischen und religiosen Fiktionen der Menschheit auf Grund'eines idealistischen Positivismus. Mit einem Anhang über Kant und Nietzsche*, 3rd edn, Leipzig: F. Meiner, 1918. Trans. 1924 C. Ogden, *Philosophy of 'As If': A System of the Theoretical, Practical and Religious Fictions of Mankind*, London: Routledge.

Volkelt, J. (1879). *Immanuel Kant's Erkenntnistheorie (Immanuel Kant's Theory of Cognition)*, Leipzig: Verlag von Leopold Voss.

Willey, T. (1987). *Back to Kant*, Detroit: Wayne State University Press.

Windelband, W. (1884). *Präludien (Preludes)*, 2 vols. Tübingen: J. C. B. Mohr.

Zeller, E. (1862). 'Über Bedeutung und Aufgabe der Erkenntnistheorie' ('On the Significance and Task of the Theory of Knowledge'), Heidelberg (Antrittsrede). Reprinted in *Vorträge und Abhandlungen*, Leipzig: Fues, 1865–84.

CHAPTER 3 IDEALISM IN BRITAIN AND THE UNITED STATES

Allard, J. (1998). 'The Essential Puzzle of Inference', *Bradley Studies* 4: 61–81.

Bosanquet, B. (1883). 'Logic as the Science of Knowledge' in A. Seth and R. B. Haldane (eds.), *Essays in Philosophical Criticism*, London: Longmans. 2nd edn 1928, corrected impression 1928.

Bosanquet, B. (1888, 1911). *Logic, or the Morphology of Knowledge*, Oxford: Clarendon Press. 2nd edn 1911.

Bosanquet, B. (1892). *A History of Aesthetic*, London: Swan Sonnenschein.

Bosanquet, B. (1899). *The Philosophical Theory of the State*, London: Macmillan. 4th edn 1923, repr. 1965.

Bosanquet, B. (1912). *The Principle of Individuality and Value, The Gifford Lectures for 1911*, London: Macmillan.

Bosanquet, B. (1913). *The Value and Destiny of the Individual, The Gifford Lectures for 1912*. London: Macmillan.

Bosanquet, B. (1920). *Implication and Linear Inference*, London: Macmillan.

Bosanquet, B. (1927). *Science and Philosophy and Other Essays*, ed. J. H. Muirhead and R. C. Bosanquet, London: Macmillan.

Bradley, F. H. (1876). *Ethical Studies*, Oxford: Clarendon Press. 2nd edn 1927.

Bradley, F. H. (1883). *The Principles of Logic*, Oxford: Clarendon Press. 2nd edn 1922; 2nd edn corrected 1928.

Bradley, F. H. (1893). *Appearance and Reality*, London: Swan Sonnenschein. 2nd edn 1897. Repr. 1930, Oxford: Clarendon Press.

Bradley, F. H. (1914). *Essays on Truth and Reality*, Oxford: Clarendon Press.

Bradley, F. H. (1935). *Collected Essays*, Oxford: Clarendon Press. New edn 1969.

Bradley, J. (1979). 'Hegel in Britain: A Brief History of British Commentary and Attitudes', *Heythrop Journal* 20: 1–24; 163–82.

Caird, E. (1877). *A Critical Account of the Philosophy of Kant*, Glasgow: Maclehose.

Caird, E. (1889). *The Critical Philosophy of Kant*, Glasgow: Maclehose.

Caird, E. (1893). *The Evolution of Religion*, Glasgow: Maclehose.

Caird, J. (1880). *Philosophy of Religion*, Glasgow: Maclehose.

Candlish, S. (1989). 'The Truth about F. H. Bradley', *Mind* 98: 331–48.

Clendenning, J. (1985). *The Life and Thought of Josiah Royce*, Madison: University of Wisconsin Press.

Cunningham, G. W. (1933). *The Idealistic Argument in Recent British and American Philosophy*, New York: Century Company.

Den Otter, S. M. (1996). *British Idealism and Social Explanation: A Study in Late Victorian Theory*, Oxford: Clarendon Press.

Eliot, T. S. (1964). *Knowledge and Experience in the Philosophy of F. H. Bradley*, London: Faber and Faber.

Freeden, M. (1996). *Ideologies and Political Theory: A Conceptual Approach*, Oxford: Clarendon Press.

Fuss, P. (1965). *The Moral Philosophy of Josiah Royce*, Cambridge, MA: Harvard University Press.

Green, T. H. (1868). 'Popular Philosophy in Relation to Life', *North British Review*, 45, 133–62. Repr. in Green (1885–9), vol. III, 92–125.

Green, T. H. (1874). 'General Introduction to Vol. I' and 'Introduction to Moral Part of the Treatise' in D. Hume, *Treatise of Human Nature* (ed. T. H. Green and T. H. Grose), London. Repr. in Green (1885–9), vol. I, 1–371.

Green, T. H. (1880). 'Review of J. Caird: *Introduction to the Philosophy of Religion*', Academy 18: 28–30. Repr. in Green 1885–9, vol. III, 138–46.

Green, T. H. (1881). *Liberal Legislation and Freedom of Contract: A Lecture*, Oxford and London: Slatter and Rose; Simpkin, Marshall. Repr. 1986 in P. Harris and J. Morrow (eds.), *T. H. Green: Lectures on the Principles of Political Obligation and Other Writings*, Cambridge: Cambridge University Press, 194–212.

Green, T. H. (1883a). *Prolegomena to Ethics*, Oxford: Clarendon Press. 5th edn 1907, Oxford: Clarendon Press.

Green, T. H. (1883b [1888]). *Witness of God and Faith: Two Lay Sermons* (ed. A. Toynbee), London: Longmans, Green.

Green, T. H. (1885–9). *Works of Thomas Hill Green*, ed. R. Nettleship, 3 vols. London: Longmans, Green.

Green, T. H. (1886). *Lectures on the Principles of Political Obligation* in R. L. Nettleship (ed.), *The Works of Thomas Hill Green*, vol. II (1888), London: Longmans, Green. Repr. 1986 in P. Harris and J. Morrow (eds.), *Lectures on the Principles of Political Obligation and Other Writings*, Cambridge: Cambridge University Press.

Greengarten, I. M. (1981). *Thomas Hill Green and the Development of Liberal-Democratic Thought*, Toronto: University of Toronto Press.

Hylton, P. (1990). *Russell, idealism, and the Emergence of Analytic Philosophy*, Oxford: Clarendon Press.

Ingardia, R. (ed.) (1991). *Bradley: A Research Bibliography*, Bowling Green: Philosophy Documentation Center.

Kempe, A. B. (1889–90). 'On the Relation between the Logical Theory of Classes and the Geometrical Theory of Points', *Proceedings of the London Mathematical Society* 21: 147–82.

Kuklick, B. (1972). *Josiah Royce: An Intellectual Biography*, Indianapolis: Bobbs-Merrill.

McBriar, A. M. (1987). *An Edwardian Mixed Doubles: The Bosanquets and the Webbs*, Oxford: Clarendon Press.

MacNiven, D. (1987). *Bradley's Moral Psychology*, Lewiston, NY: Edwin Mellen Press.

Mander, W. J. (1994). *An Introduction to Bradley's Metaphysics*, Oxford: Clarendon Press.

Mansel, H. L. (1856). *A Lecture on the Philosophy of Kant*, London: John Henry and James Parker. Reprinted 1873 in H. L. Mansel (ed. H. W. Chandler), *Letters, Lectures and Reviews*, London: John Murray.

Manser, A. (1982). *Bradley's Logic*, Totowa, NJ: Barnes and Noble.

Manser, A. and Stock, G. (eds.) (1984). *The Philosophy of F. H. Bradley*, Oxford: Clarendon Press.

Marcel, G. (1945). *La Métaphysique de Royce*, Paris: Aubier, Editions Montaigne. Trans. 1956 V. Ringer and G. Ringer, *Royce's Metaphysics*, Chicago: H. Regnery.

Masson, D. (1865). *Recent British Philosophy*, London: Macmillan. 3rd edn 1877.

Milne, A. J. M. (1962). *The Social Philosophy of English Idealism*, London: George Allen and Unwin.

Muirhead, J. H. (1931). *The Platonic Tradition in Anglo-Saxon Philosophy*, London: George Allen and Unwin and New York: Macmillan.

Nettleship, R. L. (1888). 'Memoir' in T. H. Green (ed. R. L. Nettleship), *The Works of Thomas Hill Green*, vol. III, London: Longmans, Green, xi–clxi.

Nicholson, P. P. (1978). 'A Bibliography of the Writings of Bernard Bosanquet (1848–1923)', *Idealistic Studies*, 8: 261–80.

Nicholson, P. P. (1990). *The Political Philosophy of the British Idealists*, Cambridge: Cambridge University Press.

Richter, M. (1964). *The Politics of Conscience*, London: Weidenfeld and Nicolson.

Royce, J. (1885). *The Religious Aspect of Philosophy*, Boston: Houghton Mifflin.

Royce, J. (1892). *The Spirit of Modern Philosophy*, Boston: Houghton Mifflin.

Royce, J. (1899). *The World and the Individual, First Series*, New York: Macmillan.

Royce, J. (1901). *The World and the Individual, Second Series*, New York: Macmillan.

Royce, J. (1905). 'The Relation of the Principles of Logic to the Foundations of Geometry', *Transactions of the American Mathematical Society*, 24: 353–415. Reprinted in 1951 J. Royce (D. S. Robinson, ed.), *Royce's Logical Essays*, Dubuque: Wm C. Brown.

Royce, J. (1908). *The Philosophy of Loyalty*, New York: Macmillan.

Royce, J. (1913). *The Problem of Christianity*, New York: Macmillan. Reprinted 1968, Chicago: University of Chicago Press.

Royce, J. (1970). *The Letters of Josiah Royce* (ed. J. Clendenning), Chicago: University of Chicago Press.

Seth, A. (1887). *Hegelianism and Personality*, Edinburgh: Blackwood.

Sprigge, T. L. S. (1993). *James and Bradley: American Truth and British Reality*, Chicago and La Salle, IL: Open Court.

Stirling, J. H. (1865). *The Secret of Hegel*, London: Longmans, Green. Second edn 1898, Edinburgh: Oliver and Boyd.

Stock, G. (1985). 'Negation: Bradley and Wittgenstein', *Philosophy* 60: 465–76.

Stock, G. (ed.) (1998). *Appearance Versus Reality*, Oxford: Clarendon Press.

Sweet, W. (1997). *Idealism and Rights: The Social Ontology of Human Rights in the Political Thought of Bernard Bosanquet*, Lanham, MD: University Press of America.

Thomas, G. (1987). *The Moral Philosophy of T. H. Green*, Oxford: Clarendon Press.

Vincent, A. (ed.) (1986). *The Philosophy of T. H. Green*, Aldershot: Gower.

Wallace, W. (1874). *The Logic of Hegel translated from The Encyclopaedia of Philosophical Sciences with Prolegomena*, Oxford: Clarendon Press. Second edition (2 titles): 1892, *The Logic of Hegel translated from The Encyclopaedia of Philosophical Sciences*, Oxford: Clarendon Press; 1894, *Prolegomena to the Study of Hegel's Philosophy*, Oxford: Clarendon Press.

Walsh, W. H. (1986). 'Green's Criticism of Hume' in A. Vincent (ed.), *The Philosophy of T. H. Green*, Aldershot: Gower.

Wollheim, R. (1959). *F. H. Bradley*, Baltimore: Penguin Books. 2nd edn 1969.

CHAPTER 4 IDEALISM IN RUSSIA

Berdiaev, N. A. (1901). *Sub"ektivizm i individualizm v obshchestvennoi filosofii. Kriticheskii etiud o N. K. Mikhailovskom (Subjectivism and Individualism in Social Philosophy. A Critical Study of N. K. Mikhailovskii)*, St Petersburg: Popova.

Berdiaev, N. A. (1916). *Smysl tvorchestva. Opyt opravdaniia cheloveka*, Moscow: Leman and Sakharov. Trans. D. A. Lowrie 1955, *The Meaning of the Creative Act*, New York: Harper and Bros.

Berdiaev, N. A. (1923). *Smysl istorii. Opyt filosofii chelovechekoi sud'by*, Berlin: Obelisk. Trans. G. Reavey 1936, *The Meaning of History*, London: Geoffrey Bles.

Berdiaev, N. A. (1939). *O rabstve i svobode cheloveka. Opyt personalistickeskoi filosofii*, Paris: YMCA Press. Trans R. M. French 1943, *Slavery and Freedom*, London: Geoffrey Bles.

Billington, J. H. (1958). *Mikhailovskii and Russian Populism*, Oxford: Clarendon Press.

Fateev, V. A. (ed.) (1995). *V. V. Rozanov: Pro et Contra*, St Petersburg: Izdatel'stvo russkogo Khristianskogo gumanitarnogo instituta, 2 vols.

Frank, S. L. (1950). 'Introduction' to Soloviev 1950, 9–31.

Lavrov, P. I. (1965). *Filosofiia i sotsiologiia: izbrannye proizvedeniia (Philosophy and Sociology: Selected Writings)*. Moscow: Mysl', 2 vols.

Lavrov, P. L. (1860). *Ocherki voprosov prakticheskogo filosofii (Essays on Questions of Practical Philosophy)*, St Petersburg: Glazunov.

Lavrov, P. L. (1870 [1891]). *Istoricheskie pis'ma*, Geneva. Trans. 1967 J. P. Scanlan, *Historical Letters*, Berkeley, CA: University of California Press.

Lossky, N. O. (1951). *History of Russian Philosophy*. New York: International Universities Press.

Mikhailovksii, N. K. (1869). '*Chto takoe Progress*' ('*What is Progress?*'). Trans. 1965 in J. M. Edie, J. P. Scanlan and M.-B. Zeldin, *Russian Philosophy*, vol. II, Chicago, IL: Quadrangle Books, 170–98.

Mikhailovksii, N. K. (1906–14). *Polnoe sobranie sochinenii (Complete Works)*, St Peterburg: M. M. Stanisulevich, 4th edn. 10 vols.

Naucho, F. (1966). *Berdiaev's Philosophy: The Existential Paradox of Freedom and Necessity*, Garden City, NY: Doubleday.

Novgorodstev, P. N. (ed.) (1903). *Problemy idealizma (Problems of idealism)*, Moscow: Moskovskoe psikhologicheskoe obshchestvo.

Rozanov, V. V. (1886). *O ponimanii (On Understanding)*, Moscow: E. Lissiev and Iu. Roman.

Rozanov, V. V. (1891 [1894]). *Legenda o velikom inkvizitore F. M. Dostoevskogo*, Moscow: Nikolaev; trans. (of 1906 St Petersburg edn) S. Roberts 1972, *Dostoevsky and the Legend of the Grand Inquisitor*, Ithaca, NY: Cornell University Press.

Rozanov, V. V. (1990). *V. V. Rozanov*, Moscow: Nauka, 2 vols.

Soloviev, V. S. (1874). *Krizis zapadnoi filosofii: protiv pozitivistov*, Trans. 1996 B. Jakim, *The Crisis of Western Philosophy: Against the Positivists*, West Stockbridge, MA: Lindisfarne Press.

Soloviev, V. S. (1877–81). *Chteniia o bogochelovechestve*, Trans. 1948 P. Zouboff, *Lectures on Godmanhood*, London: Dennis Dobson.

Soloviev, V. S. (1892–4). *Smysl liubvi*, Trans. 1985 T. R. Beyer, *The Meaning of Love*, West Stockbridge, MA: Lindisfarne Press.

Soloviev, V. S. (1950). *A Solovyov Anthology*. Ed. S. Frank; trans. N. Duddington, London: SCM Press.

Soloviev, V. S. (1966–70). *Sobranie sochinenii (Collected Works)*, 12 vols., Brussels.

Soloviev, V. S. (1988). *Sochinenia (Works)*, 2 vols., Moscow: Mys'l.

Trubetskoi, E. N. (1913 [1995]). *Mirosozertsanie Vl. S. Solov'ëva (Soloviev's Worldview)*, Moscow: Medium.

Vekhi. Sbornik statei o russkoi intelligentsii (1909). Moscow: I. N. Kushnerev. Trans. M. S. Shatz and J. E. Zimmerman, *Signposts. A Collection of Essays on the Russian Intelligentsia*, Irvine, CA: Charles Schlacks Jr, 1986.

Venturi, F. (1960). *Roots of Russian Populism: A History of the Populist and Socialist Movements in Nineteenth-Century Russia*. Trans. F. Haskell. New York: Knopf.

Walicki, A. (1973). *Rosyjska filozofia I mysl spaleczna od oswiexenia do marksizmu*, Warsaw: Wiedza Powszechna. Trans. 1980 H. Andrews-Rusiecka, *A History of Russian Thought from the Enlightenment to Marxism*, Oxford: Clarendon Press.

Walicki, A. (1987). *Legal Philosophies of Russian Liberalism*, Oxford: Clarendon Press.

CHAPTER 5 BERGSON

Bergson, H. (1896). *Matière et mémoire: essai sur la relation du corps à l'esprit*, Paris: Alcan. Repr. 1985 Quadrige. Paris: Presses Universitaires de France. Trans. 1911 N. M. Paul and W. Scott Palmer, *Matter and Memory*, New York: Swan Sonnenschein.

Bergson, H. (1900). *Le Rire: essai sur la signification du comique*, Paris: Alcan. Repr. 1985 Quadrige. Paris: Presses Universitaires de France. Trans. 1911 C. Brereton and F. Rothwell, *Laughter: An Essay on the Meaning of the Comic*, London: Macmillan.

Bergson, H. (1903). 'Introduction à la métaphysique', *Revue de métaphysique et de morale* 29: 1–36. Reprinted 1987 in *La Pensée et le Mouvant: Essais et conférences*, Quadrige. Paris: Presses Universitaires de France. Trans. 1912 T. E. Hulme *Introduction to Metaphysics*, New York: Putnam.

Bergson, H. (1907). *L'Évolution créatrice*, Paris: Alcan. Reprinted 1986 Quadrige. Paris: Presses Universitaires de France. Trans. 1911 A. Mitchell, *Creative Evolution*, New York: Holt and London: Macmillan.

Bergson, H. (1911). *L'Intuition philosophique*, Paris: Alcan. Repr. 1987 in *La Pensée et le mouvant: Essais et conférences*. Quadrige. Paris: Presses Universitaires de France.

Bergson, H. (1919). *L'Énergie spirituelle*, Paris: Alcan. Repr. 1985 Quadrige. Paris: Presses Universitaires de France. Trans. 1920 H. Wildon-Carr *Mind-Energy: Lectures and Essays*, New York: Holt.

Bergson, H. (1922). *Durée et Simultanéité: à propos de la théorie d'Einstein*. Paris: Alcan. Repr. 1972 in A. Robinet (ed.), *Mélanges*. Paris: Presses Universitaires de France. Trans. 1956 H. Dingle, *Duration and Simultaneity*, Indianapolis, IN: Bobbs-Merrill.

Bergson, H. (1932). *Les Deux Sources de la morale et de la religion*, Paris: Alcan. Repr. 1988 Quadrige. Paris: Presses Universitaires de France. Trans. 1935 R. A. Audra and C. Brereton, *The Two Sources of Morality and Religion*, New York: Holt.

Bergson, H. (1934). *La Pensée et le mouvant: essais et conférences*, Paris: Alcan. Repr. 1987 Quadrige. Paris: Presses Universitaires de France. Trans. 1946 M. L. Andison, *The Creative Mind*, New York: Philosophical Library.

Deleuze, G. (1966). *Le Bergsonisme*, Paris: Presses Universitaires de France. Trans. (1988). H. T. Milison and B. Habberjan, *Bergsonism*, New York: Zone Books.

Du Bos, C. (1946–61). *Journal: 1921–1939*, Paris: Corréa/Editions du Vieux Colombier.

Gouhier, H. (1964). *Bergson et le Christ des Evangiles*, Paris: Fayard.

Hude, H. (1989–90). *Bergson*, Paris: Editions Universitaires.

James, W. (1890). *The Principles of Psychology*, New York: Holt. New edn 1981, F. Bowers (ed.), Cambridge, MA: Harvard University Press.

Lacey, A. R. (1989). *Bergson*, London: Routledge.

Maire, G. (1935). *Bergson mon maître*, Paris: Grasset.

Malcolm, N. (1958). *Ludwig Wittgenstein: A Memoir*, London: Oxford University Press.

McTaggart, J. M. E. (1908). 'The Unreality of Time', *Mind*, 17: 457–74.

Moore, F. C. T. (1996). *Bergson: Thinking Backwards*, Cambridge: Cambridge University Press.

Russell, B. (1914). *The Philosophy of Bergson*, Cambridge: Bowes and Bowes.

Russell, B. and Whitehead, A. (1910–13). *Principia Mathematica*. Cambridge: Cambridge University Press.

Soulez, P. (1997). *Bergson*, Paris: Flammarion.

Worms, F. (1992). *Introduction à Bergson: l'âme et le corps*, Paris: Hatier.

CHAPTER 6 PRAGMATISM

Abel, R. (1955). *The Pragmatic Humanism of F. C. S. Schiller*, New York: King's Crown Press.

Bird, G. (1986). *William James*, London: Routledge.

Brent, J. (1993). *Charles Sanders Peirce: A Life*, Bloomington and Indianapolis: Indiana University Press.

Clifford, W. K. (1877). 'The Ethics of Belief', *Contemporary Review* 29: 283–309.

Dewey, J. (1938). *Logic: The Theory of Inquiry*, New York: Holt.

Fisch, M. (1986). *Peirce, Semeiotic and Pragmatism: Essays by Max Fisch*. Edited by K. L. Ketner and C. J. W. Kloesel. Bloomington and Indianapolis: Indiana University Press.

Ford, M. (1982). *William James's Philosophy: A New Perspective*, Amherst, MA: University of Massachusetts Press.

Hookway, C. J. (1985). *Peirce*, London: Routledge.

James, W. (1890). *The Principles of Psychology*, New York: Holt. New edn 1981, F. Bowers (ed.), Cambridge, MA: Harvard University Press.

James, W. (1897). *The Will to Believe and other Essays in Popular Philosophy*, New York: Longmans, Green. New edn 1979, ed. F. Bowers, Cambridge, MA: Harvard University Press.

James, W. (1902). *The Varieties of Religious Experience: A Study of Human Behaviour*, New York and London: Longmans, Green. New edn 1985, ed. F. Bowers, Cambridge, MA: Harvard University Press.

James, W. (1907). *Pragmatism: A New Name for some Old Ways of Thinking*, New York and London: Longman, Green & Co. New edn 1975, ed. F. Bowers, Cambridge, MA: Harvard University Press.

James, W. (1909a). *A Pluralistic Universe*, New York and London: Longmans, Green. New edn 1977, ed. F. Bowers, Cambridge, MA: Harvard University Press.

James, W. (1909b). *The Meaning of Truth*, New York: Longmans, Green. New edn 1975, ed. F. Bowers, Cambridge, MA: Harvard University Press.

James, W. (1912). *Essays in Radical Empiricism*, New York: Longmans, Green. New edn 1976, ed. F. Bowers, Cambridge, MA: Harvard University Press.

Ketner, K. (ed.) (1995). *Peirce and Contemporary Thought*, New York: Fordham University Press.

Kuklick, B. (1977). *The Rise of American Philosophy: Cambridge Massachusetts 1860–1930*, New Haven, CT: Yale University Press.

Murphey, M. (1961). *The Development of Peirce's Philosophy*, Cambridge, MA: Harvard University Press. Reissued 1993, Indianapolis: Hackett Publishing Company.

Myers, G. E. (1986). *William James: His Life and Thought*, New Haven, CT: Yale University Press.

Ogden, C. K. and Richards, I. A. (1923). *The Meaning of Meaning*, London: Kegan Paul.

Papini, G. (1913). *Pragmatismo (Pragmatism)*, Milan: Libreria Editrice Milanese.

Peirce, C. S. (1867). 'On a New List of Categories', *Proceedings of the American Academy of Arts and Sciences*, 7: 287–98. Repr. 1984 in E. C. Moore (ed.), *Writings of Charles S. Peirce: A Chronological Edition*, vol. II, Bloomington and Indianapolis, IN: Indiana University Press, 49–59.

Peirce, C. S. (1868–9). The *Journal of Speculative Philosophy* series. *Journal of Speculative Philosophy*, 2: 103–14, 140–57, 193–208. Repr. 1984 in E. C. Moore *et al.* (eds.), *Writings of Charles S. Peirce: A Chronological Edition*, vol. II, Bloomington and Indianapolis, IN: Indiana University Press, 193–272.

Peirce, C. S. (1871). 'Fraser's *The Works of George Berkeley*', *North American Review*, 113: 449–72. Repr. 1984 in E. C. Moore (ed.), *Writings of Charles S. Peirce: A Chronological Edition*, vol. II, Bloomington and Indianapolis, IN: Indiana University Press, 462–87.

Peirce, C. S. (1877–8). 'Illustrations of the Logic of Science', *Popular Science Monthly*, 12: 1–15, 286–302, 604–15, 705–18; 13: 203–17, 470–82. Repr. 1986 in C. J. W. Kloesel *et al.* (eds.), *Writings of Charles S. Peirce: A Chronological Edition*, vol. III, Bloomington and Indianapolis: Indiana University Press, 242–374.

Peirce, C. S. (1891–3). The *Monist* series on metaphysics. *The Monist*, 1: 161–76; 2: 321–37; 2: 533–59; 3: 1–22; 3: 176–200. Repr. 1992 in N. Houser and C. Kloesel (eds.), *The Essential Peirce: Selected Philosophical Writings*, vol. I (1867–93), Bloomington and Indianapolis, IN: Indiana University Press, 285–371.

Peirce, C. S. (1905–6). *Monist* papers on pragmaticism. *The Monist*, 15: 161–81; 481–99. Repr. 1998 with additional manuscript material in Peirce Edition Project (ed.), *The Essential*

Peirce: Selected Philosophical Writings, vol. II (1893–1913), Bloomington and Indianapolis, IN: Indiana University Press, 331–433.

Peirce, C. S. (1908). 'A Neglected Argument for the Reality of God', *The Hibbert Journal*, 7: 90–112. Repr. 1998 in Peirce Edition Project (ed.), *The Essential Peirce: Selected Philosophical Writings*, vol. II (1893–1913), Bloomington and Indianapolis, IN: Indiana University Press, 434–50.

Peirce, C. S. (1934). 'Lectures on Pragmatism' in C. Hartshorne and P. Weiss (eds.), *Collected Papers of Charles Sanders Peirce*, vol. V, Cambridge, MA: Harvard University Press, 13–131. Repr. 1998 as 'Harvard Lectures on Pragmatism (1903)' in Peirce Edition Project (ed.), *The Essential Peirce: Selected Philosophical Writings*, vol. II (1893–1913), Bloomington and Indianapolis, IN: Indiana University Press, 133–241.

Peirce, C. S. (1958). 'Josiah Royce, The Religious Aspect of Philosophy', in A. Burks (ed.), *Collected Papers of Charles Sanders Peirce*, vol. VIII, Cambridge, MA: Harvard University Press, 39–53. Repr. 1993 as 'An American Plato: Review of Royce's *Religious Aspect of Philosophy*', in C. J. W. Kloesel *et al.* (eds.), *Writings of Charles S. Peirce: A Chronological Edition*, vol. IV, Bloomington and Indianapolis, IN: Indiana University Press, 221–34.

Peirce, C. S. (1992). *Reasoning and the Logic of Things*, ed. K. L. Ketner, Cambridge, MA: Harvard University Press.

Putnam, R. A. (ed.) (1997). *The Cambridge Companion to William James*, Cambridge: Cambridge University Press.

Royce, J. (1885). *The Religious Aspect of Philosophy*, Boston and New York: Houghton Mifflin Company.

Schiller, F. (1891). *Riddles of the Sphinx: A Study of the Philosophy of Evolution*, London: Swan Sonnenschein.

Schiller, F. (1903). *Humanism*, London: Macmillan.

Schiller, F. (1929). *Logic for Use*, London: G. Bell.

Schiller, F. (1934). *Must Philosophers Disagree?*, London: Macmillan.

Thayer, H. S. (1968). *Meaning and Action: A Critical History of Pragmatism*, Indianapolis: Bobbs-Merrill.

Vaihinger, H. (1911). *Die Philosophie des als-ob*, Berlin: Reuther and Reichard. Trans. 1924 C. K. Ogden, *The Philosophy of As-If*, London: Kegan Paul.

Vailati, G. (1911). *Scritti (Writings)*, ed. M. Calderoni, U. Ricci, and G. Vacca. Florence: Successori B. Seeber.

CHAPTER 7 PSYCHOLOGY: OLD AND NEW

Angell, J. R. (1907). 'The Province of Functional Psychology', *Psychological Review* 14: 61–91.

Bain, A. (1855). *The Senses and the Intellect*, London: Parker & Son.

Baldwin, J. M. (1889). *Handbook of Psychology*, vol. I, *Senses and Intellect*, New York: Henry Holt.

Baldwin, J. M. (1891). *Handbook of Psychology*, vol. II, *Feeling and Will*, London: Macmillan and New York: Henry Holt.

Beneke, F. E. (1833). *Lehrbuch der Psychologie*, Berlin: Ernst Siegfried Mittler.

Beneke, F. E. (1845). *Lehrbuch der Psychologie als Naturwissenschaft*, 2nd edn, Berlin: Bosen und Bromberg.

Bonnet, C. (1755). *Essai de psychologie*, London.

Boring, E. G. (1929). *A History of Experimental Psychology*, New York: Century. 2nd edn 1950. New York: Appleton-Century-Crofts.

Brentano, F. (1874). *Psychologie vom empirischen Standpunkt*, Leipzig: Duncker and Humboldt. Trans. 1973 A. C. Rancurello, D. B. Terrell, and L. L. McAlister, *Psychology from an Empirical Standpoint*, London: Routledge.

Carpenter, W. B. (1837). 'On the Voluntary and Instinctive Actions of Living Beings', *Edinburgh Medical and Surgical Journal*, 48: 22–44.

Carpenter, W. B. (1874). *Principles of Mental Physiology*, London: King and Co., 6th edn 1881: Kegan Paul.

Carpenter, W. B. (1881). *Principles of Mental Physiology*, 6th edn, London: Kegan Paul.

Cesca, G. (1885). 'Ueber die Existenz von unbewussten psychischen Zuständen', *Vierteljahrsschrift für wissenschaftliche Philosophie* 9: 288–301.

Comte, A. (1830–42). *Cours de philosophie positive*, 6 vols., Paris: Bachelier. Trans. 1855 H. Martineau, *The Positive Philosophy*, New York: Blanchard.

Danziger, K. (1979). 'The Positivist Repudiation of Wundt', *Journal of the History of the Behavioral Sciences* 15: 205–30.

Darwin, C. (1859). *On the Origin of Species*, London: J. Murray.

Darwin, C. (1872). *The Expression of the Emotions in Man and Animals*, London: J. Murray.

Delboeuf, J. (1883a). *Eléments de psychophysique générale & spéciale*, Paris: Baillière.

Delboeuf, J. (1883b). *Examen critique de la loi psychophysique: sa base et sa signification*, Paris: Baillière.

Dewey, J. (1896). 'The Reflex Arc Concept in Psychology', *Psychological Review* 3: 357–70.

Dunn, R. (1858). 'On Mental Physiology: or, the Correlations of Physiology and Psychology', *Journal of Mental Science* 4: 343–60.

Ebbinghaus, H. (1885). *Ueber das Gedachtnis: Untersuchungen zur experimentellen Psychologie*, Leipzig: Duncker & Humboldt. Trans. 1913 H. A. Ruger and C. E. Bussenius, *Memory: A Contribution to Experimental Psychology*, New York: Teachers College, Columbia University.

Evans, R. (1984). 'The Origins of American Academic Psychology' in J. Brozek (ed.), *Explorations in the History of Psychology in the United States*, Lewisburg: Bucknell University Press, 17–60.

Fechner, G. T. (1860). *Elemente der Psychophysik*, 2 vols., Leipzig: Breitkopf and Härtel. Vol. I trans. 1966 H. E. Adler, ed. D. Howes and E. Boring, *Elements of Psychophysics*, New York: Holt, Rinehart, and Winston.

Fechner, G. T. (1882). *Revision der Hauptpunkte der Psychophysik*, Leipzig: Breitkopf and Härtel.

Hatfield, G. (1990). *The Natural and the Normative: Theories of Spatial Perception from Kant to Helmholtz*, Cambridge, MA: MIT Press.

Hatfield, G. (1997). 'Wundt and Psychology as Science: Disciplinary Transformations', *Perspectives on Science* 5: 349–82.

Hearnshaw, L. S. (1964). *A Short History of British Psychology, 1840–1940*, London: Methuen and Co.

Heidbreder, E. (1933). *Seven Psychologies*, New York: Appleton-Century.

Helmholtz, H. (1867). *Handbuch der physiologischen Optik*, Leipzig: Voss. Trans. 1924–5 J. P. C. Southall, *Treatise on Physiological Optics*, 3 vols., Milwaukee: Optical Society of America.

Herbart, J. F. (1816). *Lehrbuch zur Psychologie*, Königsberg and Leipzig: Unzer. Trans. 1891 M. K. Smith, *A Text-Book in Psychology*, New York: Appleton.

Herbart, J. F. (1824–5). *Psychologie als Wissenschaft neu gegründet auf Erfahrung, Metaphysik und Mathematik*, Königsberg: Unzer.

Hering, E. (1861–4). *Beiträge zur Physiologie (Contributions to Physiology)*, Leipzig: Engelmann.

Hering, E. (1868). *Die Lehre vom binocularen Sehen (The Theory of Binocular Vision)*, Leipzig: Engelmann.

Hilgard, E. R. (1987). *Psychology in America: A Historical Survey*, San Diego: Harcourt Brace Jovanovich.

James, W. (1890). *The Principles of Psychology*, 2 vols., New York: Holt.

Krüger, J. G. (1756). *Versuch einer Experimental-Seelenlehre*, Halle: C. H. Hemmerde.

Külpe, O. (1893). *Grundriss der Psychologie, auf experimenteller Grundlage dargestellt*, Leipzig: Engelmann. Trans. 1895 E. B. Titchener, *Outlines of Psychology, Based upon the Results of Experimental Investigation*, New York: Macmillan.

Kusch, M. (1999). *Psychological Knowledge: A Social History and Philosophy*, London: Routledge.

Ladd, George Trumbull (1887). *Elements of Physiological Psychology*, New York: Charles Scribner's Sons.

Ladd, George Trumbull (1894). *Psychology, Descriptive and Explanatory*, New York: Charles Scribner's Sons.

Ladd, George Trumbull (1895). *Philosophy of Mind: An Essay in the Metaphysics of Psychology*, New York: Charles Scribner's Sons.

Lange, F. A. (1866). *Geschichte des Materialismus und Kritik seiner Bedeutung in der Gegenwart*, 2 vols., Iserlohn and Leipzig: J. Baedeker. Trans. 1925 E. C. Thomas, *The History of Materialism and Criticism of its Present Importance*, 3rd edn, 3 vols., London: Routledge.

Lewes, G. H. (1857). *Biographical History of Philosophy*, rev. edn, London: Parker & Son.

Lewes, G. H. (1874–5). *Problems of Life and Mind, First Series, Foundations of a Creed*, 2 vols., Boston: Osgood.

Lewes, G. H. (1877). *Problems of Life and Mind, Second Series, The Physical Basis of Mind*, Boston: Osgood.

Lewes, G. H. (1879). *Problems of Life and Mind, Third Series, The Study of Psychology*, Boston: Osgood.

Lewes, G. H. (1880). *Problems of Life and Mind, Third Series, Continued*, Boston: Osgood.

Lipps, T. (1903). *Leitfaden der Psychologie*, Leipzig: Engelmann.

Loeb, J. (1900). *Comparative Physiology of the Brain and Comparative Psychology*, New York: G. P. Putnam's Sons.

Lotze, H. (1852). *Medicinische Psychologie, oder Physiologie der Seele*, Leipzig: Weidmann.

Lotze, H. (1881). *Grundzüge der Psychologie*, 3rd edn, Leipzig: S. Hürzel. Trans. 1886 G. T. Ladd, *Outlines of Psychology: Dictated Portions of the Lectures of Hermann Lotze*, Boston: Ginn and Co.

McCosh, J. (1886). *Psychology: The Cognitive Powers*, New York: Charles Scribner's Sons.

Maudsley, H. (1867). *The Physiology and Pathology of the Mind*, London: Macmillan.

Maudsley, H. (1876). *The Physiology of Mind*, London: Macmillan.

Mercier, C. (1888). *The Nervous System and the Mind: A Treatise on the Dynamics of the Human Organism*, London: Macmillan.

Mill, J. (1869). *Analysis of the Phenomena of the Human Mind*, new edn, 2 vols., London: Longmans, Green, Reader and Dyer.

Mill, J. S. (1843). *A System of Logic, Ratiocinative and Inductive*, London: John Parker. Comprises vols. VII and VIII of J. S. Mill, *Collected Works*, ed. J. M. Robson, London: Routledge and Toronto: University of Toronto Press, 1991.

Mill, J. S. (1865). *An Examination of Sir William Hamilton's Philosophy*, London: Longmans, Green; 5th edn 1878, London: Longmans, Green.

Morgan, C. Lloyd (1891). *Animal Life and Intelligence*, Boston: Ginn.

Müller, G. E. (1878). *Zur Grundlegung der Psychophysik*, Berlin: Grieben.

Müller, G. E. (1904). *Die Gesichtspunkte und die Tatsachen der psychophysischen Methodik*, Wiesbaden: Bergmann.

Müller, G. E. and Pilzecker, A. (1900). *Experimentelle Beiträge zur Lehre vom Gedächtnis. Zeitschrift für Psychologie und Physiologie der Sinnesorgane, Ergänzungsband 1*, Leipzig: Barth.

Murchison, C. (ed.) (1926). *Psychologies of 1925: Powell Lectures in Psychological Theory*, Worcester, MA: Clark University Press.

Murchison, C. (ed.) (1930). *Psychologies of 1930*, Worcester, MA: Clark University Press.

O'Donnell, J. M. (1979). 'The Crisis in Experimentalism in the 1920s: E. G. Boring and His Uses of History', *American Psychologist* 34: 289–95.

Ribot, T. (1870). *La psychologie anglaise contemporaine: Ecole expérimentale*, Paris: Ladrange. Trans. 1874, *English Psychology*, New York: Appleton.

Ribot, T. (1879). *La psychologie allemande contemporaine: Ecole expérimentale*, Paris: Baillière. Trans. 1886 J. M. Baldwin, *German Psychology of To-Day: The Empirical School*, New York: Charles Scribner's Sons.

Romanes, G. J. (1883). *Mental Evolution in Animals, with a Posthumous Essay on Instinct by Charles Darwin*, London: Kegan Paul.

Romanes, G. J. (1888). *Mental Evolution in Man, Origin of Human Faculty*, London: Kegan Paul.

Scripture, E. W. (1897). *The New Psychology*, London: Charles Scribner's Sons.

Spencer, H. (1855). *The Principles of Psychology*, 2 vols. London: Williams and Norgate. 2nd edn 1870, 3rd edn 1881.

Stout, G. F. (1896). *Analytic Psychology*, London: Swan Sonnenschein.

Stout, G. F. (1899). *A Manual of Psychology*, London and New York: University Correspondence College Press.

Sully, J. (1884). *Outlines of Psychology with Special Reference to the Theory of Education*, London: Longmans, Green.

Sully, J. (1892). *The Human Mind: A Text-Book of Psychology*, London: Longmans, Green.

Taine, H. (1870). *De l'intelligence*, 2 vols., Paris: Hachette. Trans. 1871 T. D. Haye, *On Intelligence*, London: Reeve and Co. and New York: Holt and Williams.

Titchener, E. B. (1898). 'The Postulates of a Structural Psychology', *Philosophical Review* 7: 449–65.

Titchener, E. B. (1908). *Lectures on the Elementary Psychology of Feeling and Attention*, New York: Macmillan.

Titchener, E. B. (1909a). *Lectures on the Experimental Psychology of the Thought-Processes*, New York: Macmillan.

Titchener, E. B. (1909b). *A Text-Book of Psychology*, New York: Macmillan.

Turner, R. S. (1994). *In the Eye's Mind: Vision and the Helmholtz-Hering Controversy*, Princeton, NJ: Princeton University Press.

Upham, T. C. (1841). *Elements of Mental Philosophy, Embracing the Two Departments of the Intellect and the Sensibilities*, 2nd edn, 2 vols., New York: Harper and Brothers.

Waitz, T. (1878). *Grundlegung der Psychologie*, 2nd edn, Leipzig: Siegismund and Volkening.

Ward, J. (1886). 'Psychology', in *Encyclopaedia Britannica*, 9th edn, Philadelphia: Stoddart, vol. XX, 42–90.

Weber, E. H. (1834). *De pulsu, resorptione, auditu et tactu: annotationes anatomicae et physiologicae*, Leipzig: Köhler. Trans. 1996 H. E. Ross and D. J. Murray, *E. H. Weber on the Tactile Senses*, 2nd edn, Hove: Taylor and Francis.

Wundt, W. M. (1862). *Beiträge zur Theorie der Sinneswahrnehmung*, Leipzig: Winter.

Wundt, W. M. (1863). *Vorlesungen ueber Menschen- und Thierseele*, 2 vols., Leipzig: Voss.

Wundt, W. M. (1874). *Grundzüge der physiologischen Psychologie*, Leipzig: Engelmann. 2nd edn 1880; 3rd edn 1887.

Wundt, W. M. (1883). 'Schlusswort zum ersten Band', *Philosophische Studien* 1: 615–17.

Wundt, W. M. (1886). *Eléments de psychologie physiologique*, 2 vols., Paris: Alcan.

Wundt, W. M. (1894). 'Ueber psychische Causalität und das Prinzip des psychophysischen Parallelismus', *Philosophische Studien* 10: 1–124.

Wundt, W. M. (1900–20). *Völkerpsychologie. Eine Untersuchung der Entwicklungsgesetze von Sprache, Mythus und Sitte*, 10 vols., Leipzig: Engelmann, Kröner.

Wundt, W. M. (1901). *Grundriss der Psychologie*, 4th edn, Leipzig: Engelmann. Trans. 1902 C. H. Judd, *Outlines of Psychology*, 2nd edn, Leipzig: Engelmann.
Wundt, W. M. (1908). *Logik: III.Band, Logik der Geisteswissenschaften*, 3rd edn, Stuttgart: Ferdinand Enke.
Ziehen, T. (1891). *Leitfaden der physiologischen Psychologie*, Jena: G. Fischer. Trans. 1892 C. C. van Liew and O. W. Beyer, *Introduction to Physiological Psychology*, London: Swan Sonnenschein.

CHAPTER 8 THE UNCONSCIOUS MIND

Assoun, P.-L (1976). *Freud: la philosophie et les philosophes*, Paris: Presses Universitaires de France.
Assoun, P.-L. (1980). *Freud et Nietzsche*, Paris: Presses Universitaires de France.
Baldwin, J. (1891). *Handbook of Psychology: Feeling and Will*, London: Macmillan.
Bergson, H. (1896). *Matière et mémoire: essai sur la relation du corps à l'esprit*, Paris: Presses Universitaires de France. Trans. 1991 N. Margaret Paul and W. Scott Palmer, *Matter and Memory*, New York: Zone Books.
Bergson, H. (1934). *La pensée et le mouvant: essais et conférences*, 5th edn, Paris: Alcan. Trans. M. L. Andison 1946, *The Creative Mind*, Westport, CT: Greenwood Press.
Binet, A. (1891). *Les altérations de la personnalité*, Paris: Alcan. Trans. 1896 H. Baldwin, *Alterations of Personality*, London: Chapman and Hall.
Boring, E. G. (1929). *A History of Experimental Psychology*, New York: Century, 2nd edn 1950, Englewood Cliffs, NJ: Prentice-Hall.
Bradley, F. H. (1895). 'On the supposed uselessness of the soul', Mind n.s. 4, 176–9. Repr. 1935 in *Collected Essays*, vol. I, Oxford: Clarendon Press, 343–7.
Bradley, F. H. (1902a). 'On active attention', *Mind* n.s. 11, 1–30. Repr. 1935 in *Collected Essays*, vol. II, Oxford: Clarendon Press, 408–43.
Bradley, F. H. (1902b). 'On mental conflict and imputation', *Mind* n.s. 11, 289–315. Reprinted 1935 in *Collected Essays*, vol. II, Oxford: Clarendon Press, 444–75.
Bradley, F. H. (1893). *Appearance and Reality: A Metaphysical Essay*, 1st edn, London: Swan Sonnenschein and Co., 2nd edn 1897; repr. with new pagination, Oxford: Clarendon Press, 1930.
Brandell, G. (1979). *Freud: A Man of his Century*, trans. I. White, Sussex: Harvester.
Brentano, F. (1874). *Psychologie vom empirischen Standpunkt*, Leipzig: Duncker & Humboldt. Trans. 1973 A. Rancurello, D. Terrell, and L. L. McAlister, ed. O. Kraus, *Psychology from an Empirical Standpoint*, London: Routledge.
Butler, S. (1880). *Unconscious Memory: A Comparison Between the Theory of Dr. Ewald Hering and the 'Philosophy of the Unconscious' of Dr. Edward Von Hartmann; With Translations From these Authors and Preliminary Chapters Bearing on 'Life and Habit', 'Evolution, Old and New', and Mr. Charles Darwin's Edition of Dr. Krause's 'Erasmus Darwin'*, London: David Bogue.
Carpenter, W. B. (1874). *Principles of Mental Physiology*, London: King and Co., 6th edn 1881: Kegan Paul.
Carus, C. G. (1846). *Psyche: zur Entwicklungsgeschichte der Seele*, Pforzheim: Flammer and Hoffmann. Part I trans. 1970 R. Welch, *Psyche: On the Development of the Soul*, New York: Spring Publications.
Clifford, W. K. (1878). 'On the nature of things-in-themselves', *Mind* n.s. 3, 57–67.
Dallas, E. (1866). *The Gay Science*, London: Chapman and Hall.
Darnoi, D. (1967). *The Unconscious and Eduard von Hartmann: A Historico-Critical Monograph*, The Hague: Nijhoff.
Decker, H. (1977). *Freud in Germany: Revolution and Reaction in Science, 1893–1907*, New York: International Universities Press.

Deleuze, G. (1966). *Le Bergsonisme*, Paris: Presses Universitaires de France. Trans. 1988 H. Tomlinson and B. Habberjam, *Bergsonism*, New York: Zone Books.

Ellenberger, H. (1970). *The Discovery of the Unconscious: The History and Evolution of Dynamic Psychiatry*, New York: Basic Books.

Ellenberger, H. (1993). *Beyond the Unconscious: Essays of Henri Ellenberger in the History of Psychiatry*, Princeton, NJ: Princeton University Press.

Fechner, G. T. (1860). *Elemente der Psychophysik*, Leipzig: Breitkopf and Hartel. Vol. I trans. 1966 H. Adler, ed. D. Howes and E. Boring, *Elements of Psychophysics*, New York: Holt, Rinehart, and Winston.

Foucault, M. (1966). *Les mots et les choses: une archéologie des sciences humaines*, Paris: Gallimard. Trans. 1974, *The Order of Things: An Archaeology of the Human Sciences*, London: Tavistock.

Freud, S. (1900). *Die Traumdeutung*, vols. II–III of *Gesammelte Werke*, 18 vols., Frankfurt am Main: Fischer Verlag, 1960. Trans. *The Interpretation of Dreams*, vols. IV–V of *The Standard Edition of the Complete Psychological Works of Sigmund Freud*, 24 vols., under the general editorship of J. Strachey, in collaboration with A. Freud, assisted by A. Strachey and A. Tyson, London: Hogarth Press and Institute of Psycho-Analysis, 1953–74.

Freud, S. (1904). *Zur Psychopathologie des Alltagslebens*, *Gesammelte Werke*, vol. IV, *The Psychopathology of Everyday Life*, standard edition, vol. VI.

Freud, S. (1905). *Drei Abhandlungen zur Sexualtheorie*, *Gesammelte Werke*, vol. V, 29–145. *Three Essays on the Theory of Sexuality*, *Standard Edition*, vol. VII, 123–245.

Freud, S. (1912). 'Einige Bemerkungen über den Begriff des Unbewußten in der Psychoanalyse', *Gesammelte Werke*, vol. VIII, 430–9. Trans. 'A note on the unconscious in psycho-analysis', *Standard Edition*, vol. XII, 255–66.

Freud, S. (1915). 'Das Unbewußte', *Gesammelte Werke*, vol. X, 264–303. Trans. 'The Unconscious', *Standard Edition*, vol. XVI, 159–215.

Freud, S. (1920). *Jenseits des Lustprinzips*, *Gesammelte Werke*, vol. XIII, 3–69. *Beyond the Pleasure Principle*, *Standard Edition*, vol. XVIII, 1–64.

Freud, S. (1923). *Das Ich und das Es*, *Gesammelte Werke*, vol. XIII, 237–89. *The Ego and the Id*, *Standard Edition*, vol. XIX, 1–66.

Freud, S. (1933). *Neue Folge der Vorlesungen zur Einführung in die Psychoanalyse*, *Gesammelte Werke*, vol. XV. Trans. *New Introductory Lectures on Psycho-Analysis*, *Standard Edition*, vol. XXII, pp. 1–182.

Freud, S. (1940). *Abriß der Psychoanalyse*, *Gesammelte Werke*, vol. XVII, 63–138. Trans. *An Outline of Psycho-Analysis*, *Standard Edition*, vol. XXIII, 139–207.

Freud S. (1954). *The Origins of Psycho-Analysis: Letters to Wilhelm Fließ, Drafts and Notes 1887–1902*, ed. M. Bonaparte, A. Freud, and E. Kris, trans. E. Mosbacher and J. Strachey, London: Imago.

Galton, Sir F. (1883). *Inquiries into Human Faculty and its Development*, London: Macmillan.

Gardner, S. (1999). 'Schopenhauer, Will and Unconscious' in C. Janaway (ed.), *The Cambridge Companion to Schopenhauer*, Cambridge: Cambridge University Press.

Gay, P. (1988). *Freud: A Life for Our Time*, London: Dent.

Hamilton, Sir W. (1865–6). *Lectures on Metaphysics and Logic*, 4 vols., ed. H. L. Mansel and J. Veitch, Edinburgh: William Blackwood.

Hartmann, E. von (1869). *Philosophie des Unbewußten: Versuch einer Weltanschauung. Speculative Resultate nach inductiv-naturwissenschaftlicher Methode*, Berlin: C. Duncker. Trans. 1931 W. Coupland, *Philosophy of the Unconscious: Speculative Results According to the Inductive Method of Physical Science*, London: Kegan Paul.

Hartmann, E. von (1879). *Phänomenologie des sittlichen Betwußtseins: Prolegomena zu jeder künftiger Ethik*, Berlin: C. Duncker.

Hartmann, E. von (1887). *Philosophie des Schönen: zweiter systematischer Theil der Aesthetik*, Leipzig: W. Friedrich.

Hartmann, E. von (1896). *Kategorienlehre*, Leipzig: H. Haacke.

Hartmann, E. von (1899–1900). *Geschichte der Metaphysik*, 2 vols., Leipzig: H. Haacke.

Helmholtz, H. von (1855). *Ueber das Sehen des Menschen (Ein popular-wissenschaftlicher Vortrag)*, Leipzig: Voss.

Helmholtz, H. von (1856–67). *Handbuch der Physiologischen Optik*, 3 vols., 2nd edn, Hamburg: Voss, 1896. Trans. 1924–5 J. Southall, *Treatise on Physiological Optics*, 3 vols., New York: Optical Society of America.

Helmholtz, H. von (1894). 'Über den Ursprung der richtigen Deutung unserer Sinneseindrücke', *Zeitschrift für Psychologie der Sinnesorgane* 7, 81–96. Trans. 1986 R. M. Warren and R. P. Warren, 'The Origin of the Correct Interpretation of our Sensory Impressions' in *Helmholtz on Perception: Its Physiology and Development*, New York: John Wiley, 249–60.

Henry, A. (1988). 'La réception de Schopenhauer en France' in E. Luft (ed.), *Schopenhauer: New Essays in Honour of His 200th Birthday*, New York: Edwin Mellen Press, 188–215.

Henry, M. (1985). *Généalogie de la psychanalyse: le commencement perdu*, Paris: Presses Universitaires de France. Trans. 1993 D. Brick, *The Genealogy of Psychoanalysis*, Stanford, CA: Stanford University Press.

Herbart, J. F. (1816). *Lehrbuch zur Psychologie*, Königsberg and Leipzig: Unzer. Trans. 1891 M. K. Smith, *A Text-Book in Psychology*, New York: Appleton.

Herbart, J. F. (1824). *Psychologie als Wissenschaft, neu gegründet auf Erfahrung, Metaphysik und Mathematik. (Psychology as a Science, newly founded on Experience, Metaphysics and Mathematics)*, Königsberg: Unzer.

Hering, E. (1870). *Über das Gedächtnis als eine allgemeine Funktion der organisierte Materie*, Vienna: Karl Gerold. Trans. 1880 S. Butler, 'On Memory as a Universal Function of Organised Matter' in Butler 1880, 97–133.

Hook, S. (ed.) (1964). *Psychoanalysis, Scientific Method and Philosophy*, New York: New York University Press.

Horkheimer, M. (1972). 'Schopenhauer und die Gesellschaft' in *Sozialphilosophische Studien*, Frankfurt am Main: Athenäum Fischer, 68–77.

Huxley, T. H. (1874). 'On the Hypothesis that Animals are Automata', in *Collected Essays*, 9 vols., London: Macmillan 1898, vol. I, *Methods and Results*, 199–250.

James, W. (1890). *The Principles of Psychology*, 2 vols., New York: Henry Holt. New edn 1950, New York: Dover Publications.

James, W. (1902). *The Varieties of Religious Experience*, New York: Longmans, Green. Repr. 1982, Harmondsworth: Penguin.

Janet, P. (1889). *L'Automatisme psychologique: essai de psychologie expérimentale sur les formes inférieures de l'activité humaine*, Paris: Alcan.

Janet, P. (1907–8). 'Symposium on the subconscious', *Journal of Abnormal Psychology* 2, 58–67. Repr. in Münsterberg *et al.* 1911.

Jastrow, J. (1901). *Fact and Fable in Psychology*, London: Macmillan.

Jastrow, J. (1906). *The Subconscious*, London: Archibald Constable.

Jastrow, J. (1907–8). 'Symposium on the Subconscious', *Journal of Abnormal Psychology* 2, 37–43. Repr. in Münsterberg *et al.* 1911.

Jones, E. (1953–7). *Sigmund Freud: Life and Work*, 3 vols., London: Hogarth Press.

Lange, F. A. (1866). *Geschichte des Materialismus und Kritik seiner Bedeutung in der Gegenwart*, 2 vols., 2nd edn 1887, Leipzig: Iserlohn. Trans. 1925 E. C. Thomas, *The History of Materialism and Criticism of its Present Importance*, 3rd edn, London: Routledge.

Lehrer, R. (1995). *Nietzsche's Presence in Freud's Life and Thought: On the Origins of a Psychology of Dynamic Unconscious Mental Functioning*, Albany: State University of New York Press.

Leibniz, G. W. (1765). *Nouveaux essais sur l'entendement humain*, R. E. Raspe; in *Sämtliche Schriften und Briefe*, ed. A. Robinet and H. Schepers, Berlin: Akademie-Verlag, 1962, vol. VI, 43–527. Trans. 1981 P. Remnant and J. Bennett, *New Essays on Human Understanding*, Cambridge: Cambridge University Press.

Lewes, G. H. (1874–5). 'Psychological Principles' (from *Problems of Life and Mind*, vol. I) in G. H. Lewes and J. S. Mill, *Foundations for a Science of Mind*, London: Routledge/Thoemmes Press, 1993.

Lewes, G. H. (1875). *Problems of Life and Mind*, 2 vols., 2nd edn 1883, London: Kegan Paul.

Lipps, T. (1897). 'Der Begriff des Unbewußten in der Psychologie', *Dritter Internationaler Congress für Psychologie in München vom 4. bis 7. August 1896*, Munich: J. F. Lehmann. Repr. 1974 Nendeln/Liechtenstein: Kraus.

Littman, R. (1979). 'Social and intellectual origins of experimental psychology' in E. Hearst (ed.), *The First Century of Experimental Psychology*, Hillsdale, NJ: Lawrence Erlbaum.

Lotze, R. H. (1856–64). *Mikrokosmus: Ideen zur Naturgeschichte und Geschichte der Menschen*, 3 vols., Leipzig: Hirzel. Trans. 1885 E. Hamilton and E. C. Jones, *Microcosmos: An Essay Concerning Man and his Relation to the World*, 2 vols., Edinburgh: T. & T. Clark and New York: Scribner and Welford.

Lotze, H. (1881). *Grundzüge der Psychologie*, 3rd edn, Leipzig: S. Hürzel, 1884. Trans. 1886 G. Ladd, *Outlines of Psychology: Dictated Portions of the Lectures of Hermann Lotze*, Boston: Ginn and Co.

Mandelbaum, M. (1971). *History, Man & Reason: A Study in Nineteenth-Century Thought*, Baltimore: John Hopkins Press.

Maudsley, H. (1867). *The Physiology and Pathology of the Mind*, London: Macmillan.

Merleau-Ponty, M. (1945). *Phénoménologie de la perception*, Paris: Gallimard. Trans. 1962 C. Smith, *Phenomenology of Perception*, London: Routledge.

Mill, J. S. (1843). *A System of Logic, Ratiocinative and Inductive*, London: John Parker, Comprises vols. VII and VIII of J. S. Mill, *Collected Works*, ed. J. M. Robson, London: Routledge and Toronto: University of Toronto Press, 1991.

Mill, J. S. (1865). *An Examination of Sir William Hamilton's Philosophy*, 5th edn, 1878, London: Longmans, Green.

Münsterberg, H. (1907–8). 'Symposium on the Subconscious', *Journal of Abnormal Psychology* 2: 25–33. Reprinted in Münsterberg *et al.* 1911.

Münsterberg, H., Ribot, T., Janet, P., Jastrow, J., Hart, B., and Prince, M. (1911). *Subconscious Phenomena*, London: Rebman. Reprinted in part from *Journal of Abnormal Psychology* (1907–8), 2, 22–43 and 58–80 ('A Symposium on the Subconscious').

Murray, D. (1983). *A History of Western Psychology*, Englewood Cliffs, NJ: Prentice-Hall.

Myers, F. (1892). 'The subliminal consciousness', *Proceedings of the Society for Psychical Research* 7: 298–355.

Myers, F. (1903). *Human Personality and its Survival of Bodily Death*, 2 vols., London: Longmans, Green.

Nietzsche, F. W. (1887). *Zur Genealogie der Moral: Eine Streitschrift*, Leipzig: C. G. Naumannn. Trans. 1967 W. Kaufmann and R. J. Hollingdale, *On the Genealogy of Morals*, New York: Random House.

Prince, M. (1906). *The Dissociation of a Personality*, New York and London: Longmans, Green.

Prince, M. (1907–8). 'Symposium on the subconscious', *Journal of Abnormal Psychology* 2, 22–5 and 67–80. Reprinted in Münsterberg *et al.* 1911.

Prince, M. (1914). *The Unconscious: The Fundamentals of Human Personality Normal and Abnormal*, New York: Macmillan.

Reed, E. (1997). *From Soul to Mind: The Emergence of Psychology from Erasmus Darwin to William James*, New Haven: Yale University Press.

Ricœur, P. (1965). *De l'interprétation: essai sur Freud*, Paris: Editions du Seuil. Trans. 1970 D. Savage, *Freud and Philosophy: An Essay in Interpretation*, New Haven, CT: Yale University Press.

Ribot, T. (1881). *Maladies de la mémoire*, Paris: Baillière. Trans. J. Fitzgerald 1885, *The Diseases of Memory: An Essay in Positive Psychology*, 3rd edn, London: Kegan Paul.

Ribot, T. (1889). *Psychologie de l'attention*, Paris: Alcan. Trans. 1890, *The Psychology of Attention*, London: Longmans, Green.

Ribot, T. (1907–8). 'Symposium on the subconscious', *Journal of Abnormal Psychology* 2, 33–7. Reprinted in Münsterberg *et al.* 1911.

Ribot, T. (1914). *La vie inconsciente et les mouvements*, Paris: Alcan.

Robinson, D. (1981). *An Intellectual History of Psychology*, New York: Macmillan.

Sartre, J.-P. (1943). *L'être et le néant: essai d'ontologie phénoménologique*, Paris: Gallimard. Trans. 1956 H. Barnes, *Being and Nothingness*, New York: Philosophical Library and 1957 London: Methuen.

Scheler, M. (1923). *Wesen und Formen der Sympathie*, 2nd edn, Bonn: Cohen. Trans. 1954 P. Heath, *The Nature of Sympathy*, London: Routledge.

Schelling, F. W. J. von (1800). *System des transzendentalen Idealismus*, Tübingen. Trans. 1993 P. Heath, intro. M. Vater, *System of Transcendental idealism (1800)*, Charlottesville: University Press of Virginia.

Schopenhauer, A. (1836). *Ueber den Willen in der Natur, Eine Erörterung der Bestätigungen welche die Philosophie des Verfassers seit ihrem Auftreten, durch die empirischen Wissenschaften erhalten hat*, Frankfurt on Main: Siegmund Schmerber. Trans. 1992 E. F. J. Payne, ed. D. Cartwright, *On the Will in Nature: A Discussion of the Corroborations From the Empirical Sciences that the Author's Philosophy Has Received Since its First Appearance*, Oxford: Berg.

Schopenhauer, A. (1844). *Die Welt als Wille und Vorstellung*, 2nd edn, 2 vols., Leipzig: Brockhaus. Trans. 1966 E. F. J. Payne, *The World as Will and Representation*, New York: Dover Books.

Spencer, H. (1855). *The Principles of Psychology*, 2 vols., London: Williams and Norgate. 2nd edn 1870, 3rd edn 1881.

Stewart, D. (1792). *Elements of the Philosophy of the Human Mind, Part 1*. Reprinted 1859 with Part 2, ed. G. N. Wright, London: Tegg.

Sully, J. (1884). *Outlines of Psychology: With Special Reference to the Theory of Education*, London: Longmans, Green.

Taine, H. (1870). *De l'intelligence*, Paris: Hachette. Trans. 1871 T. D. Haye, *On Intelligence*, London: Reeve and Co.

Vaihinger, H. (1911). *Die Philosophie des Als Ob. System der theoretischen, praktischen und religiösen Fiktionen der Menschheit auf Grund eines idealistischen Positivismus. Mit einem Anhang über Kant und Nietzsche*, 3rd edn, Leipzig: F. Meiner, 1918. Trans. 1924 C. Ogden, *Philosophy of 'As If': A System of the Theoretical, Practical and Religious Fictions of Mankind*, London: Routledge.

Veitch, J. (1882). *Hamilton*, Edinburgh and London: William Blackwood and Sons.

Wallace, W. (1890). *Life of Schopenhauer*, London: Walter Scott.

Ward, J. (1893). '"Modern" Psychology: a Reflexion', *Mind* n.s. 2, 54–82.

Whyte, L. L. (1979). *The Unconscious Before Freud*, London: Friedman.

Windelband, W. (1892). *Geschichte der Philosophie*, Freiburg. Trans. 1893 J. Tuffs, *A History of Philosophy With Especial Reference to the Formation and Development of its Problems and Conceptions*, New York: Macmillan.

Wollheim, R. (1991). *Freud*, 2nd edn, London: FontanaCollins.

Wollheim, R. (ed.) (1974). *Freud: A Collection of Critical Essays*, New York: Anchor Doubleday. Reprinted 1977 as *Philosophers on Freud: New Evaluations*, New York: Aronson.

Wollheim, R., and Hopkins, J. (eds.) (1982). *Philosophical Essays on Freud*, Cambridge: Cambridge University Press.

Wundt, W. (1862). *Beiträge zur Theorie der Sinneswahrnehmung*, Leipzig: C. F. Winter'sche Verlagshandlung.

CHAPTER 9 LOGIC: REVIVAL AND REFORM

Behmann, H. (1922). 'Beiträge zur Algebra der Logik, insbesondere zum Entscheidungsproblem', *Mathematische Annalen* 88: 163–229.

Bentham, G. (1827). *Outline of a New System of Logic*, London: Hunt and Clarke.

Bolzano, B. (1837). *Wissenschaftslehre*, Seidel: Sulzbach. Trans. and ed. R. George, 1972 *Theory of Science*, Oxford: Blackwell; also trans. B. Terrel, ed. J. Berg, 1973 *Theory of Science*, Dordrecht: Reidel.

Boole, G. (1847). *The Mathematical Analysis of Logic*, London: G. Bell. Repr. 1948 Oxford: Blackwell.

Boole, G. (1854). *The Laws of Thought*, London: Walton and Maberley. Repr. 1951 New York: Dover.

Bosanquet, B. (1888). *Logic or the Morphology of Knowledge*, Oxford: Clarendon Press. 2nd edn 1911.

Bradley, F. H. (1883). *The Principles of Logic*, Oxford: Clarendon Press. 2nd edn 1922.

Carroll, L. (1887). (pseud. of Charles Dodgson). *The Game of Logic*, London: Macmillan.

Carroll, L. (1895). 'What the Tortoise said to Achilles', *Mind* n.s. 4: 278–80.

Carroll, L. (1896). *Symbolic Logic, a Fascinating Recreation for the Young*, London: Macmillan.

Carroll, L. (1977). *Symbolic Logic, Parts I and II*, ed. W. W. Bartley III, Hassocks: Harvester.

De Morgan, A. (1847). *Formal Logic*, London: Taylor and Walton. Repr. 1926, London: Open Court.

De Morgan, A. (1966). *On the Syllogism and other Logical Writings*, ed. P. Heath, New Haven: Yale University Press.

Drobisch, M. (1836). *Neue Darstellung der Logik*, Leipzig: Voss.

Erdmann, B. (1892). *Logik*, Halle.

Grassmann R. (1895). *Formelbuch der Formenlehre oder Mathematik*, Stettin.

Hillebrand, F. (1891). *Die neuen Theorien der kategorischen Schlüllee. Eine logische Untersuchung* (*The New Theory of Categorical Syllogisms. A Logical Investigation*), Vienna.

Huntington, E. V. (1904). 'Sets of Independent Postulates for the Algebra of Logic', *Transactions of the American Mathematical Society* 5: 288–309.

Jevons, W. S. (1864). *Pure Logic*, London: E. Stanford.

Joseph, H. W. B. (1906). *An Introduction to Logic*, Oxford: Clarendon.

Keynes, J. N. (1884). *Studies and Exercises in Formal Logic*, London: Macmillan. 4th edn 1928.

Lotze, R. H. (1874). *Logik*, 3 vols. Leipzig: S. Hirzel. Trans. 1884–8 B. Bosanquet, Oxford: Clarendon Press.

Łukasiewicz, J. (1970). *Selected Works*, ed. L. Borkowski, Amsterdam and Warsaw: North Holland and PWN.

MacColl, H. (1877–80). 'The Calculus of Equivalent Statements', *Proceedings of the London Mathematical Society* 9 (1877–8): 9–10, 177–86; 10 (1878–9): 16–28; 11 (1879–80): 113–21.

Mill, J. S. (1843). *System of Logic*, London: Longmans, Green.

Peirce, C. S. (1933). 'On an Improvement in Boole's Calculus of Logic' in C. Hartshorne, P. Weiss, and A. W. Burks (eds.), *Collected Papers of C. S. Peirce*, vol. III, Cambridge, MA: Harvard University Press.

Schröder, E. (1877). *Operationskreis des Logikkalküls*, Leipzig: Teubner.

Schröder, E. (1890–1905). *Vorlesungen zur Algebra der Logik*, 3 vols. Leipzig: Teubner. Repr. 1966, New York: Chelsea.

Sigwart, C. (1873–8). *Logik*, 2 vols., Tübingen.

Solly, T. (1839). *A Syllabus of Logic*, Cambridge: Cambridge University Press.

Venn, J. (1881). *Symbolic Logic*, London: Macmillan. Repr. 1979, New York: Chelsea.

Whately, R. (1826). *Elements of Logic*, London.

Whitehead, A. N. (1896). *Universal Algebra*, Cambridge: Cambridge University Press.

Whitehead, A. N., and Russell, B. A. W. (1910–13). *Principia Mathematica*, 3 vols., Cambridge: Cambridge University Press.

CHAPTER 10 FOUNDATIONS OF MATHEMATICS

Bernays, P. (1922). 'Die Bedeutung Hilberts für die Philosophie der Mathematik', *Die Naturwissenschaften* 2: 93–9. Trans. 1998 P. Mancosu 'Hilbert's Significance for the Philosophy of Mathematics', in Mancosu (ed.) 1998, 189–97.

Bernays, P. (1967). 'Hilbert, David (1862–1943)' in P. Edwards (ed.), 1967, *The Encyclopedia of Philosophy*, London: Macmillan, vol. III, 496–504.

Bolzano, B. (1851). *Dr. Bernard Bolzano's Paradoxien des Unendlichen, herausgegeben aus dem schriftlichen Nachlasse des Verfassers von Dr. Fr. Prihonsky*, Leipzig: Reclam. Trans. 1950 D. A. Steele, *Paradoxes of the Infinite*, London: Routledge.

Bonola, R. (1912). *Non-Euclidean Geometry: A Critical and Historical Study of its Development*, Chicago: Open Court. Repr. 1955, New York: Dover Publications Inc.

Boolos, G. (1998). *Logic, Logic and Logic*, Cambridge, MA: Harvard University Press.

Borel, E. *et al.* (1905). 'Cinq Lettres Sur la Théorie des Ensembles', *Bulletin de la Société Mathématique de France* 33: 261–73. Trans. 1982 G. Moore, 'Five Letters on Set Theory', in Moore 1982, 311–20 or Ewald (ed.) 1996, vol. II, 1077–86.

Borel, E. (1908). *Leçons Sur la Théorie des Fonctions* [*Lectures on the Theory of Functions*], Paris: Gauthier-Villars.

Brouwer, L. E. J. (1908). 'De onbetrouwbaarheid der logische principes', *Tijdschrift voor wijsbegeerte* 2: 152–8. Trans. 1975 A. Heyting, 'The Unreliability of the Logical Principles', in L. E. J. Brouwer (ed. A. Heyting), *Collected Works. Volume 1.* Amsterdam, Oxford: North-Holland Publishing Co. (1975), 107–11.

Cantor, G. (1872). 'Über die Ausdehnung eines Satzes aus der Theorie der trigonometrischen Reihen' ('On the Expansion of a Proposition from the Theory of the Trigonometric Series'), *Mathematische Annalen* 5, 123–32. Repr. in Cantor 1932, 92–101.

Cantor, G. (1874). 'Über eine Eigenschaft des Inbegriffs aller reellen algebraischen Zahlen' ('On a Property of the Set of All Real Algebraic Numbers'), *Journal für reine und angewandte Mathematik* 77, 258–62. Repr. in Cantor 1932, 115–18.

Cantor, G. (1878). 'Ein Beitrag zur Mannigfaltigkeitslehre' ('A Contribution to the Theory of Manifolds'), *Journal für reine und angewandte Mathematik* 84, 242–58. Repr. in Cantor 1932, 119–33.

Cantor, G. (1883a). 'Über unendliche lineare Punctmannigfaltigkeiten, 5' ('On infinite linear manifolds of points'), *Mathematische Annalen* 21: 545–91. Repr. in Cantor 1932, 165–209.

Cantor, G. (1883b). *Grundlagen einer allgemeinen Mannigfaltigkeitslehre. Ein mathematisch-philosophischer Versuch in der Lehre des Unendlichen.* Leipzig: Commisonsverlag von B. G. Teubner. Trans. 1996 W. Ewald, 'Foundations of a General Theory of Manifolds: a Mathematico-Philosophical Investigation into the Theory of the Infinite' in Ewald (ed.) 1996, vol. II, 878–920.

Cantor, G. (1932). *Gesammelte Abhandlungen mathematischen und philosophischen Inhalts (Collected Memoirs on Mathematical and Philosophical Subjects)*, ed. E. Zermelo, Berlin: Springer.

Cohen, P. J. (1963–4). 'The Independence of the Continuum Hypothesis', *Proceedings of the National Academy of Science*, USA, 50: 1, 143–8, 51: 105–10.

Dedekind, R. (1854). 'Über die Einführung neuer Funktionen in der Mathematik: Habilitationsvortrag, gehalten im Hause des Prof. Hoeck, in Gegenwart von Hoeck, Gauß, Weber, Waitz, 30 Juni 1854' in Dedekind 1932, item LX, 428–38. Trans. 1996 W. Ewald, 'On the Introduction of New Functions into Mathematics', in Ewald (ed.) 1996, vol. II, 754–62.

Dedekind, R. (1872). *Stetigkeit und irrationale Zahlen*, Braunschweig: Vieweg und Sohn. (Latest reprint, 1965.) Repr. in Dedekind 1932, 315–32. Trans. 1996 W. Ewald, 'Continuity and Irrational Numbers', in Ewald (ed.) 1996, vol. II, 765–79.

Dedekind, R. (1888). *Was sind und was sollen die Zahlen?*, Braunschweig: Vieweg und Sohn. (Latest reprint, 1969.) Repr. in Dedekind 1932, 335–91. Trans. 1996 W. Ewald (with the original German title) in Ewald (ed.) 1996, vol. II, 787–833.

Dedekind, R. (1932). *Gesammelte mathematische Werke, Band 3* [*Collected Mathematical Works*, vol. III], edited by R. Fricke, E. Noether, and Öystein Ore, Braunschweig: Friedrich Vieweg and Son.

Dummett, M. (1977). *Elements of Intuitionism*, Oxford: Clarendon Press.

Dummett, M. (1991). *Frege: Philosophy of Mathematics*, London: Duckworth.

Dummett, M. (1988 [1993]). *Ursprünge der analytischen Philosophie*, Frankfurt: Suhrkamp. English Version: *The Origins of Analytic Philosophy*, London: Duckworth; Cambridge, MA: Harvard University Press 1994.

Ewald, W. (ed.) (1996). *From Kant to Hilbert: A Source Book in the Foundations of Mathematics*, vols. I and II, Oxford: Clarendon Press.

Frege, G. (1879 [1967]). *Begriffsschrift, eine der arithmetischen nachgebildete Formelsprache des reinen Denkens*, Halle an die Saale: Verlag von Louis Nebert. Trans. 1967 S. Bauer-Mengelberg, '*Begriffsschrift*, a Formula Language, Modeled on that of Arithmetic, for Pure Thought', in van Heijenoort, 1–82.

Frege, G. (1884). *Die Grundlagen der Arithmetik*, Breslau: Wilhelm Koebner. Trans. 1950, 1953 J. L. Austin, *The Foundations of Arithmetic*, Oxford: Blackwell, 2nd edn, 1953.

Frege, G. (1892). 'Über Sinn und Bedeutung', *Zeitschrift für Philosophie und philosophische Kritik* 100: 25–50. Trans. 1966 M. Black 'On Sense and Reference [Meaning]', in Frege 1984, 157–77.

Frege, G. (1893). *Grundgesetze der Arithmetik, Band 1*, Jena: Hermann Pohle.

Frege, G. (1903). *Grundgesetze der Arithmetik, Band 2*, Jena: Hermann Pohle.

Frege, G. (1976). *Nachgelassene Schriften: Zweiter Band, Wissenschaftlicher Briefwechsel*, ed. H. Hermes, F. Kambartel, and F. Kaulbach, Hamburg: Felix Meiner. Partially translated as Frege 1980.

Frege, G. (1980). *Philosophical and Mathematical Correspondence*. Oxford: Basil Blackwell. Partial trans. by H. Kaal of Frege 1976.

Frege, G. (1984). *Collected Papers on Mathematics, Logic and Philosophy*, ed. B. McGuiness, Oxford: Blackwell.

Freudenthal, H. (1957). 'Zur Geschichte der Grundlagen der Geometrie: zugleich eine Besprechung der 8. Auflage von Hilberts *Grundlagen der Geometrie* [On the History of the Foundations of Geometry, at the same time a review of the 8th Edition of Hilbert's *Foundations of Geometry*]', *Nieuw Archief voor Wiskunde* 5: 105–42.

Gödel, K. (1931). 'Über formal unentscheidbare Sätze der *Principia Mathematica* und Verwandter Systeme, I', *Monatshefte für Mathematik und Physik* 38: 173. Repr. in Gödel 1986, 144–94. Trans. J. von Heijenoort 'On Formally Undecidable Propositions of *Principia Mathematica* and Related Systems I' in Gödel 1986, 145–95.

Gödel, K. (1944). 'Russell's Mathematical Logic' in P. Schillp (ed.), *The Philosophy of Bertrand Russell*, Evanston, IL: Open Court, 1944, 125–53. Reprinted in Gödel 1990, 119–41.

Gödel, K. (1990). *Collected Works*, vol. II, ed. S. Feferman, Oxford: Clarendon Press.

Goldfarb, W. (1988). 'Poincaré Against the Logicists' in W. Aspray and P. Kitcher (eds.), *History and Philosophy of Modern Mathematics*. Minnesota Studies in the Philosophy of Science, vol. 11, Minneapolis: University of Minnesota Press, 61–81.

Goldfarb, W. (1989). 'Russell's Reasons for Ramification' in C. W. Savage and C. A. Anderson (eds.), *Rereading Russell*. Minnesota Studies in the Philosophy of Science, vol. 12, Minneapolis: University of Minnesota Press, 24–40.

Gray, J. J. (1998). 'The Foundations of Geometry and the History of Geometry', *Mathematical Intelligencer* 20, 54–9.

Hallett, M. (1984). *Cantorian Set Theory and Limitation of Size*, Oxford: Clarendon Press.

Hawkins, T. (1970). *Lebesgue's Theory of Integration*, New York: Blaisdell.

Heck, R. ed. (1997). *Language, Thought and Logic: Essays in Honour of Michael Dummett*, New York: Oxford University Press.

Heijenoort, Jean van (ed.) (1967). *From Frege to Gödel: A Source Book in Mathematical Logic*, Cambridge, MA: Harvard University Press.

Helmholtz, H. von (1870). 'Über den Ursprung und die Bedeutung geometrischen Axiome' in Helmholtz 1903, vol. II, 1–31, 381–3. Trans. W. Ewald, 'On the Origin and Significance of Geometrical Axioms' in Ewald (ed.) 1996, vol. II, 662–85.

Helmholtz, H. von (1878). 'Über den Ursprung und die Bedeutung geometrischen Axiome (II)' in H. von Helmholtz, *Wissenschaftliche Abhandlungen von Hermann Helmholtz. Drei Bände*, 1882–95 Leipzig: J. A. Barth, vol. II, 640–62. Trans W. Ewald, 'On the Origin and Significance of Geometrical Axioms (II)' in Ewald (ed.) 1996, vol. II, 685–9.

Helmholtz, H. von. (1903). *Vorträge und Reden*, 5th edn, 2 vols., Braunschweig: Friedrich Vieweg und Sohn.

Hilbert, D. (1899). 'Grundlagen der Geometrie [Foundations of Geometry]' in *Festschrift zur Feier der Enthüllung des Gauss-Weber-Denkmals in Göttingen, 1899*. Leipzig: Teubner.

Hilbert, D. (1900a). 'Über den Zahlbegriff', *Jahresbericht der deutschen Mathematiker-Vereinigung* 8: 180–4. Trans. 1996 W. Ewald, 'On the Concept of Number' in Ewald (ed.) 1996, vol. II, 1089–95.

Hilbert, D. (1900b). 'Mathematische Probleme', *Nachrichten von der königlichen Gesellschaft der Wissenschaften zu Göttingen, mathematisch-physikalische Klasse* 1900: 253–96. Trans. 1902 M. W. Newson, 'Mathematical Problems', in *Bulletin of the American Mathematical Society* (2) 8: 437–79, and repr. in F. Browder (ed.), *Mathematical Developments Arising from Hilbert Problems. Proceedings of Symposia in Pure Mathematics, Volume 28, Parts 1 and 2*, 1976, Providence, RI: American Mathematical Society. Partial reprint in Ewald (ed.) 1996, vol. II, 1096–105.

Hilbert, D. (1918). 'Axiomatisches Denken', *Mathematische Annalen* 78: 405–15. Trans. 1996 W. Ewald, 'Axiomatic Thought' in Ewald (ed.) 1996, vol. II, 1105–15.

Klein, F. (1895). 'Über die Arithmetisierung der Mathematik', *Nachrichten der königlichen Gesellschaft der Wissenschaften zu Göttingen, gesellschäftliche Mitteilungen* 1895 (2), Part 2. Trans. 1996 W. Ewald, 'The Arithmetising of Mathematics' in Ewald (ed.) 1996, vol. II, 965–71.

Kronecker, L. (1887). 'Über den Zahlbegriff', in *Philosophische Aufsätze, Eduard Zeller zu seinem fünfzigjährigen Doctorjubiläum gewidmet*, Leipzig: Fues, 261–74, also *Journal für die reine und angewandte Mathematik* 101: 337–55. Trans. 1996 W. Ewald, 'On the Concept of Number' in Ewald (ed.) 1996, vol. II, 947–55.

Mancosu, P. (ed.) (1998). *From Brouwer to Hilbert: The Debate on the Foundations of Mathematics in the 1920s*. New York: Oxford University Press.

Minkowski, H. (1905). 'Peter Gustav Lejeune Dirichlet und seine Bedeutung für die heutige Mathematik [Peter Gustav Lejeune Dirichlet and his Significance for Modern Mathematics]', *Jahresbericht der deutschen Mathematiker-Vereinigung* 14: 149–63. Reprinted in H. Minkowski (ed. D. Hilbert), *Gesammelte Abhandlungen [Collected Papers]*, vols. I and II, Leipzig: B. G. Teubner, 1911, vol. II, 447–61.

Moore, G. H. (1982). *Zermelo's Axiom of Choice: Its Origins, Development and Influence*. New York, Heidelberg, Berlin: Springer Verlag.

Nagel, E. (1939). 'The Formation of Modern Conceptions of Formal Logic in the Development of Geometry', *Osiris* 7: 142–225.

Pasch, M. (1882). *Vorlesungen über neuere Geometrie [Lectures on Recent Geometry]*, Leipzig: Teubner.

Poincaré, H. (1891). 'Les Géometries non-Euclidiennes [Non-Euclidean Geometries]', *Revue générale des sciences pures et appliquées* 2: 769–74. Repr. with small alterations in Poincaré 1902, 51–70 (English trans., 35–50).

Poincaré, H. (1902). *La Science et l'hypothèse*, Paris: Ernest Flammarion. (Latest repr., 1968.) Trans. 1905 W. J. G., *Science and Hypothesis*, London: Walter Scott Publishing Co. Repr. New York: Dover, 1952.

Poincaré, H. (1909). 'Le logique de l'infini [The Logic of the Infinite]', *Revue de métaphysique et de morale* 17: 462–82. Repr. in Poincaré 1913, 7–31.

Poincaré, H. (1913). *Dernières Pensées*. Paris: Ernest Flammarion. Trans. J. Bolduc, *Mathematics and Science: Last Essays*, New York: Dover.

Quine, W. V. O. (1963). *Set Theory and Its Logic*, Cambridge, MA: Harvard University Press.

Ramsey, F. P. (1926). 'The Foundations of Mathematics', *Proceedings of the London Mathematical Society* 25 (second series): 338–84. Reprinted 1978 in F. Ramsey (ed. H. Mellor), *Foundations: Essays in Philosophy, Logic, Mathematics and Economics*, London: Routledge, 152–212.

Richard, J. (1905). 'Les principes de mathématiques et le problème des ensembles', *Revue générale des sciences pures et appliquées* 16: 541. Trans. 1967 J. van Heijenoort, 'The Principles of Mathematics and the Problem of Sets' in van Heijenoort (ed.), 1967, 142–4.

Russell, B. A. W. (1897). *An Essay on the Foundations of Geometry*, Cambridge: Cambridge University Press. Repr. 1937, New York: Dover Publications Inc.

Russell, B. A. W. (1900). *A Critical Exposition of the Philosophy of Leibniz*, London: George Allen and Unwin. 2nd edn, 1937.

Russell, B. A. W. (1903). *The Principles of Mathematics*, vol. I, Cambridge: Cambridge University Press. 2nd edn (with a new introduction), B. A. W. Russell 1937.

Russell, B. A. W. (1906). 'On Some Difficulties in the Theory of Transfinite Numbers and Order Types', *Proceedings of the London Mathematical Society* 4 (second series): 29–53. Repr. 1973 in B. Russell (ed. D. Lackey), *Essays in Analysis*. London: George Allen and Unwin, 135–64.

Russell, B. A. W. (1908). 'Mathematical Logic as Based on the Theory of Types', *American Journal of Mathematics* 30: 222–62. Repr. (among other places) in van Heijenoort (ed.) 1967, 150–82.

Russell, B. A. W. (1919). *Introduction to Mathematical Philosophy*, London: George Allen and Unwin.

Russell, B. A. W. (1937). *The Principles of Mathematics*. 2nd edn, London: George Allen and Unwin.

Stillwell, J. (1996). *Sources of Hyperbolic Geometry*, Providence, RI: American Mathematical Society.

Tarski, A. (1933). *Pojęcie prawdy w językach nauk dedukcyjnych*, Prace Towarzystwa Nawkowego Warsawrkiego, Wydzial III Nawk Matematyczno-Fizyczych 34. Trans. J. H. Woodger (ed.), 'The Concept of Truth in Formalized Languages' in A. Tarski, *Logic, Semantics,*

Metamathematics. Papers from 1923 to 1938, Oxford: Clarendon Press. 2nd edn 1983, ed. J. Corcoran, Indianapolis, IN: Hackett.

Torretti, R. (1978). *Philosophy of Geometry from Riemann to Poincaré*, Dordrecht: Reidel.

Weyl, H. (1910). 'Über die Definition der mathematischen Grundbegriffe [On the Definition of the Fundamental Mathematical Concepts]', *Mathematisch-naturwissenschaftliche Blätter* 7: 93–5, 109–13. Repr. 1968 H. Weyl (ed. K. Chandrasekharan) *Gesammelte Abhandlungen* [*Collected Papers*], vols. I–VI, Berlin, Heidelberg, New York: Springer Verlag, vol. I, 298–304.

Weyl, H. (1917). *Das Kontinuum: kritische Untersuchungen über die Grundlagen der Analysis*, Leipzig: Veit. Trans. 1987 S. Pollard and T. Bole, *The Continuum: A Critical Examination of the Foundations of Analysis*, Kirksville, MT: The Thomas Jefferson University Press, 1987. Repr. 1994, New York: Dover Publications Inc.

Whitehead, A. N. and Russell, B. A. W. (1910–13). *Principia Mathematica*, Cambridge: Cambridge University Press. 2nd edn 1927, Cambridge: Cambridge University Press.

Wright, C. (1997). 'On the Philosophical Significance of Frege's Theorem' in Heck (ed.) 1997, 201–44.

Zermelo, E. (1908a). 'Neuer Beweis für die Möglichkeit einer Wohlordnung', *Mathematische Annalen* 65: 107–28. Trans. 1967 S. Bauer-Mengelberg, 'A New Proof of the Possibility of a Well-Ordering', in van Heijenoort (ed.) 1967, 183–98.

Zermelo, E. (1908b). 'Untersuchungen über die Grundlagen der Mengenlehre, I', *Mathematische Annalen* 65, 261–81. Trans. S. Bauer-Mengelberg, 'Investigations in the Foundations of Set Theory, I' in van Heijenoort (ed.) 1967, 199–215.

Zermelo, E. (1930). 'Über Grenzzahlen und Mengenbereiche: Neue Untersuchungen über die Grundlagen der Mengenlehre', *Fundamenta mathematicae*, 16, 29–47. Trans. 1996 M. Hallett, 'On Boundary Numbers and Domains of Sets: New Investigations in the Foundations of Set Theory', in Ewald (ed.) 1996, vol. II, 1208–33.

CHAPTER 11 THEORIES OF JUDGEMENT

Baumgartner, W. (1987). 'Die Begründung von Wahrheit durch Evidenz. Der Beitrag Brentanos' in *Gewissheit und Gewissen. Festschrift für Franz Wiedmann zum 60. Geburtstag*, Würzburg: Koenigshausen and Neumann, 93–116.

Bell, D. (1990). *Husserl*, London: Routledge.

Bergmann, J. (1879). *Allgemeine Logik*, I. *Reine Logik*, Berlin: Mittler.

Bolzano, B. (1837). *Wissenschaftslehre*, 4 vols., Sulzbach: Seidel. Trans. 1972 R. George, *Theory of Science*, Oxford: Blackwell.

Brentano, F. (1862). *Von der mannigfachen Bedeutung des Seienden nach Aristotle*, Freiburg i. B.: Herder. Trans. 1975 R. George, *On the Several Senses of Being in Aristotle*, Berkeley, CA: University of California Press.

Brentano, F. (1874). *Psychologie vom empirischen Standpunkt*, Leipzig: Duncker and Humblot: 2nd edn 1924. Trans. 1973 A. C. Rancurello, D. B. Terrell, and L. L. MacAlister, *Psychology from an Empirical Standpoint*, London: Routledge.

Brentano, F. (1928). *Vom sinnlichen und noetischen Bewusstsein*. Vol. III of *Psychologie vom empirischen Standpunkt*, Leipzig: Meiner. Trans. 1981 L. L. McAlister, *Sensory and Noetic Consciousness*, London: Routledge.

Brentano, F. (1930). *Wahrheit und Evidenz*, Leipzig: Meiner. Trans. R. M. Chisholm, I. Politzer, and K. R. Fischer, *The True and the Evident*, London: Routledge, 1966.

Brentano, F. (1933). *Kategorienlehre*, Leipzig: Meiner. Trans. 1981 R. Chisholm and N. Guterman, *The Theory of Categories*, The Hague: Nijhoff.

Brentano, F. (1956). *Die Lehre vom richtigen Urteil*, Berne: Francke.

Brentano, F. (1976). *Philosophische Untersuchungen zu Raum, Zeit, und Kontinuum*, Hamburg: Meiner. Trans. 1987 B. Smith, *Philosophical Investigations on Space, Time, and the Continuum*, London: Croom Helm.

Brentano, F. (1982). *Deskriptive Psychologie*, Hamburg: Meiner. Trans. 1995 B. Müller, *Descriptive Psychology*, London and New York: Routledge.

Cantor, G. (1895/97). 'Beiträge zur Begründung der transfiniten Mengenlehre', as reprinted in Cantor 1966. Trans. 1915 P. E. B. Jourdain, *Contributions to the Founding of the Theory of Transfinite Numbers*, New York: Dover.

Cantor, G. (1966). *Gesammelte Abhandlungen Mathematischen und Philosophischen Inhalts*, Hildensheim: Olms.

Dummett, M. (1988). *Ursprünge der analytischen Philosophie*, Frankfurt: Suhrkamp. English version: *The Origins of Analytic Philosophy*, London: Duckworth, 1993; Cambridge, MA: Harvard University Press, 1994.

Findlay, J. N. (1963). *Meinong's Theory of Objects and Values*, Oxford: Clarendon Press.

Frege, G. (1879). *Begriffsschrift*, Halle. Trans. S. Bauer-Mengelberg in J. van Heijenoort (ed.), *From Frege to Gödel. A Source Book in Mathematical Logic*, Cambridge, MA: Harvard University Press.

Grossmann, R. (1974). *Meinong*, London: Routledge.

Holenstein, E. (1975). *Roman Jakobson's Approach to Language: Phenomenological Structuralism*, Bloomington, IN: Indiana University Press.

Husserl, E. (1891). *Philosophie der Arithmetik*, Halle: C. E. M. Pfeffer.

Husserl, E. (1894). 'Intentionale Gegenstände' in *Husserliana* 22, The Hague: Nijhoff. 1979, 303–48.

Husserl, E. (1900/1). *Logische Untersuchungen*, Halle: Niemeyer. Trans. 1970 J. N. Findlay *Logical Investigations*, London: Routledge.

Husserl, E. (1913). *Ideen zu einer reinen Phänomenologie und phänomenologischen Philosophie*, in *Jahrbuch für Philosophie und phänomenologische Forschung*, vol. I, 1–323. Trans. 1982 F. Kersten, *Ideas Pertaining to a Pure Phenomenology and to a Phenomenological Philosophy*, The Hague: Nijhoff.

Husserl, E. (1929). 'Formale und transzendentale Logik' in *Jahrbuch für Philosophie und phänomenologische Forschung* 10: 1–298. Trans. 1969 D. Cairns, *Formal and Transcendental Logic*, The Hague: Nijhoff.

Husserl, E. (1931). *Meditationes cartesiennes*, Paris: Colin. Trans. 1973 D. Cairns, *Cartesian Meditations*, The Hague: Nijhoff.

Husserl, E. (1936). 'Die Krisis der europäischen Wissenschaften und die transzendentale Phänomenologie', *Philosopia* 1: 77–176. Trans. 1970 D. Carr as *The Crisis of European Sciences and Transcendental Philosophy*, Evanston: Northwestern University Press.

Kotarbiński, T. (1929). *Elementy teorii poznania, logiki formalnej i metodologii nauk*, Lvov: Ossolineum. Trans. 1966 O. Wojtasiewicz, *Gnosiology: The Scientific Approach to the Theory of Knowledge*, Oxford: Pergamon Press and Wrocław: Ossolineum.

Kotarbiński, T. (1955). *Traktat o dobrej robocie*, Warsaw: PWN. Trans. 1965 O. Wojtasiewicz, *Praxiology: An Introduction to the Science of Efficient Action*, Oxford: Pergamon Press; Warsaw: PWN.

Kotarbiński, T. (1958). 'Fazy rozwoju konkretyzmu' ('The Development Stages of Concretism'), *Studia Filozoficzne*, 4 (7), 3–13.

Leśniewski, S. (1913a). 'Czy prawda jest tylko wieczna, czy też wieczna i odwieczna?', *Nowe Tory*, 18, 493–528. Trans. 1992 S. J. Surma and J. Wójcik, 'Is All Truth Only True Eternally or Is it also true Without a Beginning' in Leśniewski 1992, 86–114.

Leśniewski, S. (1913b). 'Krytyka logicznej zasady wyłaczonego środka', *Przegląd Filozoficzny*, 16, 315–52. Trans. 1992 S. J. Surma and J. Wójcik, 'The Critique of the Logical Principle of the Excluded Middle' in Leśniewski 1992, 47–85.

Leśniewski, S. (1916). *Podstawy ogólnej teorii mnogości*, Moscow: Drukarnia Poplawskiego. Trans. 1992 D. I. Barnett, 'Foundations of the General Theory of Sets' in Leśniewski 1992, 129–73.

Leśniewski, S. (1927). 'O podstawach matematyki', *Przegląd Filozoficzny*, 30. Trans. 1992 D. I. Barnett 'On the Foundations of Mathematics', in Leśniewski 1992, 174–382.

Leśniewski, S. (1992). *Collected Works*, 2 vols., Dordrecht, London, Boston: Kluwer/PWN.

Lotze, H. (1874). *Logik: Drei Bücher vom Denken, vom Untersuchen, und vom Erkennen*, 2nd edn Leipzig: S. Hirzel. Trans. 1884 (2nd edn 1887) B. Bosanquet, *Logic in Three Books: Ontology, Cosmology and Psychology*, Oxford: Clarendon Press.

Łukasiewicz, J. (1907). 'Logika a psychologia' ('Logic and Psychology'), *Przegląd Filozoficzny*, 10, 489–92.

Łukasiewicz, J. (1909). 'O prawdopodobieństwie wniosków indukcyjnych' ('On Probability of Inductive Conclusions'), *Przegląd Filozoficzny*, 12, 209–10.

Łukasiewicz, J. (1910). *O zasadzie sprzeczności u Arystotelesa* (*On the Principle of Contradiction in Aristotle*), Cracow: PAU. New edn 1987, ed. J. Woleński, Warsaw: PWN.

Łukasiewicz, J. (1913). *Die logische Grundlagen der Wahrscheinlichkeitsrechnung*, Cracow. Trans. 1970 O. Wojtasiewicz, 'Logical Foundations of Probability Theory' in J. Łukasiewicz, *Selected Works*, Amsterdam: North-Holland Publishing Company, 1970: 16–63.

Łukasiewicz, J. (1920). 'O logice trójartościowej', *Ruch filozoficzny*, 5, 170–1. Trans. 1970 O. Wojtasiewicz, 'On Three-Valued logic' in J. Łukasiewicz, *Selected Works*, Amsterdam: North-Holland Publishing Company, 1970, 87–8.

Łukasiewicz, J. (1922). 'O determinizmie' in his (1961) *Z zagadnień logiki i filozofi*, Warsaw: PWN. Trans. 1967 Z. Jordan 'On Determinism' in S. McCall, *Polish Logic 1920–1939*, Oxford: Clarendon Press, 19–39.

Łukasiewicz, J. (1951). *Aristotle's Syllogistic from the Standpoint of Modern Formal Logic*, Oxford: Oxford University Press.

Łukasiewicz, J. and Tarski, A. (1930). 'Untersuchungen über den Aussagenkalkül' in *Comptes rendus de la Société des Sciences et des Lettres de Varsovie*, cl. Iii, 23, 1–21. Trans. 1956 J. H. Woodger, 'Investigations into the Sentential Calculus' in A. Tarski (1956), *Logic, Semantics, Metamathematics*, Oxford: Oxford University Press. New edn J. Corcoran (ed.), 1983, Indianapolis, IN: Hackett.

McAlister, L. L. (ed.) (1976). *The Philosophy of Brentano*, London: Duckworth.

Meinong, A. (1894). *Psychologisch-ethische Untersuchungen zur Werttheorie* (*Psychological-ethical investigations in value theory*), Graz: Leuscher and Lubensky.

Meinong, A. (1899). 'Über Gegenstände höherer Ordnung und deren Verhältnis zur inneren Wahrnehmung' ('Objects of higher order and their relation to inner perception') in *Zeitschrift für Psychologie und Physiologie der Sinnesorgane*, 21, 182–272.

Meinong, A. (1902). *Über Annahmen*, Leipzig: Barth. 2nd edn 1910. Trans. 1983 J. Heanue, *On Assumptions*, Berkeley, Los Angeles, London: University of California Press.

Meinong, A. (1904). 'Über Gegenstandstheorie' in A. Meinong (ed.), *Untersuchungen zur Gegenstandstheorie und Psychologie*, Leipzig: Barth. Trans. 1960 by R. Chisholm, 'The Theory of Objects' in R. Chisholm (ed.), *Realism and the Background of Phenomenology*, Glencoe, IL: Free Press, 76–117.

Meinong, A. (1915). *Über Möglichkeit und Wahrscheinlichkeit* (*On Possibility and Probability*), Leipzig: Barth.

Meinong, A. (1917). 'Über emotionale Präsentationen', *Sitzungsberichte der philosophisch-historischen Klasse der kaiserlichen Akademie der Wissenschaften in Wien*, 183/2. Trans. M.-L. Schubert-Kalsi, *On Emotional Presentations*, Evanston: Northwestern University Press, 1972.

Meinong, A. (1965). *Philosophenbriefe (Philosophical Correspondence)*, Graz: Akademische Druck- und Verlagsanstalt.

Morscher, E. (1986). 'Propositions and States of Affairs in Austrian Philosophy before Wittgenstein' in J. C. Nyiri (ed.), *From Bolzano to Wittgenstein: The Tradition of Austrian Philosophy*, Vienna: Hölder-Pichler-Tempsky, 75–85.

Mulligan, K. (ed.) (1987). *Speech Act and Sachverhalt. Reinach and the Foundations of Realist Phenomenology*, Dordrecht, Boston and Lancaster: Nijhoff.

Mulligan, K., Simons, P. M., and Smith, B. (1984). 'Truth-Makers', *Philosophy and Phenomenological Research* 44: 287–321.

Nuchelmans, G. (1973). *Theories of the Proposition. Ancient and Medieval Conceptions of the Bearers of Truth and Falsity*, Amsterdam and London: North-Holland.

Reinach, A. (1911). 'Zur Theorie des negativen Urteils' as repr. in A. Reinach, *Sämtliche Werke: Kritische Ausgabe mit Kommentar*, vol. I, 1989. Munich: Philosophia. Trans. 1982 B. Smith 'On the Theory of the Negative Judgment' in Barry Smith (ed.), *Parts and Moments: Studies in Logic and Formal Ontology*, Munich: Philosophia.

Reinach, A. (1913). 'Die apriorischen Grundlagen des bürgerlichen Rechts', *Jahrbuch für Philosophie und phänomenologische Forschung* 1: 685–847. Trans. John Crosby, 'The A Priori Foundations of the Civil Law' in *Aletheia* 3 (1983): 1–142.

Rojszczak, A. (1994). 'Wahrheit und Evidenz bei Franz Brentano' ('Brentano on Truth and Evidence'), *Brentano Studien* 5 187–218.

Rojszczak, A. (1998). 'Truth-Bearers from Twardowski to Tarski' in K. Kijania-Placek and J. Woleński (eds.), *The Lvov-Warsaw School and Contemporary Philosophy*, Dordrecht: Kluwer, 73–84.

Rojszczak, A. (1999). 'Why Should a Physical Object Take on the Role of Truth-Bearer?' in E. Köhler and J. Woleński (eds.), *Alfred Tarski and the Vienna Circle*, Dordrecht: Kluwer, 115–25.

Routley, R. (1980). *Exploring Meinong's Jungle and Beyond*, Canberra: Australian National University.

Smith, B. (1978). 'An Essay in Formal Ontology', *Grazer Philosophische Studien* 6: 39–62.

Smith, B. (ed.) (1982). *Parts and Moments. Studies in Logic and Formal Ontology*. Munich: Philosophia.

Smith, B. (ed.) (1988). *Foundations of Gestalt Theory*. Munich: Philosophia.

Smith, B. (1987). 'On the Cognition of States of Affairs' in K. Mulligan (ed.), *Speech Act and Sachverhalt: Reinach and the Foundations of Realist Phenomenology*, Dordrecht: Nijhoff: 189–225.

Smith, B. (1989a). 'On The Origins of Analytical Philosophy', *Grazer Philosophische Studien* 35: 153–73.

Smith, B. (1989b). 'Logic and Formal Ontology' in J. N. Mohanty and W. McKenna (eds.), *Husserl's Phenomenology: A Textbook*, Lanham, MD: University Press of America, 1989, 29–67.

Smith, B. (1990). 'Towards a History of Speech Act Theory' in A. Burckhardt (ed.), *Speech Acts, Meanings, and Intentions: Critical Approaches to the Philosophy of John R. Searle*, Berlin: de Gruyter, 29–61.

Smith, B. (1992). 'Sachverhalt' in J. Ritter and K. Gründer (eds.), *Historisches Wörterbuch der Philosophie*, Basle: Schwabe & Co, vol. VIII, 1102–13.

Smith, B. (1994). *Austrian Philosophy*, Chicago: Open Court.

Smith, B. (1999). 'Truthmaker Realism', *Australasian Journal of Philosophy*, 77, 274–91.

Smith, B. and Smith, D. W. (eds.) (1995). *The Cambridge Companion to Husserl*, Cambridge: Cambridge University Press.

Stumpf, C. (1873). *Über den psychologischen Ursprung der Raumvorstellung* (*The Psychological Origin of Our Presentation of Space*), Leipzig: Hirzel.

Stumpf, C. (1907). 'Zur Einteilung der Wissenschaften' ('The Classification of the Sciences') in *Abhandlungen der Königlichen Preussischen Akademie der Wissenschaften*, phil.-hist. Kl., p. 4.

Stumpf, C. (ed.) (1939/40). *Erkenntnistheorie* (*The Theory of Knowledge*), Leipzig: Barth.

Twardowski, K. (1891). *Idee und Perzeption; eine erkenntnis-theoretische Untersuchung aus Descartes* (Idea and Perception; An Epistemological inquiry into Descartes), Diss. Vienna: W. Konogen.

Twardowski, K. (1894). *Zur Lehre vom Inhalt und Gegenstand der Vorstellungen: Eine psychologische Untersuchung*, Vienna: Hölder, Trans. R. Grossmann, *On the Content and Object of Presentations*, The Hague: Nijhoff, 1977.

Twardowski, K. (1900). 'O tak zwanych prawdach względnych' ('On So-Called Relative Truths') in *Księga Pamiątkowa Uniwersytetu Lwowskiego ku uczczeniu pięćsetnej rocznicy fundacji Jagiellońskiej Uniwersytetu krakowskiego*, Lvov: Nakładem Senatu Akademickiego Uniwersytetu lwowskiego. Trans. 1998 in J. Brandl and J. Woleński (eds.), *Kasimir Twardowski. Selected Writings*, Amsterdam: Rodopi.

Twardowski, K. (1912). 'O czynnościach i wytworach' in *Księga pamiątkowa Uniwersytetu lwowskiego ku uczczeniu 250-tej rocznicy założenia Uniwersytetu Lwowskiego przez króla Jana Kazimierza*, Lvov: Uniwersytet Lwowski, 1–33. Partly trans. 1979 O. Wojtasiewicz, 'Actions and Products' in J. Pelc (ed.), *Semiotics in Poland 1894–1969*, Dordrecht: Reidel and Warsaw: PWN, 13–27. Trans. 1998 in J. Brandl and J. Woleński (eds.), *Kasimir Twardowski. Selected Writings*, Amsterdam: Rodopi.

Twardowski, K. (1919–20). 'O jasnym i niejasnym stylu filozoficznym' in *Ruch Filozoficzny*, V. Partly trans. 1979 O. Wojtasiewicz, 'On Clear and Obscure Styles of Philosophical Writings' in J. Pelc (ed.), *Semiotics in Poland 1894–1969*, Dordrecht: Reidel and Warsaw: PWN, 1–2. Trans. 1998 in J. Brandl and J. Woleński (eds.), *Kasimir Twardowski. Selected Writings*, Amsterdam: Rodopi.

Willard, D. (1984). *Logic and the Objectivity of Knowledge*, Athens, OH: University of Ohio Press.

Woleński, J. (1989). *Logic and Philosophy in the Lvov-Warsaw School*, Dordrecht/Boston/Lancaster: Kluwer.

Woleński, J. (1998). 'Theories of Truth in Austrian Philosophy' in T. Czarnecki (ed.), *Rationalistic Epistemology* (*Reports on Philosophy*, No. 18), Cracow: Jagellonian University Press.

Woleński, J. and Simons, P. (1989). 'De Veritate: Austro-Polish Contributions to the Theory of Truth from Brentano to Tarski' in K. Szaniawski (ed.), *The Vienna Circle and the Lvov-Warsaw School*, Dordrecht/Boston/London: Kluwer.

CHAPTER 12 THE LOGICAL ANALYSIS OF LANGUAGE

Ayer, A. J. (1971). *Russell and Moore: The Analytical Heritage*, London: Macmillan.

Ayer, A. J. (1972). *Russell*, London: Fontana/Collins.

Bell, D. (1979). *Frege's Theory of Judgement*, Oxford: Oxford University Press.

Bell, D. (1996). 'The Formation of Concepts and the Structure of Thoughts', *Philosophy and Phenomenological Research* 61: 583–96.

Brentano, F. (1874). *Psychologie vom empirischen Standpunkt*, Leipzig: Duncker and Humboldt. Trans. 1973 A. Rancurello, D. Terrell, and L. L. McAlister, *Psychology from an Empirical Standpoint*, London: Routledge & Kegan Paul.

Clark, R. W. (1975). *The Life of Bertrand Russell*, London: Jonathan Cape and Weidenfeld and Nicolson.

Dummett, M. A. E. (1973). *Frege: Philosophy of Language*, London: Duckworth.

Dummett, M. A. E. (1981). *The Interpretation of Frege's Philosophy*, London: Duckworth.

Dummett, M. A. E. (1988 and 1994). *Ursprünge der analytischen Philosophie*, Frankfurt: Suhrkamp. English version: *Origins of Analytical Philosophy*, London: Duckworth, 1993; Cambridge, MA: Harvard University Press, 1994.

Dummett, M. A. E. (1991). *Frege: Philosophy of Mathematics*, London: Duckworth.

Evans, G. (1982). *The Varieties of Reference*, Oxford: Oxford University Press.

Frege, G. (1892). 'Über Sinn und Bedeutung', *Zeitschrift für Philosophie und philosophische Kritik* 100: 25–50. Trans. 1984 M. Black, 'On Sense and Meaning', in G. Frege (ed. B. McGuinness), *Collected Papers on Mathematics, Logic, and Philosophy*, Oxford: Blackwell, 157–77.

Frege, G. (1879). *Begriffsschrift, eine der arithmetischen nachgebildete Formelsprache des reinen Denkens*, Halle: L. Nebert. Trans. 1972 T. W. Bynum, *Conceptual Notation and Other Articles*, Oxford: Oxford University Press.

Frege, G. (1884). *Grundlagen der Arithmetik, eine logisch-mathematische Untersuchung über den Begriff der Zahl*, Breslau: W. Koebner. Trans. with German text 1953 J. L. Austin, *The Foundations of Arithmetic*, Oxford: Blackwell.

Frege, G. (1893). *Grundgesetze der Arithmetik* (vol. I), Jena: H. Pohle. Partial trans. M. Furth 1964, *The Basic Laws of Arithmetic: Exposition of the System*, Berkeley: University of California Press.

Frege, G. (1903). *Grundgesetze der Arithmetik* (vol. II), Jena: H. Pohle. Partial trans. M. Furth 1964, *The Basic Laws of Arithmetic: Exposition of the System*, Berkeley: University of California Press.

Frege, G. (1918). 'Der Gedanke. Eine Logische Untersuchung', *Beiträge zur Philosophie des deutschen Idealismus* 1: 58–77. Trans. 1984 P. Geach and R. Stoothoff, 'Thoughts', in G. Frege (ed. B. McGuinness), *Collected Papers on Mathematics, Logic, and Philosophy*, Oxford: Blackwell, 351–72.

Hylton, P. (1990). *Russell, Idealism and the Emergence of Analytic Philosophy*, Oxford: Oxford University Press.

Kant, I. (1787). *Kritik der reinen Vernunft*, 2nd edn, Riga: Hartknoch. Trans. 1933 N. Kemp Smith, *Immanuel Kant's Critique of Pure Reason*, London: Macmillan.

Kneale, W. C. and Kneale, M. (1962). *The Development of Logic*, Oxford: Oxford University Press.

Moore, G. E. (1899). 'The Nature of Judgement', *Mind* 8: 176–93.

Orstertag, G. (ed.) (1998). *Definite Descriptions. A Reader*, Cambridge, MA: MIT Press.

Passmore, J. A. (1957). *A Hundred Years of Philosophy*, London: Duckworth.

Pears, D. F. (1967). *Bertrand Russell and the British Tradition in Philosophy*, New York: Random House.

Prior, A. N. (1976). *The Doctrine of Propositions and Terms*, London: Duckworth.

Quine, W. V. O. (1974). *Methods of Logic*, 3rd edn, London: Routledge.

Resnik, M. (1980). *Frege and the Philosophy of Mathematics*, Ithaca: Cornell University Press.

Russell, B. A. W. (1903). *The Principles of Mathematics*, Cambridge: Cambridge University Press. 2nd edn (with a new introduction) 1937, London: George Allen and Unwin.

Russell, B. A. W. (1905). 'On Denoting', *Mind* ns 14: 479–93. Repr. 1956 in B. A. W. Russell, ed. R. C. Marsh, *Logic and Knowledge*, London: George Allen and Unwin, 41–56.

Russell, B. A. W. (1912). *The Problems of Philosophy*, London: Williams and Norgate, repr. 1959 Oxford: Oxford University Press, 25–32.

Russell, B. A. W. (1913). *Theory of Knowledge*. Posthumously published 1984 in B. A. W. Russell (ed. E. R. Eames), *The Collected Papers of Bertrand Russell*, vol. VII, *Theory of Knowledge: The 1913 Manuscript*, London: George Allen and Unwin.

Russell, B. A. W. (1914a). 'On the Nature of Acquaintance', *Monist* 24: 1–16; 161–87; 435–53. Repr. 1956 in B. A. W. Russell, ed. R. C. Marsh, *Logic and Knowledge*, London: George Allen and Unwin, 127–74.

Russell, B. A. W. (1914b). *Our Knowledge of the External World as a Field for Scientific Method in Philosophy*, London: George Allen and Unwin.

Russell, B. A. W. (1918). 'The Philosophy of Logical Atomism', *Monist* 28: 495–527. Repr. 1956 in B. Russell, ed. R. C. Marsh, *Logic and Knowledge*, London: George Allen and Unwin, 177–281.

Russell, B. A. W. (1921). *The Analysis of Mind*, London: George Allen and Unwin.

Russell, B. A. W. (1927). *The Analysis of Matter*, New York: Harcourt Brace and London: Kegan Paul.

Russell, B. A. W. (1940). *An Enquiry into Meaning and Truth*, New York: Norton and London: George Allen and Unwin.

Russell, B. A. W. (1948). *Human Knowledge, Its Scope and Limits*, London: George Allen and Unwin.

Sainsbury, R. M. (1979). *Russell*, London: Routledge.

Whitaker, C. W. A. (1996). *Aristotle's 'De Interpretatione': Contradiction and Dialectic*, Oxford: Oxford University Press.

Whitehead, A. N. and Russell, B. A. W. (1910–13). *Principia Mathematica*, 3 vols., Cambridge: Cambridge University Press.

Wittgenstein, L. (1921). *Logische-philosophische Abhandlung*. Trans. with German text, 1974 D. F. Pears and B. McGuinness, *Tractatus Logico-Philosophicus*, London: Routledge.

Wittgenstein, L. (1974). *Letters to Russell, Keynes and Moore*, ed. G. H. von Wright, Oxford: Blackwell.

Wright, C. (ed.)(1983). *Frege: Tradition and Influence*, Oxford: Blackwell.

Wundt, W. (1874). *Grundzüge der physiologischen Psychologie*, Leipzig: Engelmann. Partial trans. 1904 E. B. Titchener, *Principles of Physiological Psychology*, New York: Macmillan.

CHAPTER 13 THE ATOMISM DEBATE

Boltzmann, L. (1891). *Vorlesungen über Maxwells Theorie der Elektricität und des Lichts* (*Lectures on Maxwell's Theory of Electricity and Light*), Leipzig: J. Barth.

Boltzmann, L. (1896). *Vorlesungen über Gastheorie*, Leipzig: J. Barth. Trans. 1964 S. G. Brush, *Lectures on Gas Theory*, Oxford and London: Pergamon.

Boltzmann, L. (1979). *Populäre Schriften* (*Popular Essays*), Braunschweig/Wiesbaden: Vieweg.

Brush, S. J. (1966). *Kinetic Theory*, vol. II, Oxford and London: Pergamon.

Clark, P. (1976). 'Atomism versus Thermodynamics' in C. Howson (ed.), *Method and Appraisal in the Physical Sciences*, Cambridge: Cambridge University Press.

Duhem, P. (1906). *La Théorie Physique: son Objet, sa Structure*, Paris: Marcel Rivière. Trans. 1954 P. P. Wiener, *The Aim and Structure of Physical Theory*, Princeton, NJ: Princeton University Press.

Duhem, P. (1911). *Traité d'Energétique ou de Thermodynamique Générale* (*Treatise on Energetics or General Thermodynamics*), Paris: Gauthier-Villars.

Duhem, P. (1913). *Le Système du Monde* (*The World System*), Paris: Hermann.

Mach, E. (1872). *Die Geschichte und die Wurzel des Satzes von der Erhaltung der Arbeit*, Leipzig: G. Fischer. Trans. 1910 P. E. B. Jourdain, *The History and the Root of the Principle of the Conservation of Energy*, La Salle, IL: Open Court.

Mach, E. (1883). *Die Mechanik in ihrer Entwicklung historisch-kritisch dargestellt*, Leipzig: G. Fischer. Trans. 1960 T. J. Mc.Cormack, *The Science of Mechanics: A Critical and Historical Account of its Development*, La Salle, IL: Open Court.

Mach, E. (1886). *Die Analyse der Empfindungen*, Leipzig: G. Fischer. Trans. 1959 C. M. Williams and S. Waterlow, *The Analysis of Sensations*, New York: Dover.

Mach, E. (1905). *Erkenntnis und Irrtum. Skizzen zur Psychologie der Forschung*, Leipzig: J. Barth. Trans. 1976 T. J. Mc.Cormack and P. Foulkes, *Knowledge and Error – Sketches on the Psychology of Inquiry*, Dordrecht: Reidel.

Ostwald, W. (1908). *Grundriß der Naturphilosophie (Outline of Natural Philosophy)*, Leipzig: Reclam.

Ostwald, W. (1937). *L'Energie (Energy)*, Paris: Flammarion.

Sears, W. S. (1953). *Thermodynamics, the Kinetic Theory of Gases and Statistical Mechanics*, Reading, MA: Addison-Wesley.

Sears, W. S. and Salinger, G. L. (1975). *Thermodynamics, Kinetic Theory and Statistical Thermodynamics*, Reading, MA: Addison-Wesley.

Stachel, J. (ed.) (1989). *The Collected Papers of Albert Einstein*, vol. II, Princeton, NJ: Princeton University Press.

Zahar, E. (1989). *Einstein's Revolution. A Study in Heuristic*, La Salle, IL: Open Court.

Zahar, E. (1996). 'Poincaré's Structural Realism and his Logic of Discovery' in J. L. Greffe, G. Heinzmann, and K. Lorenz, *Henri Poincaré: Science and Philosophy*, Berlin: Akademie Verlag.

Zahar, E. (1997). *Leçons d'Epistémologie (Lessons in Epistemology)*, Paris: Cahiers du CREA.

Zermelo, E. (1966). 'On the Mechanical Explanation of Irreversible Processes' in S. G. Brush (ed.), *Kinetic Theory 2*, Oxford and London: Pergamon.

CHAPTER 14 THEORIES OF SPACE-TIME IN MODERN PHYSICS

Adler, R., Bazin, M., and Schiffer, M. (1965). *Introduction to General Relativity*, San Francisco: McGraw-Hill.

Barbour, J. B. (1982). 'Relational Concepts of Space and Time', *The British Journal for the Philosophy of Science* 33: 251–74.

Bergman, P. G. (1942). *Introduction to the Theory of Relativity*, Englewood Cliffs, NJ: Prentice-Hall.

Bohm, D. (1965). *The Special Theory of Relativity*, New York: W. A. Benjamin.

Boi, L. (1995). *Le problème mathématique de l espace. Une quête de l'intelligible*, Berlin: Springer.

Boi, L. (1999). 'Some Mathematical, Epistemological and Historical Reflections on the Relationship between Geometry and Reality, Spacetime Theory and the Geometrization of Theoretical Physics, from B. Riemann to H. Weyl and Beyond', *Preprint C.A.M.S.* (EHESS, Paris) no. 176: 1–41.

Cao, T. Yu (1997). *Conceptual Developments of 20th Century Field Theories*, Cambridge: Cambridge University Press.

Cartan, E. (1923). 'Sur les variétés à connexion affine et la théorie de la relativité généralisée', *Annales de l Ecole Normale Supérieure* 40: 325–412.

Clifford, W. K. (1876). 'On the Space-Theory of Matter', *Cambridge Philosophical Society Proceedings* 2: 157–8.

Cohen-Tannoudji, G. and Spiro, M. (1986). *La matière-espace-temps*, Paris: Fayard.

Coleman, R. A. and Korté, H. (1995). 'A New Semantics for the Epistemology of Geometry. I: Modeling Spacetime Structure', *Erkenntnis* 2, 42: 141–60. (Special Issue on 'Reflections on Spacetime: Foundations, Philosophy, History', ed. U. Majer and H.-J. Schmidt.)

Damour, Th. (1995). 'General Relativity and Experiment' in D. Iagolnitzer (ed.), *Proceedings of the XIth International Congress of Mathematical Physics*, Boston: International Press, 37–46.

Earman, J., Glymour, C., and Stachel, J. (eds.) (1977). *Foundations of Space-Time Theories*, Minneapolis: University of Minnesota Press.

Eddington, A. (1924). *The Mathematical Theory of Relativity*, Cambridge: Cambridge University Press.

Ehlers, J. (1973). 'The Nature and Structure of Spacetime' in J. Mehra (ed.), *The Physicist's Conception of Nature*, Dordrecht: Reidel, 71–91.

Einstein, A. (1905). 'Zur Elektrodynamik bewegter Körper', *Annalen der Physik* 17: 891–921.

Einstein, A. (1916). 'Die Grundlagen der allgemeinen Relativitätstheorie', *Annalen der Physik* 4, 49: 769–822.

Einstein, A. (1956). *The Meaning of Relativity*, Princeton, NJ: Princeton University Press.

Einstein, A. and Infeld, L. (1938). *The Evolution of Physics*, New York: Simon and Schuster.

Ellis, G. F. R. and Williams, R. M. (1988). *Flat and Curved Space-Times*, Oxford: Clarendon Press.

Feynman, R. (1967). *The Character of Physical Laws*, Cambridge, MA: The MIT Press.

Fock, V. (1959). *The Theory of Space, Time and Gravitation*, London: Pergamon Press.

Friedman, M. (1983). *Foundations of Space-Time Theories: Relativistic Physics and the Philosophy of Science*, Princeton, NJ: Princeton University Press.

Geroch, R. P. and Horowitz, G. T. (1979). 'Global structures of spacetimes' in S. W. Hawking and W. Israel (eds.), *General Relativity. An Einstein Centenary Survey*, Cambridge: Cambridge University Press, 212–93.

Graves, J. C. (1971). *The Conceptual Foundations of Contemporary Relativity Theory*, Cambridge, MA: The MIT Press.

Grünbaum, A. (1973). *Philosophical Problems of Space and Time*, 2nd, enlarged edn. Dordrecht: Reidel.

Hawking, S. W. and Ellis, G. F. R. (1973). *The Large Scale Structure of Space-Time*, Cambridge: Cambridge University Press.

Holton, G. (1960). 'On the Origins of the Special Theory of Relativity', *American Journal of Physics* 28: 627–36.

Kanitscheider, B. (1972). 'Die Rolle der Geometrie innerhalb physikalischer Theorien', *Zeitschrift für Philosophische Forschung* 26: 42–55.

Kobayashi, S. and Nomizu, K. (1962). *Foundations of Differential Geometry*, 2 vols. New York: Wiley.

Lichnerowicz, A. (1955). *Théories relativistes de la gravitation et de l'électromagnétisme*, Paris: Masson.

Lindsay, R. B. and Margenau, H. (1957). *Foundations of Physics*, New York: Dover.

Lorentz, H. A. (1905). *Versuch einer Theorie der electrischen und optischen Erscheinungen in bewegten Körpern*, Leiden: Brill.

Lorentz, H. A., Einstein, A., Minkowski, H., and Weyl, H. (1923). *The Principle of Relativity. A Collection of Original Memoirs on the Special and General Theory of Relativity*, London: Methuen.

Mach, E. (1883). *Die Mechanik in ihrer Entwicklung historisch-kritisch dargestellt*, Leipzig: Brockhaus. Trans. 1893 T. McCormack, *The Science of Mechanics*, Chicago: Open Court.

Mainzer, K. (1994). 'Philosophie und Geschichte von Raum und Zeit', in J. Ausdretsch and K. Mainzer (eds.), *Philosophie und Physik der Raum-Zeit*, Zurich: Bibliographische Institut, 11–51.

Malamet, D. (1997). 'Causal theories of time and the conventionality of simultaneity', *Noûs* 11: 293–300.

Minkowski, H. (1909). 'Raum und Zeit', *Physikalische Zeitschrift* 10: 104–11.

Misner, C. W., K. S. Thorne, and J. A. Wheeler (1973), *Gravitation*, San Francisco: Freeman.

Paty, M. (1993). *Einstein Philosophe*, Paris: Presses Universitaires de France.

Pauli, W. (1981). *Theory of Relativity*, New York: Dover. 1st German edn 1921.

Penrose, R. (1968). 'Structure of Space-Time', in C. M. DeWitt and J. A. Wheeler (eds.), *Battelle Rencontres. 1967 Lectures in Mathematics and Physics*, New York: Benjamin, 121–235.

Petitot, J. (1992). 'Actuality of Transcendental Aesthetics for Modern Physics', in L. Boi *et al.* (eds.), *A Century of Geometry: Epistemology, History and Mathematics*, Heidelberg: Springer Verlag, 239–63.

Poincaré, H. (1902). *La Science et l'Hypothèse*, Paris: Flammarion.

Poincaré, H. (1906). 'Sur la dynamique de l'électron', *Rend. Circ. Mat. Palermo* 21: 129–75.

Regge, T. (1961). 'General relativity without coordinates', *Rivista del Nuovo Cimento* 19: 558–71.

Reichenbach, H. (1958). *The Philosophy of Space and Time*, transl. M. Reichenbach and J. Freund, New York: Dover.

Ricci, G. and Levi-Civita, T. (1901). 'Méthodes de calcul différentiel absolu et leurs applications', *Mathematische Annalen* 54: 125–201.

Riemann, B. (1867). 'Über die Hypothesen, welche der Geometrie zu Grunde liegen', *Abhandlungen der Königlichen Gesellschaft der Wissenschaften zur Göttingen* 13: 133–52.

Rindler, W. (1960). *Special Relativity*, Edinburgh: Oliver & Boyd.

Schilpp, P. A. (ed.) (1949). *Albert Einstein: Philosopher-Scientist*, Evanston, IL: The Library of Living Philosophers.

Schrödinger, E. (1954). *Space-Time Structure*, Cambridge: Cambridge University Press.

Souriau, J.-M. (1964). *Géométrie et Relativité*, Paris: Hermann.

Spivak, M. (1979). *A Comprehensive Introduction to Differential Geometry*, Berkeley, CA: Publish or Perish.

Stachel, J. (1995). 'History of Relativity' in L. M. Brown, A. Pais, and Sir B. Pippard (eds.), *Twentieth Century Physics*, vol. I, Bristol: Institute of Physics Publ., 249–356.

Stamatescu, I.-O. (1994). 'Quantum Field Theory and the Structure of Space-Time' in I.-O. Stamatescu (ed.), *Philosophy, Mathematics and Modern Physics*, Heidelberg: Springer Verlag, 67–91.

Synge, J. L. (1955). *Relativity: The Special Theory*, Amsterdam: North-Holland.

Synge, J. L. (1964). *The Petrov Classification of Gravitational Fields*, Dublin: Dublin Institute for Advanced Studies.

Torretti, R. (1996), *Relativity and Geometry*, New York: Dover (1st edn Pergamon, 1983).

Trautman, A. (1973). 'Theory of Gravitation' in J. Mehra (ed.), *The Physicist's Conception of Nature*, Dordrecht: Reidel, 179–201.

Trautman, A., Pirani, F. A. E., and Bondi, H. (1965). *Lectures on General Relativity*, Englewood Cliffs, NJ: Prentice-Hall.

Weinberg, S. (1973). *Gravitation and Cosmology. Principles and Applications of the General Theory of Relativity*, New York: Wiley.

Weinberg, S. (1918). *Raum-Zeit-Materie*, Berlin: Springer Verlag. 4th edn (1921).

Weyl, H. (1918). Transl. H. L. Brose, *Space-Time-Matter*, London: Methuen.

Wheeler, J. A. (1962). *Geometrodynamics*, New York and London: Academic Press.

Zahar, E. (1989). *Einstein's Revolution: A Study in Heuristic*, La Salle, IL: Open Court.

Zeeman, E. C. (1967). 'The Topology of Minkowski space', *Topology* 6: 161–70.

CHAPTER 15 THE GERMAN DEBATE OVER THE GEISTESWISSENSCHAFTEN
IN GERMAN PHILOSOPHY

Barth, P. (1897). *Die Philosophie der Geschichte als Soziologie, Erster Teil*, 1st edn. (*The Philosophy of History as Sociology, first part*), Leipzig: O. R. Reisland.

Barth, P. (1899). 'Fragen der Geschichtswissenschaft: I, Darstellende und begriffliche Geschichte' ('Questions of Historical Science: I, Descriptive and Conceptual History'), *Vierteljahrschrift für wissenschaftliche Philosophie* (*Quarterly for Scientific Philosophy*) 23: 322–59.

Barth, P. (1915). *Die Philosophie der Geschichte als Soziologie*, (*The Philosophy of History as Sociology*), 2nd rev. edn, Leipzig: O. R. Reisland.

Cassirer, E. (1921–9). *Philosophie der symbolischen Formen*, 3 vols., Berlin: Cassirer. Trans. 1955 R. Mannheim, *The Philosophy of Symbolic Forms*, 3 vols., New Haven, CT: Yale University Press.

Cassirer, E. (1942). *Zur Logik der Kulturwissenschaften: Fünf Studien*, in *Göteborgs Högskolas Årsskrift, Band XLVIII*, Göteborg: Wettergren and Kerbers, 2–139. Trans. 1961 C. S. Howe, *The Logic of the Humanities*, New Haven, CT: Yale University Press.

Dilthey, W. (1883). *Einleitung in die Geisteswissenschaften: Versuch einer Grundlegung für das Studium der Gesellschaft und der Geschichte, Erster Band* (1922 *Gesammelte Schriften*, vol. I), Leipzig and Berlin: B. G. Teubner. Trans. 1989 M. Neville (ed. R. Makkreel and F. Rodi) *Introduction to the Human Sciences* (*Selected Works*, vol. I), Princeton, NJ: Princeton University Press.

Dilthey, W. (1894). 'Ideen über eine beschreibende und zergliedernde Psychologie' in 1924 *Die Geistige Welt* (*Gesammelte Schriften*, vol. V), Leipzig and Berlin: B. G. Teubner. Trans. 1977 R. M. Zaner, 'Ideas Concerning and Descriptive and Analytic Psychology' in Dilthey, *Descriptive Psychology and Historical Understanding*, The Hague: Nijhoff.

Dilthey, W. (1910). 'Der Aufbau der geschichtlichen Welt in den Geisteswissenschaften' ('The Construction of the Historical World in the Human Sciences') in Dilthey 1927.

Dilthey, W. (1927). *Der Aufbau der geschichtlichen Welt in den Geisteswissenschaften* (*The Construction of the Historical World in the Human Sciences*) (*Selected Works*, vol. VII), Leipzig and Berlin: Teubner .

Erdmann, B. (1878). 'Die Gliederung der Wissenschaften' ('The Division of the Sciences'), *Vierteljahrschrift für wissenschaftliche Philosophie* (*Quarterly for Scientific Philosophy*) 2: 72–105.

Gadamer, H.-G. (1960). *Wahrheit und Methode* (*Gesammelte Werke* vol. I), Tübingen: J. C. B. Mohr. Trans. 1989 J. Weinsheimer and D. G. Marshall, *Truth and Method*, New York: Crossroad.

Heidegger, M. (1927 [1957]). *Sein und Zeit*, Tübingen: M. Niemeyer. Trans. 1962 J. Macquarrie and E. Robinson, *Being and Time*, New York: Harper and Row.

Helmholtz, H. Vōn (1865). 'Über das Verhältnis der Naturwissenschaften zur Gesamtheit der Wissenschaft' in *Populäre wissenschaftliche Vorträge, erstes Heft* (Popular Scientific Lectures, no. 1), Braunschweig: F. Vieweg, 3–29. Trans. 1971 R. Kahl, 'The Relation of the Natural Sciences to Science in General' in *Selected Writings of Hermann von Helmholtz*, Middletown, CT: Wesleyan University Press, 122–43.

Hempel, C. G. (1942). 'The Problem of Historical Knowledge', *The Journal of Philosophy* 39: 35–48.

Hempel, C. G. (1962). 'Explanation in Science and in History' in R. G. Colodny (ed.), *Frontiers of Science and Philosophy*, Pittsburgh, PA: University of Pittsburgh Press, 9–33.

Lamprecht, K. (1896). *Alte und neue Richtungen in der Geschichtswissenschaft* (*Old and New Directions in Historical Science*), Berlin: R. Gaertners.

Lamprecht, K. (1900). *Die kulturhistorische Methode* (*The Method of Cultural History*), Berlin: R. Gaertners.

Lamprecht, K. (1904 [1909]). *Moderne Geschichtswissenschaft: fünf Vorträge*, 3rd edn, Berlin: Weidmannsche. Trans. 1905 E. A. Andrews, *What is History?: Five Lectures on the Modern Science of History*, New York: Macmillan.

Lotze, H. (1874 [1880]). *Logik: Drei Bücher, vom Denken, vom Untersuchen, und vom Erkennen, zweite Auflage* (1st edn 1874), Leipzig: S. Hirzel. Trans. 1888 B. Bosanquet, *Logic in Three Books, of Thought, of Investigation, and of Knowledge*, Oxford: Clarendon Press.

Mach, E. (1903). *Populär-wissenschaftliche Vorlesungen*, 3rd edn, Leipzig: J. A. Barth. Originally published in English trans. 1894 T. J. McCormack, *Popular Scientific Lectures*, Chicago: Open Court.

Makkreel, R. A. (1975). *Dilthey, Philosopher of the Human Studies*, Princeton, NJ: Princeton University Press.

Mill, J. S. (1843). *A System of Logic Ratiocinative and Inductive, Being a Connected View of the Principles of Evidence and the Methods of Scientific Investigation* (1974 *Collected Works*, vols. VII–VIII), J. M. Robson (ed.), Toronto: University of Toronto Press.

Oakes, G. (1988). *Weber and Rickert: Concept Formation in the Cultural Sciences*, Cambridge, MA: MIT Press.

Rickert, H. (1896–1902). *Die Grenzen der naturwissenschaftlichen Begriffsbildung: eine logische Einleitung in die historischen Wissenschaften* (1929, 5th edn), Tübingen: J. C. B. Mohr. Trans. (abridged) 1986 G. Oakes, *The Limits of Concept Formation in Natural Science: A Logical Introduction to the Historical Sciences*, Cambridge: Cambridge University Press.

Rickert, H. (1898). *Kulturwissenschaft und Naturwissenschaft* (6th and 7th rev. edns, 1926), Tübingen: J. C. B. Mohr. Trans. 1962 G. Reisman, *Science and History, A Critique of Positivist Epistemology*, New York: Van Nostrand.

Rothacker, E. (1927). *Logik und Systematik der Geisteswissenschaften* (*Logic and Systematic of the Human Sciences*), Munich: R. Oldenbourg.

Sigwart, C. (1873 [1889]). *Logik, zweite durchgesehene und erweiterte Auflage*, Freiburg i.B.: J. C. B. Mohr. Trans. 1895 H. Dendy, *Logic*, 2nd edn, revised and enlarged, London: Swan Sonnenschein.

Simmel, G. (1892). *Die Probleme der Geschichtsphilosophie*, 1st edn (1989 *Gesamtausgabe*, vol. II), Frankfurt on Main: Suhrkamp.

Simmel, G. (1905). *Die Probleme der Geschichtsphilosophie*, 2nd rev. edn (1997 *Gesamtausgabe*, vol. IX), Frankfurt on Main: Suhrkamp. Trans. 1977 G. Oakes, *The Problems of the Philosophy of History: An Epistemological Essay*, New York: Macmillan.

Simmel, G. (1918). 'Vom Wesen des historischen Verstehens' Berlin: Mittler. Trans. 1980 G. Oakes, 'On the Nature of Historical Understanding', in *Essays on Interpretation in Social Science*, Totowa, NJ: Rowman and Littlefield, 97–126.

Spranger, E. (1921). *Lebensformen* (*Forms of Life*), Halle: M. Niemeyer.

Troeltsch, E. (1922). *Der Historismus und seine Probleme, erstes Buch: das logische Problem der Geschichtsphilosophie* (*Gesammelte Schriften*, vol. III) (*Historicism and its Problems*, Book I: *The Logical Problem of the Philosophy of History*), Tübingen: J. C. B. Mohr.

Weber, M. (1904). 'Die "Objectivität" im sozialwissenschaftlicher und sozialpolitischer Erkenntnis', *Archiv für Sozialwissenschaft und Sozialpolitik* 19: 22–87. Trans. 1949 E. A. Shils and H. A. Finch, ' "Objectivity" in Social Science and Social Policy', in *The Methodology of the Social Sciences*, Glencoe, IL: Free Press, 49–112.

Weber, M. (1906). 'Kritische Studien auf dem Gebiet der kulturwissenschaftlichen Logik', *Archiv für Sozialwissenschaft und Sozialpolitik* 22: 143–207. Trans. 1949 E. A. Shils and H. A. Finch, 'Critical Studies in the Logic of the Cultural Sciences: a Critique of Eduard Meyer's Methodological Views', in *The Methodology of the Social Sciences*, Glencoe, IL: Free Press, 113–88.

Weber, M. (1913). 'Über einige Kategorien der verstehenden Soziologie', *Logos* 4: 253–94. Trans. 1981 E. Graber, 'Some Categories of Interpretive Sociology', *Sociological Quarterly* 22: 145–80.

Windelband, W. (1894). 'Geschichte und Naturwissenschaft (Strassburger Rektoratsrede 1894)', in Windelband 1907, 355–79.

Windelband, W. (1907). *Präludien: Aufsätze und Reden zur Einleitung in die Philosophie*, 3rd rev. edn (1st edn 1884), Tübingen: J. C. B. Mohr.

Wundt, W. (1883). *Logik: eine Untersuchung der Prinzipien der Erkenntnis und der Methoden wissenschaftlicher Forschung, zweiter Band: Methodenlehre* (*Logic: An Investigation of the Principles of Cognition and the Methods of Scientific Research*, vol. II: *Doctrine of Method*), Stuttgart: F. Enke.

Wundt, W. (1893–5). *Logik: eine Untersuchung der Prinzipien der Erkenntnis und der Methoden wissenschaftlicher Forschung* (*Logic: An Investigation of the Principles of Cognition and the Methods of Scientific Research*), vol. I, Stuttgart: F. Enke.

Wundt, W. (1895). *Logik: eine Untersuchung der Prinzipien der Erkenntnis und der Methoden wissenschaftlicher Forschung, zweiter Band: Methodenlehre, zweite Abtheilung: Logik der Geisteswissenschaften* (*Logic: An Investigation of the Principles of Cognition and the Methods of Scientific Research, vol. II: Doctrine of Method, second part: Logic of the Human Sciences*), Stuttgart: F. Enke.

Wundt, W. (1913). *Die Psychologie im Kampf ums Dasein* (*Psychology in the Struggle for Existence*), Leipzig: Engelmann.

CHAPTER 16 FROM POLITICAL ECONOMY TO POSITIVE ECONOMICS

Black, R. D. C. (1972). 'W. S. Jevons and the Foundations of Modern Economics', *History of Political Economy* 4: 364–78.

Blaug, M. (1972). 'Was There a Marginal Revolution?', *History of Political Economy* 4: 269–80.

Caldwell, B. J. (ed.) (1990). *Carl Menger and His Legacy in Economics*, Durham, NC: Duke University Press.

Creedy, J. (1986). *Edgeworth and the Development of Neoclassical Economics*, Oxford: Blackwell.

De Marchi, N. B. (1972). 'Mill and Cairnes and the Emergence of Marginalism in England', *History of Political Economy* 4: 344–63.

Edgeworth, F. Y. (1881). *Mathematical Psychics: An Essay on the Application of Mathematics to the Moral Sciences*, London: Kegan Paul. Reprint edn 1965, New York: Augustus M. Kelley.

Edgeworth, F. Y. (1925). *Papers Relating to Political Economy*, 3 vols., New York: Burt Franklin.

Fisher, I. (1892 [1925]). *Mathematical Investigations in the Theory of Value and Prices*, New Haven, CT: Yale University Press.

Franklin, J. (1983). 'Mathematical Methods in Economics', *American Mathematical Monthly* 90: 229–44.

Gordon, H. S. (1973). 'Alfred Marshall and the Development of Economics as a Science' in R. N. Giere and R. S. Westfall (eds.), *Foundations of Scientific Method: The Nineteenth Century*, Bloomington, IN: Indiana University Press.

Hausman, D. (1992). *The Inexact and Separate Science of Economics*, Cambridge: Cambridge University Press.

Hollander, S. (1987). *Classical Economics*, Oxford: Blackwell.

Hutchison, T. W. (1978). *On Revolutions and Progress in Economic Knowledge*, Cambridge: Cambridge University Press.

Ingrao, B. and Israel, G. (1987). *La Mano Invisible*, Roma–Bari: Guis. Laterza and Figli Spa. Trans. 1990 I. McGilvray, *The Invisible Hand*, Cambridge, MA: MIT Press.

Jaffé, W. (1976). 'Jevons, Menger, and Walras De-Homogenized', *Economic Inquiry* 14: 511–24.

Jaffé, W. (1983). *William Jaffé's Essays on Walras*, Cambridge: Cambridge University Press.

Jevons, W. S. (1871 [1957]). *The Theory of Political Economy*, 5th edn (ed. H. S. Jevons) London: Macmillan. Repr. edn 1965, New York: Augustus M. Kelley.

Jevons, W. S. (1874 [1877]). *The Principles of Science*, London: Macmillan.

Keynes, J. M. (1921). *A Treatise on Probability*, London: Macmillan.

Keynes, J. N. (1890). *Scope and Method of Political Economy*, London: Macmillan.

Maloney, J. (1985). *Marshall, Orthodoxy, and the Professionalisation of Economics*, Cambridge: Cambridge University Press.

Marshall, A. (1890 [1920]). *Principles of Economics*, 8th edn, London: Macmillan. Repr. edn. 1979, London: Macmillan.

Menger, C. (1871). *Grundsätze der Volkswirtschaftslehre*. Trans. 1976 J. Dingwall and B. F. Hoselitz, *Principles of Economics*, New York: New York University Press.

Mirowski, P. (1989). *More Heat than Light: Economics as Social Physics, Physics as Nature's Economics*, Cambridge: Cambridge University Press.

Morgan, M. S. (1990). *The History of Econometric Ideas*, Cambridge: Cambridge University Press.

Newcomb, S. (1886). *Principles of Political Economy*, New York: Harper & Bros. Repr. edn 1966, New York: Augustus M. Kelley.

Pareto, V. (1909). *Manuel d'économie politique*, Paris: Giard & Brière.

Peart, S. J. (1996). *The Economics of W. S. Jevons*, London: Routledge.

Pigou, A. C. (1912). *Wealth and Welfare*, London: Macmillan.

Redman, D. A. (1997). *The Rise of Political Economy as a Science*, Cambridge, MA: MIT Press.

Rutherford, M. (1994). *Institutions in Economics: The Old and the New Institutionalism*, Cambridge: Cambridge University Press.

Schabas, M. (1990). *A World Ruled by Number: William Stanley Jevons and the Rise of Mathematical Economics*, Princeton, NJ: Princeton University Press.

Sidgwick, H. (1883). *Principles of Political Economy*, London: Macmillan.

Smith, B. (1986). 'Austrian Economics and Austrian Philosophy' in W. Grassl and B. Smith (eds.), *Austrian Economics: Historical and Philosophical Background*, London: Croom Helm.

Tarascio, V. J. (1968). *Pareto's Methodological Approach to Economics*, Chapel Hill, NC: University of North Carolina Press.

Veblen, T. (1899 [1967]). *The Theory of the Leisure Class*, Harmondsworth: Penguin.

Walras, L. (1874 [1900]). *Eléments d'économie politique pure*, 4th edn, Lausanne: F. Rouge and Paris: F. Pichon. Repr. edn 1976 Paris: R. Pichon and R. Durand-Auzias.

Weintraub, R. (1985). *General Equilibrium Analysis*, Cambridge: Cambridge University Press.

Wicksteed, P. H. (1935). *The Common Sense of Political Economy*, 2 vols. L. Robbins (ed.), London: George Routledge & Sons.

CHAPTER 17 SOCIOLOGY AND THE IDEA OF SOCIAL SCIENCE

Durkheim, E. (1895). *Les règles de la méthode sociologique*, Paris: Alcan. Trans. 1938 S. A. Solovay and J. H. Mueller, *The Rules of Sociological Method*, Chicago, IL: University of Chicago Press.

Durkheim, E. (1897). *Le Suicide: étude de sociologie*, Paris: Alcan. Trans. 1951 J. A. Spaulding and G. Simpson, *Suicide: A Study in Sociology*, Glencoe, IL: Free Press.

Durkheim, E. (1912). *Les Formes élémentaires de la vie religieuse*, Paris: Alcan. Trans. 1915 J. W. Swain, *The Elementary Forms of Religious Life*, New York: Macmillan.

Weber, M. (1904). 'Die "Objectivität" sozialwissenschaftlicher und sozialpolitischer Erkenntnis', *Archiv für Sozialwissenschaft und Sozialpolitik* 19: 22–87. Trans. 1949 E. A. Shils and H. A. Finch, ' "Objectivity" in Social Science and Social Policy' in *The Methodology of the Social Sciences*, Glencoe, IL: Free Press, 49–112.

CHAPTER 18 UTILITARIANS AND IDEALISTS

Bradley, F. H. (1927). *Ethical Studies*, 2nd edn, Oxford: Clarendon Press.

Bradley, F. H. (1893). *Appearance and Reality*, 2nd edn 1906, 9th corrected impression, Oxford: Clarendon Press.

Green, T. H. (1883). *Prolegomena to Ethics*, ed. by A. C. Bradley, Oxford: Clarendon Press.

Grote, John (1870). *An Examination of the Utilitarian Philosophy*, Cambridge: Deighton, Bell, and Co.

Huxley, T. H. (1894). *Evolution and Ethics, and Other Essays*, London: Macmillan.

Lecky, William Edward Hartpole (1869). *History of European Morals from Augustus to Charlemagne*, London: Longmans, Green.

Manser, Anthony and Stock, Guy (eds.) (1984). *The Philosophy of F. H. Bradley*, Oxford: Clarendon Press.

Nicholson, Peter P. (1990). *The Political Philosophy of the British Idealists*, Cambridge: Cambridge University Press.

Schneewind, J. B. (1977). *Sidgwick's Ethics and Victorian Moral Philosophy*, Oxford: Clarendon Press.

Schultz, Bart (ed.) (1992). *Essays on Henry Sidgwick*, Cambridge: Cambridge University Press.

Sidgwick, Henry (1874 [1907]). *The Methods of Ethics*, 7th edn, London: Macmillan.

Spencer, Herbert (1893). *The Principles of Ethics*, London: Williams and Norgate.

Spencer, Herbert (1907). *The Data of Ethics*, London: Williams and Norgate. (Original edn 1879.)

Stephen, Leslie (1882). *The Science of Ethics*, London: Smith, Elder, and Co.

Thomas, Geoffrey (1987). *The Moral Philosophy of T. H. Green*, Oxford: Clarendon Press.

CHAPTER 19 NIETZSCHE

Clark, M. (1990). *Nietzsche on Truth and Philosophy*, Cambridge: Cambridge University Press.

Danto, A. C. (1965). *Nietzsche as Philosopher*, New York: Macmillan.

Hayman, R. (1980). *Nietzsche: A Critical Life*, London: Weidenfeld and Nicolson.

Heidegger, M. (1961). *Nietzsche*, 2 vols. Pfullingen: Neske. Trans. 1979–84 D. F. Krell, *Nietzsche*, 4 vols. New York: Harper and Row.

Jaspers, K. (1936). *Nietzsche: Einführung in das Verständnis seines Philosophierens*, Berlin and Leipzig: de Gruyter. Trans. 1965 C. F. Wallraff and F. J. Schmitz, *Nietzsche: An Introduction to the Understanding of His Philosophical Activity*, Tucson: University of Arizona Press.

Kaufmann, W. (1974). *Nietzsche: Philosopher, Psychologist, Antichrist*, 4th edn Princeton, NJ: Princeton University Press.

Magnus, B. (1978). *Nietzsche's Existential Imperative*, Bloomington, IN: Indiana University Press.

Magnus, B. and Higgins, K. M. (eds.) (1996). *The Cambridge Companion to Nietzsche*, Cambridge and New York: Cambridge University Press.

Nehamas, A. (1985). *Nietzsche: Life as Literature*, Cambridge, MA: Harvard University Press.

Nietzsche, F. (1878–80). *Menschliches, Allzumenschliches*, Chemnitz: E. Schmeitzner. Trans. 1986 R. J. Hollingdale, *Human, All Too Human*, Cambridge: Cambridge University Press.

Nietzsche, F. (1881). *Die Morgenröte*, Chemnitz: E. Schmeitzner. Trans. 1982 R. J. Hollingdale, *Daybreak*, Cambridge: Cambridge University Press.

Nietzsche, F. (1882). *Die fröhliche Wissenschaft*, Chemnitz: E. Schmeitzner. Trans. 1974 W. Kaufmann, *The Gay Science*, New York: Vintage.

Nietzsche, F. (1883–5). *Also sprach Zarathustra*, Chemnitz: E. Schmeitzner. Trans. 1961 R. J. Hollingdale, *Thus Spoke Zarathustra*, Harmondsworth: Penguin.

Nietzsche, F. (1886). *Jenseits von Gut und Böse*, Leipzig: C. G. Naumann. Trans. 1973 R. J. Hollingdale, *Beyond Good and Evil*, Harmondsworth: Penguin.

Nietzsche, F. (1887). *Zur Genealogie der Moral*, Leipzig: C. G. Naumann. Trans. 1969 W. Kaufmann and R. J. Hollingdale, *On the Genealogy of Morals*, New York: Vintage.

Nietzsche, F. (1889). *Götzen-Dämmerung*, Leipzig: C. G. Naumann. Trans. 1968 R. J. Hollingdale, *Twilight of the Idols*, Harmondsworth: Penguin.

Nietzsche, F. (1908). *Ecce homo*, Leipzig: Insel-Verlag. Trans. 1979 R. J. Hollingdale, *Ecce Homo*, Harmondsworth: Penguin.

Nietzsche, F. (1980). *Sämtliche Werke: Kritische Studienausgabe*, ed. G. Colli and M. Montinari, Berlin: de Gruyter.

Nietzsche, F. (1986). *Sämtliche Briefe: Kritische Studienausgabe*, ed. G. Colli and M. Montinari, Berlin: de Gruyter.

Russell, B. (1946). *History of Western Philosophy*, London: George Allen and Unwin.

Schacht, R. (1983). *Nietzsche*, London: Routledge.

Sleinis, E. E. (1994). *Nietzsche's Revaluation of Values*, Urbana and Chicago: University of Illinois Press.

Tanner, M. (1994). *Nietzsche*, Oxford: Oxford University Press.

Young, J. (1992). *Nietzsche's Philosophy of Art*, Cambridge: Cambridge University Press.

CHAPTER 20 THE NEW REALISM IN ETHICS

Brentano, F. (1874). *Psychologie vom empirischen Standpunkt*, Leipzig: Duncker and Humblot. Trans. 1995 L. L. McAlister (ed.), *Psychology from an Empirical Standpoint*, 2nd Engl. edn, London: Routledge.

Brentano, F. (1889). *Vom Ursprung sittlicher Erkenntnis*, Leipzig: Duncker and Humboldt. Trans. 1969 R. M. Chisholm (ed.), *The Origin of Our Knowledge of Right and Wrong*, London: Routledge.

Brentano, F. (1952). *Grundlegung und Aufbau der Ethik*, Berne: Francke. Trans. 1973, E. H. Schneewind (ed.), *The Foundation and Construction of Ethics*, London: Routledge.

Brentano, F. (1966). *Die Abkehr vom Nichtrealen* (*The Turn From the Non-Real*), Berne: Francke.

Ehrenfels, C. von. (1890). 'Über Gestaltqualitäten' ('On "Gestalt qualities" '), *Vierteljahresschrift für wissenschaftliche Philosophie*, 14: 249–92.

Ehrenfels, C. von. (1897). *System der Wertheorie* (*A System of a Theory of Values*), vol. I, Leipzig. Repr. 1982 in C. von Ehrenfels (R. Fabian, ed.), *Werttheorie*, Philosophische Schriften, vol. I, Munich: Philosophia, 201–405.

James, W. (1891). 'The Moral Philosopher and the Moral Life', repr. 1956 in *The Will To Believe and Other Essays on Popular Philosophy*, New York: Dover, 184–215.

Meinong, A. (1894). *Psychologisch-ethische Untersuchungen zur Werttheorie*. Graz: Leuschner & Lubensky. Repr. 1968 in R. Haller and R. Kindinger (eds.), *Alexius Meinong Gesamtausgabe*, vol. III, *Abhandlungen zur Werttheorie*, Graz: Akademische Druck- und Verlagsanstalt, pp. 1–244.

Meinong, A. (1917). 'Über emotionale Präsentation', *Sitzungsberichte der philosophisch-historischen Klasse der Kaiserlichem Akademie der Wissenschaften in Wien*, no. 183, 2. Abhandlung. Repr. 1968 in R. Haller and R. Kindinger (eds.), *Alexius Meinong Gesamtausgabe*, vol. III, *Abhandlungen zur Werttheorie*, Graz: Akademische Druck- und Verlagsanstalt, 285–465. Transl. 1972, A. Meinong (M.-L. Schubert Kalsi, ed.), *On Emotional Presentations*, Evanston: North western University Press.

Meinong, A. (1923). *Zur Grundlegung der allgemeinen Werttheorie*, Graz: Leuschner & Lubensky. Repr. 1968 in R. Haller and R. Kindinger (eds.), *Alexius Meinong Gesamtausgabe*, vol. III, *Abhandlungen zur Werttheorie*, Graz: Akademische Druck-und Verlagsanstalt, 471–656.

Moore, G. E. (1903a). *Principia Ethica*, Cambridge: Cambridge University Press. New edition 1993, T. Baldwin (ed.), Cambridge: Cambridge University Press.

Moore, G. E. (1903b). 'Review of Franz Brentano, The Origins of the Knowledge of Right and Wrong (Engl. translation by Cecil Hague, Westminster, 1902)', *International Journal of Ethics* 14: 115–23.

Moore, G. E. (1922). 'The Conception of Intrinsic Value' in G. E. Moore, *Philosophical Studies*, London: Routledge, 253–75. Repr. 1993 in G. E. Moore (T. Baldwin, ed.), *Principia Ethica*, 280–98.

Moore, G. E. (1942). 'Reply to My Critics' in P. A. Schilpp (ed.), *The Philosophy of G. E. Mooore*, Evanston, IL: Northwestern University Press, 535–677.

Sidgwick, H. (1874) *The Methods of Ethics*, London: Macmillan. New edition 1966, New York: Dover.

Rashdell, H. (1905). *A Theory of Good and Evil*, Oxford: Clarendon Press.

Twardowski, K. (1894). *Zur Lehre vom Inhalt und Gegenstand der Vorstellungen*, Wien: Alfred Hölder. Trans. 1977 K. Twardowski (ed. R. Grossmann), *On the Content and Object of Presentations*, The Hague: Nijhoff.

CHAPTER 21 INDIVIDUALISM VS. COLLECTIVISM

Arnold, M. (1869). *Culture & Anarchy: An Essay in Political and Social Criticism*, London: Smith. New edn 1993, ed. S. Collini, Cambridge: Cambridge University Press.

Bellamy, R. (1992). *Liberalism and Modern Society: An Historical Argument*, Cambridge, MA: Polity Press.

Bosanquet, B. (1885). *Knowledge and Reality: A Criticism of Mr. F. H. Bradley's 'Principles of Logic'*, London: Kegan Paul.

Bosanquet, B. (1888). *Logic, or the Morphology of Knowledge*, 2 vols., Oxford: Clarendon Press, 2nd edn 1911.

Bosanquet, B. (1889). *Essays and Addresses*, London: Swan Sonnenschein.

Bosanquet, B. (1892). *History of Aesthetic*, London: Swan Sonnenschein, 2nd edn 1904.

Bosanquet, B. (1893). *The Civilization of Christendom and Other Studies*, London: Swan Sonnenschein.

Bosanquet, B. (1895a). *A Companion to Plato's Republic for English Readers: Being a Commentary adapted to Davies and Vaughan's Translation*, London: Rivingtons.

Bosanquet, B. (1895b). *The Essentials of Logic Being Ten Lectures On Judgement and Inference*, London and New York: Macmillan.

Bosanquet, B. (1897). *Psychology of the Moral Self*, London and New York: Macmillan.

Bosanquet, B. (1899). *The Philosophical Theory of the State*, London: Macmillan, 4th edn 1923. New edn 2001, G. F. Gaus and W. Sweet (eds.), *B. Bosanquet: The Philosophical Theory of the State and Related Essays*, South Bend, IN: St Augustine's Press.

Bosanquet, B. (1912). *The Principle of Individuality and Value: The Gifford Lectures for 1911*, London: Macmillan.

Bosanquet, B. (1913). *The Value and Destiny of the Individual: The Gifford Lectures for 1912*, London: Macmillan.

Bosanquet, B. (1915). *Three Lectures on Aesthetic*, London: Macmillan.

Bosanquet, B. (1917). *Social and International Ideals: Being Studies in Patriotism*, London: Macmillan.

Bosanquet, B. (1918). *Some Suggestions in Ethics*, London: Macmillan, 2nd edn 1919.

Bosanquet, B. (1920a). *Implication and Linear Inference*, London: Macmillan.

Bosanquet, B. (1920b). *What Religion Is*, London: Macmillan.

Bosanquet, B. (1921). *The Meeting of Extremes in Contemporary Philosophy*, London: Macmillan.

Bosanquet, B. (1927). *Science and Philosophy and Other Essays*, J. H. Muirhead and R. C. Bosanquet (eds.), London: George Allen and Unwin.

Bosanquet, B. (1999a). *The Collected Works of Bernard Bosanquet*, vol. I: *Selected Essays*, W. Sweet (ed.), Bristol: Thoemmes Press.

Bosanquet, B. (1999b). *The Collected Works of Bernard Bosanquet*, vol. XIV: *Essays on 'Aspects of the Social Problem' and Essays on Social Policy*, W. Sweet (ed.), Bristol: Thoemmes Press.

Bosanquet, H. (1924). *Bernard Bosanquet: A Short Account of his Life*, London: Macmillan.

Boucher, David and Vincent, Andrew (2000). *British Idealism and Political Theory*, Edinburgh: Edinburgh University Press.

Bradley, F. H. (1876). *Ethical Studies*, London: King, 2nd edn 1927, Oxford: Clarendon Press.

Cacoullos, A. C. (1974). *Thomas Hill Green: Philosopher of Rights*, New York: Twayne.

Carter, Matt (2003). *T. H. Green and the Development of Ethical Socialism*, Exeter: Imprint Academic.

Clarke, P. (1978). *Liberals and Social Democrats*, Cambridge: Cambridge University Press.

Collini, S. (1976). 'Hobhouse, Bosanquet and the State: Philosophical Idealism and Political Argument in England 1880–1918', *Past and Present* 72: 86–111.

Collini, S. (1979). *Liberalism and Sociology: L. T. Hobhouse and Political Argument in England 1880–1914*, Cambridge: Cambridge University Press.

Dimova-Cookson, Maria (2001). *T. H. Green's Moral and Political Philosophy: A Phenomenological Perspective*, Basingstoke: Palgrave.

Freeden, M. (1978). *The New Liberalism: An Ideology of Social Reform*, Oxford: Clarendon Press.

Freeden, M. (1996). *Ideologies and Political Theory: A Conceptual Approach*, Oxford: Clarendon Press.

Gaus, G. F. (1983). *The Modern Liberal Theory of Man*, London: Croom Helm.

Gaus, G. F. (1994). 'Green, Bosanquet and the Philosophy of Coherence' in C. L. Ten (ed.), *The Routledge History of Philosophy*, vol. VII: *The Nineteenth Century*, London: Routledge, 408–36.

Green, T. H. (1881). *Liberal Legislation and Freedom of Contract: A Lecture*, Oxford: Slatter and Rose. New edn 1986, P. Harris and J. Morrow (eds.), *T. H. Green: Lectures on the Principles of Political Obligation and Other Writings*, Cambridge: Cambridge University Press, 194–212.

Green, T. H. (1883). *Prolegomena to Ethics by the Late Thomas Hill Green*, ed. A. C. Bradley, Oxford: Clarendon Press. New edn 2003, D. Brink (ed.), Oxford: Oxford University Press.

Green, T. H. (1885–8). *Works of Thomas Hill Green*, 3 vols., ed. R. L. Nettleship, London: Longmans, Green.

Green, T. H. (1886). *Lectures on the Principles of Political Obligation*, in R. L. Nettleship (ed.), *Works of Thomas Hill Green*, vol. II: *Philosophical Works*, London: Longmans, Green. New edn 1986, P. Harris and J. Morrow (eds), *T. H. Green: Lectures on the Principles of Political Obligation and Other Writings*, Cambridge: Cambridge University Press.

Green, T. H. (1997). *Additional Writings*, ed. P. P. Nicholson, Bristol: Thoemmes Press.

Greengarten, I. M. (1981). *Thomas Hill Green and the Development of Liberal-Democratic Thought*, Toronto: University of Toronto Press.

Greenleaf, W. H. (1983). *The British Political Tradition*, 2 vols., London and New York: Methuen.

Harris, F. P. (1944). *The Neo-Idealist Political Theory: Its Continuity with the British Tradition*, New York: King's Crown Press.

Hobhouse, L. T. (1896). *The Theory of Knowledge: A Contribution to Some Problems of Logic and Metaphysics*, London: Methuen, 3rd edn 1921.

Hobhouse, L. T. (1901). *Mind in Evolution*, London: Macmillan, 3rd edn 1926.

Hobhouse, L. T. (1904). *Democracy and Reaction*, London: Fisher Unwin, 2nd edn 1909.

Hobhouse, L. T. (1906). *Morals in Evolution: A Study in Comparative Ethics*, 2 vols., London: Chapman and Hall, 3rd edn 1913.

Hobhouse, L. T. (1911a). *Liberalism*, London: Williams and Norgate. New edn 1994, J. Meadowcroft (ed.), *L. T. Hobhouse: Liberalism and Other Writings*, Cambridge: Cambridge University Press.

Hobhouse, L. T. (1911b). *Social Evolution and Political Theory*, New York: Columbia University Press. Ch. IX reprinted 1994 in J. Meadowcroft (ed.), *L. T. Hobhouse: Liberalism and Other Writings*, Cambridge: Cambridge University Press, 152–65.

Hobhouse, L. T. (1913a). *Development and Purpose: An Essay Towards a Philosophy of Evolution*, London: Macmillan, 2nd edn 1929.

Hobhouse, L. T. (1913b). 'The Historical Evolution of Property, in Fact and Idea' in C. Gore (ed.), *Property, Its Duties and Rights: Historically, Philosophically and Religiously Regarded*, London and New York: Macmillan, 1–33. Repr. 1994 in J. Meadowcroft (ed.), *L. T. Hobhouse: Liberalism and Other Writings*, Cambridge: Cambridge University Press, 175–98.

Hobhouse, L. T. (1918). *The Metaphysical Theory of the State: A Criticism*, London: George Allen and Unwin.

Hobhouse, L. T. (1921). *The Rational Good: A Study in the Logic of Practice*, London: George Allen and Unwin.

Hobhouse, L. T. (1922). *The Elements of Social Justice*, London: George Allen and Unwin.

Hobhouse, L. T. (1924). *Social Development: Its Nature and Conditions*, London: George Allen and Unwin.

Hobson, J. A. & Ginsberg, M. (1931). *L. T. Hobhouse: His Life and Work*, London: George Allen and Unwin.

Houang, F. (1954). *Le néo-hégélianisme en Angleterre: la philosophie de Bernard Bosanquet*, Paris: Vrin.

Hurka, T. (1993). *Perfectionism*, New York and Oxford: Oxford University Press.

Kloppenberg, J. T. (1986). *Uncertain Victory: Social Democracy and Progressivism in European and American Thought, 1870–1920*, New York: Oxford University Press.

Latta, R. (1905). 'Memoir' in R. Latta (ed.), *Philosophical Studies by David George Ritchie*, London and New York: Macmillan.

Lewis, H. D. (1962). *Freedom and History*, London: George Allen and Unwin.

Meadowcroft, J. (1995). *Conceptualizing the State: Innovation and Dispute in British Political Thought 1880–1914*, Oxford: Clarendon Press.

Mill, J. S. (1848). *Principles of Political Economy with Some of Their Applications to Social Philosophy*, London: Parker. New edn 1965, J. M. Robson (ed.), *Collected Works of John Stuart Mill*, vols. II–III, Toronto: University of Toronto Press and London: Routledge.

Mill, J. S. (1859). *On Liberty*, London: Parker. New edition 1977, ed. J. M. Robson, *Collected Works of John Stuart Mill*, vol. XVIII: *Essays on Politics and Society*, Toronto: University of Toronto Press and London: Routledge.

Mill, J. S. (1873). *Autobiography*, London: Longmans, Green. New edn 1981, J. M. Robson (ed.), *Collected Works of John Stuart Mill*, vol. I, Toronto: University of Toronto Press and London: Routledge.

Milne, A. J. M. (1962). *The Social Philosophy of English idealism*, London: George Allen and Unwin.

Muirhead, J. H. (1908). *The Service of the State: Four Lectures on the Political Teaching of T. H. Green*, London: John Murray.

Muirhead, J. H. (ed.) (1935). *Bernard Bosanquet and His Friends: Letters Illustrating the Sources and the Development of His Philosophical Opinions*, London: George Allen and Unwin.

Nettleship, R. L. (1888). 'Memoir' in R. L. Nettleship (ed.), *Works of Thomas Hill Green*, vol. III, *Miscellanies and Memoir*, London: Longmans, Green.

Nicholson, P. P. (1990). *The Political Philosophy of the British Idealists: Selected Studies*, Cambridge: Cambridge University Press.

Otter, S. den (1996). *British Idealism and Social Explanation: A Study in Late Victorian Thought*, Oxford: Clarendon Press.

Plamenatz, J. P. (1938). *Consent, Freedom and Political Obligation*, London: Oxford University Press, 2nd edn 1968.

Prichard, H. A. (1968). *Moral Obligation and Duty and Interest: Essays and Lectures*, London: Oxford University Press.

Pucelle, J. (1960–5). *La nature et l'esprit dans la philosophie de T. H. Green: La Renaissance de l'Idéalisme en Angleterre au XIXe siècle*, 2 vols., Paris: Beatrice Nauwelaerts.

Randall, J. H., Jr. (1966). 'Idealistic Social Philosophy and Bernard Bosanquet', *Philosophy and Phenomenological Research* 24: 473–502. Repr. 1977 in Randall (ed. B. J. Singer), *Philosophy After Darwin: Chapters for the Career of Philosophy*, vol. III, New York: Columbia University Press.

Richter, M. (1964). *The Politics of Conscience: T. H. Green and His Age*, London: Weidenfeld and Nicolson.

Ritchie, D. G. (1889). *Darwinism and Politics*, London: Swan Sonnenschein, 4th edn 1901.

Ritchie, D. G. (1891). *The Principles of State Interference: Four Essays on the Political Philosophy of Mr. Herbert Spencer, J. S. Mill, and T. H. Green*, London: Swan Sonnenschein, 4th edn 1902.

Ritchie, D. G. (1893). *Darwin and Hegel with Other Philosophical Studies*, London: Swan Sonnenschein.

Ritchie, D. G. (1894). *Natural Rights: A Criticism of Some Political and Ethical Conceptions*, London: Swan Sonnenschein and New York: Macmillan.

Ritchie, D. G. (1902). *Studies in Political and Social Ethics*, London: Swan Sonnenschein and New York: Macmillan.

Ritchie, D. G. (1905). *Philosophical Studies*, (ed.) R. Latta, London and New York: Macmillan.

Ritchie, D. G. (1998). *Collected Works of D. G. Ritchie*, vol. VI: *Miscellaneous Writings*, ed. P. P. Nicholson, Bristol: Thoemmes Press.

Sidgwick, H. (1902). *Lectures on the Ethics of T. H. Green, Mr. Herbert Spencer, and J. Martineau*, (ed.) E. E. C. Jones, London and New York: Macmillan.

Simhony, Avital and Weinstein, David (eds.) (2001). *The New Liberalism: Reconciling Liberty and Community*, Cambridge: Cambridge University Press.

Skorupski, J. (1993). *English-Language Philosophy 1750–1945*, Oxford and New York: Oxford University Press.

Spencer, H. (1884). *Man versus the State*, London: Williams and Norgate.

Sweet, W. (1997). *Idealism and Rights: The Social Ontology of Human Rights in the Political Thought of Bernard Bosanquet*, Lanham, MD: University Press of America.

Sweet, W. (1998). 'Bernard Bosanquet' in E. N. Zalta (ed.), *The Stanford Encyclopaedia of Philosophy*, Stanford, CA: CSLI.

Taylor, M. (ed.) (1996). *Herbert Spencer and the Limits of the State: The Late Nineteenth-century Debate between Individualism and Collectivism*, Bristol: Thoemmes Press.

Taylor, M. W. (1992). *Men versus the State: Herbert Spencer and Late Victorian Individualism*, Oxford: Clarendon Press.

Thomas, G. (1987). *The Moral Philosophy of T. H. Green*, Oxford: Clarendon Press.

Tyler, C. (1998). *Thomas Hill Green and the Philosophical Foundations of Politics: An Internal Critique*, Lewiston and Lampeter: Edwin Mellen Press.

Vincent, A. (ed.) (1986). *The Philosophy of T. H. Green*, Aldershot: Gower.

Vincent, A. and Plant, R. (1984). *Philosophy, Politics and Citizenship: The Life and Thought of the British Idealists*, Oxford: Blackwell.

Wempe, B. (1986). *Beyond Equality: A Study of T. H. Green's Theory of Positive Freedom*, Delft: Eburon.

Wolfe, W. (1975). *From Radicalism to Socialism: Men and Ideas in the Formation of Fabian Socialist Doctrines, 1881–1889*, New Haven, CT and London: Yale University Press.

CHAPTER 22 MARXISM AND ANARCHISM

Bakunin, M. A. (1842). 'Die Reaktion in Deutschland', *Deutsche Jahrbücher für Wissenschaft und Kunst*. Trans. and ed. 1965 J. M. Edie, J. P. Scanlon, and M.-B. Zeldin, 'The Reaction in Germany', *Russian Philosophy*, 3 vols., Chicago: Quadrangle Books, vol. I, 384–406.

Bakunin, M. A. (1873). *Gosudarstivennost' I anarkhiia*, Geneva. Trans. 1990 M. S. Shatz, *Statism and Anarchy*, Cambridge: Cambridge University Press.

Bauer, O. (1907). *Nationalitätenfrage und die Sozialdemokratie*, Vienna. Trans. 2000 J. O'Donnell, *The Question of Nationalities and Social Democracy*, Minneapolis: University of Minnesota Press.

Bottomore, Tom and Goode, Patrick (eds.) (1978). *Austro-Marxism*, Oxford: Clarendon Press.

Bourdet, Yves (1970). Introduction to R. Hilferding, *Le Capital financier*, Paris: Minuit, 9–52.

Carver, Terrell (1981). *Engels*, Oxford: Oxford University Press.

Colletti, Lucio (1972). *From Rousseau to Lenin*, London: New Left Books.

Engels, F. (1884). *Der Ursprung der Familie*, Zurich: Verlag der Schweizerischen Volksbuchhandlung. Trans. 1968 *The Origins of the Family* in K. Marx and F. Engels, *Collected Works*, London: Lawrence and Wishart.

Hilferding, Rudolf (1910). *Das Finanzkapital*, Vienna: Wiener Volksbuchhandlung. Trans. 1978 T. Bottomore, M. Watnick, and S. Gordon, *Finance Capital*, London: Routledge.

Howard, M.C. and King, J. E. (1989). *A History of Marxian Economics*, vol. I: 1882–1929, London: Macmillan.

Kautsky, Karl (1892). *Das Erfurter Programm*, Stuttgart: J. H. W. Dietz. Trans W. E. Bohm 1910, repr. 1971 *The Class Struggle*, New York: Norton.

Kautsky, Karl (1927). *Die materialistische Geschichtsauffassung*, Berlin: J. H. W. Dietz. Trans. and abr. 1988 J. H. Kautsky, *The Materialist Conception of History*, New Haven, CT: Yale University Press.

Labriola, Antonio (1896). *Saggi interno alla concezione materialistica della storia*. Trans. C. Kerr 1908 *Essays on the Materialist Conception of History*, Chicago: Charles Kerr.

Lukács, G. (1923). *Geschichte und Klassbewasstsein*, Berlin: Malik Verlag. Trans. 1971 R. Livingstone, *History and Class Consciousness Studies in Marxist Dialectics*, London: Merlin.

Marx, Karl (1871). *The Civil War in France*, London. Repr. in K. Marx and F. Engels, *Collected Works*, London: Lawrence and Wishart.

Marx, Karl and Engels, Friedrich (1975–98). *Collected Works*, 47 vols., London: Lawrence and Wishart.

Plekhanov, G. V. (1969). *Fundamental Problems of Marxism*, London: Lawrence and Wishart.

Plekhanov, G. V. (1977). *Selected Philosophical Works*, 5 vols., Moscow: Progress.

Salvadori, Massimo (1979). *Karl Kautsky and the Socialist Revolution, 1880–1938*, London: Verso.

Sorel, Georges (1908). *Réflexions sur la violence*, Paris: Editions de pages libres. Trans. T. E. Hulme repr. 1950, *Reflections on Violence*, Glencoe, IL: The Free Press.

Steenson, Gary P. (1991). *Karl Kautsky, 1854–1938*, Pittsburgh: University of Pittsburgh Press.
Walicki, Andrzy (1979). *A History of Russian Thought from the Enlightenment to Marxism*, Stanford: Stanford University Press.
Walicki, Andrzy (1995). *Marx and the Leap to the Kingdom of Freedom*, Stanford: Stanford University Press.

CHAPTER 23 LEGAL THEORY

Austin, J. (1861–3). *The Province of Jurisprudence Determined* and *Lectures on Jurisprudence*, 3 vols., London: J. Murray. Reprinted 1885, 5th edn, 2 vols., ed. Robert Campbell, London: J. Murray.
Bentham, J. (1970). *Of Laws in General*, ed. H. L. A. Hart, London: Athlone Press.
Binder, J. (1931). Review of A. Hägerström, *Der römische Obligationsrecht im Lichte der allgemeinen römischen Rechtsanschauung (The Roman Concept of Obligation in Light of the General Roman View of the Law)* (1927), *Kritische Vierteljahrsschrift für Gesetzgebung und Rechtswissenschaft*, 24: 269–315.
Buckland, W. W. (1945). *Some Reflections on Jurisprudence*, Cambridge: Cambridge University Press.
Cassirer, E. (1939). 'Axel Hägerström. Eine Studie zur schwedischen Philosophie der Gegenwart' ('Axel Hägerström. A Study of Contemporary Swedish Philosophy'), *Göteborgs Högskolas Årsskrift*, 45: 3–120.
Gierke, O. (1863–1913). *Das deutsche Genossenschaftsrecht (The German Law of Associations)*, 4 vols., Berlin: Weidmann. Trans. 1990 M. Fischer, *Community in Historical Perspective*, Cambridge: Cambridge University Press (selections from vol. I). Trans. 1900 F. W. Maitland, *Political Theories of the Middle Ages*, Cambridge: Cambridge University Press (a selection from vol. III). Trans. 1977 G. Heiman, *Associations and the Law. The Classical and Early Christian Stages*, Toronto: University of Toronto Press (another selection from vol. III). Trans. 1934 E. Barker, *Natural Law and the Theory of Society 1500 to 1800*, Cambridge: Cambridge University Press (a selection from vol. IV).
Gierke, O. (1874). 'Die Grundbegriffe des Staatsrechts und die neueren Staatsrechtstheorien' ('The Fundamental Concepts of State Law and the Newer Theories of State Law'), *Zeitschrift für die gesamte Staatswissenschaft*, 30: 153–98, 265–335. Repr. 1915 as a book, Tübingen: J. C. B. Mohr.
Gierke, O. (1880). *Johannes Althusius und die Entwicklung der naturrechtlichen Staatstheorien (Johannes Althusius and the Development of Natural Law Theories of the State)*, Breslau: M. and N. Marcus. Trans. 1939 B. Freyd, *The Development of Political Theory*, New York: W. W. Norton.
Gierke, O. (1883a). *Naturrecht und Deutsches Recht (Natural Law and German Law)*, Frankfurt: Rütter and Loening.
Gierke, O. (1883b). 'Labands Staatsrecht und die deutsche Rechtswissenschaft' ('Laband's Theory of State Law, and German Legal Science'), *Schmollers Jahrbuch für Gesetzgebung, Verwaltung und Volkswirtschaft im Deutschen Reiche*, 7: 1097–195.
Gierke, O. (1887). *Die Genossenschaftstheorie und die deutsche Rechtsprechung (The Theory of Associations, and Adjudication in Germany)*, Berlin: Weidmann.
Gierke, O. (1902). *Das Wesen der menschlichen Verbände (The Nature of Human Associations)*, Berlin: Gustav Schade.
Gierke, O. (1916–17). 'Recht und Sittlichkeit' ('The Law and Morality'), *Logos*, 6: 211–64.
Gurwitsch, G. (1922–3). 'Otto v. Gierke als Rechtsphilosoph' ('Otto v. Gierke as Legal Philosopher'), *Logos*, 11: 86–132.

Hägerström, A. (1902). *Kants Ethik im Verhältnis zu seinem erkenntnistheoretischen Grundgedanken* (*Kant's Ethics in Relation to his Fundamental Ideas in the Theory of Knowledge*), Uppsala: Almqvist and Wiksell.

Hägerström, A. (1908). *Das Prinzip der Wissenschaft, I. Die Realität* (*The Principle of Science*, vol. I: *Reality*), Uppsala: Almqvist and Wiksell.

Hägerström, A. (1910). 'Kritiska punkter i värdepsykologien' ('Critical Points in the Psychology of Valuation') in *Festskrift tillägnad E. O. Burman på hans 65–årsdag den 7 oktober 1910*, Uppsala: Akademiska bokhandeln, 17–75.

Hägerström, A. (1927). *Der römische Obligationsbegriff im Lichte der allgemeinen römischen Rechtsanschauung* (*The Roman Concept of Obligation in Light of the General Roman View of the Law*), vol. I, Uppsala: Almqvist and Wiksell.

Hägerström, A. (1929). 'Axel Hägerström' in *Die Philosophie der Gegenwart in Selbstdarstellungen* (*Contemporary Philosophy in Self-Portrayals*), ed. R. Schmidt, vol. VII, Leipzig: Felix Meiner, 111–59. Trans. 1964 R. T. Sandin, 'A Summary of My Philosophy' in A. Hägerström, *Philosophy and Religion*, London: George Allen and Unwin, 31–74.

Hägerström, A. (1935). 'Begreppet viljeförklaring på privaträttens område', *Theoria*, 1: 32–57, 121–38. Trans. 1953 C. D. Broad, 'The Conception of a Declaration of Intention in the Sphere of Private Law' in A. Hägerström, *Inquiries into the Nature of Law and Morals*, Stockholm: Almqvist and Wiksell, 299–347.

Hart, H. L. A. (1955). Review of A. Hägerström, *Inquiries into the Nature of Law and Morals* (1953), *Philosophy*, 30: 369–73.

Hart, H. L. A. (1982). *Essays on Bentham*, Oxford: Clarendon Press.

Heck, P. (1932). *Begriffsbildung und Interessenjurisprudenz*, Tübingen: J. C. B. Mohr. Trans. 1948 M. M. Schoch, 'The Formation of Concepts and the Jurisprudence of Interests' in *The Jurisprudence of Interests*, ed. M. M. Schoch, Cambridge, MA: Harvard University Press, 99–256.

Holmes, O. W. (1881). *The Common Law*, Boston: Little, Brown.

Holmes, O. W. (1896–7). 'The Path of the Law', *Harvard Law Review*, 10: 457–78. Reprinted 1920 in *Collected Legal Papers*, New York: Harcourt, Brace, and Howe, 167–202.

Holmes, O. W. (1905). *Lochner v New York* (dissenting opinion), *United States Reports*, vol. 198: 45–76, at 74–6. Reprinted 1992 in *The Essential Holmes*, ed. Richard A. Posner, Chicago: University of Chicago Press, 305–7.

Hull, N. E. H. (1997). *Roscoe Pound & Karl Llewellyn*, Chicago: University of Chicago Press.

Jhering, R. (1852–65). *Geist des römischen Rechts* (*Spirit of the Roman Law*), 3 parts (the second of which is divided into two volumes): pt 1 (1852), pt 2 (1854), pt 2.2 (1858), pt 3 (1865), Leipzig: Breitkopf and Härtel. Repr. 1891, 1894, 1898, 1906.

Jhering, R. (1872). *Der Kampf um's Recht*, Vienna: G. J. Manz. Trans. 1924 J. J. Lalor, *The Struggle for Law*, New York: Macmillan.

Jhering, R. (1877, 1884). *Der Zweck des Rechts* (*The Purpose of the Law*), 2 vols., Leipzig: Breitkopf and Härtel. Trans. 1914 I. Husik, *Law as a Means to an End* (vol. I only), Boston: Boston Book Co.

Kunkel, W. (1929). Review of A. Hägerström, *Der römische Obligationsrecht im Lichte der allgemeinen römischen Rechtsanschauung* (*The Roman Concept of Obligation in Light of the General Roman View of the Law*) (1927), *Zeitschrift der Savigny-Stiftung für Rechtsgeschichte, romanistische Abteilung*, 49: 479–90.

Maine, H. (1861). *Ancient Law*, London: J. Murray. Repr. 1963, preface by Raymond Firth, introduction and notes by Frederick Pollock, Boston: Beacon Press.

Maine, H. (1875). *Lectures on the Early History of Institutions*, London: J. Murray. Repr. 1888, London: J. Murray.

Mill, J. S. (1838). 'Bentham', *London and Westminster Review*. Repr. 1875 in J. S. Mill, *Dissertations and Discussions*, vol. I, London: Longmans, Green, 330–92.

Olivecrona, K. (1953). 'Editor's Preface' in A. Hägerström, *Inquiries into the Nature of Law and Morals*, Stockholm: Almqvist and Wiksell, x–xxvi.

Olivecrona, K. (1971). *Law as Fact*, 2nd edn, London: Steven and Sons.

Pollock, F. (1906). Maine, *Ancient Law*, with introduction and notes by Sir Frederick Pollock, London: J. Murray. Reprinted 1963, preface by Raymond Firth, Boston: Beacon Press.

Pollock, F. (1941). *The Holmes-Pollock Correspondence*, 2 vols., Cambridge, MA: Harvard University Press.

Pound, R. (1907). 'The Need of a Sociological Jurisprudence', *The Green Bag*, 19: 607–15.

Pound, R. (1908). 'Mechanical Jurisprudence', *Columbia Law Review*, 8: 605–23.

Pound, R. (1908–9). 'Liberty of Contract', *Yale Law Journal*, 18: 454–87.

Ross, J. (1893). *Three Generations of English Women* (memoirs and correspondence), revised edn, London: T. Fisher Unwin.

Schlegel, J. H. (1995). *American Legal Realism and Empirical Social Science*, Chapel Hill: University of North Carolina Press.

Stolleis, M. (1992). *Geschichte des öffentlichen Rechts in Deutschland* (*History of Public Law in Germany*), 3 vols., Munich: C. H. Beck (1988–99), vol. II: *Staatsrechtslehre und Verwaltungsrecht 1800–1914* (*Public Law Theory and Administrative Law 1800–1914*).

Vinogradoff, P. (1920). *Outlines of Historical Jurisprudence*, 2 vols., London: Oxford University Press.

Woodard, C. (1991). 'A Wake (or Awakening?) for Historical Jurisprudence' in *The Victorian Achievement of Sir Henry Maine. A Centennial Reappraisal*, ed. Alan Diamond, Cambridge: Cambridge University Press, 242–55.

CHAPTER 24 SCEPTICAL CHALLENGES TO FAITH

Barth, Karl. (1960). *Church Dogmatics III*, 2, Edinburgh: T. & T. Clark.

Bibby, Cyril. (1960). *Scientist, Humanist and Educator*, New York and London: Horizon Press.

Burrow, John W. (1996). *Evolution and Society: A Study of Victorian Social Theory*, Cambridge: Cambridge University Press, ch. 6.

Cashdollar, Charles D. (1989). *The Transformation of Theology, 1830–1890: Positivism and Protestant Thought in Britain and America*, Princeton, NJ: Princeton University Press.

Chadwick, Owen (1975). *The Secularization of the European Mind in the Nineteenth Century*, Cambridge: Cambridge University Press.

Clifford, W. K. (1879). *Lectures and Essays*, eds. F. Pollock and L. Stephens, 2 vols. Volume I includes a life of Clifford by Pollock. London: Macmillan.

Clifford, W. K. (1882). *Mathematical Papers*, ed. R. Tucker, with an introduction by H. J. S. Smith. London: Macmillan.

Clifford, W. K. (1885). *Common Sense of the Exact Sciences*, edited and partly written by Karl Pearson. London: Kegan Paul. Reissued with a preface by Bertrand Russell and a new introduction by James R. Newman (New York, 1955).

Comte, Auguste (1830–42). *Cours de philosophie positive*, 6 vols. Paris: Rouen frères. Trans. and abridged 1853 Harriet Martineau, *The Positive Philosophy of Auguste Comte*, 2 vols. London: Chapman.

Comte, Auguste (1851–4). *Système de politique positive*, 4 vols. Paris: L. Mathias. Trans. 1875–7 J. H. Bridges *et al.*, *The System of Positive Polity*, 4 vols. London: Longmans, Green.

Comte, Auguste (1852). *Catéchisme positiviste*, Paris: l'auteur. Trans. 1858 Richard Congreve, *The Catechism of Positive Religion*, London: Chapman.

Comte, Auguste (1968–70). *Oeuvres*, 13 vols. Paris.

Desmond, Adrian. (1997). *Huxley: From Devil's Disciple to Evolution's High Priest*, Reading, MA: Addison-Wesley.

Duncan, David (1908). *Life and Letters of Herbert Spencer*, 2 vols., London: Methuen.

Durkheim, Emile. (1912). *Les formes élémentaires de la vie religieuse*, Paris: Alcan. Trans. 1915 J. W. Swain, *The Elementary Forms of the Religious Life*, New York: Macmillan.

Espinasse, Francis (1895). *The Life of Ernest Renan*, London: W. Scott. Repr. 1980 Boston.

Gouhier, Henri (1965). *La vie d'Auguste Comte* (*The Life of Auguste Comte*), 2nd rev. edn, Paris: J. Vrin.

Haeckel, Ernst Heinrich (1868). *Natürliche Schöpfungsgeschichte*, Berlin: G. Reimer. Trans. 1876 E. R. Lankester, *The History of Creation*, London: Routledge.

Haeckel, Ernst Heinrich (1899). *Die Welträtsel*, Bonn: E. Strauss. Trans. 1929 Joseph McCabe, *The Riddle of the Universe*, London: Watts.

Hayman, Ronald (1980). *Nietzsche: A Critical Life*, Oxford: Oxford University Press.

Holt, N. R. (1971). 'Ernst Haeckel's Monistic Religion', *Journal of the History of Ideas* 32: 265–80.

Huxley, Leonard (ed.) (1900). *Life and Letters of Thomas Henry Huxley*, 2 vols., London: Macmillan.

Huxley, Thomas Henry (1863). *Evidence as to Man's Place in Nature*, London: Williams and Norgate.

Huxley, Thomas Henry (1879). *Hume*, London: Macmillan.

Huxley, Thomas Henry (1893–94). *Collected Essays*, 9 vols., London: Macmillan.

Huxley, Thomas Henry (1898–1902). *Scientific Memoirs*, ed. M. Foster and E. R. Lankester, 5 vols., London: Macmillan.

Kaufmann, Walter (1950). *Nietzsche: Philosopher, Psychologist, Antichrist*, Princeton, NJ: Princeton University Press. 4th edn, 1974.

Kelly, Alfred (1981). *The Descent of Darwin: The Popularization of Darwinism in Germany, 1860–1914*, Chapel Hill, NC: University of North Carolina Press.

Lightman, Bernard (1987). *The Origins of Agnosticism: Victorian Unbelief and the Limits of Knowledge*, Baltimore and London: Johns Hopkins University Press.

Livingston, James C. (1974). *The Ethics of Belief: An Essay on the Victorian Religious Conscience*, Tallahassee, FL: Scholars Press.

Lukes, Steven (1973). *Emile Durkheim: His Life and Work*, New York: Harper and Row.

Magnus, Bernd (1978). *Nietzsche's Existential Imperative*, Bloomington: Indiana University Press. Eternal Recurrence as 'countermyth' to Christianity.

McCarthy, Gerald D. (1986). *The Ethics of Belief Debate*, Atlanta: Scholars Press.

Mill, J. S. (1865). *Auguste Comte and Positivism*, London, repr. 1961 Ann Arbor: University of Michigan Press.

Newman, J. H. (1870). *An Essay in Aid of a Grammar of Assent*, London: Burnes, Oates, and Co. New edn 1985, ed. I. T. Ker, Oxford: Clarendon Press.

Nietzsche, Friedrich (1882). *Die fröhliche Wissenschaft*. Trans. 1974 Walter Kaufmann, *The Gay Science*, New York: Vintage Press.

Nietzsche, Friedrich (1883–5). *Also sprach Zarathustra*. Trans. 1961 R. J. Hollingdale, *Thus Spoke Zarathustra*, Harmondsworth: Penguin.

Nietzsche, Friedrich (1886). *Jenseits von Gut und Böse*. Trans. 1966 Walter Kaufmann, *Beyond Good and Evil*, New York: Vintage Press.

Nietzsche, Friedrich (1887). *Zur Genealogie der Moral*. Trans. 1968 Walter Kaufmann and R. J. Hollingdale, *On the Genealogy of Morals*, New York: Vintage Press.

Nietzsche, Friedrich (1889). *Die Götzen-Dämmerung*. Trans. 1968 R. J. Hollingdale, *The Twilight of the Idols*, Harmondsworth: Penguin.

Nietzsche, Friedrich (1895). *Der Antichrist*. Trans. 1968 R. J. Hollingdale, *The Anti-Christ*, Harmondsworth: Penguin.

Nietzsche, Friedrich (1906). *Der Wille zur Macht*. A collection of Nietzsche's outlines and notes of 1883–8 selected and arranged by editors. Trans. 1967 Walter Kaufmann *The Will to Power*, New York: Viking.

Nietzsche, Friedrich (1908). *Ecce Homo*. Trans. Walter Kaufmann, *Ecce Homo*, New York: Vintage Press.

Nietzsche, Friedrich (1967–84). *Werke: Kritische Gesamtausgabe* (*Complete Critical Works*), ed. G. Colli and J. Montinari, Berlin: de Gruyter.

Peel, J. D. Y. (1971). *Herbert Spencer: The Evolution of a Sociologist*, London: Heinemann.

Pickering, Mary (1993). *Auguste Comte: An Intellectual Biography*, vol. I, Cambridge: Cambridge University Press.

Pickering, W. S. F. (1984). *Durkheim's Sociology of Religion*, London: Routledge.

Pommier, Jean (1925). *La pensée religieuse de Renan*, Paris: F. Rieder.

Ratschow, Carl Heinz (1985). 'Friedrich Nietzsche' in *Nineteenth Century Religious Thought in the West*, ed. Ninian Smart *et al.*, Cambridge: Cambridge University Press.

Reardon, B. M. G. (1985). 'Ernest Renan and the Religion of Science' in *Religion in the Age of Romanticism*, Cambridge: Cambridge University Press.

Renan, Ernest (1847–61). *Oeuvres complètes*, 10 vols., ed. Henriette Psichari. Paris: Colmann–Lévy.

Renan, Ernest (1863). *Vie de Jésus*, Paris: Michel Lévy frères. Trans. 1864 C. E. Wilbour, *The Life of Jesus*, New York: Carlton.

Renan, Ernest (1863–81). *Histoire des origines du christianisme*, 7 vols., Paris: Michel-Lévy frères. Trans. 1889–90 *The History of the Origins of Christianity*, London: Mathieson and Co.

Renan, Ernest (1887–93). *Histoire du peuple d'Israël*, 5 vols., Paris: C. Lévy. Trans. 1888–96 C. B. Pitman and D. V. Bingham, *History of the People of Israel*, London: Chapman and Hall.

Renan, Ernest (1890). *L'Avenir de la science*, Paris: C. Lévy. Trans. 1891 A. D. Vandam and C. B. Pitman, *The Future of Science*, London: Chapman and Hall.

Richards, R. (1987). *Darwin and the Emergence of Evolutionary Theories of Mind and Behavior*, Chicago: University of Chicago Press.

Roberts, Tyler T. (1998). *Contesting Spirit: Nietzsche, Affirmation, Religion*, Princeton, NJ: Princeton University Press.

Spencer, Herbert (1862). *First Principles*. London: Williams and Norgate.

Spencer, Herbert (1864–7). *Principles of Biology*, 2 vols. London: Williams and Norgate.

Spencer, Herbert (1870–72). *Principles of Psychology*, 2 vols., 2nd edn, London: Williams and Norgate.

Spencer, Herbert (1876–96). *Principles of Sociology*, 3 vols. London: Williams and Norgate.

Spencer, Herbert (1893) *Principles of Ethics*, 2 vols. London: Williams and Norgate.

Spencer, Herbert (1884). *Man Versus the State*, London: Williams and Norgate.

Spencer, Herbert (1904). *An Autobiography*, 2 vols. London: Williams and Norgate.

Wallwork, Ernest (1972). *Durkheim: Morality and Milieu*, Cambridge, MA: Harvard University Press.

Wardman, H. W. (1964). *Ernest Renan: A Critical Biography*, London: Athlone Press.

Weindling, P. J. (1989). 'Ernst Haeckel's Darwinismus and the secularization of nature' in James R. Moore (ed.), *History, Humanity and Evolution*, Cambridge: Cambridge University Press, 311–29.

Wiltshire, David (1978). *The Social and Political Thought of Herbert Spencer*, Oxford: Oxford University Press.

Wright, Terence R. (1986). *The Religion of Humanity: The Impact of Comtean Positivism on Victorian Britain*, Cambridge: Cambridge University Press.

CHAPTER 25 THE DEFENCE OF FAITH

Allen, Gay Wilson (1967). *William James: A Biography*, New York: Viking.

Barth, K. (1962). 'The Principles of Dogmatics according to Wilhelm Herrmann' in *Theology and Church*, London: SCM Press.

Beintker, M. (1976). *Die Gottesfrage in der Theologie Wilhelm Herrmann* (*The Question of God in Wilhelm Herrmann's Theology*), Berlin: Evangelische Verlaganstalt.

Bergson, Henri (1889). *Essai sur les données immédiates de la perception*, Paris: Alcan. Trans. 1910 F. L. Pogson, *Time and Free Will*, London: George Allen and Unwin.

Bergson, Henri (1896). *Matière et mémoire*, Paris: Alcan. Trans. 1911 N. M. Paul and W. S. Palmer, *Matter and Memory*, London: George Allen and Unwin.

Bergson, Henri (1907). *L'évolution créatrice*, Paris: Alcan. Trans. 1911 A. Mitchell, *Creative Evolution*, London: Macmillan.

Bergson, Henri (1932). *Les Deux Sources de la morale et de la réligion*, Paris: Alcan. Trans. 1935 R. A. Audra and C. Brereton, *The Two Sources of Morality and Religion*, London: Macmillan.

Bergson, Henri (1959). *Oeuvres* (*Works*), ed. André Robinet and introduced by Henri Gouhier. Paris: Presses Universitaires de France.

Blondel, Maurice (1893). *L'Action. Essai d'une critique de la vie et d'une science de la pratique* (*Essay on a Critique of Life and a Science of Practice*), Paris: Alcan. Repr. 1950 in *Les Premiers écrits de Maurice Blondel*, vol. I, Paris: Presses Universitaires de France. Trans. 1984 Oliva Blanchette, *Action*, Notre Dame, IN: University of Notre Dame Press.

Blondel, Maurice (1896). 'Lettre sur les exigences de la pensée contemporaine en matière d'apologétique et sur la methode de la philosophie dans l'étude du problème religieux', *Annales de philosophie chrétienne* 131 and 132. Repr. Maurice Blondel 1956, *Premiers écrits*, vol. II, 5–95. Trans. 1964 A. Dru and I. Trethowan, *The Letter on Apologetics and History and Dogma*, London: Harvill Press.

Blondel, Maurice (1904). 'Histoire et dogma: Les lacunes philosophiques de l'exégesé moderne', *La Quinzaine* 56. Reprinted 1956, *Premiers écrits*, vol. II, 149 ff. Trans. 1964 A. Dru and I. Trethowan, *The Letter on Apologetics and History and Dogma*, London: Harvill Press.

Blondel, Maurice (1934). *La Pensée* (*Thought*), 2 vols., Paris: Alcan. Reprinted 1948 and 1954, Paris: Presses Universitaires de France.

Blondel, Maurice (1935). *L'Etre et les êtres* (*Being and Beings*), Paris: Alcan.

Blondel, Maurice (1936–7). *L'Action*, 2 vols., Paris: Alcan.

Blondel, Maurice (1944–6). *La philosophie et l'esprit chrétien* (*Philosophy and the Christian Spirit*), 2 vols., Paris: Presses Universitaires de France.

Boekraad, A. J. (1955). *The Personal Conquest of Truth*, Louvain: Editions Nauwelaerts.

Boekraad, A. J. and Tristram Henry. (1961). *The Argument from Conscience to the Existence of God*, Louvain: Editions Nauwelaerts.

Bouillard, Henri (1969). *Blondel and Christianity*. Trans. L. P. Caron, Washington: Corpus Books.

Boutroux, E. (1879). *De la contingence des lois de la nature*, Paris: Alcan. Trans. F. Rothwell 1916, *The Contingency of the Laws of Nature*, Chicago, IL: Open Court.

Clendenning, J. (1985). *The Life and Thought of Josiah Royce*, Madison: University of Wisconsin Press.

Copleston, Frederick (1975). *A History of Philosophy*, vol. IX, New York: Newman Press.

Daly, Gabriel (1980). *Transcendence and Immanence: A Study in Catholic Modernism and Integralism*, Oxford: Oxford University Press.

Dansette, A. (1961). *Religious History of Modern France*, vol. II, New York: Herder and Herder.

De Achaval, Hugo M. and Holmes, J. Derek (eds.) (1976). *The Theological Papers of John Henry Newman on Faith and Certainty*, Oxford: Clarendon Press.

Deegan, Daniel L. (1966). 'Wilhelm Herrmann: An Assessment', *Scottish Journal of Theology* 19.

Duméry, Henri (1948). *La Philosophie de l'action: Essai sur l'intellectualisme blondélien* (*The Philosophy of Action: An Essay on Blondelian Intellectualism*), Paris: Aubier.

Ferreira, M. Jaime (1990). *Doubt and Religious Commitment: The Role of the Will in Newman's Thought*, Oxford: Clarendon Press.

Fischer-Appelt, Peter (1965). *Metaphysik im Horizont der Theologie Wilhelm Herrmann* (*Metaphysics in the Horizon of Wilhelm Herrmann's Theology*), Munich: Kaiser Verlag.

Fisher, Simon (1988). *Revelatory Positivism? Barth's Earliest Theology and the Marburg School*, Oxford: Oxford University Press.

Fuss, Peter (1965). *The Moral Philosophy of Josiah Royce*, Cambridge, MA: Harvard University Press.

Gilley, Sheridan (1990). *Newman and His Age*, London: Darton, Longmans, and Todd.

Gregory, Frederick (1992). *Nature Lost? Natural Science and the German Theological Traditions in the Nineteenth Century*, Cambridge, MA: Harvard University Press.

Hanna, T. (ed.) (1962). *The Bergsonian Heritage*, New York: Columbia University Press.

Herrmann, Wilhelm (1876). *Die Metaphysik in der Theologie* (*Metaphysics in Theology*), Halle: Niemeyer.

Herrmann, Wilhelm (1879). *Die Religion im Verhältnis zum Welterkennen und zur Sittlichkeit* (*Religion and Its Relation to Science and Morality*), Halle: Niemeyer.

Herrmann, Wilhelm (1886). *Der Verkehr des Christen mit Gott*, Stuttgart: J. G. Cotta. Trans. 1906 R. W. Stewart, *The Communion of the Christian with God*, London: Williams and Norgate. From the 4th German edn 1903. Repr. with introduction by R. Voekel. Philadelphia: Westminster Press, 1971; London, 1972.

Herrmann, Wilhelm (1901). *Ethik*, Tübingen: J. C. B. Mohr.

Herrmann, Wilhelm (1925). *Dogmatik*, ed. M. Rade, Stuttgart: F. A. Perthes. Trans. 1927 N. Micklem and K. A. Saunders, *Systematic Theology*, London: George Allen and Unwin.

Herrmann, Wilhelm (1966–7). *Schriften zur Grundlegung der Theologie* (*Writings on Laying the Foundations of Theology*), 2 vols., Munich: Kaiser Verlag.

James, William (1975–90). *The Works of William James*, 21 vols., ed. F. H. Burkhardt, F. Bowers and I. K. Skrupskelis, Cambridge, MA: Harvard University Press.

James, William (1897). *The Will to Believe and Other Essays*, New York and London: Longmans, Green.

James, William (1902). *The Varieties of Religious Experience: A Study of Human Behaviour*, New York and London: Longmans, Green.

James, William (1907). *Pragmatism: A New Name for Some Old Ways of Thinking*, New York and London: Longmans, Green.

James, William (1909). *A Pluralistic Universe*, New York and London: Longmans, Green.

James, William (1909). *The Meaning of Truth: A Sequel to Pragmatism*, New York and London: Longmans, Green.

James, William (1912). *Essays in Radical Empiricism*, New York and London: Longmans, Green.

Jankélévitch, Vladimir (1959). *Henri Bergson*, Paris: Presses Universitaires de France.

Kant, I. (1790). *Kritik der Urteilskraft*, Berlin: Lagarde und Friederich. Trans. 1952 J. C. Meredith, *The Critique of Judgment*, Oxford: Clarendon Press.

Ker, Ian (1988). *John Henry Newman: A Biography*, Oxford: Clarendon Press. The fullest account of his life and writings.

Kolakowski, L. (1985). *Bergson*, Oxford: Oxford University Press.

Lacroix, Jean (1968). *Maurice Blondel: An Introduction to the Man and His Philosophy*. Trans. John C. Guinness, New York: Sheed and Ward.

Lambeth, David (1999). *William James and the Metaphysics of Experience*, Cambridge, MA: Harvard University Press.

Lee, Seong–Woo (1995). *Das Wesen der Religion und ihr Verhältnis zu Wissenschaft und Sittlichkeit bei Wilhelm Herrmann* (*The Essence of Religion and Its Relationship to Science and Morality in Wilhelm Herrmann*), Frankfurt-on-Main and New York: Peter Lang.

Mahlmann, Theodor (1962). 'Das Axiom des Erlebnisses bei Wilhelm Herrmann' (*The Principle of Experiences in Wilhelm Herrmann*), *Neue Zeitschrift für systematische Theologie und Religionsphilosophie* 6, 70–107.

Myers, Gerald E. (1986). *William James: His Life and Thought*, New Haven, CT: Yale University Press.

Newman, J. H. (1845). *An Essay on the Development of Christian Doctrine*, London: James Toovey. New edn 1989, Notre Dame, IN: University of Notre Dame Press.

Newman, J. H. (1852). *Discourses on the Scope and Nature of University Education: Addressed to the Catholics of Dublin*, Dublin. New edn 1976, I. T. Ker (ed.), *The Idea of a University*, Oxford: Clarendon Press.

Newman, J. H. (1864). *Apologia Pro Vita Sua*, London: Longmans. New edn 1967, Martin J. Svaglic (ed.), Oxford: Clarendon Press.

Newman, J. H. (1870). *An Essay in Aid of a Grammar of Assent*, London: Burns, Oates, and Co. New edn 1985, I. T. Ker (ed.), Oxford: Clarendon Press.

Oppenheim, F. M. (1980). *Royce's Voyage Down Under: A Journey of the Mind*, Lexington, KY: University of Kentucky Press.

Perry, Ralph Barton (1935). *The Thought and Character of William James*, 2 vols., Boston: Little, Brown. Both a biography and a study of James's thought.

Price, H. H. (1969). *Belief*, London: George Allen and Unwin.

Reardon, Bernard M. G. (1975). *Liberalism and Tradition: Aspects of Catholic Thought in the Nineteenth Century*, Cambridge: Cambridge University Press.

Royce, Josiah (1885). *The Religious Aspect of Philosophy*, Boston: Houghton Mifflin. Repr. New York: Dover, 1983.

Royce, Josiah (1897). *The Conception of God*, New York: Macmillan.

Royce, Josiah (1899–1900). *The World and the Individual*, 2 vols., New York: Macmillan. Repr. Magnolia, MA: Peter Smith, 1983.

Royce, Josiah (1908). *The Philosophy of Loyalty*, New York: Macmillan.

Royce, Josiah (1912). *The Sources of Religious Insight*, New York: Charles Scribner's Sons.

Royce, Josiah (1913). *The Problem of Christianity*, New York: Macmillan. Reprinted, Chicago: University of Chicago Press, 1968.

Sillem, E. J. (ed.) (1969). *The Philosophical Notebook of John Henry Newman*, 2 vols., Louvain: Nauwelaerts Publishing House.

Simon, Linda (1998). *Genuine Reality: A Life of William James*, Chicago: Harcourt Brace.

Smart, Ninian, *et al.* (eds.) (1985). *Nineteenth Century Religious Thought in the West*, vol. II, Cambridge: Cambridge University Press, chs. 7 and 8.

Smith, John E. (1985). 'William James and Josiah Royce' in Ninian Smart *et al.* (eds.), *Nineteenth Century Religious Thought in the West*, vol. II, Cambridge: Cambridge University Press.

Smith, John E. (1950). *Royce's Social Infinite*, New York: Library of Liberal Arts Press.

Somerville, James M. (1968). *Total Commitment: Blondel's L'Action*, Washington: Corpus Books.

Suckiel, Ellen Kappy (1996). *Heaven's Champion: William James's Philosophy of Religion*, Notre Dame, IN: University of Notre Dame Press.

Tresmontant, Claude (1963). *La métaphysique de Maurice Blondel* (*The Metaphysics of Maurice Blondel*), Paris: Editions du Seuil.

Turner, Frank M. (1974). *Between Science and Religion: The Reaction to Scientific Naturalism in Late Victorian England*, New Haven, CT: Yale University Press.

Vargish, Thomas (1970). *The Contemplation of Mind*, Oxford: Oxford University Press.

Welch, Claude (1985). *Protestant Thought in the Nineteenth Century, vol. II: 1870–1914*, New Haven, CT: Yale University Press.

CHAPTER 26 ART AND MORALITY: AESTHETICS AT 1870

Baumgarten, Alexander Gottlieb (1735). *Meditationes philosophicae de nonnullis ad poema pertinentibus*, Halle: Johann Heinrich Grunert. Modern edition with German translation 1983: Heinz Paetzold, *Philosophische Betrachtungen über einige Bedingungen des Gedichtes*, Hamburg: Felix Meiner. English translation 1954 K. Aschenbrenner and W. B. Holther, *Reflections on Poetry*, Berkeley/Los Angeles: University of California Press.

Guyer, Paul (1993). *Kant and the Experience of Freedom*, Cambridge: Cambridge University Press.

Guyer, Paul (1996). 'Pleasure and Knowledge in Schopenhauer's Aesthetics' in Jacquette (1996), 109–32.

Harrison, Charles, Wood, Paul, and Gaiger, Jason (1998). *Art in Theory 1815–1900: An Anthology of Changing Ideas*, Oxford: Blackwell.

Jacquette, Dale (ed.) (1996). *Schopenhauer, Philosophy and the Arts*. Cambridge: Cambridge University Press.

Kant, I. (1790). *Kritik der Urteilskraft*. Trans. 2000 P. Guyer and E. Matthews, *Critique of the Power of Judgment*, Cambridge: Cambridge University Press.

Landow, George P. (1985). *Ruskin*, Oxford: Oxford University Press.

Lotze, Hermann (1845). *Über den Begriff der Schönheit*. Göttingen: Vanderhoeck and Ruprecht.

Lotze, Hermann (1856–64). *Mikrokosmos: Ideen zur Naturgeschichte und Geschichte der Menschheit*, 3 vols., Leipzig: Hirzel. Trans. 1885 E. Hamilton and E. C. Jones, *Microcosmos: An Essay concerning Man and his Relation to the World*. 2 vols., Edinburgh: T. & T. Clark and New York: Scribner and Welford.

Lotze, Hermann (1868). *Geschichte der Ästhetik in Deutschland* (*History of Aesthetics in Germany*), Munich: Cotta, 1868.

Lotze, Hermann (1884). *Die Grundzüge der Ästhetik: Diktate aus den Vorlesungen*, Leipzig: Hirzel; modern edition from 1990: Hein Stünke (ed.), *Schriften zur Kunsttheorie VI*, Berlin: Alexander Verlag; English translation in 1885 by G. T. Ladd, *Outlines of Aesthetics: Dictated Portions of the Lectures of H. Lotze*, Boston: Ginn & Co.

Magee, Brian (1983). *The Philosophy of Schopenhauer*, Oxford: Clarendon Press.

Morris, William (1910–15). *The Collected Works of William Morris*, ed. May Morris, London.

Morris, William (1891). *News from Nowhere*, London: Reeves and Turner. Repr. 1995 ed. K. Kumar, Cambridge: Cambridge University Press.

Nehamas, Alexander (1985). *Nietzsche: Life as Literature*, Cambridge, MA: Harvard University Press.

Nietzsche, Friedrich (1872). *Die Geburt der Tragödie aus dem Geiste der Musik* (after 1886: *Die Geburt der Tragödie, oder Griechentum und Pessimismus*), Leipzig: E. W. Fritzsch. English translation 1867 by Walter Kaufmann, *The Birth of Tragedy*, New York: Random House.

Nietzsche, Friedrich (1886). *Jenseits von Gut und Böse*, Leipzig: C. G. Naumann; English translation 1973 by R. J. Hollingdale, *Beyond Good and Evil*, Harmondsworth: Penguin.

Pater, Walter (1873). *The Renaissance: Studies in Art and Poetry* (originally entitled *Studies in the History of the Renaissance*), London: Macmillan; modern edition, 1986, ed. Adam Phillips, Oxford: Oxford University Press.

Pater, Walter (1885). *Marius the Epicurean: His Sensations and Ideas*. London; modern edition, 1985, ed. Michael Levey, Harmondsworth: Penguin.

Pater, Walter (1973). *Essays on LIterature and Art*, ed. Jennifer Uglow. London: J. M. Dent.

Ruskin, John (1903–12). *The Library Edition of the Works of John Ruskin*, ed. E. T. Cook and Alexander Wedderburn, London.

Ruskin, John (1985). *Unto this Last and Other Writings*, ed. Clive Wilmer, Harmondsworth: Penguin.

Ruskin, John (1995). *Selected Writings: Modern Painters, The Stones of Venice, The Seven Lamps of Architecture, Praeterita*, ed. Philip Davis, London: J. M. Dent.

Ruskin, John (1996). *Lectures on Art*, ed. Bill Beckley, New York: Allworth Press.

Schiller, J. C. F. (1975). *Briefe über die Ästhetische Erziehung des Menschen*. Jena: no publisher. Repr. in K. Goedeke (ed.), *Schillers sämmtliche Schriften*, Stuttgart, 1867–76. Trans. 1967 F. M. Wilkinson and L. A. Willoughby, *On the Aesthetic Education of Men*, Oxford: Clarendon Press.

Schopenhauer, Arthur (1844). *Die Welt als Wille und Vorstellung*, 2nd edn, 2 vols. Leipzig, Brockhans; trans. 1958 E. F. J. Payne, *The World as Will and Representation*, New York: Dover.

Silk, M. S. and Stern, J. P. (1981). *Nietzsche on Tragedy*. Cambridge: Cambridge University Press.

Stansky, Peter (1983). *Morris*, Oxford: Oxford University Press.

Stolnitz, Jerome. (1961a). 'On the Origins of "Aesthetic Disinterestedness" ', *Journal of Aesthetics and Art Criticism* 20.

Stolnitz, Jerome. (1961b). 'On the Significance of Lord Shaftesbury in Modern Aesthetic Theory', *Philosophical Quarterly* 11.

Young, Julian. (1992). *Nietzsche's Philosophy of Art*. Cambridge: Cambridge University Press.

CHAPTER 27 FORM AND FEELING: AESTHETICS AT THE
TURN OF THE CENTURY

Bell, Clive (1914). *Art*, London: Chatto and Windus. Repr. New York: G. P. Putnam's Sons, 1958.

Bosanquet, Bernard (1892). *A History of Aesthetic*, London: George Unwin. 2nd edn 1904.

Bosanquet, Bernard (1915). *Three Lectures on Aesthetic*, London: Macmillan.

Bullough, Edward (1912 [1957]). *Aesthetics: Lectures and Essays*, ed. Elizabeth M. Wilkinson, Stanford: Stanford University Press.

Collingwood, R. (1924). *Speculum Mentis*, Oxford: Clarendon Press.

Croce, Benedetto (1902). *Estetica come scienza dell'espressione e linguistica generale*, Milan: Sandron. Trans. 1992 C. Lyas, *The Aesthetic as the Science of Expression and of the Linguistic in General*, Cambridge: Cambridge University Press.

Croce, Benedetto (1913). *Guide to Aesthetics*, trans. Patrick Romanell. Indianapolis: Bobbs-Merrill, 1965; repr. cited: Indianapolis: Hackett, 1995.

Dilthey, Wilhelm (1985). 'Poetry and Experience', *Selected Works*, vol. V, ed. Rudolf A. Makkreel and Frithjof Rodi, Princeton, NJ: Princeton University Press.

Fry, Roger (1920). *Vision and Design*, London: Chatto and Windus; reprint cited: Oxford: Oxford University Press, 1981.

Fry, Roger (1996). *A Roger Fry Reader*, ed. by Christopher Reed. Chicago: University of Chicago Press.

Harrison, Charles, Wood, Paul, and Gaiger, Jason (1998). *Art in Theory: 1815–1900. An Anthology of Changing Ideas*, Oxford: Blackwell.

Santayana, George (1896). *The Sense of Beauty: Being the Outline of Aesthetic Theory*, New York: Charles Scribner's Sons; reprint cited: New York: Dover Publications, 1905.

Santayana, George (1905). *Reason in Art; The Life of Reason*, vol. IV. New York: Charles Scribner's Sons; cited from *The Life of Reason, or the Phases of Human Progress*; new one-volume edition revised by the author in collaboration with Daniel Cory. New York: Charles Scribner's Sons, 1954.

Tolstoy, Leo (1898). *What is Art?* Transl. 1995 Richard Pevear and Larissa Volokhonsky. Harmondsworth: Penguin.

INTERLUDE: PHILOSOPHY AND THE FIRST WORLD WAR

Alexander, S. (1920). *Space, Time and Deity*, London: Macmillan.

Benda, J. (1927). *La Trahison des Clercs*, Paris. Trans. 1928 R. Aldington, *The Treason of the Intellectuals*, London: Routledge.

Bernhardi, Friedrich von (1912). *Germany and the Next War*, London: Edward Arnold.

Bosanquet, B. (1899). *The Philosophical Theory of the State*, London: Macmillan.

de Chardin, T. (1965). *Ecrits du temps de la guerre*, Paris: Grasset. Trans. (part only) 1968 R. Hague *Writings in Time of War*, London: Collins.

Dewey, J. (1915). *German Philosophy and Politics*, New York: Holt.

Engelmann, P. (1967). *Letters from Ludwig Wittgenstein with a Memoir*, trans. L. Furtmüller, Oxford: Blackwell.

Ferguson, N. (1998). *The Pity of War*, Harmondsworth: Penguin.

Heidegger, M. (1927). *Sein und Zeit*, Tübingen: Max Niemeyer Verlag. Trans. 1962 J. Macquarrie and E. Robinson, *Being and Time*, Oxford: Blackwell.

Hobhouse, L. T. (1918). *The Metaphysical Theory of the State*, London: George Allen and Unwin.

Jünger, E. (1920). *In Stahlgewittern*, Berlin. Trans. 1929 *The Storm of Steel*, London: Chatto and Windus.

Jünger, E. (1928). *Das Wäldchen 125*, Berlin: F. Mittler. Trans. 1930 B. Creighton, *Copse 125*, London: Chatto and Windus.

Monk, R. (1990). *Ludwig Wittgenstein: The Duty of Genius*, London: Jonathan Cape.

Monk, R. (1996). *Bertrand Russell: The Spirit of Solitude*, London: Jonathan Cape.

Muirhead, J. H. (1915). *German Philosophy in Relation to the War*, London: John Murray.

Ott, H. (1993). *Martin Heidegger: The Political Life*, London: HarperCollins.

Rhees, R. (ed.) (1984). *Recollections of Wittgenstein*, Oxford: Oxford University Press.

Ross, Sir W. D. (1930). *The Right and the Good*, Oxford: Clarendon.

Russell, B. A. W. (1914). *On Scientific Method in Philosophy*, London: Oxford University Press. Repr. 1986 in *The Collected Papers of Bertrand Russell*, vol. VIII, London: George Allen and Unwin.

Russell, B. A. W. (1916). *Principles of Social Reconstruction*, London: George Allen and Unwin.

Russell, B. A. W. (1920). *The Analysis of Mind*, London: George Allen and Unwin.

Wallace, S. (1988). *War and the Image of Germany*, Edinburgh: John Donald.

Wittgenstein, L. (1921). 'Logische-philosophische Abhandlung', in *Annalen der Naturphilosophie*. Trans. 1922 C. K. Ogden, *Tractatus Logico-Philosophicus*, London: Routledge.

Wittgenstein, L. (1961). *Notebooks 1914–16*, ed. G. H. von Wright and G. E. M. Anscombe, trans. G. E. M. Anscombe, Oxford: Blackwell.

CHAPTER 28 LOGICAL ATOMISM

Griffin, J. (1964). *Wittgenstein's Logical Atomism*, Oxford: Oxford University Press.

Moore, G. E. (1899). 'The Nature of Judgment', *Mind* n.s. 5: 176–93. Repr. 1993 in G. E. Moore (ed. T. Baldwin), *Selected Writings*, London: Routledge, 1–19.

Russell, B. A. W. (1910a). *Principia Mathematica*, vol. I, Cambridge: Cambridge University Press.

Russell, B. A. W. (1910b). 'On the Nature of Truth and Falsehood' in *Philosophical Essays*, London: George Allen and Unwin. Reprinted in Russell (1984–), vol. VI, 115–24.

Russell, B. A. W. (1911). 'Le Réalisme analytique', *Bulletin de la société française de philosophie*, 11: 282–91. Trans. in Russell (1984–), vol. VI, 133–46.

Russell, B. A. W. (1914). 'The Relation of Sense-data to Physics', *Scientia* 16, 1–27. Reprinted in Russell (1984–), vol. VIII, 5–29.

Russell, B. A. W. (1918). 'The Philosophy of Logical Atomism', *Monist* 28: 495–527; 29 (1919): 33–63, 190–222. Reprinted in Russell (1984–), vol. VIII, 160–244.

Russell, B. A. W. (1927). 'Introduction', 2nd, edn *Principia Mathematica*, Cambridge: Cambridge University Press, xiii–xlvi.

Russell, B. A. W. (1968). *The Autobiography of Bertrand Russell 1914–1944*, London: George Allen and Unwin.

Russell, B. A. W. (1984–). *The Collected Papers of Bertrand Russell*, London: Routledge.

Wittgenstein, L. (1921). *Logische-Philosophische Abhandlung*, in *Annalen der Naturphilosophie*. Trans. 1922 C. K. Ogden *Tractatus Logico-Philosophicus*, London: Routledge.

Wittgenstein, L. (1929). 'Some Remarks on Logical Form', *Proceedings of the Aristotelian Society, Supplementary volume 9*, 162–71. Reprinted in *Philosophical Occasions* (ed. J. Klagge and A. Nordmann), Indianapolis: Hackett, 29–35.

Wittgenstein, L. (1961). *Notebooks 1914–16*, ed. G. H. von Wright and G. E. M. Anscombe, trans. G. E. M. Anscombe, Oxford: Blackwell.

CHAPTER 29 THE SCIENTIFIC WORLD CONCEPTION:
LOGICAL POSITIVISM

Ayer, A. J. (1936). *Language, Truth, and Logic*, London: Gollancz.

Bell, D. and Vossenkuhl, W. (1992). *Science and Subjectivity: The Vienna Circle and Twentieth-Century Philosophy*, Berlin: Akademie.

Carnap, R. (1922). *Der Raum* (*Space*), Berlin: Reuther und Reichard.

Carnap, R. (1928a). *Der logische Aufbau der Welt*. Berlin: Weltkreis. Trans. 1967 R. George, *The Logical Structure of the World*, Berkeley and Los Angeles: University of California Press.

Carnap, R. (1928b). *Scheinproblems in der Philosophy*, Berlin: Weltkreis. Trans. 1967 R. George, *Pseudoproblems in Philosophy*, Berkeley and Los Angeles: University of California Press.

Carnap, R. (1934). *Logische Syntax der Sprache*, Vienna: Springer Verlag. Trans. 1937 A. Smeaton, *The Logical Syntax of Language*, London: Routledge.

Carnap, R. (1936). 'Von Erkenntnistheorie zur Wissenschaftslogik' ('From Epistemology to the Logic of Science'), in *Actes du Congrès Internationale de Philosophie Scientifique, Sorbonne, Paris, 1935*, vol. I, Paris: Hermann and Cie, 36–41.

Carnap, R. (1936–7). 'Testability and Meaning', *Philosophy of Science* 3: 419–71; 4: 1–40.

Carnap, R. (1942). *Introduction to Semantics*, Cambridge, MA: Harvard University Press.

Carnap, R. (1947). *Meaning and Necessity*, Chicago: University of Chicago Press.

Carnap, R. (1950). *Logical Foundations of Probability*, Chicago: University of Chicago Press.

Carnap, R. (1963). 'Intellectual Autobiography', in P. A. Schilpp (1963), 3–84.

Cartwright, N., Fleck, L., Cat, J. and Uebel, T. E. (1996). *Otto Neurath: Philosophy between Science and Politics*, Cambridge: Cambridge University Press.

Coffa, J. A. (1991). *The Semantic Tradition from Kant to Carnap: To the Vienna Station*, Cambridge: Cambridge University Press.

Dewey, J. (1938). 'Unity of Science as a Social Problem' in O. Neurath, R. Carnap, and C. W. Morris (eds.), *International Encyclopedia of Unified Science*, vol. I, no 1, Chicago: University of Chicago Press, 29–38.

Dewey, J. (1939). *Theory of Valuation*, Chicago: University of Chicago Press.

Feigl, H. (1934). 'The Logical Character of the Principle of Induction', *Philosophy of Science* 1: 20–9.

Feigl, H. (1945). 'Operationism and Scientific Method', *Psychological Review* 52: 250–9.

Friedman, M. (1987). 'Carnap's *Aufbau* Reconsidered', *Noûs* 21: 521–45.

Friedman, M. (1992). 'Epistemology in the *Aufbau*', *Synthèse* 93: 15–57.

Galison, P. (1990). '*Aufbau/Bauhaus*: Logical Positivism and Architectural Modernism', *Critical Inquiry* 16: 709–52.

Galison, P. (1996). 'Constructing Modernism: The Cultural Location of *Aufbau*' in Giere and Richardson (1996), 17–44.

Giere, R. N. and Richardson, A. W. (1996). *Origins of Logical Empiricism*, Minneapolis: University of Minnesota Press.

Haller, R. (1982). *Schlick und Neurath. Ein Symposion* (*Schlick and Neurath: A Symposium*), Amsterdam: Rodopi.

Haller, R. and Stadler, F. (1993). *Wien-Berlin-Prag: Der Aufstieg der wissenschaftlichen Philosophie* (*Vienna-Berlin-Prague: The Rise of Scientific Philosophy*), Vienna: Hölder-Pichler-Tempsky.

Hempel, C. G. (1942). 'The Function of General Laws in History', *Journal of Philosophy* 39: 35–48.

Hempel, C. G. (1945). 'Studies in the Logic of Confirmation', *Mind* 54: 1–26, 97–121.

Hintikka, J. (1975). *Rudolf Carnap, Logical Empiricist: Materials and Perspectives*, Dordrecht: Reidel.

McGuinness, B. (1985). *Zurück zu Schlick. Eine Neubewertung von Werk und Wirkung* (*Back to Schlick. A New Evaluation of his Work and Influence*), Vienna: Hölder-Pichler-Tempsky.

Morris, C. W. (1937). *Logical Positivism, Pragmatism and Scientific Empiricism*, Paris: Hermann et Cie.

Moulines, C. U. (1991). 'Making Sense of Carnap's *Aufbau*', *Erkenntnis* 35: 263–86.

Nemeth, E. (1981). *Otto Neurath und der Wiener Kreis, Wissenschaftlichkeit als revolutionärer politischer Anspruch* (*Scientific Status as Revolutionary Politics*), Frankfurt: Campus.

Nemeth, E. and Stadler, F. (1996). *Encyclopedia and Utopia: The Life and Work of Otto Neurath (1882–1945)*, Dordrecht: Kluwer.

Neurath, O. (1931). *Empirische Soziologie*, Vienna: Springer. Partial trans. 1973 P. Foulkes and M. Neurath, 'Empirical Sociology' in O. Neurath (ed. M. Neurath and R. S. Cohen), *Empiricism and Sociology*, Dordrecht: Reidel, 319–421.

Neurath, O. (1933). *Einheitswissenschaft und Psychologie*, Vienna: Gerold. Trans. 1987 H. Kraal, 'Unified Science and Psychology' in B. McGuinness (ed.), *The Unity of Science*, Dordrecht: Reidel, 1–23.

Neurath, O. (1944). *Foundations of the Social Sciences*, Chicago: University of Chicago Press.

Neurath, O., Carnap, R., and Hahn, H. (1929). *Wissenschaftliche Weltauffassung. Der Wiener Kreis*, Vienna: Wolf. Trans. 1973 P. Foulkes and M. Neurath, 'Scientific World Conception. The Vienna Circle' in O. Neurath (ed. M. Neurath and R. S. Cohen), *Empiricism and Sociology*, Dordrecht: Reidel, 299–318.

Neurath, P. and Nemeth, E. (1994). *Otto Neurath oder die Einheit von Wissenschaft und Gesellschaft* (*Otto Neurath or the Unity of Science and Society*). Vienna: Böhlau.

Oberdan, T. (1993). *Protocols, Truth and Convention*, Amsterdam: Rodopi.

Proust, J. (1986). *Questione de Forme: Logique et proposition analytique de Kant à Carnap*, Paris: Librairie Arthème Fayard. Trans. 1989 A. Brenner, *Questions of Form: Logic and the Analytic Proposition from Kant to Carnap*, Minneapolis: University of Minnesota Press.

Quine, W. V. (1936). 'Truth by Convention' in O. H. Lee (ed.), *Philosophical Essays for A. N. Whitehead*, New York: Longman, 90–124. Reprinted 1976 in W. V. Quine, *The Ways of Paradox*, Cambridge, MA: Harvard University Press, 77–106.

Quine, W. V. (1942). *Mathematical Logic*, New York: Norton.

Reichenbach, H. (1920). *Relativitätstheorie und Erkenntnis Apriori*, Berlin: Springer Verlag. Trans. 1965 M. Reichenbach, *The Theory of Relativity and A Priori Knowledge*, Berkeley and Los Angeles: University of California Press.

Reichenbach, H. (1924). *Axiomatik der relativistischen Raum-Zeit-Lehre*, Braunschweig: Vieweg. Trans. 1969 M. Reichenbach, *Axiomatization of the Theory of Relativity*, Berkeley and Los Angeles: University of California Press.

Reichenbach, H. (1928). *Philosophie der Raum-Zeit-Lehre*, Berlin: de Gruyter. Trans. 1958 M. Reichenbach and J. Freund, *The Philosophy of Space and Time*, New York: Dover.

Reichenbach, H. (1935). *Wahrscheinlichkeitslehre* (*Probability Theory*), Leiden: Sijthoff.

Reichenbach, H. (1938). *Experience and Prediction*, Chicago: University of Chicago Press.

Reichenbach, H. (1939). 'Dewey's Theory of Science' in P. A. Schilpp (ed.), *The Philosophy of John Dewey*, Evanston: Northwestern University Press, 157–92.

Reichenbach, H. (1944). *Philosophical Foundations of Quantum Mechanics*, Berkeley and Los Angeles: University of California Press.

Reichenbach, H. (1951). *The Rise of Scientific Philosophy*, Berkeley and Los Angeles: University of California Press.

Reichenbach, H. (1956). *The Direction of Time*, Berkeley and Los Angeles: University of California Press.

Reisch, G. A. (1994). 'Planning Science: Otto Neurath and the *International Encyclopedia of Unified Science*', *British Journal for the History of Science* 27: 153–75.

Richardson, A. W. (1997a). 'Toward a History of Scientific Philosophy', *Perspectives on Science* 5: 418–51.

Richardson, A. W. (1997b). 'Two Dogmas about Logical Empiricism', *Philosophical Topics* 25: 145–68.

Richardson, A. W. (1998). *Carnap's Construction of the World*, Cambridge: Cambridge University Press.

Ricketts, T. G. (1994). 'Carnap's Principle of Tolerance, Empiricism and Conventionalism' in P. Clark and B. Hale (eds.), *Reading Putnam*, Oxford: Blackwell, 176–200.

Runggaldier, E. (1984). *Carnap's Early Conventionalism: An Inquiry into the Background of the Vienna Circle*, Amsterdam: Rodopi.

Salmon, W. C. (1979). *Hans Reichenbach: Logical Empiricist*, Dordrecht: Reidel.

Salmon, W. and Wolters, G. (1994). *Logic, Language, and the Structure of Scientific Theories*, Pittsburgh: University of Pittsburgh Press.

Sauer, W. (1989). 'On the Kantian Background of Neopositivism', *Topoi* 8: 111–19.

Schilpp, P. A. (1963). *The Philosophy of Rudolf Carnap*, La Salle, IL: Open Court.

Schlick, M. (1910). 'Das Wesen der Wahrheit nach der modernen Logik', *Vierteljahrsschrift für wissenschaftliche Philosophie und Soziologie* 34: 386–477. Trans. 1979 P. Heath, 'The Nature of Truth in Modern Logic' in M. Schlick (ed. H. L. Mulder and B. F. B. van de Velde-Schlick), *Philosophical Papers*, vol. I, Dordrecht: Reidel, 41–103.

Schlick, M. (1917). *Raum und Zeit in der gegenwärtigen Physik*, Berlin: Springer Verlag. Trans. 1979 P. Heath, 'Space and Time in Contemporary Physics' in M. Schlick (ed. H. L. Mulder and B. F. B. van de Velde-Schlick), *Philosophical Papers*, vol. I, Dordrecht: Reidel, 207–69.

Schlick, M. (1918, 1925). *Allgemeine Erkenntnislehre*, Berlin: Springer. Trans. of 2nd edn 1974 A. Blumberg and H. Feigl, *General Theory of Knowledge*, La Salle, IL: Open Court.

Schlick, M. (1930). 'Die Wende der Philosophie', *Erkenntnis* 1: 4–11. Trans. 1979 P. Heath, 'The Turning-Point in Philosophy' in M. Schlick (ed. H. L. Mulder and B. F. B. van de Velde-Schlick), *Philosophical Papers*, vol. II, Dordrecht: Reidel, 154–60.

Schlick, M. (1932). 'Positivismus und Realismus', *Erkenntnis* 3: 1–31. Trans. 1979 P. Heath, 'Positivism and Realism' in M. Schlick (ed. H. L. Mulder and B. F. B. van de Velde-Schlick), *Philosophical Papers*, vol. II, Dordrecht: Reidel, 259–84.

Schlick, M. (1934). 'Über das Fundament der Erkenntnis', *Erkenntnis* 4: 79–99. Trans. 1979 P. Heath, 'On the Foundation of Knowledge' in M. Schlick (ed. H. L. Mulder and B. F. B. van de Velde-Schlick), *Philosophical Papers*, vol. II, Dordrecht: Reidel, 370–87.

Stadler, F. (1991). 'Aspects of the Social Background and Position of the Vienna Circle at the University of Vienna' in Uebel (1991), 51–77.

Stadler, F. (1993). *Scientific Philosophy: Origins and Developments*, Dordrecht: Kluwer.

Stadler, F. (1997). *Studien zum Wiener Kreis. Ursprung, Entwicklung und Wirkung des Logischen Empirismus im Kontext*, Frankfurt: Suhrkamp. Trans. 2001 C. Nielsen, *The Vienna Circle: Studies in the Origins, Development and Influence of Logical Empiricism*, Vienna: Springer.

Uebel, T. E. (1991). *Rediscovering the Forgotten Vienna Circle*, Dordrecht: Kluwer.

Uebel, T. E. (1992). *Overcoming Logical Positivism from Within: The Emergence of Neurath's Naturalism in the Vienna Circle's Protocol Sentence Debate*, Amsterdam: Rodopi.

Uebel, T. E. (1996a). 'Anti-Foundationalism and the Vienna Circle's Revolution in Philosophy', *British Journal for the Philosophy of Science* 47: 415–40.

Uebel, T. E. (1996b). 'The Enlightenment Ambition of Epistemic Utopianism: Otto Neurath's Theory of Science in Historical Perspective' in Giere and Richardson (1996), 91–112.

Zolo, D. (1989). *Reflexive Epistemology: The Philosophical Legacy of Otto Neurath*, Dordrecht: Kluwer.

CHAPTER 30 THE ACHIEVEMENTS OF THE POLISH SCHOOL OF LOGIC

Ajdukiewicz, K. (1974). *Pragmatic Logic*, Warsaw and Dordrecht: The Polish Scientific Publishers–Reidel.

Ajdukiewicz, K. (1978). *The Scientific World-Perspective and Other Essays, 1931–1963*, ed. J. Giedymin, Dordrecht: Reidel.

Bar-Hillel, Z. and Fraenkel, A. (1958). *Foundations of Set Theory*, Amsterdam: North-Holland.

Chwistek, L. (1948). *The Limits of Science: Outline of Logic and of the Methodology of the Exact Sciences*, London: Kegan Paul.

Coniglione, F., Poli, R., and Woleński, J. (eds.) (1993). *Polish Scientific Philosophy: The Lvov-Warsaw School*, Amsterdam: Rodopi.

Czeżowski, T. (1999). *Selected Papers*, ed. L. Gumański, Amsterdam: Rodopi.

Jaśkowski, S. (1934). *On the Rules of Supposition in Formal Logic*, Warsaw: Nakładem Seminarium Filozoficznego Wydziałn Matematyczno-Przyrodniczego Universy tetr Warszawskeigo. Repr. 1967 in S. McCall (ed.), *Polish Logic 1920–37*, Oxford: Clarendon Press.

Jordan, Z. (1945). *The Development of Mathematical Logic and of Logical Positivism in Poland between Two Wars*, Oxford: Oxford University Press; repr. in McCall 1967, 346–406.

Kijania-Placek, K. and Woleński, J. (eds.) (1988). *The Lvov-Warsaw School and Contemporary Philosophy*, Dordrecht: Kluwer.

Kotarbiński, T. (1966). *Gnosiology. The Scientific Approach to the Theory of Knowledge*, Wrocław: Ossolineum and Oxford: Pergamon Press.

Leśniewski, S. (1988). *Lecture Notes in Logic*, ed. J. T. J. Srzednicki and Z. Stachniak, Dordrecht: Kluwer.

Leśniewski, S. (1992). *Collected Works*, vols. I–II, ed. S. J. Surma, J. T. J. Srzednicki, D. I. Barnett, and V. T. Rickey, Dordrecht: Kluwer.

Luschei, E. (1962). *The Logical Systems of Leśniewski*, Amsterdam: North-Holland Publishing Company.

Łukasiewicz, J. (1957). *Aristotle's Syllogistic from the Standpoint of Modern Formal Logic*, Oxford: Clarendon Press.

Łukasiewicz, J. (1970). *Selected Works*, ed. L. Borkowski, Warsaw: Polish Scientific Publishers and Amsterdam: North-Holland Publishing Company.

Łukasiewicz, J. (forthcoming). *Collected Works*, ed. J. T. J. Srzednicki, A. LeBlanc, G. Malinowski, and J. Woleński, Aldershot: Ashgate.

Łukasiewicz, J. and Tarski, A. (1930). 'Untersuchungen über den AussagenKalkül', *Comptes Rendus des Séances de la Société des Sciences et des Lettres de Varsovie* (Classe 3) 23: 30–50. Trans. 'Investigations into the Sentential Calculus' in Łukasiewicz 1970 and Tarski 1956.

McCall, S. (ed.) (1967). *Polish Logic 1920–1939*, Papers by Ajdukiewicz, Chwistek, Jaśkowski, Jordan, Leśniewski, Łukasiewicz, Słupecki, Sobociński, and Wajsberg, Oxford: Clarendon Press.

Mostowski, A. (1948). *Logika matematyczna (Mathematical Logic)*, Warsaw: Monografie Matematyczne.

Mostowski, A. (1967). 'Tarski, Alfred' in P. Edwards (ed.), *The Encyclopedia of Philosophy*, vol. VIII, New York: Macmillan, 77–81.

Mostowski, A. (1979). 'Foundational Studies', *Selected Works*, vols. I–II, Warsaw: Polish Scientific Publishers and Amsterdam: North Holland Publishing Company.

Sierpiński, W. (1965). *Cardinal and Ordinal Numbers*, Warsaw: Polish Scientific Publishers.

Sinisi, V. and Woleński, J. (eds.) (1994). *The Heritage of Kazimierz Ajdukiewicz*, Amsterdam: Rodopi.

Skolimowski, H. (1967). *Polish Analytical Philosophy*, London: Routledge.

Srzednicki, J. T. J., Rickey, V. F., and Czelakowski, J. (eds.) (1984). *Leśniewski's Systems: Ontology and Mereology*, The Hague: Martinus Nijhoff and Wrocław: Ossolineum.

Srzednicki, J. T. J. and Stachniak, Z. (eds.) (1998). *Leśniewski's System: Protothetic*, Dordrecht: Kluwer.

Tarski, A. (1956). *Logic, Semantics, Metamathematics Papers from 1923–1939*, Oxford: Oxford University Press; 2nd edn 1984, J. Corcoran, Indianapolis: Hackett Publishing Company.

Tarski, A. (1986). *Collected Papers*, vols. I–IV, ed. R. S. Givant and R. M. McKenzie, Basle: Birkhäuser Verlag.

Twardowski, K. (1977). *On the Content and Object of Presentation. A Psychological Investigation*, The Hague: Nijhoff.

Twardowski, K. (1999). *Selected Philosophical Papers*, ed. J. Brandl and J. Woleński, Amsterdam: Rodopi.

Wajsberg, M. (1977). *Logical Works*, ed. S. J. Surma, Wrocław: Ossolineum.

Woleński, J. (1989). *Logic and Philosophy in the Lvov-Warsaw School*, Dordrecht: Kluwer.

Woleński, J. (ed.) (1990). *Kotarbiński: Logic, Semantics and Ontology*, Dordrecht: Kluwer.

Zawirski, Z. (1994). *Selected Writings on Time, Logic and the Methodology of Science*, ed. I. Szumilewicz-Lachman, Dordrecht: Kluwer.

CHAPTER 31 LOGIC AND PHILOSOPHICAL ANALYSIS

Ayer, A. J. (1936). *Language, Truth and Logic*, London: Gollancz. New edn 1971, Harmondsworth: Penguin.

Carnap, R. (1934). 'On the Character of Philosophical Problems', *Philosophy of Science* 1: 5–19. Repr. 1967 in R. Rorty (ed.), *The Linguistic Turn*, Chicago: Chicago University Press, 54–62.

Carnap, R. (1950). 'Empiricism, Semantics and Ontology', *Revue Internationale de Philosophie* 4: 20–40.

Kant, I. (1781(A), 1787(B)). *Kritik der reinen Vernuft*, Riga. Trans. 1929 N. Kemp Smith, *Critique of Pure Reason*, London: Macmillan.

Lewis, C. I. (1929). *Mind and World-Order*, New York: Charles Scribner's.

Lewis, C. I. and Langford, C. H. (1932). *Symbolic Logic*, New York: Appleton Century.

Moore, G. E. (1899). 'The Nature of Judgement', *Mind* 8: 176–93. Repr. 1993 in G. E. Moore (ed. T. Baldwin), *Selected Writings*, London: Routledge, 1–19.

Moore, G. E. (1903). *Principia Ethica*, Cambridge: Cambridge University Press. Rev. edn 1993 (ed. T. Baldwin) Cambridge: Cambridge University Press.

Russell, B. A. W. (1905). 'On Denoting', *Mind* 14: 479–93. Repr. 1994 in A. Urquart (ed.), *The Collected Papers of Bertrand Russell*, vol. IV, London: Routledge, 415–27.

Russell, B. A. W. (1914). *Our Knowledge of the External World*, London: Open Court.

Russell, B. A. W. (1918–19). 'The Philosophy of Logical Atomism', *The Monist* 28: 495–527, 29: 32–63, 190–222, 345–80. Repr. 1986 in J. Slater (ed.), *The Collected Papers of Bertrand Russell*, vol. VIII, London: George Allen and Unwin, 160–244.

Russell, B. A. W. (1959). *My Philosophical Development*, London: George Allen and Unwin. Repr. 1995, London: Routledge.

Wisdom, J. (1934). *Problems of Mind and Matter*, Cambridge: Cambridge University Press.

Wittgenstein, L. (1921). 'Logische-philosophische Abhandlung', *Annalen der Naturphilosophie*. Trans. 1922 C. K. Ogden, *Tractatus Logico-Philosophicus*, London: Routledge.

CHAPTER 32 THE CONTINUING IDEALIST TRADITION

Alexander, S. (1920). *Space, Time and Deity*, 2 vols., London: Macmillan.

Armour, Leslie and Trott, Elizabeth (1981). *The Faces of Reason: Philosophy and Culture in English Canada, 1850–1950*, Waterloo, Ontario: Wilfrid Laurier University Press.

Ayer, A. J. (1936). *Language Truth and Logic*, London: Gollancz. 2nd edn 1946, London: Gollancz.

Bhattacharyya, K. C. (1976). *The Search for the Absolute in Neo-Vedanta*, ed. G. Bosworth Burch, Honolulu: University of Hawaii Press.

Blanshard, B. (1939). *The Nature of Thought*, London: George Allen and Unwin.

Bogumil, Gacka (1994). *Bibliography of American Personalism*, Lublin: Oficyna Wydawnicza, Czas.

Bogumil, Gacka (1995). *American Personalism*, Lublin: Oficyna Wydawnicza, Czas.

Boodin, J. E. (1921). 'Notes on Science and Life', appended to a typescript of an Aristotelian Society Paper read at 21 Gower Street, London, 7 March 1921, Boodin Archive, University of California at Los Angeles.

Boodin, J. E. (1925). *Cosmic Evolution*, New York: Macmillan.

Boodin, J. E. (1934). *God: A Cosmic Philosophy of Religion*, New York: Macmillan.

Boodin, J. E. (1939). *The Social Mind*, New York: Macmillan.

Bosanquet, B. (1889). *The Philosophical Theory of the State*, London: Macmillan.

Bosanquet, B. (1920). *Implication and Linear Inference*, London: Macmillan.

Bosanquet, B. (1923). *The Meeting of Extremes in Contemporary Philosophy*, London: Macmillan.

Bosanquet, B. (1934). *A History of Aesthetics*, London: George Allen and Unwin.

Bowne, B. P. (1908). *Personalism*, Boston: Houghton Mifflin.

Bradley, F. H. (1893). *Appearance and Reality*, London: Swan Sonnenschein. 2nd edn 1897 repr. 1969 with a new pagination, Oxford: Clarendon Press.

Brightman, E. S. (1930). *The Problem of God*, New York: Abingdon.

Brightman, E. S. (1940). *A Philosophy of Religion*, New York: Prentice-Hall.

Brunschvicg, Léon (1939). *La Raison et la religion*, Paris: Presses Universitaires de France.

Cassirer, Ernst (1923–96). *Philosophie der Symbolischen Formen*, Berlin: B. Cassirer, and Darmstadt: Wissenschaftliche Buchgesellschaft. Trans. 1955–7 Ralph Manheim, *The Philosophy of Symbolic Forms*, 4 vols., New Haven, CT: Yale University Press.

Collingwood, R. G. (1919). 'Lectures on the Ontological Argument', Bodleian Modern Manuscripts, Collingwood deposit 2, Film 12/1.

Collingwood, R. G. (1924). *Speculum Mentis*, Oxford: Clarendon Press.

Collingwood, R. G. (1928). Letter to Samuel Alexander July 30, 1928, Alexander Archive, The John Rylands Library, Manchester.

Collingwood, R. G. (1933). 'Lectures on Ethics', Bodleian Library Modern Manuscripts, Deposit 8, Film 12/2.

Collingwood, R. G. (1935). Correspondence with Gilbert Ryle, letter of 9 May, 1935, Bodleian MS. Eng. Lett. d.194.

Collingwood, R. G. (1938a). *An Autobiography*, Oxford: Clarendon Press.

Collingwood, R. G. (1938b). *The Principles of Art*, Oxford: Oxford University Press.

Collingwood, R. G. (1940). *An Essay on Metaphysics*, Oxford: Clarendon Press.

Collingwood, R. G. (1942). *The New Leviathan*, Oxford: Clarendon Press. 2nd edn ed. David Boucher 1998, Oxford: Clarendon Press.

Collingwood, R. G. (1946). *The Idea of History*, Oxford: Oxford University Press.

Croce, Benedetto (1920). *Nuovi Saggi di Estetica* (*New Essays on Aesthetics*), Bari: Laterza and Figli.

Cunningham, G. W. (1916–24). Correspondence with Richard Burdon Haldane (Viscount), Watts Cunningham Archives, Cornell University, Ithaca, NY.

Cunningham, G. W. (1933). *The Idealistic Argument in Recent British and American Philosophy*, New York: Century.

Dray, William (1998). *History as Reenactment*, Oxford: Oxford University Press.

Eddington, A. S. (1920). *Space, Time and Gravitation*, Cambridge: Cambridge University Press.

Eddington, A. S. (1928). *The Nature of the Physical World*, Cambridge: Cambridge University Press.

Eddington, A. S. (1929). *Science and the Unseen World*, New York: Macmillan.

Eddington, A. S. (1939). *The Philosophy of the Physical Sciences*, Cambridge: Cambridge University Press.

Ewing, A. C. (1933). *Idealism: A Critical Survey*, London: Methuen.

Ewing, A. C. (1957). *The Idealist Tradition from Berkeley to Blanshard*, Glencoe, IL: The Free Press.

Flewelling, R. T. (1926). *Creative Personality*, New York: Macmillan.

Flewelling, R. T. (1935). Letter of March 5, 1934 to Norbert Oldgeering, Catholic University of America, University of Southern California, Flewelling Archive.

Flewelling, R. T. (1952). *The Person or the Significance of Man*, Los Angeles: Ward Ritchie Press.

Gentile, Giovanni (1920). *Teoria Generale Dello Spirito come Atto Puro*, third edition, Bari: Laterza and Figli, 1920. Trans. 1922 H. Wildon Carr, *The Theory of Mind as Pure Act*, London: Macmillan.

Guitton, Jean (1939). *Le Problème de la connaissance et la pensée religieuse*, Paris: Aubier.

Haack, Susan (1993). *Evidence and Inquiry: Towards Reconstruction in Epistemology*, Oxford: Blackwell.

Haldane, R. B. (Viscount) (1921). *The Reign of Relativity*, London: John Murray.

Hocking, W. E. (1912). *The Meaning of God in Human Experience*, New Haven, CT: Yale University Press.

Hocking, W. E. (1940). *Living Religions and a World Faith*, New York: Macmillan.

Hoernlé, R. F. Alfred (1920). *Studies in Contemporary Metaphysics*, New York: Harcourt Brace.

Hoernlé, R. F. Alfred (1927). *Idealism as a Philosophy*, New York: Harcourt Brace.

Hoernlé, R. F. Alfred (1939). *South African Native Policy and the Liberal Spirit*, Capetown: University of Capetown Press.

Jeans, Sir James (1930). *The Mysterious Universe*, Cambridge: Cambridge University Press. New edn 1937, Harmondsworth: Pelican.

Jones, Sir H. and Muirhead, J. H. *The Life and Philosophy of Edward Caird*, Glasgow: Maclehose Jackson, and Co.

Joseph, H. W. B. (1916). *An Introduction to Logic* (2nd edn), Oxford: Clarendon Press.

Joseph, H. W. B. (1931). 'Short Treatise on Propositional Functions', New College Archives, Oxford, PA/J/2 10/5 (there are two versions of the treatise).

Joseph, H. W. B. (1932). 'Lectures on Internal and External Relations and the Philosophy of Analysis' (subtitled inside the notes 'Lectures on Logical Atomism'), New College Archives, Oxford, PA/J/2 3/3.

Le Senne, René (1930). *Le Devoir*, Paris: Alcan.

Lodge, R. (1937). *The Questioning Mind*, New York: E. P. Dutton.

Luce, A. A. (1954). *Sense Without Matter*, Edinburgh: Nelson.

McTaggart, J. M. E. (1921–7). *The Nature of Existence*, 2 vols., Cambridge: Cambridge University Press.

Marshall, Bruce (1963). *The Month of the Falling Leaves*, London: Constable.

Metz, Rudolph (1938). *A Hundred Years of British Philosophy*, London: George Allen and Unwin.

Meyerson, Emile (1931). *Du Cheminement de la pensée*, 3 vols. Paris: Alcan.

Moore, G. E. (1903). 'The Refutation of Idealism', *Mind* 12, 433–53.

Muirhead, J. H. (1931). *The Platonic Tradition in Anglo-Saxon Philosophy*, London: George Allen and Unwin.

Mure, G. R. G. (1958). *Retreat From Truth*, Oxford: Blackwell.

Mure, G. R. G. (1978). *Idealist Epilogue*, Oxford: Clarendon Press.

Paton, H. J. (1955). *The Modern Predicament: A Study in the Philosophy of Religion*, London: George Allen and Unwin.

Radhakrishnan, Sarvepalli (1932). *An Idealist View of Life*, New York: Macmillan.

Sharif, M. M. (1966). *In Search of Truth*, Lahore: Institute of Islamic Culture.

Sinclair, M. (1917). *A Defence of Idealism*, New York: Macmillan, p. v.

Smith, J. A. (1914–16).The Hibbert Lectures. The second series of these unpublished essays is in the archives of Magdalen College, Oxford (Magdalen MSS. 1026 I–3). There are notes by R. G. Collingwood in the Bodleian Library, Modern Manuscripts.

Smith, J. A. (1926). Letter of 18 February to Samuel Alexander, Alexander Archive, John Rylands Library, Manchester.

Smith, J. A. (1929–30). Gifford Lectures. Syllabi and fragments remain in the Magdalen College, Oxford archives (Magdalen MSS. 1026 II–27).

Spirito, U. (1974). *L'idealismo italiano e suoi critici*, 2nd. edn Rome: Bulzoni.

Stebbing, L. S. (1937). *Philosophy and the Physicists*, London: Methuen.

Streeter, B. H. (1927). *Reality*, London: Macmillan.

Taylor, A. E. (1932). *The Faith of a Moralist*, 2 vols., London: Macmillan.

Temple, W. (1934). *Nature, Man and God*, London: Macmillan.

Watson, J. (1897). *Christianity and Idealism*, with an introductory essay by George Holmes Howison, New York: Macmillan.

Watson, J. (1919). *The State in Peace and War*, Glasgow: Maclehose.

Whitehead, A. N. (1929). *Process and Reality*, New York: Macmillan and Cambridge: Cambridge University Press.

Wilson, J. Cook (1926). *Statement and Inference*, ed. A. S. L. Farquharson, 2 vols., Oxford: Clarendon Press.

CHAPTER 33 TRANSFORMATIONS IN SPECULATIVE PHILOSOPHY

Alexander, Samuel (1920). *Space Time and Deity*, 2 vols., London: Macmillan.

Bergson, H. (1889). *Quid Aristoteles de Loco Senserit*. Doctoral thesis. Trans. into French 1949 R. Mosse-Bastide, *L'Idée de lieu chez Aristote, Les Etudes bergsoniennes*, vol. II.

Bergson, H. (1889). *Essai sur les donnes immédiates de la conscience*, Paris: Presses Universitaires de France. Trans. 1910 F. L. Pogson, *Time and Free Will: An Essay on the Immediate Data of Consciousness*, London: George Allen and Unwin.

Bergson, H. (1903). 'Introduction à la métaphysique', *Revue de la metaphysique et de morale*, 11: 1–36. Trans. 1913 T. E. Hulme, *An Introduction to Metaphysics*, Indianapolis, IN: Bobbs-Merrill, 1985.

Bergson, H. (1907). *L'Evolution créatrice*, Paris: Presses Universitaires de France. Trans. 1911 A. Mitchell, *Creative Evolution*, London: Macmillan.

Bradley, J. (1996). 'Act, Event, Series: Metaphysics, Mathematics, and Whitehead', *Journal of Speculative Philosophy* 10: 233–48.

Cassirer, E. (1910). *Substanzbegriff und Funktionsbegriff*, Berlin: Cassirer. Trans. 1923 W. C. Swabey and M. C. Swabey, *Substance and Function*, Chicago: Open Court.

Cassirer, E. (1923–9). *Philosophie der symbolischen Formen*, 3 vols., Berlin: Bruno Cassirer. Trans. 1955–7 R. Manheim, *The Philosophy of Symbolic Forms*, 3 vols., New Haven: Yale University Press.

Collingwood, R. G. (1940). *An Essay on Metaphysics*, Oxford: Clarendon Press.

Crocker, S. (1997). 'The Oscillating Now: Heidegger on the Failure of Bergson', *Philosophy Today* 41: 405–23.

Deleuze, G. (1966). *Le Bergsonisme*, Paris: Presses Universitaires de France. Trans. 1988 H. Tomlinson, *Bergsonism*, New York: Zone Books.

Dewey, J. (1929). *Experience and Nature*, Chicago: Open Court. New edn, 1958, New York: Dover.

Hampe, M. and Maasen, H. (1991). *Prozess, Gefuhl und Raum-Zeit: Materialien zu Whiteheads Prozess und Realität, Die Gifford Lectures und ihre Deutung: Materialien zu Whiteheads 'Prozess und Realität'*, 2 vols., Frankfurt: Suhrkamp.

Harris, P. (1997). *Creation in Time: Philosophy, Theology and the Event in the Later Heidegger*, St. John's, Newfoundland: privately published.

Heidegger, M. (1927). *Sein und Zeit*, Tübingen: Niemeyer Verlag. Trans. 1962 J. Macquarrie and E. Robinson, *Being and Time*, Oxford: Blackwell.

Heidegger, M. (1960). *Der Ursprung des Kunstwerkes*, Stuttgart: Reclam. Lecture first delivered Freiburg, 1935. Trans. 1971 A. Hofstadter, 'The Origin of the Work of Art' in *Poetry, Language, Thought*, New York: Harper and Row, 15–88.

Heidegger, M. (1969). 'Zeit und Sein' in *Zur Sache des Denkens*, Tübingen: Niemeyer 1–26. Lecture delivered Freiburg, 1962. Trans 1972. J. Stambaugh, 'Time and Being' in *On Time and Being*, New York: Harper and Row, 1–24.

Heidegger, M. (1975). *Die Grundprobleme der Phänomenologie (Gesamtausgabe, vol. XXIV)* Frankfurt: V. Klostermann. Lectures delivered Marburg, 1927. Trans. 1982 A. Hofstadter, *The Basic Problems of Phenomenology*, Bloomington, IN: Indiana University Press.

Heidegger, M. (1978). *Metaphysische Anfangsgrunde der Logik (Gesamtausgabe, vol. XXVI)*, Frankfurt: V. Klostermann. Lectures delivered Marburg, 1928. Trans. 1984 M. Heim, *The Metaphysical Foundations of Logic*, Bloomington, IN: Indiana University Press.

Bibliography

Heidegger, M. (1989). *Beiträge zur Philosophie (vom Ereignis)*, (*Gesamtausgabe*, vol. LXV) Frankfurt: V. Klostermann. Writings, 1936–9.

Husserl, E. (1928). 'Vorlesungen zur Phenomenologie des inneren Zeitbewusstseins', (ed. M. Heidegger), *Jahrbuch fur Philosophie und phänomenologische Forschung*, 9: 367–498. Trans. 1964 J. W. Churchill, *The Phenomenology of Internal Time Consciousness*, Bloomington: Indiana University Press.

James, W. (1916). *Some Problems of Philosophy*, New York: Longmans, Green. New edn 1979 ed. F. Bowers, Cambridge, MA: Harvard University Press.

Ketner, K. L. (1977). *A Comprehensive Bibliography and Index of the Published Works of Charles Sanders Peirce with a Bibliography of Secondary Studies*, Greenwich, CT: Johnson Associates.

Lowe, V. (1966). *Understanding Whitehead*, Baltimore, MD: Johns Hopkins Press.

Lowe, V. (1985, 1990). *Alfred North Whitehead: The Man and His Work*, 2 vols., Baltimore, MD: Johns Hopkins University Press.

McTaggart, J. M. E. (1921, 1927). *The Nature of Existence*, 2 vols., Cambridge: Cambridge University Press.

McTaggart, J. M. E (1908). 'The Unreality of Time', *Mind* 17, 457–74. Reprinted 1934 *Philosophical Studies*, London: Edward Arnold, 110–31.

Nietzsche, F. (1901). *Nachgelassene Werke: Der Wille zur Macht*, vol. XV, Leipzig: C. G. Naumann. Trans. 1967 W. Kaufmann, *The Will to Power*, London: Weidenfeld and Nicolson.

Peirce, C. S. (1931–68). *Collected Papers of Charles Sanders Peirce*, 8 vols., ed. C. Hartshorne, P. Weiss, and A. Books, Cambridge, MA: Harvard University Press.

Roberts, J. (1992). *The Logic of Reflection: German Philosophy in the Twentieth Century*, New Haven, CT: Yale University Press.

Royce, J. (1913). *The Problem of Christianity*, New York: Macmillan, 2 vols. New edn, 1967, New York: Archon Books.

Rubinoff, L. (1970). *Collingwood and the Reform of Metaphysics: A Study in the Philosophy of Mind*, Toronto: University of Toronto Press.

Russell, B. A. W. (1915). 'On the Experience of Time', *Monist* 25: 212–33.

Skolem, T. (1923). 'Begrundung der elementaren Arithmetik durch rekurrierende Denkweise ohne Anwendung Scheinbarer Veranderlichen mit unendlichem Ausdehnungsbereich', *Videnskapsselskapets skrifter*, I, *Matematisk-naturvidenskabelig Klasse*, n. 6. Trans. 1967 J. van Heijenoort, 'The Foundations of Elementary Arithmetic established by means of the Recursive Mode of Thought, without Use of Apparent Variables ranging over Infinite Domains', *From Frege to Godel. A Sourcebook in Mathematical Logic*, 1879–1931, Cambridge, MA: Harvard University Press, 303–33.

Whitehead, A. N. (1898). *A Treatise on Universal Algebra*, Cambridge: Cambridge University Press.

Whitehead, A. N. and Russell, B. A. W. (1910–13). *Principia Mathematica*, 3 vols., Cambridge: Cambridge University Press.

Whitehead, A. N. (1911). *Introduction to Mathematics*, new edn 1958, New York: Oxford University Press.

Whitehead, A. N. (1917). *The Aims of Education and Other Essays*, London: Williams and Norgate. 2nd edn 1950, London: Ernest Benn.

Whitehead, A. N. (1919). *Enquiry Concerning the Principles of Natural Knowledge*, Cambridge: Cambridge University Press.

Whitehead, A. N. (1920). *The Concept of Nature*, Cambridge: Cambridge University Press.

Whitehead, A. N. (1922). *The Principle of Relativity*, Cambridge: Cambridge University Press.

Whitehead, A. N. (1926). *Religion in the Making*, Cambridge: Cambridge University Press.

Whitehead, A. N. (1926). *Science and the Modern World*, Cambridge: Cambridge University Press. New edn 1967, New York: The Free Press.

Whitehead, A. N. (1928). *Symbolism: Its Meaning and Effect*, Cambridge: Cambridge University Press. New edn 1959, New York: G. P. Putnam's Sons.

Whitehead, A. N. (1929a). *Process and Reality: An Essay in Cosmology*, Cambridge: Cambridge University Press. Corrected edn 1978, New York: The Free Press.

Whitehead, A. N. (1929b). *The Function of Reason*, Princeton, NJ: Princeton University Press. New edn 1958, Boston: The Beacon Press.

Whitehead, A. N. (1933). *Adventures of Ideas*, Cambridge: Cambridge University Press. New edn 1967, New York: The Free Press.

Whitehead, A. N. (1938). *Modes of Thought*, Cambridge: Cambridge University Press. New edn 1968, New York: The Free Press.

Whitehead, A. N. (1947). *Essays in Science and Philosophy*, New York: Philosophical Library.

Woodbridge, B. A. (1977). *Alfred North Whitehead: A Primary-Secondary Bibliography*, Bowling Green, OH: Philosophy Documentation Center.

CHAPTER 34 REALISM, NATURALISM, AND PRAGMATISM

Blau, Joseph (1952). *Men and Movements in American Philosophy*, New Jersey: Prentice Hall.

Cohen, Morris (1931). *Reason and Nature: An Essay on the Meaning of Scientific Method*, New York: Harcourt Brace.

Cohen, Morris (1933). *Law and the Social Order: Essays in Legal Philosophy*, New York: Harcourt Brace.

Cohen, Morris and Nagel, Ernest (1934). *An Introduction to Logic and the Scientific Method*, New York: Harcourt Brace.

Delaney, C. F. (1969). *Mind and Nature: A Study of the Naturalistic Philosophies of Cohen, Woodbridge, and Sellars*, Notre Dame: University of Notre Dame Press.

Dewey, John (1922). *Human Nature and Conduct*, New York: Henry Holt.

Dewey, John (1925). *Experience and Nature*, Chicago: Open Court.

Dewey, John (1927). 'Half-Hearted Naturalism', *The Journal of Philosophy* 24: 57–64.

Dewey, John (1938). *Logic: The Theory of Inquiry*, New York: Henry Holt.

Drake, Durant *et al.* (1920). *Essays in Critical Realism: A Cooperative Study of the Problem of Knowledge*, New York: Macmillan.

Flower, Elizabeth and Murphy, Murray (1977). *A History of Philosophy in America*, 2 vols., New York: Capricorn Books.

Holt, Edwin *et al.* (1912). *The New Realism: Cooperative Studies in Philosophy*, New York: Macmillan.

Hook, Sidney (1927). *The Metaphysics of Pragmatism* Chicago: Open Court.

Hook, Sidney (1934). 'What is Materialism?' *The Journal of Philosophy* 24: 235–42.

Hook, Sidney (1944). 'Is Physical Realism Sufficient?' *The Journal of Philosophy* 41, 544–51.

Krikorian, Y. H. (1944). *Naturalism and the Human Spirit*, New York: Columbia University Press.

Kuklick, Bruce (1977). *The Rise of American Philosophy, Cambridge Massachusetts 1860–1930*, New Haven: Yale University Press.

Lewis, C. I. (1918). *A Survey of Symbolic Logic*, Berkeley: University of California Press.

Lewis, C. I. (1929). *Mind and the World Order*, New York: Charles Scribner's.

Lewis, C. I. (1950). *An Analysis of Knowledge and Valuation*, La Salle, IL: Open Court.

Lovejoy, A. D. (1930). *The Revolt Against Dualism*, Chicago: Open Court.

Mead, George Herbert (1934). *Mind, Self and Society*, Chicago: University of Chicago Press.

Mead, George Herbert (1938). *The Philosophy of the Act*, Chicago: University of Chicago Press.

Mead, George Herbert (1959). *The Philosophy of the Present*, La Salle, IL: Open Court.

Miller, David (1973). *George Herbert Mead: Self, Language and the World*, Austin: University of Texas Press.

Morris, C. W. (1937). *Logical Positivism, Pragmatism and Scientific Empiricism*, Paris: Herman.

Ryan, Alan (1995). *John Dewey and the High Tide of American Liberalism*, New York: W. W. Norton.

Santayana, George (1905). *The Life of Reason*, 5 vols. New York: Charles Scribner's.

Santayana, George (1923). *Skepticism and Animal Faith,* New York: Charles Scribner's.

Santayana, George (1925). 'Dewey's Naturalistic Metaphysics', *The Journal of Philosophy* 22: 673–88.

Santayana, George (1927–40). *The Realms of Being*, New York: Charles Scribner's.

Scheffler, Israel (1974). *Four Pragmatists*, London: Routledge.

Sellars, Roy Wood (1916). *Critical Realism: A Study of the Nature and Conditions of Knowledge*, Chicago: Rand McNally.

Sellars, Roy Wood (1922). *Evolutionary Naturalism*, Chicago: Open Court.

Sellars, Roy Wood (1932). *The Philosophy of Physical Realism*, New York: Macmillan.

Sellars, Roy Wood (1943). 'Dewey on Materialism', *Philosophy and Phenomenological Research*, 111: 381–92.

Sellars, Roy Wood (1944). 'Does Naturalism Need Ontology?' *The Journal of Philosophy* 41: 686–94.

Sellars, Roy Wood (1944). 'Is Naturalism Enough?' *The Journal of Philosophy* 41: 533–44.

Sprigge, T. L. S. (1995). *Santayana*, London: Routledge.

Thayer, Henry S. (1968). *Meaning and Action: A Critical History of American Pragmatism*, Indianapolis: Bobbs-Merrill.

Tiles, J. E. (1988). *Dewey*, London: Routledge.

Woodbridge, F. J. E. (1926). *The Realm of Mind: An Essay on Metaphysics*, New York: Columbia University Press.

Woodbridge, F. J. E. (1937). *Nature and Mind: Selected Essays*, New York: Columbia University Press.

CHAPTER 35 FRENCH CATHOLIC PHILOSOPHY

Bars, H. (1959). *Maritain en notre temps*, Paris: Grasset.

Bars, H. (1962). *La politique selon Jacques Maritain*, Paris: Editions ouvrières.

Blondel, Maurice (1948, 1954). *La Pensée*, 2 vols., Paris: Alcan. 2nd edn, Paris: Presses Universitaires de France, vol. I, 1948, vol. II, 1954.

Blondel, Maurice (1944). *La Philosophie et l'Esprit chrétien*, Paris: Alcan. 2nd edn, Paris: Presses Universitaires de France, 1950.

Blondel, Maurice (1949, 1963). *L'Action*, 2 vols., Paris: Alcan, 1936–7. Second edition, Paris: Presses Universitaires de France, vol. I, 1949, vol. II, 1963.

Blondel, Maurice (1893). *L'Action: essai d'une critique de la vie et d'une science de la pratique*, Paris: Alcan. Further edns, Paris: Presses Universitaires de France, 1950 and 1973.

Blondel, Maurice (1893). *Le lien substantiel et la substance composée d'après Leibniz* (Latin text 1893), trans. C. Troisfontaines, Paris–Louvain: Béatrice Nauwelaerts, 1972.

Blondel, Maurice (1932). *Le Problème de la philosophie catholique*, Paris: Bloud et Gay.

Blondel, Maurice (1935). *L'Etre et les Etres*, Paris: Alcan. 2nd edn, Paris: Presses Universitaires de France 1963.

Claudel, P. *et al.* (1948). *Le Mal est parmi nous: un problème actuel*, Paris: Plon.

Cornati, D. (1998). *L'ontologia implicita nell'Action (1893) di Maurice Blondel*, Milan: Glossa.

Coutagne, M.-J. (ed.) (1994). *L'Action: une dialectique du salut, Actes du colloque du centenaire (Aix-en-Provence, March 1993)*, Paris: Beauchesne.

Doering, B. E. (1983). *J. Maritain and the French Catholic Intellectuals*, Notre Dame, IN: Notre Dame University Press.

Favraux, P. (1987). *Une philosophie du Médiateur: Maurice Blondel*, Paris–Naumur: Lethielleux.

Fecher, Ch. A. (1953). *The philosophy of J. Maritain*, Westminster: Newman Press, 1953.

Fessard, G. (1936). *Pax Nostra*, Paris, Grasset

Fessard, G. (1956). *La Dialectique des exercices spirituels de Saint Ignace de Loyola*, Paris: Aubier.

Fessard, G. (1990). *Hegel, le christianisme et l'histoire*, ed. M. Sales, Paris: Presses Universitaires de France.

Fessard, G. (1997). *Le mystère de la Société: recherches sur le sens de l'histoire*, ed. Sales, M. (S. J.), Namur: Culture et Vérité.

Gilson, E. and Maritain, J. (1991). *Deux approches de l'être. Correspondence 1923–71, Etienne Gilson, Jacques Maritain*, ed. G. Prouvost, Paris: Vrin.

Hersch, J., Lévinas, E., Ricoeur, P., and Tilliette, X. (1976). *Jean Wahl et Gabriel Marcel*, Paris: Beauchesne.

Lapointe, F. H. and C. (1977). *Gabriel Marcel and his Critics, International Bibliography (1928–1976)*, New York and London: Garland.

Leduc-Fayette, D. (ed.) (1986, 1987). *Colloque Maurice Blondel (Centre d'Etudes des Philosophes Français – Sorbonne), 'Revue philosophique de la France et de l'étranger'* 1986 (IV) and 1987 (I).

Lubac, H. de, Rougier, M. and Sales, M. (1985). Introd. by X. Tilliette, *Gabriel Marcel et Gaston Fessard, correspondance*, Paris: Beauchesne.

MacNeill, J.-J. (1966). *The Blondelian Synthesis: A Study of the Influence of German Philosophy Sources on the Formation of Blondel's Method and Thought*, Leiden: Brill.

Marcel, Gabriel (1927). *Journal Métaphysique*, Paris: Gallimard. Trans. 1952 G. Wall, *Metaphysical Journal*, London: Rockcliff.

Marcel, Gabriel (1935). *Etre et Avoir*, Paris: Aubier. Trans. 1949 K. Farrer, *Being and Having*, London: Dacre Press.

Marcel, Gabriel (1940). *Du Refus à l'invocation*, Paris: Gallimard.

Marcel, Gabriel (1945a). *Homo viator*, Paris: Aubier. Trans. 1951 E. Craufurd, *Homo Viator*, London: Gollancz.

Marcel, Gabriel (1945b). *La métaphysique de Royce (The Metaphysics of Royce)*. Paris: Aubier.

Marcel, Gabriel (1951). *Le Mystère de l'être*, Paris, Aubier Trans. 1950 G. S. Fraser and R. Hague, *The Mystery of Being*, London: Harvill Press.

Maritain, Jacques (1914). *La philosophie bergsonienne: études critiques*, Paris: Marcel Rivière, New edn, Paris: Téqui, 1927.

Maritain, Jacques (1920). *Art et scolastique*, Paris: Art catholique. New edn 1927.

Maritain, Jacques (1930). *Le Docteur angélique*, Paris: Desclée de Brouwer. Trans. 1931 J. F. Scamlan, *St. Thomas Aquinas: Angel of the Schools*, London: Sheed and Ward.

Maritain, Jacques (1932a). *De la philosophie chrétienne*, Milan: Rivista de neo-scolastica.

Maritain, Jacques (1932b). *Les degrés du savoir: distinguer pour unir*, Paris: Desclée de Brouwer.

Maritain, Jacques (1934). *Sept leçons sur l'Etre et les premiers principes de la raison spéculative*, Paris: Téqui.

Maritain, Jacques (1935). *Science et sagesse*, Paris: Labergerie Trans. 1940 B. J. Wall, *Science and Wisdom*, London: Geoffrey Bles.

Maritain, Jacques (1936). *L'Humanisme intégral*, Paris: Aubier, 1936.

Maritain, Jacques (1939). *Quatre essais sur l'esprit dans sa condition charnelle*, Paris: Desclée de Brouwer. New edn 1956, Paris: Alsatia.

Maritain, Jacques (1942). *Saint Thomas and the problem of Evil*, Milwaukee: Marquette University Press.

Maritain, Jacques (1944). *De Bergson à Thomas d'Aquin*, New York: Editions de la Maison Française.

Maritain, Jacques (1947). *Court traité de l'existence et de l'existant*, Paris: P. Hartmann. Trans. 1987 L. Galantiere and G. B. Phelan, *Existence and the existent*, Lanham, MD: University Press of America.

Maritain, R. (1949a). *Jacques Maritain, son oeuvre philosophique*, Paris: Desclée de Brouwer.

Maritain, R.(1949b). *Les grandes amitiés*, Paris: Desclée de Brouwer.

Perico, Y. (1991). *Maurice Blondel: genèse du sens*, Paris: Editions Universitaires.

Plourde, S. (1985). *Vocabulaire philosophique de Gabriel Marcel*, Paris: Cerf.

Ricoeur, P. (1948). *Gabriel Marcel et Karl Jaspers, deux maîtres de l'existentialisme*, Paris: Temps présent.

Sacquin, M. (ed.) (1988). *Colloque Gabriel Marcel*, Paris: Bibliothèque nationale, 1988.

Schillp, P. A. and Hahn, L. E. (eds.) (1984). *The Philosophy of Gabriel Marcel*, La Salle, IL: Library of Living Philosophers, vol. XXII.

Smith, B. W. (1976). *J. Maritain: anti-modern or ultramodern? An Historical Analysis of his Critics, his Thought and his Life*, New York and Amsterdam: Elsevier.

Tilliette, X. (1989). *Filosofi davanti a cristo: Maurice Blondel e il pancritismo*, Brescia: Quiriniana.

Tilliette, X. (1990). *Le Christ de la philosophie*, Paris: Cerf.

Tilliette, X. (1993). *Le Christ des philosophes*, Namur: Culture et Vérité.

Virgoulay, R. and Troisfontaines, C. (1975–6). *Maurice Blondel: bibliographie analytique et critique*. I. *Oeuvres de M. B. (1880–1973)*, II. *Etudes sur M. B. (1893–1913)*, Louvain: Peeters.

Virgoulay, R. (1980). *Blondel et le modernisme, la philosophie de l'action et les sciences religieuses*, Paris: Cerf.

CHAPTER 36 SPANISH PHILOSOPHY

Abellán, J. L. (1979–92). *Historia crítica del pensamiento español (A Critical History of Spanish Thought)*, Madrid: Espasa Calpe.

Alonso Gamo, J. Mª. (1966). *Un español en el mundo: Santayana (A Spaniard in the World: Santayana)*, Madrid: Ediciones Cultura Hispánica.

Araya, G. (1971). *Claves filológicas para la comprensión de Ortega (Philological Keys for Ortega's Understanding)*, Madrid: Gredos.

Ferrater Mora, J. (1957). *Ortega y Gasset: an Outline of his philosophy*, Cambridge: Bowes and Bowes and New Haven, CT: Yale University Press.

Ferrater Mora, J. (1962). *Unamuno*, Berkeley: University of California Press.

Ganivet, A. (1897). *Idearium español*, Granada. Trans. *Spain. An Interpretation*, London: Eyre & Spottiswoode, 1946.

García Bacca, D. (1934). *Introducció a la logística amb applications a la filosofia i a les matemàtiques (Introduction to the Logistic with Applications to the Philosophy and the Mathematics)*, Barcelona: Institut d'Estudis Catalans.

Gracia Guillén, D. (1986). *Voluntad de verdad (The Will to Truth)*, Barcelona: Labor.

Guy, A. (1983). *Histoire de la philosophie espagnole (History of Spanish Philosophy)*, Toulouse: Publications de l'Université.

Izuzquiza, I. (1984). *El proyecto filosófico de Juan David García Bacca (The Philosophical Project of Juan David García Bacca)*, Barcelona: Anthropos.

Jiménez-Landi, A. (1996). *La Institución Libre de Enseñanza (The Institute of Free Education)* 4 vols., Madrid: Editorial Complutense.

López-Morillas, J. (1956). *El krausismo español. Perfil de una aventura intelectual (Spanish Krausism. Outline of an Intellectual Adventure)*, Madrid: F.C.E.; 2nd augmented edn 1980.

Marías, J. (1962). *Ortega. I. Circunstancia y vocación* (*Ortega. I. Circumstance and Vocation*), Madrid: Revista de Occidente.

Marías, J. (1983). *Ortega. II. Las trayectorias* (*Ortega. II. The Trajectories*), Madrid: Alianza Editorial.

Morán, G. (1998). *El maestro en el erial: Ortega y Gasset y la cultura del franquismo* (*The Master in the Uncultivated Land: Ortega y Gasset and the Culture of Franquism*), Barcelona: Tusquets.

Nozick, M. (1971). *Miguel de Unamuno*, New York: Twayne.

Olmedo, M. (1965). *El pensamiento de Ganivet* (*The Thought of Ganivet*), Madrid: Revista de Occidente and Granada: Diputación Provincial, 1998.

Orringer, N. (1979). *Ortega y sus fuentes germánicas* (*Ortega and his German Sources*) Madrid: Gredos.

Orringer, N. (1985). *Unamuno y los protestantes liberales* (*Unamuno and Liberal Protestants*), Madrid: Gredos.

Ors, E. d' (1911). *La ben plantada* (*The Good-Looking Wife*), Barcelona: Lib. Alvar Verdaguer and Ed. Selecta Catalònia, 1980.

Ors, E. d' (1947). *El secreto de la filosofía* (*The Secret of Philosophy*), Madrid: Editorial Iberia; new repr. in Madrid: Tecnos, 1998.

Ors, E. d (1987–). *Obra catalana d'Eugeni d'Ors* (*Complete Catalan Works*), Madrid. Ediciones dels Quaderns Crema, 15 vols. (incomplete).

Ortega y Gasset, J. (1914). *Meditaciones del Quijote*, Madrid: Ediciones de la Residencia de Estudiantes; *Meditations on Quixote*, New York: Norton, 1961.

Ortega y Gasset, J. (1921). *España invertebrada*, Madrid: Espasa Calpe; *Invertebrate Spain*, London: George Allen and Unwin and New York: Norton, 1937.

Ortega y Gasset, J. (1923). *El tema de nuestro tiempo*, Madrid: Espasa Calpe; *The Modern Theme*, London: C. W. Daniel, 1931 and New York: Norton, 1933, repr. 1961.

Ortega y Gasset, J. (1929). *La rebelión de las masas*, Madrid: Revista de Occidente, 1929; *The Revolt of the Masses*, London: George Allen and Unwin and New York: Norton, 1932.

Ortega y Gasset, J. (1935). *Historia como sistema: Del Imperio Romano*, Madrid: Revista de Occidente. Trans. 1941 H. Weyl and W. Attenson, 'History as System' in *Philosophy and History*, Oxford: Clarendon Press.

Ortega y Gasset, J. (1946–83). *Obras completas* (*Complete Works*), Madrid: Revista de Occidente, vols. I–XI, 1946–69; Madrid: Alianza Editorial, vols. I–XII, 1983.

Ortega y Gasset, J. (1959). *En torno a Galileo*, Madrid: Revista de Occidente; *Man and Crisis*, New York: Norton, 1958; London: George Allen and Unwin, 1959.

Ortega y Gasset, J. (1957). *El hombre y la gente*, Madrid: Revista de Occidente, 1957; *Man and People*, New York: Norton, 1957.

Ortega y Gasset, J. (1958). *La idea de principio en Leibniz y la evolución de la teoría deductiva*, Madrid: Revista de Occidente. *The Idea of Principle in Leibniz and the Evolution of Deductive Theory*, New York, 1971.

Ortega y Gasset, J. (1958). *Prólogo para alemanes*, Madrid: Taurus.

Rius, M. (1991). *La filosofía d'Eugeni d'Ors* (*The Philosophy of Eugeni d'Ors*), Barcelona: Curial Edicions Catalanes.

Russell, B. A. W. (1940). 'The Philosophy of Santayana' in P. A. Schilpp (ed.), *The Philosophy of George Santayana*, La Salle, IL: Open Court; 2nd printing 1971, 451–74.

Sánchez Barbudo, A. (1968). *Estudios sobre Galdós, Unamuno y Machado* (*Studies on Galdós, Unamuno and Machado*), Madrid, Guadarrama; new edn Barcelona: Lumen, 1981.

Santayana, G. (1925). *Dialogues in Limbo*, London: Constable.

Santayana, G. (1940a). 'A General Confession' in P. A. Schilpp (ed.), *The Philosophy of George Santayana*, La Salle, IL: Open Court; 2nd printing 1971, 1–30.

Santayana, G. (1942). *Realms of Being*, New York: Scribner.

Unamuno, M. de (1895). *En torno al casticismo* (*On Authentic Tradition*), Madrid: La España Moderna.

Unamuno, M. de (1905). *Vida de Don Quijote y Sancho* (*The Life of Don Quijote and Sancho*), Madrid: Renacimiento. *Our Lord Don Quixote and Sancho with Related Essays*, Princeton, NJ: Princeton University Press, 1967.

Unamuno, M. de (1913). *Del sentimiento trágico de la vida en los hombres y en los pueblos*, Madrid: Renacimiento. *The Tragic Sense of Life in Men and in Peoples*, Princeton, NJ: Princeton University Press, 1972.

Unamuno, M. de (1925). *La agonía del cristianismo*, Paris: Editorial Excelsior. *The Agony of Christianity and Essais of Faith*, Princeton, NJ: Princeton University Press, 1974.

Unamuno, M. de (1933). *San Manuel Bueno, mártir*, Madrid, Espasa Calpe. 'Saint Emmanuel the Good, Martyr' in *Abel Sánchez and Other Histories*, Chicago: Regnery, 1956.

Unamuno, M. de (1959–64). *Obras completas* (*Complete Works*), Madrid: Vergara, 16 vols.; repr. Madrid: Escelicer, 1966, 9 vols.

Zubiri, X. (1944). *Naturaleza, Historia, Dios*, Madrid: Editora Nacional. *Nature, History, God*, Washington DC: University of America Press, 1981.

CHAPTER 37 THE PHENOMENOLOGICAL MOVEMENT

Brentano, F. (1874). *Psychologie vom empirischen Standpunkt*, Leipzig: Duncker and Humblot. 2nd edn by O. Kraus, 1924, Leipzig: Meiner. Trans. 1973 A.C. Rancurello, D. B. Terrell, and L. L. MacAlister, *Psychology from an Empirical Standpoint*, London: Routledge.

Frings, M. S. (ed.) (1974). *Max Scheler (1874–1928) Centennial Essays*, The Hague: Nijhoff.

Guignon, Ch. (ed.) (1993). *The Cambridge Companion to Heidegger*, Cambridge and New York: Cambridge University Press.

Heidegger, M. (1927). *Sein und Zeit*, Tübingen: Max Niemeyer Verlag. Trans. 1962 J. Macquarrie and E. Robinson, *Being and Time*, Oxford: Blackwell.

Heidegger, M. (1947). *Brief über den 'Humanismus'*, Berne: A. Franke Verlag. Reprinted 1976 in *Wegmarken* (*Gesamtausgabe*, vol. IX), Frankurt on Main: V. Klostermann. Trans. 1998 F. A. Capuzzi 'Letter on Humanism' in *Pathmarks*, ed. W. McNeill, Cambridge: Cambridge University Press.

Heidegger, M. (1953). *Einführung in die Metaphysik*, Tubingen: M. Niemayer. Trans. 1959 R. Manheim, *An Introduction to Metaphysics*, New Haven, CT: Yale University Press.

Héring, J. (1925). *Phénoménologie et philosophie religieuse* (*Phenomenology and Religions Philosophy*), Paris: 1926.

Howells, Ch. (ed.) (1992). *The Cambridge Companion to Sartre*, Cambridge and New York: Cambridge University Press.

Husserl, E. (1891). *Philosophie der Arithmetik*, Halle: C. E. M. Pfeffer. Repr. 1970 in *Husserliana* XII, The Hague: Nijhoff.

Husserl, E. (1900–1). *Logische Untersuchungen*, Halle: M. Niemayer. Repr. 1975, 1984 in *Husserliana* XVIII, XIX, The Hague: Nijhoff. Trans. J. N. Findlay 1970, *Logical Investigations*, London: Routledge.

Husserl, E. (1913). *Ideen zu einer reinem Phänomenlogie und phänomenologischen Philosophie* I, in *Jahrbuch für Philosophie und phänomenologische Forschung* I, 1–323. Reprinted 1950 in *Husserliana*, vol. III, The Hague: Nijhoff. Trans. 1982 F. Kersten, *Ideas Pertaining to a Pure Phenomenology and to a Phenomenological Philosophy* I, The Hague: Nijhoff.

Husserl, E. (1929). 'Formale und transcendentale Logik' in *Jahrbuch für Philosophie und phänomenologische Forschung* 10, 1–298. Reprinted 1974 in *Husserliana* XVII, The Hague: Nijhoff. Trans. 1969 D. Cairns, *Formal and Transcendental Logic*, The Hague: Nijhoff.

Husserl, E. (1931). *Méditations cartésiennes*, trans. G. Pfeiffer and E. Levinas, Paris: Colin. German version reprinted 1950 in *Husserliana*, I, The Hague: Nijhoff. Trans. 1973 D. Cairns, *Cartesian Meditations*, The Hague: Nijhoff.

Husserl, E. (1936). 'Die Krisis der europäischen Wissenschaften und die transzendentale Phänomenologie', *Philosophia 1: 77–176*. Repr Inted. 1954 in *Husserliana* VI, The Hague: Nijhoff. Trans. 1970 D. Carr *The Crisis of European Sciences and Transcendental Philosophy*, Evanston, IL: Northwestern University Press.

Kojève, A. (1947). *Introduction à la lecture de Hegel*, Paris: Gallimard. Trans. (part only) 1969 J. H. Nichols, *Introduction to the Reading of Hegel*, New York: Basic Books.

Lapointe, F. and Lapointe, C. (eds.) (1976). *Maurice Merleau-Ponty and His Critics (1942–1976)*, New York and London: Garland Publishing Inc.

Levinas, E. (1930). *La Théorie de l'intuition dans la phénoménologie de Husserl*, Paris: Alcan. Trans. 1973 A. Orianne, *The Theory of Intuition in Husserl's Phenomenology*, Evanston, IL: Northwestern University Press.

Merleau-Ponty, M. (1942). *La Structure de comportment*, Paris: Presses Universitaires de France. Trans. 1963 A. Fisher, *The Structure of Behavior*, Boston, MA: Beacon Press.

Merleau-Ponty, M. (1945). *Phénoménologie de la perception*, Paris: Gallimard. Trans. 1962 C. Smith *The Phenomenology of Perception*, London: Routledge.

Merleau-Ponty, M. (1955). *Les Aventures de la dialectique*, Paris: Gallimard. Trans. 1974 J. Bien, *Adventures of the Dialectic*, London: Heinemann.

Sartre, J.-P. (1936a). *L'Imagination*, Paris: Alcan. Trans. 1962 F. Williams, *Imagination*, Ann Arbor, MI: University of Michigan Press.

Sartre, J.-P. (1936b). 'La Transcendence de l'ego', *Recherches Philosophiques* 6. Trans. 1962 F. Williams and R. Kirkpatrick, *The Transcendence of the Ego*, New York: Noonday.

Sartre, J.-P. (1939). *Esquisse d'une théorie des émotions*, Paris: Hermann. Trans. 1962 P. Mairet, *Sketch for a Theory of the Emotions*, London: Methuen.

Sartre, J.-P. (1940). *L'Imaginaire*, Paris: Gallimard. Trans. 1948 B. Frechtman, *The Psychology of the Imagination*, New York: Philosophical Library.

Sartre, J.-P. (1943). *L'Etre et le néant*, Paris: Gallimard. Trans. 1956 H. Barnes, *Being and Nothingness*, New York: Philosophical Library, London: Methuen, 1957.

Scheler, M. (1913, 1916). *Der Formalismus in der Ethik und die materiale Wertethik*, 2 vols. Halle: M. Niemayer. Trans. 1973 M. S. Frings and R. Funk, *Formalism in Ethics and Non-Formal Ethics of Values*, Evanston, IL: Northwestern University Press.

Scheler, M. (1923). *Wesen und Formen der Sympathie*, Bonn: F. Cohen. Trans. 1954 P. Heath, *The Nature of Sympathy*, London: Routledge.

Smith, B. and Smith, D. W. (eds.) (1995). *The Cambridge Companion to Husserl*, Cambridge and New York: Cambridge University Press.

CHAPTER 38 HEIDEGGER

Adorno, T. (1964). *Jargon der Eigentlichkeit*, Frankfurt: Suhrkamp. Trans. 1973 K. Tarnowski and F. Will, *Jargon of Authenticity*, London: Routledge.

Adorno, T. (1966). *Negative Dialektik*, Frankfurt: Suhrkamp. Trans. 1973 E. B. Ashton, *Negative Dialectics*, London: Routledge.

Ferry, L. and Renaut, A. (1988). *Heidegger et les modernes*, Paris: Grasset. Trans. 1990 F. Philip, *Heidegger and Modernity*, Chicago: University of Chicago Press.

Guignon, C. (ed.) (1993). *Cambridge Companion to Heidegger*, Cambridge: Cambridge University Press.

Heidegger, M. (1927). *Sein und Zeit* in *Jahrbuch für Philosophie und phänomenologische Forschung* 8, Halle: Niemeyer. Trans. 1962 J. Macquarrie and E. Robinson, *Being and Time*, New York: Harper and Row.

Heidegger, M. (1929). *Kant und das Problem der Metaphysik*, Bonn: Friedrich Cohen. Trans. 1990 R. Taft, *Kant and the Problem of Metaphysics*, Bloomington, IN: Indiana University Press.

Heidegger, M. (1950). *Holzwege*, Frankfurt on Main: Vittorio Klostermann. Trans. 2002 J. Young and K. Haynes, *Off the Beaten Track*, Cambridge: Cambridge University Press.

Heidegger, M. (1953). *Einführung in die Metaphysik*, Tübingen: Max Niemeyer. Trans. 1959 R. Manheim, *Introduction to Metaphysics*, New Haven, CT: Yale University Press.

Heidegger, M. (1959). *Gelassenheit*, Pfullingen: Günther Neske. Trans. 1966 J. M. Anderson and E. H. Freund, *Discourse on Thinking*, New York: Harper and Row.

Heidegger, M. (1961). *Nietzsche*, Pfullingen: Günther Neske, 2 vols. Trans. 1979–87, D. F. Krell and F. Capuzzi, *Nietzsche*, New York: Harper and Row, 4 vols.

Heidegger, M. (1967). *Wegmarken*, Frankfurt on Main: Vittorio Klostermann. Trans. 1997 D. F. Krell, W. McNeill, and J. Sallis, *Pathmarks*, Cambridge: Cambridge University Press.

Heidegger, M. (1975–). *Gesamtausgabe*, Frankfurt on Main: Vittorio Klostermann.

Heidegger, M. *et al.* (1976). *Nur noch ein Gott kann uns retten* in *Der Spiegel*, 30. Jg., Nr. 23, 31 May 1976. Trans. 1990 L. Harries in *Martin Heidegger and National Socialism*, ed. G. Neske and E. Kettering, New York: Paragon House.

Kisiel, T. (1993). *The Genesis of Heidegger's Being and Time*, Berkeley, CA: University of California Press.

Löwith, K. (1984). *Heidegger: Denker in dürftiger Zeit: Zur Stellung der Philosophiein 20. Jahrhundert*, Stuttgart: Metzler.

Merker, B. (1988). *Selbsttäuschung und Selbsterkenntnis: Zu Heideggers Transformation der Phänomenologie Husserls*, Frankfurt on Main: Suhrkamp.

Ott, H. (1988). *Martin Heidegger: Unterwegs zu seiner Biographie*, Frankfurt on Main: Campus. Trans. 1994 A. Blunden, *Martin Heidegger: A Political Life*, London: Fontana.

Pöggeler, O. (1983). *Der Denkweg Martin Heideggers*, Pfullingen: Max Neske. Trans. 1987 D. Margushak and S. Barber, *Martin Heidegger's Path of Thinking*, Atlantic Highlands, NJ: Humanities Press.

Schnädelbach, H. (1983). *Philosophie in Deutschland 1831–1933*, Frankfurt on Main: Suhrkamp. Trans. 1984 E. Matthews, *Philosophy in Germany 1983–1933*, Cambridge: Cambridge University Press.

Young, J. (2002). *Heidegger's Later Philosophy*, Cambridge: Cambridge University Press.

Zimmermann, M. (1990). *Heidegger's Confrontation with Modernity: Technology, Politics, Art*, Bloomington, IN: Indiana University Press.

CHAPTER 39 LATIN AMERICAN PHILOSOPHY

Astrada, C. (1933). *El juego existencial* (*The Existential Game*), Buenos Aires: El Ateneo.

Bello, Andrés (1880). *Filosofía del entendimiento* (*Philosophy of Understanding*). Originally written in 1854, published posthumously in 1880. Repr. 1946, México: Fondo de Cultura Económica.

Caso, Antonio (1943). *La existencia como economía, como desinterés y como caridad* (*Existence as Economy, as Unselfishness and as Charity*). Third Edition. México, Secretaría de Educación Pública.

Crawford, William Rex (1944). *A Century of Latin American Thought*. Cambridge: Cambridge University Press.

Guy, Alain (1989). *Panorama de la philosophie ibéro-americaine. Du XVIe siècle a nos jours* (*Overview of Ibero-American Philosophy. From XVI Century to the Present*), Génova: Patiño.

Ingenieros, José (1919). *Principios de Psicología (Principles of Psychology)*, *Obras completas (Complete Works)*, vol. IX, Buenos Aires: Elmer Editor, 1956. A first version (1910) was entitled *Principios de Psicología biológica (Principles of Biological Psychology)*.

Mariátegui, J. C. (1928). *Siete ensayos sobre la realidad peruana (Seven Essays on Peruvian Reality)*. *Obras Completas (Complete Works)* (1969), vol. II. Lima: Empresa Editora Amauta.

Mariátegui, J. C. (H. Neira ed.) (1973). *José Carlos Mariátegui en sus textos (José Carlos Mariátegui in his Essays)*. Lima: PEISA. Biblioteca Peruana.

Romero, Francisco (1951). 'Latin American's Twentieth-century Sages'. *Américas*, III.

Salazar Bondy, A. (1968) *¿Existe una filosofía de nuestra américa? (Is There a Philosophy of our America?)* Mexico City: Siglo Veitiuno Editores.

Sanchez Reulet, A. (1954). *Contemporary Latin American Philosophy*. Mexico City: University of New Mexico.

Soler, Ricaurte (1968). *El positivismo argentino (Argentine Positivism)*. Buenos Aires: Paidós.

Vaz Ferreira, C. (1920). *Lógica Viva (Live Logic)*, Montevideo: Talleres graficos A. Barreiro y Ramos.

Woodward, R. L. (ed.) (1971). *Positivism in Latin America*. Lexington, MA, Heath.

Zea, L. (1942). 'En torno a la filosofía americana' ('On (Latin) American Philosophy'), in *Ensayos sobre filosofía de la historia (Essays on the Philosophy of History)*, Mexico.

Zea, L. (1968). *El positivismo en México (Positivism in Mexico)*. Mexico: Fondo de Cultura Económica. Trans. 1974 O. Schutte, *Positivism in Mexico*. Austin: University of Texas Press.

Zea, L. (ed.) (1980). '*El pensamiento positivista latinoamericano' (Latin American Positivist Thought)*, Caracas: Biblioteca Ayacucho.

CHAPTER 40 JAPANESE PHILOSOPHY

Carter, Robert E. (1997). *The Nothingness Beyond God: An Introduction to the Philosophy of Nishida Kitarō*, 2nd edn, St. Paul, MN: Paragon House.

Dilworth, David A. and Viglielmo, Valdo H. with Zavala, Agustin Jacinto (1998). *Sourcebook for Modern Japanese Philosophy: Selected Documents*, London: Greenwood Press.

Heisig, James W. and Maraldo, John C. (eds.) (1994). *Rude Awakenings: Zen, The Kyoto School, and the Question of Nationalism*, Honolulu: University of Hawaii Press.

Jacinto Zavala, Agustin (ed.) with Tamiyo Kambe ohara (2 vols.: 1995, 1997). *Textos de la Filosofia Japonesa Moderna: Antologia, Zamora, Michacán:* El Colegio de Michoacán.

Nishida, Kitarō (1911). *Zen no kenkyū*, Tokyo: Iwanami shoten. Trans. 1992 Masao Abe and Christover Ives, *An Inquiry into the Good*, New Haven, CT: Yale University Press.

Nishida, Kitarō (1927). *Hataraku mono kara miru mono e (From the Acting to the Seeing)*, Tokyo: Iwanami shoten.

Nishida, Kitarō (1929). *Ippansha no jikakuteki taikei (The Self-Conscious System of the Universal)*, Tokyo: Iwanami shoten.

Nishida, Kitarō (1934). *Tetsugaku no kompon mondai*, Tokyo: Iwanami shoten. Trans. 1970 David A. Dilworth, *Fundamental Problems of Philosophy*, Tokyo: Sophia University Press.

Nishitani, Keiji (1985). *Nishida Kitarō: sono hito to shisō*, Tokyo: Chikuma Shobō. Trans. 1991 Yamamoto Seisaku and James W. Heisig, *Nishida Kitarō*, Berkeley: University of California Press.

Ohashi, Ryōsuke (ed.) (1990). *Die Philosophie der Kyôto Schule: Texte und Einführung*, Munich and Freiburg: Verlag Karl Alber.

Piovesana, Gino K. (1997). *Recent Japanese Philosophical Thought 1862–1996: A Survey Including a New Survey by Naoshi Yamawaki 'The Philosophical Thought of Japan from 1963–1996'*, Richmond, Surrey: Japan Library (Curzon Press Ltd).

Tanabe, Hajime (1946). *Zangedō to shite no tetsugaku*, Tokyo: Iwanami shoten. Trans. 1988
    Takeuchi Yoshinori, with Valdo H. Viglielmo and James W. Heisig, *Philosophy as Meta-
    noetics*, Berkeley: University of California Press, 1986.
Unno, Taitetsu (ed.) (1990). *The Religious Philosophy of Tanabe Hajime: The Metanoetic Imperative*,
    Berkeley, CA: University of California Press.
Watsuji, Tetsurō (1952). *Nihon rinri shisōshi (A History of Japanese Ethical Thought)*, Tokyo: Iwanami
    shoten.
Watsuji, Tetsurō (1935). *Fudo*, Tokyo: Iwanami shoten. Trans. 1961 Geoffrey Bownas, *Climate
    and Culture: A Philosophical Study*, Tokyo: Hokuseido Press. Repr. 1988, Westport, CT:
    Greenwood Press.
Watsuji, Tetsurō (3 vols: 1937, 1942, 1949). *Rinrigaku (Ethics)*, Tokyo: Iwanami shoten. Partial
    trans. 1996 Yamamoto Seisaku and Robert E. Carter, *Rinrigaku: Ethics in Japan*, Albany,
    NY: State University of New York Press.

CHAPTER 41 SENSIBLE APPEARANCES

Anscombe, G. E. M. (1965). 'The Intentionality of Sensation: A Grammatical Feature' in R. J.
    Butler (ed.), *Analytical Philosophy* (2nd series), Oxford: Blackwell.
Austin, J. L. (1962). *Sense and Sensibilia*, Oxford: Oxford University Press.
Ayer, A. J. (1940). *The Foundations of Empirical Knowledge*, London: Macmillan.
Baldwin, T. (1990). *G. E. Moore*, London: Routledge.
Barnes, W. H. (1945). 'The Myth of Sense-Data', *Proceedings of the Aristotelian Society* 45.
    Reprinted 1965 in R. Swarz (ed.), *Perceiving, Sensing, and Knowing*, New York: Doubleday,
    138–67.
Brentano, F. (1874). *Psychologie vom empirischen Standpunkt*, vol. I, edited by Oskar Kraus in 1924,
    Hamburg: Felix Meiner Verlag. Trans. 1973 A. Rancurello, D. Terrell, and L. McAlister,
    Psychology from an Empirical Standpoint, London: Routledge.
Broad, C. D. (1914). *Perception, Physics and Reality*, Cambridge: Cambridge University Press.
Broad, C. D. (1923). *Scientific Thought*, London: Kegan Paul.
Broad, C. D. (1925). *Mind and its Place in Nature*, London: Kegan Paul.
Burnyeat, M. (1979). 'Conflicting Appearances', *Proceedings of the British Academy* 65: 69–111.
Dawes Hicks, G. (1917). 'Are the Materials of Sense Affections of the Mind?', *Proceedings of the
    Aristotelian Society* 17: 434–45.
Drake, Durant et al. (1920). *Essays in Critical Realism: A Cooperative Study of the Problem of
    Knowledge*, New York: Macmillan.
Ducasse, C. J. (1942). 'Moore's Refutation from idealism' in P. A. Schilpp (ed.), *The Philosophy
    of G. E. Moore*, Evanston, IL: Northwestern University Press, 223–52.
Heidegger, M. (1927). *Sein und Zeit*, Tübingen: Niemeyer. Trans. 1962 J. Macquarrie and
    E. Robinson, *Being and Time*, Oxford: Blackwell.
Husserl, E. (1900/1). *Logische Untersuchungen*. Halle: M. Niemayer. Reprinted 1975, 1984 in
    Husserliana XVIII, XIX, The Hague: Nijhoff. Trans. 1970 J. N. Findlay, *Logical Investigations*,
    London: Routledge.
Husserl, E. (1913). *Ideen zu einer reinem Phänomenlogie und phänomenologischen Philosophie* I,
    in *Jahrbuch für Philosophie und phänomenologische Forschung* I 1–323. Reprinted 1950 in
    Husserliana, vol. III, The Hague: Nijhoff. Trans. 1982 F. Kersten, *Ideas Pertaining to a Pure
    Phenomenology and to a Phenomenological Philosophy*, vol. I, The Hague: Nijhoff.
Lewis, C. I. (1929). *Mind and the World-Order*, New York: Charles Scribner's.
Marion, M. (2000). 'Oxford Realism: Knowledge and Perception', *British Journal for the History
    of Philosophy* 8–9: 299–338, 485–519.

Merleau-Ponty, M. (1942). *La Structure de comportement*, Paris: Presses Universitaires de France. Trans. 1963 A. Fisher, *The Structure of Behavior*, Boston, MA: Beacon Press.

Merleau-Ponty, M. (1945). *Phénoménologie de la perception*, Paris: Gallimard. Trans. 1962 C. Smith, *The Phenomenology of Perception*, London: Routledge.

Moore, G. E. (1903). 'The Refutation of Idealism', *Mind* 12: 433–53.

Moore, G. E. (1909). 'The Subject-Matter of Psychology', *Proceedings of the Aristotelian Society* 10: 36–62.

Moore, G. E. (1914). 'The Status of Sense-Data', *Proceedings of the Aristotelian Society* 14: 355–406.

Moore, G. E. (1925). 'A Defence of Common Sense' in J. H. Muirhead (ed.), *Contemporary British Philosophy* (2nd series), London: George Allen and Unwin, 193–223. Reprinted in T. Baldwin (ed.), *G. E. Moore: Selected Writings*, London: Routledge, 106–33.

Moore, G. E. (1942). 'A Reply to my Critics: 10. Subjectivity of sense-data', in P. A. Schilpp (ed.), *The Philosophy of G. E. Moore*, Evanston, IL: Northwestern University Press, 653–60.

Paul, G. A. (1936). 'Is there a Problem about Sense-Data?', *Aristotelian Society Supplementary Volume* 15, 61–77.

Price, H. H. (1932). *Perception*, London: Methuen.

Prichard, H. (1909). *Kant's Theory of Knowledge*, Oxford: Oxford University Press.

Prichard, H. (1950). *Knowledge and Perception*, Oxford: Oxford University Press.

Russell, B. A. W. (1912). *The Problems of Philosophy*, London: Williams and Norgate.

Russell, B. A. W. (1914). *Our Knowledge of the External World*, Chicago and London: Open Court.

Russell, B. A. W. (1921). *The Analysis of Mind*, London: George Allen and Unwin.

Sartre, J.-P. (1940). *L'Imaginaire*, Paris: Gallimard. Trans. 1948 B. Frechtman, *The Psychology of the Imagination*, New York: Philosophical Library.

Sartre, J.-P. (1943). *L'être et le néant*, Paris: Gallimard. Trans. 1956 H. Barnes, *Being and Nothingness*, New York: Philosophical Library; 1957 London: Methuen.

Searle, J. R. (1983). *Intentionality*, Cambridge: Cambridge University Press.

Sellars, W. (1956). 'Empiricism and the Philosophy of Mind', in H. Feigl and M. Scriven (eds.), *Minnesota Studies in the Philosophy of Science* 1, Minneapolis: Minnesota University Press, 253–329. Repr. 1963 in W. Sellars *Science, Perception and Reality*, London: Routledge, 127–96.

CHAPTER 42 THE RENAISSANCE OF EPISTEMOLOGY

Albert, H. (1978). 'Science and the Search for Truth', *Boston Studies in the Philosophy of Science* 58: 203–20.

Albert, H. (1985). *Treatise on Critical Reason*, Princeton, NJ: Princeton University Press.

Apel, K. O. (1975). 'The Problem of Philosophical Fundamental-Grounding in Light of a Transcendental Pragmatic of Language', *Man & World* 8: 239–75.

Blanshard, B. (1939). *The Nature of Thought*, New York: Macmillan.

Bosanquet, B. (1888). *Logic, or the Morphology of Knowledge*, 2nd edn 1911, Oxford: Clarendon Press.

Bosanquet, B. (1920). *Implication and Linear Inference*, London: Macmillan.

Bradley, F. H. (1883). *The Principles of Logic*, Oxford: Clarendon Press. 2nd edn 1922.

Bradley, F. H. (1893). *Appearance and Reality*, London: Swan Sonnenschein. 2nd edn. 1897. Repr. 1930, Oxford: Clarendon Press.

Bradley, F. H. (1914). *Essays on Truth and Reality*, Oxford: Clarendon Press.

Carnap, R., Morris, C., and Neurath, O. (eds.) (1938–70). *International Encyclopedia of Unified Science*, Chicago, IL: University of Chicago Press.

Chisholm, R. (1973). 'The Problem of the Criterion', *The Aquinas Lecture*, Marquette University. Repr. 1982 in R. Chisholm, *The Foundations of Knowing*, Brighton: The Harvester Press, ch. 5.

Chisholm, R. (1989). *Theory of Knowledge*, 3rd edn, Englewood Cliffs, NJ: Prentice-Hall.

Dewey, J. (1925). *Experience and Nature*, Chicago, IL and London: Open Court.

Dewey, J. (1929). *The Quest for Certainty*, New York: Minton Balch.

Dewey, J. (1938). *Logic: The Theory of Inquiry*, New York: Holt.

Ducasse, C. J. (1942). 'Moore's Refutation of Idealism' in P. A. Schilpp (ed.), *Philosophy of G. E. Moore*, Chicago, IL: Northwestern University Press, 225–51.

Fries, J. F. (1807, 1828–31). *Neue oder anthropologische Kritik der Vernunft*, Heidelberg: Bey Mohr and Zimmer.

Gettier, E. L. (1963). 'Is Justified True Belief Knowledge?', *Analysis* 23: 121–3.

Haller, R. (1974). 'Über die Möglichkeit der Erkenntnistheorie' ('On the Possibility of a Theory of Knowledge') in P. Schroeder (ed.), *Vernunft Erkenntnis Sittlichkeit* (*Reason, Knowledge, Ethics*), Hamburg: Felix Meiner V. 37–54.

Hegel, G. W. F. (1802). *On the Relationship of Scepticism with Philosophy*. Trans. 1985 in G. Di Giovanni and H. S. Harris (eds.), *Between Kant and Hegel, Texts in the Development of Post-Kantian Idealism*, New York: Suny Press, 311–62.

Husserl, E. (1950). *Die Idee der Phaenomenologie, Funf Vorlesungen*, in *Gesammelte Werke*, vol. II, ed. Walter Biemel, The Hague: Nijhoff. These are five lectures delivered by Husserl in Göttingen in 1907. Trans. 1964 W. P. Alston and G. Nakhinian, *The Idea of Phenomenology*, The Hague: Nijhoff.

Joachim, H. H. (1906). *The Nature of Truth: An Essay*, 2nd edn 1939, Oxford: Clarendon Press.

Lakatos, I. (1978). 'Infinite Regress and Foundations of Mathematics' in *Philosophical Papers II*, ed. J. Worrall and G. Currie, Cambridge: Cambridge University Press, 3–23.

Mercier, D. (1923). *Critériologie Générale ou Théorie Générale de la Certitude*, 8th edn, Louvain: Institut supérieur de philosophie and Paris: Alcan.

Moore, G. E. (1925). 'A Defence of Common-Sense' in *Contemporary British Philosophy*, 2nd series, ed. J. H. Muirhead, London: George Allen and Unwin. Repr. 1959 in *Philosophical Papers*, London: George Allen and Unwin and in 1993 *Selected Writings*, ed. T. Baldwin, London: Routledge.

Moore, G. E. (1939). 'Proof of an External World', *Proceedings of the British Academy* 25: 273–300. Repr. 1959 in *Philosophical Papers*, London: George Allen and Unwin and in 1993, *Selected Writings*, ed. T. Baldwin, London: Routledge.

Nelson, L. (1930). 'Über das Sogenannte Erkenntnisproblem' ('On the So-called Problem of Knowledge'), *Abhandlungen der Fries'schen Schule*, n.s. 1: 444–6.

Nelson, L. (1965). 'The Impossibility of the "Theory of Knowledge"', English trans. in *Socratic Method and Critical Philosophy, Selected Essays* by T. K. Brown III, foreword by B. Blanshard, introd. by J. Kraft, New York: Dover, 185–205.

Nelson, L. (1971). *Progress and Regress in Philosophy, From Hume and Kant to Hegel and Fries*, ed. Julius Kraft, English trans. Humphrey Palmer, Oxford: Blackwell.

Neurath, O. (1983). *Philosophical Papers 1913–1946*, ed. R. S. Cohen and M. Neurath, Dordrecht: Reidel.

Peirce, C. S. (1931–58). *Collected Papers of C. S. Peirce*, ed. C. Hortshorne, P. Weiss, and A. Burks, Cambridge, MA: Harvard University Press.

Popper, K. R. (1962). *The Logic of Scientific Discovery*, London: Hutchinson (1st edn 1934).

Popper, K. R. (1979). *Die beiden Grundprobleme der Erkenntnistheorie*, Tübingen: J. C. B. Mohr.

Quine, W. V. (1969). 'Epistemology Naturalized', in *Ontological Relativity and Other Essays*, New York: Columbia University Press.

Quine, W. V. (1992). *Pursuit of Truth*, Cambridge, MA: Harvard University Press.

Ramsey, F. P. (1931). *The Foundations of Mathematics*, ed. R. B. Braithwaite, London: Kegan Paul.

Rorty, R. (1979). *Philosophy and the Mirror of Nature*, Princeton, NJ: Princeton University Press.

Russell, B. A. W. (1912). *The Problems of Philosophy*, London: Williams and Norgate.

Russell, B. A. W. (1914). *Our Knowledge of the External World*, Chicago and London: Open Court.

Russell, B. A. W. (1921). *The Analysis of Mind*, London: George Allen and Unwin.

Russell, B. A. W. (1927). *The Analysis of Matter*, London: George Allen and Unwin.

Russell, B. A. W. (1948). *Human Knowledge. Its Scope and Limits*, London: George Allen and Unwin.

Russell, B. A. W. (1984). *Collected Papers*, vol. VII, ed. E. R. Eames, London: George Allen and Unwin.

Schlick, M. (1925). *General Theory of Knowledge*, English trans. 1974 by A. E. Blumberg, Vienna and New York: Springer Verlag.

Schlick, M. (1979). *Philosophical Papers*, ed. H. Mulder and B. F. B. van de Velde-Schlick, 2 vols., Dordrecht: Reidel.

Sellars, W. S. (1963). *Science, Perception and Reality*, London and New York: Routledge. Repr. 1991, Atascadero, CA: Ridgeview.

Sextus Empiricus (1976), *Outlines of Pyrrhonism*, English trans. R. G. Bury, Cambridge, MA: Harvard University Press.

Wittgenstein, L. (1969). *On Certainty*, ed. G. E. M. Anscombe and G. H. von Wright, trans. D. Paul and G. E. M. Anscombe, Oxford: Blackwell.

CHAPTER 43 THE SOLIPSISM DEBATES

Bell, D. (1996). 'Solipsism and Subjectivity', *European Journal of Philosophy* 4: 155–74.

Braithwaite, R. B. (1933). 'Solipsism and the "Common Sense View of the World" ', *Analysis* 1: 13–15.

Cornforth, M. (1933). 'Is Solipsism Compatible with Common Sense?', *Analysis* 1: 21–6.

Craig, E. J. (1998). 'Solipsism', in E. J. Craig (ed.), *Routledge Encyclopedia of Philosophy*, London: Routledge, vol. IX, 25–26.

Descartes, R. (1954). *Meditations on First Philosophy* in G. E. M. Anscombe and P. T. Geach (eds.), *Descartes: Philosophical Writings*, London: Thomas Nelson.

Heidegger, M. (1927). *Sein und Zeit*. Trans. 1967 J. Macquarrie and E. Robinson, *Being and Time*, Oxford: Blackwell.

Husserl, E. (1931). *Méditations cartésiennes*, Paris: Armand Colin. Trans. 1973 D. Cairns, *Cartesian Meditations*, The Hague: Nijhoff.

Husserl, E. (1954). *Die Krisis der europäischen Wissenschaften und die transzendentale Phänomenologie*, The Hague: Nijhoff. Trans. 1970 D. Carr, *The Crisis of European Sciences and Transcendental Phenomenology*, Evanston: Northwestern University Press.

Merleau-Ponty, M. (1945). *Phénoménologie de la perception*, Paris: Gallimard. Trans. 1962 C. Smith, *The Phenomenology of Perception*, London: Routledge.

Miller, R. W. (1980). 'Solipsism in the *Tractatus*', *Journal of the History of Ideas* 18: 142–66.

Moore, G. E. (1925). 'A Defence of Common Sense' in J. H. Muirhead (ed.), *Contemporary British Philosophy*, second series, London: George Allen and Unwin, 93–223.

Russell, B. A. W. (1927). *An Outline of Philosophy*, London: George Allen and Unwin.

Russell, B. A. W. (1948). *Human Knowledge: Its Scope and Limits*, London: George Allen and Unwin.

Sartre, J.-P. (1943). *L'être et le néant*, Paris: Gallimard. Trans. 1956 H. E. Barnes, *Being and Nothingness*, New York: Philosophical Library, 1957 and London: Methuen.

Schopenhauer, A. (1844). *Die Welt als Wille und Vorstellung*, 2nd edn Berlin: H. Bohm. Trans. 1969 E. F. J. Payne, *The World as Will and Representation*, New York: Dover.

Stebbing, L. S. (1933). 'Concerning Solipsism: Reply to Braithwaite', *Analysis* 1: 26–8.

Wisdom, J. O. (1933). 'Solipsism', *Analysis* 1: 17–21.

Wittgenstein, L. (1921). 'Logische-philosophische Abhandlung', *Annalen der Naturphilosophie*. Trans. 1922. C. K. Ogden, *Tractatus Logico-Philosophicus*, London: Routledge. Rev. trans. 1961 D. F. Pears and B. F. McGuiness: Routledge.

Wittgenstein, L. (1953). *Philosophical Investigations*. Trans. G. E. M. Anscombe, Oxford: Blackwell.

Wittgenstein, L. (1958). *The Blue and Brown Books*, Oxford: Blackwell.

Wittgenstein, L. (1961). *Notebooks 1914–1916*. Ed. G. H. von Wright and G. E. M. Anscombe, trans. G. E. M. Anscombe, Oxford: Blackwell.

Wittgenstein, L. (1968). 'Notes for Lectures on "Private Experience" and "Sense Data"', *Philosophical Review* 77.

Wittgenstein, L. (1975). *Philosophical Remarks*. Ed. R. Rhees, trans. R. Hargreaves and R. White, Oxford: Blackwell.

Wittgenstein, L. (1979). *Wittgenstein's Lectures. Cambridge 1932–1935*. Ed. A. Ambrose, Oxford: Blackwell.

CHAPTER 44 LANGUAGE

Aler, J. (1972). 'Heidegger's Conception of Language in *Being and Time*' in Kocklemans 1972, 33–62.

Ayer, A. J. (1936). *Language Truth and Logic*, London: Gollancz.

Ayer, A. J. (ed.) (1959). *Logical Positivism*, Glencoe, IL: The Free Press.

Bell, D. (1990). *Husserl*, London: Routledge.

Biemel, W. (1972). 'Poetry and Language in Heidegger' in Kockelmans 1972: 65–105.

Biemel, W. (1977). *Martin Heidegger: An Illustrated Study*, trans. J. L. Mehta, London: Routledge, chs. 4 and 6.

Black, M. (1954). 'Carnap on Semantics and Logic' in M. Black, *Problems of Analysis*, London: Routledge, 255–90.

Black, M. (1966). *Language and Philosophy*, Ithaca, NY: Cornell University Press.

Carnap, R. (1932a). 'Die physikalische Sprache als Universalsprache der Wissenschaft', *Erkenntis*, 432–65. Trans. 1934 M. Black, *The Unity of Science*, London: Kegan Paul. Repr. in part in Hanfling 1981a, 150–60.

Carnap, R. (1932b). 'Uberwindung der Metaphysik durch logische Analyse der Sprache', *Erkenntnis*, 2, 219–41. Trans. 1959 A. Pap, 'The Elimination of Metaphysics Through Logical Analysis' in Ayer 1959, 60–81.

Carnap, R. (1934a). 'On the Character of Philosophical Problems', *Philosophy of Science* 1, 5–19. Repr. in Rorty 1967, 54–62.

Carnap, R. (1934b). *Logische Syntax Der Sprache*, Vienna: Springer Verlag. Trans. 1937 Amethe Smeaton, *The Logical Syntax of Language*, London: Kegan Paul.

Carnap, R. (1938). 'Logical Foundations of the Unity of Science' in O. Neurath, R. Carnap, and Charles Morris (eds.), *International Encyclopedia of Unified Science*, vol. I, no. 1, Chicago: Chicago University Press, 42–62. Repr. in Hanfling 1981a, 112–29.

Carnap, R. (1942). *Introduction to Semantics*, Cambridge, MA: Harvard University Press.

Carnap, R. (1963). 'Intellectual Autobiography', in P. A. Schilpp (ed.), *The Philosophy of Rudolf Carnap*, La Salle, IL: Open Court, 3–84.

Dreyfus, H. L. (ed.) (1982). *Husserl, Intentionality and Cognitive Science*, Cambridge Mass.: MIT Press.

Dreyfus, H. L. (1995). *Being-in-the-World: A Commentary on Heidegger's* Being and Time, *Division I*, Cambridge, MA.: MIT Press.

Fogelin, R. J. (1976). *Wittgenstein*, London: Routledge.

Hanfling, O. (1981a) *Logical Positivism*, Oxford: Blackwell.

Hanfling, O. (ed.) (1981b). *Essential Readings in Logical Positivism*, Oxford: Blackwell.

Heidegger, M. (1927). *Sein und Zeit, Jahrbuch fur Philosophie und phänomenologische Forschung*, vol. VIII, Halle: Max Niemayer. Trans. 1962 J. McQuarrie and E. Robinson, *Being and Time*, New York: Harper and Row.

Hempel, C. G. (1950). 'Problems and Changes in the Empiricist Criterion of Meaning', *Revue International de Philosophie*, 11. Repr. in Linsky 1952, 163–88.

Holdcroft, D. (1991). *Saussure: Signs, System and Arbitrariness*, Cambridge: Cambridge University Press.

Husserl, E. (1900–1). *Logische Untersuchungen*, Halle a.d.S.: Max Niemeyer. 2nd edn in two parts 1913–22. Trans. 1957 J. N. Findlay, *Logical Investigations*, London: Routledge.

Husserl, E. (1913). 'Ideen zur einer reinen Phänomenologie und phänomenologischen Philosophie', *Jahrbuch fur Philosophie und phänemenologische Forschung*, 1: 1–323. Trans. 1982 F. Kersten, *Ideas Pertaining to a Pure Phenomenology and to a Phenomenological Philosophy. First Book: General Introduction to a Pure Phenomenology*, The Hague: Nijhoff.

Jager, R. (1972). *The Development of Bertrand Russell's Philosophy*, London: George Allen and Unwin.

Kenny, A. J. (1973). *Wittgenstein*, Harmondsworth: Penguin.

Kockelmans, J. J. (ed.) (1972). *On Heidegger and Language*, Evanston, IL: Northwestern University Press.

Linsky, L. (ed.) (1952). *Semantics and the Philosophy of Language*, Urbana, IL: University of Illinois Press.

Mohanty, J. N. (1995). 'The Development of Husserl's Thought' in Smith and Smith 1995, 45–77.

Moore, G. E. (1954). 'Wittgenstein's Lectures in 1929–33', *Mind* 63: 1–15, 289–316, and (1955) *Mind* 64, 1–27.

Morris, C. W. (1938). 'Foundations of the Theory of Signs' in O. Neurath, R. Carnap and Charles Morris (eds.), *International Encyclopedia of Unified Science*, vol. I, no. 2, Chicago: Chicago University Press, 1–59.

Ogden, C. K. and Richards, I. A. (1923). *The Meaning of Meaning: A Study of The Influence of Language upon Thought and of The Science of Symbolism*, London: Routledge.

Passmore, J. (1978). *A Hundred Years of Philosophy*, Harmonsdworth: Penguin.

Pears, D. F. (1972). 'Russell's Logical Atomism', in D. F. Pears (ed.), *Bertrand Russell: A Collection of Critical Essays*, Garden City, New York: Doubleday Anchor Books.

Quine, W. V. O. (1951). 'Two Dogmas of Empiricism', *Philosophical Review*, 60, 20–43. Repr. in W. V. O. Quine (1961), *From a Logical Point of View*, Cambridge, MA: Harvard University Press.

Rescher, N. (1995). 'The Rise and Fall of Analytic Philosophy', in N. Rescher 1993, *Essays in the History of Philosophy*, Aldershot: Avebury, 327–37.

Rorty, R. (ed.) (1967). *The Linguistic Turn*, Chicago: University of Chicago Press.

Rorty, R. (1993). 'The Reification of Logic' in C. B. Guignan (ed.) 1993, *The Cambridge Companion to Heidegger*, Cambridge: Cambridge University Press.

Russell, B. A. W. (1918). 'The Philosophy of Logical Atomism', *The Monist* 28, 495–527, and (1919) 29, 32–63, 190–222, 345–80. Repr. in Russell 1956, 175–282.

Russell, B. A. W. (1921). *An Analysis of Mind*, London: George Allen and Unwin, ch. 10.

Russell, B. A. W. (1924). 'Logical Atomism' in ed. J. H. Muirhead, *Contemporary British Philosophy*, vol. I, xxx. Reprinted in Russell 1956, 321–43.

Russell, B. A. W. (1956). *Logic and Knowledge*, ed. R. C. Marsh, London: George Allen and Unwin.

Russell, B. A. W. (1959). *My Philosophical Development*, London: George Allen and Unwin.

Sainsbury, M. (1979). *Russell*, London: Routledge.

Saussure, Ferdinand de (1916). *Cours de linguistique generale*, ed. C. Bally and A. Sechehaye, Lausanne and Paris: Payot. Trans. 1977 Wade Baskin, *Course in General Linguistics*, Glasgow: Fontana/Collins.

Schlick, M. (1979). *Philosophical Papers*, 2 vols., ed. H. L. Mulder and B. F. B. van de Velde-Schlick. Trans. P. Heath, Dordrecht: Reidel.

Simons, P. (1995). 'Meaning and Language' in Smith and Smith 1995, 106–37. An account of Husserl's theory.

Smith, B. and Smith, D. W. (1995). *Introduction* in B. Smith and D. W. Smith (ed.), *The Cambridge Companion to Husserl*, Cambridge: Cambridge University Press, 1–44.

Smith, B. (1994). 'Husserl's Theory of Meaning and Reference' in L. Haaparanta (ed.), *Mind, Meaning and Mathematics*, Dordrecht: Kluwer, 163–84.

Stevenson, C. L. (1937). 'The Emotive Meaning of Ethical Terms', *Mind* 14–31. Reprinted in Ayer 1959, 264–81.

Tarski, A. (1936). 'Der Wahrheitsbegriff in den formalisierten Sprachen', *Studia Philosophica* 1, 261–405. There is an English version with replies to criticisms, 'The Semantic Conception of Truth', *Philosophy and Phenomenological Research*, 4, 341–75. Repr. in Linsky 1952, 13–49.

Urmson, J. O. (1956). *Philosophical Analysis: Its Development Between the Two World Wars*, Oxford: Clarendon Press.

Waissman, F. (1965). *The Principles of Linguistic Philosophy*, ed. R. Harre, London: Macmillan.

Waissman, F. (1967). *Wittgenstein und der Wiener Kreis*, ed. B. F. McGuiness, Oxford: Blackwell.

Warnock, M. (1960). *Ethics Since 1900*, London: Oxford University Press.

Wittgenstein, L. (1922). *Tractatus Logico-Philosophicus*, trans. C. K. Ogden, London: Routledge.

Wittgenstein, L. (1929). 'Some Remarks on Logical Form', *Proceedings of the Aristotelian Society*, suppl. vol. IX, 162–71.

Wittgenstein, L. (1953). *Philosophical Investigations*, ed. G. E. M. Anscombe and R. Rhees, trans. G. E. M. Anscombe, Oxford: Blackwell.

Wittgenstein, L. (1958). *The Blue and Brown Books*, Oxford: Blackwell.

CHAPTER 45 THE END OF PHILOSOPHY AS METAPHYSICS

Austin, J. L. (1979). 'Ifs and Cans' in *Philosophical Papers*, Oxford: Oxford University Press.

Derrida, J. (1993). 'On a Newly Arisen Apocalyptic Tone in Philosophy', trans. J. Leavey, Jr in P. Fenves (ed.), *Raising the Tone of Philosophy*, Baltimore: Johns Hopkins University Press, 117–71.

Glendinning, S. (1998). *On Being With Others*, London: Routledge.

Hacker, P. M. S. (1986). *Insight and Illusion: Themes in the Philosophy of Wittgenstein*. Rev. edn, Oxford: Clarendon Press.

Heidegger, M. (1969). 'Das Ende der Philosophie und die Aufgabe des Denkens' in *Zur Sache des Denkens*, Tübingen: Niemeyer. Trans. 1977 D. Farrell Krell, 'The End of Philosophy and the Task for Thinking' in D. Farrell Krell, *Basic Writings*, London: Routledge, 427–49.

Heidegger, M. (1975). *Die Grundprobleme der Phänomenologie (Gesamtausgabe* vol. XXIV), Frankfurt: V. Klosterman. Trans. 1982 A. Hofstadter, *The Basic Problems of Phenomenology*, Bloomington, IN: Indiana University Press.

Heidegger, M. (1927). *Sein und Zeit*, Halle: Niemeyer. Trans. 1962 J. Macquarrie and E. Robinson, *Being and Time*, Oxford: Blackwell.

Heidegger, M. (1967). 'Was ist Metaphysik?' in *Wegmarken*, Frankfurt on Main: Vittorio Klostermann Verlag. Trans. 1977 D. Farrell Krell, 'What is Metaphysics?' in D. Farrell Krell (ed.), *Basic Writings*, London: Routledge, 89–110.

Husserl, (1913). *Ideen zu einer Reinen Phänomenologie und Phänomenologischen Philosophie*, Halle: Niemeyer. Trans. 1931 W. R. Boyce Gibson, *Ideas toward a Pure Phenomenology and Phenomenological Philosophy*, London: George Allen and Unwin.

Kant, I. (1787). *Kritik der Reinen Vernunft*, Riga: J. F. Hartknoch. Trans. 1933 N. Kemp Smith, *The Critique of Pure Reason*, London: Macmillan.

McManus, D. (1995). 'Philosophy in Question: *Philosophical Investigations* 133', *Philosophical Investigations* 18: 4 348–61.

Moore, G. E. (1953). *Some Main Problems of Philosophy*, London: George Allen and Unwin.

Rorty, R. (1982). 'Pragmatism and Philosophy', Introduction to *Consequences of Pragmatism*, Brighton: Harvester, xiii–xlvii.

Ryle, G. (1971). 'Phenomenology versus *The Concept of Mind*' in *Collected Papers*, London: Hutchinson.

Wittgenstein, L. (1981). *Zettel*, trans. G. E. M. Anscombe, Oxford: Blackwell.

Wittgenstein, L. (1953). *Philosophical Investigations*, trans. G. E. M. Anscombe, Oxford: Blackwell.

Wittgenstein, L. (1969). *The Blue and Brown Books*, Oxford: Blackwell.

CHAPTER 46 FIRST-ORDER LOGIC AND ITS RIVALS

Barcan, R. (1946a). 'A Functional Calculus of First-order Based on Strict Implication', *The Journal of Symbolic Logic* 11: 1–16.

Barcan, R. (1946b). 'The Deduction Theorem in a Functional Calculus of First Order Based on Strict Implication', *The Journal of Symbolic Logic* 11: 115–18.

Barcan, R. (1947). 'The Identity of Individuals in a Strict Functional Calculus of Second Order', *The Journal of Symbolic Logic* 12: 12–15.

Brouwer, L. E. J. (1948). 'Consciousness, Philosophy and Mathematics', *Proceedings of the 10th International Congress of Philosophy, Amsterdam, 1948*, 1235–49. Repr. 1975 in L. E. J. Brouwer, *Collected Works*, ed. A. Heyting, vol. I, Amsterdam: North-Holland, 480–94.

Gödel, K. (1929). 'Über die Vollstandigkeit des Logikkalküls', doctoral dissertation, University of Vienna. Trans. 1986 S. Bauer-Mengelberg and J. van Heijenoort, 'On the completeness of the Calculus of Logic' in K. Gödel, *Collected Works*, ed. S. Feferman *et al.*, vol. I, New York: Oxford University Press, 60–101.

Gödel, K. (1932). 'Zum intuitionistischen Aussagenkalkül', *Anzeigen der Akademie der Wissenschaften in Wien* 69: 65–6. Trans. 1986 J. Dawson, 'On the Intuitionistic Propositional Calculus' in K. Gödel, *Collected Works*, ed. S. Feferman *et al.*, vol. I, New York: Oxford University Press, 222–5.

Gödel, K. (1933). 'Eine Interpretation des intuitionistischen Aussagenkalküls', *Ergebnisse eines mathematischen Kolloquiums*, 4: 39–40. Trans. 1986 J. Dawson, 'An Interpretation of the Intuitionistic Propositional Calculus', in K. Gödel, *Collected Works*, ed. S. Feferman *et al.*, vol. I, New York: Oxford University Press, 300–3.

Heyting, A. (1930a). 'Die formalen Regeln der intuitionistischen Logik', *Sitzungsberichte der preussischen Akademie der Wissenschaften, Physikalisch-mathematische Klasse*, 16: 42–56.

Heyting, A. (1930b). 'Die formalen regeln der intuitionistischen Mathematik', *Sitzungsberichte der preussischen Akademie der Wissenschaften, Physikalisch-mathematische Klasse*, 16: 57–71, 158–69.

Hilbert, D. and Ackermann, W. (1928). *Grundzüge der theoretischen Logik*, Berlin: Springer. 2nd edn 1938. Trans. 1950 L. M. Hammond *et al.*, ed. R. E. Luce, *Principles of Mathematical Logic*, New York: Chelsea.

Kleene, S. (1945). 'On the Interpretation of Intuitionistic Number Theory', *The Journal of Symbolic Logic*, 10: 109–24.

Kripke, S. (1959). 'A Completeness Theorem in Modal Logic', *The Journal of Symbolic Logic*, 24: 1–14.

Lewis, C. I. (1912). 'Implication and the Algebra of Logic', *Mind* 21: 522–31.

Lewis, C. I. (1918). *A Survey of Symbolic Logic*, Berkeley: University of California Press.

Lewis, C. I. and Langford, C. H. (1932). *Symbolic Logic*, New York: The Century Co.

Łukasiewicz, J. (1930). 'Philosophische Bemerkungen zu mehrwertigen System des Aussagenkalküls', *Comptes rendus des séances de la Société de Sciences et des Lettres de Varsovie*, 23: cl. iii, 51–77. Trans. 1970 H. Weber, 'Philosophical Remarks on Many-valued Systems of Propositional Logic' in J. Łukasiewicz, *Selected Works*, ed. L. Borkowski, Amsterdam: North-Holland, 153–78.

Łukasiewicz, J. (1953). 'A System of Modal Logic', *The Journal of Computing Systems* 1: 111–49.

Quine, W. V. (1939). 'Designation and Existence', *The Journal of Philosophy* 36: 701–9.

Quine, W. V. (1947). 'The Problem of Interpreting Modal Logic', *The Journal of Symbolic Logic* 12: 43–8.

Russell, B. A. W. (1914). *Our Knowledge of the External World*, Chicago and London: Open Court.

Shapiro, S. (1985). 'Second-order Languages and Mathematical Practice', *The Journal of Symbolic Logic*, 50: 714–42.

Skolem, T. (1920). 'Logisch-kombinatorische Untersuchungen über die Erfüllbarkeit und Beweisbarkeit mathematischen Sätze nebst einem Theorem über dichte Mengen', *Skrifer utgi av Videnkapsselkapet I Kristiana, I. Matematisk-naturvidenskabelig klasse*, no. 4: 1–36. Partial trans. 1967 S. Bauer-Mengelberg, 'Logico-combinatorial Investigations in the Satisfiability or Provability of Mathematical Propositions: A Simplified Proof of a Theorem by L. Lowenheim and Generalizations of the Theorem' in J. van Heijenoort (ed.), *From Frege to Gödel: A Sourcebook in Mathematical Logic*, Cambridge, MA: Harvard University Press, 254–63.

Skolem, T. (1923). 'Einige Bemerkungen zur Axiomatischen Begründen der Mengenlehre', *Matematischerkongressen in Helsingfors 4–7 Juli 1922, Den femte skandinaviska Matematikerkongressen, Redogörelse*, Helsinki: Akademiska Bokhandeln, 217–32. Trans. 1967 S. Bauer-Mengelberg, 'Some Remarks on Axiomatized Set Theory' in J. van Heijenoort (ed.), *From Frege to Gödel: A Sourcebook in Mathematical Logic*, Cambridge, MA: Harvard University Press, 291–301.

Skolem, T. (1930). 'Einige Bemerkungen zu der Abhandlung von E. Zermelo: "Über die Definitheit in der Axiomatik" ', *Fundamenta Mathematicae* 15: 337–41. Repr. 1970 in T. Skolem (ed. J. E. Fenstad), *Selected Works in Logic*, Oslo: Universitetsforlaget, 275–9.

Skolem, T. (1934). 'Über die Nichtcharakterisierbarkeit der Zahlenreihe mittels endlich oder abzählbar unendlich vieler Aussagen mit ausschliesslich Zahlenvariablen', *Fundamenta Mathematicae* 23: 150–61. Repr. 1970 in T. Skolem (ed. J. E. Fenstad), *Selected Works in Logic*, Oslo: Universitetsforlaget, 355–66.

Whitehead, A. N. and Russell, B. A. W. (1910–13). *Principia Mathematica*, vols. I–III, Cambridge: Cambridge University Press. 2nd edn 1925.

Zermelo, E. (1908). 'Untersuchungen über die Grundlagen der Mengenlehre, I', *Mathematische Annalen* 65, 261–81. Trans. 1967 S. Bauer-Mengelberg, 'Investigations in the Foundations of Set Theory I' in J. van Heijenoort (ed.), *From Frege to Gödel: A Sourcebook in Mathematical Logic*, Cambridge, MA: Harvard University Press, 200–15.

CHAPTER 47 THE GOLDEN AGE OF MATHEMATICAL LOGIC

Ackermann, W. (1928). 'Zum Hilbertschen Aufbau der reellen Zahlen', *Mathematische Annalen* 99: 118–33. Trans. S. Bauer-Mengelberg, 'On Hilbert's Construction of the Real Numbers', in van Heijenoort 1967, 493–507.

Ackermann, W. (1954). *Solvable Cases of the Decision Problem*, Amsterdam: North-Holland.

Anderson, C. A. (1998). 'Alonzo Church's contributions to philosophy and intensional logic', *The Bulletin of Symbolic Logic* 4: 129–71.

Barendregt, H. (1997). 'The Impact of the Lambda Calculus in Logic and Computer Science', *The Bulletin of Symbolic Logic* 3: 181–215.

Bernays, P. (1926). 'Axiomatische Untersuchung des Aussagen-Kalküls der *Principia Mathematica*' ('Axiomatic Investigation of the Propositional Calculus of *Principia Mathematica*'), *Mathematische Zeitschrift* 25: 305–20.

Bernays, P. (1967). 'Hilbert, David' (1862–43) in P. Edwards, (ed.) *Encyclopedia of Philosophy*, vol. III: 496–504. New York: Macmillan and Free Press.

Browder, F. E. (ed.) (1976). *Mathematical Developments Arising from Hilbert Problems*. Proceedings of Symposia in Pure Mathematics, XXVIII. Providence: American Mathematical Society.

Church, A. (1935). 'An Unsolvable Problem of Elementary Number Theory', *Bulletin of the American Mathematical Society* 41: 332–3.

Church, A. (1936a). 'An Unsolvable Problem of Elementary Number Theory', *American Journal of Mathematics* 58: 345–63. Repr. in Davis 1965, 88–107.

Church, A. (1936b). 'A Note on the Entscheidungsproblem', *The Journal of Symbolic Logic* 1: 40–1 and 101–2. Repr. in Davis 1965, 110–15.

Church, A. (1936c). 'A Bibliography of Symbolic Logic', *The Journal of Symbolic Logic* 1: 121–216. Additions and corrections 3: 178–92.

Church, A. (1941). *The Calculi of Lambda Conversion*. Princeton, NJ: Princeton University Press.

Davis, M. (ed.) (1965). *The Undecidable: Basic Papers on Undecidable Propositions, Unsolvable Problems, and Computable Functions*, Hewlett, NY: Raven Press.

Dawson, J. W., Jr. (1993). 'The Compactness of First-order Logic: From Gödel to Lindström', *History and Philosophy of Logic* 14: 15–37.

Dawson, J. W., Jr. (1997). *Logical Dilemmas: The Life and Work of Kurt Gödel*. Wellesley, MA: A. K. Peters, Ltd.

Dedekind, R. (1888). *Was sind und was sollen die Zahlen?*, Braunschweig: Vieweg. Trans. 1996 W. Ewald in W. Ewald (ed.) *From Kant to Hilbert: A Source Book in the Foundation of Mathematics*, vol. II, Oxford: Clarendon Press.

Dreben, B. and Goldfarb, W. D. (1979). *The Decision Problem: Solvable Classes of Quantificational Formulas*, Reading, MA: Addison-Wesley.

Enderton, H. B. (1998). 'Alonzo Church and the Reviews', *The Bulletin of Symbolic Logic* 4: 181–203.

Gandy, R. (1988). 'The Confluence of Ideas' in R. Herken (ed.), *The Universal Turing Machine*, Oxford: Oxford University Press, 55–111.

Gentzen, G. (1936). 'Die Widerspruchsfreiheit der reinen Zahlentheorie', *Mathematische Annalen* 112: 493–565. Trans. 1969 M. E. Szabo, 'The Consistency of Pure Number Theory' in

G. Gentzen (ed. M. E. Szabo), *The Collected Papers of Gerhard Gentzen*, Amsterdam: North-Holland, 68–131.

Gödel, K. (1929). *Über die Vollständigkeit des Logikkalküls*, doctoral dissertation, University of Vienna. Repr. in Gödel 1986, 60–100. Trans. S. Bauer-Mengelberg and J. van Heijenoort, *On the Completeness of the Calculus of Logic* in Gödel 1986, 61–101.

Gödel, K. (1930). 'Die Vollständigkeit der Axiome des logischen Funktionenkalküls', *Monatshefte für Mathematik und Physik* 37: 349–60. Repr. in Gödel 1986, 102–22. Trans. S. Bauer-Mengelberg, 'The Completeness of the Axioms of the Functional Calculus of Logic', in Gödel 1986, 103–23.

Gödel, K. (1931). 'Über formal unentscheidbare Sätze der *Principia Mathematica* und verwandter Systeme, I', *Monatshefte für Mathematik und Physik* 38: 173. Repr. in Gödel 1986, 144–94. Trans. J. van Heijenoort, 'On Formally Undecidable Propositions of *Principia Mathematica* and Related Systems, I' in Gödel 1986, 145–95.

Gödel, K. (1934). 'On Undecidable Propositions of Formal Mathematical Systems', mimeographed notes by S. C. Kleene and J. B. Rosser. Repr. in Gödel 1986, 346–71.

Gödel, K. (1938). 'Vortrag bei Zilsel', shorthand lecture draft. Transcribed C. Dawson, in Gödel 1995, 86–112. Trans. C. Parsons, 'Lecture at Zilsel's' in Gödel 1995, 87–113.

Gödel, K. (1940). *The Consistency of the Axiom of Choice and of the Generalized Continuum Hypothesis with the Axioms of Set Theory*, Princeton, NJ: Princeton University Press. Reprinted in Gödel 1990, 33–101.

Gödel, K. (1941). 'In What Sense is Intuitionistic Logic Constructive?', manuscript lecture notes, first published in Gödel 1995, 189–200.

Gödel, K. (1949). 'An Example of a New Type of Cosmological Solutions of Einstein's Field Equations of Gravitation', *Reviews of Modern Physics* 21: 447–50.

Gödel, K. (1986). *Collected Works*, vol. I: *Publications 1929–1936*, New York and Oxford: Oxford University Press.

Gödel, K. (1990). *Collected Works*, vol. II: *Publications 1938–1974*, ed. S. Feferman *et al.*, New York and Oxford: Oxford University Press.

Gödel, K. (1995). *Collected Works*, vol. III: *Unpublished Essays and Lectures*, ed. S. Feferman *et al.*, New York and Oxford: Oxford University Press.

Goldfarb, W. D. (1979). 'Logic in the Twenties: The Nature of the Quantifier', *The Journal of Symbolic Logic* 44: 351–68.

Henkin, L. (1949). 'The Completeness of the First-order Functional Calculus', *The Journal of Symbolic Logic* 14: 159–66.

Herken, R., (ed.) (1988). *The Universal Turing Machine*, Oxford: Oxford University Press.

Hilbert, D. (1899). *Grundlagen der Geometrie*, Leipzig: Teubner. Trans. 1971 L. Unger and P. Bernays, *Foundations of Geometry*, La Salle, IL: Open Court.

Hilbert, D. (1900). 'Mathematische Probleme. Vortrag, gehalten auf dem internationalen Mathematiker-Kongress zu Paris 1900', *Nachrichten von der Königlichen Gesellschaft der Wissenschaften zu Göttingen*, 253–97. Trans. 1902 M. W. Newson, 'Mathematical Problems. Lecture Delivered Before the International Congress of Mathematicians at Paris in 1900', *Bulletin of the American Mathematical Society* 8: 437–79. Repr. 1976 in F. Browder (ed.), *Mathematical Developments Arising from Hilbert Problems* (Proceedings of Symposia in Pure Mathematics 28:1), Providence: American Mathematical Society, 1–34.

Hilbert, D. (1926). 'Über das Unendliche', *Mathematische Annalen* 95: 161–90. Trans. S. Bauer-Mengelberg, 'On the Infinite' in van Heijenoort 1967, 367–92.

Hilbert, D. (1935). *Gesammelte Abhandlungen*, 3 vols., Berlin: Springer Verlag.

Hilbert, D. (1968). *Grundlagen der Geometrie*, 10th edn, Leipzig: Teubner.

Hilbert, D. and Ackermann, W. (1928). *Grundzüge der theoretischen Logik* (*Fundamentals of Theoretical Logic*), Berlin: Springer Verlag.

Hilbert, D. and Bernays, P. (1934). *Grundlagen der Mathematik* (*Foundations of Mathematics*), Berlin: Springer Verlag.

Hilbert, D. and Bernays, P. (1939). *Grundlagen der Mathematik*, vol. II, Berlin: Springer Verlag.

Hodges, A. (1983). *Alan Turing: The Enigma*. New York: Simon and Schuster.

Kleene, S. C. (1935). 'λ Theory of Positive Integers in Formal Logic', *American Journal of Mathematics* 57: 153–73.

Kleene, S. C. (1936a). 'λ-definability and Recursiveness', *Duke Mathematical Journal* 2: 340–53.

Kleene, S. C. (1936b). 'General Recursive Functions of Natural Numbers', *Mathematische Annalen* 112: 727–42.

Kleene, S. C. (1981). 'Origins of Recursive Function Theory', *Annals of the History of Computing* 3: 52–67.

Lindenbaum, A. and Tarski, A. (1926). 'Communication sur les recherches de la théorie des ensembles' ('Report on Research in the Theory of Sets'), *Comptes Rendus des séances de la Société des Sciences et des Lettres de Varsovie, Classe III, Sciences mathématiques et physiques* 19: 299–330.

Löwenheim, L. (1915). 'Über Möglichkeiten im Relativkalkül', *Mathematische Annalen* 76: 447–70. Trans. S. Bauer-Mengelberg, 'On Possibilities in the Calculus of Relatives' in van Heijenoort 1967, 228–51.

Moore, G. H. (1982). *Zermelo's Axiom of Choice, Its Origins, Development, and Influence*. New York: Springer Verlag.

Post, E. L. (1921). 'Introduction to a General Theory of Elementary Propositions', *American Journal of Mathematics* 43: 163–85. Repr. in van Heijenoort 1967, 265–283.

Reid, C. (1970). *Hilbert*, New York: Springer Verlag.

Richard, J. (1905). 'Les principes de Mathématiques et la problème des ensembles', *Revue générale des sciences pures et appliquées* 16. 541. Trans. 1967 J. van Heijenoost, 'The Principles of Mathematics and the Problem of Sets' in van Heijenoort (ed.) 1967, 142–4.

Rosser, J. B. (1936). 'Extensions of Some Theorems of Gödel and Church', *The Journal of Symbolic Logic* 1: 87–91. Repr. in Davis 1965, 230–5.

Russell, B. A. W. (1903). *The Principles of Mathematics*, London: George Allen and Unwin.

Russell, B. A. W. and Whitehead, A. (1910–13). *Principia Mathematica*, Cambridge: Cambridge University Press.

Shanker, S. G. (ed.) (1988). *Gödel's Theorem in Focus*, London: Croom Helm.

Sieg, W. (1988). 'Hilbert's program sixty years later', *The Bulletin of Symbolic Logic* 2: 338–48.

Sieg, W. (1997). 'Step by Recursive Step: Church's Analysis of Effective Calculability', *The Bulletin of Symbolic Logic* 3: 154–80.

Skolem, T. (1920). 'Logisch-kombinatorische Untersuchungen über die Erfüllbarkeit oder Beweisbarkeit mathematischer Sätze nebst einem Theorem über dichte Mengen', *Skrifter utgit av Videns-kapsselslapet i Kristiania, I. Matematisk-naturvidenskabelig klasse* 4: 1–36. Partial trans. S. Bauer-Mengelberg, 'Logico-combinatorial Investigations in the Satisfiability or Provability of Mathematical Propositions: A Simplified Proof of a Theorem by L. Löwenheim and Generalizations of the Theorem' in van Heijenoort 1967, 254–63.

Skolem, T. (1923a). 'Begründung der elementaren Arithmetik durch die rekurrierende Denkweise ohne Anwendung scheinbarer Veränderlichen mit unendlichem Ausdehnungsbereich', *Skrifter utgit av Videnskapsselskapet i Kristiana, I. Matematisk-naturvidenskabelig klasse* 6: 1–38. Trans. S. Bauer-Mengelberg, 'The Foundations of Elementary Arithmetic Established by Means of the Recursive Mode of Thought, Without the Use of Apparent Variables Ranging over Infinite Domains' in van Heijenoort 1967, 303–33.

Skolem, T. (1923b). 'Einige Bemerkungen zur axiomatischen Begründung der Mengenlehre', *Matematikerkongressen i Helsingfors 4–7 Juli 1922, Den femte skandinaviska matematikerkongressen,*

Redogörelse, Helsinki: Akademiska Bokhandlen, 217–32. Trans. S. Bauer-Mengelberg, 'Some Remarks on Axiomatized Set Theory' in van Heijenoort 1967, 291–301.

Skolem, T. (1933). 'Über die Unmöglichkeit einer vollständigen Charakterisierung der Zahlenreihe mittels eines endlichen Axiomensystems', *Norsk matematisk forenings skrifter* 2 (10): 73–82. Reprinted in Skolem 1970, 345–54.

Skolem, T. (1934). 'Über die Nicht-charakterisierbarkeit der Zahlenreihe mittels endlich oder abzählbar unendlich vieler Aussagen mit ausschliesslich Zahlenvariablen' ('On the Non-characterisability of the Number Sequence by Means of Finitely or Countably Infinitely Many Propositions Containing Only Variables for Numbers'), *Fundamenta Mathematicae* 23: 150–61. Reprinted 1970 in T. Skolem, *Selected Works in Logic*, Oslo: Universitetsforlaget, 355–66.

Skolem, T. (1970). *Selected Works in Logic*, ed. J. Fenstad, Oslo: Universitetsforlaget.

Tarski, A. (1933). *Pojecie prawdy w jezykach nauk dedukcyjnych*, Prace Towarzystwa Naukowego Warszawskiego, wydial III, no. 34. Trans. 1956 J. H. Woodger (ed.), 'The Concept of Truth in Formalized Languages' in A. Tarski, *Logic, Semantics, Metamathematics. Papers from 1923 to 1938*, Oxford: Clarendon Press. 2nd edn, 1983 ed. J. Corcoran, Indianapolis, IN: Hackett.

Turing, A. M. (1937). 'On Computable numbers, with an Application to the Entscheidungsproblem', *Proceedings of the London Mathematical Society* 2, 42: 230–65; correction, 43: 544–6. Reprinted in Davis 1965, 116–54.

van Heijenoort, J. (ed.) (1967). *From Frege to Gödel: A Source Book in Mathematical Logic, 1879–1931*, Cambridge, MA: Harvard University Press.

van Rootselaar, B. (1981). 'Zermelo, Ernst Riedrich Ferdinand', *Dictionary of Scientific Biography*, vol. XIV, 613–16. New York: Charles Scribner's.

Zermelo, E. (1904). 'Beweis, dass jede Menge wohlgeordnet werden kann (Aus einem an Herrn Hilbert gerichteten Briefe)', *Mathematische Annalen* 59: 514–16. Trans. S. Bauer-Mengelberg, 'Proof that Every Set Can Be Well-ordered', in van Heijenoort 1967, 139–41.

Zermelo, E. (1908). 'Untersuchungen über die Grundlagen der Mengenlehre. I' *Mathematische Annalen* 65: 261–81. Trans. S. Bauer-Mengelberg, 'Investigations in the Foundations of Set Theory, I' in van Heijenoort 1967, 199–215.

Zermelo, E. (1930). 'Über Grenzzahlen und Mengenbereiche: Neue Untersuchungen über die Grundlagen der Mengenlehre' ('On Limit Numbers and Set Domains: New Investigations Concerning the Foundations of Set Theory'), *Fundamenta Mathematicae* 16: 29–47.

CHAPTER 48 GENERAL RELATIVITY

Barbour, J. (1999). 'The Development of Machian Themes in the Twentieth Century' in J. Butterfield (ed.), *The Arguments of Time*, Oxford: Clarendon Press, 83-109.

Barbour, J. B. and Pfister, H. (eds.) (1995). *Mach's Principle; From Newton's Bucket to Quantum Gravity*, Boston-Basle-Berlin: Birkhäuser.

Bergmann, P. (1965). 'Physics and Geometry' in Y. Bar-Hillel, *Logic, Methodology and Philosophy of Science; Proceedings of the 1964 International Congress*, Amsterdam: North-Holland Publishers, 343–46.

Bergmann, P. (1980). Remarks in 'Open Discussion' following papers by S. Hawking and W. Unruh in H. Woolf (ed.), *Some Strangeness in the Proportion*, Reading, MA: Addison-Wesley Publishers, 156.

Earman, J. (1995). *Bangs, Crunches, Whimpers, and Shrieks: Singularities and Acausalities in Relativistic Spacetimes*, New York: Oxford University Press.

Eddington, A. S. (1930). 'On the Instability of the Einstein World', *Monthly Notices of the Royal Astronomical Society* 90: 668–78.

Einstein, A. (1916). *Die Grundlagen der allgemeinen Relativitätstheorie*, Leipzig: J. Barth; trans. 1923 W. Perrett and G. B. Jeffrey 'The Foundation of the General Theory of Relativity', in H. A. Lorentz, A. Einstein, H. Minkowski, and H. Weyl, *The Principle of Relativity*; repr. New York: Dover, 1952, 111–64.

Einstein, A. (1917). 'Kosmologische Betrachtungen zur allgemeinen Relativitätstheorie', *Sitzungsberichte der Preußischen Akademie der Wissenschaften. Math.-Phys. Kl.*; trans. 1952 W. Perrett and G. B. Jeffrey, 'Cosmological Considerations on the General Theory of Relativity', in H. A. Lorentz, A. Einstein, H. Minkowski, and H. Weyl, *The Principle of Relativity*, 1923; repr. New York: Dover, 1952, 175–88.

Einstein, A. (1918). 'Prinzipielles zur allgemeinen Relativitätstheorie', *Annalen der Physik* 55: 241–4.

Einstein, A. (1921). 'Geometrie und Erfahrung', *Sitzungsberichte der Preußischen Akademie der Wissenschaften. Math.-Phys. Kl.*; separately issued in expanded form and trans. 1923 W. Perrett and G. B. Jeffrey, 'Geometry and Experience' in *Sidelights on Relativity*, New York: E. P. Dutton, 27–56.

Einstein, A. (1949). 'Autobiographical Notes' in P. A. Schilpp (ed.), *Albert Einstein, Philosopher-Scientist*, Evanston, IL: Northwestern University Press, 1–95.

Einstein, A. (1952). 'Relativity and the Problem of Space', Appendix V, 135–57, in A. Einstein, *Relativity: The Special and General Theory*, 15th edn, New York: Crown Publishers, 1961.

Friedman, M. (1983). *Foundations of Space-Time Theories: Relativistic Physics and Philosophy of Science*, Princeton, NJ: Princeton University Press.

Hoffman, B. (1972). *Albert Einstein – Creator and Rebel* (written in collaboration with Helen Dukas), New York: Viking Press.

Holton, G. (1986). *The Advancement of Science, and its Burdens*, New York: Cambridge University Press.

Hubble, E. (1929). 'A Relation Between Distance and Radial Velocity Among Extra-galactic Nebulae', *Proceedings of the National Academy of Science (USA)* 15: 168–73.

Kretschmann, E. (1917). 'Über den physikalischen Sinn der Relativitätspostulate, A. Einstein's neue und seine ursprüngliche Relativitätstheorie', *Annalen der Physik* 53: 575–614.

Norton, J. D. (1989). 'How Einstein Found his Field Equations' in D. Howard and J. Stachel (eds.), *Einstein and the History of General Relativity*, Boston-Basle-Berlin: Birkhäuser, 101–59.

Norton, J. D. (1993). 'General Covariance and the Foundations of General Relativity: Eight Decades of Dispute', *Reports on Progress in Physics* 56: 791–858.

Pais, A. (1982). *'Subtle is the Lord': The Life and Science of Albert Einstein*, New York: Oxford University Press.

Reichenbach, H. (1928). *Philosophie der Raum-Zeit Lehre*, Berlin and Leipzig: de Gruyter; trans. *The Philosophy of Space and Time*, New York: Dover, 1957.

Ryckman, T. A. (1992). '(P)oint-(C)oincidence Thinking', *Studies in History and Philosophy of Science* 23: 471–97.

Ryckman, T. A. (2004). *The Reign of Relativity: Philosophy in Physics, 1915–25,* New York: Oxford University Press.

Smolin, L. (1992). 'Space and Time in the Quantum Universe' in A. Ashtekar and J. Stachel (eds.), *Conceptual Problems of Quantum Gravity*, Boston-Basle-Berlin: Birkhäuser, 228–88.

Sommerfeld, A. (1949). 'To Albert Einstein's Seventieth Birthday' in P. A. Schilpp (ed.), *Albert Einstein, Philosopher-Scientist*, Evanston, IL: Northwestern University Press, 99–105.

Stachel, J. (1986). 'What a Physicist Can Learn from the Discovery of General Relativity' in R. Ruffini (ed.), *Proceedings of the Fourth Marcel Grossmann Meeting on General Relativity*, Amsterdam: North Holland Publishers, 1857–62.

Stachel, J. (1989). 'Einstein's Search for General Covariance, 1912–1915' in D. Howard and J. Stachel (eds.), *Einstein and the History of General Relativity*, Boston-Basle-Berlin: Birkhäuser, 63–100. (Based on a paper circulating privately since 1980.)

Weinberg, S. (1989). 'The Cosmological Constant Problem', *Reviews of Modern Physics*: 61, 1–23.

Weyl, H. (1918). *Raum-Zeit-Materie*, Berlin: Springer Verlag. 4th edn 1921, trans. 1922 H. Brose, *Space-Time-Matter*, London: Methuen.

CHAPTER 49 SCIENTIFIC EXPLANATION

Bachelard, Gaston (1929). *Valeur inductive de la relativité (The Inductive Value of Relativity)*, Paris: J. Vrin.

Bachelard, Gaston (1933). *Les intuitions atomistiques: essai de classification (Atomistic Intuitions: A Classification)*, Paris: Vrin.

Bachelard, Gaston (1969). *Essai sur la connaissance approchée (Essay on the Approach to Knowledge)*, Paris: Vrin. Trans. in Jones (1991).

Bachelard, Gaston (1973). *Le Nouvel Esprit scientifique (The New Scientific Spirit)*, Paris: Presses Universitaires de France. Trans. in Jones (1991).

Berkeley, George (1901). *De Motu*, vol. III, §37, in A. C. Fraser (ed.), *Works*, Oxford: Oxford University Press.

Bridgman, P. W. (1927). *The Logic of Modern Physics*, New York: Macmillan.

Bridgman, P. W. (1936). *The Nature of Physical Theory*, Princeton, NJ: University Press.

Bridgman, P. W. (1955). *Reflections of a Physicist*, New York: Philosophical Library.

Brunschvicg, Léon (1905). *L'idéalisme contemporain (Contemporary idealism)*, Paris: Alcan.

Brunschvicg, Léon (1931). *De la connaissance de soi (On Self-consciousness)*, Paris: Alcan.

Campbell, N. R. (1920). *Physics: The Elements*, Cambridge: Cambridge University Press.

Campbell, N. R. (1921). *What is Science?* Cambridge: Cambridge University Press.

Carnap, R. (1928). *Der logische Aufbau der Welt*, Berlin: Weltkreis-Verlag. Trans. 1967 R. George, *The Logical Structure of the World*, Berkeley, CA: University of California Press.

Carnap, R. (1932). 'Überwindung der Metaphysik durch logische Analyse der Sprache', *Erkenntnis* 2: 219–41. Trans. 1959 A. Pap, 'The Elimination of Metaphysics Through the Logical Analysis of Language' in A. J. Ayer (ed.), *Logical Positivism*, Glencoe, IL: Free Press, 60–81.

Duhem, P. (1905–6). *Les origines de la statique. Les sources des théories physiques*, 2 vols., Paris: A. Hermann. Trans. 1991 G. H. Leneaux, V. N. Vagliente, and G. H. Wagener, *The Origins of Statics: the sources of physical theory*, Dordrecht: Kluwer.

Duhem, P. (1906). *La théorie physique. Son objet et sa structure*, Paris: Chevalier et Rivière. Trans. 1954 P. Wiener, *The Aim and Structure of Physical Theory*, Princeton, NJ: Princeton University Press.

Duhem, P. (1913–59). *Le système du monde. Histoire des doctrines cosmologiques de Platon à Copernic (The System of the World: A History of Cosmological Doctrines from Plato to Copernicus)*, 10 vols. Paris: A. Hermann.

Gale, George (1984). 'Science and the Philosophers', *Nature* 312: 491–5.

Hempel, C. G. and Oppenheim, Paul (1939). 'Studies in the Logic of Explanation', *Philosophy of Science* 15: 135–75.

Hesse, Mary (1966). *Models and Analogies in Science*, South Bend: Notre Dame Press.

Jones, M. M. (1991). *Gaston Bachelard, Subversive Humanist: Texts and Readings*, Madison: University of Wisconsin Press.

Leibniz, G. W. (1860). *Mathematische Schriften*, vol. VI, ed. C. I. Gerhardt, Halle.

Meyerson, E. (1908). *Identité et Réalité*, Paris: Alcan. Trans. 1930 K. Loewenberg, *Identity and Reality*, New York: Macmillan.

Meyerson, E. (1921). *De l'explication dans les sciences*, 2 vols. Paris: Payot. Trans. 1991 D. A. and M.-A. Sipfle, *Explanation in the Sciences*, Boston Studies in the Philosophy of Science 128, Dordrecht: Kluwer.

Meyerson, E. (1925). *La deduction rélativiste*, Paris: Payot. Trans. 1985 D. A. Sipfle and M.-A. Sipfle, *The Relativistie Deduction*, Boston Studies in the Philosophy of Science 83, Dordrecht: Reidel.

Meyerson, E. (1929). 'Explanation', *Encyclopedia Britannica*, 14th edn, 984–5.

Meyerson, E. (1931). *Du cheminement de la pensée* (*The Ways of Thought*), 3 vols. Paris: Alcan.

Neurath, Otto (1932). 'Protokolsätze', *Erkenntnis* 3: 204–14. Trans. 1959 'Protocol Sentences' in A. J. Ayer (ed.), *Logical Positivism*, Glencoe, IL: Free Press, 199–207.

Poincaré, H. (1889). *Leçons sur la théorie mathématique de la lumière* (*Lessons on the Mathematical Theory of Light*), Paris: G. Carré.

Poincaré, H. (1902a). 'La valeur objective de la science' (*The Objective Value of Science*), *Revue de métaphysique* 10: 265.

Poincaré, H. (1902b). *La Science et l'hypothèse,* Paris: Flammarion. Trans. 1905 W. J. G., *Science and Hypothesis*, London: Walter Scott Publishing Co. Repr. New York: Dover Publications, 1952.

Poincaré, H. (1904). *La Valeur de la science*, Paris: Flammarion. Trans. 1907 by G. B. Halstead, *The Value of Science*, London: Walter Scott.

Poincaré, H. (1908). *Science et méthode*, Paris: Flammarion. Trans. 1914 F. Maitland, *Science and Method*, London: Nelson.

Suppe, Frederick (1977). *The Structure of Scientific Theories*. 2nd edn, Urbana, IL: University of Illinois Press.

Taine, Hippolyte (1897). *De l'intelligence*. Paris: Hachette, vol. II. Trans. 1899 T. D. Haye, *On Intelligence*, New York: Holt.

Whitehead, A. N. and Russell, B. A. W. (1910–13). *Principia Mathematica*, Cambridge: Cambridge University Press.

CHAPTER 50 THE RISE OF PROBABILISTIC THINKING

van Brakel, J. (1985). 'The Possible Influence of the Discovery of Radio-active Decay on the Concept of Physical Probability', *Archive for History of Exact Sciences*, 31, 369–85.

Exner, F. (1919). *Vorlesungen über die physikalischen Grundlagen der Naturwissenschaften* (*Introduction to the Physical Foundations of the Natural Sciences*), Vienna: Franz Deuticke.

Feller, W. (1968). *An Introduction to Probability Theory and Its Applications*, vol. I, New York: Wiley.

de Finetti, B. (1931). 'Sul significato soggettivo della probabilità' ('On the Subjective Significance of Probability'), *Fundamenta Mathematicae*, vol. XVII, 298–329.

de Finetti, B. (1937). 'La Prévision: ses lois logiques, ses sources subjectives', *Annales de l'Institut Henri Poincaré*, 7, 1–68. Trans. 1964, 'Foresight: Its Logical Laws, Its Subjective Sources' in H. Kyburg and H. Smokler (eds.), *Studies in Subjective Probability*, New York: Wiley.

Heidelberger, M. (1987). 'Fechner's Indeterminism: From Freedom to Laws of Chance' in Krüger 1987, vol. I, 117–56.

Hilbert, D. (1899). *Grundlagen der Geometrie*, Leipzig: Teubner.

Howson, C. and Urbach, P. (1989). *Scientific Reasoning: The Bayesian Approach*, La Salle, IL: Open Court.

Jeffreys, H. (1939). *Theory of Probability*, Oxford: Oxford University Press.

Kolmogorov, A. (1933). *Grundbegriffe der Wahrscheinlichkeitsrechnung*, Berlin: Springer-Verlag. Trans. 1950 N. Morrison, *Foundations of the Theory of Probability*, New York: Chelsea.

von Kries, J. (1886). *Die Principien der Wahrscheinlichkeits-Rechnung* (*The Principles of Probability*), Freiburg: J. C. B. Mohr.

Krüger, L. *et al.* (1987). *The Probabilistic Revolution*, 2 vols., Cambridge, MA: MIT Press.

Maxwell, J. C. (1873). 'Does the Progress of Physical Science Tend to Give Any Advantage to the Opinion of Necessity (or Determinism) over that of the Contingency of Events and the Freedom of the Will' in L. Campbell and W. Garnett 1882, *The Life of James Clerk Maxwell*, London, 434–44.

von Mises, R. (1928). *Wahrscheinlichkeit, Statistik und Wahrheit*, Vienna: Springer-Verlag. Trans. 1957 J. Bernstein and R. G. Newton, *Probability, Statistics, and Truth*, New York: Dover.

von Plato, J. (1994). *Creating Modern Probability: Its Mathematics, Physics and Philosophy in Historical Perspective*, Cambridge: Cambridge University Press.

Poincaré, H. (1912). *Calcul des probabilités* (*The Probability Calculus*), 2nd edn, Paris: Gauthier Villars.

Ramsey, F. (1931). '*The Foundations of Mathematics and other Logical Essays*, ed. R. Braithwaite, London: Kegan Paul.

Reichenbach, H. (1915). *Der Begriff der Wahrscheinlichkeit für die mathematische Darstellung der Wirklichkeit* (*The Concept of Probability for the Mathematical Representation of Reality*), Leipzig: Barth.

Reichenbach, H. (1935). *Wahrscheinlichkeitslehre*, Leiden: Sijthoff's. Trans. 1949 E. Hutton and M. Reichenbach, *The Theory of Probability*, Berkeley, CA: University of California Press.

CHAPTER 51 VITALISM AND EMERGENCE

Alexander, S. (1920). *Space, Time, and Deity*, 2 vols., London: Macmillan.

Asimov, I. (1964). *A Short History of Biology*, Garden City, NY: The Natural History Press.

Bakhtin, M. (1926). 'Contemporary Vitalism', *Chelovek I Priroda* (*Man and Nature*), vols. I and II (published under the name I. Kanaev). Trans. 1992 in F. Burwick and P. Douglass (eds.), *The Crisis in Modernism*, Cambridge: Cambridge University Press, 1992, 76–97.

Bechtel, W. and Richardson, R. C. (1993). *Discovering Complexity: Decomposition and Localization as Strategies in Scientific Research*, Princeton, NJ: Princeton University Press.

Bechtel, W. and Richardson, R. C. (1998). 'Vitalism' in *Routledge Encyclopedia of Philosophy*, vol. IX, ed. E. Craig, London: Routledge, 639–43.

Beckner, M. (1972). 'Vitalism' in *The Encyclopedia of Philosophy*, vol. VIII, ed. P. Edwards, New York: Macmillan, 253–56.

Beckermann, A., Flohr, H., and Kim, J. (eds.) (1992). *Emergence or Reduction? Essays on the Prospects of Nonreductive Physicalism*, Berlin: Walter de Gruyter.

Beckerman, A. (1992). 'Supervenience, Emergence, and Reduction' in A. Beckermann *et al.*, Berlin: Walter de Gruyter, 94–118.

Bergson, H. (1907). *L'Evolution créatrice*, Paris: Alcan. Trans. 1911 A. Mitchell, *Creative Evolution*, New York: Holt.

Blitz, D. (1992). *Emergent Evolution: Qualitative Novelty and the Levels of Reality*, Dordrecht: Kluwer.

Broad, C. D. (1925). *The Mind and Its Place in Nature*, London: Kegan Paul.

Burwick, F. and Douglass, P. (eds.) (1992). *The Crisis in Modernism*, Cambridge: Cambridge University Press.

Burwick, F. and Douglass, P. (1922). 'Introduction' in F. Burwick and P. Douglass (eds.) (1992), 1–14.

Driesch, H. (1905). *Der Vitalismus als Geshichte und als Lehre*, Leipzig. Trans. 1914 C. K. Ogden, *The History and Theory of Vitalism*, London: Macmillan.

Driesch, H. (1908). *The Science and Philosophy of the Organism*, London: Adams and Charles Black. Trans. 1909 *Philosophie des Organischen*, 2 vols. Leipzig.

Feldman, F. (1995). 'Life', 'Vitalism' in J. Kim and E. Sosa (eds.), *A Companion to Metaphysics*, Oxford: Blackwell, 272–4, 508–9.

Haldane, J. S. (1923). *Mechanism, Life, and Personality*, New York: Dutton.

Kamenka, E. (1972). 'Communism, Philosophy under' in P. Edwards (ed.), *Encyclopedia of Philosophy*, New York: Macmillan.

Kim, J. (1992). 'Downward Causation in Emergence and Nonreductive Physicalism' in A. Beckermann, *et al.* (eds.) (1992), 119–38.

Lehan, R. (1992). 'Bergson and the Discourse of the Moderns' in F. Burwick and P. Douglass (eds.) (1992), 277–305.

Lewes, G. H. (1875). *Problems of Life and Mind*, vol. II, London: Kegan Paul.

Lovejoy, A. O. (1911). 'The Import of Vitalism', *Science* 34: 75–80.

Lovejoy, A. O. (1912). 'The Meaning of Driesch and the Meaning of Vitalism' *Science* 36: 672–5.

Lovejoy, A. O. (1926). 'The Meaning of "Emergence" and its Modes' in *Proceedings of the Sixth International Congress of Philosophy*, New York, 20–33.

McLaughlin, B. P. (1992). 'The Rise and Fall of British Emergentism' in A. Beckermann *et al.* (eds.) (1992), 49–93.

McLaughlin, B. P. (1992). 'Epiphenomenalism' in S. Guttenplan (ed.), *A Companion to the Philosophy of Mind*, Oxford: Blackwell, 277–88.

McLaughlin, B. P. (1997). 'Emergence and Supervenience', *Intellectica* 25: 25–43.

McLaughlin, B. P. (1999). 'Emergentism' in R. A. Wilson and F. C. Keil, *The MIT Encyclopedia of the Cognitive Sciences*, Cambridge, MA: MIT, 267–8.

Mill, J. S. (1843). *A System of Logic*, London: Longmans, Green. 8th edn 1872.

Morgan, C. Lloyd (1912). *Instinct and Experience*, London: Methuen.

Morgan, C. Lloyd (1923). *Emergent Evolution*, London: Williams and Norgate.

Morris, C. R. (1926). 'The Notion of Emergence', *Proceedings of the Aristotelian Society*, suppl. vol. VI, 49–55.

Nagel, E. (1951). 'Mechanist Biology and Organismic Biology', *Philosophy and Phenomenological Research* 2: 327–38.

Nagel, E. (1961). *The Structure of Science*, New York: Harcourt, Brace, and World.

Pappas, G. S. (1995). 'Mechanism' in J. Kim and E. Sosa (eds.), *A Companion to Metaphysics*, Oxford: Blackwell, 304–5.

Passmore, J. (1957). *A Hundred Years of Philosophy*, London: Duckworth.

Pepper, S. (1926). 'Emergence', *Journal of Philosophy* 3: 241–5.

Riddel, J. N. (1992). 'Bergson and the discourse of the moderns' in F. Burwick and P. Douglass (eds.) (1992), 330–67.

Rousseau, G. (1992). 'The Perceptual Crises of Modernism and the Traditions of Enlightenment Vitalism: With a Note on Mikhail Bakhtin' in F. Burwick and P. Douglass (1992), 15–75.

Smuts, J. C. (1926). *Holism and Evolution*, London: Macmillan.

Stace, W. T. (1939). 'Novelty, Indeterminism, and Emergence', *Philosophical Review* 48: 295–310.

Stephan, A. (1992). 'Emergence – A Systematic View of its Historical Facets' in A. Beckermann *et al.* (eds.) (1992), 25–48.

Wolsky, M. I. and Wolsky, A. A. (1992): 'Bergson's Vitalism in the Light of Modern Biology' in F. Burwick and P. Douglass (1992), 153–70.

CHAPTER 52 BEHAVIOURISM AND PSYCHOLOGY

Amundson, R. (1983). 'E. C. Tolman and the Intervening Variable: A Study in the Epistemological History of Psychology', *Philosophy of Science*, 50: 268–82.

Amundson, R. and Smith, L. D. (1984). 'Clark Hull, Robert Cummins, and Functional Analysis', *Philosophy of Science*, 51: 657–66.

Angell, J. R. (1913). 'Behavior as a Category of Psychology', *Psychological Review* 20: 255–70.

Bergmann, G. and Spence, K. W. (1941). 'Operationism and Theory in Psychology', *Psychological Review* 48: 1–14. Reprinted 1960 in K. W. Spence, *Behavior Theory and Learning: Selected Papers*, Englewood Cliffs, NJ: Prentice-Hall, 3–16.

Bridgman, P. W. (1927). *Logic of Modern Physics*, New York: Macmillan.

Carnap, R. (1932). 'Psychologie in physikalischer Sprache', *Erkenntnis* 3: 107–42. Trans. 1959 G. Schick, 'Psychology in Physical Language', in A. J. Ayer (ed.), *Logical Positivism*, New York: Free Press, 165–97.

Carnap, R. (1935). *Philosophy and Logical Syntax*, London: Kegan Paul.

De Laguna, G. A. (1916). 'Sensation and Perception', *Journal of Philosophy, Psychology and Scientific Methods* 13: 533–47, 617–30.

De Laguna, G. A. (1918). 'Dualism in Animal Psychology', *Journal of Philosophy, Psychology and Scientific Methods* 15: 617–27.

Dewey, J. (1896). 'The Reflex Arc Concept in Psychology', *Psychological Review* 3: 357–70.

Dewey, J. (1911). 'Brief Studies in Realism, I', *Journal of Philosophy, Psychology and Scientific Methods* 8: 393–400.

Dewey, J. (1914). 'Psychological Doctrine and Philosophical Teaching', *Journal of Philosophy, Psychology and Scientific Methods* 11: 505–11.

Dewey, J. (1925). *Experience and Nature*, Chicago: Open Court.

Dewey, J., Hook, S., and Nagel, E. (1945). 'Are Naturalists Materialists?', *Journal of Philosophy* 42: 515–30.

Feigl, H. (1951). 'Principles and Problems of Theory Construction in Psychology', in W. Dennis, R. Leeper, H. F. Harlow, J. J. Gibson, D. Krech, D. M. Rioch, W. S. McCulloch, and H. Feigl, *Current Trends in Psychological Theory*, Pittsburgh: University of Pittsburgh Press, 179–213.

Ferster, C. B. and Skinner, B. F. (1957). *Schedules of Reinforcement*, New York: Appleton-Century-Crofts.

Harrell, W. and Harrison, R. (1938). 'Rise and Fall of Behaviorism', *Journal of General Psychology* 18: 367–421.

Heidbreder, E. (1933). *Seven Psychologies*, New York: Century.

Hempel, C. G. (1935). 'Analyse logique de la psychologie', *Revue de synthèse* 10: 27–42. Trans. 1949 W. Sellars, 'Logical Analysis of Psychology' in H. Feigl and W. Sellars (eds.), *Readings in Philosophical Analysis*, New York: Appleton-Century-Crofts, 373–84.

Holt, E. B. (1915). 'Response and Cognition', *Journal of Philosophy, Psychology and Scientific Methods* 12: 365–73, 393–409. Repr. 1915 in E. B. Holt, *The Freudian Wish and Its Place in Ethics*, New York: Holt, 153–208.

Holt, E. B. *et al.* (1912). *The New Realism: Cooperative Studies in Philosophy*, New York: Macmillan.

Hull, C. L. (1930). 'Simple Trial-and-Error Learning: A Study in Psychological Theory', *Psychological Review* 37: 241–56.

Hull, C. L. (1937). 'Mind, Mechanism, and Adaptive Behavior', *Psychological Review* 44: 1–32.

Hull, C. L. (1943). *Principles of Behavior: An Introduction to Behavior Theory*, New York: Appleton-Century.

Hull, C. L. (1952). *A Behavior System: An Introduction to Behavior Theory Concerning the Individual Organism*, New Haven: Yale University Press.

Hull, C. L. (1984). *Mechanisms of Adaptive Behavior: Clark L. Hull's Theoretical Papers, With Commentary* in A. Amsel and M. E. Rashotte (eds.), New York: Columbia University Press.

Jennings, H. S. (1906). *Behavior of the Lower Organisms*, New York: Macmillan.

Koch, S. (1954). 'Clark L. Hull' in A. T. Poffenberger (ed.), *Modern Learning Theory*, New York: Appleton-Century-Crofts, 1–176.

Loeb, J. (1900). *Comparative Physiology of the Brain and Comparative Psychology*, New York: G. P. Putnam's Sons.

MacCorquodale, K. and Meehl, P. E. (1948). 'On a Distinction between Hypothetical Constructs and Intervening Variables', *Psychological Review* 55: 95–107. Repr. 1953, 'Hypothetical Constructs and Intervening Variables' in H. Feigl and M. Brodbeck, *Readings in the Philosophy of Science*, New York: Appleton-Century-Crofts, 596–611.

Mach, E. (1912). *Mechanik in ihrer Entwicklung historisch-kritisch dargestellt*, 7th edn, Leipzig: Brockhaus. Trans. 1919 T. J. McCormack, *Science of Mechanics: A Critical and Historical Account of Its Development*, 4th edn, Chicago: Open Court.

McDougall, W. (1905). *Physiological Psychology*, London: Dent.

McDougall, W. (1911). *Body and Mind: A History and a Defense of Animism*, New York: Macmillan.

McDougall, W. (1912). *Psychology: The Study of Behavior*, New York: Holt.

O'Neil, W. M. (1995). 'American Behaviorism: A Historical and Critical Analysis', *Theory & Psychology* 5: 285–305.

Pepper, S. C. (1923). 'Misconceptions Regarding Behaviorism', *The Journal of Philosophy* 20: 242–4.

Perry, R. B. (1909). 'The Mind Within and the Mind Without', *Journal of Philosophy, Psychology and Scientific Methods* 6: 169–75.

Perry, R. B. (1912). *Present Philosophical Tendencies*, London: Longmans, Green.

Perry, R. B. (1918). 'Docility and Purposiveness', *Psychological Review* 25: 1–20.

Perry, R. B. (1921a). 'A Behavioristic View of Purpose', *Journal of Philosophy* 18: 85–105.

Perry, R. B. (1921b). 'The Cognitive Interest and its Refinements', *Journal of Philosophy* 18: 365–75.

Pillsbury, W. B. (1911). *Essentials of Psychology*, New York: Macmillan.

Poincaré, H. (1902). *Science et l'hypothèse*, Paris: Flammarion. Trans. 1905 G. B. Halsted, *Science and Hypothesis*, New York: Science Press.

Quine, W. V. O. (1985). *Time of My Life: An Autobiography*, Cambridge, MA: MIT Press.

Roback, A. A. (1923). *Behaviorism and Psychology*, Cambridge, MA: University Book Store.

Russell, B. (1921). *Analysis of Mind*, London: George Allen and Unwin.

Russell, B. (1927). *Philosophy*, New York: Norton.

Santayana, G. (1905). *Life of Reason: Or the Phases of Human Progress*, New York: Charles Scribner's Sons.

Santayana, G. (1920). 'Three Proofs of Realism' in *Essays in Critical Realism: A Co-Operative Study of the Problem of Knowledge*, London: Macmillan, 163–84.

Sellars, R. W. (1916). *Critical Realism: A Study of the Nature and Conditions of Knowledge*, New York: Rand, McNally.

Sellars, R. W. (1922). *Evolutionary Naturalism*, Chicago: Open Court.

Singer, E. A. (1911). 'Mind as an Observable Object', *Journal of Philosophy, Psychology and Scientific Methods* 8: 180–6.

Skinner, B. F. (1938). *Behavior of Organisms: An Experimental Analysis*, New York: Appleton-Century.

Skinner, B. F. (1945). 'Operational Analysis of Psychological Terms', *Psychological Review* 52: 270–7, 291–4. Repr. 1972 in B. F. Skinner, *Cumulative Record: A Selection of Papers*, 3rd edn, New York: Appleton-Century-Crofts, 370–84.

Skinner, B. F. (1976). *Particulars of My Life*, New York: Knopf.

Smith, L. D. (1986). *Behaviorism and Logical Positivism: A Reassessment of the Alliance*, Stanford: Stanford University Press.

Spence, K. W. (1944). 'The Nature of Theory Construction in Contemporary Psychology', *Psychological Review* 51: 47–68. Repr. 1960 in K. W. Spence, *Behavior Theory and Learning: Selected Papers*, Englewood Cliffs, NJ: Prentice-Hall, 17–38.

Thorndike, E. L. (1898). *Animal Intelligence: An Experimental Study of the Associative Process in Animals*. Psychological Review Monograph Supplement no. 8, New York: Macmillan.

Titchener, E. B. (1914). 'On "Psychology As the Behaviorist Views It"', *Proceedings of the American Philosophical Society* 53: 1–17.

Tolman, E. C. (1926). 'A Behavioristic Theory of Ideas', *Psychological Review* 33: 352–69.

Tolman, E. C. (1927). 'A Behaviorist's Definition of Consciousness', *Psychological Review* 34: 433–9.

Tolman, E. C. (1932). *Purposive Behavior in Animals and Men*, New York: Century.

Tolman, E. C. (1938). 'Determiners of Behavior at a Choice Point', *Psychological Review* 45: 1–41.

Tolman, E. C. (1949). 'Discussion: Interrelationships between Perception and Personality', *Journal of Personality* 18: 48–50.

Tolman, E. C. (1951a). *Collected Papers in Psychology*, Berkeley: University of California Press.

Tolman, E. C. (1951b). 'A Psychological Model' in T. Parsons and E. A. Shils (eds.), *Toward a General Theory of Action*, Cambridge, MA: Harvard University Press, 279–361.

Warren, H. C. (1914). *Human Psychology*, New York: Houghton Mifflin.

Washburn, M. F. (1908). *The Animal Mind: A Text-book of Comparative Psychology*, New York: Macmillan.

Watson, J. B. (1913a). 'Image and Affection in Behavior', *Journal of Philosophy, Psychology and Scientific Methods* 10: 421–8.

Watson, J. B. (1913b). 'Psychology as the Behaviorist Views It', *Psychological Review* 20: 158–77.

Watson, J. B. (1914). *Behavior: An Introduction to Comparative Psychology*, New York: Holt.

Watson, J. B. (1919). *Psychology from the Standpoint of a Behaviorist*, Philadelphia: Lippincott.

Watson, J. B. (1924). *Behaviorism*, New York: People's Institute Publishing Co.

Williams, K. A. (1931). 'Five Behaviorisms', *Americal Journal of Psychology* 43: 337–60.

Woodbridge, F. J. E. (1909). 'Consciousness, the Sense Organs, and the Nervous System', *Journal of Philosophy, Psychology and Scientific Methods* 6: 449–55.

Woodbridge, F. J. E. (1913). 'Belief in Sensations', *Journal of Philosophy, Psychology and Scientific Methods* 10: 599–608.

Woodbridge, F. J. E. (1921). 'Mind Discerned', *The Journal of Philosophy* 18: 337–47.

Woodbridge, F. J. E. (1925). 'Behavior', *The Journal of Philosophy* 22: 402–11.

Woodworth, R. S. (1948). *Contemporary Schools of Psychology*, rev. edn, New York: Ronald Press.

Yerkes, R. M. (1907). *The Dancing Mouse: A Study in Animal Behavior*, New York: Macmillan.

Yerkes, R. M. (1917). 'Behaviorism and Genetic Psychology', *Journal of Philosophy, Psychology and Scientific Methods* 14: 154–60.

CHAPTER 53 GESTALT PSYCHOLOGY

Ash, M. G. (1995). *Gestalt Psychology in German Culture, 1890–1967: Holism and the Quest for Objectivity*, Cambridge: Cambridge University Press.

Ellis, W. D. (ed.) (1938). *A Sourcebook of Gestalt Psychology*, London: Routledge.

Harrington, A. (1996). *Reenchanted science: Holism in German culture from Wilhelm II to Hitler*. Princeton, NJ: Princeton University Press.

Henle, M. (ed.) (1961). *Documents of Gestalt Psychology*, Berkeley: University of California Press.

Hochberg, J. (1974). 'Organization and the Gestalt tradition' in E. C. Carterette and M. P. Friedman (eds.), *Handbook of Perception, vol I: Historical and Philosophical Roots of Perception*. New York: Academic, 180–211.

James, W. (1890). *The Principles of Psychology*, New York: Henry Holt and Co.

Koffka, K. (1922). 'Perception: An Introduction to *Gestalt-theorie*', *Psychological Bulletin* 19: 531–85. Available at: http://psychclassics.yorku.ca/Koffka/Perception/perception.htm.

Koffka, K. (1935). *Principles of Gestalt Psychology*, New York: Harcourt, Brace, and World.

Köhler, W. (1913). 'Über unbemerkte Empfindungen und Urteilstäuschungen', *Zeitschrift für Psychologie* 66: 51–80.

Köhler, W. (1927). *Intelligenzprüfungen an Menschenaffen*. Trans. 1938 *The mentality of apes*, New York: Liveright.

Köhler, W. (1947). *Gestalt Psychology: An Introduction to New Concepts in Modern Psychology*, New York: Liveright.

Köhler, W. (1959). 'Gestalt psychology today', *American Psychologist* 14: 727–34. Repr. 1978 in E. R. Hilgard (ed.), *American Psychology in Historical Perspective: Addresses of the Presidents of the American Psychological Association*, Washington, DC: American Psychological Association, 251–63.

Köhler, W. (1967 [1971]). 'Gestalt Psychology', *Psychologische Forschung*, 31, xviii–xxx. Reprinted in Köhler 1971, 108–22.

Köhler, W. (1971). *The Selected Papers of Wolfgang Köhler*, New York: Liveright.

Leahey, T. H. (2003). *A History of Psychology; Main Currents in Psychological Thought*, 56th edn, Upper Saddle River, NJ: Prentice-Hall.

Lewin, K. (1936). *Principles of Topological Psychology*, New York: McGraw-Hill.

Smith, B. (ed.) (1988). *Foundations of Gestalt Psychology*, Munich: Philosophia.

Sokal, M. (1984). 'The Gestalt Psychologists in behaviourist America', *American Historical Review*, 89, 1240–63.

Wertheimer, M. (1912). 'Experimentelle Studien über das Sehen von Bewegung' ('Experimental Studies on the Seeing of Movement'), *Zeitschrift für Psychologie*, 161–265. Abbreviated translation published in T. Shipley (ed.), *Classics in Psychology*, New York: Philosophical Library, 1032–89.

Wertheimer, M. (1923). 'Untersuchungen zur Lehre von der Gestalt II' ('Laws of Organisation in Perceptual Forms') *Psychologische Forschung* 4, 301–50. Translation published in Ellis, 1938, 71–88. Available at: http://psychclassics.yorku.ca/Wertheimer/Forms/forms.htm.

Wertheimer, M. (1945). *Productive Thinking*, New York: Harper and Row.

CHAPTER 54 WITTGENSTEIN'S CONCEPTION OF MIND

Anscombe, G. E. M. (1971). *An Introduction to Wittgenstein's Tractatus*, London: Hutchinson.

Budd, M. (1989). *Wittgenstein's Philosophy of Psychology*, London: Routledge.

Cavell, S. (1979). *The Claim of Reason: Wittgenstein, Skepticism, Morality and Tragedy*, Oxford: Oxford University Press.

Child, W. (1996). 'Solipsism and First Person/Third Person Asymmetries', *European Journal of Philosophy* 4, no. 2: 137–54.

Hacker, P. M. S. (1986). *Insight and Illusion*, Oxford: Clarendon Press.

Hacker, P. M. S. (1990). *Wittgenstein: Meaning and Mind*, vol. III, Oxford: Blackwell.

Hertzberg, L. (1994). ' "The Kind of Certainty is the Kind of Language Game" ' in *The Limits of Experience, Acta Philosophica Fennica*, vol. 56.

Jacquette, D. (1998). *Wittgenstein's Thought in Transition*, Indianapolis, IN: Purdue University Press.

Johnston, P. (1993). *Wittgenstein: Rethinking the Inner*, London: Routledge.

Kenny, A. (1984). 'Wittgenstein's Early Philosophy of Mind' in *The Legacy of Wittgenstein*, Oxford: Blackwell: 1–9.

McDowell, J. H. (1982). 'Criteria, Defeasibility and Knowledge', *Proceedings of the British Academy* 68: 455–80.

McDowell, J. H. (1998). 'Intentionality and Interiority in Wittgenstein' in *Mind, Value and Reality*, Cambridge, MA: Harvard University Press.

McGinn, M. E. (1997). *Wittgenstein and the Philosophical Investigations*, London: Routledge.

Mulhall, S. (1990). *On Being in the World*, London: Routledge.

O'Brien, L. F. (1996). 'Solipsism and Self-Reference', *European Journal of Philosophy* 4, no. 2: 175–94.

Pears, D. F. (1987). *The False Prison*, 2 vols. Oxford: Oxford University Press.

Pears, D. F. (1996). 'The Originality of Wittgenstein's Investigation of Solipsism', *European Journal of Philosophy* 4, no. 2: 124–36.

Schulte, J. (1993). *Experience and Expression: Wittgenstein's Philosophy of Psychology*, Oxford: Oxford University Press.

Stern, D. G. (1995). *Wittgenstein on Mind and Language*, Oxford: Oxford University Press.

Sullivan, P. M. (1996). 'The "Truth" in Solipsism, and Wittgenstein's Rejection of the A Priori', *European Journal of Philosophy* 4, no. 2: 195–219.

Wittgenstein, L. (1921). 'Logische-philosophische Abhandlung', *Annalen der Naturphilosophie*. Trans. 1922 C. K. Ogden, *Tractatus Logico-Philosophicus*, London: Routledge; revised trans. 1961 tr. D. F. Pears and B. F. McGuiness, London: Routledge.

Wittgenstein, L. (1953). *Philosophische Untersuchungen*, ed. G. E. M. Anscombe and R. Rhees, trans. G. E. M. Anscombe, *Philosophical Investigations*, Oxford: Blackwell.

Wittgenstein, L. (1958). *The Blue and Brown Books* (dictated 1933–4), Oxford: Blackwell.

Wittgenstein, L. (1968). 'Wittgenstein's Notes for Lectures on "Private Experience" and "Sense Data" ' (notes made 1936), ed. R. Rhees, *The Philosophical Review* 77, 275–320. Reprinted in Wittgenstein 1993a: 202–88.

Wittgenstein, L. (1974). *Philosophische Grammatik* (notes made 1932–4), ed. R. Rhees, trans. A. J. P. Kenny, *Philosophical Grammar*, Oxford: Blackwell.

Wittgenstein, L. (1975). *Philosophische Bemerkungen* (notes made 1929–30), ed. R. Rhees, trans. R. Hargreaves and R. White, *Philosophical Remarks*, Oxford: Blackwell.

Wittgenstein, L. (1978). *Bemerkungen zu den Grundlagen der Mathematik* (notes made 1937–44), ed. G. H. von Wright, R. Rhees, and G. E. M. Anscombe, trans. G. E. M. Anscombe, *Remarks on the Foundations of Mathematics*, Oxford: Blackwell.

Wittgenstein, L. (1979). *Notebooks 1914–1916*, ed. G. E. M. Anscombe and G. H. von Wright, trans. G. E. M. Anscombe, Oxford: Blackwell.

Wittgenstein, L. (1984). 'The Language of Sense Data and Private Experience', *Philosophical Investigations* 7, 2–45 and 101–40. Repr. in Wittgenstein (1993a), 290–367.

Wittgenstein, L. (1993a). *Philosophical Occasions* (reprinted versions of Wittgenstein's shorter published works), ed. James Klagge and Alfred Nordmann, Indianapolis, IN: Hackett.

Wittgenstein, L. (1993b). 'Notes for the Philosophical Lecture', ed. D. Stern, in Wittgenstein 1993a, 447–58.

Wright, C. (1989). 'Wittgenstein's Later Philosophy of Mind: Sensation, Privacy, and Intention', *The Journal of Philosophy* 86.

CHAPTER 55 THE METHODOLOGY OF THE SOCIAL SCIENCES

Bell, D. (1990). *Husserl*, London: Routledge.

Cartwright, N., Cat, J., Fleck, B., and Uebel, T. (1995). *Between Science and Politics: The Philosophy of Otto Neurath*, Cambridge: Cambridge University Press.

Collingwood, R. G. (1940). *An Essay on Metaphysics*, Oxford: Oxford University Press.

Collingwood. R. G. (1946). *The Idea of History*, Oxford: Oxford University Press.

Cook, G. A. (1993). *George Herbert Mead: The Making of a Social Pragmatist*, Urbana, IL: University of Illinois Press.

Dewey, J. (1927). *The Public and Its Problems*, New York: Henry Holt. Repr. 1984 in J. A. Boydston (ed.), *John Dewey: The Later Works*, vol. II, Carbondale: Southern Illinois University Press.

Dewey, J. (1935). *Liberalism and Social Action*, New York: Henry Holt. Repr. 1987 in J. A. Boydston (ed.) *John Dewey: The Later Works*, vol. XI, Carbondale: Southern Illinois University Press.

Dewey, J. (1938). *Logic: The Theory of Inquiry*, New York: Henry Holt. Repr. 1988 in J. A. Boydston (ed.) *John Dewey: The Later Works*, vol. XII, Carbondale: Southern Illinois University Press.

Dreyfus, Hubert (1991). *Being-in-the-World*, Cambridge, MA: MIT Press.

Dussen, W. J. van der (1981). *History as a Science: The Philosophy of R.G. Collingwood*, Oxford: Oxford University Press.

Factor, R. and Turner, S. (1984). *Max Weber and the Dispute Over Reason and Value*, London: Routledge, 1984.

Habermas, J. (1967). 'Zur Logik der Sozialwissenschaften', *Philosophisches Rundschau* 5. Trans. 1988 S. Nicholson and J. Stark, *On the Logic of The Social Sciences*. Cambridge, MA: Polity Press/MIT Press.

Habermas, J. (1968). *Erkenntnis und Interesse*, Frankfurt: Suhrkamp. Trans. 1971 J. Shapiro, *Knowledge and Human Interest*, Boston: Beacon Press.

Heidegger, M. (1927). *Sein und Zeit*, Tübingen: Max Niemayer Verlag. Trans. 1962 J. Macquarrie and E. Robinson, *Being and Time*, New York: Harper and Row.

Held, D. (1984). *Introduction to Critical Theory*, Berkeley: University of California Press.

Horkheimer, M. (1931). 'Die gegenwärtige Lage der Sozialphilosophie und die Aufgaben eines Instituts für Sozialforschung', *Frankfurter Universitätsreden* 27, 1–26. Trans. 1993 G. F. Hunter, M. Kramer, and J. Torpey, *Between Philosophy and Social Science*, Cambridge MA: MIT Press, 1–14.

Horkheimer, M. (1937). 'Traditionelle und kritische Theorie', *Zeitschrift für Sozialforschung* 6: 2, 245–83. Trans. 1982 M. O'Connell, *Critical Theory*, New York: Continuum, 188–244.

Horkheimer, M. and Adorno, T. W. (1944). *Dialektik der Aufklärung (The Dialectic of Enlightenment)*, Amsterdam: Quierdo. Trans. 1969 J. Cumming, New York: Continuum.

Husserl, E. (1936/1954). *Krisis der europäischen Wissenschaften und die transzendentale Phänomenologie, Husserliana*, vol. VI. Trans. 1970 David Carr, *The Crisis of the European Sciences and Transcendental Phenomenology*, Evanston: Northwestern University Press.

Joas, H. (1980). *Praktische Intersubjektivität: Die Entwicklung des Werkes von George Herbert Mead*, Frankfurt: Suhrkamp. Trans. 1985 R. Meyer, *George Herbert Mead: A Contemporary Reexamination of his Thought*, Cambridge, MA: MIT Press.

Mead, G. H. (1934). *Mind, Self and Society*, Chicago: University of Chicago Press.

Mink, L. (1969). *Mind, History and Dialectic*, Bloomington, IN: Indiana University Press.

Natanson, M. (1986). *Anonymity: A Study in the Philosophy of Alfred Schütz*, Bloomington: Indiana University Press.

Neurath, O. (1910). 'Zur Theorie der Sozialwissenschaften', *Jahrbuch für Gesetzgebung, Verwaltung und Volkswirtschaft im Deutschen Reich* 34, 37–67. Repr. 1981, ed. R. Haller and H. Rütte, *Gesammelte philosophische und methodologische Schriften*, Vienna: Hölder, Pichler, Tempsky, 23–46.

Neurath, O. (1913–46). *Philosophical Papers 1913–1946*. Trans. and ed. 1983 R. Cohen and M. Neurath, Dordrecht: Reidel.

Neurath, O. (1932). 'Protocolsätze', *Erkenntnes* 3: 204–14. Transl. in Neurath (1913–46).

Neurath, O. (1944). *Foundations of the Social Sciences*, International Encyclopedia of Unified Science, vol. II, no. 1, Chicago: University of Chicago Press.

Rouse, Joseph (1988). *Knowledge and Power*, Ithaca: Cornell University Press.

Ryan, A. (1996). *John Dewey and the High Tide of American Liberalism*, New York: Norton.

Schütz, A. (1932). *Der sinnhafte Aufbau der sozialen Welt*, Vienna: Springer-Verlag. Trans. 1967 G. Walsh and F. Lehnert, *The Phenomenology of the Social World*, Evanston: Northwestern University Press.

Schütz, A. (1964). *Collected Papers*, vol. II, The Hague: Njihoff.

Spiegelberg, Herbert. (1960). *The Phenomenological Movement: An Historical Introduction*, *Phenomenologica 5/6*, vols. I and II, The Hague: Njihoff.

Uebel, T. (1992). *Overcoming Logical Positivism from Within: The Emergence of Neurath's Naturalism in the Vienna Circle's Protocol Sentence Debate*, Amsterdam: Rodopi.

Wagner, H. (1983). *Alfred Schütz: An Intellectual Biography*, Chicago: University of Chicago Press.

Weber, Max (1921). *Gesammelte politische Schriften*. Munich: Drei Masken Verlag. Ed. H. H. Gerth and C. W. Mills, 1946 *From Max Weber*, Oxford: Oxford University Press.

Weber, Max (1922a). *Gesammelte Aufsätze zur Wissenschaftslehre*, Tübingen: J. C. B. Mohr. Trans. and ed. 1949 E. Shils and H. A. Finch, *The Methodology of the Social Sciences*, New York: Free Press.

Weber, Max (1922b). *Wirtschaft und Gesellschaft*, Tübingen: J. C. B. Mohr. Trans. 1978 G. Roth and C. Wittich, *Economy and Society*, Berkeley: University of California Press.

Westbrook, Robert (1991). *John Dewey and American Democracy*, Ithaca: Cornell University Press.

Wiggershaus, Rolf (1986). *Die Frankfurter Schule*, Munich: Hanser Verlag, 1986. Trans. 1994 M. Robertson, *The Frankfurt School: Its Histories, Theories and Political Significance*, Cambridge, MA: Polity Press/MIT Press.

CHAPTER 56 THE RISE OF SOCIAL ANTHROPOLOGY

Benedict, R. (1934). *Patterns of Culture*, New York: Houghton-Mifflin.

Boas, F. (1940). *Race, Language and Culture*, New York: The Free Press.

Durkheim, E. (1895). *Les règles de la méthode sociologique*, Paris: Alcan. Trans. 1938 Sarah A. Solovay and John H. Mueller, *The Rules of Sociological Method*, Chicago, IL: University of Chicago Press.

Engels, F. (1884). *Der Ursprung der Familie, des Privateigentums und des Staat*, Zurich: Hottingen. Trans. 1968 *The Origins of the Family, Private Property, and the State* in K. Marx and F. Engels, *Selected Works*, London: Lawrence and Wishart.

Evans Pritchard, E. E. (1964). *Social Anthropology and Other Essays*, Glencoe, IL: The Free Press.

Fortes, M. (1953). *Social Anthropology at Cambridge since 1900: An Inaugural Lecture*, Cambridge: Cambridge University Press.

Frazer, J. G. (1890). *The Golden Bough*, London: Macmillan; 3rd edn 1907–15, 12 vols. London: Macmillan.

Kuklick, H. (1991). *The Savage Within: The Social History of British Anthropology, 1885–1945*. Cambridge: Cambridge University Press.

Mach, E. (1886). *Beiträge zur Analyse der Empfindungen*, Jena. Trans. 1914 C. Williams, *Analysis of Sensations and the Relation of the Physical to the Psychical*, La Salle, IL: Open Court.

Malefijt, A. deW. (1974). *Images of Man*, New York: Alfred A. Knopf.

Malinowski, B. (1929). *The Sexual Life of Savages in North-Western Melanesia*, London: Routledge.
Malinowski, B. (1944). *A Scientific Theory of Culture and Other Essays*, New York: Oxford University Press.
Malinowski, B. (1954). *Magic, Science and Religion and Other Essays*, Garden City, NY: Doubleday and Company.
Mead, M. (1928). *Coming of Age in Samoa*, New York: William Morrow and Company.
Montesquieu, C. de (1748). *L'Esprit des Lois*. Trans. 1966 T. Nugent, *The Spirit of Laws*. New York: Hafner Publishing Company.
Morgan, L. H. (1870). *Systems of Consanguinity and Affinity in the Human Family*, Washington DC: The Smithsonian Institution.
Radcliffe-Brown, A. R. (1952). *Structure and Function in Primitive Society*, Glencoe, IL: The Free Press.
Russell, B. A. W. (1914). *Our Knowledge of the External World*, New York: W.W. Norton and Company.
Salmon, Merrilee H. (1997). 'Ethical Considerations in Anthropology and Archaeology, or Relativism and Justice for All', *Journal of Anthropological Research* 53: 47–63.
Sapir, E. (1921). *Language*, New York: Harcourt, Brace, and Company.
Tylor, E. B. (1871). *Primitive Culture*, London: Murray.
Tylor, E. B. (1889). 'On a Method of Investigating the Development of Institutions; Applied to the Laws of Marriage and Descent', *Journal of the Royal Anthropological Institute of Great Britain and Ireland* 18: 245–72.
Whorf, B. (1956). *Language, Thought and Reality*, ed. John B. Carroll, New York: John Wiley and Sons.

CHAPTER 57 WESTERN MARXISM AND IDEOLOGY CRITIQUE

Adorno, Theodor W. (1955). *Prismen*, Berlin: Suhrkamp. Trans. 1967 S. and S. Weber, *Prisms*, London: Spearman.
Anderson, Perry (1976). *Considerations on Western Marxism*, London: New Left Books.
Arato, Anthony and Breines, Paul (1979). *The Young Lukács and the Origins of Western Marxism*, London: Pluto.
Eagleton, Terry (1991). *Ideology*, London: Verso.
Horkheimer, Max (1995). *Between Philosophy and Social Science: Early Selected Writings*. Trans. G. Frederick Hunter, M. S. Kramer, and J. Torpey, Cambridge, MA: MIT Press.
Horkheimer, Max (1972). *Critical Theory: Selected Essays*, ed. M. J. O'Connell *et al.*, New York: Seabury Press.
Jay, Martin (1973). *The Dialectical Imagination*, London: Heinemann.
Kettler, David, Meja, Volker, and Stehr, Nico (1984). *Karl Mannheim*, London: Tavistock.
Löwy, Michael (1979). *Georg Lukács – From Romanticism to Bolshevism*, London: Verso.
Lukács, Georg, (1923). *Geschichte und Klassbewusstsein*, Frankfurt: Malik Verlag. Trans. 1971 R. Livingstone, *History and Class Consciousness*, London: Merlin.
Mannheim, Karl (1929). *Ideologie und Utopie*, Bonn: Friedrich Cohen. Trans. 1936 L. Wirth and E. Shils, *Ideology and Utopia*, London: Routledge.
Mannheim, Karl (1984). *Konservatismus*, Frankfurt: Suhrkamp. Trans. 1986 D. Kettler, V. Meja, and E. R. King, *Conservatism*, London: Routledge.
Rees, John (1998). *The Algebra of Revolution*, London: Routledge.
Rosen, Michael (1996). *Of Voluntary Servitude*, Cambridge, MA: Polity.
Stedman-Jones, Gareth (1972). 'The Marxism of the Early Lukács', *New Left Review*, 70, 27–64.
Wiggershaus, Rolf (1994). *The Frankfurt School*, Cambridge, MA: MIT Press.

CHAPTER 58 FROM INTUITIONISM TO EMOTIVISM

Ayer, A. J. (1936). *Language, Truth and Logic*, London: Gollancz.

Barnes, W. H. F. (1934). 'A Suggestion about Values', *Analysis* 1: 45–6.

Barnes, W. H. F. (1948). 'Ethics without Propositions', *Proceedings of the Aristotelian Society*, supp. vol. XXII: 1–30.

Braithwaite, R. B. (1928). 'Verbal Ambiguity and Philosophical Analysis', *Proceedings of the Aristotelian Society* 28: 135–54.

Broad, C. D. (1928). 'Analysis of Some Ethical Concepts', *Journal of Philosophical Studies (Philosophy)* 3; reprinted in Broad 1971, 63–81.

Broad, C. D. (1930). *Five Types of Ethical Theory*, London: Kegan Paul.

Broad, C. D. (1934). 'Is "Goodness" a Name of a Simple Non-Natural Quality?', *Proceedings of the Aristotelian Society* 34; reprinted in Broad 1971, 106–23.

Broad, C. D. (1945). 'Some Reflections on Moral-Sense Theories in Ethics', *Proceedings of the Aristotelian Society* 45; reprinted in Broad 1971, 188–222.

Broad, C. D. (1971). *Broad's Critical Essays in Moral Philosophy*, ed. D. Cheney, London: George Allen and Unwin.

Carnap, R. (1935). *Philosophy and Logical Syntax*, London: Kegan Paul.

Carritt, E. F. (1928). *The Theory of Morals*, London: Oxford University Press.

Carritt, E. F. (1935). *Morals and Politics*, London: Oxford University Press.

Carritt, E. F. (1947). *Ethical and Political Thinking*, Oxford: Clarendon Press.

Dewey, J. (1899–1924). *The Middle Works: 1899–1924*, 15 vols., ed. J. A. Boyston, Carbondale: Southern Illinois University Press (1976–83).

Dewey, J. (1922). *Human Nature and Conduct*, New York: Holt (*Middle Works*, vol. XIV).

Dewey, J. (1925–53). *The Later Works: 1925–1953*, 17 vols., ed. J. A. Boyston, Carbondale: Southern Illinois University Press (1976–83).

Dewey, J. (1929). *The Quest for Certainty*, New York: Milton, Balch and Co. (*Later Works*, vol. IV).

Dewey, J. (1939). *The Theory of Valuation*, Chicago: University of Chicago Press (*Later Works*, vol. XIII).

Dewey, J. and Tufts, J. H. (1932). *Ethics*, rev. edn, New York: Holt (*Later Works*, vol. VII).

Edwards, P. (1955). *The Logic of Moral Discourse*, Glencoe, IL: The Free Press.

Ewing, A. C. (1929). *The Morality of Punishment*, London: Kegan Paul.

Ewing, A. C. (1947). *The Definition of Good*, London: Routledge.

Ewing, A. C. (1953). *Ethics*, London: English Universities Press, Teach Yourself Books.

Ewing, A. C. (1959). *Second Thoughts in Moral Philosophy*, London: Routledge.

Festenstein, M. (1997). *Pragmatism and Political Theory*, Oxford: Polity.

Gouinlock, J. (1972). *John Dewey's Philosophy of Value*, New York: Humanities Press.

Hägerström, A. (1911). 'Om Moraliska Föreställningars Sanning'. Trans. 1964 R. T. Sandin, *Philosophy and Religion*, London: George Allen and Unwin.

Hägerström, A. (1938). *Inquiries into the Nature of Laws and Morals*, trans. C. D. Broad, Stockholm: Almqvist and Wiksell.

Hurley, P. E. (1988). 'Dewey on Desires: The Lost Argument', *Transactions of the Charles S. Peirce Society* 24: 509–19.

Joseph, H. W. B. (1931). *Some Problems in Ethics*, Oxford: Clarendon Press.

Mackie, J. L. (1946). 'A Refutation of Morals', *Australian Journal of Psychology and Philosophy* 24: 77f.

Moore, G. E. (1903). *Principia Ethica*, Cambridge: Cambridge University Press; rev. edn, ed. T. Baldwin 1993.

Moore, G. E. (1912). *Ethics*, London: Home University Library.

Moore, G. E. (1952). 'A Reply to my Critics' in P. A. Schilpp ed., *The Philosophy of G. E. Moore*, New York: Tudor Publishing Co., 533–677.

Ogden, C. K. and Richards, I. A. (1923). *The Meaning of Meaning*, London: Routledge.

Prichard, H. A. (1912). 'Does Moral Philosophy Rest on a Mistake?', *Mind* 21: 21–37. Repr. in Prichard 1968, 1–17.

Prichard, H. A. (1928). 'Duty and Interest'; inaugural lecture, repr. in Prichard 1968, 203–38.

Prichard, H. A. (1932). 'Duty and Ignorance of Fact', *Proceedings of the British Academy*: 67–92; repr. with endnotes in Prichard 1968, 18–39.

Prichard, H. A. (1968). *Moral Obligation*, ed. J. O. Urmson, Oxford: Clarendon Press.

Rashdall, H. (1907). *The Theory of Good and Evil*, Oxford: Clarendon Press.

Robinson, R. (1948). 'The Emotive Theory of Ethics', *Proceedings of the Aristotelian Society*, supp. vol. XXII: 79–106.

Ross, W. D. (1930). *The Right and The Good*, Oxford: Clarendon Press.

Ross, W. D. (1939). *Foundations of Ethics*, Oxford: Clarendon Press.

Russell, B. A. W. (1936). *Religion and Science*, New York: Holt.

Selby-Bigge, L. A. (1897). *British Moralists*, Oxford: Clarendon Press.

Stevenson, C. L. (1937). 'The Emotive Meaning of Ethical Terms', *Mind* 46: 14–31. Repr. in Stevenson 1963, 10–31.

Stevenson, C. L. (1938). 'Persuasive Definitions', *Mind* 47: 331–50. Repr. in Stevenson 1963, 32–54.

Stevenson, C. L. (1944). *Ethics and Language*, Yale: Yale University Press.

Stevenson, C. L. (1948). 'The Nature of Ethical Disagreement', *Sigma* 8–9. Repr. in Stevenson 1963, 1–9. This piece was written in 1941.

Stevenson, C. L. (1963). *Facts and Values*, New Haven, CT: Yale University Press.

Stratton, G. M. (1903). 'A Psychological Test of Virtue', *International Journal of Ethics* 11: 200–13.

Urmson, J. O. (1968). *The Emotive Theory of Ethics*, London: Hutchinson.

Urmson, J. O. (1975). 'A Defence of Intuitionism', *Proceedings of the Aristotelian Society* 75: 111–19.

Welchman, J. (1995). *Dewey's Ethical Thought*, Ithaca: Cornell University Press.

Wittgenstein, L. (1921). *Logische-philosophische Abhandlung*, in *Annalen der Natur Philosophie*. Trans. 1961 D. F. Pears and B. F. McGuinness, *Tractatus Logico-Philosophicus*, London: Routledge.

Wittgenstein, L. (1965). 'Lecture on Ethics', *Philosophical Review* 74: 3–12.

CHAPTER 59 PHILOSOPHY OF RELIGION

Alexander, Samuel (1920). *Space, Time and Deity* (Gifford Lectures 1916–18), London: Macmillan.

Andresen, Carl (ed.) (1985ff.). *Handbuch der Dogmen- und Theologiegeschichte*, 3 vols. Berlin: de Gruyter.

Ayer, A. J. (1936). *Language, Truth and Logic*, London: Victor Gollancz.

Barth, K. (1922). *Der Römerbrief*, Zurich. Trans. 1933 E. Hoskyns, *The Epistle to the Romans*, London: Oxford University Press.

Barth, K. (1932–67). *Die kirchliche Dogmatik*, Munich. Trans. 1936–69 G. Thomson *et al.*, *Church Dogmatics*, Edinburgh: T. & T. Clark.

Barth, K. (1947). *Die protestantische Theologie im 19 Jahrhundert*, Zurich. Trans. 1972 B. Cozens and J. Bowden, *Protestant Theology in the Nineteenth Century*, London: SCM.

Brunner, E. (1927). *Die Religionsphilosophie evangelischer Theologie*, Munich: Oldenburg. Trans. 1937 *The Philosophy of Religion from the standpoint of Protestant Theology*, London: Ivor Nicholson and Watson.

Brunner, E. (1941). *Offenbarung und Vernunft*, Zurich: Zwingli. Trans. 1947 *Revelation and Reason*, London: SCM.

Buber, M. (1923). *Ich und Du*, in *Das dialogische Prinzip*, Heidelberg. Trans. 1937 R. Smith, *I and Thou*, Edinburgh: T. &T. Clark.

Collingwood, R. G. (1916). *Religion and Philosophy*, London: Macmillan.

Collingwood, R. G. (1940). *An Essay on Metaphysics*, Oxford: Oxford University Press.

Dalferth, I. U. (1981). *Religiose Rede von Gott*, Munich: Kaiser.

Dilthey, W. (1883). *Einleitung in die Geisteswissenschaften*, Leipzig. Trans. 1989 J. R. Betanzons *Introduction to the Human Sciences: An Attempt to Lay the Foundation for the Study of Society and History*, London: Harvester Wheatsheaf.

Emmet, D. (1936). *Philosophy and Faith*, London: SCM.

Emmet, D. (1945). *The Nature of Metaphysical Thinking*, London: Macmillan.

Farrer, A. M. (1943). *Finite and Infinite*, London: Dacre.

Gestrich, Christoff (1977). *Neuzeitliches Denken und die Spaltung der dialektischen Theologie*, Tübingen: J. C. B. Mohr (Paul Siebeck).

Guttman, Julius (1964). *Philosophies of Judaism: The History of Jewish Philosophy from Biblical Times to Franz Rosenzweig*, London: Routledge.

Hartshorne, C. (1941). *Man's Vision of God, and the Logic of Theism*, New York.

Hartshorne, C. (1948). *The Divine Relativity: A Social Conception of God*, New Haven: Yale University Press.

Hodgson, L. (1930). *Essays in Christian Philosophy*, London: Longmans, Green.

Hodgson, Leonard (1943). *Towards a Christian Philosophy*, London: Nisbet.

Hugel, Fr. von (1921, 1926). *Essays and Addresses*, series I, II, London: Dent.

Husserl, E. (1936). 'Die Krisis der europäischen Wissenschaften und die transzendentale Phänomenologie', *Philosophia* 1: 77–176. Repr. 1954 in *Husserliana*, vol. VI, trans. 1970 David Carr, The Hague: Nijhoff. *The Crisis of the European Sciences and Transcendental Philosophy*, Evanston, IL: Northwestern University Press.

Langford, T. A. (1969). *In Search of Foundations: English Theology 1900–1920*, Nashville: Abingdon Press.

MacKinnon, D. M. (1940). 'What is a Metaphysical Statement?' *Proceedings of the Aristotelian Society* XLI.

Maréchal, J. (1923–49). *Le point de départ de la métaphysique*, Bruges.

Pailin, D. (1986). *Groundwork of Philosophy of Religion*, London: Epworth.

Pringle-Pattison, A. Seth (1917). *The Idea of God in Recent Philosophy*, Gifford Lectures (1912–13), Aberdeen.

Rahner, K. (1939). *Geist in Welt*, Leipzig. Trans. 1968 W. Dych, *Spirit in the World*, London: Sheed & Ward.

Roberts, R. H. (1990). *Hope and its Hieroglyph: A Critical Decipherment of Ernst Bloch's 'Principle of Hope'*, Atlanta: Scholars Press.

Roberts, R. H. (1992). *A Theology on Its Way? Essays on Karl Barth*, Edinburgh: T. & T. Clark.

Roberts, R. H. (1996). 'Theology and Social Science' in D. Ford (ed.), *The Modern Theologians*, Oxford: Blackwell (2nd rev. edn, 1996), 700–19.

Scholder, K. (1977–85). *Die kirchen im dritten Reich*, 2 vols., Berlin. Trans. 1987–8 *The Churches and the Third Reich*, London: SCM.

Sell, A. P. F. (1988). *The Philosophy of Religion 1875–1980*, Bristol: Thoemmes Press.

Smart, N. et al. (1985ff.). *Nineteenth Century Religious Thought in the West*, 3 vols., Cambridge: Cambridge University Press.

Smith, R. (1997). *Fontana History of the Human Sciences*, London: Fontana Press.

Streeter, B. H. (ed.) (1912). *Foundations*, London: Macmillan.

Temple, W. (1934). *Nature, Man and God* (Gifford Lectures 1932–4), London: Macmillan.

Tennant, R. F. (1928, 1930). *Philosophical Theology*. Cambridge: Cambridge University Press.

Tillich, P. (1988–). *Main Works*, Berlin: de Gruyter.

van der Leeuw, G. (1933). *Phänomenologie der Religion*, Tübingen. Trans. 1938 J. E. Turner, *Religion in essence and manifestation: a study in phenomenology*, London: George Allen and Unwin.

von Balthasar, H. U. (1947). *Prometheus; Studien zur Geschichte des deutschen Idealismus*, Heidelberg: F. H. Kerle Verlag.

Webb, C. C. J. (1918–20). *God and Personality*, 2 vols. (Gifford lectures 1918–19), Aberdeen.

Webb, C. C. J. (1925). 'Outline of a philosophy of religion' in J. H. Muirhead (ed.), *Contemporary British Philosophy*, London: George Allen and Unwin.

Webb, C. C. J. (1933). *A Study of Religious Thought in England from 1850*, Oxford: Clarendon Press.

Welch, C. (1972). *Protestant Thought in the Nineteenth Century*, 2 vols. New Haven: Yale University Press.

Whitehead, A. N. (1926). *Religion in the Making*, Cambridge: Cambridge University Press.

Whitehead, A. N. (1929). *Process and Reality*, Cambridge: Cambridge University Press.

CHAPTER 60 LITERATURE AS PHILOSOPHY

Bersani, Leo (1965). *The Fictions of Life and of Art*, New York and London: Oxford University Press.

Bowie, Malcolm (1998). *Proust among the Stars*, London: HarperCollins.

Goldthorpe, Rhiannon (1991). *La Nausée* (Unwin Critical Library), London: HarperCollins.

Mann, Thomas (1924). *Der Zauberberg*, in *Gesammelte Werke*, 13 vols, vol. III (1960), Frankfurt on Main: Fischer Verlag. Trans. 1960 H. T. Lowe-Porter, *The Magic Mountain*, Harmondsworth: Penguin.

Minden, Michael (ed.) (1995). *Thomas Mann*, London: Longmans.

Murdoch, Iris (1953). *Sartre: Romantic Rationalist*, Cambridge: Bowes and Bowes. Reprinted, with a new introduction, 1989, Harmondsworth: Penguin.

Proust, Marcel (1913–27). *A la recherche du temps perdu*. New edition 1987–9, ed. Jean-Yves Tadié, 4 vols., Paris Gallimard (Pléiade). Trans. 1992 C. K. Scott Moncrieff and Terence Kilmartin, revised by D. J. Enright, *In Search of Lost Time*, 6 vols., London: Chatto and Windus. Repr. in paperback 1996, London: Vintage.

Reed, T. J. (1974). *Thomas Mann. The Uses of Tradition*, Oxford: Clarendon Press.

Sartre, Jean-Paul (1938). *La Nausée*. New edition 1981 in *Œuvres romanesques*, ed. Michel Contat and Michel Rybalka, Paris: Gallimard (Pléiade). Trans. 1965 Robert Baldick, *Nausea*, Harmondsworth: Penguin.

CHAPTER 61 AESTHETICS BETWEEN THE WARS: ART AND LIBERATION

Ayer, Alfred Jules (1946). *Language, Truth and Logic*, 2nd edn, London: Gollancz.

Benjamin, Walter (1968). *Illuminations*, ed. with an introduction by Hannah Arendt, New York: Harcourt, Brace, and World.

Benjamin, Walter (1978). *Reflections: Essays, Aphorisms, Autobiographical Writings*, ed. Peter Demetz, New York: Harcourt Brace Jovanovich.

Cassirer, Ernst (1944). *An Essay on Man*, New Haven: Yale University Press.

Collingwood, R. G. (1925). *Outlines of a Philosophy of Art*, London: Oxford University Press.

Collingwood, R. G. (1938). *The Principles of Art*, Oxford: Clarendon Press.

Danto, A. (1964). 'The Artworld', *Journal of Philosophy* 61, 571–84.

Dewey, John (1934). *Art as Experience*, New York: Milton Balch.

Goodman, N. (1968). *The Languages of Art*, Indianapolis, IN: Hackettt.

Harrison, Charles and Wood, Paul (eds.) (1992). *Art in Theory 1900–1990: An Anthology of Changing Ideas*, Oxford: Blackwell.

Heidegger, M. (1950), *Holzwege (Forest Paths)*, Frankfurt: Vittorio Klosterman.

Hofstadter, Albert and Kuhns, Richard (eds.) (1964). *Philosophies of Art and Beauty: Selected Readings from Plato to Heidegger*, New York: The Modern Library.

Ingarden, R. (1931). *Das Literarische Kunstwark*, Halle: Niemeyer. Trans. 1973 G. G. Grabowicz, *The Literary Work of Art*, Evanston, IL: Northwestern University Press.

Kelly, Michael, ed. (1998). *Encyclopedia of Aesthetics*, New York: Oxford University Press.

Langer, Suzanne K. (1942). *Philosophy in a New Key: A Study in the Symbolism of Reason, Rite and Art*, Cambridge, MA: Harvard University Press.

Lukács, G. (1916). *Die Theorie des Romans*, Berlin: Paul Cassirer. Trans. A. Bostock 1978 *The Theory of the Noval*, London: Merlin.

Taylor, Ronald (ed.) (1977). *Aesthetics and Politics: The Key Texts of the Classic Debate within German Marxism*, London: Verso.

Wittgenstein, Ludwig (1966). *Lectures & Conversations on Aesthetics, Psychology and Religious Belief*, ed. Cyril Barrett, Oxford: Blackwell.

CHAPTER 62 HANS KELSEN AND NORMATIVE LEGAL POSITIVISM

Alexy, R. (1992). *Begriff und Geltung des Rechts (Concept and Validity of the Law)*, Freiburg and Munich: Karl Alber. Trans. 2002 S. L. Paulson and B. L. Paulson, *The Argument from Injustice. A Reply to Legal Positivism*, Oxford: Clarendon Press.

Hart, H. L. A. (1957–8). 'Positivism and the Separation of Law and Morals', *Harvard Law Review* 71: 593–629. Repr. 1983 in H. L. A. Hart, *Essays in Jurisprudence and Philosophy*, Oxford: Clarendon Press, 49–87.

Kant, I. (1781, 1787). *Kritik der reinen Vernunft*, Riga: Hartknoch. Trans. 1998 P. Guyer and A. W. Wood, *Critique of Pure Reason*, Cambridge: Cambridge University Press.

Kant, I. (1797). *Die Metaphysik der Sitten, Erster Theil, metaphysische Anfangsgründe der Rechts-lehre* (First Part, *Metaphysical First Principles of the Theory of Law*), Königsberg: Friedrich Nicolovius. Trans. 1991 M. Gregor, *The Metaphysics of Morals*, Cambridge: Cambridge University Press, 33–177.

Kelsen, H. (1911). *Hauptprobleme der Staatsrechtslehre (Main Problems in the Theory of Public Law)*, Tübingen: J. C. B. Mohr, 2nd printing (1923) with new foreword. Trans. of 'Foreword' in S. L. Paulson and B. L. Paulson (eds. and trans.) (1998), 3–22.

Kelsen, H. (1920). *Das Problem der Souveränität und die Theorie des Völkerrechts (The Problem of Sovereignty and the Theory of International Law)*, Tübingen: J. C. B. Mohr.

Kelsen, H. (1922a). *Das soziologische und das juristische Staatsbegriff (The Sociological and the Legal Concept of the State)*, Tübingen: J. C. B. Mohr.

Kelsen, H. (1922b). 'Rechtswissenschaft und Recht' ('Legal Science and the Law'), *Zeitschrift für öffentliches Recht*, 3: 103–235.

Kelsen, H. (1923–4). 'Die Lehre von den drei Gewalten oder Funktionen des Staates' ('The Doctrine of the Three Powers or Functions of the State'), *Archiv für Rechts-und Wirtschafts-philosophie*, 17: 374–408.

Kelsen, H. (1925). *Allgemeine Staatslehre (General Constitutional Theory)*, Berlin: Springer Verlag.

Kelsen, H. (1928). *Die philosophischen Grundlagen der Naturrechtslehre und des Rechtspositivis-mus*, Charlottenburg: Pan-Verlag Rolf Heise. Trans. 1945 W. H. Kraus as an appendix to H. Kelsen, *General Theory of Law and State*, Cambridge, MA: Harvard University Press, 389–446.

Kelsen, H. (1934). *Reine Rechtslehre* (*Pure Theory of Law*) 1st edn, Leipzig and Vienna: Deuticke. Trans. 1992 B. L. Paulson and S. L. Paulson, *Introduction to the Problems of Legal Theory* (the subtitle of the original work), Oxford: Clarendon Press.

Kelsen, H. (1941–2). 'The Pure Theory of Law and Analytical Jurisprudence', *Harvard Law Review* 55: 44–70. Repr. 1957 (with omissions) in H. Kelsen, *What is Justice?*, Berkeley and Los Angeles: University of California Press, 266–87, 390 (notes).

Kelsen, H. (1945). *General Theory of Law and State*, trans. H. Wedberg, Cambridge, MA: Harvard University Press.

Kelsen, H. (1960). *Reine Rechtslehre*, 2nd edn, Vienna: Franz Deuticke. Trans. 1967 M. Knight, *The Pure Theory of Law*, Berkeley and Los Angeles: University of California Press.

Kelsen, H. (1979). K. Ringhofer and R. Walter (eds.), *Allgemeine Theorie der Normen*, Vienna: Manz. Trans. 1991 M. Hartney, *General Theory of Norms*, Oxford: Clarendon Press.

Maihofer, W. (ed.) (1962). *Naturrecht oder Rechtspositivismus?* (*Natural Law or Legal Positivism?*), Darmstadt: Wissenschaftliche Buchgesellschaft.

Merkl, A. J. (1917). *Das Recht im Lichte seiner Anwendung* (*The Law in Light of its Application*), Hanover: Helwing.

Merkl, A. J. (1931). 'Prolegomena einer Theorie des rechtlichen Stufenbaus' ('Prolegomena to a Theory of the Hierarchical Structure of the Law') in A. Verdross (ed.), *Gesellschaft, Staat und Recht. Untersuchungen zur Reinen Rechtslehre. Festschrift Hans Kelsen zum 50. Geburtstage gewidmet* (*Society, State, and the Law. Investigations into the Pure Theory of Law. Festschrift Dedicated to Hans Kelsen on his Fiftieth Birthday*), Vienna: Springer Verlag, 252–94.

Paulson, S. L. (1992). 'The Neo-Kantian Dimension of Kelsen's Pure Theory of Law', *Oxford Journal of Legal Studies* 12: 311–32.

Paulson, S. L. (1996). 'Hans Kelsen's Earliest Legal Theory: Critical Constructivism', *The Modern Law Review* 59: 797–812. Repr. (with revisions) in S. L. Paulson and B. L. Paulson (eds.) (1998), 23–43.

Paulson, S. L. (2003). 'Legal Theory, 1870–1914', chapter 23 in this volume.

Paulson, S. L. and Paulson, B. L. (eds.) (1998). *Normativity and Norms. Critical Perspectives on Kelsenian Themes*, Oxford: Clarendon Press.

Pound, R. (1933–4). 'Law and the Science of Law in Recent Theories', *Yale Law Journal* 43: 525–36.

Raz, J. (1974). 'Kelsen's Theory of the Basic Norm', *The American Journal of Jurisprudence* 19: 94–111. Repr. (with revisions) in S. L. Paulson and B. L. Paulson (eds.) (1998), 47–67.

Raz, J. (1981). 'The Purity of the Pure Theory', *Revue internationale de philosophie* 138: 441–59. Repr. in S. L. Paulson and B. L. Paulson (eds.) (1998), 237–52.

Ross, A. (1961). 'Validity and the Conflict between Legal Positivism and Natural Law', *Revista Jurídica de Buenos Aires*, no. 4: 46–93 (bilingual printing). Repr. in S. L. Paulson and B. L. Paulson (eds.) (1998), 147–63.

von Wright, G. H. (1963). *Norm and Action*, London: Routledge.

CHAPTER 63 THE LIBERAL DEMOCRATIC STATE: DEFENCES AND DEVELOPMENTS

Beetham, D. (1985). *Max Weber and the Theory of Modern Politics*, 2nd edn, Cambridge: Polity.

Bellamy, R. P. (1992). *Liberalism and Modern Society: A Historical Argument*, Cambridge: Polity.

Bellamy, R. P. (2000). *Rethinking Liberalism*, London: Pinter.

Beveridge, W. (1945). *Why I am a Liberal*, London: Herbert Jenkins.

Calogero, G. (1940–5). *Difesa del liberalsocialismo ed altri saggi* (*A Defence of Liberal Socialism and Other Writings*), repr. 1968, ed. M. Sciavone and D. Cofrancesco, Milan: Marzorati.

Croce, B. (1928). 'Liberismo e liberalismo' ('Free Trade and Liberalism'), *Atti dell'Accademia di scienze morale e politiche della società reale di Napoli* 51, 75–9. Reprinted 1973, B. Croce, *Etica e politica*, Bari: Laterza, 263–8.

Croce, B. (1943). 'Revisione filosofica dei concetti di "Liberta" e "Giustizia"' ('Philosophical Re-readings of the Concepts of Liberty and Justice'), *La Critica* 40 (1943), 276–84.

De Ruggiero, G. (1925). *Storia del liberalismo europeo*. Bari: Laterza. Trans 1927 R. G. Collingwood, *The History of European Liberalism*, Oxford: Clarendon Press.

De Ruggiero, G. (1946) *Il ritorno alla ragione* (*The Return to Reason*), Bari: Laterza.

Dewey, J. (1927). *The Public and its Problems*, New York: Henry Holt. Repr. 1984 in J. A. Boydston (ed.), *John Dewey: The Later Works*, Carbondale, IL: Southern Illinois University Press, vol II, 253–372.

Dewey, J. (1935). *Liberalism and Social Action*, New York: G. P. Putnam's Sons. Repr. 1987 in J. A. Boydston (ed.), *John Dewey: The Later Works*, Carbondale, IL: Southern Illinois University Press, vol. XI, 1–65.

Dewey, J. (1939). 'The Economic Basis of the New Society' in J. Ratner, *Intelligence in the Modern World*, New York: Modern Library, 1939. Repr. 1988 in J. A. Boydston (ed.), *John Dewey: The Later Works*, Carbondale, IL: Southern Illinois University Press, 416–38.

Einaudi, L. (1928). 'Di concetti di liberismo economico, e di borghesia e sulle origini materialistiche della guerra', *La riforma sociale*, 35, vol. 39, nos. 9–10 September-October, 501–16. Repr. 1973 in L. Einaudi, *Il buongoverno*, Bari: Laterza, vol. I, 196–218.

Freeden, M. (1986). *Liberalism Divided: A Study in British Political Thought 1914–39*, Oxford: Clarendon Press.

Harris, J. (1977). *William Beveridge: A Biography*, Oxford: Clarendon Press.

Hayek, F. A. (1935) (ed.). *Collectivist Economic Planning*, London: Routledge.

Hayek, F. A. (1944). *The Road to Serfdom*, London: Routledge.

Hetherington, H. J. W. and Muirhead, J. H. (1918). *Social Purpose: A Contribution to a Philosophy of Civic Society*, London: George Allen and Unwin.

Hirst, P. Q. (ed.) (1989). *The Pluralist Theory of the State: Selected Writings of G. D. H. Cole, J. N. Figgis and H. J. Laski*, London: Routledge.

Hobhouse, L. T. (1911). *Liberalism*, London: Williams and Norgate. New edn 1964, Oxford: Oxford University Press.

Hobhouse, L. T. (1918). *The Metaphysical Theory of the State*, London: George Allen and Unwin.

Hobson, J. A. (1934). *Democracy and a Changing Civilisation*, London: John Lane The Bodley Head Ltd.

Keynes, J. M. (1919). *The Economic Consequences of the Peace*, London: Macmillan.

Keynes, J. M. (1925). 'Am I a Liberal?', *Nation and Atheneum*, 8 and 15 August. Repr. 1972 in *Essays in Persuasion, Collected Writings of John Maynard Keynes*, vol. IX, London: Macmillan, 295–306.

Keynes, J. M. (1926). *The End of Laissez-Faire*. London: Hogarth Press. Repr. 1972 in *Essays in Persuasion, Collected Writings of John Maynard Keynes*, vol. IX, London: Macmillan, 272–94.

Keynes, J. M. (1927). 'Liberalism and Industry', in H. L. Nathan and H. Heathcote Williams (eds.), *Liberal Points of View*, London: Ernest Benn, 205–19. Repr. 1981 in D. Moggridge (ed.), *Activities 1922–29, Collected Writings of John Maynard Keynes*, vol. XIX, London: Macmillan, 638–48.

Keynes, J. M. (1936). *The General Theory of Employment, Interest and Money*, London: Macmillan. Repr. 1973 in D. Moggridge and A. Robinson (eds.), *The Collected Works of John Maynard Keynes*, vol. VIII, London Macmillan.

Kloppenberg, J. T. (1986). *Uncertain Victory: Social Democracy and Progressivism in European and American Thought 1700–1920*, New York: Oxford University Press.

Lavoie, D. (1985). *Rivalry and Central Planning: The Socialist Calculation Debate Reconsidered.* Cambridge: Cambridge University Press.

Mosca, G. (1923). *Elementi di scienza politica*, 2nd edn, Turin: Fratelli Bocca. Trans. 1939 Hannah D. Kahn, *The Ruling Class*, ed. A Livingston, New York: McGraw-Hill.

Pareto, V. (1902–3). *Les systèmes socialistes*, 2 vols. Paris: V. Girard and E. Brière.

Pareto, V. (1916). *Trattato di sociologia generale*, 2 vols., Florence: Barbera. Trans. 1935 A. Livingston and A. Bongiorno, *The Mind and Society*, 4 vols., New York.

Pareto, V. (1921). *La trasformazione della democrazia*, Milan: Carbaccio.

Russell, B. A. W. (1916). *Principles of Social Reconstruction*, London: George Allen and Unwin.

Ryan, A. (1995). *John Dewey and the High Tide of American Liberalism*, New York: W. W. Norton & Co.

Schumpeter, J. A. (1943). *Capitalism, Socialism and Democracy*, London: George Allen and Unwin.

Skidelsky, R. (1983). *John Maynard Keynes: Hopes Betrayed 1883–1920*, London: Allen Lane.

Skidelsky, R. (1994). *John Maynard Keynes: The Economist as Saviour 1921–46*, London: Macmillan.

Von Mises, L. (1927). *Liberalismus*, Jena: G. Fischer. Trans. 1985 R. Raico, *Liberalism in the Classic Tradition*, San Francisco: Cobden Press.

Von Mises, L. (1932). *Die Gemeinwirtschaft*, 2nd edn (1st edn 1922), Jena: G. Fischer. Trans. 1936 J. Kahane, *Socialism: An Economic and Sociological Analysis*, London: Jonathan Cape.

Weber, M. (1918a). *Parlament und Regierung im neugeordneten Deutschland. Zür politischen Kritik des Beamtentums und Parteiwesens*, Munich and Leipzig: Duncker and Humblot. Trans. 1994 as 'Parliament and government in Germany under a New Political Order: Towards a Critique of Officialdom and the Party System' in P. Lassman and R. Speirs, *Weber: Political Writings*, Cambridge: Cambridge University Press, 130–271.

Weber, M. (1918b). *Der Sozialismus*, Vienna: 'Phöbus' Kommissions-verlag Dr. Viktor Pimmer o.J. Trans. 1994 as 'Socialism' in P. Lassman and R. Speirs, *Weber: Political Writings*, Cambridge: Cambridge University Press, 272–303.

Weber, M. (1919). 'Politik als Beruf', *Geistige Arbeit als Beruf. Vier Vorträge vor dem Freistudentischen Bund*, Munich and Leipzig: Duncker and Humblot. Trans. 1994 as 'The Profession and Vocation of Politics' in P. Lassman and R. Speirs, *Weber: Political Writings*, Cambridge: Cambridge University Press, 309–69.

CHAPTER 64 THE LIBERAL DEMOCRATIC STATE: CRITICS

Adamson, W. L. (1980). *Hegemony and Revolution: Antonio Gramsci's Political and Cultural Theory*, Berkeley and Los Angeles: University of California Press.

Adorno, T. W. (1970). *Ästhetische Theorie (Gesammelte Schriften*, vol. VI), Frankfurt: Suhrkamp. Trans. 1997 R. Hullot-Kentor, *Aesthetic Theory*, Minneapolis: University of Minnesota Press.

Adorno, T. W. (1973). *Negative Dialektik (Gesammelte Schriften*, vol. VI), Frankfurt: Suhrkamp. Trans. E. B. Ashton, *Negative Dialectics*, London: Routledge.

Adorno, T. W. and Horkheimer, M. (1944). *Dialektik der Aufklärung*, New York: Social Studies Association. Trans. 1972 J. Cunning, *Dialectic of Enlightenment*, New York: Herder and Herder.

Arato, A. and Breines, P. (1979). *The Young Lukács and the Origins of Western Marxism*, New York: Seabury Press.

Bellamy, R. and Schecter, D. (1993). *Gramsci and the Italian State*, Manchester: Manchester University Press.

Bendersky, J. (1983). *Carl Schmitt: Theorist for the Reich*, Princeton, NJ: Princeton University Press.

Benhabib, S., Bonss, W., and McCole, J. (1993). *On Max Horkheimer: New Perspectives*, Cambridge, MA: MIT Press.

Buck-Morss, S. (1977). *The Origin of Negative Dialectics: Theodor W. Adorno, Walter Benjamin, and the Frankfurt Institute*, New York: Free Press.

Calandra, G. (1987). *Gentile e il fascismo*, Rome and Bari: Laterza.

Dallmayr, F. (1993). *The Other Heidegger*, Ithaca, NY: Cornell University Press.

Femia, J. (1981). *Gramsci's Political Thought: Hegemony, Consciousness and the Revolutionary Process*, Oxford: Oxford University Press.

Gentile, G. (1915). *Teoria generale dello spirito come atto puro*, Bari: Laterza. Trans. 1922 H. W. Carr, *The Theory of Mind as Pure Act*, London: Macmillan.

Gentile, G. (1927). 'The Philosophic Basis of Fascism', *Foreign Affairs* 6: 290–304.

Gentile, G. (1937). *Fondamenti della filosofia del diritto*, 3rd edn, Florence: Sansoni.

Gluck, M. (1985). *Georg Lukács and His Generation 1900–1918*, Cambridge, MA: Harvard University Press.

Gottfried, P. E. (1990). *Carl Schmitt: Politics and Theory*, New York: Greenwood Press.

Gramsci, A. (1948–51). *Quaderni del carcere*, ed. F. Platone, 6 vols., Turin: Einaudi. Rev. complete edn 1975 ed. V. Gerratana, Turin: Einaudi. Trans. 1971 (incomplet) Q. Hoare and G. Smith, *Selections from the Prison Notebooks*, London: Lawrence and Wishart.

Gramsci, A. (1982). *La città futura*, ed. S. Caprioglio, Turin: Einaudi. Trans. 1994 V. Cox, *Pre-prison Writings*, Cambridge: Cambridge University Press.

Heidegger, M. (1953). *Einführung in die Metaphysik* (*Gesamtausgabe* vol. XL), Frankfurt: V. Klosterman. Trans. 1961 R. Manheim, *An Introduction to Metaphysics*, New York: Anchor Books.

Heidegger, M. (1954). *Die Frage nach der Technik* (*Vorträge und Aufsätze*, 13–44), Pfullingen: Verlag Günter Neske. Trans. 1977 W. Lovitt, *The Question Concerning Technology* (*Basic Writings*, 283–317), New York: Harper and Row.

Horkheimer, M. (1947). *The Eclipse of Reason*, New York: Oxford University Press.

Jay, M. (1984a). *Adorno*, Cambridge, MA: Harvard University Press.

Jay, M. (1984b). *Max Horkheimer and the Retreat from Hegelian Marxism* in *Marxism and Totality: The Adventures of a Concept from Lukács to Habermas*, Berkeley and Los Angeles: University of California Press.

Kadarkay, A. (1991). *Georg Lukács: Life, Thought, and Politics*, Oxford: Blackwell.

Lukács, G. (1910). *A lélek és a formák*, Budapest: Franklin. Trans. 1974 A. Bostock, *Soul and Form*, Cambridge, MA: MIT Press.

Lukács, G. (1920). *Die Theorie des Romans*, Berlin: Paul Cassirer. Trans. 1971 A. Bostock, *Theory of the Novel*, Cambridge, MA: MIT Press.

Lukács, G. (1923). *Geschichte und Klassenbewusstsein: Studien über Marxistische Dialektik*, Berlin: Malik Verlag. Trans. 1971 R. Livingstone, *History and Class Consciousness: Studies in Marxist Dialectics*, Cambridge, MA: MIT Press.

Lukács, G. (1924). *Lenin: Studie über den Zusammenhang seiner Gedanken*, Berlin: Malik Verlag. Trans. 1971 N. Jacobs, *Lenin: A Study on the Unity of His Thought*, Cambridge, MA: MIT Press.

Maier, C. (1975). *Recasting Bourgeois Europe: Stabilization in France, Germany and Italy in the Decade After the First World War*, Princeton, NJ: Princeton University Press.

McCormick, J. (1997). *Carl Schmitt's Critique of Liberalism: Against Politics as Technology*, Cambridge: Cambridge University Press.

Mommsen, W. (1959). *Max Weber und die deutsche Politik, 1890–1920*, Tübingen: J. C. B. Mohr. Trans. 1984 M. Steinberg, *Max Weber and German Politics, 1890–1920*, Chicago: University of Chicago Press.

Prezzolini, G. (1909). 'Relazione del primo anno della Voce', *La Voce* I:1.

Romano, S. (1984). *Giovanni Gentile: La filosofia al potere*, Milan: Bompiani.

Rose, G. (1978). *The Melancholy Science: An Introduction to the Thought of Theodor W. Adorno*, New York: Columbia University Press.

Safranski, R. (1994). *Ein Meister aus Deutschland: Heidegger und seine Zeit*, Munich: Carl Hanser Verlag. Trans. 1998 E. Osers, *Martin Heidegger: Between Good and Evil*, Cambridge, MA: Harvard University Press.

Schmitt, C. (1925a). *Politische Romantik*, Berlin: Duncker and Humboldt. Trans. 1986 G. Oakes, *Political Romanticism*, Cambridge, MA: MIT Press.

Schmitt, C. (1925b). *Römischer Katholizismus und politsche Form*, Munich: Theatiner-Verlag. Trans. 1996 G. Ulmen, *Roman Catholicism and Political Form*, Westport, CT: Greenwood.

Schmitt, C. (1934). *Politische Theologie: Vier Kapitel zur Lehre von der Souveränität*, Munich: Duncker and Humblot. Trans. 1985 G. Schwab, *Political Theology: Four Chapters on the Concept of Sovereignty*, Cambridge, MA: MIT Press.

Schmitt, C. (1963a). 'Das Zeitalter der Neutralisierungen und Entpolitisierungen' in *Der Begriff des Politischen*, Berlin: Duncker and Humboldt. Trans. 1993 M. Konzett and J. McCormick, 'The Age of Neutralisations and Depoliticisations', *Telos* 96.

Schmitt, C. (1963b). *Der Begriff des Politischen: Text von 1932 mit einem Vorwort und drei Corollarien*, Berlin: Duncker and Humboldt. Trans. 1976 G. Schwab, *The Concept of the Political*, New Brunswick, NJ: Rutgers University Press.

Stirk, P. (1992). *Max Horkheimer: A New Interpretation*, Lanham, MD: Barnes and Noble.

Veneruso, D. (1984). *Gentile e il primato della tradizione culturale italiana: Il dibattito politico all'interno del fascismo*, Rome: Edizioni Studium.

Wolin, R. (1990). *The Politics of Being: The Political Thought of Martin Heidegger*, New York: Columbia University, Press.

Zimmerman, M. (1990). *Heidegger's Confrontation with Modernity: Technology, Politics, and Art*, Bloomington, IN: Indiana University Press.

INDEX

Page numbers in italics refer to entries in the biobibliography